2002

Collins Road Atlas

BRITAIN & IRELAND

CONTENTS

ii - iii	Key to map symbols	220-223	London urban maps
iv - ix	Route planning maps	224-225	London central map
x - xi	Motorway junctions with limited access	226-243	Urban area maps
xii - xiii	Motorway services information	244-247	Ireland road maps & city centre plans
2-203	Road map section	248-252	Index to London street names
204-219	City & town centre plans	253-284	Index to place names in Britain / Ireland

2002 Edition

Published by Collins
An imprint of HarperCollins*Publishers*
77-85 Fulham Palace Road
Hammersmith
London W6 8JB

The Bartholomew website address is: www.bartholomewmaps.com

Printed in Italy ISBN 0 00 711615 2 OC10861 MDC

e-mail: roadcheck@harpercollins.co.uk

HarperCollins*Publishers*

Key to map symbols

Route planning maps (pages iv-ix)

full S M25 Fleet S limited	Motorway with service area	dual A894 single	'A' Road		Ferry route / International airport
full 4 5 limited	Motorway junction		'B' Road	886	Summit height in metres
dual A82 single	Primary route		Road under construction		International / National boundary
Oxford	Primary route destination		Gradient / Toll / Tunnel		National / Forest park

Road maps (pages 2-203)

ROAD INFORMATION

M4	Motorway
30 29	Motorway junction with full / limited access
Maidstone Birch Sarn	Motorway service area with off road / full / limited access
A48	Primary dual / single carriageway
	With passing places
A30	'A' road dual / single carriageway
	With passing places
B1403	'B' road dual / single carriageway
	With passing places
	Minor road
	Restricted access due to road condition or private ownership
	Road projected or under construction
	Multi-level junction(occasionally with junction number)
	Roundabout
10	Road distance in miles
	Road tunnel
	Steep hill (arrows point downhill)
Toll	Level crossing / Toll

OTHER TRANSPORT INFORMATION

Poole 2½ hrs (3 hrs)	Car ferry route with journey times; daytime and (night-time)
	Railway line / Station / Tunnel
	Airport with scheduled services
H	Heliport
P	Park and Ride site*

CITIES , TOWNS & VILLAGES

	Built up area
	Town / Village / Other settlement
Peterhead	Primary route destination
St Ives	Seaside destination

OTHER FEATURES

	National boundary
	County / Unitary Authority boundary
	National / Regional park
	Forest park boundary
Danger Zone	Military range
	Woodland
468	Spot height in metres
941	Summit height in metres
	Lake / Dam / River / Waterfall
	Canal / Dry canal / Canal tunnel
	Beach
14	Adjoining page indicator

TOURIST INFORMATION

A selection of tourist detail is shown on the mapping.
It is advisable to check with the local tourist information office regarding opening times and facilities available.

i i	Tourist information office (all year / seasonal)
	Preserved railway
1738	Battlefield
	Ancient monument
	Ecclesiastical building
	Castle
	Historic house (with or without garden)
	Garden
	Museum / Art gallery
£	Factory shop village
	Theme park
	Major sports venue
	Motor racing circuit
	Racecourse
	Country park
	Nature reserve
	Wildlife park or Zoo
	Other interesting feature
	Golf course
(NT) (NTS)	National Trust property / National Trust for Scotland
(MNT)	Manx National Trust (Isle of Man)

	land below	0	165	490	985	1640	2295	2950	feet
water	sea level	0	50	150	300	500	700	900	metres

City and town centre plans (pages 204-219)

- Motorway
- Primary route
- 'A' road
- 'B' road
- Through route
- Other road
- Footpath / Footbridge
- Restricted access
- Pedestrian street
- Tourist building
- Important building
- Higher education building
- Hospital
- Cemetery
- Recreational area / Open space
- One way street
- Tourist information centre
- Car park
- Park and Ride site*
- Railway line / Station
- Underground / Metro / Light rail station
- Foot ferry
- Ecclesiastical building
- North arrow

London central map (pages 224-225)

- Primary route
- 'A' road
- 'B' road
- Other road
- Street market / Pedestrian street
- Track / Path
- One way street / Access restriction
- Ferry
- Borough boundary
- Postal district boundary
- Main / Other railway station
- LRT / DLR / Bus or coach station
- Leisure and tourism
- Shopping
- Administration and law
- Health and welfare
- Education
- Industry and commerce
- Public open space
- Park / Garden / Sports ground
- Tourist information centre
- Cinema / Theatre
- Major hotel
- Embassy
- Church
- Mosque
- Synagogue
- Other place of worship
- Car park / Public toilet
- Police station / Fire station / Post office

Urban area maps (pages 220-223 & 226-243)

- Motorway number
- Motorway junctions with full access
- Motorway junctions with limited access
- Motorway service area with full / limited / off road access
- Primary route number
- Dual carriageway
- Single carriageway
- 'A' road number
- Dual carriageway
- Single carriageway
- 'B' road number
- Dual carriageway
- Single carriageway
- Minor road dual carriageway
- Minor road single carriageway
- Road under construction
- Road tunnel
- Roundabout / Toll
- One way street / Level crossing
- Car ferry with destination
- Railway line / Station / Tunnel
- Underground station
- Light rail station
- Park and Ride site*
- Airport with scheduled services
- County / Unitary Authority boundary
- District boundary
- Public building
- Spot height in metres
- Woodland
- Park

*PARK AND RIDE SITES SHOWN IN THIS ATLAS OPERATE A MINIMUM OF 5 DAYS A WEEK

To Dublin & Dún Laoghaire
Holyhead
Anglesey
Holy Island
Llandudno
Conwy
Colwyn Bay
Rhyl
Prestatyn
Bangor
Caernarfon
Caernarfon Bay
Snowdon (Yr Wyddfa)
Snowdonia
Betws-y-coed
Llŷn Peninsula
Pwllheli
Porthmadog
Tremadoc Bay
Harlech
Bala
Aberdaron
Bardsey
Barmouth
Dolgellau
Machynlleth
Cardigan Bay
Aberdyfi
Aberystwyth
Cambrian Mountains
St George's Channel
New Quay
Cardigan
Fishguard
Pembrokeshire Coast National Park
St David's
Haverfordwest
Milford Haven
Pembroke Dock
Tenby
To Rosslare
Carmarthen
Llanelli
Swansea
Port Talbot
Neath
Bridgend
Cardiff
Newport
Cardiff International
Barry
Brecon
Brecon Beacons National Park
Black Mountains
Merthyr Tydfil
Abergavenny
Monmouth
Chepstow
Hereford
Leominster
Worcester
Gloucester
Bristol
Kingswood
Bath
Weston-super-Mare
Bristol Channel
To Cork
Worms Head
Caldey Island
St Govan's Head
Lundy Island
Exmoor National Park
Minehead
Ilfracombe
Barnstaple
Bideford
Hartland Point
Bridgwater
Taunton
Glastonbury
Wells
Frome
Yeovil
Exeter
Exmouth
Dartmoor National Park
Okehampton
Tavistock
Bodmin Moor
Bodmin
Launceston
Bude
Newquay
Liskeard
Plymouth
Torquay
Paignton
St Austell
Truro
Redruth
Falmouth
Penzance
Helston
Land's End
Lizard Point
Isles of Scilly
Hugh Town
St. Mary's
To Santander (summer only)
To Roscoff
Weymouth
Dorchester
Bill of Portland
To Channel Islands
CHANNEL ISLANDS
Alderney
Guernsey
St Peter Port
Sark
Jersey
St Helier
To Poole, Weymouth & Portsmouth
Shrewsbury
Telford
Wolverhampton
Dudley
BIRMING
Stourbridge
Kidderminster
Stafford
Stoke-
Newcastle-under-Lyme
Crewe
Chester
Wrexham
Oswestry
Llangollen
LIVERPOOL
Birkenhead
Runcorn
Widnes
Warrington
Ellesmere Port
Macclesfield
Congleton
Cannock
Halesowen
Bromsgrove
Newtown
Welshpool
Llandrindod Wells
Builth Wells
Rhayader
Llangurig
Llandovery
Llandeilo
Cwmbran
Pontypool
Caerphilly
Pontypridd
Ebbw Vale
Stroud
Chipping Sodbury
Trowbridge
Shepton Mallet
Blandford Forum
Honiton
Cullompton

V
ENGLISH CHANNEL
SCALE
0 10 20 30 40 miles
0 10 20 30 40 50 60 km
1:1,350,000 (approx) 22 miles to 1 inch / 13.5 km to 1 cm
LONDON
Sheffield
Lincoln
Skegness
Boston
Nottingham
Derby
Leicester
Grantham
Peterborough
King's Lynn
Norwich
Great Yarmouth
Lowestoft
Coventry
Northampton
Cambridge
Ipswich
Felixstowe
Harwich
Colchester
Chelmsford
Southend-on-Sea
Oxford
Reading
Luton
St Albans
Watford
Slough
Guildford
Crawley
Brighton
Eastbourne
Hastings
Maidstone
Canterbury
Dover
Folkestone
Margate
Ramsgate
Southampton
Portsmouth
Bournemouth
Poole
Winchester
Salisbury
Swindon
Milton Keynes
Bedford
Isle of Wight
The Wash
North Downs
South Downs
Channel tunnel
Strait of Dover
Calais
Dieppe
To Esbjerg
To Hamburg
To Hoek van Holland
To Oostende
To Dieppe (Summer only)
To Caen & Le Havre
To St. Malo & Cherbourg
To Bilbao & Channel Islands
To Cherbourg, Channel Islands & St. Malo

Colonsay
Scalasaig
Jura
Islay
Port Askaig
Bowmore
Portnahaven
Port Ellen
Mull Of Oa
Tarbert
Lochgilphead
Tayvallich
Ardrishaig
Kilmartin
Gigha
Tayinloan
Kintyre
Carradale
Campbeltown
Machrihanish
Southend
Mull of Kintyre
Kilbrannan Sound
Claonaig
Lochranza
Arran
Brodick
Lamlash
Lagg
Rothesay
Bute
Sound of Bute
Dunoon
Gourock
Greenock
Port Glasgow
Helensburgh
Dumbarton
Alexandria
Clydebank
Paisley
GLASGOW
Johnstone
Coatbridge
Airdrie
Hamilton
Motherwell
Wishaw
East Kilbride
Kilmarnock
Irvine
Ardrossan
Saltcoats
Stevenston
Kilwinning
Largs
Troon
Prestwick
Ayr
Galston
Mauchline
Cumnock
New Cumnock
Maybole
Turnberry
Girvan
Ailsa Craig
Colmonell
Ballantrae
Cairnryan
Kirkcolm
Stranraer
Portpatrick
Glenluce
Sandhead
Luce Bay
Port William
Drummore
Mull of Galloway
Whithorn
Burrow Head
Wigtown
Wigtown Bay
Newton Stewart
Gatehouse of Fleet
Kirkcudbright
Castle Douglas
Dalbeattie
Dundrennan
Galloway Forest Park
Bargrennan
New Galloway
Dalmellington
Moniaive
Sanquhar
Kirkconnel
Thornhill
Dumfries
Lochmaben
Lockerbie
Moffat
Beattock
Annan
Gretna
Gretna Green
Ecclefechan
Langholm
Newcastleton
SOUTHERN UPLANDS
Lowther Hills
Pentland Hills
Moorfoot Hills
Lammermuir Hills
Cheviot
Solway Firth
Stirling
Alloa
Clackmannan
Kincardine
Falkirk
Grangemouth
Bo'ness
Denny
Kilsyth
Cumbernauld
Kirkintilloch
Linlithgow
Broxburn
Bathgate
Livingston
Whitburn
West Calder
Dunfermline
Inverkeithing
Kirkcaldy
Burntisland
Firth of Forth
North Berwick
Dunbar
Edinburgh
Musselburgh
Dalkeith
Bonnyrigg
Penicuik
Haddington
Gifford
Humbie
Lauder
Stow
Galashiels
Peebles
Innerleithen
Melrose
Selkirk
Newtown St Boswells
Earlston
Gordon
Greenlaw
Jedburgh
Hawick
Bonchester Bridge
Teviotdale
Eskdalemuir
Biggar
Lanark
Carluke
Carstairs
Carnwath
Douglas
Abington
Elvanfoot
Rigside
Strathaven
West Linton
Blyth Bridge
Rathlin Island
Ballycastle
Bushmills
Armoy
Cushendun
Cushendall
Ballymoney
Garvagh
Kilrea
Ballymena
Broughshane
Carnlough
Larne
Maghera
Randalstown
Antrim
Moneymore
Ballyclare
Whitehead
Carrickfergus
Newtownabbey
Belfast
Belfast Lough
Bangor
Donaghadee
Dundonald
Newtownards
Comber
Lough Neagh
Crumlin
Dunmurry
Lisburn
Lurgan
Craigavon
Portadown
Dromore
Ballynahinch
Saintfield
Killinchy
Kirkcubbin
Portavogie
Ards Peninsula
Strangford Lough
Crossgar
Portaferry
Strangford
Downpatrick
Ardglass
Banbridge
Tandragee
Markethill
Rathfriland
Ballyward
Dundrum
Newcastle
Slieve Donard
Mourne Mountains
Newry
Warrenpoint
Annalong
Kilkeel
North Channel
Isle of Man
Point of Ayre
Andreas
Ramsey
Ramsey Bay
Kirk Michael
Peel
Laxey
Laxey Bay
Foxdale
Onchan
Douglas
Dalby
Port Erin
Port St Mary
Castletown
Calf of Man
Douglas (summer only)
(summer only)
IRISH SEA
Dundalk (Dun Dealgan)
Dundalk Bay
Castlebellingham
Ardee
Dunleer
Drogheda (Droichead Átha)
Slane
Balbriggan
Skerries
Rush
Ashbourne
Swords
Malahide
Lambay Island
Howth
Lucan
Dublin (Baile Átha Cliath)
Dublin Bay
Dún Laoghaire
Bray (Bré)
Enniskerry
Blessington
Djouce Mt
Wicklow Mts National Park
Wicklow Mountains
Lugnaquilla Mt
Wicklow (Cill Mhantáin)
Wicklow Head
Rathdrum
Aughrim
Arklow (An tInbhear Mór)
Inch
Gorey
Craanford
Ferns
Enniscorthy (Inis Corthaidh)
Blackwater
Amlwch
Moelfre
Holyhead
Holy Island
Anglesey
Llannerch-y-medd
Valley
Pentraeth
Llangefni
Beaumaris
Llanfairpwllgwyngyll
Menai Bridge
Bangor
Caernarfon
Caernarfon Bay
Llanberis
Snowdon (Yr Wyddfa)
Snowdonia National Park
Llanwnda
Llandwrog
Llanllyfni
Llanaelhaearn
Nefyn
Lleyn Peninsula
Beddgelert
Blaenau Ffestiniog
Ffestiniog
Tremadog
Porthmadog
Tremadog Bay
Criccieth
Pwllheli
Llanbedrog
Abersoch
Aberdaron
Bardsey
Harlech
Trawsfynydd
Llanuwchllyn
Bala
Llyn Tegid (Bala Lake)
Dolgellau
Barmouth
Llanelltyd
Mallwyd
Corris
Tywyn
Llangelynin
Machynlleth
Aberdyfi
Cardigan Bay
Eglwys Fach
Llandudno
Conwy
Conwy Bay
Rhôs-on-Sea
Colwyn Bay
Abergele
Rhyl
Prestatyn
Llanfairfechan
Glan Conwy
Llanrwst
Betws-y-coed
Capel Curig
Pentrefoelas
St Asaph (Llanelwy)
Denbigh
Ruthin
Mold
Flint
Holywell
Connah's Quay
Hawarden
Buckley
Chester
Wrexham
Llangollen
Ruabon
Chirk
Oswestry
Llanfyllin
Welshpool
Shrewsbury
Montgomery
Newtown
Llanwnog
Cambrian Mountains
Cumbrian Mountains
Lake District National Park
Carlisle
Brampton
Longtown
Wigton
Abbeytown
Aspatria
Maryport
Cockermouth
Workington
Seaton
Great Clifton
Distington
Whitehaven
St Bees Head
St Bees
Egremont
Cleator Moor
Frizington
Keswick
Buttermere
Derwent Water
Ullswater
Patterdale
Penrith
Shap
Orton
Tebay
Grasmere
Ambleside
Troutbeck
Windermere
Kendal
Coniston
Seascale
Gosforth
Broughton in Furness
Newby Bridge
Millom
Ulverston
Dalton-in-Furness
Barrow-in-Furness
Isle of Walney
Morecambe
Morecambe Bay
Heysham
Lancaster
Carnforth
Milnthorpe
Kirkby Lonsdale
Cockerham
Garstang
Fleetwood
Cleveleys
Thornton
Poulton-le-Fylde
Blackpool
Lytham St Anne's
Freckleton
Kirkham
Preston
Leyland
Chorley
Tarleton
Southport
Burscough Bridge
Formby
Ormskirk
Skelmersdale
Wigan
Crosby
Kirkby
Bootle
St Helens
Wallasey
Birkenhead
LIVERPOOL
West Kirby
Bebington
Heswall
Ellesmere Port
Widnes
Runcorn
Warrington
Frodsham
Weaverham
Winsford
Nantwich
Whitchurch
Ellesmere
Wem

N O R T H
S E A
SCALE
0 10 20 30 40 miles
0 10 20 30 40 50 60 km
1:1,350,000 (approx) 22 miles to 1 inch / 13.5 km to 1 cm
To Stavanger Haugesund & Bergen
To Göteborg & Kristiansand
To Amsterdam
To Rotterdam & Zeebrugge
Berwick-upon-Tweed
Holy Island or Lindisfarne
Farne Islands
Bamburgh
North Sunderland
Alnwick
Northumberland National Park
Morpeth
Ashington
Blyth
Cramlington
Whitley Bay
Tynemouth
South Shields
Newcastle upon Tyne
Gateshead
Sunderland
Hexham
Durham
Hartlepool
Bishop Auckland
Middlesbrough
Stockton-on-Tees
Darlington
Redcar
Whitby
Robin Hood's Bay
North York Moors
North York Moors National Park
Scarborough
Filey
Flamborough Head
Bridlington
Yorkshire Dales National Park
Ripon
Harrogate
York
Leeds
Bradford
Halifax
Huddersfield
Wakefield
Pontefract
Selby
Goole
Kingston upon Hull
Holderness
Withernsea
Spurn Head
Grimsby
Cleethorpes
Scunthorpe
Doncaster
Barnsley
Rotherham
Sheffield
Oldham
Rochdale
Manchester
Salford
Stockport
Lincoln
Lincolnshire Wolds
Skegness
Boston
The Wash
Nottingham
Derby
Mansfield
Chesterfield
Stoke-on-Trent
Grantham
Leicester
Peterborough
King's Lynn
Cromer
Norwich
Walsall
Wolverhampton
Birmingham

ATLANTIC
OCEAN
WESTERN ISLES (NA H-EILEANAN AN IAR)
Lewis (Eilean Leodhais)
North Harris (Ceann a Tuatha Hearadh)
South Harris
North Uist (Uibhist a' Tuath)
Benbecula (Beinn na Faoghla)
South Uist (Uibhist a' Deas)
Barra (Eilean Barraigh)
Vatersay (Bhatarsaigh)
Pabaigh (Pabaigh)
Mingulay (Miughalaigh)
Eriskay (Eiriosgaigh)
Lochboisdale (Loch Baghasdail)
Castlebay (Bagh a' Chaisteil)
Lochmaddy (Loch na Madadh)
Heisker or Monach Islands
Stornoway (Steornabhagh)
Rubha Robhanais
Port Nis
Barabhas
Tolsta Head
Carlabhagh
Port nan Giuran
Miavaig
Gearraidh na h-Aibhne
Scarp
Kebock Head
An Tairbeart
Scalpay (Eilean Scalpaigh)
Shiant Islands
Taobh Tuath
Pabbay
Roghadal
Baile Mhartainn
The Minch
Little Minch
Summer Isles
Point of Stoer
Rubha Reidh
Rubha Hunish
Skye
Kilmaluag
Uig
Dunvegan
Portree
Borve
Bracadale
Sligachan
Cuillin Hills
Raasay
Rona
Scalpay
Kyle of Lochalsh
Kyleakin
Broadford
Soay
Elgol
Canna
Rum (Rhum)
Eigg
Muck
Mallaig
Morar
Arisaig
Sound of Arisaig
Knoydart
Coll
Tiree
Mull
Ulva
Iona
Fionnphort
Pennyghael
Tobermory
Salen
Craignure
Lochaline
Kilchoan
Strontian
Colonsay
Scalasaig
Oronsay
Jura
Tarbert
Islay
Port Askaig
Bowmore
Portnahaven
Port Ellen
Mull Of Oa
Gigha
Kintyre
Campbeltown
Machrihanish
Southend
Mull of Kintyre
Rathlin Island
Arran
Brodick
Lamlash
Lagg
Bute
Rothesay
Cape Wrath
Durness
Tongue
Bettyhill
Strathy Point
Dounreay
Scrabster
Thurso
Rhiconich
Laxford Bridge
Scourie
Ben Hope
Altnaharra
Sutherland
Caithness
Forsinard
Kinbrace
Helmsdale
Unapool
Lochinver
Ledmore
Elphin
Lairg
Invercassley
Pittentrail
Brora
Golspie
Bonar Bridge
Ardgay
Ullapool
Dornoch Firth
Tain
Tarbat Ness
Portmahomack
Hill of Fearn
Balintore
Easter Ross
Wester Ross
Aultbea
An Teallach
Poolewe
Gairloch
Kinlochewe
Achnasheen
Liathach
Torridon
Shieldaig
Craig
Lochcarron
Stromeferry
Dornie
Garve
Strathpeffer
Dingwall
Invergordon
Balnapaling
Cromarty
Black Isle
Conon Bridge
Fortrose
Rosemarkie
Ardersier
Nairn
Forres
Findhorn
Hopeman
Burghead
Kinloss
Moray Firth
Muir of Ord
Beauly
Inverness
Dores
Glen Cannich
Cannich
Glen Affric
Drumnadrochit
Glen Mor
Foyers
Invermoriston
Fort Augustus
Glen Shiel
Glen Garry
Invergarry
Monadhliath Mountains
Tomatin
Dava
Grantown-on-Spey
Dulnain Bridge
Carrbridge
Boat of Garten
Aviemore
Kincraig
Kingussie
Newtonmore
Cairngorm Mountains
Ben Macdui
Laggan
Dalwhinnie
Spean Bridge
Roybridge
Glen Spean
Glenfinnan
Fort William
Ben Nevis
Kinlochleven
Glen Coe
Ballachulish
Bidean Nam Bian
Rannoch Moor
Rannoch Station
Kinloch Rannoch
Grampian Mountains
Blair Atholl
Killiecrankie
Pitlochry
Kirkmichael
Spittal of Glenshee
Grandtully
Aberfeldy
Kenmore
Ballinluig
Dunkeld
Ben Lawers
Killin
Portnacroish
Bridge of Orchy
Tyndrum
Crianlarich
Dalmally
Oban
Taynuilt
Lismore
Loch Linnhe
Firth of Lorn
Kilmelford
Argyll
Inveraray
Kilmartin
Lochgilphead
Tayvallich
Ardrishaig
Luing
Scarba
Clachan
Arrochar
Lochgoilhead
Argyll Forest Park
Ben Lomond
Aberfoyle
Queen Elizabeth Forest Park
Loch Lomond
Lochearnhead
Comrie
Crieff
Strathyre
Callander
Methven
Auchterarder
Gleneagles
Doune
Dunblane
Bridge of Allan
Stirling
Alloa
Kincardine
Tillicoultry
Dollar
Clackmannan
Grangemouth
Bo'ness
Denny
Falkirk
Kilsyth
Cumbernauld
Linlithgow
Kirkintilloch
Bathgate
Livingston
Drymen
Garelochhead
Helensburgh
Alexandria
Dumbarton
Greenock
Gourock
Port Glasgow
Dunoon
Milngavie
Bearsden
Clydebank
Coatbridge
Airdrie
Whitburn
West Calder
Calderpruix
Harthill
GLASGOW
Paisley
Johnstone
Wemyss Bay
Largs
Millport
Barrhead
Newton Mearns
East Kilbride
Hamilton
Motherwell
Wishaw
Carluke
Carnwath
Lanark
Carstairs
Strathaven
Beith
Dunlop
Dalry
West Kilbride
Stewarton
Kilwinning
Ardrossan
Stevenston
Saltcoats
Irvine
Kilmarnock
Galston
Troon
Prestwick
Glasgow Prestwick International
Ayr
Mauchline
Muirkirk
Cumnock
New Cumnock
Douglas
Abington
Kirkconnel
Sanquhar
Dalmellington
Maybole
Turnberry
Ailsa Craig
Girvan
Colmonell
Ballantrae
Galloway Forest
Loch Doon
Moniaive
Thornhill
Lowther Hills
SOUTHERN UPLANDS
Elvanfoot
Kilchattan
Claonaig
Carradale
Tayinloan
Kilbrannan Sound
Sound of Bute
Firth of Clyde
Malin Head
Ballygorman
Inishowen
Carndonagh
Moville
Drumfree
Buncrana
Carrowkeel
Portsalon
Lough Swilly
Lough Foyle
Milford
Inishtrahull Sound
Portrush
Portstewart
Coleraine
Bushmills
Ballycastle
Armoy
Cushendun
Cushendall
Ballymoney
Limavady
Pentland Firth

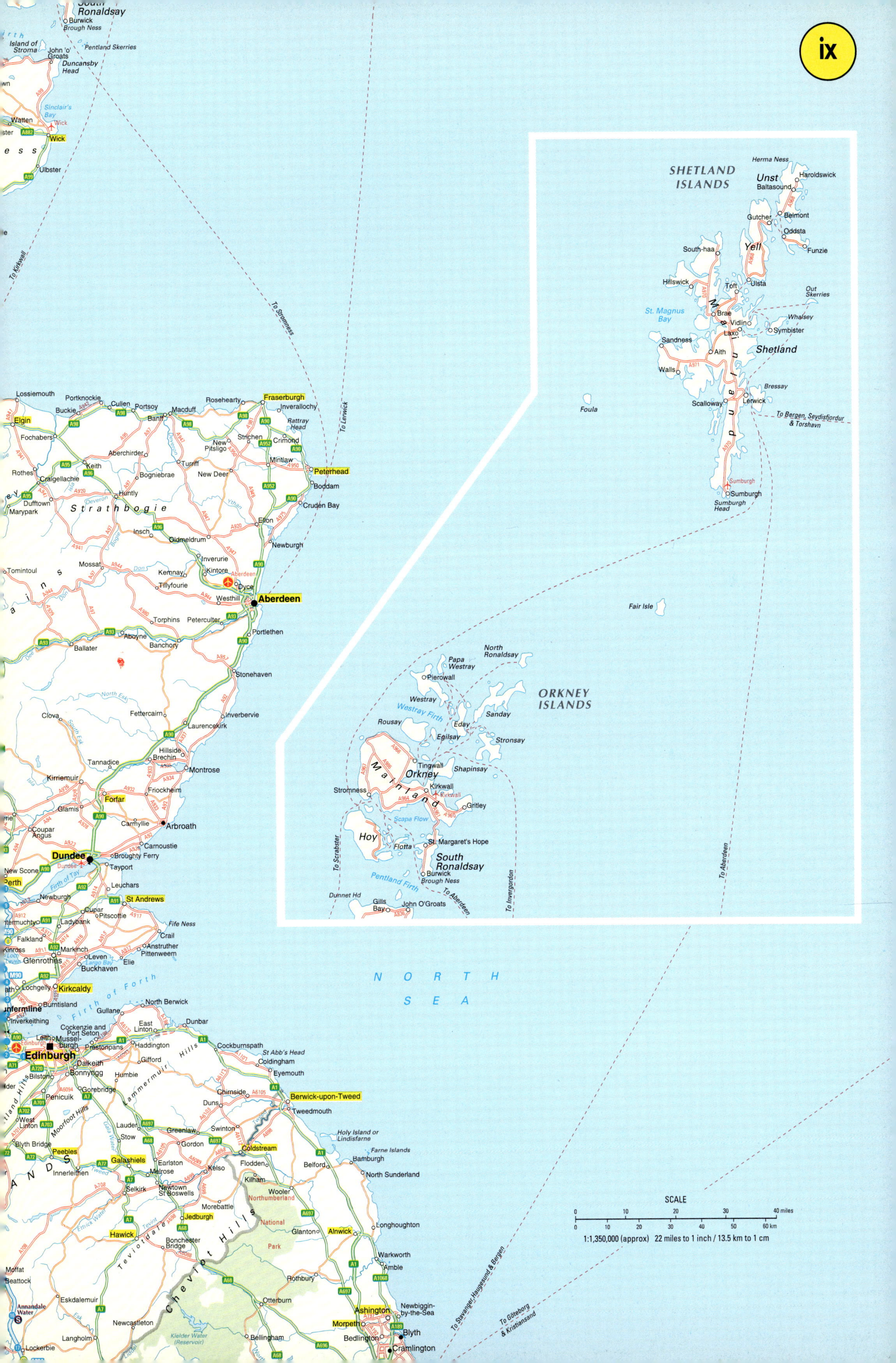
SHETLAND ISLANDS
Herma Ness
Haroldswick
Unst
Baltasound
Gutcher
Belmont
Oddsta
Yell
Funzie
South-haa
Hillswick
Toft
Ulsta
Out Skerries
St. Magnus Bay
Brae
Vidlin
Whalsey
Laxo
Symbister
Sandness
Aith
Shetland
Mainland
Walls
Bressay
Scalloway
Lerwick
Foula
To Bergen, Seydisfjordur & Torshavn
Sumburgh
Sumburgh Head
Fair Isle
ORKNEY ISLANDS
North Ronaldsay
Papa Westray
Pierowall
Westray
Westray Firth
Sanday
Rousay
Eday
Egilsay
Stronsay
Tingwall
Shapinsay
Orkney
Mainland
Stromness
Kirkwall
Gritley
Scapa Flow
Hoy
Flotta
St. Margaret's Hope
South Ronaldsay
Burwick
Brough Ness
Pentland Firth
Dunnet Hd
Gills Bay
John O'Groats
To Scrabster
To Aberdeen
To Invergordon
NORTH SEA
Island of Stroma
John 'o' Groats
Duncansby Head
Pentland Skerries
Sinclair's Bay
Watten
Wick
Ulbster
To Kirkwall
To Stromness
To Lerwick
Lossiemouth
Portknockie
Buckie
Cullen
Portsoy
Banff
Macduff
Rosehearty
Fraserburgh
Inverallochy
Rattray Head
Elgin
Fochabers
Aberchirder
New Pitsligo
Strichen
Crimond
Turriff
Mintlaw
Peterhead
Rothes
Keith
Craigellachie
Bogniebrae
New Deer
Boddam
Dufftown
Huntly
Marypark
Strathbogie
Cruden Bay
Ellon
Insch
Oldmeldrum
Newburgh
Inverurie
Tomintoul
Mossat
Kemnay
Kintore
Aberdeen
Tillyfourie
Dyce
Westhill
Aberdeen
Torphins
Peterculter
Portlethen
Aboyne
Banchory
Ballater
Stonehaven
Fettercairn
Clova
Inverbervie
Laurencekirk
Tannadice
Hillside
Brechin
Montrose
Kirriemuir
Friockheim
Forfar
Glamis
Carmyllie
Arbroath
Coupar Angus
Carnoustie
Dundee
Broughty Ferry
Tayport
New Scone
Perth
Firth of Tay
Leuchars
Newburgh
St Andrews
Cupar
Pitscottie
Ladybank
Fife Ness
Falkland
Crail
Markinch
Anstruther
Pittenweem
Glenrothes
Leven
Elie
Largo Bay
Buckhaven
Lochgelly
Kirkcaldy
Firth of Forth
Burntisland
North Berwick
Gullane
Dunfermline
Inverkeithing
East Linton
Dunbar
Cockenzie and Port Seton
Leith
Musselburgh
Prestonpans
Haddington
Cockburnspath
Edinburgh
Gifford
St Abb's Head
Dalkeith
Coldingham
Bonnyrigg
Humbie
Eyemouth
Bilston
Gorebridge
Lammermuir Hills
Chirnside
Penicuik
Duns
Berwick-upon-Tweed
Tweedmouth
Moorfoot Hills
West Linton
Lauder
Greenlaw
Swinton
Holy Island or Lindisfarne
Stow
Blyth Bridge
Peebles
Galashiels
Gordon
Coldstream
Farne Islands
Earlston
Bamburgh
Innerleithen
Melrose
Kelso
Flodden
Belford
North Sunderland
Selkirk
Newtown St Boswells
Kilham
Wooler
Northumberland National Park
Morebattle
Jedburgh
Hawick
Teviotdale
Bonchester Bridge
Cheviot Hills
Glanton
Alnwick
Longhoughton
Warkworth
Amble
Moffat
Beattock
Eskdalemuir
Rothbury
Otterburn
Ashington
Newbiggin-by-the-Sea
Morpeth
Newcastleton
Blyth
Langholm
Bellingham
Bedlington
Cramlington
Kielder Water (Reservoir)
Annandale Water
Lockerbie
To Stavanger, Haugesund & Bergen
To Göteborg & Kristiansand
SCALE
0
10
20
30
40 miles
0
10
20
30
40
50
60 km
1:1,350,000 (approx) 22 miles to 1 inch / 13.5 km to 1 cm

Motorway junctions with limited access

A1(M) LONDON TO NEWCASTLE

2
Northbound : No access
Southbound : No exit
3
Southbound : No access
5
Northbound : No exit
Southbound : No access
: No exit
44
Northbound : No exit to M1 Westbound
Dishforth
Southbound : No access from A168 Eastbound
57
Northbound : No access
: Exit only to A66(M) Northbound
Southbound : Access only from A66(M) Southbound
: No exit
65
Northbound : No access from A1
Southbound : No exit from A1

A3(M) PORTSMOUTH

1
Northbound : No exit
Southbound : No access
4
Northbound : No access
Southbound : No exit

A38(M) BIRMINGHAM

Victoria Road
Northbound : No exit
Southbound : No access

A48(M) CARDIFF

M4 29
Westbound : No access from M4 29 Eastbound
Eastbound : No exit to M4 29 Westbound
29A
Westbound : No exit to A48 Eastbound
Eastbound : No access to A48 Westbound

A57(M) MANCHESTER

Brook Street
Westbound : No exit
Eastbound : No access

A58(M) LEEDS

Westgate
Southbound : No access
Woodhouse Lane
Westbound : No exit

A64(M) LEEDS

Claypit Lane
Eastbound : No access

A66(M) DARLINGTON

A1(M)
Northbound : No access from A1(M) Southbound
: No exit
Southbound : No access
: No exit to A1(M) Northbound

A167(M) NEWCASTLE

Campden Street
Northbound : No exit
Southbound : No access
: No exit

M1 LONDON TO LEEDS

2
Northbound : No exit
Southbound : No access
4
Northbound : No exit
Southbound : No access
6A
Northbound : Access only from M25 21
: No exit
Southbound : No access
: Exit only to M25 21
7
Northbound : Access only from M10
: No exit
Southbound : No access
: Exit only to M10
17
Northbound : No access
: Exit only to M45
Southbound : Access only from M45
: No exit
19
Northbound : Exit only to M6
Southbound : Access only from M6
21A
Northbound : No access
Southbound : No exit
23A
Northbound : No access from A453
Southbound : No exit to A453
24A
Northbound : No exit
Southbound : No access
35A
Northbound : No access
Southbound : No exit
43
Northbound : No access
: Exit only to M621
Southbound : No exit
: Access only from M621
48
Northbound : No exit to A1 Southbound
: Access only from A1 Northbound
Southbound : Exit only to A1 Southbound
: No access

M2 ROCHESTER TO CANTERBURY

1
Westbound : No exit to A2 Eastbound
Eastbound : No access from A2 Westbound

M3 LONDON TO WINCHESTER

8
Westbound : No access
Eastbound : No exit
10
Northbound : No access
Southbound : No exit
13
Southbound : No exit A335 Eastbound
: No access
14
Westbound : No access
Eastbound : No exit

M4 LONDON TO SWANSEA

1
Westbound : No access from A4 Eastbound
Eastbound : No exit to A4 Westbound
2
Westbound : No access from A4 Eastbound
: No exit to A4 Eastbound
Eastbound : No access from A4 Westbound
: No exit to A4 Westbound
21
Westbound : No access M48 Eastbound
Eastbound : No exit M48 Westbound
23
Westbound : No exit M48 Eastbound
Eastbound : No access M48 Westbound
25
Westbound : No access
Eastbound : No exit
25A
Westbound : No access
Eastbound : No exit
29
Westbound : No access
: Exit only to A48(M)
Eastbound : Access only from A48(M) Eastbound
: No exit
38
Westbound : No access
39
Westbound : No exit
Eastbound : No access
: No exit
41
Westbound : No exit
Eastbound : No access

M5 BIRMINGHAM TO EXETER

10
Northbound : No exit
Southbound : No access
11A
Northbound : No access from A417 Eastbound
Southbound : No exit to A417 Westbound
12
Northbound : No access
Southbound : No exit

M6 COVENTRY TO CARLISLE

M1
Northbound : No access from M1 19 Southbound
Southbound : No exit to M1 19 Northbound
4A
Northbound : No access from M42 8 Northbound
: No exit
Southbound : No access
: Exit only to M42 8
5
Northbound : No access
Southbound : No exit
10A
Northbound : No access
: Exit only to M54
Southbound : Access only from M54
: No exit
20
Northbound : No exit to M56 Eastbound
Southbound : No access from M56 Westbound
20A
Northbound : No exit
: No access
24
Northbound : No exit
Southbound : No access
25
Northbound : No access
Southbound : No exit
30
Northbound : Access only from M61 Northbound
: No exit
Southbound : No access
: Exit only to M61 Southbound
31A
Northbound : No access
Southbound : No exit

M8 EDINBURGH TO GLASGOW

8
Westbound : No access from M73 2 Southbound
: No access from A8 Eastbound
: No access from A89 Eastbound
Eastbound : No access from A89 Westbound
: No exit to M73 2 Northbound
9
Westbound : No exit
Eastbound : No access
14
Westbound : No exit
Eastbound : No access
16
Westbound : No access
Eastbound : No exit
17
Eastbound : Access only from A82, not central Glasgow
: Exit only to A82, not central Glasgow
18
Westbound : No access
Eastbound : No access
19
Westbound : Access only from A814 Eastbound
Eastbound : Exit only to A814 Westbound, not central Glasgow
20
Westbound : No access
Eastbound : No exit
21
Westbound : No exit
Eastbound : No access
22
Westbound : No access
: Exit only to M77 Southbound
Eastbound : Access only from M77 Northbound
: No exit
: No exit to M77
23
Westbound : No access
Eastbound : No exit
25
Westbound : No access from A739 Northbound
: No exit to A739 Southbound
Eastbound : No access from A739 Northbound
: No exit to A739 Southbound
25A
Eastbound : No exit
Westbound : No access
28
Westbound : No access
Eastbound : No exit
28A
Westbound : No access
Eastbound : No exit

M9 EDINBURGH TO STIRLING

1A
Westbound : No access
Eastbound : No exit
2
Westbound : No exit
Eastbound : No access
3
Westbound : No access
Eastbound : No exit
6
Westbound : No exit
Eastbound : No access
8
Westbound : No access
: No access from M876 Eastbound
Eastbound : No access to M876 Westbound
: No exit

M10 ST ALBANS

M1
Northbound : No access
: Exit only to M1 7 Northbound
Southbound : Access only from M1 7 Southbound
: No exit

M11 LONDON TO CAMBRIDGE

4
Northbound : No access from A1400 Westbound
: No exit
Southbound : No access
: No exit to A1400 Eastbound
5
Northbound : No access
Southbound : No exit
9
Northbound : No access
Southbound : No exit
13
Northbound : No access
Southbound : No exit
14
Northbound : No access from A428 Eastbound
: No exit to A428 Westbound
: No exit to A1307
Southbound : No access from A428 Eastbound
: No access from A1307
: No exit

M20 LONDON TO FOLKESTONE

2
Westbound : No exit
Eastbound : No access
3
Westbound : No access
: Exit only to M26 Westbound
Eastbound : Access only from M26 Eastbound
: No exit
11A
Westbound : No exit
Eastbound : No access

M23 LONDON TO CRAWLEY

7
Northbound : No exit to A23 Southbound
Southbound : No access from A23 Northbound
10A
Southbound : No access from B2036
Northbound : No exit to B2036

M25 LONDON ORBITAL MOTORWAY

1B
Northbound : No exit
Southbound : No access
5
Clockwise : No exit to M26 Eastbound
Anticlockwise : No access from M26 Westbound

Spur of M25 (5)

Clockwise : No access from M26 Westbound
Anticlockwise : No exit to M26 Eastbound

(19)

Clockwise : No access
Anticlockwise : No exit

(21)

Clockwise : No access from M1 (6A) Northbound
: No exit to M1 (6A) Southbound
Anticlockwise : No access from M1 (6A) Northbound
: No exit to M1 (6A) Southbound

(31)

Clockwise : No exit
Anticlockwise : No access

M26 SEVENOAKS

M25 (5)

Westbound : No exit to M25 Anticlockwise
: No exit to M25 spur
Eastbound : No access from M25 Clockwise
: No access from M25 spur

M20

Westbound : No access from M20 (3) Eastbound
Eastbound : No exit to M20 (3) Westbound

M27 SOUTHAMPTON TO PORTSMOUTH

(4) West

Westbound : No exit
Eastbound : No access

(4) East

Westbound : No access
Eastbound : No exit

(10)

Westbound : No access
Eastbound : No exit

(12) West

Westbound : No exit
Eastbound : No access

(12) East

Westbound : No access from A3
Eastbound : No exit

M40 LONDON TO BIRMINGHAM

(3)

Westbound : No access
Eastbound : No exit

(7)

Eastbound : No exit

(13)

Northbound : No access
Southbound : No exit

(14)

Northbound : No exit
Southbound : No access

(16)

Northbound : No exit
Southbound : No access

M42 BIRMINGHAM

(1)

Northbound : No exit
Southbound : No access

(7)

Northbound : No access
: Exit only to M6 Northbound
Southbound : Access only from M6 Northbound
: No exit

(7A)

Northbound : No access
: Exit only to M6 Eastbound
Southbound : No access
: No exit

(8)

Northbound : Access only from M6 Southbound
: No exit
Southbound : Access only from M6 Southbound
: Exit only to M6 Northbound

M45 COVENTRY

M1

Westbound : No access from M1 (17) Southbound
Eastbound : No exit to M1 (17) Northbound

M49 BRISTOL

(18A)

Northbound : No access from M5 Southbound
Southbound : No access from M5 Northbound

M53 BIRKENHEAD TO CHESTER

(11)

Northbound : No access from M56 (15) Eastbound
: No exit to M56 (15) Westbound
Southbound : No access from M56 (15) Eastbound
: No exit to M56 (15) Westbound

M54 WOLVERHAMPTON TO TELFORD

M6

Westbound : No access from M6 (10A) Southbound
Eastbound : No exit to M6 (10A) Northbound

M56 STOCKPORT TO CHESTER

(1)

Westbound : No access from M60 Eastbound
: No access from A34 Northbound
Eastbound : No exit to M60 Westbound
: No exit to A34 Southbound

(2)

Westbound : No access
Eastbound : No exit

(3)

Westbound : No exit
Eastbound : No access

(4)

Westbound : No access
Eastbound : No exit

(7)

Westbound : No access
Eastbound : No exit

(8)

Westbound : No exit
Eastbound : No access

(9)

Westbound : No exit to M6 Southbound
Eastbound : No access from M6 Northbound

(15)

Westbound : No access
: No access from M53 (11)
Eastbound : No exit
: No exit to M53 (11)

M57 LIVERPOOL

(3)

Northbound : No exit
Southbound : No access

(5)

Northbound : Access only from A580 Westbound
: No exit
Southbound : No access
: Exit only to A580 Eastbound

M58 LIVERPOOL TO WIGAN

(1)

Westbound : No access
Eastbound : No exit

M60 MANCHESTER

(2)

Westbound : No exit
Eastbound : No access

(3)

Westbound : No access from M56 (1)
: No access from A34 Southbound
: No exit to A34 Northbound
Eastbound : No access from A34 Southbound
: No exit to M56 (1)
: No exit to A34 Northbound

(4)

Westbound : No access
Eastbound : No exit to M56

(5)

Westbound : No access from A5103 Southbound
: No exit to A5103 Southbound
Eastbound : No access from A5103 Northbound
: No exit to A5103 Northbound

(7)

Westbound : No access from A56 Southbound
: No exit to A56 Northbound
Eastbound : No exit to A56 Southbound
: No access from A56 Northbound

(14)

Westbound : No access from A580
: No exit to A580 Eastbound
Eastbound : No access from A580 Westbound
: No exit to A580

(16)

Westbound : No access
Eastbound : No exit

(20)

Westbound : No access
Eastbound : No exit

(22)

Westbound : No access

(25)

Westbound : No access

(26)

Eastbound : No access
: No exit

(27)

Westbound : No exit
Eastbound : No access

M61 MANCHESTER TO PRESTON

(2)

Northbound : No access from A580 Eastbound
: No access from A666
Southbound : No exit to A580 Westbound

(3)

Northbound : No access from A580 Eastbound
: No access from A666
Southbound : No exit to A580 Westbound

M6

Northbound : No exit to M6 (30) Southbound
Southbound : No access from M6 (30) Northbound

M62 LIVERPOOL TO HULL

(23)

Westbound : No exit
Eastbound : No access

M65 BURNLEY

(9)

Westbound : No exit
Eastbound : No access

(11)

Westbound : No access
Eastbound : No exit

M66 MANCHESTER TO EDENFIELD

(1)

Northbound : No access
Southbound : No exit

M67 MANCHESTER

(1)

Westbound : No exit
Eastbound : No access

(2)

Westbound : No access
Eastbound : No exit

M69 COVENTRY TO LEICESTER

(2)

Northbound : No exit
Southbound : No access

M73 GLASGOW

(2)

Northbound : No access from M8 (8) Eastbound
Southbound : No exit to M8 (8) Westbound

(3)

Northbound : No exit to A80 Southbound
Southbound : No access from A80 Northbound

M74 GLASGOW

(2)

Westbound : No access
Eastbound : No exit

(3)

Westbound : No exit
Eastbound : No access

(7)

Northbound : No exit
Southbound : No access

(9)

Northbound : No access
: No exit
Southbound : No access

(10)

Southbound : No exit

(11)

Northbound : No exit
Southbound : No access

(12)

Northbound : Access only from A70 Northbound
Southbound : Exit only to A70 Southbound

(18)

Northbound : No access
Southbound : No exit

M77 GLASGOW

M8

Northbound : No exit to M8 (22) Westbound
Southbound : No access from M8 (22) Eastbound

(4)

Northbound : No exit
Southbound : No access

M80 STIRLING

(3)

Southbound : No access

(5)

Northbound : No access
: No access from M876
Southbound : No exit
: No exit to M876

M90 EDINBURGH TO PERTH

(2A)

Northbound : No access
Southbound : No exit

(7)

Northbound : No exit
Southbound : No access

(8)

Northbound : No access
Southbound : No exit

(10)

Northbound : No access from A912
: No exit to A912 Southbound
Southbound : No access from A912 Northbound
: No exit to A912

M180 SCUNTHORPE

(1)

Westbound : No exit
Eastbound : No access

M606 BRADFORD

Straithgate Lane

Northbound : No access

M621 LEEDS

(2A)

Northbound : No exit
Southbound : No access

(4)

Southbound : No access

(5)

Northbound : No access
Southbound : No exit

(6)

Northbound : No exit
Southbound : No access

M876 FALKIRK

M80

Westbound : No exit to M80 (5) Northbound
Eastbound : No access from M80 (5) Southbound

M9

Westbound : No access
: No access from M9 (7) (8) Eastbound
Eastbound : No exit
: No exit to M9 (7) (8) Westbound

(2)

Northbound : No access
Southbound : No exit

Motorway services information

Motorway Number	Junction	Service Provider	Service Name	On-site Services							
A1(M)	1	Welcome Break	South Mimms	✓	✓	✓	✓		✓	✓	✓
A1(M)	10	Extra	Baldock	✓	✓	✓	✓	✓	✓	✓	✓
A1(M)	17	Extra	Peterborough	✓	✓	✓	✓	✓	✓	✓	✓
A1(M)	34	Moto	Blyth	✓	✓	✓	✓	✓	✓	✓	
A1(M)	61	RoadChef	Durham	✓	✓	✓	✓		✓		
A1(M)	64	Moto	Washington	✓	✓	✓	✓	✓	✓	✓	
M1	2–4	Welcome Break	London Gateway	✓	✓	✓	✓		✓		✓
M1	11–12	Moto	Toddington	✓	✓	✓	✓	✓	✓	✓	
M1	14–15	Welcome Break	Newport Pagnell	✓	✓	✓	✓		✓		✓
M1	15A	RoadChef	Rothersthorpe	✓	✓	✓	✓				
M1	16–17	RoadChef	Watford Gap	✓	✓	✓	✓		✓		
M1	21–21A	Welcome Break	Leicester Forest East	✓	✓	✓	✓		✓		✓
M1	22	Moto	Leicester	✓	✓	✓	✓	✓	✓	✓	
M1	23A	Moto	Donington Park	✓	✓	✓	✓	✓	✓	✓	✓
M1	25–26	Moto	Trowell	✓	✓	✓	✓	✓	✓	✓	
M1	28–29	RoadChef	Tibshelf	✓	✓	✓	✓		✓	✓	
M1	30–31	Welcome Break	Woodall	✓	✓	✓	✓		✓		✓
M1	38–39	Moto	Woolley Edge	✓	✓	✓	✓	✓	✓	✓	
M2	4–5	Moto	Medway	✓	✓	✓	✓	✓	✓	✓	
M3	4A–5	Welcome Break	Fleet	✓	✓	✓	✓		✓		✓
M3	8–9	RoadChef	Winchester	✓	✓	✓	✓		✓	✓	
M4	3	Moto	Heston	✓	✓	✓	✓	✓	✓	✓	✓
M4	11–12	Moto	Reading	✓	✓	✓	✓	✓	✓	✓	✓
M4	13	Moto	Chieveley	✓	✓	✓	✓	✓	✓	✓	
M4	14–15	Welcome Break	Membury	✓	✓	✓	✓		✓		✓
M4	17–18	Moto	Leigh Delamere	✓	✓	✓	✓	✓	✓	✓	✓
M4	23A	First Motorway	Magor	✓	✓	✓	✓	✓	✓		
M4	30	Moto	Cardiff Gate	✓	✓	✓	✓		✓		
M4	33	Moto	Cardiff	✓	✓	✓	✓	✓	✓	✓	✓
M4	36	Welcome Break	Sarn Park	✓	✓	✓	✓		✓		✓
M4	47	Moto	Swansea	✓	✓	✓	✓	✓	✓	✓	
M4	49	RoadChef	Pont Abraham	✓	✓	✓	✓	✓		✓	
M5	3–4	Moto	Frankley	✓	✓	✓	✓	✓	✓	✓	
M5	8	RoadChef	Strensham (South)	✓	✓	✓	✓				
M5	8	RoadChef	Strensham (North)	✓	✓	✓	✓		✓	✓	
M5	13–14	Welcome Break	Michael Wood	✓	✓	✓	✓		✓		✓
M5	19	Welcome Break	Gordano	✓	✓	✓	✓		✓		✓
M5	21–22	RoadChef	Sedgemoor (South)	✓	✓	✓	✓				
M5	21–22	Welcome Break	Sedgemoor (North)	✓	✓	✓	✓		✓		✓
M5	24	First Motorway	Bridgwater	✓	✓	✓	✓		✓		
M5	25–26	RoadChef	Taunton Deane	✓	✓	✓	✓		✓	✓	
M5	28	Moto	Cullompton	✓	✓	✓	✓				
M5	29–30	Moto	Exeter	✓	✓	✓	✓	✓	✓	✓	✓

On-site Services: Fuel · Information · Disabled facilities · Accommodation · Food · Other shops · Service shops · Conference facilities

Motorway Number	Junction	Service Provider	Service Name	On-site Services
M6	3–4	Welcome Break	Corley	Fuel, Disabled facilities, Food, Service shops, Accommodation
M6	10–11	Moto	Hilton Park	Fuel, Disabled facilities, Food, Service shops, Information, Accommodation, Other shops
M6	14–15	RoadChef	Stafford (South)	Fuel, Disabled facilities, Food, Service shops, Accommodation, Other shops
M6	14–15	Moto	Stafford (North)	Fuel, Disabled facilities, Food, Service shops, Information, Other shops, Conference facilities
M6	15–16	Welcome Break	Keele	Fuel, Disabled facilities, Food, Service shops
M6	16–17	RoadChef	Sandbach	Fuel, Disabled facilities, Food, Service shops
M6	18–19	Moto	Knutsford	Fuel, Disabled facilities, Food, Service shops, Information, Other shops
M6	27–28	Welcome Break	Charnock Richard	Fuel, Disabled facilities, Food, Service shops, Accommodation
M6	32–33	Moto	Lancaster	Fuel, Disabled facilities, Food, Service shops, Information, Accommodation, Other shops
M6	35A–36	Moto	Burton-in-Kendal	Fuel, Disabled facilities, Food, Service shops, Information, Accommodation, Other shops
M6	36–37	RoadChef	Killington Lake	Fuel, Disabled facilities, Food, Service shops, Accommodation
M6	38–39	Westmorland	Tebay	Fuel, Disabled facilities, Food, Service shops, Accommodation, Conference facilities
M6	41–42	Moto	Southwaite	Fuel, Disabled facilities, Food, Service shops, Information, Accommodation, Other shops
M8	4–5	RoadChef	Harthill	Fuel, Disabled facilities, Food, Service shops, Conference facilities
M9	9	Moto	Stirling	Fuel, Disabled facilities, Food, Service shops, Information, Accommodation, Other shops
M11	8	Welcome Break	Birchanger Green	Fuel, Disabled facilities, Food, Service shops, Accommodation, Conference facilities
M18	5	Moto	Doncaster North	Fuel, Disabled facilities, Food, Service shops, Information, Accommodation, Other shops
M20	8	RoadChef	Maidstone	Fuel, Disabled facilities, Food, Service shops, Information, Accommodation
M23	11	Moto	Pease Pottage	Fuel, Disabled facilities, Food, Service shops, Information, Accommodation, Other shops
M25	5–6	RoadChef	Clacket Lane	Fuel, Disabled facilities, Food, Service shops, Accommodation
M25	30	Moto	Thurrock	Fuel, Disabled facilities, Food, Service shops, Information, Accommodation, Other shops
M27	3–4	RoadChef	Rownhams	Fuel, Disabled facilities, Food, Service shops, Accommodation
M40	8	Welcome Break	Oxford	Fuel, Disabled facilities, Food, Service shops, Accommodation, Conference facilities
M40	10	Moto	Cherwell Valley	Fuel, Disabled facilities, Food, Service shops, Information, Accommodation, Other shops, Conference facilities
M40	12–13	Welcome Break	Warwick	Fuel, Disabled facilities, Food, Service shops, Accommodation, Conference facilities
M42	2	Welcome Break	Hopwood Park	Fuel, Disabled facilities, Food, Service shops, Other shops
M42	10	Moto	Tamworth	Fuel, Disabled facilities, Food, Service shops, Information, Accommodation, Other shops, Conference facilities
M48	1	Moto	Severn View	Fuel, Disabled facilities, Food, Service shops, Information, Accommodation, Other shops
M50	4	Welcome Break	Ross Spur	Fuel, Disabled facilities, Food, Service shops
M56	14	RoadChef	Chester	Fuel, Disabled facilities, Food, Service shops, Information, Accommodation
M61	6–7	First Motorway	Bolton West	Fuel, Disabled facilities, Food, Service shops, Accommodation, Conference facilities
M62	7–9	Welcome Break	Burtonwood	Fuel, Disabled facilities, Food, Service shops, Accommodation
M62	18–19	Moto	Birch	Fuel, Disabled facilities, Food, Service shops, Information, Accommodation, Other shops, Conference facilities
M62	25–26	Welcome Break	Hartshead Moor	Fuel, Disabled facilities, Food, Service shops, Accommodation, Conference facilities
M62	33	Moto	Ferrybridge	Fuel, Disabled facilities, Food, Service shops, Information, Other shops
M74	4–5	RoadChef	Bothwell	Fuel, Disabled facilities, Food, Service shops
M74	5–6	RoadChef	Hamilton	Fuel, Disabled facilities, Food, Service shops, Information, Accommodation, Conference facilities
M74	11–12	Cairn Lodge	Happendon	Fuel, Disabled facilities, Food, Service shops, Conference facilities
M74	12–13	Welcome Break	Abington	Fuel, Disabled facilities, Food, Service shops, Accommodation, Conference facilities
M74	16	RoadChef	Annandale Water	Fuel, Disabled facilities, Food, Service shops, Accommodation
M74	22	Welcome Break	Gretna Green	Fuel, Disabled facilities, Food, Service shops, Accommodation, Conference facilities
M90	6	Moto	Kinross Sevices	Fuel, Disabled facilities, Food, Service shops, Information, Accommodation, Other shops

All Granada motorway services have been renamed Moto from the end of July 2001

A
B
C
D
1
2
3
4
5
3.2 miles to 1 inch
0 2 4 6 8 10 miles
0 2 4 6 8 10 km
2 km to 1 cm
Crane Islands
Godrevy Island
Navax Point
Tehidy
Coombe
Gwithian
Kehelland
Tuckingmill
Camborne
Roseworthy
Barbara Hepworth Museum
The Island
Tate St Ives
St Ives
St Ives Bay
Carn Naun Pt
The Carrack's
Gurnard's Head
Porthmeor
Trendrine Hill
247
Zennor
Halsetown
Towednack
Carbis Bay
A3074
Phillack
Hayle
Lelant
Connor Downs
Angarrack
Barripper
Gwinear
Rosewarne
Carnhell Green
Praze-an-Beeble
Amalebra
Cripplesease
Trencrom Hill
Fort (NT)
Chysauster Ancient Village
Nancledra
Pendeen Watch
Lower Boscaswell
Morvah
252
Bojewyan
Pendeen
Levant Steam Engine (NT)
Trewellard
Botallack
Carnyorth
Cape Cornwall
The Brisons
St Just
Carn Leskys
New Mill
Whitecross
Canon's Town
St Erth
St Erth Praze
Fraddam
Leedstown
Crowan
Townshend
Crowlas
Ludgvan
A30
Madron
Heamoor
Gulval
Penzance
Trengwainton (NT)
A3071
Newbridge
Tremethick Cross
Longrock
Chyandour
St Hilary
Relubbus
Godolphin House
Godolphin Cross
Goldsithney
Trescowe
Nancegollan
Crowntown
Bosavern
Kelynack
Carn Euny Ancient Village
Sancreed
Drift Resr
Penzance
Buryas Bridge
Tredavoe
Newlyn
St Michael's Mount (NT)
Marazion
Perranuthnoe
Germoe
Tregonning Hill
A394
Breage
Sithney
Ashton
Rinsey
Praa Sands
Cudden Point
Trewavas Head
Porthleven
Land's End
Brane
Catchall
Lower Drift
Kerris
Paul
Whitesand Bay
Sennen Cove
A30
Crows-an-wra
Mousehole
St Clement's Isle
Land's End
Longships
Sennen
Trevescan
Land's End
St Buryan
Boleigh
Burial Chamber
Lamorna Cove
MOUNT'S BAY
Minack Theatre Visitor Centre
Porthcurno
Treen
St Levan
Cribba Head
Gwennap Head
Logan Rock
Bereppe
Gunwalloe
Poldhu Cove
Poldhu Point
Porth Mellin
Mullion Cove
Mullion Island
Predannack Wollas
Wolf Rock
B3306
B3311
B3309
B3315
B3283
B3301
B3302
B3303
B3280
B3304
A
B
C
D

D
E
F
G
3
Newquay
Towan Head
Fistral Bay
Newquay Bay
Sea Life Centre
Newquay Zoo
Porth
Newquay Cornwall
Trebudannon
Colan
Mountjoy
Quintrell Downs
Newquay Pearl
Kestle Mill
Retyn
Columb Major
Castle-an-Dinas
Victoria
Roche
Bodwen
Bilberry
Bugle
Luxulyan
Stenalees
Penwithick
Carthew
Ruddlemoor
Ruthvoes
Trevarren
St Columb Road
Indian Queens
Fraddon
Blue Anchor
Retew
Treviscoe
St Dennis
Hensbarrow Downs
Nanpean
Foxhole
Wheal Martyn
Eden Project
St Blazey
Boscoppa
High Street
Trewoon
St Mewan
ST AUSTELL
Polgooth
Sticker
Hewas Water
St Stephen
Coombe
Scarcewater
Brighton
New Mills
Mitchell
Summercourt
Chapel Town
St Enoder
Pentire
West Pentire
Crantock
Holywell Bay
Penhale Point
Holywell
Carines
Ligger Pt
Holywell Bay Fun Park
Cubert
Penhale Sands
Mount
Ligger or Perran Bay
Rejerrah
Newlyn East
Lappa Valley Rly
Newlyn Downs
Carland Cross
Trerice (NT)
Rose
Perranporth
Goonhavern
Bolingey
Perranzabuloe
Zelah
Bawden Rocks or Man and his Man
St Agnes Head
Trevellas
St Agnes
Penhallow
Callestock Cider Farm
Callestick
Mithian
St. Agnes Leisure Park
Goonbell
Truthan
St Allen
Trispen
St Erme
Tregear
Ladock
Trelassick
Grampound Road
Grampound
Creed
Trewithen
Probus
Tresillian
St Ewe
Lost Gardens of Heligan
Polmassick
Trenarren
Pentewan
Penare Point
Mevagissey
Chapel Point
Porthtowan
Mount Hawke
Shortlanesend
Kenwyn
Three Burrows
Tregavethan
Portreath
Mawla
Blackwater
Bridge
Illogan
Threemilestone
Gloweth
Cornwall County Mus
Cathedral
Truro
St Clement
Merther
Scorrier
Chacewater
Baldhu
Cornish Goldsmiths
Redruth
St Day
Twelveheads
Cross Lanes
Kea
Malpas
Playing Place
Lamorran
St Michael Penkevil
Old Kea
Trewarthenick
Tregony
Ruan Lanihorne
Trevarrick
St Michael Caerhays
Portholland
Gorran Churchtown
Gorran Haven
Maenease Point
Boswinger
Penare
Dodman Point
Veryan Bay
Portloe
Veryan
Carne
Gerrans Bay
Nare Head
Pool
Carn Brea
Pennance
Lanner
Carharrack
Gwennap
Bissoe
Carnon Downs
Perranwell Sta.
Cornish Engines (NT)
Four Lanes
Penhalvean
Perranarworthal
Ponsanooth
Devoran
Carclew
Penpol
Trelissick (NT)
Trelissick
Philleigh
Feock
Troon
CORNWALL
Stithians
Stithian's Resr
Mylor Bridge
Carrick Roads
St Just in Roseland
Trewithian
Portscatho
Gerrans
Greeb Point
Burras
Porkellis
Rame
Long Downs
Mabe Burnthouse
Penryn
Mylor
Flushing
St. Mawes Castle
St Mawes
Pendennis
Pendennis Point
Falmouth
Budock Water
Treverva
Penjerrick
Falmouth Bay
Bohortha
St Anthony
Zone Point
Edgcumbe
Seworgan
Wendron
Brill
Constantine
Mawnan Smith
Glendurgan (NT)
Maen Porth
Rosemullion Head
Mawnan
Helston
Gweek
Cornish Seal Sanctuary
Porth Navas
Trebah Garden
Helford
Trelowarren
Mawgan
Garras
Manaccan
St Anthony
Nare Point
St Martin
Tunnel
Tregidden
Newtown in St Martin
Porthallow
Porthoustock
Manacle Point
The Manacles
St Keverne
Traboe
Tumuli
St. Winwaloe
Crosslanes
Cury
Goonhilly Downs
Mullion
Penhale
Lowland Pt
Coverack
Gwenter
Ruan Major
Kuggar
Ruan Minor
Black Head
Cadgwith
Grade
Toll
Kynance Cove
Landewednack
Lizard
Hot Point
Lizard Point
A30
A39
A390
A391
A392
A393
A394
A3047
A3058
A3075
A3076
A3078
A3083
B3274
B3279
B3275
B3285
B3284
B3277
B3287
B3273
B3289
B3297
B3298
B3300
B3280
B3291
B3293
B3296
1
2
3
4
5

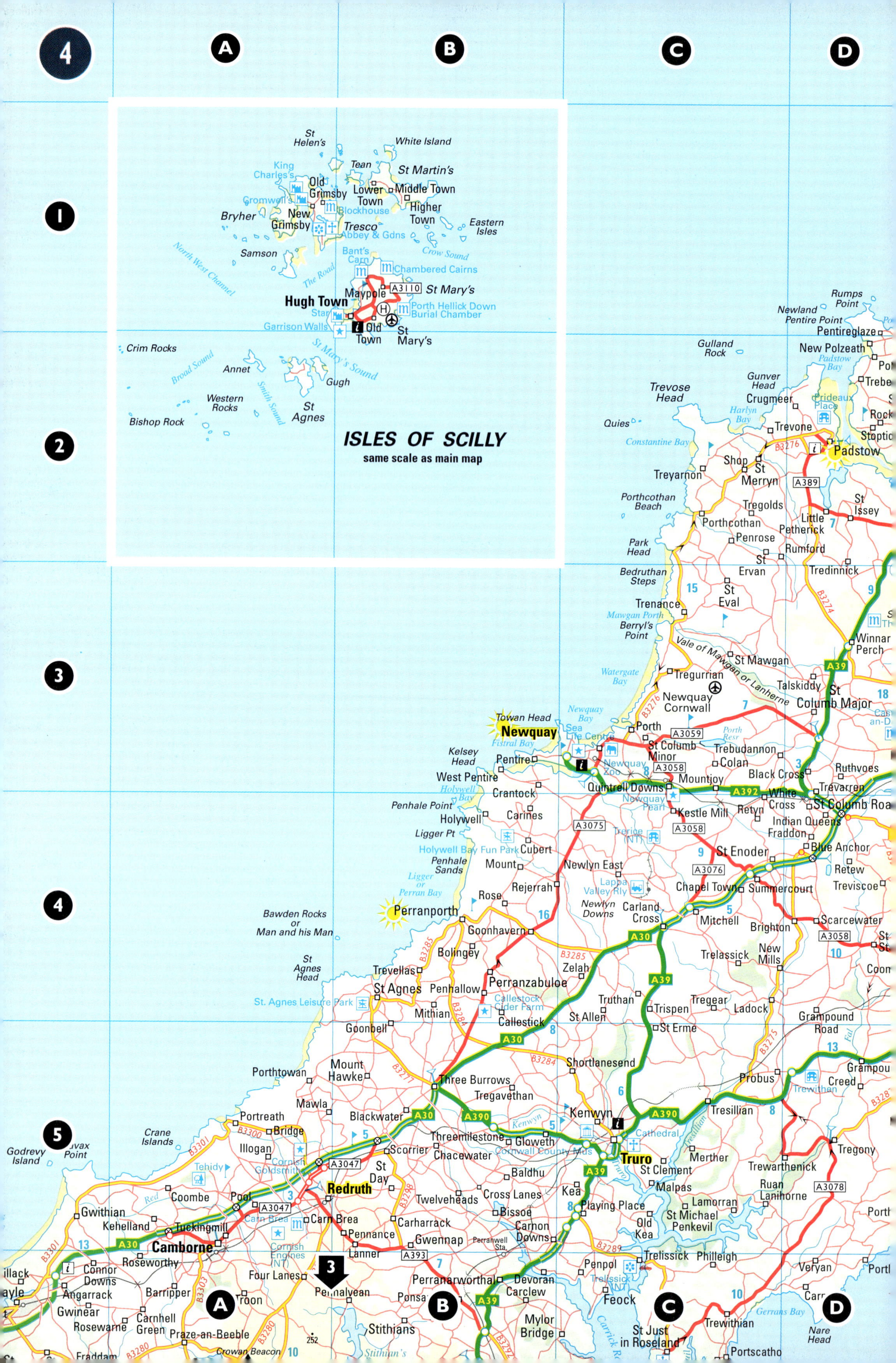
4
A
B
C
D
1
2
3
4
5
ISLES OF SCILLY
same scale as main map
St Helen's
White Island
Tean
St Martin's
King Charles's
Old Grimsby
Lower Town
Middle Town
Higher Town
Cromwell's
Blockhouse
Bryher
New Grimsby
Tresco
Abbey & Gdns
Eastern Isles
Samson
North West Channel
Crow Sound
Bant's Carn
Chambered Cairns
The Road
Maypole
A3110
St Mary's
Hugh Town
Star
Porth Hellick Down Burial Chamber
Garrison Walls
Old Town
Crim Rocks
St Mary's Sound
Broad Sound
Annet
Gugh
Western Rocks
Smith Sound
St Agnes
Bishop Rock
Rumps Point
Newland
Pentire Point
Pentireglaze
Gulland Rock
New Polzeath
Padstow Bay
Gunver Head
Trevose Head
Crugmeer
Prideaux Place
Harlyn Bay
Quies
Trevone
Constantine Bay
B3276
Padstow
Shop
St Merryn
Treyarnon
A389
Porthcothan Beach
Tregolds
St Issey
Porthcothan
Little Petherick
Penrose
Park Head
Rumford
St Ervan
Tredinnick
Bedruthan Steps
St Eval
B3274
Trenance
Mawgan Porth
Berryl's Point
Winnar Perch
Vale of Mawgan or Lanherne
St Mawgan
Watergate Bay
A39
Tregurrian
Newquay Cornwall
Talskiddy
St Columb Major
B3276
Towan Head
Newquay Bay
Newquay
Sea Life Centre
Porth
A3059
Fistral Bay
St Columb Minor
Trebudannon
Kelsey Head
Pentire
Newquay Zoo
A3058
Colan
Black Cross
Ruthvoes
West Pentire
Quintrell Downs
Mountjoy
A392
White Cross
Trevarren
St Columb Road
Holywell Bay
Crantock
Newquay Pearl
Kestle Mill
Retyn
Indian Queens
Penhale Point
Holywell
Cubert
Carines
A3075
Trerice (NT)
A3058
Fraddon
Blue Anchor
Ligger Pt
St Enoder
Holywell Bay Fun Park
Penhale Sands
Mount
Newlyn East
A3076
Retew
Ligger or Perran Bay
Rejerrah
Lappa Valley Rly
Chapel Town
Summercourt
Treviscoe
Rose
Newlyn Downs
Carland Cross
Mitchell
Perranporth
Brighton
Scarcewater
Bawden Rocks or Man and his Man
Goonhavern
A30
A3058
Bolingey
B3285
Zelah
Trelassick
New Mills
St Agnes Head
B3285
Trevellas
Perranzabuloe
A39
St Agnes
Penhallow
Callestock Cider Farm
Truthan
Tregear
Ladock
St. Agnes Leisure Park
Mithian
St Allen
Trispen
Grampound Road
Callestick
Goonbell
B3284
St Erme
B3284
A30
B3275
Porthtowan
Mount Hawke
Shortlanesend
Grampound
B3277
Three Burrows
Probus
Creed
Tregavethan
Trewithen
Mawla
Portreath
Blackwater
A30
A390
Kenwyn
A390
Tresillian
Crane Islands
B3300
Bridge
Threemilestone
Gloweth
Cathedral
Godrevy Island
Navax Point
Illogan
B3301
Scorrier
Chacewater
Cornwall County Mus
Truro
Merther
Tregony
A3047
St Day
Tehidy
Cornish Goldsmiths
Baldhu
A39
St Clement
Trewarthenick
Redruth
Coombe
Pool
B3298
Twelveheads
Cross Lanes
Kea
Malpas
Ruan Lanihorne
A3078
Gwithian
A3047
Carn Brea
Bissoe
Playing Place
Lamorran
Kehelland
Tuckingmill
Carn Brea
Carharrack
Carnon Downs
Old Kea
St Michael Penkevil
Camborne
Pennance
Gwennap
Perranwell Sta.
B3289
A30
Cornish Engines (NT)
Lanner
A393
Trelissick
Philleigh
Connor Downs
Roseworthy
Penpol
Veryan
Angarrack
Four Lanes
Perranarworthal
Devoran
Trelissick Gdn
Gwinear
Barripper
Troon
Ponsa
Carclew
Feock
Carrick Roads
Gerrans Bay
Rosewarne
Carnhell Green
Praze-an-Beeble
Pennance
Stithians
Mylor Bridge
St Just in Roseland
Trewithian
Nare Head
Fraddam
B3280
Crowan Beacon
252
Stithians Res
Portscatho
B3303
B3297
3

D
E
F
G
5
Fire Beacon Point
Tresparrett Posts
Collamoor Head
Langdon
South Wheatley
Caudwor
Maxworthy
Troswell
West Curry
Clubworthy
Bennacott
Luffincott
Chapmans Well
North
East
Boscastle Pottery
Boscastle
Marshgate
Lesnewth
Otterham
Treias
6
irbstow
Canworthy Water
Brazacott
Giles on the Heath
Trevalga
Tintagel Head
Tintagel Old Post Office (NT)
Bossiney
Tintagel
B3263
B3266
B3262
Hallworthy
Treneglos
Tremaine
North Petherwin
Polapit Tamar
Ladycross
Werrington
Yeolmbridge
Lawrence House (NT)
Treknow
Trewarmett
Davidstow
Trewassa
Tremail
Tresmeer
Egloskerry
Langore
St Stephens
Start Point
Trebarwith
B3314
A39
A395
17
Tregeare
Launceston Steam Rly
Red Down
Kensey
Ottery
Delabole
Rockhead
Camelford
St Clether
Laneast
Downhead
Trewen
Pipers Pool
Launceston
1
Tregadillett
Kennards House
Treligga
Westdowns
Port Isaac Bay
Valley Truckle
Lanteglos
Trewalder
Helstone
Tresinney
Lower Moor
New Park
Buttern Hill 346
Bray Down 346
Polyphant
A30
Altarnun
Fivelanes
Lewannick
South Petherwin
Port Isaac
Port Gaverne
Port Quin
Long Cross Victorian Gdns
St Teath
Rough Tor 400
Brown Willy 420
Garrow Tor
369
Trelights
Pendoggett
Tregeare Rounds
Michaelstow
Codda
B3257
Lezant
Trekenner
Trebullett
Congdon's Shop
St Endellion
B3314
Allen
De Lank
B O D M I N
M O O R
Bolventor
Smallacombe Downs
Trebartha
North Hill
Coad's Green
Inny
St Kew
Trelill
11
13
St Breward
Row
St Tudy
St Kew Highway
Kilmar Tor 390
15
2
Windmill
Chapel Amble
C O R N W A L L
Treworнан
Bodieve
Kelly
St Mabyn
Blisland
Dozmary Pool
Camel Trail
Trevanson
Wadebridge
Egloshayle
21
Temple
Brown Gelly Downs 342
Siblyback Resr
Henwood
Bathpool
Rillaton Mill
Linkinhorne
Bray Shop
South Hill
Upton
Upton Cross
St Breock
Inscribed Stone
A389
Pencarrow
Camel
Hellandbridge
Helland
Cardinham Moor
Colliford Reservoir
Hurlers Stone Circle
Minions
Caradon Hill
Common Moor
B3254
Golberdon
Haye
Burlawn
Washaway
Maidenwell
Warleggan
Darite
Trevigro
Monolith
Lane-end
Dunmere
Bodmin
Cardinham
Mount
St Neot
King Doniert's Stone
Trethevy Quoit
Middlehill
Tremar
St Breock Downs
Fiddler
Ruthernbridge
Nanstallon
St Lawrence
St Cleer
St Ive
A390
Dobwalls Family Adventure Park
Ley
8
Withiel
Bodmin & Wenford Rly
A389
12
A38
Liskeard
Merrymeet
Pengover Green
3
St Wenn
Lanivet
Bodmin Parkway Sta.
Doublebois
Dobwalls
Trevelmond
Tregonetha
A30
Trebyan
Lanhydrock House
West Taphouse
East Taphouse
Seaton
Menheniot
B3266
Fowey
A390
Braddock Down 1643
St Pinnock
East Looe
Lamellion
Blunts
B3274
Victoria
13
Lockengate
Sweetshouse
Restormel
Boconnoc
Horningtops
Roche
Bodwen
Redmoor
B3359
St Keyne
B3254
Trewidland
Bylane End
A38
Bilberry
Lostwithiel
Bridgend
Herodsfoot
Bugle
Lanlivery
Couch's Mill
Bocaddon
Duloe
Trerulefoot
St Dennis
Luxulyan
A387
Widegates
11
Tredinnick
B3274
Hensbarrow Downs
Stenalees
Lerryn
West Looe
Lanreath
Sandplace
Morval
Hessenford
Polbathic
Nanpean
Carthew
Penwithick
Penpillick
A390
Muchlarnick
B3253
9
B3247
Ruddlemoor
A391
Trethurgy
St Blazey
Tywardreath Highway
St Veep
Pelynt
St Martin
Seaton
4
Foxhole
Wheal Martyn
Eden Project
St Blazey Gate
Golant
Penpoll
Looe
Downderry
Portwrinkle
Tywardreath
High Street
Boscoppa
Par
A3082
Lescrow
Trenewan
A387
Looe Bay
Trewoon
Holmbush
A3082
Polkerris
Bodinnick
Porthallow
West Looe
East Looe
St Mewan
ST AUSTELL
A390
Carlyon Bay
Charlestown
St Austell Bay
Fowey
Lansallos
St George's or Looe Island
Whitsand
A390
Menabilly
Polruan
Lantivet Bay
Polperro
Sticker
Polgooth
Porthpean
St Catherine's
Pencarrow Head
Hewas Water
Gribbin Head
5
Trenarren
Black Head
B3273
Pentewan
8
St Ewe
Lost Gardens of Heligan
Penare Point
Mevagissey Bay
3.2 miles to 1 inch
0 2 4 6 8 10 miles
0 2 4 6 8 10 km
2 km to 1 cm
5
Mevagissey
Trevarrick
St Michael Caerhays
Chapel Point
Gorran Churchtown
Gorran Haven
Maenease Point
Boswinger
Penare
Veryan Bay
Dodman Point
D
E
F
G

A
B
C
D
20
1
2
3
4
5
Helebridge
Marhamchurch
Widemouth Bay
Bridgerule
Pyworthy
Rydon
Chasty
Yeomadon
Week Orchard
Coppathorne
Dizzard Point
Poundstock
Tregole
Treskinnick Cross
Tinney
Herdicott
Corfcott Green
Whitstone
Week St Mary
North Tamerton
Crackington Haven
Cambeak
St Gennys
Trewint
A39
Jacobstow
Wainhouse Corner
Crackington
Trebarrow
Tetcott
Tamar
19
15
Tresparrett Posts
West Curry
Luffincott
Chapmans Well
South Wheatley
Fire Beacon Point
Collamoor Head
Langdon
Caudworthy
Maxworthy
Clubworthy
Trespparett
B3263
Marshgate
Troswell
Bennacott
Boyton
Boscastle
Boscastle Pottery
Lesnewth
Canworthy Water
Otterham
Trelash
Warbstow
Brazacott
Tintagel Head
Trevalga
Tintagel Old Post Office (NT)
Bossiney
Tintagel
Tremaine
Treneglos
Hallworthy
North Petherwin
Ladycross
Polapit Tamar
Werrington
Treknow
Trewarmett
Davidstow
Tresmeer
Egloskerry
Langore
Yeolmbridge
Start Point
Trebarwith
Trewassa
Tremail
17
Tregeare
Launceston Steam Rly
St Stephens
Newport
Lawrence House (NT)
B3314
B3266
Delabole
Rockhead
Camelford
A395
Red Down
St Clether
Pipers Pool
Launceston
Treligga
Westdowns
Port Isaac Bay
Valley Truckle
Lower Moor
New Park
Laneast
Downhead
Trewen
Tregadillett
Kennards House
Port Isaac
Port Quin
Port Gaverne
Trewalder
Lanteglos
Tresinney
Bray Down
Buttern Hill
346
Polyphant
South Petherwin
Long Cross Victorian Gdns
Helstone
Rough Tor
400
Altarnun
Fivelanes
Lewannick
Trelights
Pendoggett
St Teath
St Endellion
Tregeare Rounds
Michaelstow
Garrow Tor
Brown Willy
420
369
A30
Codda
Congdon's Shop
Lezant
Trekenner
Trebullett
Trelill
11
St Kew
St Breward
13
B O D M I N
Bolventor
Trebartha
North Hill
Coad's Green
M O O R
Smallacombe Downs
Kilmar Tor
390
St Kew Highway
St Tudy
Row
C O R N W A L L
Chapel Amble
Bodieve
Kelly
St Mabyn
Henwood
Bathpool
Linkinhorne
Rilla Mill
Bray Shop
South Hill
Camel Trail
Trevanson
Wadebridge
Blisland
Temple
Brown Gelly Downs
342
Dozmary Pool
Siblyback Resr
Upton
Upton Cross
St Breock
Egloshayle
Camel
Cardinham Moor
Colliford Reservoir
Hurlers Stone Circle
A389
Pencarrow
Hellandbridge
Helland
Maidenwell
Minions
Common Moor
Caradon Hill
Golberdon
Haye
Inscribed Stone
Burlawn
5
Washaway
7
Lane-end
Warleggan
Darite
Pensilva
Trevigro
Monolith
Cardinham
Middlehill
King Doniert's Stone
Trethevy Quoit
Dunmere
Bodmin
Mount
St Neot
Tremar
St Ive
Rutherbridge
Nanstallon
St Cleer
A390
St Lawrence
Withiel
St Wenn
Bodmin & Wenford Rly
Ley
Dobwalls Family Adventure Park
Liskeard
Merrymeet
Quethiock
12
A38
Doublebois
Dobwalls
Pengover Green
Lanivet
Bodmin Parkway Sta.
East Taphouse
West Taphouse
Trevelmond
Menheniot
Tregonetha
Trebyan
Lanhydrock House
St Pinnock
Lamellion
Blunts
Victoria
Restormel
Braddock Down 1643
Roche
Lockengate
Sweetshouse
Redmoor
Boconnoc
Horningtops
Bodwen
B3359
Trewidland
Bylane End
Bilberry
Lostwithiel
Bridgend
Herodsfoot
St Keyne
Duloe
Treruletoot
Bugle
Luxulyan
Lanlivery
Couch's Mill
Bocaddon
Widegates
Tredinnick
St Dennis
Hensbarrow Downs
Stenalees
A387
Hessenford
Polbathic
Nanpean
Carthew
A391
Penwithick
Lerryn
Lanreath
Sandplace
Morval
Trethurgy
Penpillick
Muchlarnick
Ruddlemoor
St Blazey
Tywardreath Highway
Golant
St Veep
Pelynt
St Martin
Seaton
Foxhole
Eden Project
Wheal Martyn
St Blazey Gate
Tywardreath
Penpoll
Looe
Looe Bay
Downderry
Portwrinkle
High Street
Boscoppa
Par
A3082
Lescrow
Trenewan
Trewoon
Holmbush
Polkerris
Bodinnick
Porthallow
West Looe
East Looe
St Mewan
St Austell
Carlyon Bay
Charlestown
St Austell Bay
Menabilly
Fowey
Polruan
Lansallos
Polperro
St George's or Looe Island
Whitsand Bay
Sticker
Polgooth
Porthpean
St. Catherine's
Pencarrow Head
Lantivet Bay
Hewas Water
Gribbin Head
Trenarren
Pentewan
Black Head
Lost Gardens of Heligan
St Ewe
Penare Point
Mevagissey Bay
Mevagissey

Anvil Corner
Dunsland Cross
Brandis Corner
Highampton
Hatherleigh
Lydacott
Basset's Cross
Halwill Forest
Graddon Moor
Exbourne
Honeychurch
North Tawton
Jacobstowe
Sampford Courtenay
Nymet Tracey
Halwill
Halwill Junction
Beaworthy
Inwardleigh
Clawton
Northlew
Oak Cross
Ashbury
Itton
Upcott
Quoditch
Broadbury
Folly Gate
Belstone Corner
Taw Green
Spreyton
Okehampton
Ashwater
Henford
Eworthy
Germansweek
Southcott
South Tawton
Sticklepath
Thorndon Cross
Yelland
Boasley Cross
Belstone
Okehampton Camp
Finch Foundry
South Zeal
Whiddon Down
Virginstow
Hewton
Roadford Resr
Bratton Clovelly
Meldon
Cawsand Hill
Throwleigh
Drewsteignton
Castle Drogo
Gridley Corner
Bridestowe
Sourton
Yes Tor
High Willhays
Wonson
Broadwoodwidger
Cross Green
Gidleigh
Easton
Murchington
Thrushelton
Stowford
Bridestowe & Stourton Common
Okement Hill
Hangingstone Hill
Chagford
Lewdown
Lewtrenchard
Shortacombe
Cranmere Pool
Great Kneeset
Frenchbeer
Moretonhampstead
Lifton
Tinhay
Portgate
Allerford
Lydford
Amicombe Hill
Whitehorse Hill
DEVON
Downton
Danger Zone
Black Ridge
Fernworthy Resr
Coryton
Lydford Gorge (NT)
Beardon
Sittaford Tor
Lettaford
Marystow
Cut Hill
Easdon Tor
Lawhitton
Kelly
North Brentor
Settlements
White Ridge
Chillaton
Black Down
Willsworthy
Warren House
Grimspound
Bradstone
Brent Tor
Lynch Tor
DARTMOOR
Felldownhead
Horndon
Hameldown Tor
Cowsic Head
South Brentor
Blackdown
Cocks Hill
Rough Tor
Postbridge
Hamel Down
Dunterton
Milton Abbot
Mary Tavy
Higher White Tor
Longcross
Cudlipptown
Treburley
Rezare
Lamerton
Peter Tavy
Bellever
Widecombe in the Moor
Cox Tor
Great Mis Tor
Cator Court
Church House (NT)
Bonehill Down
Sydenham Damerel
Cholwell
Horsebridge
Merrivale
Rundlestone
Two Bridges
Babeny
Corndon Tor
Stoke Climsland
Tavistock
Merrivale Prehistoric Settlement
Princetown
Downgate
Luckett
Latchley
Gulworthy
Sampford Spiney
High Moorland Visitor Centre
Royal Hill
Ponsworthy
Dartmeet
Buckland in the Moor
Chilsworthy
Whitchurch
Gunnislake
Walkhampton Common
Hexworthy
Poundsgate
Kelly Bray
Kit Hill
Hingston Down
Higher Walreddon
Whiteworks
Harrowbarrow
St Ann's Chapel
Albaston
Morwellham Quay Mus.
Horrabridge
DARTMOOR NATIONAL PARK
Ryder's Hill
River Dart
Dupath Well
Morwellham
Walkhampton
Callington
Cotehele (NT)
Buckland Monachorum
Dousland
Burrator Resr
Cater's Beam
Holne
Calstock
The Garden House
Yelverton
Sheepstor
Scorriton
Abbey
Ashton
St Dominick
Crapstone
Meavy
Buckfast
Bere Alston
Buckland Abbey (NT)
Dean Moor
Buckfastleigh
St Mellion
Milton Combe
Maristow House
Clearbrook
Pillaton
Cadover Bridge
Brent Moor
Dean
Shaugh Prior
Shell Top
Stall Moor
Shipley Bridge
Penn Moor
Harford Moor
Ugborough Moor
Cargreen
Bere Ferrers
Bickleigh
Harbourneford
Hatt
Roborough
Didworthy
Landulph
Tamerton Foliot
Lee Moor
Botusfleming
Plymouth City
South Brent
Landrake
Carkeel
Trematon
PLYMOUTH
Cornwood
Harford
Saltash
Plym Forest
Lutton
Lincombe
Markwell
St Stephens
St Budeaux
Crownhill
Plym Bridge
Drakeland Corner
Dartmoor Wildlife Park
Ugborough Beacon
Avonwick
St Germans
Egg Buckland
Sparkwell
Bittaford
Diptford
Antony Ho. (NT)
Crabtree
Ivybridge
Ugborough
Sheviock
Devonport
Lee Mill Bridge
North Huish
Torpoint
Plympton
Antony
Royal Citadel
Saltram (NT)
Crafthole
St John
Stonehouse
Westlake
Bickham
Cremyll
National Marine Aquarium
Oreston
Elburton
Brownston
Gara Bridge
Danger Zone
Drake's Island
Turnchapel
Plymstock
Sequer's Bridge
Ermington
Freathy
Millbrook
Mount Edgcumbe
Brixton
Yealmpton
Modbury
Topsham Bridge
Hooe
Goosewell
Dunstone
Kingsand
The Sound
Staddiscombe
Kitley
Ford
Flete
Cawsand Bay
Torr
Rame
Cawsand
Plymouth Breakwater
Down Thomas
Knighton
Holbeton
Ashford
Loddiswell
Woodleigh
Penlee
Heybrook Bay
Wembury Bay
Wembury
Battisborough Cross
St Ann's Chapel
Rame Head
Great Mew Stone
Worswell
Kingston
Aveton Gifford
Gara Pt
Houghton
Noss Mayo
Ringmore
Venn
Netton
Bigbury
Churchstow
Stoke Point
Beacon
A3072
A3079
A386
A30
A388
A390
A38
A3064
A374
A379
A3121
A382
B3260
B3212
B3357
B3362
B3257
B3413
B3416
B3247
B3186
B3196
B3216
B3217
B3219
B3215
7
8
10
21

8
A
B
C
D
1
2
3
4
5
7
Tavistock
Gulworthy
A390
Latchley
Whitchurch
Prehistoric Settlement
Sampford Spiney
Princetown
High Moorland Visitor Centre
Royal Hill
407
445
Walkhampton Common
Hexworthy
Whiteworks
Dartmeet
Ponsworthy
Poundsgate
Tor
Chilsworthy
Gunnislake
Kingston Down
Harrowbarrow
St Ann's Chapel
Albaston
Morwellham Quay
Morwellham
Higher Walreddon
Horrabridge
Walkhampton
Dousland
Yelverton
Sheepstor
Burrator Resr
Meavy
Dupath Well
Cotehele (NT)
Calstock
Buckland Monachorum
The Garden House
Crapstone
DARTMOOR
NATIONAL PARK
Ryder's Hill
Cater's Beam
River Dart
Holne
Scorriton
Abbey
Buckfast
Buckfastleigh
Dean Moor
Ashton
St Dominick
St Mellion
Pillaton
A388
Bere Alston
Buckland Abbey (NT)
Milton Combe
Maristow House
Clearbrook
A386
Shaugh Prior
Cadover Bridge
Shell Top
475
Penn Moor
468
480
Stall Moor
Harford Moor
Ugborough Moor
Brent Moor
Shipley Bridge
Harbourneford
Didworthy
South Brent
Dean
Cargreen
Bere Ferrers
Hatt
Landulph
Tamerton Foliot
Bickleigh
Roborough
Plymouth City
Lee Moor
Botusfleming
A38
Landrake
Trematon
Saltash
St Stephens
Toll
Markwell
St Germans
A374
PLYMOUTH
DEVON
Plym Forest
Plym Bridge
Drakeland Corner
Sparkwell
Lutton
Cornwood
Harford
Dartmoor Wildlife Park
Ugborough Beacon
Bittaford
Ivybridge
Ugborough
Lincombe
Avonwick
Diptford
North Huish
Bickham
St Budeaux
A3064
Crownhill
B3413
A386
Egg Buckland
Crabtree
B3416
Plympton
Lee Mill Bridge
A3121
Antony Ho. (NT)
Devonport
Torpoint
Antony
St John
St John's Lake
Stonehouse
Cremyll
Royal Citadel
A374
Saltram (NT)
National Marine Aquarium
Oreston
Elburton
A379
Plymstock
Brixton
Westlake
Sequer's Bridge
Ermington
Brownston
Gara Bridge
Modbury
Topsham Bridge
Danger Zone
Freathy
B3247
Millbrook
Drake's Island
Turnchapel
Mount Edgcumbe
The Sound
Hooe
Goosewell
Staddiscombe
Kitley
Yealmpton
Dunstone
Ford
Torr
Flete
Holbeton
Kingsand
Cawsand Bay
Cawsand
Rame
Plymouth Breakwater
Down Thomas
Knighton
Wembury
B3186
Rame Head
Penlee Point
Heybrook Bay
Wembury Bay
Great Mew Stone
Worswell
Gara Pt
Noss Mayo
Newton Ferrers
Netton
Battisborough Cross
Stoke Point
Kingston
Houghton
Ringmore
B3392
St Ann's Chapel
Bigbury
A379
Ashford
Loddiswell
Aveton Gifford
Venn
Churchstow
Woodleigh
Beacon Pt
Bigbury-on-Sea
Burgh Island
Bantham
Cookworthy
Kingsbridge
Buckland
Upton
West Alvington
Thurlestone
South Huish
South Milton
Bigbury Bay
Galmpton
A381
Hope
Bolt Tail
Malborough
Bolberry
Salcombe
Soar
Overbeck's Garden (NT)
Overbeck's Museum (NT)
Bolt Head
Santander 24 hrs (summer only)
Roscoff 6-7½ hrs
CHANNEL ISLANDS
location map
Alderney
Guernsey
Herm
Sark
Jersey
same scale as main map
JERSEY
Grosnez (ruins)
Plemont Pt
Greve de Lecq Bay
B55
B33
St John
149
Bouley Bay
Dolmen
Battle of Flowers Museum
St Ouen
56
B31
Carrefour Selous
La Mielle de Morville
St Ouen's Bay
St Peter
B27
German Underground Hosp
Zoo
St Martin
St Catherine's Bay
Mt Orgueil
A12
A10
A8
A9
Dolmen
Maufant
Jersey
A11
67
Five Oaks
A6
B35
B41
A2
A1
Gorey
A13
Corbière Lighthouse
St Brelade
St Aubin
St Aubin's Bay
Peoples Park
La Hougue Bie
A3
Grouville
La Cotte
Elizabeth
ST HELIER
A5
A4
St Peter Port 1hr, Poole 3¼ hrs
Portsmouth 10hrs, Weymouth 3¼ hrs
Noirmont Pt
St Malo 1¼ hrs
La Rocque Pt

9
D
E
F
G
10
Sigford
Bickington
Teigngrace
Kingsteignton
Bishopsteignton
Teignmouth
Ashburton
Combe Cross
West Ogwell
East Ogwell
Bradley Manor
NEWTON ABBOT
Netherton
Shaldon
Combeinteignhead
Stokeinteignhead
Wolborough
Milber
Haccombe
Lower Gabwell
Higher Gabwell
Maidencombe
Babbacombe Bay
Woodland
Denbury
Abbotskerswell
Coffinswell
Daccombe
Barton
Forder Green
Torbryan
Kingskerswell
Landscove
Broadhempston
Woolston Green
Ipplepen
North Whilborough
Edginswell
Babbacombe Model Village
St Marychurch
Buckfast Butterfly & Dartmoor Otter Sanctuary
Compton
Shiphay
Babbacombe
Kent's Cavern
Staverton
Cockington Court
Torre Abbey
TORQUAY
Red Post
Marldon
Cockington
Dartington
Littlehempston
Berry Pomeroy
TORBAY
Blagdon
Shinner's Bridge
Cott
Motor Museum
Totnes
Tigley
Pier
Paignton
Tor Bay
Collaton St Mary
Belsford
Harberton
Bowden
Sharpham House
Zoo
Goodrington
Stoke Gabriel
Ashprington
Bow
Berry Head
Cornworthy
Galmpton
Harbertonford
Tuckenhay
Washbourne
East Cornworthy
Dittisham
Churston Ferrers
Brixham
St Mary's Bay
Sharkham Point
Higher Brixham
Hillhead
Paignton & Dartmouth Steam Railway
Allaleigh
Capton
Downton
Halwell
Hemborough Post
Woodhuish
Woodlands Leisure Park
Dartmouth
Boohay
Scabbacombe Head
Coleton Fishacre (NT)
Blackawton
Kingswear
East Allington
Millcombe
Dartmouth Pottery
Mew Stone
River Dart (Dart Pleasure Craft)
Bowden
Coombe
Stoke Fleming
3.2 miles to 1 inch
0 2 4 6 8 10 miles
0 2 4 6 8 10 km
2 km to 1 cm
Cole's Cross
Merrifield
Strete
Buckland-tout-Saints
Slapton
Start Bay
Slapton Ley
Slapton Sands
Sherford
Stokenham
Frogmore
Chillington
East Charleton
Torcross
Ford
Beeson
Beesands
Dunstone
South Pool
Kellaton
Chivelstone
South Allington
Hallsands
East Prawle
Start Point
Lannacombe Bay
Prawle Point
A38
A383
A381
A380
A3022
A379
A384
A385
A3122
B3205
same scale as main map
ALDERNEY
The Swinge
Fort Quesnard
St Anne
Alderney
same scale as main map
Portsmouth 6½ hrs
Poole 2½ hrs, Weymouth 2½ hrs
GUERNSEY
Grand Havre
Dolmen
Bordeaux
L'Islet
Vale (ruins)
St Sampson
Herm
Saumarez Park & Folk Mus
Vazon Bay
Guernsey Museum
Cas. Cornet
Lihou
Dolmen
St Peter Port
Jethou
Sark
Rocquaine Bay
St Saviour
King's Mill
German Underground Military Hosp
Fort Grey
Guernsey
Sausmarez Manor
La Seigneurie
Brecqhou
110
79
Pleinmont Pt
German Occupation Mus
St Martin
Jerbourg Pt
St Helier 1 hr
St Malo 2 hrs
Little Sark
1
2
3
4
5

10
22
21
7
9
Clapworthy
Bishop's Nympton
George Nympton
Alswear
Mariansleigh
Ash Mill
Knowstone
Rackenford Moor
Romansleigh
King's Nympton
Rowley
Meshaw
Creacombe
Rackenford
Head Bridge
Cadbury Barton
Newhouse Moor
Week
Kings Nympton Sta.
Elstone
Witheridge
Nomansland
Little Dart
Dalch
Cheldon
West Worlington
East Worlington
Thelbridge Barton
Washford Pyne
Chawleigh
Lake
Hele Lane
Cruwys Morchard
Puddington
Pennymoor
Way Village
Ashley
Eggesford
Filleigh
Forches Cross
Eastington
Black Dog
Poughill
Woolfardisworthy
Upham
Cadeleigh
Well Town
Brushford
Coldridge
Nymet Rowland
Lapford
Morchard Bishop
Oldborough
Kennerleigh
Stockleigh English
East Village
Cheriton Fitzpaine
Taw
Bondleigh
Morchard Road Sta.
Ash Bullayne
East Leigh
Down St Mary
Zeal Monachorum
Copplestone Sta.
Copplestone
Upton Hellions
Sandford
Creedy Park
Stockleigh Pomeroy
North Tawton
Bow
Clannaborough Barton
Broadnymett
Nymet Tracey
Coleford
Knowle
Colebrooke
Crediton
Shobrooke
Efford
Thorverton
Itton
Yeoford
Uton
Hookway
Newton St Cyres
Brampford Speke
Upton Pyne
Spreyton
Court Barton
Oldridge
Cowley
Hittisleigh
Tedburn St Mary
South Zeal
Whiddon Down
Cheriton Bishop
Cheriton Cross
Crockernwell
Pathfinder Village
Whitestone
Throwleigh
Drewsteignton
Longdown
Pocombe Bridge
Castle Drogo (NT)
Wonson
Gidleigh
Easton
Dunsford
Murchington
Chagford
Doccombe
Bridford
Dunchideock
Doddiscombsleigh
Shillingford St George
Frenchbeer
Moretonhampstead
Lettaford
North Bovey
Sandluck
Christow
Coombe
Higher Ashton
Lower Ashton
Trusham
Canonteign Falls
Easdon Tor
Manaton
Lustleigh
Becky Falls
Hennock
Grimspound
Hameldown Tor
Hamel Down
Hound Tor Medieval Village
Yarner Wood
House of Marbles & Teign Valley Glass
Haytor Vale
Bovey Tracey
Devon Guild of Craftsmen
Chudleigh
Chudleigh Knighton
Ugbrooke
Widecombe in the Moor
Bonehill Down
Cator Court
Church House (NT)
Dunstone
Rippon Tor
Ilsington
Brimley
Heathfield
Cardew Design
Liverton
Coldeast
Stover
Trago Mills
Preston
Sandygate
Horridge
Sigford
Ponsworthy
Buckland in the Moor
Dartmeet
Poundsgate
Bickington
Teigngrace
Kingsteignton
Highweek
Hedgehog Hospital and Farm
Newton Abbot
Caton
Rew
Combe Cross
Bradley Manor
Ashburton
River Dart
Holne
West Ogwell
East Ogwell
Wolborough
Scorriton
Woodland
Denbury
Abbotskerswell
Buckfast
Abbey
Forder Green
Torbryan
Buckfastleigh
Landscove
Broadhempston
Woolston Green
Ipplepen
North Whilborough
Compton
Edginswell
Dean Moor
Kingskerswell
Daccombe
Barton
Babbacombe Model Village
St Marychurch
Babbacombe Bay
Maidencombe
Higher Gabwell
Stokeinteignhead
Combeinteignhead
Shaldon
Netherton
Teignmouth
Grand Pier
Bishopsteignton
Holcombe
Dawlish
Luton
Little Haldon
Ideford
Ashcombe
Langdon House
Mamhead
Dawlish Warren
Dawlish Warren Sta.
Cockwood
Starcross
Kenton
Powderham
Powderham Castle
Kenn
Kennford
Exminster
Bickham House
Devon and Exeter
Great Haldon
Exmouth
Littleham
Withycombe Raleigh
Lympstone
A La Ronde
Stuart Line Cruises
Exton
Ebford
Topsham
Woodbury
Yettington
Black Hill
Woodbury Salterton
Clyst St George
Westpoint Exhibition Centre
Exeter Ship Canal
Exe
Alphington
Countess Wear
Ide
Exeter
Whipton
Pinhoe
Exwick
Sowton
Clyst Honiton
Exeter Airport
Aylesbeare
Crealy Park
Clyst St Mary
Farringdon
White Cross
Half Way Inn
Rockbeare
Whimple
Broadclyst
Clyst St Lawrence
Westwood
Dog Village
Poltimore
Stoke Canon
Rewe
Nether Exe
Killerton (NT)
Budlake
Up Exe
Silverton
Hele
Bradninch
Langford
Mutterton
Westcott
Plymtree
Clyst
Aunk
Ravenshayes
Fursdon
Cadbury
Bickleigh
Bickleigh Castle
Colebrooke
Cullompton
Butterleigh
Withleigh
Tiverton
Grand Western Houseboat Co.
Brithem Bottom
Ash Thomas
Halberton
Sampford Peverell
Tiverton Parkway Sta.
Templeton
Templeton Bridge
Calverleigh
Loxbeare
Washfield
Bolham
Knightshayes Court (NT)
Exe Valley
Chettiscombe
Chevithorne
Uplowman
East Mere
Pitt
Whitnage
Stoodleigh Beacon
Stoodleigh
Cove
Oakfordbridge
Oakford
Huntsham
Hockworthy
Bampton
Shillingford
Clayhanger
Petton
M5
A361
A377
A30
A38
A380
A3072
A396
A379
A382
A383
A381
A3022
A376
A3052
B3137
B3042
B3220
B3219
B3212
B3193
B3344
B3387
B3192
B3181
B3183
B3182
B3178
B3179
B3391
B3227
B3226
B3096
B3131
B3199

TAUNTON
Bathealton
Chipley
Langford Budville
Bishop's Hull
Rumwell
Bradford-on-Tone
Wilton
Trull
Ruishton
Henlade
Thornfalcon
Greenway
Moor
Drayton
Swell
Isle
Hambridge
Isle Abbotts
Isle Brewers
Curry Mallet
Wrantage
West Hatch
Hatch Beauchamp
Beercrocombe
Hatch Green
23
Staple Fitzpaine
Bickenhall
Pitminster
Corfe
Poundisford Park
Blagdon Hill
Angersleigh
Orchard Portman
Thurlbear
Appley
Greenham
Runnington
Thorne St Margaret
Wellington
West Buckland
Taunton Deane
Rockwell Green
Holywell Lake
Holcombe Rogus
Sampford Arundel
Wrangway
Blackmoor
Ford Street
Wellington Monument (NT)
Burlescombe
Nicholashayne
Black Down Hills
Clayhidon
Rosemary Lane
Churchstanton
SOMERSET
Fyfett
Curland
Staple Hill
Windmill Hill
Ashill
Broadway
Horton
Horton Cross
Puckington
Ilton
Stocklinch
Westport
Barrington Court (NT)
Barrington
Shepton Beauchamp
East Lambrook
West Lambrook
South Petherton
Whitelackington
Seavington St Mary
Ilminster
Donyatt
Kingstone
Dinnington
Lopen
Merriott
Hinton St George
Dowlish Wake
Cricket Malherbie
Chillington
Cudworth
Crewkerne
Appledore
Waterloo Cross
Culmstock
Culm Valley
Hemyock
Hackpen Hill
Stapley
Uffculme
Craddock
Ashill
Bolham Water
Churchingford
Bishopswood
Buckland St Mary
Crock Street
Combe St Nicholas
Northay
Whitestaunton
Wadeford
Chaffcombe
Cricket St Thomas
Smeatharpe
Madford
Marsh
Howley
Newcott
Yarcombe
A303
A30
A358
A35
A38
A373
A375
A3052
M5
Chard
Hewish
Blackborough
Sheldon
Kentisbeare
Dunkeswell
Luppitt
Upottery
Rawridge
Beacon
Wambrook
Forton
Tatworth
South Chard
Winsham
Wayford
Clapton
Clapton Court
Cricket St Thomas
Crinkley Bottom
Forde Abbey
Chard Junction
Kerswell
Broadhembury
Colliton
Luton
Upton
Payhembury
Higher Tale
Colestocks
Monkton
Combe Raleigh
Awliscombe
Godford Cross
Buckerell
Stockland
Stockland Hill
Furley
Membury
Cotleigh
Chardstock
Tytherleigh
Alston
Holditch
Thorncombe
Blackdown
Burstock
Broadwindsor
Pilsdon Pen
Birdsmoor Gate
Marshwood
Bettiscombe
Fishpond Bottom
Marshwood Vale
12
South Bowood
Dalwood
Smallridge
Weycroft
Hawkchurch
Axminster
Wilmington
Widworthy
Loughwood Meeting House (NT)
Honiton
Hamlet
Gittisham
Offwell
Feniton
Higher Cheriton
Fenny Bridges
Alfington
Escot
Shute
Kilmington
Raymond's Hill
Wootton Fitzpaine
Charmouth
Whitchurch Canonicorum
Ryall
Morcombelake
Symondsbury
Chideock
Seatown
Golden Cap
Eype
Broadoak
Fairmile
Cadhay
Ottery St Mary
Farnwood
West Hill
Wiggaton
Tipton St John
Venn Ottery
Harpford
Bowd
Newton Poppleford
Church Green
Putts Corner
Farway
Northleigh
Seaton Junction
Whitford
Musbury
Colyton
Seaton Tramway
Colyford
Combpyne
Rousdon
Uplyme
Lyme Regis
Axmouth
Dowlands
Pinhay
Southleigh
Broad Down
Blackbury Camp
Sand
Sidbury
Sidford
Harcombe
Weston
Salcombe Regis
Donkey Sanctuary
Branscombe
Old Bakery (NT)
Vicarage
Beer
Seaton
Seaton Bay
Marine House
Beer Head
Sidmouth
Pinn
Bicton Park
Otterton
East Budleigh
Fairlynch Arts Centre & Museum
Budleigh Salterton
LYME BAY
3.2 miles to 1 inch
2 km to 1 cm
10 miles
10 km
D
E
F
G
1
2
3
4
5

12
24
11
A
B
C
D
1
2
3
4
5
SOMERSET
DORSET
BLACKMOOR VALE
Drayton
Long Load
Thorney
Kingsbury Episcopi
Stapleton
Ash
Coat
Hambridge
Isle Brewers
Westport
East Lambrook
Martock
West Lambrook
Bower Hinton
Barrington
Barrington Court (NT)
Stocklinch
Shepton Beauchamp
South Petherton
Stoke sub Hamdon
Norton-sub-Hamdon
Priory (NT)
Ham Hill
Montacute
Montacute Ho. (NT)
Tintinhull
Tintinhull Ho. (NT)
Ilchester
Fleet Air Arm Museum
Bridgehampton
Northover
Ashington
Chilthorne Domer
Yeovil Marsh
Mudford
Chilton Cantelo
Marston Magna
Queen Camel
Preston Plucknett
YEOVIL
Odcombe
Chiselborough
Seavington St Michael
Over Stratton
Lopen
Kingstone
Dinnington
Merriott
West Chinnock
East Chinnock
West Coker
North Coker
East Coker
Barwick
Stoford
Hardington Mandeville
Dowlish Wake
Cricket Malherbie
Hinton St George
Chillington
Cudworth
Haselbury Plucknett
Pendomer
Closworth
Sutton Bingham Res
Crewkerne
Cricket St Thomas
Hewish
Crinkley Bottom
Misterton
North Perrott
Hardington Marsh
Halstock
Wayford
Winsham
Clapton
Clapton Court
Seaborough
Drimpton
South Perrott
Mosterton
Whetley Cross
Chedington
Corscombe
East Chelborough
West Chelborough
Ford Abbey
Blackdown
Burstock
Broadwindsor
Pilsdon Pen
Birdsmoor Gate
Marshwood
Pilsdon
Bettiscombe
Fishpond Bottom
Marshwood Vale
Beaminster
Toller Whelme
Stoke Abbott
Parnham
Netherbury
South Bowood
Mapperton
Melplash
Waytown
Salwayash
Broadoak
Whitchurch Canonicorum
Dottery
Ryall
Morcombelake
Symondsbury
Chideock
Charmouth
Lyme Regis
Golden Cap
Seatown
Bridport
Bothenhampton
Eype
West Bay
Walditch
North Hill
Burton Bradstock
Shipton Gorge
Bradpole
Uploders
Loders
Nettlecombe
Powerstock
West Milton
North Poorton
Eggardon Hill
Askerswell
Chilcombe
Puncknowle
Swyre
West Bexington
Kingston Russell Stone Circle
White Hill
Abbotsbury
Abbotsbury Swannery
Abbotsbury Sub-tropical Gardens
Abbey
St. Catherine's Chapel
Chesil Beach
West Fleet
East Fleet
Long Bredy
Litton Cheney
Poor Lot Barrows
Littlebredy
Kingston Russell
Compton Valence
West Compton
Toller Porcorum
Toller Fratrum
Wynford Eagle
Hooke
Higher Kingcombe
Lower Kingcombe
Chilfrome
Lower Wraxall
Cattistock
Chalmington
Rampisham
Uphall
Toller Down Gate
Benville Lane
Evershot
Holywell
Melbury Sampford
Melbury Bubb
Melbury Osmond
Stockwood
Chetnole
Leigh
Yetminster
Ryme Intrinseca
Beer Hackett
Bradford Abbas
Thornford
Lillington
Longburton
Over Compton
Nether Compton
Compton House
Trent
Adber
Rimpton
Sandford Orcas
Corton Denham
Charlton Horethorne
Sutton Montis
The Manor
Poyntington
Milborne Wick
Oborne
Sherborne
Old Castle
Abbey
North Wootton
Folke
Alweston
Caundle Marsh
Holnest
Sandhills
Hermitage
Middlemarsh
Hilfield
Batcombe
Frome St Quentin
Minterne Magna
Minterne
Up Cerne
Up Sydling
Lyon's Gate
Buckland Newton
Alton Pancras
The Giant (NT)
Cerne Abbas
Sydling St Nicholas
Godmanstone
Maiden Newton
Frampton
Grimstone
Forston
Stratton
Bradford Peverell
Charminster
Wolfeton
Tutankhamun Exhibition
Dinosaur Mus
Dorset County Mus
Dorchester
Burton
Stinsford
Hardy's Cottage (NT)
Lower Bockhampton
West Stafford
Winterbourne Abbas
Winterbourne Steepleton
Nine Stones
Martinstown
Hardy Monument
Maiden Castle
Winterborne Came
Whitcombe
Winterborne Monkton
Black Down
Bronkham Hill
Portesham
Rodden
Langton Herring
Chickerell
Charlestown
Upwey
Broadwey
Bincombe
Sutton Poyntz
White Horse
Osmington
Preston
Jordan Hill Roman Temple
Radipole
Overcombe
Osmington Mills
Sea Life Centre
Weymouth Bay
Melcombe Regis
Westham
WEYMOUTH
Brewers Quay
The Timewalk
Nothe Fort
Wyke Regis
Ferry Bridge
Portland Harbour
West Bay
Portland
Fortuneswell
Grove
Easton
Weston
Southwell
Isle of Portland
Bill of Portland
Guernsey 2 hrs, Jersey 3½ hrs & St Malo 5¼ hrs
Stowell
Templecombe
Horsington
Cheriton
Abbas Combe
Yenston
Stowell Hill
Henstridge
Henstridge Ash
Henstridge Marsh
Milborne Port
Purse Caundle
Goathill
Haydon
Stalbridge
Stourton Caundle
Bishop's Caundle
Holwell
Crouch Hill
King's Stag
Kingston
Pulham
Glanvilles Wootton
Hazelbury Bryan
Dunstish
Mappowder
Folly
Plush
Piddletrenthide
White Lackington
Nether Cerne
Piddlehinton
Puddletown
Broadmayne
3.2 miles to 1 inch
0 2 4 6 8 10 miles
0 2 4 6 8 10 km
2 km to 1 cm
A303
A356
A3088
A37
A30
A352
A357
A3030
A3066
A35
A354
A359
A378
B3165
B3162
B3163
B3164
B3157
B3159
B3143
B3146
B3148
B3168

13
D
E
F
G
1
2
3
4
5
26
14
Knap Corner
A30
Donhead St Mary
White Hill
Alvediston
Ebbesborne Wake
A354
Bowerchalk
Woodminton
Shaft
East Stour
Cann
Ludwell
Charlton
Cann Common
Stour Provost
Stour Row
Fifehead Magdalen
Guy's Marsh
Todber
Marnhull
Margaret Marsh
Melbury Abbas
Twyford
A350
Compton Abbas
Ashmore
Chase
Tollard Royal
Deanland
Sixpenny Handley
Woodyates
Martin Drove End
Martin
Tidpit
Rockbourne
Whitsbury
Rockbourne Roman Villa
Damerham
Pentridge
Pentridge Hill
Bedchester
East Orchard
West Orchard
Sutton Waldron
Fontmell Magna
Cranborne
Woodcutts
Dean
Farnham
B3081
B3091
B3092
Hinton St Mary
Manston
Hammoon
Sturminster Newton
Iwerne Minster
Stubhampton
Minchington
Chettle
Monkton Up Wimborne
Boveridge
Cranborne Manor
Cranborne
Sandleheath
Lower Burgate
Fordingbridge
Ashford
Daggons
Alderholt
Fiddleford Manor
A357
Child Okeford
Shroton (Iwerne Courtney)
Tarrant Gunville
Cashmoor
Gussage St Michael
Gussage All Saints
Wimborne St Giles
Edmondsham House
Edmondsham
Cranborne Common
B3078
Fifehead Neville
Shillingstone
Okeford Fitzpaine
Tarrant Hinton
Pimperne Down
Church & Earthworks
Knowlton
Sutton Holms
Romford
Harbridge
Hod Hill
Stourpaine
Long Crichel
Tarrant Launceston
Verwood
Ringwood Forest
Ellingham
Durweston
Pimperne
Woodlands
Whitmore
Ibberton
Turnworth
Woolland
Stoke Wake
Blandford Forum
Blandford Camp
Tarrant Monkton
Manswood
Moor Crichel
Horton Inn
Horton
Horton Common
Bryanston
Tarrant Rawston
Tarrant Rushton
Witchampton
Hinton Martell
Uppington
Chalbury Common
Mannington
Moors Valley Railway
Ashley Heath
St Ives
Blashford
Langton Long Blandford
Blandford St Mary
Bulbarrow Hill
Winterborne Stickland
Charlton Marshall
Tarrant Keyneston
Badbury Rings (NT)
Stanbridge
Gaunt's Common
Three Legged Cross
Holt
Holt Heath
St Leonards
Moors Valley
Highbury
Ansty
Winterborne Houghton
Hilton
Milton Abbas
Milton Abbey
Winterborne Clenston
Thornicombe
Tarrant Crawford
Spetisbury
A350
B3082
Shapwick
Clapgate
Broom Hill
West Moors
Tadden
Colehill
Canford Bottom
Ferndown
A31
Trickett's Cross
Avon Heath
A338
Higher Whatcombe
A354
Charlton Down
Kingston Lacy (NT)
Pamphill
Priest's House
B3073
Stapehill
Knoll Gardens
Winterborne Whitechurch
Sturminster Marshall
Wimborne Minster
Stapehill Abbey Crafts & Garden
Hampreston
Parley Common
Dewlish
Almer
Winterborne Kingston
Winterborne Zelston
A31
Canford Magna
Longham
Dudsbury
Parley Cross
Bournemouth International
Milborne St Andrew
Anderson
Corfe Mullen
East End
A349
A341
A347
West Parley
Hurn
Lytchett Matravers
Bearwood
Kinson
POOLE
Canford Heath
Alice in Wonderland Maze
Athelhampton House
A35
Tolpuddle
Bere Regis
Bloxworth
Morden
East Morden
Hill View
Beacon Hill
Broadstone
A348
A3049
Holdenhurst
Wallisdown
Moordown
Winton
Burleston
Affpuddle
Briantspuddle
Turners Puddle
Slepe
Lytchett Minster
Upton
Waterloo
Upton Park
Newtown
A3040
A3049
A347
CHRISTCHURCH
Pokesdown
Lane End
Bloxworth Heath
Gore Heath
A351
Holton Heath
Hamworthy
Longfleet
Branksome
Parkstone
Westbourne
Boscombe
Southbourne
Woodsford
Wareham Forest
Gallows Hill
Clouds Hill (NT)
Trigon Hill
Holton Heath Sta.
POOLE
Poole Arts Centre
Guildhall
Pottery
Compton Acres
Branksome Park
Lilliput
Russell-Cotes Art Gallery & Museum
BOURNEMOUTH
Moreton Sta.
Moreton
Bovington Camp
Tank Museum
Monkey World Ape Rescue Centre
Sandford
Wareham
Arne
Poole Harbour
Canford Cliffs
Crossways
East Burton
A352
Stokeford
Brownsea Island
Sandbanks
Winfrith Heath
Wool
Bindon Abbey
Holmebridge
Stoborough
Hartland Moor
Poole Bay
Toll
Warmwell
Owermoigne
East Stoke
West Holme
Stoborough Green
Ridge
Studland Bay
East Knighton
Coombe Keynes
Middlebere Heath
Wytch Heath
Newton Heath
Winfrith Newburgh
Isle of Purbeck
Holworth
Chaldon Herring or East Chaldon
Lulworth
Grange Heath
Danger Zone
East Creech
Norden
Church Knowle
Corfe (NT)
Corfe Castle
Studland
The Foreland or Handfast Point
B3351
Lulworth Camp
East Lulworth
Purbeck Hills
Steeple
Nine Barrow Down
Ballard Down
Ballard Point
Harman's Cross
Ulwell
Chaldon Down
West Lulworth
Corfe Castle Mus
Swanage Bay
Lulworth Cove Heritage Cen
Lulworth Cove
Worbarrow Bay
Tyneham
Kimmeridge
Kingston
Swanage Rly
Peveril Point
Broad Bench
Toll
Smedmore
B3069
Langton Matravers
Herston
Swanage
Durlston Bay
Durlston Country Park Visitor Centre
Durlston
Durlston Head
Worth Matravers
Tilly Whim Caves
Seacombe Cliff
St Aldhelm's or St Alban's Head
Guernsey 2¼ hrs & Jersey 3¼ hrs
Cherbourg 2¼-4¼ hrs (5¼ hrs) & St. Malo 4¼ hrs (Summer only)
D
E
F
G

14
26
13
A
B
C
D
1
2
3
4
5
Wick Down
Wick
Downton
Redlynch
Morgan's Vale
Woodfalls
Lover
Newhouse
Newton
Melchet Court
Sherfield English
East Wellow
West Wellow
Newtown
Awbridge
Earls
Abbottswood
Romsey
Ampfield
Otterbourne
Chandler's Ford
North Baddesley
Chilworth
Toothill
Lee
Upton
Rownhams
Nursling
Bassett
Testwood
Calmore
Totton
Eling
Millbrook
Freemantle
Northam
SOUTHAMPTON
Hounsdown
Colbury
Pooksgreen
Ashurst
Lyndhurst Rd. Sta.
Marchwood
Dibden
Hythe
Dibden Purlieu
Hardley
Holbury
Blackfield
Fawley
Beaulieu
Beaulieu Rd. Sta.
Beaulieu Heath
East Boldre
Buckler's Hard Maritime Museum
Bucklers Hard
Exbury
St Leonards Grange
Norleywood
East End
Pilley
Portmore
Walhampton
Lymington Pier Sta.
LYMINGTON
Boldre
Battramsley
Setley
Brockenhurst
Balmerlawn
Lyndhurst
New Forest Museum & Information Centre
Bank
Emery Down
Newtown
Minstead
Bartley
Cadnam
Copythorne
Winsor
Netley Marsh
Woodlands
Ower
Paulton's Park
Canada
Plaitford
Landford
Hamptworth
Nomansland
Bramshaw
Newbridge
Brook
Fritham
Stoney Cross
Furzey
THE NEW FOREST
Bolderwood
Linwood
Linford
Poulner
Picket Post
Ringwood
Crow
Burley Street
Burley
Bisterne Close
Bisterne
Kingston
Moyles Court
Blashford
Ellingham
Harbridge
Ibsley
North Gorley
South Gorley
Hungerford
Frogham
Blissford
Stuckton
Godshill
Fordingbridge
Upper Burgate
Woodgreen
Breamore
North Charford
Hale
Upper Street
Whitsbury
Rockbourne
Rockbourne Down
Rockbourne Roman Villa
Tidpit
Martin
Martin Drove End
Damerham
Sandleheath
Ashford
Bickton
Alderholt
Daggons
Cranborne
Cranborne Common
Edmondsham
Edmondsham House
Sutton Holms
Romford
Whitmoor
Verwood
Ringwood Forest
Horton Common
Mannington
Three Legged Cross
Holt Heath
Ashley Heath
St Ives
St Leonards
Moors Valley Railway
Moors Valley
Highbury
West Moors
Ferndown
Avon Heath
Trickett's Cross
Stapehill
Knoll Gardens
Hampreston
Dudsbury
Parley Cross
West Parley
Hurn
Bournemouth International
Alice in Wonderland Maze
Kinson
Holdenhurst
Sopley
Winkton
Ripley
Avon
Bransgore
Shirley
Thorney Hill
Neacroft
Hinton Admiral
Hinton
Burton
Macpenny's
Bashley
Wootton
Tiptoe
Sway
New Milton
Hordle
Ashley
Highcliffe
Everton
Downton
Lower Pennington
Lymore
Keyhaven
Milford on Sea
Barton on Sea
Mudeford
Christchurch
CHRISTCHURCH
Wick
Southbourne
Pokesdown
Boscombe
Russell-Cotes Art Gallery & Museum
Westbourne
Branksome Park
Canford Cliffs
BOURNEMOUTH
Winton
Wallisdown
Christchurch Bay
Hengistbury Head
Tumuli
Poole Bay
The Foreland or Handfast Point
Ballard Point
Swanage
Peveril Point
Durlston Head
Hurst
Sconce Point
Fort Victoria
Yarmouth
Colwell Bay
Totland
Totland Bay
Norton
Norton Green
Freshwater
Needles Pleasure Park
Alum Bay
The Needles
The Needles Old Battery (NT)
Freshwater Bay
Compton Bay
Easton
Thorley
Thorley Street
Wellow
Hamstead
Newtown
Newtown Bay
Cranmore
Shalfleet
Ningwood
Newbridge
Calbourne
Shalcombe
Brighstone Forest
Brook Down
Brook
Mottistone
Moortown
Brighstone
Limerstone
Brighstone Bay
The Undercliff
Atherfield Point
A354
A36
A27
A3090
A337
A336
A326
A35
A31
A338
A347
A3060
A3049
A3040
A3054
A3055
A33
M3
M27
M271
B3078
B3080
B3079
B3081
B3072
B3073
B3347
B3058
B3055
B3056
B3054
B3399
B3401
B3322
Deadman Hill
3.2 miles to 1 inch
0 2 4 6 8 10 miles
0 2 4 6 8 10 km
2 km to 1 cm

15
28
16
D
E
F
G
1
2
3
4
5
HAMPSHIRE
WEST SUSSEX
Petersfield
Owslebury
Colden Common
Fisher's Pond
Hensting
Marwell Zoo
Upham
Corhampton Down
Corhampton
Exton
Meonstoke
West Meon
Warnford
East Meon
Langrish
Stroud
Weston
Ramsdean
Butser Hill
War Down
Nursted
Buriton
Queen Elizabeth
Rogate
Chithurst
West Harting
Nyewood
South Harting
East Harting
Elsted
Treyford
Didling
North Marden
Uppark (NT)
Compton
Up Marden
West Marden
East Marden
Chilgrove
Bishopstoke
Crowdhill
Fair Oak
Lower Upham
Dean
EASTLEIGH
Stoneham
Southampton International
Horton Heath
Wintershill
Newtown
Bishop's Waltham
Palace
Droxford
Brockbridge
Chidden
Clanfield
Soberton
Durley
Swanmore
Hillpound
Itchen Valley
Long Common
Waltham Chase
Shirrell Heath
Soberton Heath
Hambledon
Catherington
Chalton
West End
Curdridge
Shedfield
Hoe Gate
Anthill Common
Horndean
Blendworth
Finchdean
Forestside
Thornhill
Botley
Newtown
Lovedean
Cowplain
Hedge End
Manor Farm
Curbridge
Wickham
Worlds End
Denmead
Rowland's Castle
Walderton
Stoughton
Kingley Vale
Sholing
Burridge
Hundred Acres
Forest of Bere
WATERLOOVILLE
Stansted Park
Old Netley
Bursledon
Swanwick
North Boarhunt
Red Hill
Lower Swanwick
Whiteley
Southwick
Woodend
Hound
Park Gate
Sarisbury
Funtley
Boarhunt
Purbrook
HAVANT
New Brighton
Funtington
East Ashling
West Stoke
Hamble-le-Rice
Royal Victoria
Locks Heath
Titchfield Abbey
Wallington
FAREHAM
Ports Down
Bedhampton
Denvilles
Westbourne
Woodmancote
West Ashling
Warsash
Titchfield
Portchester
Port Solent
Wymering
Cosham
Drayton
Langstone
Emsworth
Hermitage
Hambrook
Southbourne
Nutbourne
Broadbridge
Fishbourne
CHICHESTER
Fawley
Meon
Horsea Island
Hilsea
PORTSMOUTH
Northney
North Hayling
Thorney Island
Chidham
Bosham
Holy Trinity
Roman Palace
Calshot
Stubbington
Hill Head
Bridgemary
Rowner
Portsmouth Harbour
Whale Island
North End
Portsea Island
Langstone Harbour
Stoke
West Thorney
Hayling Island
Lee-on-the-Solent
Brockhurst
Hardway
Fort
Historic Dockyard
Fratton
West Town
Chichester Harbour
West Itchenor
Birdham
Calshot Foreshore
GOSPORT
Portsea
Cath.
Eastney
South Hayling
Eastoke
Stone Point
Alverstoke
Southsea
Stokes Bay
Hayling Bay
West Wittering
Windmill
Highleigh
Somerley
Gilkicker Point
PORTSMOUTH
Cowes
Cowes Roads
THE SOLENT
East Cowes
Gurnard
Maritime Museum
Osborne
Osborne Bay
East Wittering
Earnley
Northwood
Whippingham
Ryde Roads
RYDE
Quarr Hill
Fishbourne
Wootton Bridge
Binstead
Brickfields Horse Country
Nettlestone Point
Seaview
Bracklesham Bay
Selsey
Parkhurst
Parkhurst Forest
Mildred
Isle of Wight Steam Rly
Haylands
Flamingo Park
Nettlestone
Wootton Common
NEWPORT
Havenstreet
St Helens
Bembridge Point
Hunny Hill
Gunville
Staplers
Robin Hill
East Ashey
Bembridge
Foreland
Carisbrooke
Carisbrooke Castle & Mus
Downend
Nunwell
Brading
Windmill (NT)
Hillway
Whitecliff Bay
Arreton
Roman Villa
Isle of Wight Zoo
Gatcombe
Blackwater
Alverstone
Yaverland
Culver Cliff
Merstone
Newchurch
Geology Mus
Chillerton
Rookley
Isle of Wight (Sandown)
Sandown
Shorwell
Rookley
Branstone
ISLE OF WIGHT
Apse Heath
Sandown Bay
Kingston
Godshill
Sandford
Whiteley Bank
Shanklin Chine
Shanklin
Chale Green
Appuldurcombe
Little Atherfield
Roud
Wroxall
Luccombe Village
Pyle
Stenbury Down
Dunnose
Bierley
Whitwell
Bonchurch
Ventnor
Chale
Niton
St Lawrence
Ventnor Botanic Gardens
Blackgang
Blackgang Chine
The Undercliff
Rocken End
St. Catherine's Point
Guernsey 6½ hrs & Jersey 10 hrs
Bilbao 35 hrs
St. Malo 8¾ hrs (10½ hrs)
Cherbourg 2¾ hrs-5 hrs (7 hrs)
Caen 6 hrs & Le Havre 5½ hrs
M27
M275
A3(M)
A3
A27
A32
A272
A334
A3051
A3024
A3025
A259
A286
A288
A2030
A3023
A3054
A3020
A3021
A3055
A3056
B3333
B3385
B3334
B2177
B2149
B2148
B2146
B2147
B2141
B2178
B2179
B2198
B3395
B3330
B3399
B3323

16
A
B
C
D
1
2
3
4
5
29
15
WEST SUSSEX
S O U T
Whitehill
Passfield
Bramshott
Haslemere
Educational Museum
Lythe Hill
Ramsnest Common
Alfold
Bucks Green
Rudgwick
Conford
Danger Zone
Liphook
Shottermill
Hammer
Camelsdale
Linchmere
Fisherstreet
Loxwood
Ifold
Plaistow
The Haven
Slinfold
Longmoor Camp
Liss Forest
Liss
Black Down
Northchapel
Buckman Corner
Five Oaks
Itchingfield
Langley
East Liss
Rake
Fernhurst
Roundstreet Common
Newpound Common
Barns Green
Lurgashall
Kirdford
Fishers Farm Park
Billingshurst
Milland
Balls Cross
Wisborough Green
Southwater
Marsh
Hill Brow
Redford
Lickfold
Henley
Brooks
Sheet
Petersfield
Rogate
Robins
Strood Green
Coneyhurst
Chithurst
Woolbeding
Lodsworth
Upperton
Gunter's Bridge
Burdocks
Adversane
Iping
Easebourne
River
Coolham
Trotton
Stedham
Midhurst
Cowdray House (ruins)
Tillington
Petworth House (NT)
Petworth
North Heath
Broadford Bridge
West Harting
Nyewood
South Harting
East Harting
West Lavington
South Ambersham
Selham
Coultershaw Bridge
Byworth
Egdean
Stopham
Codmore Hill
Gay Street
Broomer's Corner
Elsted
Fittleworth
Nutbourne
West Chiltington
Dial Post
Treyford
Didling
Bepton
Heyshott
Graffham
Coates
Pulborough
Pulborough Brooks R.S.P.B. Nature Reserve
Thakeham
Uppark (NT)
Linch Down
Cocking
Duncton
Coldwaltham
Hardham
Wiggonholt
West Chiltington Common
Warminghurst
Abingworth
Ashington
North Marden
East Lavington
Waterfield
East Marden
Chilgrove
Barlavington
Greatham
Rackham
Storrington
Cootham
Hole Street
West Marden
Up Marden
Sutton
Bignor
Parham
Sullington
Washington
Forestside
Bow Hill
Singleton
Charlton
East Dean
Upwaltham
West Burton
Bury
Amberley
Kithurst Hill
Stansted Park
West Dean
Weald & Downland Open Air Museum
Goodwood
Slindon Estate (NT)
Houghton
Amberley Museum
Amberley Sta.
Walderton
Stoughton
Kingley Vale
Madehurst
North Stoke
South Stoke
Harrow Hill
North End
Findon
Woodend
Mid Lavant
Goodwood House
Halnaker Hill
Eartham
Dale Park
Arundel Park
Burpham
Funtington
West Stoke
East Lavant
Halnaker
Slindon
St. Nicholas Cathedral
Wildfowl Trust
Wepham
Woodmancote
East Ashling
West Ashling
Strettington
Priory
Denmans
Arundel
Warningcamp
Patching
Clapham
Westbourne
Boxgrove
Fontwell
Crossbush
High Salvington
Emsworth
Hambrook
Westhampnett
Tangmere
Walberton
Binsted
Poling Corner
Hammerpot
Durrington
Salvington
CHICHESTER
Aldingbourne
Norton
Fontwell Park
Eastergate
Tortington
Poling
Highdown Hill (NT)
Broadwater
Southbourne
Nutbourne
Broadbridge
Oving
Nyton
Westergate
Lyminster
Body Shop Visitor Cen
Angmering
Thorney Island
Chidham
Fishbourne
Bosham
Roman Palace
Tangmere Military Aviation Museum
Woodgate
Barnham
Yapton
Ford
Wick
West Tarring
Apuldram
Merston
Burndell
Clymping
Toddington
Goring-by-Sea
West Thorney
Donnington
Runcton
Berri Court
Colworth
Shripney
Bilsham
East Preston
Ferring
West Worthing
West Itchenor
Hunston
North Mundham
Flansham
Rustington
Kingston
Chichester Harbour
South Mundham
North Bersted
Ancton
Harbour Park Amusements
Littlehampton
Shipton Green
Birdham
Street End
South Bersted
Middleton-on-Sea
Felpham
West Wittering
Highleigh
Windmill
Butlins Family Entertainment Resort, Bognor Regis
Somerley
Sidlesham
Nyetimber
Aldwick
BOGNOR REGIS
East Wittering
Earnley
Pagham
Norton
Church Norton
Bracklesham Bay
Selsey
Selsey Bill
A3
A272
A286
A283
A29
A264
A281
A285
A24
A280
A27
A259
A284
A2032
A2031
B3004
B2131
B2070
B2146
B2141
B2147
B2178
B2138
B2139
B2133
B2132
B2233
B2166
B2179
B2198
B2145
B2201
B2187
B2140
280
255
238

17
D
E
F
G
1
2
3
4
5
30
18
Faygate
A264
Buchan
Pease Pottage
Holmbush
Colgate
Roffey
Pease Pottage
St Leonard's Forest
High Beeches
Balcombe
Selsfield Common
Millennium Seed Bank
Wakehurst Place (NT)
West Hoathly
Sharpthorne
Highbrook
Weir Wood Resr
Spring Hill Wildfowl Park
Kidbrooke Park
Coleman's Hatch
Hartfield
Friar's Gate
Crowborough
Steel Cross
Ashdown
Forest
Jarvis Brook
Poundgate
A26
Denne Park
Ashfold Crossways
Handcross
Nymans (NT)
Mannings Heath
Monk's Gate
Staplefield
Ardingly
Ardingly Resr
Horsted Keynes Sta.
Horsted Keynes
Chelwood Gate
Duddleswell
A22
Danehill
Nutley
Heron's Ghyll
Slaugham
Brook Street
Borde Hill
Paxhill Park
Lower Beeding
Warninglid
Nuthurst
A24
Leonardslee
A23
A275
Fairwarp
High Hurstwood
Copsale
Crabtree
Whitemans Green
Cuckfield
Lindfield
Bluebell Railway
Sheffield Green
Sheffield Park (NT)
Five Ash Down
Maresfield
Five Ash Down
Maplehurst
Haywards Heath
Scayne's Hill
Sheffield Park Sta.
Fletching
A272
Pound Green
Hadlow Down
Bolney
Ansty
A273
Buxted
Piltdown
Ringles Cross
Cowfold
Sandrocks
North Chailey
Newick
Uckfield
Blackboys
Framfield
Stonebridge
Waldron
A281
Wineham
Hickstead
A2300
Twineham
Wivelsfield
Wivelsfield Sta.
Wivelsfield Green
Beeches Farm
New Town
Ridgewood
West Grinstead
Partridge Green
Burgess Hill
Chailey
South Street
Newick Park
Horsted Place
Ditchling Common
Little Horsted
Sayers Common
A273
Plumpton Green
South Common
Spithurst
Isfield
Bines Green
Albourne
Bentley Motor Museum
Halland
Henfield
Hurstpierpoint
EAST
Barcombe Cross
Shortgate
Ashurst
Blackstone
Hassocks
Keymer
Plumpton
Streat
Wildfowl Park
Danny
Ditchling
East Chiltington
Barcombe
Whitesmith
Laughton
Woodmancote
Middleton
Clayton
Westmeston
Cooksbridge
New Hall
Oreham Common
A281
Pyecombe
Ditchling Beacon
Plumpton
Hamsey
Holme's Hill
SUSSEX
Small Dole
Poynings
Offham
South Malling
Ringmer
A2037
Mount Harry
Lewes 1264
Cliffe Hill
Glyndebourne
Steyning
Edburton
Fulking
Lewes
Bramber
Upper Beeding
DOWNS
Stanmer
Mount Caburn
Glynde Place
Chalvington
Upper Dicker
The Dicker
St Mary's
Botolphs
Patcham
A27
Falmer
Glynde
Middle Farm & English Farm Cider Centre
Mus.of Sussex Archaeology
Foredown Tower
Coldean
Hollingbury
Kingston near Lewes
Beddingham
Coombes
A270
Newmarket Hill
Iford
A26
West Firle
Firle Place
Charleston Farmhouse
Selmeston
A283
British Engineerium
Moulsecoomb
Rodmell
Kingston by Sea
Hangleton
Preston
Bevendean
Preston Manor
Firle Beacon
Alciston
Berwick
North Lancing
West Blatchington
Woodingdean
Monk's House
Marlipins
Portslade
Southease
A27
Shoreham
Royal Pavilion
Brighton
Southwick
HOVE
Drusillas Park
Lancing
A259
Kemp Town
Tarring Neville
Alfriston
Priory
Shoreham-by-Sea
Portslade-by-Sea
South Lancing
BRIGHTON
Ovingdean
Telscombe
South Heighton
Old Clergy House
WORTHING
BRIGHTON & HOVE
Rottingdean
Grange Art Gal. & Mus.
Piddinghoe
Denton
Paradise Family Leisure Park
Palace Pier
Volks Electric Rly
Saltdean
Newhaven
Litlington
Telscombe Cliffs
A259
Bishopstone
Charleston Manor
Peacehaven
East Blatchington
A259
Westdean
Seaford
Seven Sisters
East Dean
Dieppe 2hrs (summer only)
3.2 miles to 1 inch
0
2
4
6
8
10 miles
0
2
4
6
8
10 km
2 km to 1 cm

18
Crowborough
Friar's Gate
Boarshead
Steel Cross
Jarvis Brook
Poundgate
Heron's Ghyll
Fairwarp
High Hurstwood
Five Ash Down
Maresfield
Buxted
Pound Green
Hadlow Down
Ringles Cross
Uckfield
New Town
Framfield
Blackboys
Ridgewood
Horsted Place
Halland
Shortgate
East Hoathly
Whitesmith
Laughton
Holme's Hill
Golden Cross
Chiddingly
Muddles Green
Ringmer
Glyndebourne
Glynde
Ripe
Chalvington
The Dicker
Upper Dicker
Lower Dicker
Middle Farm & English Farm Cider Centre
Michelham Priory
Arlington
Arlington Resr
Berwick Sta.
West Firle
Firle Place
Charleston Farmhouse
Selmeston
Alciston
Berwick
Polegate
Wilmington
Folkington
Drusillas Park
Alfriston
Old Clergy House
Wannock
Willingdon
Ring Neville
South Heighton
Paradise Family Leisure Park
Denton
Bishopstone
Litlington
Jevington
Charleston Manor
Filching Manor
Lullington Heath
Willingdon Hill
Blatchington
Seaford
Westdean
Seven Sisters
Friston
East Dean
Birling Gap
Beachy Head
Holywell
EASTBOURNE
Eastbourne Pier & Glass Studio
Fort Fun
Sovereign Harbour
Langney Point
Hampden Park
Langney
Stone Cross
Friday Street
Westham
Pevensey
Pevensey Bay
Hankham
Pevensey Levels
Norman's Bay
Cooden
BEXHILL
Little Common
Hooe
Hooe Common
Sidley
Bulverhythe
St Leonards
HASTINGS
Clambers Play
Silverhill
Hollington
St Helen's
Baldslow
Westfield
The Moor
Telham
Beaufort Park
Battle
Hastings 1066
Yesterday's World
Buckleys
Abbey
Catsfield
Henley's Down
Crowhurst
Ninfield
Lower Street
Lunsford's Cross
Boreham Street
Wartling
Windmill Hill
Herstmonceux
Herstmonceux Castle
Stunts Green
Magham Down
Hailsham
Upper Horsebridge
Lower Horsebridge
Hellingly
Lealands
Cowbeech
Foul Mile
Bodle Street Green
Ashburnham Place
Ponts Green
Penhurst
Burlow
Horam
Vine's Cross
Foxhunt Green
Maynard's Green
Warbleton
Rushlake Green
Cups Corner
Three Cups Corner
Dallington
Netherfield
Whatlington
Sedlescombe
Sedlescombe Street
Kent Street
Cripp's Corner
Vinehall Street
John's Cross
Mountfield
Brightling
Darwell Resr
Darvell
Robertsbridge
Salehurst
Silver Hill
Hurst Green
Swiftsden
Cooper's Corner
Boarzell
Etchingham
Haremere Hall
Burwash
Bateman's (NT)
Burwash Weald
Burwash Common
Witherhurst
Witherenden Hill
Oxley's Green
Punnett's Town
Heathfield
Chapel Cross
Cade Street
Cross in Hand
Broad Oak
Little London
Waldron
Stonebridge
Possingworth Park
Five Ashes
Butcher's Cross
Mayfield
Coggins Mill
Rotherfield
Town Row
Mark Cross
Tidebrook
Stonegate
Stonegate Sta.
Ticehurst
Shover's Green
Three Leg Cross
Wadhurst
Cousley Wood
Sparrow's Green
Durgates
Beech Hill
Bewl Water
Bedgebury National Pinetum
Bedgebury Forest
Flimwell
Gill's Green
Hawkhurst
High Street
The Moor
Four Throws
Iden Green
Benenden
Rolvenden
Great Maytham Hall
Sandhurst
Linkhill
Bodiam
Bodiam (NT)
Kent & East Sussex Rly
Ewhurst
Great Dixter
Northiam
Staplecross
Millcorner
Horns Cross
Broad Oak
Cackle Street
Brede
Sedlescombe
EAST SUSSEX
31
17
A
B
C
D
1
2
3
4
5
A21
A26
A22
A27
A267
A265
A268
A229
A272
A271
A295
A259
A2100
A2101
A2036
A269
A28
A2021
B2100
B2099
B2101
B2102
B2192
B2124
B2104
B2103
B2095
B2182
B2204
B2096
B2089
B2165
B2092
B2093
B2244
3.2 miles to 1 inch
0 2 4 6 8 10 miles
0 2 4 6 8 10 km
2 km to 1 cm

CHANNEL TUNNEL MAPS

Eurotunnel: Access from the UK

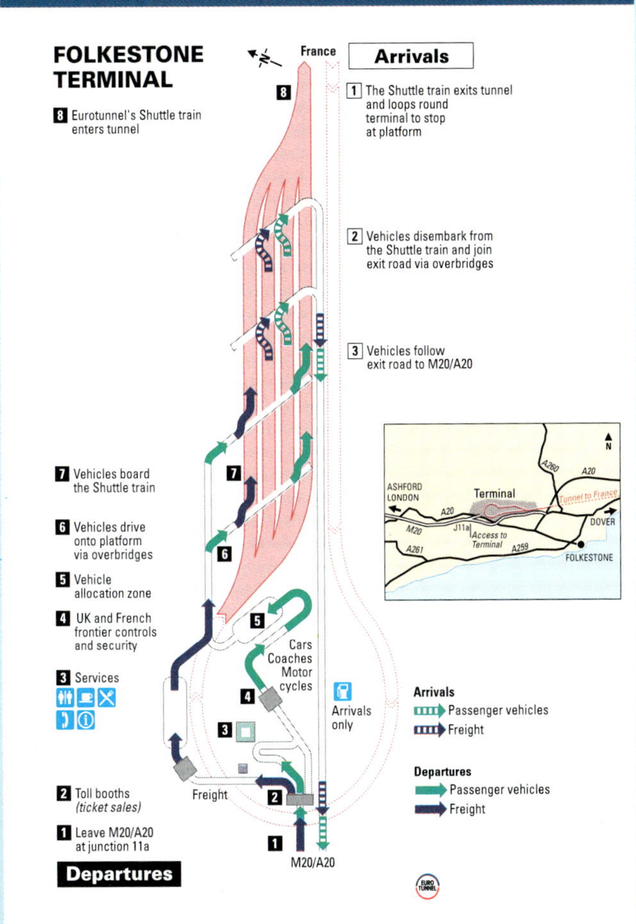

Eurotunnel: Access from France

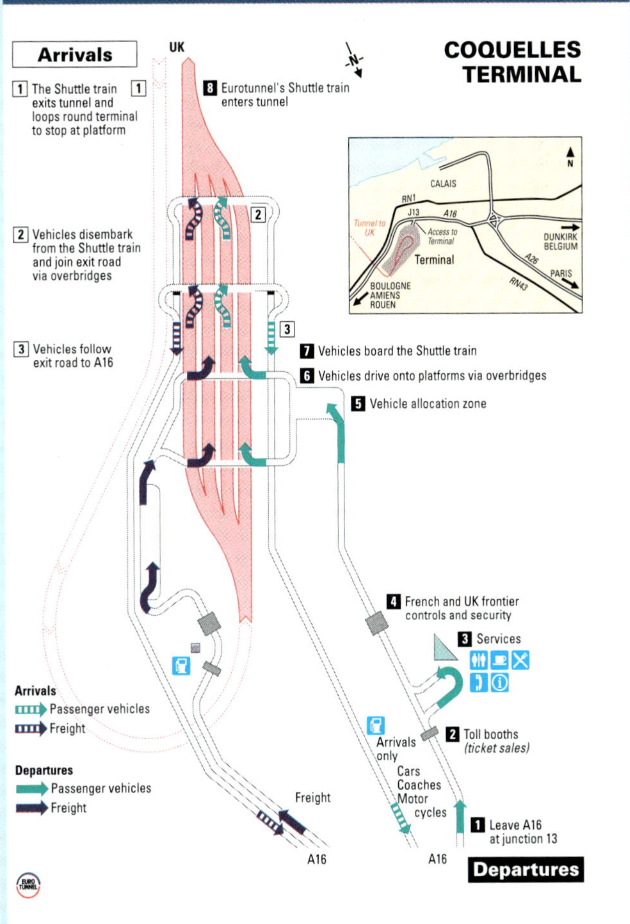

1
2
3
4
5

D E F G

A
B
C
D
1
2
3
4
5
North West Point
Lundy
Rat Island
Shutter Rock
3.2 miles to 1 inch
0 2 4 6 8 10 miles
0 2 4 6 8 10 km
2 km to 1 cm
B A R N S
O
B I D E
B
Hartland Point
Titchberry
Windbury Point
Gallantry Bower
Hartland Abbey
Clovelly
Hartland Quay
Stoke
Hartland
B3248
Dyke
Buck's M
Milford
Philham
A39
Clovelly Cross
Milky Way Adventure Park
Elmscott
Edistone
Tosberry
Woolfardisworthy
South Hole
Knaps Longpeak
Welcombe
Ashmansworthy
Meddon
Gooseham
Kismeldon
East Youlstone
Eastcott
Morwenstow
Dinworthy
Higher Sharpnose Point
Shop
Bradwo
14
Woodford
Lower Sharpnose Point
Taylors Cross
Upper Tamar Lake
Alfardisworthy
Coombe
Kilkhampton
Lower Tamar Lake
Stibb
B3254
Youldonmoor Cross
Soldon C
CORNWALL
Youldon
Hols
Stratton 1643
Poughill
Flexbury
Hersham
Grimscott
Bude Haven
Bude
Stratton
Launcells
Launcells Cross
Chilsworthy
Bude Bay
A3072
Pancrasweek
Historical & Folk Museum
Red Post
Helebridge
Marhamchurch
Rydon
Chasty
Widemouth Bay
Bridgerule
Pyworthy
Titson
Yeomadon
Coppathorne
Week Orchard
Herdicott
Dizzard Point
Poundstock
Tinney
Corfcott
Tregole
Treskinnick Cross
Trewint
North Tamerton
Crackington Haven
Cambeak
Tetcot
Jacobstow
Trebarrow
6

D
E
F
G
The Valley of Rocks
Lynmouth Cliff Rly
Lynmouth Bay
Lynmouth
Lynton
Heddon's Mouth
Woody Bay
Trentishoe
Martinhoe
Hunter's Inn
Heale
Barbrook
Hillsford Bridge
Cheriton
Furzehill
Shallowford
Widmouth Head
Watermouth Castle
Combe Martin Bay
Ilfracombe
Hele
Berrynarbor
Combe Martin
Combe Martin Wildlife & Dinosaur Park
Bull Point
Lee Bay
Lee
Rockham Bay
Morte Point
Mortehoe
Slade
Chambercombe Manor
Sterridge
Parracombe
Churchtown
Mullacott Cross
Trimstone
Woolacombe
Morte Bay
Kentisbury
Blackmoor Gate
Hoaroak Hill
Challacombe Common
Pinkworthy Pond
Kentisbury Ford
West Down
Berry Down Cross
Patchole
Arlington Beccott
Arlington
Bittadon
East Down
Pickwell
North Buckland
Baggy Point
Putsborough
Croyde Bay
Croyde
Georgeham
Challacombe
Arlington Court (NT)
Milltown
Loxhore
Knightacott
Muddiford
Bratton Fleming
Halsinger
Marwood
Marwood Hill
Shirwell Cross
Shirwell
Leworthy
Knowle
Pippacott
Kingsheanton
Saunton
Saunton Sands
Braunton
Heanton Punchardon
Prixford
Benton
Lydcott
Span Head
Wrafton
Ashford
Goodleigh
Stoke Rivers
Brayford
Braunton Burrows
Toll
Pilton
St. Anne's Chapel Heritage Centre
Northleigh
Gunn
High Bray
Charles
North Heasley
Heasley Mill
Barnstaple
Newport
Bickington
The Neck
Yelland
Fremington
Landkey
Swimbridge Newland
West Buckland
Yarnacott
East Buckland
Northam Burrows
Appledore
North Devon Maritime Mus.
Instow
Bickleton
Tawstock
Bishop's Tawton
Swimbridge
Westward Ho!
Tapeley Park
St John's Chapel
Northam
Tapeley
Westleigh
Eastleigh
Horwood
Lower Lovacott
Newton Tracey
Filleigh
North Molton
Burton Art Gallery
East-the-Water
Herner
Cobbaton
Abbotsham
Big Sheep
Bideford
Hiscott
Ensis
Chittlehampton
South Molton
Quince Honey Farm
Woodtown
Alverdiscott
Fairy Cross
Ford
Gammaton Moor
Fishleigh Barton
Hudscott
Clapworthy
Umberleigh
Horns Cross
Littleham
Yeo Vale
Landcross
Yarnscombe
Atherington
Goldworthy
Langridgeford
Langridge
Warkleigh
Satterleigh
George Nympton
Alswear
Parkham
Buckland Brewer
Weare Giffard
Huntshaw Cross
Parkham Ash
Monkleigh
High Bullen
Sherwood Green
High Bickington
Chittlehamholt
Romansleigh
Great Torrington
St Giles in the Wood
Portsmouth Arms Sta.
King's Nympton
Rowley
Melbury
Frithelstock Stone
Frithelstock
Dartington Crystal
Head Bridge
Powler's Piece
Taddiport
Rosemoor
Kingscott
Northcote Manor
Cadbury Barton
East Putford
Little Torrington
Roborough
Burrington
Kings Nympton Sta.
Week
Elstone
Langtree
Colleton Mills
West Putford
Villavin
Beaford
D E V O N
Stibb Cross
Chulmleigh
Riddlecombe
Bulkworthy
Peters Marland
Winswell
Ashreigney
Copy Lake
Cheldon
Brendon
Abbots Bickington
Woollaton
Dolton
Chawleigh
Sutcombe
Newton St Petrock
Merton
Heanton Satchville
Ashley
Milton Damerel
Huish
Hollacombe
Eggesford Barton
Dowland
Forches Cross
North Town
Wembworthy
Shebbear
Buckland Filleigh
Petrockstow
Thornbury
Ash Barton
Iddesleigh
Winkleigh
Coldridge
Lapford
Nymet Rowland
Brushford
Bradford
Meeth
Sheepwash
Cookbury
Taw Bridge
Hele Bridge
Broadwood Kelly
Black Torrington
Monkokehampton
Bondleigh
Anvil Corner
Highampton
East Leigh
Down St Mary
Holsworthy
Dunsland Cross
Brandis Corner
Hatherleigh
Zeal Monachorum
Hollacombe
Lydacott
Basset's Cross
Graddon Moor
Honeychurch
North Tawton
Exbourne
Bow
Halwill Forest
Jacobstowe
Broadnymett
Shilstone
Sampford Courtenay
Halwill Junction
Nymet Tracey
Clawton
Halwill
Beaworthy
Inwardleigh
Northlew
Oak
Belstone Corner
Itton
Ashbury
Folly Gate
Upcott
Quoditch
Broadbury
Taw Green
Spreyton
Okehampton
Bristol Channel (A P L E)
B A R N S T A P L E O R F O R D B A Y
A39
A361
A399
A3123
A377
A386
A388
A3072
A3079
B3343
B3230
B3231
B3233
B3236
B3227
B3232
B3226
B3220
B3217
B3216
B3219
B3215
B3042
B3096
B3358
22
7
10
1
2
3
4
5
480
473
439

3.2 miles to 1 inch
0 2 4 6 8 10 miles
0 2 4 6 8 10 km
2 km to 1 cm
A
B
C
D
1
2
3
4
5
37
21
10
B R I S T O L C H A N
Tusker Rock
Southerndown
Pitcot
St Brides Major
Llysworney
Cowbridge
Llanblethian
Llandow
Wick
Broughton
Llandough
Llanmihangel
St Mary Church
Treguff
Flemingston
Llanmaes
Marcross
Llantwit Major
Boverton
Eglwys-Brewis
Gileston
St Donats
Nash Point
St Athan
East Aberthaw
West Aberthaw
Breaksea Pt
VALE
GLAMO
Foreland Point
Countisbury Cove
Lynmouth Bay
Lynton & Lynmouth Cliff Rly
The Valley of Rocks
Woody Bay
Lynton
Lynmouth
Countisbury
Watersmeet Ho (NT)
Martinhoe
Hunter's Inn
Toll
Barbrook
Hillsford Bridge
Brendon
Malmsmead
Tippacott
Oare
Cheriton
Furzehill
Brendon Common
Culbone Hill
Culbone
Porlock Weir
Porlock Bay
Bossington
Selworthy Beacon
West Porlock
Porlock
Allerford
Selworthy
North Hill
Minehead
Butlins Family Entertainment Resort
Dunster Sta
Blue Anchor Bay
Alcombe
Marsh Street
Blue Anchor
Luccombe
Wootton Courtenay
South Common
Dunster
Dunster Castle & Mill (NT)
Carhampton
Old Cleeve
Timberscombe
Withycombe
Bilbrook
Cleeve Abbey
Dunkery Hill
Dunkery Beacon
519
Codsend Moors
Croydon Hill
Rodhuish
Orchard Wyndham
Shallowford
Blackmoor Gate
Hoaroak Hill
Pinkworthy Pond
473
480
Challacombe Common
E X M O O R
Dry Hill
444
Dure Down
Challacombe
Shoulsbarrow Common
Simonsbath
Barle
Exe
EXMOOR
Exford
Quarme
Luckwell Bridge
Cutcombe
Wheddon Cross
Luxborough
Roadwater
Nettlecombe
Kingsbridge
Lype Hill
423
BRENDON HILLS
Treborough
Leworthy
Lydcott
Span Head
439
Kinsford Water
409
Long Holcombe
NATIONAL PARK
Withypool Common
Withypool
Winsford
Winsford Hill
Exton
Withiel Florey
Raleigh's Cross
High Bray
Charles
North Radworthy
Worth Hill
North Heasley
Heasley Mill
South Radworthy
Dane's Brook
Liscombe
Bridgetown
S O M E R
Brompton Regis
Clatworthy Reservoir
East Buckland
Molland Common
Hawkridge
Twitchen
317
Huish Champflower
North Molton
Filleigh
Molland
Wimbleball Lake
Upton
Dulverton
Haddon Hill
Bury
Skilgate
D E V O N
West Anstey
Battleton
Chipstable
Waterrow
South Molton
Bish Mill
Quince Honey Farm
East Anstey
Nightcott
Brushford
Oldways End
Exebridge
Morebath
Petton
Clapworthy
Bishop's Nympton
Shillingford
Satterleigh
George Nympton
Alswear
Crooked Oak
Ash Mill
Knowstone
Bampton
Clayhanger
Mariansleigh
Rose Ash
Rackenford Moor
Oakfordbridge
Oakford
Huntsham
Romansleigh
King's Nympton
Head Bridge
Rowley
Meshaw
Creacombe
Stoodleigh
Cove
Hockworthy
Newhouse Moor
Stoodleigh Beacon
Cadbury Barton
Rackenford
Kings Nympton Sta.
Elstone
Colleton Mills
Week
Loxbeare
Washfield
Knightshayes Court (NT)
East Mere
Uplowman
Pitt
A39
A399
A396
A361
A48
B3223
B3358
B3224
B3222
B3190
B3227
B3226
B3137
B3191
B4270
B4265

23
38
24
11
D
E
F
G
1
2
3
4
5
Grangetown
Twyn-yr-odyn
St Nicholas
Leckwith
Wenvoe
St Lythans
Llandough
Michaelston-le-Pit
Dinas Powys
Cogan
PENARTH
Wales Millennium Centre
Pleasure Steamers Waverley & Balmoral
Lower Penarth
St Andrews Major
St. Lythans Burial Chamber
Palmerston
Merthyr Dyfan
Colcot
Cadoxton
Sully
Cosmeston
Lavernock
Lavernock Point
Swanbridge
Sully Island
Rhoose
Porthkerry
Porthkerry Park
Barry Island Pleasure Park
BARRY
Barry Island
Whitmore Bay
Penmark
Flat Holm
MOUTH OF THE SEVERN
WESTON-SUPER-MARE
Steep Holm
Weston Bay
Clevedon
Clevedon Pier
Manor House
Kenn
Middle Hope (NT)
Woodspring Priory
Sand Point
Sand Bay
Kingston Seymour
North End
Yatton
Icelton
Wick St Lawrence
Kewstoke
Bourton
St Georges
Hewish
Puxton
Congresbury
Toll
Milton
Worle
West Wick
East Rolstone
NORTH SOMERSET
Locking
Sandford
Churchill
Banwell
Sidcot
Star
Hutton
Uphill
Brean Down
Christon
Bleadon
Bleadon Hill
Loxton
Winscombe
Compton Bishop
Cross
Axbridge
Cheddar Reservoir
King John's Hunting Lodge (NT)
Brean
Berrow Flats
Lympsham
Eastertown
Lower Weare
Weare
Biddisham
Sedgemoor
Tarnock
Badgworth
Berrow
Gore Sand
East Brent
Rooks Bridge
Brent Knoll Hillfort
Brent Knoll
Stone Allerton
Clewer
Chapel Allerton
Burnham-on-Sea
Edithmead
Mark Causeway
Mark
Stoughton
Blackford
Wedmore
Stert Island
Highbridge
Watchfield
Heath House
Westham
Bason Bridge
River Bridge
Cote
Burtle
Westhay
BRIDGWATER BAY
Hinkley Pt
Stert Flats
Stolford
Steart
Huntspill
West Huntspill
East Huntspill
Huntspill Level
Stretcholt
Puriton
Woolavington
Watchet
Doniford
East Quantoxhead
Kilton
Lilstock
Knighton
Burton
Shurton
Stockland Bristol
Otterhampton
Kilve
Stringston
Stogursey
St Decumans
St Audries
West Quantoxhead
Williton
Holford
Dodington
Coleridge Cottage
Coultings
Fiddington
Combwich
Pawlett
Down End
Dunball
Knowle Hall
Cossington
Rodway
Cannington
Sampford Brett
Bicknoller
Nether Stowey
Over Stowey
QUANTOCK HILLS
Vellow
Halsway Manor
Chilton Trinity
Bawdrip
Stawell
Chilton Polden
Edington
Catcott
Shapwick
Monksilver
Stogumber
Four Forks
Charlinch
Spaxton
Wembdon
BRIDGWATER
Chedzoy
Sutton Mallet
Moorlinch
Greinton
Crowcombe
Flaxpool
Quantock Forest
Hawkridge Resr
Durleigh Resr
Admiral Blake Mus
Church House
Combe Sydenham Hall
West Somerset Rly
Lower Vexford
Bagborough Hill
Lower Aisholt
Barford Park
Enmore
Durleigh
Sedgemoor 1685
Westonzoyland
Elworthy
Willett
West Bagborough
Merridge
Courtway
Goathurst
Woolmersdon
Huntworth
Northmoor Green or Moorland
Middlezoy
Greylake
Compton Ralph
Tolland
Lydeard St Lawrence
Cothelstone
Toulton
Fyne Court (NT)
Broomfield
North Petherton
Thorngrove
Othery
Henley
Clatworthy
Gaulden Manor
Combe Florey
East Combe
Pitsford Hill
Tarr
Cushuish
Thurloxton
North Newton
Maunsel
Burrow Bridge
Pathe
High Ham
Langley Marsh
Bishop's Lydeard
Fulford
Kingston St Mary
Lyng
Athelney
Aller
Low Ham
Maundown
Ford
Fitzhead
Ash Priors
Hestercombe
Adsborough
Hedging
Stathe
Wearne
Halse
West Monkton
Durston
East Lyng
West Lyng
Curload
VALE OF TAUNTON DEANE
Cheddon Fitzpaine
Monkton Heathfield
Creech Heathfield
Stoke St Gregory
Langport
Huish Episcopi
Heathfield
Norton Fitzwarren
Staplegrove
Mare Green
Nunnington Park
Milverton
Hillfarrance
Somerset County Mus
Bathpool
Creech St Michael
West Curry Rivel
Oake
Bishop's Hull
Ham
Knapp
North Curry
Sedge Moor
Much Drayton
Priest's House
Bathealton
Chipley
Ruishton
Henlade
Thornfalcon
Greenway
Langford Budville
Rumwell
Wilton
TAUNTON
Stoke St Mary
Swell
Thorney
Nynehead
Bradford-on-Tone
Trull
Orchard Portman
Wrantage
Fivehead
Isle Abbotts
Hambridge
Kingsbury Episcopi
Kittisford
Appley
Runnington
Thorne St Margaret
West Buckland
Taunton Deane
Thurlbear
West Hatch
Hatch Court
Curry Mallet
Isle Brewers
Greenham
Wellington
Hatch Beauchamp
Beercrocombe
Holywell Lake
Rockwell Green
Poundisford Park
Corfe
Green
Westport
Barrington Court (NT)
East Lambrook
Blackmoor
Pitminster
Staple Fitzpaine
Bickenhall
Kingston
West Lambrook
Sampford Arundel
Wrangway
Angersleigh
Blagdon Hill
Curland
Barrington
South Petherton
Burlescombe
Luxhay Resr
Windmill Hill
Ashill
Stocklinch
Shepton Beauchamp
Nicholashayne
Blackdown Hills
Clayhidon
Horton Cross
Staple Hill
M5
A38
A39
A358
A370
A371
A368
A303
A372
A378
A361
A3065
A3259
A4050
A4055
A4160
A4232
A4226
A4267
B3139
B3140
B3141
B3151
B3168
B3187
B3188
B3224
B3227

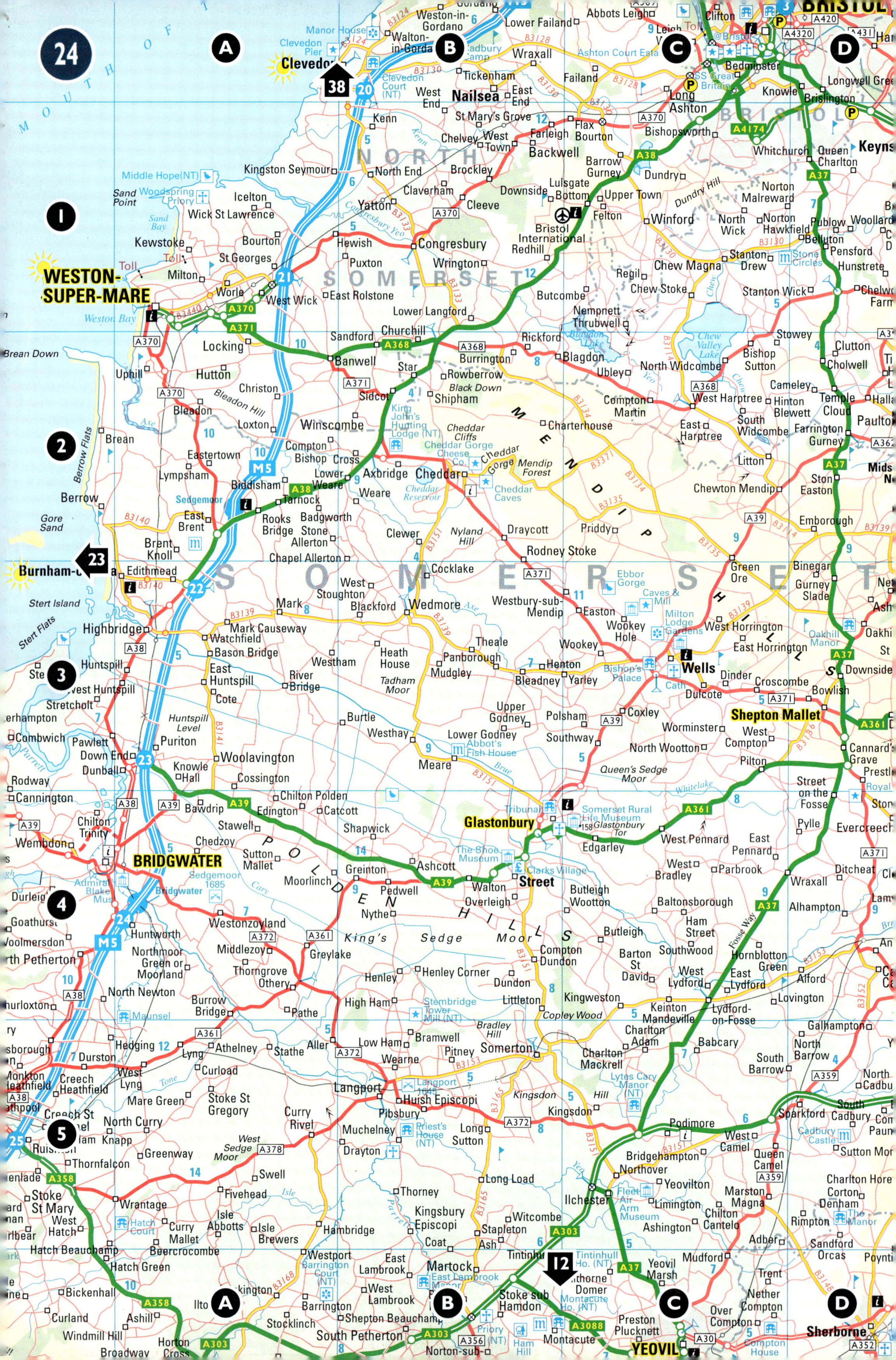

24
A
B
C
D
1
2
3
4
5
MOUTH OF
Weston-in-Gordano
Walton-in-Gordano
Manor House
Clevedon Pier
Clevedon
Clevedon Court (NT)
38
20
Lower Failand
Abbots Leigh
Wraxall
Tickenham
Failand
Ashton Court Estate
Leigh Woods
Clifton
BRISTOL
Bedminster
SS Great Britain
Long Ashton
Knowle
Brislington
Longwell Green
West End
Nailsea
East End
St Mary's Grove
Flax Bourton
Bishopsworth
Whitchurch
Queen Charlton
Keynsham
Kenn
Chelvey
West Town
Farleigh
Backwell
Barrow Gurney
Dundry
Dundry Hill
Norton Malreward
Kingston Seymour
North End
Brockley
NORTH SOMERSET
Middle Hope (NT)
Woodspring Priory
Sand Point
Sand Bay
Icelton
Wick St Lawrence
Yatton
Claverham
Cleeve
Downside
Lulsgate Bottom
Upper Town
Felton
Winford
North Wick
Norton Hawkfield
Publow
Woollard
Belluton
Pensford
Kewstoke
Bourton
Congresbury
Hewish
Bristol International
Redhill
Wrington
Puxton
St Georges
Toll
Milton
WESTON-SUPER-MARE
Worle
West Wick
East Rolstone
Weston Bay
SOMERSET
Butcombe
Regil
Chew Magna
Chew Stoke
Stanton Drew
Stone Circles
Hunstrete
Stanton Wick
Chelwood
Farm
Lower Langford
Nempnett Thrubwell
Blagdon Lake
Sandford
Churchill
Rickford
Blagdon
Ubley
Chew Valley Lake
Bishop Sutton
Stowey
Clutton
Cholwell
Brean Down
Locking
Banwell
Burrington
Rowberrow
Star
North Widcombe
Hutton
Uphill
Christon
Bleadon Hill
Sidcot
Shipham
Black Down
Compton Martin
West Harptree
Cameley
Hinton Blewett
Temple Cloud
Hallatrow
Paulton
Bleadon
Loxton
Winscombe
King John's Hunting Lodge (NT)
Cheddar Cliffs
Cheddar Gorge Cheese Co.
Charterhouse
MENDIP HILLS
East Harptree
South Widcombe
Farrington Gurney
Litton
Brean
Berrow Flats
Eastertown
Compton Bishop
Cross
Axbridge
Cheddar
Gorge
Mendip Forest
Cheddar Reservoir
Cheddar Caves
Midsomer Norton
Lympsham
Biddisham
Tarnock
Lower Weare
Weare
Chewton Mendip
Ston Easton
Berrow
Sedgemoor
East Brent
Rooks Bridge
Badgworth
Stone Allerton
Clewer
Nylland Hill
Draycott
Priddy
Emborough
Gore Sand
Brent Knoll
Chapel Allerton
Rodney Stoke
Green Ore
Binegar
Gurney Slade
Burnham-on-Sea
Edithmead
Cocklake
West Stoughton
Blackford
Wedmore
Westbury-sub-Mendip
Easton
Ebbor Gorge
Caves & Mill
Milton Lodge Gardens
Wookey Hole
West Horrington
East Horrington
Oakhill Manor
Stert Island
Stert Flats
Mark
Mark Causeway
Highbridge
Watchfield
Bason Bridge
Westham
Heath House
Panborough
Theale
Wookey
Wells
Bishop's Palace
Cath
Dinder
Croscombe
Downside
Huntspill
West Huntspill
East Huntspill
Cote
River Bridge
Tadham Moor
Mudgley
Bleadney
Henton
Yarley
Dulcote
Bowlish
Shepton Mallet
Stretcholt
Combwich
Pawlett
Huntspill Level
Puriton
Woolavington
Burtle
Westhay
Upper Godney
Lower Godney
Polsham
Coxley
Worminster
West Compton
Cannard's Grave
Down End
Dunball
Knowle Hall
Cossington
Abbot's Fish House
Meare
Southway
North Wootton
Pilton
Queen's Sedge Moor
Rodway
Cannington
Bawdrip
Chilton Polden
Edington
Catcott
Shapwick
Glastonbury
Tribunal
Somerset Rural Life Museum
Glastonbury Tor
Street on the Fosse
Royal
Chilton Trinity
Wembdon
Stawell
Chedzoy
Sutton Mallet
POLDEN HILLS
Edgarley
West Pennard
East Pennard
Pylle
Evercreech
BRIDGWATER
Sedgemoor 1685
Moorlinch
Greinton
Ashcott
The Shoe Museum
Clarks Village
Street
West Bradley
Parbrook
Ditcheat
Durleigh
Admiral Blake Mus
Pedwell
Walton
Overleigh
Butleigh Wootton
Baltonsbury
Wraxall
Alhampton
Goathurst
Westonzoyland
Nythe
Ham Street
Fosse Way
Huntworth
Middlezoy
Greylake
King's Sedge Moor
Butleigh
Barton St David
Southwood
Hornblotton Green
North Petherton
Northmoor Green or Moorland
Thorngrove
Othery
Henley
Henley Corner
Compton Dundon
West Lydford
East Lydford
Alford
North Newton
Burrow Bridge
Dundon
Littleton
Kingweston
Keinton Mandeville
Lydford-on-Fosse
Lovington
Thurloxton
Maunsel
Pathe
High Ham
Stembridge Tower Mill (NT)
Copley Wood
Charlton Adam
Galhampton
Hedging
Athelney
Stathe
Aller
Low Ham
Bramwell
Bradley Hill
Somerton
Babcary
North Barrow
Durston
Lyng
West Lyng
Wearne
Pitney
Charlton Mackrell
South Barrow
Creech Heathfield
Curload
Langport
Langport 1645
Lytes Cary Manor (NT)
North Cadbury
Mare Green
Stoke St Gregory
Curry Rivel
Huish Episcopi
Kingsdon
Hill
South Cadbury
Creech St Michael
North Curry
Knapp
Pibsbury
Long Sutton
Sparkford
Podimore
Cadbury Castle
Ruishton
Greenway
West Sedge Moor
Muchelney
Priest's House (NT)
Drayton
Bridgehampton
West Camel
Queen Camel
Sutton Montis
Thornfalcon
Swell
Long Load
Northover
Yeovilton
Charlton Horethorne
Henlade
Wrantage
Fivehead
Thorney
Ilchester
Fleet Air Arm Museum
Limington
Marston Magna
Corton Denham
Stoke St Mary
West Hatch
Hatch Court
Curry Mallet
Isle Abbotts
Isle Brewers
Hambridge
Kingsbury Episcopi
Witcombe
Stapleton
Ashington
Chilton Cantelo
Rimpton
The Manor
Hatch Beauchamp
Beercrocombe
Westport
Barrington Court (NT)
East Lambrook
Coat
Ash
Tintinhull
Tintinhull Ho. (NT)
Yeovil Marsh
Mudford
Adber
Sandford Orcas
Hatch Green
Martock
East Lambrook Manor
Thorne
Trent
Bickenhall
Ilton
Kingstone
West Lambrook
Stoke sub Hamdon
Montacute Ho. (NT)
Nether Compton
Curland
Ashill
Barrington
Shepton Beauchamp
Preston Plucknett
Over Compton
Sherborne
Windmill Hill
Stocklinch
South Petherton
Priory (NT)
Ham Hill
Montacute
YEOVIL
Compton House
Broadway
Horton Cross
Norton-sub-Hamdon
12
23

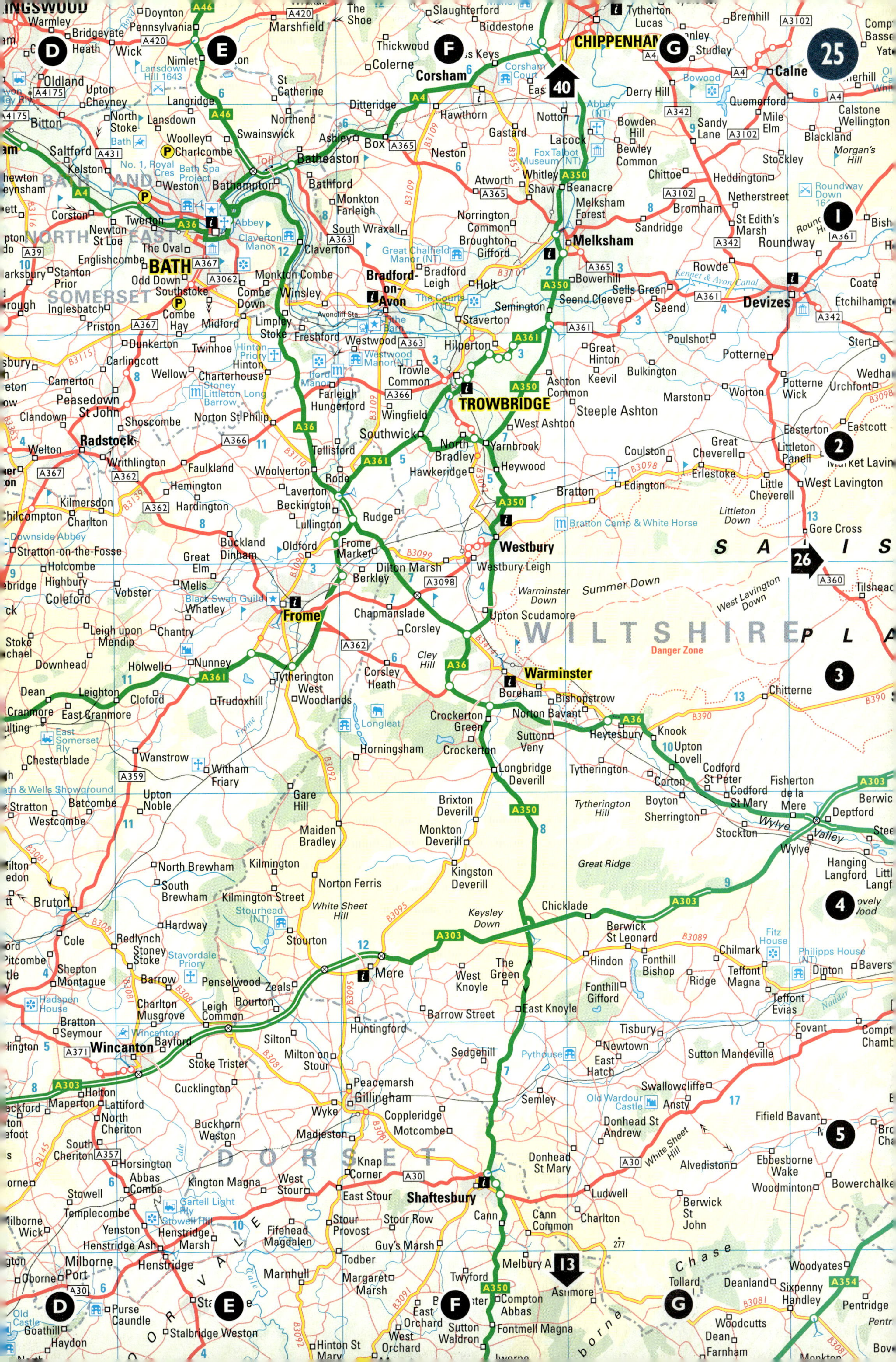
25
CHIPPENHAM
Calne
Corsham
Bath
BATH AND NORTH EAST SOMERSET
Melksham
Devizes
Bradford-on-Avon
TROWBRIDGE
Westbury
Frome
Warminster
WILTSHIRE
SALISBURY PLAIN
Danger Zone
Radstock
Mere
Wincanton
Gillingham
Shaftesbury
DORSET
VALE
Chase
40
26
13
Warmley
Doynton
Pennsylvania
Marshfield
The Shoe
Slaughterford
Biddestone
Tytherton Lucas
Bremhill
Bridgeyate
Heath
Wick
Nimlet
Thickwood
Colerne
Studley
Oldland
Upton Cheyney
Lansdown Hill 1643
Langridge
St Catherine
Ditteridge
Hawthorn
Corsham Court
Derry Hill
Bowood
Quemerford
Bitton
North Stoke
Lansdown
Woolley
Charlcombe
Northend
Swainswick
Ashley
Box
Gastard
Notton
Lacock
Bowden Hill
Bewley Common
Sandy Lane
Mile Elm
Calstone Wellington
Blackland
Morgan's Hill
Saltford
Kelston
Batheaston
Bathford
Neston
Fox Talbot Museum (NT)
Stockley
Chittoe
Heddington
Roundway Down 1643
Weston
Bath Spa Project
Bathampton
Monkton Farleigh
Atworth
Whitley
Shaw
Beanacre
Melksham Forest
Bromham
Netherstreet
St Edith's Marsh
Roundway
Corston
Newton St Loe
Twerton
Abbey
Claverton Manor
Claverton
South Wraxall
Norrington Common
Broughton Gifford
Sandridge
Englishcombe
The Oval
Great Chalfield Manor (NT)
Rowde
Stanton Prior
Odd Down
Southstoke
Monkton Combe
Combe Down
Winsley
Bradford Leigh
Holt
Bowerhill
Sells Green
Seend
Kennet & Avon Canal
Coate
Etchilhampton
Inglesbatch
Combe Hay
Priston
Midford
Limpley Stoke
Avoncliff Sta.
The Courts (NT)
Semington
Seend Cleeve
Staverton
Dunkerton
Twinhoe
Hinton Priory
Freshford
Westwood
Westwood Manor (NT)
Hilperton
Great Hinton
Poulshot
Potterne
Stert
Carlingcott
Hinton Charterhouse
Iford Manor
Trowle Common
Keevil
Bulkington
Potterne Wick
Urchfont
Wedhampton
Camerton
Wellow
Stoney Littleton Long Barrow
Farleigh Hungerford
Ashton Common
Worton
Marston
Peasedown St John
Clandown
Shoscombe
Norton St Philip
Wingfield
Steeple Ashton
West Ashton
Easterton
Eastcott
Welton
Southwick
North Bradley
Yarnbrook
Coulston
Great Cheverell
Littleton Panell
Market Lavington
West Lavington
Writhlington
Faulkland
Tellisford
Woolverton
Rode
Hawkeridge
Heywood
Erlestoke
Little Cheverell
Kilmersdon
Hemington
Laverton
Bratton
Edington
Littleton Down
Chilcompton
Charlton
Hardington
Beckington
Lullington
Rudge
Bratton Camp & White Horse
Gore Cross
Downside Abbey
Stratton-on-the-Fosse
Buckland Dinham
Oldford
Frome Market
Holcombe
Great Elm
Dilton Marsh
Westbury Leigh
Highbury
Coleford
Mells
Berkley
Warminster Down
Summer Down
West Lavington Down
Tilshead
Vobster
Black Swan Guild
Whatley
Chapmanslade
Corsley
Upton Scudamore
Leigh upon Mendip
Chantry
Stoke St Michael
Downhead
Holwell
Nunney
Cley Hill
Corsley Heath
Boreham
Bishopstrow
Chitterne
Dean
Leighton
Cloford
Tytherington
West Woodlands
Trudoxhill
Cranmore
East Cranmore
East Somerset Rly
Longleat
Crockerton Green
Norton Bavant
Heytesbury
Knook
Upton Lovell
Sutton Veny
Chesterblade
Horningsham
Crockerton
Codford St Peter
Codford St Mary
Fisherton de la Mere
Wanstrow
Witham Friary
Longbridge Deverill
Corton
Boyton
Sherrington
Deptford
Berwick
Upton Noble
Batcombe
Gare Hill
Brixton Deverill
Tytherington Hill
Stockton
Wylye
Wylye Valley
Stratton
Westcombe
Maiden Bradley
Monkton Deverill
Hanging Langford
North Brewham
South Brewham
Kilmington
Norton Ferris
Kingston Deverill
Great Ridge
Bruton
Kilmington Street
Stourhead (NT)
White Sheet Hill
Keysley Down
Chicklade
Cole
Hardway
Redlynch
Stoney Stoke
Stavordale Priory
Stourton
Berwick St Leonard
Hindon
Fonthill Bishop
Chilmark
Fitz House
Philipps House (NT)
Teffont Magna
Dinton
Baverstock
Shepton Montague
West Knoyle
The Green
Fonthill Gifford
Ridge
Teffont Evias
Barrow
Penselwood
Zeals
Hadspen House
Charlton Musgrove
Bourton
Leigh Common
Barrow Street
East Knoyle
Bratton Seymour
Wincanton
Bayford
Silton
Huntingford
Tisbury
Newtown
Fovant
Sutton Mandeville
Stoke Trister
Milton on Stour
Sedgehill
Pythouse
East Hatch
Holton
Cucklington
Peacemarsh
Swallowcliffe
Maperton
Lattiford
Wyke
Coppleridge
Semley
Old Wardour Castle
Ansty
North Cheriton
Motcombe
Donhead St Andrew
Fifield Bavant
South Cheriton
Buckhorn Weston
Madjeston
White Sheet Hill
Horsington
Abbas Combe
Kington Magna
West Stour
Knap Corner
Donhead St Mary
Alvediston
Ebbesborne Wake
Stowell
Templecombe
Carsall Light Rly
East Stour
Ludwell
Woodminton
Bowerchalke
Stowell Hill
Yenston
Henstridge Marsh
Fifehead Magdalen
Stour Provost
Stour Row
Cann
Cann Common
Charlton
Berwick St John
Milborne Wick
Henstridge Ash
Guy's Marsh
Milborne Port
Henstridge
Marnhull
Todber
Melbury Abbas
Twyford
Tollard Royal
Deanland
Sixpenny Handley
Woodyates
Oborne
Margaret Marsh
East Orchard
Compton Abbas
Ashmore
Purse Caundle
Stalbridge
Stalbridge Weston
Sutton Waldron
Fontmell Magna
West Orchard
Hinton St Mary
Haydon
Goathill
Woodcutts
Dean
Farnham
Pentridge
Old Castle
A46
A420
A4
A4175
A431
A36
A39
A367
A3062
A363
A365
A350
A342
A3102
A361
A366
A362
A3098
A359
A371
A303
A357
A30
A354
A360
B3109
B3353
B3107
B3115
B3139
B3110
B3099
B3090
B3414
B390
B3092
B3095
B3081
B3089
B3145
B3091
B3098
B3116
Toll
No. 1, Royal Cres

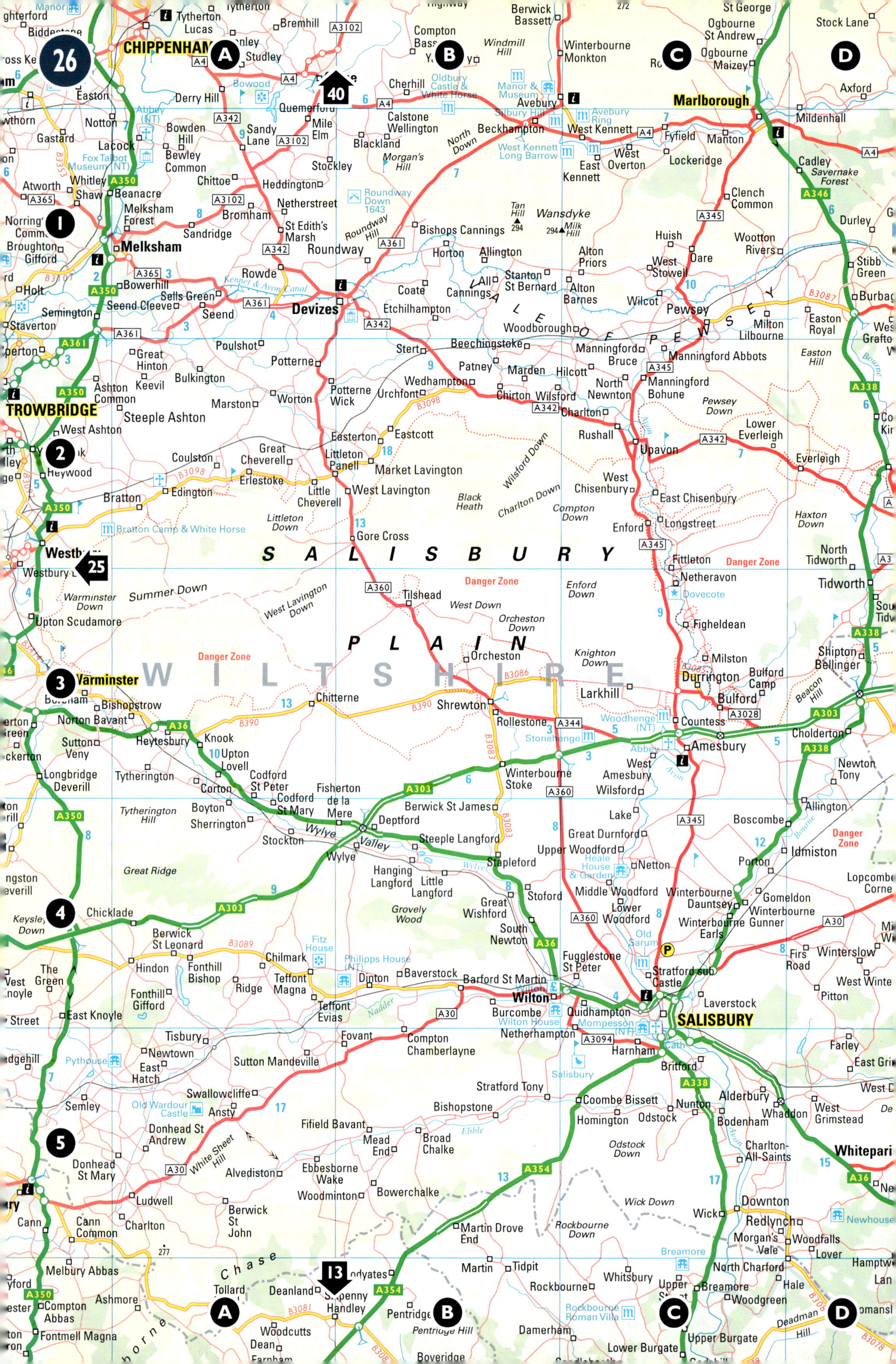

26
CHIPPENHAM
A
B
C
D
40
Tytherton Lucas
Bremhill
Studley
Bowood
Derry Hill
Quemerford
Calne
Compton Bassett
Windmill Hill
Cherhill
Oldbury Castle & White Horse
Calstone Wellington
Blackland
Berwick Bassett
Winterbourne Monkton
Manor & Museum
Avebury
Silbury Hill
Avebury Ring
Beckhampton
West Kennett
West Kennett Long Barrow
East Kennett
West Overton
Fyfield
St George
Ogbourne St Andrew
Ogbourne Maizey
Stock Lane
Axford
Marlborough
Mildenhall
Manton
Lockeridge
Cadley
Savernake Forest
Clench Common
Durley
Easton
Notton
Gastard
Lacock
Fox Talbot Museum (NT)
Bowden Hill
Bewley Common
Sandy Lane
Mile Elm
Stockley
Morgan's Hill
North Down
Atworth
Whitley
Shaw
Beanacre
Melksham Forest
Chittoe
Heddington
Netherstreet
Bromham
Sandridge
Roundway Down 1643
Roundway Hill
St Edith's Marsh
Roundway
Tan Hill
294
Wansdyke
Milk Hill
Bishops Cannings
Horton
Allington
Alton Priors
Huish
Oare
Wootton Rivers
Stibb Green
Burbage
Norrington Common
Broughton Gifford
Melksham
Bowerhill
Rowde
Kennet & Avon Canal
Sells Green
Seend Cleeve
Seend
Devizes
Holt
Semington
Staverton
Coate
All Cannings
Stanton St Bernard
Alton Barnes
Etchilhampton
West Stowell
Wilcot
Pewsey
Milton Lilbourne
Easton Royal
VALE OF PEWSEY
Woodborough
Beechingstoke
Manningford Bruce
Manningford Abbots
Manningford Bohune
Easton Hill
Grafton
Trowbridge
TROWBRIDGE
Great Hinton
Keevil
Ashton Common
Bulkington
Poulshot
Potterne
Potterne Wick
Worton
Marston
Stert
Urchfont
Wedhampton
Patney
Marden
Hilcott
North Newnton
Chirton
Wilsford
Charlton
Pewsey Down
Steeple Ashton
West Ashton
Heywood
Coulston
Great Cheverell
Erlestoke
Easterton
Eastcott
Littleton Panell
Market Lavington
Rushall
Upavon
Lower Everleigh
Everleigh
Wilsford Down
Bratton
Edington
Little Cheverell
West Lavington
Black Heath
Charlton Down
Compton Down
West Chisenbury
East Chisenbury
Longstreet
Enford
Haxton Down
Bratton Camp & White Horse
Littleton Down
Gore Cross
North Tidworth
Westbury
25
SALISBURY
PLAIN
Danger Zone
Fittleton
Netheravon
Dovecote
Tidworth
Tilshead
West Down
Enford Down
Orcheston Down
Figheldean
Warminster Down
Summer Down
West Lavington Down
Upton Scudamore
Orcheston
Knighton Down
Milston
Shipton Bellinger
WILTSHIRE
Warminster
Bishopstrow
Chitterne
Shrewton
Larkhill
Durrington
Bulford Camp
Bulford
Beacon Hill
Norton Bavant
Heytesbury
Knook
Rollestone
Stonehenge
Woodhenge (NT)
Countess
Amesbury
Cholderton
Sutton Veny
Upton Lovell
Codford St Peter
Codford St Mary
Corton
Tytherington
Winterbourne Stoke
West Amesbury
Wilsford
Newton Tony
Longbridge Deverill
Boyton
Sherrington
Fisherton de la Mere
Berwick St James
Deptford
Tytherington Hill
Wylye Valley
Stockton
Wylye
Steeple Langford
Lake
Great Durnford
Upper Woodford
Heale House & Garden
Netton
Boscombe
Allington
Idmiston
Porton
Great Ridge
Hanging Langford
Little Langford
Stapleford
Stoford
Great Wishford
Grovely Wood
South Newton
Middle Woodford
Lower Woodford
Winterbourne Dauntsey
Gomeldon
Winterbourne Gunner
Winterbourne Earls
Lopcombe Corner
Chicklade
Keysley Down
Berwick St Leonard
Hindon
Fonthill Bishop
Fonthill Gifford
Chilmark
Fitz House
Philipps House (NT)
Teffont Magna
Teffont Evias
Dinton
Baverstock
Barford St Martin
Wilton
Burcombe
Wilton House
Quidhampton
Fugglestone St Peter
Old Sarum
Stratford sub Castle
Laverstock
SALISBURY
Firs Road
Winterslow
West Winterslow
Pitton
Ridge
East Knoyle
West Knoyle
The Green
Tisbury
Newtown
East Hatch
Pythouse
Fovant
Compton Chamberlayne
Netherhampton
Mompesson
Harnham
Britford
Farley
East Grimstead
Sutton Mandeville
Swallowcliffe
Semley
Old Wardour Castle
Ansty
Donhead St Andrew
Donhead St Mary
Stratford Tony
Bishopstone
Coombe Bissett
Homington
Odstock
Nunton
Alderbury
Whaddon
West Grimstead
Bodenham
Charlton-All-Saints
Odstock Down
Whiteparish
Fifield Bavant
Mead End
Broad Chalke
Ebble
White Sheet Hill
Alvediston
Ebbesborne Wake
Woodminton
Bowerchalke
Wick Down
Wick
Downton
Redlynch
Morgan's Vale
Woodfalls
Newhouse
Lover
Ludwell
Charlton
Berwick St John
Cann
Cann Common
Martin Drove End
Rockbourne Down
Breamore
North Charford
Hale
Melbury Abbas
Chase
13
Tollard
Deanland
Sixpenny Handley
Martin
Tidpit
Rockbourne
Whitsbury
Upper Street
Breamore
Woodgreen
Ashmore
Compton Abbas
Pentridge
Pentridge Hill
Rockbourne Roman Villa
Damerham
Deadman Hill
Fontmell Magna
Woodcutts
Dean
Farnham
Boveridge
Lower Burgate
Upper Burgate
A4
A342
A350
A361
A365
A3102
A345
A346
A338
A360
A344
A303
A36
A30
A354
A3028
A3094
B3098
B3086
B390
B3089
B3081
B3087
B3083
1
2
3
4
5

27
D
E
F
G
I
2
3
4
5
41
28
15
M4
M3
A34
A303
A339
A31
A343
A338
A4
A30
A272
A3057
A3090
A335
A27
A36
A337
A35
WEST BERKS
HAMPSHIRE
NEWBURY
Thatcham
ANDOVER
BASINGSTOKE
WINCHESTER
EASTLEIGH
Romsey
Hungerford
Kintbury
Whittonditch
Knighton
Chilton Foliat
Shefford Woodlands
Hungerford Newtown
Wickham
Wickham Heath
Eddington
Froxfield
Chisbury
Little Bedwyn
Great Bedwyn
Avington
Halfway
Stockcross
Speen
Marsh Benham
Enborne
Hamstead Marshall
Chieveley
Welford
Weston
Boxford
Bagnor
Donnington
Newbury II 1644
Newbury I 1643
Curridge
Hermitage
Little Hungerford
Yattendon
Bradfield
Southend
Stanford Dingley
Bucklebury
Cold Ash
Chapel Row
Upper Bucklebury
Midgham
Beenham
Woolhampton
Aldermaston Wharf
Sulhamstead
Ufton Nervet
Aldermaston
Brimpton
Crookham
Wasing
Greenham
Shaw
Bagshot
Shalbourne
Ham
Inkpen
Upper Green
West Woodhay
Walbury Hill
Combe
East Woodhay
North End
Ball Hill
Broad Laying
Wash Common
Woolton Hill
East End
Highclere
Highclere Castle
Newtown
Burghclere
Sandham Mem Chapel (NT)
Headley
Plastow Green
Ashford Hill
Heath End
Fair Oak
Baughurst
Tadley
Pamber Heath
Pamber Green
Pamber End
Little London
Silchester
Mortimer West End
Aldermaston Soke
Wilton
Rivar
Buttermere
Marten
East Grafton
Oxenwood
Tidcombe
Fosbury
Vernham Street
Linkenholt
Faccombe
Vernham Dean
Haydown Hill
Chute Causeway
Ashmansworth
Sidown Hill
Crux Easton
Whitway
Ecchinswell
Kingsclere
Sydmonton
Old Burghclere
Wolverton
Ramsdell
Charter Alley
Monk Sherborne
Sherborne St John
Upton
Upper Chute
Chute Standen
Chute Cadley
Lower Chute
Tangley
Ibthorpe
Hurstbourne Tarrant
Doles Wood
Woodcott
Binley
Litchfield
Egbury
Hannington
North Oakley
Ibworth
Upper Wootton
Wootton St Lawrence
Ludgershall
Wildhern
Hatherden
Stoke
Little London
Swampton
St Mary Bourne
Enham Alamein
Smannell
Clanville
Penton Mewsey
Appleshaw
Weyhill
Charlton
Kimpton
Fyfield
Thruxton
Mus of the Iron Age
Finkley Down Farm Park
Picket Piece
Andover Down
Whitchurch
Whitchurch Silk Mill
Freefolk
Laverstoke
Overton
Quidhampton
Ashe
Oakley
Deane
Southington
East Oakley
Steventon
Kempshott
Cliddesden
Dummer
North Waltham
Farleigh Wallop
Ellisfield
Nutley
Axford
Popham
Woodmancott
Preston Candover
Chilton Candover
Brown Candover
Bradley
Upper Wield
Totford
Northington
Hattingley
The Grange
Monxton
Amport
Quarley
Anna Valley
Upper Clatford
Abbotts Ann
Bury Hill
Goodworth Clatford
Grateley
Harewood Forest
Longparish
Middleton
Forton
Barton Stacey Camp
Barton Stacey
Hurstbourne Priors
Tufton
Micheldever Sta.
Palestine
Wherwell
Newton Stacey
Bullington
Egypt
Hunton
West Stratton
East Stratton
Micheldever Forest
Micheldever
Micheldever Wood
Fullerton
Chilbolton
Sutton Scotney
Wonston
Stoke Charity
Over Wallop
Middle Wallop
Nether Wallop
Longstock
Leckford
Stockbridge
Crawley Down
Crawley
South Wonston
Roman Road
Worthy Down
Kings Worthy
Winchester
Old Alresford
Bighton
Alresford
Itchen Abbas
Itchen Stoke
Martyr Worthy
Avington Park
Easton
Avington
Ovington
New Alresford
Bishop's Sutton
Ropley
Gundleton
Broughton
Houghton Lodge
Houghton
Whiteshoot Hill
The Common
West Tytherley
Bossington
Horsebridge
King's Somborne
Little Somborne
Up Somborne
Ashley
Littleton
Headbourne Worthy
Sparsholt
East Tytherley
Brook
Farley Down
Farley Mount
Pitt Down
Pitt
Oliver's Battery
Standon
Chilcomb
Intech 2000
Tichborne
Cheriton
Cheriton 1644
New Cheriton
Bramdean
Hinton Ampner
Beauworth
Kilmeston
Brockwood Park
Longwood Warren
Morestead
Mottisfont
Mottisfont Abbey Gardens (NT)
Michelmersh
Braishfield
Hursley
Compton
Shawford
Twyford
Owslebury
West Meon
Warnford
Lockerley
East Dean
Carter's Clay
Kent's Oak
Newtown
Awbridge
Timsbury
Stanbridge Earls
Abbottswood
Sir Harold Hillier Gdns
Ampfield
Otterbourne
Colden Common
Hensting
Marwell Zoo
Upham
Corhampton Down
Corhampton
Exton
Meonstoke
Melchet Court
Sherfield English
Romsey Abbey
Broadlands
East Wellow
West Wellow
Plaitford
North Baddesley
Chandler's Ford
Fisher's Pond
Crowdhill
Bishopstoke
Fair Oak
Lower Upham
Dean
Toothill
Lee
Chilworth
Canada
Paulton's Park
Ower
Calmore
Upton
Rownhams
Nursling
Testwood
Bassett
North Stoneham
Southampton International
Itchen Valley
Horton Heath
Wintershill
Durley
Bishop's Waltham
Palace
Swanmore
Droxford
Brockbridge
Soberton
Newbridge
Newtown
Swaythling

28
A
B
C
D
1
2
3
4
5
42
27
15
READING
NEWBURY
BASINGSTOKE
WINCHESTER
Wokingham
Woodley
Tilehurst
Thatcham
Theale
Tadley
Hook
Odiham
FLEET
FARNBO
Alton
Bordon
Petersfield
Sandhurst
Yateley
Bishop's Waltham
Bishopstoke
EASTLEIGH
W BERKS
WOKINGHAM
HAMPSHIRE
NORTH
Chieveley
Hermitage
Bucklebury
Bradfield
Englefield
Calcot
Earley
Lower Earley
Winnersh
Shinfield
Burghfield
Spencers Wood
Mortimer
Aldermaston
Greenham
Kingsclere
Burghclere
Overton
Oakley
Old Basing
Whitchurch
Stacey Camp
Micheldever
Popham
Dummer
New Alresford
Four Marks
Chawton
Selborne
Liss
Greatham
Whitehill
Headley
Stockbridge
Twyford
Colden Common
Upham
Droxford
Swanmore
Meonstoke
Corhampton
Exton
West Meon
East Meon
Chalton
Chidden
Clanfield
Soberton
Horton Heath
Fair Oak
Southampton International
M4
M3
A3
A31
A33
A34
A303
A339
A272
A32
A30
A327
A329(M)

29
43
30
16
D
E
F
G
1
2
3
4
5
Hawthorn Hill
Maiden's Green
Warfield
Winkfield
Winkfield Row
Newell Green
Windsor Forest
Windsor Great Park
Cranbourne
Cooper's Hill
Englefield Green
Woodside
Wraysbury
Hythe End
Stanwell
Stanwell Moor
East Bedfont
Feltham
Ashford
HOUNSLOW
Twickenham
Teddington
Ham
RICHMOND UPON THAMES
Richmond Park
KINGSTON UPON THAMES
Wimbledon
Norbiton
New Malden
BRACKNELL
North Ascot
Ascot
Burleigh
Cheapside
Sunninghill
Sunningdale
South Ascot
Virginia Water
Thorpe
STAINES
Laleham
Littleton
Sunbury
Hanworth
West Molesey
East Molesey
Hampton
Hampton Court Palace
Surbiton
Upper Halliford
Shepperton
Chertsey
WALTON-ON-THAMES
Weybridge
Molesey
Weston Green
Thames Ditton
Long Ditton
Tolworth
Worcester Park
Look Out Discovery Park
Surrey Hill
Bagshot
Crowthorne
Windlesham
Chobham Common
Longcross
Lyne
Addlestone
New Haw
Row Town
Woodham
Ottershaw
Hersham
West End
ESHER
Claygate
Hook
Chessington
Ewell
EPSOM
Whiteley Village
Brooklands
Claremont Landscape Garden (NT)
Malden Rushett
Oxshott
Chessington World of Adventures
Horton Park Farm
CAMBERLEY
Blackwater
Lightwater
Burrowhill
Chobham
Bagshot Heath
Donkey Town
Bisley
Knaphill
Horsell
St John's
Byfleet
West Byfleet
Wisley
Pyrford
WOKING
Cobham
Stoke D'Abernon
Downside
Martyr's Green
Ashtead
FRIMLEY
Frimley Green
Deepcut
Brookwood
Mytchett
Farnborough
Pirbright
Ripley
Ockham
Old Woking
Mayford
Send
Send Marsh
Sutton Green
Fetcham
LEATHERHEAD
Little Bookham
Great Bookham
Effingham
Givons Grove
Mickleham
Tadworth
Headley
Walton on the Hill
The Hermitage
Pebble Coombe
Box Hill (NT)
Danger Zone
Henley Park
Worplesdon
Pitch Place
Stoughton
West Clandon
East Horsley
West Horsley
Hatchlands (NT)
Polesden Lacey (NT)
Westhumble
Denbies Wine Centre
Chapel Farm Animal Trail
Buckland
Betchworth
North Camp
Ash Vale
Normandy
Wood Street Village
Burpham
Merrow
East Clandon
Clandon Park (NT)
Newland's Corner
North Town
Ash
Flexford
Wanborough
Tongham
Badshot Lea
Onslow Village
GUILDFORD
Guildford House Gallery
Dorking
Brockham
South Park
REIGATE
Hog's Back
Seale
Puttenham
Compton
Shere
Gomshall
Albury
Albury Park
Wotton
Abinger Hammer
Westcott
Runfold
FARNHAM
The Sands
Shalford
Chilworth
Wonersh
Blackheath
Farley Green
Sutton Abinger
Abinger Common
Friday Street
North Holmwood
South Holmwood
Leigh
Dovers Green
Lower Bourne
Waverley Abbey
Shackleford
Hurtmore
Farncombe
Bramley
Shamley Green
Peaslake
Holmbury St Mary
Leith Hill
Coldharbour
Beare Green
Parkgate
Norwood Hill
Charleshill
Tilford
Elstead
Peper Harow
Eashing
Godalming
Busbridge
Hurtwood Common
Stroud Common
Forest Green
Newdigate
Charlwood
Millbridge
Frensham Little Pond
Frensham
Milford
Witley Common (NT)
Winkworth Arboretum (NT)
Thorncombe Street
Rowly
Grafham
Hascombe
Ewhurst
Jayes Park
Capel
Ockley
Gatwick Zoo
Rushmoor
Thursley
Bowlhead Green
Wheelerstreet
Witley
Hydestile
Hambledon
Ewhurst Green
Cranleigh
Loxhill
Ifieldwood
Rusper
Beacon Hill
Brook
Wormley
Sandhills
Walliswood
Oakwoodhill
Kingsfold
Lambs Green
Hindhead
Gibbet Hill
Grayshott
Grayswood
Chiddingfold
Dunsfold
Alfold Crossways
Alfold
Ellen's Green
Bucks Green
Rudgwick
Rowhook
Warnham
Faygate
Buchan
Haslemere
Shottermill
Hammer
Camelsdale
Linchmere
Educational Museum
Lythe Hill
Ramsnest Common
Fisherstreet
Kingsley Green
Plaistow
Loxwood
Ifold
The Haven
Slinfold
Broadbridge Heath
HORSHAM
Holmbush
Roffey
Colgate
St Leonard's Forest
Black Down
Northchapel
Buckman Corner
Roundstreet Common
Five Oaks
Itchingfield
Christ's Hosp. Sta.
Denne Park
Ashfold Crossways
Mannings Heath
Monk's Gate
Fernhurst
Lurgashall
Kirdford
Newpound Common
Fishers Farm Park
Barns Green
Lower Beeding
Henley
Lickfold
Balls Cross
Wisborough Green
Billingshurst
Southwater
Nuthurst
Copsale
Brooks Green
Coneyhurst
Strood Green
Maplehurst
The Bar
Woolbeding
Lodsworth
Upperton
Gunter's Bridge
Adversane
Burdocks
Easebourne
River
Tillington
Petworth House (NT)
Petworth
Broadford Bridge
North Heath
Coolham
Shipley
Cowfold
Midhurst
Cowdray House (ruins)
South Ambersham
Selham
Byworth
Egdean
Gay Street
Broomer's Corner
Dial Post
West Grinstead
Partridge Green
Wineham
West Lavington
Coultershaw Bridge
Fittleworth
Stopham
Codmore Hill
Nutbourne
West Chiltington
Bepton
Cocking
Heyshott
Graffham
Duncton
Coates
Pulborough
Ham
Wiggonholt
Pulborough Brooks R.S.P.B. Nature Reserve
Thakeham
Warminghurst
West Chiltington Common
Abingworth
Ashington
Bines Green
Henfield
Coldwaltham
Watersfield
East Lavington
Didling
SURREY
DOWNS
WEST SUSSEX
M25
M3
A3
A24
A272
A29
A281
A283

A
B
C
D
1
2
3
4
5
44
29
17
Wembley
Willesden
Harlesden
CAMDEN
HACKNEY
TOWER HAMLETS
Barking
Greenford
Perivale
Yeading
EALING
Hayes
Southall
Hanwell
Acton
HAMMERSMITH & FULHAM
CITY OF WESTMINSTER
CITY OF LONDON
Shoreditch
Finsbury
Marylebone
Stepney
Poplar
Beckton
Hyde Park
West Drayton
Norwood Green
Chiswick
KENSINGTON & CHELSEA
Bermondsey
Sipson
Harmondsworth
Heston
Brentford
Deptford
Charlton
Cranford
Osterley
Barnes
Fulham
Battersea
SOUTHWARK
Camberwell
GREENWICH
Kidbrooke
Blackheath
Isleworth
Kew
Mortlake
Putney
WANDSWORTH
Clapham
LEWISHAM
Eltham
Stanwell
HOUNSLOW
RICHMOND UPON THAMES
Roehampton
LAMBETH
Dulwich
Hither Green
East Bedfont
Feltham
Twickenham
Richmond Park
Catford
Ashford
Ham
Teddington
Wimbledon Common
Upper Tooting
West Norwood
Sydenham
Grove Park
Mottingham
Streatham
Crystal Palace
Hanworth
KINGSTON UPON THAMES
Wimbledon
Penge
Chislehurst
Upper Norwood
Beckenham
Bickley
Littleton
Sunbury
West Molesey
Hampton
Norbiton
Mitcham
South Norwood
BROMLEY
Upper Halliford
East Molesey
Surbiton
New Malden
MERTON
Morden
Eden Park
West Wickham
Hayes
Orpington
Weston Green
Thames Ditton
Long Ditton
Tolworth
Worcester Park
The Wrythe
Beddington Corner
Beddington
Shirley
Addington
Locksbottom
WALTON-ON-THAMES
ESHER
Hook
Carshalton
Wallington
CROYDON
Keston
Farnborough
Hersham
West End
Claygate
Chessington
Ewell
Cheam
SUTTON
Whiteley Village
South Beddington
Belmont
Selsdon
New Addington
Leaves Green
Malden Rushett
EPSOM
Purley
Sanderstead
London Biggin Hill
Oxshott
Woodmansterne
Coulsdon
Kenley
Farleigh
Byfleet
Cobham
Stoke D'Abernon
BANSTEAD
Chipstead
Biggin Hill
Downside
Ashtead
Epsom
Whyteleafe
Chelsham
Warlingham
Martyr's Green
LEATHERHEAD
Burgh Heath
Tatsfield
Fetcham
Tadworth
Kingswood
Hooley
Chaldon
Woldingham
Little Bookham
Great Bookham
Headley
Walton on the Hill
Caterham
Titsey
East Horsley
Effingham
Givons Grove
Mickleham
The Hermitage
Merstham
Limpsfield
West Horsley
Pebble Coombe
Godstone
Oxted
East Clandon
Westhumble
Buckland
Nutfield
Hurst Green
Tandridge
Holland
Betchworth
REIGATE
Redhill
Bletchingley
Dorking
Brockham
South Park
South Nutfield
South Godstone
Shere
Gomshall
Wotton
Westcott
Abinger Hammer
Doversgreen
Ridge Green
Crowhurst Lane End
Crowhurst
Marlpit Hill
Albury
North Holmwood
Leigh
Sidlow
Redhill Aerodrome & Heliport
The Grange
Blindley Heath
Friday Street
Abinger Common
Salfords
Haxted
Peaslake
South Holmwood
Outwood
Holmbury St Mary
Leith Hill
Coldharbour
Beare Green
Parkgate
Norwood Hill
Horley
Horne
Smallfield
Lingfield
Hookwood
Povey Cross
Felcourt
Forest Green
Newdigate
Charlwood
Gatwick (London)
Burstow
Newchapel
Dormansland
Jayes Park
Capel
Tinsley Green
Shipley Bridge
Dormans Park
Ewhurst
Lowfield Heath
Copthorne
Felbridge
Ockley
Ewhurst Green
County Oak
Ifieldwood
East Grinstead
Hammerwood
Walliswood
Rusper
Ifield
Three Bridges
Pound Hill
Crawley Down
Brockhurst
Sunnyside
Oakwoodhill
Kingsfold
Lambs Green
Gossops Green
CRAWLEY
Crabbet Park
Saint Hill
Brambletye
Ashurstwood
Worth
Turners Hill
Forest Row
Rowhook
Faygate
Rudgwick
Warnham
Bucks Green
Selsfield Common
Colgate
Holmbush
Pease Pottage
Broadbridge Heath
Roffey
Sharpthorne
West Hoathly
St Leonard's Forest
Wych Cross
The Haven
Slinfold
HORSHAM
Balcombe
Highbrook
Buckman Corner
Handcross
Ashfold Crossways
Ardingly
Horsted Keynes
Five Oaks
Itchingfield
Denne Park
Mannings Heath
Staplefield
Chelwood Gate
Newpound Common
Barns Green
Monk's Gate
Dan
Lower Beeding
Brook Street
Paxhill Park
Billingshurst
Nuthurst
Warninglid
Southwater
SURREY
WEST SUSSEX
GREATER LONDON
NORTH
M4
M3
M25
M23
A40
A4
A3
A24
A23
A22
A264
A217
A25
A29
A281

31
THURROCK
MEDWAY
DOWNS
KENT
WEALD
EAST SUSSEX
45
32
18
D
E
F
G
I
2
3
4
5
CANVEY ISLAND
Corringham
Stanford-le-Hope
Thames Haven
South Ockendon
South Hornchurch
Dagenham
Rainham
Wennington
Aveley
Purfleet
Thamesmead
Erith Marshes
Erith
Belvedere
Abbey Wood
East Wickham
Bexleyheath
Slade Green
DARTFORD
Crayford
Greenhithe
West Thurrock
GRAYS
Tilbury
East Tilbury
Chadwell St Mary
Linford
Swanscombe
GRAVESEND
NORTHFLEET
Stone
Bluewater
Wilmington
Hawley
Darenth
Sutton at Hone
Hextable
Swanley
Crockenhill
St Mary Cray
St Paul's Cray
Foots Cray
North Cray
Coldblow
South Darenth
Horton Kirby
Farningham
Eynsford
Fawkham Green
Hartley
Longfield
New Barn
Istead Rise
Cobham
Shorne
Higham
Cliffe
Cliffe Woods
Cooling
Hoo
High Halstow
Chattenden
Upper Upnor
Frindsbury
Strood
ROCHESTER
CHATHAM
GILLINGHAM
Brompton
Luton
Rainham
Wigmore
Walderslade
Capstone
Lidsing
Bredhurst
Stockbury
Borstal
Wouldham
Burham
Blue Bell Hill
Eccles
Aylesford
Boxley
Detling
Thurnham
MAIDSTONE
Bearsted
Sandling
Ditton
Larkfield
East Malling
West Malling
Leybourne
New Hythe
Snodland
Halling
Cuxton
Luddesdown
Meopham
Meopham Green
Culverstone Green
Vigo Village
Wrotham
Wrotham Heath
Borough Green
Platt
Ightham
Ivy Hatch
Stone Street
Seal
Kemsing
Heaverham
Otford
Shoreham
West Kingsdown
Knockholt
Halstead
Badgers Mount
Chevening
Dunton Green
Riverhead
Sevenoaks
Chipstead
Sundridge
Brasted
Westerham
Ide Hill
Toy's Hill
Sevenoaks Weald
Underriver
Shipbourne
Plaxtol
Dunk's Green
Mereworth
West Peckham
Wateringbury
Teston
Barming
East Barming
Tovil
Loose
Coxheath
East Farleigh
West Farleigh
Nettlestead
Nettlestead Green
Yalding
Hunton
Linton
Boughton Monchelsea
Chart Sutton
Sutton Valence
Langley
Otham
Leeds
Hildenborough
Hadlow
Golden Green
East Peckham
Hale Street
Beltring
Laddingford
Tonbridge
Tudeley
Five Oak Green
Capel
Paddock Wood
Collier Street
Marden
Marden Beech
Marden Thorn
Staplehurst
Headcorn
Frittenden
Brenchley
Horsmonden
Matfield
Pembury
Kipping's Cross
Lamberhurst
Lamberhurst Quarter
Goudhurst
Kilndown
Bedgebury Cross
Cranbrook
Sissinghurst
Benenden
Hawkhurst
Flimwell
Ticehurst
Wadhurst
Cousley Wood
Durgates
Stonegate
Mayfield
Rotherfield
Crowborough
Jarvis Brook
Frant
Eridge Green
Groombridge
Langton Green
Rusthall
ROYAL TUNBRIDGE WELLS
Southborough
Bidborough
Penshurst
Leigh
Chiddingstone
Chiddingstone Causeway
Hever
Markbeech
Cowden
Hartfield
Ashurst
Speldhurst
Fordcombe
Etchingham
Hurst Green
M25
M26
M20
M2
A2
A20
A21
A25
A26
A227
A228
A229
A13
A282
A249
A264
A267

A
B
C
D
SOUTHEND-ON-SEA
46
Shoeburyness
Chapman Sands
Leigh Beck
CANVEY ISLAND
Sea Life Centre
Southend Pier
Peter Pan's Adventure Island
Allhallows-on-Sea
Allhallows
Halstow Marshes
St Mary's Marshes
St Mary's Hoo
Isle of Grain
Grain
Lower Stoke
Northward Hill
Stoke
Stoke Saltings
Wallend
Halstow
Hoo
Kingsnorth Power Station
Queenborough
Sheerness
West Minster
Halfway Houses
Minster
Eastchurch
Warden Point
Warden
Leysdown-on-Sea
ISLE OF SHEPPEY
Elmley Island
Kingshill
Eastchurch Marshes
Isle of Harty
Chetney Marshes
MEDWAY
Upnor
Upper Upnor
Chatham Historic Dockyard & World Naval Base
Brompton
Grange
GILLINGHAM
Luton
Upchurch
Iwade
Lower Halstow
Kemsley
Swale Sta.
The Swale
Shell Ness
WHITSTABLE
Swalecliffe
Chestfield
Seasalter
Rainham
Wigmore
Walderslade
Newington
Hartlip
Bobbing
Milton Regis
Sittingbourne & Kemsley Lt Rly
Conyer
Uplees
Murston
SITTINGBOURNE
Borden
Lidsing
Bredhurst
Stockbury
Oad Street
Tunstall
Teynham Sta.
Teynham
Bapchild
Rodmersham
Luddenham Court
Oare
Graveney
Yorkletts
Clapham Hill
Pean Hill
Faversham
Goodnestone
Hernhill
Dargate
Honey Hill
Tyler Hill
Blean
Preston
Maison Dieu
Ospringe
Lynsted
Highsted
Bredgar
Kit's Coty House
Little Kit's Coty
31
Abbey
Boxley
Sandling
Allington
Detling
Thurnham
Hucking
Bicknor
Wormshill
Broad Street
Frinsted
Milstead
Newnham
Doddington
Whitehill
North Street
Brogdale Horticultural Trust
Boughton Street
Dunkirk
Rough Common
Harbledown
Thanington
Hales Place
Overslean
Chartham Hatch
Sheldwich
Selling
Eastling
Wichling
MAIDSTONE
Maidstone
Eyhorne Manor
Bearsted
Hollingbourne
Eyhorne Street
West Street
Frith
Throwley
Badlesmere
Leaveland
Shottenden
Chilham
Old Wives Lees
Shalmsford Street
Chartham
Street End
Otterden Place
Warren Street
NORTH DOWNS
Chilham Castle
Stalisfield Green
Molash
Godmersham
Petham
Upper Hardres Court
Stoneacre (NT)
Shepway
Leeds
Otham
Leeds Castle & Gdns
Harrietsham
Lenham
Langley
Langley Heath
Broomfield
Kingswood
Sandway
Loose
Boughton Green
Chart Corner
Five Wents
Lenham Heath
Charing
Challock
Eastwell Park
Boughton Aluph
Bilting
Crundale
Sole Street
Waltham
Bossingham
Boughton Monchelsea Place
Warmlake
Chart Sutton
Sutton Valence
Liverton Street
Ulcombe
Grafty Green
Boughton Malherbe
Egerton
Charing Heath
Westwell Leacon
Westwell
Boughton Lees
Wye
Hassell Street
Bodsham Green
Stelling Minnis
Cross-at-Hand
Milebush
Egerton Forstal
Little Chart
Pluckley
Pluckley Thorne
Pluckley Sta.
Ram Lane
Hothfield
Kennington
Brook
National Nature Trails
Hastingleigh
Lymbridge Green
Sixmile
Headcorn
Staplehurst
Marden Thorn
ASHFORD
Willesborough Lees
Stowting
Rhodes Minnis
Maltman's Hill
Great Chart
Hinxhill
Smarden
Haffenden Quarter
Wick Hill
Frittenden
Sissinghurst Castle (NT)
Ashford
South Willesborough
Willesborough
Sevington
Brabourne
Brabourne Lees
Mersham
Smeeth
Standen
Bethersden
Bull Green
Curteis' Corner
Kingsnorth
Cheeseman's Green
Swanton Mill
Sellindge
Stanford
Beachborough
Postling
Cranbrook Common
Three Chimneys
Biddenden
High Halden
Shadoxhurst
Stonestreet Green
Aldington
Westenhanger Sta.
Folkestone
Sissinghurst
Wilsley Green
Cranbrook
East End
London Beach
St Michaels
Hengherst
Bromley Green
Redbrook Street
Sugarloaf
Stone Cross
Bonnington
Court-at-Street
Lympne
Port Lympne
West Hythe
Benenden
Hole Park
Tenterden
Brook Street
Woodchurch
The Leacon
Hamstreet
Ruckinge
Bilsington
Romney Marsh
Gill's Green
Iden Green
Hawkhurst
Four Throws
Rolvenden
Rolvenden Sta.
Great Maytham Hall
Rolvenden Layne
Leigh Green
Ashenden
Smallhythe Place (NT)
Small Hythe
Shirley Moor
Reading Street
Kenardington
Warehorne
Appledore Heath
Appledore
Appledore Sta.
Snave
Newchurch
Burmarsh
Romney, Hythe & Dymchurch Railway
Dymchurch
Martello Tower
St Mary in the Marsh
St Mary's Bay
19
The Moor
Sandhurst
Linkhill
Wittersham Rd. Sta.
Wittersham
Stone
Snargate
Brenzett
Ivychurch
New Romney
The Stocks
Brookland
Bodiam (NT)
Bodiam
Kent & East Sussex Rly
M2
M20
A2
A20
A28
A249
A229
A262
A268
A274
A250
A251
A252
A259
A261
A290
A299
A2070
A228
A231
A278
A2045
B2000
B2001
B2004
B2008
B2231
B2205
B2067
B2068
B2080
B2082
B2085
B2086
B1014
B1016

D
E
F
G
47
3.2 miles to 1 inch
0 2 4 6 8 10 miles
0 2 4 6 8 10 km
2 km to 1 cm
1
2
3
4
5
MARGATE
South Channel
Long Nose Spit
Dreamland
Foreness Point
Tudor House
Cliftonville
White Ness
Westgate on Sea
Kingsgate
North Foreland
Salmeston Grange
St Peter's
Bleak House
BROADSTAIRS
Dickens House
RAMSGATE
Birchington
Quex House & Gdns
RAF Manston Spitfire & Hurricane Memorial Bldg
Isle of Thanet
Acol
Manston
Minster
Monkton
Cliffs End
Abbey
St Augustine's Cross
Pegwell Bay
Sandwich Flats
HERNE BAY
Reculver
Towers & Roman Fort
Hillborough
Beltinge
Broomfield
St Nicholas at Wade
Herne
Hunters Forstal
Highstead
Boyden Gate
Sarre
Gore Street
Maypole
Chislet
Hoath
Upstreet
West Stourmouth
East Stourmouth
Westmarsh
Roman Road
Grove
Stodmarsh
Hersden
Westbere
Preston
Richborough Castle
Stonar Cut
Great Stonar
Sandwich
Sandwich Bay
Ware
Elmstone
Stodmarsh
Great Stour
Hoaden
Cop Street
Bird Park
Roman Amphitheatre
Wickhambreaux
Littlebourne
Ickham
Ash
Salutation Gdn
Toll
Howletts Wild Animal Park
Wingham
Marshborough
Woodnesborough
Staple
Bramling
Bekesbourne
Patrixbourne
Worth
Goodnestone Park
Goodnestone
Eastry
Ham
Hacklinge
Bridge
Adisham
Chillenden
Knowlton
Finglesham
Hardres
Aylesham
Nonington
Betteshanger
Sholden
DEAL
Deal
Kingston
Easole Street
Tilmanstone
Northbourne
Great Mongeham
Barham
Womenswold
Elvington
East Studdal
Walmer
Ripple
Walmer Castle & Garden
Derringstone
Barfrestone
Eythorne
Sutton
Kingsdown
Woollage Green
Shepherdswell (Sibertswold)
Ashley
West Langdon
Ringwould
Breach
Denton
Lydden
Bladbean
Wingmore
Coldred
Martin Mill Sta.
East Langdon
Wootton
Lydden
Whitfield
Guston
St Margaret's at Cliffe
Selstead
West Cliffe
St Margaret's Bay
The Pines
Elham
Temple Ewell
Acrise Place
Ewell Minnis
South Foreland
Ottinge
Swingfield Minnis
Alkham
Buckland
Dover
DOVER
St Radigund's Abbey
Lyminge
Densole
Drellingore
De Bradelei Wharf
Paddlesworth
Hawkinge
Maxton
West Hougham
Farthingloe
Knights Templar Church
Etchinghill
Capel le Ferne
Channel Tunnel Terminal
Channel Tunnel
Calais 1/2 hr-1 1/4 hrs, Oostende 2 hrs
Newington
East Wear Bay
Cheriton
FOLKESTONE
Sandgate
Rotunda Amusement Park
Hythe
STRAIT OF DOVER
A28
A299
A253
A256
A257
A258
A254
A255
A2
A20
A260
A291
B2046
B2011
B2050
B2052

A
B
C
D
1
2
3
4
5
48
David's (Tyddewi)
St Non's Chapel
Solva
Green Scar
Dinas Fawr
Brawdy
Penycwm
Llethr
Newgale Sands
Ramsey Sound
Ynys Bery
Dudwell Mountain
178
Mountain Water
Treffgarne
Leweston
Spittal
Upper Scolton
Walton East
Wolfsdale
Scolton Manor
Rudbaxton
Clarbeston
Clarbeston Road
Roch
Folly
Camrose
Keeston
Tangiers
Poyston Cross
Crundale
Wiston
Rickets Head
Nolton
Pelcomb Cross
Pelcomb Bridge
Lambston
Druidston
Prendergast
ST BRIDE'S BAY
Sutton
Castle Mus & Art Gallery
Haverfordwest (Hwlffordd)
The Rhos
Haroldston West
Portfield Gate
Priory
Uzmaston
Picton
Broad Haven
Dreenhill
Merlin's Bridge
Broadway
Pope Hill
Woodbine
Boulston
Stack Rocks
Little Haven
Walton West
Ratford Bridge
Lower Freystrop
Landshipping
Talbenny
Rosepool
North Johnston
Hook
Western Cleddau
The Nab Head
Walwyn's Castle
Freystrop Cross
Garland Stone
St Brides
Robeston Cross
Tiers Cross
Johnston
Llangwm
Skomer Island
Wooltack Point
Hasguard
PEMBROKESHIRE
Deer Park
Marloes
Sandy Haven
Thornton
Rosemarket
Sardis
Newton Mountain
Mew Stone
Herbrandston
Steynton
Lawrenny
Cresswell Quay
Gateholm Island
St Ishmael's
Houghton
Broad Sound
Hoopers Point
Honeyborough
Llanstadwell
Waterston
Milford Haven (Aberdaugleddau)
Dale
Burton
The Stack
Dale Point
Neyland
Toll
Upton
Carew
Newton
The Head
Skokholm Island
MILFORD HAVEN
Cosheston
Rosslare 3¼ hrs
Thorn I.
Pembroke Dock (Doc Penfro)
Waterloo
Milton
Angle
Angle Bay
Pwllcrochan
St Ann's Head
Rhoscrowther
Sheep Island
Hundleton
Pembroke (Penfro)
Lamphey
Newton
Maiden Wells
Kingsfold
Hodgeston
Freshwater West
Ruins
Castlemartin
Warren
St Twynnells
Freshwater East
PEMBROKESHIRE COAST NATIONAL PARK
Blucks Pool
St Petrox
Cheriton
Trewent Point
Linney
Merrion
Linney Head
Danger Zone
Stackpole
Crow Rock
Bosherston
Toes
Buckspool
The Wash
Stackpole Head
Broad Haven
Saddle Head
Chapel
St Govan's Head
A487
A40
A4076
A477
A4075
B4330
B4329
B4341
B4327
B4325
B4322
B4320
B4319
3.2 miles to 1 inch
0 2 4 6 8 10 miles
0 2 4 6 8 10 km
2 km to 1 cm

35
49
36
D
E
F
G
D
E
F
G
2
3
4
5
Llanycefn
Login
Mynach
Maesgwynne
Gellywen
Abernant
Newchurch
Llanboidy
Bletherston
Llandissilio
Henllan Amgoed
Castell Gorfod
Meidrim
Merthyr
Tre-vaughan
Carmarthen (Caerfyrddin)
Rhydywrach
Llanfallteg
Llanfallteg West
Cwmfelin Boeth
Llangynin
Bron-y-Gaer
Sarnau
Johnstown
Llanllwch
Pensarn
Clynderwen
Gelly
Bethesda
Llanddewi Velfrey
Whitland Abbey
Whitland
Pwll Trap
Bancyfelin
Cwmffrwd
Llawhaden
Robeston Wathen
A40
Trevaughan
Llwyn-y-brain
St Clears
Llangynog
Llangain
Croesyceiliog
Canaston Bridge
Narberth (Arberth)
Redstone Bank
Crinow
Lampeter Velfrey
CARMARTHENSHIRE
A4075
Cold Blow
Brandy Hill
Llanddowror
A4066
A484
Llangendeirne
Oakwood Leisure Park
Princes Gate
Taverenspite
B4328
Cwmllyfri
Pontantwn
Cross Hands
A4115
Templeton
B4314
A477
Red Roses
Llandeilo Abercywyn
Llanybri
Llandefaelog
Ludchurch
Llanteg
Llandawke
Laugharne
Llansteffan
A478
Folly Farm
Llansadurnen
Broadway
Ferryside
Reynalton
Thomas Chapel
Colby Woodland Garden (NT)
Marros
Brook
Cliff
Wharley Point
Broadlay
Broadway
Loveston
Amroth
Pendine
Llanmiloe
East Marsh
Laugharne Burrows
Llansaint
Mynydd-y-Garreg
Begelly
Kilgetty
Stepaside
Ginst Point
St Ishmael
Kidwelly (Cydweli)
A4075
Cresselly
Jeffreyston
B4586
Pendine Sands
Laugharne Sands
Gwendraeth
Pentlepoir
B4316
Saundersfoot
Saundersfoot Bay
East Williamston
Redberth
Welsh Motor Sports Centre
Sageston
Monkstone Point
B4318
New Hedges
Tenby Roads
Pembrey Forest
Burry Port
Gumfreston
Tenby (Dinbych-y-Pysgod)
Cefn Sidan Sands
Pembrey
St Florence
St Catherine's Island
Manorbier Sta.
Tudor Merchant's House (NT)
Jameston
Penally
Lydstep
Giltar Point
B4585
Caldey Sound
St Margaret's Island
Monastery
Old Castle Head
Caldey Island
Priory
Chapel Point
CARMARTHEN BAY
Llanmadoc
Burry Holms
Cheriton
Llangennith
Rhossili Bay
Rhossili Downs
Rhossili
Worms Head
Middleton
(NT)

36
A
B
C
D
1
2
3
4
5
50
35
Carmarthen
(Caerfyrddin)
Johnstown
Llanllwch
Pensarn
Tanerdy
Ffynnon-ddrain
Abergwili
White Mill
Nantgaredig
Llanfihangel uwch-gwili
Pontargothi
Llanegwad
Felindre
Court Henry
Pentrefelin
Broadoak
Llangathen
Dryslwyn
Llandeilo
Dinefwr Park (NT)
Ffairfach
Gelli Aur
Maerdy
Llangunnor
Capel Dewi
Llanarthney
Golden Grove
Nantycaws
National Botanic Garden of Wales
Penrhiwgoch
Trap
Carreg Cennen
Trichrung
Capel Gwynfe
Pont Clydach
Carreg Lwyd
Tair Carn Isaf
Bylchau Rhos-fain
Cwmffrwd
Croesyceiliog
Llangain
Llanddarog
Cwmisfael
Porthyrhyd
Heol-ddu
Maesybont
Carmel
Llyn Llech Owain
Pentre Gwenlais
Derwydd
Blaengweche
Llandybie
BLACK MOUNTAIN
CARMARTHENSHIRE
Llangendeirne
Crwbin
Mynydd Cerrig
Drefach
Cefneithin
Gorslas
Penygroes
Saron
Tir-y-dail
Glanaman
Brynamman
Lower Brynamman
Tairgwaith
Gwaun-Cae-Gurwen
Garnant
Pontamman
Ammanford
(Rhydaman)
Betws
Mynydd y Betws
Banc Cwmhelen
Cwmgors
Penlle'rfedwen
Pontyffynnon
Tycroes
Capel Hendre
Cross Hands
Tumble
Pontantwn
Llandefaelog
Bancffosfelen
Meinciau
Pontyberem
Ferryside
Cliff
Broadway
Broadlay
Llansaint
Mynydd-y-Garreg
Four Roads
Pontyates
Pont-Henri
Cynheidre
Llannon
Mynydd Sylen
Sylen
Pont Abraham
Garnswllt
Graig Fawr
Mynydd Garn-fach
Mynydd y Gwair
Cefn Gwrhyd
Godre'r-graig
Rhyd-y-fro
Llangiwg
Ynysmeudwy
Kidwelly
(Cydweli)
Gwendraeth
Carway
Llandyry
Five Roads
Horeb
Waun y Clyn
Trimsaran
Fforest
Pentrebach
Cefn Drum
Hendy
Pontarddulais
Pontardawe
Alltwen
Trebanos
Craig-cefn-parc
Felindre
Welsh Motor Sports Centre
Pembrey Forest
Cefn Sidan Sands
Mynydd Pen-bre
Burry Port
Pembrey
Dyfatty
Pwll
Felinfoel
Llangennech
Bolgoed
Pontlliw
Vardre
Clydach
Pant-lasau
Ynystawe
Glais
Bryn-côch
Rhyddin
Dafen
Bryn
Llwynhendy
Grovesend
Swansea
Cefn Padrig
Llanelli Coastal Park
LLANELLI
Bynea
Bynea Sta
Gorseinon
Penllergaer
Llangyfelach
Llansamlet
Birchgrove
Skewen
Loughor
Tirdeunaw
Cadle
Morriston
Trallwn
Melincryddan
Whitford Point
Llanrhidian Sands
Crofty
Pen-clawdd
Gowerton
Waunarlwydd
Fforest-fach
Landore
Winsh-wen
Bon-y-maen
Pentre-Dwr
Pentre-chwyth
Kilvey Hill
Windmill
Broughton Bay
Whitford Burrows
Llanmorlais
Poundffald
Three Crosses
Dunvant
Cockett
Llanmadoc
Cheriton
Landimore
Burry Holms
Llangennith
Weobley
Llanrhidian
Oldwalls
Fairyhill
Killay
Sketty
Upper Killay
Clyne Valley
Clyne Common
SWANSEA
(Abertawe)
PORT TALBOT
GOWER
Rhossili Bay
Rhossili Downs
Llanddewi
Reynoldston
Cefn Bryn
Knelston
Le Breos Burial Chamber
Parc
Ilston
Pennard
Parkmill
Penmaen
Bishopston
Black Pill
West Cross
The Mumbles
Mumbles Head
Rhossili
Middleton
Worms Head
Penrice
Scurlage
Nicholaston
Southgate
Oystermouth
Newton
Langland Bay
SWANSEA BAY
Oxwich
Oxwich Bay
Oxwich Green
Pwlldu Head
Port Eynon
Horton
Port Eynon Bay
Overton
Culver Hole
Port Eynon Point
Cork 10 hrs
(summer only)
3.2 miles to 1 inch
0 2 4 6 8 10 miles
0 2 4 6 8 10 km
2 km to 1 cm
A40
A48
A483
A484
A476
A4138
A474
A4069
A4068
A4067
A4240
A4216
A4118
A4217
A483
M4
B4300
B4310
B4312
B4306
B4309
B4317
B4308
B4297
B4556
B4296
B4295
B4271
B4436
B4247
B4620
B4489
B4603
B4291
B4290
49
48
47
46
45
44
43
42

37
51
38
22
D
E
F
G
BRECON BEACONS NATIONAL PARK
FOREST FAWR
POWYS
NEATH
PORT TALBOT
AFAN FOREST PARK
RHONDDA
CYNON
TAFF
MERTHYR TYDFIL
BRIDGEND
VALE OF GLAMORGAN
CARDIFF
VALE OF NEATH
Glasfynydd Forest
Moel Feity
Cnewr
Heol Senni
Fan Bwlch Chwyth
Pen Milan
Pen y Fan
Llansantffraed
Talybont-on-Usk
Bwlch
Coed-yr-ynys
Garreg Las
Fan Hir
Fan Gyhirych
Fan Fawr
Fan Nedd
Fan Llia
Beacons Reservoir
Ystradfellte Reservoir
Cwm Crew
Craig Fan Ddu
Neuadd Reservoirs
Talybont Reservoir
Torpantau
Abercynafon
Twyn-du
Garn Caws
Cefn Carn Fadog
Carreg Lem
Carreg Goch
Castell y Geifr
Cefn Mawr
Dan-yr-Ogof Caves
Penwyllt
Craig-y-nos
Carreg-lwyd
Bryn Bugeiliaid
Pen-y-cae
Aber-llia
Ystradfellte
Gwaun Nant Ddu
Waun Lysiog
Nant-ddu
Cantref Resr
Pentwyn Reservoir
Pontsticill Reservoir
Twyn Croes
Garn Ddu
Pontsticill
Brecon Mountain Rly
Cader Fawr
Llwyn-on Reservoir
Caer-Lan
Abercraf
Caehopkin
Coelbren
Penrhos
Ystradgynlais
Onllwyn
Cwmgiedd
Gurnos
Dyffryn Cellwen
Mynydd y Drum
Seven Sisters
Varteg Hill
Pant Sychbant
Onllwyn
Cefn-coed-y-cymmer
Vaynor
Trefil
Tafarnaubach
Princetown
Dukestown
Llechryd
Rhymney
Penderyn
Mynydd-y-glog
Pontbren Llwyd
Pont Nedd Fechan
Glynneath (Glyn-Nedd)
Aberpergwm
Morfa Glas
Pont Walby
Rhigos
Hirwaun
Cyfarthfa
MERTHYR TYDFIL
Pontlottyn
Fochriw
Crynant
Hirfynydd
Pentreclwydau
Blaengwrach
Cwmgwrach
Rheola Forest
Mynydd Marchywel
Hirwaun Common
Penywaun
Llwydcoed
Ochr-y-Mynydd
Mynydd Aberdar
Abercanaid
Pentrebach
Aber-nant
Mynydd Merthyr
Troedyrhiw
Tirphil
Aberdulais Falls & Historic Site (NT)
Cilfrew
Resolven
Melincourt
Mynydd Resolfen
Cefn Grug
Craig y Llyn
Cefntyle-brych
Rhondda Fach
Trecynon
Cwmdare
Dare Valley
Aberdare
Aberaman
Cwmbach
Aberfan
Bedlinog
Deri
Aberdulais
Cadoxton-Juxta-Neath
Tonna
Moel yr Hyrddod
Carn Caglau
Blaencwm
Blaenrhondda
Tynewydd
Treherbert
Abercwmboi
Cwmaman
St Gwynno Forest
MOUNTAIN ASH
Miskin
Merthyr Vale
Cefn Merthyr
BARGOED
Gilfach
Gelli-gaer Common
Glyncorrwg
NEATH (Castell-nedd)
Cefn Morfudd
Blaengwynfi
Abergwynfi
TREORCHY
Cwm-parc
Maerdy
Cefn y Rhondda
Ferndale
Penrhiwceiber
Treharris
Trelewis
GELLIGAER
Penybryn
Nelson
Llanwonno
Ynysboeth
Abercynon
Ynysybwl
Cymmer
Duffryn
Croeserw
Caerau
Mynydd Caerau
Moel Trawsnant
Afan Argoed
Dyffryn
Pontrhydyfen
Foel Fynyddau
Briton Ferry
Llansawel
Pentre
Ton Pentre
Ystrad
Penrhys
Pontygwaith
Wattstown
Ynyshir
Clydach Vale
Tonypandy
Llwynypia
Trealaw
Nant-y-moel
Werfa
Mynydd Llangeinwyr
Cefn Gwyngul
Glyncoch
Trehafod
Porth
Cilfynydd
Ystrad Mynach
Mynydd Eglwysilan
Senghenydd
Llanbradach
Pwll-y-glaw
Cwmafan
Mynydd Dinas
Bryn
Nantyffyllon
Blaengarw
Pontycymer
Wyndham
Price Town
Mynydd Maes-teg
Penygraig
Cymmer
Hopkinstown
PONTYPRIDD
Abertridwr
MAESTEG
Garth
Glanllynfi
Ogmore Vale
Ogmore Forest
Trebanog
Treforest
Glyntaff
Rhydyfelin
Goytre
Taibach
Mynydd Margam
Llangynwyd
Pont Rhyd-y-cyff
Gilfach Goch
Tonyrefail
Pen-y-coedcae
Upper Boat
Treforest Ind. Est.
Margam
Moel Ton-mawr
Llangeinor
Betws
Glynogwr
Blackmill
Mynydd y Gaer
Mynydd Maendy
Coedely
Castellau
Llantwit Fardre
Ton-teg
Church Village
Beddau
Coytrahen
Mynydd Baedan
Bryngarw
Brynmenyn
Abergarw
Bryncethin
Heol-y-Cyw
Efail Isaf
Taff's Well (Ffynnon Taf)
Gwaelod-y-garth
Margam Burrows
Kenfig Burrows
Kenfig Hill
Cefn Cribwr
Aberkenfig
Tondu
Sarn
Hirwaun Common
Cefn Hirgoed
Brynna
Llanharan
Talbot Green
LLANTRISANT
Cross Inn
Pentyrch
Creigiau
Tongwynlais
Kenfig Pool
Mawdlam
Pyle
North Cornelly
Kenfig
Cefn Cross
Pen-y-fai
McArthurGlen
Penprysg
Bryncae
Llanharry
Tyle-garw
Pontyclun
Miskin
Groes-faen
Radyr
Coity
Pencoed
Llanilid
Brynsadler
BRIDGEND (Pen-y-Bont ar Ogwr)
Coychurch
South Cornelly
Laleston
Newcastle
Tythegston
Nottage
Merthyr Mawr
Newton
Porthcawl
Castle & Stepping Stones
Treoes
St Mary Hill
Llangan
Graig Penllyn
Llansannor
Ystradowen
St Bride's-super-Ely
St Fagans
Ewenny
Ewenny Priory
Corntown
Ogmore
Colwinston
Penllyn
Maendy
Pendoylan
Peterston-super-Ely
St George's
Ely
Caerau
Culverhouse Cross
Ogmore-by-Sea
St Brides Major
Southerndown
Tusker Rock
Pitcot
Llysworney
Aberthin
Cowbridge
Welsh St Donats
Bonvilston
St Nicholas
Twyn-yr-odyn
Wenvoe
Michaelston-le-Pit
Llandow
Wick
Llanblethian
Nash
Llandough
Sigingstone
Llanmihangel
St Hilary
Llantrithyd
Old Beaupre
Tregoff
Tinkinswood Burial Chamber
St Lythans
Dyffryn
St. Lythans Burial Chamber
Broughton
Monknash
Mary Church
Llancarfan
Llanbethery
Flemingston
Eglwys-Brewis
St Athan
Penmark
Merthyr Dyfan
Colcot
Cadoxton
Marcross
Nash Point
St Donats
Llantwit Major
Boverton
Llan
Gileston
West Aberthaw
Cardiff International Airport
Rhoose
Porthkerry
Barry Island Pleasure Park
BARRY
Sully
East

NATIONAL PARK
POWYS
BLAENAU
GWENT
MERTHYR TYDFIL
CAERPHILLY
TORFAEN
MONMOUTH
NEWPORT
CARDIFF
MOUTH OF THE SEVERN
A
B
C
D
1
2
3
4
5
52
37
23
Llansantffraed
Cwmdu
Pen Cerrig-calch
Patrishow
Cwmyoy
Hoaldalbert
Bwlch
Gaer
Tretower
Myarth
Coed-yr-ynys
Llangynidr
Crickhowell
Llanbedr
Llanfihangel Crucorney
Llangattock Lingoed
Bont
Cross Ash
Upper Green
Newcastle
Twyn-du
Talybont Reservoir
Ffawyddog
Llangattock
Llangenny
Sugar Loaf
Blaenawey
Mynydd Pen-y-fal
Rholben
Deri
Ysgyryd Fawr
Llanvetherine
White Castle
Llangattock-Vibon-Avel
Abercynafon
Dyffryn Crawnon
Garn Caws
Cefn Onneu
Cwrt-y-gollen
Glangrwyne
Llantilio Pertholey
Mardy
Hen Gwrt
Llantilio Crossenny
Pentwyn Reservoir
Pontsticill Reservoir
Mynydd Llangynidr
Mynydd Llangatwg
Llanelly
Gilwern
Govilon
Abergavenny (Y Fenni)
Croes Hywel
Llanvapley
Llanddewi Rhydderch
Trefil
Rassau
Blackrock
Clydach
Llanfoist
Blorenge
Wernyrheolydd
Coed Morgan
Penrhos
Tregare
Tafarnaubach
Princetown
Beaufort
Brynmawr
Llanelly Hill
Pontypool & Blaenavon Steam Rly
Blaenavon Ironworks
Llanellen
Llanarth
Great Oak
Dukestown
Sirhowy
Ebbw Vale
Newtown
Nantyglo
Blaenavon
Coedcae
The Bryn
Llanvihangel Gobion
Bryngwyn
Raglan
Brecon Mountain Rly
Llechryd
Bryn Bach
Tredegar
Mynydd Carn-y-Cefn
Coalbrookvale
Big Pit Mining Museum
Maerdy
Clytha Hill
Rhymney
Festival Pk
Blaina
Coity Mountain
Rhyd-y-meirch
Llanover
Pen-groes-oped
Nant-y-derry
Twyn-y-Sheriff
Kingcoed
Merthyr Tydfil
Pontlottyn
Cefn yr Arail
Gwastad
Cwmtillery
Varteg
Mynydd Garnclochdy
Goetre
Bettws Newydd
Gwehelog
Kemeys Commander
Llandenny
Fochriw
Abertysswg
Cefn Manmoel
Cwm
Abertillery
Penperlleni
Croes-y-pant
Mamhilad
Manmoel
Abersychan
Monkswood
Llancayo
Llansoy
Gwernesney
Troedyrhiw
New Tredegar
Tirphil
Hollybush
Llanhilleth
Cwm Ffrwd-oer
Pontnewynydd
Trevethin
Little Mill
Glascoed
Usk
Bedlinog
Deri
Aberbeeg
St Illtyd
Aberfan
Markham
Bedwellty
Argoed
Aber Bargoed
Glandwr
Trinant
Tranch
Pontypool
The Valley Inheritance
Llanbadoc
Llangwm-isaf
Merthyr Vale
Mountain Ash
Bargoed
Oakdale
Rock
Croespenmaen
Swffryd
Crumlin
Griffithstown
New Inn
Llandegfedd Reservoir
Coed-y-paen
Llanllywel
Penrhiwceiber
Gelli-gaer Common
Gilfach
Trelewis
Pengam
Newbridge (Cefn Bychan)
Mynydd Maen
Upper Cwmbran
Sebastopol
Pontrhydyrun
Llantrisant
Newchurch
Gaerllwyd
Treharris
Gelligaer
Penybryn
Fleur-de-lis
Blackwood
Greenmeadow Community Farm
Croesyceiliog
Llangybi
Abercynon
Ynysybwl
Nelson
Cefn Hengoed
Hengoed
Pontllanfraith
Ystrad Mynach
Maesycwmmer
Abercarn
Cefn Rhyswg
Cwmbran
Pontnewydd
Llandegveth
Tredunnock
Newbridge-on-Usk
Pen-y-cae-mawr
Earlswood
Wentwood
Cilfynydd
Wyllie
Ynysddu
Cwmcarn
Pontywaun
Henllys
Llantarnam
Llanfrechfa
Ponthir
Llanhennock
Parc-Seymour
Glyncoch
Mynydd Eglwysilan
Senghenydd
Cwmfelinfach
Crosskeys
Risca
Castell-y-bwch
Croes-y-mwyalch
Kemeys Inferior
Llanvaches
Trehafod
Llanbradach
Wattsville
Sirhowy Valley
Pontymister
Bettws
Malpas
Caerleon
Roman Fort
Christchurch
Llanbeder
Penhow
St Brides Netherwent
Llanmartin
Abertridwr
Glyntaff
Rhydyfelin
Bedwas
Machen
Rogerstone
Milton
Underwood
Llanwern
Wilcrick
Magor
Upper Boat
Caerphilly
Lower Machen
Rhiwderin
Liswerry
Bishton
Steel Works
Langstone
Llandevenny
Pen-y-coedcae
Church Village
Tonteg
Treforest Ind. Est.
Nantgarw
Glan-y-llyn
Draethen
Rudry
Parc Cefn Onn
Pentre-Poeth
Bassaleg
Gaer
Newport (Casnewydd)
Pye Corner
Broadstreet Common
Caldicot Level
Summerleaze
Redwick
Efail Isaf
Gwaelod-y-garth
Thornhill
Taff's Well (Ffynnon Taf)
Michaelston-y-Fedw
Began
Tredegar
Maesglas
Coedkernew
Whitson
Nash
Llantrisant
Cross Inn
Pentyrch
Tongwynlais
Castell Coch
Lisvane
Llanedeyrn
Castleton
Marshfield
St Brides Wentlooge
Goldcliff
Creigiau
Radyr
Pentwyn
Llanishen
St Mellons
Blacktown
Groes-faen
Birchgrove
Llanrumney
Whitchurch
Rumney
Peterstone Wentlooge
Llandaff North
Roath
St Bride's-super-Ely
Peterston-super-Ely
St Georges
St Fagans
Museum of Welsh Life
Llandaff
Ely
Canton
Cardiff (Caerdydd)
Caerau
Grangetown
Wales Millennium Centre
Millennium Stadium
Portishead
Redcliff Bay
Walton-in-Gordano
Manor House
Clevedon Pier
Clevedon
Clevedon Court (NT)
Weston in Gordano
Tinkinswood Burial Chamber
St Nicholas
Twyn-yr-odyn
Wenvoe
Leckwith
Llandough
Cogan
Pleasure Steamers Waverley and Balmoral
Dyffryn
St Lythans Burial Chamber
St Lythans
Michaelston-le-Pit
Dinas Powys
St Andrews Major
Penarth
Llancarfan
Colcot
Palmerstown
Lower Penarth
Merthyr Dyfan
Cadoxton
Sully
Lavernock
Lavernock Point
Cardiff International
Porthkerry Park
Rhoose
Porthkerry
Barry
Swanbridge
Sully Island
Barry Island Pleasure Pk.
Barry Island
Middle Hope (NT)
Sand Point
Woodspring Priory
Kingston Seymour
Icelton
Kenn
North End
Clavedon
Yatton
A40
A479
A465
A4077
A4047
A4048
A4046
A4049
A4043
A467
A469
A472
A4042
A4051
A4054
A470
A4058
A4059
A4060
A473
A468
A48
A455
A48(M)
M4
A4119
A4232
A4161
A4160
A4055
A4050
A4226
A4231
A449
B4558
B4560
B4521
B4233
B4598
B4246
B4248
B4486
B4254
B4251
B4263
B4262
B4591
B4239
B4487
B3124
B3133
23A
24
25
25A
26
27
28
29
29A
30
32
33
34
20

39
D
E
F
G
1
2
3
4
5
53
40
25
GLOUCESTER
BRISTOL
KINGSWOOD
GLOUCESTERSHIRE
SOUTH GLOUCESTERSHIRE
NORTH SOMERSET
DEAN FOREST AND WYE VALLEY
Forest of Dean
VALE OF BERKELEY
VALE OF GLOUCESTER
SEVERN
Monmouth (Trefynwy)
Chepstow
Caldicot
Avonmouth
Ross-on-Wye
Cinderford
Coleford
Lydney
Mitcheldean
Newnham
Berkeley
Dursley
Thornbury
Yate
Chipping Sodbury
Patchway
Filton
Frampton Cotterell
Winterbourne
Mangotsfield
Portishead
Nailsea
Long Ashton
Keynsham
Nailsworth
Stonehouse
Wotton-under-Edge
Severn Beach
Severn Road Bridge
Severn View
Severn Tunnel
Oldbury-on-Severn
Lydney Sand
The Noose
New Grounds
Frampton on Severn
Westbury-on-Severn
Michael Wood
Battery Point
Chepstow Park Wood
St Weonards
Peterstow
Tretire
Skenfrith
Broad Oak
Llangarron
Llangrove
Marstow
Whitchurch
Goodrich
Welsh Bicknor
Symonds Yat
English Bicknor
Ruardean
Drybrook
Longhope
Huntley
Hartpury
Highnam
Churcham
Minsterworth
Elmore
Quedgeley
Hardwicke
Longney
Frampton
Saul
Whitminster
Eastington
Frocester
Coaley
Cam
Uley
Kingscote
Slimbridge
Sharpness
Purton
Blakeney
Awre
Newerne
Aylburton
Alvington
Woolaston
Tidenham
Tutshill
Sedbury
Beachley
Mathern
Crick
Portskewett
Sudbrook
Rogiet
Caerwent
Shirenewton
Mynydd-bach
Itton Common
St Arvans
Devauden
Trellech
Tintern Parva
Llandogo
Whitebrook
St Briavels
Hewelsfield
Bream
Parkend
Yorkley
Pillowell
Whitecroft
Ruspidge
Littledean
Flaxley
Blaisdon
Elton
Arlingham
Rodley
Tortworth
Charfield
Kingswood
Cromhall
Wickwar
Hawkesbury
Hawkesbury Upton
Horton
Little Sodbury
Old Sodbury
Badminton
Acton Turville
Tormarton
Dodington
Codrington
Pucklechurch
Wick
Marshfield
Cold Ashton
Lansdown
Batheaston
Bathampton
Saltford
Bitton
Oldland
Hanham
Warmley
Siston
Soundwell
Fishponds
Stapleton
Horfield
Henbury
Westbury on Trym
Shirehampton
Pill
Easton-in-Gordano
Abbots Leigh
Portbury
Clifton
Redland
Bedminster
Knowle
Brislington
Whitchurch
Queen Charlton
Hallen
Easter Compton
Almondsbury
Pilning
Olveston
Alveston
Tockington
Rudgeway
Elberton
Aust
Littleton-upon-Severn
Rockhampton
Falfield
Stone
Woodford
Newport
Stinchcombe
North Nibley
Leighterton
Didmarton
Sopworth
Luckington
Alderton
Littleton Drew
Grittleton
Nettleton
Castle Combe
West Kington
North Wraxall
Ford
The Shoe
Thickwood
Colerne
Box
Bathford
Monkton
Glasshouse Hill
Kent's Green
Tibberton
Bulley
Rudford
Lassington
Highleadon
Sandhurst
Barnwood
Hempsted
Whaddon
Brookthorpe
Haresfield
Harescombe
Pitchcombe
Stroud Green
Whiteshill
Randwick
Leonard Stanley
King's Stanley
Woodchester
Amberley
Horsley
Newington Bagpath
Lasborough
Ozleworth
Tresham
Alderley
Hillesley
Knockdown
M4
M5
M48
M49
M32
A40
A48
A38
A46
A4
A37
A4174
A403
A432
A420
A431
A4135
A4136
A466
A4151
A419
A430
A417
A4137
A369
A370
A4018
A4162
A4320
A4175
A365
A433

40
54
39
25
A
B
C
D
1
2
3
4
5
GLOUCESTER
CHELTENHAM
STROUD
Cirencester
Nailsworth
Dursley
Tetbury
Malmesbury
CHIPPENHAM
Corsham
Calne
SWINDON
Wootton Bassett
Highleadon
Sandhurst
Maisemore
Highnam
Churcham
Norton
Staverton
Down Hatherley
Staverton Bridge
Golden Valley
Gloucestershire
Up Hatherley
Leckhampton
Prestbury
Charlton Kings
Longford
Churchdown
Badgeworth
Shurdington
Barnwood
Hucclecote
Brockworth
Bentham
Crickley Hill
Little Witcombe
Great Witcombe
Pilley
Whittington
Dowdeswell
Andoversford
Kilkenny
Foxcote
Seven Springs
Ullenwood
Coberley
Upper Coberley
Cowley
Birdlip
Brockhampton
Sevenhampton
Syreford
Shipton
Hazleton
Charlton Abbots
Hawling
Salperton
Notgrove
Naunton
Turkdean
Compton Abdale
Withington
Withington Woods
Chedworth
Chedworth Woods
Chedworth Roman Villa (NT)
Yanworth
Stowell
Hampnett
Northleach
Eastington
Colesbourne
Elkstone
Fossebridge
Coln St Dennis
Coln Rogers
Foss Cross
Rendcomb
Minsterworth
Elmore Back
Elmore
Tuffley
Robinswood Hill
Hempsted
Quedgeley
Whaddon
Hardwicke
Longney
Moreton Valence
Brookthorpe
Matson
Upton St Leonards
Prinknash Abbey
Prinknash Park
Cranham
Brimpsfield
Syde
Whiteway
Winstone
Haresfield
Harescombe
Sheepscombe
Edge
Painswick
The Camp
Miserden
Misarden Park Gardens
Sudgrove
Duntisbourne Abbots
Duntisbourne Leer
Woodmancote
North Cerney
Calmsden
Bagendon
Edgeworth
Duntisbourne Rouse
Daglingworth
Baunton
Stratton
Putloe
Wheatenhurst
Whitminster
Pitchcombe
Stroud Green
Slad
Whiteshill
Randwick
Stonehouse
Rodborough
Eastcombe
Bisley
Bournes Green
Oakridge Lynch
Bussage
Chalford
Sapperton
Frampton Mansell
Thrupp
Brimscombe
Hyde
Leonard Stanley
King's Stanley
Frocester
Woodchester
Coaley
Amberley
Nympsfield
Minchinhampton
Box
Uley
Cam
Horsley
Barton End
Avening
Tiltups End
Cherington
Rodmarton
Tarlton
Coates
Siddington
Kingscote
Newington Bagpath
Beverstone
Lasborough
Ozleworth
Tetbury Upton
Culkerton
Ashley
Kemble
Ewen
South Cerney
Shorncote
Poole Keynes
Somerford Keynes
Cotswold Water Park
Cerney Wick
Latton
Ashton Keynes
Oaksey
Chelworth
Crudwell
Eastcourt
Chedglow
Long Newnton
Wortley
Tresham
Leighterton
Doughton
Westonbirt
Westonbirt Arboretum
Brokenborough
Shipton Moyne
Knockdown
Willesley
Oldbury on the Hill
Didmarton
Sopworth
Hawkesbury Upton
Easton Grey
Foxley
Sherston
Norton
Luckington
Little Badminton
Badminton
Alderton
Acton Turville
Littleton Drew
Grittleton
Hullavington
Corston
Rodbourne
Startley
Lower Seagry
Upper Seagry
Little Somerford
Great Somerford
Dauntsey
Brinkworth
Lea
Cleverton
Garsdon
Charlton
Charlton Park
Hankerton
Upper Minety
Minety
Leigh
Cricklade
Purton Stoke
Purton
Blunsdon St Andrew
Lydiard Millicent
Lydiard Mansion
Callow Hill
Hook
Grittenham
Tockenham
Tockenham Wick
Lyneham
Bradenstoke
Church End
Preston
Bushton
Clyffe Pypard
Goatacre
Broad Town
Broad Hinton
Uffcott
Elcombe
Clevancy
Hilmarton
Highway
Winterbourne Bassett
Berwick Bassett
Compton Bassett
Yatesbury
Windmill Hill
Cherhill
Oldbury Castle & White Horse
Winterbourne Monkton
Avebury
Beckhampton
West Kennett
East Kennett
Calstone Wellington
Blackland
Morgan's Hill
Stockley
Quemerford
Mile Elm
Heddington
Netherstreet
Roundway Down 1643
Bremhill
Spirthill
Charlcutt
East Tytherton
Tytherton Lucas
Stanley
Studley
Derry Hill
Bowood
Sandy Lane
Bowden Hill
Bewley Common
Lacock
Fox Talbot Museum (NT)
Whitley
Shaw
Beanacre
Melksham
Atworth
Gastard
Easton
Corsham Court
Hawthorn
Ditteridge
Box
Ashley
Batheaston
Bathford
Monkton
Swainswick
Northend
St Catherine
Colerne
Thickwood
Cross Keys
Biddestone
Slaughterford
Sheldon Manor
Hardenhuish
Ford
Yatton Keynell
Kington St Michael
Leigh Delamere
Stanton St Quintin
Sutton Benger
Christian Malford
Foxham
Kington Langley
Langley Burrell
Burton
Nettleton
Castle Combe
West Kington
North Wraxall
Upper Wraxall
The Shoe
Marshfield
West Littleton
Tormarton
G L O U C E S T E R S H I R E
C O T S W O L D H I L L S
W I L T S H I R E
M5
M4
A40
A38
A46
A417
A419
A429
A433
A435
A436
A4135
A350
A4
A3102
A420
A365
A342
A4019
A4173
A430
A4361
B4008
B4014
B4040
B4042
B4058
B4069
B4070
B4073
B4425
B4696
B4068
B3109

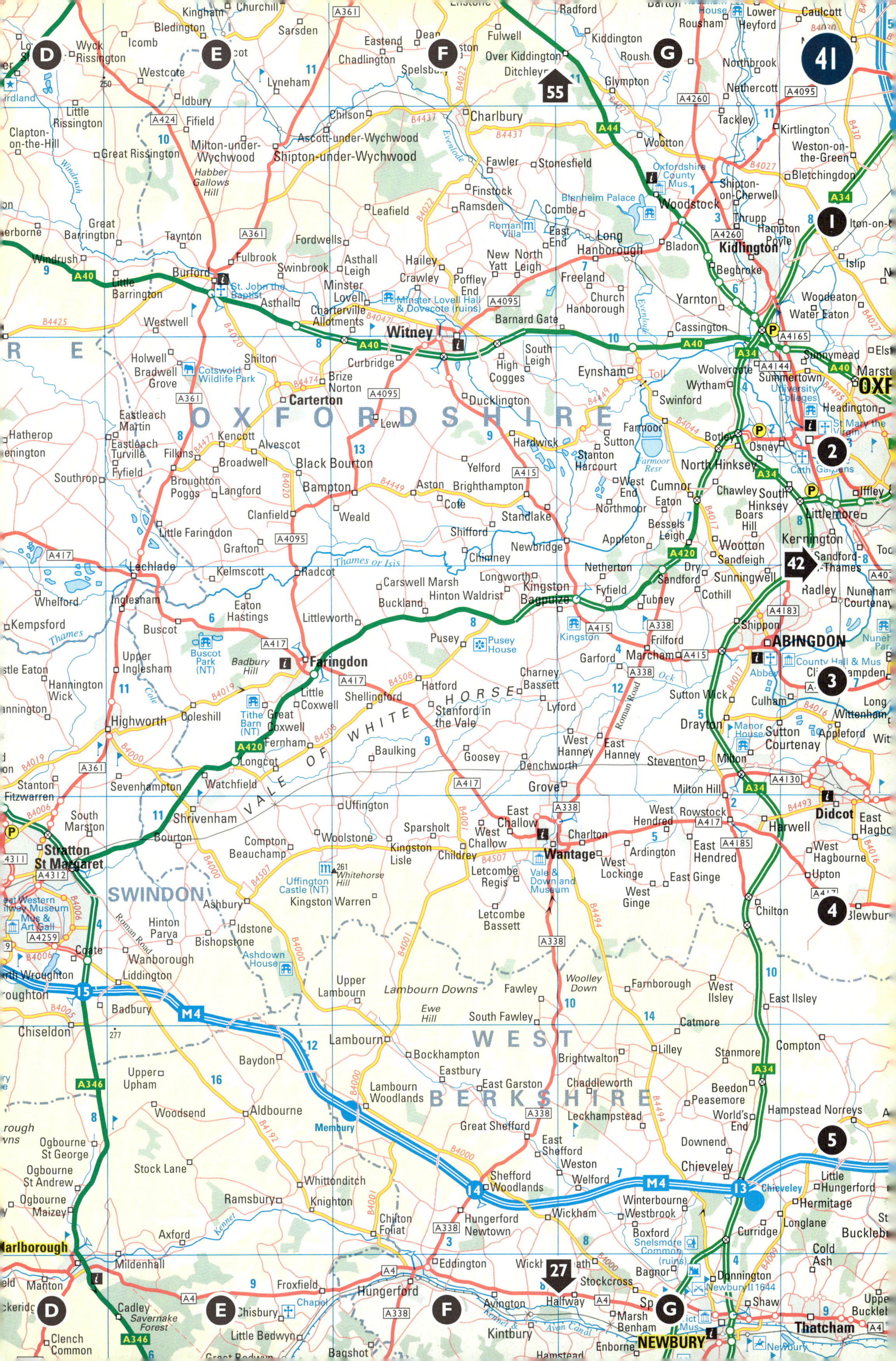
OXFORDSHIRE
SWINDON
WEST BERKSHIRE
VALE OF WHITE HORSE
Kingham
Churchill
Bledington
Icomb
Wyck Rissington
Sarsden
Chadlington
Eastend
Dean
Spelsbury
Fulwell
Over Kiddington
Ditchley
Radford
Kiddington
Rousham
Lower Heyford
Caulcott
Northbrook
Nethercott
Westcote
Lyneham
Idbury
Fifield
Little Rissington
Clapton-on-the-Hill
Great Rissington
Milton-under-Wychwood
Ascott-under-Wychwood
Shipton-under-Wychwood
Chilson
Charlbury
Habber Gallows Hill
Fawler
Stonesfield
Finstock
Glympton
Tackley
Kirtlington
Wootton
Weston-on-the-Green
Bletchingdon
Oxfordshire County Mus.
Shipton-on-Cherwell
Thrupp
Hampton Poyle
Woodstock
Blenheim Palace
Combe
Ramsden
Leafield
Roman Villa
East End
Long Hanborough
Bladon
Kidlington
Begbroke
Islip
Great Barrington
Taynton
Fordwells
Asthall Leigh
Hailey
Poffley End
New Yatt
North Leigh
Freeland
Church Hanborough
Yarnton
Woodeaton
Water Eaton
Windrush
Little Barrington
Burford
Fulbrook
Swinbrook
Minster Lovell
Crawley
St. John the Baptist
Asthall
Charterville Allotments
Minster Lovell Hall & Dovecote (ruins)
Barnard Gate
Cassington
Witney
Westwell
Shilton
Curbridge
Brize Norton
South Leigh
High Cogges
Eynsham
Toll
Wolvercote
Wytham
Summertown
University Colleges
Swinford
Headington
Holwell
Bradwell Grove
Cotswold Wildlife Park
Carterton
Ducklington
Hatherop
Eastleach Martin
Eastleach Turville
Fyfield
Kencott
Alvescot
Filkins
Broadwell
Lew
Hardwick
Farmoor
Sutton
Stanton Harcourt
Farmoor Resr
Botley
Osney
North Hinksey
St Mary the Virgin
Cath
Southrop
Black Bourton
Yelford
Broughton Poggs
Langford
Bampton
Aston
Brighthampton
Cote
West End
Cumnor
Chawley
South Hinksey
Iffley
Littlemore
Northmoor
Eaton
Boars Hill
Weald
Standlake
Bessels Leigh
Clanfield
Shifford
Appleton
Wootton
Kennington
Little Faringdon
Grafton
Newbridge
Chimney
Sandleigh
Sandford-on-Thames
Thames or Isis
Lechlade
Kelmscott
Radcot
Carswell Marsh
Longworth
Netherton
Dry Sandford
Sunningwell
Radley
Nuneham Courtenay
Whelford
Inglesham
Eaton Hastings
Buckland
Hinton Waldrist
Kingston Bagpuize
Fyfield
Tubney
Cothill
Kempsford
Thames
Buscot
Littleworth
Shippon
ABINGDON
Pusey
Pusey House
Kingston
Frilford
Garford
Marcham
County Hall & Mus
Upper Inglesham
Buscot Park (NT)
Badbury Hill
Faringdon
Charney Bassett
Abbey
Hannington Wick
Little Coxwell
Shellingford
Hatford
Lyford
Roman Road
Ock
Sutton Wick
Culham
Long Wittenham
Highworth
Coleshill
Tithe Barn (NT)
Great Coxwell
Stanford in the Vale
Drayton
Manor House
Sutton Courtenay
Appleford
Fernham
Baulking
West Hanney
East Hanney
Goosey
Steventon
Milton
Longcot
Denchworth
Stanton Fitzwarren
Sevenhampton
Watchfield
Grove
Milton Hill
South Marston
Shrivenham
Uffington
Sparsholt
East Challow
West Challow
West Hendred
Rowstock
Didcot
East Hagbourne
Harwell
Stratton St Margaret
Bourton
Compton Beauchamp
Woolstone
Kingston Lisle
Childrey
Wantage
Charlton
Ardington
East Hendred
West Hagbourne
Upton
Great Western Railway Museum
Mus & Art Gall
Ashbury
Uffington Castle (NT)
Whitehorse Hill
Kingston Warren
Letcombe Regis
Vale & Downland Museum
West Lockinge
East Ginge
West Ginge
Blewbury
Hinton Parva
Idstone
Bishopstone
Letcombe Bassett
Chilton
Coate
Wanborough
Ashdown House
Wroughton
Liddington
Upper Lambourn
Lambourn Downs
Fawley
Woolley Down
Farnborough
West Ilsley
East Ilsley
Badbury
Ewe Hill
South Fawley
Chiseldon
Catmore
Lambourn
Bockhampton
Brightwalton
Lilley
Stanmore
Compton
Baydon
Eastbury
East Garston
Chaddleworth
Beedon
Peasemore
Upper Upham
Lambourn Woodlands
Woodsend
Aldbourne
Membury
Great Shefford
Leckhampstead
World's End
Hampstead Norreys
Ogbourne St George
East Shefford
Downend
Stock Lane
Weston
Chieveley
Ogbourne St Andrew
Whittonditch
Shefford Woodlands
Welford
Little Hungerford
Ogbourne Maizey
Ramsbury
Knighton
Winterbourne
Hermitage
Westbrook
Wickham
Chilton Foliat
Hungerford Newtown
Boxford
Snelsmore Common
Longlane
Curridge
Bucklebury
Axford
Kennet
Cold Ash
Marlborough
Mildenhall
Eddington
Wickham Heath
Stockcross
Bagnor
Donnington
Newbury 1644
Manton
Froxfield
Hungerford
Halfway
Shaw
Cadley
Savernake Forest
Chisbury
Chapel
Avington
Marsh Benham
Thatcham
Clench Common
Little Bedwyn
Kintbury
Avon Canal
Enborne
NEWBURY
Bagshot
Hamstead
Great Bedwyn
M4
A40
A34
A44
A420
A338
A346
A417
A415
A361
A424
A4095
A4260
A4165
A4144
A4183
A4130
A4185
A4312
A4259
A4
B4022
B4437
B4027
B4425
B4020
B4477
B4449
B4044
B4017
B4019
B4000
B4508
B4507
B4001
B4494
B4009
B4192
B4005
B4006
B4493
B4016
B4030
B430
42
55
27

42
A
B
C
D
56
41
28
I
2
3
4
5
Bicester
Bicester Village
Lower Heyford
Caulcott
Middleton Stoney
Rousham
Northbrook
Nethercott
Chesterton
Launton
Charndon
Marsh Gibbon
Edgcott
Calvert
Botolph Claydon
Granborough
North Marston
Dunton
Grendon Underwood
Pitchcott
Oving
Whitchurch
Quainton
Aston Abbots
Hardwick
Weedon
Tackley
Kirtlington
Ambrosden
Wendlebury
Blackthorn
Kingswood
Weston-on-the-Green
Bletchingdon
Ludgershall
Waddesdon
Akeman Street
Westcott
Wotton Underwood
Waddesdon Manor (NT)
Shipton-on-Cherwell
Hampton Poyle
Merton
Upper Arncott
Piddington
Fencott
Charlton-on-Otmoor
Murcott
Duck Decoy (NT)
Woodstock
Kidlington
Begbroke
Islip
Oddington
Ot Moor
Noke
Boarstall
Dorton
Ashendon
Upper(Over) Winchendon
AYLESBURY
Brill
Horton-cum-Studley
Hartwell
Stone
Lower(Nether) Winchendon
Yarnton
Cassington
Woodeaton
Water Eaton
Beckley
Oakley
Chilton
Upton
Dinton
Bishopstone
Stoke Mandeville
Wolvercote
Sunnymead
Summertown
Elsfield
Easington
Long Crendon
Chearsley
Cuddington
Westlington
Ford
Wytham
Marston
Stanton St John
Forest Hill
Worminghall
Notley Abbey (ruins)
Haddenham
Kimble Wick
Little Kimble
OXFORD
University Colleges
Headington
St Mary the Virgin
Botanic Gardens
Osney
Holton
Courthouse (NT)
Ickford
Shabbington
Aston Sandford
Nash Lee
Ellesborough
North Hinksey
South Hinksey
Shotover
Wheatley
Waterperry
Waterstock
Thame
Kingsey
Owlswick
Meadle
Great Kimble
Chawley
Iffley
Cowley
Horspath
Tiddington
Rycote Chapel
Moreton
Towersey
Longwick
Askett
Monks Risborough
Princes Risborough
Boars Hill
Littlemore
Cuddesdon
Great Milton
Ilmer
Pitch Green
Chinnor & Princes Risborough Rly
Wootton
Sandford-on-Thames
Kennington
Garsington
Denton
Great Haseley
Tetsworth
Emmington
Sydenham
Henton
Bledlow
Saunderton
Loosley Row
Lacey Green
Sunningwell
Toot Baldon
Marsh Baldon
Little Milton
Little Haseley
Chinnor
Cothill
Radley
Nuneham Courtenay
Chislehampton
Stoke Talmage
Postcombe
Adwell
South Weston
Aston Rowant
Kingston Blount
Bledlow Ridge
Bradenham
Shippon
ABINGDON
Nuneham Park
Stadhampton
Chalgrove 1643
Lewknor
The City
Stokenchurch
Marcham
Abbey
County Hall & Mus
Clifton Hampden
Berinsfield
Drayton St Leonard
Chalgrove
Newington
Easington
Pyrton
Shirburn
West Wycombe
Sutton Wick
Culham
Burcot
Abbey Church
Brightwell Baldwin
Cuxham
Watlington
Christmas Common
Beacon's Bottom
West Wycombe Park (NT)
Drayton
Long Wittenham
Dorchester
Warborough
Berrick Salome
Britwell Salome
Northend
Ibstone
Manor House
Sutton Courtenay
Appleford
Little Wittenham
Shillingford
Benson
Cadmore End
Bolter End
Lane End
HIGH WYCOMBE
Milton
OXFORDSHIRE
CHILTERN
Ewelme
Swyncombe
Greenfield
Turville Heath
Turville
Fingest
Booker
Milton Hill
Didcot
East Hagbourne
Brightwell
Wallingford
Cookley Green
Pishill
Frieth
Rowstock
Harwell
North Moreton
Crowmarsh Gifford
Russell's Water
Park Corner
Stonor Park
Skirmett
East Hendred
West Hagbourne
Upton
South Moreton
Cholsey
Cholsey & Wallingford Rly
Nuffield
Maidensgrove
Stonor
Rockwell End
East Ginge
Chilton
Blewbury
Aston Upthorpe
Aston Tirrold
North Stoke
Hailey
Huntercombe End
Fawley
Lower Woodend
Marlow
Nettlebed
Middle Assendon
Hambleden
Mill End
Bisham Abbey N.S.C.
Ipsden
Moulsford
Highmoor Cross
Bix
Greenlands
Fawley Court
Aston
Remenham
Remenham Hill
Medmenham
Hurley
Hurley Bottom
Lower Assendon
Greys Court (NT)
Stoke Row
Shepherd's Green
Greys Green
Henley-on-Thames
River & Rowing Mus
West Ilsley
East Ilsley
Streatley
South Stoke
Checkendon
Exlade Street
Rotherfield Greys
Burchett's Green
Woodcote
Cleeve
Rotherfield Peppard
Harpsden
Cockpole Green
Ashley Hill
Goring
Cray's Pond
Gallowstree Common
Sonning Common
Crazies Hill
Warren Row
Catmore
Compton
Knowl Hill
Stanmore
Aldworth
Basildon
Beale Park
Cane End
Kidmore End
Lower Shiplake
Shiplake
Wargrave
WEST
BERKS
Beedon
Basildon Park (NT)
Whitchurch Hill
Whitchurch-on-Thames
Tokers Green
Mapledurham
Dunsden Green
Binfield Heath
Kiln Green
Peasemore
World's End
Hampstead Norreys
Ashampstead
Emmer Green
Sonning Eye
Hare Hatch
Upper Basildon
Pangbourne
Mapledurham House & Mill
Caversham
Play Hatch
Sonning
Ruscombe
Twyford
Chieveley
Yattendon
Tidmarsh
Purley on Thames
Museum of Reading
READING
Woodley
Whistley Green
Shurlock Row
Little Hungerford
Sulham
Tilehurst
Dinton Pastures
Hermitage
Frilsham
Bradfield
Englefield
North Street
Calcot
Earley
Hurst
Snelsmore Common
Longlane
Stanford Dingley
Theale
Lower Earley
Winnersh
Binfield
Curridge
Bucklebury
Southend
Whitley
Sindlesham
Popeswood
Cold Ash
Upper Bucklebury
Chapel Row
Beenham
Sulhamstead
Sheffield Bottom
Reading
Burghfield
Shinfield
Wokingham
Donnington
Shaw
Thatcham
Midgham
Beenham Hill
Woolhampton
Aldermaston Wharf
Ufton Nervet
Burghfield Hill
Burghfield Common
Three Mile Cross
Grazeley
Spencers Wood
Arborfield
Arborfield Cross
Barkham
Arborfield Garrison
Eastheath
NEWBURY
Newbury
Midgham Sta.
Padworth
Wokefield Park
Swallowfield
M40
M4
A329(M)
A34
A40
A41
A44
A418
A4095
A4421
A413
A4260
A4165
A4144
A4142
A420
A415
A4074
A4183
A329
A4130
A4185
A417
A4155
A321
A4
A339
A340
A3290
A4010
B4027
B4011
B4009
B4015
B4016
B4493
B480
B481
B482
B4526
B471
B3024
B3018
B3030
B3349
B3270
B3034

STEVENAGE
LUTON
DUNSTABLE
Leighton Buzzard
Houghton Regis
HARPENDEN
Welwyn
HEMEL HEMPSTEAD
ST ALBANS
Hatfield
Berkhamsted
Tring
Wendover
CHESHAM
AMERSHAM
WATFORD
Borehamwood
Radlett
Abbots Langley
Kings Langley
Rickmansworth
Chorleywood
Beaconsfield
Hazlemere
HARROW
UXBRIDGE
HILLINGDON
BRENT
EALING
HAMMERSMITH & FULHAM
MAIDENHEAD
SLOUGH
WINDSOR
Eton
HOUNSLOW
RICHMOND UPON THAMES
KINGSTON UPON THAMES
STAINES
BRACKNELL
Ascot
Egham
Ashford
WALTON-ON-THAMES
Chertsey
London Heathrow
London Luton
B E D S
H E R T S
B U C K S
C H I L T E R N
S O U T H B U C K S
W I N D S O R & M A I D E N H E A D
M1
M10
M25
M4
M3
M40
A1(M)
44
57
29

44
58
43
30
A
B
C
D
1
2
3
4
5
STEVENAGE
LUTON
HARPENDEN
WELWYN GARDEN CITY
HERTFORD
Ware
Hoddesdon
Cheshunt
Waltham Abbey
HEMEL HEMPSTEAD
ST ALBANS
Hatfield
Potters Bar
Abbots Langley
Radlett
WATFORD
Borehamwood
BARNET
ENFIELD
Chingford
WALTHAM FOREST
HARROW
HARINGEY
HILLINGDON
BRENT
CAMDEN
ISLINGTON
HACKNEY
TOWER HAMLETS
NEWHAM
EALING
HAMMERSMITH & FULHAM
CITY OF WESTMINSTER
CITY OF LONDON
KENSINGTON & CHELSEA
SOUTHWARK
GREENWICH
LEWISHAM
WANDSWORTH
LAMBETH
HOUNSLOW
RICHMOND UPON THAMES
KINGSTON UPON THAMES
BROMLEY
Sunbury
WALTON-ON-THAMES
Wimbledon
Welwyn
Knebworth
Stanstead Abbotts
Hatfield House
Shenley
Bushey
Edgware
Stanmore
Finchley
Hendon
Wembley
Southall
Hayes
Heston
Twickenham
Teddington
Mitcham
Croydon
Sydenham
Ware
Harlow
Epping
Loughton
Woodford
Walthamstow
Barking
Leyton
Stoke Newington
Tottenham
Wood Green
Hornsey
Golders Green
Hampstead
Willesden
Paddington
Marylebone
Finsbury
Stepney
Poplar
Beckton
Bermondsey
Deptford
Catford
Chislehurst
Eltham
Charlton
Barnes
Fulham
Putney
Roehampton
Chiswick
Brentford
Acton
Hanwell
Greenford
Northolt
Ruislip
Pinner
Northwood
Rickmansworth
Chorleywood
Kings Langley
Redbourn
Wheathampstead
Sandridge
Colney Heath
London Colney
South Mimms
Cuffley
Northaw
Brookmans Park
Welham Green
Essendon
Bayford
Broxbourne
Wormley
Nazeing
Roydon
Hunsdon
Widford
Standon
Puckeridge
Much Hadham
Watton at Stone
Benington
Walkern
Datchworth
Codicote
Kimpton
M1
M10
M25
A1(M)
M4
M3
A10
A406
A41
A40
A4
A3
A23
A20
A2
A12
A13
A205

D
E
F
G
45
59
I
2
46
3
4
5
31
Birchanger
Stansted
Takeley
Great Dunmow
Stebbing
Braintree
Rayne
Felsted
Great Notley
Black Notley
Witham
Pattiswick
Coggeshall Hamlet
Silver End
Cressing
Rivenhall
Faulkbourne
Terling
Little Braxted
Wickham Bishops
Hatfield Peverel
Great Totham
Boreham
Langford
Maldon
Heybridge
Danbury
Little Baddow
Woodham Walter
Chelmsford
Moulsham
Great Baddow
Galleywood
Sandon
Writtle
Broomfield
Great Waltham
Little Waltham
Pleshey
Roxwell
Chignall St James
Good Easter
Mashbury
High Easter
Hatfield Broad Oak
Hatfield Heath
Sheering
Harlow
Matching
Matching Tye
Abbess Roding
Leaden Roding
Margaret Roding
White Roding
Aythorpe Roding
Beauchamp Roding
Berners Roding
The Rodings
Church Langley
Potter Street
Threshers Bush
Magdalen Laver
High Laver
Little Laver
Moreton
Fyfield
Willingale
Shellow Bowells
Bobbingworth
Tyler's Green
Norton Mandeville
Norton Heath
Shelley
Chipping Ongar
High Ongar
North Weald Bassett
Toot Hill
Greensted
Epping
Fiddlers Hamlet
Stanford Rivers
Stapleford Tawney
Blackmore
Stondon Massey
Nine Ashes
Margaretting
Ingatestone
Fryerning
Mill Green
Kelvedon Hatch
Doddinghurst
Mountnessing
Pilgrims Hatch
Navestock
Navestock Side
Coxtie Green
Stock
West Hanningfield
South Hanningfield
East Hanningfield
Rettendon
Woodham Ferrers
Bicknacre
Howe Green
Hanningfield Resr
Ramsden Heath
Downham
Billericay
Shenfield
Hutton
Brentwood
South Weald
Tye Common
Ingrave
Herongate
Little Burstead
Great Burstead
South Green
Ramsden Bellhouse
Crays Hill
Wickford
Shotgate
Nevendon
Runwell
Rawreth
Battlesbridge
Hockley
Rayleigh
South Woodham
Thundersley
Hadleigh
Daws Heath
Basildon
Pitsea
Vange
Laindon
Langdon Hills
Dunton Wayletts
North Benfleet
Bowers Gifford
South Benfleet
Canvey Island
Leigh Beck
Corringham
Fobbing
Coryton
Stanford-le-Hope
Mucking
Thames Haven
Horndon on the Hill
Orsett
Bulphan
West Horndon
East Horndon
Childerditch
Little Warley
Great Warley
Brook Street
Harold Wood
Harold Hill
Noak Hill
Havering-atte-Bower
Romford
Gidea Park
Hornchurch
Cranham
Upminster
Havering
Elm Park
Dagenham
South Hornchurch
Rainham
Wennington
Aveley
North Ockendon
South Ockendon
Baker Street
North Stifford
West Thurrock
Thurrock
Purfleet
Grays
Tilbury
East Tilbury
West Tilbury
Chadwell St Mary
Linford
Little Thurrock
Lakeside
Abridge
Passingford Bridge
Stapleford Abbotts
Lambourne End
Chigwell Row
Hainault
Collier Row
Marks Gate
Rush Green
Becontree
Creekmouth
Thamesmead
Erith
Belvedere
Abbey Wood
East Wickham
Slade Green
Crayford
Bexleyheath
Dartford
Greenhithe
Stone
Swanscombe
Gravesend
Northfleet
Bean
Wilmington
Hawley
Sutton at Hone
Darenth
South Darenth
Horton Kirby
Swanley
Hextable
Crockenhill
Farningham
Fawkham Green
Longfield
Hartley
New Barn
Southfleet
Betsham
Istead Rise
Cobham
Sole Street
Meopham
Luddesdown
Shorne
Shorne Ridgeway
Higham
Lower Higham
Chalk
Singlewell or Ifield
Thong
Strood
Rochester
Chatham
Gillingham
Frindsbury
Upper Upnor
Upnor
Wainscott
Chattenden
Cliffe
Cliffe Woods
Cooling
Church Street
High Halstow
Hoo
St Mary's Hoo
Allhallows
Kingsnorth Power Station
Medway
Borstal
Cuxton
Luton
Brompton
Rainham
Thames
M11
M25
M20
M2
A12
A13
A127
A130
A120
A414
A1114
A128
A1089
A282
A2
A226
A289
28
29
30
31
7
6/27
3/1
1A
1B
2
8

46
59
45
32
A
B
C
D
1
2
3
4
5
BRAINTREE
Rayne
Great Notley
Black Notley
Young's End
Bocking
Stane Street
Freeport
Tye Green
Bradwell
Pattiswick
Broad Green
Coggeshall
Coggeshall Hamlet
Paycocke's (NT)
Little Tey
Marks Tey
Stanway
Copford Green
Heckfordbridge
Easthorpe
Hardy's Green
Birch
Beacon
Shrub End
Old Heath
Rowhedge
Blackheath
Gryme's Dyke
Fingringhoe
Layer de la Haye
Abberton
Abberton Reservoir
Langenhoe
Danger Zone
Peldon
Great Wigborough
Mersea Island
West Mersea
Virley Channel
Cobmarsh Island
Great Cob I.
Salcott Channel
Virley
Salcott
Tolleshunt D'Arcy
Tolleshunt Knights
Oxley Green
Layer Breton
Layer Marney
Layer Marney Tower
Birch Green
Smythe's Green
Shalom Hall
Messing
Feering
Kelvedon
Inworth
Tiptree
Tiptree Heath
Silver End
Hawbush Green
Rivenhall
Rivenhall End
Great Braxted
Little Braxted
Witham
Wickham Bishops
Great Totham
Little Totham
Tolleshunt Major
Tollesbury
Tollesbury Fleet
The Nass
Heybridge
Heybridge Basin
Northey Island
Osea Island
Goldhanger
Broad Street Green
Blackwater
Bradwell Waterside
Bradwell-on-Sea
Sales Point
St Peter's
Ramsey Island
St Lawrence
Tillingham
Dengie
Dengie Marshes
Ray Sand
Asheldham
Steeple
Mayland
Maylandsea
Mundon
Latchingdon
Southminster
Althorne
Mangapps Farm Railway Museum
Stoneyhills
Ostend
Burnham-on-Crouch
Old Montsale
Deal Hall
Holliwell Point
Crouch
Courtsend
Churchend
Foulness Island
Wallasea Island
Paglesham Churchend
Paglesham Eastend
Potton Island
Havengore Island
Maplin Sands
Barling
Little Wakering
Great Wakering
North Shoebury
Shoeburyness
Shoebury Ness
Southchurch
Thorpe Bay
Sea Life Centre
Southend Pier
SOUTHEND-ON-SEA
Chapman Sands
Westcliff-on-Sea
Peter Pan's Adventure Island
Leigh-on-Sea
Leigh Beck
CANVEY ISLAND
Hadleigh
Daws Heath
Prittlewell
Prittlewell Priory
Kid's Kingdom
Mr B's Amusements
Central Mus
SOUTHEND
Eastwood
London Southend
Rochford
Great Stambridge
Ballards Gore
Ashingdon
Canewdon
Hawkwell
Hockley
RAYLEIGH
Weir
Rawreth
Hullbridge
South Fambridge
Bridgemarsh Island
Battlesbridge
South Woodham Ferrers
Marsh Farm
Stow Maries
Cold Norton
Purleigh
Rudley Green
Great Canney
Cock Clarks
Hazeleigh
Woodham Mortimer
Danbury
Danbury Park
Runsell Green
Maldon
Maldon 991
Woodham Walter
Langford
Ulting
Little Baddow
Nounsley
Hatfield Peverel
Crix
Boreham
Terling
Gamble's Green
Fairstead
Faulkbourne
White Notley
Chipping Hill
Rank's Green
Great Leighs
Little Leighs
Fuller Street
Willows Green
Cobler's Green
Felsted
Little Dunmow
Bannister Green
Blake End
Stebbing Green
Hartford End
Littley Green
Pleshey
Great Waltham
Little Waltham
Broomfield
St James
CHELMSFORD
Writtle
Moulsham
Great Baddow
Galleywood
Galleyend
Sandon
Bicknacre
Howe Green
East Hanningfield
Woodham Ferrers
Rettendon
Hyde Hall
Rettendon Place
West Hanningfield
South Hanningfield
Hanningfield Resr
Downham
Ramsden Heath
Norsey Wood
Stock
Ingatestone
Runwell
Wickford
Shotgate
Nevendon
Ramsden Bellhouse
South Green
Barleylands Farm Mus
Crays Hill
Little Burstead
Great Burstead
North Benfleet
BASILDON
Laindon
Langdon Hills
Dry Street
Vange
Pitsea
Bowers Gifford
Thundersley
Hope's Green
SOUTH BENFLEET
Pitsea Hall
Wat Tyler
Corringham
Fobbing
Coryton
Stanford-le-Hope
Mucking
Thames Haven
THAMES
Blythe Sands
Linford
East Tilbury
Halstow Marshes
St Mary's Marshes
St Mary's Hoo
Allhallows-on-Sea
Allhallows
Isle of Grain
Grain
Lower Stoke
Stoke
Stoke Saltings
Wallend
Northward Hill
Cliffe
Cooling
Church Street
High Halstow
Cliffe Woods
Lower Higham
Chalk
Higham
Shorne
Shorne Ridgeway
Thong
Chattenden
Hoo
Kingsnorth Power Station
MEDWAY
Upnor
Upper Upnor
Wainscott
Frindsbury
Strood
ROCHESTER
Chatham Historic Dockyard & World Naval Base
Brompton
GILLINGHAM
Grange
CHATHAM
Borstal
Cuxton
Luddesdown
Sole Street
Cobham Hall
Luton
Rainham
Upchurch
Lower Halstow
Iwade
Bobbing
Kemsley
Swale Sta.
Chetney Marshes
Queenborough
Sheerness
West Minster
Minster
Halfway Houses
Eastchurch
Warden
Warden Point
Leysdown-on-Sea
ISLE OF SHEPPEY
Eastchurch Marshes
Isle of Harty
Elmley Island
The Swale
KENT
ESSEX
A12
A120
A130
A131
A138
A414
A1060
A1114
A1016
A132
A127
A129
A1015
A13
A176
A1235
A1321
A1014
A1013
A228
A289
A226
A231
A230
A229
A2
M2
A249
A250
A1124

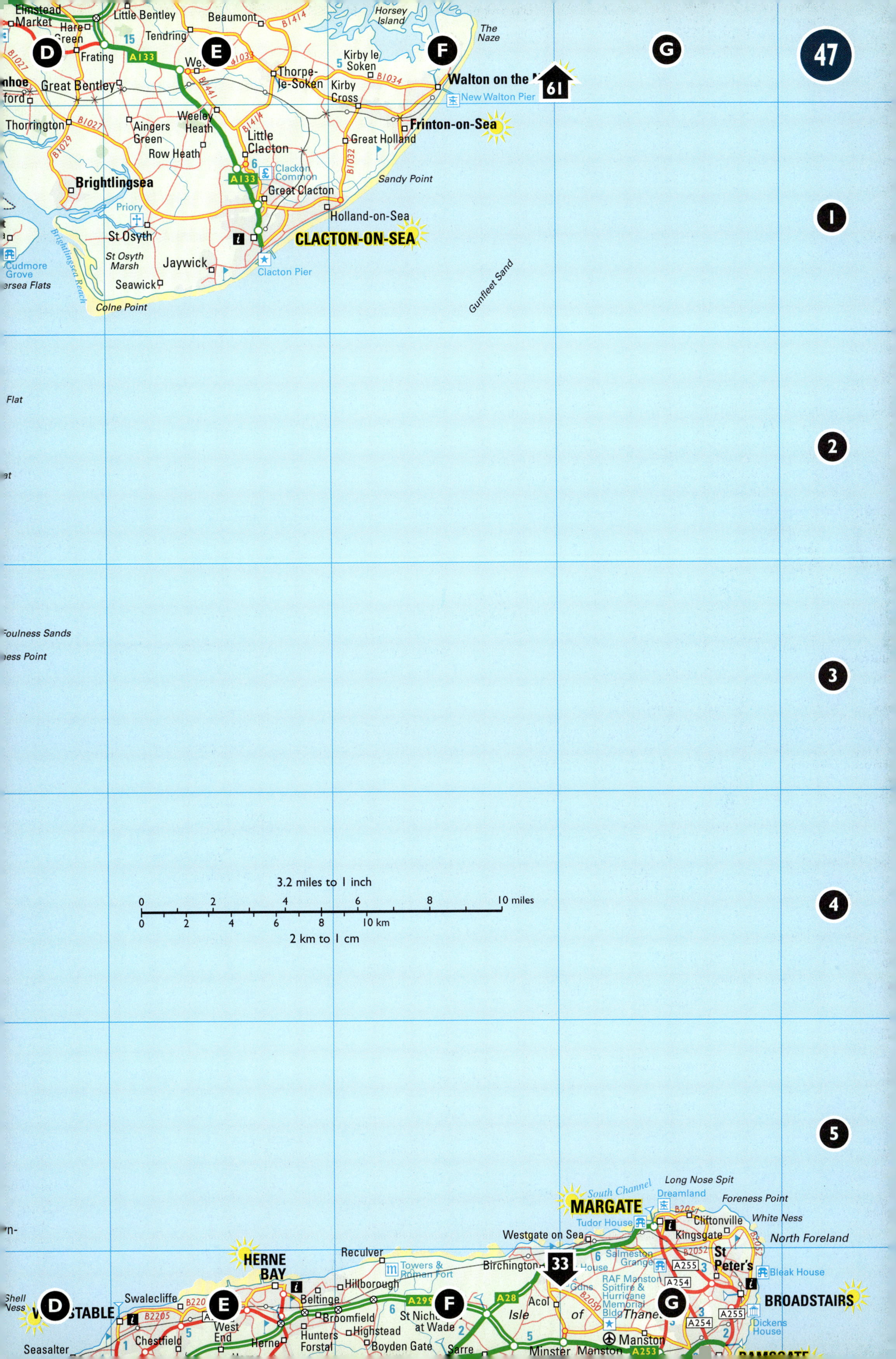
Elmstead Market
Hare Green
Little Bentley
Beaumont
Horsey Island
The Naze
Tendring
Frating
A133
Kirby le Soken
Thorpe-le-Soken
Walton on the
61
New Walton Pier
Great Bentley
Kirby Cross
Thorrington
Aingers Green
Weeley Heath
Little Clacton
Frinton-on-Sea
Great Holland
Row Heath
Clacton Common
Sandy Point
Brightlingsea
Great Clacton
Priory
Holland-on-Sea
St Osyth
CLACTON-ON-SEA
Cudmore Grove
St Osyth Marsh
Jaywick
Clacton Pier
Seawick
Brightlingsea Reach
Colne Point
Gunfleet Sand
Flat
Foulness Sands
Point
3.2 miles to 1 inch
0 2 4 6 8 10 miles
0 2 4 6 8 10 km
2 km to 1 cm
South Channel
Long Nose Spit
MARGATE
Dreamland
Foreness Point
White Ness
Tudor House
Cliftonville
Westgate on Sea
Kingsgate
North Foreland
HERNE BAY
Reculver
Towers & Roman Fort
Birchington
33
Salmestone Grange
St Peter's
Bleak House
RAF Manston Spitfire & Hurricane Memorial Bldg
Hillborough
Swalecliffe
Beltinge
Acol
Isle of Thanet
BROADSTAIRS
Shell Ness
WHITSTABLE
Broomfield
St Nicholas at Wade
Dickens House
Chestfield
West End
Herne
Hunters Forstal
Highstead
Boyden Gate
Sarre
Minster
Manston
Seasalter
A28
A299
A253
A254
A255
B2205

A
B
C
D
1
2
3
4
5
3.2 miles to 1 inch
0 2 4 6 8 10 miles
0 2 4 6 8 10 km
2 km to 1 cm
Rosslare 1¾–3½ hrs
Strumble Head
Tresinwen
Carregwastad Point
Crincoed Point
Fishguard Bay
Dinas Head
Newport Bay
Dinas Island
Cwm-yr-Eglw
Bryn-henllan
Dinas Cross
Parrog
Pen Brush
Pen Caer
Llanwnda
Goodwick (Wdig)
Fishguard (Abergwaun)
A487
Trefasser
Penbwchdy
Dyffryn
Lower Town
A487
St Nicholas
Manorowen
Mynydd Melyn
307
Mynydd Carregog
Llanychaer Bridge
Cilrhedyn Bridge
PEMBROKESHIRE
COAST
NATIONAL PARK
Penmorfa
10
Scleddau
8
Pontfaen
Ynys Deullyn
Granston
Cwm Gwaun
Abercastle
Jordanston
Trecwn
Mynydd Cilciffeth
334
Penclegyr
Porthgain
Trevine
Mathry
Castle Morris
Newbridge
Llanrhian
A487
A40
Morvil
Abereiddy
Penparc
B4331
Mynydd Castlebythe
347
Carreg-gwylan-fach
Penclegyr
Berea
Croesgoch
Letterston
Little Newcastle
Puncheston
Penllechwen
Treglemais
Llanreithan
Tre-ddiog
Castlebythe
North Bishop
St David's Head
Treleddyd-fawr
Tretio
Rhodiad-y-Brenin
Treffynnon
15
St Dogwells
Tufton
Whitesands Bay or Porth-mawr
6
B4330
Welsh Hook
B4583
A487
Caerfarchell
Newton
Carreg
Point St John
Cathedral
Bishop's Palace
Whitchurch
Middle Mill
Llandeloy
Wolf's Castle
Rinaston
Wallis
Ambleston
Woodstock
Rhosson
St David's (Tyddewi)
Ford
Hayscastle
14
Trefgarn Owen
Hayscastle Cross
Llys-y-frân Resr
Bishops and Clerks
St Non's Chapel
Solva
A487
Brawdy
Mountain Water
12
Walton East
Ramsey Sound
Dudwell Mountain
178
Treffgarne
Spittal
Green Scar
Penycwm
Llethr
A40
Upper Scolton
Ramsey Island
Dinas Fawr
Newgale
Leweston
Newgale Sands
PEMBROKESHIRE
Ynys Bery
16
Wolfsdale
Scolton Manor
Clarbeston
Roch
Folly
Rudbaxton
Clarbeston Road
B4329
Camrose
34
Keeston
Poyston Cross
ST BRIDE'S BAY
Rickets Head
Nolton
B4330
Tangiers
Crundale
Pelcomb Cross
Wis
Druidston
Lambston
Pelcomb Bridge
Prendergast
Castle Mus & Art Gallery
Sutton
A40

D
E
F
G
I
New Quay Head
New Quay Bay
New Quay (Ceinewydd)
Ffos-y-ffin
Llwyn-onn
Gilfachrheda
Llanarth
Cwmtudu
Nanternis
Cross Inn
Ynys-Lochtyn
Llwyndafydd
Synod Inn
Llangranog
Wervil Brook
Plwmp
Pentregat
Pencribach
Penbryn
Parcllyn
Aberporth
Tresaith
Brynhoffnant
Sarnau
Talgarreg
50
Wstrws
Capel Cynon
Cardigan Island
Cemaes Head
Gwbert
Ferwig
Blaenannerch
Tan-y-groes
Tremain
Blaenporth
Glynarthen
Pen-yr-afr
Pwllygranant
Cippyn
Cardigan (Aberteifi)
St Dogmaels
Ceibwr Bay
Tre-Rhys
Abbey
Penparc
CEREDIGION
Bettws Evan
Rhydlewis
Ffostrasol
Castell Howell
Llangoedmor
Noyadd Trefawr
Beulah
Brongest
Hawen
Penrhiw-pal
Maesllyn
Tre-groes
Pontshaen
Moylgrove
Monington
Cardigan
Pantgwyn
Ponthirwaun
Troedyraur
Croes-lan
Pren-gwyn
Llechryd
Llandygwydd
Capel Tygwydd
(NT)
Teifi
Glanrhyd
Cilgerran
Manordeifi
Cwmcoy
Pont Ceri
Llandyfriog
Teifi Valley
Aber-banc
Penrhiw-llan
Horeb
Llandysul
Tredrissi
Llantood
Bridell
Berry Hill
Trewilym
Rhos-hill
Pentre Mansion
Cenarth
Abercych
Newcastle Emlyn (Castell Newydd Emlyn)
Llanfair-Orllwyn
Bangor Teifi
Henllan
Nevern
Newport
Velindre
Eglwyswrw
Newchapel
Clynfyw
Penrherber
Aberarad
Welsh Woollen Industry
Pentrecagal
Llangeler
Pontwelly
Pentre Ifan Burial Chamber
Llanfair-Nant-Gwyn
Boncath
Cilwendeg
Felindre
Drefach
Pentre-cwrt
Glynteg
Saron
Banc-y-ffordd
Carningli Common
Cilgwyn
Crosswell
Whitechurch
Blaenffos
Glaspant
Capel Iwan
Moelfre
Cwmpengraig
Penboyr
Bwlch-clawdd
Rhos
Brynberian
Freni-fawr
Bwlch-y-groes
Star
Clydey
Cilrhedyn
Cwm-Morgan
Tafarn-y-bwlch
PRESCELLY MTS (MYNYDD PRESELI)
Crymych
Taf
Tegryn
Gorllwyn
Foel Eryr
Foel Cwmcerwyn
Hermon
Llanfyrnach
Cwmduad
Hermon
Mynachlogddu
Foel Drych
Pentre Galar
Trelech
Dinas
Greenway
Rosebush
Glandwr
Esgair
Llanpumsaint
Hebron
Blaenwaun
Blaen-y-coed
Cynwyl Elfed
Maenclochog
Llangolman
Post House
Trelech a'r Betws
Gwili
Llanglydwen
Llanwinio
New Moat
Efailwen
Cefn-y-pant
Via Julia
Cwmfelin Mynach
Cwmbach
Talog
Bwlchnewydd
Newchurch
Gellywen
Maesgwynne
Llys-y-fran
Llanycefn
Login
Llandre
Llanboidy
Abernant
Nant Cynnen
Ffynnon-ddrain
Pen-ffordd
CARMARTHENSHIRE
Tre-vaughan
Tanerdy
Llandissilio
Castell Gorfod
Meidrim
Merthyr
Bletherston
Rhydywrach
Henllan Amgoed
Carmarthen (Caerfyrddin)
Johnstown
Clynderwen
Llanfallteg
Llanfallteg West
Llangynin
35
Bron-y-Gaer
Sarnau
Pensarn
Gelly
Cwmfelin Boeth
Llanllwch
Llanddewi Velfrey
Whitland Abbey
Pwll Trap
Bancyfelin
Cwmffrwd
Llawhaden
Whitland
Llangynog
Llangain
Croesyceiliog
Robeston Wathen
Trevaughan
St Clears
Redstone Bank
A487
A484
A486
A475
A478
A40
A485
B4342
B4321
B4334
B4338
B4548
B4546
B4570
B4571
B4333
B4582
B4332
B4329
B4313
B4299
B4298
B4301
B4312
B4459
B4476

A
B
C
D
62
49
36
Carreg Ti-pw
Llanddeiniol
Rhos-y-garth
Llanafan
Ysbyty
Mynydd Bach
Llangwyryfon
Lledrod
Tynygraig
Llanrhystud
Trefenter
Bronnant
Ystrad Meurig
Ffair Rhos
Pontrhydfendigaid
Strata Florida
Llansantffraid
Llanon
Rhyd-rosser
Llyn Eiddwen
Swyddffynnon
Cors-goch Glan Teifi
MYNYDD BACH
Nebo
Blaenpennal
Aberarth
Aberaeron
Cross Inn
Bethania
Pennant
Monachty
Penuwch
Carn Gron
New Quay Head
New Quay Bay
New Quay
Ceinewydd
Ffos-y-ffin
Llanaeron
Llanerchaeron (NT)
Cilcennin
Llangeitho
Sarn Helen
Tregaron
Y Drum
Llwyn-onn
Gilfachrheda
Llwyncelyn
Bwlch-llan
Parcrhydderch
Esgair Fraith
Ciliau-Aeron
Capel Betws Lleucu
Llanarth
Neuadd
Oakford
Brynog
Trefilan
Gartheli
Cross Inn
Ystrad Aeron
Tal-sarn
Abermeurig
Llyn Berwyn
Bryn Rhudd
Dihewyd
Mydroilyn
Llanddewi-Brefi
Synod Inn
CEREDIGION
Temple Bar
Esgair Llethr
Llethr Llwyd
Plwmp
Caledrhydiau
Bettws Bledrws
Llangybi
Pentregat
Bryn Brawd
Cribyn
Silian
Llanfair Clydogau
Talgarreg
Gorsgoch
Capel St Silin
Carn Nant-yr-ast
Cefn Gwenffrwd
Wstrws
Capel Cynon
Aber
Lampeter
Cellan
Pentrefelin
Craig Twrch
Craig Siarls
Castell Howell
Cwrt-newydd
Ffostrasol
Llanwnen
Cwmann
Garthynty
Cwmsychbant
Alltyblaca
Ram
Pontshaen
Llanwenog
Dre-fach
Llanycrwys
Rhydowen
Pencarreg
Ffarmers
Tre-groes
Mynydd Mallaen
Croes-lan
Pren-gwyn
Highmead
Llanybydder
Pen Tas-eithin
Capel Dewi
Rock Mill Woollen and Water Mill
Mynydd Pencarreg
Penrhiw-llan
Horeb
Llandre
Rhyd Galed
Llanfair-Orllwyn
Abergiar
Bangor Teifi
Llandysul
Maesycrugiau
Pumsaint
Dolaucothi Gold Mines (NT)
Cilycwm
Henllan
Llanllwni
Caio
Llangeler
Pontwelly
Llanfihangel ar-arth
Aber Bowlan
Drefach
Pentre-cwrt
Mynydd Llanllwni
Mynydd Llanybydder
Rhydcymerau
Saron
Banc-y-ffordd
Crugybar
Porthyrhyd
Lllidiadnenog
Bwlch-clawdd
Pencader
New Inn
Llansawel
Penboyr
Gwyddgrug
Dol-gran
Gwernogle
Abergorlech
Edwinsford
Llandovery
Blaenos
Gorllwyn
Talley
Abbey
Llwyn-y-brain
Cwmduad
Alltwalis
Pen-y-garn
Mynydd Cynros
Waunclynda
Llansadwrn
Llanwrda
Dolgarreg
Halfway
Mynydd Figyn
Cwmdu
Llanllawddog
Brechfa
Cilgwyn
Esgair
Llanpumsaint
CARMARTHENSHIRE
Soar
Pontarsais
Llanfynydd
Capel Isaac
Maerdy
Llangadog
Cynwyl Elfed
Felindre
Gwili
Plas
Salem
Rhydargaeau
Manordeilo
Newchurch
Rhiwe
Felingwmuchaf
Pen-y-banc
Rhosmaen
Bethlehem
Dyffryn Ceidrych
Twynllanan
Llanfihangel uwch-gwili
DYFFRYN TYWI
Court Henry
Pentrefelin
Llandeilo
Trichrung
Fynnon-ddrain
Capel Gwyn
Broadoak
Dinefwr Park (NT)
Pont Aber
Tre-vaughan
Nantgaredig
Pontargothi
Llangathen
Tanerdy
Abergwili
White Mill
Felindre
Ffairfach
Capel Gwynfe
Carmarthen (Caerfyddin)
Llanegwad
Dryslwyn
Gelli Aur
Johnstown
Llangunnor
Llanarthney
Maerdy
Pensarn
Capel Dewi
Golden Grove
Trap
Carreg Cennen
Pont Clydach
Carreg-lwyd
Llanllwch
Nantycaws
National Botanic Garden of Wales
Penrhiwgoch
Tair Carn Isaf
BLACK MOUNTAIN
Cwmffrwd
Derwydd
Gwynfe
Pentre Gwenlais
Carmel
Llangain
Croesyceiliog
Llanddarog
Cwmisfael
Porthyrhyd
Maesybont
Heol-ddu
Llyn Lech Owain
Llandybie
Bylchau Rhos-fain

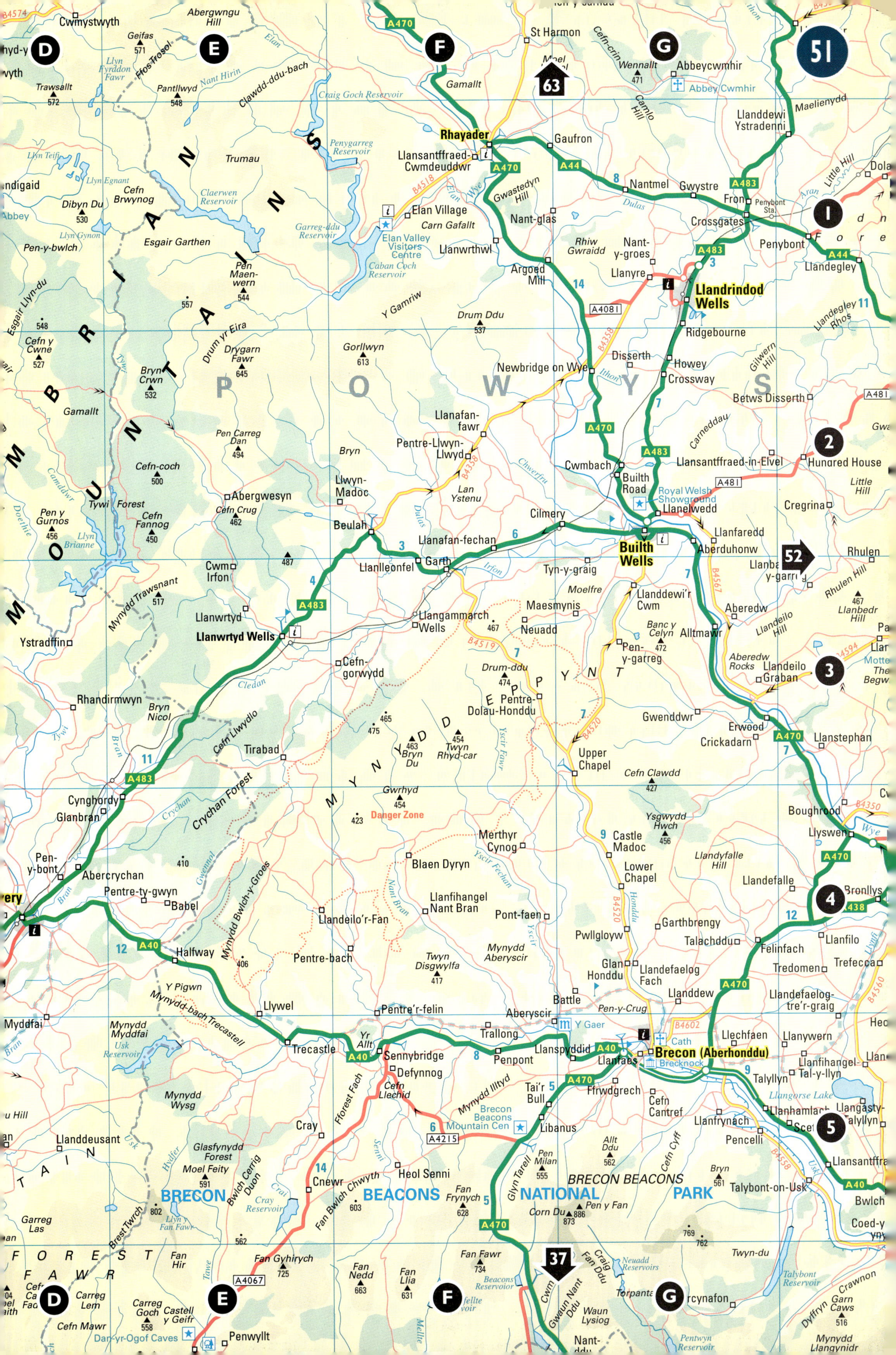
Cwmystwyth
Abergwngu Hill
Geifas 571
Trawsallt 572
Llyn Fyrddon Fawr
Ffos Trosol
Pantllwyd 548
Nant Hirin
Clawdd-ddu-bach
Craig Goch Reservoir
A470
St Harmon
Cefn-crin
Wennallt 471
Abbeycwmhir
Abbey Cwmhir
Moel
63
Gamallt
Rhayader
Gaufron
Llanddewi Ystradenni
Maelienydd
Penygarreg Reservoir
Llyn Teifi
Trumau
Llansantffraed-Cwmdeuddwr
Elan
Wye
A44
8
Nantmel
Gwystre
A483
Fron
Penybont
Little Hill
Llyn Egnant
Cefn Brwynog
Dibyn Du 530
Claerwen Reservoir
Garreg-ddu Reservoir
Elan Village
Carn Gafallt
Gwastedyn Hill
Nant-glas
Dulas
Crossgates
Aran
Llyn Gynon
Pen-y-bwlch
Esgair Garthen
Elan Valley Visitors Centre
Caban Coch Reservoir
Llanwrthwl
Rhiw Gwraidd
Nant-y-groes
Penybont
Llandegley
Pen Maen-wern 544
Argoed Mill
14
Llanyre
Llandrindod Wells
Esgair Llyn-du
548
557
Y Gamriw
Drum Ddu 537
A4081
Llandegley Rhos
11
Cefn y Cwne 527
Drum yr Eira
Drygarn Fawr 645
Gorllwyn 613
B4358
Ridgebourne
Disserth
Howey
Crossway
Gilwern Hill
Tywi
Bryn Crwn 532
Newbridge on Wye
Ithon
P O W Y S
Betws Disserth
A481
C A M B R I A N M O U N T A I N S
Gamallt
Llanafan-fawr
Carneddau
Pen Carreg Dan 494
Bryn
Pentre-Llwyn-Llwyd
Llansantffraed-in-Elvel
2
Hundred House
Cefn-coch 500
Llwyn-Madoc
Cwmbach
Builth Road
Chwefru
Lan Ystenu
Little Hill
Camddwr
Tywi Forest
Abergwesyn
Cefn Crug 462
Royal Welsh Showground
Llanelwedd
Cregrina
Pen y Gurnos 456
Cefn Fannog 450
Llyn Brianne
Doethie
Beulah
Dulas
Cilmery
Llanfaredd
Aberduhonw
52
Rhulen
3
Llanafan-fechan
6
Builth Wells
487
Cwm Irfon
Llanlleonfel
Garth
Irfon
Tyn-y-graig
Llanbadarn-y-garreg
Rhulen Hill
Mynydd Trawsnant
517
4
Moelfre
B4567
467 Llanbedr Hill
Maesmynis
Llanddewi'r Cwm
Aberedw
Llanwrtyd
A483
Llangammarch Wells
467
Neuadd
Banc y Celyn 472
Alltmawr
Llandeilo Hill
Ystradffin
Llanwrtyd Wells
Cefn-gorwydd
B4519
7
Pen-y-garreg
Aberedw Rocks
Llandeilo Graban
3
Cleddan
Drum-ddu 474
E P P Y N T
Rhandirmwyn
Pentre-Dolau-Honddu
Bryn Nicol
465
475
Gwenddwr
Erwood
Cefn Llwydlo
463 Bryn Du
454 Twyn Rhyd-car
Ysgir Fawr
Crickadarn
A470
Llanstephan
Tywi
Bran
Tirabad
B4520
Upper Chapel
11
A483
M Y N Y D D
Cefn Clawdd 427
Gwrhyd 454
Crychan Forest
Cynghordy
Glanbran
Crychan
423
Danger Zone
Boughrood
B4350
Ysgwydd Hwch 456
Merthyr Cynog
9
Castle Madoc
Llyswen
Wye
410
Gwennol
Pen-y-bont
Blaen Dyryn
Ysgir Fechan
Lower Chapel
Landyfalle Hill
A470
Abercrychan
Llandefalle
Mynydd Bwlch-y-Groes
Nant Bran
Bronllys
4
A438
Pentre-ty-gwyn
Babel
Llanfihangel Nant Bran
Honddu
12
Llandeilo'r-Fan
Pont-faen
Garthbrengy
Llanfilo
Talachddu
12
A40
Halfway
406
Pentre-bach
Mynydd Aberyscir
Ysgir
Pwllgloyw
Felinfach
Twyn Disgwylfa 417
Trefecca
Y Pigwn
Glan Honddu
Llandefaelog Fach
Tredomen
B4560
Mynydd-bach Trecastell
Llywel
Battle
Llanddew
A470
Llandefaelog-tre'r-graig
Myddfai
Pentre'r-felin
Aberyscir
Pen-y-Crug
Mynydd Myddfai
Y Gaer
B4602
Llechfaen
Llanywern
Usk Reservoir
Yr Allt
Trallong
Cath
Trecastle
A40
Sennybridge
8
Penpont
Llanspyddid
A40
Llanfaes
Brecon (Aberhonddu)
Brecknock
9
Talyllyn
Llanfihangel-Tal-y-llyn
Defynnog
Tai'r Bull
5
Ffrwdgrech
Llangorse Lake
Cefn Llechid
Mynydd Illtyd
A470
Cefn Cantref
Llanhamlach
Llangasty-Talyllyn
Mynydd Wysg
Fforest Fach
Brecon Beacons Mountain Centre
Libanus
Llanfrynach
Scethrog
5
Cray
6
A4215
Pencelli
Llanddeusant
Usk
Allt Ddu 562
Cefn Cyff
B4558
Llansantffraed
Glasfynydd Forest
Senni
Pen Milan 555
Glyn Tarell
Bryn 561
Usk
A40
Moel Feity 591
Bwlch Cerrig Duon
14
Cnewr
Heol Senni
BRECON BEACONS NATIONAL PARK
Talybont-on-Usk
Hydfer
Crai
Fan Bwlch Chwyth
Fan Frynych 628
5
Corn Du 886
Pen y Fan
873
Bwlch
Cray Reservoir
603
Garreg Las
802
Llyn y Fan Fawr
Brest Twrch
A470
Coed-y-
769
762
562
Fan Hir
Fan Gyhirych 725
Fan Fawr 734
37
Craig Fan Ddu
Neuadd Reservoirs
Twyn-du
F O R E S T F A W R
Tawe
A4067
Fan Nedd 663
Fan Llia 631
Beacons Reservoir
Talybont Reservoir
Crawnon
Carreg Lem
Carreg Goch 558
Castell y Geifr
Llwyn-on Reservoir
Cwm
Gwaun Nant Ddu
Torpantau
Waun Lysiog
Garn Caws 516
Dyffryn Crawnon
Cefn Mawr
Dan-yr-Ogof Caves
Penwyllt
Mellte
Nant-ddu
Pentwyn Reservoir
Mynydd Llangynidr
D
E
F
G
I
2
3
4
5

A
B
C
D
64
51
38
1
2
3
4
5
Llanbister
Crug
Llangunllo
Llanbister Rd Sta.
Llangynllo Sta.
Panpunton
Stowe
Bucknell
Buckton
Leintwardine
Walford
Milebrook
A4113
Bryan
Letton
Adforton
Abbey Cwmhir
Maelienydd
Llanddewi Ystradenni
Glog Hill
Bleddfa
Rhos-y-Meirch
A488
B4356
B4355
B4357
Pilleth
Whitton
Norton
Llan-wen Hill
Birtley
Newton
Harley's Mtn
Lingen
Wigmore
Leinthall Earls
Ongar Street
Lower Lye
Yatton
A4110
Aymestrey
Gwystre
A483
Penybont
Penybont Sta.
Dolau
Little Hill
Fforest-fach
Black Mixen
Llanfihangel Rhydithon
Radnor Forest
Great Rhos
660
Pentre
Cascob
Pilleth 1402
Maes-Treylow
Discoed
Offa's Dyke
Presteigne
Stapleton
Kinsham
Combe
Byton
Mortimer's Cross
Lucton
Llandrindod Wells
Llandegley
A44
Llandegley Rhos
Egairnantau
Fron Hill
Bache Hill
610
Kinnerton
New Radnor
B4372
Evenjobb
Rodd
Nash
Coombes Moor
B4362
Wapley Hill
Shobdon
Ledicot
Kingsland
Ridgebourne
Howey
Crossway
Gilwern Hill
Wolfpits
Old Radnor
Walton
Knill
Titley
Stansbatch
Staunton on Arrow
Shirl Heath
Burlingjobb
Bradnor Hill
Eywood
Pembridge
Eardisland
Burton Court
Llanfihangel-nant-Melan
Yardro
Dolyhir
B4355
Kington
Marston
Lower Barewood
Sollers Dilwyn
Stretford Court
Betws Disserth
Bryn-y-maen
Gwaithla
Hergest Ridge
Hergest Croft
Lower Hergest
Moorcot
Barewood
Luntley
Dilwyn Common
Dilwyn
A481
Gwaunceste Hill
542
Colva Hill
Gladestry
Lyonshall
Holme Marsh
Broxwood
Haven
Llansantffraed-in-Elvel
Hundred House
Glascwm
Colva
Hengoed
Upper Hergest
Kingswood
A480
A4112
Knapton Green
Royal Welsh Showground
Little Hill
Glascwm Hill
524
Huntington
Woonton
Llanelwedd
Cregrina
POWYS
Veaullt
Brilley Mountain
Michaelchurch-on-Arrow
Upper Welson
Lower Welson
Almeley
Weobley
Weobley Marsh
Upcott
Sarnesfield
HER
Llanfaredd
Newchurch
Red Hill
509
A4111
Ledgemoor
Aberduhonw
Rhulen
Llanbadarn-y-garreg
Bryngwyn
Dolleycanney
Brilley
Hurstway Common
Eardisley
Kinnersley
Norton Wood
B4230
Canon Pyon
Rhosgoch
Rhulen Hill
467
Llanbedr Hill
Aberedw
Clyro Hill
Rhydspence
Whitney
A438
Winforton
Willersley
Ailey
Calver Hill
Norton Canon
Wormsley
Yarsop
Foxley
Alltmawr
Llandeilo Hill
Toll
Letton Lake
Letton
Moorhampton
Staunton on Wye
Yazor
Mansell Lacy
Llanbedr
Painscastle
B4594
Clifford
Bronydd
Priory Wood
Merbach
Bredwardine
Mansell Gamage
Aberedw Rocks
Llandeilo Graban
Motte & Bailey
The Begwns
B4352
Pen-y-Park
Brobury
Portway
Bishopstone
Clyro
Hardwicke
Arthur's Stone
Moccas Court
Monnington on Wye
A438
Erwood
Crickadarn
A470
Llanstephan
Llowes
Hay-on-Wye
B4350
B4348
The Bage
Moccas
Preston on Wye
Byford
Bridge Sollers
The Weir (NT)
Canon Bridge
Cusop
Dorstone
Blakemere
Ploughfield
Lulham
Cwmbach
Boughrood
Glasbury
Llanigon
Cefn Hill
486
Snodhill
Tyberton
Madley
Pipton
Tregoyd
Vagar Hill
Hinton
Peterchurch
Llyswen
A4079
Three Cocks
Craswall Priory (ruins)
Urishay Common
Golden Valley
Shenmore
Llandyfalle Hill
Velindre
Hay Bluff
677
Turnastone
Vowchurch
Webton
Kingstone
Clehonger
A4078
Upper Maes-coed
Llandefalle
Bronllys
Twmpa
690
Craswall
A438
Talgarth
Llanelieu
St Margarets
Kerry's Gate
Thruxton
Michaelchurch Escley
Escley Brook
Olchon
Felinfach
Llanfilo
Rhos Dirion
713
Middle Maes-coed
Whitfield
Talachddu
Tredomen
Trefecca
A479
Olchon Valley
Monnow
Bacton
Didley
Pen y Manllwyn
Capel-y-ffin
Llanveynoe
Abbey Dore
Abbey Dore Court
Wormbridge
Llandefaelog-tre'r-graig
Pengenffordd
Waun Fach
811
Grwyne Fawr Res
Lower Maes-coed
Abbey (ruins)
Kilpeck
Brecon (Aberhonddu)
Heol Lly Goden
BRECON BEACONS
Longtown
Howton
Llanywern
800
Mynydd Troed
Priory
Ewyas Harold
Kenderchurch
Llechfaen
Llanfihangel-Tal-y-llyn
Grwyne Fechan
Mynydd Merddin
A40
Talyllyn
Llangorse
Mynydd Llysiau
Llanthony
Clodock
Pontrilas
Pen Twyn Mawr
Rowlstone
Llanhamlach
Llangorse Lake
Llangasty-Talyllyn
Mynydd Llangorse
B4560
MOUNTAINS
Hatterrall Hill
Llangua
Kentchurch
Scethrog
Cathedine
Pen Allt-mawr
Pen Gwyllt Meirch
Walterstone
Oldcastle
Grosmont
366
Cwmdu
NATIONAL PARK
Cwmyoy
A465
Hoaldalbert
Bryn
561
Talybont-on-Usk
Llansantffraed
A479
Pen Cerrig-calch
701
Crug Mawr
550
Patrishow
Pandy
Graig Syfyrddin
Bwlch
Gaer
Tretower
Tretower Court
Llanfihangel Crucorney
Llanfihangel Court
Llangattock Lingoed
Skenfrith
Coed-yr-ynys
Myarth
Llanbedr
Bryn arw
Bont
769
762
Twyn-du
Mynydd Pen-y-fal
Blaenawey
Sugar Loaf
596
Upper Green
Cross Ash
Llangynidr
B4558
Ffawydd
Crickhowell
MONMOUTHSHIRE
Talybont Reservoir
Crawnon
Llangattock
Llanbedr
Deri
Llantilio Pertholey
486
Ysgyryd Fawr
Llanvetherine
White Castle
Abercynafon
Garn Caws
516
Glangrwyne
Cefn Onneu
Cwrt-y-gollen
Dyffryn
Mynydd Llangynidr
Pentwyn Resr
A4077
Mynydd Llanwenarth
Rholben
Mardy
Hen Gwrt
Llangattock-Vibon-Avel

53
65
54
39
D
E
F
G
I
2
3
4
5
WORCESTERSHIRE
HEREFORDSHIRE
GLOS
Ludford
Overton
Caynham Camp
Caynham
Whitton
Hope Bagot
Nash
Coreley
Milson
Neen Sollars
Bayton
Mamble
Clows Top
Pound Bank
Callow Hill
Bliss Gate
Rock
Ribbesford
Stourport-on-Severn
Areley Kings
Hartlebury Common
Ashford Carbonel
Ashford Bowdler
Greete
Boraston
Frith Common
Richard's Castle
Woofferton
Tenbury Wells
Newnham
Lindridge
Eardiston
Pensax
Abberley
Dunley
Astley Cross
Crossway Green
Lincomb
The Burf
Orleton Common
Comberton
Wyson
Little Hereford
Brimfield
Burford
Rochford
Upper Rochford
Stockton on Teme
Orleton
Hanley William
Stanford on Teme
Abberley Hill
Abberley Hall
Astley
Noutard's Green
Sytchampton
Callows Grave
Bircher
Middleton on the Hill
St Michaels
Broadheath
Stanford Bridge
Great Witley
Eastgrove Cottage Garden
Frog Pool
Woodbury Hill
Moreton
Eye
Ashton
Berrington Hall (NT)
Leysters
Hanley Child
Kyre Park
Sapey Common
Shelsley Walsh
Witley Court
Little Witley
Holt Fleet
Holt Heath
Luston
Stoke Bliss
Bank Street
Garmsley Camp
Upper Sapey
Shelsley Beauchamp
Kimbolton
Wolferlow
Clifton upon Teme
Holt
Sinton Green
Hawford
Grimley
Stockton
Whyle
Grafton
Collington
High Lane
Harpley
Wichenford
Martley
Eyton
Bach Camp
Hatfield
Thornbury
Wall Hills
Edvin Loach
Tedstone Wafre
Tedstone Delamere
Wichenford Dovecote (NT)
Moseley
Shoulton
Hallow Heath
Hallow
Cholstrey
Leominster
Pudleston
Grendon Green
Edwyn Ralph
Horsham
Berrow Green
Peachley
Monkland
Ivington
Stoke Prior
Steen's Bridge
Docklow
Whitbourne
Broad Green
Lower Broadheath
Broadwas
Brierley
Wharton
Humber
Bredenbury
Bromyard Downs
Brockhampton Hall
Knightwick
Lulsley
Cotheridge
WORCESTER
Aulden
Risbury
Marston Stannett
Bromyard
Rushwick
St John's
Hope under Dinmore
Upper Hill
Birley
Bowley
Linley Green
Alfrick
Leigh
Bransford
Bransford Bridge
Pencombe
Suckley Hills
Suckley
Queenswood
Westhope
Dinmore Manor
Bodenham
Maund Bryan
Little Cowarne
Munderfield Row
Stanford Bishop
Smith End Green
Collett's Green
Powick
Leigh Sinton
Bodenham Moor
Ullingswick
Munderfield Stocks
Stoke Lacy
Acton Beauchamp
Acton Green
Longley Green
Callow End
Urdimarsh
The Vault
Felton
Bishop's Frome
Stifford's Bridge
Storridge
Newland
Wellington
Walker's Green
Preston Wynne
Burley Gate
Moreton Jeffries
Evesbatch
Cradley
Malvern Link
Madresfield
Wellington Marsh
Marden
Much Cowarne
Five Bridges
Ridgeway Cross
West Malvern
GREAT MALVERN
Sutton Walls
Moreton on Lugg
Ocle Pychard
Castle Frome
Fromes Hill
Pow Green
Mathon
Barnard's Green
Guarlford
Rhydd
Burghill
Sutton St Nicholas
Newtown
Lower Egleton
Westhide
Stretton Grandison
Canon Frome
Lower Wyche
Upper Wyche
Hanley Swan
Pipe and Lyde
Shelwick
Withington
Bosbury
Coddington
Three Counties Showground
Stretton Sugwas
Holmer
Shucknall
Yarkhill
Roman Road
Ashperton
Colwall Stone
Malvern Hills
Hagley
Weston Beggard
Staplow
Colwall Green
Malvern Wells
Lugwardine
Bartestree
Munsley
Little Malvern
Wellington Heath
Welland
Upton upon Severn
White Cross
HEREFORD
Dormington
Tarrington
Waller's Green
Little Welland
Breinton
Tupsley
Prior's Frome
Trumpet
Cath
Rotherwas Chapel
Checkley
Belmont Abbey
Lower Bullingham
Hampton Bishop
Aylton
Newtown
Ledbury
Hollybush
Castlemorton
Grafton
Dinedor
Holme Lacy
Mordiford
Putley
Little Marcle
Eastnor
Birts Street
Longdon
Fiddler's Green
Allensmore
Woolhope
Chase End Street
Camer's Green
Callow
Twyford Common
Rushall
Ledstock
Preston
St. John Baptist
Fownhope
King's Green
Dewsall Court
Aconbury
Bolstone
Sollers Hope
Hellen's
Donnington
Bromsberrow Heath
Tillers' Green
Broom's Green
Pendock
Forthampton
Ryton
Kingsthorne
Little Birch
Little Dewchurch
Ballingham
Much Marcle
Redmarley D'Abitot
Eldersfield
Much Dewchurch
Brockhampton
How Capel Court
Dymock
Wye
Wormelow Tump
Much Birch
Carey
Yatton Wood
How Caple
St. Mary's Church
Kempley
Kempley Green
Poolhill
Corse Lawn
Staunton
Orcop Hill
Hoarwithy
Penalt
Fawley Chapel
Foy
Hole-in-the-Wall
Old Gore
Brand Green
Corse
Tirley
Llandinabo
Harewood End
Kings Caple
Baysham
Upton Bishop
Botloe's Green
Upleadon
Hasfield
Llanwarne
Sellack
Brampton Abbotts
Crow Hill
Gorsley Common
Newent
Blackwells End
Ashleworth
Nup End
White End
Pencoyd
Gorsley
Hartpury
Orcop
Sandyway
Michaelchurch
Bridstow
Linton
Kilcot
Ross Spur
Rudhall
Little Gorsley
Highleadon
Sandhurst
St Weonards
St Owen's Cross
Tretire
Peterstow
Ross-on-Wye
Bromsash
Aston Crews
Aston Ingham
Clifford's Mesne
Kent's Green
Nature in Art
Twigworth
Weston under Penyard
Hom Green
Glewstone
Pencraig
Hillcourt
Coughton
Pontshill
Lea
May Hill
Taynton
Tibberton
Rudford
Maisemore
Lassington
Longford
Llangarron
Broad Oak
Goodrich
Walford
Flanesford Priory
Hope Mansell
Glasshouse Hill
Bulley
Highnam
Skenfrith
Pembridge
Llangrove
Marstow
Kerne Bridge
Puddlebrook
Longhope
Huntley
Birdwood
Churcham
Welsh Newton
Whitchurch
Welsh Bicknor
Ruardean
Mitcheldean
Oakle
GLOUCESTER
Barn
Ganarew
Ruardean Woodside
Lower Lydbrook
Blaisdon
Minsterworth
Hempsted
Symonds Yat
Nailbridge
Northwood
Elmore Back
Monnow
Severn
Leadon
Lodon
Frome
Teme
Rea
A456
A443
A451
A4025
A449
A49
A4112
A44
A4440
A465
A417
A4103
A438
A4104
A4172
A4137
A40
A48
A4136
A430
A38
A466
M50
B4361
B4362
B4214
B4204
B4202
B4203
B4197
B4196
B4195
B4190
B4204
B4203
B4220
B4214
B4224
B4399
B4349
B4348
B4521
B4347
B4234
B4228
B4229
B4221
B4222
B4224
B4215
B4216
B4208
B4211
B4209
B4218
B4232
B4503
B4424
B4024
275
340
286
296
425

54
66
53
40
A
B
C
D
1
2
3
4
5
BROMSGROVE
REDDITCH
WORCESTER
GREAT MALVERN
WORCESTERSHIRE
Droitwich
Pershore
Evesham
Alcester
Tewkesbury
CHELTENHAM
GLOUCESTER
Bishop's Cleeve
Winchcombe
Broadway
VALE OF EVESHAM
COTSWOLD HILLS
GLOUCESTERSHIRE
M5
M42
M50
A38
A44
A46
A40
A417
A435
A441
A448
A449
A422
A4538
A4104
A438
A4019
A4013
A436
A429
A4440
A4103
Ribbesford
Shenstone
Mustow Green
Corbett
Bournheath
Catshill
Barnt Green
Weatheroak Hill
Upper Mitton
Wilden
Hartlebury
Rushock
Dodford
Lickey End
Blackwell
Alvechurch
Portway
Wood End
Tutnall
Hewell Lane
Branson's Cross
Beoley
Holt End
Tanworth in Arden
Finstall
Aston Fields
Tardebigge
Hewell Grange
Gorcott Hill
Dunley
Astley Cross
Crossway Green
Norchard
Elmley Lovett
Cutnall Green
Elmbridge
Lincomb
The Burf
Acton
Upton Warren
Stoke Prior
Avoncroft Museum of Buildings
Ullenhall
Oldberrow
Astley
Noutard's Green
Dunhampton
Hampton Lovett
Webheath
Sytchampton
Doverdale
Wychbold
Woodgate
Headless Cross
Mappleborough Green
Witley
Frog Pool
Walkwood
Beaudesert
Eastgrove Cottage Garden
Shrawley
Oldfield
Hanbury Hall (NT)
Crabbs Cross
Witley Court
Little Witley
Uphampton
Ombersley
Hanbury
Ham Green
Hunt End
Morton Bagot
Holt Fleet
Holt Heath
The Jinney Ring Craft Centre
Woolmere Green
Studley Common
Studley
Holt
Salwarpe
Hadzor
Astwood Bank
Hawford Dovecote (NT)
Bradley Green
Feckenham
Sambourne
Wichenford
Sinton Green
Hawford
Coughton Court (NT)
Great Alne
Martley
Grimley
Fernhill Heath
Martin Hussingtree
Earl's Common
Holberrow Green
New End
Coughton
Moseley
Hallow Heath
Claines
Oddingley
Himbleton
Stock Green
Stock Wood
Cookhill
King's Coughton
Wichenford Dovecote (NT)
Shoulton
Hindlip
Sale Green
Hallow
Tibberton
Huddington
Grafton Flyford
Inkberrow
Walcote
Broad Green
Peachley
Lower Broadheath
Warndon
Crowle Green
Crowle
Arrow
Haselor
Billesley
Broadwas
The Greyfriars
Bredicot
Broughton Hackett
Flyford Flavell
Kington
Abbots Morton
Weethley
Oversley Green
Red Hill
Exhall
Temple Grafton
Henwick
Cathedral
St John's
Spetchley
Churchill
Upton Snodsbury
North Piddle
Ragley Hall
Rushwick
Leigh
Bransford
Bransford Bridge
Commandery
Spetchley Park
Sneachill
White Ladies Aston
Naunton Beauchamp
Abberton
Rous Lench
Dunnington
Wixford
Ardens Grafton
Broom
Bidford-on-Avon
Worcester 1651
Whittington
Iron Cross
Smith End Green
Collett's Green
Powick
Norton
A4538 Peopleton
Bishampton
Atch Lench
Church Lench
Salford Priors
Welford-on-Avon
Barton
Leigh Sinton
Callow End
Kempsey
Littleworth
Stoulton
Throckmorton
Harvington
Abbot's Salford
Dorsing
Newland
Drakes Broughton
Pinvin
Cleeve Prior
Long Marston
Malvern Link
Madresfield
Draycott
Hawbridge
Norton
North Littleton
Pershore Sta.
Lenchwick
Evesham Country Park Shopping & Garden Centre
Clevelode
Pirton
Wadborough
Wyre Piddle
Lower Moor
Tithe Barn (NT)
Middle Littleton
Pebworth
Guarlford
Rhydd
Kerswell Green
Clifton
High Green
Abbey
Wick
Fladbury
Evesham 1265
Offenham
Broad Marston
Severn Stoke
Pershore Bridge Picnic Site
Charlton
Cropthorne
South Littleton
Wyche
Hanley Swan
Besford
Pensham
Aldington
Bretforton
Kinnersley
Defford
Birlingham
Little Comberton
Hampton
Honeybourne
Three Counties Showground
Earl's Croome
Great Comberton
Bricklehampton
Badsey
Malvern Wells
Hanley Castle
Baughton
Eckington
Elmley Castle
Netherton
Fleece Inn (NT)
Weston Subedge
Welland
Upton upon Severn
Holly Green
Strensham
Bredon Hill 293
Hinton on the Green
Wickhamford
Willersey
Little Welland
Naunton
Stratford
Bredon's Norton
Ashton under Hill
Sedgeberrow
Childswickham
Saintbury
Uckinghall
Ripple
Twyning Green
Tithe Barn (NT)
Kemerton
Overbury
Conderton
Aston Somerville
Broad Campden
Hollybush
Castlemorton
Longdon
Twyning
Bredon's Hardwick
Bredon
Elaine Rippon Hand Painted Silk
Beckford
Dumbleton
Wormington
Laverton
Buckland
Broadway Hill 309
Broadway Tower
Birts Street
Sledge Green
Shuthonger
The Mythe
Northway
Aston Cross
Great Washbourne
Stanton
Rectory
Snowshill Manor (NT)
Snowshill
Bushley
Pamington
Alderton
Toddington
New Town
Stanway
Pendock
Forthampton
Ashchurch
Walton Cardiff
Teddington
Alstone
Didbrook
Eldersfield
Chaceley
Oxenton
Dixton
Hailes
Hailes Abbey (NT)
Corse Lawn
Tewkesbury 1471
Deerhurst
Fiddington
Gotherington
Gretton
Greet
Cutsdean
Staunton
Tredington
Glos. & Warwicks. Rly
Farmcote
Ford
Apperley
Odda's Chapel
Stoke Orchard
Langley Hill
Temple Guiting
Condicote
Corse
Tirley
Hardwicke
Cleeve Hill
Sudeley
Kineton
Hasfield
Lower Apperley
Elmstone Hardwicke
Woodmancote
Roman Villa
Cotswold Farm Park
Nup End
White End
Coombe Hill
Southam
Guiting Power
Barton
Ashleworth
Ashleworth Tithe Barn (NT)
The Leigh
Boddington
Uckington
Swindon Village
Cheltenham 330
Belas Knap Long Barrow
Highleadon
Sandhurst
Nature in Art
Norton
Staverton
Staverton Bridge
Prestbury
Charlton Abbots
Hawling
Naunton
Dovecote
Down Hatherley
Golden Valley
Twigworth
Gloucestershire
Innsworth
Sevenhampton
Brockhampton
Rudford
Maisemore
Lassington
Longford
Up Hatherley
Whittington
Syreford
Dowdeswell
Andoversford
Salperton
Notgrove
Bourton-on-the-Water
Bulley
Highnam
Churchdown
Leckhampton
Charlton Kings
Cold Aston
Nat. Waterways Mus.
Badgeworth
Shurdington
Pilley
Kilkenny
Shipton
Hazleton
Turkdean
Barnwood
Brockworth
Bentham
Crickley Hill
Foxcote
Hempsted
Ullenwood
Seven Springs
Compton Abdale
Elmore Back
Matson
Upton St Leonards
Coberley
Upper Coberley
Withington
Hampnett
Farmington

55
67
56
41
D
E
F
G
I
2
3
4
5
M40
A46
A429
A423
A44
A45
A452
A361
A422
A34
WARWICKSHIRE
OXFORDSHIRE
Kenilworth
Stoneleigh
Bubbenhall
Stretton-on-Dunsmore
Bourton on Dunsmore
Dunsmore
Bilton
Dunchurch
Thurlaston
Draycote
Barby
Hockley Heath
Chadwick End
Baddesley Clinton (NT)
Wroxall
Beausale
Castle End
Lapworth
Turner's Green
Rowington Green
Rowington
Ashow
Weston under Wetherley
Princethorpe
Wappenbury
Eathorpe
Frankton
Marton
Birdingbury
Draycote Water
Woolscott
Kites Hardwick
Leek Wootton
Old Milverton
Cubbington
Hunningham
Leamington Hastings
Grandborough
Willoughby
Lowsonford
Shrewley
Haseley
Hatton
Lord Leycester Hospital
ROYAL LEAMINGTON SPA
Long Itchington
Broadwell
Henley-in-Arden
Pinley Green
Preston Bagot
Hatton Country World
Budbrooke
Jephson Gardens
Offchurch
Wolfhampcote
Claverdon
Hampton on the Hill
Warwick
Radford Semele
Whitnash
Bascote
Stockton
Lower Shuckburgh
Flecknoe
Langley
Wolverton
Norton Lindsey
Warwickshire County Mus
Longbridge
Bishop's Tachbrook
Ufton
Southam
Napton on the Hill
Napton Hill
Staverton
Edstone
Bearley
Sherbourne
Barford
Harbury
Ladbroke
Cantlow
Snitterfield
Wasperton
Chesterton Green
Bishop's Itchington
Catesby
Hellidon
Arbury Hill
Wilmcote
Shakespeare's Birthplace
Ingon
Hampton Lucy
Newbold Pacey
Ashorne
Charlecote Park (NT)
Charlecote
Moreton Morrell
Priors Marston
Priors Hardwick
Alveston
Tiddington
Wellesbourne
Lighthorne
Heritage Motor Centre
Knightcote
Shottery
Anne Hathaway's Cottage
Stratford-upon-Avon
Harvard House
Shire Horse Centre
Gaydon
Wormleighton
Upper Boddington
Byfield
Walton
Loxley
Chadshunt
Northend
Burton Dassett Hills
Fenny Compton
Lower Boddington
Hinton
West Farndon
Clifford Chambers
Atherstone on Stour
Preston on Stour
Combrook
Kineton
Little Kineton
Avon Dassett
Claydon
Aston le Walls
Eydon
Farnborough Hall (NT)
Farnborough
Chipping Warden
Wimpstone
Lower Quinton
Alderminster
Ettington
Butlers Marston
Edgehill 1642
Radway
Edge Hill
Pillerton Hersey
Pillerton Priors
Ratley
Mollington
Warmington
Cropredy Bridge 1644
Edgcote 1469
Wardington
Upper Wardington
Upper Quinton
Meon Hill
Admington
Newbold on Stour
Fulready
Halford
Armscote
Oxhill
Lower Tysoe
Shotteswell
Cropredy
Williamscot
Great Bourton
Upton (NT)
Hornton
Kiftsgate Court
Ilmington
Blackwell
Idlicote
Tredington
Whatcote
Upper Tysoe
Middle Tysoe
Brook Cottage
Horley
Hanwell
Chacombe
Middleton Cheney
Marston St Lawrence
Hidcote Manor (NT)
Darlingscott
Honington
Shenington
Alkerton
Wroxton
Drayton
Wroxton Abbey
Thenford
Hidcote Boyce
Ebrington
Shipston on Stour
Balscote
Grimsbury
Warkworth
Charingworth
Barcheston
Upper Brailes
Winderton
Epwell
Shutford
BANBURY
North Newington
Broughton
Farthinghoe
Stretton-on-Fosse
Willington
Lower Brailes
Brailes Hill
Tidmington
Burmington
Sibford Gower
Sibford Ferris
Tadmarton
Swalcliffe
Broughton Castle
Bodicote
Upper Astrop
Newbottle
Paxford
Aston Magna
Sutton-under-Brailes
Stourton
Cherington
Todenham
Twyford
King's Sutton
Draycott
Batsford Park Arboretum
Batsford
Little Wolford
Great Wolford
Tadmarton Heath
Ascott
Whichford
Milcombe
Bloxham
Milton
Adderbury
Lower Lemington
Long Compton
Barford St John
Aynho
Bourton-on-the-Hill
Moreton-in-Marsh
Barton-on-the-Heath
Wigginton
Hook Norton
South Newington
Barford St Michael
Deddington
Clifton
Sezincote
Rollright Stones
Swerford
Hempton
Aynhoe Park
Souldern
Longborough
Little Compton
Great Rollright
Nether Worton
Deddington Castle
Evenlode
Chastleton
Great Tew
Over Worton
North Aston
Fritwell
Donnington
Adlestrop
Over Norton
Little Tew
Duns Tew
Somerton
Baynards Green
Stow 1646
Broadwell
Salford
Heythrop
Ledwell
Middle Aston
Fewcott
Upper Swell
Stow-on-the-Wold
Cornwell
Chipping Norton
Sandford St Martin
Ardley
Lower Swell
Daylesford
Church Enstone
Gagingwell
Middle Barton
Steeple Aston
Maugersbury
Upper Oddington
Lower Oddington
Churchill
Lidstone
Westcott Barton
Enstone
Steeple Barton
Hopcrofts Holt
Upper Heyford
Kingham
Rousham House
Lower Heyford
Icomb
Bledington
Sarsden
Radford
Rousham
Caulcott
Lower Slaughter
Wyck Rissington
Foscot
Eastend
Chadlington
Dean
Taston
Fulwell
Kiddington
Rousham Gap
Middleton Stoney
Westcote
Lyneham
Spelsbury
Over Kiddington
Ditchley
Glympton
Northbrook
Birdland
Idbury
Upper Rissington
Little Rissington
Fifield
Milton-under-Wychwood
Chilson
Ascott-under-Wychwood
Charlbury
Nethercott
Tackley
Kirtlington
Clapton-on-the-Hill
Great Rissington
Shipton-under-Wychwood
Stonesfield
Wootton
Weston-on-the-Green
Bletchingdon
Hawk Gallows Hill
Finstock
Ramsden
Blenheim Palace
Combe
Woodstock
Shipton-on-Cherwell

56
68
55
42
A
B
C
D
1
2
3
4
5
NORTHAMPTONSHIRE
OXFORDSHIRE
BUCKINGHAMSHIRE
NORTHAMPTON
MILTON KEYNES
Daventry
Towcester
Brackley
Buckingham
Bicester
Wolverton
Hillmorton
Dunchurch
Thurlaston
Kilsby
Crick
West Haddon
Winwick
Cottesbrooke
Creaton
Hollowell
Teeton
Coton Manor Wildlife Garden
Ravensthorpe
Hollowell Resr
Ravensthorpe Resr
Brixworth
Scaldwell
Old
Walgrave
Pitsford Reservoir Nature Reserve
Hannington
Pitsford Reservoir
Holcot
Pitsford
Spratton
Barby
Woolscott
Kites Hardwick
Grandborough
Willoughby
Ashby St Ledgers
Watford
Watford Gap
Long Buckby
East Haddon
Holdenby
Holdenby House
Broadwell
Braunston
Wolfhampcote
Welton
Buckby Wharf
Great Brington
Whilton
Althorp
Chapel Brampton
Church Brampton
Harlestone
Kingsthorpe
Boughton
Moulton
Boothville
Sywell
Overstone
Sywell Resr
Flecknoe
Lower Shuckburgh
Napton on the Hill
Daventry Resr
Norton
Borough Hill
Brockhall
Little Brington
Nobottle
New Duston
Dallington
Weston Favell
Great Billing
Little Billing
Ecton
Staverton
Dodford
Flore
Harpole
Duston
Upton
Catesby
Newnham
Upper Weedon
Weedon Bec
Kislingbury
Far Cotton
Little Houghton
Cogenhoe
Hellidon
Arbury Hill
Badby
Nene
Church Stowe
Upper Stowe
Nether Heyford
Bugbrooke
Rothersthorpe
Wootton
Northampton 1460
Hardingstone
Great Houghton
Brafield-on-the-Green
Priors Marston
Hardwick
Everdon
Charwelton
Preston Capes
Farthingstone
Gayton
Milton Malsor
Collingtree
Preston Deanery
Hackleton
Boddington
Byfield
Litchborough
Foster's Booth
Pattishall
Eastcote
Blisworth
Quinton
Horton
Piddington
Grimscote
Cold Higham
Astcote
Courteenhall
Roade
Salcey Forest
Lower Boddington
Hinton
Woodford Halse
West Farndon
Maidford
Adstone
Foxley
Duncote
Tiffield
Greens Norton
Waterways
Stoke Bruerne
Eakley
Aston le Walls
Claydon
Eydon
Canons Ashby
Priory (ruins)
Blakesley
Moreton Pinkney
Woodend
Shutlanger
Ashton
Hartwell
Ravenstone
Cropredy Bridge 1644
Chipping Warden
Edgcote 1469
Culworth
Bradden
Stoke Park Pavilions
Long Street
Stoke Goldington
Cropredy
Wardington
Upper Wardington
Weston
Weedon Lois
Slapton
Abthorpe
Wood Burcote
Alderton
Grafton Regis
Hanslope
Williamscot
Thorpe Mandeville
Sulgrave Manor
Sulgrave
Wappenham
Plumpton End
Pury End
Paulerspury
Yardley Gobion
Little Linford
Watling Street
Chacombe
Middleton Cheney
Marston St Lawrence
Helmdon
Silverstone
Whittlebury
Whittlewood Forest
Potterspury
Castlethorpe
Haversham
Newport Pagnell
Greatworth
Thenford
Grimsbury
Warkworth
Radstone
Crowfield
Syresham
Lillingstone Lovell
Old Stratford
Stony Stratford
Old Wolverton
Cosgrove
New Bradwell
Halse
Biddlesden
Deanshanger
Passenham
Farthinghoe
Steane
Whitfield
Wicken
Calverton
Bradwell
The Stadium
Upper Astrop
Turweston
Dadford
Lillingstone Dayrell
Leckhampstead
Akeley
Upper Weald
Loughton
Newbottle
Stowe School
Shalstone
Chackmore
Foxcote Reservoir
Maids' Moreton
Beachampton
Shenley Church End
Twyford
King's Sutton
Charlton
Hinton-in-the-Hedges
Evenley
Westbury
Great Ouse
Thornton
Shenley Brook End
Adderbury
Radclive
Whaddon
Nash
Bletchley
Aynho
Croughton
Mixbury
Water Stratford
Thornborough
Whaddon Chase
Deddington
Clifton
Finmere
Tingewick
Chantry Chapel (NT)
Gawcott
Barton Hartshorn
Newton Purcell
Aynhoe Park
Souldern
Cottisford
Preston Bissett
Padbury
Great Horwood
Little Horwood
Newton Longville
Deddington Castle
North Aston
Fritwell
Hardwick
Hethe
Chetwode
Priory House
Hillesden
Adstock
Drayton Parslow
Somerton
Baynards Green
Cherwell Valley
Stoke Lyne
Fringford
Steeple Claydon
Addington
Winslow Hall
Mursley
Swanbourne
Winslow
Middle Aston
Fewcott
Ardley
Stratton Audley
Twyford
Middle Claydon
Steeple Aston
Upper Heyford
Roman Road
North End
Lower Heyford
Bucknell
Poundon
East Claydon
Granborough
Hoggeston
Claydon (NT)
Rousham
Rousham House
Caulcott
Caversfield
Charndon
Calvert
Botolph Claydon
Dunton
Middleton Stoney
Marsh Gibbon
Edgcott
North Marston
Cublington
Bicester Village
Northbrook
Launton
Oving
Nethercott
Chesterton
Grendon Underwood
Quainton
Pitchcott
Whitchurch
Tackley
Kirtlington
Ambrosden
Wendlebury
Blackthorn
Kingswood
Aston Abbotts
Hardwick
Weston-on-the-Green
Ludgershall
Bletchingdon
Merton
Upper Arncott
Piddington
Westcott
Waddesdon
Oxfordshire County Museum
Shipton-on-Cherwell
Fencott
Wotton
Akeman Street
M1
M45
M40
A5
A45
A43
A361
A425
A426
A428
A422
A421
A4421
A413
A41
A34
A4095
A4260
A508
A5199
A5076
A5095
A5123
A4500
A4071
B4429
B4036
B5385
B4525
B4031
B4100
B4030
B430
B4033
B4011
B4027
B526

D
E
F
G
I
2
3
4
5
69
58
43
CAMBS
BEDFORDSHIRE
HERTS
MILTON KEYNES
LUTON
Isham
Finedon
Little Addington
Raunds
Catworth
Leighton Bromswold
Woolley
Great Stukeley
Huntingdon
Hartford
Spaldwick
Ellington
Easton
Brampton
Hinchingbrooke House
Godmanchester
Great Harrowden
Irthlingborough
Stanwick
Hargrave
Covington
Chelveston
Tilbrook
Grafham
Grafham Water
Buckden
Wellingborough
Higham Ferrers
Caldecott
Shelton
Lower Dean
Upper Dean
Kimbolton
Stonely
West Perry
Offord Cluny
Offord D'Arcy
Diddington
Rushden
Irchester
Wilby
Earls Barton
Great Doddington
Yielden
Newton Bromswold
Swineshead
Melchbourne
Pertenhall
Staughton Green
Staughton Highway
Great Staughton
Southoe
Wymington
Farndish
Wollaston
Podington
Knotting
Riseley
Knotting Green
Top End
Keysoe
Little Staughton
Great Paxton
Graveley
Hail Weston
Little Paxton
Toseland
Lower End
Strixton
Hinwick
Souldrop
Keysoe Row
Staploe
Duloe
St Neots
Whiston
Grendon
Santa Pod
Bushmead Priory
Eaton Ford
Eaton Socon
Croxton
Castle Ashby
Bozeat
Sharnbrook
Bletsoe
Bolnhurst
Eynesbury
Easton Maudit
Thurleigh
Colmworth
Yardley Hastings
Odell
Felmersham
Radwell
Harrold
Harrold-Odell
Milton Ernest
Duck's Cross
Wyboston
Chawston
Little Barford
Abbotsley
Carlton
Pavenham
Colesden
Wilden
Warrington
Lavendon
West End
Oakley
Ravensden
Roxton
Tempsford
Waresley
Renhold
Green End
Cleat Hill
Turvey
Stevington
Clapham
Salph End
Church End
Great Barford
Tetworth
Olney
Cold Brayfield
Great Ouse
Bromham
Bedford
Goldington
Everton
Cowper & Newton
Clifton Reynes
Newton Blossomville
Willington
Blunham
Sandy
Weston Underwood
Emberton
Stagsden
Box End
Biddenham
Cecil Higgins Mus & Art Gall
Priory Park Marina
Mogerhanger
Girtford
Potton
Cople
Thorncote Green
Beeston
Hatch
Kempston Church End
Kempston
Cardington
Sutton
Wrestlingworth
Hardmead
Astwood
Sherington
Wood End
Keeley Green
Harrowden
Lower Caldecote
Elstow
Moot Hall
Cotton End
Northill
Ickwell Green
Upper Caldecote
Biggleswade
Chicheley
North Crawley
Kempston Hardwick
Herring's Green
Swiss Garden
Lathbury
Bourne End
Wootton
Wootton Green
Wilstead
Old Warden
Broom
Newport Pagnell
Lower Shelton
Upper Shelton
Broad Green
Moulsoe
Cranfield
Stewartby Lake
Stewartby
How End
Houghton Conquest
Haynes
Haynes Church End
Southill
Stanford
Edworth
Willen
Marston Moretaine
Langford
Hinxworth
Broughton
Salford
Milton Keynes Village
Brogborough
Lidlington
Millbrook
Houghton House
Chicksands
Shefford
Clifton
Astwick
Caldecote
Woolstone
Woughton on the Green
Maulden
Clophill
Henlow
Ampthill
Campton
Stotfold
Walton
Wavendon
Aspley Guise
Ridgmont
Flitton
Silsoe
Meppershall
Upper Stondon
Church End
Arlesey
Simpson
Woburn Sands
Husborne Crawley
Steppingley
Greenfield
Wrest Park
Upper Gravenhurst
Flitwick
Bow Brickhill
Fenny Stratford
Aspley Heath
Safari Park
Pulloxhill
Upton End
Lower Stondon
Shillington
Standalone Farm
Norton
Woburn
Eversholt
Woburn Abbey
Westoning
Apsley End
Holwell
Higham Gobion
Little Brickhill
Tingrith
Pirton
Ickleford
Letchworth
Barton-le-Clay
Great Brickhill
Milton Bryan
Harlington
Sharpenhoe
Hexton
Walsworth
Willian
Stoke Hammond
Stockgrove
Potsgrove
Toddington
Sundon Hills
Barton Hills
Hitchin
Great Wymondley
Little Wymondley
Heath and Reach
Battlesden
Streatley
Mus & Art Gallery
Graveley
Soulbury
Fancott
Upper Sundon
Charlton
Gosmore
St Ippollitts
Hockliffe
Wingfield
Lower Sundon
Warden Hill
Lilley
Great Offley
Stewkley
Leighton Buzzard
Tebworth
Chalton
Sundon Park
Leighton Buzzard Lt Rly
Linslade
Eggington
Houghton Regis
Limbury
Ley Green
Preston
Burcott
Stanbridge
Tilsworth
Leagrave
Stopsley
Cockernhoe
King's Walden
Ascott (NT)
Wing
Billington
Dunstable
Mus & Art Gall
Luton
Breachwood Green
St Paul's Walden
Langley
Eaton Green
Ledburn
Slapton
Totternhoe
Church End
London Luton
Whitwell
Bendish
Stockwood Craft Mus & Gdns
Knebworth House
Mentmore
Eaton Bray
Dunstable Downs
Caddington
The Node
Old Knebworth
Nup End
Wingrave
Horton
Edlesborough
Kensworth
Slip End
New Mill End
Peter's Green
Kimpton
Codicote
Ivinghoe
Whipsnade
Whipsnade Wild Animal Pk
Whipsnade Park
Woodside Farm
Luton Hoo
East Hyde
Ayot St Lawrence
Cheddington
Markyate
Shaw's Corner (NT)
Hulcott
Long
Kinsbourne
Marshall's
Welwyn
Ayot
A14
A1
A6
A509
A510
A45
A428
A421
A603
A5134
A422
A600
A6001
A507
A5130
A4012
A5120
A505
A4146
A5
A5065
A418
A1081
A602
A1072
A1(M)
M1
B663
B660
B645
B661
B571
B569
B573
B574
B5388
B565
B531
B530
B1046
B1040
B1042
B658
B655
B656
B4032
B4540
B4541
B489
B488
B579
B653
B652
B651
B197

58
70
57
44
A
B
C
D
1
2
3
4
5
Woolley
Great Stukeley
Huntingdon
Wyton
Houghton
St Ives
Earith
Ouse Fen
Aldreth
Wilburton
Stretham
Brampton
Hinchingbrooke House
Godmanchester
Hemingford Abbots
Hemingford Grey
Island Hall
Holywell
Church End
Over
Willingham
Smithey Fen
North Fen
Upware
Chittering
Grafham
Buckden
Offord Cluny
Offord D'Arcy
Wood Green Animal Shelter
Fenstanton
Fen Drayton
Swavesey
Rampton
Cottenham
Denny Abbey
River Bank
Boxworth End
Longstanton
Hilton
Conington
Westwick
Waterbeach
Southoe
Great Paxton
Graveley
Papworth St Agnes
Elsworth
Boxworth
Lolworth
Oakington
Landbeach
Impington
Papworth Everard
Bar Hill
Histon
Milton
Horningsea
Lode
Little Paxton
Toseland
Yelling
Knapwell
Dry Drayton
Girton
Stow cum Quy
Anglesey Abbey (NT)
Duloe
St Neots
Eaton Ford
Eaton Socon
Eynesbury
Croxton
Caxton Gibbet
Eltisley
Cambourne
Caxton
Highfields
Hardwick
Madingley
Cambridge American Cemetery & Memorial
Coton
King's Coll Chapel
Chesterton
Fen Ditton
Teversham
Cambridge
CAMBRIDGE
Little Wilbraham
Abbotsley
Little Barford
Great Gransden
Little Gransden
Bourn
Caldecote
Comberton
Toft
Barton
Univ Botanic Gardens
Grantchester
Church End
Cherry Hinton
Fulbourn
Longstowe
Kingston
Great Eversden
Trumpington
Gog Magog Hills
Wandlebury
Tempsford
Waresley
CAMBRIDGESHIRE
Tetworth
Gamlingay
Hatley St George
Little Eversden
Frog End
Harlton
Haslingfield
Hauxton
Great Shelford
Stapleford
Worsted Lodge
Everton
East Hatley
Wimpole Hall (NT)
Arrington
Roman Road
Orwell
Harston
Little Shelford
Babraham
Little Abington
Sandy
Potton
Cockayne Hatley
Croydon
Wimpole
Barrington
Newton
Sawston
Great Abington
Wimpole Home Farm (NT)
Shepreth
Foxton
Duxford Chapel
Whittlesford
Pampisford
Beeston
Hatch
Caldecote
Sutton
Wrestlingworth
Tadlow
Wendy
Shingay
Docwra's Manor
Whaddon
Thriplow
BEDS
Eyeworth
Guilden Morden
Abington Pigotts
Whaddon Gap
Meldreth
Fowlmere
Duxford
Imperial War Museum
Hinxton
Stump Cross
Linton Zoo & Gdns
Biggleswade
Dunton
Broom
Kneesworth
Melbourn
Bassingbourn
Litlington
Flint Cross
Bridgefoot
Ickleton
Chrishall Grange
Great Chesterford
Little Chesterford
Stanford
Steeple Morden
Edworth
Hinxworth
Royston
Heydon
Elmdon
Strethall
Littlebury
Langford
Audley End
Ashwell
Barley
Great Chishall
Chrishall
Littlebury Green
Clifton
Henlow
Astwick
Caldecote
Ashwell & Morden Sta.
Icknield Way
Slip End
Therfield
Little Chishall
Pond Street
Audley End
Wendens Ambo
Audley End Sta.
Church End
Arlesey
Stotfold
Newnham
Baldock
Bygrave
Reed
Duddenhoe End
Upper Stondon
Radwell
Kelshall
Barkway
Nuthampstead
Upper Green
Arkesden
Shortgrove
Lower Stondon
Standalone Farm
Norton
Baldock
Wallington
Sandon
Langley
Newport
Holwell
Buckland
Roe Green
Mill End
Quin
Wicken Bonhunt
LETCHWORTH
Clothall
Chipping
Anstey
Meesden
Clavering
Pirton
Ickleford
Rushden
Wyddial
Rickling
HERTFORDSHIRE
Walsworth
Willian
Weston
Throcking
Starling's Green
Quendon
Prior's Hall Barn
HITCHIN
Great Wymondley
Hall's Green
Cromer
Cottered
Buntingford
Great Hormead
Hare Street
Brent Pelham
Berden
Rickling Green
Art Gallery
Little Wymondley
Graveley
Hare Street
Aspenden
Little Hormead
Furneux Pelham
Stocking Pelham
Ugley
Charlton
Ardeley
Westmill
Barleycroft End
East End
Ugley Green
Great Offley
Gosmore
St Ippollitts
Hay Street
Manuden
Wood End
Walkern
Patmore Heath
Farnham Green
Farnham
Stansted Mountfitchet
Preston
STEVENAGE
Aston End
Great Munden
Nasty
Braughing
Albury
King's Walden
Shephall
Fairlands Valley Park
Benington
Hazel End
St Paul's Walden
Benington Lordship
Haultwick
Puckeridge
Little Hadham
Birchanger
Whitwell
Langley
Aston
Hebing End
Green End
Standon
Hadham Ford
BISHOP'S STORTFORD
Bendish
Broadwater
Bragbury End
Collier's End
Bury Green
Birchanger Green
Knebworth House
Dane End
Much Hadham
Thorley Street
Great Hallingbury
Hatfield Forest
The Node
Old Knebworth
Knebworth
Datchworth
Sacombe
Woolmer Green
Watton at Stone
High Cross
Thorley
Kimpton
Codicote
Datchworth Green
Wadesmill
Hadham Cross
Perry Green
Spellbrook
Little Hallingbury
Blackmore End
Ayot St Lawrence
Shaw's Corner (NT)
Bull's Green
Stapleford
Tonwell
Thundridge
Baker's End
Allen's Green
Adventure Island Playbarn
Welwyn
Burnham Green
Chapmore End
Paynes
A1
A14
A141
A1123
A1096
A1198
A428
A603
A1307
A1134
A1301
A10
A505
A11
A6001
A507
A600
A6141
A602
A1072
A1155
A1(M)
A120
A119
A1184
M11
B1040
B1050
B1049
B661
B1046
B1042
B1039
B1368
B1386
B1383
B1052
B1038
B658
B197
B656
B655
B1037
B651
B652
B1184
Great Ouse
Cam
Kym
Ivel
Hiz
Rhee
Granta
Ash
Rib
Ermine Street
Grafham Water

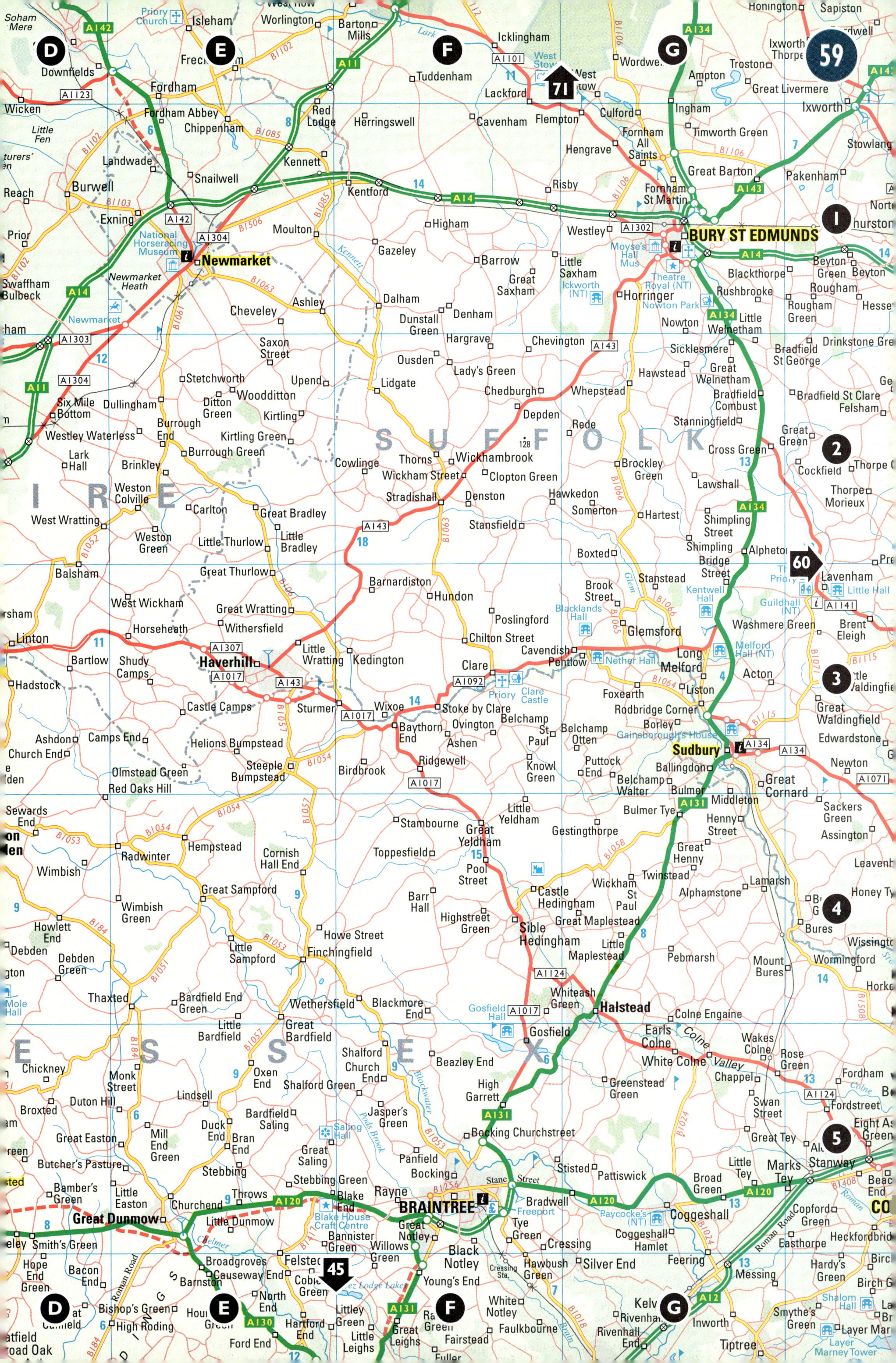

59
71
60
45
D
E
F
G
I
2
3
4
5
SUFFOLK
ESSEX
Soham Mere
Priory Church
Isleham
Worlington
Barton Mills
Icklingham
West Stow
West Stow
Wordwell
Honington
Sapiston
Ixworth Thorpe
Troston
Ampton
Great Livermere
Ixworth
Downfields
Freckenham
Tuddenham
Lackford
Flempton
Culford
Ingham
Timworth Green
Stowlangtoft
Wicken
Little Fen
Fordham
Fordham Abbey
Chippenham
Red Lodge
Herringswell
Cavenham
Hengrave
Fornham All Saints
Great Barton
Pakenham
Landwade
Kennett
Snailwell
Burwell
Kentford
Risby
Fornham St Martin
Reach
Exning
Higham
Westley
Prior
National Horseracing Museum
Newmarket
Moulton
Gazeley
Barrow
Little Saxham
Great Saxham
Moyse's Hall Mus
Theatre Royal (NT)
BURY ST EDMUNDS
Blackthorpe
Beyton Green
Beyton
Swaffham Bulbeck
Newmarket Heath
Ickworth (NT)
Horringer
Nowton Park
Rushbrooke
Rougham
Rougham Green
Hessett
Newmarket
Cheveley
Ashley
Dalham
Dunstall Green
Denham
Nowton
Little Welnetham
Saxon Street
Hargrave
Chevington
Sicklesmere
Bradfield St George
Drinkstone Green
Ousden
Lady's Green
Great Welnetham
Stetchworth
Upend
Lidgate
Chedburgh
Whepstead
Hawstead
Bradfield Combust
Bradfield St Clare
Felsham
Six Mile Bottom
Dullingham
Ditton Green
Woodditton
Kirtling
Depden
Rede
Stanningfield
Great Green
Westley Waterless
Burrough End
Burrough Green
Kirtling Green
Cowlinge
Thorns
Wickhambrook
Wickham Street
Clopton Green
Brockley Green
Cross Green
Lawshall
Cockfield
Thorpe Morieux
Lark Hall
Brinkley
Weston Colville
Stradishall
Denston
Hawkedon
Somerton
Hartest
Shimpling Street
Shimpling
West Wratting
Carlton
Great Bradley
Stansfield
Boxted
Alpheton
Weston Green
Little Thurlow
Little Bradley
Bridge Street
Balsham
Great Thurlow
Barnardiston
Hundon
Brook Street
Stanstead
Kentwell Hall
Lavenham
Little Hall
West Wickham
Great Wratting
Withersfield
Poslingford
Blacklands Hall
Glemsford
Guildhall (NT)
Washmere Green
Brent Eleigh
Horseheath
Chilton Street
Cavendish
Linton
Bartlow
Shudy Camps
Haverhill
Little Wratting
Kedington
Clare
Pentlow
Nether Hall
Long Melford
Melford Hall (NT)
Acton
Little Waldingfield
Hadstock
Castle Camps
Sturmer
Wixoe
Priory
Clare Castle
Foxearth
Liston
Great Waldingfield
Stoke by Clare
Belchamp St Paul
Belchamp Otten
Rodbridge Corner
Borley
Gainsborough's House
Edwardstone
Ashdon
Camps End
Helions Bumpstead
Baythorn End
Ovington
Ashen
Sudbury
Church End
Steeple Bumpstead
Birdbrook
Ridgewell
Knowl Green
Puttock End
Ballingdon
Newton
Olmstead Green
Belchamp Walter
Bulmer
Great Cornard
Red Oaks Hill
Little Yeldham
Middleton
Sewards End
Stambourne
Great Yeldham
Gestingthorpe
Bulmer Tye
Henny Street
Sackers Green
Assington
Hempstead
Toppesfield
Wimbish
Radwinter
Cornish Hall End
Pool Street
Great Henny
Twinstead
Lamarsh
Leavenheath
Great Sampford
Barr Hall
Castle Hedingham
Wickham St Paul
Alphamstone
Honey Tye
Bures
Wimbish Green
Highstreet Green
Sible Hedingham
Great Maplestead
Howlett End
Debden
Howe Street
Little Sampford
Finchingfield
Little Maplestead
Pebmarsh
Mount Bures
Wissington
Wormingford
Debden Green
Thaxted
Bardfield End Green
Wethersfield
Blackmore End
Whiteash Green
Halstead
Colne Engaine
Horkesley
Mole Hall
Little Bardfield
Great Bardfield
Gosfield Hall
Gosfield
Earls Colne
Wakes Colne
Colne Valley
Chickney
Monk Street
Oxen End
Shalford Church End
Beazley End
White Colne
Chappel
Rose Green
Fordham
Broxted
Duton Hill
Lindsell
Shalford Green
High Garrett
Greenstead Green
Fordstreet
Swan Street
Eight Ash Green
Mill End Green
Duck End
Bran End
Bardfield Saling
Jasper's Green
Saling Hall
Great Easton
Bocking Churchstreet
Great Tey
Butcher's Pasture
Stebbing
Great Saling
Panfield
Bocking
Stisted
Pattiswick
Little Tey
Marks Tey
Stanway
Bamber's Green
Little Easton
Churchend
Throws
Stebbing Green
Blake End
Rayne
Stane Street
Broad Green
Smith's Green
Great Dunmow
Little Dunmow
Blake House Craft Centre
BRAINTREE
Freeport
Bradwell
Paycocke's (NT)
Coggeshall
Copford Green
Great Notley
Bannister Green
Willows Green
Tye Green
Cressing
Coggeshall Hamlet
Heckfordbridge
Easthorpe
Hope End Green
Bacon End
Broadgroves
Causeway End
Felsted
Black Notley
Hawbush Green
Silver End
Feering
Messing
Hardy's Green
Birch Green
Barnston
Cobbler's Green
Young's End
Bishop's Green
North End
Littley Green
White Notley
Kelvedon
Rivenhall
Inworth
Smythe's Green
Shalom Hall
Layer Marney
High Roding
Hartford End
Rayne Green
Faulkbourne
Rivenhall End
Layer Marney Tower
Great Leighs
Little Leighs
Fairstead
Ford End
Tiptree
Fuller Street
Roman Road
A11
A14
A142
A1123
A1304
A1303
A1101
A134
A143
A1302
A1307
A1017
A1092
A1141
A131
A1124
A120
A12
A130
B1102
B1085
B1506
B1103
B1063
B1061
B1106
B1066
B1065
B1064
B1071
B1115
B1052
B1054
B1057
B1053
B1058
B1051
B1184
B1256
B1417
B1018
B1024
B1508
B1408

72
59
46
A
B
C
D
1
2
3
4
5
Honington
Sapiston
Hepworth
Wattisfield
Eye
Stradbroke
Bardwell
Stanton
Little Green
Gislingham
Thornham Parva
Ixworth Thorpe
Walsham le Willows
Cranmer Green
Braiseworth
Redlingfield
Athelington
Great Livermere
Four Ashes
Thornham Magna
Occold
Fingal Street
Ixworth
Crowland
Finningham
Wickham Street
Stoke Ash
Langham
Westhorpe
Wickham Skeith
Thorndon
Rishangles
Bedingfield
Southolt
Tannington
Timworth Green
Badwell Ash
Wyverstone Street
Wyverstone
Thwaite
Stowlangtoft
Hunston
Long Thurlow
Brockford Street
Wetheringsett
Bedfield
Saxtead Little Green
Great Barton
Pakenham
Stanton Street
Great Ashfield
Bacton
Cotton
Mid Suffolk Light Railway Museum
Kenton
Monk Soham
Earl Soham
Earl's Green
Mendlesham
Post Mill
Norton
Ward Green
Aspall
Thurston
BURY ST EDMUNDS
Haughley Green
Gipping
Wetherup Street
Debenham
Ashfield
Tostock
Elmswell
Old Newton
Mendlesham Green
Mickfield
Beyton Green
Beyton
Wetherden
Blackthorpe
Woolpit
Haughley
Haughley New Street
Middlewood Green
Winston
Roman Road
Rushbrooke
Rougham
Hessett
Drinkstone
Rougham Green
Little Welnetham
Little Stonham
Stonham Aspal
Harleston
Stowupland
Stowmarket
Forward Green
Earl Stonham
Stonham Barns Craft Centre
Pettaugh
Framsden
Cretingham
Bradfield St George
Drinkstone Green
Great Welnetham
Rattlesden
Mus of East Anglian Life
Creeting St Mary
Gedding
Buxhall
Bradfield Combust
Bradfield St Clare
Felsham
Poystreet Green
Great Finborough
Combs Ford
Combs
Crowfield
Helmingham Hall
Helmingham
Otley Hall
Charsfield
Stanningfield
Great Green
High Street Green
Badley
Gosbeck
Ashbocking
Otley
Little Finborough
Needham Market
Battisford
Coddenham
Cockfield
Thorpe Green
Brettenham
Lawshall
Thorpe Morieux
Charles Tye
Battisford Tye
Hemingstone
Swilland
Shimpling Street
Cross Green
Ringshall
Barking
Witnesham
Burgh
Shimpling
Wattisham
Barham
Henley
Grundisburgh
Bridge Street
Hitcham
Great Bricett
Ringshall Stocks
Willisham
Baylham
Great Bealings
Preston
Lavenham
Little Hall
Kettlebaston
Bildeston
Nedging Tye
Naughton
Offton
Nettlestead
Great Blakenham
Claydon
Culpho
Kentwell Hall
Chelsworth
Somersham
Little Blakenham
Blakenham Woodland Gdn
Akenham
Tuddenham
Little Bealings
Guildhall (NT)
Washmere Green
Brent Eleigh
Monks Eleigh
Whitton
Westerfield
Playford
Whatfield
Flowton
Bramford
Castle Hill
Rushmere St Andrew
Melford Hall (NT)
Milden
Semer
Elmsett
Christchurch Mansion
Kesgrave
Martlesham Heath
Little Waldingfield
Lindsey
Aldham
Burstall
Sproughton
IPSWICH
Liston
Wolves Wood
Great Waldingfield
Kersey
St. James's Chapel
Hintlesham
Chattisham
Copdock
Chantry
Sudbury
Guildhall
Edwardstone
Hadleigh
Groton
Newton
Boxford
Layham
Belstead
Wherstead
Nacton
Great Cornard
Middleton
Sackers Green
Little Wenham
Henny Street
Assington
Polstead
Shelley
Raydon
Great Wenham
Capel St Mary
Freston
Woolverstone
Levington
Trimley
Alton Water Reservoir
Tattingstone
Chelmondiston
Leavenheath
Holton St Mary
Lamarsh
Honey Tye
Stoke-by-Nayland
Thorington Street
Higham
East Bergholt
Bentley
Holbrook
Alphamstone
Bures Green
Bures
Stratford St Mary
East End
Stutton
Harkstead
Erwarton
Shotley
Nayland
Dedham Art & Craft Cen
Flatford Mill & Bridge Cott (NT)
Brantham
Upper Street
Lower Holbrook
Wissington
Langham
Boxted
Castle Ho
Cattawade
Holbrook Bay
Shop Corner
Mount Bures
Wormingford
Little Horkesley
Boxted Cross
Blacksmith's Corner
Dedham
Mistley Towers
Wrabness
Great Horkesley
Manningtree Sta.
Manningtree
New Mistley
Colne Engaine
Lamb Corner
Bradfield
Parkeston
Langham Moor
Lawford
St. Mary's Church (Remains of)
Bradfield Heath
Ramsey
Upper Dovercourt
Wakes Colne
Rose Green
Horkesley Heath
Ardleigh Reservoir
Ardleigh
Colne Valley
Chappel
Fordham
West Bergholt
Little Bromley
Horsleycross Street
Wix
Little Oakley
Swan Street
Fordstreet
Mile End
High Woods
Fox Street
Horsley Cross
Great Oakley
Eight Ash Green
Go Bananas
Great Bromley
Great Tey
Aldham
Crockleford Heath
Stones Green
Little Tey
Marks Tey
Stanway
Elmstead Market
Hare Green
Little Bentley
Beaumont
Horsey Island
Broad Green
Beacon End
Shrub End
Zoo
Old Heath
Beth Chatto
Tendring
Hamford Water
Coggeshall
Copford Green
St Botolph's Priory
COLCHESTER
Bourne Mill (NT)
Frating
Great Bentley
Weeley
Thorpe-le-Soken
Kirby le Soken
Heckfordbridge
Blackheath
Rowhedge
Wivenhoe
Kirby Cross
Easthorpe
Gryme's Dyke
Alresford
Messing
Hardy's Green
Birch
Layer de la Haye
Danger Zone
Fingringhoe
Thorrington
Aingers Green
Weeley Heath
Birch Green
Abberton
Row Heath
Great Holland
Shalom Hall
Langenhoe
Little Clacton
Clacton Common
Inworth
Smythe's Green
Layer Marney
Abberton Reservoir
Brightlingsea
Sandy Point
Great Clacton
Tiptree
Layer Marney Tower
Peldon
Priory
S U F F O L K
E S S E X
A134
A1088
A143
A14
A140
A1120
A1141
A1071
A1214
A1156
A12
A137
A131
A1124
A120
A1232
A133

D
E
F
G
73
Huntingfield
Walpole
Thorington
Bramfield
A144
Laxfield
Heveningham
Ubbeston Green
Poys Street
Dunwich
Darsham Sta.
Darsham
Brundish
Peasenhall
A1120
Sibton
Yoxford
Westleton
Middleton
Badingham
A12
Dunwich Heath (NT)
B1122
Bruisyard
Bruisyard Street
Vineyard & Winery
Theberton
East Bridge
Kelsale
Brabling Green
Cransford
Rendham
Carlton
Leiston Abbey
Framlingham
Sweffling
Saxmundham
B1119
Sizewell
Leiston
Great Glemham
Sternfield
Coldfair Green
Knodishall
Parham
Farnham
Aldringham
B1353
Thorpe Ness
Kettleburgh
Glemham Hall
Stratford St Andrew
Friston
Thorpeness
The Meare
Easton
Easton Farm Park
Hacheston
Marlesford
Gromford
Church Common
A1094
Little Glemham
Snape
Moot Hall
Campsey Ash
Blaxhall
B1069
Aldeburgh
Iken
Wickham Market
Wickham Market Sta.
B1078
High Street
Slaughden
Aldeburgh Bay
Pettistree
Tunstall
Rendlesham
Tunstall Forest
Sudbourne
Ufford
A1152
Chillesford
Eyke
Butley
B1084
Melton
Bromeswell
Orford
Rendlesham Forest
Orford Ness
Sutton Hoo Tumuli
Tide Mill
B1083
Capel St Andrew
Gedgrave Hall
Orford Beach
Boyton
Sutton
Shottisham
Waldringfield
Hollesley
Shingle Street
Hollesley Bay
3.2 miles to 1 inch
0 2 4 6 8 10 miles
0 2 4 6 8 10 km
2 km to 1 cm
Newbourne
Hemley
Ramsholt
Alderton
Bawdsey
Kirton
Falkenham
A14
Felixstowe Ferry
Trimley St Mary
Trimley Marshes
Walton
Old Felixstowe
FELIXSTOWE
Manning's Amusement Park
Harwich Harbour
Landguard Fort
Harwich
Landguard Point
Esbjerg 19 hrs
Hamburg 20 hrs
Hoek Van Holland 3¾ hrs
The Naze
Walton on the Naze
New Walton Pier
47

A
B
C
D
1
2
3
4
5
75
50
CARDIGAN BAY
Barmouth Bay
Llanenddwyn
Ystumgwern
Dyffryn Ardudwy Sta.
Dyffryn Ardudwy
Llanddwywe
Tal-y-bont
Dyffryn Burial Chamber
A496
Diffwys
Craig-y-cae
Ganllwyd
Y Garn
Uwch-mynydd
Precipice Walk
Nannau
Taicynhaeaf
Llanelltyd
A496
Cymer Abbey
A470
Bontddu
Pen-y-bryn
Toll
Caerdeon
Llanaber
Panorama Walk
Abergwynant
Penmaenpool
Dolgellau
Cutiau
A493
Islawr-dref
Barmouth (Abermaw)
The Bar
Mawddach
Arthog
Morfa Mawddach Sta.
GWYNEDD
SNOWDONIA
CADAIR IDRIS
Mynydd Moel
Penygadair
Llyn Cau
Fairbourne & Barmouth Rly
Fairbourne
Friog
Pen y Garn
Mynydd Pennant
Mynydd Pencoed
Tal-y-llyn Lake
Llwyngwril
Llanfihangel-y-pennant
Tal-y-llyn
Esgair Berfa
Castell y Bere (Ruin)
Corris Uchaf
Graig Goch
Llangelynin
Dysynni
PARK
Abergynolwyn
Tarren-y-Gesail
Rhoslefain
A493
Llanegryn
Peniarth
Foel Wyllt
Mynydd Tan-y-coed
Foel y-Geifr
Llanfendigaid
B4405
Dolgoch
Pantperthog
Tonfanau
Tarrenhendre
Bryncrug
Aber Dysynni
Pandy
Pen Trum-gwr
Rhyd-yr-onnen
Trum Gelli
Tywyn
Talyllyn Rly
Pennal
Cwrt
DYFI
Caethle Farm
A493
Derwenlas
Glaspwll
Aberdyfi Bar
Aberdovey (Aberdyfi)
Eglwys Fach
Ysgubor-y-coed
Furnace
Dyfi Furnace
Pen Carreg Gopa
Twyni Bach
Traeth Maelgwyn
Dyfi (Dovey)
Cwm Einion
Fochno
Ynyslas
B4353
Tre'r-ddol
Foel Goch
Angler's Retreat
Moel-y-Llyn
Llancynfelyn
Cors
Taliesin
Cletwr
Cwm Ceulan
Leri
Borth
Talybont
Upper Borth
B4353
Dolybont
Llandre
A487
Nant-y-moch Resr
CEREDIGION
Sarn Cynfelyn
Bont-goch (Elerch)
B4572
Bow Street
Penrhyn-coch
Salem
Llyn Syfydrin
Disgwylfa Fawr
Llangorwen
Great Aberystwyth Camera Obscura
Clarach
Plas Gogerddan
Cwmsymlog
Cliff Railway
Aberystwyth Arts Centre
National Library of Wales
Pen-bont Rhydybeddau
Aberystwyth
Capel Dewi
Waun Fawr
A4159
Old Goginan
Goginan
Ponterwyd
The Bar
Ceredigion
Llanbadarn Fawr
Capel Bangor
A44
Cwmbrwyno
Penparcau
(Summer Only)
Vale of Rheidol Rly
Rhydyfelin
Aberffrwd
Rheidol Falls
Capel Seion
Llanfarian
A4120
Rheidol
Gors
Allt Wen
New Cross
Devil's Bridge (Pontarfynach)
Llanfihangel-y-Creuddyn
Abermad
Blaenplwyf
Llanilar
Ystwyth
Cnwch Coch
B4340
Rhodmad
A485
B4575
Rhos-y-garth
B4576
A487
Llanafan
Ystwyth
Llanddeiniol
Carreg Ti-pw
Wyre
Llangwyryfon
Mynydd Bach
Ysbyty
Llanrhystud
Lledrod
Tynygraig
B4340
B4343
Trefenter
MYNYDD BACH
Llansantffraid
Rhyd-rosser
Llyn Eiddwen
Ystrad Meurig
Llanon
Swyddffynnon
Pont
Nebo

63
D
E
F
G
I
2
3
4
5
76
64
51
Llanfyllin
Hirnant
Penygarnedd
Aber-Nai
Tycrwyn
Rhiwargor
Alltforgan
Cedig
Tyuchaf
Lake Vyrnwy
Llanwddyn
Abertridwr
Llanfihangel-yng-Ngwynfa
Llwydiarth
Pont Llogel
Dolanog
Pontrobert
Llangadfan
Foel
Pen-y-bont
Llanerfyl
Four Crosses
Heniarth
Llangyniew
Melin-y-ddol
Melin-y-grug
Llanfair Caereinion
Manafon
Pant-y-ffridd
Stingwern Hall
Llanllugan
Adfa
Llanwyddelan
New Mills
Gregynog
Tregynon
Bettws Cedewain
Dolfor
Bwlch-y-ffridd
Llanllwchaiarn
Rhydlydan
Aberhafesp
Caersws
Llanwnog
Clatter
Carno
Plas Llysyn
Talerddig
Newtown (Y Drenewydd)
Textile Mus
Mochdre
Llandinam
Trefeglwys
Dolfor
Pentre
Kerry Hill
Cilfaesty Hill
Llyn-dwr Hill
Llaithddu
Bryn Gydfa
Llanbadarn Fynydd
Red Lion Hill
Moel Wilym
Gorslydan
Moelfre Hill
Ddyle
Llanbister
Abbeycwmhir
Abbey Cwmhir
Llanddewi Ystradenni
Maelienydd
Little Hill
Fron
Gwystre
Nantmel
Gaufron
Rhayader
Llansantffraed-Cwmdeuddwr
Gwastedyn Hill
Gamallt
St Harmon
Moel Hywel
Wennallt
Camlo Hill
Cefn-crin
Bwlch-y-sarnau
Pant-y-dwr
Drysgol
Cefn Cenarth
Pistyll
Bryn Titley
Dolfach
Foel Gurig
Tylwch
Oldchapel Hill
Llangurig
Cwmbelan
Llanidloes
Coed-y-gaer
Y Foel
Dethenydd
Hengwm-wydd-fawr
Rhyddhywel
Oakley Park
Y Fan
Fan Hill
Bryn Tail Lead Mine Buildings
Llyn Clywedog Reservoir
Llawryglyn
Bryn Crugog
Gors Goch
Waun Garno
Staylittle
Bryn yr Oerfa
Trannon
Pont Crugnant
Dylife
Bryn y Fedwen
Pennant
Moelfre
Bryn Amlwg
Llanbrynmair
Tafolwern
Llan
Bont Dolgadfan
Tal-y-wern
Mynydd Tyr-sais
Darowen
Abercegir
Commins Coch
Cemmaes Road (Glantwymyn)
Cemmaes
Cwm-Llinau
Aberangell
Mallwyd
Dinas-Mawddwy
Minllyn
Cwm-Cewydd
Foel Dugoed
Nant-y-dugoed
Mynydd Llyn Coch-hwyad
Esgair Ddu
Mynydd y Cemais
Tafolog
Mynydd Rhiw-Saeson
Dol Fawr
Pentre-celyn
Plas-rhiw-Saeson
Pandy
Esgair Priciau
Tir y mynach
Nant yr Eira
Bryn y Castell
Ffridd-Rhyd-Dhu
Twmpath Melyn
Rhyd
Esgair Cwmowen
Mynydd Clogau
Mynydd y Gribin
Mynydd Waun Fawr
Dolwen
Pen Coed
Moel y Llyn
Carreg y Frân
Tir Rhiwiog
Hen Gerrig
Pen y Ffridd Gownwy
Penisarcwn
Dyfnant Forest
Mynydd y Gadfa
Pren Croes
Llanymawddwy
Foel Rhudd
Bwlch y groes
Dyrysgol
Drws-y-nant
Rhydymain
Bont Newydd
Brithdir
Torrent Walk
Craig y Ffynnon
Bwlch y Fign
Y Gribin
Bwlch yr Oerddrws
Foel Benddin
Aber Cywarch
Foxes
Cribin Fawr
Cae Afon
Waun-oer
Mynydd Dolgoed
Tal y Mieryn
Foel-y-ffridd
Dyfi Forest
Mynydd Ceiswyn
Garneddwen
Corris
Corris Craft Centre
Esgairgeiliog
Plas Llwyngwern
Cen for Alternative Technology
Llanwrin
Abergwydol
Penegoes
Machynlleth
Aberhosan
Dylife
Bryn Moel
Glaslyn
Pen Pumlumon-Arwystli
Blaenhafren Source of River Severn
Source of River Wye
PLYNLIMON
Mynydd y Groes
Esgair y Maesnant
Tor Du
Geufron
Eisteddfa Gurig
Drum Peithnant
Dyffryn Castell
Pant Mawr
Tyn-y-Cwm
Esgair Ychion
Banc Nant-Rhys
Ysbyty Cynfyn
Pen y Garn
Bryn Garw
Yr Allt
Esgair Elan
Llaniwared
Cwmystwyth
Abergwngu Hill
Geifas
Ffos Trosol
Llyn Fyrddon Fawr
Pantllwyd
Nant Hirin
Clawdd-ddu-bach
Craig Goch Reservoir
Penygarreg Reservoir
Trawsallt
Claerwen Reservoir
Cefn Brwynog
Dibyn Du
Llyn Egnant
Pontrhydfendigaid
CAMBRIAN MOUNTAINS
POWYS
A470
A458
A489
A483
A44
A494
A495
B4393
B4382
B4395
B4389
B4385
B4518
B4569
B4568
B4355
B4343
B4574
B4404
B4396
B4580

A
B
C
D
1
2
3
4
5
77
63
52
Penygarnedd
Bwlch-y-ddar
Pen-y-bont
Llanyblodwel
Porth-y-waen
Llynclys
Crickheath
Pant
Woolston
Weirbrook
Knockin
Stanwardine in the Fields
Myddle
Ruyton-XI-Towns
Dovaston
Kinnerley
Milford
Little Ness
Prescott
Walford
Aber-Naint
Llanfechain
Llansantffraid-ym-Mechain
Llanymynech
Maesbrook
Llanfyllin
Tycrwyn
Llandysilio
Domgay
Four Crosses
Crosslanes
Edgerley
Kinton
Wilcott
Nesscliffe
Yeaton
Grafton
Great Ness
Godor
Bwlch-y-cibau
Deuddwr
Llandrinio
Melverley Green
Melverley
Pentre
Felton Butler
Ensdon
Forton
Montford Bridge
Llanfihangel-yng-Ngwynfa
Waen-fach
Sarnau
Trefnanney
Arddlin
Criggion
Crewgreen
Breidden Hill
365
Alberbury
Alberbury Priory
Shrawardine
Montford
Ford
Allt y Main
356
Pentre'r beirdd
Geuffordd
Middletown Hill
364
Moel y Golfa
404
Meifod
Broniarth Hill
Pontrobert
Groes-lwyd
Guilsfield (Cedigfa)
Pool Quay
Trewern
Middletown
Wollaston
Rowton
Halfway House
Cardeston
Shoot Hill
Garreg Bank
Stretton Heath
Yockleton
Nox
Trelydan Hall
Powysland Mus
Frochas
Vennington
Westbury
Stoney Stretton
Cruckton
Cruckmeole
Hanwood
Four Crosses
Llangyniew
Heniarth
Cyfronydd
Welshpool (Y Trallwng)
Welshpool & Llanfair Lt. Rly
Buttington
Edge
Lea
Farley
Hinton
Annscroft
Long Mountain
Roman Road
Lower Wallop
Westley
Asterley
Pleeley
Melin-y-ddol
Llanfair Caereinion
Castle Caereinion
Powis (NT)
Hope
Leighton
Rowley
Aston Rogers
Rea Brook
Pontesbury
Pontesford
Short Cross
Brockton
Worthen
Minsterley
Oaks
Llwynderw
Fron
Trelystan
Binweston
Leigh
Wrentnall
Manafon
Pant-y-ffridd
Stingwern Hill
Kingswood
Marton
Ploxgreen
Habberley
Church Pulverbatch
Llanllugan
Llanwyddelan
New Mills
Forden
Betton
Snailbeach
Pulverbatch
Meadowtown
Hope
Perkins Beach
Cothercott
Berriew (Aberriw)
Vaynor Park
Woodmoor
Wotherton
Rorrington
Gravels
Pennerley
Pick
Woo
Brooks
Garthmyl
Middleton
Black Marsh
Shelve
Stiperstones
Tregynon
Gregynog
Chirbury
Stone Circle
Priestweston
The Marsh
513
Corndon Hill
Black Rhadley Hill
The Bog
Ratlinghope
Bridges
Long Mynd
Bettws Cedewain
Montgomery (Trefaldwyn)
Llandyssil
Cefn-y-coed
POWYS
SHROPSHIRE
Dolforwyn
Abermule
Church Stoke
Hyssington
Linley Hill
Carding Mill Valley & Long Mynd (NT)
516
All Stretton
Bwlch-y-ffridd
Rhydlydan
Llanllwchaiarn
Llanmerewig
Pentreheyling
Linley
Norbury
Wentnor
Little Stretton
Textile Museum
Newtown (Y Drenewydd)
Pentre
Snead
More
Asterton
Minton
Sarn
Lydham
Kerry
Glanmule
Bishop's Castle
Lea
Myndtown
Eaton
Marshbrook
Mochdre
Cefn-gwyn
Edenhope Hill
Mainstone
Plowden
Whittingslow
Eyton
Woolston
Dolfor
Clun Forest
Colebatch
Lydbury North
Upper
Cefn Einion
Edgton
Horderley
Pentre
Kerry Hill
Anchor
Brockton
Wistanstow
Hall of the Forest
Bryn
Acton
Lower Down
Walcot
Cheney Longville
Cilfaesty Hill
528
Kempton
Hopesay
Sibdon Carwood
Bicton
Whitcott Keysett
Newcastle
Little Brampton
Aston on Clun
Craven Arms
Felindre
Bettws-y-crwyn
Clunton
Purslow
Stokesay
Clun
Quabbs
Llwyn
Woodside
Clunbury
Clunbury Hill
Broome
Bryn Gydfa
Black Hill
441
Beguildy
Hurgin
Llanfair Hill
Twitchen
Clungunford
Moel Wilym
469
Black Mountain
Offa's Dyke
Hobarris
Hopton Castle
Hopton Titterhill
396
Shelderton
Llanbadarn Fynydd
Red Lion Hill
Gorslydan
Beacon Hill
547
Dutlas
Llanfair Waterdine
Purlogue
Chapel Lawn
Obley
Hoptonheath
Moelfre Hill
Pool Hill
Lloyney
Five Turnings
New Invention
Redlake
Bedstone
Kinton
Ddyle
Knucklas
Brynmelyn
Llanbister
Lanlluest
Llangynllo Sta.
Panpunton
Stowe
Bucknell
Buckton
Leintwardine
Downton on the Rock
Crug
Knighton
Milebrook
Walford
Brampton Bryan
Burrington
Abbeycwmhir
Abbey Cwmhir
Llangunllo
Llanbister Rd Sta.
Bailey Hill
Rhos-y-Meirch
Letton
Adforton
Maelienydd
HEREFORDSHIRE
Llanddewi Ystradenni
Cilog Hill
Bleddfa
Llan-wen Hill
Birtley
Newton
Wigmore
Leinthall Starkes
Pilleth
Harley's
Whitton
Little Hill
Fforest-fach
Pentre
Norton
Lingen
Ongar Street
Yatton
Gwystre
Dol
Llanfihangel Rhydithon
Black Mixen
Pilleth 1402
Cascob
Lower Lye
Croft (NT)
Fron
Penybont
Stapleton
A5
A483
A488
A489
A490
A495
A458
A4113
A4110
B4396
B4391
B4580
B4393
B4392
B4382
B4390
B4389
B4385
B4388
B4386
B4387
B4499
B4368
B4568
B4355
B4356
B4357
B4367
B4370
B4397
B4398
Tanat
Cain
Vyrnwy
Severn
Montgomery Canal
Rhiw
Mule
Camlad
Ithon
Teme
Clun
Onny
Lugg
Morda
Aran

SHREWSBURY
TELFORD
BRIDGNORTH
Ludlow
Newport
Church Stretton
Bewdley
Stourport-on-Severn
Cleobury Mortimer
Tenbury Wells
Much Wenlock
Ironbridge
Wellington
Oakengates
Shifnal
Donnington
Hadley
Madeley
Broseley
Albrighton
Bayston Hill
Wroxeter
Atcham
Cressage
Coalbrookdale
Buildwas
Lilleshall
Edgmond
Crudgington
Rodington
Withington
Upton Magna
Uffington
Battlefield
Albrighton
Bomere Heath
Preston Gubbals
Hadnall
Shawbury
Astley
Great Wytheford
Poynton Green
Osbaston
Walton
High Ercall
Roden
Rowton
Ellerdine Heath
High Hatton
Waters Upton
Cherrington
Tibberton
Howle
Sambrook
Pickstock
Weston Jones
Norbury
Forton
Sutton
Aqualate Mere
Gnosall Heath
Bromstead Heath
Church Aston
Chetwynd Aston
Longford
Adeney
Kynnersley
Preston upon the Weald Moors
Eyton upon the Weald Moors
Sleapford
Long Waste
Longdon upon Tern
Marsh Green
Rushmoor
Isombridge
Admaston
Wrockwardine
Arleston
Leegomery
Trench
Woodcote
Heath Hill
Weston Heath
Sheriffhales
Crackleybank
Great Chatwell
Orslow
Brineton
Marston
Blymhill
Weston-under-Lizard
Bishop's Wood
Kiddemore
Tong Norton
Tong
Shackerley
Cosford
Boningale
Redhill
Hollinswood
Oldpark
Lawley
Dawley
Horsehay
Stirchley
The Wyke
Telford International Centre
Kemberton
Grindle
Ryton
Beckbury
Brockton
Sutton Maddock
Coalport
Norton
Stockton
Badger
Burnhill Green
Ackleton
Chesterton
The Walls
Worfield
Wyken
Hilton
Upper Ludstone
Claverley
Upper Aston
Roughton
Allscot
Swancote
Heathton
Halfpenny Green
Bobbington
Highgate Common
Six Ashes
Quatt
Quatford
Eardington
Oldbury
Woodlands
Dudmaston Hall (NT)
Glazeley
Chelmarsh
Hampton
Deuxhill
Sidbury
Middleton Scriven
Billingsley
Chorley
Stottesdon
Woodhill
Highley
Alveley
Birdsgreen
Romsley
Enville
Gallowstree Elm
Potter's Cross
Kinver
Kingsford
Shatterford
Upper Arley
Trimpley
Habberley
Blakebrook
Wribbenhall
Franche
Wolverley
Blakeshall
Buttonoak
Wyre Forest
Kinlet
Baveney Wood
Far Forest
Callow Hill
Fingerpost
Ribbesford
Lem Hill
Pound Bank
Bayton
Clows Top
Bliss Gate
Rock
Areley Kings
Dunley
Astley Cross
Lincomb
Crossway Green
The Burf
Noutard's Green
Sychampton
Frog Pool
Great Witley
Abberley
Abberley Hall
Pensax
Stanford on Teme
Stockton on Teme
Orleton
Hanley William
Lindridge
Newnham
Rochford
Upper Rochford
Broadheath
Frith Common
Neen Sollars
Mamble
Milson
Coreley
Hints
Hopton Wafers
Doddington
Neen Savage
Catherton
Cleeton St Mary
Silvington
Oreton
Farlow
Titterstone Clee Hill
Cleehill
Knowle
Hope Bagot
Whitton
Nash
Greete
Boraston
Caynham
Knowbury
Farden
Snitton
Bitterley
Middleton
Henley
Ludford
Bromfield
Stanton Lacy
Overton
Ashford Carbonel
Ashford Bowdler
Richard's Castle
Woofferton
Brimfield
Comberton
Orleton
Wyson
Bircher
Burford
Callows Grave
St Michaels
Middleton on the Hill
Brown Clee Hill
Abdon
Tugford
Holdgate
Upper Heath
Bouldon
Peaton
Clee St Margaret
Diddlebury
Munslow
Aston Munslow
Corfton
Westhope
Seifton
Culmington
Vernolds Common
Lower Hayton
Upper Hayton
Hayton's Bent
Great Sutton
Stoke St Milborough
Cleedownton
Hopton Cangeford
Weston Hill
Loughton
Wheathill
Burwarton
Aston Botterell
Cleobury North
Neenton
Ditton Priors
Middleton Priors
Chetton
Upton Cressett
Aston Eyre
Monkhopton
Morville
Tasley
Lane Head
Cross
Astley Abbotts
Nordley
The Smithies
Haughton
Acton Round
Barrow
Willey
Wyke
Benthall
Homer
Wenlock Priory
Sheinton
Leighton
Little Wenlock
Upper Longwood
Rushton
Eaton Constantine
Dryton
Donnington
Uppington
Aston
The Wrekin
Walcot
Norton
Cross Houses
Berrington
Condover
Cantlop
Great Ryton
Pitchford
Golding
Upper Cound
Cound
Acton Pigott
Acton Burnell
Frodesley
Longnor
Ruckley
Kenley
Harley
Broomcroft
Stretton Westwood
Church Preen
Hughley
Presthope
Bourton
Easthope
Longville in the Dale
Brockton
Weston
Shipton
Stanton Long
Broadstone
Wilderhope Manor (NT)
Plaish
Gretton
Cardington
Caer Caradoc
East Wall
Wall under Heywood
Wall Bank
Rushbury
Hope Bowdler
Ticklerton
Hatton
Acton Scott
Eaton
Middlehope
Harton
Enchmarsh
Leebotwood
Dorrington
Hook-a-Gate
Great Lyth
Meole Brace
Shelton
Sutton
Alderton
Yorton
Grinshill
Clive
Merrington
Harmer Hill
Muckleton
Edgebolton
Moreton Corbet
Great Bolas
Haughmond Abbey
Attingham Park (NT)
Viroconium Roman Town
Ironbridge Gorge Mus
Benthall Hall (NT)
Buildwas Abbey
Acton Burnell
Severn Valley Railway
Severn Valley Rly
Cliff Rly
Lilleshall N.S.C.
Weston Park
White Ladies Priory
Aerospace Museum
Boscobel
Boldsall Wood
Nurton
Pattingham
Trysull
Lower Penn
WOLVERHAMPTON
KIDDERMINSTER
Wilden
Upper Mitton
Hartlebury Common
Leapgate
West Midland Safari Park
Kingsford Country Park
Fishery & Wildlife Sanctuary
Kinlet
Shipton Hall
Hope Bowdler Hill
Ape Dale
Wenlock Edge
Hope Dale
Corve Dale
Rea Brook
Borle Brook
Chelmarsh Resr
Worfe
Severn
Tern
Roman Road
TELFORD & WREKIN
SHROPSHIRE
WORCESTERSHIRE
M54
A5
A41
A49
A53
A442
A458
A518
A5223
A4169
A464
A4117
A456
A443
A451
A449
A454
A4025
A519
A528
A5112
B4380
B4371
B4368
B4364
B4363
B4376
B4378
B4375
B4373
B4379
B4176
B4555
B4194
B4202
B4214
B4361
B4362
B4365
B4386
B4394
B5061
B5062
B5063
B5067
B5060
B4203
B4190
B4196
B4195
B5314
79
53
66

A
B
C
D
1
2
3
4
5
79
65
54
STAFFORD
Tixall
Great Haywood
Little Haywood
Colwich
Milford
Walton-on-the-Hill
Weeping Cross
Castle Bank
Brocton
Bednall
Acton Trussell
Dunston
Coppenhall
Hyde Lea
Levedale
Penkridge
Cannock Chase
Brindley Heath
Pye Green
Hednesford
Huntington
CANNOCK
Hatherton
Four Crosses
Bridgtown
Cheslyn Hay
Great Wyrley
Landywood
Norton Canes
Chasetown
Burntwood
Hammerwich
LICHFIELD
RUGELEY
Brereton
Armitage
Handsacre
Longdon
Upper Longdon
Blithbury
Colton
Hamstall Ridware
Hill Ridware
Mavesyn Ridware
Pipe Ridware
King's Bromley
Rileyhill
Elmhurst
Farewell
Chorley
Gentleshaw
Cannock Wood
Hazelslade
Littleworth
Wimblebury
Heath Hayes
Chase Terrace
Edial
Burntwood Green
Wall
Shenstone
Weeford
Stonnall
Chesterfield
BROWNHILLS
Clayhanger
Shire Oak
Walsall Wood
Vigo
Pelsall
BLOXWICH
Shelfield
Rushall
ALDRIDGE
Little Aston
Shenstone Woodend
Little Hay
Roughley
Four Oaks
Streetly
Mere Green
SUTTON COLDFIELD
WALSALL
Maw Green
Gnosall
Gnosall Heath
Haughton
Ranton
Coton
Derrington
Shut Heath
Norbury
Forton
Allimore Green
Church Eaton
Bradley
Bromstead Heath
Chetwynd Aston
Orslow
High Onn
Mitton
Whiston
Bickford
Marston
Great Chatwell
Brineton
Blymhill
Weston-under-Lizard
Wheaton Aston
Lapley
Stretton
Gailey
Weston Heath
Bishop's Wood
Kiddemore Green
Brewood
Horsebrook
Four Ashes
Standeford
Shareshill
Coven
Featherstone
Tong Norton
Tong
Shifnal
Shackerley
Cosford
Codsall Wood
Codsall
Bilbrook
Oaken
Albrighton
Boningale
Grindle
Ryton
Beckbury
Burnhill Green
Badger
Ackleton
Pattingham
Nurton
Perton
Wergs
Tettenhall
Tettenhall Wood
WOLVERHAMPTON
Trescott
Lower Penn
Penn
Bradmore
Blakenhall
Ettingshall
Bilston
Essington
New Invention
Wood Hayes
WEDNESFIELD
Willenhall
Oxley
Bushbury
Heath Town
Monmore Green
Darlaston
Moxley
King's Hill
Wednesbury
Bradley
Coseley
Princes End
Tipton
Upper Gornal
Sedgley
Gospel End
The Walls
Chesterton
Worfield
Shipley
Seisdon
Trysull
Upper Ludstone
Claverley
Upper Aston
Roughton
Wombourne
The Bratch
Heathton
Halfpenny Green
Himley
Swindon
Gornalwood
DUDLEY
Dudley Port
Bobbington
Wall Heath
Kingswinford
Pensnett
Woodside
Brierley Hill
Netherton
Rowley Regis
Quarry Bank
Merry Hill
Blackheath
Old Hill
OLDBURY
SMETHWICK
WEST BROMWICH
Great Barr
Hamstead
Handsworth
Queslett
Kingstanding
Perry Barr
Short Heath
Erdington
Tyburn
Walmley
Wylde Green
Aston
Saltley
Ward End
BIRMINGHAM
Gravelly Hill
Castle Bromwich
Yardley
Hay Mills
South Yardley
Acock's Green
Olton
Kineton Green
Hall Green
SOLIHULL
Shirley
Chad Valley
Edgbaston
Harborne
Selly Oak
Moseley
Bournbrook
King's Heath
Stirchley
Bournville
Cotteridge
Springfield
Solihull Lodge
Northfield
King's Norton
West Heath
Longbridge
Rubery
Rednal
Drakes Cross
Whitlock's End
Wythall
Earlswood
Hopwood
Weatheroak Hill
Cofton Hackett
Barnt Green
Lickey
Blackwell
Alvechurch
Rowney Green
Portway
Branson's Cross
Wood End
Tanworth in Arden
Holt End
Beoley
Gorcott Hill
REDDITCH
Hewell Lane
Hewell Grange
Webheath
Headless Cross
Walkwood
Mappleborough Green
Oldberrow
Beaudesert
Quinton
Woodgate
Frankley
Illey
Romsley
Hasbury
Cradley
HALESOWEN
Lye
Old Swinford
Pedmore
Hagley
West Hagley
Clent
Holy Cross
Clent Hills
Belbroughton
Bell End
Drayton
Fairfield
Upper Catshill
Catshill
Bournheath
Dodford
Sidemoor
Lickey End
BROMSGROVE
Finstall
Tutnall
Aston Fields
Tardebigge
Stoke Prior
Upton Warren
Wychbold
Woodgate
Elmbridge
Cutnall Green
Elmley Lovett
Hampton Lovett
Doverdale
Rushock
Chaddesley Corbett
Harvington
Stone
Shenstone
Mustow Green
Hartlebury
Torchard
Crossway Green
Dunhampton
Sytchampton
Noutard's Green
The Burf
Astley
Astley Cross
Lincomb
Dunley
Areley Kings
Stourport-on-Severn
Upper Mitton
Wilden
Ribbesford
Bewdley
Wribbenhall
Blakebrook
KIDDERMINSTER
Franche
Habberley
Low Habberley
Trimpley
Upper Arley
Wolverley
Cookley
Caunsall
Blakeshall
Churchill
Broome
Blakedown
Kingsford
Shatterford
Romsley
Kinver
Potter's Cross
Whittington
Norton
Wollaston
STOURBRIDGE
Stourton
Amblecote
Wordsley
Enville
Gallowstree Elm
Six Ashes
Quatt
Witley
Frog Pool
SAFFS
WEST MIDLANDS
M6
M54
M5
M42
A38(M)

67
81
68
55
BURTON UPON TRENT
SWADLINCOTE
Ashby de la Zouch
COALVILLE
Shepshed
LEICESTERSHIRE
TAMWORTH
Atherstone
HINCKLEY
NUNEATON
BEDWORTH
WARWICKSHIRE
COVENTRY
Kenilworth
ROYAL LEAMINGTON SPA
RUGBY
Knowle
Earl Shilton
Narborough
Market Bosworth
Polesworth
Hartshill
Castle Gresley
Linton
Overseal
Moira
Measham
Ibstock
Markfield
Groby
Ratby
Kirby Muxloe
Desford
Newbold Verdon
Barwell
Burbage
Stoney Stanton
Sapcote
Broughton Astley
Wolvey
Bulkington
Binley
Balsall Common
Meriden
Coleshill
Kingsbury
Fazeley
Dordon
Baddesley Ensor
Mancetter
Fillongley
Corley
Berkswell
Stoneleigh
Dunchurch
Long Lawford
Brandon
Wolston
Ryton-on-Dunsmore
Bubbenhall
Cubbington
Hockley Heath
Dorridge
Bentley Heath
Elford
Harlaston
Clifton Campville
Netherseal
Appleby Magna
Twycross
Sheepy Magna
Fenny Drayton
Higham on the Hill
Stoke Golding
Sutton Cheney
Thornton
Bagworth
Nailstone
Barlestone
Osbaston
Hathern
Long Whatton
Belton
Thringstone
Whitwick
Swannington
Coleorton
Packington
Woodville
Hartshorne
Newhall
Branston
Barton-under-Needwood
Walton-on-Trent
Rosliston
Croxall
Edingale
Whittington
Hopwas
Wishaw
Curdworth
Water Orton
Marston Green
Hampton in Arden
Elmdon
Bickenhill
Birmingham International
Fen End
Honiley
Haseley
Old Milverton
Leek Wootton
Charnwood Forest
Leicester Forest East
Thurlaston
Huncote
Croft
Cosby
Sharnford
Frolesworth
Claybrooke Magna
Ullesthorpe
Pailton
Monks Kirby
Withybrook
Shilton
Ansty
Brinklow
Churchover
Harborough Magna
Clifton upon Dunsmore
Hillmorton
Bilton
Thurlaston
Draycote
Marton
Birdingbury
Long Itchington
Broadwell
Grandborough
Willoughby
Barby
Woolscott
M1
M6
M42
M69
M45
M40
A5
A444
A42
A511
A38
A46
A45
A452
A4177
A47
A426
A428
A4114
A4600
A4082

68
A
B
C
D
82
Long Whatton
Normanton on Soar
Hoton
Wymeswold
Old Dalby
Wartnaby
Scalford
Chadwell
Stonesby
Holwell
Ab Kettleby
Stanford on Soar
Prestwold
Grimston
Saxelbye
Thorpe Arnold
Garthorpe
Shepshed
LOUGHBOROUGH
Cotes
Burton on the Wolds
Walton on the Wolds
Ragdale
Asfordby Hill
Freeby
Saxby
Thorpe Acre
Great Central Rly
Asfordby
Melton Mowbray
Brentingby
Wymondham
Melton Carnegie Museum
Stapleford
Woodthorpe
Nanpantan
Seagrave
Fosse Way
Hoby
Frisby on the Wreake
Kirby Bellars
Burton Lazars
Quorn
Barrow upon Soar
Brooksby
Rotherby
Beacon Hill
Thrussington
Sileby
Woodhouse
Ratcliffe on the Wreake
Great Dalby
Broombriggs Farm
Mountsorrel
Rearsby
Whissendine
Ulverscroft
Woodhouse Eaves
Cossington
East Goscote
Little Dalby
Swithland
Gaddesby
Copt Oak
Rothley
Queniborough
Ashby Folville
Burrough Hill Hillfort
Syston
Thorpe Satchville
Somerby
Pickwell
Markfield
Bradgate Park
Thurcaston
Watermead
Cropston
Wanlip
Cropston Resr
South Croxton
Barsby
Twyford
Burrough on the Hill
Cold Overton
Stanton
Bardon
Newtown Linford
Field Head
Barkby
Birstall
Thurmaston
Barkby Thorpe
Anstey
Baggrave Hall
Owston
Knossington
Oakham
Rutland County Museum
Thornton Resr
Beeby
Hungarton
Lowesby
Marefield
Braunston
Groby
National Space Science Centre
Belgrave
Belgrave Hall
Keyham
Whatborough Hill
230
Quenby Hall
Cold Newton
Glenfield
Humberstone
Scraptoft
Halstead
Withcote
Ratby
Wygston's Ho
LEICESTER
Tilton on the Hill
Launde Abbey
Newtown
Dane Hills
Kirby Muxloe
Bushby
Eye Brook
Desford
Braunstone
Stoneygate
Thurnby
Houghton on the Hill
Loddington
Ridlington
Leicester Forest East
Evington
Billesdon
Skeffington
Belton
Aylestone
Knighton
Stoughton
Leicester
Farmworld
East Norton
Peckleton
Gaulby
Rolleston
Tugby
67
Enderby
Oadby
King's Norton
Allexton
Thurlaston
Little Stretton
Glen Parva
WIGSTON
Great Glen
Illston on the Hill
Goadby
Earl Shilton
Huncote
South Wigston
Newton Harcourt
Carlton Curlieu
Noseley
Stockerston
Narborough
Whetstone
Blaby
Burton Overy
Hallaton
Horninghold
Shangton
Sence
LEICESTERSHIRE
Glooston
Croft
Cosby
Countesthorpe
Kilby
Kibworth Harcourt
Stonton Wyville
Cranoe
Blaston
Stoney Stanton
Sutton in the Elms
Fleckney
Kibworth Beauchamp
Langton Hall
Tur Langton
Slawston
Nevill Holt
Sapcote
Aston Flamville
Primethorpe
Peatling Magna
Church Langton
Medbourne
Great Easton
Broughton Astley
Arnesby
Smeeton Westerby
Willoughby Waterleys
East Langton
Thorpe Langton
Welham
Drayton
Sharnford
Saddington
Saddington Resr
Welland
Frolesworth
Dunton Bassett
Ashby Magna
Shearsby
Weston by Welland
Ashley
Cottingham
Wigston Parva
Foxton
Leire
Peatling Parva
Bruntingthorpe
Foxton Canal
Great Bowden
Sutton Bassett
Middleton
East Carlton
Claybrooke Magna
Gumley
Claybrooke Parva
Ashby Parva
Gilmorton
Mowsley
Laughton
Harborough
Brampton Ash
Wilbarston
Ullesthorpe Parva
Wibtoft
Lubenham
Dingley
Stoke Albany
Walton
Little Bowden
Market Harborough
Willey
Kimcote
Theddingworth
Marston Trussell
Bitteswell
Lutterworth
East Farndon
Pipewell
Misterton
Husbands Bosworth
Braybrooke
Shire Falconry Centre
Monks Kirby
Newnham Paddox
Walcote
North Kilworth
NORTHAMPTONSHIRE
Cotesbach
Sibbertoft
Great Oxendon
Desborough
Pailton
Rushton Triangular Lodge
Swift
Sulby Resr
Clipston
Stretton under Fosse
Churchover
South Kilworth
Rothwell
Arthingworth
Shawell
Welford
Naseby 1645
Easenhall
Swinford
Stanford Hall
Kelmarsh
Harrington
Harborough Magna
Stanford on Avon
Orton
Newbold on Avon
Newton
Naseby
Thorpe Malsor
Catthorpe
Little Lawford
Lilbourne
Clay Coton
Loddington
Naseby Resr
Haselbech
Clifton upon Dunsmore
Long Lawford
Maidwell
Great Cransley
Watling Street
Cold Ashby
Thornby
Draughton
Brampton Valley Way
Faxton
Rugby
Yelvertoft
WARKS
Hillmorton
Lamport
Bilton
Winwick
Hollowell Resr
Guilsborough
Cottesbrooke
Old
Walgrave
Dunchurch
Crick
Coton Manor Wildlife Garden
Coton
Creaton
Scaldwell
Pitsford Reservoir Nature Reserve
Kilsby
West Haddon
Hollowell
Ravensthorpe Resr
Brixworth
Hannington
Thurlaston
Barby
Teeton
Ravensthorpe
Spratton
Woolscott
Ashby St Ledgers
Watford
Long Buckby
Holcot
Kites Hardwick
East Haddon
Pitsford Reservoir
Pitsford
Grandborough
Willoughby
Watford Gap
Holdenby House
Holdenby
Sywell
Overstone
Broadwell
Braunston
Chapel Brampton
M1
M6
M69
M45
A42
A6
A60
A6006
A46
A606
A607
A512
A6004
A50
A563
A47
A594
A5460
A5199
A6030
A5
A426
A4303
A4304
A508
A427
A14
A428
A4071
A361
A43
A45
B676
B5366
B582
B6047
B664
B669
B4429
B4027
B4112
B4455
B4669
B581
B578
B5414
B5380
B591

LINCOLNSHIRE
RUTLAND
PETERBOROUGH
CAMBS
NORTHAMPTONSHIRE
Spalding
Sproxton
Woolsthorpe Manor (NT)
Buckminster
Colsterworth
Swayfield
Elsthorpe
Hanthorpe
Morton Fen
West
Stainby
North Witham
Swinstead
Grimsthorpe
Dyke
Bourne North Fen
Twenty
Sewstern
Gunby
Scottlethorpe
Cawthorpe
Bourne
83
Eastgate
South Witham
Creeton
Castle Bytham
Little Bytham
Careby
Toft
Lound
Northorpe
Thurlby
Baston Common
Deeping Fen
Thistleton
Edmondthorpe
Market Overton
Clipsham
Witham on the Hill
Manthorpe
Teigh
Stretton
Carlby
Deeping St Nicholas
Barrow
Greetham
Pickworth
Wilsthorpe
Baston
Ashwell
Braceborough
Langtoft
Cottesmore
Essendine
Greatford
Crowland Common
Vale of Catmose
Exton
Ryhall
Barholm
Market Deeping
Crowland
Barleythorpe
Burley
Great Casterton
Little Casterton
Belmesthorpe
Tallington Lakes Leisure Centre
Deeping Gate
Tickencote
Tallington
West Deeping
Deeping St James
Whitwell
Empingham
Uffington
Maxey
Northborough
Borough Fen
Upper Hambleton
Stamford
Peakirk Wildfowl Refuge
Egleton
Tinwell
Burghley
Etton
Glinton
Peakirk
Rutland Water
Normanton
Bainton
Helpston
Newborough
Brooke
Edith Weston
Ketton
Easton on the Hill
Pilsgate
Barnack
Ufford
Gwash
North Luffenham
Southorpe
Eye Green
Manton
Lyndon
Werrington
Eye
Preston
Pilton
Collyweston
Walton
Wing
Wittering
Marholm
South Luffenham
Morcott
Duddington
Thornhaugh
New England
Glaston
Tixover
Upton
Newark
Barrowden
70
PETERBOROUGH
Bisbrooke
Wakerley
Ailsworth
Longthorpe Tower
Wansford
Sutton
Castor
Longthorpe
Seaton
Stibbington
Nene Valley Rly
Peterborough Green Wheel
Lyddington
Bede House
Harringworth
Ferry Meadows
Woodston
Yarwell
Sibson
Water Newton
Old Fletton
Thorpe by Water
Laxton
King's Cliffe
Nassington
Alwalton
Orton Waterville
Orton Longueville
Stanground
Blatherwycke
Apethorpe
Chesterton
Farcet
Bulwick
Big Sky Adventure Play
Hampton
Gretton
Woodnewton
Fotheringhay
Elton
Peterborough
Caldecott
Deene
Elton Hall
Kirby Hall
Deene Hall
Deenethorpe
Haddon
Farcet Fen
Yaxley
Morborne
Rockingham
Willow Brook
Southwick
Tansor
Eaglethorpe
Warmington
Norman Cross
Whittlesey Mere
CORBY
Weldon
Upper Benefield
Glapthorn
Cotterstock
Folksworth
Stilton
Lower Benefield
Oundle
Caldecote
Ashton
Denton
Holme
Barnwell
Lutton
Polebrook
Stanion
Brigstock
Stoke Doyle
Great Oakley
Little Oakley
Lyveden New Bield (NT)
Armston
Hemington
Glatton
Conington
Luddington in the Brook
Lilford Park
Barnwell St Andrew
Barnwell All Saints
Pilton
Newton
Geddington
Cross
Wadenhoe
Thurning
Great Gidding
Sawtry
Achurch
Wigsthorpe
Sudborough
Boughton
Aldwincle
Little Gidding
Steeple Gidding
Grafton Underwood
Lowick
Thorpe Waterville
Winwick
Woodwalton
Weekley
Clopton
Coppingford
Warkton
Slipton
Islip
Titchmarsh
Hamerton
Roman Road
KETTERING
Twywell
Thrapston
Upton
Alconbury Hill
Barton Seagrave
Cranford St Andrew
Woodford
Alconbury Weston
Cranford St John
Old Weston
Buckworth
Burton Latimer
Great Addington
Denford
Bythorn
Brington
Molesworth
Alconbury
Wicksteed Park
Ringstead
Keyston
Barham
Leighton Bromswold
Great Stukeley
Isham
Woolley
Little Addington
Catworth
Spaldwick
Huntingdon
Finedon
Raunds
Easton
Ellington
Stanwick
Stow Longa
Brampton
Great Harrowden
Irthlingborough
Hargrave
Hinchingbrooke House
Godmanchester
Chelveston
Covington
Grafham
Higham Ferrers
Caldecott
Shelton
Lower Dean
Tilbrook
57
Grafham Water
Buckden
RUSHDEN
Upper Dean
Kimbolton
Stonely
West Perry
Offord Cluny
Wilby
Irchester
Yielden
Swineshead
Diddington
Nene
Welland
Glen
A1
A1(M)
A6
A14
A15
A16
A43
A45
A47
A151
A427
A509
A510
A605
A606
A1073
A1179
A1260
A4300
A6003
A6014
A6116
A6121
B645
B660
B662
B663
B664
B668
B670
B672
B1081
B1090
B1091
B1095
B1166
B1176
B1443
B1524
B1525
B571
B574
B569

70
84
69
58
A
B
C
D
1
2
3
4
5
LINCOLNSHIRE
CAMBRIDGESHIRE
PETERBOROUGH
PETERBOROUGH (North Level)
Bedford
Bedford (Middle Level)
Bedford (South
Spalding
West
Pode Hole
Little London
Twenty
Weston Hills
Moulton
Whaplode
Whaplode Fen
Moulton Chapel
Whaplode St Catherine
Holbeach St Johns
Hargate
Fleet
Gedney
Gedney Broadgate
Delph Bank
Little London
Long Sutton
Sutton Bridge
Sutton Crosses
South Holland Main Drain
Wingland Marsh
Walpole Cross Keys
Terrington
Sutton St James
Tydd St Mary
Tydd Gote
Four Gotes
Tydd St Giles
Walpole St Andrew
Walpole St Peter
Terrington St John
Cowbit
Deeping Fen
North Drove Drain
Deeping St Nicholas
Moulton Fen
Aswick Grange
Great
Postland
Whaplode Drove
Holbeach Drove
Gedney Hill
Sutton St Edmund
Tydd St Giles Fen
Newton
Fitton End
Gorefield
Leverington
West Walton
West Walton Highway
Walpole Highway
Marshland
St John's Fen End
Wisbech
Walsoken
New Walsoken
Crowland
Common
Crowland
Crowland Abbey
Shepeau Stow
Market Deeping
Deeping Gate
Deeping St James
Peakirk Wildfowl Refuge
Borough Fen
Peakirk
Glinton
North Fen
Church End
Parson Drove
Peckover House (NT)
Wisbech & Fenland
Wisbech St Mary
Murrow
Tholomas Drove
Emneth
Emneth Hungate
Elm
Holly End
Morris Fen
Wryde Croft
Newborough
Thorney
Level
Eye Green
Eye
Werrington
Walton
Adventurers' Land
Guyhirn
Waldersey
Friday Bridge
Outwell
Upwell
Ring's End
Coldham
Laddus Fens
North District
Nordelph
Three Holes
Newark
PETERBOROUGH
Priors Fen
Hobbs Lots Bridge
Twenty Foot River
Euximoor Fen
North Side
Morton's Leam
Eldernell
White Moor
Westry
Longthorpe
Woodston
Old Fletton
Peterborough Green Wheel
Eastrea
Coates
Whittlesey
March
Binnimoor Fen
Christchurch
South District
Orton
Orton Longueville
Stanground
King's Delph
West Fen
Town End
Lakesend
Upwell Fen
Welney
Big Sky Adventure Play
Hampton
Farcet
Flag Fen
Glass Moor
White Fen
Wimblington
Ranson Moor
Gold Hill
Yaxley
Farcet Fen
Pondersbridge
Sixteen Foot Drain
Norman Cross
Whittlesey Mere
Benwick
Doddington
Wimblington Fen
Manea
The Herne
Middle Moor
Mere Side
Ramsey Mereside
Holme
Ramsey St Mary's
Ramsey Forty Foot
Forty Foot or Vermuden's Drain
West Moor
Purls Bridge
Fodder Fen
Chatteris
Horseway
Langwood Fen
Welches Dam
Pymore
New Bedford River
Glatton
Conington
Ramsey Heights
Ramsey
Ramsey Hollow
Ramsey Abbey Gatehouse (NT)
Little Downham
Sawtry
Roman Road
Tick Fen
Bury
Upwood
Somersham High North Fen
Horseley Fen
Wardy Hill
Coveney
West Fen
Gidding
Woodwalton
Great Raveley
Wistow
Pidley Fen
Chatteris Fen
Mepal
Warboys
Fenton
Witcham
Ely
Upton
Wennington
Little Raveley
Abbots Ripton
Broughton
Pidley
Somersham
Sutton
Wentworth
Witchford
Alconbury
Alconbury Hill
Alconbury Weston
North Fen
Old Bedford River
Stuntney
Little Thetford
Oldhurst
Woodhurst
Kings Ripton
Hill Row Doles
Haddenham
Little Stukeley
Colne
Bluntisham
Great Stukeley
Earith
Wilburton
Stretham
Woolley
Huntingdon
Hartford
Aldreth
Cromwell Mus
Wyton
Houghton
Ouse Fen
Great Ouse
Needingworth
Brampton
Hinchingbrooke House
Houghton Mill (NT)
St Ives
Holywell
Church End
Willingham
Smithey Fen
North Fen
Chittering
Upware
Grafham
Hemingford Abbots
Hemingford Grey
Godmanchester
Island Hall
Over
Swavesey
Denny Abbey
Buckden
Wood Green Animal Shelter
Fenstanton
Rampton
Cottenham
Boxworth End
Longstanton
Offord Cluny
Offord D'Arcy
Diddington
Conington
A1(M)
A1
A14
A15
A16
A17
A47
A141
A142
A605
A1073
A1101
A1123
A1139
A1179
A1260
A1421
A10
A151
A1198

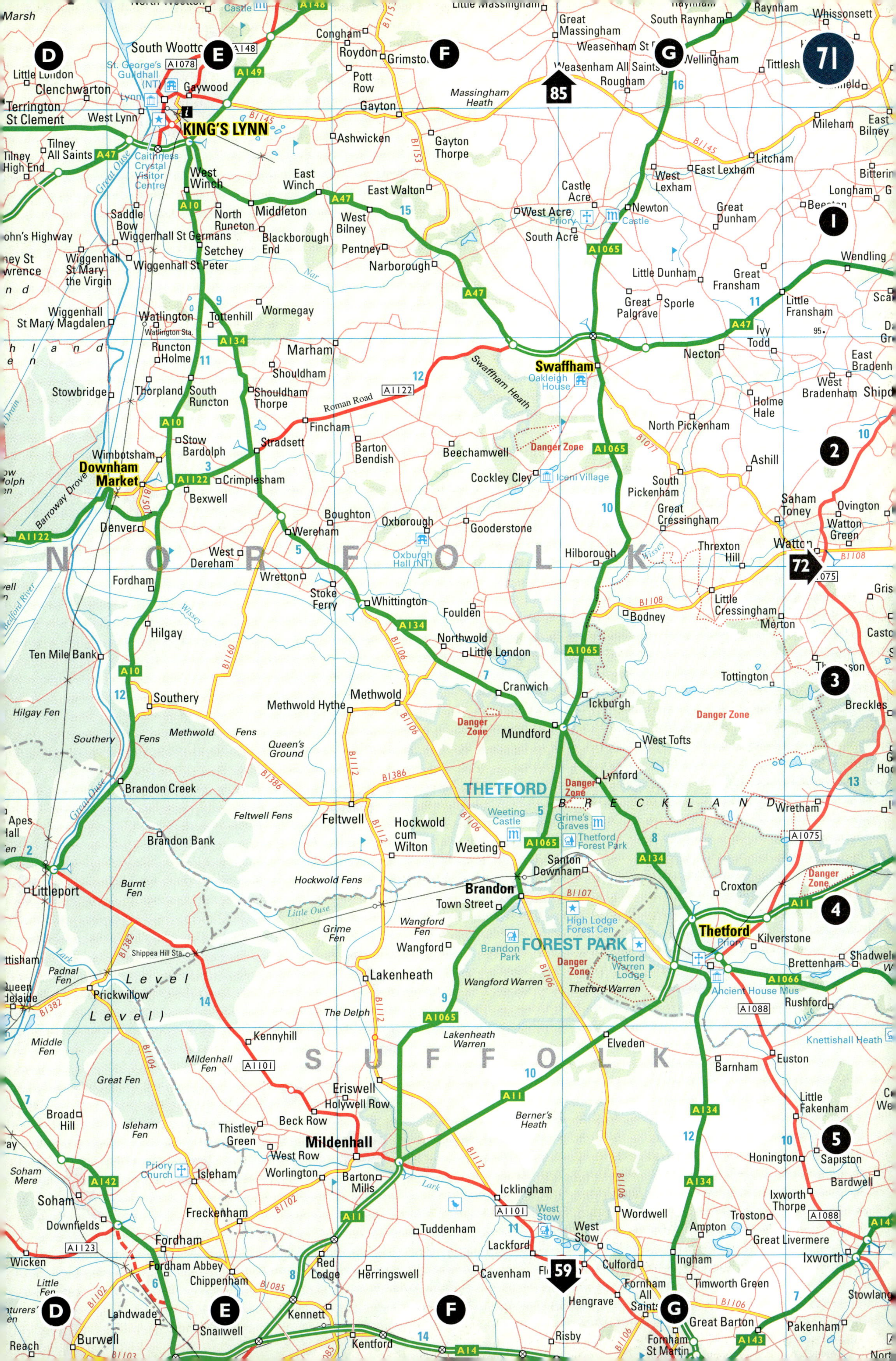
71
D
E
F
G
I
85
72
59
KING'S LYNN
South Wootton
Gaywood
St. George's Guildhall (NT)
Lynn Mus
West Lynn
Clenchwarton
Little London
Terrington St Clement
Tilney All Saints
Tilney High End
Caithness Crystal Visitor Centre
Great Ouse
West Winch
North Runcton
Middleton
East Winch
East Walton
West Bilney
Pentney
Narborough
Nar
Ashwicken
Gayton
Gayton Thorpe
Grimston
Congham
Roydon
Pott Row
Massingham Heath
Little Massingham
Great Massingham
Weasenham St Peter
Weasenham All Saints
Rougham
South Raynham
Raynham
Wellingham
Whissonsett
Tittleshall
Mileham
East Bilney
Litcham
East Lexham
West Lexham
Longham
Beeston
Great Dunham
Newton
Castle Acre
Priory
Castle
West Acre
South Acre
Little Dunham
Great Fransham
Little Fransham
Wendling
Great Palgrave
Sporle
Ivy Todd
Necton
East Bradenham
West Bradenham
Holme Hale
Swaffham
Oakleigh House
Swaffham Heath
Roman Road
Marham
Shouldham
Shouldham Thorpe
Fincham
Barton Bendish
Beechamwell
Danger Zone
Cockley Cley
Iceni Village
North Pickenham
South Pickenham
Ashill
Saham Toney
Ovington
Watton
Watton Green
Great Cressingham
Threxton Hill
Little Cressingham
Hilborough
Gooderstone
Oxborough
Oxburgh Hall (NT)
Boughton
Wereham
Stradsett
Crimplesham
Bexwell
Downham Market
Wimbotsham
Stow Bardolph
Barroway Drove
Denver
Saddle Bow
Wiggenhall St Germans
Setchey
Wiggenhall St Mary the Virgin
Wiggenhall St Peter
Blackborough End
Wormegay
Tottenhill
Watlington
Wiggenhall St Mary Magdalen
Runcton Holme
Thorpland
South Runcton
Stowbridge
John's Highway
West Dereham
Wretton
Stoke Ferry
Whittington
Foulden
Northwold
Little London
Cranwich
Bodney
Merton
Tottington
Ickburgh
Mundford
Fordham
Hilgay
Wissey
Ten Mile Bank
Southery
Hilgay Fen
Southery Fens
Methwold Fens
Methwold Hythe
Methwold
Queen's Ground
Feltwell
Feltwell Fens
Hockwold cum Wilton
Weeting
Weeting Castle
Grime's Graves
Thetford Forest Park
Santon Downham
THETFORD
BRECKLAND
West Tofts
Lynford
Wretham
Croxton
Thetford
Priory
Kilverstone
Brettenham
Shadwell
Rushford
Ancient House Mus
Knettishall Heath
Euston
Barnham
Little Fakenham
Honington
Sapiston
Bardwell
Ixworth Thorpe
Ixworth
Troston
Great Livermere
Ampton
Ingham
Timworth Green
Culford
Fornham All Saints
Fornham St Martin
Great Barton
Pakenham
Stowlangtoft
Brandon Creek
Brandon Bank
Littleport
Burnt Fen
Hockwold Fens
Little Ouse
Brandon
Town Street
Wangford Fen
Wangford
Brandon Park
FOREST PARK
High Lodge Forest Cen
Thetford Warren Lodge
Thetford Warren
Wangford Warren
Lakenheath
Grime Fen
Shippea Hill Sta.
Padnal Fen
Prickwillow
Level
The Delph
Lakenheath Warren
Elveden
Kennyhill
Mildenhall Fen
Great Fen
Eriswell
Holywell Row
Beck Row
Thistley Green
Isleham Fen
Mildenhall
West Row
Berner's Heath
Broad Hill
Middle Fen
Priory Church
Isleham
Worlington
Barton Mills
Icklingham
Lark
Soham Mere
Soham
Freckenham
Downfields
Fordham
Fordham Abbey
Chippenham
Wicken
Little Fen
Landwade
Snailwell
Burwell
Reach
Red Lodge
Herringswell
Tuddenham
Cavenham
West Stow
Lackford
Flempton
Hengrave
Wordwell
Risby
Kentford
Kennett
NORFOLK
SUFFOLK
A47
A149
A148
A1078
A10
A134
A1122
A1065
A1075
A11
A1066
A1088
A1101
A142
A1123
A14
A143
B1145
B1153
B1077
B1108
B1160
B1106
B1112
B1386
B1107
B1382
B1104
B1102
B1085
B1507

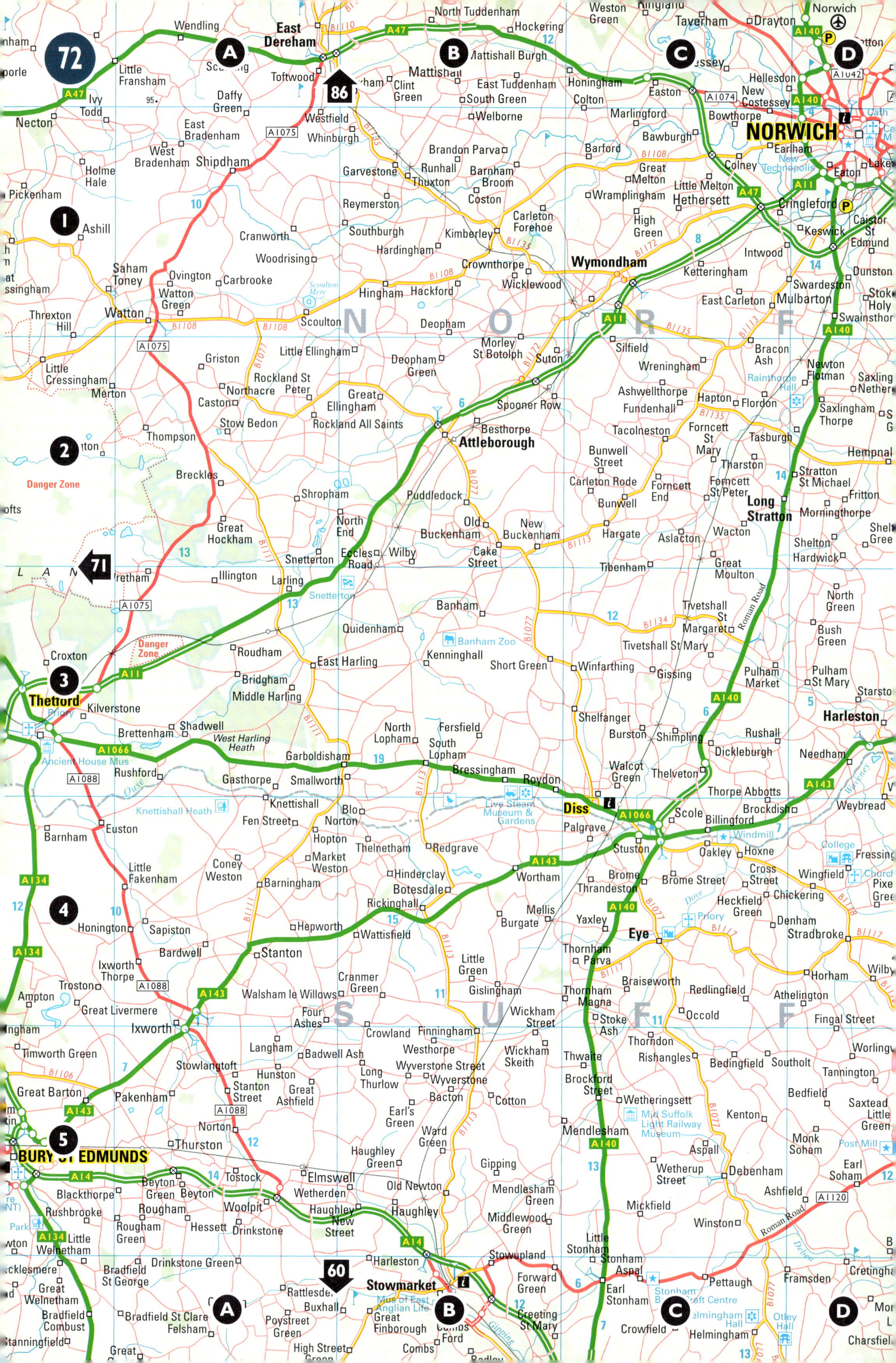
72
Wendling
East Dereham
A47
North Tuddenham
Hockering
Weston Green
Taverham
Drayton
Norwich
Little Fransham
Scarning
Toftwood
86
Mattishall
Mattishall Burgh
Clint Green
East Tuddenham
Honingham
Easton
Hellesdon
New Costessey
Ivy Todd
Necton
Daffy Green
Westfield
Whinburgh
South Green
Welborne
Colton
Marlingford
Bowthorpe
NORWICH
East Bradenham
West Bradenham
Shipdham
A1075
Brandon Parva
Barford
Bawburgh
Earlham
Holme Hale
Garvestone
Runhall
Thuxton
Barnham Broom
Coston
Great Melton
Colney
New Technopolis
Eaton
Pickenham
Reymerston
Wramplingham
Little Melton
Hethersett
Cringleford
Ashill
Cranworth
Southburgh
Kimberley
Carleton Forehoe
High Green
Keswick
Caistor St Edmund
Woodrising
Hardingham
Intwood
Saham Toney
Ovington
Carbrooke
Watton Green
Crownthorpe
Wymondham
Ketteringham
Dunston
Hingham
Hackford
Wicklewood
Swardeston
Threxton Hill
Watton
Scoulton
Scoulton Mere
Deopham
East Carleton
Mulbarton
Swainsthorpe
Morley St Botolph
Suton
Silfield
Bracon Ash
Little Cressingham
Griston
Little Ellingham
Deopham Green
Wreningham
Newton Flotman
Saxlingham Nethergate
Merton
Northacre
Rockland St Peter
Great Ellingham
Rainthorpe Hall
Caston
Ashwellthorpe
Fundenhall
Hapton
Flordon
Saxlingham Thorpe
Stow Bedon
Rockland All Saints
Spooner Row
Besthorpe
Attleborough
Tacolneston
Forncett St Mary
Tasburgh
Thompson
Hempnall
Danger Zone
Bunwell Street
Tharston
Stratton St Michael
Breckles
Shropham
Puddledock
Carleton Rode
Forncett End
Forncett St Peter
Long Stratton
Fritton
Morningthorpe
Great Hockham
North End
Old Buckenham
New Buckenham
Bunwell
Hargate
Aslacton
Wacton
Shelton
Hardwick
Eccles Road
Wilby
Cake Street
Great Moulton
Snetterton
Illington
Larling
Tibenham
71
North Green
Banham
Tivetshall St Margaret
Roman Road
Bush Green
Quidenham
Banham Zoo
Tivetshall St Mary
Croxton
Roudham
Kenninghall
Short Green
Winfarthing
Gissing
Pulham Market
Pulham St Mary
Thetford
Bridgham
East Harling
Kilverstone
Middle Harling
A140
Harleston
Priory
Shadwell
West Harling Heath
Brettenham
Shelfanger
Burston
Shimpling
Rushall
A1066
North Lopham
Fersfield
South Lopham
Dickleburgh
Needham
Ancient House Mus
Rushford
Garboldisham
Walcot Green
Thelveton
A1088
Gasthorpe
Smallworth
Bressingham
Roydon
Thorpe Abbotts
Brockdish
Weybread
A143
Knettishall Heath
Knettishall
Blo Norton
Live Steam Museum & Gardens
Diss
Scole
Billingford
Palgrave
Fen Street
Euston
Hopton
Thelnetham
Redgrave
Stuston
Windmill
Oakley
Hoxne
Barnham
Market Weston
Coney Weston
Hinderclay
Wortham
Brome
Brome Street
Cross Street
Wingfield
College
Fressingfield
Little Fakenham
Barningham
Botesdale
Thrandeston
Dove
Church
Rickinghall
Mellis
Heckfield Green
Chickering
A134
Yaxley
Priory
Denham
Honington
Sapiston
Hepworth
Wattisfield
Burgate
Eye
Stradbroke
Bardwell
Stanton
Little Green
Thornham Parva
Horham
Ixworth Thorpe
Troston
Cranmer Green
Gislingham
Braiseworth
Redlingfield
Athelington
Ampton
Great Livermere
Walsham le Willows
Thornham Magna
Occold
Four Ashes
Wickham Street
Stoke Ash
Fingal Street
Ixworth
Crowland
Finningham
Thorndon
Worlingworth
Langham
Westhorpe
Wickham Skeith
Thwaite
Rishangles
Bedingfield
Southolt
Timworth Green
Badwell Ash
Stowlangtoft
Hunston
Long Thurlow
Wyverstone Street
Wyverstone
Brockford Street
Tannington
Great Barton
Pakenham
Stanton Street
Great Ashfield
Bacton
Cotton
Wetheringsett
Bedfield
Mid Suffolk Light Railway Museum
Kenton
Saxtead Little Green
Earl's Green
Norton
Mendlesham
BURY ST EDMUNDS
Thurston
Ward Green
Monk Soham
Post Mill
Haughley Green
Aspall
Gipping
Tostock
Elmswell
Wetherup Street
Debenham
Earl Soham
Beyton Green
Beyton
Old Newton
Mendlesham Green
Ashfield
Blackthorpe
Woolpit
Wetherden
Haughley New Street
Haughley
Mickfield
A1120
Rushbrooke
Rougham
Middlewood Green
Rougham Green
Hessett
Drinkstone
Little Welnetham
Winston
Little Stonham
Stonham Aspal
Stowupland
Drinkstone Green
Harleston
Cretingham
Bradfield St George
Great Welnetham
60
Stowmarket
Forward Green
Earl Stonham
Stonham Barns Craft Centre
Pettaugh
Framsden
Rattlesden
Buxhall
Mus of East Anglian Life
Creeting St Mary
Helmingham Hall
Otley Hall
Bradfield Combust
Bradfield St Clare
Felsham
Poystreet Green
Great Finborough
Combs Ford
Gipping
Crowfield
Helmingham
Charsfield
High Street Green
Combs
Stanningfield
N O R F O L K
S U F F O L K

D
E
F
G
87
1
2
3
4
5
Salhouse
Panxworth
Fairhaven
Burgh St Margaret
Filby Broad
Bygone Village
Billockby
Filby
Roman Site
Caister-on-Sea
South Walsham
Upton
Upton Green
A1064
Caister Castle
Mautby
New Rackheath
Little Plumstead
Hemblington
Thrigby Hall Wildlife Gdns
West Caister
Great Plumstead
North Burlingham
Acle
Stokesby
Runham
Yarmouth
Thorpe End Garden Village
Thorpe St Andrew
Blofield
Lingwood
Damgate
A47
A149
Brundall
Beighton
Tunstall
Postwick
Strumpshaw
Moulton St Mary
THE BROADS
Halvergate Marshes
Halvergate
Greyfriar's Cloisters
Old Merchant's House & Row 111 House
Sea Life Centre
GREAT YARMOUTH
Pleasure Beach
Trowse Newton
Kirby Bedon
Surlingham
Buckenham
South Burlingham
Freethorpe
Berney Arms Sta.
Berney Arms Mill
Burgh Castle
Southtown
A146
Bramerton
Hassingham
Southwood
Wickhampton
Freethorpe Common
Roman Fort
Gorleston on Sea
Rockland St Mary
Cantley
Pettitts Animal Adventure Park
Limpenhoe
Framingham Pigot
Framingham Earl
Hellington
Claxton
Bradwell
Belton
A143
Hobland Hall
Poringland
Yelverton
Ashby St Mary
Hardley Street
Reedham
Alpington
Bergh Apton
Thurton
Langley Street
Norton Marshes
St Olaves Priory
Fritton
Fritton Lake
Hopton
Howe
Brooke
Chedgrave
Norton Subcourse
Lower Thurlton
Heckingham
Thurlton
Lound
Sisland
Loddon
Seething
Mundham
The Laurels
Hales
Hales Hall
Thorpe
Herringfleet
Somerleyton
Blundeston
Corton
A12
Kirstead Green
Raveningham
Haddiscoe
Pleasurewood Hills Theme Park
Maypole Green
Oulton
Lowestoft End
Lowestoft Ness
Kirby Cane
Toft Monks
Wheatacre
Camps Heath
East Point Pavilion
Woodton
Thwaite St Mary
Stockton
Aldeby
Burgh St Peter
LOWESTOFT
Topcroft
Hedenham
Ellingham
Kirby Row
Gillingham
Oulton Broad
Kirkley
Topcroft Street
Hempnall Green
Ditchingham
Broome
Geldeston
Beccles
Shipmeadow
Barnby
Pakefield
Great Green
Earsham
Mettingham
Barsham
Worlingham
North Cove
Transport Museum
Carlton Colville
Bungay
Ringsfield
Beccles Heliport
Mutford
Gisleham
Denton
The Otter Trust
Ilketshall St Andrew
Rushmere
Flixton
Ringsfield Corner
Ellough
Hulver Street
Henstead
Kessingland
Kessingland Beach
Suffolk Wildlife & Country Park
Ilketshall St Margaret
Stone Street
A145
Homersfield
St Margaret South Elmham
Sotterly
Benacre
Redenhall
St Michael South Elmham
Ilketshall St Lawrence
Redisham
Brampton Sta.
Shadingfield
St Cross South Elmham
Stone Street
West End
Mendham
All Saints South Elmham
Cox Common
Brampton
Wrentham
Covehithe
Frostenden
Stoven
Rumburgh
Clay Common
South Cove
St James South Elmham
A144
Spexhall
Westhall
Metfield
Uggeshall
Wissett
Broadway
Wangford
Mount Pleasant
Little Whittingham Green
Chediston
Holton
Reydon
A1095
Blackwater
Linstead Parva
Halesworth
Blyford
Southwold
Silverley's Green
Wenhaston
Blythburgh
Walberswick
Cratfield
Cookley
Huntingfield
Walpole
Blackheath
Thorington
Bramfield
Laxfield
Heveningham
Dunwich
Brundish Street
Ubbeston Green
Poys Street
Darsham Sta.
Brundish
Peasenhall
Sibton
Darsham
A1120
Westleton
Badingham
Yoxford
Middleton
Dunwich Heath (NT)
Dennington
Bruisyard
Theberton
East Bridge
Bruisyard Street
Vineyard & Winery
Kelsale
Saxtead Green
Brabling Green
Cransford
Rendham
Carlton
Leiston Abbey
Framlingham
Sweffling
Saxmundham
Sizewell
Great Glemham
Sternfield
Leiston
Coldfair Green
Knodishall
Parham
Farnham
Aldringham
Thorpe Ness
Kettleburgh
Glemham Hall
Friston
Thorpeness
The Meare
61
Hoo
Easton
Hacheston
Stratford St Andrew
Church Common
A1094
Easton Farm Park
Marlesford
Gromford
Snape
Moot Hall
Little Glemham
Campsey Ash
Blaxhall
Aldeburgh
Iken
Wickham Market

A
B
C
D
1
2
3
4
5
3.2 miles to 1 inch
0 2 4 6 8 10 miles
0 2 4 6 8 10 km
2 km to 1 cm
88
CAERNARFON
BAY
Cymyran Bay
Rhosneigr
A4080
Ty Newydd Burial Chamber
Burial Chamber
Cerrigceinwen
Llangris
Gawres
rclodiad y
ered Cairn
Bethel
Trefdraeth
Llyn Coron
Llangadwaladr
Aberffraw
Hermon
Malltraeth
Aberffraw Bay
Bodorgan
Malltraeth Sands
B4422
B4421
A4080
Newborough (Niwbwrch)
16
Newborough Warren
Malltraeth Bay
Llanddwyn Island
Llanddwyn Bay
Abermenai Point
The Bar
Foryd Bay
Dinas Dinlle
Llandwrog
Pontllyfni
Trwyn Maen Dylan
Aberdesach
Capeluchaf
Clynnog-fawr
Gyrn Goch
10
Bwlch Mawr
509
Gyrn Ddu
522
Trefor
A499
Trwyn y Gorlech
Yr Eifl
564
Llanaelhaearn
Pen-sarn
Llithfaen
B4417
6
Cefn-caer-Ferch
Carreg Ddu
Pistyll
Porth-Dinllaen
Pencaenewydd
St Cybi's Well
Morfa Nefyn
Nefyn
Llwyndyrys
Llangybi
Groesffordd
Edern
B4412
Garn Boduan
Fron
Y Ffôr
B4354
Llanarmon
Tan-y-graig
Rhos-fawr
Chwilog
Penarth Fawr Medieval Hall
Porth Ysgadan
Rhos-y-llan
Ceidio Fawr
Bodfuan
Llannor
Tudweiliog
7
Abererch
A497
Penychain
Efailnewydd
Denio
Dinas
14
Carn Fadryn
B4415
Penllech
Garnfadryn
371
A497
Rhyd-y-clafdy
Pwllheli
Porth Colmon
Porth Colmon
Llaniestyn
Carreg yr Imbill
Llangwnnadl
Penrhos
Sarn-Meyllteyrn
Penrhyn Mawr
Rhedyn
Y Gamlas
Porth Oer
Bryncroes
16
B4413
Llanbedrog
Ty-hen
Botwnnog
Nanhoron
A499
Methlem
Rhydlios
Llandegwning
Mynytho
Trwyn Llanbedrog
Mynydd Rhiw
305
Llangian
Capel Carmel
Rhoshirwaun
Llawr-y-dref
Abersoch
Braich Anelog
Rhiw
Plas-yn-Rhiw (NT)
Rhydolion
St Tudwal's Road
Anelog
Mynydd Anelog
191
Llanengan
Llanfaelrhys
Porth Neigwl or Hell's Mouth
Pwlldefaid
Aberdaron
Sarn Bach
Braich y Pwll
Aberdaron Bay
Bwlchtocyn
St Tudwal's Islands
Uwchmynydd
Ynys Gwylan-fawr
Trwyn yr Wylfa
Pen y Cil
Porth Ceiriad
Cilan Uchaf
Bardsey Sound (Swnt Enlli)
Trwyn Cilan
Bardsey Island (Ynys Enlli)
St. Mary's Abbey
LLEYN PENINSULA
GW
ANG
ISL

75
89
76
62
D
E
F
G
D
E
F
G
I
2
3
4
5
Menai Bridge
Bangor
Llanfairpwllgwyngyll
Llanddaniel Fab
Bryn Celli Ddu Burial Chamber
Plas Newydd (NT)
Bodowyr Burial Chamber
Brynsiencyn
Y Felinheli
Anglesey Sea Zoo
Menai Strait
Port Penrhyn
Penrhyn (NT)
Abergwyngregyn
Llandygai
Glanadda
Penrhos-garnedd
Tal-y-bont
Crymlyn
Aber Falls
Moel Wnion
580
Gorddinog
Garreg Fawr
Pandy
Moelfre
435
Henryd
Tal-y-fan
610
Ty'n-y-groes
Caerhun
Tal-y-cafn
Eglwysbach
Llanbedr-y-cennin
Tal-y-bont
Vale of Conwy
Dolgarrog
Pont Dolgarrog
Trefriw
Trefriw Woollen Mill
Llanrwst
Gwydir
Gwydir Uchaf Chapel
Llanddoged
Pentre-tafarn-y-fedw
Melin-y-coed
Oerfa
Oakland
Capel Garmon
Chambered Long
Rhydlanfair
Glan Conwy
Ysbyty Ifan
Rhos-y-mawr
Mwdwl Eithin
Llanllechid
Rachub
Bethesda
Tregarth
Gerlan
Braichmelyn
Glasinfryn
Tal-y-Cae
Waen-wen
Seion
Pentir
Rhiwlas
Llanddeiniolen
Penisa'r Waun
Saron
Bethel
Waterloo Port
Caernarfon
Segontium Roman Fort
Caeathro
Llanrug
Pont-rug
Brynrefail
Clwt-y-bont
Deiniolen
Fachwen
Cwm-y-glo
Dinorwig
Llanberis
Llanberis Lake Rly
Welsh Slate Mus
Dolbadarn
Llyn Padarn
Llyn Peris
Bontnewydd
Waunfawr
Welsh Highland Rly
Betws Garmon
Snowdon Mountain Rly
Nant Peris
Rhostryfan
Rhosgadfan
Moel Eilio
726
Salem
Dinas
Llanwnda
Groeslon
Carmel
Moel Tryfan
Mynydd Mawr
698
Llyn Cwellyn
Nantlle
Talysarn
Llanllyfni
Penygroes
Llyn Nantlle Uchaf
Y Garn
634
Rhyd-Ddu
Trum y Ddysgl
709
Craig Cwm Silyn
734
Ffridd Uchaf
Beddgelert Forest
Nebo
Nasareth
Garneddgoch
700
Pant-Glas
608
Beddgelert
Pass of Aberglaslyn
Moel Hebog
782
Pont Aberglaslyn
Nantmor
Cae Ddafydd
Croesor
Llanfihangel-y-pennant
Bryncir
Garndolbenmaen
Cennin
Glan-Dwyfach
Dolbenmaen
Golan
Moel-ddu
552
Llyn Cwmystradllyn
Penmorfa
Tremadog
Prenteg
Tan-lan
Garreg
Rhyd
Llanfrothen
Rhoslan
Pentrefelin
Gell
Llanystumdwy
Criccieth
Lloyd George Museum
Porthmadog
Moel-y-Gest
Morfa Bychan
Borth-y-Gest
Black Rock Sands
Harlech Point
Minffordd
Penrhyndeudraeth
Portmeirion Village
Talsarnau
Traeth Bach
Ynys
Eisingrug
Glyn-Cywarch
Morfa Harlech
Harlech
Llanfair
Llandanwg
Pen-sarn
Llanbedr
Pentre Gwynfryn
Morfa Dyffryn
Coed Ystumgwern
Llanenddwyn
Dyffryn Ardudwy
Dyffryn Burial Chamber
Llanddwywe
Tal-y-bont
Llanaber
Barmouth (Abermaw)
Panorama Walk
Caerdeon
Bontddu
Taicynhaeaf
Pen-y-bryn
Penmaenpool
Islawr-dref
Dolgellau
Cross Foxes Inn
Llanelltyd
Cymer Abbey
Nannau
Foel Offrwm
404
Precipice Walk
Bont Newydd
Torrent Walk
Brithdir
Rhydymain
Drws-y-nant
Llanfachreth
Ganllwyd
Cefndeuddwr
COED Y BRENIN
FOREST PARK
Moel Hafodowen
435
Rhobell Fawr
734
Moel Cors-y-garnedd
Dduallt
657
Dyrysgol
Craig-y-cae
Y Garn
629
Uwch-mynydd
Diffwys
750
Llyn Bodlyn
Moelfre
589
Y Llethr
754
Rhinog Fach
711
Rhinog Fawr
720
Llyn Hywel
Roman Steps
Llyn Cwm Bychan
Craig Ddrwg
Moel Ysgyfarnogod
623
Crawcwellt
Bronaber
Mynydd Bach
Moel y Feidiog
563
Mynydd Bryn-llech
SNOWDONIA
NATIONAL
PARK
Trawsfynydd
Llyn Trawsfynydd
Cwm Prysor
Tomen-y-mur Roman Fort
Gellilydan
Craig Gyfynys
Maentwrog
Vale of Ffestiniog
Ffestiniog
Cynfal Falls
Graig Wen
Moel Llyfnant
750
Arenig Fawr
854
Llyn Arenig-Fawr
Craig yr Hyrddod
Ffridd Trawsgoed
Arenig Fach
689
Carnedd Iago
538
Migneint
Bethania
Tanygrisiau
Ffestiniog Rly
Moelwyn Mawr
770
Moelwyn Bach
711
Blaenau Ffestiniog
Llechwedd Slate Caverns
Rhiwbryfdir
Glanaber Terrace
Moel Penamnen
Cnicht
689
Bwlch y Gorddinan (Crimera Pass)
Blaenau Dolwyddelan
Dolwyddelan
Pentre-bont
Y Ro Wen Gwydyr Forest
Ty Mawr (NT)
Pont-y-pant
Mynydd Cribau
GWYDYR FOREST PARK
Betws-y-coed
Fairy Glen
Carnedd Moel-siabod
872
Pen-y-Gwryd Hotel
Capel Curig
Pont Cyfyng
Llynnau Mymbyr
Glyn
Ty Hyll
Swallow Falls
Plas Gwynant
Llyn Gwynant
Llyn Dinas
Yr Aran
747
Snowdon (Yr Wyddfa)
1085
Llyn Llydaw Resr
898
Glaslyn
Pass of Llanberis
356
S N O W D O N I A
Glyder Fawr
999
Glyder Fach
994
Y Garn
946
Foel Goch
831
Elidyr Fawr
923
Mynydd Perfedd
812
Nant Ffrancon
Pont Pen-y-benglog
Llyn Ogwen
Carnedd Dafydd
1044
Carnedd Llywelyn
1064
Foel Grach
Garnedd Uchaf
926
Foel-Fras
942
Drosgl
758
Llwytmor
849
Drum
770
Pen Llithrig y-wrach
Llyn Cowlyd Reservoir
Llyn Eigiau Reservoir
Llyn Crafnant
Llyn Geirionydd
Llyn Dulyn Resr
C O N W Y
Pen y Bedw
Llyn Conwy
504
Penmachno
Machno
A5025
A545
A487
A4087
A5
A55
A4080
A4086
A4085
A499
A498
A497
A496
A470
A4212
A4086
A548
A494
A493
B4366
B4547
B4409
B4418
B4410
B4391
B4407
B4406
B4573
B4416
B5106
B5113
B5427

76
89
75
63
A
B
C
D
1
2
3
4
5
CONWY
GWYNEDD
SNOWDONIA
NATIONAL
PARK
GWYDYR
FOREST
PARK
COED Y BRENIN
FOREST PARK
Henryd
Moelfre
Gorddinog
Tal-y-fan
610
Ty'n-y-groes
Caerhun
Bodnant (NT)
Graig
glwysbach
Mynydd Llanelian
Mynydd Branar
Moel Gyffylog
Moelfre Uchaf
Betws-yn-Rhos
A548
Moelfre Isaf
Groesffordd Marli
Llannefydd
Plas-yn-Cefn
Trefnant
Llanfair Talhaiarn
Pentre Isaf
Gell
Mwdwl Eithin
Llangernyw
Hafodunos
Tre-pys-llygod
Pen y Mwdwl
Plasisaf
Henllan
Llansannan
Deunant
Rhos-y-mawn
Wenlli
Pandy Tudur
Tan-y-fron
Bylchau
Groes
Gwaynynog
A543
A544
B5382
B5384
B5428
Drum
770
Llwytmor
849
Foel-Fras
942
Drosgl
758
Garnedd Uchaf
926
Foel Grach
1064
Carnedd Dafydd
1044
Llanbedr-y-cennin
Tal-y-bont
Dolgarrog
Pont Dolgarrog
Vale of Conwy
Llyn Eigiau Reservoir
Pen Llithrig y-wrach
Llyn Cowlyd Reservoir
Trefriw
Trefriw Woollen Mill
A470
Llanddoged
A548
Pentre-tafarn-y-fedw
Llanrwst
Gwydir
Melin-y-coed
Oerfa
424
Gwytherin
Nantglyn
Pant-pastynog
378
Sportsman's Arms
Gorsedd Bran
518
Pentre Saron
Bryn Trillyn
466
Aled Isaf Resr
Llyn Brenig
Pont Pen-y-benglog
314
Glyder Fach
994
Capel Curig
Pont Cyfyng
A5
Glyn
Ty-Hyll
Swallow Falls
Gwydir Uchaf Chapel
Oaklands
Cefn rhudd
468
Moel Seisiog
Moel Llyn
Llyn Aled
Mynydd Hiraethog
Nilig
519
A4086
Pen-y-Gwryd Hotel
Carnedd Moel-siabod
872
Betws-y-coed
Mynydd Cribau
Pont-y-pant
Capel Garmon
Nebo
Chambered Long Cairn
Llyn Alwen
A543
532
Llyn Brenig Visitor Centre
Pentre-llyn-cymmer
Clocaenog Forest
Craig Bron-banog
501
Dolwyddelan
A498
Blaenau Dolwyddelan
Dolwyddelan
Pentre-bont
Ty Mawr (NT)
Fairy Glen
Rhydlanfair
Glan Conwy
Pentrefoelas
Hafod-Dinbych
Alwen Reservoir
475
Pont yr Alwen
Cefn-brith
Y Ro Wen
Gwydyr Forest
594
Penmachno
371
Rhydlydan
Glasfryn
Llanfihangel Glyn Myfyr
Bwlch y Gorddinan (Crimea Pass)
385
Moel Penamnen
Llechwedd Slate Caverns
Ysbyty Ifan
Garn Prys
534
447
Cerrigydrudion
B5105
Mwdwl-eithin
470
Bettws Gwerfil Goch
Rhiwbryfdir
Blaenau Ffestiniog
Glanaber Terrace
Pen y Bedw
504
Ty-Mawr
A470
Moelwyn Mawr
770
Tanygrisiau
658
661
Llyn Conwy
Gylchedd
628
669
Carnedd y Filiast
Cadair Benllyn
Gellioedd
Llangwm
Ty-nant
Maerdy
A496
Bethania
Migneint
B4407
B4501
Four Crosses
Moelwyn Bach
711
Ffestiniog
B4391
Arenig Fach
689
Capel Celyn
Foel Goch
611
Wenallt
Glan-yr-afon
Moel Emoel
Glan-yr-afon
A494
Vale of Ffestiniog
Maentwrog
Cynfal Falls
Carnedd Iago
538
A4212
Llyn Celyn
Ciltalgarth
Fron-goch
Bethel
Gellilydan
Craig Gyfynys
Graig Wen
Tomen-y-mur Roman Fort
Craig yr Hyrddod
Llidiardau
Sarnau
Cefn-ddwysarn
Mynydd Mynyllod
Llyn Trawsfynydd
Llyn Arenig-Fawr
Arenig Fawr
854
Rhyd-uchaf
A4212
Rhiwlas
Llandderfel
Crogen
Trawsfynydd
A4212
Cwm Prysor
552
Moel Llyfnant
750
Gwastadros
Bala
Llanfor
B4401
Pale
Moel y farnogo
623
667
Llanycil
Rhos-y-gwaliau
Cefn Coch
Ffridd Trawsgoed
Parc
Llyn Tegid (Bala Lake)
B4391
Rhiwaedog-is-afon
Foel Cwm-Sian-Llwyd
648
Dinam
A470
Bronaber
Mynydd Bach
Moel y Feidiog
563
Mynydd Bryn-llech
Llangower
B4403
Hirnant Pass
Pont Cwm Pydew
Milltir Gerrig
425
Llanuwchllyn
Pentre-piod
Crawcwellt
Bala Lake Rly.
Rhyd-wen
Foel Figenau
Eirth
720
Rhinog Fawr
Rhinog Fach
711
Dyrysgol
Pont Rhyd-sarn
Y Bryn
Foel y Geifr
626
Cyrniau Nod
666
Pencraig
Y Llethr
754
Cefndeuddwr
Moel Hafodowen
435
Dduallt
657
Rhobell Fawr
734
Pant Gwyn
Talardd
Ty-nant
Cwm Cynllwyd
Pennant Melangell
Diffwys
750
Ganllwyd
Moel Cors-y-garnedd
Foel Ddu
465
Roman Road
Aran Benllyn
884
Cwm Croes
Rhiwargor
Alltforgan
Craig-y-cae
Y Garn
629
Llanfachreth
A494
Drws-y-nant
Creiglyn Dyfi
Foel Rhudd
Bwlch y groes
Cedig
Uwch-mynydd
Precipice Walk
Foel Offrwm
404
Nannau
Bont Newydd
Rhydymain
Aran Fawddwy
905
Dyrysgol
731
Ty-uchaf
B4393
Lake Vyrnwy
Taicynhaeaf
Llanelltyd
Cymer Abbey
Torrent Walk
Brithdir
Craig y Ffynnon
779
Llanymawddwy
Llanwddyn
Bontddu
Pen-y-bryn
A496
A470
Penmaenpool
Dolgellau
A470
Bwlch yr Oerddrws
359
Bwlch y Fign
655
Benddin
Aber Cywarch
Pen y Ffridd Gownwy
Penisarcwn
497
Dyfnant Forest
Abergwynant
A493
Islawr-dref
Cross Foxes Inn
A470
Llwydiarth

77
91
78
64
FLINTSHIRE
DENBIGHSHIRE
WREXHAM
CHESHIRE
SHROPSHIRE
CLWYDIAN RANGE
VALE OF CLWYD
BERWYN
D
E
F
G
I
2
3
4
5
Tremeirchion
Caerwys
Babell
Brynford
Bedol
Flint (Y Fflint)
Flint (ruins)
White Sands
Burton
Puddington
Ledsham
Capenhurst
Little Stanney
Thornton-le-Moors
Graig
Afonwen
Ysceifiog
Pentre Halkyn
Lixwm
Walwen
Halkyn
Halkyn Mountain
Flint Mountain
Connah's Quay
Shotwick
Saughall
Backford
Mollington
Bodfari
Moel y Parc
Ddol
Nannerch
Rhes-y-cae
Northop
Northop Hall
Rhosesmor
Wepre
Shotton
Garden City
Queensferry
Sealand
Blacon
Upton
Hoole
Friary (ruins)
Moel Llys-y-coed
Rhydymwyn
Soughton
Ewloe
Ewloe (ruins)
Aston
Mancot Royal
Sandycroft
Hawarden
CHESTER
Saltney
Waen
Llangwyfan
Cilcain
Gwernaffield
Mold (Yr Wyddgrug)
Buckley (Bwcle)
Drury
Llandyrnog
Ffordd-las
Moel Famau
Loggerheads
Cadole
Prenbrigog
Llong
Bretton
Broughton
Eccleston
Llanrhaeadr
Llangynhafal
Gwernymynydd
Padeswood
Penyffordd
Lower Kinnerton
Dodleston
Eaton Hall
Saighton
Rowton Heath 1645
Llanynys
Tafarn-y-Gelyn
Moel Findeg
Maeshafn
Nercwys
Rhos-y-brwyner
Cuckoo's Nest
Bruera
Rhewl
Hirwaen
Llanferres
Pontblyddyn
Plas Teg
Llanbedr-Dyffryn-Clwyd
Leeswood
Pontybodkin
Hope
Burton Green
Pulford
Aldford
Ruthin (Rhuthun)
Ruthin Craft Centre
Eryrys
Treuddyn
Waun-y-Llyn
Caergwrle
Rossett
Lavister
Trevalyn
Bontuchel
Llanfwrog
Llanfair Dyffryn Clwyd
Llanarmon-yn-Ial
Graianrhyd
Pantyffordd
Llanfynydd
Ffrith
Cefn-y-bedd
Llay
Marford
Churton
Efenechtyd
Llyn Gweryd
Llyn Cyfynwy
Rhydtalog
Gelli Gynan
Summerhill
Gresford
Farndon
Holt
Crewe
Clocaenog
Clawdd-newydd
Graig-fechan
Moel y Waun
Bwlchgwyn
Brymbo
Moss
Brynteg
Gwersyllt
Borras Head
Llan-y-pwll
Pentre-celyn
Llandegla
Moel Garegog
Minera
Southsea
Rhos-ddu
Hugmore
Ridleywood
Cefn Coch
Derwen
Nant y Garth Pass
Pen-y-stryt
Esclusham Mountain
Coedpoeth
New Broughton
Rhosnesni
WREXHAM (Wrecsam)
Wrexham Industrial Estate
Llanelidan
Mynydd Cricor
Cyrn-y-Brain
Rhos-berse
Bersham
Rhostyllen
Pentre Maelor
Shocklach
Ty-mawr
Pentre-bwlch
World's End
Talwrn
Erddig Hall (NT)
Marchwiel
Bowling Bank
Gwyddelwern
Bryneglwys
Moel y Gamelin
Maesyrychen Mt
Horseshoe Pass
Eglwyseg Mountain
Rhosllanerchrugog
Ruabon Mountain
Stryt-issa
Johnstown
Stryt-yr-hwch
Cross Lanes
Llantysilio Mountain
Moel Morfydd
Pentredwr
Eliseg's Pillar
Valle Crucis Abbey (ruins)
Pant
Gyfelia
Eyton
Bangor-is-y-coed
Bangor-on-Dee
Caer Drewyn
Carrog
Rhewl
Llantysilio
Llangollen Rly
Castell Dinas Bran (ruins)
Penycae
Acrefair
Ruabon
Wat's Dyke
Threapwood
Haughton Mill
Tyn-y-cefn
Corwen
Glyndyfrdwy
Garth
Trevor
Cefn-mawr
Wynnstay Park
Overton
Isaf
Cynwyd
Llangollen
Froncysyllte
Newbridge
Pentre
Erbistock
Lightwood Green
Horseman's Green
Moel Fferna
Moel yr Henfaes
Y Foel
Shellbrook Hill
Sodylt Bank
Trench
Penley
Pontfadog
Halton
Knolton
Park Lane
Plas Nantyr
Glyn Ceiriog
Chirk (NT)
Chirk
Street Dinas
Dudleston Heath
Pen-plaenau
Bryn Du
Dolywern
Llwynmawr
Bronygarth
Gledrid
Rhyn
Ifton Heath
Cadair Bronwen
Pandy
Tyn-y-Rhos
Preesgweene
St Martin's
Elson
The Grange
Welshampton
Foel Wen
Tregeiriog
Llechrydau
Pen y Gwely
Craignant
Weston Rhyn
Rhewl
New Marton
Ellesmere
Colemere
Llanarmon Dyffryn Ceiriog
Selattyn
Gobowen
Perthy
Moel Sych
Cadair Berwyn
Mynydd Tarw
Cefn Hir-fynydd
Foel Rhiwlas
Rhiwlas
Hengoed
Old Oswestry Hill Fort
Hindford
Welsh Frankton
Tetchill
Lee
White Mere
Garneddwen
Tyn-y-ffridd
Llangadwaladr
Llawnt
Brogyntyn
Whittington
Hordley
Crose Mere
Rhydycroesau
Babbinswood
Kenwick
Tan-y-pistyll
Mynydd Mawr
Gyrn Moelfre
Lledrod
Middleton
Moel Hen-fache
Llyn Moelfre
Oswestry
Lower Hordley
Cockshutt
Y Clogydd
Craig Rhiwarth
Glan-hafon
Tai-bach
Moelfre
Croesau Bach
Transport Museum
Rednal
Bagley
Llansilin
Morda
Queen's Head
Haughton
Cefn-coch
Llanrhaeadr-ym-Mochnant
Trefonen
Ball
Grimpo
Petton
Llangynog
Treflach
Maesbury Marsh
West Felton
Weston Lullingfields
Pentre
Penybontfawr
Nantmawr
Llynclys
Morton
Eardiston
Woolston
Weirbrook
Pentrefelin
Llangedwyn
Stanwardine in the Fields
Penygarnedd
Bwlch-y-ddar
Pen-y-bont
Porth-y-waen
Llanyblodwel
Crickheath
Knockin
Baschurch
Montgomery Canal
Pant
Kinnerley
Ruyton-XI-Towns
Prescott
Aber-Naint
Llanfechain
Llansantffraid-ym-Mechain
Llanymynech
Maesbrook
Dovaston
Milford
Little Ness
Walford
Llandysilio
Crosslanes
Kinton
Nesscliffe
Yeaton
Tycrwyn
Llanfyllin
Bwlch-y-cibau
Four Crosses
Domgay
Edgerley
Wilcott
Great Ness
Grafton
Llanfihangel-yng-Ngwynfa
Godor
Waen-fach
Llandrinio
Melverley Green
Melverley
Pentre
Felton Butler
Ensdon
Sarnau
Arddlin
Shrawardine
Forton
POWYS
A5026
A5119
A548
A55
A494
A541
A5104
A549
A550
A5118
A483
A525
A542
A5152
A534
A528
A539
A5
A495
A4080
A490
A5116
A41
A5268
M56
M53
A543
B5122
B5123
B5125
B5129
B5101
B5102
B5373
B5445
B5130
B5430
B5431
B5429
B5437
B5426
B5605
B5069
B5070
B5068
B5009
B4500
B4579
B4580
B4396
B4391
B4393
B4398
B4397
B5401
B4401

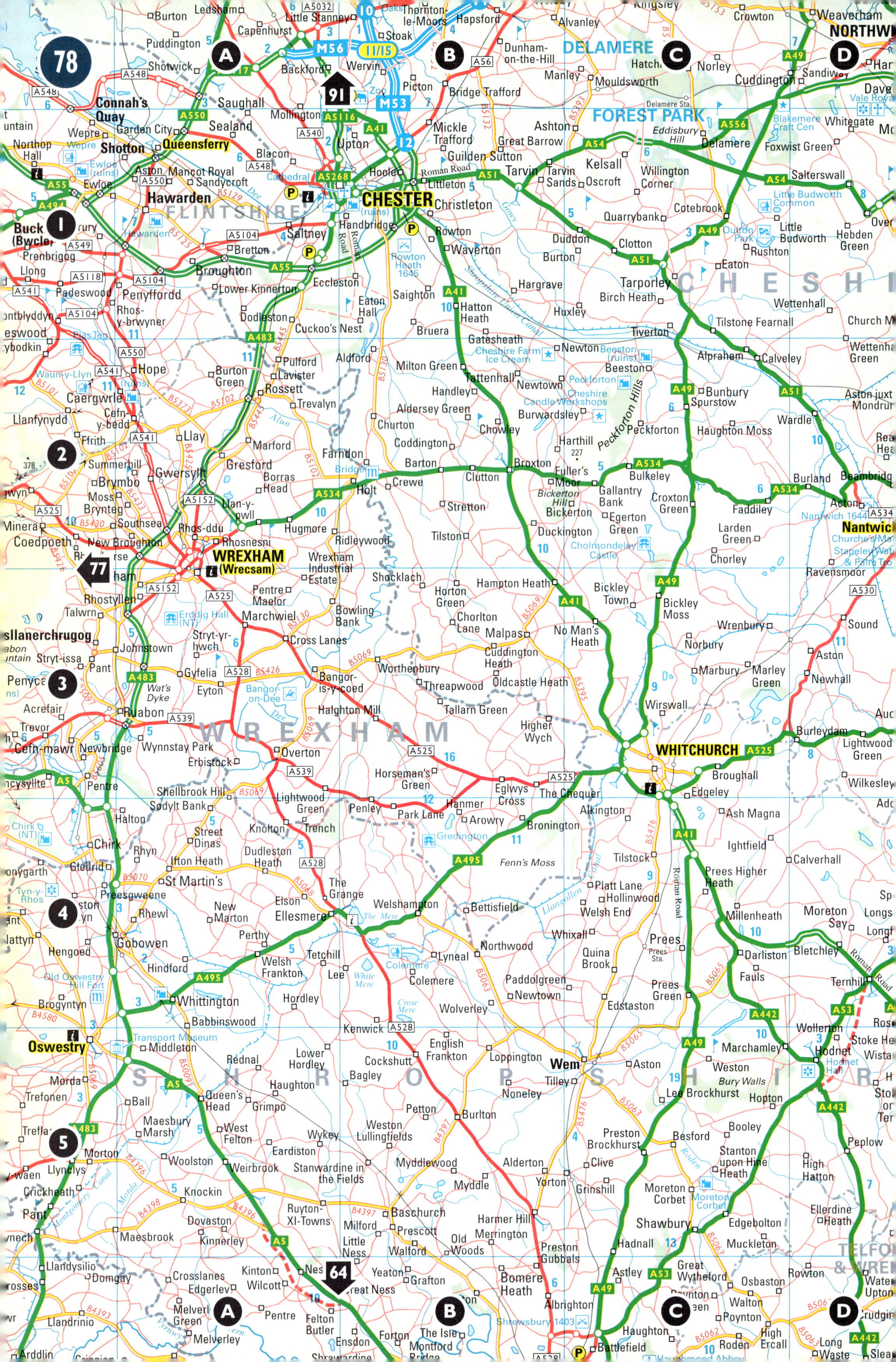

Burton
Ledsham
Little Stanney
Thornton-le-Moors
Hapsford
Alvanley
Kingsley
Crowton
Weaverham
NORTHWICH
Puddington
Capenhurst
Stoak
Dunham-on-the-Hill
DELAMERE
Hatchmere
Norley
Cuddington
Sandiway
Shotwick
Backford
Wervin
Picton
Bridge Trafford
Manley
Mouldsworth
Delamere Sta.
Connah's Quay
Saughall
Mollington
Mickle Trafford
Ashton
FOREST PARK
Eddisbury Hill
Delamere
Blakemere Craft Cen
Whitegate
Vale Royal
Wepre
Garden City
Sealand
Upton
Great Barrow
Foxwist Green
Northop Hall
Shotton
Queensferry
Blacon
Guilden Sutton
Tarvin
Kelsall
Willington Corner
Salterswall
Ewloe
Aston
Mancot Royal
Sandycroft
Cathedral
Hoole
Littleton
Tarvin Sands
Oscroft
Little Budworth Common
Hawarden
FLINTSHIRE
CHESTER
Christleton
Quarrybank
Cotebrook
Buckley (Bwcle)
Saltney
Handbridge
Rowton
Little Budworth
Oulton Park
Hebden Green
Prenbrigog
Bretton
Waverton
Duddon
Clotton
Rushton
Llong
Broughton
Rowton Heath 1645
Burton
Eaton
Padeswood
Penyffordd
Lower Kinnerton
Eccleston
Hargrave
Tarporley
Birch Heath
CHESHIRE
Wettenhall
Rhos-y-brwyner
Eaton Hall
Saighton
Hatton Heath
Huxley
Tilstone Fearnall
Church Minshull
Dodleston
Cuckoo's Nest
Bruera
Tiverton
Wettenhall Green
Gatesheath
Cheshire Farm Ice Cream
Newton
Beeston (ruins)
Beeston
Alpraham
Calveley
Hope
Pulford
Lavister
Aldford
Milton Green
Tattenhall
Newtown
Peckforton Cheshire Candle Workshops
Burton Green
Rossett
Bunbury
Spurstow
Caergwrle
Trevalyn
Handley
Aston juxta Mondrum
Llanfynydd
Cefn-y-bedd
Aldersey Green
Burwardsley
Peckforton Hills
Peckforton
Wardle
Haughton Moss
Ffrith
Churton
Chowley
Harthill
Llay
Marford
Coddington
Farndon
Summerhill
Gresford
Barton
Broxton
Fuller's Moor
Bulkeley
Burland
Brymbo
Gwersyllt
Borras Head
Holt
Crewe
Clutton
Bickerton Hill
Gallantry Bank
Croxton Green
Faddiley
Moss
Brynteg
Llan-y-pwll
Stretton
Bickerton
Egerton Green
Acton
Nantwich 1644
Minera
Southsea
Rhos-ddu
Hugmore
Larden Green
Coedpoeth
New Broughton
Rhosnesni
Ridleyway
Tilston
Duckington
Cholmondeley Castle
Chorley
WREXHAM (Wrecsam)
Wrexham Industrial Estate
Shocklach
Hampton Heath
Bickley Town
Ravensmoor
Rhostyllen
Pentre Maelor
Horton Green
Bickley Moss
Talwrn
Erddig Hall (NT)
Marchwiel
Bowling Bank
Chorlton Lane
Malpas
No Man's Heath
Wrenbury
Sound
Llanerchrugog
Stryt-yr-hwch
Cross Lanes
Cuddington Heath
Norbury
Stryt-issa
Johnstown
Pant
Worthenbury
Aston
Gyfelia
Bangor-is-y-coed
Marbury
Marley Green
Newhall
Wat's Dyke
Eyton
Bangor-on-Dee
Threapwood
Oldcastle Heath
Acrefair
Ruabon
Halghton Mill
Tallarn Green
Wirswall
Trevor
WREXHAM
Higher Wych
Burleydam
Cefn-mawr
Newbridge
Wynnstay Park
Overton
WHITCHURCH
Lightwood Green
Erbistock
Horseman's Green
Broughall
Wilkesley
Shellbrook Hill
Lightwood Green
Eglwys Cross
The Chequer
Edgeley
Pentre
Sodylt Bank
Penley
Hanmer
Park Lane
Arowry
Alkington
Ash Magna
Halton
Street Dinas
Knolton
Trench
Gredington
Bronington
Ightfield
Chirk
Rhyn
Ifton Heath
Dudleston Heath
Fenn's Moss
Tilstock
Calverhall
Gledrid
St Martin's
The Grange
Prees Higher Heath
Preesgweene
Elson
Welshampton
Platt Lane
Hollinwood
Tyn-y-Rhos
Bettisfield
Welsh End
Millenheath
Moreton Say
Rhewl
New Marton
Ellesmere
The Mere
Whixall
Prees
Hengoed
Gobowen
Perthy
Tetchill
Northwood
Quina Brook
Darliston
Bletchley
Hindford
Welsh Frankton
Lee
Lyneal
Colemere
Paddolgreen
Fauls
Old Oswestry Hill Fort
Whittington
Hordley
Newtown
Prees Green
Ternhill
Brogyntyn
Babbinswood
Cross Mere
Wolverley
Edstaston
Oswestry
Transport Museum
Middleton
Kenwick
English Frankton
Loppington
Wem
Aston
Wollerton
Hodnet
Stoke Heath
Rednal
Lower Hordley
Cockshutt
Bagley
Tilley
Marchamley
Weston
Bury Walls
Morda
Trefonen
Queen's Head
Haughton
Noneley
Lee Brockhurst
Hopton
Ball
Grimpo
Petton
Burlton
SHROPSHIRE
Maesbury Marsh
West Felton
Weston Lullingfields
Wykey
Preston Brockhurst
Booley
Peplow
Trefla
Morton
Eardiston
Clive
Stanton upon Hine Heath
Llynclys
Woolston
Weirbrook
Stanwardine in the Fields
Myddlewood
Alderton
Yorton
Grinshill
High Hatton
Crickheath
Knockin
Myddle
Moreton Corbet
Ellerdine Heath
Pant
Dovaston
Ruyton-XI-Towns
Baschurch
Harmer Hill
Shawbury
Edgebolton
Maesbrook
Kinnerley
Milford
Prescott
Merrington
Old Woods
Hadnall
Muckleton
Little Ness
Walford
Preston Gubbals
Llandysilio
Domgay
Crosslanes
Kinton
Nesscliffe
Great Ness
Yeaton
Grafton
Bomere Heath
Astley
Great Wytheford
Osbaston
Rowton
Edgerley
Wilcott
Albrighton
Walton
Poynton
Upton
Melverley Green
Pentre
Felton Butler
Shrewsbury 1403
Haughton
High Ercall
Crudgington
Llandrinio
Melverley
Ensdon
Forton
The Isle
Montford Bridge
Battlefield
Roden
Long Waste
Arddlin
Shrawardine
TELFORD & WREKIN
A B C D
1 2 3 4 5

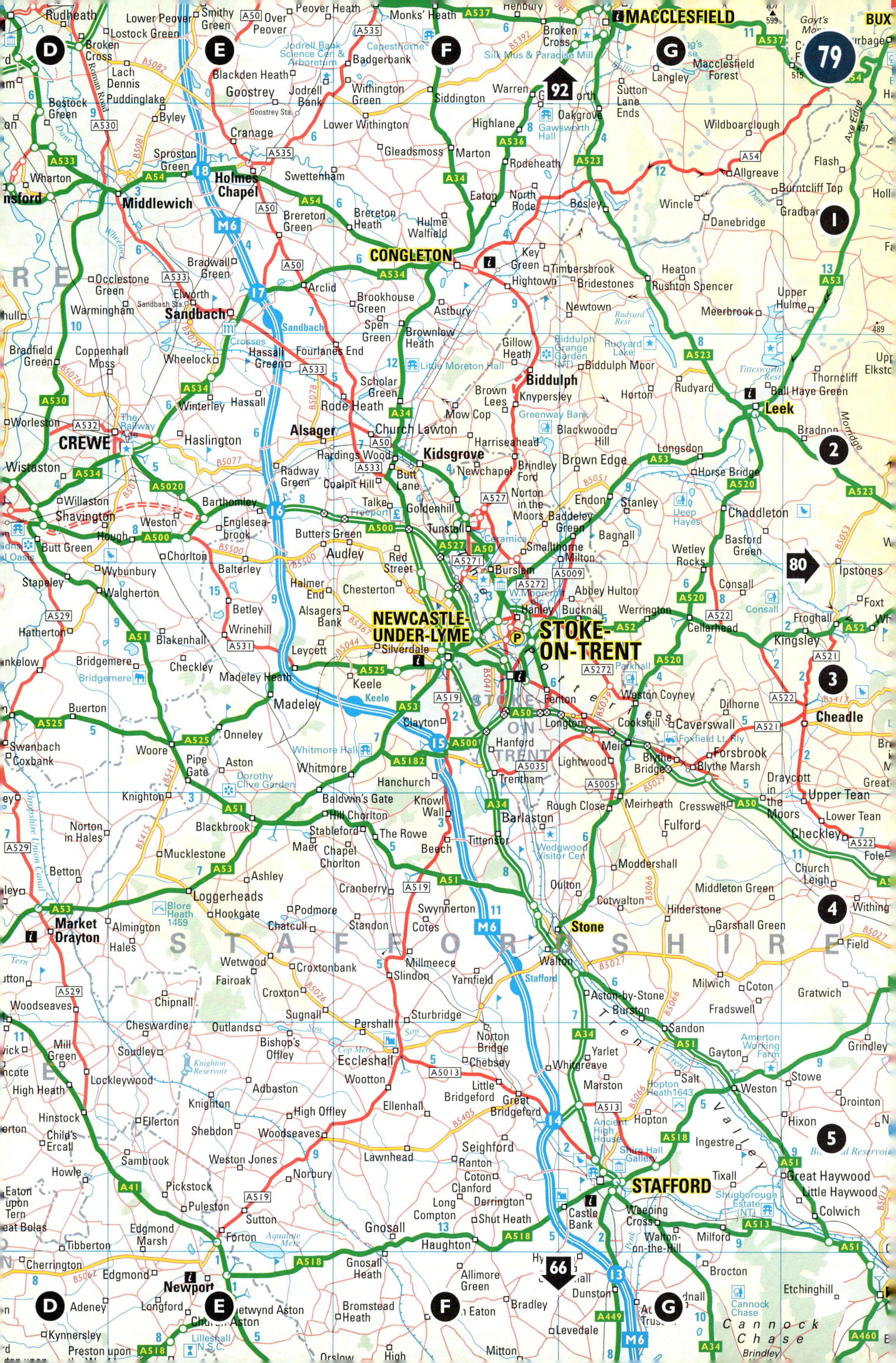
79
80
92
66
D
E
F
G
I
2
3
4
5
MACCLESFIELD
Macclesfield Forest
Rudheath
Lower Peover
Smithy Green
Over Peover
Peover Heath
Monks' Heath
Henbury
Broken Cross
Lostock Green
Lach Dennis
Jodrell Bank Science Cen & Arboretum
Capesthorne
Badgerbank
Silk Mus & Paradise Mill
Blackden Heath
Goostrey
Jodrell Bank
Withington Green
Siddington
Warren
Sutton Lane Ends
Langley
Bostock Green
Puddinglake
Byley
Cranage
Lower Withington
Highlane
Oakgrove
Gawsworth Hall
Wildboarclough
Wharton
Sproston Green
Holmes Chapel
Swettenham
Gleadsmoss
Marton
Rodeheath
Allgreave
Flash
Burntcliff Top
Middlewich
Brereton Green
Brereton Heath
Eaton
North Rode
Bosley
Wincle
Gradbach
Danebridge
Hulme Walfield
Bradwall Green
CONGLETON
Key Green
Timbersbrook
Hightown
Bridestones
Heaton
Rushton Spencer
Upper Hulme
Occlestone Green
Elworth
Arclid
Brookhouse Green
Astbury
Newtown
Meerbrook
Warmingham
Sandbach
Spen Green
Brownlow Heath
Gillow Heath
Biddulph Grange Garden
Rudyard Lake
Crosses
Hassall Green
Fourlanes End
Little Moreton Hall
Biddulph Moor
Bradfield Green
Coppenhall Moss
Wheelock
Scholar Green
Biddulph
Knypersley
Brown Lees
Horton
Rudyard
Tittesworth Resr
Thorncliff
Ball Haye Green
Winterley
Hassall
Rode Heath
Mow Cop
Greenway Bank
Leek
Worleston
The Railway Age
Alsager
Church Lawton
Blackwood Hill
Bradnop
CREWE
Haslington
Harriseahead
Kidsgrove
Hardings Wood
Newchapel
Longsdon
Brown Edge
Horse Bridge
Wistaston
Radway Green
Butt Lane
Brindley Ford
Coalpit Hill
Willaston
Shavington
Barthomley
Talke
Goldenhill
Norton in the Moors
Endon
Stanley
Deep Hayes
Cheddleton
Weston
Englesea-brook
Freeport
Tunstall
Baddeley Green
Bagnall
Basford Green
Hough
Butters Green
Ceramica
Smallthorne
Wetley Rocks
Butt Green
Chorlton
Audley
Red Street
Burslem
Milton
Ipstones
Stapeley
Wybunbury
Balterley
Halmer End
Chesterton
Abbey Hulton
Consall
Walgherton
Betley
W. Moorcroft
Bucknall
Werrington
Foxt
Alsagers Bank
Hanley
Cellarhead
Froghall
Hatherton
Wrinehill
NEWCASTLE-UNDER-LYME
STOKE-ON-TRENT
Kingsley
Blakenhall
Leycett
Silverdale
Bridgemere
Checkley
Madeley Heath
Keele
Parkhall
Weston Coyney
Dilhorne
Fenton
Cookshill
Caverswall
Cheadle
Buerton
Madeley
Clayton
Longton
Foxfield Lt. Rly
Forsbrook
Swanbach
Coxbank
Woore
Onneley
Hanford
Meir
Blythe Bridge
Blythe Marsh
Pipe Gate
Aston
Whitmore Hall
Whitmore
Lightwood
Draycott in the Moors
Dorothy Clive Garden
Trentham
Upper Tean
Knighton
Hanchurch
Baldwin's Gate
Knowl Wall
Rough Close
Meirheath
Cresswell
Lower Tean
Norton in Hales
Blackbrook
Hill Chorlton
Barlaston
Fulford
Checkley
Stableford
The Rowe
Maer
Chapel Chorlton
Beech
Tittensor
Wedgwood Visitor Cen
Church Leigh
Mucklestone
Moddershall
Betton
Ashley
Cranberry
Oulton
Middleton Green
Loggerheads
Blore Heath 1459
Hookgate
Cotwalton
Hilderstone
Withington
Podmore
Swynnerton
Garshall Green
Market Drayton
Almington
Hales
Chatcull
Standon
Cotes
Stone
S T A F F O R D S H I R E
Field
Wetwood
Millmeece
Walton
Slindon
Fairoak
Croxtonbank
Yarnfield
Stafford
Milwich
Coton
Croxton
Aston-by-Stone
Gratwich
Woodseaves
Chipnall
Sugnall
Sturbridge
Burston
Fradswell
Cheswardine
Outlands
Pershall
Sandon
Bishop's Offley
Norton Bridge
Amerton Working Farm
Grindley
Mill Green
Soudley
Cop Mere
Eccleshall
Chebsey
Yarlet
Gayton
Lockleywood
Knighton Reservoir
Wootton
Whitgreave
Stowe
High Heath
Adbaston
Little Bridgeford
Marston
Salt
Weston
Drointon
Knighton
Great Bridgeford
Hopton Heath 1643
Hinstock
Ellerton
High Offley
Ellenhall
Hixon
Child's Ercall
Shebdon
Woodseaves
Seighford
Hopton
Ingestre
Sambrook
Weston Jones
Lawnhead
Ranton
Ancient High House
Shire Hall Gallery
Howle
Norbury
Coton Clanford
Tixall
Great Haywood
Little Haywood
Pickstock
STAFFORD
Shugborough Estate (NT)
Puleston
Long Compton
Derrington
Eaton upon Tern
Weeping Cross
Colwich
Sutton
Gnosall
Shut Heath
Castle Bank
Edgmond Marsh
Forton
Aqualate Mere
Haughton
Walton-on-the-Hill
Milford
Tibberton
Gnosall Heath
Cherrington
Edgmond
Newport
Allimore Green
Dunston
Brocton
Etchinghill
Adeney
Longford
Church Aston
Chetwynd Aston
Bromstead Heath
Bradley
Cannock Chase
Kynnersley
Lilleshall N.S.C.
Levedale
Preston upon
Orslow
High
Mitton
Brindley
Trent
Trent Valley
Potteries
Sandbach Sta.
Goostrey Sta.
Wheelock
Dane
Sow
Penk
Shropshire Union Canal
A537
A50
A535
A34
A536
A523
A54
A530
A533
A532
A534
A5020
A500
A529
A51
A531
A525
A53
A527
A5271
A5272
A5009
A520
A522
A52
A521
A5005
A5035
A519
A5182
A5013
A513
A518
A41
A449
A460
M6
B5082
B5081
B5079
B5078
B5077
B5076
B5071
B5500
B5044
B5367
B5041
B5039
B5029
B5051
B5053
B5417
B5027
B5066
B5026
B5405
B5062
B5415
B5392
Sandbach Services
Keele Services
Stafford Services
18
17
16
15
14
13
12
11
10
9
8
7
6
5
4
3
2
1

80
93
79
66
A
B
C
D
1
2
3
4
5
CHESHIRE
STAFFORDSHIRE
PEAK
DISTRICT
NATIONAL
PARK
MACCLESFIELD
BUXTON
Bakewell
Leek
Biddulph
STOKE-ON-TRENT
Cheadle
Ashbourne
Uttoxeter
Stone
STAFFORD
BURTON UPON TRENT
Rugeley
Henbury
Broken Cross
Warren
Gawsworth
Oakgrove
Highlane
Marton
Rodeheath
Eaton
North Rode
Bosley
Key Green
Timbersbrook
Hightown
Bridestones
Newtown
Gillow Heath
Biddulph Grange Garden (NT)
Biddulph Moor
Rudyard Lake
Rudyard
Horton
Brown Lees
Knypersley
Greenway Bank
Blackwood Hill
Brown Edge
Newchapel
Brindley Ford
Norton in the Moors
Baddeley Green
Endon
Stanley
Bagnall
Milton
Burslem
Hanley
Bucknall
Abbey Hulton
Werrington
Cellarhead
Langley
Macclesfield Forest
Sutton Lane Ends
Wildboarclough
Allgreave
Wincle
Danebridge
Heaton
Rushton Spencer
Meerbrook
Upper Hulme
Tittesworth Resr
Longsdon
Horse Bridge
Cheddleton
Deep Hayes
Wetley Rocks
Basford Green
Consall
Goyt's Moss
Cat and Fiddle Inn
Burbage
Harpur Hill
Pavilion Gardens
Micrarium
Flash
Burntcliff Top
Gradbach
Axe Edge
Brand Side
Hollinsclough
Longnor
Fawfieldhead
Newtown
Upper Elkstone
Thorncliff
Ball Haye Green
Bradnop
Morridge
Warslow
Butterton
Onecote
Thor's Cave
Grindon
Wetton
Alstonefield
Ecton
Hulme End
Brund
Sheen
Hartington
Pilsbury
Crowdecote
Earl Sterndale
King Sterndale
Wormhill
Miller's Dale
Blackwell
Taddington
Chelmorton
Flagg
Little Longstone
Great Longstone
Ashford in the Water
Rowland
Sheldon
Monyash
Over Haddon
Youlgreave
Alport
Middleton
Arbor Low Stone Circle & Gibb Hill Barrow
Nine Ladies Stone Circle
Elton
Winster
Heathcote
Biggin
Pikehall
Market House (NT)
Grangemill
Aldwark
Longcliffe
Alsop en le Dale
Ballidon
Brassington
Parwich
Carsington
Bradbourne
Tissington
Fenny Bentley
Kniveton
Ilam
Thorpe
Ilam Park (NT)
Blore
Dove Dale
Waterfall
Waterhouses
Winkhill
Calton
Cauldon
Ipstones
Foxt
Froghall
Whiston
Kingsley
Near Cotton
Weaver Hills
Ramshorn
Stanton
Mayfield
Hanging Bridge
Swinscoe
Mapleton
Atlow
Hulland
Bradley
Clifton
Osmaston
Edlaston
Wyaston
Commonside
Shirley
Ednaston
Snelston
Ellastone
Norbury
Roston
Yeaveley
Rodsley
Oakamoor
Farley
Alton
Alton Towers Leisure Park
Wootton
Bradley in the Moors
Greatgate
Croxden Abbey
Croxden
Denstone
Rocester
Great Cubley
Little Cubley
Alkmonton
Hollington
Longford
Thurvaston
Marston Montgomery
Waldley
Somersal Herbert
Boylestone
Sutton on the Hill
Church Broughton
Doveridge
Sudbury
Sudbury Hall (NT)
Foston
Scropton
Hatton
Marchington
Coton in the Clay
Tutbury
Rolleston
Hanbury
Hanbury Woodend
Anslow
Horninglow
Anslow Gate
Bass Mus of Brewing
Needwood Forest
Rangemore
Tatenhill
Dunstall
Branston
Barton-under-Needwood
Branston Water Park
Walton-on-Trent
Rosliston
Catton Hall
Woodhouses
Yoxall
Hadley End
Hoar Cross
Hoar Cross Hall
Newborough
Draycott in the Clay
Marchington Woodlands
Bagot's Park
Abbots Bromley
Kingstone
Grindley
Stowe
Drointon
Newton
Blithfield Reservoir
Admaston
Blithbury
Colton
Hamstall Ridware
Hill Ridware
Morrey
Pipe Ridware
Mavesyn Ridware
King's Bromley
Orgreave
Handsacre
Armitage
Brereton
Etchinghill
Cannock Chase
Brocton
Milford
Walton-on-the-Hill
Weeping Cross
Great Haywood
Little Haywood
Colwich
Shugborough Estate (NT)
Tixall
Ingestre
Hixon
Weston
Salt
Gayton
Amerton Working Farm
Sandon
Hopton
Hopton Heath 1643
Marston
Yarlet
Whitgreave
Aston-by-Stone
Burston
Trent Valley
Walton
Stafford
Yarnfield
Norton Bridge
Chebsey
Little Bridgeford
Great Bridgeford
Seighford
Ranton
Coton Clanford
Derrington
Shut Heath
Castle Bank
Ancient High House
Shire Hall Gallery
Hyde Lea
Coppenhall
Dunston
Allimore Green
Bradley
Church Eaton
Levedale
Mitton
Acton Trussell
Bednall
Brindley
Fradswell
Coton
Milwich
Gratwich
Field
Bramshall
Blount's Green
Uttoxeter
Withington
Church Leigh
Stramshall
Beamhurst
Fole
Checkley
Lower Tean
Upper Tean
Draycott in the Moors
Cresswell
Meirheath
Fulford
Hilderstone
Garshall Green
Middleton Green
Moddershall
Cotwalton
Oulton
Barlaston
Tittensor
Wedgwood Visitor Cen
Rough Close
Trentham
Hanford
Lightwood
Meir
Blythe Bridge
Forsbrook
Blythe Marsh
Foxfield Lt. Rly
Caverswall
Dilhorne
Cookshill
Longton
Fenton
Weston Coyney
Parkhall
Potteries
Cheadle
Ceramica
M6
A537
A536
A523
A54
A53
A520
A52
A521
A522
A5272
A50
A500
A34
A51
A513
A518
A449
A460
A515
A6
A619
A6020
A5012
A517
A511
A38
A5270
A5035
A5005
A527
A5271
A5009
B5053
B5054
B5055
B5056
B5035
B5032
B5033
B5030
B5027
B5017
B5013
B5234
B5066
B5029
B5039
B5051
B5016
B5014
B5018
B5041
B5405
B6049
B6465
B5417
Roman Road

CHESTERFIELD
Over End
Cutthorpe
Old Brampton
Linacre Reservoirs
Wadshelf
Chatsworth Farmyard & Adventure Playground
Brampton
Holymoorside
Walton
Calow
Arkwright
Brimington
Brimington Common
Woodthorpe
Shuttlewood
Long Duckmanton
Bolsover
Castle
Creswell
Welbeck Abbey
Elmton
Whaley
Norton
Nether Langwith
Cuckney
Cuckney Hill
Budby
Meden Vale
Church Warsop
Sherwood Forest Amusement Pk
Market Warsop
Shirebrook
Upper Langwith
Scarcliffe
Palterton
Carr Vale
Hills Town
Hasland
Cock Alley
Sutton Scarsdale
Temple Normanton
Heath
Doe Lea
Glapwell
Stony Houghton
Grassmoor
Wingerworth
Beeley
Rowsley
Caldwell's Mill
Nether Moor
Old Tupton
Tupton
Holmewood
Williamthorpe
North Wingfield
Ault Hucknall
Rowthorne
New Houghton
Pleasley
Sherwood Forest Rare Breeds
Old Clipstone
Edwinstowe
Clipstone Forest
Clipstone
Mansfield Woodhouse
MANSFIELD
Forest Town
Ratcher Hill
Darley Dale
Two Dales
Kelstedge
Alton
Clay Cross
Ashover
Fallgate
Danesmoor
Hardstoft
Hardwick Hall (NT)
Teversal
Pilsley
Lane End
Tibshelf
Stretton
Milltown
Upper Hackney
Matlock Bank
Matlock
Tansley
Brightgate
Matlock Bath
Bonsall
Peak Rail
Ogston Reservoir
Morton
Higham
Stonebroom
Shirland
Stanton Hill
Skegby
Huthwaite
Sutton in Ashfield
Blackwell
Brackenfield
Wessington
Lea
Cromford
Black Rocks
Middleton
Bolehill
Holloway
South Wingfield
Fourlane Ends
National Tramway Mus
Westhouses
South Normanton
Alfreton
McArthurGlen
Kirkby in Ashfield
NOTTS
Rainworth
Blidworth
Ravenshead
Wonderland Pleasure Park
White Post Modern Farm Centre
Haywood Oaks
Wirksworth
Whatstandwell
Alderwasley
Crich
Crich Carr
Hopton
Carsington Water
Alport Height
Fritchley
Somercotes
Pinxton
Swanwick
Pentrich
Riddings
Annesley Woodhouse
Annesley
Newstead Abbey
Newstead
Selston
Ironville
Midland Rly
Butterley
Ambergate
Heage
Ripley
Codnor
Bagthorpe
Underwood
Linby
Papplewick
Burntstump
Patchings Art
Oxton
Kirk Ireton
Idridgehay
Shottle
Belper Lane End
Mount Pleasant
White Moor
Denby Pottery
Cross Hill
Loscoe
Langley Mill
New Brinsley
Brinsley
HUCKNALL
Butler's Hill
Bestwood Lodge
Calverton
Dorket Head
Woodborough
Cross o' the Hands
Shottlegate
BELPER
De Bradelei
Turnditch
Windley
Hazelwood
Kilburn
Denby
HEANOR
Eastwood
Moorgreen
Watnall
Redhill
Arnold
Lambley
Holbrook
Horsley
Horsley Woodhouse
Marlpool
Langley
Kimberley
Nuthall
Bulwell
Highbury Vale
Old Basford
Windley Meadows
Milford
Smalley
Shipley
American Adventure
Awsworth
Burton Joyce
DERBYSHIRE
Mugginton
Weston Underwood
Duffield
Coxbench
Stanley Common
Mapperley
Cossall
Bilborough
NOTTINGHAM
Carlton
Gedling
Netherfield
Colwick
Royal Concert Hall & Theatre Royal
National Ice Centre
Holme Pierrepont
Little Eaton
Quarndon
Kedleston
Morley
West Hallam
High Lane
ILKESTON
Trowell
Wollaton Hall
Kirk Langley
Langley Green
Allestree
Breadsall
Stanley
Kirk Hallam
Stanton by Dale
Dale
Chaddesden
DERBY
Mackworth
Markeaton Craft Village
Radbourne Common
Radbourne
Stapleford
Bramcote
Beeston
West Bridgford
Trent Bridge
Wilford
Gamston
Bassingfield
Cotgrave Country Park
Cotgrave
Spondon
Ockbrook
Risley
Sandiacre
Borrowash
Elvaston
Littleover
Mickleover
Normanton
Osmaston
Crewton
Alvaston
Breaston
Toton
Clifton
Attenborough
Ruddington
Edwalton
Plumtree
Normanton-on-the-Wolds
Dalbury
Burnaston
Etwall
Findern
Draycott
Elvaston
Thulston
LONG EATON
Barton in Fabis
New Sawley
Sawley
Thrumpton
Thrumpton Hall
Gotham
Nottingham Heritage Centre
Rushcliffe
Bradmore
Keyworth
Chellaston
Barrow upon Trent
Shardlow
Bunny
Stanton-on-the-Wolds
Egginton
Willington
Twyford
Repton
Swarkestone
Aston on Trent
Lockington
Hemington
Castle Donington
Ratcliffe on Soar
Kingston on Soar
Widmerpool
Stanton by Bridge
Weston-on-Trent
Donington Park
Kegworth
Wysall
Milton
Ingleby
King's Newton
East Midlands International
Sutton Bonington
West Leake
East Leake
Costock
Willoughby-on-the-Wolds
Newton Solney
Melbourne
Melbourne Hall
Isley Walton
Diseworth
Long Whatton
Rempstone
Foremark Reservoir
Ticknall
Staunton Harold Reservoir
Wilson
Tonge
Normanton on Soar
Winshill
Bretby
Breedon on the Hill
LEICS
Hathern
Hoton
Wymeswold
Prestwold
Calke Abbey (NT)
Newhall
Hartshorne
Goseley Dale
Ferrers Centre for Arts & Crafts
Staunton Harold Hall
Belton
Worthington
Stanford on Soar
Cotes
Burton on the Wolds
SWADLINCOTE
Church Gresley
Smisby
Woodville
Osgathorpe
Shepshed
Thorpe Acre
LOUGHBOROUGH
Great Central Rly
Walton on the Wolds
Ski Centre
Ashby de la Zouch
Thringstone
Barrow upon Soar
Blackfordby
Norris Hill
National Forest Millennium Discovery Centre
Coleorton
Woodthorpe
Nanpantan
Seagrave
Swannington
Whitwick
Quorn
Moira
Charnwood Forest
Fosse Way
Sherwood Forest
94
82
67

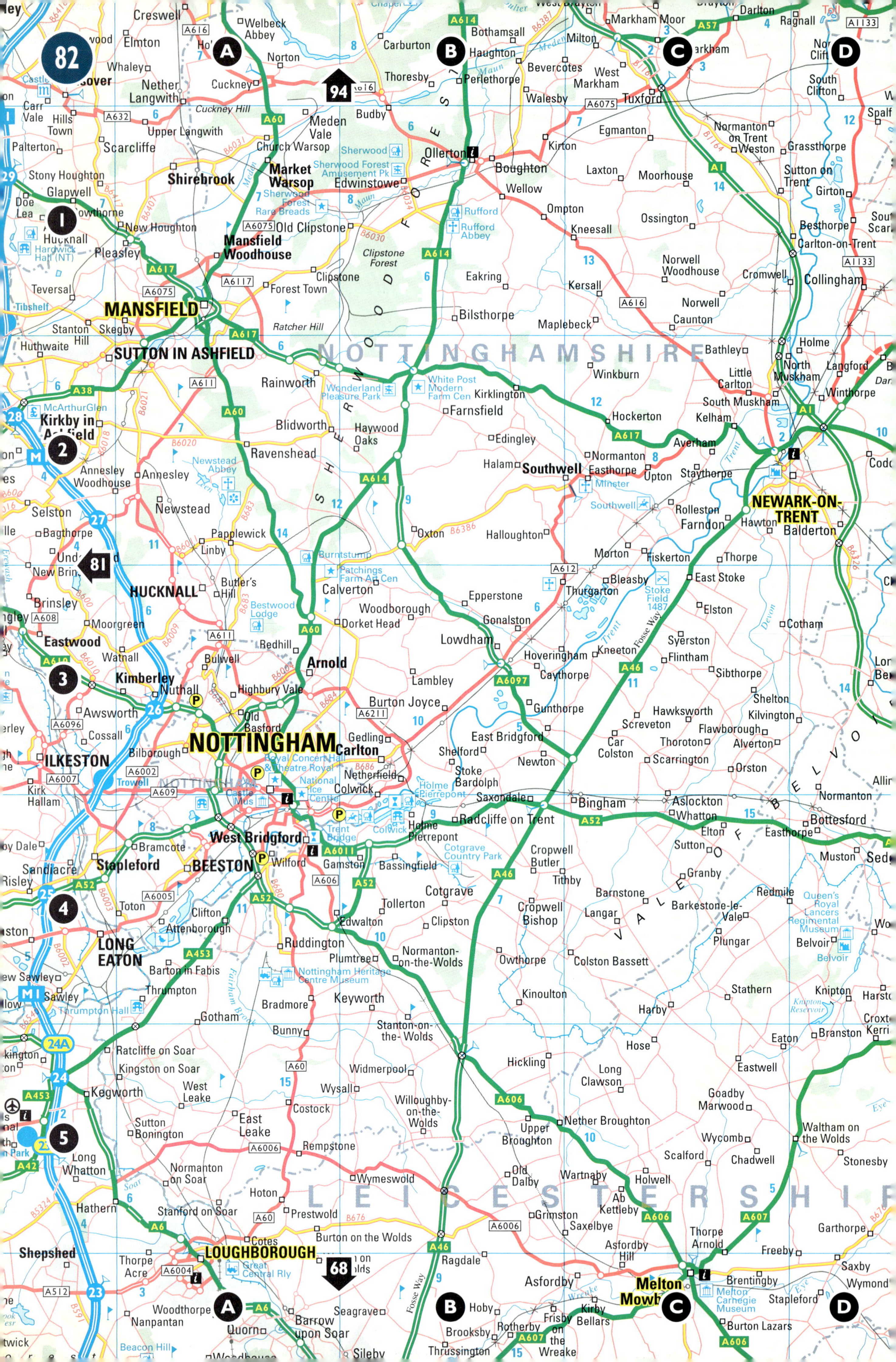
82
94
81
68
A
B
C
D
NOTTINGHAMSHIRE
LEICESTERSHIRE
SHERWOOD FOREST
VALE OF BELVOIR
Creswell
Welbeck Abbey
Elmton
Whaley
Norton
Carburton
Bothamsall
Haughton
Perlethorpe
Markham Moor
Darlton
Ragnall
Milton
West Markham
Tuxford
Walesby
Bevercotes
South Clifton
Spalford
Nether Langwith
Cuckney
Cuckney Hill
Thoresby
Budby
Carr Vale
Hills Town
Upper Langwith
Meden Vale
Scarcliffe
Palterton
Church Warsop
Sherwood
Sherwood Forest Amusement Pk
Ollerton
Boughton
Kirton
Egmanton
Normanton on Trent
Weston
Grassthorpe
Sutton on Trent
Girton
Stony Houghton
Glapwell
Shirebrook
Market Warsop
Edwinstowe
Wellow
Laxton
Moorhouse
Doe Lea
Rowthorne
Ault Hucknall
Hardwick Hall (NT)
New Houghton
Pleasley
Sherwood Forest Rare Breeds
Old Clipstone
Rufford
Rufford Abbey
Ompton
Kneesall
Ossington
Besthorpe
Carlton-on-Trent
Mansfield Woodhouse
Clipstone Forest
Clipstone
Eakring
Kersall
Norwell Woodhouse
Norwell
Cromwell
Collingham
Teversal
Tibshelf
MANSFIELD
Forest Town
Ratcher Hill
Bilsthorpe
Maplebeck
Caunton
Stanton Hill
Skegby
Huthwaite
SUTTON IN ASHFIELD
Rainworth
Wonderland Pleasure Park
White Post Modern Farm Cen
Kirklington
Winkburn
Bathley
Holme
Little Carlton
North Muskham
Langford
South Muskham
Winthorpe
McArthurGlen
Kirkby in Ashfield
Blidworth
Haywood Oaks
Farnsfield
Hockerton
Kelham
Averham
Edingley
Halam
Southwell
Normanton
Easthorpe
Upton
Staythorpe
Annesley Woodhouse
Annesley
Newstead Abbey
Ravenshead
Minster
Southwell
Rolleston
NEWARK-ON-TRENT
Farndon
Hawton
Balderton
Selston
Newstead
Papplewick
Linby
Oxton
Halloughton
Morton
Fiskerton
Thorpe
Bagthorpe
Underwood
New Brinsley
Burntstump
Patchings Farm Art Cen
Calverton
Epperstone
Bleasby
Thurgarton
Stoke Field 1487
East Stoke
Brinsley
HUCKNALL
Butler's Hill
Bestwood Lodge
Woodborough
Dorket Head
Gonalston
Elston
Cotham
Moorgreen
Eastwood
Watnall
Bulwell
Redhill
Lowdham
Hoveringham
Kneeton
Syerston
Flintham
Kimberley
Nuthall
Highbury Vale
Arnold
Lambley
Caythorpe
Sibthorpe
Awsworth
Old Basford
Burton Joyce
Gunthorpe
Shelton
Hawksworth
Kilvington
Cossall
Bilborough
NOTTINGHAM
Gedling
Carlton
East Bridgford
Screveton
Flawborough
Car Colston
Thoroton
Alverton
ILKESTON
Royal Concert Hall & Theatre Royal
Netherfield
Shelford
Newton
Scarrington
Orston
Kirk Hallam
Trowell
National Ice Centre
Colwick
Holme Pierrepont
Stoke Bardolph
Saxondale
Bingham
Aslockton
Whatton
Normanton
Castle Mus
Trent Bridge
Radcliffe on Trent
Elton
Bottesford
Stapleford
Bramcote
West Bridgford
Holme Pierrepont
Cotgrave Country Park
Cropwell Butler
Tithby
Sutton
Granby
Easthorpe
Muston
Sandiacre
Risley
BEESTON
Wilford
Gamston
Bassingfield
Cotgrave
Barnstone
Langar
Barkestone-le-Vale
Redmile
Queen's Royal Lancers Regimental Museum
Toton
Clifton
Attenborough
Tollerton
Edwalton
Clipston
Cropwell Bishop
Plungar
Belvoir
LONG EATON
Ruddington
Plumtree
Normanton-on-the-Wolds
Owthorpe
Colston Bassett
Barton in Fabis
Nottingham Heritage Centre Museum
Stathern
Knipton
Knipton Reservoir
Sawley
Thrumpton
Thrumpton Hall
Bradmore
Keyworth
Kinoulton
Harby
Gotham
Bunny
Stanton-on-the-Wolds
Hose
Eaton
Branston
Ratcliffe on Soar
Kingston on Soar
Widmerpool
Hickling
Long Clawson
Eastwell
Kegworth
West Leake
Wysall
Willoughby-on-the-Wolds
Goadby Marwood
Costock
East Leake
Upper Broughton
Nether Broughton
Sutton Bonington
Rempstone
Wycomb
Waltham on the Wolds
Long Whatton
Normanton on Soar
Scalford
Chadwell
Stonesby
Wymeswold
Old Dalby
Wartnaby
Holwell
Hathern
Hoton
Prestwold
Grimston
Ab Kettleby
Saxelbye
Thorpe Arnold
Garthorpe
Stanford on Soar
Shepshed
Cotes
LOUGHBOROUGH
Burton on the Wolds
Ragdale
Asfordby Hill
Freeby
Thorpe Acre
Great Central Rly
Asfordby
Melton Mowbray
Brentingby
Saxby
Wymond
Melton Carnegie Museum
Stapleford
Woodthorpe
Nanpantan
Quorn
Barrow upon Soar
Seagrave
Hoby
Brooksby
Rotherby
Frisby on the Wreake
Kirby Bellars
Burton Lazars
Beacon Hill
Sileby
Thrussington
Fosse Way
A614
A57
A1133
A616
A60
A632
A6075
A1
A617
A6117
A611
A38
A612
A608
A610
A6097
A46
A6211
A6096
A6002
A6007
A609
A52
A6011
A606
A6005
A453
A6006
A60
A6004
A6
A512
A607
A606
M1
B6020
B6386
B6030

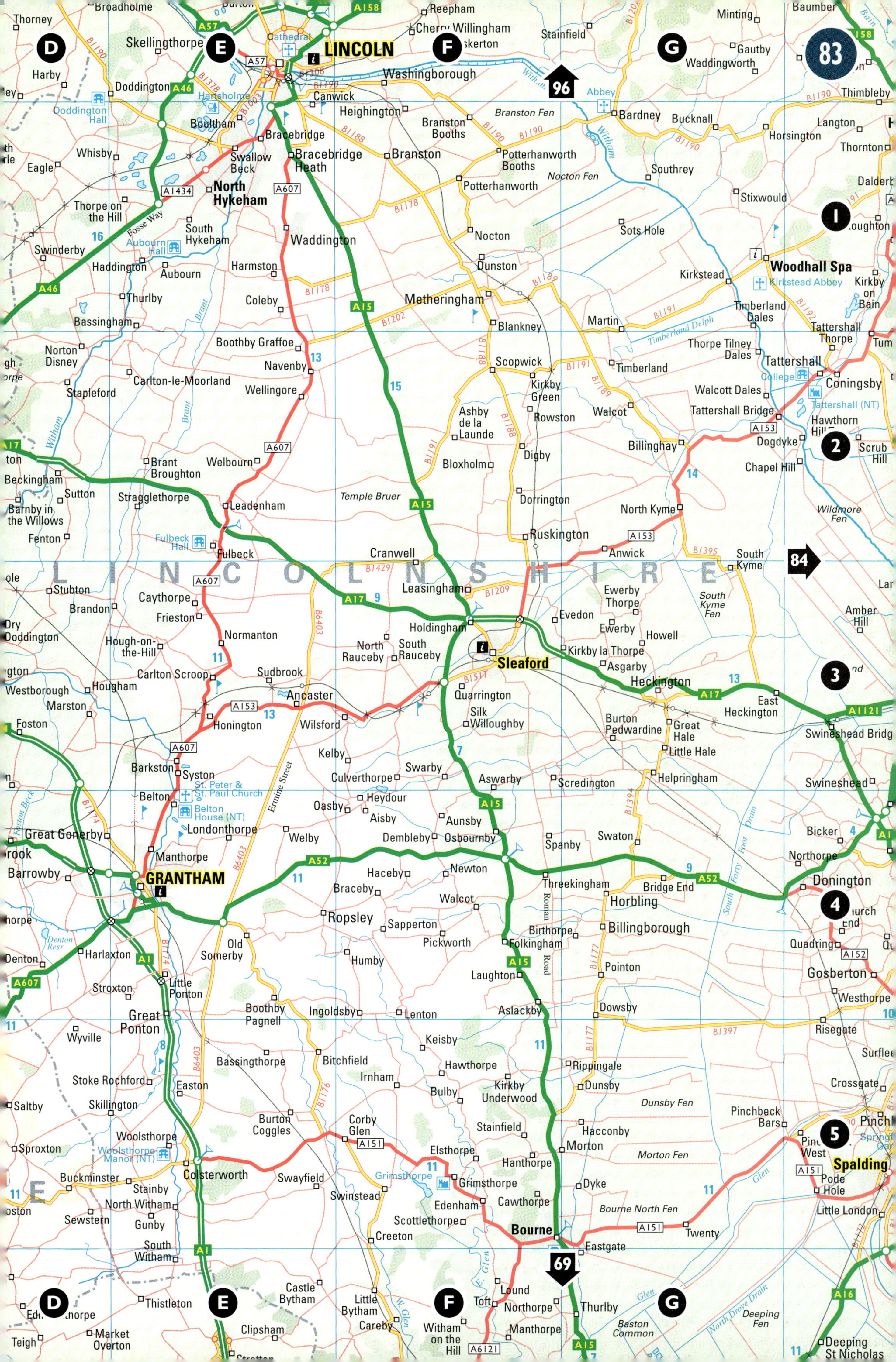
D
E
F
G
LINCOLN
96
84
69
I
2
3
4
5
L I N C O L N S H I R E
Thorney
Broadholme
Skellingthorpe
Reepham
Cherry Willingham
Stainfield
Minting
Gautby
Waddingworth
Baumber
Thimbleby
Harby
Doddington
Doddington Hall
Hartsholme
Canwick
Washingborough
Heighington
Branston Booths
Branston Fen
Bardney
Bucknall
Horsington
Langton
Thornton
Whisby
Eagle
Boultham
Bracebridge
Bracebridge Heath
Branston
Potterhanworth Booths
Nocton Fen
Southrey
Swallow Beck
North Hykeham
Potterhanworth
Stixwould
Dalderby
Thorpe on the Hill
Fosse Way
South Hykeham
Aubourn Hall
Swinderby
Waddington
Nocton
Sots Hole
Woodhall Spa
Kirkstead
Kirkstead Abbey
Kirkby on Bain
Haddington
Aubourn
Harmston
Dunston
Thurlby
Coleby
Metheringham
Bassingham
Blankney
Martin
Timberland Delph
Timberland Dales
Tattershall Thorpe
Norton Disney
Boothby Graffoe
Navenby
Scopwick
Timberland
Thorpe Tilney Dales
Tattershall
College
Coningsby
Stapleford
Carlton-le-Moorland
Wellingore
Kirkby Green
Walcott Dales
Tattershall (NT)
Ashby de la Launde
Rowston
Walcot
Tattershall Bridge
Hawthorn Hill
Billinghay
Dogdyke
Scrub Hill
Brant Broughton
Welbourn
Digby
Chapel Hill
Beckingham
Bloxholm
Sutton
Stragglethorpe
Leadenham
Temple Bruer
Dorrington
North Kyme
Wildmore Fen
Barnby in the Willows
Fulbeck Hall
Ruskington
Fenton
Fulbeck
Cranwell
Anwick
South Kyme
Stubton
Leasingham
Ewerby Thorpe
South Kyme Fen
Amber Hill
Brandon
Caythorpe
Evedon
Frieston
Holdingham
Ewerby
Howell
Dry Doddington
Normanton
North Rauceby
South Rauceby
Kirkby la Thorpe
Hough-on-the-Hill
Sleaford
Asgarby
Carlton Scroop
Sudbrook
Heckington
Westborough
Hougham
Ancaster
Quarrington
East Heckington
Marston
Silk Willoughby
Burton Pedwardine
Great Hale
Foston
Honington
Wilsford
Little Hale
Swineshead Bridge
Kelby
Barkston
Syston
Swarby
Culverthorpe
Aswarby
Helpringham
Scredington
Swineshead
St. Peter & St. Paul Church
Belton
Belton House (NT)
Heydour
Oasby
Aisby
Ermine Street
Aunsby
Great Gonerby
Londonthorpe
Welby
Dembleby
Osbournby
Spanby
Swaton
Bicker
Northorpe
Manthorpe
GRANTHAM
Barrowby
Haceby
Newton
Threekingham
Bridge End
Donington
Braceby
Horbling
Walcot
Ropsley
Billingborough
Church End
Denton Resr
Old Somerby
Sapperton
Birthorpe
Folkingham
Quadring
Harlaxton
Denton
Humby
Pickworth
Roman Road
Pointon
Laughton
Gosberton
Stroxton
Little Ponton
Westhorpe
Great Ponton
Boothby Pagnell
Ingoldsby
Lenton
Aslackby
Dowsby
Risegate
Wyville
Keisby
Surfleet
Bassingthorpe
Bitchfield
Hawthorpe
Rippingale
Stoke Rochford
Easton
Irnham
Bulby
Kirkby Underwood
Dunsby
Dunsby Fen
Crossgate
Saltby
Skillington
Burton Coggles
Corby Glen
Stainfield
Hacconby
Pinchbeck Bars
Woolsthorpe
Woolsthorpe Manor (NT)
Elsthorpe
Morton
Morton Fen
Pinchbeck West
Spalding
Sproxton
Colsterworth
Swayfield
Grimsthorpe
Hanthorpe
Pode Hole
Buckminster
Stainby
Swinstead
Dyke
Cawthorpe
Edenham
Bourne North Fen
North Witham
Sewstern
Gunby
Scottlethorpe
Little London
Creeton
Bourne
Twenty
Eastgate
South Witham
Castle Bytham
Little Bytham
Lound
Toft
Northorpe
Thurlby
Baston Common
Deeping Fen
North Drove Drain
Thistleton
Carlby
Witham on the Hill
Manthorpe
Market Overton
Teigh
Clipsham
Deeping St Nicholas
Stretton
Witham
Brant
Glen
Bain
South Forty Foot Drain
A57
A158
A46
A1434
A607
A15
A153
A17
B1429
B1209
B1517
B6403
A52
A1121
A1
A151
A6121
A16
A152
B1190
B1378
B1003
B1188
B1178
B1202
B1191
B1189
B1192
B1395
B1394
B1177
B1397
B1176
B1174
B1308
Abbey
Cathedral

84
Minting
Baumber
West Ashby
Fulletby
Tetford
Salmonby
Ashby Puerorum
Brinkhill
Somersby
Ulceby Cross
Ulceby
Cumberworth
Hog
Willoughby
Wispington
Edlington
A158
A16
A1028
A52
A153
A155
A17
A1121
A151
A1101
A152
B1190
B1191
B1192
B1195
B1183
B1184
B1395
B1391
B1397
B1356
B1357
B1180
B1515
B1165
B1168
B1173
B1172
B1359
B1390
Harrington
Harrington Hall
Enderby
Langton
Aswardby
Claxby
Sloothby
Thimbleby
Low Toynton
High Toynton
Greetham
96
Winceby 1643
Hagworthingham
Sausthorpe
Skendleby
Welton le Marsh
Addlethorpe
Bucknall
Langton
Horsington
Horncastle
Thornton
Mareham on the Hill
Hameringham
Lusby
Raithby
Partney
Scremby
Candlesby
Orby
Orby Marsh
Burgh Marsh
Burgh le Marsh
Dalderby
Stixwould
Asgarby
Claxby Pluckacre
Hareby
Mavis Enderby
Hundleby
Spilsby
Ashby by Partney
Gunby Hall (NT)
Bratoft
Roughton
Moorby
Miningsby
Old Bolingbroke
Halton Holegate
Great Steeping
Irby in the Marsh
Church Farm Museum
Haltham
Wood Enderby
West Keal
East Keal
Toynton All Saints
Steeping
Firsby
Kirkstead
Woodhall Spa
Kirkstead Abbey
Kirkby on Bain
Mareham le Fen
East Kirkby
Hagnaby
Toynton St Peter
Little Steeping
Croft
Timberland Dales
Revesby
Keal Cotes
Toynton Fen Side
Thorpe St Peter
Stickford
Fendike Corner
Thorpe Culvert
Tattershall Thorpe
Tumby
Havenhouse Sta.
Thorpe Tilney Dales
Tattershall
Moor Side
LINCOLNSHIRE
New Bolingbroke
Wainfleet Bank
Wainfleet All Saints
College
Coningsby
Midville
New Leake
Eastville
Key's Toft
Walcott Dales
Tumby Woodside
Tattershall (NT)
Tattershall Bridge
Hawthorn Hill
Stickney
Friskney Eaudyke
Dogdyke
Scrub Hill
New York
Carrington
East Fen
Friskney
Wainfleet Sand
Chapel Hill
West Fen
Lade Bank
Northlands
Wildmore Fen
Leake Common Side
Trader Windmill
Wrangle
Wrangle Lowgate
Friskney Flats
Gipsey Bridge
Frithville
Sibsey
Old Leake
83
South Kyme Fen
Langrick
Fishtoft Drove
Leake Hurn's End
Langriville
Hobhole Drain
Amber Hill
Anton's Gowt
Hill Dyke
Leverton
Leverton Outgate
BOSTON
Long Sand
Witham
Frith Bank
Brothertoft
Benington
Benington Sea End
Holland Fen
St. Botolph
Butterwick
Hubbert's Bridge
Guildhall
Haltoft End
East Heckington
Fydell
Skirbeck
Butterwick Low
Roger Sand
Great Hale
Little Hale
Swineshead Bridge
Kirton Holme
Frampton West End
Freiston
Freiston Shore
Fishtoft
Fenhouses
Kirton End
Toft Sand
Scrane End
Black Buoy Sand
Swineshead
Wyberton
The Haven
Frampton
Gat Sand
Drayton
THE
The Scalp
Mare Tail
Bicker
Kirton
Sandholme
Hoffleet Stow
Northorpe
Skeldyke
Wigtoft
Forty Foot Drain
Donington
Sutterton
Algarkirk
Old South
Church End
Quadring
Quadring Eaudike
Fosdyke
Bicker Haven
Holbeach St Matthew
Old Lynn Channel
Gosberton
Holbeach St Marks
Westhorpe
Whaplode Marsh
Dawsmere
Risegate
Holbeach Marsh
Gedney Marsh
Gedney Drove End
Surfleet
Surfleet Seas End
Holbeach Clough
Moulton Seas End
Saracen's Head
Holbeach Hurn
Crossgate
Holbeach Bank
Lutton Marsh
Spalding Marsh
Pinchbeck Bars
Pinchbeck
Loosegate
Weston
Holbeach
Gedney Dyke
Lutton
Guy's Head
Springfields Gardens
Fleet Hargate
Chapelgate
Pinchbeck West
Fun Farm
Moulton
Whaplode
Gedney
Little London
Terrington
Spalding
Fleet
Glen
Pode Hole
Long Sutton
Nene
Gedney Broadgate
Sutton Bridge
Wingland Marsh
Delph Bank
Little London
Weston Hills
Sutton Crosses
Twenty
Walpole Cross Keys
South Holland Main Drain
Whaplode Fen
Moulton Chapel
70
Whaplode St Catherine
Tydd Gote
Tydd St Mary
North Drove Drain
Deeping Fen
Holbeach St Johns
Sutton St James
Walpole St Andrew
Moulton Fen
Walpole St Peter
Four Gotes
Tydd St Giles
Deeping St Nicholas
Terrington St John

D
E
F
G
97
t Leonards
Ingoldmells
Ingoldmells Point
Fantasy Island
Butlins Family Entertainment Resort, Skegness
A52
Skegness
Skegness Natureland Seal Sanctuary
Gibraltar Point
Gibraltar
3.2 miles to 1 inch
0 2 4 6 8 10 miles
0 2 4 6 8 10 km
2 km to 1 cm
1
2
3
4
5
LYNN DEEPS
DEEPS
WASH
Seal Sand
Peter Black Sand
Bulldog Sand
Ongar Hill
Marsh
Brancaster Bay
Holkham Bay
Norton
Holme next the Sea
Thornham
A149
Brancaster
Titchwell
Burnham Deepdale
Burnham Norton
Burnham Market
Burnham Overy
Overy Staithe
Holkham
Wells-nex
Holkham Hall
Burnham Thorpe
Sea Life Centre
Hunstanton
Ringstead
Summerfield
Creake Abbey
Wells & Walsingham Lt Rly
Heacham
Norfolk Lavender
Sedgeford
Docking
B1454
B1155
Stanhoe
North Creake
South Creake
Shirehall Museum
Egmere
Shrine of Our Lady of Walsingham
North Barsham
East Barsham
West Barsham
Snettisham
Fring
Bircham Newton
Southgate
Shernborne
Ingoldisthorpe
Great Bircham
Bircham Tofts
Bagthorpe
Barmer
Syderstone
Sculthorpe
NORFOLK
Dersingham
Anmer
Tattersett
A148
Dunton
Shereford
86
Fakenham
Hempton
Sandringham House
Sandringham
Houghton Hall
Wolferton
West Newton
St Mary Magdalene Chapel
New Houghton
East Rudham
West Rudham
Tatterford
Helhoughton
Toftrees
Colkirk
A1065
Flitcham
Harpley
Castle Rising
Trinity Hospital
Castle
Hillington
A148
North Wootton
Little Massingham
Great Massingham
West Raynham
South Raynham
East Raynham
Whissonsett
Congham
Roydon
Grimston
South Wootton
A1078
Weasenham St Peter
Wellingham
Horningtoft
Weasenham All Saints
Rougham
Tittleshall
Stanfield
Little London
Clenchwarton
St George's Guildhall (NT)
Gaywood
A149
Pott Row
Massingham Heath
Terrington St Clement
West Lynn
Gayton
KING'S LYNN
71
Ashwicken
Gavton
Mileham
East Bilney
Tilney All Saints
A47
Caithness Crystal Visitor Centre
East Winch
East Walton
Castle Acre
East Lexham
Litcham
Lexham
Bitteri
Longham
A47
A10
B1145
B1153
B1440
B1439
B1355
B1105
B1146
Babingley
Great Ouse

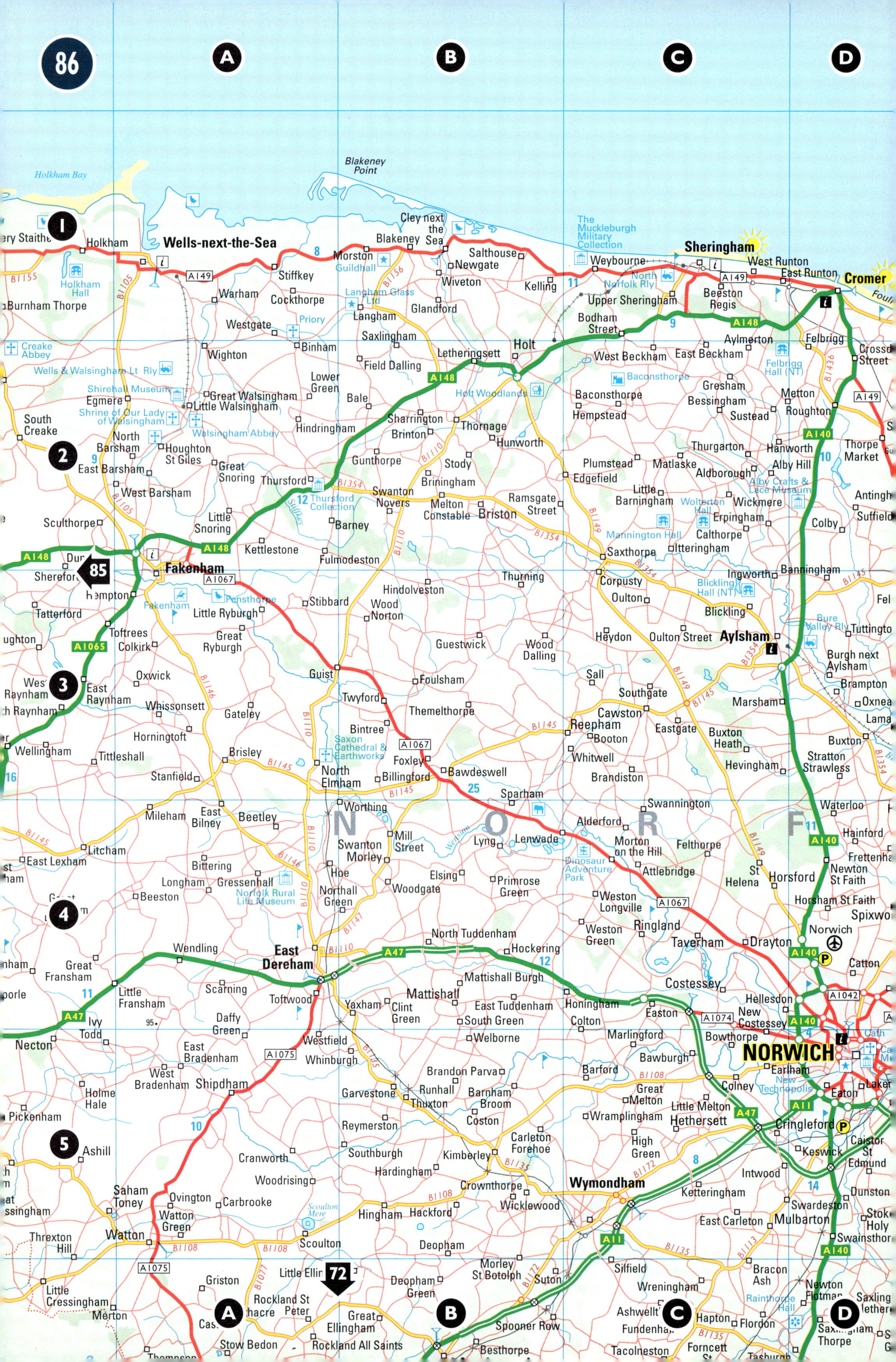
A
B
C
D
Holkham Bay
Blakeney Point
1
Holkham
Wells-next-the-Sea
Cley next the Sea
Blakeney
Morston
Guildhall
Salthouse
Newgate
Wiveton
Kelling
The Muckleburgh Military Collection
Sheringham
Weybourne
North Norfolk Rly
West Runton
East Runton
Cromer
A149
B1155
Holkham Hall
Burnham Thorpe
B1105
Warham
Stiffkey
Cockthorpe
Langham Glass Ltd
Langham
Glandford
B1156
Upper Sheringham
Beeston Regis
Bodham Street
A148
Aylmerton
Felbrigg
Cross Street
Creake Abbey
Wighton
Westgate
Priory
Binham
Saxlingham
Field Dalling
Letheringsett
Holt
West Beckham
East Beckham
Wells & Walsingham Lt Rly
Shirehall Museum
Egmere
Great Walsingham
Little Walsingham
Lower Green
Bale
Holt Woodlands
Baconsthorpe
Gresham
Bessingham
Felbrigg Hall (NT)
Metton
Roughton
South Creake
Shrine of Our Lady of Walsingham
Walsingham Abbey
Hindringham
Sharrington
Brinton
Thornage
Hunworth
Hempstead
Sustead
B1436
2
North Barsham
Houghton St Giles
East Barsham
Great Snoring
Thursford
Gunthorpe
B1110
Stody
Briningham
Plumstead
Matlaske
Thurgarton
Hanworth
Alby Hill
Aldborough
Alby Crafts & Lace Museum
Edgefield
Thorpe Market
Antingham
West Barsham
B1354
Swanton Novers
Melton Constable
Briston
Ramsgate Street
Little Barningham
Wolterton Hall
Wickmere
Erpingham
Calthorpe
Suffield
Colby
Sculthorpe
Little Snoring
12
Thursford Collection
Barney
Mannington Hall
Itteringham
Saxthorpe
Dunton
Fakenham
Kettlestone
Fulmodeston
85
Shereford
Hempton
Fakenham
A1067
Pensthorpe
Stibbard
Hindolveston
Wood Norton
Thurning
Corpusty
Oulton
Ingworth
Blickling Hall (NT)
Banningham
Tatterford
Little Ryburgh
Great Ryburgh
Toftrees
Colkirk
A1065
Guestwick
Wood Dalling
Heydon
Oulton Street
Blickling
Aylsham
Bure Valley Rly
Tuttington
Burgh next Aylsham
3
West Raynham
East Raynham
Oxwick
B1146
Guist
Foulsham
Sall
Southgate
Brampton
Oxnead
Whissonsett
Gateley
Twyford
Themelthorpe
Cawston
Reepham
Booton
Eastgate
Buxton Heath
Marsham
Lamas
Buxton
Wellingham
Horningtoft
Tittleshall
Stanfield
Brisley
B1145
Bintree
Saxon Cathedral & Earthworks
North Elmham
Foxley
Billingford
Bawdeswell
Whitwell
Brandiston
Hevingham
Stratton Strawless
16
Mileham
East Bilney
Beetley
Worthing
25
Sparham
Swannington
Waterloo
Litcham
N
O
R
F
Swanton Morley
Mill Street
Lyng
Lenwade
Alderford
Morton on the Hill
Felthorpe
Hainford
East Lexham
Bittering
Hoe
Elsing
Primrose Green
Dinosaur Adventure Park
Attlebridge
St Helena
Horsford
Newton St Faith
Frettenham
4
Longham
Beeston
Gressenhall
Norfolk Rural Life Museum
Northall Green
Woodgate
Weston Longville
Horsham St Faith
Spixworth
Wendling
East Dereham
North Tuddenham
Hockering
Weston Green
Ringland
Taverham
Drayton
Norwich
A140
A47
Great Fransham
Little Fransham
11
Scarning
Toftwood
Mattishall Burgh
Mattishall
Clint Green
East Tuddenham
Honingham
Costessey
Hellesdon
Catton
A1042
Ivy Todd
Daffy Green
Yaxham
South Green
Colton
Easton
A1074
New Costessey
Necton
East Bradenham
West Bradenham
Westfield
Whinburgh
A1075
Welborne
Marlingford
Bowthorpe
Bawburgh
NORWICH
Holme Hale
Shipdham
Brandon Parva
Runhall
Garvestone
Thuxton
Barnham Broom
Coston
Barford
Great Melton
Earlham
New Technopolis
Colney
Eaton
Pickenham
10
Reymerston
Wramplingham
Little Melton
Hethersett
A11
Cringleford
Keswick
Caistor St Edmund
5
Ashill
Cranworth
Southburgh
Kimberley
Carleton Forehoe
High Green
Intwood
Woodrising
Hardingham
Crownthorpe
Wymondham
Ketteringham
Dunston
Saham Toney
Ovington
Carbrooke
Watton Green
Scoulton Mere
Hingham
Hackford
Wicklewood
Swardeston
East Carleton
Mulbarton
Swainsthorpe
Threxton Hill
Watton
B1108
Scoulton
Deopham
B1135
B1172
Silfield
Bracon Ash
Little Cressingham
Griston
Little Ellingham
72
Deopham Green
Morley St Botolph
Suton
Wreningham
Newton Flotman
Saxlingham Nethergate
Merton
Rockland St Peter
Great Ellingham
Ashwellthorpe
Hapton
Flordon
Rainthorpe Hall
Stow Bedon
Rockland All Saints
Spooner Row
Besthorpe
Fundenhall
Tacolneston
Forncett St
Tasburgh
Saxlingham Thorpe

D
E
F
G
3.2 miles to 1 inch
0 2 4 6 8 10 miles
0 2 4 6 8 10 km
2 km to 1 cm
1
2
3
4
5
Overstrand
Sidestrand
Trimingham
Gimingham
Mundesley
Trunch
Knapton
Paston
Bacton
Edingthorpe
Keswick
Walcott
Bradfield
Swafield
North Walsham
Witton Bridge
Ridlington
Happisburgh
Spa Common
Crostwight
Whimpwell Green
Hempstead
Happisburgh Common
Lessingham
Sea Palling
Waxham
Honing
East Ruston
Bengate
Westwick
Worstead
Stalham
Ingham
Stalham Green
Dilham
Smallburgh
Low Street
Sutton
Hickling
Hickling Green
Hickling Heath
Horsey
Horsey Windpump (NT)
Sloley
Fairstead
Scottow
Market Street
Sco Ruston
Beeston St Lawrence
Beeston Hall
Barton Common
Barton Turf
Clearwater 2000
Catfield
Tunstead
Ashmanhaugh
Wroxham Barns
Neatishead
Irstead
Potter Heigham
Coltishall
Hoveton
NORFOLK
BROADS
Ludham
West Somerton
East Somerton
Winterton-on-Sea
Hemsby Hole
Belaugh
Wroxham
Horning
Upper Street
Bastwick
Martham
Hemsby
Newport
Repps
Thurne
Crostwick
Rackheath
Salhouse
Woodbastwick
St. Helen
Ranworth
Rollesby
Ormesby St Margaret
Scratby
California
Clippesby
Burgh St Margaret
Ormesby St Michael
Filby Broad
Fairhaven
Panxworth
Billockby
Bygone Village
Thrigby
Filby
Caister Castle
Roman Site
Caister-on-Sea
New Rackheath
South Walsham
Upton
Upton Green
Mautby
West End
West Caister
Thrigby Hall Wildlife Gdns
Sprowston
Little Plumstead
Hemblington
Stokesby
Runham
Yarmouth
Thorpe End Garden Village
Great Plumstead
North Burlingham
Acle
Thorpe St Andrew
Blofield
Lingwood
Damgate
Tunstall
Greyfriar's Cloisters
Old Merchant's House & Row 111 House
Sea Life Centre
GREAT YARMOUTH
Pleasure Beach
Brundall
Beighton
Moulton St Mary
Halvergate Marshes
Halvergate
THE BROADS
Postwick
Strumpshaw
South Burlingham
Breydon Water
Thorpe Newton
Kirby Bedon
Surlingham
Buckenham
Freethorpe
Berney Arms Mill
Burgh Castle
Southtown
Bramerton
Hassingham
Southwood
Wickhampton
Roman Fort
Gorleston on Sea
Rockland St Mary
Cantley
Freethorpe Common
Framingham Pigot
Claxton
Limpenhoe
Pettitts Animal Adventure Park
Bradwell
Hellington
Yelverton
Delton
Hobland Hall
Earl Poringland
Ashby St Mary
Hardley Street
Alpington
Bergh Apton
Thurton
Reedham
Langley Street
Norton Marshes
St. Olaves Priory
Fritton
Fritton Lake
Hopton
Howe
Brooke
Chedgrave
Norton Subcourse
Lower Thurlton
Heckingham
Thurlton
Sisland
Loddon
Seething
Hales
Thorpe
Herringfleet
Blundeston
Kirstead Green
Hales Hall
Raveningham
Haddiscoe
Somerleyton
Pleasurewood Hills Theme Park
A149
A1151
A1062
A1064
A47
A146
A143
A12
A1242
B1159
B1145
B1150
B1151
B1152
B1140
B1136
B1074
B1332
B1354
73

A
B
C
D
1
2
3
4
5
The Skerries
West Mouse
Middle Mouse
Carmel Head
Cemlyn Bay
Cemaes Bay
Porth Wen Bay
Bull Bay
Point Lynas
Llanbadrig
Amlwch
Amlwch Port
Cemaes
Neuadd
Burwen
Llaneilian
Tregele
Pengorffwysfa
Llanfairynghornwy
Llanfechell
Bodewryd
Pen-y-sarn
Nebo
Ynys Dulas
(NT)
Llanrhyddlad
Carreg-lefn
Rhos-goch
Parys Mountain
Dulas
Dulas Bay
Church Bay
Rhyd-wyn
Llanfflewyn
Rhos-y-bol
A5025
HOLYHEAD
BAY
ISLE OF
City Dulas
Brynrefail
Lligwy Bay
Capel Lligwy
Llanfaethlu
Llanbabo
Llyn Alaw
Capel Parc
Din Lligwy
Moelfre
Lligwy Burial Chamber
Ceidio
Llandyfrydog
Dublin 1¼-3½ hrs & Dún Laoghaire 1¼ hr
Windmill
Llanddeusant
Elim
Llanallgo
North Stack
Llanfwrog
Llannerch-y-medd
Maenaddwyn
Marian-Glas
Holyhead Mountain
220
Holyhead (Caergybi)
Roman Fort
Salt Island
Llanfigael
B5112
B5111
ANGLESEY
17
South Stack
Llaingoch
Llanfachraeth
Standing Stone
Carmel
Capel Coch
Bryn-teg
Benllech
Kingsland
Pen-llyn
Llyn Llywenan
B5110
B5108
Hut Circles
Standing Stones
Penrhos
Llanynghenedl
B5109
ANGLESEY
Llechcynfarwy
Red Wharf
A5
3
Bodedern
Burial Chambers
Llanbedrgoch
Burial Chamber
Valley (Dyffryn)
Trefor
Llangwyllog
Tregaian
Penrhyn Mawr
Trearddur
A55
(YNYS MÔN)
Llanddyfnan
Caergeiliog
Llynfaes
Pentraeth
B4545
Four Mile Bridge
Llanfair-yn-neubwll
4
Rhosmeirch
Bryngwran
Llyn Frogwy
Cefni Resr
Talwrn
Gwalchmai
Bodffordd
HOLY ISLAND
Bodior
Capel Gwyn
5
6
Llangefni
A5025
Rhoscolyn
Heneglwys
A4080
B4422
A5114
Braint
Tywyn Trewan
Ceint
Cymyran Bay
B5420
Ty Newydd Burial Chamber
Cerrigceinwen
Penmynydd
Rhosneigr
Llangristiolus
A4080
Llanfaelog
Pentre Berw
Llanfairpwllgwyngyll
Ty Croes Sta.
Gaerwen
Menai Bri
(Porthaethw
Barclodiad y Gawres Chambered Cairn
B4422
Cefni Malltraeth Marsh
B4419
Bethel
Trefdraeth
Llanddaniel Fab
Llyn Coron
Bryn Celli Ddu Burial Chamber
Plas Newydd (NT)
74
Aberffraw
Llangadwaladr
Hermon
Malltraeth
Llangaffo
Bodowyr Burial Chamber
Castell Bryn-gwyn
Aberffraw Bay
Bodorgan
B4421
Brynsiencyn
A4080
Malltraeth Sands
Newborough
Dwyran
B4419
Llanddaniolen
Menai Strait

D
E
F
G
1
2
3
4
5
3.2 miles to 1 inch
0
2
4
6
8
10 miles
0
2
4
6
8
10 km
2 km to 1 cm
90
Great Ormes Head
Great Orme
Cable Car
North Wales Theatre
Toll
Llandudno
Little Ormes Head
Gogarth
Penrhyn-side
Great Orme Tramway
B5115
Penrhyn Bay (Bae Penrhyn)
A546
Conwy Sands
Rhôs-on-Sea
Ocean
Kinmel
Suspension Bridge (NT)
Llanrhos
Llandrillo-yn-Rhôs
COLWYN BAY
(Bae Colwyn)
Deganwy
Mochdre
Abergele Roads
Pensar
Aberconwy House (NT)
A55
Llanddulas
A547
Old Colwyn
Abergele
Conwy
Llandudno Junction
Gyffin
Llysfaen
Gwrych
Dwygyfylchi
Capelulo
Conwy
Llansanffraid Glan Conwy
Rhyd-y-foel
Foel Lus
Penmaenmawr
Llanelian-yn-Rhôs
B5383
B5381
Bryn-y-maen
Dolwen
Betws-yn-Rhos
Puffin Island (Priestholm)
St. Seirol's Well
Penmon
Llanddona
Llangoed
B5109
Penmaen Swatch
CONWY BAY
Llan-faes
Beaumaris
Beaumaris (Biwmaris)
Llansadwrn
Llandegfan
A545
Llanfairfechan
Nant-y-Pandy
Moelfre
435
C O N W Y
Henryd
Pentrefelin
Mynydd Llanelian
Dawn
B5381
A548
Garth
Port Penrhyn
Penrhyn (NT)
Gorddinog
Garreg Fawr
Tal-y-fan
610
Rowen
B5106
A470
Bodnant (NT)
Hafod-lom
Mynydd Branar
Bangor
A5
A55
Abergwyngregyn
Crymlyn
Ty'n-y-groes
Graig
Moel Gyffylog
Caerhun
Tal-y-cafn
Eglwysbach
Glanadda
Llandygai
Aber Falls
Anafon
Llanfair Talhaiarn
Tal-y-bont
Moel Wnion
580
G W Y N E D D
849
Drum
770
Llanbedr-y-cennin
Tal-y-bont
76
Gell
Pentre Isaf
A544
Waen-
Glasinfryn
A5
Llanllechid
Llwytmor
Drosgl
758
Foel-Fras
942
Mwdwl Eithin
B5113
Tre-pys-llygod
Pen y Mwdwl
Tal-y-Cae
Tregarth
Rachub
Bethesda
Garnedd Uchaf
926
Dulyn
Dolgarrog
Dolgarrog Sta.
A548
Pentir
Gerlan
SNOWDONIA
Rhiwlas
Braichmelyn
Dulyn Resr
Porth-llwyd
Pont Dolgarrog
Vale of Conwy
Rhos-y-mawn
12
B5382
Llans
A5
B4409

A
B
C
D
1
2
3
4
5
3.2 miles to 1 inch
0 2 4 6 8 10 miles
0 2 4 6 8 10 km
2 km to 1 cm
Douglas, Isle of Man 2½ - 4 hrs
Form
89
Belfast 8½ hrs, Dublin 3¼ - 8 hrs
LIVERPOOL BAY
East Hoyle Bank
Meols Sta.
Hoylake
A553
Manor Rd. Sta.
Saughall Massie
Hilbre Island
West Kirby
Frankby
B5139
Caldy
A540
Thurstaston
The Wirral (NT)
Dawpool Bank
Welsh Channel
Point of Ayr
Talacre
Prestatyn
RHYL
Sky Tower
Sea Life Centre
Ocean Beach Amusement Park
A548
Gronant
Mostyn Bank
Ffynnongroyw
Gwespyr
Llanasa
Mostyn Quay
A547
Gwaenysgor
Gyrn
Kinmel Bay (Bae Cinmel)
Meliden (Gallt Melyd)
Gop Hill
Trelogan
Towyn
A525
B5119
Mostyn
Glan-y-don
Abergele Roads
Pensarn
Trelawnyd
Llannerch-y-Môr
Maen Achwyfaen
Downing
Holywell Bank
Llanddulas
Morfa Rhuddlan
Plas Llwyd
Rhuddlan
Dyserth
Whitford (Chwitffordd)
Mertyn
Basingwerk Abbey
Greenfield Valley
Abergele
Bodrhyddan Hall
Greenfield (Maes-Gl
Rhuddlan Castle & Twt Hill
Marian Cwm
A5151
Lloc
A5026
Carmel
COLWYN BAY (Bae Colwyn)
A55
Old Colwyn
Llysfaen
Gwrych
Rhyd-y-foel
Cwm
Llyn Helyg
St Winifred's Holy Well & Ch
Pengwern
Roman Road
Gorsedd
Llanelian-yn-Rhôs
Gele
St George
Bodelwyddan
Pantasaph
Walwen
Holywell (Treffynnon)
Dolwen
Betws-yn-Rhos
DENBIGHSHIRE
Rhuallt
Pen-y-cefn
Brynford
Bagillt
St Asaph (Llanelwy)
Groesffordd
Babell
A5026
Bedol
Dawn
B5381
A548
Moelfre Isaf
Marli
Tremeirchion
FLINTSHIRE
Flint (Y Fflint)
Mynydd Bodrochwyn
Elwy
Cefn Meiriadog
Caerwys
Aifonwen Craft & Antique Centre
Pentre Halkyn
Mynydd Branar
CONWY
VALE OF CLWYD
Graig
Llannerch
Afon-wen
Llannefydd
A541
Ysceifiog
Lixwm
Halkyn Mountain
A5119
Llanfair Talhaiarn
Plas-yn-Cefn
A525
Trefnant
Moel y Parc
398
Ddôl
Walwen
Halkyn
Pentre Isaf
A544
Tre-pys-llygod
Aled
76
Bodfari
B5428
A541
A525
Nannerch
Rhes-y-cae
Northop
Llangernyw
Plasisaf
Henllan
A543
Pen y Mwdwl
Friary (ruins)
Dinbych Llanfair
A548
B5382
Denbigh (Dinbych)
Waen
Llangwyfan
Moel Llys-y-coed
Rhydymwyn
A5119
Llansannan
A541
(Bae Penrhyn)
-on-Sea
o-yn-Rhôs

91
D
E
F
G
100
92
78
SOUTHPORT
Southport Pier
Pleasureland
Zoo
Trans Pennine Trail
Birkdale
Ainsdale
Horse Bank
Angry Brow
Banks
Crossens
Marshside
Churchtown
Mere Brow
Martin Mere
Holmeswood
Tarleton
Becconsall
Hundred End
Hesketh Bank
Much Hoole
Bretherton
Croston
Sollom
Rufford
Rufford Old Hall (NT)
Leyland
Farington
Clayton-le-Woods
Whittle-le-Woods
Euxton
CHORLEY
Astley Hall
Eccleston
Camelot Theme Park
Heskin Green
Charnock Richard
Coppull
Coppull Moor
Adlington
Rivington
Heapey
White Coppice
Anglezarke Moor
Limbrick
Botany Bay Villages
Brinscall
Grimeford V
Blackrod
Standish
Shevington Moor
Shevington
Red Rock
Haigh
Aspull
Wrightington Bar
Parbold
Mawdesley
Newburgh
Appley Bridge
Dalton
Roby Mill
Gathurst
Marylebone
WIGAN
Wigan Pier
Orrell
Up Holland
Ince-in-Makerfield
Hindley
Platt Bridge
Abram
Westleigh
Pennington Flash
Bryn
Bryn Gates
Ashton-in-Makerfield
Golborne
Lowton
Lane Head
Kenyon
NEWTON-LE-WILLOWS
Croft
Winwick
Burtonwood
WARRINGTON
Fearnhead
Orford
Martins
Great Sankey
Penketh
Latchford
Stockton Heath
Lower Walton
Higher Walton
Moore
Appleton
Thorn
Stretton
Hatton
Walton Hall
Daresbury
Preston on the Hill
Preston Brook
Higher Whitley
Lower Whitley
Comberbach
Dutton
Aston
Sutton Weaver
Frodsham
Netherton
Helsby
Alvanley
Newton
Kingsley
Crowton
Acton Bridge
Little Leigh
Weaverham
Northwich
Norley
Cuddington
Sandiway
Hatchmere
DELAMERE
FOREST PARK
Delamere
Whitegate
Foxwist Green
Salterswall
Winsford
Kelsall
Willington Corner
Cotebrook
Little Budworth Common
Tarvin Sands
Tarvin
Oscroft
Great Barrow
Mickle Trafford
Guilden Sutton
Littleton
Christleton
Hoole
Upton
CHESTER
Saltney
Hawarden
Ewloe
Aston
Sandycroft
Mancot
Queensferry
Sealand
Blacon
Shotton
Connah's Quay
Garden City
Wepre
Northop Hall
Saughall
Mollington
Backford
Picton
Bridge Trafford
Dunham-on-the-Hill
Manley
Mouldsworth
Hapsford
Thornton-le-Moors
Elton
Ince
Ince Banks
Stoak
Little Stanney
Wervin
Blue Planet Aquarium
Cheshire Oaks
Whitby
ELLESMERE PORT
Overpool
Great Sutton
Capenhurst
Ledsham
Puddington
Shotwick
Burton
Ness
Botanic Gardens
Neston
Little Neston
Parkgate
Willaston
Childer Thornton
Little Sutton
Hooton
Mount Manisty
Eastham
Eastham Woods
Bromborough
Raby
Thornton Hough
Brimstage
Barnston
Storeton
Gayton
Heswall
Pensby
Irby
Greasby
Woodchurch
Upton
Prenton
Oxton
BIRKENHEAD
Bidston
Seacombe
Leasowe
WALLASEY
New Brighton
New Palace & Adventureland
Rock Ferry
New Ferry
Port Sunlight
Lady Lever Art Gallery
BEBINGTON
Voirrey Embroidery
LIVERPOOL
Lime St Sta
Central Sta
RC Cathedral
Cathedral
HM Customs National Museum
Sudley Art Gal & Mus
Aigburth
Grassendale
Allerton
Garston
Speke
Speke Hall (NT)
Liverpool
Hunt's Cross
Halewood
Hough Green
Ditton
Hale
Hale Bank
WIDNES
RUNCORN
Halton
Norton
Norton Priory
Weston Point
Weston
Keckwick
HALTON
Farnworth
Cronton
Gateacre
Woolton
Childwall
Mossley Hill
National Wildflower Centre
Huyton
Roby
Knotty Ash
West Derby
Croxteth Hall
Knowsley
Knowsley Safari Park
Prescot
Whiston
Rainhill
Rainhill Stoops
Bold Heath
Clock Face
Sutton Leach
ST HELENS
Thatto Heath
West Park
Eccleston
Transport Mus
World of Glass
Haydock
Earlestown
Collins Green
Garswood
Crank
Moss Bank
Billinge
Rainford
Crawford
Bickerstaffe
Barrow Nook
Melling Mount
Melling
KIRKBY
Aintree
LITHERLAND
Ford
Netherton
Sefton
Seaforth
Waterloo
BOOTLE
Walton
CROSBY
Great Crosby
Little Crosby
Hall Road Sta
Thornton
Lunt
Maghull
Lydiate
Ince Blundell
Hightown
Great Altcar
Formby
Freshfield
Formby Hills
Downholland Cross
Haskayne
Barton
Halsall
ORMSKIRK
Aughton Park
Aughton
Town Green
Scarth Hill
SKELMERSDALE
Westhead
Digmoor
Scarisbrick
Shirdley Hill
Bescar
Brown Edge
Snape Green
Tarlscough
New Lane
Burscough Bridge
Burscough
Pinfold
Danger Zone
Mad Wharf
Crosby Channel
LANCASHIRE
GREATER MANCHESTER
MERSEYSIDE
WIRRAL
MERSEY
CHESHIRE
Manchester Ship Canal
Weaver
M6
M61
M58
M57
M62
M56
M53
A59
A565
A570
A580
A57
A5209
A49
A6
A577
A58
A5080
A5300
A562
A561
A533
A557
A556
A54
A51
A41
A550
A5117
A540
A494
A548
A5268
A5116
A552
A554
A551
A553
A5027
A5036
A566
A506
A5058
A506
A5207
A5147
A5267
A581
A573
A574
A559
A5061
A56
A5032
A5117
Toll

92
100
91
79
A
B
C
D
1
2
3
4
5
BLACKBURN WITH DARWEN
LANCS
GREATER MANCHESTER
WARRINGTON
CHESHIRE
Withnell
Darwen
Hoddlesden
Haslingden
RAWTENSTALL
Bacup
Clough Foot
Britannia
Whelton
Heapey
Brinscall
Ryal Fold
Tockholes
Helmshore
Waterfoot
Shawforth
Euxton
CHORLEY
White Coppice
Anglezarke Moor
Turton Moor
Edenfield
Whittle Hill
Whitworth
Calderbrook
Limbrick
Belmont
Edgworth
Stubbins
Ramsbottom
Shuttleworth
Wardle
Charnock Richard
Winter Hill
Turton Bottoms
Chapeltown
Cheesden
Broadley
Healey
Coppull
Rivington
Egerton
Summerseat
Wolstenholme
Smallbridge
Sykes
Adlington
Grimeford Village
Toppings
Greenmount
Walmersley
Shawclough
Firgrove
Eagley
Astley Bridge
Tottington
ROCHDALE
Milnrow
Coppull Moor
Bradshaw
Harwood
Limefield
Newhey
Shevington Moor
Horwich
Blackrod
Standish
BOLTON
HEYWOOD
Castleton
Red Rock
Ainsworth
BURY
Fishpool
Haigh
Aspull
Lostock Junction
Hollins
Slattocks
Shevington
Daubhill
RADCLIFFE
Birch
Marylebone
Wingates
Little Lever
Whitefield
Royton
WIGAN
Westhoughton
FARNWORTH
Prestolee
MIDDLETON
Chadderton
Hindley
Hindley Green
Kearsley
Ashton-in-Makerfield
Platt Bridge
Little Hulton
Walkden
Higher Blackley
Atherton
PRESTWICH
Failsworth
Bryn
Bryn Gates
Abram
Tyldesley
Swinton
Harpurhey
LEIGH
Worsley
Pendlebury
Boothstown
Lower Broughton
Cheetham Hill
ASHTON-UNDER-LYNE
Higher Green
SALFORD
Golborne
Lately Common
Astley Green
ECCLES
Droylsden
Lowton
Lowton Common
Lane Head
Glazebury
Barton
Trafford Centre
MANCHESTER
Audenshaw
NEWTON-LE-WILLOWS
Twiss Green
Chat Moss
Trafford Park
Gorton
Denton
HYDE
Kenyon
Culcheth
URMSTON
STRETFORD
Rusholme
Levenshulme
Croft
Irlam
Flixton
Chorlton-cum-Hardy
Reddish
Haughton Green
Burtonwood
Winwick
Risley
Carrington
Withington
Heaton Moor
Cadishead
Carrington Moss
Ashton upon Mersey
SALE
Burnage
Bredbury
Fearnhead
Birchwood
Partington
Didsbury
Romiley
Orford
Martinscroft
Hollins Green
Great Sankey
Woolston
Warburton
Broadheath
Baguley
STOCKPORT
WARRINGTON
Heatley
ALTRINCHAM
Timperley
CHEADLE
Heaviley
Offerton
Statham
Lymm
Dunham Town
Bowdon
GATLEY
Latchford
Thelwall
Grappenhall
Hale
Cheadle Hulme
HAZEL GROVE
Stockton Heath
Little Bollington
Halebarns
Heald Green
Bramhall
Lower Walton
Walton
Broomedge
Moss Nook
Appleton Thorn
Sworton Heath
High Legh
Ashley
Manchester
Styal
Handforth
Poynton
Keckwick
Hatton
Stretton
Rostherne
Daresbury
Tatton Park
Morley Green
Woodford
Preston on the Hill
Preston Brook
Higher Whitley
Arley
Mere
WILMSLOW
Dean Row
Adlington
Over Tabley
Knolls Green
Dutton
Antrobus
Bate Heath
Mobberley
Mottram St Andrew
Lower Whitley
Great Budworth
Knutsford
Alderley Edge
Bollington
Aston
Comberbach
Pickmere
Prestbury
Ollerton
Little Leigh
Marthall
Kerridge
Anderton
Marston
Plumley
Nether Alderley
Tytherington
Barnton
Wincham
Lostock Gralam
Chelford
Monks' Heath
Hurdsfield
Crowton
Weaverham
Smithy Green
Lower Peover
Over Peover
Henbury
Northwich
Rudheath
Peover Heath
Capesthorne
Broken Cross
MACCLESFIELD
Norley
Lostock Green
Jodrell Bank Science Cen & Arboretum
Badgerbank
Cuddington
Sandiway
Hartford
Broken Cross
Blackden Heath
Lach Dennis
Langley
Davenham
Puddinglake
Goostrey
Withington Green
Siddington
Warren
Gawsworth
Sutton Lane Ends
Whitegate
Moulton
Byley
Jodrell Bank
Lower Withington
Oakgrove
Delamere
Bostock Green
Cranage
Highlane
Foxwist Green
Gleadsmoss
Marton
Rodeheath
Salterswall
Winsford
Wharton
Sproston Green
Holmes Chapel
Swettenham
Little Budworth Common
Over
Middlewich
Brereton
Eaton
North Rode
Bosley
M6
M61
M62
M60
M602
M66
M56
A627(M)
A6144(M)

Mankinholes
Cragg
Sowerby Bridge
Southowram
Liversedge
Heckmondwike
Kirkhamgate
Turley Holes Edge
Sowerby
Triangle
Norland Town
BRIGHOUSE
Rastrick
Roberttown
DEWSBURY
Ravensthorpe
Ossett
Lumb
Mill Bank
Greetland
Elland
Soyland Moor
Ripponden
Barkisland
Holywell Green
Stainland
Lindley
Upper Hopton
Whitley Lower
Thornhill
Horbury
Netherton
Middlestown
Crigglestone
Rishworth Moor
Rishworth
Booth Wood
Outlane
Quarmby
Kirkheaton
National Coal Mining Museum of England
Grange Moor
Flockton Green
Flockton
Hill Top
HUDDERSFIELD
Golcar
Milnsbridge
Linthwaite
Cowmes
Lepton
Almondbury
Midgley
West Bretton
Woolley Edge
Woolley
Moselden Height
Pole Moor
Moss Moor
WEST YORKS
Slaithwaite
Netherton
Farnley Tyas
Highburton
Kirkburton
Emley
Yorkshire Sculpture Park
Denshaw
Crompton Fold
Castleshaw Moor
Huddersfield Narrow Canal and The Standedge Experience
Close Moss
Marsden
Meltham
Butterley Resr
Honley
Brockholes
Shelley
Kirklees Lt. Rly
Skelmanthorpe
Clayton West
High Hoyland
Kexbrough
Darton
Staincross
Mapplewell
Bleak Hey Nook
Diggle
Marsden Moor Estate
Netherthong
Thurstonland
New Mill
Shepley
Cannon Hall
Cannon Hall Farm
Moorside
Strinesdale Countryside Area
Delph
Wessenden Moor
Upperthong
Holmfirth
Lane Head
Denby Dale
Cawthorne
Gawber
BARNSLEY
Dobcross
Uppermill
Austonley
Scholes
Hepworth
Upper Denby
Silkstone
Ingbirchworth
Hoyland Swaine
Silkstone Common
Saddleworth Moor
Holme
Black Hill
OLDHAM
Grasscroft
Greenfield
Alphin Pike
Dovestone Resr
Chew Resr
Mossley
Micklehurst
SOUTH
Wentworth Castle
Penistone
Thurlstone
Heyden
Moor
Carlecotes
Thurlstone Moors
Dunford Bridge
Oxspring
Birdwell
Featherbed Moss
Windleden Resrs
YORKSHIRE
Thurgoland
Pilley
Tankersley
Langsett
Upper Midhope
Midhopestones
Walkerwood Res
Longdendale
Salter's Brook Bridge
Featherbed Moss
Langsett Resr
Midhope Moors
Stocksbridge
Wortley
STALYBRIDGE
Torside Resr
Deepcar
Bolsterstone
Broomhead Resr
High Green
Newton
Hollingworth
Tintwistle
Howden Moors
Bleaklow Hill
Margery Hill
Wightwizzle
Ewden Village
Broomhead Moor
Mottram in Longdendale
Hadfield
Dinting Sta.
Old Glossop
Whar Side
Grenoside
Gee Cross
Glossop
Doctor's Gate
Oughtibridge
Werneth Low
Broadbottom
Charlesworth
Snake Pass
PEAK
Howden Resr
Abbey Brook
Bradfield Moors
High Bradfield
Agden Resr
Birley Carr
Chisworth
Etherow
Hope Woodlands
Chunal
Featherbed Top
Derwent Dale
Strines Resr
Low Bradfield
Worrall
Damflask Resr
Compstall
Derwent Resr
Upper Derwent Reservoirs
Ladybower Resr
The Edge
Marple
Mellor
Kinder Reservoir
Kinder Scout
Totley Moor
Loxley
Stannington
Little Hayfield
High Peak
DERBYSHIRE
The Peak
Edale Moor
Edale
Thornsett
Birch Vale
Hayfield
Kinder Low
Edale Cross
DISTRICT
Win Hill
High Neb
Stanage Edge
Redmires Reservoirs
Fulwood
Newtown
Disley
Low Leighton
New Mills
Brown Knoll
Barber Booth
Vale of Edale
Lose Hill
Aston
Thornhill
Bamford
Chinley Head
Mam Tor
Treak Cliff Cavern
Castleton
Hope
Furness Vale
Black Hill
Chinley
Rushup Edge
Hope Valley
Brough
Burbage Moor
Whaley Bridge
Buxworth
Slackhall
Peak Cavern
Peveril Castle
Speedwell Cavern (NT)
Hathersage
Carl Wark
Dore
Beauchief
Totley
Horwich End
Lower Crossings
Chapel-en-le-Frith
Sparrowpit
Eldon Hill
Bradwell
St. Michael
Kettleshulme
Coplow Dale
Abney
Nether Padley
Longshaw Estate
Shrigley
Taxal
Combs Reservoir
Combs
NATIONAL
Little Hucklow
Peak Forest
Eyam Moor Tumulus & Stone Circle
Great Hucklow
Dronfield Woodhouse
Stubley
Fernilee
Fernilee Resr
Hob Tor
Dove Holes
Grindlow
Grindleford
Lidgate
Holmesfield
Rainow
Peak Dale
Wheston
Foolow
Eyam
Froggatt
St. Lawrence
Barbrook Reservoir
Common Side
Goyt's Bridge
Shining Tor
Errwood Resr
Upper End
Tideswell
Litton
Stoney Middleton
White Edge
Curbar
Moorhall
Barlow
BUXTON
Wormhill
Wardlow
Calver
Cutthorpe
MACCLESFIELD
Fairfield
Micrarium
Miller's Dale
Linacre Reservoirs
Macclesfield Forest
Goyt's Moss
Burbage
Blackwell
Great Longstone
Rowland
Baslow
Over End
Robin Hood
Old Brampton
Cat and Fiddle Inn
Pavilion Gardens
King Sterndale
Little Longstone
Hassop
Nether End
Wadshelf
Buxton
Harpur Hill
Taddington
Pilsley
Chatsworth Farmyard & Adventure Playground
Edensor
Chatsworth
Holymoorside
EAST MOOR
Chelmorton
PARK
Wildboarclough
Axe Edge
Sheldon
Flagg
Bakewell
Beeley
Flash
Earl Sterndale
Burntcliff Top
Monyash
Haddon Hall
Over Haddon
Rowsley
Caudwell's Mill
Hollinsclough
Gradbach
Wincle
102
94
80

WAKEFIELD
Normanton
Altofts
Outwood
Wrenthorpe
Ossett
Horbury
Netherton
Middlestown
Crigglestone
Walton
Crofton
Sharlston
Featherstone
PONTEFRACT
Ackton
Purston Jaglin
Carleton
Darrington
East Hardwick
West Hardwick
Ackworth
Wentbridge
Thorpe Audlin
Badsworth
Ackworth Moor Top
Fitzwilliam
Kinsley
Hemsworth
South Hiendley
Ryhill
Wintersett
Notton
Woolley
West Bretton
Clayton West
Darton
Kexbrough
Mapplewell
Staincross
Royston
Carlton
Cudworth
Shafton
Brierley
Grimethorpe
South Kirkby
North Elmsall
South Elmsall
Upton
Hampole
Adwick le Street
Clayton
Hooton Pagnell
Brodsworth
Great Houghton
Thurnscoe
Billingley
Darfield
Goldthorpe
Barnburgh
Hickleton
Marr
BARNSLEY
Gawber
Dodworth
Silkstone
Silkstone Common
Penistone
Oxspring
Thurgoland
Wentworth Castle
Worsbrough
Wombwell
Ardsley
Birdwell
Pilley
Hoyland
Jump
Tankersley
Wortley
Elsecar
Brampton
Wath upon Dearne
West Melton
Swinton
Mexborough
Denaby
Conisbrough
Kilnhurst
Bolton upon Dearne
Adwick upon Dearne
High Melton
Sprotbrough
Cadeby
Warmsworth
DONCASTER
BENTLEY
Arksey
Armthorpe
Cantley
Bessacarr
Edlington
New Edlington
Loversall
Wadworth
Rossington
New Rossington
Carcroft
Skellow
Burghwallis
Campsall
Norton
Askern
Sutton
Womersley
Little Smeaton
Kirk Smeaton
Walden Stubbs
Cridling Stubbs
Whitley
Eggborough
Hensall
Great Heck
Pollington
Fenwick
Moss
Braithwaite
Kirk Bramwith
Thorpe in Balne
Barnby Dun
Kirk Sandall
Edenthorpe
Dunsville
Nutwell
Auckley
Ferrybridge
Deepcar
Stocksbridge
Chapeltown
High Green
Wentworth
Nether Haugh
Thorpe Hesley
Greasbrough
Rawmarsh
Parkgate
Thrybergh
Ravenfield
Dalton
ROTHERHAM
Wickersley
Bramley
Braithwell
Maltby
Hooton Levitt
Stainton
Tickhill
Bawtry
Harworth
Styrrup
Oldcotes
Firbeck
Laughton en le Morthen
Thurcroft
Brampton en le Morthen
Ulley
Aughton
Whiston
Brinsworth
Tinsley
Catcliffe
Treeton
Ecclesfield
Grenoside
Oughtibridge
Wharncliffe Side
Bradfield
High Bradfield
Low Bradfield
Worrall
Wadsley Bridge
Wincobank
Meadowhall
Fir Vale
Stannington
Darnall
Handsworth
SHEFFIELD
Fulwood
Intake
Woodhouse
Aston
Hackenthorpe
Beighton
Heeley
Gleadless
Beauchief
Norton
Dore
Totley
Greenhill
Highlane
Ridgeway
Mosborough
Halfway
Killamarsh
Eckington
Marsh Lane
Spinkhill
Coal Aston
Dronfield
Dronfield Woodhouse
Apperknowle
Stubley
Holmesfield
Lidgate
Unstone
West Handley
Middle Handley
Renishaw
Barlborough
Whitwell
Hodthorpe
Staveley
Whittington
Common Side
Barlow
Moorhall
Cutthorpe
Newbold
CHESTERFIELD
Old Brampton
Wadshelf
Brimington
Brimington Common
Arkwright
Calow
Duckmanton
Woodthorpe
Clowne
Creswell
Elmton
Holbeck
Whaley
Bolsover
Nether Langwith
Upper Langwith
Shuttlewood
Carr Vale
Hills Town
Palterton
Scarcliffe
Stony Houghton
Glapwell
Ault Hucknall
Shirebrook
Market Warsop
Church Warsop
Meden Vale
Cuckney
Norton
Welbeck Abbey
Carburton
Budby
Edwinstowe
Thoresby
Dinnington
North Anston
South Anston
Todwick
Kiveton Park
Wales
Harthill
Thorpe Salvin
Shireoaks
Netherthorpe
Rhodesia
WORKSOP
Gateford
Woodsetts
Gildingwells
Letwell
Langold
Carlton in Lindrick
North Carlton
Wigthorpe
Scofton
Blyth
Holymoorside
Walton
Beeley
Rowsley
Wingerworth
Grassmoor
Temple Normanton
Heath
Sutton Scarsdale
Holmewood
Williamthorpe
Tupton
Old Tupton
Nether Moor
Hasland
Cock Alley
Doe Lea
Brampton
WEST YORKSHIRE
NORTH YORKS
SOUTH YORKSHIRE
DERBYSHIRE
The Dukeries
Burbage Moor
EAST MOOR
M1
M18
M62
A1(M)
A1

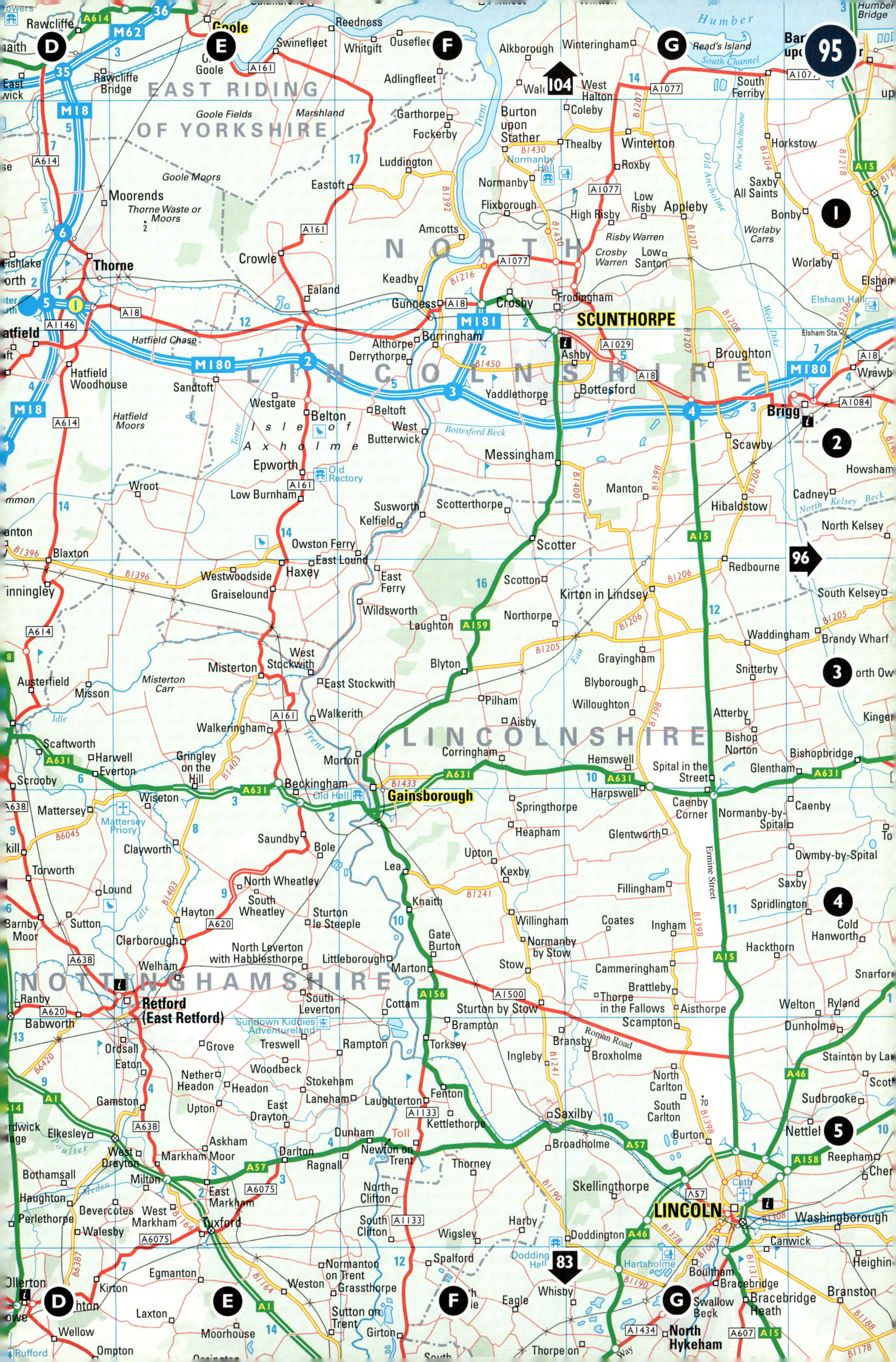
Rawcliffe
Goole
Reedness
Swinefleet
Whitgift
Ousefleet
Humber
Read's Island
South Channel
Alkborough
Winteringham
West Halton
Coleby
South Ferriby
Horkstow
Rawcliffe Bridge
EAST RIDING OF YORKSHIRE
Goole Fields
Marshland
Adlingfleet
Garthorpe
Fockerby
Trent
Burton upon Stather
Thealby
Winterton
Roxby
Normanby Hall
Luddington
Normanby
Flixborough
Eastoft
Goole Moors
Moorends
Thorne Waste or Moors
Thorne
Crowle
Amcotts
NORTH
High Risby
Low Risby
Appleby
Risby Warren
Crosby Warren
Low Santon
Saxby All Saints
Bonby
Worlaby Carrs
Worlaby
Elsham
Elsham Hall
Old Ancholme
New Ancholme
Keadby
Gunness
Crosby
Frodingham
SCUNTHORPE
Ealand
Hatfield
Hatfield Chase
Burringham
Althorpe
Derrythorpe
Ashby
Broughton
Hatfield Woodhouse
Sandtoft
LINCOLNSHIRE
Yaddlethorpe
Bottesford
Brigg
Wrawby
Westgate
Belton
Beltoft
West Butterwick
Bottesford Beck
Isle of Axholme
Hatfield Moors
Messingham
Scawby
Howsham
Epworth
Old Rectory
Manton
Cadney
Wroot
Low Burnham
Susworth
Kelfield
Scotterthorpe
Hibaldstow
North Kelsey Beck
North Kelsey
Scotter
Blaxton
Owston Ferry
East Lound
Haxey
Westwoodside
Graiseloud
Redbourne
East Ferry
Scotton
Kirton in Lindsey
South Kelsey
Wildsworth
Laughton
Northorpe
Waddingham
Brandy Wharf
West Stockwith
Misterton
Blyton
Grayingham
Snitterby
Austerfield
Misson
Misterton Carr
East Stockwith
Blyborough
Willoughton
Walkerith
Pilham
Aisby
Atterby
Bishop Norton
Walkeringham
Scaftworth
Harwell
Everton
Gringley on the Hill
Morton
Corringham
Hemswell
Spital in the Street
Glentham
Bishopbridge
Scrooby
Beckingham
Old Hall
Gainsborough
Harpswell
Caenby Corner
Normanby-by-Spital
Caenby
Wiseton
Mattersey
Mattersey Priory
Springthorpe
Heapham
Glentworth
Ermine Street
Clayworth
Saundby
Bole
Upton
Kexby
Owmby-by-Spital
Torworth
Lound
North Wheatley
Lea
Fillingham
Saxby
South Wheatley
Knaith
Spridlington
Hayton
Sturton le Steeple
Barnby Moor
Sutton
Gate Burton
Willingham
Coates
Ingham
Cold Hanworth
Clarborough
North Leverton with Habblesthorpe
Littleborough
Marton
Normanby by Stow
Hackthorn
Welham
Stow
NOTTINGHAMSHIRE
Cammeringham
Snarford
Ranby
Retford (East Retford)
South Leverton
Cottam
Sturton by Stow
Thorpe in the Fallows
Brattleby
Aisthorpe
Welton
Ryland
Babworth
Sundown Kiddies Adventureland
Brampton
Scampton
Dunholme
Ordsall
Grove
Treswell
Rampton
Torksey
Bransby
Roman Road
Broxholme
Stainton by Langworth
Eaton
Woodbeck
Ingleby
North Carlton
Nether Headon
Headon
Stokeham
South Carlton
Sudbrooke
Gamston
Upton
East Drayton
Laneham
Laughterton
Fenton
Saxilby
Burton
Nettleham
Elkesley
Askham
Dunham
Toll
Kettlethorpe
Broadholme
Reepham
West Drayton
Markham Moor
Darlton
Newton on Trent
Thorney
Cherry Willingham
Bothamsall
Milton
Ragnall
Skellingthorpe
Cath
LINCOLN
Haughton
East Markham
North Clifton
Washingborough
Perlethorpe
Bevercotes
West Markham
Tuxford
South Clifton
Harby
Doddington
Canwick
Walesby
Wigsley
Dodding Hall
Hartsholme
Heighington
Ollerton
Egmanton
Normanton on Trent
Spalford
Boultham
Bracebridge
Kirton
Weston
Grassthorpe
Whisby
Eagle
Swallow Beck
Bracebridge Heath
Branston
Laxton
Sutton on Trent
North Hykeham
Wellow
Moorhouse
Girton
Thorpe on the Hill
Ompton
Rufford
M62
M18
M180
M181
A614
A161
A1077
A18
A1146
A1029
A1084
A159
A631
A638
A620
A156
A1500
A1133
A57
A6075
A46
A15
A158
A1434
A607
A1
B1430
B1392
B1216
B1450
B1207
B1204
B1218
B1206
B1208
B1398
B1400
B1396
B1205
B1403
B1433
B1241
B6045
B6420
B6387
B1164
B1190
B1378
B1003
B1131
B1308
B1188
B1178
104
96
83

A
B
C
D
104
95
83
1
2
3
4
5
Humber
Barton-upon-Humber
New Holland
East Halton Skitter
Paull Holme Sands
Cherry Cobb Sands
Foulholme Sands
Patrington
Haven Side
EAST RIDING OF YORKSHIRE
Sunk Island
Old Hall
Sunk Island Sands
South Ferriby
Barrow upon Humber
Goxhill
South End
East Halton
Thornton Abbey
Thornton Curtis
NORTH LINCOLNSHIRE
Horkstow
Saxby All Saints
Bonby
Worlaby Carrs
Worlaby
Burnham
Wootton
North Killingholme
South Killingholme
Immingham Dock
MOUTH OF THE HUMBER
Ulceby
Immingham
Habrough
Brocklesby Sta.
Elsham
Elsham Hall
Croxton
Kirmington
Brocklesby
Stallingborough
Healing
NORTH EAST LINCOLNSHIRE
West Marsh
Great Coates
Wellholme Galleries
GRIMSBY
National Fishing Heritage Centre
CLEETHORPES
Elsham Sta.
Melton Ross
Humberside International
Keelby
Broughton
M180
Wrawby
Barnetby le Wold
Great Limber
Aylesby
Brigg
Bigby
Riby
Laceby
Bradley
Scartho
Humberston
Searby
Owmby
Grasby
Irby upon Humber
Waltham
New Waltham
Howsham
Cadney
Hibaldstow
North Kelsey Beck
Swallow
Barnoldby le Beck
Holton le Clay
Brigsley
Ashby cum Fenby
Tetney
North Cotes
Tetney Lock
North Kelsey
Roman Road
Caistor
Cabourne
Beelsby
Hatcliffe
Cuxwold
Nettleton
Rothwell
Grainsby
Moortown
South Kelsey
East Ravendale
Holton le Moor
North Thoresby
Thornton le Moor
Waddingham
Brandy Wharf
Thoresway
Thorganby
Wold Newton
Churchthorpe
Fulstow
Swinhope
Ludborough
North Owersby
Covenham St Bartholomew
Normanby le Wold
Stainton le Vale
Claxby
Usselby
Kirmond le Mire
Binbrook
Utterby
Atterby
Bishop Norton
Kingerby
Kirkby
Osgodby
Osgodby Moor
Walesby
North Ormsby
Fotherby
Little Grimsby
North Elkington
Bishopbridge
Glentham
Tealby
Kelstern
Caenby
Normanby-by-Spital
West Rasen
Middle Rasen
Market Rasen
Ludford Parva
Ludford Magna
Welton le Wold
South Elkington
Keddington
Louth
Toft next Newton
North Willingham
Burgh on Bain
Newton by Toft
Owmby-by-Spital
Linwood
Sixhills
Hallington
Saxby
Legsby
Gayton le Wold
Spridlington
Faldingworth
Hainton
LINCOLNSHIRE
THE WOLDS
Raithby
Cold Hanworth
Lissington
East Torrington
South Willingham
Donington on Bain
Tathwell
Hackthorn
Friesthorpe
Wickenby
West Torrington
Benniworth
Snarford
Holton cum Beckering
East Barkwith
Stenigot
Haugham
Cawthorpe
Welton
Ryland
Snelland
West Barkwith
Market Stainton
Cadwell Park
Dunholme
Fulnetby
Rand
Panton
Sotby
Cawkwell
Asterby
Maidenwell
Goulceby
Stainton by Langworth
Langton by Wragby
Wragby
Ranby
Scamblesby
Farforth
Great Sturton
Oxcombe
Scothern
Sudbrooke
Langworth
Hatton
Flint Hill
Kingthorpe
Nettleham
Barlings
Apley
Hemingby
Belchford
Reepham
Baumber
Cherry Willingham
Stainfield
Minting
West Ashby
Fulletby
Tetford
Salmonby
Fiskerton
Gautby
Wispington
Low Toynton
LINCOLN
Washingborough
Waddingworth
Edlington
Ashby Puerorum
Canwick
Branston Booths
Thimbleby
Greetham
Boultham
Heighington
Bardney
Bucknall
Horsington
Langton
Horncastle
High Toynton
Winceby 1643
Bracebridge
Bracebridge Heath
Branston
Potterhanworth Booths
Thornton
Mareham on the Hill
Hameringham
Swallow Beck
Nocton Fen
Southrey
Potterhanworth
Dalderby
Asgarby
Hareby
Stixwould
Claxby Pluckacre
Witham
Ermine Street
Abbey
A15
A18
A46
A160
A180
A1173
A1077
A1084
A1103
A631
A157
A158
A153
A16
A1098
A1031
A1136
A1033
M180

D
E
F
G
105
Holmpton
Out Newton
Weeton
Skeffling
Easington
Skeffling Clays
Kilnsea
Kilnsea Clays
Spurn Head
3.2 miles to 1 inch
0 2 4 6 8 10 miles
0 2 4 6 8 10 km
2 km to 1 cm
1
2
3
4
5
ORPES
Marsh Chapel
Eskham
Wragholme
Grainthorpe
Meals
North Somercotes
Donna Nook
Ludney
Conisholme
Church End
A1031
South Somercotes
Saltfleet
Skidbrooke
Saltfleetby St Clements
Alvingham
Saltfleetby All Saints
North Cockerington
South Cockerington
Saltfleetby St Peter
Theddlethorpe St Helen
Grimoldby
B1200
Theddlethorpe All Saints
Manby
Little Carlton
Great Carlton
Great Eau
Mablethorpe
Legbourne
South Reston
Gayton le Marsh
A1104
Trusthorpe
North Reston
Strubby
Withern
A157
Thorpe
A52
Sutton on Sea
Authorpe
Tothill
Maltby le Marsh
B1373
Muckton
Beesby
Sutton le Marsh
Sandilands
Burwell
Claythorpe
Markby
Hannah
A16
Belleau
Aby
Saleby
A1111
White Pit
Swaby
A1104
Ketsby
South Thoresby
Bilsby
B1449
Huttoft
Alford
Rigsby
Anderby
Farlesthorpe
Mumby
Well
Authorpe Row
Brinkhill
Driby
Cumberworth
Ulceby Cross
B1196
Chapel St Leonards
Hogsthorpe
Ulceby
Harrington
Harrington Hall
Willoughby
Claxby
Langton
Sloothby
Aswardby
Skendleby
A1028
Welton le Marsh
Sausthorpe
Addlethorpe
Fantasy Island
Ingoldmells Point
85
Partney
A158
Ashby by Partney
Candlesby
Orby
Butlins Family Entertainment Resort, Skegness
Hundleby
Orby Marsh
Burgh Marsh
Spilsby
Mavis Enderby
Gunby Hall (NT)
Burgh le Marsh
Winthorpe
Great
Bratoft

A B C D

ISLE OF MAN
1
2
3
4
5
Point of Ayre
The Ayres
A16
Rue Point
Visitors Centre
Smeale
Farm
Glentruan
Cranstal
The Lhen
A10
Dhowin
A17
Bride
A19
Andreas
Sartfield
Jurby Head
Jurby
Jurby West
Jurby East
B3
A9
Shellag Point
Ballasalla
Sandygate
A17
B14
B7
Regaby
A13
Ballachurry Fort
Crawyn
The Cronk
The Curraghs
A14
St Judes
Dhoor
Ramsey Bay
A13
B9
Sulby
A3
Ramsey
A10
Churchtown
1079
Orrisdale
A3
Ballaugh
Glen Auldyn
Port e Vullen
Orrisdale Head
A18
A15
Maughold Head & Brooghs (MNT)
Maughold Head
Ravensdale
Dreemskerry
Maughold
T.T. Course
North Barrule
565
Ballajora
Kirk Michael
Slieau Curn
I S L E
Glen Auldyn
Corrany
Port Mooar
Slieau Managh
Slieau Dhoo
Clagh Ouyr
Ballacarnane Beg
A3
Sileau Freoaghane
488
A14
Manx Electric Rly
Snaefell
621
Glen Mona
Barregarrow
Sulby Resr
A2
Gob y Deigan
Shoughlaige-e-Caine
Sartfell
Slieau Lhean
Port Cornaa
Dhoon
B10
Knocksharry
A4
Little London
Beinn-y-Phott
546
Snaefell Mountain Rly
St. German's Cath
Peel
Cronk-y-Voddy
O F
Bulgham Bay
St Patrick's Isle
Ballagyr
Lambfell Moar
Injebreck
B11
Peel Castle & Round Tower
Neb
Colden
487
Injebreck Resr
Laxey Glen
Ballaheannagh
House of Manannan
A20
Laxey
Laxey Head
Contrary Head
A1
Tynwald
Ballig
Ballacannell
Sileau Ruy
478
A18
B12
Laxey Bay
Knockaloe Moar
A30
St John's
Greeba Mountain
Baldwin
Baldrine
Garwick Bay
Patrick
M A N
A27
T.T. Course
B21
B22
B20
Clay Head
333
A3
A1
A23
Hillberry
Glenmaye
Crosby
A2
Belfast 2 1/2 hrs (summer only)
Dalby Point
Glen Vine
A22
Onchan
A11
Dalby
Foxdale
Eairy
Garth
Port Groudle
Niarbyl Island
Dalby Mountain
A36
A24
Union Mills
Strang
B35
A26
B32
Onchan Head
Niarbyl Bay
South Barrule
483
B36
Braaid
Manx Mus
Douglas Bay
Close Clark
Stuggadhoo
A24
Strioh Vuigh
341
A27
B39
A41
DOUGLAS
Ballamodha
B35
B37
Quine's Hill
A37
Douglas Head
Newtown
Heysham 3 1/2 hrs
Ronague
A3
St Mark's
B29
Lingague
Grenaby
A26
Ballaveare
Little Ness
Liverpool 2 1/2 - 4 hrs
Fleshwick Bay
B44
A5
A25
Isle of Man Steam Rly
A36
Ballakilpheric
B40
Rushen
10
B25
Ballabeg
Bradda
Colby
A7
Ballafesson
Ballasalla
Bradda Head
A32
B53
Santon Head
Port Erin
Croit e Caley
Port Grenaugh
A3
Balladoole
Isle of Man
Meayl Circle
Nautical Mus
Derbyhaven
Calf of Man
Cregneash
The Howe
Port St Mary
Bay ny Carrickey
Rushen
Derby Fort
A31
Castletown
St Michael's Island
(MNT)
Spanish Head
Perwick Bay
Castletown Bay
Langness
Chicken Rock
Dreswick Point
Dublin 2 1/2 - 4 1/2 hrs (summer only)
same scale as main map

A B C D

D
E
F
G
107
Furness
Little Urswick
Stainton with Adgarley
Hawcoat
Newton
Dendron
Scales
Baycliff
Aldingham
A590
Furness Abbey
Newbarns
Gleaston
A5087
North Scale
Furness Mus
Leece
Dock Museum
Roosecote
Vickerstown
BARROW-IN-FURNESS
Newbiggin
A590
Tummer Hill Scar
CUMBRIA
Biggar
Rampside
Roa Island
Sheep Island
Foulney Island
ISLE OF WALNEY
Piel
Piel Island
South End
Piel Bar
Hilpsford Point
M O R E C A M B E
Cartmel Wharf
B A Y
Lancaster Sound
Mort Bank
Humphrey Head Point
Warton Sands
Yeoman Wharf
MORECAMBE
I
Heysham
Sandylands
A5105
B5273
Oxcliffe Hill
HEYSHAM
Heaton
A683
Middleton
Overton
Heysham Lake
Douglas, Isle of Man 3½ hrs
Belfast 4 hrs
Sunderland Bank
Glasson
Sunderland Point
2
Cockersand Abbey
Larne 8 hrs
Bernard Wharf
A588
100
North Wharf
Pilling Lane
Pilling
Fisher's Row
Rossall Point
FLEETWOOD
Knott End-on-Sea
Preesall
Stake Pool
Freeport
22
Stalmine
Wyre
LANCS
3
Burn Naze
A587
Staynall
A588
Hambleton Moss Side
Cleveleys
Trunnah
Hambleton
Ratten Row
Little Bispham
Thornton
Out Rawcliffe
Norbreck
Whin Lane End
Toll
Bispham
Carleton
A585
Great Eccleston
A586
North Shore
A587
Poulton-le-Fylde
Singleton
BLACKPOOL
A584
A587
B5266
Thistleton
Elswick
A585
BLACKPOOL
Normoss
Staining
B5260
Esprick
Greenhalgh
Blackpool Tower
Sea Life Centre
Blackpool Zoo
Great Marton
Weeton
4
A5073
A583
M55
South Shore
South Pier
Common Edge
Great Plumpton
Wesham
Pleasure Beach
A5230
A583
Kirkham
Squires Gate
Westby
Blackpool
Wrea Green
13
Higher Ballam
Moss Side
B5259
B5261
St Anne's
LYTHAM ST ANNE'S
Ansdell
Saltcotes
Warton
Freckleton
Lytham
Lytham
12
Salter's Bank
Ribble
3.2 miles to 1 inch
0 2 4 6 8 10 miles
0 2 4 6 8 10 km
2 km to 1 cm
Banks Sands
5
Hesketh Bank
Becconsall
Hundred End
Banks
Horse Bank
Crossens
9
Marshside
A565
91
Hungry Brow
Southport Pier
Churchtown
Mere Brow
SOUTHPORT
Pleasureland
Zoo
Martin Mere
Trans Pennine Trail
Holmeswood
Birkdale
Birkdale
Brown Edge
Bescar Lane Sta.
Tarlscough
A5267

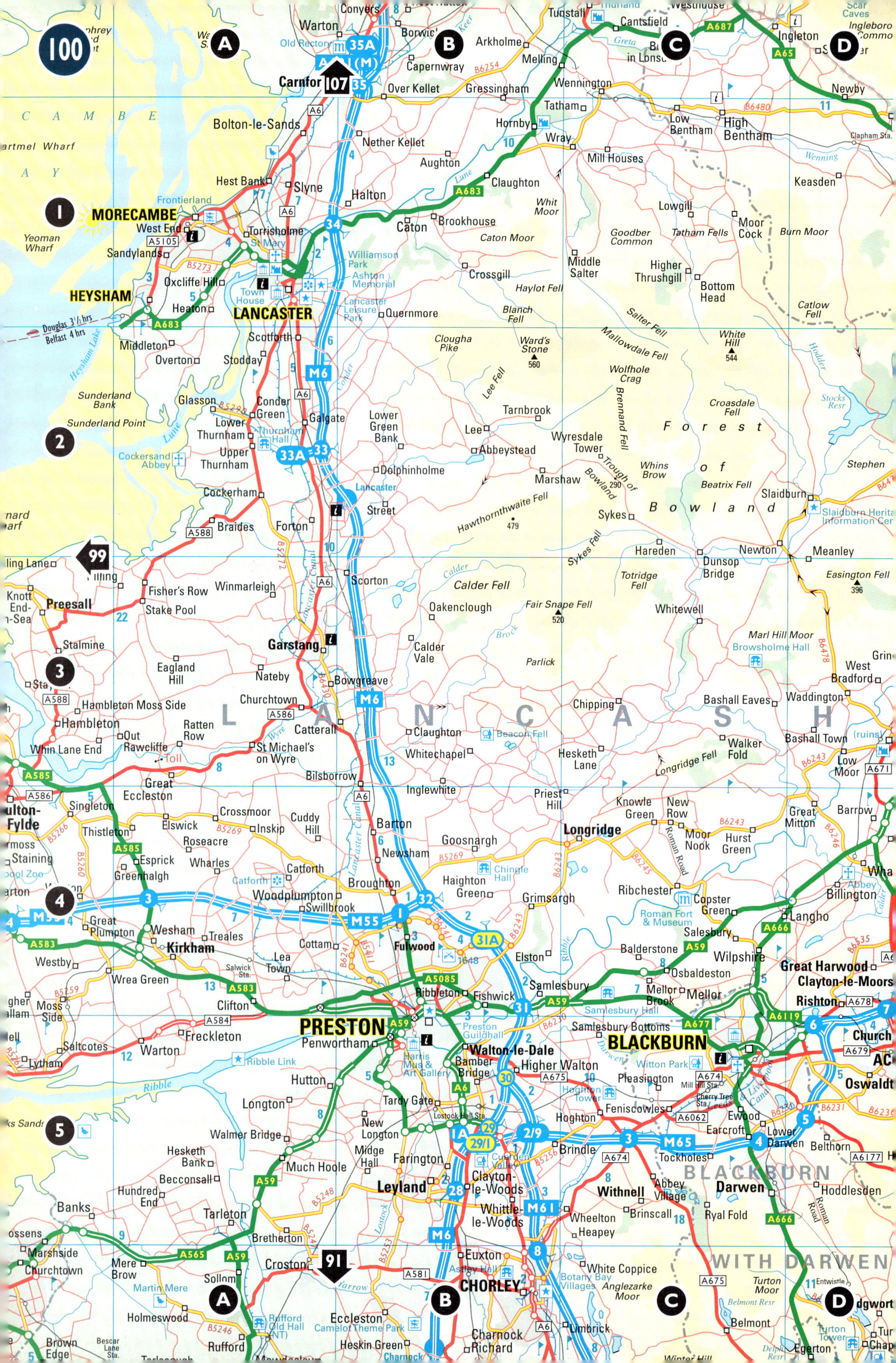

100
107
99
91
A
B
C
D
1
2
3
4
5
MORECAMBE
HEYSHAM
LANCASTER
PRESTON
BLACKBURN
CHORLEY
Carnforth
Warton
Bolton-le-Sands
Hest Bank
Slyne
Halton
Nether Kellet
Over Kellet
Capernwray
Borwick
Arkholme
Melling
Gressingham
Hornby
Wray
Wennington
Tatham
Tunstall
Cantsfield
Ingleton
Newby
Low Bentham
High Bentham
Mill Houses
Claughton
Aughton
Caton
Brookhouse
Caton Moor
Keasden
Lowgill
Tatham Fells
Moor Cock
Burn Moor
Goodber Common
Whit Moor
Middle Salter
Higher Thrushgill
Bottom Head
Crossgill
Haylot Fell
Blanch Fell
Catlow Fell
Quernmore
Williamson Park
Ashton Memorial
Lancaster Leisure Park
Town House
Frontierland
West End
Sandylands
Torrisholme
Oxcliffe Hill
Heaton
Yeoman Wharf
Douglas 3½ hrs
Belfast 4 hrs
Heysham Lake
Middleton
Overton
Stodday
Scotforth
Sunderland Bank
Sunderland Point
Glasson
Conder Green
Galgate
Lower Thurnham
Upper Thurnham
Thurnham Hall
Cockersand Abbey
Cockerham
Braides
Forton
Lower Green Bank
Dolphinholme
Lancaster
Street
Clougha Pike
Ward's Stone
560
Lee Fell
Tarnbrook
Lee
Abbeystead
Wyresdale Tower
Marshaw
Trough of Bowland
Hawthornthwaite Fell
479
Salter Fell
Mallowdale Fell
Wolfhole Crag
Brennand Fell
White Hill
544
Croasdale Fell
Forest of Bowland
Whins Brow
Beatrix Fell
Slaidburn
Slaidburn Heritage Information Centre
Stephen
Sykes
Sykes Fell
Hareden
Newton
Meanley
Dunsop Bridge
Easington Fell
396
Totridge Fell
Whitewell
Marl Hill Moor
Browsholme Hall
West Bradford
Waddington
Bashall Eaves
Bashall Town
Low Moor
Walker Fold
Chipping
Longridge Fell
Hesketh Lane
Beacon Fell
Calder Fell
Oakenclough
Fair Snape Fell
520
Calder Vale
Parlick
Scorton
Garstang
Bowgreave
Preesall
Stalmine
Fisher's Row
Stake Pool
Winmarleigh
Eagland Hill
Nateby
Churchtown
Hambleton Moss Side
Hambleton
Out Rawcliffe
Ratten Row
Catterall
St Michael's on Wyre
Bilsborrow
Whin Lane End
LANCASHIRE
Claughton
Whitechapel
Inglewhite
Priest Hill
Knowle Green
New Row
Longridge
Moor Nook
Hurst Green
Great Mitton
Barrow
Great Eccleston
Singleton
Thistleton
Elswick
Crossmoor
Inskip
Cuddy Hill
Roseacre
Wharles
Esprick
Greenhalgh
Catforth
Barton
Newsham
Goosnargh
Chingle Hall
Haighton Green
Woodplumpton
Swillbrook
Broughton
Grimsargh
Ribchester
Roman Fort & Museum
Copster Green
Salesbury
Langho
Billington
Great Plumpton
Wesham
Kirkham
Treales
Cottam
Fulwood
Lea Town
Westby
Wrea Green
Clifton
Elston
Samlesbury
Balderstone
Osbaldeston
Mellor Brook
Mellor
Wilpshire
Great Harwood
Clayton-le-Moors
Rishton
Church
Oswaldtwistle
Freckleton
Warton
Lytham
Saltcotes
Moss Side
Ribble Link
Ribble
Penwortham
Ribbleton
Fishwick
Preston Guildhall
Samlesbury Hall
Samlesbury Bottoms
Walton-le-Dale
Higher Walton
Harris Mus & Art Gallery
Bamber Bridge
Witton Park
Pleasington
Hoghton Tower
Hoghton
Feniscowles
Cherry Tree
Ewood
Earcroft
Lower Darwen
Belthorn
Hutton
Longton
Tardy Gate
Lostock Hall
New Longton
Walmer Bridge
Midge Hall
Farington
Much Hoole
Hesketh Bank
Becconsall
Hundred End
Banks
Tarleton
Leyland
Clayton-le-Woods
Cuerden Valley
Whittle-le-Woods
Brindle
Withnell
Abbey Village
Tockholes
Darwen
Hoddlesden
Wheelton
Heapey
Brinscall
Ryal Fold
BLACKBURN WITH DARWEN
Bretherton
Croston
Marshside
Churchtown
Mere Brow
Sollom
Martin Mere
Holmeswood
Euxton
Astley Hall
White Coppice
Botany Bay Villages
Anglezarke Moor
Turton Moor
Belmont
Entwistle
Turton Tower
Rufford
Rufford Old Hall
Eccleston
Camelot Theme Park
Heskin Green
Charnock Richard
Limbrick
Egerton
M6
M55
M61
M65
A6
A683
A687
A65
A585
A586
A588
A583
A584
A59
A5085
A677
A666
A6119
A675
A674
A6062
A565
A581
A5105
B5273
B6254
B6480
B6478
B6243
B6246
B5269
B6242
B6241
B6244
B5411
B6230
B5256
B5248
B5247
B5253
B5246
B6231

D
E
F
G
I
101
109
102
93
2
3
4
5
NATIONAL
PARK
N O R T H
Y O R K S H I R E
WEST
YORKSHIRE
Houses
Ghent
694
Heselden
Littondale
Ribblesdale
Fountains Fell
668
Darnbrook Fell
Arn
Kettlewell
Riggs Moor
Stean
Lofthouse
Hamblet
Moughton Fell
Studfold
Arncliffe Cote
Hawkswick
Stean Moor
Meugher
Ramsgill
Wharfe
Helwith Bridge
Austwick
Feizor
Stainforth Bridge (NT)
Stainforth
538
Kilnsey
Conistone
Grassington Moor
Heathfield Moor
Malham Tarn
Hebden Moor
Appletreewick
Pateley Bridge
Eldroth
Stackhouse
Watershed Mill Visitor Centre
Langcliffe
Bordley
Green Hill
Moor
Giggleswick
Settle
553
Kirkby Fell
Malham
Threshfield
Grassington
Grimwith Resr
Grassington National Park Centre
Linton
Hebden
Wham
Giggleswick Sta.
Malham National Park Centre
Burnsall
Cleatop
Black Hill
Rathmell
Mearbeck
Kirkby Malham
Hanlith
Winterburn Resr
Way Gill
Threapland
Cracoe
Thorpe
Appletreewick
Howgill
Pock Stones Moor
Simon's Seat
Long Gill
Long Preston
Airton
Calton
Hetton
Rylstone
506
Drebley
Barden Fell
Brown Bank Head
410
Brayshaw
Otterburn
Winterburn
Earl Seat
Thruscross Resr
West End
Tosside
Wigglesworth
Hellifield
Bell Busk
Eshton
Flasby
Barden Resrs
Eller Beck
Embsay Moor
Halton West
Coniston Cold
Gargrave
Eastby
Halton East
Bolton Abbey Estate
Priory (rems. of)
Hill End
Round Hill
409
Moor
Nappa
Embsay Steam Rly
Embsay
Bolton Abbey
Bolton Bridge
Beamsley Beacon
Paythorne Moor
Bank Newton
Thorlby
Stirton
Draughton
Beamsley
Paythorne
Newsholme
East Marton
Broughton
Holy Trinity
Chelker Resr
Langbar
March Ghyll Resr
Horton
West Marton
Skipton
Carleton
Addingham
Middleton
Holden
Bolton by Bowland
Gisburn
Elslack
Ravenshaw
Low Bradley
Bracewell
Thornton-in-Craven
Pinhaw
388
Cononley
Ilkley
Sawley
Sawley Abbey
Newby
Rimington
Barnoldswick
Earby
Silsden
Kildwick
Rombalds Moor
Manor House
Ilkley Moor
402
Salterforth
Downham
Kelbrook
Lothersdale
Cross Hills
Glusburn
Steeton
Weets Hill
Whitemoor Resr
Greystone
Sutton-in-Craven
Worston
Clitheroe
Foulridge
Cowling
Utley
Riddlesden
East Morton
Airedale
Pendle Hill
557
Blacko
Laneshaw Resr
Cliffe Cas. Art Gall & Mus
East Riddlesden Hall (NT)
Laycock
KEIGHLEY
Barley
Roughlee
Ogden Resrs
Laneshawbridge
Eldwick
Pendleton
Barrowford
Colne
Winewall
Keighley & Worth Valley Rly
Newchurch
Wheatley Lane
Pendle Heritage Centre
Trawden
Wycoller
443
Keighley Moor
Oakworth
Ingrow
BINGLEY
Oldfield
Harden
1853 Gallery
Sabden
The Forest of Pendle
Fence
NELSON
The Forest of Trawden
Haworth
Bronte Weaving Shed
Cullingworth
Stanbury
Higham
Brierfield
Catlow
Boulsworth Hill
518
Haworth Moor
Bronte Parsonage
Wilsden
Simonstone
Read
Gawthorpe Hall (NT)
Harle Syke
Haggate
Penistone Hill
Oxenhope
Sandy Lane
Padiham
Widdop
Walshaw Dean Resrs
Wadsworth Moor
Leeming
Denholme
BRADFORD
Altham
Forest of Burnley
Worthorne
Thornton
Denholme Clough
451
BURNLEY
Towneley Hall Art Gall & Mus
Hurstwood Resr
Hurstwood
Gorple Resrs
Hebden Water
Clayton
Ogden Water
Warley Moor Resr
Hapton
Huncoat
Hardcastle Crags
Heptonstall Moor
Ogden
Queensbury
Walk Mill
Calder
Pecket Well
Buttershaw
Great Hameldon
409
Hameldon Hill
Holme Chapel
High Gate
479
Wainstalls
Illingworth
Shelf
Dunnockshaw
Clowbridge Resr
Redmires Dam
Blackshaw Head
Old Grammar School Mus
Heptonstall
Hebden Bridge
Mount Tabor
Holmfield
Northowram
Love Clough
Heald Moor
Cornholme
Mytholm
Walkley Clogs
Midgley
Ovenden
Boothtown
Baxenden
Forest of Rossendale
Water
Lydgate
Eastwood
Walkley's Canalside Mill
Mytholmroyd
Luddenden
Acre
Crawshawbooth
Weir
Todmorden
Warley Town
HALIFAX
Shibden Eureka
Haslingden
Grane
RAWTENSTALL
Bacup
Clough Foot
Mankinholes
Cragg
Sowerby Bridge
Southowram
Newchurch
Stacksteads
Lumbutts
Withens Clough Resr
Sowerby
BRIGHOUSE
Helmshore
Ogden Resr
E. Lancs Rly
Waterfoot
Britannia
Gorpley Resr
Walsden
Rochdale Canal Restoration
Turley Holes Edge
Triangle
Norland Town
454
Shawforth
Warland Resr
Lumb
Mill Bank
Greetland
Brandwood Moor
Warland
Elland
Edenfield
Whittle Hill
468
Cowm Resr
Calderbrook
Soyland Moor
Ripponden
Barkisland
Holywell Green
418
Whitworth
Summit
Stainland
Lindley
Watergrove Resr
Clough
Rishworth
Rishworth Moor
Outlane
Ramsbottom
Shuttleworth
Spring Mill Resr
Wardle
Quarmby
Booth Wood
Cheesden
Naden Resrs
Broadley
Healey
Littleborough
472
Smithy Bridge Sta.
Hollingworth Lake
Summerseat
Ashworth Moor Resr
Greenbooth
Moselden
Pole Moor
HUDDERSFIELD
A65
A59
A682
A56
A6068
A629
A6069
A6131
A6034
A650
A6114
A646
A678
A679
A680
A671
A681
A6033
A647
A644
A6036
A58
A6026
A6025
A643
A640
A6033
A672
A56
M65
B6480
B6160
B6265
B6251
B6252
B6383
B6250
B6143
B6429
B6144
B6145
B6141
B6138
B6113
B6114
B6382
B6380
B6238
B6527
B6214

110
101
93
NORTH YORKSHIRE
WEST YORKSHIRE
Lofthouse
Hambleton Hill
Ramsgill
Bouthwaite
Dallowgill Moor
Greygarth
Laverton
Galphay
Winksley Banks
Grange
Hutton Conyers
Sharow
Ripon
Dishforth
Cundall
Norton-le-Clay
Grantley
Studley Royal
Studley Roger
Aldfield
Risplith
Fountains Abbey (NT)
Eavestone
Sawley
Markenfield Hall
Ingerthorpe
Gouthwaite Reservoir
Wath
Heathfield Moor
Pateley Moor
Pateley Bridge
Appletreewick
Greenhow Hill
Beverley
Wilsill
Glasshouses
Smelthouses
Brimham Rocks (NT)
Bishop Thornton
Markington
Bishop Monkton
Littlethorpe
Bridge Hewick
Copt Hewick
Newby Hall
Skelton
Langthorpe
Boroughbridge
Roecliffe
Aldborough
Isurium Roman Town
Kirby Hill
Helperby
Myton
Minskip
Lower Dunsforth
Grafton
Marton
Great Ouseburn
Guise Cliff
Low Laithe
Summer Bridge
Dacre Banks
Shaw Mills
South Stainley
Burton Leonard
Copgrove
Staveley
Heyshaw
Dacre
Burnt Yates
Clint
Ripley
Nidd
Brearton
Ferrensby
Farnham
Arkendale
Clareton
Coneythorpe
Allerton Park
Whixley
Flaxby
Pock Stones Moor
Simon's Seat
Howgill
Earl Seat
Barden Fell
Brown Bank Head
Thruscross Reservoir
Padside
Thornthwaite
West End
Darley
Birstwith
Hampsthwaite
Killinghall
Scotton
Scriven
Knaresborough
Mother Shipton's Cave
Swincliffe
Kettlesing Bottom
Kettlesing
Forest Moor
Bilton
HARROGATE
High Harrogate
Goldsborough
Kirk Hammerton
Hunsingore
Cowthorpe
Little Ribston
North Deighton
Blubberhouses
Fewston Reservoir
Fewston
Harlow Carr
Beckwithshaw
Pannal
Follifoot
Spofforth
Hill End
Bolton Abbey
Bolton Bridge
Round Hill
Beamsley Beacon
Beamsley
Langbar
Timble
Swinsty Resr
Bland Hill
Jack Hill
March Ghyll Reservoir
Chelker Resr
Lindley Wood Reservoir
Middleton
Denton
North Rigton
Stainburn
Huby
Weeton Sta.
Kirkby Overblow
Stockeld Park
Kirk Deighton
Wetherby
Bickerton
Walton
ILKLEY
Manor House
Ilkley Moor
Askwith
Weston
Farnley
Leathley
Dunkeswick
Weeton
Sicklinghall
Clap Gate
Linton
Netherby
Collingham
Thorp Arch
Boston Spa
Burley in Wharfedale
Otley
Pool
Arthington
Harewood
Harewood House
East Keswick
Bardsey
East Rigton
Clifford
Bramham
The Chevin
Chevin Forest Park
Menston
Rombalds Moor
Riddlesden
East Riddlesden Hall (NT)
East Morton
Hawksworth
Guiseley
Leeds Bradford International
Bramhope
Golden Acre Park
Eccup
Eccup Resr
Scarcroft
Thorner
Bramham Park
Eldwick
Keighley & Worth Valley Rly
BINGLEY
Baildon
Yeadon
Rawdon
Tinshill
Adel
Alwoodley Gates
Tropical World
Kiddal Lane End
Harden
1853 Gallery
SHIPLEY
Horsforth
Moor Allerton
Roundhay
Barwick in Elmet
Aberford
Cullingworth
Wilsden
Calverley
Kirkstall Abbey
Gledhow
Chapel Allerton
Scholes
Roman Ridge
Seacroft
Denholme
Sandy Lane
Allerton
Bradford Cathedral
Farsley
Kirkstall
Headingley
Harehills
Cross Gates
LEEDS
Whitkirk
Temple Newsam
West Garforth
Garforth
Old Micklefield
Cock Beck
BRADFORD
Thornton
Clough
PUDSEY
Royal Armouries Museum
Ogden Water
Ogden
Clayton
Bolling Hall
Dudley Hill
Tong Street
New Farnley
Beeston
Swillington
Kippax
Queensbury
Wibsey
Buttershaw
Bierley
Westgate Hill
Adwalton Moor 1643
Drighlington
Gildersome
Churwell
Middleton Rly
Middleton
ROTHWELL
Woodlesford
Oulton
Great Preston
Allerton Bywater
Holmfield
Shelf
Oakenshaw
Birkenshaw
Adwalton
MORLEY
Thorpe on the Hill
Robin Hood
Carlton
Methley
Mickletown
Castleford
Ovenden
Boothtown
Northowram
Wyke
Gomersal
Oakwell Hall
Tingley
Lofthouse
HALIFAX
Shibden Hall
Eureka
Hipperholme
Cleckheaton
Hartshead Moor
Birstall Smithies
BATLEY
East Ardsley
STANLEY
Altofts
Whitwood
Pontefract
Sowerby Bridge
Southowram
Liversedge
Heckmondwike
Kirkhamgate
Wrenthorpe
Outwood
Normanton
Norland Town
BRIGHOUSE
Rastrick
Roberttown
Greetland
Elland
Holywell Green
Barkisland
Stainland
Mirfield
Ravensthorpe
DEWSBURY
Ossett
WAKEFIELD
Warmfield
Ackton
Purston Jaglin
Featherstone
Sharlston
Nostell Priory (NT)
West Hardwick
Outlane
Lindley
Quarmby
HUDDERSFIELD
Kirkheaton
Upper Hopton
Whitley Lower
National Coal Mining Museum for England
Grange Moor
Horbury
Netherton
Middlestown
Flockton Green
Crofton
Pugneys
Crigglestone
Walton
Anglers
Wintersett
Fitzwilliam
Ackworth
Calder
Aire
M1
M62
M621
M606
A1(M)
A61
A59
A658
A661
A65
A660
A6120
A64
A650
A629
A641
A643
A644
A62
A638
A642
A639
A63
A656
A655
A645
A653
A6110
A647
A6177
A6036
A58
A168
A6055
B6265
B6165
B6161
B6162
B6451
B6160
B6382
B6429
B6144
B6145
B6380
B6154
B6157
B6123
B6128
B6117
B6134
B6133
B6135
B6137
B6118
B6114
B6112
B6113

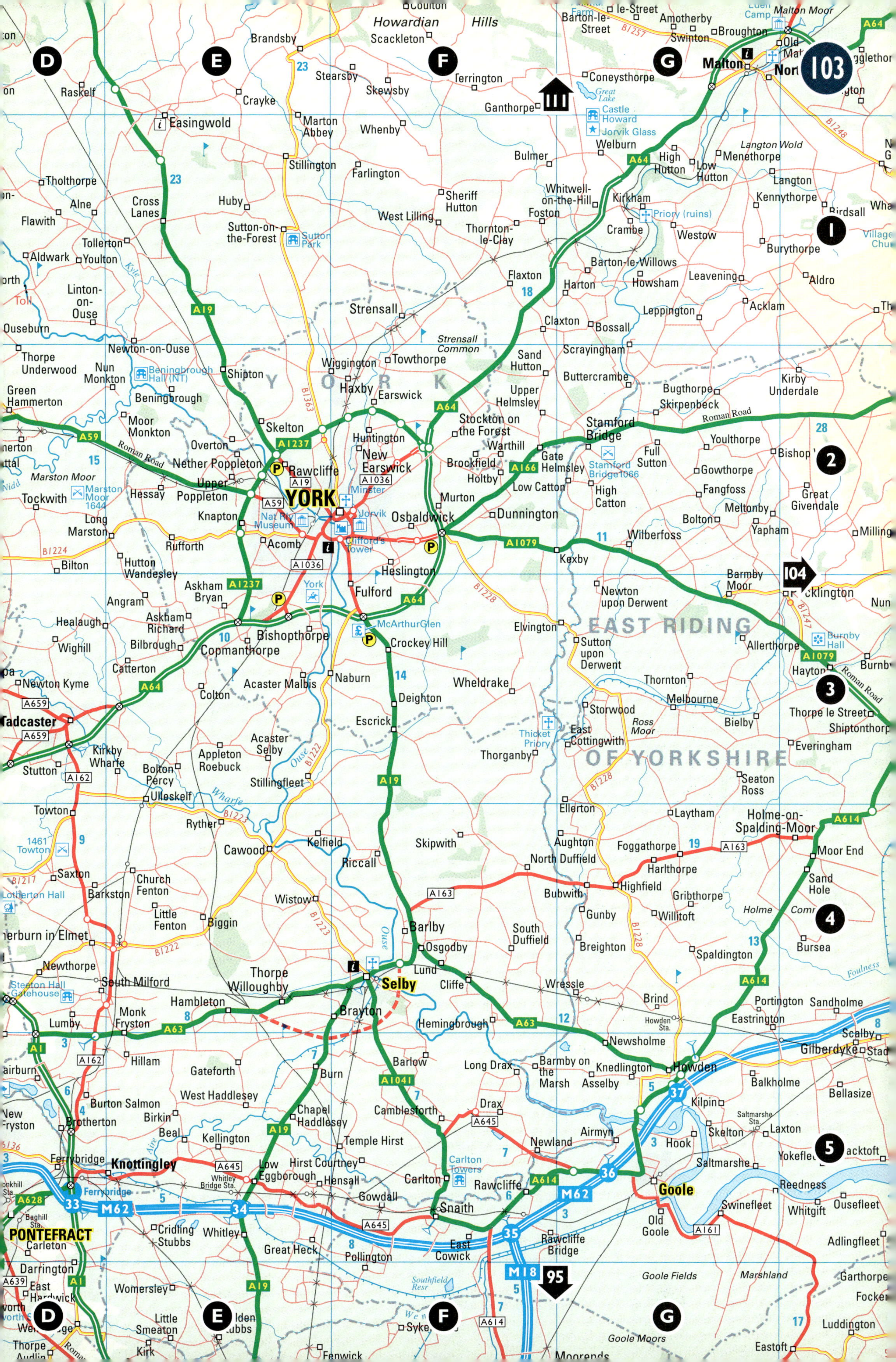

Howardian Hills
Coulton
Brandsby
Scackleton
Barton-le-Street
Amotherby
Swinton
Broughton
Malton Moor
Eden Camp
A64
103
Malton
Old Malton
Norton
Raskell
Crayke
Stearsby
Skewsby
Terrington
Coneysthorpe
Great Lake
Castle Howard
Jorvik Glass
Ganthorpe
Easingwold
Marton Abbey
Whenby
Welburn
Bulmer
High Hutton
Low Hutton
Langton Wold
Menethorpe
Langton
Kennythorpe
Birdsall
Stillington
Farlington
Sheriff Hutton
Whitwell-on-the-Hill
Foston
Kirkham
Priory (ruins)
Crambe
Westow
Burythorpe
Aldro
Tholthorpe
Alne
Flawith
Cross Lanes
Huby
Sutton-on-the-Forest
Sutton Park
West Lilling
Thornton-le-Clay
Tollerton
Youlton
Aldwark
Linton-on-Ouse
Kyle
Flaxton
Barton-le-Willows
Harton
Howsham
Leavening
Acklam
Leppington
Claxton
Bossall
Strensall
Strensall Common
Ouseburn
Newton-on-Ouse
Thorpe Underwood
Nun Monkton
Beningbrough Hall (NT)
Beningbrough
Shipton
Wiggington
Towthorpe
Sand Hutton
Scrayingham
Buttercrambe
Kirby Underdale
Green Hammerton
YORK
Haxby
Earswick
Upper Helmsley
Bugthorpe
Skirpenbeck
Roman Road
Moor Monkton
Skelton
A1237
Huntington
Stockton on the Forest
Stamford Bridge
Youlthorpe
28
Bishop
A59
Overton
New Earswick
Warthill
Gate Helmsley
Full Sutton
Gowthorpe
15
Nether Poppleton
Rawcliffe
Brockfield
A166
Stamford Bridge 1066
Fangfoss
Great Givendale
Marston Moor
Upper Poppleton
A19
A1036
Holtby
Low Catton
High Catton
Meltonby
Tockwith
Marston Moor 1644
Hessay
A59
Minster
Murton
Dunnington
Bolton
Yapham
Long Marston
Knapton
Nat Rly Museum
Jorvik
Osbaldwick
Wilberfoss
Milling
B1224
Rufforth
Acomb
Clifford's Tower
A1079
11
Kexby
Bilton
Hutton Wandesley
A1036
Heslington
Barmby Moor
104
Pocklington
Askham Bryan
A1237
York
Fulford
B1228
Newton upon Derwent
Nun
Angram
A64
Healaugh
Askham Richard
Bishopthorpe
McArthurGlen
Elvington
EAST RIDING
Burnby Hall
Wighill
Bilbrough
10
Copmanthorpe
Crockey Hill
Sutton upon Derwent
Allerthorpe
A1079
Catterton
14
Hayton
Newton Kyme
A64
Acaster Malbis
Naburn
Wheldrake
Thornton
Melbourne
3
Roman Road
A659
Colton
Deighton
Storwood
Thorpe le Street
Tadcaster
A659
Escrick
Ross Moor
Bielby
Shiptonthorpe
Kirkby Wharfe
Acaster Selby
Thicket Priory
East Cottingwith
Everingham
Stutton
Bolton Percy
Appleton Roebuck
Ouse
B1222
Thorganby
OF YORKSHIRE
A162
Stillingfleet
A19
Seaton Ross
Towton
Ulleskelf
Wharfe
B1228
Ryther
B1223
Ellerton
Laytham
Holme-on-Spalding-Moor
A614
1461 Towton
9
Cawood
Kelfield
Skipwith
Aughton
Foggathorpe
19
A163
Moor End
North Duffield
Harlthorpe
B1217
Saxton
Church Fenton
Riccall
Sand Hole
Lotherton Hall
Barkston
Wistow
A163
Bubwith
Highfield
Gribthorpe
Little Fenton
Biggin
Gunby
Willitoft
Holme
Comm
4
Sherburn in Elmet
B1223
Ouse
Barlby
South Duffield
Breighton
B1228
Spaldington
13
Bursea
Osgodby
B1222
Newthorpe
Thorpe Willoughby
Lund
Foulness
South Milford
Selby
Cliffe
Wressle
Brind
A614
Steeton Hall Gatehouse
Hambleton
Portington
Sandholme
Monk Fryston
8
Brayton
Hemingbrough
A63
12
Howden Sta.
Eastrington
Lumby
A63
Newsholme
Scalby
A1
3
A162
Hillam
Barlow
Long Drax
Barmby on the Marsh
Knedlington
Howden
Gilberdyke
Stad
Sherburn
Gateforth
Burn
A1041
Asselby
Balkholme
7
West Haddlesey
Camblesforth
Drax
5
37
Kilpin
Bellasize
New Fryston
Burton Salmon
Brotherton
Birkin
Chapel Haddlesey
A645
Saltmarshe Sta.
Laxton
Skelton
Beal
Kellington
Temple Hirst
Newland
Airmyn
3
Hook
5
Blacktoft
Yokefleet
Aire
A19
B6136
Ferrybridge
Knottingley
A645
Whitley Bridge Sta.
Low Eggborough
Hirst Courtney
Hensall
Carlton Towers
Carlton
7
Rawcliffe
A614
36
Saltmarshe
Reedness
Goole
Knottingley Sta.
A628
33
Ferrybridge
M62
5
34
Gowdall
6
M62
3
Swinefleet
Whitgift
Ousefleet
Baghill Sta.
PONTEFRACT
Cridling Stubbs
Whitley
A645
Snaith
35
Old Goole
A161
Carleton
Great Heck
8
Pollington
East Cowick
Rawcliffe Bridge
Adlingfleet
Darrington
A639
M18
95
Goole Fields
Marshland
Garthorpe
East Hardwick
A1
Womersley
Southfield Resr
5
Fockerby
Went
Wentbridge
Little Smeaton
Balne
Norton
Sykehouse
A614
7
17
Luddington
Thorpe Audlin
Roman
Kirk Smeaton
Stubbs Walden
Fenwick
Moorends
Goole Moors
Eastoft
D
E
F
G
I
2
3
4
5
Y O R K

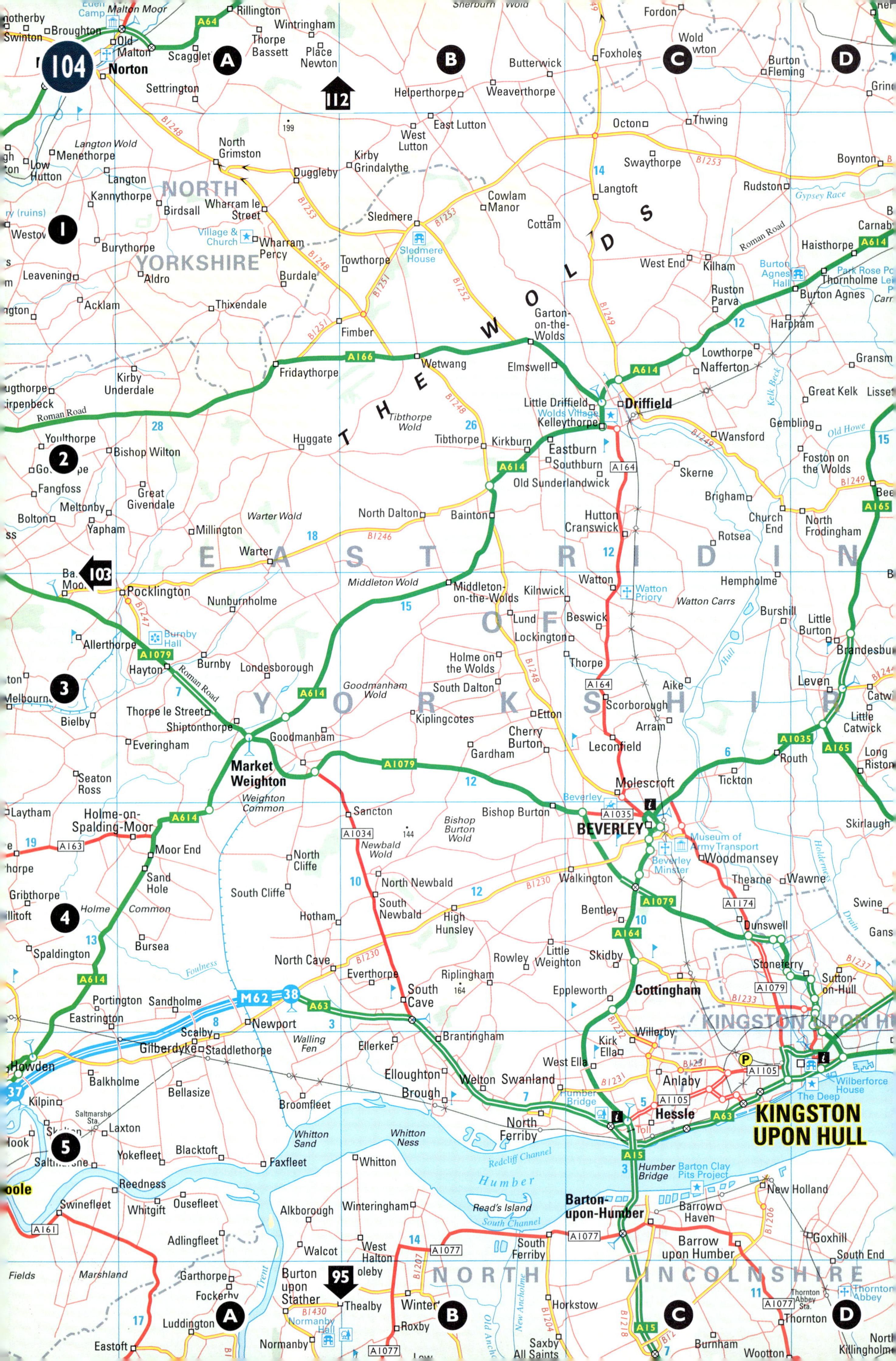

104
112
103
95
A
B
C
D
1
2
3
4
5
Malton Moor
Rillington
Wintringham
Thorpe Bassett
Place Newton
Broughton
Swinton
Old Malton
Scagglethorpe
Norton
Settrington
Sherburn
Fordon
Foxholes
Wold Newton
Burton Fleming
Butterwick
Helperthorpe
Weaverthorpe
East Lutton
West Lutton
Octon
Thwing
Langton Wold
Menethorpe
Low Hutton
Langton
North Grimston
Kirby Grindalythe
Duggleby
Swaythorpe
Boynton
Langtoft
Rudston
Gypsey Race
NORTH
Kennythorpe
Birdsall
Wharram le Street
Sledmere
Cowlam Manor
Cottam
Westow
Village & Church
Wharram Percy
Sledmere House
Burythorpe
YORKSHIRE
Aldro
Towthorpe
Burdale
West End
Kilham
Carnaby
Haisthorpe
Roman Road
Burton Agnes Hall
Park Rose
Thornholme
Burton Agnes
Ruston Parva
Leavening
Acklam
Thixendale
Fimber
Garton-on-the-Wolds
THE WOLDS
Harpham
Lowthorpe
Nafferton
Gransmoor
Kirby Underdale
Fridaythorpe
Wetwang
Elmswell
Driffield
Little Driffield
Wolds Village
Kelleythorpe
Great Kelk
Gembling
Wansford
Foston on the Wolds
Kelk Beck
Old Howe
Roman Road
Youlthorpe
Bishop Wilton
Huggate
Tibthorpe Wold
Tibthorpe
Kirkburn
Eastburn
Southburn
Skerne
Fangfoss
Great Givendale
Meltonby
Bolton
Yapham
Millington
Warter Wold
North Dalton
Bainton
Old Sunderlandwick
Hutton Cranswick
Brigham
Church End
North Frodingham
Rotsea
Warter
EAST RIDING OF YORKSHIRE
Pocklington
Nunburnholme
Middleton Wold
Middleton-on-the-Wolds
Kilnwick
Watton
Watton Priory
Watton Carrs
Hempholme
Burshill
Little Burton
Brandesburton
Burnby Hall
Allerthorpe
Hayton
Burnby
Londesborough
Lund
Beswick
Lockington
Holme on the Wolds
Thorpe
Hull
Leven
Melbourne
Bielby
Goodmanham Wold
South Dalton
Aike
Catwick
Little Catwick
Roman Road
Thorpe le Street
Shiptonthorpe
Kiplingcotes
Etton
Scorborough
Arram
Everingham
Goodmanham
Cherry Burton
Gardham
Leconfield
Routh
Long Riston
Seaton Ross
Market Weighton
Weighton Common
Molescroft
Tickton
Laytham
Holme-on-Spalding-Moor
Sancton
Bishop Burton
Bishop Burton Wold
Beverley
BEVERLEY
Skirlaugh
Moor End
North Cliffe
Newbald Wold
Museum of Army Transport
Beverley Minster
Woodmansey
Sand Hole
South Cliffe
North Newbald
South Newbald
Walkington
Thearne
Wawne
Gribthorpe
Holme Common
Hotham
High Hunsley
Bentley
Swine
Dunswell
Ganstead
Bursea
Spaldington
North Cave
Everthorpe
Rowley
Little Weighton
Skidby
Stoneferry
Sutton-on-Hull
Foulness
South Cave
Riplingham
Eppleworth
Cottingham
KINGSTON UPON HULL
Portington
Sandholme
Eastrington
Newport
Walling Fen
Scalby
Gilberdyke
Staddlethorpe
Brantingham
Ellerker
Kirk Ella
Willerby
West Ella
Howden
Balkholme
Bellasize
Elloughton
Brough
Welton
Swanland
Anlaby
Wilberforce House
The Deep
Kilpin
Saltmarshe Sta.
Laxton
Broomfleet
Humber Bridge
Hessle
North Ferriby
Skelton
Hook
Whitton Sand
Whitton Ness
Toll
KINGSTON UPON HULL
Saltmarshe
Yokefleet
Blacktoft
Faxfleet
Whitton
Redcliff Channel
Humber
Humber Bridge
Barton Clay Pits Project
Goole
Reedness
New Holland
Swinefleet
Whitgift
Ousefleet
Alkborough
Winteringham
Read's Island
South Channel
Barton-upon-Humber
Barrow Haven
Adlingfleet
Walcot
West Halton
South Ferriby
Goxhill
Barrow upon Humber
South End
Fields
Marshland
Garthorpe
Fockerby
Trent
Burton upon Stather
Coleby
Winterton
NORTH LINCOLNSHIRE
Thornton Abbey Sta.
Thornton Abbey
Thornton
Luddington
Normanby Hall
Thealby
Roxby
Horkstow
New Ancholme
Old Ancholme
Eastoft
Normanby
Saxby All Saints
Burnham
Wootton
North Killingholme

105
Crab Rocks
Buckton
Bempton
113
Flamborough Head
Sewerby Hall
Sewerby
BRIDLINGTON
Hilderthorpe
A165
B1255
B1229
Moor
Fraisthorpe
BRIDLINGTON
BAY
Barmston
Ulrome
Skipsea
B1242
Dunnington
Atwick
3.2 miles to 1 inch
0 2 4 6 8 10 miles
0 2 4 6 8 10 km
2 km to 1 cm
Hornsea
Trans Pennine Trail
Freeport
Hornsea Freeport
Hornsea Mere
Seaton
B1244
Sigglesthorne
Goxhill
Rolston
Mappleton
Great Hatfield
Rise
Great Cowden
31
Withernwick
New Ellerby
Marton
West Newton
Old Ellerby
Aldbrough
Burton Constable Hall
Flinton
B1238
Garton
Coniston
Sproatley
Humbleton
Lelley
Bilton
Owstwick
Tunstall
Elstronwick
B1240
B1239
Burton Pidsea
Roos
Preston
Waxholme
20
B1362
Wadworth Hill
Rimswell
Withernsea
A1033
Hedon
Burstwick
Halsham
Thorngumbald
Paull
17
Keyingham
Ottringham
Winestead
Hollym
4
East Halton Skitter
Paull Holme Sands
Holmpton
Patrington
B1445
Cherry Cobb Sands
Salthaugh Grange
Out Newton
Rotterdam 14 hrs
Zeebrugge 14 hrs
Haven Side
Welwick
7
Weeton
Foulholme Sands
97
Easington
Sunk Island
MOUTH
Old Hall
Skeffling Clays
Immingham Dock
South Killingholme
Sunk Island Sands
Kilnsea
D E F G
1 2 3 4 5

A
B
C
D
1
2
3
4
5
116
99
Harrington
Distington
Ullock
Lorton
Whinlatter Pass
300
Whinlatter Forest
Grisedale Pike
790
Braithwaite
Mockerkin
Gilgarran
Moresby
Pica
16
Hopegill Head
Causey Pike
Brackenthwaite Fell
Grasmoor
851
Stair
Asby
Parton
Lamplugh
Loweswater
Loweswater
Blake Fell
572
Cogra Moss
Murton Fell
Loweswater Fell
Crummock Water
Little Town
Derwent Fells
WHITEHAVEN
Arlecdon
Rowrah
Kirkland
Croasdale
B5289
Robinson
737
Saltom Bay
Hensingham
B5295
B5294
Frizington
A5086
Scale Force
Buttermere
340
Great Borne
616
Dale Head
754
St Bees Head
Sandwith
6
Cleator Moor
A595
Ennerdale Bridge
Ehen
Keekle
Buttermere
Red Pike
High Stile
806
Honister Pass
358
Moor Row
Wath Brow
Ennerdale Water
Bigrigg
B5345
Cleator
Liza
Scarth Gap Pass
Hay Stacks
Ennerdale Fell
Rottington
Lank Rigg
Kirk Beck
Pillar
892
St Bees
Egremont
Wilton
Steeple
841
Black Sail Pass
Caw Fell
Haycock
797
LAKE
Kirk Fell
Great Gable
899
How Man
Snellings
Worm Gill
Sty Head
Wasdale Head
Haile
Lingmell
Middletown
Seatallan
692
Great End
Esk Hause
Nethertown
Ehen
Calder Bridge
Calder
Scafell Pike
977
Sca Fell
964
Beckermet
Bleng
Copeland Forest
C U M B R I A N
Braystones Sta.
Sellafield Visitors Cen.
Ponsonby
Calder Abbey
Wast Water
Wellington
Sellafield
Gosforth
Nether Wasdale
Burnmoor Tarn
Eskdale Fell
Whillan Beck
Whin Rigg
Sellafield Sta.
C
U
M
Hardknott Roman Fort
Hardknott Pass
393
B5344
NATIONAL
Irt
Seascale
Santon Bridge
Boot
Holmrook
Eskdale Green
Eskdale
Drigg
Gubbergill
Mite
Beckfoot
Stanley Force
Harter Fell
649
Duddon
Ravenglass & Eskdale Rly Mus
Roman Bath House
Esk
Kokoarrah
Devoke Water
Ravenglass & Eskdale Rly
Muncaster Castle
Third Millennium Project
Ravenglass
Muncaster
Woodend
Seathwaite
Ulpha Fell
Hall
Broad Oak
Stainton Fell
Dunnerdale
Caw
529
Lane End
Whitfell
573
Bigert Mire
Ulpha
Hoses
20
Corney
Prior Park
Ulpha Park
Broughton Mills
Stub Place
Selker Bay
Stoneside Hill
Hycemoor
Bootle
Bank End
Duddon Bridge
Lower Hawthwaite
Hyton
Bootle Fell
Broughton in Furness
Broadgate
9
Annaside
White Combe
Black Combe
600
Lady Hall
Foxfield
Grizebeck
Whitbeck
7
Green Road Sta.
A595
Whicham
A5093
Sand Side
Kirkby-in-Furness Sta.
Dalton (NT)
Silecroft
Millom
Millom Folk Museum
Soutergate
Kirksanton
Millom
15
Haverigg
A595
Haverigg Point
Duddon Sands
Askam in Furness
Ireleth
Marton
Lindal in Furness
3.2 miles to 1 inch
0
2
4
6
8
10 miles
0
2
4
6
8
10 km
2 km to 1 cm
Dalton-in-Furness
A590
Stainton with Adgarley
Hawcoat
Newton
Furness Abbey
Dendron
Newbarns
North Scale
Dock Museum
Furness Museum
Vickerstown
Leece
Roosecote
A590
BARROW-IN-FURNESS
Tummer Hill Scar
Biggar

107
D
E
F
G
I
118
108
100
1
2
3
4
5
MOUNTAINS
DISTRICT
PARK
LAKE
LANCS
MORECAMBE
BAY
Latrigg
Castlerigg Stone Circle
Keswick
Great Dodd
856
Stybarrow Dodd
840
High Seat
608
Watendlath
Rosthwaite
Borrowdale
Stonethwaite
Thirlmere
Helvellyn
949
Striding Edge
Wythburn
Wythburn Fells
Dollywagon Pike
Ullscarf
726
Fairfield
873
Seat Sandal
Dunmail Raise
High Raise
762
Stake Pass
Langdale Pikes
Dungeon Ghyll Force
Grasmere
Dove Cottage
Rydal Fell
Rydal Mount
Rydal
Chapel Stile
Elterwater
Adrian Sankey Glassmakers
Stockghyll Force
Clappersgate
Ambleside
Skelwith Bridge
Waterhead
Stagshaw (NT)
Pike of Blisco
702
Wrynose Pass
390
Crags
Cockley Beck
Furness Fells
Wray Castle
Outgate
High Wray
Hawkshead Courthouse (NT)
Hawkshead
The Old Man of Coniston
803
Dow Crag
Coniston
Bowmanstead
Steam Yacht Gondola (NT)
Brantwood
Torver
Claife Heights
Hill Top (NT)
Near Sawrey
Esthwaite Water
Grizedale Forest Park
Grizedale
GRIZEDALE FOREST PARK
Satterthwaite
Sunny Bank
Blawith Fells
255
Force Forge
Grathwaite
High Nibthwaite
Water Yeat
Blawith
Woodland Fell
Oxen Park
Rusland
Thwaite Head
Finsthwaite
Lakeside
Aquarium of the Lakes
Lakeside & Haverthwaite Rly
Stott Park Bobbin Mill
Newby Bridge
Staveley-in-Cartmel
Fell Foot Park (NT)
Lowick
Colton
Spark Bridge
Bouth
Gawthwaite
Haverthwaite
Penny Bridge
Greenodd
Low Wood
Backbarrow
Ayside
High Newton
Stribers
Broughton Beck
Mansriggs
Arrad Foot
Ulverston
Field Broughton
Cartmel Priory (NT)
Cartmel
Holker
Allithwaite
Cark
Flookburgh
Cartmel Sands
Grange-over-Sands
Kents Bank
Holme Island
Lindale
Meathop
Colony Gift Corporation
Great Urswick
Little Urswick
Bardsea
Scales
Baycliff
Gleaston
Aldingham
Newbiggin
Mort Bank
Cartmel Wharf
Humphrey Head Point
Warton Sands
Matterdale End
Little Mell Fell
Wreay
Watermillock
Ulcat Row
Dockray
Aira Force (NT)
Dowthwaitehead
Ullswater
Sandwick
Loadpot Hill
671
Glenridding
Place Fell
657
Patterdale
Martindale Common
Dale Head
Bampton Common
Beda Fell
Bridgend
Hartsop
Brothers Water
Hayeswater
High Raise
803
Kidsty Pike
High Street
829
Haweswater Resr
Mardale Common
Kirkstone Pass
454
Middle Dodd
776
Nan Bield Pass
Harter Fell
765
Gatescarth Pass
Kentmere Resr
Ill Bell
755
Sadgill
Kentmere
Applethwaite Common
Troutbeck
Long Sleddale
Staveley Head Fell
Nat Pk Visitor Centre
Troutbeck Bridge
Windermere Steamboat Mus
Windermere
World of Beatrix Potter
Ings
Staveley
Bowness-on-Windermere
Mitchelland
Crook
Windermere Lake Cruises
Winster
Underbarrow
Crosthwaite
Grigghall
Bowland Bridge
Row
Low Howe
Lyth Valley
Whitbarrow Scar
Cartmel Fell
Pool Bank
Witherslack Hall
Witherslack
Town End
Levens
Brigsteer
Sizergh (NT)
Cotes
Askham
Lowther
Helton
Whale
Lowther Wildlife Park
Barton Fell
Bampton
Rosgill
Hackthorpe
Great Strickland
Little Strickland
Morland
Newby
Sleagill
Bolton
Reagill
Maulds Meaburn
Wickerslack
Shap Abbey
Shap
Keld
Ralfland Forest
Wet Sleddale Resr
Seat Robert
Cros Ravensworth
Shap Summit
316
Crosby Ravensworth Fell
Orton
Tebay
Greenholme
Bretherdale Head
Borrowdale
Great Yarlside
Shap Fells
426
Forest Hall
Whinfell Beacon
Langdale
Uldale Head
Garnett Bridge
Watchgate
Grayrigg
Lowgill
Beck Foot
Burneside
Meal Bank
Firbank
Lambrigg Fell
Fisher Tarn Resr
KENDAL
Abbot Hall Art Gall & Mus.
Castle
K Village
New Hutton
Killington Lake
Garths
Millholme
Middleshaw
Oxenholme
Natland
Old Hutton
Killington
Harprigg
Middleton
Sedgwick
Stainton
Gatebeck
Endmoor
Rigmaden Park
Levens
Hincaster
Woodhouse
Crooklands
Leasgill
Heversham
Warth Hill
Scout Hill
Nook
Old Town
Mansergh
Barbon
Lupton
Farleton
Milnthorpe
Storth
Beetham
Kearstwick
Kirkby Lonsdale
Casterton
Roman Road
Holme
Clawthorpe
Hutton Roof
Moor End
Burton-in-Kendal
Whittington
Newton
Arnside
Silverdale
Yealand Redmayne
Silverdale Sta.
Leighton
Yealand Conyers
Priest Hutton
Warton
Borwick
Tunstall
Arkholme
Cantsfield
Thurland
Burrow
Cowan Bridge
Leck Fell
Old Rectory
Capernwray
Melling
Carnforth
Over Kellet
Gressingham
Wennington
Tatham
Hornby
Wray
Nether Kellet
Bolton-le-Sands
Hest Bank
Slyne
Halton
Claughton
Mill Houses
Greta
Lune
Ingmire Hall
Kent
M6
A6
A591
A592
A593
A5084
A5092
A590
A5087
A5074
A685
A684
A683
A65
A6070
A601(M)
A5105
B5289
B5322
B5343
B5285
B5286
B5284
B5278
B5277
B5271
B5282
B6384
B6385
B6254
B6257
B6260
B6261
35
35A
36
37
38
39

108
A
B
C
D
1
2
3
4
5
Pooley Bridge
Askham
Castle
Lowther
Hackthorpe
Helton
Whale
Lowther Wildlife Park
Great Strickland
Morland
Bolton
Kings Meaburn
Brampton
Crackenthorpe
Appleby-in-Westmorland
Murton
Little Fell
745
Danger Zone
Burton Fell
Little Strickland
Newby
Sleagill
118
Colby
Hilton
Warcop Fell
Burrells
Coupland
Brackenber
Iron Band
562
Loadpot Hill
671
Bampton
Rosgill
Reagill
Hoff
B6260
A66
Great Ormside
Sandford
Warcop
Hillbeck
B6276
Brough
North
Bampton Common
Shap Abbey
Shap
M6
Maulds Meaburn
Wickerslack
Crosby Ravensworth
Drybeck
Great Asby
Bleatarn
Little Musgrave
Great Musgrave
Verteris Roman Fort
Brough Sowerby
Kaber
Argill Beck
Haweswater Reservoir
Keld
Ralfland Forest
Swindale Beck
Wet Sleddale Resr
Shap Summit
316
39
Mardale Common
Seat Robert
CUMBRIA
A6
Soulby
A685
Winton
Crosby Ravensworth Fell
Grange Scar
Crosby Garrett
Waitby
Kirkby Stephen
Hartley
Harter Fell
765
Gatescarth Pass
Great Yarlside
Shap Fells
Birk Beck
Orton
B6261
Tebay
Raisbeck
Smardale
Nettle Hill
Begin Hill
Winton Fell
Bastifell
Nateby
Nine Standards Rigg
662
Tailbridge Hill
426
Greenholme
Sadgill
Kentmere
Long Sleddale
Bretherdale Head
38
Kelleth
Newbiggin-on-Lune
Ash Fell
A683
Southwaite
Ravenstonedale
B6270
Birkdale
Borrowdale
West Fell
Outhgill
B6259
High Seat
710
Staveley Head Fell
Forest Hall
Whinfell Beacon
Langdale Fell
Simon's Seat
587
Uldale Head
Ravenstonedale Common
Harter Fell
522
107
Garnett Bridge
Watchgate
Yarlside
Wild Boar Fell
708
Mallerstang
Common
A591
Staveley
Grayrigg
Lowgill
The Calf
676
Uldale House
Swarth Fell
Burneside
Meal Bank
Beck Foot
Bluecaster
Low Haygarth
West Baugh Fell
Holmes Moss
Abbotside Common
Brant Fell
Cautley
Underbarrow
Lambrigg Fell
Fisher Tarn Resr
Firbank
B6257
Baugh Fell
Cotterdale
KENDAL
A684
37
Ingmire Hall
Sedbergh
Knoutberry Haw
676
East Baugh Fell
Garsdale Head
Clough
Garsdale Sta.
Mid Mossdale
Grigghall
Abbot Hall Art Gall & Mus.
Castle
New Hutton
Killington Lake
Killington Resr
Millthrop
Garsdale
West Mostard
Mossdale Moor
Hardr
Garths
Millholme
Oxenholme
Middleshaw
Brigsteer
Row
Low Howe
Lyth Valley
Sizergh (NT)
Natland
Old Hutton
Killington
Dee
Aye Gill Pike
556
Great Knoutberry Hill
672
Widdale Fell
Cotes
Sedgwick
Harprigg
Gawthrop
Dent
Dentdale
Middleton Fell
Cowgill
Dent Sta.
Lea Yeat
Levens
Stainton
A65
Gatebeck
Middleton
Calf Top
609
Stone House
Wold Fell
557
B6255
Dodd Fell
668
Black Hall
A590
Endmoor
B6254
Rigmaden Park
Deepdale
Hincaster
Woodhouse
Warth Hill
Crag Hill
682
YORKS
Leasgill
Heversham
Crooklands
Scout Hill
Old Town
Mansergh
Barbon
Blea Moor
Oughtershaw Moss
36
Nook
Lupton
Bullpot Farm
Whernside
736
Gayle Moor
Milnthorpe
B6385
Farleton
Far Gearstones
Cam Fell
Storth
B5282
Beetham
Kearstwick
Roman Road
Casterton
Kirkby Lonsdale
627
Langstrothdale
NATIONAL PARK
Ribblehead Sta.
Sike Moor
Holme
Hutton Roof
Leck Beck
Weathercote
B6479
Moor End
Leck Fell
Scales Moor
Cam Beck
High Birkwith
Clawthorpe
Chapel-le-Dale
Burton-in-Kendal
Leck
Cowan Bridge
Ireby
Selside
Horton Moor
Yealand Redmayne
Silverdale Sta.
Whittington
White Scar Caves
Ingleborough
724
Simon Fell
Leighton
Yealand Conyers
A6070
Newton
Nether Burrow
Westhouse
Skirwith
New Houses
Pen-y-Ghent
694
Priest Hutton
Tunstall
Thurland
Ingleborough Common
Warton
Borwick
Cantsfield
A687
Ingleton
Horton in Ribblesdale
Old Rectory
35A
Arkholme
Burton in Lonsdale
Slatenber
Moughton Fell
A601(M)
Capernwray
Greta
Melling
A65
Studfold
Carnforth
35
Over Kellet
B6254
Gressingham
Wennington
Low Bentham
Newby
Helwith Bridge
LANCS
100
Hornby
High Bentham
B6480
Clapham
Wharfe
Bolton-le-Sands
M6
Nether Kellet
Wray
Clapham Sta.
Austwick
Feizor
Aughton
Mill Houses
Wenning
Stainforth
A5105
A683
Claughton
Lune
Keasden
Lawkland
Lune Forest
790

109
119
110
101
D
E
F
G
1
2
3
4
5
DURHAM
NORTH YORKSHIRE
DALES
PARK
A66
A67
A688
A684
A6108
A6136
A1(M)
A1
A68
B6276
B6277
B6278
B6279
B6274
B6275
B6270
B6271
B6160
B6265
Lune Moor
Thringarth
Lunedale
Grassholme
Selset Reservoir
Romaldkirk
Hunderthwaite
Hury
Mickleton Moor
Hunderthwaite Moor
Blackton Resr
Hury Resr
Baldersdale
Balderhead Resr
Clove Lodge
Cotherstone Moor
Cotherstone
Lartington
Barnard Castle
Startforth
Bowes Museum
Stainton
Staindrop
Raby
Burnt Houses
Cleatlam
Little Newsham
Winston
Gainford
Piercebridge
Headlam
Summerhouse
Langton
Ingleton
Killerby
Hilton
Bolam
Redworth
Denton
Walworth
Archdeacon Newton
High Coniscliffe
Low Coniscliffe
Manfield
Cleasby
Dere Street
Deep Dale
Deepdale Beck
Beldoo Hill
Boldron
Westwick
Egglestone
Whorlton
Wycliffe
Ovington
Caldwell
Eppleby
Forcett
Aldbrough St John
Stanwick Camp
Bowes
Gilmonby
Greta Bridge
Brignall
Barningham
Scargill
Hutton Magna
Lane Head
West Layton
East Layton
Newsham
Bowes Moor
Stainmore Forest
Scargill High Moor
Barningham Moor
Kaber Fell
Sleightholme Moor
Cleasby Hill
Taylor Rigg
Tan Hill
Hope Moor
Dalton
Ravensworth
Gayles
Roman Road
Melsonby
Barton
Kirby Hill
Whashton
Gilling West
Middleton
Corner
Arkengarthdale Moor
Water Crag
Stonesdale Moor
Rogan's Seat
Whaw
Kexwith Moor
Holgate Moor
Hurst Moor
Great Pinseat
Markse Moor
High Moor
Skeeby
West Stonesdale
Melbecks Moor
Langthwaite
Arkengarthdale
Hurst
Washfold
Marrick Moor
Georgian Theatre
Richmond
Keld
Calver Hill
Skelton
Marske
Hudswell
Uckerby
Brompton
Catterick
Catterick Camp
Hipswell Moor
Thwaite
Muker
Ivelet
Gunnerside
Blades
Low Row
Feetham
Kearton
Healaugh
Reeth
Fremington
Grinton
Harkerside Moor
Ellerton Priory
Marrick
Downholme
Butter Tubs Pass
Crackpot
Oxnop Ghyll
Gibbon Hill
Stainton Moor
Scotton
Tunstall
East Appleton
Redmire Moor
Preston Moor
Bellerby Moor
East Bolton Moor
Barden
East Hauxwell
Hackforth
Arrathorne
Hunton
Askrigg Common
High Shaw
Castle Bolton
Leyburn Moor
Bellerby
Bolton
Preston-under-Scar
Redmire
Hardraw
Sedbusk
Askrigg
Newbiggin
Wensleydale
Woodhall
Low Bolton
Leyburn
Constable Burton
Patrick Brompton
Finghall
Bainbridge
Carperby
Aysgarth Falls
National Park Cen
Swinithwaite
Wensley
Harmby
Spennithorne
Newton-le-Willows
Bedale Hall
Hawes
Ropemaker
Wensleydale Cheese Visitor Centre
Burtersett
Countersett
Thornton Rust
Aysgarth
West Burton
West Witton
Middleham
Thornton Resr
Thornton Steward
Cowling
Rookwith
Burrill
Wether Fell
Marsett
Semer Water
Thoralby
Penhill
Agglethorpe
Abbey (rems. of)
Braithwaite Hall (NT)
East Witton
Jervaulx Abbey
Brymor High Jervaulx Farm
Thirn
Stalling Busk
Stake Fell
Bishopdale Beck
Newbiggin
Melmerby
Coverham
Caldbergh
Ellingstring
High Ellington
High Burton
Fleet Moss
Harland Hill
Carlton Moor
Carlton
Walden
West Scrafton
Black Sheep Brewery Visitors Centre
Masham
Cragdale Moor
Kidstones
Gammersgill
Coverdale
Colsterdale
Fearby
Oughtershaw
Middle Tongue
Horsehouse
Colsterdale Moor
Healey
Walden Head
Deepdale
Bradley
Arkleside
Langstrothdale Chase
Yockenthwaite
Cray
Buckden Pike
Cover Head Bents
Woodale
Hindlethwaite Moor
Great Haw
Leighton
Ilton
Swinton
Aldburgh
Hubberholme
Buckden
Masham Moor
Leighton Resr
Little Whernside
Scar House Reservoir
Brown Ridge
Roundhill Resr
Mickley
Grewelthorpe
Foxup
Halton Gill
Angram Resr
Nidderdale
Starbotton
Litton
Great Whernside
Middlesmoor
Kirkby Malzeard Moor
Nether Heselden
Littondale
Wharfe
How Stean Beck
Lofthouse
Hambleton Hill
Riggs Moor
Stean
Fountains Fell
Darnbrook Fell
Skirfare
Kettlewell
Arncliffe
Wharfedale
Dallowgill Moor
Greygarth
Laverton
Laver
Stean Moor
Ramsgill
Bouthwaite
Lumley Moor Resr
Hawkswick
Conistone Moor
Meugher
Grantley
Arncliffe Cote
Gouthwaite Resr
Risplith
Eavestone
Kilnsey
Grassington Moor
Malham Tarn
Conistone
Heathfield Moor
Pateley Moor
Appletreewick Moor
Pateley Bridge
Hebden Moor

110
109
120
102
A
B
C
D
1
2
3
4
5
DURHAM
DARLINGTON
STOCKTON-ON-TEES
MIDD
NORTH
YORK
Burnt Houses
Raby
Staindrop
Bolam
Hilton
Ingleton
Heighington
Houghton Bank
Houghton-le-Side
Aycliffe
Brafferton
Coatham Mundeville
Great Stainton
Little Stainton
Whitton
Thorpe Thewles
Carlton
Redmarshall
Langton
Summerhouse
Denton
Walworth
Archdeacon Newton
Headlam
Cleatlam
Little Newsham
Gainford
Winston
Stainton
Barnard Castle
Bowes Museum
Westwick
Whorlton
Ovington
Egglestone
Wycliffe
Caldwell
Eppleby
Piercebridge
High Coniscliffe
Low Coniscliffe
Mowden
DARLINGTON
Haughton Le Skerne
Barmpton
Great Burdon
Sadberge
Eastbourne
Hartburn
Elton
Longnewton
Preston Hall Museum
Urlay Nook
Teesside Airport Sta.
Allens West Sta.
Eaglescliffe
Ingleby Barwick
Middleton St George
Dinsdale Sta.
Teesside International
Aislaby
Yarm
Greta Bridge
Brignall
Barningham
Hutton Magna
Lane Head
West Layton
East Layton
Forcett
Aldbrough St John
Stanwick Camp
Manfield
Cleasby
Stapleton
Blackwell
Middleton One Row
Hurworth-on-Tees
Neasham
Low Dinsdale
Eryholme
Croft-on-Tees
Newton Morrell
Barton
Dalton-on-Tees
Croft
Sockburn
Girsby
Low Worsall
Kirklevington
Picton
Newsham
Dalton
Ravensworth
Gayles
Kirby Hill
Whashton
Melsonby
Gilling West
Scotch Corner
Middleton Tyas
Low Entercommon
High Entercommon
Hornby
Appleton Wiske
Great Smeaton
West Rounton
East Rounton
Welbury
Holgate Moor
Washfold
High Moor
Marske Moor
Skeeby
Moulton
North Cowton
Atley Hill
East Cowton
Birkby
Deighton
Georgian Theatre
Richmond
Uckerby
Scorton
Bolton-on-Swale
Hutton Bonville
Ingleby Arncliffe
East Harlsey
Marske
Hudswell
Brompton on Swale
Catterick
Whitwell
Streetlam
Danby Wiske
Oaktree Hill
Northallerton
Mount Grace Priory (NT)
Marrick
Ellerton Priory
Catterick Camp
Hipswell Moor
Downholme
Ellerton
Kiplin
Great Langton
Stainton
Stainton Moor
Scotton
Tunstall
East Appleton
Kirby Fleetham
Yafforth
Brompton
Ellerbeck
Kirby Sigston
Barden
East Hauxwell
Hornby
Hackforth
Great Fencote
Little Fencote
Romanby
Northallerton
Crosby Court
Preston Moor
Bellerby Moor
Bellerby
Arrathorne
Leyburn Moor
Preston-under-Scar
Burton Hall
Hunton
Langthorne
Scruton
Thrintoft
Ainderby Steeple
Morton-on-Swale
Warlaby
Thornton-le-Beans
Leyburn
Constable Burton
Patrick Brompton
Little Holtby
Kirkbridge
North Otterington
Wensley
Harmby
Finghall
Little Crakehall
Great Crakehall
Leeming Bar
Leeming
Borrowby
Spennithorne
Newton-le-Willows
Aiskew
Londonderry
Thornton-le-Moor
Bedale Hall
Bedale
Middleham
Thornton Resr
Abbey (rems of)
Cowling
Burrill
Exelby
Gatenby
Newby Wiske
Maunby
South Otterington
Thornton-le-Street
Agglethorpe
Thornton Steward
Rookwith
Thirn
Theakston
North Kilvington
Coverham
East Witton
Thornton Watlass
Thorp Perrow Arboretum
Braithwaite Hall (NT)
Jervaulx Abbey
Brymor High Jervaulx Farm
Burneston
Kirby Wiske
Newsham
Carthorpe
Pickhill
West Scrafton
Ellingstring
Snape
High Burton
Thirsk
High Ellington
Low Burton
Well
Dere Street
Sinderby
Sandhutton
Black Sheep Brewery Visitors Centre
Masham
Fearby
Colsterdale
Colsterdale Moor
Kirklington
Ainderby Quernhow
Carlton Miniott
World of James Herriot Museum
Nosterfield
Howe
Healey
Thornborough
Baldersby
Skipton-on-Swale
Swinton
Binsoe
Middleton Quernhow
Great Haw
Leighton
Leighton Reservoir
Ilton
Sutton Howgrave
Catton
Masham Moor
Aldburgh
West Tanfield
Brown Ridge
Mickley
Wath
Melmerby
Roundhill Reservoir
Grewelthorpe
North Stainley
Topcliffe
Asenby
Dalton
Lightwater Village
Lightwater Valley Park
Norton Conyers
Rainton
Kirkby Malzeard
Kirkby Malzeard Moor
Nunwick
Lofthouse
Hambleton Hill
Azerley
Sutton Grange
Dishforth
Cundall
Stean
Laverton
Galphay
Hutton Conyers
Sharow
Greygarth
Norton-le-Clay
Stean Moor
Ramsgill
Dallowgill Moor
Winksley Banks
Winksley
Ripon
Cathedral
Copt Hewick
Marton-le-Moor
Bouthwaite
Lumley Moor Reservoir
Grantley
Studley Royal
Studley Roger
Ripon
Bridge Hewick
Kirby Hill
Helperby
Gouthwaite Reservoir
Aldfield
Fountains Abbey (NT)
Littlethorpe
Newby
Skelton
Boroughbridge
Risplith
Markenfield Hall
Langthorpe
Boroughbridge
Heathfield Moor
Pateley Moor
Ingerthorpe
Bishop Monkton
Aldborough
Appletreewick
Pateley Bridge
Roecliffe
Lower Dunsforth
A1(M)
A66(M)
A1
A66
A67
A68
A167
A1150
A6108
A6136
A684
A61
A168
A19
A135
A1044
A177
A1027
B6279
B6275
B6274
B6271
B6280
B1263
B1264
B6268
B6285
B6267
B6265
B1448
544
429
406

III
121
112
103
D
E
F
G
1
2
3
4
5
Marske-by-the-Sea
Saltburn-by-the-Sea
Haverton Hill
Port Clarence
Dormanstown
Kirkleatham
Kirkleatham Old Hall Museum
New Marske
BROUGH
MIDDLESBROUGH
Cargo Fleet
Grangetown
South Bank
Eston
Lazenby
Yearby
Wilton
Upleatham
Dunsdale
North Ormesby
Ormesby
Normanby
Acklam
Nature's World
Stewart Park
Capt. Cook Birthplace Mus
Flatts Lane Woodland Country Park
Marton
Tollesby
Hemlington
Thornton
Stainton
Coulby Newham
Nunthorpe
Maltby
Newby
Hilton
Seamer
Tanton
Middleton-on-Leven
Stokesley
Great Ayton
Little Ayton
Pinchinthorpe
Newton under Roseberry
Roseberry Topping
Guisborough
Gisborough Moor
Easby Moor
Easby
REDCAR AND CLEVELAND
Brotton
Skelton
Skelton Green
North Skelton
Carlin How
Loftus
Mining Mus
Kilton
Easington
Boosbeck
Margrove Park
Lingdale
Stanghow
Moorsholm
Liverton
Boulby
Staithes
Dalehouse
Port Mulgrave
Hinderwell
Roxby
Runswick
Runswick Bay
Kettleness
Newton Mulgrave
Borrowby
Ellerby
Roxby Low Moor
Scaling
Scaling Resr
Mickleby
East Barnby
West Barnby
Ugthorpe
Roxby High Moor
Lockwood Beck Resr
Freebrough Hill
Moorsholm Moor
Commondale Moor
Commondale
Danby Low Moor
Danby Beacon
Lealholm Moor
Danby
Moors Centre
Houlsyke
Lealholm
Egton Low Moor
Egton
North Yorkshire Moors Rly
Grosmont
Egton Bridge
Glaisdale
Esk Dale
Ainthorpe
Castleton
Kildale
Kildale Moor
Battersby
Baysdale Beck
Baysdale
NORTH YORK MOORS NATIONAL PARK
Westerdale
Baysdale Moor
Westerdale Moor
Castleton Ridge
Danby High Moor
Glaisdale Rigg
Street
Glaisdale Moor
Egton High Moor
Pike Hill Moss
Beck Hole
Goathland
Thomason Foss
Hunt House
Wheeldale Moor
Wheeldale Moor Roman Road
Rudby
Sexhow
Kirkby
Great Broughton
Ingleby Greenhow
Great Busby
Enterpen
Potto
Carlton-in-Cleveland
Faceby
Whorlton
Swainby
CLEVELAND HILLS
Urra
Round Hill
Bilsdale East Moor
Seave Green
Chop Gate
Cockayne Ridge
Farndale Moor
Rosedale Moor
Whorlton Moor
Osmotherley
Bilsdale West Moor
Snilesworth Moor
Arnsgill Ridge
Cow Ridge
Grange
Cockayne
Rudland Rigg
Church Houses
Farndale
Blakey Ridge
Thorgill
Rosedale Abbey
ROSEDALE
BRANSDALE
Hodge Beck
Low Mill
Fangdale Beck
Cropton Forest
NORTH RIDING FOREST PARK
Stape
Keldy Castle
Spaunton Moor
Over Silton
Nether Silton
Arden Great Moor
Helmsley Moor
HAMBLETON HILLS
Kepwick
Hawnby
Gillamoor
Fadmoor
Hutton-le-Hole
Ryedale Folk Museum
Lastingham
Spaunton
Appleton-le-Moors
Newton-on-Rawcliffe
Newton Dale
Levisham
Lockton
Cropton
Boltby Moor
Kirby Knowle
Boltby
Old Byland
Wether Cote Fm
Carlton
Pockley
Kirkbymoorside
Keldholme
Kirkby Mills
Sinnington
Wrelton
Aislaby
Middleton
Pickering
Thirlby
Cold Kirby
Rievaulx
Rievaulx Terrace (NT)
Abbey
Scawton
Beadlam
Nawton
Wombleton
Great Edstone
Marton
Sutton-under-Whitestonecliffe
Duncombe Park
Helmsley
Scawton Moor
Rye Dale
Harome
Sproxton
Vale of Pickering
Normanby
Muscoates
Salton
Flamingo Land
Thornton Dale
Osgodby Hall
Bagby
High Kilburn
Kilburn
Thirkleby
Little Thirkleby
Oldstead
Byland Abbey
Wass
Ampleforth College
Ampleforth
Shandy Hall
Oswaldkirk
Nunnington Hall (NT)
Nunnington
West Ness
East Ness
Great Barugh
Little Barugh
Kirby Misperton
Brawby
Butterwick
Low Marishes
Stonegrave
Gilling East
Gilling
Cawton
Hovingham
Hutton Sessay
Coxwold
Newburgh Priory
Thorpe Hall
Carlton Husthwaite
Husthwaite
Thormanby
Oulston
Yearsley
Little Habton
Great Habton
Ryton
Fryton
Slingsby
Wyville Animal Farm
Appleton-le-Street
Barton-le-Street
Amotherby
Swinton
Broughton
Eden Camp
Old Malton
Malton
Norton
Scagglethorpe
Settrington
Howardian Hills
Coulton
Scackleton
Brandsby
Stearsby
Skewsby
Terrington
Coneysthorpe
Great Lake
Castle Howard
Jorvik Glass
Raskelf
Crayke
Ganthorpe
Easingwold
Marton Abbey
Whenby
Bulmer
Welburn
Langton Wold
Menethorpe
Low Hutton
Langton
Kennythorpe
Birdsall
Stillington
Farlington
Sheriff Hutton
Whitwell-on-the-Hill
Kirkham
Priory (ruins)
Foston
Huby
Alne
Cross Lanes
West Lilling
A19
A170
A171
A172
A174
A64
A169
B1257
B1363
B1248
B1266
B1366

A
B
C
D
Saltburn-by-the-Sea
Brotton
Skinningrove
Skelton
Mining Mus
Carlin How
Loftus
North Skelton
Kilton
Easington
Boulby
Staithes
Dalehouse
A174
Port Mulgrave
Hinderwell
Runswick Bay
Runswick
Kettle Ness
Kettleness
Goldsborough
REDCAR AND CLEVELAND
Lingdale
Liverton
Roxby
Borrowby
Newton Mulgrave
Moorsholm
Roxby Low Moor
B1366
Scaling
Scaling Resr
Freebrough Hill
Moorsholm Moor
A171
22
B1266
Ellerby
16
Lythe
Sandsend Ness
Sandsend
East Barnby
West Barnby
Mickleby
Roxby High Moor
Commondale
Danby Low Moor
Ugthorpe
Dunsley
Whitby
Lifeboat Mus
St. Mary's
Saltwick Bay
Abbey
Capt.Cook Memorial Museum
Newholm
Danby Beacon
Danby
Moors Centre
Lealholm Moor
Houlsyke
Castleton
Ainthorpe
Esk Dale
Lealholm
Egton Low Moor
Aislaby
Ruswarp
Stainsacre
High Hawsker
Sleights
Egton
North Yorkshire Moors Rly
Ugglebarnby
Sneaton
Low Hawsker
B1447
Ness Point or North Cheek
Robin Hood's Bay
Glaisdale
Grosmont
Egton Bridge
Street
Glaisdale Rigg
Sneatonthorpe
Raw
Fylingthorpe
Littlebeck
B1416
Danby High Moor
Sleights Moor
Falling Foss
Low Moor
Old Peak or South Cheek
Ravenscar
Beck Hole
NORTH YORK MOORS
Thomason Foss
Goathland
Glaisdale Moor
Egton High Moor
Pike Hill Moss
A169
Flask Inn
20
Farndale Moor
Mallyan Spout
NATIONAL PARK
Rosedale Moor
Hunt House
Fylingdales Moor
292
Burn Howe Rigg
Staintondale
Wheeldale Moor
NORTH
Church Houses
Farndale
ROSEDALE
Wheeldale Moor Roman Road
Thorgill
Blakey Ridge
Allerston High Moor
Lockton High Moor
Rosedale Abbey
Harwood Dale
Low Mill
Crompton Forest
NORTH RIDING FOREST PARK
Toll
Saltergate
Cloughton Ness
Broxa Forest
Cloughton
Spaunton Moor
Stape
Lockton Low Moor
Black Beck
Burniston
Keldy Castle
North Riding Forest Park
Silpho
Broxa
Suffield
Levisham
Langdale End
Lastingham
Gillamoor
Hutton-le-Hole
Spaunton
Newton-on-Rawcliffe
Newton Dale
Lockton
Stain Dale
Hackness
A165
Fadmoor
Ryedale Folk Museum
Sea Life Centre
Cropton
Everley
Scalby
Appleton-le-Moors
NORTH RIDING FOREST PARK
Dalby Forest
Wykeham Forest
Irton Moor
Falsgrave
Kirkbymoorside
Keldholme
Sinnington
Wrelton
Aislaby
Kirkby Mills
A170
13
Middleton
West Ayton
East Ayton
Nawton
Sawdon
Hutton Buscel
Great Edstone
Toll
Wombleton
YORKSHIRE
Marton
Pickering
Ebberston Hall
Wilton
Ruston
Wykeham
Irton
Thornton-le-Dale
Allerston
Ebberston
Snainton
17
Brompton
Wykeham Abbey
Seamer
Normanby
Vale of Pickering
B1415
Wilton Carr
A64
Muscoates
Salton
Flamingo Land
Priory
Nunnington Hall (NT)
Great Barugh
Little Barugh
Kirby Misperton
Yedingham
THE CARRS
Staxton
Flixton
West Ness
East Ness
Brawby
7
Low Marishes
B1258
East Heslerton
Sherburn
Ganton
Willerby
Butterwick
Little Habton
Great Habton
Derwent
East Knapton
West Knapton
West Heslerton
Ryton
Fryton
Slingsby
Wyville Animal Farm
Appleton-le-Street
Scampston
Wykeham
Old Malton Moor
Sherburn Wold
B1249
5
Hills
Barton-le-Street
B1257
Amotherby
Eden Camp
Rillington
Wintringham
Swinton
Broughton
Old Malton
Thorpe Bassett
Place Newton
Foxholes
Malton
Norton
Scagglethorpe
Butterwick
Terrington
Coneysthorpe
Great Lake
Settrington
Helperthorpe
Weaverthorpe
Ganthorpe
Castle Howard
Jorvik Glass
B1248
199
104
West Lutton
East Lutton
Octon
Welburn
Langton Wold
Menethorpe
North Grimston
Kirby Grindalythe
Bulmer
A64
Low Hutton
Duggleby
Langton
Whitwell-on-the-Hill
Kirkham
Kennythorpe
Birdsall
Wharram le Street
B1253
Cowlam Manor
Sledmere
Langtoft
Sheriff Hutton
Foston
Priory (ruins)
1
2
3
4

D
E
F
G
1
2
3
4
5
3.2 miles to 1 inch
0 2 4 6 8 10 miles
0 2 4 6 8 10 km
2 km to 1 cm
SCARBOROUGH
South Bay
Spa Complex
Black Rocks
A165
Cayton Bay
Cayton
The Wyke
Gristhorpe
Lebberston
Filey Brigg
Filey
Hertford
A1039
Folkton
Muston
Filey Bay
Hunmanby
Reighton Sands
Reighton
Speeton
Crab Rocks
Buckton
10
Burton Fleming
Bempton
B1229
Flamborough Head
Grindale
Flamborough
Sewerby Hall
Thwing
B1255
Sewerby
Boynton
Rudston
Gypsey Race
BRIDLINGTON
Bessingby
105
D
E
F
G

114
122
A
B
C
D
1
2
3
4
5
Knocknain
Leswalt
Soleburn Bridge
Innermessan
Lochinch Castle
New Luce
Tarf Bridge
Loch Ronald
Shennanton
Galdenoch
Craig Fell
Black Loch
Castle Kennedy
White Loch
Stranraer
Broadsea Bay
Portslogan
Loch Magillie
Soulseat Loch
Dunragit Moor
Abbey
Carscreugh
Barlae
Craighlaw
Kirkcowan
Whitecairn
DUMFRIES
Dunragit
Whitecrook
Glenluce
Whiteleys
Lochans
Genoch
Knock Moss
Dernaglar Loch
Knock Fell
Black Head
Cairn Pat
Kildrochet House
Genoch Square
Castle of Park
Whitefield Loch
Dinvin
Colfin
Portpatrick
Dunskey
Awhirk
Stoneykirk
THE RINNS OF GALLOWAY
Sands of Luce
Crow's Nest
Auchenmalg
Fell Loch
Old Place of Mochrum
Castle Loch
Culmalzie
Mochrum Loch
Water of Malzie
Port of Spittal Bay
Auchenmalg Bay
Culshabbin
Balgreggan
Sandhead
Alticry
Kirkmadrine Stones
Cairngarroch Bay
Chapel Finian
Elrig Loch
Loch Head
Money Head
Elrig
Clachanmore
Ardwell House
Ardwell
LUCE BAY
Chapel Rossan
Ardwell Bay
Barr Point
Port William
Drumbreddan Bay
Logan
Balgowan
New England Bay
Mull of Logan
Logan Botanic Gardens
Port Logan
Terally
Danger Zone
Barsalloch Point
Monreith
Kilstay
Clanyard Bay
Laggantalluch Head
Kirkmaiden
Drummore
Damnaglaur
Cailiness Point
Maryport
Crammag Head
Dunman
Portankill
Nick of Kindram
East Tarbert
West Tarbert
Mull of Galloway
A75
A77
A716
A747
B7043
B737
B7077
B7084
B7042
B7065
B7041
B7005
B735

Benfield
A75
Barhoi
D
Nether Barr
Palnure
E
Cairnsmore
F
Darngarroch
G
A762
Threave
Rhonehouse or Kelton Hill
B795
Barraer
Baltersan
6
A75
Spittal
123
B796
Castramont
Loch Whinyeon
Glengap
Bridge of Dee
Dildawn
Argrennan
Causeway End
7
Barholm Mains
Creetown
Gem Rock Museum
Glenquicken Moor
Skyre Burn
Rusko
Low Barlay
Ringford
A711
Tongland Loch
Carsegowan
A N D G A L L O W A Y
Cassencarie
Glen
Lauchentyre
Gatehouse of Fleet
Barcaple
10
Stone Circle
A714
Wigtown Sands
Cairnharrow
456
Anwoth
Cardoness Castle
Valleyfield
Culquhirk
Martyrs' Monument
Chambered Cairns
Ardwall
Barwhinnock
A762
B733
B7005
Carsluith
B727
9
Twynholm
Tongland
B7052
Bladnoch
Wigtown
Carsluith
11
Cardoness
Girthon
A75
Dam
B7005
Baldoon Sands
Kirkdale House
A75
Barharrow
9
Cumstoun
Langlands
Broughton House & Garden
11
Sandgreen
A755
Fleet Bay
Lennox Plunton
High Borgue
Kirkcudbright
Maclellan's Castle (ruin)
Stewartry Museum
B727
B7052
Barnbarroch
B7085
Kirkinner
Orchardton Bay
Innerwell Port
Murray's Isles
Islands of Fleet
Whauphill
Stewarton
Ardwall Island
Barlocco Island
Knockbrex
B727
Bombie
Bankhead
12
A746
B7004
B727
St Mary's Isle
Borgue
Auchnabony
Motte of Druchtag
Kirkland of Longcastle
B7052
Eggerness
Kirkandrews
A711
Dundrennan
Airyhassen
Sorbie
B7052
Garlieston
W I G T O W N
Senwick
Townhead
Kirkcudbright Bay
B7085
T H E
12
Galloway House
Cruggleton Bay
B A Y
Ringdoo Point
Borness
2
Standing Stones
M A C H A R S
Ross
Balmae
Barwinnock
White Loch
Castlewigg
Cults
B7004
(ruin)
Little Ross
B7021
Port Allen
Fort
Monreith
Craigdhu
Rispain Camp
Whithorn
Priory
B7063
Bay
A747
116
Cairndoon
10
Glasserton
Portyerrock
Fell of Carleton
B7004
3
Kidsdale
Isle of Whithorn
St Ninian's Cave
Port Castle Bay
St. Ninian's Chapel
3
Cutcloy
Devil's Bridge
Burrow Head
3.2 miles to 1 inch
0
2
4
6
8
10 miles
0
2
4
6
8
10 km
2 km to 1 cm
4
5
D
E
F
G

116
A
B
C
D
1
2
3
4
5
124
115
A713
A711
A745
A710
A75
A762
B795
B736
B727
B794
B793
A597
A596
A66
A595
B5295
B5294
A5086
B5345
Hillowton
Motte of Urr
Castle Douglas
Buchan
Threave
Threave (NTS)
Carlingwark Loch
Bridge of Dee
Rhonehouse or Kelton Hill
Dildawn
Argrennan
Breoch
Gelston
Craignair
Dalbeattie
Loch Fern
Cuil Hill
Loch Kindar
fell
569
Carse Bay
Kirkbean
Carsethorn
Cavens
Borron Point
Arbigland
Southwick Burn
Dalbeattie Forest
Palnackie
Barnbarroch
Caulkerbush
Mainsriddle
Ringford
Barcaple
Valleyfield
Tongland Loch
Netherthird
Airieland
Screel Hill
Kippford or Scaur
Fairgirth
Orchardton Tower
(NTS)
White Loch
Douglas Hall
Preston Merse
Gillfoot Bay
Southerness
Southerness Point
Mersehead Sands
Twynholm
Tongland
Dam
Bengairn
391
DUMFRIES & GALLOWAY
Rough Firth
Rockcliffe
Colvend
Port o' Warren
Cumstoun
Langlands
Broughton House & Garden
Kirkcudbright
Maclellan's Castle (ruin)
Stewartry Museum
Castlehill Point
Auchencairn
Auchencairn Bay
Almorness Point
Hestan Island
Barnhourie Sands
Balcary Point
Bombie
St Mary's Isle
Bankhead
Hazlefield
Rascarrel
Auchnabony
Dundrennan
Townhead
Abbey
Orroland
Rascarrel Bay
Barlocco Bay
Kirkcudbright Bay
Port Mary
Balmae
Little Ross
Abbey Head
SOLWAY FIRTH
Blackshaw Bank
Cross
Maryport
Ellenborough
Broughton Moor
Flimby
Camerton
Seaton
Great Clifton
WORKINGTON
Westfield
High Harrington
Distington
Gilgarran
Moresby
Pica
Keekle
Parton
WHITEHAVEN
Saltom Bay
Hensingham
Frizington
Cleator Moor
St Bees Head
Sandwith
Moor Row
Wath Brow
Bigrigg
Cleator
Rottington
St Bees
Egremont
Wilton
Kirk Beck
How Man
Snellings
Middletown
Nethertown
Ehen
Haile
Beckermet
Braystones
Sellafield
Ponsonby
3.2 miles to 1 inch
0 2 4 6 8 10 miles
0 2 4 6 8 10 km
2 km to 1 cm

117
D
E
F
G
Bowness-on-Solway
Torduff Point
Rockcliffe Marsh
Burgh Marsh
126
Glasson
Drumburgh
Hadrian's Wall
Burgh by Sands
Beaumont
Cargo
Kingstown
Houghton
Todhills
Harker
Scaleby
Linstock
Crosby
Cardurnock
Bowness Common
Anthorn
Easton
Boustead Hill
Longburgh
Monkhill
Grinsdale
Kirkandrews-upon-Eden
Gateway City Project
Border Regiment Mus
Stanwix
Grune Point
Whitrigg
Moricambe
Angerton
Fingland
Kirkbampton
Studholme
Thurstonfield
Moorhouse
CARLISLE
Skinburness
Newton Arlosh
Kirkbride
Oughterby
Little Bampton
Great Orton
Little Orton
Tullie House
Scotby
Silloth
Calvo
Seaville
Causewayhead
Wedholme Flow
Aikton
Newby West
Cummersdale
Carleton
Blitterlees
Biglands
Wiggonby
Carlisle
Gamelsby
Baldwinholme
Durdar
Brisco
Abbeytown
Kelsick
Oulton
Micklethwaite
A596
A595
Thursby
Dalston
Beckfoot
Highlaws
Lessonhall
Dundraw
Pelutho
Waverbridge
Wigton
West Curthwaite
Buckabank
Wreay
M6
Blencogo
Waverton
Red Dial
Gaitsgill
Mawbray
Bromfield
Langrigg
Aikshaw
Warblebank
Rosley
Raughton Head
Stockdalewath
Edderside
Westnewton
Bolton Low Houses
Westward
Welton
Allonby
Fletchertown
Brocklebank
Ivegill
Allonby Bay
Hayton
Aspatria
Baggrow
Mealsgate
Sebergham
Low Braithwaite
Blennerhasset
Faulds Brow
Inglewood
Sowerby Row
118
Boltongate
Whelpo
Caldbeck
Allerby
Plumbland
Torpenhow
Hesket Newmarket
Hutton End
Arkleby
Parsonby
Bothel
Whitrigg
Ireby
Parkend
Crosby
Gilcrux
High Ireby
Millhouse
Moota Hill
Ruthwaite
Uldale
Branthwaite
Dearham
Sunderland
Longlands
Lamonby
Unthank
Tallentire
Blindcrake
Binsey
Caldbeck Fells
Bewaldeth
High Pike 658
Skelton
Bridekirk
CUMBRIA
Hutton Roof
Dovenby
Uldale Fells
Carrock Fell
Mosedale
Johnby
Broughton
Papcastle
Bassenthwaite
Knott 710
Greystoke Forest
Great Broughton
Cockermouth
Embleton
Great Calva 690
Greystoke
Wordsworth House (NT)
Berrier Hill
Brigham
Mungrisdale
Greysouthen
Skiddaw Forest
Skiddaw 931
Saddleback or Blencathra 868
Eaglesfield
WHINLATTER FOREST PARK
Bassenthwaite Lake
Mirehouse
Motherby
Thornthwaite Forest
Scales
A66
Penruddock
Deanscales
Lord's Seat
Millbeck
Hutton
Dean
Pardshaw
Lorton Vale
High Lorton
Thornthwaite
Applethwaite
Threlkeld
Great Mell Fell
Ullock
Whinlatter Pass
Latrigg
Matterdale End
Little Mell Fell
Wreay
Whinlatter Forest
Portinscale
Castlerigg Stone Circle
Mockerkin
Grisedale Pike 790
Braithwaite
Keswick
Cumberland Pencil Mus.
Clough Head 726
Watermillock
Ulcat Row
Hopegill Head
Matterdale Common
Dockray
Loweswater
Brackenthwaite Fell
Causey Pike
Stair
Derwent Water
Great Dodd 856
Dowthwaitehead
Aira Force (NT)
Lamplugh
Grasmoor 851
Blake Fell 572
Little Town
Sandwick
Murton Fell
Loweswater Fell
Crummock Water
Derwent Fells
Stybarrow Dodd 840
High Seat 608
Ullswater
Kirkland
Croasdale
Scale Force
Buttermere
Robinson 737
Grange
Glenridding
Place Fell 657
Great Borne 616
Borrowdale
Watendlath
Thirlmere
Patterdale
Ennerdale Bridge
Red Pike
Buttermere
High Stile 806
Dale Head 754
Rosthwaite
Helvellyn 949
Striding Edge
Honister Pass 358
Seatoller
Borrowdale
Wythburn
Bridgend
Hartsop
Ennerdale Water
Scarth Gap Pass
Hay Stacks
Dollywaggon Pike
Grisedale
Ennerdale Fell
Stonethwaite
Borrowdale Fells
Ullscarf 726
Wythburn Fells
Lank Rigg
Pillar 892
Black Sail Pass
Steeple 841
Seathwaite
Fairfield 873
Seat Sandal
Dunmail Raise
Caw Fell
Haycock 797
LAKE
Kirk Fell
Great Gable 899
Glaramara
DISTRICT
Sty Head
High Raise 762
107
Wasdale Head
Allen Crags
Stake Pass
Rydal Fell
Middle Dodd 776
Kirkstone Pass 454
Lingmell
Great End
Esk Hause
Scafell Pike 977
Sca Fell 964
Langdale Pikes
Dungeon Ghyll Force
Grasmere
Rydal Mount
Rydal
Bow Fell 902
Copeland Forest
Calder Abbey
CUMBRIAN MOUNTAINS
B5307
B5302
B5300
B5301
B5299
B5304
B5305
B5291
B5292
B5289
B5322
B5343
B6264
A591
A594
A5086
A5091
A592
A6
1
2
3
4
5

118
126
117
108
A
B
C
D
1
2
3
4
5
Moat
Easton
Chapeltown
Netherby
Crofthead
Longtown
A6071
A7
Roman Road
Kirklinton
Smithfield
Todhills
Scaleby
Scalebyhill
Laversdale
Irthington
Blackford
Harker
Houghton
Kingstown
Cargo
Grinsdale
Stanwix
Linstock
Low Crosby
Newby East
Little Corby
Warwick
Warwick Bridge
Wetheral
Great Corby
Heads Nook
Scotby
Carleton
Cummersdale
Carlisle
Tullie House
Gateway City Project
Border Regiment Mus
Durdar
Brisco
Dalston
Cumwhinton
Cumwhitton
Corby Castle
Priory
Cotehill
Wreay
M6
Southwaite
Low Hesket
High Hesket
Aiketgate
Armathwaite
Ainstable
Ruckcroft
Staffield
Kirkoswald
Lazonby
Glassonby
Gaitsgill
Raughton Head
Stockdalewath
Ivegill
Low Braithwaite
Sebergham
Sowerby Row
Calthwaite
Inglewood Forest
Hutton End
Plumpton
Plumpton Head
New Rent
Unthank
Lamonby
Skelton
Ellonby
Hutton-in-the-Forest
Hutton Roof
Johnby
Laithes
Catterlen
Blencow
Greystoke Forest
Greystoke
Berrier Hill
Newton Reigny
Penrith
Newbiggin
Motherby
Penruddock
Hutton
Dacre
Dalemain
Stainton
Eamont Bridge
Brougham
Brocavum Roman Fort
Clifton
Tirril
Ullswater Steamers
Pooley Bridge
Lowther Castle
Askham
Lowther
Helton
Whale
Lowther Wildlife Park
Hackthorpe
Great Strickland
Melkinthorpe
Little Strickland
Sleagill
Newby
Morland
Cliburn
Temple Sowerby
Whinfell Forest
Roman Road
A66
A592
A5091
Great Mell Fell
Matterdale End
Little Mell Fell
Wreay
Watermillock
Ulcat Row
Dockray
Aira Force (NT)
Dowthwaitehead
Matterdale Common
Ullswater
Sandwick
Loadpot Hill 671
Martindale Common
Dale Head
Bampton Common
Barton Fell
Glenridding
Place Fell 657
Patterdale
Rosgill
Shap
Shap Abbey
Reagill
Maulds Meaburn
Wickerslack
Hoff
Burrells
Coupland
Colby
Appleby-in-Westmorland
Crackenthorpe
Kings Meaburn
Bolton
Long Marton
Brampton
Kirkby Thore
Murton
Hilton
Brackenber
Great Ormside
Sandford
Warcop
Dufton
Knock
Keisley
Backstone Edge
Milburn
Acorn Bank (NT)
Culgaith
Newbiggin
Blencarn
Kirkland
Skirwith
Langwathby
Edenhall
Winskill
Hunsonby
Little Salkeld
Great Salkeld
Salkeld Dykes
Ousby
Row
Melmerby
Gamblesby
Melmerby Fell 710
Ousby Fell
Green Fell
Cross Fell 893
Great Dun Fell 847
Knock Fell
Milburn Forest
Round Hill
Fiend's Fell
Hartside Height
580
A686
Gilderdale Forest
Black Fell 661
Renwick Fell
Renwick
Haresceugh
Scale Houses
Watch Hill
Croglin
Croglin Fell
Croglin Water
Grey Nag 656
Newbiggin
Cumrew
Holmwrangle
Hornsby
Hornsby Gate
Hall's Tenement
Castle Carrock
Faugh
How
Hayton
Talkin
Farlam
Talkin Tarn
Hallbankgate
Tindale
Tindale Tarn
Tindale Fells
Forest Head
Cold Fell 621
King's Forest of Geltsdale
Geltsdale Middle
Glendue Fell
Burnstones
Knarsdale
Slaggyford
Kirkhaugh
Williamston Common
Whitfield Law
Ayle
Alston
Raise
Bayles
Leadgate
Garrigill
Alston Moor
Rotherhope Fell
South Tynedale Rly
Ashholme Common
Stonehouse
Lambley
Halton Lea Gate
Midgeholme
A689
Featherstone Castle
Rowfoot
Plenmeller
Plenmeller Common
Denton Fell
Haltwhistle
Melkridge
Greenhead
Gilsland
Gilsland Spa
Poltross Burn Milecastle
Birdoswald (Camboglanna)
Roman Army Museum
Roman Fort
Roman Camps
Hadrian's Wall
Thirlwall Common
Whiteside
NORTHUMBERLAND
Black Fell
Butterburn
Deer Hill
Spadeadam Forest
Danger Zone
King Water
Green Rigg
Wiley Sike
Spadeadam
West Hall
Kirkcambeck
Lyneholmeford
Stapleton
Boltonfellend
Hethersgill
Hether Burn
Walton
Lanercost Priory
Naworth
Banks
Low Row
Newtown
Brampton
A69
A689
Milton
CUMBRIA
NORTHUMBERLAND

119
128
120
109
NATIONAL PARK
H U M B E R L A N D
D U R H A M
Haughton Common
Simonburn
Nunwick
Barrasford
Choll
Humshaugh
Chollerford
Walwick
Low Brunton
Brocolitia
Chesters (Cilurnum)
Turret
Wall
Hadrian's Wall
Housesteads (Vercovicium)
Once Brewed Visitor Centre
Chesterholm (Vindolanda)
Stanegate
Newbrough
Fourstones
Warden
Acomb
Bardon Mill
Haydon Bridge
Henshaw
South Tyne
Low Gate
Hexham
Sandhoe
Aydon
Corbridge
Corstopitum
Tyne Green
Dilston
Sunnyside
Linnels
Newbiggin
Hexham Levels 1464
Dipton Wood
West Dipton Burn
Riding Mill
Broomhaugh
Newton
Ovington
Ovingham
Prudhoe
Mickley Square
Stocksfield
Painshawfield
Coalburns
Leadgate
High Spen
Hedley on the Hill
Chopwell
Hamsterley
Stamfordham
Heugh
Fenwick
Hawkwell
Ouston
Grindstonelaw
Bingfield
Great Whittington
Little Whittington
Hadrian's Wall (Course of)
Harlow Hill
Rudchester
Stagshaw Bank
Halton
Horsley
Wylam
Stephenson's Birthplace
Crawcrook
Calleton Lane
Ryal
Dotland
Dalton
Whitley Chapel
Slaley Forest
Slaley
Healey
Dere Street
Whittonstall
Newlands
Ebchester
Kiln Pit Hill
Barleyhill
Shotleyfield
Shotley Bridge
Derwent Walk
Carterway Heads
Derwent Resr
Pow Hill
Ruffside
Edmundbyers
Muggleswick
Allensford
Castleside
Consett
Delves
Knitsley
Rowley
Healeyfield
Leadgate
Catton
Whitfield
Bearsbridge
Allendale Town
Studdon
Ninebanks
Hexhamshire Common
Broadwell House
Blanchland Moor
Hangman Hill
Devil's Water
Hope Fell
Blanchland
Abbey
Sinderhope
Allendale Common
Mohope Moor
Hartley Moor
Spartylea
Carr Shield
Green Hill
Hunstanworth
Nookton Fell
Cross Rigg
Muggleswick Common
Smiddy Shaw Resr
Skaylock Hill
Waskerley
Waskerley Resr
Waskerley Beck
Butsfield
Satley
Cornsay
Nenthall
Nenthead
Coalcleugh
Allenheads
Killhope Moor
Killhope Lead Mining Centre
Bolt's Law
561
Redburn Common
Rookhope
Rookhope Burn
Middlehope Moor
Stanhope Common
Collier Law 516
Wolsingham Park Moor
Tunstall Resr
Cornriggs
Cowshill
Wearhead
Burnhope Reservoir
Ireshopeburn
Westgate
Eastgate
Crawleyside
Stanhope
Tow Law
Weardale
St John's Chapel
Daddry Shield
Brotherlee
Frosterley
Wolsingham
Thornley
Burnhope Seat 746
Ireshope Moor
Chapel Fell
Chapelfell Top 699
Hill End
Harvey Hill
Knitsley Fell
Bellbeaver Rigg
Three Pikes
Westernhope Moor
Snowhope Hill
Bollihope
Common
Viewing Hill
Harwood
Langdon Common
Outberry Plain
675
Pikeston Fell
St Johns Hall
Pawlaw Pike
Langdon Beck
Newbiggin Common
Middleton Common
Carrs Hill
Redford
Bedburn
Hamsterley
Bedburn Beck
Hamsterley Common
Cow Green Reservoir
Widdybank Fell
Forest-in-Teesdale
High Force
Monks Moor
Euden Beck
Hamsterley Forest
Dufton Fell
Newbiggin
Bowlees Picnic Area
Eggleston Common
Woodland
Morley
Cronkley Fell
Holwick Fell
Holwick
Middleton-in-Teesdale
Butterknowle
Woodland Fell
Copley
Langleydale Common
Mickle Fell 790
Lune Forest
Bowbank
Mickleton
Eggleston
Burnt Houses
Lune Moor
Thringarth
Lunedale
Romaldkirk
Raby
Fish Lake
Little Fell 745
Danger Zone
Burton Fell
Grassholme
Grassholme Resr
Selset Reservoir
Mickleton Moor
Hunderthwaite
Hury
Kinninvie
Staindrop
Warcop Fell
Hunderthwaite Moor
Blackton Resr
Hury Resr
Balderhead Resr
Baldersdale
Cotherstone
Cotherstone Moor
Stainton
Cleatlam
Little Newsham
Iron Band 562
Stainmore Common
Hillbeck
Brough
North Stainmore
Barnard Castle
Startforth
Bowes Museum
Westwick
Whorlton
Winston
Deep Dale
Balder
Tees
Lune
A68
A69
A695
A6079
A686
A689
A692
A688
A67
B6318
B6320
B6319
B6305
B6306
B6307
B6309
B6321
B6528
B6530
B6278
B6295
B6277
B6276
B6262
B6279
B6282
B6297
B6301
B6274

120
NORTHUMBERLAND
128
119
110
A
B
C
D
1
2
3
4
5
WHITLEY BAY
TYNEMOUTH
NORTH SHIELDS
SOUTH SHIELDS
NEWCASTLE UPON TYNE
GATESHEAD
Gosforth
Longbenton
Wallsend
Jarrow
Hebburn
FELLING
BOLDON
Cleadon
Whitburn
Marsden
SUNDERL
Newburn
Ryton
Blaydon
Prudhoe
WHICKHAM
Rowlands Gill
Metrocentre
Dunston
Team Valley
Sunniside
Lamesley
Springwell
Birtley
WASHINGTON
STANLEY
Annfield Plain
CONSETT
CHESTER-LE-STREET
Pelton
Great Lumley
Plawsworth
Sacriston
Witton Gilbert
Framwellgate Moor
HOUGHTON LE SPRING
Hetton-le-Hole
Murton
South Hetton
Easington
Haswell
DURHAM
Shincliffe
Sherburn
Shadforth
Thornley
Cassop
Wheatley Hill
Bowburn
Coxhoe
Crook
Willington
Spennymoor
Ferryhill
Bishop Auckland
Shildon
Newton Aycliffe
Aycliffe
Sedgefield
Tow Law
Wolsingham
St Helen Auckland
West Auckland
Staindrop
DARLINGTON
STOCKTON-ON-TEES
STOCKTON-ON-TEES
MIDDLE
Billingh
Wolviston
Wynyard
Trimdon
Fishburn
Bishop Middleham
Chilton
Rushyford
Kelloe
Wingate
Station Town
Castle Eden
Hutton Henry
Peterlee
Shotton
Shotton Colliery
Seaham
Ryhope
Silksworth
New Silksworth
Herrington
Penshaw
Fatfield
Fence Houses
Bournmoor
Lanchester
Langley Park
Esh Winning
Brancepeth
Brandon
Ushaw Moor
Bearpark
Satley
Butsfield
Cornsay
Quebec
Hamsterley
Witton-le-Wear
Evenwood
Cockfield
Headlam
Gainford
Piercebridge
Winston
Barnard Castle
Heighington
Redworth
Middridge
Coundon
Westerton
Kirk Merrington
Dean Bank
Cornforth
Croxdale
Tudhoe
Sunderland Bridge
Hett
Ovington
Ovingham
Stocksfield
Mickley Square
Crawcrook
Greenside
Winlaton
Swalwell
Heddon-on-the-Wall
Throckley
Wylam
Horsley
Rudchester
Ponteland
Dinnington
Seaton Burn
Wide Open
Killingworth
Backworth
Earsdon
Shiremoor
New York
Cullercoats
Preston
Benton Square
Forest Hall
Fawdon
Kenton
Jesmond
Heaton
Byker
Walker
Pelaw
Monkton
West Boldon
East Boldon
Hylton
Southwick
Castletown
South Hylton
Fulwell
Monkwearmouth
Hendon
Ouston
Beamish
Tanfield
Burnopfield
Kibblesworth
Wrekenton
Shiney Row
A1(M)
A194(M)
A1
A19
A68
A167
A688
A689
A690
A691
A692
A693
A694
A695
A696
A1018
A1231
A1300
A184
A66
A67
A1150
A177
A181
A182
A183
A186
A187
A189
A191
A193
A194
A195
A1027
DURHAM
STOCKTON-ON-TEES
DARLINGTON
TYNE & WEAR

D
E
F
G
1
2
3
4
5
Amsterdam 15 hrs
3.2 miles to 1 inch
0 2 4 6 8 10 miles
0 2 4 6 8 10 km
2 km to 1 cm
Blackhall Colliery
Blackhall Rocks
Dene Mouth
Turning the Tide
Crimdon Park
Hart
Hartlepool Historic Ships
The Headland
Jackson's Landing
Historic Quay & Museum of Hartlepool
Hartlepool Bay
HARTLEPOOL
Elwick
Dalton Piercy
Seaton Carew
Tees Bay
Greatham
Newton Bewley
Seal Sands
Tees Mouth
Cowpen Bewley
Haverton Hill
Port Clarence
Coatham
Redcar
Warrenby
Dormanstown
Kirkleatham Old Hall Museum
Kirkleatham
Marske-by-the-Sea
Saltburn-by-the-Sea
REDCAR & CLEVELAND
New Marske
Yearby
Wilton
Upleatham
Grangetown
Lazenby
South Bank
North Ormesby
Eston
Normanby
Dunsdale
Flatts Lane Woodland Country Park
Ormesby
MIDDLESBROUGH
Marton
Tollesby
Suzy Project
Pinchinthorpe
Guisborough
Margrove Park
Lingdale
Stanghow
Skelton
North Skelton
Brotton
Warsett Hill
Skinningrove
Mining Museum
Loftus
Liverton
Boulby
Staithes
Dalehouse
Roxby
Port Mulgrave
Hinderwell
Runswick Bay
Runswick
Newton
Kettle Ness
A1086
A179
A1049
A689
B1277
A178
A1185
A1046
A19
A1032
A172
A171
A66
A174
A1085
A1042
B1380
B1269
A173
A174
A171

A
B
C
D
131
Ailsa Craig
1
3.2 miles to 1 inch
0 2 4 6 8 10 miles
0 2 4 6 8 10 km
2 km to 1 cm
2
3
4
5
A77
Dipple
Chapeldonan
Craighead
Grangeston
Old Dai
Girvan
Saugh Hill
Glendoune
Black Neuk
Glendrissaig
Pinminnoch
Ardwell
Kennedy's Pass
Grey Hill
297
A714
Pinmore
B734
Lendalfoot
Motte
Water of Lendal
Carleton Fishery
Aldons
Daljarrock
Poundland
Pinwherry
Bennane Head
Colmonell
Dalreoch
Stinchair
Craigneil
Glenduisk
Ballantrae Bay
Knockdolian
B7044
Mains of Tig
Ballochmorrie
Water of Tig
Auchairne
Balkissock
Ballantrae
Barrhill
Shiel Hill
Glenapp Castle
Smyrton
Downan Point
Kilantringan Loch
Craigie Fell
Beneraird
439
Cross Water
Carlock Hill
Milljoan Hill
Altimeg Hill
Chirmorrie
Glen App
Larne 1-2¼ hrs, Belfast 1½-3¼ hrs
Finnarts Point
Milleur Point
Markdhu
Corsewall Point
Miltonise
Standing Stones
Barnhills
Glenwhilly
Dalnigap
North Cairn
DUMFRIES
LOCH RYAN
B738
Corsewall
Kirkcolm
Cairnryan
Cairn Point
South Cairn
Dounan Bay
Main Water of Luce
Cross Water of Luce
Airies
Loch Connell
Ervie
A718
Artfield Fell
Portobello
B798
St Mary's Croft
Braid Fell
Beoch
Burn
Soleburn Bridge
Knocknain
Leswalt
New Luce
Tarf Bridge
Innermessan
B7043
THE RHINNS OF GALLOWAY
Auchmantle
Lochnaw
Lochinch Castle
Galdenoch
A751
Black Loch
Castle Kennedy
Craig Fell
Stranraer
White Loch
Carscreugh
B737
Broadsea Bay
Portslogan
Loch Magillie
Castle Kennedy
Dunragit Moor
Whitecairn
Piltanton Burn
A77
Soulseat Loch
A75
Abbey
Whiteleys
Dunragit
Lochans
Whitecrook
Glenluce
Black Head
Genoch
Cairn Pat
Castle of Park
Dinvin
Kildrochet House
B7077
Genoch Square
A747
A77
Colfin
B7084
Portpatrick
A716
Sands of Luce
Awhirk
Dunskey
Stoneykirk
Crow's Nest
Port of Spittal Bay
B7042
Auchenmalg Bay
Balgreggan
Sandhead
Cairngarroch Bay
Kirkmadrine Stones
114
Money Head
Clachanmore
Ardwell House
Ardwell
Ardwell Bay
LUCE BAY

D
E
F
G
132
124
115
I
2
3
4
5
SOUTH
CARRICK
AYRSHIRE
GALLOWAY FOREST PARK
GALLOWAY
WIGTOWN BAY
THE
Kirk Hill
Craigoch
Kilkerran
Craig
Tairlaw
Maratz Hill
Ness Glen
Todden Hill
Water of Deugh
Dailly
Bargany
Hadyard Hill
Garleffin Fell
429
Loch Bradan Reservoir
Loch Finlas
Loch Doon
Eriff
Benbrack
Drumjohn
Cairnsmore of Carsphairn
797
Dodd Hill
Black Shoulder
Linfern Loch
Glengennet
North Balloch
South Balloch
Changue Forest
Nick of the Balloch Pass
341
Barr
Shiel Hill
Loch Riecawr
Waterhead
Craiglee
Loch Doon
Starr
Loch Head
Lamloch
A713
Brochloch
Coran of Portmark
Garryhorn
Garryhorn Burn
Carsphairn
Craig of Knockgray
Knockgray
Marscalloch Hill
B729
Water of Deugh
Kendoon Loch
Bardennoch
Shalloch
565
Polmaddie Hill
479
Shalloch on Minnoch
Loch Macaterick
Meaul
695
Dalshangan
Polmaddy Burn
Carlin's Cairn
Corserine
813
Kirriereoch Hill
786
Kirriereoch Loch
Merrick
843
Elgin Lane
Loch Moan
Garwall Hill
Black Clauchrie
Loch Harrow
Forrest Lodge
Burnhead
B7000
Polharrow Burn
Knocknalling
12
Rhinns of Kells
Millfire
716
Loch Dungeon
Loch Enoch
Craignaw
Loch Neldricken
Meikle Millyea
746
Earlstoun Loch
Palgowan
Water of Minnoch
Buchan Burn
Buchan Hill
Loch Valley
Cooran Lane
Garroch Burn
Garroch
St John's Town of Dalry
Feoch Burn
Loch Goosey
Eldrick
Corwar House
Glen Trool Lodge
Loch Trool
1307
Darrou
Loch Dee
Glenlee
A762
Bennan
22
A714
Glentrool
Water of Trool
Mulldonoch
Clatteringshaws Loch
Bruce's Stone
Craigencallie
New Galloway
A712
Drumlamford Loch
B7027
Drumlamford Ho.
Loch Dornal
Bargrennan
Lamachan Hill
716
Larg Hill
Millfore
Darnaw
Cairnsmore of Dee
Clatteringshaws
Kenmure
Pulniskie Burn
Clachaneasy
Larg
Loch Ochiltree
Loch Maberry
Polbae
Forest Drive (summer only)
Black Water of Dee
Shaw Hill
Garlick Hill
Knockville
19
Wild Goat Park
Round Fell
Fell of Fleet
471
Knowe
Urrall Fell
Black Burn
Penninghame
Garlies Castle
Penkiln Burn
Dallash
Palnure Burn
Cairnsmore Burn
Craignelder
Loch Grannoch
Loch Fleet
Auchencloy Hill
Airie Hill
Loch Skerrow
Glenrazie
Boreland
Cumloden
Carseriggan
Challoch
Minnigaff
711
Bargaly
Little Water of Fleet
Culvennan Fell
Loch Ronald
Newton Stewart
Blackcraig
Cairnsmore of Fleet
Door of Cairnsmore
White Top of Culreoch
Darngarroch
Benfield
Shennanton
A75
Nether Barr
Palnure
Cairnsmore
Linn of Barhoise
B735
6
B796
15
Barlae
Craighlaw
Kirkcowan
Barraer
Baltersan
Spittal
Castramont
Loch Whinyeon
7
Causeway End
Barholm Mains
Creetown
Gem Rock Museum
Glenquicken Moor
Skyre Burn
Rusko
Low Barlay
B733
Carsegowan
Dernaglar Loch
Spittal
Stone Circle
Bladnoch
A714
Culquhirk
Cassencarie
Wigtown Sands
Glen
Lauchentyre
Gatehouse of Fleet
Cairnharrow
456
Anworth
Cardoness Castle
Martyrs' Monument
B733
B7005
Wigtown
Bladnoch
Carsluith
Chambered Cairns
Ardwall
Fell Loch
Old Place of Mochrum
B7052
Water of Malzie
Carsluith
Cardoness
Girthon
Barharrow
Baldoon Sands
Kirkdale House
11
9
Castle Loch
Culmalzie
Sandgreen
Fleet Bay
Mochrum Loch
B7005
Culshabbin
B7052
Barnbarroch
B7085
Kirkinner
Orchardton Bay
Lennox Plunton
B727
Murray's Isles
Islands of Fleet
Ardwall Island
Barlocco Island
Knockbrex
Alticry
Elrig Loch
Chapel Finian
A747
Loch Head
Elrig
Whauphill
Stewarton
A746
B7004
Innerwell Port
Kirkland of Longcastle
Eggerness
Kirkandrews
Senwick
Barr Point
Mochrum
Airyhassen
B7085
Sorbie
Garlieston
B7052
Galloway House
Cruggleton Bay
Ringdoo Point
Borness

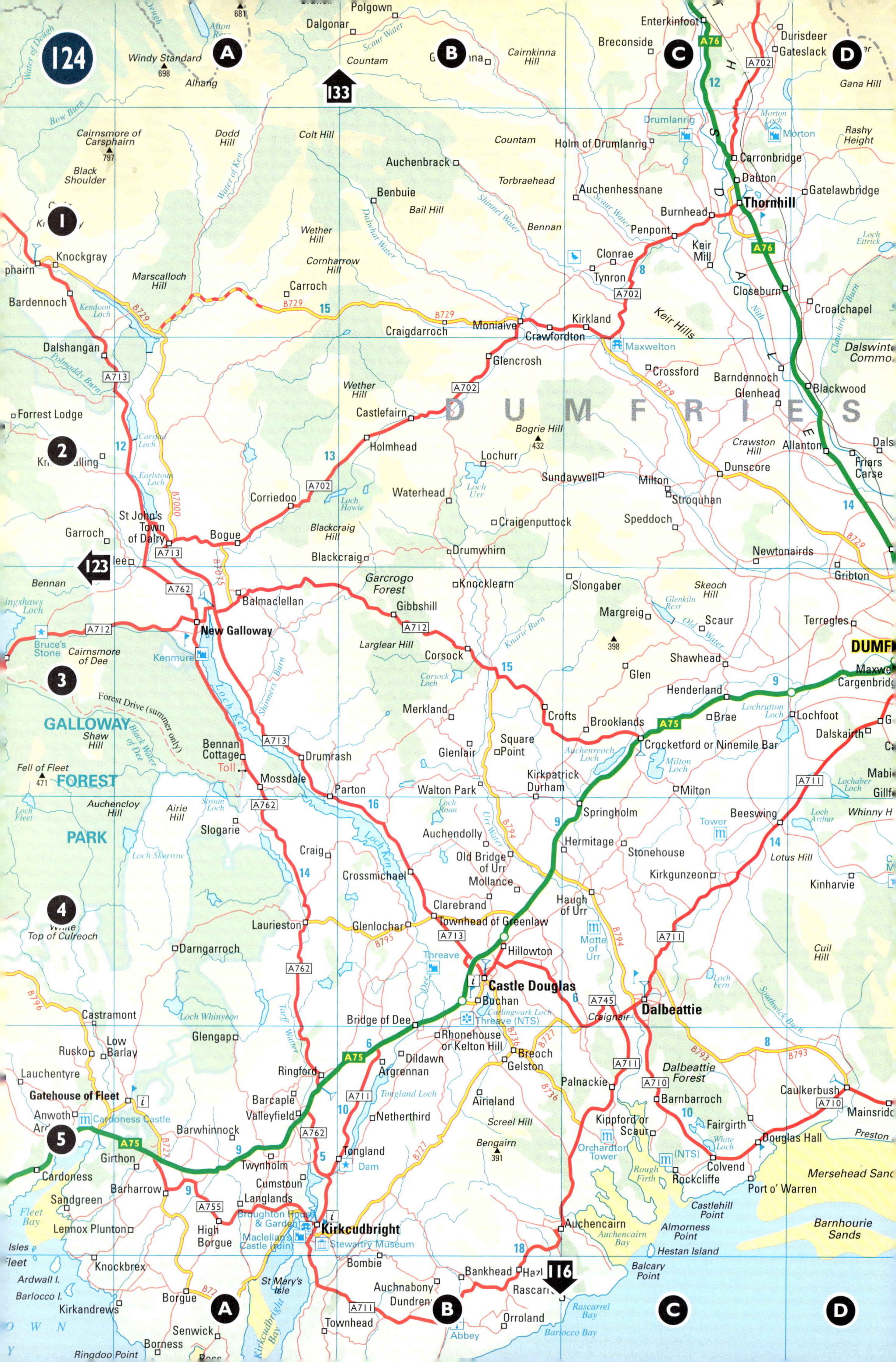

124
A
B
C
D
1
2
3
4
5
133
123
116
Windy Standard
698
681
Afton Res
Alhang
Polgown
Dalgonar
Scaur Water
Countam
Cairnkinna Hill
Enterkinfoot
Breconside
A76
A702
Durisdeer
Gateslack
Gana Hill
Bow Burn
Cairnsmore of Carsphairn
797
Black Shoulder
Dodd Hill
Colt Hill
Countam
Holm of Drumlanrig
Drumlanrig
Morton Loch
Morton
Rashy Height
Water of Ken
Auchenbrack
Torbraehead
Carronbridge
Dabton
Gatelawbridge
Benbuie
Bail Hill
Shinnel Water
Auchenhessnane
Scaur Water
Thornhill
Burnhead
Penpont
Bennan
Dalwhat Water
Wether Hill
Cornharrow Hill
Knockgray
phairn
Marscalloch Hill
Clonrae
Tynron
Keir Mill
Loch Ettrick
Carroch
B729
15
Bardennoch
Kendoon Loch
Closeburn
Croalchapel
Craigdarroch
Moniaive
Kirkland
Crawfordton
Keir Hills
Maxwelton
Dalswinton Common
Dalshangan
Polmaddy Burn
A713
Glencrosh
Crossford
Barndennoch
Glenhead
Blackwood
Wether Hill
Castlefairn
DUMFRIES
Forrest Lodge
Carsfad Loch
Bogrie Hill
432
Allanton
Crawston Hill
Dalswinton
Friars Carse
12
Holmhead
13
Lochurr
Sundaywell
Milton
Dunscore
Earlstoun Loch
B7000
Loch Urr
Waterhead
Stroquhan
Corriedoo
Loch Howie
Craigenputtock
Speddoch
14
Garroch
St John's Town of Dalry
Bogue
Blackcraig Hill
Drumwhirn
Newtonairds
Blackcraig
Gribton
Bennan
A762
Garcrogo Forest
Knocklearn
Slongaber
Skeoch Hill
ingshaws Loch
Balmaclellan
Gibbshill
Glenkiln Resr
Margreig
Scaur
A712
Bruce's Stone
New Galloway
Larglear Hill
Old Water
Terregles
Cairnsmore of Dee
Kenmure
Corsock
Knarie Burn
398
Shawhead
DUMFRIES
Corsock Loch
15
Glen
Maxwelltown
Cargenbridge
Forest Drive (summer only)
Shirmers Burn
9
Henderland
GALLOWAY
Loch Ken
Merkland
Crofts
Brooklands
Brae
Lochrutton Loch
Lochfoot
Shaw Hill
Black Water of Dee
A75
Dalskairth
Bennan Cottage
Square Point
Auchenreoch Loch
Crocketford or Ninemile Bar
Toll
Glenlair
Drumrash
Fell of Fleet
471
FOREST
Mossdale
Kirkpatrick Durham
Milton Loch
A711
Lochaber Loch
Mabie
Gillfoot
Parton
Walton Park
Milton
Loch Roan
Springholm
Loch Fleet
Auchencloy Hill
Airie Hill
Stroan Loch
16
Tower
Beeswing
Loch Arthur
Whinny Hill
Slogarie
Urr Water
B794
PARK
Auchendolly
Hermitage
Stonehouse
14
Loch Skerrow
Craig
Old Bridge of Urr
Lotus Hill
Crossmichael
Kirkgunzeon
Mollance
Kinharvie
Haugh of Urr
Clarebrand
White Top of Culreoch
Laurieston
Glenlochar
Townhead of Greenlaw
B795
Motte of Urr
Darngarroch
Threave
Hillowton
Cuil Hill
Castle Douglas
Loch Fern
Buchan
Dalbeattie
Carlingwark Loch
Threave (NTS)
Craignair
A745
Southwick Burn
B796
Castramont
Loch Whinyeon
Bridge of Dee
Glengap
Tarff Water
Rhonehouse or Kelton Hill
B736
B727
Breoch
8
Gelston
B793
Rusko
Low Barlay
Dildawn
Argrennan
Dalbeattie Forest
Palnackie
Lauchentyre
Ringford
A710
Barnbarroch
Caulkerbush
Gatehouse of Fleet
Tongland Loch
Airieland
Mainsriddle
Barcaple
Valleyfield
Netherthird
Kippford or Scaur
Fairgirth
Anwoth
Cardoness Castle
Screel Hill
White Loch
Preston
Barwhinnock
Orchardton Tower
Douglas Hall
Girthon
Bengairn
391
(NTS)
Colvend
Mersehead Sands
Cardoness
Twynholm
Tongland
Dam
Rough Firth
Rockcliffe
Port o' Warren
Barharrow
Cumstoun
Sandgreen
A755
Langlands
Castlehill Point
Fleet Bay
Broughton House & Garden
Kirkcudbright
Auchencairn
Almorness Point
Barnhourie Sands
Lennox Plunton
High Borgue
Auchencairn Bay
Isles of Fleet
Maclellan's Castle (ruin)
Stewartry Museum
Hestan Island
18
Bombie
Knockbrex
Balcary Point
Ardwall I.
St Mary's Isle
Bankhead
Barlocco I.
Auchnabony
Rascarrel
Kirkandrews
Borgue
Dundrennan
Rascarrel Bay
Kirkcudbright Bay
Townhead
Orroland
Senwick
Abbey
Borness
Barlocco Bay
Ringdoo Point

125
134
126
117
D
E
F
G
I
2
3
4
5
ANNANDALE
DUMFRIES AND GALLOWAY
SOLWAY FIRTH
CUMBRIA
Dumcrieff
Beattock
Kinnelhead
Craighoar Hill
Queensberry
697
Wee Queensberry
Minnygap Height
Holehouse Hill
Forest of Ae
Whitefauld Hill
Great Hill
Poldean
Laverhay Height
Laverhay
Milne Height
Fingland Fell
Newton
St Ann's
Johnstonebridge
Annandale Water
Dinwoodie Mains
Hangingshaw
Sibbaldbie
Blackacre
Kirkland
Parkgate
Ae Village
Nethermill
Cumrue
Templand
Millhousebridge
Glenae
Duncow
Kirkton
Amisfield
Tinwald
Lochmaben
Lockerbie
Locharbriggs
Torthorwald
Rammerscales
Carthat Hill
Heck
Hightae
Castlemilk
Kettleholm
Collin
Noblehill
Robert Burns Centre
Camera Obscura
Kingholm Quay
Woodside
Racks
Cleughbrae
Mouswald
Dalton
Carrutherstown
Netherwood
Kelton
Lochar Moss
Glencaple
Kirkconnell
Shambellie Grange
Sweetheart Abbey
New Abbey
Bankend
Shearington
Comlongon
Brow Well
Clarencefield
Ruthwell
Cross
Kinmount
Cummertrees
Powfoot
Caerlaverock
Blackshaw
Merse
Blackshaw Bank
Annan
Eastriggs
Dornock
Rigg
Gretna
Gretna Green
Gretna Gateway
Springfield
Blacksmith's Shop
Kirkpatrick-Fleming
Hollee
Nutberry Moss
Creca
Brydekirk
Kirtlebridge
Ecclefechan
Carlyle's Birthplace (NTS)
Middlebie
Roman Fort
Springkell
Eaglesfield
Chapelknowe
Waterbeck
Wallacehall
Solwaybank
Burnswark
Howat's Hill
Roman Camp
Tundergarth Mains
Bankshill
Grange Fell
Dunnabie
Debate
Paddockhole
Callisterhall
Bigholms
Raes Knowes
Gillenbie
Corrie Common
Heithat
Corsehill
Boreland
Hart Fell
The Shin
Telford Memorial
Calkin Rig
450
Craigcleuch
Glentenmont Height
Bentpath
Castle O'er
Castle O'er Forest
The Knock
Billholm
Allangillfoot
Hog Hill
Eskdalemuir
Holm
Jamestown
Causeway Grain Head
White Hope
Dinnings Hill
Black Esk Resr
Garwald
Garwaldwaterfoot
Davington
Fingland
Lamblair Knowe
Blaeberry Hill
Stock Hill
Jock's Shoulder
Black Hill
Cowan Fell
Crumpton Hill
Milltown
Kirkbean
Carsethorn
Cavens
Borron Point
Arbigland
Carse Bay
Southerness
Southerness Point
Gillfoot Bay
Criffell
569
Torduff Point
Rockcliffe Marsh
Bowness-on-Solway
Port Carlisle
Glasson
Drumburgh
Hadrian's Wall
Burgh Marsh
Burgh by Sands
Easton
Boustead Hill
Longburgh
Monkhill
Bowness Common
Cardurnock
Anthorn
Whitrigg
Grune Point
Moricambe
Angerton
Kirkbride
Fingland
Kirkbampton
Studholme
Thurstonfield
Oughterby
Little Bampton
Great Orton
Newton Arlosh
Skinburness
Silloth
Calvo
Seaville
Causewayhead
Blitterlees
Wedholme Flow
Aikton
Biglands
Gamelsby
Wiggonby
Baldwinholme
Micklethwaite
Thursby
Kelsick
Oulton
Lessonhall
Abbeytown
Highlaws
Beckfoot
Pelutho
Blencogo
Waverton
Waverbridge
Wigton
West Curthwaite
Bromfield
Langrigg
Red Dial
Mawbray
Aikshaw
Dubmill Point
Warblebank
Rosley
M74
A701
A709
A780
A75
A710
A596
A595
B7020
B7076
B7068
B725
B723
B722
B724
B6357
B721
B709
B5307
B5302
B5301
B5305

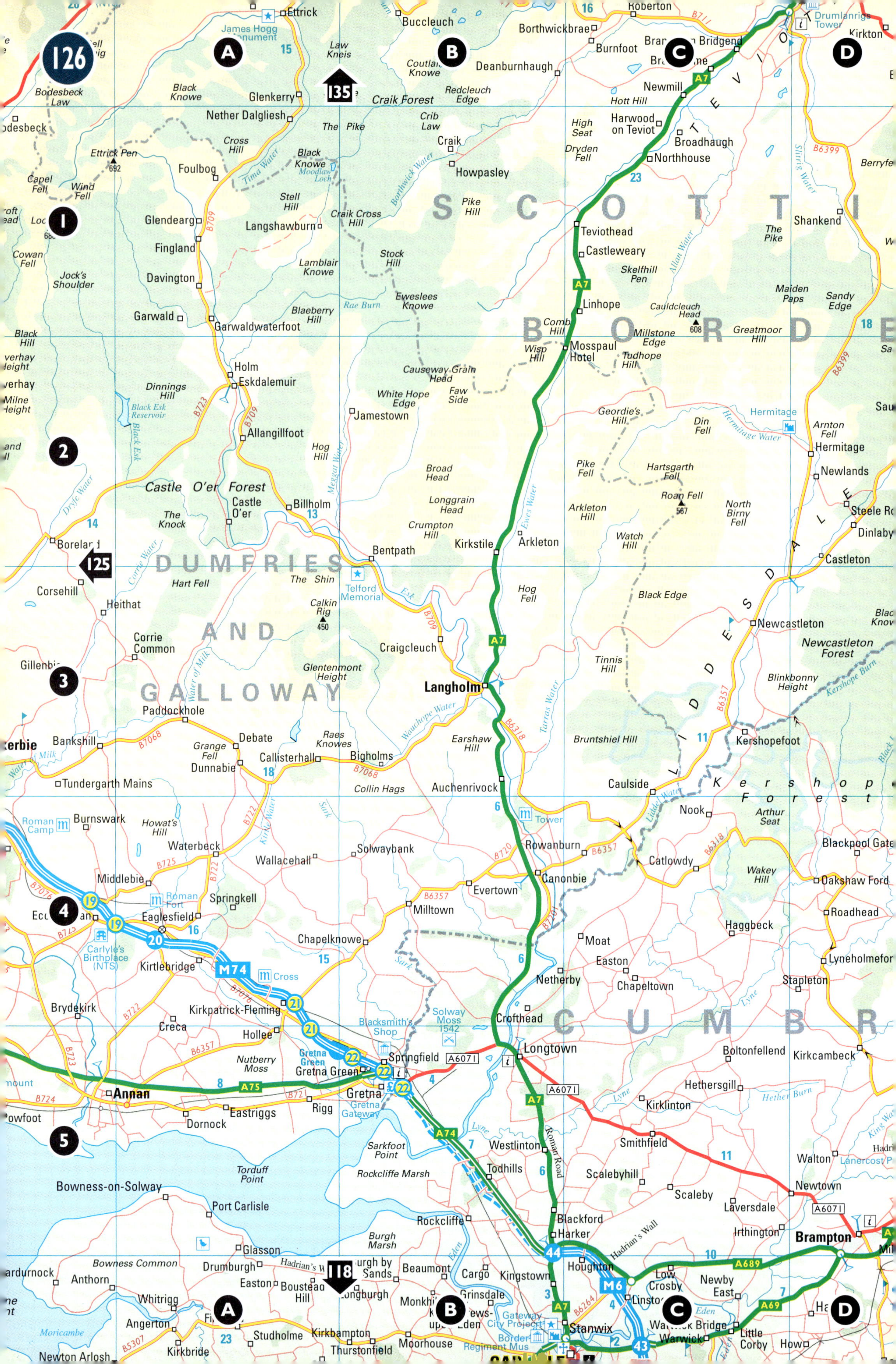

126
135
125
118
A
B
C
D
1
2
3
4
5
Ettrick
James Hogg Monument
Buccleuch
Borthwickbrae
Roberton
Burnfoot
Bridgend
Drumlanrig's Tower
Kirkton
Bodesbeck Law
Law Kneis
Coutlair Knowe
Deanburnhaugh
Newmill
Hott Hill
Black Knowe
Glenkerry
Craik Forest
Redcleuch Edge
Nether Dalgliesh
Crib Law
High Seat
Harwood on Teviot
The Pike
Craik
Broadhaugh
Dryden Fell
Northhouse
Ettrick Pen
692
Cross Hill
Foulbog
Tima Water
Black Knowe
Moodlaw Loch
Howpasley
Capel Fell
Wind Fell
Stell Hill
Borthwick Water
Pike Hill
SCOTTISH
Shankend
Berryfell
Glendearg
Langshawburn
Craik Cross Hill
Teviothead
The Pike
Cowan Fell
Fingland
Castleweary
Lamblair Knowe
Stock Hill
Skelfhill Pen
Allan Water
Jock's Shoulder
Davington
Maiden Paps
Sandy Edge
Eweslees Knowe
Linhope
Garwald
Rae Burn
Cauldcleuch Head
608
Blaeberry Hill
Garwaldwaterfoot
Comb Hill
Black Hill
Millstone Edge
Greatmoor Hill
BORDERS
Wisp Hill
Mosspaul Hotel
Tudhope Hill
Holm
Eskdalemuir
Causeway Grain Head
Dinnings Hill
Faw Side
White Hope Edge
Geordie's Hill
Hermitage
Black Esk Reservoir
Black Esk
Jamestown
Din Fell
Hermitage Water
Arnton Fell
Allangillfoot
Hermitage
Hog Hill
Megget Water
Broad Head
Pike Fell
Hartsgarth Fell
Newlands
Castle O'er Forest
Roan Fell
567
Dryfe Water
Longgrain Head
Arkleton Hill
North Birny Fell
Steele Road
The Knock
Castle O'er
Billholm
Crumpton Hill
Dinlaby
Borelan
Kirkstile
Arkleton
Watch Hill
Castleton
DUMFRIES
Bentpath
Corrie Water
Hart Fell
The Shin
Telford Memorial
Esk
Hog Fell
Black Edge
Corsehill
Heithat
Calkin Rig
450
LIDDESDALE
Newcastleton
Newcastleton Forest
Corrie Common
AND
Craigcleuch
Tinnis Hill
Gillenbie
Water of Milk
Glentenmont Height
Blinkbonny Height
Kershope Burn
GALLOWAY
Langholm
Paddockhole
Wauchope Water
Tarras Water
Bankshill
Raes Knowes
Earshaw Hill
Bruntshiel Hill
Kershopefoot
Grange Fell
Debate
Callisterhall
Bigholms
Dunnabie
Collin Hags
Tundergarth Mains
Auchenrivock
Caulside
Liddel Water
Kershope Forest
Roman Camp
Burnswark
Kirtle Water
Sark
Tower
Nook
Arthur Seat
Howat's Hill
Waterbeck
Solwaybank
Rowanburn
Catlowdy
Blackpool Gate
Wallacehall
Middlebie
Canonbie
Wakey Hill
Oakshaw Ford
Roman Fort
Springkell
Evertown
Milltown
Roadhead
Ecclefechan
Eaglesfield
Haggbeck
Carlyle's Birthplace (NTS)
Chapelknowe
Moat
Lyneholmeford
Kirtlebridge
M74
Cross
Easton
Netherby
Chapeltown
Stapleton
Brydekirk
Kirkpatrick-Fleming
Solway Moss 1542
CUMBRIA
Creca
Hollee
Blacksmith's Shop
Crofthead
Longtown
Boltonfellend
Kirkcambeck
Nutberry Moss
Gretna Green
Springfield
Gretna Green
Annan
Gretna
Gretna Gateway
Rigg
Eastriggs
Dornock
Kirklinton
Hethersgill
Hether Burn
Powfoot
Sarkfoot Point
Westlinton
Roman Road
Smithfield
Walton
Lanercost Priory
Torduff Point
Rockcliffe Marsh
Todhills
Scalebyhill
Bowness-on-Solway
Scaleby
Newtown
Port Carlisle
Laversdale
Rockcliffe
Blackford
Harker
Irthington
Brampton
Burgh Marsh
Hadrian's Wall
Glasson
Drumburgh
Burgh by Sands
Beaumont
Cargo
Kingstown
Houghton
Low Crosby
Newby East
Bowness Common
Easton
Boustead Hill
Longburgh
Grinsdale
Linstock
Cardurnock
Anthorn
Monkhill
Eden
Whitrigg
Angerton
Newtown
Gateway City Project
Warwick Bridge
Little Corby
Moricambe
Kirkbampton
Stanwix
Warwick
How
Border Regiment Mus
Studholme
Newton Arlosh
Kirkbride
Thurstonfield
Moorhouse
A7
A74
A75
A6071
A689
A69
M6
B709
B723
B7068
B6357
B6318
B6399
B711
B7076
B725
B722
B724
B721
B6264
B5307
B720

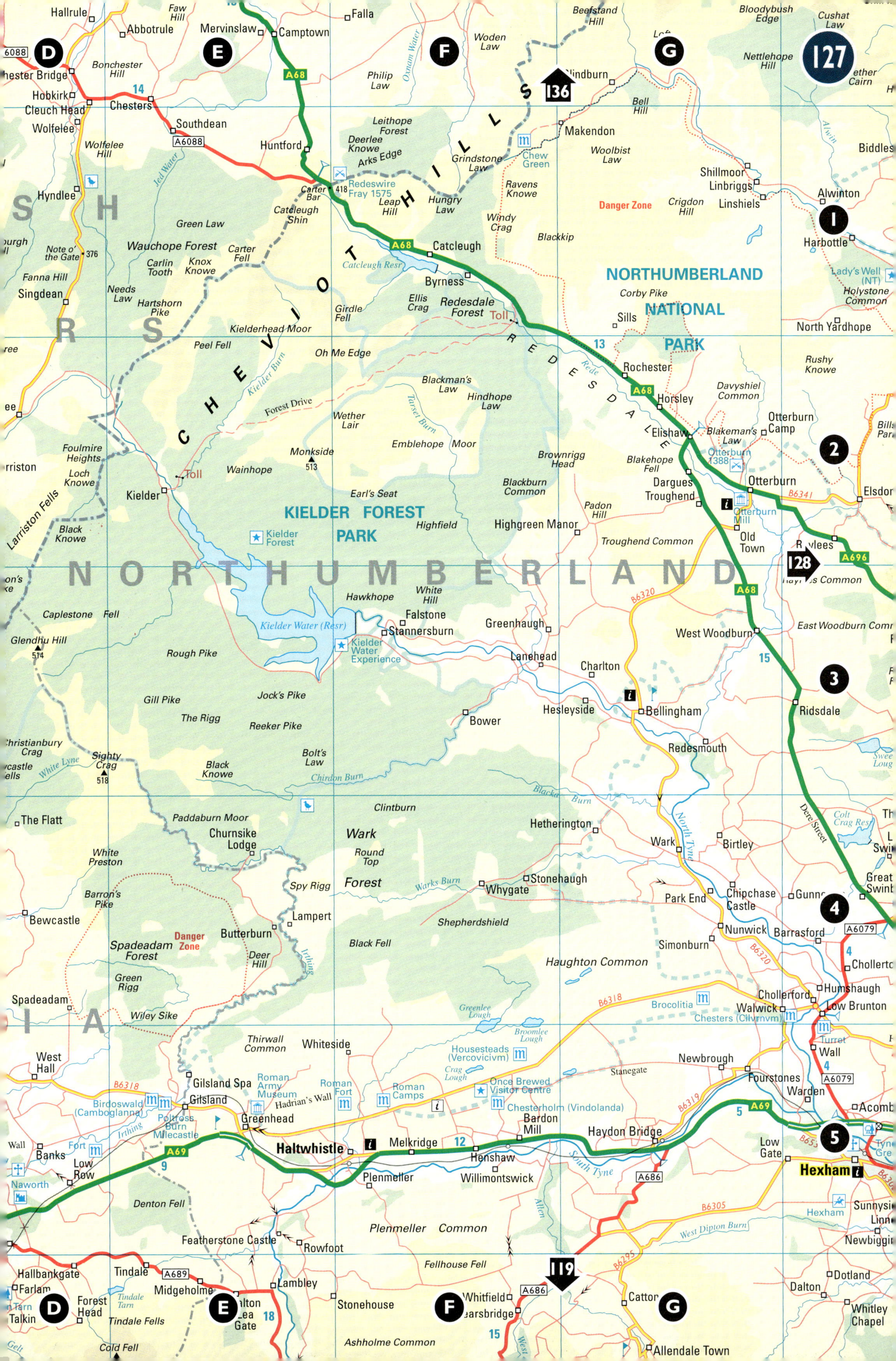
127
136
128
119
D
E
F
G
I
2
3
4
5
Hallrule
Faw Hill
Abbotrule
Mervinslaw
Camptown
Falla
Woden Law
Beefstand Hill
Bloodybush Edge
Cushat Law
Nettlehope Hill
Bonchester Hill
Hobkirk
Cleuch Head
Wolfelee
Chesters
Southdean
A6088
Wolfelee Hill
Huntford
A68
Philip Law
Oxnam Water
Leithope Forest
Deerlee Knowe
Arks Edge
Grindstone Law
Makendon
Chew Green
Woolbist Law
Bell Hill
Shillmoor
Linbriggs
Linshiels
Alwinton
Biddlestone
Hyndlee
Jed Water
Carter Bar
418
Redeswire Fray 1575
Leap Hill
Hungry Law
Ravens Knowe
Windy Crag
Danger Zone
Crigdon Hill
Harbottle
Green Law
Catcleugh Shin
Wauchope Forest
Carter Fell
Catcleugh
Catcleugh Resr
Blackkip
Note o' the Gate
376
Carlin Tooth
Knox Knowe
Byrness
Fanna Hill
Singdean
Needs Law
Hartshorn Pike
Ellis Crag
Girdle Fell
Redesdale Forest
Toll
NORTHUMBERLAND NATIONAL PARK
Corby Pike
Sills
Lady's Well (NT)
Holystone Common
North Yardhope
Kielderhead Moor
Peel Fell
Oh Me Edge
13
Rochester
Rushy Knowe
CHEVIOT HILLS
REDESDALE
Blackman's Law
Hindhope Law
Horsley
Davyshiel Common
Kielder Burn
Forest Drive
Tarset Burn
Wether Lair
Emblehope Moor
Elishaw
Blakeman's Law
Otterburn Camp
Foulmire Heights
Monkside
513
Wainhope
Toll
Brownrigg Head
Blakehope Fell
Otterburn 1388
Loch Knowe
Larriston Fells
Kielder
Earl's Seat
Blackburn Common
Dargues
Troughend
Otterburn
B6341
Elsdon
Padon Hill
Otterburn Mill
Old Town
KIELDER FOREST PARK
Kielder Forest
Highfield
Highgreen Manor
Troughend Common
Black Knowe
Rayleees
A696
NORTHUMBERLAND
Hawkhope
White Hill
B6320
A68
Caplestone Fell
Falstone
Greenhaugh
West Woodburn
East Woodburn Common
Kielder Water (Resr)
Stannersburn
Glendhu Hill
514
Kielder Water Experience
Rough Pike
Lanehead
Charlton
15
Gill Pike
Jock's Pike
Hesleyside
Bellingham
Ridsdale
The Rigg
Reeker Pike
Bower
Christianbury Crag
Sighty Crag
518
Bolt's Law
Redesmouth
White Lyne
Black Knowe
Chirdon Burn
Blacka Burn
The Flatt
Clintburn
Paddaburn Moor
Churnsike Lodge
Hetherington
Colt Crag Resr
Dere Street
Wark
White Preston
Round Top
Wark Forest
North Tyne
Birtley
Spy Rigg
Warks Burn
Stonehaugh
Whygate
Park End
Chipchase Castle
Barron's Pike
Great Swinburne
Lampert
Shepherdshield
Bewcastle
Butterburn
Nunwick
Barrasford
A6079
Danger Zone
Spadeadam Forest
Deer Hill
Irthing
Black Fell
Simonburn
Haughton Common
B6320
Chollerton
Green Rigg
Humshaugh
Spadeadam
B6318
Greenlee Lough
Brocolitia
Chollerford
Walwick
Low Brunton
Wiley Sike
Chesters (Cilurnvm)
Broomlee Lough
Thirlwall Common
Whiteside
Turret
Wall
West Hall
Housesteads (Vercovicivm)
Newbrough
Stanegate
Crag Lough
Fourstones
Gilsland Spa
Roman Army Museum
Roman Fort
Roman Camps
Once Brewed Visitor Centre
Warden
A6079
B6318
Birdoswald (Camboglanna)
Gilsland
Hadrian's Wall
Chesterholm (Vindolanda)
B6319
A69
Acomb
Poltross Burn Milecastle
Greenhead
Bardon Mill
Haydon Bridge
Wall
Fort
Banks
Haltwhistle
Melkridge
12
Henshaw
Low Gate
A69
Low Row
9
Plenmeller
Willimontswick
South Tyne
A686
Hexham
Naworth
Denton Fell
Allen
B6305
Hexham
Sunnyside
Linnels
West Dipton Burn
Newbiggin
Featherstone Castle
Rowfoot
Plenmeller Common
Hallbankgate
Tindale
A689
Fellhouse Fell
B6295
Dotland
Farlam
Midgeholme
Lambley
Whitfield
A686
Dalton
Tindale Tarn
Talkin
Forest Head
Tindale Fells
Alston Lea Gate
18
Stonehouse
Cupola Bridge
Catton
Whitley Chapel
15
West Allen
Cold Fell
Ashholme Common
Allendale Town
Gelt

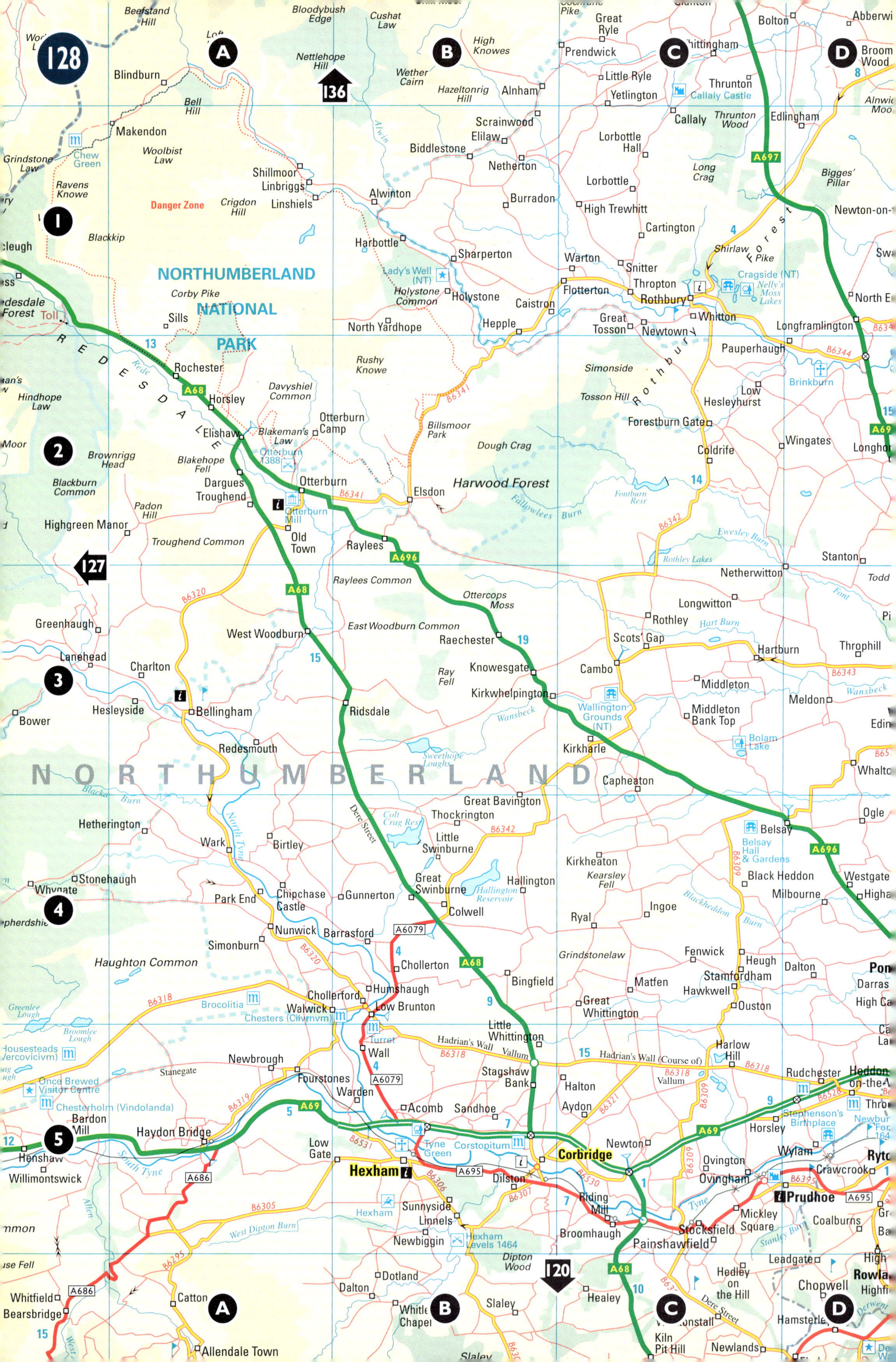
A
B
C
D
136
127
120
1
2
3
4
5
NORTHUMBERLAND NATIONAL PARK
NORTHUMBERLAND
Danger Zone
Beefstand Hill
Bloodybush Edge
Cushat Law
High Knowes
Great Ryle
Prendwick
Bolton
Abberwick
Broome Wood
Nettlehope Hill
Wether Cairn
Hazeltonrig Hill
Alnham
Little Ryle
Yetlington
Whittingham
Thrunton
Callaly Castle
Callaly
Thrunton Wood
Edlingham
Alnwick Moor
Blindburn
Bell Hill
Makendon
Chew Green
Grindstone Law
Woolbist Law
Ravens Knowe
Crigdon Hill
Shillmoor
Linbriggs
Linshiels
Scrainwood
Elilaw
Biddlestone
Netherton
Lorbottle Hall
Lorbottle
Long Crag
Bigges' Pillar
Alwinton
Burradon
High Trewhitt
Cartington
Newton-on-the-Moor
Blackkip
Harbottle
Sharperton
Shirlaw Pike
Rothbury Forest
Lady's Well (NT)
Holystone Common
Holystone
Warton
Snitter
Thropton
Rothbury
Cragside (NT)
Nelly's Moss Lakes
North Elyham
Whitton
Caistron
Flotterton
Hepple
Great Tosson
Newtown
Longframlington
North Yardhope
Corby Pike
Sills
Rochester
Redesdale
Rede
Pauperhaugh
Brinkburn
Rushy Knowe
Simonside
Tosson Hill
Low Hesleyhurst
Forestburn Gate
Davyshiel Common
Horsley
Hindhope Law
Elishaw
Blakeman's Law
Otterburn Camp
Billsmoor Park
Dough Crag
Coldrife
Wingates
Longhorsley
Brownrigg Head
Blakehope Fell
Otterburn 1388
Harwood Forest
Fontburn Resr
Blackburn Common
Dargues
Troughend
Otterburn
Elsdon
Otterburn Mill
Padon Hill
Highgreen Manor
Troughend Common
Old Town
Raylees
Fallowlees Burn
Ewesley Burn
Rothley Lakes
Stanton
Netherwitton
Todd
Raylees Common
Ottercops Moss
Longwitton
Greenhaugh
West Woodburn
East Woodburn Common
Rothley
Hart Burn
Raechester
Scots' Gap
Hartburn
Throphill
Lanehead
Charlton
Ray Fell
Knowesgate
Cambo
Middleton
Kirkwhelpington
Wallington Grounds (NT)
Middleton Bank Top
Meldon
Wansbeck
Bower
Hesleyside
Bellingham
Ridsdale
Sweethope Loughs
Bolam Lake
Kirkharle
Redesmouth
Capheaton
Whalton
Great Bavington
Blacka Burn
Thockrington
Colt Crag Resr
Ogle
Hetherington
Dere Street
Belsay
Belsay Hall & Gardens
Little Swinburne
Wark
North Tyne
Birtley
Kirkheaton
Kearsley Fell
Black Heddon
Westgate
Milbourne
High Callerton
Stonehaugh
Whygate
Great Swinburne
Hallington
Hallington Reservoir
Park End
Chipchase Castle
Gunnerton
Colwell
Ingoe
Blackheddon Burn
Ryal
Nunwick
Barrasford
Simonburn
Grindstonelaw
Fenwick
Heugh
Dalton
Ponteland
Chollerton
Haughton Common
Bingfield
Stamfordham
Hawkwell
Darras Hall
Matfen
Greenlee Lough
Brocolitia
Chollerford
Humshaugh
Great Whittington
Ouston
Walwick
Low Brunton
Chesters (Cilurnum)
Broomlee Lough
Housesteads (Vercovicium)
Turret
Wall
Little Whittington
Hadrian's Wall
Vallum
Hadrian's Wall (Course of)
Harlow Hill
Rudchester
Heddon-on-the-Wall
Newbrough
Stanegate
Fourstones
Once Brewed Visitor Centre
Warden
Stagshaw Bank
Halton
Chesterholm (Vindolanda)
Bardon Mill
Acomb
Sandhoe
Aydon
Throckley
Stephenson's Birthplace
Horsley
Newburn Ford
Haydon Bridge
Low Gate
Tyne Green
Corstopitum
Newton
Wylam
Henshaw
South Tyne
Hexham
Corbridge
Ovington
Ovingham
Crawcrook
Ryton
Willimontswick
Dilston
Prudhoe
Riding Mill
Mickley Square
Coalburns
Allen
Sunnyside
Hexham Levels 1464
Linnels
Broomhaugh
Stocksfield
Painshawfield
Stanley Burn
West Dipton Burn
Newbiggin
Dipton Wood
Leadgate
Highfield
Rowlands Gill
Dotland
Hedley on the Hill
Chopwell
Dalton
Whitfield
A686
Catton
Bearsbridge
Healey
Whitley Chapel
Slaley
Minsteracres
Hamsterley
Derwent
Kiln Pit Hill
Newlands
Allendale Town
A68
A69
A696
A697
A6079
A695
B6341
B6342
B6320
B6318
B6319
B6321
B6305
B6295
B6306
B6307
B6309
B6343
B6344
B6530
B6531
B6528
B6395

D
E
F
G
137
121
1
2
3
4
5
3.2 miles to 1 inch
0 2 4 6 8 10 miles
0 2 4 6 8 10 km
2 km to 1 cm
Alnwick
Boulmer Haven
Hawkhill
Lesbury
Alnmouth Sta.
Bilton
Alnmouth
Alnmouth Bay
High Buston
Shilbottle
Birling
Eastfield Hall
Warkworth
Amble
Coquet Island
Moor
Gloster Hill
Guyzance
Morwick Hall
North Togston
Hauxley
Hauxley Haven
Old Swarland
Acklington
Radcliffe
Togston
Broomhill
Hadston Carrs
Felton
South Broomhill
Chevington Drift
East Thirston
Red Row
Druridge Bay
Eshott
West Chevington
Druridge Bay
Widdrington
Causey Park
Widdrington Sta.
The Scars
Cresswell
Earsdon Moor
Snab Point
Fenrother
Tritlington
Ulgham
Ellington
Espley Hall
Lynemouth
Beacon Point
Hebron
Longhirst
Queen Elizabeth II
Woodhorn
Morpeth Chantry
Pegswood
ASHINGTON
Newbiggin-by-the-Sea
Northumbria Craft Centre
Bothal
Hirst
Mitford
Wansbeck
Morpeth
Sheepwash
North Seaton
Shadfen
Guide Post
Stakeford
Cambois
Hepscott
Scotland Gate
Tranwell
Clifton
East Sleekburn
Nedderton
BLYTH
Bedlington
Cowpen
Bebside
Plessey Woods
Saltwick
East Hartford
Newsham
Stannington
Shankhouse
Nelson Village
Cramlington
New Hartley
Seaton Sluice
Seaton
Hartley
Berwick Hill
Brenkley
Seaton Delaval
St Mary's or Bait Island
Dykes
Horton Grange
Dudley
Seghill
WHITLEY BAY
Seaton Burn
Spanish City
Dinnington
Wide Open
Burradon
Earsdon
Prestwick
Hazlerigg
Camperdown
Backworth
Shiremoor
Monkseaton
Newcastle International
Killingworth
Marden
Cullercoats
New York
TYNEMOUTH
Black Callerton
Forest Hall
Benton Square
Preston
Fawdon
Longbenton
NORTH SHIELDS
Willington
Gosforth
Kenton
SOUTH SHIELDS
North Tyneside Steam Rly
Wallbottle
Blakelaw
Jesmond
Wallsend
Royal Quays
Harton
Newburn
NEWCASTLE UPON TYNE
Heaton
Bede's World
Marsden Bay
Lemington
Jarrow
Marsden
Stella
Walker
Hebburn
International Centre for Life
Byker
Blaydon
Monkton
Whitburn
Swalwell
Winlaton
Metrocentre
Dunston
Pelaw
Cleadon
BOLDON
GATESHEAD
FELLING
West Boldon
WHICKHAM
East Boldon
Whitburn Bay
Team Valley
Roker
Winlaton Mill
Southwick
Gibside Chapel
Wrekenton
Hylton
Gill
Sunniside
Springwell
Castletown
Monkwearmouth
Marley Hill
National Glass Centre
Lamesley
Angel of the North
Birtley
SUNDERLAND
Burnopfield
Kibblesworth
Tanfield Rly
Hobson
Tanfield
Beamish
WASHINGTON
Hendon
Tyne
Wear
A1
A1068
A189
A197
A196
A1147
A193
A192
A1061
A1171
A19
A190
A1056
A191
A186
A1058
A167
A6085
A695
A694
A692
A167(M)
A184
A185
A194
A1300
A1018
A183
A194(M)
A195
A1290
A1231
A690
B6345
B1339
B1330
B1337
B1331
B1505
B1325
B1318
B1505
B1297
B1298
B1291
B1426
B6324
Stavanger 19 hrs, Haugesund 21½ hrs & Bergen 22-26 hrs
Kristiansand 17 hrs & Göteborg 25 hrs
Amsterdam 15 hrs

130
139
A
B
C
D
1
2
3
4
5
GIGHA ISLAND
Tarbert
Creag Bhan 100
Ardaily
Ardminish
Achamore Gardens
Craro Island
Cara Island
Mull of Cara
Sound of Gigha
Ronachan
Corriechrevie
Auchinafaud
Cruach Mhic-Gougain
Rhunahaorine Point
Rhunahaorine
Tayinloan
Killean
Beacharr
Muasdale
Achaglass
Carradale Forest
Belloch
Glenbarr
Arnicle
ARGYLL AND BUTE
KINTYRE
Bellochantuy
Killocraw
Corrylach
Tangy
Westport
Low Ballevain
Kilchenzie
East Darlochan
Campbeltown (Machrihanish)
Machrihanish Bay
Kilmichael
Drumore
Campbeltown
Machrihanish
Witchburn
Drumlemble
Dalivaddy
Chiscan
Knocknaha
Kilchrist
Kilkerran
Davaar Island
Davaar
Glenramskill
New Orleans
Killellan
Largybaan
Brecklate
Keprigan
Kildavie
Carrine
Keil
Southend
Machrarioch
Garveld
Feorlan
Mull of Kintyre
Sanda Island
Sheep Island
Sanda Sound
Crossa
Cour
Sunadale
Grogport
Carradale
Dippen
Torrisdale
Whitestone
Saddell
Bunlarie
Ballochgair
Drumgarve
Calliburn
Peninver
KILBRANNAN SOUND
A83
B842
B843

SOUND OF BUTE
D
E
F
G
Cock of Arran
Newton
Loch Ranza
Lochranza
A841
Catacol Bay
Rubha Airigh Bheirg
Glen Catacol
Glen Chalmadale
North Glen Sannox
14
Craw
Lenimore
Thundergay
Beinn Bhreac 573
Beinn Tarsuinn
Beinn Bhreac 711
Mullach Buidhe 721
Caisteal Abhail 859
Cir Mhor 798
Glen Sannox
Cioch-na-h-Oighe
Mid Sannox
Sannox Bay
Corrie
Pirnmill
Loch Tanna
Goat Fell 874
Beinn Tarsuinn 825
Imachar
Beinn Bharrain
Glen Rosa
Ballikine
17
Beinn Nuis 792
Brodick (NTS)
Merkland Point
NORTH
Glen Iorsa
Iorsa Water
A841
Dougarie
Brodick Garden (NTS)
Brodick Castle (NTS)
A R R A N
Heritage Museum
Brodick Bay
Brodick
361
An Tunna
Glencloy
Auchgallon Stone Circle
Chambered Cairn
Strathwhillan
Glaister
Tarsnacraig
South Corrygills
Machrie
5
A'Chruach 404
A841
Machrie Bay
Machrie Water
B880
Ard Bheinn 512
Clauchlands Point
A841
Machrie Moor Stone Circles
Beinn Bhreac 503
Margnaheglish
Tormore
Ballymichael
11
Benlister Glen
Lamlash
Lamlash Bay
Holy Island
King's Cave
Hut Circles
Cnoc a'Chapuill 417
Glenkiln
Torbeg
Shiskine
Fort
AYRSHIRE
Tighvein 458
Kingscross Point
Kingscross
Blackwaterfoot
Drumadoon Bay
Knockenkelly
Whiting Bay
Kilpatrick
Kiscadale
Brown Head
Glen Scorrodale
Glen Ashdale
Whiting Bay
Largymore
Corriecravie
Largybeg
Largybeg Point
Torr a' Chaisteil
Sliddery
Dippin
20
Levencorroch
Dippin Head
Lagg
Kilmory Water
A841
Shannochie
Kildonan
Chambered Cairns
Bennan Head
Sound of Pladda
Pladda
1¼ hr Claonaig (summer only)
St Blane's Church
B881
Dunagoil Bay
Torr Mor
Garrochty
Garroch Head
140
Little Cumbrae
Millport Bay
Kaim Hill 387
Inner Brigurd Point
Hunterston
A78
Gull Point
Crosbie
12
Portencross
B7048
West Kilbride
Munnoch
Farland Head
Ardneil Bay
Seamill
Munnoch Resr
B780
1
Ardrossan
Horse Isle
Saltcoats
Rothesay 1½ hrs (summer only)
1 hr
2
FIRTH OF CLYDE
132
3
4
Dunure
Dunure Mains
Culzean Bay
Culzean Castle & Country Park (NTS)
Maidenhead Bay
Morriston
Maidens
11
Turnberry
12
Turnberry Bay
Turnberry
5
A77
Dowhill
Dipple
Low Craighead
Chapeldonan
Grangeston
Killochan
Old Dailly
Penkill
Saugh Hill
Girvan
Glendoune
Black Neuk
Ailsa Craig
122
3.2 miles to 1 inch
0 2 4 6 8 10 miles
0 2 4 6 8 10 km
2 km to 1 cm

132
A
B
C
D
1
2
3
4
5
141
131
123
NORTH AYRSHIRE
CUNNINGHAME
EAST AYRSHIRE
AYR
SOUTH AYRSHIRE
Kaim Hill 387
South Hourat
Glengarnock
Beith
Gateside
Caldwell
Lugton
Gabroc Hill
Windy Yet
Hunterston
Crosbie
West Kilbride
Portencross
Farland Head
Seamill
Giffordland
Munnoch
Munnoch Resr
Caaf Resr
Dalry
Blair
The Den
Barrmill
Burnhouse
Dunlop
Fullwood
Kingsford
Auchentiber
Stewarton
Kingswell
Ballageich Hill 330
Dalgarven
Kilwinning
Montgreenan
Eglinton
Cunninghamhead
Kilmaurs
Fenwick
Waterside
Tayburn
Moscow
Loudon Castle Park
Ardrossan
Horse Isle
Stevenston
Saltcoats
1 hr Brodick
Perceton
IRVINE
Springside
Knockentiber
Dreghorn
Crosshouse
KILMARNOCK
Dick Institute
Newmilns
Galston
The Big Idea Exhibition
Scottish Maritime Museum
Irvine Bay
Gatehead
Drybridge
Riccarton
Crookedholm
Hurlford
Dundonald
Crossroads
Sornhill
Milrig
Middleyard
Bogend
Coodham
Craigie
Boydston
Barassie
Loans
Symington
Whitelees
Adamhill
Lochlea
Crosshands
Belfast 2½ hrs (summer only)
Troon
Lady Isle
Rosemount
Monkton
Fail
Tarbolton
Bachelor's Club (NTS)
Mossgiel
Mauchline
Ballochmyle
Prestwick
Prestwick International
Mossblown
Failford
Barskimming
Catrine
Ayr Bay
Whitletts
St Quivox
Auchincruive
Annbank
Stair
Trabboch
AYR
Wallace Tower
Seafield
Loudoun Hall
Belston
Holmston
Sundrum Mains
Schaw
Ochiltree
Joppa
Coylton
Drongan
Burns' Cottage
Craig Tara
Heads of Ayr
Alloway
Maclaurin Gallery & Rozelle House
Tam O'Shanter Experience
Burns National Heritage Park
Burnton
Sinclairston
Skares
Lagg
Fisherton
Dunure
Brown Carrick Hill 287
Dunduff
Nether Auchendrane
Mount Oliphant
Hollybush
Littlemill
Dunure Mains
Sauchrie
Minishant
Culroy
Dalrymple
Skeldon
Rankinston
Stannery Knowe
Electric Brae
Knoweside
Culzean Bay
Culzean Castle & Country Park (NTS)
Pennyglen
Grimmet
Dalvennan
Patna
Lethanhill
Kilmein Hill 429
Maybole
Kirkmichael
Loch Spallander Reservoir
Keirs Hill
Waterside
Benbeoch
Maidenhead Bay
Morriston
Maidens
Kirkoswald
Crossraguel Abbey
Turnberry
Turnberry Bay
Souter Johnnie's Cottage (NTS)
Crosshill
Blairquhan
Burnton
Clawfin
Dalmellington
Cloyntie
Gass
Straiton
Windy Standard
Kirk Hill
Craigoch
Dalcairnie
Wallacetown
Kilkerran
Craig
Craigengillan
Dowhill
Dipple
Deil's Elbow
Maratz Hill
Ness Glen
Chapeldonan
Low Craighead
Bargany Mains
Dailly
Tairlaw
Eriff
Benbrack
Grangeston
Killochan
Bargany
Old Dailly
Penkill
Hadyard Hill
Garleffin Fell 429
Loch Doon
Loch Bradan Reservoir
Drumjohn
Girvan
Saugh Hill
Linfern Loch
Craiglee
Glendoune
Glengennet
North Balloch
Waterhead
Lamloch
A78
A737
A736
A735
A738
A71
A759
A719
A77
A76
A79
A713
A70
B7048
B781
B780
B785
B777
B706
B707
B778
B769
B751
B7038
B7081
B7064
B7080
B730
B739
B744
B743
B705
B7037
B7036
B742
B7024
B7034
B7045
B7023
B741
B764

KILBRIDE
Jackton
Calder Glen
Polnoon
Crutherland
A726
Auldhouse
Rutherend
Shawtonhill
Melowther Hill
Chapelton
Corse Hill 376
Laird's Seat
Ardochrig
Meikle Earnock
Low Waters
Chatelherault
Eddlewood
Quarter
A723
Limekilnburn
Fairholm
Larkhall
Machan
Overtown
Waterloo
Law
Carluke
Forth
Hare Hill
Netherton
Ashgill
Rosebank
Milton Lockhart
A721
Kilncadzow
Braidwood
Harelaw
142
Netherburn
Glassford
Udstonhead
Stonehouse
Netherfield
A71
Strathaven
Craignethan
Crossford
Hazelbank
Draffan
Cleghorn
A706
A70
Carstairs
Jerviswood
Lanstruth
Blackwood
Nemphlar
Auchenheath
Black Hill Fort
A72
Lanark
Kirkfieldbank
Kirkmuirhill
New Lanark
New Lanark World Heritage Village
Falls of Clyde
Hyndford Bridge
A73
Cairngryffe Hill
Sandford
Boghead
Deadwaters
B7086
Caldermill
Moss
Hareshaw
West Cauldcoats
S O U T H
Lesmahagow
Hawksland
Birkwood
Kype Muir
Kype Water
A70
Harleyholm
Darvel
Priestland
Drumclog
Dungavel
1307
Auchlochan
Logan Water
L A N A R K S H I R E
Stone Hill
Changue Hill
Auchingilloch
Douglas Water
Mill Rig
Goodbush Hill
Cumberhead
Coalburn
Braehead
Rigside
Glengavel Reservoir
Nutberry Hill 522
Bankend
Happendon
Uddington
Distinkhorn
Robert Law
Newton
Garf Water
B7055
Wedder Hill 434
Priesthill Height
St Bride's Church
Douglas
New Mains
Scaur Hill
Dungavel 510
Middlefield Law
134
Mid Hill
Dun Rig
Glenbuck
Black Hill
Parish Holm
Hazelside
Glespin
Redshaw
Wildshaw Hill
Roberton
Netherwood
Greenock Water
M74
Muirkirk
Smallburn
Carmacoup
Abington
Nethershield
Kames
Gilmilnscroft
Nether Wellwood
Glentaggart
Airds Moss
Boghead
Cairn Table 593
Dryrigs Hill
Crawfordjohn
Duneaton Water
S H I R E
Wardlaw Hill
Cronberry
Carbellow
Auchinleck
Lugar
Stony Hill
Glespin Burn
Drake Law
Abington
A702
Logan
Gass Water
Lettershaws
Cumnock
Netherthird
Dalblair
Mount Stuart
Glenmuir Water
Duneaton Water
Wellgrain Dod
B7040
Fingland
Spango Water
L O W T H E R H I L L S
Craigdullyeart Hill
Corsebank
Lochhill
Cocker Hill
Hallmerk Hill
Wanlock Water
Leadhills
Watchman Hill
Elvan Water
Pathhead
Lagrae
Kirkland
Wanlock Dod
Carco
New Cumnock
D U M F R I E S
Connel Park
Wanlockhead
Museum of Scottish Lead Mining
Beam Engine
Afton Bridgend
A76
Kirkconnel
732 Green Lowther
Burnside
Laight
Willowgrain Hill
Kelloholm
Drumbuie
Crawick
Mennock Pass 329
Lowther Hill
Roman Road
Sanquhar
Mennock Water
Hare Hill
Kello Water
Ulzieside
Mennock
Dalveen Pass 277
Enoch Hill 569
Blackcraig Hill 700
A N D
Eliock
Craigdarroch
Euchan Water
Glengenny Muir
Ardoch
Ballencleuch Law 691
Cloud Hill
Blacklorg Hill 681
Afton Resr
Cruffell
Wether Hill
Polgown
Dalgonar
Enterkinfoot
Durisdeer
Breconside
Scaur Water
Cairnkinna Hill
Wedder Law
Windy Standard 698
Countam
Glenmanna
Gateslack
Alhang
G A L L O W A Y
Gana Hill
Cairnsmore of Carsphairn 797
Colt Hill
124
Drumlanrig
Drumlanrig
Morton Loch
Morton
Rashy Height
Countam
Black Shoulder
Auchenbrack
Benbuie
Torbraehead
Bail Hill
Auchenhessnane
Dabton
Gatelawbridge
Burnhead
Thornhill

134
143
133
125
A
B
C
D
Carluke
Forth
Auchengray
Stobwood
Hare Hill
Springfield Reservoir
Braehead
Netherton
Kilncadzow
Harelaw
West End
Carnwath
Cleghorn
Carstairs
Carstairs Junction
Ravenstruther
Lanark
New Lanark
Falls of Clyde
Hyndford Bridge
Pettinain
Libberton
Whitecastle
Newbigging
Walston
Elsrickle
Dunsyre
Dolphinton
Black Mount
Left Law
Bleak Law
White Craig
Catstone
West Water Resr
Mendick Hill
West Linton
Lady Gifford's Well
Whim
Lamancha
Halmyre Mains
Mountain Cross
Romannobridge
Wether Law
Blyth Bridge
Kirkdean
Castlecraig
Cringletie
Crailzie Hill
White Meldon
Black Meldon
Lyne
Lyne Station
Cross Kirk
Neidpath
Broughton Heights
Candy Mill
Ewe Hill
Skirling
Penvalla
Trahenna Hill
Stobo
Kirkton Manor
Cademuir Hill
Broughton
Biggar
Gladstone Court
Covenanters' House
Coulter Motte
Goseland Hill
John Buchan Centre
Rachan
Drumelzier
Tinnis
Dawyck Arboretum
Whitelaw Hill
Carnwath
Cairngryffe Hill
SOUTH
LANARKSHIRE
Covington
Quothquan
Thankerton
Harleyholm
Douglas Water
Stone Hill
St John's Kirk
Symington
Coulter
Fort & Settlement
Common Law
Tinto
707
Uddington
Robert Law
Scaur Hill
Newton
Wiston
Lamington
Dungavel Hill
510
Snaip Hill
Culter Allers Farm
Blakehope Head
Worm Hill
Drumelzier Law
Pykestone Hill
737
Horse Hope Hill
Wildshaw Hill
Roberton
Broad Hill
Culter Fell
748
Culter Waterhead Resr
Glenlood Hill
Stanhope
Taberon Law
Blackhouse Heights
Dollar Law
Black Law
Abington
Wandel
Hudderstone
Gathersnow Hill
690
Glenwhappen Rig
Oliver
Hearthstane
Crawfordjohn
Cold Chapel
Arbory Hill
Rome Hill
Duncangill Head
Camps Resr
Coomb Dod
Culter Cleuch Shank
Tweedsmuir
Glenmuck Height
Broad Law
840
830
Deer Law
Drake Law
Glenbreck
Meggethead
Talla Linnfoots
Talla Reservoir
Megget Reservoir
Cappercleuch
Lettershaws
Crawford
Craigmaid
Fruid Resr
Molls Cleuch Dod
Lochcraig Head
800
Birkhill
Herman Law
Muchra
Wellgrain Dod
Harleburn Head
Clyde Law
Elvanfoot
Gameshope Loch
Cape Law
Loch Skeen
White Coomb
822
Grey Mare's Tail (NTS)
Watchman Hill
Glenochar
Beattock Summit
Tweed's Well
Hart Fell
808
Saddle Yoke
Bell Craig
Wanlockhead
Museum of Scottish Lead Mining
Beam Engine
Green Lowther
732
Watermeetings
Devil's Beef Tub
Mennock Pass
329
Lowther Hill
Tomont Hill
Wintercleuch Fell
Wintercleugh
Swatte Fell
Ericstane
Bodesbeck Law
Black Knowe
Greenhillstairs
Granton House
Capplegill
Bodesbeck
Daer Resr
Dalveen Pass
277
Comb Law
Auldton Fell
Ettrick Pen
692
Foulbog
Gallow Hill
Capel Fell
Wind Fell
Ballencleuch Law
691
Moffat
Craigieburn
Croft Head
Loch Fell
688
Glendearg
Whiteside Hill
Dumcrieff
Cowan Fell
Fingland
Durisdeer
Gateslack
Wedder Law
Craighoar Hill
Beattock
Jock's Shoulder
Davington
Earncraig Hill
Kinnelhead
DUMFRIES AND GALLOW
Garwald
Gana Hill
Queensberry
697
Poldean
Black Hill
Laverhay Height
Morton Loch
Morton
Rashy Height
Wee Queensberry
Minnygap Height
Carronbridge
Dabton
Thornhill
Gatelawbridge
Tower
Black Esk Reservoir
M74
A702
A70
A73
A721
A706
A72
A701
A708
A76
B7016
B7055
B7078
B7040
B797
B719
B7059
B712
B709

135
D
E
F
G
144
126
136
1
2
3
4
5
Torfichen Hill
Gladhouse Reservoir
MOORFOOT
Westloch
Portmore Loch
Heriot
Heriot Water
Oxton
Carfraemill
Collie Law
Edgarhope Wood
Scoured Rig
Westruther
Dun Law
Dewar
Dewar Burn
Blackhope Scar
651
Fountainhall
Torquhan
Inchkeith Hill
Thirlestane
Lauder
Thirlestane
Whiteburn
Houndslow
Ladyside Height
Lauder Common
Galabank
Killochyett
Stow
Leithen Water
Totto Hill
Eastside Heights
Whitehope Law
Dunslair Heights
Windlestraw Law
659
Torsonce
Nether Blainslie
Legerwood
Huntlywood
Greenknowe Tower
Glentress Forest
Black Law
Black Knowe
Colquhar
Yardstone Knowe
Great Law
Birkhill
Lauder Water
Fans
Peebles
Seathope Law
Glentress
Priesthope Hill
Caddon Water
William Law
Langshaw
Cardrona
Lee Pen
Buckholm
Earlston
Mellerstain
Kailzie
Kirkburn
Walkerburn
Knowes Hill
Torwoodlee
Galashiels
Glendearg
Innerleithen
Thornylee
Clovenfords
Woollen Mill
Cardrona Forest
Elibank and Traquair Forest
Meigle Hill
Gattonside
Drygrange
Redpath
Wallace's Hill
Ashiestiel
Caddonfoot
Gala Hill
Abbey
Newstead
Traquair House
Traquair
Ashiestiel Hill
Yair Hill Forest
Abbotsford
Melrose
Scott's View
Glenkinnon Burn
Boleside
Darnick
Priorwood (NTS)
Eildon Hills
422
Bemersyde
Wallace Monument
Quair Water
Minch Moor
567
Tweed
Cauldshiels Loch
Newtown St Boswells
Clintmains
Mertoun
Glensax Burn
SCOTTISH
BORDERS
FOREST
Broomy Law
Peat Law
Lindean
Cauldshiels Hill
Bowden
Dryburgh Abbey
St B
Rutherford
Blake Muir
Broadmeadows
Selkirk Glass
Deuchar Law
Yarrowford
Yarrow Kirk
Selkirk
Sir Walter Scott's Courtroom
Charlesfield
Douglas Burn
Yarrow
Yarrow Water
Fastheugh Hill
Bowhill
1645
Philiphaugh
Halliwell's House Mus
Midlem
Longnewton
Ancrum Moor 1545
Yarrow Feus
Aikwood Tower
New Belses
Mountbenger
Sundhope
Ettrickbridge
Clerklands
Lilliesleaf
Riddell
Old Belses
Ancrum
Dryhope
Sundhope Height
Kirkhope
Ettrick Water
Black Knowe Head
Gilmanscleuch
Shaw's Hill
Woll
Ashkirk
Minto Hills
Chesters
Lanton
The Wiss
Altrieve Lake
Akermoor Loch
Jedburgh
Newburgh
Hassendean
Minto
Newton
Shaws Under Loch
Groundistone Heights
Crosslee
Mossbrae Height
Langhope Burn
Clarilaw
Knowetownhead
Dunion Hill
Abbey
Cacrabank
Drinkstone Hill
Ashybank
Denholm
Bedrule
Hundalee
Hopehouse
Esdale Law
Hellmoor Loch
Appletreehall
Burnfoot
TEVIOTDALE
Rubers Law
Home Law
Hawick Mus & Scott Gallery
Hawick
Bairnkin
Borthwickshiels
Alemoor Loch
Ale Water
Wilton
Drumlanrig's Tower
Faw Hill
Ettrick
Rankle Burn
Roberton
Hallrule
Buccleuch
Borthwickbrae
Kirkton
Abbotrule
James Hogg Monument
Law Kneis
Burnfoot
Branxholm Bridgend
White Hill
Bonchester Hill
Coutlair Knowe
Deanburnhaugh
Branxholme
Bonchester Bridge
Hobkirk
Glenkerry
Sauchie Law
Craik Forest
Redcleuch Edge
Newmill
Hott Hill
Cleuch Head
Chesters
Ettrick Water
The Pike
Crib Law
Harwood on Teviot
High Seat
Wolfelee
Southdean
Tima Water
Black Knowe
Moodlaw Loch
Craik
Broadhaugh
Dryden Fell
Northhouse
Slitrig Water
Wolfelee Hill
Howpasley
Berryfell Hill
Borthwick Water
Stell Hill
Pike Hill
Hyndlee
Jed Water
Craik Cross Hill
Shankend
Langshawburn
Teviothead
The Pike
Green Law
Wauchope Forest
Stock Hill
Castleweary
Wyndburgh Hill
Lamblair Knowe
Skelfhill Pen
Allan Water
Note o' the Gate
376
Carlin Tooth
Fanna Hill
Needs Law
Hartshorn Pike
Eweslees Knowe
Maiden Paps
Sandy Edge
Singdean
Blaeberry Hill
Rae Burn
Linhope
Cauldcleuch Head
608
Eskdalemuir
Comb Hill
Millstone Edge
Greatmoor Hill
Saughtree Fell
Holm
Causeway Grain
Wisp Hill
Mosspaul Hotel
Tudhope Hill
Saughtree
White Hope Edge
Jamestown
Geordie's Hill
Din Fell
Hermitage
Hermitage Water
Arnton Fell
Allangillfoot
A7
A72
A68
A697
A6089
A6105
A6091
A698
A699
A707
A708
A6088
B709
B7062
B7060
B7009
B6362
B6374
B6360
B6359
B6398
B6404
B6356
B6397
B6400
B6453
B6405
B6358
B6357
B6399
B6456
B711
B710
9
11
7
12
15
6
8
5
10
16
14
23
18

136
145
144
135
127
A
B
C
D
1
2
3
4
5
LAMMERMUIR
LAUDERDALE
SCOTTISH BORDERS
CHEVIOT HILLS
NORT
Whiteadder Resr
Faseny Water
Hopes Water
Penshiel Hill
Cranshaws Hill
Cranshaws
Whiteadder Water
Abbey St B
Abbey & Trout Farm
Ellemford
Meikle Says Law
Meikle Law
Seenes Law
Wrunk Law
Cockburn Law
Edin's Hall Broch
Drakemire
A6112
B6438
Horseley Hill
Cairncross
20
A1
Reston
Auchencrow
Ayton
Marygold
Millerton Hill
B6437
B6355
Hunt Law
495
Dye Water
Blythe Edge
Watch Water Resr
Longformacus
Dirrington Great Law
Lintlaw
Preston
B6365
Edrom Norman Arch
Edrom
Chirnsidebridge
Chirnside
Whiteadder Water
A6105
Foulden
Tithe Barn
Mordi
Hold
Clap
Lar
Duns
Manderston
Allanton
Hutton
Paxton
Dirrington Little Law
Wedderlie Burn
Cheeklaw
Whitelaw
Blackadder
B6460
Sunwick
Paxton House
Fishwick
Union Bridge
Gavinton
B6456
Choicelee
Polwarth
Sinclair's Hill
Whitsome
B6461
Horncliffe
Scoured Rig
arhope Wood
Westruther
Hule Moss
Greenlaw Moor
Fogo Church
Fogo
Fogorig
Leet Water
Horndean
Lady Kirk Church
Thornton Park
Thirlestane
Whiteburn
A697
Houndslow
16
Greenlaw
Blackadder Water
Swinton
Ladykirk
Norham
Upsettlington
Shoresw
Shoresc
A6089
Eden Water
Purves Hall
Swintonmill
Simprim
Grindon
Felkington
Greenknowe Tower
24
A6105
B6364
Leitholm
Tweed
Legerwood
Huntlywood
Gordon
Easter Howlaws
Orange Lane
Duddo
Hume
Humehall
Eccles
The Hirsel
Lennel
A698
Castle Heaton
Fans
Legars
Sweethope Hill
Bircham
Coldstream
Coldstream Museum
Cornhill on Tweed
Etal
Leader Water
Mellerstain
Earlston
B6461
Carham
Wark
B6350
Pallinsburn House
Crookham
Stichill
Nenthorn
Ednam
Hendersyde Park
East Learmouth
Branxton
Flodden 1513
A68
B6356
B6397
Smailholm
Kelso
Hadden
Pressen
Flodden
Kimmers
Redpath
Smailholm Tower
Scott's View
Floors
Sprouston
Downham
Howtel
B6352
Milfield
Newstead
A6091
Bemersyde
Wallace Monument
B6404
Kelso Abbey
B6396
Mindrum
Housedon Hill
Newtown St Boswells
Clintmains
Makerstoun
Trows
A699
Maxwellheugh
Lempitlaw
Pawston
Kilham
Dryburgh Abbey
Mertoun
Teviot
Blakelaw
Kilham Hill
Lanton
St Boswells
Rutherford
Roxburgh
Heiton
B6436
Westnewton
Coupland
Glen
B6398
Shotton
Charlesfield
Maxton
Bowmont Forest
Vencheh Hill
Gipsy Palace
Kirknewton
Ancrum Moor 1545
Frogden
Linton Hill
Coldsmouth Hill
Hethpool
Yeavering Bell
Longnewton
Fairnington
Kirk Yetholm
Town Yetholm
Waterloo Monument
Peniel Heugh
Kale Water
White Law
College Burn
Newton Tors
New Belses
Nisbet
Eckford
Linton
Old Belses
B6400
Crailing
B6401
Morebattle
Crookedshaws Hill
Preston Hill
Ancrum
Harestanes (Woodlands Centre)
Cessford
The Curr
Chesters
Bonjedward
Crailinghall
Gateshaw
Hownam Law
The Schil
Langleeford
Minto Hills
Lanton
Hartrigge
Mowhaugh
Sourhope
The Cheviot
815
Newton
Jedburgh
Hownam Mains
Minto
Mary Queen of Scots House
Shibden Hill
Hownam
Hedgehope Hill
B6405
B6358
Dunion Hill
Abbey
Chatto
Craik Moor
Bowmont Water
Cock Law
12
Bedrule
Hundalee
Oxnam
Comb Fell
Denholm
Langlee
Swinside Hall
Swanlaws
Rubers Law
Bairnkine
Mossburnford
Windy Gyle
619
Bream
Shill
B6357
Hallrule
Faw Hill
Falla
Beefstand Hill
Bloodybush Edge
Cushat Law
Abbotrule
Mervinslaw
Camptown
Woden Law
Loft Hill
A6088
Oxnam Water
Nettlehope Hill
Bonchester Hill
Philip Law
Blindburn
Wether Cairn
chester Bridge
14
Hobkirk
Cleuch Head
Chesters
Bell Hill
Wolfelee
Southdean
Leithope Forest
Deerlee Knowe
Arks Edge
Makendon
Woolbist Law
Wolfelee Hill
Huntford
Chew Green
Jed Water
Carter Bar
418
Redeswire Fray 1575
Ravens Knowe
Shillmoor
Linbriggs
Alwin
Biddle
Alwinton
Hyndlee
Catcleugh
Leap Hill
Hungry Law
Danger Zone
Crigdon Hill
Linshiels

3.2 miles to 1 inch
0 2 4 6 8 10 miles
0 2 4 6 8 10 km
2 km to 1 cm
D
E
F
G
1
2
3
4
5
Burnmouth
Hilton Bay
Lamberton Beach
Needles Eye
Halidon Hill
Halidon Hill 1333
Sharper's Head
Ravensdown Barracks
Berwick-upon-Tweed
Berwick (ruins)
Tweedmouth
East Ord
Spittal
Redshin Cove
A1167
Longridge Towers
Scremerston
Murton
Cheswick Black Rocks
Allerdeanmill Burn
Cheswick
West Allerdean
Goswick
Ancroft
Berrington
Emmanuel Head
St. Mary
Holy Island or Lindisfarne
Beal
West Mains
Holy Island
Lindisfarne (NT) Castle Point
Priory
Holy Island Sands
Haydon Dean
Bowsden
Burrows Hole
Guile Point
Fenham Flats
Barmoor Lane End
West Kyloe
Fenwick
Lowick
Kyloe Hills
Buckton
Longstone
Staple Sound
Farne Islands
Farne Island
Ross
Budle Bay
Budle Point
Grace Darling Museum
Bamburgh
Inner Sound
Holburn
Detchant
Middleton
Elwick
Easington
Budle
Cockenheugh 211
Waren Mill
Glororum
Bamburgh
Monks House Rocks
Fenton
North Hazelrigg
Belford
Spindlestone
Seahouses
Nesbit
Doddington
Roman Road
South Hazelrigg
Bradford
Burton
North Sunderland
Ewart Newtown
East Horton
Bellshill
Elford
West Horton
Warenton
Adderstone
Lucker
Beadnell
Homildon Hill 1402
Newham Hall
Twizell House
Warenford
Benthall
Beadnell Bay
Wandon
Chatton
Greendykes
Newham
West Fleetham
Swinhoe
Swinhoe Burn
Humbleton
Wooler
Newstead
Chathill
High Newton by-the-Sea
Snook Point
Earle
Haugh Head
Chillingham
Chillingham Park
Rosebrough
Tughall
Middleton Hall
Newtown
315
Ellingham
Preston
Newton Haven or St Mary's
Lilburn Tower
Hepburn
Wandylaw
Preston Tower
Brunton
Low Newton-by-the-Sea
East Lilburn
Brownieside
Embleton Bay
Cateran Hill
Middle Moor
Christon Bank
Embleton
Ilderton
Old Bewick
Bewick Moor
North Charlton
Dunstanburgh (NT)
Langlee Crags
Roseden
West Ditchburn
South Charlton
Craster
Roddam
New Bewick
Rock
Dunstan
Wooperton
Eglingham
Rennington
Stamford
Cullernose Point
1464
Beanley
Howick Hall
Howick
Dunmoor Hill
Brandon
East Bolton
Shipley
Littlehoughton
Reaveley
Powburn
Hulne Priory
Howick Haven
Ingram
Branton
Longhoughton Steel
Longhoughton
Hulne Park
1093
Denwick
Boulmer
Cochrane Pike
Glanton
Alnwick Abbey
Boulmer Haven
Great Ryle
Bolton
Abberwick
Alnwick
Hawkhill
High Knowes
Whittingham
Prendwick
Broome Wood
Barter Books
Lesbury
Little Ryle
Thrunton
Alnmouth Sta.
Alnham
Yetlington
Callaly Castle
Alnwick Moor
Bilton
Alnmouth
Alnmouth Bay
Scrainwood
Callaly
Thrunton Wood
Edlingham
Buston
Elilaw
Lorbottle Hall
Shilbottle
Long Crag
Biggies' Pillar
Lorbottle
Burradon
Eastfield Hall
Warkworth
HUMBERLAND
128
A1
A697
A1068
B6461
B6354
B6525
B6353
B6349
B6348
B1342
B1340
B1341
B1339
B6347
B6346
B6341
Aln
14
9
10
15
17
8

A
B
C
D
1
2
3
4
5
146
3.2 miles to 1 inch
0
2
4
6
8
10 miles
0
2
4
6
8
10 km
2 km to 1 cm
Port Mor
Machrins
Scalasaig
B8086
B8085
Loch Staosnaig
Port L
Balerominduhb
Rubha Dubh
Garvard
Balerominmore
Eilean Mhucaig
Rubha Ban
Priory
Oronsay
Dubh Eilean
Eilean nan Ron
Caolas Mor
Eilean Ghaoideamal
Shian Bay
Sgeir Mhor a'Bhrein-phuirt
1 1/4 hrs
Rubh' an t-Sailein
Loch Tarbert
Rubh' a'Chrois-aoinidh
Glenbatrick
Rubh a'Mhail
Scrinadle
Beinn Bhrea
439
Rubha Bholsa
Sgarbh Breac
364
Jura Forest
Beinn an Oir
785
Beinn Shiantaidh
755
Na Peileirean
Nave Island
Ardnave Point
Gortantaoid Point
Margadale Hill
Bunnahabhainn Bay
Beinn a'Chaolais
734
Paps of Jura
Corran
Loch a'Chnuic Bhric
Loch an t-Siob
Killinallan Point
Ardnave
Tayovullin
Kilnave
Ardnave Loch
Carraig Bhan
Ton Mhor
Sanaigmore
316
Bunnahabhainn
Giur-bheinn
Killinallan
Beinn Bhreac
286
Ardnahoe
Loch Staoisha
Gleann Asdale
Knockr
Leargybreck
Glas Bheinn
561
Loch Gruinart
A R G Y L L
Eilean Mor
Braigo
Leckgruinart
Balulive
Port Askaig
Feolin Ferry
Feolin
Rubha Lamanais
Smaull
Keills
Dubh Bheinn
Keils
Ballinaby
Carnduncan
B8017
Aoradh
Craigens
Loch Finlaggan
Craighouse
Saligo Bay
Grainel
Gruinart Flats
Ballygrant
Loch Ballygrant
Brat Bheinn
342
Crackaig
Loch Gorm
B8018
I S L A Y
Loch Cam
8
A846
A846
Coul Point
Machrie
Aruadh
Lyrabus
Moin'a'choire
Loch Lossit
Cabrach
Sannaig
Rockside
Foreland
Esknish
Ardfin
Machir Bay
Kilchoman
Blackrock
Redhouses
Beinn Dubh
Jura Ho.
Rubha na Traille
Islay Ho.
Am Fraoch Eilean
Brosdale Island
Conisby
Bridgend
Sgorr nam Faoileann
Bruichladdich
Cachlaidh Mhor
Barr
Kilchiaran
Gartnatra
Neriby
Beinn na Caillich
Kilchiaran Bay
Bowmore
Cattadale
McArthur's Head
15
Glas Bheinn
471
Tormisdale
Gearach
Port Charlotte
Ronnachmore
Cluanach
Gartbreck
Cruach
Proaig
Carn
Kilennan
Beinn Tart a'Mhill
232
Laggan
Lossit
elsay
RINNS OF ISLAY
A847
LOCH INDAAL
Laggan
Beinn Bhan
471
Beinn Bheigeir
491
Rubha Liath
Nerabus
Rubha na Faing
Duich
Ardtalla
Beinn Uraraidh
454
13
11
Easter Ellister
B8016
Loch Uraraidh
Claggain Bay
Portnahaven
A846
Trudernish
Kintour
Port Wemyss
Laggan Bay
Islay
Sgorr Bhogachain
Loch Uigeadail
Kintour
Orsay
Rinns Point
Glenegedale
Kildalton Church & Crosses
Ardmore
Ardmore Point
Machrie
Beinn Sholum
347
2 1/4 hrs
Leorin
Eilean a'Chuirn
Kintra
Machrie
Leorin Lochs
Eilean Bhride
Rubha Mor
Maol Buidhe
165
Cornabus
Port Ellen
Lagavulin
Ardbeg
Rubha na Gainmhich
Carnmore
Laphroaig
THE OA
Risabus
The Ard
Caolas an Eilein
Lower Killeyan
Port Chubaird
Texa
Loch Kinnabus
Inerval
Mull Of Oa
Rubha nan Leacan

D
E
F
G
147
Lealt
Beinn Bhreac
467
Corpach Bay
Dubh Bheinn
JURA
Rainberg Mor
453
Cruach Sganadail
Tramiag Bay
Ardlussa
Inverlussa
Lussa Point
Eilean an Rubha
Lussagiven
A846
Glenn Aoistail
Gleann Dorch
Beinn Sgaillinish
Tarbert
Tarbert Bay
Creag Nam Fiadh Mor
Lagg
Rubh' a'Chamais
Gate House
A846
Beinn Tarsuinn
Achamore
24
Ardmenish
An Dunan
Rubh 'an Leim
Lowlandman's Bay
Sron Garbh
Rubh 'an Leanachais
Eilean Bhride
Small Isles
Eilean Gabhar
Na Caillich
Na Cuiltean
SOUND OF JURA
Ardnoe Point
Crinan
Rubha nam Barr
Cnoc Reamhar
265
Bellanoch
B8025
Dunadd Fort
Cup & Ring Marks
Moine Mhor
B841
Kilmichael Glassary
Bridgend
Achnashelloch
Craigans
Loch Glashan
A83
Ardnackaig
Arichonan
Cairnbaan
Craigglas
A816
Achnabreck Cup & Ring Marks
Badden
Lochgair
Loch Gair
Gallchoille
Arinafad Beg
Gariob
Knapdale Forest
Auchindarrach
Lochgilphead
Middle Kames
Carsaig Island
Carsaig Bay
Scotnish
Seafield
Eilean Dubh
Tayvallich
Achnamara
Cruach Breacain
360
Brackley
Carrick
Achnaba
Turbiskill
Eilean Loain
Kilmichael of Inverlussa
Cam Loch
Ardrishaig
Loch Gilp
Castleton
Silvercraigs
Otter Ferry
Ashfield
Caolard Rubha
Eilean Mor
Ballimore
Barrahormid
Kilmory
Daltote
Cruach Lusach
466
Beinn Bheag
B8000
Taynish
Ulva Islands
Auchbraad
Keillmore
New Ulva
Dunrostan
Inverneil
Fearnoch
Loch na Cille
Loch Sween
B8024
Sròndoire
Rubha Beag
Otter
Sween
14
Kilfinan Bay
Danna Island
Abhainn Mor
Achahoish
Loch Fuar Bheinne
St Columba's Cave
A83
Corr Eilean
Eilean Mor
Ellary
Cruach a'Phubuill
477
Port Leatham
12
Eilean Mor Chapel
Chapel
Kilmory
Clachbreck
2
Erines
Auchalick Bay
Lower Auchalick
Kilmory Bay
Ballyaurgan
Stob Odham
562
Meall Mor
Loch Caolisport
Baile Boidheach
Cnoc a Bharaille
Point of Knap
Stonefield
Barmore Island
Loch Chaorunn
Ashens
Derybruich
140
Druimdrishaig
Dubh Chreag
480
ARGYLL AND BUTE
Larach na Gaibhre
Meall Reamhar
Barfad
East Loch Tarbert
½ hr (summer only)
Portavadie
Dubhchladach
Tarbert
Mealdarroch Point
Cretshengan
Loch nan Torran
Meall Reamhar
Loch a'Chaoruinn
Escart
West Tarbert
Asgog Bay
Coulaghailtro
Corranbuie
Cruach an t-Sorchain
3
KNAPDALE
Achaglachgach Forest
Kilberry
Achadacaie
377
Rubha Lagganroa
Kilberry Head
Crosses
Cruach Airde
Cruach Doire Leithe
422
Camas na Ceardaich
B8024
5
Kennacraig
Redhouse
Cnoc a'Bhaile-shios
Carse
Dunmore
West Loch Tarbert
Whitehouse
Coire nan Capull
Rubha Cruitiridh
Loch Stornoway
Ardpatrick
Achadh-chaorrunn
Culindrach
B8001
Gartnagrenach
Gartavaich
Glenrisdell
KINTYRE
Skipness
Skipness Point
2 hrs
Ardpatrick Point
Portachoillan
Cruach nam Fiadh
269
Claonaig
B8001
Auchameanach
Quinhill
Clachan
Rockfield
Ronachan Point
4
Port Mor
Ronachan
B842
SOUND
West Tarbert Bay
East Tarbert Bay
Corriechrevie
Loch Ciaran
Eascart Farm
Port Fada
½ hr (summer only)
Tarbert
Ballochroy
Crossaig
Creag Bhan
100
Auchinafaud
Loch Garasdale
Loch Ranza
Newton
Druimyeon Bay
Ardailly
Cruach Mhic-Gougain
Lochranza
GIGHA ISLAND
Rhunahaorine Point
A83
Catacol Bay
Ardminish
Ardminish Bay
Cnoc-an t-Samhlaidh
Rubha Airigh Bheirg
Glen Catacol
Craro Island
Achamore Gardens
Rhunahaorine
Narachan Hill
285
Cour Bay
Cour
Craw
Lenimore
Thundergay
½ hr
Cnoc Reamhar
21
Grob Bagh
Sound of Gigha
Tayinloan
Carradale Water
Sunadale
KILBRANNAN SOUND
5
Beinn Bhreac
573
Cara Island
Killean
Deucheran Hill
329
Grogport
Beinn Bhreac
711
Beinn Tarsuinn
Mull of Cara
Pirnmill
Loch Tanna
Beacharr
Cruach Mhic-an-t-Saoir
364
Mullach Buidhe
721
Whitefarland Point
Cruach nan Gabhar
354
Clachaig Water
Imachar
Beinn Bharrain
Achaglass
Carradale Forest
Muasdale
130
Balliekine
17
Diollaid Mhor
33
Beinn Bhreac
Rhonadale
Carradale
Dougarie Point
A841
Glen Iorsa
Iorsa Water
Belloch
Arnicle
Beinn an Tuirc
Dippen
Carradale Garden
Dougarie
Barr Water
Torrisdale
Glenbarr
Carradale

140
148
139
131
A
B
C
D
1
2
3
4
5
FOREST PARK
ARGYLL AND BUTE
NORTH AYRSHIRE
SOUND OF BUTE
FIRTH OF CLYDE
LOCH FYNE
Kilmichael Glassary
Craigans
Loch Glashan
Minard Castle
Barnacarry
Cruach an Lochain
Caol Ghleann
Stuck
Cruach a'Bhuic
Carrick
Corran
Beinn Bheag 618
Ardnahein
Portincaple
Achnabreck Cup & Ring Marks
Asknish
Lochgair
Loch Gair
Lephinmore
Cruach Fasgach
Lephinch
Kilbridemore
Dunans
Creag Tharsuinn
Beinn Mhor 742
Bernice
Sligrachan Hill
Creachan Mor 657
Glen Finart
Garelochhead
Glenald
Badden
Lochgilphead
Middle Kames
Goirtein
Garvie
Conchra
Meall Dubh
Sron Mhor
A815
Barnacabber
Mambeg
Faslane Bay
Carrick
Cruach Chuilceachan 435
Glendaruel
A886
Clach Bheinn
Coylet
Coulport
Garrachra
Glen Massan
Younger Botanic Gdns
Stronchullin Hill 548
Ardentinny
Meikle Rahane
Achnaba
Largiemore
Ardacheranmor
Stronlonag
Glen Tarsan
Ardpeaton
Gairletter Point
Port Ann
Camquhuart
Cruach nan Cuilean
Meall an Fharaidh
Sgorach Mor 601
Benmore
Uig
Cnoc a'Mhadaidh 470
Clynder
Castleton
Silvercraigs
Ardachearanbeg
Clachan of Glendaruel
Loch Tarsan
Rosneath
Caolard Rubha
Eilean Mor
Otter Ferry
Ballimore
Ballochandrain
Craigendive
Glenlean
Ballochyle Hill
Ardbeg
Orchard
Blairmore
Cove
Auchnaha
Ardtaraig
Oalinlongart
A880
Kilmun
Strone
Strone Point
Holy Loch
Sandbank
Ardnadam
Kilcreggan
Ormsdale
Cruach nan Caorach 458
Auchenbreck
Cruach Neuran
Clachaig
B836
Fearnoch
Lindsaig
Rubha Beag
Ard a'Chapuill
Cruach nan Capull
Glenkin
Hunter's Quay
Otter
Kilfinan
Springfield
Invervegain
Leacann nan Gall
Dunloskin
Loch Loskin
Kirn
Kilfinan Bay
Beinn Bhreac 454
A8003
Bishop's Seat
Dunoon
Gourock
A83
Acharosson
Fearnoch
Beinn Bhreac 507
Black Craig 522
A770
Cloch Point
McLean Art
Port Leatham
Drum
Beinn Capuill
Troustan
Inverchaolain
Bullwood
Castle Levan
Melldalloch
West Glen
Buttock Point
Colintraive
Blairbuie
Ardhallow
Chrisswell
A78
Auchalick Bay
Lower Auchalick
Port Driseach
Coustonn
Kilmarnock Hill
Corlarach Hill
Lunderston Bay
Ardgowan
Tighnabruaich
Rhubodach
Kyles of Bute
South Hall
Glaic
Beinn Ruadh
Inverkip
Stonefield
Barmore Island
Craignafeoch
Auchenlochan
Kames
Derybruich
Shalunt
Strone Point
Knockdow
Ardyne Burn
Dunan
Wemyss Point
Millhouse
Asgog Loch
Portavadie
Blair's Ferry
Glenmore
Stuck
Ardmaleish Point
Innellan
Wemyss Bay
Leap Moor
Barfad
East Loch Tarbert
½ hr (summer only)
Tarbert
Mealdarroch Point
West Tarbert
Low Stillaig
Cnoc na Carraige 207
Kilbride Farm
Glecknabae
Kames Hill
Ardmaleish
Ardyne Point
Toward
Upper Skelmorlie
Kilbride
Kames Bay
Port Bannatyne
Toward Point
Skelmorlie
CLYDE
Asgog Bay
Kilbride Bay
Carry
Ardlamont
Blindman's Bay
Drumachloy
B875
Ardbeg
Ardbeg Point
Rothesay Bay
Bogany Point
Craigmore
Knockencorsan
Cruach Doire Leithe 422
377
Ettrick Bay
A844
Rothesay
Ardencraig Gardens
Meigle Bay
REGION
Rubha Lagganroaig
Ardlamont Bay
Ardlamont Point
Upper Ardroscadale
Orcadia
Bute Museum
Camas na Ceardaich
B878
St Mary's Chapel
Ascog
Routenburn
Rowantree Hill
Noddsdale
Noddsdale Water
Cnoc a'Bhaile-shios
St Ninian's Point
Loch Fad
Loch Ascog
Meikle Kilmory
Netherhall
The Vikingar Experience
Coire nan Capull
Kerrycroy
Largs
Tomont End
Gogo Water
Inchmarnock
Midpark
Meikle Grenach
Mountstuart
Culindrach
Loch Quien
B881
Skelmorlie Aisle
Glenrisdell
Ambrismore
Great Cumbrae
Ballochmartin
B896
B899
Skipness
Skipness Point
Ardscalpsie
Piperhall
A760
Claonaig
B8001
Auchameanach
Scalpsie Bay
Stravanan
Kingarth
Kelburn Country Centre
Stravanan Bay
Kilchattan Bay
Kilchattan
Millport
Millport Bay
Fairlie
Fairlie Roads
Port Fada
St Blane's Church
Kaim Hill 387
Dunagoil Bay
Little Cumbrae
Torr Mor
Cock of Arran
Garrochty
Inner Brigurd Point
Garroch Head
Hunterston
Loch Ranza
Newton
Lochranza
A841
Gull Point
Crosbie
Catacol Bay
Glen Catacol
Glen Chalmadale
Portencross
West Kilbride
Farland Head
B7048
B781
Rubha Airigh Bheirg
North Glen Sannox
Ardneil Bay
Munnoch Resr
Craw
Seamill
Lenimore
Thundergay
Beinn Bhreac 573
Mid Sannox
Sannox Bay
Glen Sannox
Beinn Tarsuinn
Caisteal Abhail 859
1¼ hrs (summer only)
B780
Pirnmill
Beinn Bhreac 711
Mullach Buidhe 721
Loch Tanna
Cir Mhor 798
Cioch-na-h-Oighe
Corrie
Ardrossan
Horse Isle
Stevenston
Saltcoats
Imachar
Beinn Bharrain
Goat Fell 874
Beinn Tarsuinn 825
ARRAN
Glen Rosa
Balliekine
Beinn Nuis 792
Brodick (NTS)
Merkland Point
1 hr
Dougarie Point
Glen Iorsa
Iorsa Water
Brodick Garden (NTS)
Brodick Castle
Brodick Bay
Dougarie
361
An Tunna
Heritage Museum
Brodick
Glencloy
Auchagallon

Inchlonaig
Cashel Farm
Edentaggart
Loch Lomond Park Centre
PARK
Milarrochy
Luss
Camstraddan House
Inchconnachan
Aldochlay
Balmaha
Pass of Balmaha
149
Inchmoan
Inchcailloch
Gartachoil
Buchlyvie
Arngibbon
141
Balafark
Garadhban Forest
Milton
Buchanan Castle
Drymen
Balfron Station
Balfron
Endrick Water
Boquhan
Gartness
STIRLING
Killearn
George Buchanan Monument
Fintry
Culcreuch
Craigton
Corrie of Balglass
Gonachan Cottage
Rossdhu House
LOCH LOMOND
Inchmurrin
Ross Priory
Torrinch
Gartocharn
Lorn
Duncryne
Caldarvan
Craighat
Baptiston
Earl's Seat
578
CAMPSIE FELLS
Strathblane Hills
Dumgoyne
Blairquhosh
Hart Hill
Strathblane
Fin Glen
Queen's View
Blanefield
Clachan of Campsie
Haughhead
Lennoxtown
Lennox Forest
Carbeth
Strathblane
Beinn Laorach
713
Beinn Ruisg
593
Beinn Tharsuinn
Glen Luss
Inchtavannach
Faslane
Auchinvennal
Blairnairn
Shantron
Glen Fruin
Shandon
Blairvadach
Inverlauren
Hill House (NTS)
Daligan
Blarglas
Arden
Dumfin
Balloch Castle
Rhu
Helensburgh
Craigendoran
Rosneath Bay
Cameron
Balloch
Jamestown
WEST
Finnich Glen
Mill of Camsail
Rosneath Point
Camis Eskan
Colgrain
Keppoch
Alexandria
Bonhill
Loch Lomond
Dumbarton Muir
DUNBARTONSHIRE
Ardmore
Renton
Cardross
Townend
Crosslet
Kilpatrick Hills
401
EAST
DUNBARTONSHIRE
Mugdock
Kinkell
GREENOCK
FIRTH OF CLYDE
DUMBARTON
Loch Humphrey
Cochno
Edinbarnet
Milngavie
Art Gallery
Balderneck
Dougalston
Torrance
Balmore
KIRKINTILLOCH
Drumfrochar
PORT GLASGOW
Newark
Dumbarton
Milton
Bowling
Old Kilpatrick
Faifley
Duntocher
BEARSDEN
Cadder
INVERCLYDE
Lurg Moor
Gryfe Reservoirs
Finlaystone (NTS)
Langbank
M8
Toll
Erskine
Drumchapel
Bishopton
M898
Garvock
Auchenfoyle
Cairncurran Hill
Strath Gryfe
Auchenbothie
Kilmacolm
CLYDEBANK
Maryhill
Bishopbriggs
142
Springburn
GLASGOW
Corkney Top
Cairncurran
Southbar
Inchinnan
Yoker
Creuch Hill
441
Duchal Moor
Duchal
Georgetown
Renfrew
Glasgow
Botanic Gdns
Partick
MUIRSHIEL REGIONAL PARK
North Burnt Hill
Black Fell
Quarrier's Village
Houston
Bridge of Weir
Crosslee
Govan
Glasgow Science Centre
GLASGOW
People's Palace
Mill Burn
Carruthmuir
Linwood
PAISLEY
Queenside Muir
Hill of Stake
522
Muirshiel
Weaver's Cott. (NTS)
Kilbarchan
Johnstone
Elderslie
Millikenpark
Crookston
Museum of Education
Burrell
RENFREWSHIRE
Slaty Law
Misty Law
Locher Water
Collegiate Church
Johnstone Castle
Gleniffer Braes
Pollok
Pollokshaws
RUTHERGLEN
Irish Law
484
Black Law
Castle Semple Water
Castle Semple Loch
Howwood
Gleniffer Braes
Nitshill
Castlemilk
Lochwinnoch
Caplaw
Barrhead
Balgray Resr
Thornliebank
Giffnock
M77
Neilston
Clarkston
Carmunnock
Nerston
Whitehill
Camphill Resr
Woodside
Corkindale Law
Loch Libo
EAST RENFREWSHIRE
Malletsheugh
Newton Mearns
Busby
Cock Law
Kilbirnie
Lochlands Hill
Hall
Uplawmoor
Neilston Pad
Mearns
Waterfoot
Thorntonhall
South Hourat
Glengarnock
Beith
Kilbirnie Loch
Caldwell
Gateside
Lugton
Long Loch
Harelaw Dam
Earn Water
Jackton
Eaglesham
Polnoon
Gabroc Hill
Windy Yet
Highfield
The Den
Barrmill
Burnhouse
Bennan Loch
Ballageich Hill
330
Dunwan Dam
Auldhouse
Dalry
Fullwood
Dunlop
EAST
AYRSHIRE
Melowther Hill
Lochgoin Reservoir
Blair
Kingsford
Kingswell
Lochgoin
Corse Hill
376
Laird's Seat
Dusk Water
Auchentiber
CUNNINGHAME
Stewarton
Dalgarven
Fenwick
Waterside
Tayburn
Kilwinning
Montgreenan
Eglinton
Rowallan
Stevenston
Cunninghamhead
Kilmaurs
Pley Moss
Polbaith Burn
Hareshaw
Perceton
Moscow
Loudon Castle Park
132
IRVINE
Dreghorn
Springside
Knockentiber
Dean
KILMARNOCK
Newmilns
Darvel
Priestland
The Big Idea Exhibition
Crosshouse
Scottish Maritime Museum
Gatehead
Crookedholm
Hurlford
Galston
Greenholm
Irvine
Drybridge
Riccarton
A811
A82
A875
A81
A809
A891
A814
A813
A8
A761
A726
A77
A737
A760
A736
A735
A719
A78
A738
A71
A803
A879
A807
A8014
A739
A730
A74
M8
M77
M898
B837
B818
B834
B822
B821
B831
B8050
B8049
B788
B789
B790
B786
B776
B777
B784
B780
B771
B706
B707
B778
B769
B764
B767
B759
B785
B751
B7038
B7081
B7080
B730
B7064
B7073

A
B
C
D
1
2
3
4
5
150
141
133
STIRLING
Alloa
Clackmannan
South Alloa
Kennet
Dunmore
Airth
Cambus
Sauchie
Bannockburn
St Ninians
Cowie
Plean
Torwood
Glenbervie
Dunipace
Denny
Larbert
Stenhousemuir
Carronshore
Carron
Bainsford
Skinflats
Grangemouth
Bonnybridge
FALKIRK
Camelon
Laurieston
Polmont
Brightons
Dennyloanhead
Longcroft
Haggs
High Bonnybridge
Banknock
Castlecary
Kilsyth
Banton
Dullatur
Croy
Twechar
Queenzieburn
Balloch
CUMBERNAULD
Carbrain
Condorrat
Luggiebank
Abronhill
Old Shields
Jawcraig
Slamannan
Shieldhill
California
Maddiston
Blackbraes
Standburn
Avonbridge
Westfield
Binniehill
Limerigg
Greengairs
Wattston
Longriggend
Armadale
Caldercruix
Plains
Blackridge
Westrigg
Forrest
Harthill
Eastfield
West Benhar
Kirk of Shotts
Salsburgh
Shotts
Fauldhouse
Jersay
Dykehead
Stane
Allanton
Hartwood
Newmains
Bonkle
Murdostoun
Morningside
Cambusnethan
Wishaw
Waterloo
Overtown
Law
Carluke
Netherton
Dalserf
Rosebank
Braidwood
Milton Lockhart
Crossford
Hazelbank
Nemphlar
Kirkfieldbank
New Lanark
Lanark
Hyndford Bridge
Kilncadzow
Harelaw
Clegorn
Carstairs
Ravenstruther
Jerviswood
Kirkmuirhill
Blackwood
Auchenheath
Boghead
Lesmahagow
Birkwood
Auchlochan
Hawksland
Douglas Water
Harleyholm
Clydesdale
Mossend
Holytown
Newarthill
Cleland
Bellside
Bellshill
Viewpark
Tannochside
Uddingston
MOTHERWELL
HAMILTON
Bothwell
Calderglen
Stonefield
High Blantyre
EAST KILBRIDE
Meikle Earnock
Low Waters
Eddlewood
Quarter
Limekilnburn
Larkhall
Machan
Ashgill
Fairholm
Netherburn
Glassford
Udstonhead
Netherfield
Stonehouse
Strathaven
Sandford
Deadwaters
COATBRIDGE
AIRDRIE
Chapelhall
Calderbank
Whifflet
Rawyards
Glenmavis
Glenboig
Moodiesburn
Chryston
Muirhead
Gartcosh
Stepps
Mollinsburn
Riggend
Stand
GLASGOW
Bishopbriggs
Springburn
Maryhill
Partick
Govan
Shettleston
Tollcross
Carmyle
Cambuslang
Flemington
RUTHERGLEN
Castlemilk
Carmunnock
Nerston
Lymekilns
Pollokshaws
Thornliebank
Giffnock
Clarkston
Busby
Waterfoot
Jackton
Eaglesham
Polnoon
Torrance
Crutherland
Auldhouse
Rutherend
Shawtonhill
Chapelton
Ardochrig
Caldermill
Hareshaw
West Cauldcoats
Drumclog
Darvel
Priestland
Dungavel
Auchingilloch
KIRKINTILLOCH
Lenzie
Waterside
Auchinloch
Cadder
Balmore
Torrance
Bardowie
Milngavie
Kinkell
Lennoxtown
Milton of Campsie
Lennox Forest
Haughhead
Clachan of Campsie
Blanefield
Strathblane
Fintry
Craigton
Gonachan Cottage
Balafark
Arngibbon
Garden
Buchlyvie
Cauldhame
Leckie
Gargunnock House
Gargunnock Hills
Touch Hills
North Third
Easter Buckieburn
Carron Bridge
Muirmill
Tomtain
Earl's Seat
Meikle Bin
Lecket Hill
Kilsyth Hills
CAMPSIE FELLS
STIRLING
FALKIRK
NORTH LANARKSHIRE
EAST DUNBARTONSHIRE
SOUTH LANARKSHIRE
M80
M9
M876
M73
M8
M74
A80
A73
A71
A8

D
E
F
G
I
FIFE
DUNFERMLINE
Cowdenbeath
Lochgelly
KIRKCALDY
Kinghorn
Burntisland
Aberdour
Inverkeithing
Rosyth
Dalgety Bay
North Queensferry
Firth of Forth
Inchkeith
Inchcolm
Bo'ness
Linlithgow
South Queensferry
EDINBURGH
Leith
Musselburgh
Portobello
Kirkliston
Broxburn
Livingston
Bathgate
Whitburn
West Calder
East Calder
Mid Calder
Currie
Balerno
Dalkeith
Lasswade
Bonnyrigg
Loanhead
Roslin
Penicuik
PENTLAND HILLS REGIONAL PARK
EDINBURGH
PENTLAND HILLS
MIDLOTHIAN
West Linton
Carnwath
Peebles
SCOTTISH BORDERS
Innerleithen
Biggar
Skirling
Broughton
Stobo
Kirkton Manor
Eddleston
Leadburn
Lamancha
Howgate
Carlops
Romannobridge
Blyth Bridge
Dolphinton
Newbigging
Libberton
Quothquan
Thankerton
Covington
M90
M9
M8
A823(M)
A90
A720
A71
A702
A701
A703
A72
2
3
4
5

151
144
134

144
A
B
C
D
152
143
135
FIRTH OF FORTH
Dysart
Pathhead
Church
KIRKCALDY
A921
B923
Kinghorn
Pettycur
Inchkeith
Fidra
Lamb
Craigleith
North Berwick
Scottish Seabird Centre
Yellowcraig
Bass Rock
Tantallon
St Baldred's Boat
Auldhame
Dirleton
Muirfield
Gullane Bay
Gullane Bents
Gullane Point
Gullane
North Berwick Law
A198
Kingston
Whitekirk
B1347
B1345
Aberlady Bay
Luffness
Aberlady
Craigielaw Point
EAST LOTHIAN
Drem
East Fortune
B1377
Tyninghame House
Tyninghame
St Baldred's
Mungoswells
Chesters Hill Fort
Church of Plaque
Museum of Flight
Preston
Preston Mill & Phantassie Doocot (NTS)
East Linton
Friary
Gosford House
Gosford Bay
Ballencrieff
Spittal
A6137
Athelstaneford
B1343
Longniddry Bents
Collegiate Church
Garleton Hills
Traprain
Hailes
Biel Water
Pitcox
Royal Yacht Britannia
Black Rocks
Leith
A199
A900
A1
Portobello
Cockenzie and Port Seton
Prestonpans 1745
Prestonpans
Longniddry
B1348
Seton Tower & Hamilton House (NTS)
St. Mary's Church
Church
Stenton
Musselburgh
Levenhall
Meadowmill
Elvingston
Haddington
Palace of Holyroodhouse
Duddingston
Arthur's Seat
Joppa
Newcraighall
Niddrie
Craigmillar
Inveresk
Wallyford
Tranent
A199
Macmerry
Gladsmuir
Traprain Law Fort
Papple
Pressmennan Lake
Deuchrie Dod
Whitelaw Hill
Garvald
Nunraw Abbey
Pinkie 1547
B6414
B6355
B6363
B6368
B6369
B6370
Lennoxlove
Samuelston
Bolton
Gifford Church
Carfrae
Dunbar Common
Craighall
Danderhall
Royal Observatory
Whitecraig
New Winton
A6093
New Town
Elphinstone
Carberry Tower
Crossgatehall
Winton House
Market Cross
Dalkeith Park
Gilmerton
Millerhill
Ormiston
Pencaitland
West Saltoun
East Saltoun
Gifford
Danskine
Clints Dod
White
Rangely Kip
Liberton
B701
A701
A720
Kaimes
Eskbank
Dalkeith
A6124
Cousland
Peastonbank
Gilchrist
Birns Water
Longyester
Whiteadder Water
B6355
Straiton
Lasswade
Bonnyrigg
Newbattle
Easthouses
Oxenford
A68
B6371
Peaston
Newlands Hill
Loanhead
Polton
Mayfield
B6482
B6372
Ford
Pathhead
Humbie
Fasney Water
Whiteadder Resr
Penshiel Hill
Rosslyn
Roslin
Roslin Glen
Newtongrange
Arniston Engine
Newlandrig
Vogrie
Fala Dam
Lammer Law
528
Hopes Resr
Hopes Water
Meikle Says Law
535
Auchendinny
Rosewell
A7
South Esk
B6367
Crichton
B6457
Fala
MIDLOTHIAN
A6094
Carrington
Gorebridge
Crichton
Crib Law
West Hill
Seenes Law
Meikle Law
Penicuik
Borthwick
Borthwick
North Middleton
Tynehead
B6458
Dean Burn
Soutra Hill
LAMMERMUIR
Edgelaw Resr
Cauldhall Moor
Temple
Middleton
Fala Moor
Dun Law
363
Soonhope Burn
Hunt Law
495
Dye Water
Falahill
Gilston
Blythe Edge
B6372
Rosebery Resr
B7007
B6368
Turf Law
A68
Hogs Law
MOORFOOT HILLS
Torfichen Hill
Gladhouse Reservoir
Heriot
Oxton
Carfraemill
Earnscleugh Water
Westloch
B709
Heriot Water
Gala Water
SCOTTISH BORDERS
Collie Law
A697
Scoured Rig
Edgarhope Wood
Wedderlie Burn
Portmore Loch
Inchkeith Hill
Westruther
Dewar
Dun Law
Blackhope Scar
651
Fountainhall
Thirlestane
Thirlestane
B6456
Lauder
Houndslow
Whiteburn
A697
Ladyside Height
Torquhan
Cockholm Burn
Lauder Common
B6362
Dewar Burn
Leithen Water
Totto Hill
Eastside Heights
Galabank
A6089
Eden Water
Killochyett
Stow
Lugate Water
LAUDERDALE
Dunslair Heights
Whitehope Law
Windlestraw Law
659
Torsonce
Nether Blainslie
Greenknowe Tower
Legerwood
Huntlywood
Glentress Forest
Black Law
Black Knowe
Yardstone Knowe
Great Law
Birkhill
Leader Water
A6105
Colquhar
Seathope Law
Peebles
A72
Glentress
Priesthope Hill
Fans
Cardrona
Lee Pen
Kailzie
Kirkburn
William Law
Buckholm
Langshaw
Torwoodlee
Caddon Water
Earlston
Mellerstain
Knowes Hill
Galashiels
Glendearg
B6397
Cardrona Forest
B7062
Innerleithen
Walkerburn
Thornylee
Clovenfords
Meigle Hill
Woollen Mill
B6374
B6356
Drygrange
Redpath
Elibank and

D
E
F
G
I
2
3
4
5
3.2 miles to 1 inch
0
2
4
6
8
10 miles
0
2
4
6
8
10 km
2 km to 1 cm
Dunbar
West Barns
A1087
Broxburn
Dunbar 1650
Barns Ness
Skateraw Harbour
Skateraw
Spott
Doonhill Homestead
Thorntonloch
Innerwick
Brunt Hill
Cocklaw Hill
Bilsdean
Reed Point
Pease Bay
Siccar Point
Wheat Stack
Fast
Telegraph Hill
St Abb's Head
Dunglass Church
Cove
Cockburnspath
Oldhamstocks
Bransly Hill
Monynut Edge
Ecclaw
Ecclaw Hill
Blackburn Rig
Meikle Black Law
A1107
Lumsdaine
Coldingham Loch
Cross Law
Coldingham Moor
Northfield
St Abbs
Coldingham Bay
Coldingham
Priory
Press
Eyemouth Museum
Eyemouth
Heart Law
Laughing Law
Grantshouse
Houndwood
Cairncross
Abbey & Trout Farm
Abbey St Bathans
Cranshaws Hill
Cranshaws
Horseley Hill
Reston
Ayton
Burnmouth
Ellemford
Cockburn Law
Drakemire
Auchencrow
Hilton Bay
Wrunk Law
Edin's Hall Broch
A6112
Marygold
Millerton Hill
Ayton Hill
Lamberton Beach
LAMMERMUIR HILLS
Longformacus
Preston
Lintlaw
Lamberton
Tithe Barn
Mordington Holdings
Dirrington Great Law
Edrom Norman Arch
Edrom
Chirnsidebridge
Chirnside
Whiteadder Water
A6105
Foulden
Halidon Hill
Needles Eye
Clappers
Halidon Hill 1333
Sharpe Head
Ravensdown Barracks
Duns
Manderston
Allanton
Berwick-upon
Dirrington Little Law
Cheeklaw
Blackadder
Hutton
Paxton
Berwick (ruins)
Gavinton
Whitelaw
Sunwick
Paxton House
Tweedmouth
East Ord
Spittal
Choicelee
Polwarth
Fishwick
Union Bridge
Redshin Cove
Sinclair's Hill
Whitsome
Horncliffe
Longridge Towers
A1167
Hule Moss
Fogo Church
Fogo
Horndean
Thornton Park
Murton
Scremerston
Greenlaw Moor
Fogorig
Lady Kirk Church
Norham
Swinton
Ladykirk
Thornton
Shoreswood
Cheswick
Greenlaw
Swintonmill
Simprim
Upsettlington
Shoresdean
West Allerdean
Purves Hall
Grindon
Ancroft
Felkington
Leitholm
Berrington
Easter Howlaws
Duddo
Bowsden
Orange Lane
NORTHUMBERLAND
BORDERS
Hume
Humehall
A697
Eccles
The Hirsel
Lennel
A698
Castle Heaton
Coldstream Museum
Barmoor Lane End
Legars
Coldstream
Etal
Lowick
Sweethope Hill
Birgham
Cornhill on Tweed
Carham
Pallinsburn House
Crookham
Wark
Stichill
Ednam
Branxton
Hendersyde Park
Kelso
Learmouth
Flodden 1513
Hadden
Pressen
Flodden
Kimmerston
A6089
136

A
B
C
D
1
2
3
4
5
154
138
Cairn na Burgh More
Burgh Beg
Fladda
Sgeir a Chaisteil
Lunga
Loch Tuath
Rubha Chulinish
Fanmore
Gometra Ho.
Gometra
Bearnus
Beinn Chreagach
Rubha Maol na Mine
Beinn Eolasary
ULVA
A'Chrannag
Maisgeir
Bac Mor or Dutchman's Cap
Bac Beag
Little Colonsay
Staffa
Eilean Dubh
Staffa (NTS)
Fingal's Cave
Chapel
Inch Kenneth
Erisgeir
Balmea
Creach Bheinn
491
Ardmeanach
Bearraich
Aird na h-Iolaire
Burg (NTS)
Carraig Mhic Thomais
Reidh Eilean
Eilean Chalbha
Port an Duine Mhairbh
Dun I
Maclean's Cross
Iona Abbey
Baile Mòr
Iona (NTS)
Rubha nan Cearc
Kintra
Beinn Chladan
Stac an Aoineidh
Ruanaich
Iona
Fionnphort
Aridhglas
A849
Loch na Lathaich
Erraibus
Ardtun
Bunessan
Ardchrishnish
Port an Aird Fhada
LOCH
Lee
Loch Assapol
Cruach
Rubha na Carraig-geire
Sound of Iona
Fidden
Ross of Mull
Knockvologan
Ardalanish
Uisken
Scoor
Soa Island
Erraid
Eilean Dubh
Torr Fada
Ardchiavaig
Port Mor
Aird Mor
Eilean a'Chalmain
Eilean Mor
Rubh' Ardalanish
Dearg Sgeir
Torran Rocks
Na Torrain
Ruadh Sgeir
West Reef
McPhail's Anvil
Torran Sgoilte
Sgeir Ghobhlach
Otter Rock
Dubh Artach
Eilean Dubh
Balnahard
Rubh' a'Geodha
Kiloran Bay
Port Ceann a'Gharraidh
COLONSAY
Loch an Sgoltaire
Kiloran
Kiloran Gardens
Colonsay
B8086
B8087
Upper Kilchattan
Lower Kilchattan
L. Fada
Scalasaig
Port Mor
Machrins
B8085
Port Lotha
Balerominduhb
Sguide Loinne
Garvard
Balerominmore
Port Askaig 1½ hrs
Eilean Mhucaig
Priory
Rubha Ban
Dubh Eilean
Oronsay
Eilean nan Ron
Caolas Mor
Eilean Ghaoideamal
3.2 miles to 1 inch
0 2 4 6 8 10 miles
0 2 4 6 8 10 km
2 km to 1 cm

147
155
148
139
D
E
F
G
I
2
3
4
5
MULL
ARGYLL AND BUTE
JURA
FIRTH OF LORN
Salen Bay
Lochaline
Glais Bheinn
479
Mam a' Chullaich
An Sleaghach
513
481
Eignaig
Inninbeg
Inninmore Bay
Rubha an Ridire
Lynn of Morven
Lismore
Bernera
Achadun (ruin)
Kilcheran
Eilean Dubh
Pladda Island
Salen
A849
Pennygown
Fishnish
Ardtornish Point
Killiechronan
Cruach Torran Lochain
Kellan
Killbeg
Balmeanach
Garmony
B8073
B8035
Lagganulva
Killiemor
Gruline
Beinn Bhuidhe
412
Glen Forsa
Beinn Chreagach Mhor
579
Salen Forest
Scallastle Bay
Scallastle
Craignure Bay
Craignure
Mull & West Highland Railway
Torosay Castle
Duart Bay
Duart
Duart Point
Eilean Musdile
Lady's Rock
Sound of Ulva
Loch Na Keal
Knock
Loch Ba
Na Binneinean
Gaodhail
Beinn Mheadhon
637
Dun da Ghaoithe
766
Maol nan Uan
Eorsa
Beinn a'Ghraig
591
Beinn na Duatharach
Clachandhu
Dhiseig
Beinn Fhada
702
Gortenbuie
Beinn Talaidh
761
Sgurr Dearg
741
Lochdon
Coirc Bheinn
561
Ben More
966
Cruachan Dearg
704
Beinn Chaisgidle
504
Corra-bheinn
704
Oakbank
Gorten
Loch Don
Maiden Island
Rubh' a'Bhearnaig
Eilean nan Gamhna
Guibean Uluvalt
Cruach Choireadail
Ishriff
A849
Ardachoil
Ardnadrochit
Grass Point
Maol na Coille Moire
Glen More
Dererach
Uluvalt
Craig
15
Ardura
Cruach Ardura
Auchnacraig
Carn Ban
Port Donain
Ruba na Lice
Ardantrive
Balevulin
Beinn Fhada
Glas Bheinn
Barr-nam-boc Bay
Balliemore
Kerrera
Upper Gylen
Aird of Kinloch
Loch Beg
Creag na h-Iolaire
Loch Airdeglais
Creach Beinn
698
Fellonmore
Kilfinichen Bay
Cruach nan Con
Ben Buie
717
Loch Spelve
Croggan
Rubha na Faoilinn
Ardmore
Gylen
Maol nan Uan
Pennyghael
Loch Fuaron
Kinlochspelve
Dalnaha
Portfield
Bach Island
Rubha Seanach
Dubh Sgeir
Minard Point
Ardentallan
Killunaig
A849
Beinn na Croise
503
Lochbuie
Loch Uisg
Creag nam Fitheach
Brolass
Leidle
Glenbyre
Loch Buie
Maol Ban
Barnacarry Bay
Barnacarry
Druim Fada
405
Beinn Chreagach
376
Carsaig
Beinn a'Bhainne
Eilean Duin
Kilninver
Rubha Garbh Airde
Nun's Pass
Carsaig Bay
Rubha Dubh
Creachan Mor
Port Ohirnie
Ardencaple House
Frank Lockwood's Island
Insh Island
Sound of Insh
Ardfad
B844
Clachan-Seil
An Cala Garden
Malcolm's Point
Dun-Mor
Seil
Ardshellach
Folk Museum
Easdale
Balvicar
Caddleton
Henderson's Rock
B8003
Cuan Sound
Seil Sound
Garvellachs
Isles of the Sea
Cullipool
Torsay Island
Kilchoan
Ardanstur
Melfort
Belnahua
Degnish
Loch Melfort
Tullich
Garbh Eileach
Glas Eilean
Ardinamar
Eilean Gamhna
Degnish Point
A'Chuli
Kames
Monastery (ruin)
Eilean Dubh Mor
Luing
Arduaine
Arduaine Garden (NTS)
Tom Soilleir
365
Eileach an Naoimh
Lunga
Sound of Luing
Toberonochy
Black Mill Bay
Shuna
Asknish Bay
Barravullin
Eilean Arsa
Craobh Haven
Guirasdeal
Shuna Sound
Lunga
Shuna Point
Gemmil
Kintraw
Cruach Scarba
449
Ardfern
A816
Eilean Mhic Chrion
Barrackan
Scarba
Bagh Ban
B8002
Corranmore
Tibertich
Bagh Gleann a'Mhaoil
Rubha Righinn
Reisa Mhic Phaidean
Craignish
Carnassarie
Str. of Corryvreckan
Eilean Righ
Old Poltalloch
Sculptured Stones
Kirkton
Carnassarie
2½ hrs
Beinn nan Capull
Reisa an t-Sruith
Kilmartin
Kinuachdrachd
Sculptured Stones
Glengarrisdale Bay
Craignish Point
Island Macaskin
Stone Circle
Slockavullin
Kinuachdrach Harbour
Ri Cruin Cairn
Cruach na Seilcheig
Bagh Gleann Speireig
Glengarrisdale
Poltalloch
Rubha Garbh-ard
Barsloisnoch
Glendebadel Bay
Crinan Loch
Ben Garrisdale
365
Lealt Burn
Ardnoe Point
Crinan
B8025
Cruach Ionnastail
Dunadd Fort
Bellanoch
Cup & Ring Marks
Lussa
Rubha nam Barr
Cnoc Reamhar
265
6
Moine Mhor
Corpach Bay
Beinn Bhreac
467
Lealt
B841
Cairnbaan
Ardnackaig
Arichonan
Gallchoille
Gariob
Craigglas
Dubh Bheinn
Carsaig Island
Arinafad Beg
Knapdale Forest
Tarbert Bay
Ardlussa
Carsaig Bay
Auchindar
Seafield
Shian Bay
Crauch Sganadail
Lussagiven
Eilean Dubh
Tayvallich
Achnamara
Brackley
Cruach Breacain
360
Lussa Point
Eilean an Rubha
Aoistail
Turbiskill
Kilmichael

148
156
147
140
A
B
C
D
1
2
3
4
5
Eignaig
An Sleaghach
Morven
Bachuil
Lismore
Achnacroish
Baligrundle
Bernera
Achadun (ruin)
Kilcheran
Balure
Eilean Dubh
Pladda Island
Duart
Lady's Rock
Eilean Musdile
West Highland Railway
Appin Rocks
Eriska
Eilean Dubh
North Shian
South Shian
South Creagan
Barcaldine
A828
Achacha
Kiel Crofts
Culcharan
Benderloch
Ledaig
South Ledaig
Rubha Garbh-aird
Ardmucknish Bay
Eilean Mor
Dunstaffnage
North Connel
Connel
Achnacairn
Ardchattan Priory
Achnacloich
Creach Bheinn
810
Beinn Bhreac
708
Beinn Molurgainn
690
Beinn Mheadhonach
714
Cadderlie
B845
Dail
Ardmaddy
Meall an Fheuraich
Inverliver
Glen Kinglass
Beinn nan Lus
709
Beinn Trilleachan
839
Stob Duine Ruaidh
822
Acharn
Glennoe
Glen Noe
Glen Liver
Beinn a'Chochuil
980
Beinn Eunaich
988
Craig
Bonawe Quarries
Loch Etive
Airds Point
Airds Bay
Bonawe
Balure
Bonawe Furnace (iron works)
Ben Cruachan
1126
Stob Diamh
998
Beinn a'Bhuiridh
Cruachan Power Station Visitor Centre
Pass of Brander
Falls of Cruachan
Lochawe
A85
Dunbeg
Pennyfuir
Cuil-uaine
Culnadalloch
Fearnoch Forest
Ardchonnel
Black Lochs
Dailnamac
Balindore
Taynuilt
Glen Nant
Fanans
Tailor's Leap
Dunollie
Ganavan Bay
Maiden Island
Rubh' a'Bhearnaig
Eilean nan Gamhna
Glencruittein
Oban
Ardantrive
Ruba na Lice
Barr-nam-boc Bay
Balliemore
Kerrera
Upper Gylen
Ardmore
Gylen
Soroba
A816
Strontoiller
Barguillean Garden
Glenamachrie
Loch Nell
Cruach Airdeny
Beinn Ghlas
515
LORN
Shellachan
Trevine
Ardanaiseig
Barachander
Loch an Leoid
Loch Tromlee
Loch Nant
Sior Loch
Hayfield
Inishail
Innis Chonain
Achlian
Inistrynich
Kilchrenan
Annat
Taychreggan
Cladich
Ardbrecknish
Upper Sonachan
Portsonachan
Bach Island
Sgeir
Rubha Seanach
Minard Point
Kilbride
Gallanach
Lerags
Dunach
Cleigh
Kilmore
Ardentallan
Loch Feochan
Glenfeochan
Knipoch
Barnacarry Bay
Barrnacarry
Eilean Duin
Rubha Garbh Airde
Duachy
Kilninver
A'Chruach
368
Musdale
Lower Achachenna
Coillaig
Glen Euchar
Scammadale
Bragleenbeg
Shellachan
Loch Scamadale
Beinn Chapull
515
ARGYLL
AND
BUTE
Inverinan
Abhainn Fionain
Accurrach
Taynafead
Beinn Ghlas
550
A819
Clachan-Seil
Ardshellach
Seil
Balvicar
B8003
Caddleton
Corrielorne
Loch Tralaig
Loch na Sreinge
Inverinan Forest
Ballimeanoch
Tullich
Ladyfield
Cruach nam Fearna
332
Melfort
Pass of Melfort
Drissaig
Narrachan
Loch Avich
Allt Beochlich
Cruach Mhor
589
Stuc Scardan
Glen Shira
Torsay Island
Kilchoan
Ardanstur
Loch a' Phearsain
Kilmelford
Maolachy
Dalavich
Eredine Forest
Drimfern
Glen Aray
Kilblaan
Elrig
Degnish
Degnish Point
Ardinamar
Eilean Gamhna
Loch Melfort
Tullich
Lagalochan
Ardchonnell
Sallachry
Barr Mor
Portinnisherrich
High Balantyre
Dun Corr-bhile
Dubh Loch
Drishaig
Kames
Arduaine
Arduaine Garden (NTS)
Tom Soilleir
365
Carn Duchan
491
Lochan a'Bhruic
Inverliever Forest
Cam Loch
Beinn Bhreac
526
Lochan Long
Inveraray
Inveraray Jail
Asknish Bay
Shuna
Eilean Arsa
Craobh Haven
Barravullin
Gleann Domhain
Cruach an Eachlaich
Kilmaha
Eredine
Durran
B840
An Suidhe
514
Douglas Water
Am Buachaille
Auchnabreac
Creag a'Phuill
Wildlife Park
Strone Point
Dundarave Point
St Catherines
Cruach nan Capull
Shuna Point
Lunga
Gemmil
Ardfern
Inverliever
Arichamish
Torran
Loch Fyne
Kintraw
Auchnangoul
Dalchenna
Ardnagowan
Eilean Mhic Chrion
Barrackan
Ford
Fincharn
Beinn Dearg
Killean
Claonairigh
Hazelbank
Creagan an Eich
Bagh Ban
B8002
Corranmore
Tibertich
Auchindrain
Museum of Country Life
Loch Ederline
Fincharn Loch
Creggans
Clachan Strachur
Succoth
Carnassarie
Eilean Righ
Kirkton
Old Poltalloch
Beinn Laoigh
433
Brenachoille
A83
Kenmore
Dun Leacainn
Strachur Bay
Mid Letter
Balliemeanoch
Goatfield
Furnace
Eurach
Loch Gaineamhach
Barmolloch
Carnassarie Castle
Kilmartin
Kilmartin House
Beinn Bhan
319
Sculptured Stones
Stone Circle
Carron
Beinn Ghlas
420
Stuckreoch
Glensluain
A815
Carnach Mor
Island Macaskin
Slockavullin
Ri Cruin Cairn
Loch Leathan
Knockalava
Gleann Airigh
Feorlin
Crarae Woodland Garden
Leahd
Balliemore
Cruach nan Capull
Glenbranter
Inverncaden
Baluachraig
Crarae
Newton
Minard
Leanach
Glenshellish
ARGYLL FOREST PARK
Poltalloch
Poltalloch Monuments
Ballymeanoch
Leckuary
Minard Forest
Rubha Garbh-
Barsloisnoch
Lachlan
A886
Garbhallt
Crinan
Drimvore
Tullochgorm
Cruach an Lochain
508
Dunadd Fort
Kilmichael Glassary
Birdfield
Minard Castle
Stuck
Beinn Bheag
618
Bellanoch
B8025
Bridgend
Craigans
Loch Glashan
Barnacarry
Lephinmore
Cup & Ring Marks
Moine Mhor
Cruach Fasgach
Caol Ghleann
Cnoc Reamhar
265
B841
Achnashelloch
Asknish
B8000
Kilbridemore
Creag Tharsuinn
Bernice
Beinn Mhor
742
Arichonan
Cairnbaan
Achnabreck Cup & Ring Marks
Lochgair
Lephinchapel
Dunans
Gariob
Craigglas
Badden
Loch Gair
Meall Dubh
Knapdale Forest
Auchindrain
Middle Kames
Goirtein
Garvie
Sron Mhor
Coylet
Seafield
Lochgilphead
Carrick
Cruach Chuilceachan
435
Glendaruel
Conchra
Garrachra
Glen Massan
Achnamara
Cruach Breacain
360
Brackley
Achnaba
Largiemore
Ardacheranmor
Stronlonag
Glen Tarsan

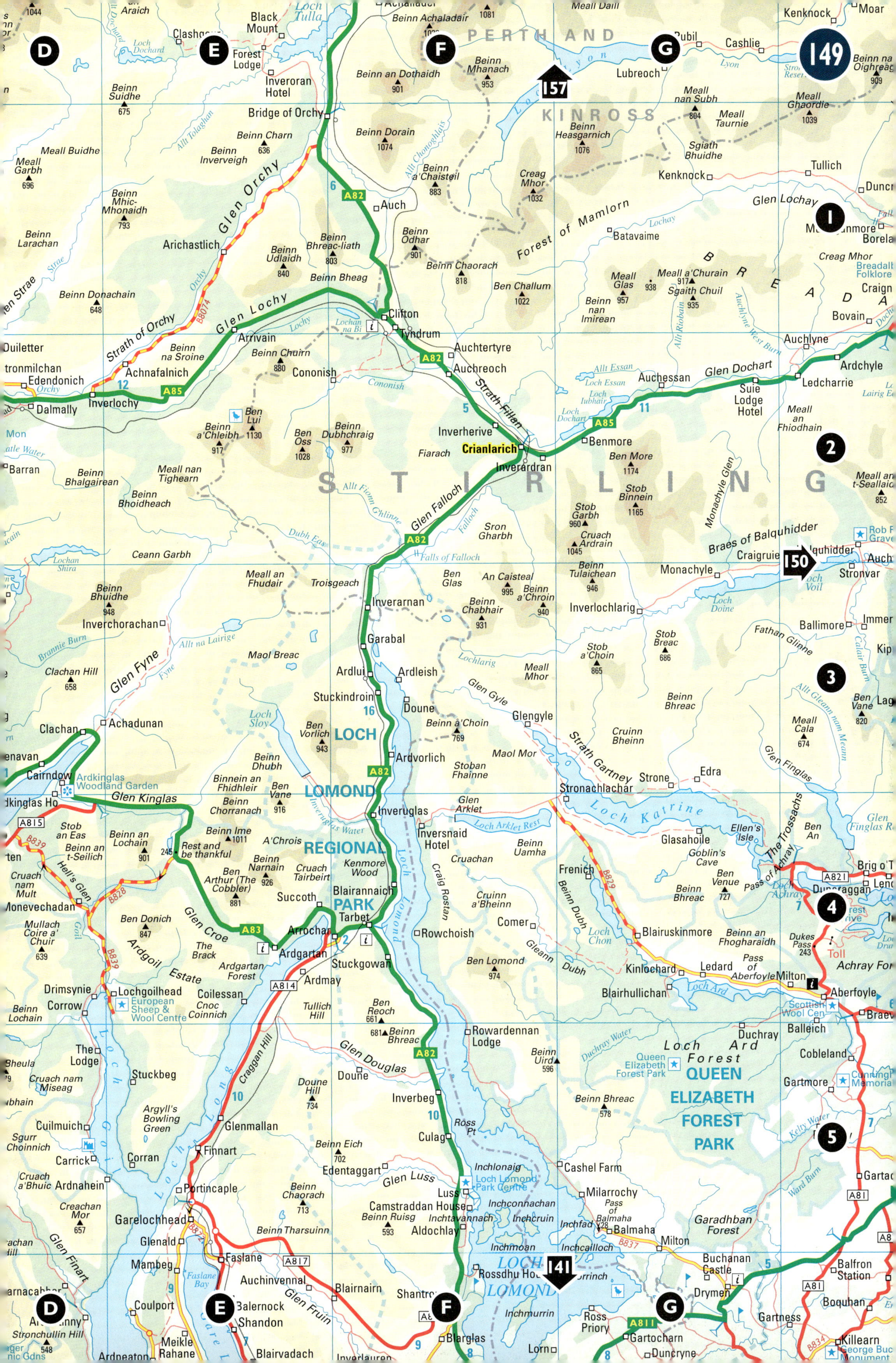
149
157
150
141
D
E
F
G
I
2
3
4
5
PERTH AND KINROSS
STIRLING
LOCH LOMOND REGIONAL PARK
QUEEN ELIZABETH FOREST PARK
Loch Ard Forest
Forest of Mamlorn
BREADALBANE
Black Mount
Loch Tulla
Clashgour
Forest Lodge
Inveroran Hotel
Bridge of Orchy
Loch Dochard
Beinn Suidhe 675
Meall Buidhe
Meall Garbh 696
Beinn Mhic-Mhonaidh 793
Beinn Larachan
Beinn Charn 636
Beinn Inverveigh
Glen Orchy
Arichastlich
Beinn Udlaidh 840
Beinn Bhreac-liath 803
Beinn Bheag
Beinn Donachain 648
Strath of Orchy
Glen Lochy
Arrivain
Beinn na Sroine
Achnafalnich
Duiletter
Edendonich
Inverlochy
Dalmally
Beinn Achaladair
Beinn an Dothaidh 901
Beinn Mhanach 953
Beinn Dorain 1074
Beinn a'Chaisteil 883
Auch
Beinn Odhar 901
Beinn Chaorach 818
Clifton
Tyndrum
Auchtertyre
Auchreoch
Strath Fillan
Beinn Chuirn 880
Cononish
Ben Lui 1130
Beinn a'Chleibh 917
Ben Oss 1028
Beinn Dubhchraig 977
Inverherive
Crianlarich
Inverardran
Fiarach
Lubreoch
Pubil
Cashlie
Meall nan Subh 804
Meall Taurnie
Sgiath Bhuidhe
Beinn Heasgarnich 1076
Creag Mhor 1032
Kenknock
Tullich
Glen Lochay
Batavaime
Meall Glas 957
Meall a'Churain
Sgaith Chuil 935
Beinn nan Imirean
Ben Challum 1022
Meall Ghaordie 1039
Beinn na Oighreag 909
Kenknock
Moar
Creag Mhor
Breadalbane Folklore
Craign
Bovain
Auchlyne
Ardchyle
Ledcharrie
Glen Dochart
Auchessan
Suie Lodge Hotel
Loch Iubhair
Loch Essan
Benmore
Ben More 1174
Stob Binnein 1165
Meall an Fhiodhain
Monachyle Glen
Braes of Balquhidder
Craigruie
Monachyle
Stronvar
Loch Voil
Loch Doine
Ballimore
Glen Falloch
Falls of Falloch
Sron Gharbh
Stob Garbh 960
Cruach Ardrain 1045
Beinn Tulaichean 946
An Caisteal 995
Beinn a'Chroin 940
Beinn Chabhair 931
Ben Glas
Inverlochlarig
Stob a'Choin 865
Stob Breac 686
Fathan Glinne
Beinn Bhreac
Meall Cala 674
Ben Vane 820
Glen Finglas
Barran
Beinn Bhalgairean
Meall nan Tighearn
Beinn Bhoidheach
Ceann Garbh
Meall an Fhudair
Troisgeach
Beinn Bhuidhe 948
Inverchorachan
Maol Breac
Clachan Hill 658
Glen Fyne
Clachan
Achadunan
Cairndow
Ardkinglas Woodland Garden
Ardkinglas Ho
Inverarnan
Garabal
Ardlui
Ardleish
Stuckindroin
Doune
Meall Mhor
Glen Gyle
Glengyle
Beinn a'Choin 769
Loch Sloy
Ben Vorlich 943
Ardvorlich
Stoban Fhainne
Maol Mor
Cruinn Bheinn
Strath Gartney
Strone
Edra
Stronachlachar
Loch Katrine
Ellen's Isle
The Trossachs
Glasahoile
Goblin's Cave
Ben Venue 727
Beinn Bhreac
Pass of Achray
Loch Achray
Duncraggan
Brig o'Turk
Ben An
Glen Kinglas
Beinn Dhubh
Binnein an Fhidhleir
Ben Vane 916
Beinn Chorranach
Beinn Ime 1011
A'Chrois
Inveruglas
Inveruglas Water
Glen Arklet
Loch Arklet Res
Inversnaid Hotel
Cruachan
Beinn Uamha
Frenich
Beinn Dubh
Stob an Eas
Beinn an Lochain 901
Beinn an t-Seilich
Rest and be thankful
Beinn Narnain 926
Ben Arthur (The Cobbler) 881
Cruach Tairbeirt
Kenmore Wood
Blairannaich
Craig Rostan
Cruinn a'Bheinn
Comer
Loch Chon
Blairuskinmore
Beinn an Fhogharaidh
Pass of Aberfoyle
Dukes Pass 243
Achray Forest
Hell's Glen
Cruach nam Mult
Lonevechadan
Succoth
Tarbet
Arrochar
Ardgartan
Rowchoish
Ben Lomond 974
Gleann Dubh
Kinlochard
Ledard
Milton
Aberfoyle
Blairhullichan
Loch Ard
Scottish Wool Centre
Ben Donich 847
Glen Croe
The Brack
Ardgartan Forest
Ardgoil Estate
Mullach Coire a' Chuir 639
Drimsynie
Lochgoilhead
European Sheep & Wool Centre
Corrow
Beinn Lochain
Coilessan
Cnoc Coinnich
Ardmay
Stuckgowan
Tullich Hill
Ben Reoch 661
Beinn Bhreac 681
Rowardennan Lodge
Beinn Uird 596
Duchray Water
Duchray
Balleich
Cobleland
Gartmore
Cunninghame Memorial
The Lodge
Loch Goil
Stuckbeg
Cruach nam Miseag
Craggan Hill
Glen Douglas
Doune
Doune Hill 734
Inverbeg
Ross Pt
Queen Elizabeth Forest Park
Beinn Bhreac 578
Kelty Water
Cuilmuich
Argyll's Bowling Green
Glenmallan
Loch Long
Sgurr Choinnich
Carrick
Corran
Finnart
Beinn Eich 702
Culag
Edentaggart
Glen Luss
Luss
Loch Lomond Park Centre
Inchlonaig
Cashel Farm
Milarrochy
Pass of Balmaha
Balmaha
Inchcailloch
Garadhban Forest
Gartach
Ward Burn
Cruach a'Bhuic
Ardnahein
Creachan Mor 657
Portincaple
Beinn Chaorach 713
Camstraddan House
Beinn Ruisg 593
Inchtavannach
Inchconnachan
Inchcruin
Aldochlay
Inchfad
Garelochhead
Beinn Tharsuinn
Glen Finart
Glenald
Mambeg
Faslane
Faslane Bay
Auchinvennal
Inchmoan
Rossdhu House
Inchmurrin
Loch Lomond
Milton
Buchanan Castle
Drymen
Balfron Station
Boquhan
Gartness
Killearn
George Buchanan Monument
Coulport
Balernock
Shandon
Glen Fruin
Blairnairn
Shantron
Ross Priory
Gartocharn
Duncryne
Stronchullin Hill 548
Meikle Rahane
Ardpeaton
Blairvadach
Inverlauren
Blarglas
Lorn
A82
A85
A83
A814
A815
A817
A811
A81
B8074
B839
B828
B829
B837
B834

150
158
149
142
A
B
C
D
1
2
3
4
5
Pubil
Kenknock
Moar
Meall Luaidhe 780
a' Choire Leith 926
Meall Garbh 1118
Meall Greigh 1001
A827
Remony
Acharn
Ben Oighreag 909
Lairig Breisleich
550
Meall Corranaich 1069
Ben Lawers 1214
Lawers Burn
Ardradnaig
Meall nan Subh 804
Stronuich Reservoir
Meall Ghaordie 1039
Lochan na Lairige
Beinn Ghlas 1013
Cragganruar
Beinn Bhreac
Creag an Sgliata
Meall Taurnie
Meall Glass
Meall nan Tarmachan 1043
Ben Lawers (NTS)
Meall Odhar
Lawers
Ardtalnaig
Quaich
Garrow
Auchnacloich
Sgiath Bhuidhe
Carie
Loch Tay
Creagan na Beinne 888
Acharn Burn
Meall nam Fuaran 805
Tullich
Milton Morenish
A827
Kiltyrie
Glen a' Chilleine
Tullich Hill
enknock
Duncroist
Morenish
Ardeonaig
Glen Lochay
Murlaganmore
Camusurich
Achnafree Craig
Falls of Lochay
Boreland
Finlarig
Cloichran
Creag Mhor
Finlarig
Dalriech
Auchnafree
Almond
Breadalbane Folklore Cen
Killin
Achmore
Creag Uchdag 879
Glen Almond
eall a' Churain 917
Kinnell
Sgaith Chuil 935
Craignavie
Lochan Breaclaich
Creag Gharbh
Ruadh Mheall
Finglen Burn
Auchnafree Hill
BREADALBANE
Ben Chonzie 931
Bovain
Dochart
Mid Lix
Loch Lednock Resr
Loch Turret Resr
Auchlyne
Auchlyne West Burn
ssan
Glen Dochart
Ardchyle
Beinn Leabhain
Spout Rolla
Glen Lednock
Invergeldie
Carn Chois
A85
Suie Lodge Hotel
Ledcharrie
Lairig Eala
Glen Ogle
Beich Burn
Glen Tarken
Meall nam Fiadh
Glen Turret
Meall an Fhiodhain
Meall a' Mhadaidh
Glen Beich
Sron Mor 672
Loch Boltachan
Carroglen
Glenbeich
Ardveich
A85
Creag Each
Creag Liath
Falls of Turret
Melville's Mon
Monachyle Glen
A85
Auchraw
Dalveich
Derry
St Fillans
13
Dunira
Deil's Caldron
Ochtertyre
Meall an t-Seallaidh 852
Lochearnhead
Loch Earn
Ardtrostan
Comrie
Lawers
Edinchip
Edinample
Ardvorlich
Tullybannocher
Quoig
Rob Roy's Grave
A84
Meall Reamhar 678
Ross
Dalginross
Braes of Balquhidder
Balquhidder
Auchtubh
Kingshouse
Ben Halton 620
STRATHEARN
Lochlane
onachyle
Loch Voil
Stronvar
Strathyre Forest
Glen Ample
Ben Vorlich 985
All Srath a' Ghlinne
Cultybraggan Camp
Mill of Fortune
The Balloch
Loch Doine
Forest of Glenartney
Water of Ruchill
Torlum
Torlum Wood
Ballimore
Immeroin
Stuc a' Chroin 972
Glen Artney
B827
Culloch
Tighnablair
Craggan
Ochte
Fathan Glinne
Kipp
Strathyre
Dalchruin
Machany Water
Calair Burn
14
Findhuglen
Knaik
Dunruchan Hill
Beinn Bhreac
Runacraig
Meall Odhar
Auchinner
Ben Clach
Creag Beinn nan Eun
Findhu Glen
Langside
Ben Vane 820
Laggan
Ardchullarie More
Allt Gleann nam Meann
A84
Greenscares
Meall Cala 674
Ardnandave Hill
Loch Lubnaig
Meall Leathan Dhail
Beinn Odhar 632
Coire Nochd Mor
Glenlichorn
B827
Garric
STIRLING
Glen Finglas
Uamh Bheag 665
Cromlet
Edra
Braeleny
Slymaback
Gleann Casaig
Ben Ledi 879
Anie
Pass of Leny
Bullie Burn
Kilmahog Woollen Mill
Bracklinn Falls
Cambushinn Hill
Loch Katrine
Glen Finglas Resr
Kilmahog
Ellen's Isle
Ben An
The Trossachs
Bochastle
Callander
B8033
Glasahoile
Goblin's Cave
Milton of Callander
Coilantogle
Rob Roy & Trossachs Visitor Centre
Muckle Burn
STRATHALLAN
Ben Venue
Brig o' Turk
10
Drummond
Keltie Water
Pass of Achray
Duncraggan
Lendrick Lodge
A821
Loch Venachar
Loch Mahaick
Ardoch Burn
Beinn Bhreac
Loch Achray
Easter Dullater
A84
Braes of Doune
Kinbuck
Balhaldie
Forest Drive
West Dullater
12
Invertrossachs
6
Drumvaich
Glassingall
A821
Loch Drunkie
A81
Loch Rusky
Argaty
Ashfield
Sheriffmuir 1715
skinmore
Beinn an Fhogharaidh
Dukes Pass 243
Menteith Hills
Beinn Dearg
B822
B8032
Burn of Cambus
Allan Water
Toll
Stockbridge
Ledard
Pass of Aberfoyle
Milton
Achray Forest
Port of Menteith
Torrie Forest
Teith
Doune
A820
Dunblane
Loch Ard
Aberfoyle
A81
Blairhoyle
Easter Borland
Deanston
Pisgah
Wharry
Scottish Wool Centre
Malling
Inchmahome Priory
Ruskie
A873
Thornhill
Gartincaber
B826
Doune
Inverardoch Mains
Cauldhame
Balleich
Braeval
Kippenross Ho
Duchray
Tamavoid
Goodie Water
Blair Drummond
B824
QUEEN ELIZABETH FOREST PARK
Loch Ard Forest
Cobleland
Lake of Menteith
Flanders Moss
12
Safari Park
Keir House
Sunnylaw
Cunninghame Graham Memorial (NTS)
B8031
Bridge of Allan
Gartmore
Dykehead
Forth
Easter Poldar
B8075
Nyadd
Ochtertyre
M9
A9
Blairlogie
Menst
B8034
B823
A84
Dalmary
B822
Causewayhead
Kelty Water
Drip Moss
Wallace Mon
Garden
Arngomery
A811
19
B835
Arnprior
B8037
Kippen
Gargunnock
Smith Art Gallery & Museum
Stirling Bridge 1297
Cambuskenneth Abbey
Cambu
Buchlyvie
Cauldhame
Leckie
Gargunnock House
A91
Gartachoil
Arngibbon
STIRLING
Ward Burn
Argyll & Sutherland Highlanders Museum
Royal Burgh of Stirling Visitor Centre
A81
Wrightpark
Cambusbarron
Touch Hills
Garadhban Forest
485
St Ninians
1314
Fallin
A905
ilton
A875
B822
Gargunnock Hills
Bannockburn Heritage Cen (NTS)
Bannockburn
Balafark
Bannock Burn
Buchanan Castle
A811
Balfron Station
Ling Hill
Earl's Hill
North Third
Cow
5
North Third Resr
A9
Balfron
Drymen
511
Fintry Hills
Earl's Hill
9
Gartness
Boquhan
B818
Culcreuch
Craigton
Loch Coulter Resr
Stirlin
Loup of Fintry
A872
Killearn
B834
George Buchanan
Corrie of
Fintry
Gonachan
Cairnoch Hill 413
Easter Buckieburn
Plean
M

151
159
152
143
D
E
F
G
I
2
3
4
5
PERTH
AND
KINROSS
CLACKMANNANSHIRE
FIFE
STRATHBRAAN
Logiealmond
STRATHMORE
SIDLAWS
Braes of the Carse
CARSE
OCHIL HILLS
Blairgowrie
Rosemount
Dunkeld
Birnam
Inver
Little Dunkeld
Concraigie
Clunie
Craigie
Muirton of Ardblair
Kirkton of Lethendy
Spittalfield
Thornton
Stenton
Caputh
Delvine
Meikleour
Coupar Angus
Keithick
Markethill
Kinclaven
Woodside
Burrelton
Campmuir
Scotston
Amulree
Achnafauld
Corrymuckloch
Ballinlick
Trochry
Aldville
Milton
Drumour
Newton
Gellyburn
Murthly
Ardoch
Waterloo
Upper Obney
Laguna
Cargill
Bankfoot
Airntully
Stanley
West Tofts
Craigieholm
Whitefield
Springfield
Tullybelton
Wolfhill
Saucher
Dunsinnan
Kinrossie
Collace
Kirkton of Collace
Guildtown
Harrietfield
Chapelhill
Moneydie
Newmiln
Colenden
Luncarty
St Martins
Balbeggie
Tulchan
Buchanty
Pickston
Busby
Methven
Pitcairngreen
Almondbank
Scones Lethendy
Old Scone
Kinnaird
Rait
Kilspindie
Pitroddie
New Scone
Bridgend
Huntingtower
PERTH
Tibbermore
Newmiln
Keillour
Fowlis Wester
Forebrae
Braegrum
Monzie
Gilmerton
Glenturret Distillery
Stuart Strathearn Crystal
Crieff Visitors Centre
Keillour Forest
Madderty
Inchaffray Abbey
Dubheads
Clathy
Findo Gask
Crossgates
Milltown of Aberdalgie
Aberdalgie
Friarton
Craigend
Tarsappie
Rhynd
Moncreiffe
Elcho
Balthayock
Kinfauns
Glendoick
Glencarse
Chapelhill
Inchyra
Port Allen
Newburgh
St David's
Kirkton
Gask
Chapelbank
Kinkell Bridge
Millearne
Broom of Dalreach
Forteviot
Forgandenny
Bridge of Earn
Kintillo
Muthill
Machany
Aberuthven
Duncrub
Dunning
Invermay
Garvock
Glenearn
Dron
Aberargie
Abernethy
Glenfoot
Ayton
Pitcairlie
Pleasance
Westerton
Auchterarder
Damside
Pitcairns
Kippen
Path of Condie
Rossie Ochill
Balmanno Hill
Pitmedden Forest
Muirtown
Gleneagles Hotel
Gleneagles
Blackford
Gleneagles House
Newton of Balcanquhal
Auchtermuchty
Glenfarg
Arngask
Duncrievie
Gateside
Strathmiglo
Nether Urquhart
Falkland
Middleton
Burnside
Craigow
Upper Tillyrie
Dalqueich
Arlary
Milnathort
Balgedie
Kinnesswood
Pitkevy
Leslie
Glendevon
Glen Devon
Burnfoot
Carnbo
Warroch
Kinross
Loch Leven
Scotlandwell
Auchmuirbridge
Yetts o' Muckhart
Pool of Muckhart
Crook of Devon
Drum
Coldrain
Gairney Bank
Kinglassie
Tillicoultry
Dollar
Alva
Devonside
Dollarbeg
Rumbling Bridge
Powmill
Cleish
Ballingry
Lochore
Crosshill
Auchterderran
Tullibody
Coalsnaughton
Sauchie
Blairingone
Solsgirth
Hill End
Blairadam Forest
Kelty
Glencraig
Lochgelly
Alloa
Clackmannan
Forest Mill
Balgonar
Saline
Lassodie
Lower Oakfield
Lumphinnans
Cowdenbeath
South Alloa
Kennet
Bogside
Bowershall
Kingseat
Hill of Beath
Auchtertool
Dunmore
Blairhall
Carnock
Gowkhall
Oakley
Milesmark
Wellwood
Crossgates
Fordell
Donibristle
Airth
Valleyfield
Cairneyhill
Bowtrees
M90
A9
A93
A94
A85
A91
A92
A822
A823
A824
A826
A912
A922
A923
A977
A984
A985
A907
A908
A909
A911
A994
A921

152
160
151
144
A
B
C
D
1
2
3
4
5
Blairgowrie
Rosemount
Meigle
Kinloch
Kirkinch
Eassie and Nevay
Milton
Inverarity
Whigstreet
Lochlair
Muirton of Ardblair
Arthurstone
Newbigging
Auchtertyre
Ark
Nether
Kinpurney Hill
Gallow Hill
Gateside
Gallowfauld
Kirkbuddo
Carrot
Hayhillock
Keillor
Auchterhouse Hill
Craigowl Hill
Carrot Hill
Greenburn
Crombie
Coupar Angus
Keithick
Markethill
Kettins
Bonnyton
Kirkton of Auchterhouse
Kirkton of Tealing
Balgray
Todhills
Newton of Affleck
Affleck
Monikie
Kirkton of Monikie
Campmuir
Leys
Thriepley
Auchterhouse
Dovecot & Earth House
Newbigging
Wellbank
Craigton
Woodside
Burrelton
Pitcur
Lundie
Leoch
East March
Bucklerheads
Upper Victoria
PERTH
ANGUS
Dronley
Kirkton of Strathmartine
Drumsturdy
Newbigging
Springfield
Muirhead
Kellas
Laws
Murroes
Barry
Hallyburton Forest
Littleton
Blacklaw Hill
Fowlis
Birkhill
Clatto
Burnside of Duntrune
Mains of Ardestie
King's Seat
Saucher
Liff
Camperdown
Downfield
DUNDEE
Baldovie
Wolfhill
Dunsinnan
Kinrossie
Collace
Kirkton of Collace
Abernyte
Knapp
Benvie
Lochee
Douglas and Angus
Claypotts
Monifieth
Buddon
Barry
Pitmiddle Wood
Rossie Priory
Denhead
Broughty Ferry
Invergowrie
DUNDEE
Ballindean
Longforgan
Kingoodie
Dundee Contemporary Arts
Toll
Tay Road Bridge
Broughty
Tayport
Balbeggie
Braes of the Carse
Kinnaird
Craigdallie
Inchture
Dundee
Discovery Point & R.R.S. Discovery
Newport-on-Tay
Tentsmuir Point
KINROSS
Rait
CARSE OF GOWRIE
FIRTH OF TAY
Tay Bridge
Woodhaven
Tentsmuir
Forest
Kilspindie
Pitrodie
Grange
Dog Bank
Wormit
Pickletillem
Megginch Castle
Balmerino
Kirkton
Bottomcraig
Abbey (NTS)
Gauldry
Kinfauns
Glendoick
Errol
Carthagena Bank
Coultra
Cruivie
Carrick
Kinfauns Forest
Kilmany
Lucklawhill
RAF Memorial
Earlshall
Glencarse
Port Allen
Chapelhill
Balhelvie
Hazelton Walls
Balmullo
Leuchars
Eden Mouth
Elcho
Norman's Law
Brunton
Creich
Rathillet
Forret Hill
Logie
Mugdrum Island
North Deep
Glenduckie Hill
Luthrie
Craigsanquhar
Guardbridge
Out Head
Newburgh
South Deep
Glenduckie
Norman's Hill
Dairsie
Kincaple
St Andrews
British Golf Museum
St Andrews Bay
Sea Life Centre
Abernethy
Lindores Abbey
Dunbog
Moonzie
Lindores
Lindifferon
Cairney Lodge
Strathkinness
Aberargie
Round Tower
Ormiston Hill
Grange of Lindores
Mount Hill
Kemback
Blebocraigs
Cunnoquhie
Fernie
Scottish Deer Centre
Cupar
Magus Muir
Pitcairley Hill
Letham
Dura
Craigtoun
Prior Muir
Monimail
Over Rankeilour
Hill of Tarvit (NTS)
Denhead
Pitmedden Forest
Pleasance
Collessie
Cupar Muir
Pitscottie
Balvaird
Bow of Fife
Springfield
Bridgend
Cameron Burn
Auchtermuchty
Beins Law
Kinloch
Scotstarvit Tower
Ceres
Baldinnie
Cameron Resr
Stravithie
Dunshelt
Craigrothie
Fife Folk Museum
Craighall
Lathockar
Kinaldy
Howe of Fife
Ladybank
Gateside
Strathmiglo
Lathrisk
Pitlessie
Struthers
FIFE
Peat Inn
West Lingo
Falkland Palace (NTS)
Kingskettle
Falfield
Kinaldy Burn
Nether Urquhart
Newton of Falkland
Balmalcolm
Teasses
New Gilston
Lathones
Falkland
Kettlebridge
Woodside
Largoward
Lochty
West Lomond
Lomond Hills
Montrave
Kellie Law
Carnbee
FIFE REGIONAL PARK
Freuchie
Clatto Hill
Pratis
Balhousie
Lathallan Mill
East Lomond
Glasslie
Arncroach
Muirhead
Langdyke
Largo Law
Wester Newburn
Charleton
Kellie (NTS)
Bishop Hill
Pitkevy
New Inn
Kilmux
Upper Largo
Grangemuir
Kinnesswood
Bandon
Bonnybank
Colinsburgh
Holl Resr
Balbirnie
Star
Kennoway
Lower Largo
Drumeldrie
Abercrombie
Scotlandwell
Auchmuirbridge
Leslie
Cadham
Markinch
Kingsdale
Lundin Links
Kilconquhar
Balcurvie
Largo Bay
Ruddons Point
St Monans
GLENROTHES
Woodside
Milton of Balgonie
Windygates
Leven
Earlsferry
Innerleven
Elie
Kinglassie
Coaltown of Balgonie
Methil
Kincraig Point
Chapel Ness
Saucher Point
Benarty Hill
Ballingry
Dogton Stone
Buckhaven
Thornton
Lochore
Lochore Meadows
Macduff's Castle
Crosshill
Auchterderran
East Wemyss
Cluny
Coaltown of Wemyss
Cardenden
West Wemyss
Lochgelly
Chapel
FIRTH OF FORTH
Gallatown
Dysart
Pathhead
Lumphinnans
Church
Museum & Art Gallery
Ravenscraig
KIRKCALDY
Auchtertool
Linktown
Tiel Burn
Fordell
Donibristle
Cullaloe Hills
Dunearn
The Binn
Kinghorn
Burntisland
Pettycur
Aberdour
Yellowcraig
Lamb
A90
A92
A91
A93
A94
A923
A984
A85
A914
A913
A916
A915
A917
A955
A910
A909
A921
A911
A912
A928
A930
B961
B978
B9127
B954
B953
B946
B945
B939
B940
B941
B942
B9131
B936
B937
B9130
B981
B921
B922
B9097
B920
B919
B925
B9157
B927
B996
B966

Redford
Marywell
Meg's Craig
A933
A92
St Vigeans
Carlingheugh Bay
Guynd
B9127
Arbirlot
Elliot Water
The Deil's Heid
Abbey
Arbroath
Bonnyton
Easter Knox
A92
Wormiehills
Salmond's Muir
East Haven
Panbride
Carnoustie
Inchcape or Bell Rock
Buddo Ness
Babbet Ness
A917
Cambo Ness
Kingsbarns
North Carr
Tullybothy Craigs
Craighead
Fife Ness
Wormiston
B940
B9171
Crail
Spalefield
West Ness
Innergellie
Kilrenny
Cellardyke
Anstruther
Scottish Fisheries Museum
North Ness
Isle of May
Chapel
South Ness
3.2 miles to 1 inch
10 miles
10 km
2 km to 1 cm
Bass Rock
Scottish Seabird Centre
D
E
F
G
1
2
3
4
5
161
145

A
B
C
D
163
146
1
2
3
4
5
SEA OF THE
HEBRIDES
INNER HEBRIDES
ARGYLL
AND
BUTE
same scale as main map
Calgary Point
Caolas Ban
Gunna
Port a'Mh
Urvaig
Miodar
Sgeir Bharrach
Salum Bay
Rubha Dubh
Caolas
Vaul
Balephetrish Bay
Balephetrish Hill
B8069
Ruaig
The Green
Brock
Port Ban
Gott Bay
Rubha Liath
Hough Bay
TIREE
Tiree
Scarinish
Soa
Kilkenneth
Moss
B8068
B8065
Crossapoll
Heanish
Saundaig
Heylipoll
Baugh
Hynish Bay
Barrapoll
Balemartine
B8067
Mannel
Balephuil
Rinn Thorbhais
Hynish
Skerryvore Museum
Rubha Sgor an t-Snidhe
Ruinsival
528
Ainshval
781
Sgurr nan Gillean
764
Rubha nam Meirleach
SOUND OF
Rubha an Fhasaidh
Sound of Eigg
Eilean nan Each
Godag
Rubh' Leam na Laraich
Beinn Airein
137
Port M
Muck
H I G
Sanna Point
Sanna Bay
Point of Ardnamurchan
Port Min
Grigadale
Oban-Lochboisdale 5-7hrs
Oban-Castlebay 5¼ hrs
Eag na Maoile
Eilean Mor
Rubha Mor
Bousd
Rubha Sgor-Innis
Rubh' a'Bhinnein
B8072
Sorisdale
Loch Fada
Torastan
Bagh na Coille
Cliad Bay
Grishipoll
Arnabost
Grishipoll Bay
B8071
Clabhach
Ben Hogh
104
73
Ballyhaugh
Loch Cliad
Hogh Bay
Arinagour
Totamore
Totronald
COLL
B8070
Loch Eatharna
Arileod
Acha
Feall Bay
Port Mine
Uig
Eilean Ornsay
Calgary Point
Crossapol
Gorton
Crossapol Bay
Loch Breachacha
Friesland Bay
Gunna
Caolas Ban
Rubha Fasachd
Port a'Mhurain
Soa
Urvaig
Miodar
Salum Bay
Rubha Dubh
Caolas
Ruaig
Brock
Port Ban
Gott Bay
Rubha Liath
anish
1¼ hrs
Oban 2¾ hrs
Sorne Point
Quinish Point
Quinish
Caliach Point
Port na Ba
Sunipol
Langamull
Croig
Mornish
Cruach Sleibhe
166
Frachadil
Dervai
Rubha nan Oirean
Calgary
B8073
Calgary Bay
Treshnish Point
Treshnish
Ensay
Carn Mor
342
Cruachan Ceann a'Ghair
261
Beinn Duill
191
Cruachan Odhar
256
Beinn nan Clach
315
Rubh' a'Chaoil
Kilninian
Rubh' an t-Suibhein
Tostarie
Normann's Ruh
Port Burg
Loch Tuath
Cairn na Burgh More
Cairn na Burgh Beg
Fanmore
Treshnish Isles
Sgeir a Chaisteil
Fladda
Rubha Chulinish
Ballygown Bay
Eilean Dioghlum
Gometra Ho.
Rubha nan Gall
Lunga
Gometra
Bearnus
Beinn Chreagach
Rubha Maol na Mine
Beinn Eolasary
ULVA
Bac Mor or Dutchman's Cap
Maisgeir
A'Chranna
Beag
Little Colonsay
Staffa
Eilean Dubh
Chapel

155
D
E
F
G
164
156
147
A830
Morar
Loch a' Ghille Ghobaich
Bracora
Bracora
Stoul
Kyleskonoydart
Tarbet
Swordland
Eilean a' Phidhir
NORTH MORAR
Loch Morar
SOUTH MORAR
Cleadale
An Cruachan 299
Bay of Laig
Laig
EIGG
An Sgurr 393
Kildonnan
Galmisdale
Portnaluchaig
Back of Keppoch
Eilean Ighe
ARISAIG
Arisaig
Luinga Mhor
Loch nan Ceall
Rhumach
Rubh' Arisaig
Morroch
Druimindarroch
Cruach Doire 'n Dobhrain 103
Carn a' Mhadaidh-ruaidh 503
Lettermorar
Loch a' Choire Riabhaich
Sidhean Mor 599
Glen Beasdale
Beinn nan Cabar 574
Meoble
Meith Bheinn 710
Druim a' Chuirn
The Prince's Cairn
L. Beag
Loch nan Uamh
Arnipol
Arienskill
Lochailort
Ranochan
Inverailort
Loch Doir a' Ghearrain
Loch Ailort
Loch Eilt
Sgurr na Pai
Rubha Chaolais
Eilean nan Gobhar
Ardnish
Sound of Arisaig
An Stac 814
Druim Fiaclach 869
Samalaman Island
Glenuig Bay
Roshven
Rois-Bheinn 882
Croit Bheinn 663
Smirisary
Glenuig
A861
Cruach Bhrochdadail 357
Sgurr Dhomhnuill Mor 713
HIGHLAND
Glenuig Hill
Kylesbeg
Eilean Shona 265
Bailetonach
Shona Beag
Beinn Gaire 666
MOIDART
Brunery Hill
Glen Forslan
Gaskan
Kinlochmoidart
Loch Moidart
Tioram
Rubha Aird Druimnich
Carn Mor
Ardtoe
Beinn Bhreac 240
Ardmolich
Glen Moidart
Gorstanvorran
Loch Shiel
Ockle Point
Ockle
Newton of Ardtoe
Shielfoot
Cruach a' Ghaill 371
Fascadale
Achateny
Kilmory
Swordle
Beinn Bhreac 357
Kentra
Cliff
A861
Dalnabreck
Dalelia
Branault
Kentra Bay
B8044
Achnaha
Meall nan Con 437
Gorteneorn
Arivegaig
Acharacle
Polloch
Beinn an Leathaid
Meall an Tarmachain 404
Loch Mudle
Ardshealach
Claish Moss
Achnanellan
Kinlochan
B8007
ARDNAMURCHAN
Leac Shoilleir 440
SUNART
Beinn Resipol 845
Camphouse
Beinn nan Losgann 313
Salen
Resipole
Beinn na Seilg 342
Kilchoan
Ben Hiant 528
Lochan nam Fiann
Tarbert
Scotstown
Mingary
Beinn Bhuidhe 278
Loch Laga
Ardery
Kilchoan Bay
Glenbeg
Natural History Centre
Ben Laga 512
Loch Sunart
Anaheilt
Drumnatorran
Sron Bheag
Maclean's Nose
Ardslignish
Glenborrodale
B8007
Gearr Chreag 340
Ranachan
Woodend
Strontian
Ardnastang
Eilean Mor
Laga
Eilean Mor
Ardmore Point
Oronsay
Risga
Carna
Glencripesdale
Meall a' Bhroin
Liddesdale
Achleek
Bloody Bay
Auliston Point
A884
Meall an Inbhire
Beinn Ghormaig 452
Taobh Dubh 352
Glas Bheinn 620
Rahoy
Loch Teacuis
Meall a' Chaise 522
Achagavel
Tobermory
Tobermory Bay
Calve Island
Beinn Iadain 571
Lochuisge
Barr
Kinloch
Gleann Dubh
Achleanan
Ardantiobairt
Loch Uisge
'S Airdhe Beinn
A848
Drimnin
MORVERN
Beinn na h-Uamha 464
Beinn Chlaonleud 475
Beach
Meall a' Chaorainn Loch Uisge
Sgurr Shalachain
B8043
Beinn Bhuidhe 451
Mishnish Lochs
B849
Sidhean na Raplaich 550
Durinemast
Loch Arienas
Clounlaid
Beinn Mheadhoin 739
Aros
Rhemore
A884
Allt Geal
Alltachonaich
Sgurr a' Bhuic 569
Caol Lochan
Loch Frisa
Speinne Mor 444
Killundine
Beinn an t-Sruthain 267
Claggan
Ardtornish
Gleann Geal
Ardnacross
Creag Bhan Ard 339
Beinn Bhan 400
Larachbeg
Braigh na Glaice Moire
Meall Damh
Lettermore
SOUND OF MULL
Kinlochaline
Ardtornish
Beinn a' Chaisil 437
Glensanda
Achnacraig
Salen Forest
Meall na Caorach
Funary Forest
Loch Teàrnait
Bellart
Fiunary
Rannoch
Druim an Fhraoich Mhin 318
Ledmore
Tenga
A848
Tighachnoic
Loch nan Clach
Glen Aros
Aros
Eileanan Glasa
Achnaha
Meall a' Chaorainn 481
Beinn Bhuidhe 387
Meall an Fhiar Mhaim 309
Salen Bay
Lochaline
Glais Bheinn 479
Mam a' Chullaich 462
An Sleaghach 513
Eignaig
Beinn na Drise 424
Salen
A849
Fishnish Bay
Fishnish Point
Inninbeg
Beinn nan Carn 333
Pennygown
Fishnish
Ardtornish Point
Lynn of Morven
Killiechronan
B8035
B8073
Cruach Torran Lochain
Killbeg
MULL
Lagganulva
Kellan
Balmeanach
Inninmore Bay
Killiemor
Gruline
Beinn Bhuidhe 412
Glen Forsa
Beinn Chreagach Mhor 579
Garmony
Rubha an Ridire
Lismore
Loch Na Keal
Loch Ba
Salen Forest
Bernera
Achadun (ruin)
Kilcheran
Knock
Na Binneinean
Gaodhail
Scallastle
Craignure
Craignure Bay
Loch Fiart
Eilean Dubh
Beinn na Duatharach
Dun da Ghaoithe 766
Maol nan Uan
Mull & West Highland Railway
Pladda Island
591
LOCH LINNHE

156
165
155
148
A
B
C
D
1
2
3
4
5
Kylesknoydart
Kylesmorar
Tarbet
Swordland
NORTH MORAR
SOUTH MORAR
Kinlochmorar
Sgurr na h-Aide
859
Upper Glendessarry
Glen Dessarry
Glendessary
Murlaggan
Loch Arkaig
Monadh Gorm
470
Strathan
Kinlocharkaig
Glen Pean
Pean
Ardachy
Ardrac
Druim a' Chuirn
An Stac
718
Sgurr an Ursainn
817
Sgurr nan Coireachan
956
Sgurr Thuilm
963
Mullach Choire nan Geur-oirean
727
Locheil Forest
Glen Mallie
Inver Mallie
Beinn nan Cabar
574
Meoble
Meith Bheinn
710
Loch Beoraid
Kinlochbeoraid
Braigh nan Uamhachan
765
Gulvain
987
962
Streap
909
Stob Coire nan Cearc
887
Meall a' Phubuill
774
Druim Gleann Laoigh
698
Beinn Bhan
796
771
HIGHLAND
Sron Thoraraidh
383
Glas-charn
633
Sgurr an Utha
796
Sgurr a' Mhuidhe
Beinn an Tuim
810
Na h-Uamhachan
691
Glen Finnan
Gleann Dubh Lighe
Gleann Fionnlighe
Gleann Suileag
Coille Mhor
635
729
Stob a'Ghrianain
744
Glen Loy
Strone
Arienskill
Lochailort
Inverailort
Ranochan
Loch Eilt
A830
14
Glenfinnan
Glenfinnan Monument (NTS)
Sgurr na Paite
Druim Fada
An Stac
814
Druim Fiaclach
869
Beinn Odhar Mhor
870
Beinn Odhar Bheag
882
Meall a' Bhainne
559
Drumfern
Kinlocheil
Fassfern
Locheilside Sta
Loch Eil
Loch Eil Outward Bound
Meall Bhanabhie
326
Torcastle
Torlundy
s-Bheinn
882
Croit Bheinn
663
Loch Shiel
Garvan
Duisky
Blaich
A861
11
Corpach
Banavie
Neptune's Staircase
Caol
Sgorr Craobh a' Chaorainn
775
Glen Garvan
Achaphubuil
Camusnagaul
Trislaig
Old Inverlochy
Claggan
Fort William
Achintee
West Highland Museum
Glenaladale
Gaire
666
Glen Forslan
Gaskan
Sgurr Ghiubhsachain
Meall nan Damh
723
Sron an t-Sluichd
367
Meall an Fheidh
423
Meall an Doire Shleaghaich
407
Ceann Caol
488
Meall an t-Slamain
467
Stob Coire a' Chearcaill
770
Sgurr an Lubhair
722
Carn an Daimh
Glen Nevis
Ho
Gorstanvorran
Scamodale
Meall Mor
759
Stob Mhic Bheathain
721
Cona Glen
Corrlarach
Goirtean a'Chladaich
Nevis Forest
Cruach Ghaill
371
Sgurr na Greine
497
Sgurr an Tarmachain
756
Resourie
Carn na Nathrach
786
Druim Leathad nam Fias
21
Druimarbin
Blarmachfoldach
Polldubh
Achriabhach
Polloch
Achnanellan
Glen Hurich
Druim Garbh
Sgurr Dhomhnuill
888
Glen Scaddle
Tighnacomaire
Creagbheitheachain
Aryhoulan
Inverscaddle Bay
12
LOCH LINNHE
Kiachnish
Glenhurich
Kinlochan
ARDGOUR
Sgorr a' Chaorainn
477
Sgurr na h-Eanchainne
730
Corrychurrachan
Blar a' Chaorainn
Mullach nan Coirean
939
Lundavra
Lochan Lunn Da Bhra
Beinn na Gucaig
616
Doire Ban
566
Lairigmor
Strontian
Glen Gour
Sgurr nan Cnamh
701
Scotstown
Ardery
Sallachan
Clovullin
Corran
Keppanach
Glenrigh Forest
Anaheilt
Drumnatorran
Garbh Bheinn
885
Beinn Leamhain
502
Corran Narrows
Abhainn Righ
Mam na Gualainn
796
Ranachan
Woodend
Ardnastang
Strontian
Achnalea
Gearradh
Sallachan Point
Onich
A82
North Ballachulish
9
Caolasnacon
Loch Leven
Eilean Mor
Liddesdale
Achleek
7
Glen Tarbert
6
Inversanda
Inversanda Bay
Rubh' a' Bhaid Bheithe
South Ballachulish
3
Ballachulish
Glencoe
Pap of Glencoe
742
Sgorr na Fiannaidh
966
Glen Coe
Glencoe (NTS)
A884
Taobh Dubh
352
Meall a' Choirein Luachraich
Creach Bheinn
853
Glas Bheinn
620
Fuar Bheinn
765
Meall nan Each
591
Maol Odhar
B8043
Kentallen
Lochuisge
Loch Uisge
Beinn Na Cille
651
13
Kilmalieu
Rubha Mor
Cuil Bay
A828
Auchindarroch
Glenduror Forest
Sgorr Dhonuil
1001
Sgorr Dhearg
1024
Beinn a' Bheithir
Gleann an Fhiodh
Sgorr a' Choise
663
Meall Mor
676
1692
Bidean nam Bian
1150
Meall a' Chaorainn
Loch Uisge
Glengalmadale
Am Broilein
Camasnacroise
Loch a' Choire
Eilean Balnagowan
Keil
Duror
Glen Duror
Laroch
Meall an Aodainn
679
Meall Lighiche
772
Sgor na h-Ulaidh
994
Beinn Maol Chaluim
847
Beach
Sgurr Shalachain
Beinn Mheadhoin
739
Dalnatrat
Achvlair
Salachan Glen
Bealach
Fraochaidh
Salachail
Alltachonaich
Ceanna Mor
Sgurr a' Bhuic
569
32
Lurignich
Polanach
Meall Ban
655
Beinn Mhic na Ceisich
Barnamuc
Beinn Fhionnlaidh
959
Beinn a' Chaisil
437
Shuna Island
Sound of Shuna
Appin Ho
North Dallens
APPIN
Elleric
Glenure
Glen Creran
Invercharnan
Glensanda
Portnacroish
Stalker
Kinlochlaich
Tynribbie
Fasnacloich
Loch Baile Mhic Chailein
Glen Ure
Gualachulain
Eilean Loch Oscair
Eilean Ramsay
Ardtur
Strath of Appin
Glasdrum
Invercreran
Taraphocain
Beinn Sgulaird
932
Kinlochetive
Port Ramsay
Port Appin
Inver
Druimavuic
Beinn Trilleachan
839
Ben Starav
1078
Stob an Duine Ruaidh
822
481
An Sleaghach
513
Eignaig
Bachuil
Clachan
Appin Rocks
Airds Bay
Eriska
North Shian
Eilean Dubh
South Creagan
ARGYLL
Creach Bheinn
810
Loch Creran
South Shian
Sea Life Centre
Barcaldine
Lynn of Morven
Lynn of Lorn
Achnacroish
Lismore
B8045
8
Seabank
A828
Achacha
Beinn Bhreac
708
Beinn Molurgainn
690
Allt Easach
Abhainn Dalach
Achadun (ruin)
Baligrundle
Culcharan
Benderloch
Dail
Bernera
Kilcheran
Lorn
Balure
Loch Fiart
Eilean Dubh
Pladda Island
Benderloch
Ledaig
B845
Beinn Mheadhonach
714
Cadderlie
Ardmaddy
Meall an Fheuraich
Inverliver
Glen Kinglass
West Highland Railway
Rubha Garbh-aird
South Ledaig

157
166
158
149
D
E
F
G
I
2
3
4
5
Meall na Teanga 917
935
637
636
Letter Finlay
Altura
Loch Lochy
Glen Gloy
Turret Bridge
Carn Liath 1006
Sherramore
Comra
Kinloch Laggan
Achnasaul
Clunes
Bunarkaig
Invergloy
Leana Mhor 685
Glen Roy
Carn Dearg 834
Leana Mhor
Burn of Agie
Loch Sguadaig
Stob Poite Coire Ardair 1053
Creag Meagaidh 1130
Coille Coire Chrannaig
Aberarder
Loch Laggan
Ardverikie
Coire Ceirsle Hill 654
Beinn Teallach 915
Beinn a'Chaorainn 1050
An Cearcallach 993
A82
A86
B8005
B8004
Rathliesbeag
Stronenaba
Gairlochy
Bohuntine Hill
Bohuntine
Moy Forest
Commando Memorial
Spean Bridge Woollen Mill
Creag Dhubh 658
Bohenie
Binnein Shuas
Creag Pitridh 924
Geal Charn 1049
Brackletter
Spean Bridge
Tirindrish
Inverroy
Roybridge
Murlaggan
Roughburn
Craigbeg
Moy
Lochan na h-Earba
Cruim Leacainn 228
Killiechanate
Braes o' Lochaber
Tulloch Sta
Loch Moy
Tom an Teine 187
GLEN SPEAN
Leanachan Forest
1688
Meall Liath Mor
Ardverikie
Forest
Beinn Chlianaig 721
Nevis Range Ski Development
Aonach Mor Mountain Gondola & Nevis Range Ski Centre
Fersit
Beinn a'Chlachair 1087
An Lairig
Carn Dearg 1034
Sgurr Finnisg-aig 663
Killiechonate Forest
Stob Choire Claurigh 1177
Stob Coire an Laoigh 1115
Stob Ban 977
Stob a'Choire Mheadhoin 1106
Stob Coire Easain 1116
Stob Coire Sgriodain 976
Chno Dearg 1047
Loch Guilbinn
Aonach Beag 1114
Geal Charn 1132
Loch an Sgoir
Ben Alder Forest
Carn Mor Dearg 1223
Aonach Mor 1219
Aonach Beag 1236
Sgurr Choinnich Mor 1095
Ben Nevis 1344
Lairig Leacach
Loch Treig
Beinn Eibhinn 1101
Beinn a'Chumhainn
Ben Alder 1148
Beinn Bheoil 1019
Garbh Bheinn 858
Strath Ossian
Meall a'Bhuirich 840
Beinn na Lap 937
Corrour Shooting Lodge
Loch Ossian
Corrour Forest
Sgor Gaibhre 952
Meall a'Bhealaich
Ben Alder Cottage
Prince Charlie's Cave
Loch Ericht
Stob Aonaich 855
Water of Nevis
Abhainn Rath
Luibeilt
Binnein Beag 940
An Gearanach 982
Sgurr a'Mhaim 1098
Stob Coire a'Chairn 981
Binnein Mor 1128
Na Gruagaichean 1005
Sgurr Eilde Mor 1008
Am Bodach 1032
Sgorr an Iubhair 1001
Loch Eilde Beag
Loch Eilde Mor
Glas Bheinn 789
Corrour Sta
Loch na Sgeallaig
Carn Dearg 939
Rannoch Forest
Ciaran Water
Leum Uilleim 906
Beinn Pharlagain 807
Kinlochmore
Kinlochleven
Meall na Duibhe 570
Allt Eigheach
Lochan Loin nan Donnlaich
Blackwater Reservoir
Black Water
Leven
Garbh Bheinn 867
Meall Dearg 951
The Chancellor
Devil's Staircase
Beinn Bheag
Meall Bhalach 708
Meall nan Ruadhag 646
Black Corries
Stob na Cruaiche 739
PERTH
Rannoch Sta
B846
Bridge of Ericht
Killichonan
Loch Rannoch
Finnart
Camghouran
Bridge of Gaur
Gaur
Loch Eigheach
Gleann Duibhe
Aonach Eagach
The Study
Altnafeadh
Beinn a'Chrulaiste 857
Black Corries Lodge
A Chruach
Loch Laidon
Ossian's Cave
Three Sisters
Pass of Glen Coe
Kingshouse Hotel
Stob Dearg 1022
Stob Dubh 958
Buachaille Etive Beag
Royal Forest
Buachaille Etive Mor
955
Lochan Gainmhich
Rannoch Moor
AND
RANNOCH
Meall a'Bhobuir
Glen Etive
Glencoe (Whitecorries) Chairlift & Ski Area
348
Beinn Mhic Chasgaig 843
Sròn na Creise 1100
Meall a'Bhuiridh 1108
Beinn Chaorach
Lochan na Stainge
Loch Ba
Meall Buidhe 931
Cam Chreag 860
Stob Dubh
Beinn Ceitlein
Clach Leathad 1098
KINROSS
Meall Garbh 701
Aonach Mor
Black Mount
Lochan na h-Achlaise
Abhainn Duibhe
Meall Cruinn
Meall Odhar 876
Stob Ghabhar 1087
Stob a'Choire Odhair 947
Water of Tulla
Eas Daimh
Loch an Daimh
Meall Buidhe 907
Stuchd an Lochain 960
Stob Coir' an Albannaich 1044
Meall nan Eun 926
Meall an Araich
Loch Tulla
Achallader
Beinn a'Chreachain 1081
Beinn Achaladair 1038
Meall Daill
Kenknock
Moar
Loch Dochard
Clashgour
Black Mount
Forest Lodge
Pubil
Cashlie
Lyon
Loch Lyon
Lubreoch
Stronuich Reservoir
Beinn nan Oighreag 909
AND
Beinn Suidhe 675
Inveroran Hotel
Beinn an Dothaidh 901
Beinn Mhanach 953
BUTE
Meall nan Subh 804
Meall Taurnie
Meall Ghaordie 1039
Bridge of Orchy
Beinn Dorain 1074
Beinn Heasgarnich 1076
Sgiath Bhuidhe
Kenknock
Tullich
Beinn Charn 636
Creag Mhor 1032
Glen Lochay
Dunc
Meall Buidhe
Glen Orchy
Beinn Mhic-Mhonaidh
A82
Auch
Beinn a'Chaisteil 883
696
6
27
29
8
3

158
167
157
150
A
B
C
D
1
2
3
4
5
GRAMPIAN
HIGHLAND
MOUNTAINS
PERTH AND KINROSS
Forest of Atholl
TAY FOREST PARK
Garvamore
Sherramore
Crathie
Balgowan
Spey
Phones
Loch Crunachdan
Black Craig 565
Falls of Truim
Etteridge
Garbh Mheall Mor 593
Allt Crunachdain
Druban Beag
Meallach Mor 768
Mor 857
Liath 1006
A86
Comra
Kinloch Laggan
Coille Coire Chrannaig
Loch Laggan
Linn of Pattack
Loch Caoldair
Glen Truim
A889
Loch Cuaich
Allt Cuaich
Meall Chuaich 951
Bogha-cloiche 897
Loch an t-Seilich
Aberarder
Ardverikie
Allt an t-Sluic
Dalwhinnie
A9
Beinn Eilde
Gaick Lodge
Gaick Forest
Lochan na h-Earba
Binnein Shuas
Loch Ericht Forest
Loch Bhrodainn
Allt Gharbh Ghaig
Creag Pitridh 924
Geal Charn 1049
Meall Cruaidh 897
Carn na Caim 941
Ardverikie Forest
Creagan Mor
Meall a'Chaorainn
Cama Choire
Loch an Duin
Beinn a'Chlachair 1087
Allt Cam
Loch Pattack
Ben Alder Lodge
Geal Charn 917
424
A'Bhuidheanach Bheag 936
Sronphadruig Lodge
Dalnamein Forest
An Lairig
Carn Dearg 1034
Ben Alder Forest
An Torc
Glas Mheall Mor 928
Allt Glas Choire
Allt Dearg
Sron a'Chleirich 816
Aonach Beag 1114
Loch an Sgoir
A'Mharconaich 975
Dalnacardoch Forest
Glen Bruar
Bruar Water
Eibhinn 1101
Beinn Udlamain 1010
Sgairneach Mhor 991
Sow of Atholl
Pass of Drumochter
Badnambiast
Ben Alder 1148
Beinn Bheoil 1019
18
Beinn a'Chumhainn
Stob an Aonaich Mhoir 855
An Cearcall
Meall na Leitreach 775
Allt a'Chireachain
Meall a'Bhealaich
Prince Charlie's Cave
Craiganour Forest
Glen Garry
Craig Bhagailteach
Ben Alder Cottage
Loch Ericht
Loch Garry
Loch Con
Sron Choin
Meall a'Chathaidh
Fair Bhuidhe
Falls of the Bruar
Pitagowan
Duinish
Allt Shallainn
Beinn Mholach 841
Allt Sleibh
Calvine
Struan
Loch Forest
Sron a'Chlaonaidh
Talla Bheith Forest
Creag a'Mhadaidh
Loch Errochty
Trinafour
Dalchalloch
10
B847
Allt Ghlas
Allt Ruighe nan Saorach
Errochty Water
Glen Errochty
Sron Bheag
Aulich Burn
Beinn a'Chuallaich 891
Torr Dubh
Craig nan Caisean
Lochan Loin nan Donnlaich
Tressait
Balmore
Dunalastair
B846
B8019
Loch Tummel
Bridge of Ericht
Talladh-a-Bheith
Aulich
20
Killichonan Burn
Killichonan
Loch Rannoch
Kinloch Rannoch
Dunalastair Resr
Tummel Bridge
Foss
Inverhadden
Tempar
Lassintullich
Finnart
Carie
Bridge of Gaur
Camghouran
Rannoch School
Braes of Foss
Gleann Duibhe
Leagag
Schiehallion 1083
Loch Kinardochy
388
Meall Tairneachan 787
Farragon Hill 780
Geal Charn
Allt Camghouran
Allt Mor
Deer Park
14
Strath of Appin
Meall a'Bhobuir
Meall a'Mhuic 745
Meall Garbh 968
Carn Mairg 1042
Weem Hill
Black Wood Mem
Meall Buidhe 931
Beinn Dearg
Carn Gorm 1029
Creag Mhor 981
Menzies
Camserney
Coshieville
Keltneyburn
Dull
Weem
Cam Chreag 860
Meall Cruinn
Invervar
Balintyre
Woodend
Ancient Yew
A827
Bolfracks
Glen Lyon
Innerwick
Camusvrachan
Lyon
Drummond Hill
Fortingall
Stix
Loch an Daimh
Bridge of Balgie
Taymouth
Allt Conait
Kenmore
25
Fearnan
Craig Hill
Urlar Burn
Moar
Gleann Da-Eig
Allt Bail a'Mhuilinn
Meall Luaidhe 780
Meall a'Choire Leith 926
Meall Garbh 1118
Meall Greigh 1001
Gleann Da-ghob
Remony
Kenknock
Acharn
Pubil
Cashlie
Falls of Acharn
Beinn nan Oighreag 909
Stronuich Reservoir
Lairig Breisleich
550
Ben Lawers 1214
Meall Corranaich 1069
Ardradnaig
Loch Tay
Cragganruar
Beinn Bhreac
Creag an Sgliata
Meall nan Subh 804
Meall Ghaordie 1039
Lochan na Lairige
Beinn Ghlas 1013
Ben Lawers (NTS)
Lawers
Quaich
Garrow
Meall Glass
Meall nan Tarmachan 1043
Meall Odhar
Ardtalnaig
Auchnacloich
Meall Taurnie
Sgiath Bhuidhe
Carie
Achann Burn
Tullich
Duncroist
Milton Morenish
Kiltyrie
Gleann a'Chilleine
Kenknock
Tullich Hill
Meall nam Fuaran 805
Glen Lochay
Sron 888
29
12
9
912
4

Mullach Clach a' Bhlair
1019
Glenfeshie Forest
Glen Dee
Sgor Mor
813
Mar Forest
168
Cairn Geldie
623
Feshie
Drochaide
818
617
Inver
Inverg
159
Invercauld Bridge
Braemar
Kindrochit
Bridge of Dee
Allanaquoich
Creag Bhalg
Mar Lodge
(NTS)
Linn of Quoich
Linn of Dee
Dee
Muir
Inverey
Linn of Corriemulzie
Morrone Hill
859
Falls of Garbh Allt
Ballochbuie Forest
Auchallater
Carn Liath
818
Allt Connie
Ey Burn
The Colonel's Bed
Newbigging
A B E R D E E N S H I R E
Glen Ey Forest
Cac Carn Beag
Lochna
1155
Carn an t Sagairt Mor
1047
1110
White
Loch Callater
Glen Callater
Creag nan Gabhar
Cairn Bannoch
1012
Broad Cairn
998
Carn an Fhidhleir (Carn Ealar)
994
An Sgarsoch
1006
Geldie Burn
Carn Bhac
946
920
Glen Ey
Sgor Mor
887
Clunie Water
Baddoch Burn
G L E N C L U N I E
Beinn Bhreac
Falls of Tarf
Allt Garbh Buidhe
Ey Burn
An Socach
944
938
16
Carn an Tuirc
1019
Tolmount
958
Loch Mhairc
Tarf Water
Beinn Iutharn Mhor
1045
Beinn Iutharn Bheag
953
Carn Aosda
917
A93
Cairn of Claise
1064
Tom Buidhe
957
Braigh Sron Ghorm
879
An Sligearnach
786
Carn an Righ
1029
Glenshee Chairlifts & Ski Centre
933
Carn a'Gheoidh
975
The Cairnwell
Devil's Elbow
665
Glas Maol
1068
Caenlochan
Dearg
Carn a'Chlamain
963
Glas Tulaichean
1051
Gleann Mor
Loch Loch
Glen Loch
Creag Leacach
987
Monega Hill
Caenlochan Forest
Finalty Hill
Mayar
928
Beinn a'Chait
899
Forest Lodge
Glen Tilt
Tilt
Carn nan Gabhar
1121
Braigh Coire Chruinn-bhalgain
1069
Glen Lochsie
Gleann Beag
Carn Alt
864
A N G U S
Beinn a'Ghlo
Fender Burn
Meall a'Choire Bhuidhe
868
Ben Gulabin
Dalmunzie Hotel
Carn an Daimh
755
Monamenach
807
H O L L
all Reamhar
565
Carn Liath
975
Ben Earb
801
Spittal of Glenshee
Auchavan
160
Croftmore
Gleann Fearnach
Shee Water
Loch Beanie
Meall Breac
Badandun Hill
Cairn Daunie
Meall Uaine
794
G L E N S H E E
Mealna Letter or Duchray Hill
G L E N I S L A
Glen Finlet
Blair
Loch Moraig
Creag an -t Sithein
Finegand
Bridge of Tilt
B8079
Glen Girnaig
Dalnaglar Castle
Forter
3
Blair Atholl
12
Aldclune
Tarvie
Straloch
13
Lamh Dhearg
Lair
Cray
B951
Folda
Glenisla Forest
Garry
1689
Killiecrankie
Pass of Killiecrankie
Ben Vrackie
841
Dalnacarn
Glen Brerachan
Kindrogan Field Centre
Ennochdhu
Balvarran
Allt Menach
Mount Blair
744
Alrick
Bridge of Brewlands
Hare Cairn
lach Hill
The Soldier's Leap
141
Linn of Tummel (NTS)
Pass of Killiecrankie Visitor Centre
Badyo
Creag Dhubh
A924
Meall Mor
Queen's View Centre
B8019
Craigower
Craigower (NTS)
A924
Kirkmichael
Blacklunans
Kirkton of Glenisla
Falls of Tummel
B8079
Moulin
Pitlochry
Loch Faskally
Port na Craig
B950
Ballinluig
Dalrulzian
Cairn Gibbs
Bellaty
S T R A T H A R D L E
en's View
Cammoch Hill
Loch Broom
Knock of Balmyle
Druim Dearg
inn Eagagach
Hydro-Electric Visitor Centre & Fish Ladder
Edradour Distillery
Knockton
20
Dunfallandy Stone
5
Meall Reamhar
Balmyle
Forest of Alyth
13
Alyth Burn
Lochbroom Burn
Tummel
Ballintuim
Creag nam Mial
561
Loch erculich
Milton of Dalcapon
Persie House
Drumderg
4
Bridge of Craigisla
Strathtay
Pitnacree
Ballechin
S T R A T H T A Y
Grandtully
A827
Ballinluig
Tulliemet
A924
Ashmore
Edradynate
Little Ballinluig
Balnaguard
Logierait
Blackcraig Hill
12
Balduff Hill
Tullymurdoch
Tay
Forest of Clunie
Netherton
Bamff
Grandtully
B898
A9
Loch Ordie
Loch Benachally
Ardle
Bridge of Cally
Rochallie
10
Balnaguard Burn
Bishopric
Balmacneil
Blackcraig Forest
Hill of Alyth
Aberfeldy
Kindallachan
Guay
Benachally
A93
Tullyfergus
Alyth
Gatehouse
Grandtully Hill
Kincraigie
Dowally
Deuchary Hill
Buckny Burn
Cochrage Muir
Lornty Burn
Loch Skiach
Elrick More
Riechip
Arlick
Middleton
New Alyth
A826
Meall Reamhar
Dalguise
Craigvinean Forest
8
Butterstone
12
Achalader
Lornty
Parkhill
A926
Loch na Craige
9
Loch Kennard
Craig a Barns
A923
Loch of Butterstone
Forneth
Loch of Clunie
A923
Kinloch
Rattray
Blairgowrie
5
Monadh nam Mial
Dalmarnock
Creag an Eunaich
Loch of Craiglush
Concraigie
Craigie
Rosemount
Ericht
Balintoan Burn
Dunkeld
Loch of Lowes
Clunie
Loch of Drumellie
Muirton of Ardblair
A923
Loch Hoil
Scotston
Druim Mor
Tombane Burn
The Hermitage (NTS)
Little Dunkeld
Newtyle Hill
Kirkton of Lethendy
B947
Lunan Burn
Stormont Loch
Meall Dearg
690
Glen Cochill
Inver
Birnam
A94
Loch Fender
Ballinlick
Dunkeld & Birnam Sta
Thornton
Spittalfield
A984
Trochry
A984
Delvine
A984
Coupar Angus
8
Birnam Hill
Stenton
Caputh
11
Aldville
A822
Drumour
A9
151
Meikleour
Marketh
A826
Milton
S T R A T H B R A A N
Gellyburn
Tay
Isla
Keithick
A923
Kett
aig Hulich
A822
Ardoch
Kinclaven
A93
A94
Campmuir
Amulree
Braan
Creag Liath
Obney Hills
Muir of Thorn
B9099
Woodside
Burrelton
Findowie Hill
Upper Obney
Laguna
Cargill
Achnafauld
Meall nan
Creag na Criche

160
169
159
152
A
B
C
D
1
2
3
4
5
Braemar
Kindrochit
Bridge of Dee
Inver
Balmoral
Clachanturn
Birkhall
Aucholzie
The Coyles of Muick
Creag nan Gall
601
Cairn Leuchan
669
Red Craig
640
Yell
Craigmahandle
Ballochan
Carnferg
Linn of Muick Cottage
Falls of Garbh Allt
Ballochbuie Forest
Balmoral Forest
Inchnabobart
Conachcraig
Glen Muick
Cac Carn Beag
Lochnagar
1155
Carn a' Coire Bhoidheach
1110
Carn an t-Sagairt Mor
1047
Creag nan Gabhar
Callater
White Mounth
Dubh Loch
Loch Muick
Spittal of Glenmuick
Fasheilach
721
Mount Keen
939
Braid Cairn
887
Hill of Saughs
Cock Cairn
727
Hill of Cat
742
White Hill
Cock Hill
Mudlee Bracks
688
Glen Tennet
Water of Tarf
Cairn Bannoch
1012
Broad Cairn
998
Carn an Tuirc
1019
Tolmount
958
Black Hill of Mark
774
Glen Mark
Water of Lee
Glen Lee
Easter Balloch
Water of Mark
Burn of Branny
Monawee
Glenlee
Auchronie
Tarfside
Mid Cairncross
Loch Lee
Inchgrundle
Glen Effock
GLEN ESK
Cairn of Claise
1064
Tom Buidhe
957
Lair of Aldararie
832
W. of Unich
Craig Mellon
Glendoll Lodge
Glen Doll
White Water
Caenlochan
Braedownie
Glas Maol
1068
Monega
Caenlochan Forest
Creag Leacach
987
Finalty Hill
Mayar
928
Driesh
947
Hill of Strone
850
Green Hill
870
Loch Brandy
Muckle Cairn
Ben Tirran
896
Loch Wharral
Cruys
741
West Knock
691
Hill of Wirren
678
Bulg
607
White Hill
778
Clova
GLEN CLOVA
B955
Hunt Hill
734
Cairn Baddoch
Cairn of Barns
651
Mount Bouie
585
Wheen
Rottal
The Drums
Finbracks
Dog Hillock
722
Hill of Glansie
726
Water of Saughs
Hill of Berran
Hill of Formal
Burn of Calletar
Monamenach
807
Auchavan
Mid Hill
ANGUS
Hill of Garbet
Peat Hill
Bridgend
Tillyarblet
Badandun Hill
Cairn Daunie
GLEN PROSEN
Runtaleave
Glen Logie
Balnaboth
Glenprosen Village
Clachnabrain
Auld Darkney
Glen Ogil
Cruick Water
Paphrie Burn
Hill of Menmuir
Eskielawn
Corwharn
Hill of Couternach
Glenarm
Glenmoy
Naked Tam
Pinderachy
Auchnacree
Tullo Hill
Kirkton of Menmuir
Glen Finlet
Glen Damff
GLEN ISLA
Folda
B951
Mount Blair
744
Glenisla Forest
Tomnun
Glen Uig
Redheugh
Glenogil
Mains of Balhall
Balnamoon
Alrick
Bridge of Brewlands
Hare Cairn
Glenhead Farm
Easter Lednathie
Prosen Water
Benscravie
Horniehaugh
Falls of Drumly Harry
Deuchar Hill
Fern
Meall Mor
Backwater Resr
Cat Law
678
Tulloch Hill
Glenquiech
Ogil
Newmill of Inshewan
Noranside
Blacklunans
Kirkton of Glenisla
Dykehead
Pearsie
Cortachy
Memus
Careston
Noran Water
Bellaty
Cairn Gibbs
Druim Dearg
Creigh Hill
Carity Burn
Balloch
Inverquharity
Tannadice
Knockton
Dykends
Mile Hill
Ascreavie
Shielhill
Murthill
Finavon
Doocot (Dovecot)
Marcus
Oathlaw
Forest of Alyth
Melgam Water
Loch of Lintrathen
B951
Kinnordy
Northmuir
B957
Parkford
Hill of Finavon
Aberlemno
Sculptured Stones
Bridge of Craigisla
Bridgend of Lintrathen
Kirkton of Kingoldrum
Kirriemuir
Barrie's House (NTS)
A90
Pitkennedy
Reekie Linn
Isla
Baldovie
Westmuir
Southmuir
Mosside of Ballinshoe
Turin Hill
Turin
Balduff Hill
Kirkton of Airlie
A926
A928
Lunanhead
B9134
Rescobie
Tullymurdoch
Bamff
PERTH AND KINROSS
B954
Lindertis
Logie
Padanaram
Restenneth Priory
Reswallie
Rescobie Loch
Hill of Alyth
Shanzie
Craigton
Mains of Ballindarg
Forfar
Loch of Forfar
Meffan Institute
Burnside
Balmadies
A93
Tullyfergus
Alyth
Leys of Cossans
Eassie Sculptured Stone
Drumgley
St Orland's Stone
A932
Kingsmuir
B9128
Dunnichen
Letham
New Alyth
Jordanstone
Ruthven
Dean Water
Glamis
Angus Folk Museum
A94
Douglastown
Caldhame
Lownie Moor
Idvies
Balhary
Balendoch
Kinnettles
Craichie
Parkhill
A926
Castleton
Glamis
Thornton
Kirkton
Wester Foffarty
B9127
Lour
Fothringham Hill
Tulloes
Blairgowrie
Rattray
Sculptured Stones
Charleston
Kincaldrum
Inverarity
Whigstreet
Lochlair
Leitfie
Kinloch
Meigle
Balkeerie
Eassie and Nevay
Kirkinch
Milton
Ogilvy
Gateside
Kirkbuddo
Greystone
Rosemount
Ericht
Arthurstone
Ark Hill
Nether Handwick
Glen Ogilvy
Hayhillock
B9127
A923
Ardler
Newbigging
Newtyle
Kinpurney Hill
Gallow Hill
Gallowfauld
Carrot
Crombie
Stormont Loch
A984
A94
Auchtertyre
Keillor
Auchterhouse Hill
Craigowl Hill
455
A928
Carrot Hill
B978
Greenburn
Coupar Angus
Keithick
Markethill
A923
Kettins
Bonnyton
Kirkton of Auchterhouse
Kirkton of Tealing
Balgray
Todhills
Affleck
Newton of Affleck
Kirkton of Monikie
A94
Campmuir
Thriepley
Dovecot & Earth House
Newbigging
Monikie
Craigton
Woodside
Burrelton
Pitcur
Lundie
B954
Leoch
Kirkton of Strathmartine
East March
Bucklerheads
Drumsturdy
Newbigging
Upper Victoria
A92

161
170
153
A B E R D E E N S H I R E
Stonehaven
Laurencekirk
Inverbervie
Montrose
Brechin
Arbroath
Finzean
Baulds
Blackhall Forest
Scolty
Auchattie
Blackness
Strachan
Invery Ho.
Crossroads
Durris Forest
Upper Burnhaugh
Netherley
Cammachmore
Drumhead
Bridge of Bogendreip
Greendams
Water of Feugh
Blairydry
Darnford
Cairn-mon-earn
Westerton
Borrowfield
Craiggie
Meikle Carewe Hill
Cookney
Muchalls
Bridge of Muchalls
Newbigging
Union Croft
Doonie Point
Castle Rock of Muchalls
Mongour
Mergie
Rickarton
Mowtie
New Mains of Ury
Cowie
Garron Point
Craig of Dalfro
Peter Hill
Kerloch
Fetteresso Forest
Burn of Sheeoch
Hill of Trusta
Cowie Water
Redcloak
Strathlethan Bay
Glendye Lodge
Clachnaben
Hill of Edendocher
Water of Aven
Water of Dye
Bridge of Dye
Tipperweir
Hill of Hobseat
Leachie Hill
Tewel
Kirktown of Fetteresso
Castle Haven
Dunnottar
Carron Water
Carmont
Brae of Glenbervie
Tannachie
Newmill
Glen Dye
Hill of Fingray
Meluncart
Goyle Hill
Water of Charr
Cairn o' Mount
Tipperty
Mains of Dillavaird
Thornyhive Bay
Chapelton
Trelung Ness
Herscha Hill
Glenbervie
Drumlithie
Bruxie Hill
Midtown of Barras
Mill of Uras
Crawton
Crawton Bay
Nether Pitforthie
Hound Hillock
Strath Finella
Finella Forest
Drumtochty
Sturdy Hill
Clatterin Brig
Glensaugh
Strathfinella Hill
Auchenblae
Bervie Water
Fawsyde
Catterline
Braidon Bay
Todhead Point
North Esk
Fasque House
Thainston
East Cairnbeg
Fordoun
Parkneuk
Roadside of Kinneff
Slains Park
Phesdo
Arbuthnott House
Arbuthnott
Allardice
Kinneff
Auchmull
Fettercairn
the Mearns
Scotston
Burn Farm
The Burn
Thornyhill
Howe of the Mearns
Dalbog
Mains of Thornton
Easter Tulloch
Bervie Bay
Meikle Strath
Gannochy
Inch of Arnhall
Garvock
Redford
Knox Hill
Gourdon
Edzell
Arnhall
Sauchieburn
Luther Water
Johnston Mains
Benholm
Dunlappie
Luthermuir
Dykelands
Feus of Caldhame
Inglismaldie Forest
Brown Caterthun (fort)
White Caterthun (fort)
Johnshaven
Gallery
Marykirk
Kirktonhill
Ecclesgreig
Inchbare
Stracathro
Pert
Logie Pert
Craigo
Lochside
St Cyrus
Milton Ness
Newtonmill
Belliehill
Keithock
Muirton of Ballochy
Morphie
Logie
Pathhead
Templewood
Little Brechin
Trinity
Hillside
Dun's Dish
House of Dun (NTS)
Kirkhill
Dun
Tayock
Round Tower
Arrat
Bridge of Dun
Caledonian Rly
Montrose Basin
Montrose Museum & Art Gallery
Scurdie Ness
Middle Drums
Melgund
Barnhead
Inchbraoch
Ferryden
Farnell
Bonnyton
Maryton
Kirkton of Craig
Carcary
Rossie Moor
Fishtown of Usan
Montreathmont Moor
Westerton
Long Craig
Wuddy Law
Boddin Point
Rossie Farm School
Bolshan
Dubton
Braehead of Lunan
Lunan
Glasterlaw
Red Castle
Lunan Bay
Guthrie
Friockheim
Kinnell
Redcastle
Pitmuies
Boysack
Lunan Water
Inverkeilor
Middleton
Chapelton
Lang Craig
Inchock
Cauldcots
Red Head
Leysmill
Ethie Mains
Kinblethmont
Drunkendub
Parkhill
Colliston
Auchmithie
Redford
Marywell
Meg's Craig
Denhead of Arbirlot
St Vigeans
Carlingheugh Bay
Guynd
The Deil's Heid
Elliot Water
Arbirlot
Abbey
Bonnyton
Easter Knox
Wormiehills
Salmond's Muir
East Haven
3.2 miles to 1 inch
10 miles
10 km
2 km to 1 cm

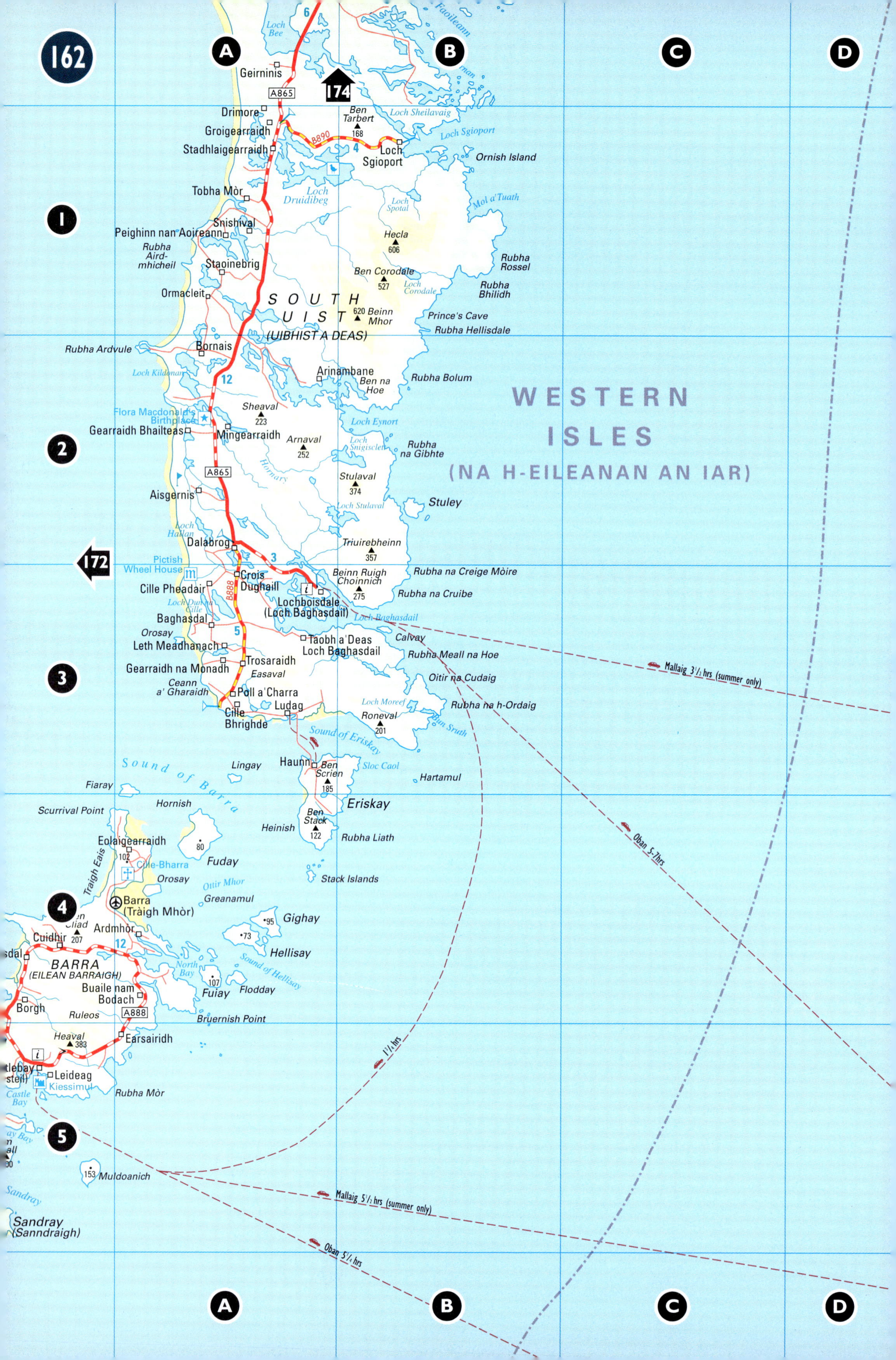

A
B
C
D
1
2
3
4
5
174
172
Loch Bee
Faoileann
Geirninis
A865
Drimore
Groigearraidh
Stadhlaigearraidh
Ben Tarbert
168
Loch Sheilavaig
B890
Loch Sgioport
Loch Sgioport
Ornish Island
Tobha Mòr
Loch Druidibeg
Loch Spotal
Mol a' Tuath
Snishival
Peighinn nan Aoireann
Rubha Aird-mhicheil
Hecla
606
Staoinebrig
Ben Corodale
527
Loch Corodale
Rubha Rossel
Rubha Bhilidh
Ormacleit
SOUTH UIST
(UIBHIST A DEAS)
620 Beinn Mhor
Prince's Cave
Rubha Hellisdale
Rubha Ardvule
Bornais
Loch Kildonan
12
Arinambane
Ben na Hoe
Rubha Bolum
WESTERN ISLES
(NA H-EILEANAN AN IAR)
Flora Macdonald's Birthplace
Sheaval
223
Gearraidh Bhailteas
Mingearraidh
Loch Eynort
Arnaval
252
Loch Smigiscleit
Rubha na Gibhte
A865
Hornary
Stulaval
374
Aisgernis
Loch Stulaval
Stuley
Loch Hallan
Dalabrog
Triuirebheinn
357
3
Pictish Wheel House
Beinn Ruigh Choinnich
275
Rubha na Creige Mòire
Cille Pheadair
Crois Dughaill
B888
Lochboisdale (Loch Baghasdail)
Rubha na Cruibe
Loch Dun na Cille
Baghasdal
Loch Baghasdail
Orosay
5
Taobh a'Deas Loch Baghasdail
Calvay
Leth Meadhanach
Rubha Meall na Hoe
Gearraidh na Monadh
Trosaraidh
Easaval
Mallaig 3½ hrs (summer only)
Oitir na Cudaig
Ceann a' Gharaidh
Poll a'Charra
Loch Moreef
Rubha na h-Ordaig
Cille Bhrighde
Ludag
Roneval
201
Bun Sruth
Sound of Eriskay
Sound of Barra
Lingay
Haunn
Ben Scrien
185
Sloc Caol
Hartamul
Fiaray
Eriskay
Hornish
Scurrival Point
Ben Stack
122
Heinish
Rubha Liath
Eolaigearraidh
102
80
Traigh Eais
Cille-Bharra
Fuday
Oban 5-7hrs
Orosay
Stack Islands
Oitir Mhor
Barra (Tràigh Mhòr)
Greanamul
Gighay
95
Ben Cliad
207
Ardmhòr
73
Cuidhir
12
Hellisay
North Bay
Sound of Hellisay
BARRA
(EILEAN BARRAIGH)
107
Buaile nam Bodach
Fuiay
Flodday
Borgh
Ruleos
A888
Bruernish Point
Heaval
383
Earsairidh
1½ hrs
Leideag
Kiessimul
Castle Bay
Rubha Mòr
153
Muldoanich
Mallaig 5½ hrs (summer only)
Sandray
Sandray
(Sanndraigh)
Oban 5½ hrs

Ramasaig Bay
Ramasaig
The Hoe
233
Lorgill
468
Healabhal Bheag (Macleod's Table South)
488
Orbost
Roag
Vatten
Harlosh
Balmore
Loch Varkasaig
Harlosh Point
175
Ose
Glen
Beinn na Cloiche
232
Loch Connan
Ben Connan
244
Beinn na Boineid
371
Ben Idrigill
340
Harlosh Island
Tarner Island
A863
Dun Beag
Bracadale
Ullinish
Struan
Coillore
B885
Allt Mor
Ben Duagrich
304
Loch Duagrich
Mugeary
Glenmore
S K Y E
An Dubh Sgeir
MacLeod's Maidens
Idrigill Point
Loch Bracadale
Wiay
Oronsay
Ardtreck Point
A863
Beinn Totaig
7
Portnalong
Loch Harport
Fernilea
Rubha nan Clach
Broc-b
Arnaval
369
Carbost
6
Drynoch
A863
B8009
Gleann Oraid
Talisker
Talisker Bay
Talisker
Stockval
416
Beinn Bhreac
370
Glen D
Biod Mor
383
Beinn Bhreac
445
Eynort
Beinn a'Bhraghad
461
Cuillin
M i n g i n i s h
Loch Eynort
Beinn Staic
411
879
Sgurr a'Ghreadaidh
An Cruachan
435
Brittle
965
Sgurr Dearg (Inaccessible Pinnacle)
986
Glenbrittle
Bualintur
Sgurr Alasdair
Beinn an Eoin
312
Culnamean
164
Rubha Thearna Sgurr
Loch Brittle
Ceann na Beinne
Rubh' an Dunain
Soay Sound
Soay
I N N E R   H E B R I D E S
S E A   O F   T H E   H E B R I D E S
H I G H L A N D
C U I L L I N   S O U N D
CANNA
Carn a'Ghaill
210
Compass Hill
140
Camas Tharbernish
Canna (NTS)
A'Chill
Garrisdale Point
Canna Harbour
Sron Ruail
Tarbert Bay
Sanday
Rubha Shamhnan Insir
Sound of Canna
Kilmory
Kilmory
Sgaorishal
278
Mullach Mor
304
Rubha na Roinne
Humla
Bloodstone Hill
388
A'Bhrideanach
National Nature Reserve
Kinloch
Kinloch
Orval
571
Sgor Reidh
R U M
Barkeval
591
An Dornabac
263
Bagh na h-Uamha
Harris
Hallival
723
Askival
812
Garbh Sgeir
Oigh-sgeir
Rubha Sgor an t-Snidhe
Ruinsival
528
Ainshval
781
Sgurr nan Gillean
764
Rubha nam Meirleach
S O U N D   O F   R
Rubha an Fhasaidh
154
D
E
F
G
1
2
3
4
5
9

164
176
163
155
A
B
C
D
1
2
3
4
5
Portree
Raasay
SOUND
INNER
Applecross
Milton
Camusteel
Camusterrach
Culduie
Sron na h-Airde Baine
Toscaig
Uags
Crowlin Islands
Eilean Meadhonach
Eilean Mor
Caolas Mor
Beinn na Greine
417
Am Maol
212
Loch Connan
Glenmore
Mugeary
Stroc-bheinn
400
Penifiler
Ben Tianavaig
413
Balachuirn
385
Dun Caan
443
Rubha na' Leac
Camastianavaig
Holoman Bay
Oskaig Point
Oskaig
Clachan
Inverarish
Beinn na'Leac
319
Lower Ollach
Upper Ollach
The Braes
Narrows of Raasay
Suisnish Point
East Suisnish
Ben Lee
445
Peinchorran
Loch Sligachan
Sconser
A87
B883
Bracadale
Coillore
Ben Duagrich
304
Loch Duagrich
A863
Beinn Totaig
Roineval
439
Meall an Fhuarain
Broc-bheinn
Glen Varragill
Loch Harport
Fernilea
Carbost
Drynoch
B8009
Glen Drynoch
Sligachan
Glamaig
775
Meall a' Mhaoil
284
Kyle More
Rubh' an Lochain
Scalpay
Mullach na Carn
396
Longay
Camas na Fisteodh
Pabay
Kyle of Lochalsh
Kyle Akin
Kyleakin
Caolas Scalpay
Loch Ainort
Luib
Dunan
Beinn Bhreac
370
Allt Dearg Mor
Glen Sligachan
Biod Mor
383
SKYE
Eynort
Beinn a'Bhraghad
461
Cuillin Hills
Am Basteir
935
Sgurr nan Gillean
965
Bruach na Frithe
958
Beinn Dearg
Marsco
736
Glas Bheinn Mhor
570
Strath Mor
Belig
Beinn Dearg Mhor
709
Beinn na Caillich
732
Broadford Bay
Broadford
Corry
Lower Breakish
Upper Breakish
Harrapool
Skulamus
A851
Cnoc Glac na Luachrach
Glen Arroch
Beinn Staic
411
Sgurr Thuilm
879
Sgurr a'Mhadaidh
918
Harta Corrie
Sgurr a'Ghreadaidh
973
Sgurr na Banachdich
965
An Cruachan
435
Sgurr Dearg (Inaccessible Pinnacle)
986
Sgurr Mhic Choinnich
948
Glenbrittle
Brittle
Bualintur
Culnamean
Sgurr Alasdair
993
Sgurr Dubh Mor
944
Sgurr nan Eag
924
Gars-bheinn
895
Loch Coruisk
Druim Hain
Garbh-bheinn
806
Bla Bheinn (Blaven)
928
Loch na Creitheach
Sgurr na Stri
497
Strathaird
Camasunary
Torrin
Kilbride
Loch Cill Chriosd
Strath Suardal
B8083
Ben Suardal
283
Beinn nan Carn
301
Heast
Beinn Bhuidhe
277
Loch Slapin
Ceann na Beinne
Loch Brittle
Camas Fhionnairigh
Loch na Cuilce
Kilmarie
Kirkibost
Ben Meabost
346
Drinan
Elgol
Prince Charles's Cave
Spar Cave
Glasnakille
Rubha na h-Easgainne
Rubh' an Dunain
Leac nam Faoileann
Soay Sound
Beinn Bhreac
141
Soay
Mol-chlach
Camas nan Gall
Loch Scavaig
Rubha Suisnish
Loch Eishort
Eilean Heast
Drumfearn
Sgorach Breac
299
Ord
Duisdealmor
Eilean Iarmain (Isleornsay)
Isle Ornsay
Ardnameacan
Dunsgaith
Tokavaig
Camus Croise
Beinn na Seamraig
561
Beinn Bhreac
436
Loch na Dal
CUILLIN SOUND
Tarskavaig Bay
Tarskavaig
Sgurr na h-Iolaire
292
Achnacloich
Loch nam Uamh
Teangue
Knock
Knock Bay
Kilmore
SLEAT
Sgurr Breac
249
Kilbeg
Loch a' Ghlinne
Inver Dalavil
Gleann Meadhonach
Clan Donald Centre
Armadale Bay
Armadale
Ardvasar
Sgurr nan Caorach
280
Calligarry
Geur Rubha
Aird of Sleat
Ard Thurinish
Point of Sleat
SOUND OF SLEAT
Rubh Ard Slisneach
Inverguseran
Airor
Druim na Roinn na Beinne
Sandaig
441
Sandaig Bay
Rubha Raonuill
Lochboisdale 3½ hrs (summer only)
Rubha na Roinne
Mullach Mor
304
Kilmory
Kinloch
National Nature Reserve
RUM
Barkeval
591
Hallival
723
Askival
812
Ainshval
781
Sgurr nan Gillean
764
Bagh na h-Uamha
SOUND OF RUM
Rubha nam Meirleach
Mallaigvaig
Mallaigmore
Mallaig
Glasnacardoch
Sgurr an Eilein Ghiubhais
522
Carn a'Ghobhair
547
Sgurr Bhuidhe
440
A830
Morar
Loch an Nostarie
Loch a'Ghille Ghobaich
Bracora
Bracorina
Eilean a'Phidhir
Portnaluchaig
Back of Keppoch
Eilean Ighe
Carn a'Mhadaidh-ruaidh
503
Lettermorar
Loch a'Cho Riabhaich
ARISAIG
Arisaig
Loch nan Ceall
Rhumach
Luinga Mhor
Morroch
Glen Beasdale
Castlebay 5¼ hrs (summer only)
Rubha an Fhasaidh
Bay of Laig
Laig
Cleadale
An Cruachan
299
315
EIGG
Kildonnan

165
D
E
F
G
177
166
156
I
2
3
4
5
A890
A896
A87
Sgurr a' Chaorachain
Meall Gorm
710
792
Russel
Coultrie
a Gharaidh
730
Achintee
Strathcarron Sta
Beinn Tharsuinn
863
West Monar Forest
Loch an Laoigh
Sgurr a' Chaorachain
Sheasgaich
945
Lurg Mhor
986
Loch Monar
Ardarroch
Lochcarron
An Sgurr
392
Achintraid
Loch Kishorn
Sgeir Fhada
Loch Carron
Attadale
Carn Geuradainn
594
Uisage Dubh
An Gead Loch
Loch Calavie
Loch an Tachdaidh
Beinn Bheag
619
Mealian Buidhe
555
Beinn Dronaig
Attadale Forest
Airigh-drishaig
Bad a' Chreamha
395
Stromemore
Ardnarff
Carn nan Iomairean
485
Loch an Iasaich
Ling
Carn na Sean Luibe
582
Loch Cruoshie
An Cruachan
706
An bhachan
1129
L. Reraig
Ardaneaskan
Strome (NTS)
Stromeferry
Achmore
Strath Ascaig
Glen Ling
Plockton
Bagh an t-Srathaidh
Loch Lundie
Beinn Raimh
447
Loch Achaidh na h-Inich
Gleann Udalain
Aonach Buidhe
899
An Socach
1069
Faochaig
868
Drumbuie
Duirinish
Sallachy
Ben Killilan
753
Sguman Coinntich
879
Killilan
Killilan Forest
Loch Mhoicean
Erbusaig
Allt-na-subh
Badicaul
Auchtertyre Hill
452
Loch Long
Conchra
Camus-luinie
Coille-righ
Glen Elchaig
Carnach
Gleann Sithidh
Beinn Fhionnlaidh
1005
Coire Lochan
Balmacara Estate (NTS)
Kirkton
Ardelve
Bundalloch
Elchaig
Loch na Leitreach
Falls of Glomach (NTS)
Mullach na Dheiragain
982
Carn Eighe
1183
Mam Sodhail
Balmacara
Nostie
Dornie
Loch nan Eun
Caisteal Maol
Loch Alsh
Eilean Donan
Glas Eilean
Boc Mor
631
Gleann a' Choilich
na Beiste
Beinn na Caillich
Ardintoul Point
Ardintoul
Letterfearn
Keppoch
Coire Dhuinnid
Beinn Bhuide
Sgurr nan Ceathreamhnan
1151
An Socach
920
A' Ghlas-bheinn
918
Loch Duich
Sgurr an Airgid
841
Dorusduain
Loch Gaorsaic
Sgurr na Coinnich
739
Kyle Rhea
Glas Bheinn
394
Beinn a' Chuirn
603
Inverinate
Lienassie
Loch a' Bhealaich
Alltbeithe
Kylerhea
Bernera
Galltair
Ault a' chruinn
Morvich
Beinn Fhada or Ben Attow
1032
(NTS)
Gleann Gniomhaidh
Affric
Glenelg Bay
Bernera Barracks
Scallasaig
Glen More
339
Invershiel
Sgurr na Moraich
876
Kintail Forest
H
L
A
N
D
Glenelg
Beinn a' Chaoinich
408
Shiel Bridge
Eilanreach
Port a' Gharaidh
Glenelg Brochs
Sgurr Mhic Bharraich
781
Croe
Ciste Dhubh
982
Mullach Fraoch-choire
1102
Balvraid
Sgurr a' Ghaorachain
Sgurr Fhuaran
1068
Five Sisters
Glen Shiel
Gleann Beag
a' Gharg Gharaidh
681
Sgurr na Ciste Duibhe
1027
Saileag
959
Sgurr a' Bhealaich Dheirg
1038
Sail Chaorainn
A' Chralaig
1120
Beinn a' Chapuill
742
Meall Buidhe
486
Glenshiel
1719
Aonach Meadhoin
1003
Beinn Aoidhdailean
633
Sandaig Islands
Sandaig
Beinn Mhialairigh
548
Beinn Sgritheall
981
Beinn nan Caorach
773
Spidean Dhomhuill Bhric
940
The Saddle
1010
Sgurr na Sgine
945
Creag nan Damh
918
Sgurr an Lochain
1004
Sgurr an Doire Leathain
1010
Cluanie Forest
Glen Cluanie
Lundie
Loch Cluanie
Beinn Clachach
617
Arnisdale
Loch Hourn
Glen Arnisdale
Corran
Druim Fada
614
713
Buidhe Bheinn
879
Maol Chinn-dearg
981
Aonach air Chrith
1021
Druim Shionnach
987
Creag a' Mhaim
947
Druim nan Cnamh
Na Cruachan
583
Beinn na Caillich
785
Kinloch Hourn
Sgurr a' Mhaoraich
1027
GLEN
Loyne
Gleann na Guiserein
Barrisdale Bay
Carn Mairi
502
Meall nan Eun
666
Sgurr Sgiath Airigh
881
Glen Quoich
Gleouraich
1035
Spidean Mialach
996
Glenquoich Forest
Druim na h-Achla
540
Ladhar Bheinn
1020
Barrisdale
Glen Barrisdale
Slat Bheinn
701
Sgurr a' Chlaidheimh
Loch Fearna
Aonach Sgoilte
849
Sgurr a' Choire-bheithe
913
Gleann Cosaidh
Druim Chosaidh
Loch Quoich
Coille Mhorgil
Tomdoun
Knoydart
Sgurr Coire na Coinnich
796
Luinne Bheinn
939
Beinn Bheag
329
Aultvoulin
Inverie
Inverie Bay
Gleann Meadail
Loch an Dubh Lochain
Meall Buidhe
946
Gairich
919
Glen Kingie
Kingie
Glas Bheinn
656
Allt Choire a' Bhalachain
A' Chruach
395
Sgurr Coire nan Gobhar
739
Ben Aden
885
Sgurr Mor
1003
Sgurr an Fhuarain
LOCHABER
Beinn Bhuidhe
865
Camusrory
Sgurr na Ciche
1040
1013
Sgurr nan Coireachan
953
Kinbreack
Lochan Dubh
Meall a' Bhlair
656
Loch Nevis
Garbh Chioch Mhor
Druim a' Chuirn
817
Sgurr Mhurlagain
880
Loch a' Bhlair
Fraoch Bheinn
866
Kylesknoydart
Upper Glendessarry
Sgurr na h-Aide
859
Glen Dessarry
Kylesmorar
Sgurr Breac
728
Beinn Chra
616
Tarbet
Glendessary
Murlaggan
NORTH MORAR
Monadh Gorm
470
Strathan
Loch Arkaig
Ardach
Swordland
Kinlochmorar
Carn Mor
829
Glen Pean
Kinlocharkaig
Loch Morar
Pean
Mullach Choire nan Geur-oirean
727
Locheil Forest
Inver Mallie
Druim a' Chuirn
An Stac
718
Sgurr nan Coireachan
956
Sgurr Thuilm
963
Gulvain
987
Glen Mallie
SOUTH MORAR
Meoble
Beinn na Cabar
574
Meith Bheinn
710
Sgurr an Ursainn
817
Braigh nan Uamhachan
765
Streap
909
Stob
962
Meall a' Phubuill
Druim Gleann Laoigh
Beinn Bhan

A
B
C
D
178
West Forest
East Monar Forest
Loch Monar
Lurg Mhor 986
An Gead Loch
Loch an Tachdaidh
Beinn Bheag 619
Allt Riabhachain
Meallan Buidhe 555
Meallan Odhar
Uisge Misgeach
Inchvuilt
Ardchuilk
Glen Strathfarrar
Loch a' Mhuillidh
Sgor na Diollaid
Loch Beannacharan
Eiteige 882
Fhuar-thuill 1049
Sgurr a'Choire Ghlais 1083
Sgurr na Muice 891
992
Sgurr na Ruaidhe 993
Beinn a'Bha'ach Ard 862
Carn Ban 736
Culligran
Culligran Falls
Farrar
Struy
Erchless Castle
A831
Eskadale
Mauld
Struy Forest
Crelevan
Carn a' Mhuilt 662
Carn Gorm 676
Glassburn
Carnoch
Loch Neaty
Strathglass
Carn nam Bad 457
Balmore
Glass
8
A831
Cannich
Muchrachd
Liatrie
Loch Carrie
Meallan Odhar 694
Creag Dubh
Glencannich Forest
Carn nan Gobhar 992
Sgurr na Lapaich 1150
An Riabhachan 1129
Braigh a'Choire Bhig 1011
Loch Cruoshie
An Cruachan 706
I
An Socach 1069
Loch Mhoicean
Loch Mullardoch
Fasnakyle Forest
Millness
Buntait
Grange
Chambered Cairn
Mony's Stone
Corrimony
Bearnock
Balnain
12
Glen
Lochan an Tairt
Glen Cannich
Beinn Fhionnlaidh 1005
Coire Lochan
Toll Creagach 1054
Doire Tana
Tom a'Choinich 1111
Gleann Sithidh
Mullach na Dheiragain
Carn Eighe 1183
Mam Sodhail 1180
Gleann nam Fiadh
Gleann a'Choilich
2
Sgurr na Lapaich 1036
An Socach 920
Beinn a'Mheadhoin 611
Loch Beinn a'Mheadhoin
Fasnakyle
Affric
Knockfin
Tomich
Enrick
Beinn Mhor 401
Abhainn Deabhag
Suidhe Ghuirmain 578
Glenurquhart Forest
Loch Meiklie
Balmacaan Forest
Coiltie
Plodda Falls
Guisachan Forest
Glen Affric
Loch Affric
Creag nan Caiman 661
Cougie
Meall a'Chrathaich
Loch nam Meur
Loch nam Breac Dearga
Loch ma Stac
Loch nan Eun
Loch a'Chrathaich
Alltbeithe
165
Affric
Allt Garbh
Aonach Shasuinn 889
Carn a' Choire Bhuidhe 847
Allt Riabhach
Carn a'Chaochain 706
Loch na Beinne Baine
Carn Mhic an Toisich 680
Allt Bhlaraidh
Levishie Forest
Levishie
Ciste Dhubh 982
Mullach Fraoch-choire 1102
Doe
Meallan Odhar 611
Meall Cuileig 443
Dundreggan Forest
A887
Invermoriston
A82
Sail Chaorainn 1002
Beinn an t-Sidhein 508
Allt na Muic
Dundreggan
16
Portclair Forest
3
A'Chralaig 1120
Sgurr nan Conbhairean 1110
Ceannacroc Forest
HIGH
Burach 607
6
Carn Ghluasaid 957
Carn nam Feuaich 732
Torgyle
Dalchreichart
Inverwick Forest
Tomchrasky
Moriston
Glen Moriston
Loch Ness
22
Lundie
A87
A887
Roderick Mackenzie's Memorial
Allt Phocachain
Inchnacardoch Hotel
Great Glen Exhibition Centre
Beinn a'Bhacaidh
393
Loch Tarff
Glen Cluanie
Loch Cluanie
Bunloinn Forest
Bun Loyne
Ceann a'Mhaim 671
Carn Mhic Raonuill 568
Fort Augustus
Abbey
Visitors Cen
Glendoebeg
Druim Shionnach 987
Creag a'Mhaim 947
Druim nan Cnamh
Beinn Loinne
Beinneun Forest
Meall Dubh 788
Oich
Caledonian Canal
Glen Doe
Lochan na Stairne
Glen Loyne
Loyne
Mullach Coire Ardachaidh 539
A82
7
Newtown
Glen Tarff
Glendoe Forest
Spidean Mialach 996
4
Glenquoich Forest
Loch Loyne
Druim na h-Achlaise 540
Cnocan Dubh 342
Loch a'Bhainne
Loch Lundie
Munerigie
Aberchalder
Carn a'Chuilinn 816
A87
14
Coille Mhorgil
Tomdoun
Inchlaggan
Loch Garry
Invergarry
Greenfield
Mandally
Beinn Bheag 329
Glen Garry
Invergarry
Corrieyairack Hill 896
Glengarry Forest
Laggan Swing Bridge
Kingie
Glas Bheinn 656
Allt Choir a'Bhalachain
Loch Oich
Culachy Forest
Corrieyairack Pass
Carn Leac 884
Ben Tee 901
Laggan
Carn Dearg 816
Corrieyairack Forest
Meall Tarsuinn 660
Allt a'Choire Ghlais
Kilfinnan
5
Sgurr Choinich 747
Meall Coire nan Saobhaidh 821
Geal Charn 803
Sron a'Choire Ghairbh 935
A82
Leacann Doire Bainneir 637
Turret
16
Glen Albyn
Meall na Teanga 917
Beinn Chraoibh 616
Leckroy
Roy
Glas Bheinn
Gleann Cia-Aig
Turret Bridge
Loch Lochy
636
Glen Gloy
Loch Arkaig
Ardachvie
Letter Finlay
Beinn Iaruinn
Achnasaul
Altura
157
Stob Poite Coire Ardair 1053
Locheil Forest
Clunes
Carn Dearg 834
Burn of Agie
Inver Mallie
Glen Mallie
A
Bunarkaig
B8005
Invergloy
B
Leana Mhor 685
Glen Roy
Leana Mhor
C
Loch Squadaig
Creag Meagaidh
D
Coire Ceirsle Hill
Beinn Bhan
Beinn Teallach 915
An Cearcallach
A82
Bohuntine

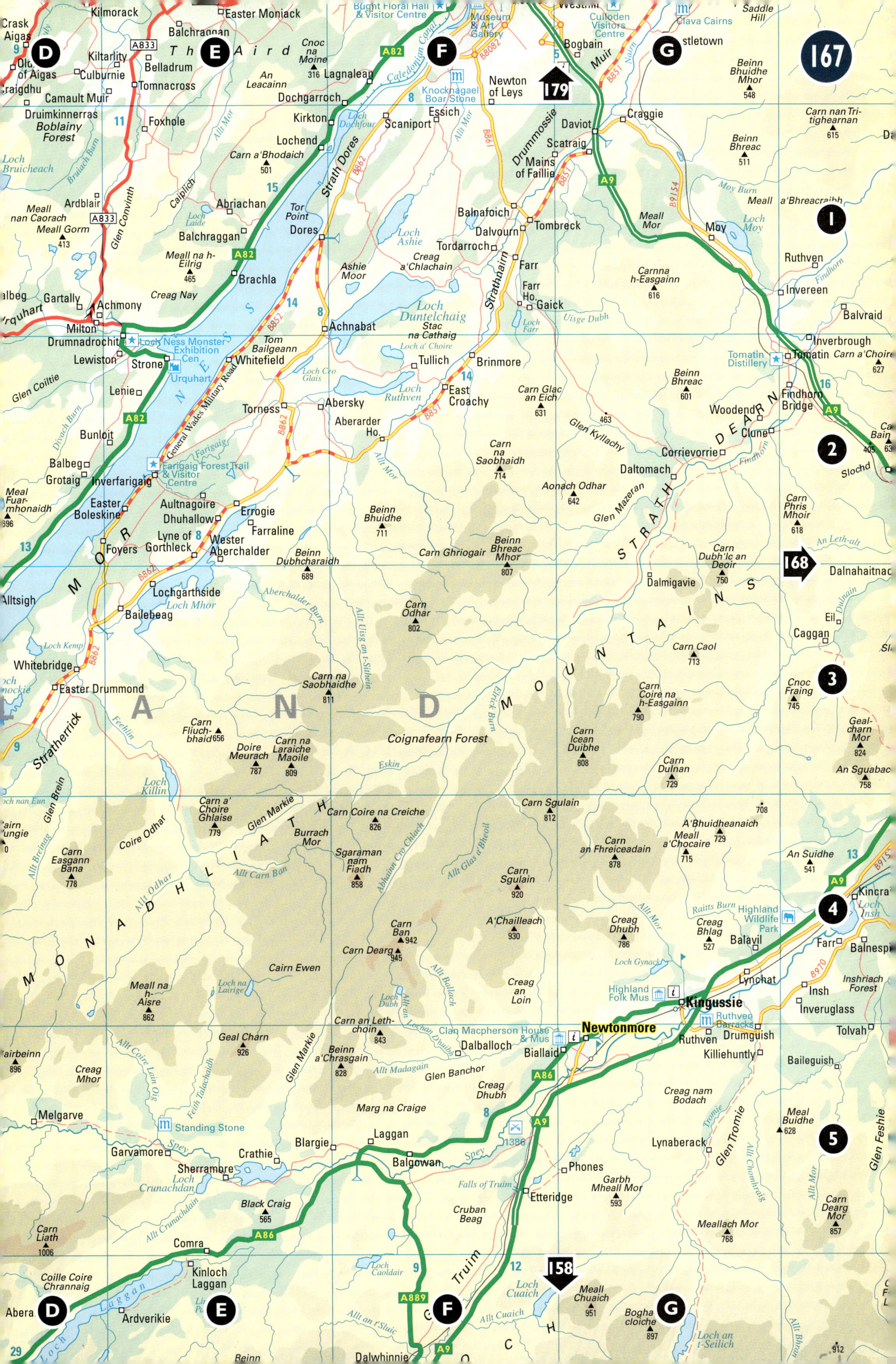

167
179
168
158
D
E
F
G
I
2
3
4
5
Kilmorack
Easter Moniack
Crask Aigas
Balchraggan
A833
The Aird
Cnoc na Moine 316
Lagnalean
A82
Caledonian Canal
Bught Floral Hall & Visitor Centre
Museum & Art Gallery
B8082
Culloden Visitors Centre
Clava Cairns
Saddle Hill
Old of Aigas
Kiltarlity
Culburnie
Belladrum
Tomnacross
An Leacainn
Dochgarroch
Knocknagael Boar Stone
Newton of Leys
Bogbain
Muir
B851
Nairn
stletown
Beinn Bhuidhe Mhor 548
Craigdhu
Camault Muir
Druimkinnerras
Boblainy Forest
Foxhole
Kirkton
Loch Dochfour
Scaniport
Essich
Allt Mor
B861
Drummossie
Daviot
Craggie
Carn nan Tri-tighearnan 615
Lochend
Carn a'Bhodaich 501
Strath Dores
B862
Scatraig
Mains of Faillie
A9
Beinn Bhreac 511
Loch Bruicheach
Bruiach Burn
Allt Mor
Caiplich
Abriachan
Tor Point
Dores
Loch Laide
Loch Ashie
Balnafoich
Tombreck
Dalvourn
B9154
Moy Burn
Meall a'Bhreacraibh
Meall Mor
Moy
Loch Moy
Meall nan Caorach
Ardblair
A833
Glen Convinth
Meall Gorm 413
Balchraggan
Meall na h-Eilrig 465
Brachla
Tordarroch
Creag a'Chlachain
Ashie Moor
Strathnairn
Farr
Farr Ho.
Gaick
Ruthven
Carnna h-Easgainn 616
Invereen
Findhorn
Creag Nay
Gartally
Achmony
Urquhart
Milton
Drumnadrochit
Loch Ness Monster Exhibition Cen.
Lewiston
Strone
Urquhart
Tom Baigeann
Whitefield
Achnabat
Loch Duntelchaig
Stac na Cathaig
Loch a' Choire
Loch Farr
Uisge Dubh
Balvraid
Inverbrough
Tomatin Distillery
Tomatin
Carn a'Choire 627
Glen Coiltie
Lenie
Loch Ceo Glais
Tullich
Brinmore
Beinn Bhreac 601
Loch Ruthven
East Croachy
Carn Glac an Eich 631
Findhorn Bridge
Woodend
Clune
Divach Burn
Bunloit
Torness
Abersky
Aberarder Ho.
B851
Glen Kyllachy
463
Corrievorrie
Balbeg
Grotaig
Inverfarigaig
Farigaig
Farigaig Forest Trail & Visitor Centre
General Wades Military Road
Allt Mor
Carn na Saobhaidh 714
Daltomach
Aonach Odhar 642
Glen Mazeran
Slochd
Meal Fuar-mhonaidh 696
Easter Boleskine
Aultnagoire
Dhuhallow
Errogie
Farraline
Beinn Bhuidhe 711
Carn Phris Mhoir 618
An Leth-allt
Lyne of Gorthleck
Western Aberchalder
Foyers
Beinn Dubhcharaidh 689
Carn Ghriogair
Beinn Bhreac Mhor 807
Carn Dubh'Ic an Deoir 750
Dalnahaitnac
Dalmigavie
Alltsigh
Lochgarthside
Loch Mhor
Aberchalder Burn
Bailebeag
Carn Odhar 802
Allt Uisg an t-Sithein
Caggan
Eil
Loch Kemp
Carn Caol 713
Whitebridge
B862
Easter Drummond
Carn na Saobhaidhe 811
Elrick Burn
Carn Coire na h-Easgainn 790
Cnoc Fraing 745
Stratherrick
Feehlin
Carn Fliuch-bhaid 656
Doire Meurach 787
Carn na Laraiche Maoile 809
Coignafearn Forest
Carn Icean Duibhe 808
Geal-charn Mor 824
Eskin
Loch Killin
Carn Dulnan 729
An Sguabac 758
Glen Brein
Carn a' Choire Ghlaise 779
Glen Markie
Carn Coire na Creiche 826
Carn Sgulain 812
708
A'Bhuidheanaich 729
Meall a'Chocaire 715
Burrach Mor
Coire Odhar
Carn Easgann Bana 778
Allt Breinag
Allt Carn Ban
Sgaraman nam Fiadh 858
Abhainn Cro Chlach
Allt Glas a'Bheoil
Carn an Fhreiceadain 878
Carn Sgulain 920
An Suidhe 541
Kincraig
Loch Insh
Raitts Burn
Highland Wildlife Park
Allt Odhar
A'Chailleach 930
Creag Dhubh 786
Creag Bhlag 527
Balavil
Farr
Balnespick
Carn Ban 942
Carn Dearg 945
Allt Mor
Loch Gynack
B970
Cairn Ewen
Meall na h-Aisre 862
Loch na Lairige
Allt Ballach
Creag an Loin
Highland Folk Mus
Kingussie
Lynchat
Insh
Inshriach Forest
Inveruglass
Carn an Leth-choin 843
Loch Dubh
Allt an Lochain Duibh
Clan Macpherson House & Mus
Newtonmore
Ruthven Barracks
Ruthven
Drumguish
Tolvah
Geal Charn 926
Beinn a'Chrasgain 828
Dalballoch
Allt Madagain
Glen Banchor
Biallaid
Killiehuntly
Baileguish
Creag Mhor
Allt Coire Lain Oig
Feith Talachaidh
Glen Markie
A86
Creag Dhubh
Creag nam Bodach
Meal Buidhe 628
Glen Feshie
Glen Tromie
Allt Chomhraig
Melgarve
Standing Stone
Marg na Craige
Garvamore
Spey
Crathie
Blargie
Laggan
1386
Lynaberack
Sherramore
Loch Crunachdan
Balgowan
Spey
Phones
Garbh Mheall Mor 593
Allt Mor
Carn Dearg Mor 857
Falls of Truim
Etteridge
Black Craig 565
Allt Crunachdain
Cruban Beag
Meallach Mor 768
Carn Liath 1006
A86
Comra
Coille Coire Chrannaig
Kinloch Laggan
Loch Caoldair
Truim
Loch Cuaich
Meall Chuaich 951
Bogha cloiche 897
Abera
Loch Laggan
Ardverikie
A889
Allt an t-Sluic
Allt Cuaich
Loch an t-Seilich
Allt Bhran
912
Beinn
Dalwhinnie
A9

A
B
C
D
180
167
159
Clava Cairns
Saddle Hill
Castleton
Carn a'Chrasgie
401
Carn Sgumain
Carnoch
Dulsie
Milltown
Banchor
Cairn Duhie
A939
A940
Knock of Braemoray
456
Aitnoch
Hill of Aitnoch
Carn Kitty
521
Sliabh Bainneach
483
Larig Hill
545
Carn Shalag
Paul's Hill
Roy's Hill
516
Glen Gheallaidh
548
Carn nan Tri-tighearnan
615
Daless
Streens
Carn na Sguabaich
466
Rhilean Burn
Leonach Burn
Lochindorb
Dava
Dava Moor
Carn Ruighe an Uain
546
Glen Tulchan
Carne na Loine
549
Gallow Hill
374
Beinn Bhreac
511
B9154
Moy Burn
Meall a'Bhreacraibh
Loch Moy
B9007
Tomlachlan Burn
Carn Ruigh Charrach
Old Military Road
Carn Bad na Caorach
477
Toremore
Advie
Ruthven
Invereen
Findhorn
Carn an t-Sean-liathanaich
635
Anaboard
Auchnagallin
Knock of Auchnahannet
334
Upper Derraid
Lettoch
Duiar
B9102
Glaschoil
Camerory
Cottartown
Creag Liath
Grant
Tomvaich
Dellefure
Charn a'Ghille Chear
710
Balvraid
Inverbrough
Tomatin Distillery
Tomatin
Carn a'Choire Mhoir
627
Carn Glas-choire
659
Beinn Mhor
Glenbeg
A939
A95
Cromdale
Carn Eachie
1690
Beinn Bhreac
601
Findhorn Bridge
A9
Woodend
Clune
Achnahannet
Grantown-on-Spey
Tullochgribban High
Dulnain Bridge
Gaich
Speybridge
Congash
Haughs of Cromdale
Hills of Cromdale
Carn nam-Bain Tighearna
634
405
Slochd
Mor
A938
Duthil
Duthil Burn
Skye of Curr
Speyside Heather Centre
A939
Lynemore
Creagan a'Chaise
722
Carn Tuairneir
693
Bogroy
Carrbridge
Landmark Visitor Centre & Sculpture Park
B970
Carn na Loinne
459
Sgor Gaoithe
628
Dirdhu
Bridge of Brown
Burn of Lochy
Carn Phris Mhoir
618
Sluggan
An Leth-allt
B9153
Drumuillie
A95
Cullachie
Nethy Bridge
Sliemore
A939
Carn Dubh'lc an Deoir
750
Dalnahaitnach
Boat of Garten
Loch Garten
Lettoch
Baddoch
Lainchoil
Tom an t-suidhe Mhor
Glen Brown
Beinn Ghuilbin
Kinveachy
Loch Vaa
Dell Lodge
Carn Meadhon
Eil
Caggan
Avielochan
Tore Hill
Abernethy Forest
Carn Caol
713
Carn Sleamhuinn
677
Allt Lorgy
Loch Mallachie
Aundorach
Braes of Abernethy
Dorback Burn
Carn Tuadhan
607
Carn na Farraidh
688
Auchgourish
Strathspey Rly
Cnoc Fraing
745
Carn Dearg Mor
712
Granish
Loch Pityoulish
Sluggan Pass
Tulloch
Carn na h-Ailig
Craigowrie
686
Geal Charn
821
Geal-charn Mor
824
Craigellachie
B9152
Aviemore
Aviemore Centre
The Queen's Forest
Meall a'Bhuachaille
810
Carn Bheadhair
803
HIGHLAND
An Sguabach
758
Coylumbridge
GLENMORE
Reindeer House
FOREST
PARK
Glenmore Lodge
An Lurg
753
Doune
Inverdruie
Polchar
Luineag
Loch Morlich
Glen More
Lairig Pass
708
A'Bhuidheanaich
729
Meall Chocaire
715
Alvie
Loch Alvie
Kinrara
Visitor Centre & Forest Trail
Castle (ruins)
Rothiemurchus
Mam Suim
Carn na Feannaige
Burn of Loin
An Suidhe
541
13
B9152
Loch Gamhna
Loch an Eilein
Castle Hill
Bynack More
1090
Water of Ailnack
GLEN AVON
The Bruach
714
Kincraig
Loch Insh
Highland Wildlife Park
Creag Bhlag
527
A9
Feshiebridge
Creag Dhubh
848
Gleann Einich
Carn Eilrig
Cairngorm Chairlift & Ski Centre
Garbh Allt
Forest of Glenavon
Balavil
Farr
Balnespick
Cairn Gorm
1245
Loch Avon
Beinn Mheadhoin
1182
Beinn a'Chaorainn
1082
Stob an t-Sluichd
Leabaidh an Daimh Bhuidhe
1171
Ben Avon
B970
Lynchat
Inshriach Forest
CAIRNGORM MOUNTAINS
Lairig Ghru
Shelter Stone
Kingussie
Insh
Inveruglass
Allt Ruadh
Pools of Dee
Loch Etchachan
North Top
1197
Ruthven Barracks
Ruthven
Drumguish
Sgoran Dubh Mor
1111
Braeriach
1296
Ben Macdui
1309
Beinn a'Bhuird
Carn Eas
1089
Tolvah
Sgor Gaoith
1118
Loch Einich
Cairngorms Nature Reserve
Derry Cairngorm
1155
Dubh Ghleann
South Top
1179
Killiehuntly
Baileguish
Achlean
Carn Ban Mor
1052
Cairn Toul
1291
Glen Derry
Beinn Bhreac
931
Meall Buidhe
628
Glen Feshie
Meall Dubhag
998
The Devil's Point
1004
Carn a'Mhaim
1037
Carn Crom
890
Glen Quoich
Monadh Mor
1113
Eidart
Derry Burn
Carn na Drochaide
818
Allt Chomhraig
Mullach Clach a'Bhlair
1019
Beinn Bhrotain
1157
Glen Dee
Sgor Mor
813
Mar Forest
Lui Water
Glen Lui
Quoich Water
Carn Dearg Mor
857
Creag Bhlag
Linn of Quoich
Allanaquoich
Meallach Mor
768
Glenfeshie Forest
GRAMPIAN
Mar Lodge
(NTS)
Linn of Dee
Dee
Muir
Inverey
Linn of Corriemulzie
Morrone Hill
859
Auchallater
Carn an Fhidhleir
Feshie
Carn Liath
818
Allt Connie
Ey Burn
The Colonel's Bed
Newbigging
Loch an t-Seilich
912
Allt Bhran
1
2
3
4
5

MORAY
ABERDEENSHIRE
CAIRNGORMS
Glenlivet
Aberlour (Charlestown of Aberlour)
Dufftown
Huntly
Upper Knockando
Knockando
Cardow
Archiestown
Carron
Spey
Daugh of Kinermony
Milltown of Edinvillie
Sheandow
Tullich
Parkmore
Balvenie
Glenfiddich Distillery
Milltown of Auchindoun
Aultnapaddock
Braehead
Daugh of Carron
Marypark
Glenfarclas Distillery
Bellehiglash
Baby's Hill
Beatshach
Meikle Conval
Ben Rinnes
Glen Rinnes
Mortlach Church
Auchindoun
Keithmore
Bakebare
Haugh of Glass
Dumeath
Beldorney
Backside
Succoth
Drumdelgie
Daugh of Cairnborrow
Milton of Cairnborrow
Torry
Cairnargat
Clashmach Hill
Bailiesward
Muckle Long Hill
Bridgend
Tillathrowie
Coynachie
Kirkstile
Culdrain
Bridge of Avon
Craigroy Farm
Dalchirach
Cairnacay
Favillar
Achnastank
Laggan
Brigehaugh
Glen Fiddich
The Scalp
Glacks of Balloch Pass
Ballochford
Carn Chrom
Laird's Seat
Tomnaven
Clashindarroch Forest
Cransmill Hill
Quarry Hill
Kirkney
Gartly
Clashindarroch
Newnoth
Cults
Craggan
Tervieside
Drumin
Hill of Achmore
Glen Fiddich Forest
Bridgend
Inverharroch
Ardwell
Black Hill
Glenlivet Distillery & Visitor Centre
Shenval
Glenlivet
Auchbreck
Carn a' Bhodaich
Corryhabbie Hill
Cook's Cairn
Meikle Firbriggs
Auchmair
Mount of Haddoch
Tap o' Noth
Kennethmont
Milton of Noth
Bruntland
Belhinnie
Rhynie
Towie
Cottown
Carn Liath
Cairn Muldonich
Tomnavoulin
Carn an t-Suidhe
Glen Suie
Round Hill
Aldunie
Aldivalloch
Cabrach
Elrick
Longlands
Wheedlemont
Craik
Craig
St Mary's Kirk
Blackwater Forest
Distillery
Carn Daimh
Knockandhu
Cairn Ellick
Cairnbrallan
Bracklach
The Buck
Mire of Midgates
Hill of Three Stones
Round Hill
Clova
Lumsden
Correen Hills
Glenconglass
Clashnoir
Braes of Glenlivet
Geal Charn
Letterach
Sand Hill
Mount Meddin
Hill of John's Cairn
Brux Hill
Tepersie Castle
Chapeltown
Creag an Fumn
Peat Hill
Edinbanchory
Lord Arthur's Cairn
Tullyness
Tomintoul
Findron
Lagganvoulin
Breac Leathad
Carn Mor
Ladder Hills
Badenyon
Dulax
Mossat
Kildrummy
Moss Hill
Rinmore
Glencuie
Kildrummy Castle Gardens
Delphorrie
Milltown
Coiliochbhar Hill
Bridge of Alford
Auchintoul
Badnafrave
Blairnamarrow
Monadh Fergie
Carn Liath
Water of Nochty
Ladylea Hill
Torrancroy
Kirkton of Glenbuchat
Glenbuchat
Mains of Glenbuchat
The Socach
Lecht Ski Centre
Torbain
Beinn a' Chruinnich
Carn Ealasaid
Breagach Hill
Bellabeg
Forbestown
Strathdon
Glenkindie
Fichlie
Sinnahard
Hillockhead
Towie
Milltown of Towie
Craig Veann
Cairn Vachich
Geal Charn
Glen Ernan
Waterside
Heughhead
Tornashean Forest
Boultenstone Hotel
Scar Hill
Milton of Cushnie
Leochel-Cushnie
Frosty Hill
Craig of Bunzeach
Bogston
Badernonach Hill
Broom Hill
Pressendye
Cock Bridge
Corgarff
Colnabaichin
Tornahaish
Fleuchats
Hillockhead
Allt Tuileach
Inchrory
Tillypronie
East Davoch
Bogfields
Bogfern
Oldmill
Carn Leac Saighdeir
Cairn Mona Gowan
Migvie
Melgum
Douneside
Craiglich
Coynach
Brown Cow Hill
Carn a' Bhacain
Deskry Water
Morven
Logie Coldstone
Corrachree
Tarland
Culsh Earth House
Milton of Auchinhove
Loch Builg
Glen Fenzie
Leys
Tomnaverie Stone Circle
Coull
Mortlich
Davan
Ordie
Scar Hill
Daldownie
Gairnshiel Lodge
Dalfad
Lary
Peter's Hill
Culblean Hill
Loch Davan
Loch Kinord
Cromar
Heugh-head
Culardoch
Braenaloin
Rinloan
Torbeg
Candacraig
Cambus o' May
Dinnet
Aboyne
Carn Liath
Duchrie Burn
Geallaig Hill
Culsh
Bridge of Gairn
Milton of Tullich
Muir of Dinnet
Oldhall
Birsemore
Glascorrie
Deecastle
Bridge o' Ess
Forest of Glentanar
Bush Crathie
Balmoral
Crathie
Greystone
Strathgirnock
Ballater
Ballaterach
Glen Tanar
Cauld Forest
Meall Gorm
Easter Balmoral
Clachanturn
Birkhall
Pannanich Hill
Black Craig
Bridge of Muick
The Fungle Road
Carnferg
Forest of Birse
Inver
Invergelder
Invercauld Bridge
Braemar
Kindrochit
Bridge of Dee
Creag nan Gall
Cairn Leuchan
Clachan
Yell
Red Craig
Craigmahandle
Aucholzie
The Coyles of Muick
Ballochan
Falls of Garbh Allt
Ballochbuie Forest
Linn of Muick
Muick Cottage
Cock Cairn
White Hill
Balmoral Forest
Inchnabobart
Mount Keen
Braid Cairn
Hill of Cat
Cock Hill
Cac Carn Beag
Lochnagar
Conachcraig
Glen Muick
Fasheilach
Hill of Saughs
Mudlee Bracks
A941
A95
B9102
B9009
B9008
A920
A96
A97
B9002
A944
A939
B9119
A93
B976
B9094
B9119
181
170
160
D
E
F
G
I
2
3
4
5

170
182
169
161
A
B
C
D
1
2
3
4
5
Huntly
Milton
Cairnborrow
Cairnargat
Clashmach Hill
Strathbogie
Mosshead
Brideswell
Slioch
Beggshill
Denend
Thomastown
Millburn
Ythanwells
Logie Newton
Bainshole
Glens of Foudland
Skares
Hill of Foudland
Kirkton of Culsalmond
Colpy
Largie
Wrangham
The Bin
Bin Forest
Cobairdy
Corse of Kinnoir
Cruchie
Lessendrum
Drumblade
Frendraught
Conland
Drumblair
Feith-hill
Auchamie
Denmoss
Nether Lenshie
Dykeside
Towie Barclay
Kirktown of Auchterless
Inverythan
Macterry
Gourdas
Darnabo
North Millbrex
Lethenty
Monkshill
Tifty
Cottown
Backhill
Fyvie Castle (NTS)
Fyvie
Woodhead
Badenscoth
Gordonstown
Rothiebrisbane
Rothienorman
Fisherford
Hill of Tillymorgan
Redhill
Blackford
Petty
Greenmyre
Crofts of Haddo
Collynie
St Katherines
Cromblet
Springleys
Barthol Chapel
Hillbrae
South Flobbets
The Banking
Silvermoss
Core Hill
Folla Rule
Cross of Jackson
Newseat
South Blackbog
Balgove
Tulloch
Jackston
Meikle Wartle
Tocher
Cairnhill
Bonnyton
Kirkton of Rayne
Pitinnan
Formartine
Mounie Castle
Glengarioch Distillery
Whitefield
Fingask
Oldmeldrum
Hill of Barra
Mill of Kingoodie
Kirkton of Bourtie
Hattoncrook
Daviot
Mains of Glack
Loanhead Stone Circle
Durno
Whiteford
Pitcaple
Milton of Inveramsay
Maiden Stone
Chapel of Garioch
Balhalgardy
Inverurie
Hillbrae
Newmill
Nether Crimond
Easter Aquorthies Stone Circle
Port Elphinstone
Kinmuck
Balbithan
Denmill
Pittodrie Ho.
Mither Tap
Garioch
Old Rayne
Ardoyne
Westhall
Oyne
Archaeolink Prehistory Park
Insch
Greenhall
Picardy Stone
Aulton
Glanderston
Leith Hall (NTS)
Slack
Wardhouse
Cults
Kirkney
Gartly
Culdrain
Backburn
Winds Eye
Wishach Hill
Knockandy Hill
Kirkstile
Clashindarroch Forest
Quarry Hill
Clashindarroch
Newnoth
Kirkney Water
Tap o' North
Kennethmont
Milton of Noth
Rhynie
Cottown
Towie
Clatt
Ardlair
Duncanston
Hill of Christ's Kirk
New Leslie
Old Leslie
Leslie
Kirkton
Auchleven
Gadie Burn
Mire of Midgates
Suie Hill
Knock Saul
Millburn
Old Military Road
Muckletown
Whitehaugh Forest
Black Hill
Bennachie
Glenton
Redhouse
Correen Hills
Brux Hill
Tepersie Castle
Lumsden
St Mary's Kirk
Craig
Craik
Bellabeg
Mossat
Lord Arthur's Cairn
Tullynessle
ABERDEENSHIRE
Millstone Hill
Woodend
Keig
Rorandle
Cairn William
Pitfichie
Bankhead
Montgarrie
Grampian Transport Mus.
Haughton House
Bridge of Alford
Alford
Howe of Alford
Auchintoul
Delphorrie
Milltown
Coiliochbhar Hill
Asloun
Dorsell
Kingsford
Gateside
Whitehouse
Pitmunie
Monymusk
Todlachie
Pitfichie Forest
Kirkton
Tillyfourie
Little Ley
Ardgowse
Tillycairn Castle
Ordhead
Sauchen
Fraser (NTS)
Bograxie
Kemnay Forest
Burnhervie
Overton
Grantlodge
Fetternear Ho.
Thainstone House
Dalmadilly
Clovenstone
Kinkell Church
Balbithan
Tavelty
Kintore
Kemnay
Cottown
Wester Fintray
Hatton of Fintray
Denhead
Craigearn
Leschangie
Lauchintilly
Leylodge
Kinellar
Tyrebagger Hill
Blackburn
Burnside
Blackchambers
Clinterty
Achath
Lyne of Skene
Dunecht
East Auchronie
Kirkton of Skene
Westhill
Elrick
Loch of Skene
Old Kinnernie
Lyne
Mains of Linton
Barmekin Hill
Echt
Garlogie
Cairnie
Lapidary Workshops
Redhill
Wester Ord
Easter Ord
Benthoul
Contlaw
South Kirkton
Landerberry
Midmar Forest
The Birks
Milton of Cullerlie
Cullerlie Stone Circle
Hardgate
Craigton
Milltimber
Fichlie
Sinnahard
Milltown of Towie
Hillockhead
Scar Hill
Milton of Cushnie
Leochel-Cushnie
Ley
Bridgeton
Muir of Fowlis
Muirhead
Craigievar (NTS)
Kintocher
Tillyfour
Correnie Moor
Correnie Forest
Benaquhallie
Shiels
Corsindae
Bankhead
Comers
Tillybirloch
Tom Burn
Broom Hill
Pressendye
East Davoch
Bogfields
Bogfern
Oldmill
Collmuir
Craiglich
Tullochvenus
Glenshalg
Melgum
Douneside
Craskins
Perkhill
Wartle
Tornaveen
Drumlasie
Auchorrie
Cromar
Tarland
Culsh Earth House
Milton of Auchinhove
Lumphanan
Cairnbeathie
Peel Ring
East Learney
Hill of Fare
Leys
Tomnaverie Stone Circle
Coull
Mortlich
Tarland Burn
Craigmyle Ho.
Torphins
Beltie Burn
Milton of Campfield
Raemoir Ho.
Scar Hill
Mid Beltie
Hirn
Glashmore
Drum (NTS)
Peterculter
Mains of Drum
Heugh-head
Rosehill
Kincardine O'Neil
Glassel
Kennerty
Brathens
East Mains
Upper Lochton
Crathes (NTS)
The Neuk
Myrebird
West Park
Drumoak
Crathes
Craiglug
Aboyne
Oldhall
Birsemore
Dee
Water of Tanar
Bridge o'Ess
Forest of Glentanar
Birse
Balfour
Ballogie
Allancreich
Potarch
Cordach
Tillydrine
Bridge of Canny
Backhill of Trustach
Inchmarlo
Maryhill
Banchory
Bridge of Dee
Auchattie
Bridge of Feugh
Kirkton of Durris
Upper Muirskie
Denside
Glen Tanar
The Fungle Road
Carnferg
Glencat
Lamahip
Finzean
Bauls
Tom's Cairn
Hill of Goauch
Blackhall Forest
Scolty
Invery Ho.
Crossroads
Durris Forest
Upper Burnhaugh
Borrowfield
Forest of Birse
Drumhead
Percie
Whitestone
Blackness
Strachan
Blairydryne
Darnford
Cairn-mon-earn
Craiggiecat
Meikle Carewe Hill
Newbigging
Water of Feugh
Bridge of Bogendreip
Westerton
Yell
Craigmahandle
Ballochan
Greendams
Craig of Dalfro
Mongour
Union Croft
Mergie
Rickarton
Mowtie
Mount Battock
White Hill
Peter Hill
Cock Hill
Water of Aven
Hill of Cat
Mudlee Bracks
Hill of Edendocher
Clachnaben
Glendye Lodge
Water of Dye
Bridge
Kerloch
Tipperweir
Fetteresso Forest
Burn of Sheeoch
Hill of Hobseat
Hill of Trusta
Tewel
Redcloak
A96
A97
A920
A941
A944
A980
A93
A947
A957
B9002
B9001
B992
B9005
B9170
B993
B9119
B977
B9125
B976
B974
B9077
B994
B979
B9126
B990

D
E
F
G
1
2
3
4
5
183
Moss of Belnagoak
Nethermuir
Clola
Little Dens
Burnhaven
Invernettie
Sandford Bay
Knaven
Kinnadie
Nether Kinmundy
Blackhill
Stirling
Sandfordhill
Skelmuir
Newton
Cairnorrie
South Upper Barrack
Mill of Elrick
Skelmuir Hill
Kinknockie
Smallburn
Moss of Cruden
Monteach
Hill of Skilmafilly
Aldie
Gask
Murdoch Head
Skelmonae
Inkhorn
Upper Hawkhillock
Ardallie
Teuchan
Loanhead
Greenheads
North Haven
Quilquox
Milton of Coldwells
Hill of Dudwick
Muirtack
Auchiries
Bullers of Buchan
Methlick
Drumwhindle
Hatton
Errollston
Cruden Bay
Arthrath
Mains of Dudwick
Waterloo
Chapel Hill
Slains (ruins)
Tanglandford
Blindburn
Port Erroll
Haddo House (NTS)
Craigie Brae
Bearnie
Toll of Birness
Bogbrae
Bay of Cruden
Inverebrie
Hilton Croft
Kiplaw Croft
The Skares
Whinnyfold
Vedderlairs
Cookston
Raxton
Broomfield
Leask
The Veshels
Artrochie
Kinharrachie
Ellon
Auchmacoy
Meikle Loch
Clochtow
Ythsie
Ythan
Esslemont
Kirkton of Logie Buchan
Kirktown of Slains
Collieston
St Catherine's Dub
Tolquhon
Pitmedden (NTS)
Bronie Burn
Cairnhill
Meikle Tarty
Waterside
Forvie Ness or Hackley Head
Pitmedden
Tipperty
Sands of Forvie
Udny Green
Old Craig
Tarty Burn
Kincraig
Newburgh
Newburgh Bar
Udny Station
Foveran Burn
Foveran House
Pettymuick
Cultercullen
Tillycorthie
Minnes
Blairythan Cottage
Affleck
Drums
Tillygreig
Tillery
Delfrigs
Menie Ho.
Whitlam
Beauty Hill
Causeyend
Newmachar
Craigie
Orrok Ho.
Blackbraes
Whitecairns
Belhelvie
Balmedie
Longdrum
Middleton of Potterton
Millden
Cothall
Potterton
Skelly Rock
Corby Loch
Blackdog
Overton
Dyce Symbol Stones
Blackdog Rock
Mundurno
North Tarbothill
Dyce
Aberdeen
ABERDEEN
Cloverhill
Stoneywood
Middleton Park
Aberdeen Exhibition & Conference Centre
Craibstone
Danestone
Bankhead
Woodside
Bridge of Don
Bucksburn
St Machar's Cathedral
Northfield
Old Aberdeen
Maritime Museum
Kingswells
Mastrick
Aberdeen Art Gallery
Provost Skene's House
Hazelhead
Girdle Ness
Torry
Nigg Bay
Gordon Highlanders Regimental Mus
Mannofield
Duthie Park & Winter Gardens
Ruthrieston
Greg Ness
Bieldside
Bridge of Dee
Nigg
Altens
Loirston
Cults
Kincorth
Souter Head
Dee
Banchory-Devenick
Cove Bay
Heathcot
Charlestown
Storybook Glen
Auchlunies
Sunnyside
Hillside
Marywell
Earnsheugh Bay
Hill of Auchlee
Findon
Findon Ness
Westside
Portlethen
Berry Top
Portlethen Village
Mill of Monquich
Downies
Cammachmore
Netherley
Newtonhill
Cookney
Muchalls
Bridge of Muchalls
Doonie Point
Castle Rock of Muchalls
Garron Point
Cowie
Strathlethan Bay
Stonehaven
Stromness, Orkney Is. 8-14hrs, Lerwick, Shetland Is. 14hrs, Bergen (summer only) 30hrs
A90
A952
A948
A975
A920
A947
A96
A956
B9005
B9170
B999
B9000
B979
B977
B997
B9119
B9077
B9003
3.2 miles to 1 inch
0 2 4 6 8 10 miles
0 2 4 6 8 10 km
2 km to 1 cm

WESTERN ISLES
(NA H-EILEANAN AN IAR)
3.2 miles to 1 inch
0 2 4 6 8 10 miles
0 2 4 6 8 10 km
2 km to 1 cm
SOUTH UIST
(UIBHIST A DEAS)
Peighinn nan Aoireann
Rubha Aird-mhicheil
Stadhebrig
Ormacleit
Hecla
606
Ben Corodale
620 Beinn Mhor
Rubha Ardvule
Bornais
Loch Kildonan
12
Arinambane
Ben na Hoe
Flora Macdonald's Birthplace
Sheaval
223
Loch Eynort
Gearraidh Bhailteas
Mingearraidh
Arnaval
252
Loch Snigiscleit
Rubha na Gibhte
Hornary
A865
Stulaval
374
Stuley
Aisgernis
Loch Stulaval
Loch Hallan
Dalabrog
Triuirebheinn
357
Pictish Wheel House
3
Crois Dughaill
Beinn Ruigh Choinnich
275
Cille Pheadair
B888
Loch Dun na Cille
Lochboisdale
(Loch Baghasdail)
Loch Baghasdail
Baghasdal
Orosay
5
Taobh a'Deas Loch Baghasdail
Calvay
Rubha
Leth Meadhanach
Trosaraidh
Gearraidh na Monadh
Easaval
Ceann a' Gharaidh
Poll a'Charra
Cille Bhrighde
Ludag
Loch Moreef
Roneval
201
Sound of Eriskay
Sound of Barra
Lingay
Haunn
Ben Scrien
185
Sloc Caol
Hartamul
Fiaray
Hornish
Eriskay
Scurrival Point
Heinish
Ben Stack
122
Rubha Liath
Eolaigearraidh
102
80
Fuday
Cille-Bharra
Traigh Eais
Orosay
Stack Islands
Ottir Mhor
Barra
(Tràigh Mhòr)
Greanamul
Greian Head
Ben Cliad
207
Ardmhòr
95
Gighay
73
Cuidhir
12
Hellisay
Allathasdal
BARRA
(EILEAN BARRAIGH)
Sound of Hellisay
North Bay
Borve Point
107
Buaile nam Bodach
Fuiay
Flodday
Borgh
Ruleos
A888
Bruernish Point
162
Doirlinn Head
Ben Tangaval
333
Heaval
383
Earsairidh
Castlebay
Aird a'Chaolais
(Bagh a'Chaisteil)
Leideag
Kiessimul
Caolas
Heishival Mor
Castle Bay
Rubha Mòr
190
Vatersay
(Bhatarsaigh)
Vatersay Bay
Am Meall
100
Vatersay
Lochboisdale 1¾ hrs
153
Muldoanich
Sound of Sandray
Mallaig 5½ hrs (summer only)
Flodday
Cairn Galtair
207
Sandray
(Sanndraigh)
Oban 5½ hrs
Lingay
Sound of Pabbay
Pabbay
(Pabaigh)
The Hoe
171
Sound of Mingulay
Guarsay Mor
Macphee's Hill
224
Mingulay
(Miughalaigh)
Carnan
273
Mingulay Bay
Sron an Duin
Sound of Berneray
Skate Point
191
Nisam Point
Bearnaraigh
A B C D
1 2 3 4 5

D
E
F
G
WESTERN ISLES
(NA H-EILEANAN AN IAR)
Shillay
Sound of Shillay
Beinn a'Charnain
196
Baile-na-Cille
Quinish
Pabbay
SOUND
Sound of Pabbay
Berneray
(Eilean Bhearnaraigh)
Borve Hill
85
Ruisigearraidh
Borgh
Bays Loch
Boreray
Caolas a' Mhorain
Sound of Berneray
Haskeir Island
Haskeir Eagach
Huilish Point
Veilish Point
Lingay
Port nan Long
Baile Mhic Phail
Aird Thorn
Beinn Mhòr
190
Stromay
Oronsay
Griminis Point
Vallay
Vallay Strand
Scolpaig
A865
Ceathramh Meadhanach
Trumaisge Arraidh
B893
Solas
Greinetobht
Balmartin
(Baile Mhartainn)
Balelone
Loch Hosta
Malacleit
Crogary Mòr
Maari
171
180
Loch nan Geireann
Manish Point
Botarua
Hosta
NORTH UIST
(UIBHIST A TUATH)
Keallasay More
Lochportain
Tigh a'Gearraidh
Blathaisbhal
Keallasay Beg
Hogha Gearraidh
Aird an Runair
Causamul
Loch Fada
174
Marrival
230
Loch Scadavay
Loch Skealtar
Rubha Port Scolpaig
Baile Raghaill
Ceann a'Bhàigh
Lochmaddy
(Loch na Madadh)
Loch nan Eun
Paibeil
Baile Mòr
Cladach a'Chaolais
Oitir Mhòr
Loch Hunder
Loch a' Bharpa
North Lee
250
Deasker
Rubha Raouill
A867
Cladach Chircebost
Loch Scadavay
Sound of Monach
Kirkibost Island
Langais
Loch Hunder
Huskeiran
Loch Euphoirt
Ceann Iar
Hearnish
Stockay
A865
B894
Saighdinis
Rubha Mhor Gille-mhicheil
Shillay
Heisker or Monach Islands
Ceann Ear
Scrot Mòr
Teanamachar
Samhla
Coroena (Corunna)
Loch Caravat
Loch Obisary
Eigneig Mhòr
Eachkamish
Eaval
347
Baleshare
Teampull na Trionaid
Cairinis
Eigneig Bheag
Oitir Mhòr
Baile Glas
Floddaybeg
Grimsay
(Griomasaigh)
Beinn a'Charnain
115
Floddaymore
Benbecula
(Baile a'Mhanaich)
Uachdar
Eilean Flodaigh
Ceallan
Beinn Roagrich
99
Aird
Balivanich
(Baile a'Mhanaich)
Gramsdal
Loch Olavat
Rubha na Rodagrich
Baile nan Cailleach
Garry-a-siar
Rueval
124
BENBECULA
(BEINN NA FAOGHLA)
Griminis
A865
Torlum
Loch Uisgebhagh
B892
Loch Olavat
Lionacleit
Uisgebhagh
Gualann
Creag Ghoraidh
B891
Hornish Point
Baile Gharbhaidh
Rubha Cam nan Gall
Ardivachar Point
Clachan
Iochdar
Aird a'Mhachair
Loch a'Laip
102
Wiay
Bagh Nam Faoileann
Loch Bee
Loch Carnan
Geirninis
A865
Drimore
Loch Sheilavaig
162
168
Groigearraidh
B890
Loch Sgioport
Stadhlaigearraidh
Loch Sgioport
Ornish Island
Loch Druidibeg
Loch Spotal
Tobha Mòr
Mol a'Tuath
SOUTH UIST
D
E
F
G

A
B
C
D
1
2
3
4
5
184
173
162
Toe Head
Chaipaval
339
365
Traigh na Cleavag
Northton (Taobh Tuath)
Maodal
251
Loch Langavat
398
Shillay
Sound of Shillay
Beinn a'Chàrnain
196
Baile-na-Cille
Quinish
Pabbay
SOUND OF HARRIS
Carminish Islands
Loch Steisevat
Ensay
Leverburgh (An T-òb)
A859
459
Cairminis
Strondev
Strannda
211
Rodel (Roghadal)
Killegray
Sound of Pabbay
Berneray (Eilean Bhearnaraigh)
Massacamber
Borve Hill
Ruisigearraidh
Borgh
85
Bays Loch
Boreray
Caolas a' Mhorain
Sound of Berneray
Groay
Gilsay
Lingay
Scaravay
Huilish Point
Veilish Point
Lingay
Port nan Long
Baile Mhic Phail
Aird Thormaid
Oronsay
Beinn Mhòr
190
Vallay
Griminis Point
Scolpaig
Vallay Strand
Ceathramh Meadhanach
Trumaisge Arraidh
Stromay
A865
Greinetobht
Solas
Crogary Mor
Hermetray
Balelone
Malacleit
Maari
171
180
Loch Aulasary
Balmartin (Baile Mhartainn)
Loch Hosta
Loch nan Geireann
Leac na Hoe
Manish Point
Botarua
Loch na Dubhcha
Hosta
Keallasay More
Lochportain
Tigh a'Gearraidh
NORTH UIST (UIBHIST A TUATH)
Keallasay Beg
Scarts Rock
Hogha Gearraidh
Blathaisbhal
Loch Portain
Aird
WESTERN ISLES (NA H-EILEANAN AN IAR)
Loch Fada
Marrival
230
Loch Scadavay
Loch Skealtar
Baile Raghaill
Ceann a'Bhàigh
Lochmaddy (Loch na Madadh)
Loch na Madadh
Rubha Port Scolpaig
Loch nan Eun
Paibeil
Baile Mòr
Cladach a'Chaolais
Loch Hungi
Oitir Mhòr
Loch a' Bharpa
A867
North Lee
250
South Lee
281
Rubha Raouill
Cladach Chirceboist
Loch Scadavay
Loch Hunder
Kirkibost Island
Langais
Loch Euphoirt
Stockay
A865
B894
Saighdinis
Rubha Mhic Gille-mh'cheil
Heisker or Monach Islands
Teanamachar
Samhla
Coroena (Corunna)
Loch Caravat
Loch Obisary
Eigneig Mhòr
Eachkamish
Eaval
347
Baleshare
Teampull na Trionaid
Cairinis
Eigneig Bheag
Oitir Mhòr
Floddaybeg
Baile Glas
Grimsay (Griomasaigh)
Beinn a'Charnain
Floddaymore
Benbecula (Baile a'Mhanaich)
Uachdar
Eilean Flodaigh
115
Ceallan
Ronay (Ronaigh)
Beinn Roagrich
99
Aird
Gramsdal
Balivanich (Baile a'Mhanaich)
Loch Olavat
Baile nan Cailleach
Garry-a-siar
Rueval
124
Rubha na Rodagrich
BENBECULA (BEINN NA FAOGHLA)
Griminis
A865
Loch Uisgebhagh
Torlum
B892
Loch Olavat
Uisgebhagh
Lionacleit
Gualann
Creag Ghoraidh
B891
LITTLE MINCH
Hornish Point
Baile Gharbhaidh
Rubha Cam nan Gall
Ardivachar Point
Clachan
Iochdar
102
Loch a' Laip
Aird a'Mhachair
Wiay
Bagh Nam Faoileann
Loch Bee
Loch Carnan
Geirninis
A865
Drimore
Loch Sheilavaig
Groigearraidh
Loch Sgioport
168
B890
Loch Sgioport
Ornish Island
Loch Druidibeg
Loch Spotal
Mol a'Tuath
Tobha Mòr
SOUTH UIST

D
E
F
G
I
185
Kennavay
Meall Challibost
Heileasbhal
An Coileach
386
Aird Mhige
Liceasto
Greosabhagh
Leac a'Li
Scadabhagh
Rubha Bocaig
Cluer
Loch Grosebay
Rubha Cluer
ANN A DEAS NA HEARADH
Aird Leimhe
Manais
Ard Manish
Fleoideabhagh
L. Fleoideabhagh
Cuidhtinis
Mhighe
Boirseam
Loch Finsbay
Rubha Quidnish
Ceann a'Bhàigh
Lingarabay Island
St Clement's Church
Rubha Vallarip
Point
Fladda-chuain
Gaeilavore Island
Gearran Island
Tarbert 1½ hrs
1¾ hrs
Rubha Hunish
Loch Hunish
Duntulm Bay
Tulm Island
2
Kilmaluag
Duntulm
Score Bay
19
Skye Cottage Museum
Ru Bornaskitaig
Camas Mor
Kilmuir
Hunglader
176
Kilvaxter
Balgown
Loch Sheosdal
Meall na Suiramach
543
350
Monkstadt
Whitewave Activities
Kilbride Point
Linicro
Bioda Buidhe
466
Stack of Skudiburgh
A855
3
Ben Gorm
Idrigil
Rubha Idrigil
Uig
Uig Bay
Balnaknock
Ascrib Islands
South Ascrib
Rubha Chorachan
Earlish
LOCH SNIZORT
TROTTERNISH
Vaternish Point
Sron Ochrulan
251
Ben Geary
284
Geary
Trumpan
Ardmore Bay
Ardmore Point
Halistra
Hallin
Gillen
Loch Losait
Stac a' Bhothain
Cuidrach
Poll na h-Ealaidh
A87
Peinlich
Glenuachdarach
VATERNISH
Biod nan Laogh
Lyndale Point
Greshornish Point
Isay
Mingay Island
Rubha Maol
Stein
Lusta
B886
Ben Diubaig
214
Loch Greshornish
Loch Snizort Beag
Lynedale Ho.
Kingsburgh
Beinn a'Sga
452
4
11
Dunvegan Head
313
Galtrigill
Ben Skriaig
Boreraig
Lampay Islands
Lovaig Bay
Loch Bay
Claigan
Beinn Bhreac
327
Beinn Chreagach
Greshornish
Flashader
A850
Treaslane
Eyre
The Aird
Carn Liath
Kensaleyre
Uig
Husabost
Totaig
Loch Dunvegan
Loch Pooltiel
Milovaig
Feriniquarrie
B884
Oisgill Bay
Colbost Croft Museum
Colbost
Dunvegan
Ben Horneval
264
14
Edinbane
Bernisdale
Ben Uigshader
246
HIGHLAND
Tote
A87
Skeabost
Carbost
Loch Mor
296
Waterstein Head
Neist Point
Moonen Bay
Skinidin
Beinn na Creiche
Uiginish
A850
Glen Dale
Kilmuir
Lonmore
Ben Sca
286
Cruachan Beinn a'Chearcaill
271
Ben Aketil
265
Drumuie
Uigshader
Beinn a'Ghlinne Bhig
208
5
Healabhal Mhor (Macleod's Table North)
468
A863
Roskhill
Roag
Vatten
SKYE
Ben Corkeval
Ramasaig Bay
Ramasaig
Hoe Rape
The Hoe
233
Lorgill
Orbost
Healabhal Bheag (Macleod's Table South)
488
Harlosh
Loch Vatten
Loch Varkasaig
Balmore
Glen Ose
Ose
Beinn na Cloiche
232
Loch Connan
Am Maol
212
Snizort
Ben Connan
244
Harlosh Point
Loch Caroy
B885
Beinn na Boineid
371
Harlosh Island
163
Tarner Island
A863
Dun Beag
Bracadale
Loch Duagrich
Ben Duagrich
304
Mugeary
Ben Idrigill
340
Ullinish
Coillore
Beinn Totaig
An Dubh Sgeir
Loch Bracadale
MacLeod's Maidens
Idrigill Point
Wiay
Ardtreck Point

A
B
C
D
1
2
3
4
5
3.2 miles to 1 inch
0 2 4 6 8 10 miles
0 2 4 6 8 10 km
2 km to 1 cm
Rubha Reidh
Melvaig
North Erradale
Big S
Longa Island
Fladda-chuain
Gearran Island
Eilean Trodday
Rubha Hunish
Loch Hunish
Rubha na h-Aiseig
Kilmaluag Bay
The Aird
Duntulm
Duntulm Bay
A855
Kilmaluag
Score Bay
Galta Mor
Sgeir Eirin
Skye Cottage Museum
Flodigarry
Eilean Flodigarry
Staffin Bay
Hunglader
Kilmuir
Camas Mor
175
Kilvaxter
Balgown
Meall na Suiramach
543
Quirang
The Needle
Digg
Staffin Island
Loch Sheoidal
Suidh a'Mhinn
350
Rubha Garbhaig
Stenscholl
Staffin
Monkstadt
Bioda Buidhe
466
Loch Cleap
Elishader
Linicro
Whitewave Activities
Kilbride Point
Stack Skudiburgh
Ben Gorm
Maligar
Loch Mealt
Rubha nam Brathairean
Idrigil
Uig
Balnaknock
Beinn Edra
611
Marishader
Garros
Rubha Idrigil
Uig Bay
Culnaknock
Chorachan
Earlish
Lealt
Loch a'Bhraige
Rubha na Fearn
Fearnmore
Fearnbeg
TROTTERNISH
Cuidrach
Poll na h-Ealaidh
A87
Peinlich
Glenuachdarach
Creag a'Lain
608
Baca Ruadh
637
RONA
Dry Harbour
125
Leac Tressirnish
Cuaig
Arinacrinachd
Lyndale Point
Beinn a'Sga
452
Hartaval
Rigg
Kingsburgh
Kyle Rona
Callakille
Treaslane
The Storr
719
A855
Eilean Tigh
111
Flashader
Eyre
Bearreraig Bay
Lonbain
An Garbh-mheall
493
Carn Liath
Kensaleyre
Loch a'Sguirr
Eilean Fladday
Edinbane
The Aird
Ben Dearg
552
Loch Leathan
Beinn na h-Iolaire
254
Meall na Fhuaid
518
Bernisdale
Ben Uigshader
246
Tote
Torran
626
Loch Fada
A87
Borve
Manish Point
Loch Arnish
Arnish
Skeabost
Carbost
Prince Charles's Cave
Cruachan Beinn 'Chearcaill
271
Drumuie
SOUND OF RAASAY
INNER SOUND
Brochel
Sithean Bhealaich Chumhaing
392
Hartfield
Applecross
Uigshader
Beinn a'Ghlinne Bhig
208
Glengrasco
Torvaig
RAASAY
Applecross
Milton
Portree
Loch Portree
Loch Connan
SKYE
Beinn na Cloiche
232
Am Maol
212
Beinn na Greine
417
Penifiler
Glame
385
Camusteel
Camusterrach
Ben Tianavaig
413
Poll Creadha
Culduie
Glenmore
Balachuirn
B885
Loch Duagrich
Stroc-bheinn
400
Camastianavaig
Dun Caan
443
Sron na h-Airde Baine
Rubha na' Leac
Bracadale
Ben Duagrich
304
Mugeary
164
A87
Holoman Bay
Toscaig
Coillore
Beinn Totaig
Lower Ollach
Clachan
Beinn na'Leac
319
Loch Toscaig
Loch Airigh
352
Upper Ollach

177
188
178
165
D
E
F
G
I
2
3
4
5
Gruinard Bay
Achgarve
Laide
Mellon Charles
Ormiscaig
Bualnaluib
Aultbea
Drumchork
Isle of Ewe
Cove
Loch an Draing
Inverasdale
Midtown
Naast
Loch Ewe
Loch Thurnaig
Tuirnaig
Boor
Poolewe
Londubh
Inverewe (NTS)
Cnoc Breac 293
Second Coast
Coast
Little Gruinard
Mungasdale
Durnamuck
Badcaul
Cnoc a' Bhaid-rallaich 545
Badrallach
Loch Broom
Ardessie
Camusnagaul
Dundonnell
Eilean Darach
Dundonnell House
Strath Beag
Gruinard Forest
An Teallach
Bidein a'Ghlas Thuill 1062
Sgurr Fiona 1059
Strathnasheallag Forest
Dundonnell Forest
Fain
Loch na Sealga
Fisherfield Forest
Beinn Dearg Mhor 908
Beinn a'Chaisgein Beag 680
Beinn a'Chaisgein Mor 857
Meall na Meine 251
Fionn Loch
Creag-mheall Beag 347
Carn nam Buailtean 384
Sail Mhor
Strath na Sealga
Beinn a'Chlaidheimh 914
Meall an t-Sithe 601
Creag Rainich 807
Mial
Gairloch
Auchtercairn
Gairloch Heritage Museum
Charlestown
Strath Bay
Loch Gairloch
Meall A'irigh Mhic Craidh 349
Badachro
Kerrysdale
Meall Aundrary 329
Shieldaig
Slattadale
Victoria Falls
Talladale
Eilean Ruairidh Mor
Eilean Suthainn
Letterewe
Furnace
Loch Maree
Beinn Airigh Charr 791
Meall Mheannaidh
Beinn Lair 860
Ruadh Stac Mor 918
A'Mhaighdean 967
Sgurr Ban 989
Mullach Coire Mhic Fhearchair 1019
Beinn Tarsuinn 936
Lochan Fada
Beinn Bheag
Groban 748
A'Chailleach 999
Slioch 980
Mullach nan Cadhaichean 294
H I G H L A N D
W E S T E R R O S S
Meall na h-Uamha 288
Craig
Lower Diabaig
Upper Diabaig
Baosbheinn 875
Shieldaig Forest
Beinn Bhreac 624
An Ruadh-mheallan 672
Sgurr Mhor 985
Beinn Alligin 922
Beinn Dearg 914
Loch na h-Oidhche
Beinn an Eoin 855
Beinn a'Chearcaill
Strath Lungard
Meall a' Ghiubhais
Beinn Eighe Nature Reserve
Taagan
Kinlochewe
Beinn a'Mhuinidh 692
Kinlochewe Forest
Heights of Kinlochewe
Leckie
Gleann na Muice
Gleann Tanagaidh
Carn a'Ghlinne 539
Ruadh-stac Mor 1010
Sail Mhor 981
Beinn Eighe
Glen Torridon
Glen Docherty
Badavanich
Lubmore
Achnasheen
Loch a'Chroisg
An Liathanach
Ledgowan Forest
Carn Beag 550
Carn Loisgte
Alligin Shuas
Inveralligin
Fasag
Torridon
Upper Loch Torridon
Liathach
Mullach an Rathain 1023
Spidean a'Choire Leith 1054
Sgurr Dubh 782
Seana Mheallan 436
Torridon Visitor Centre (NTS)
Coulin Forest
Ardheslaig
Shieldaig Island (NTS)
Rubha na Feola
Inverbain
Shieldaig
Balgy
Annat
Ben Shieldaig 516
Ben-damph Forest
Beinn na h-Eaglaise 737
Beinn Liath Mhor 925
876
Carn Breac 678
Croic-bheinn 493
An Fur 387
Glenshieldaig Forest
Loch Damh
Beinn Damh 902
Maol Chean-dearg 933
Sgorr Ruadh 960
Fuar Tholl 907
Glen Carron
Moruisg 928
Carn Gorm
Carn Liath 857
An Staonach 513
Meall na Saobhaidhe 368
An Ruadh-stac 892
Achnashellach Sta
Craig
Achnashellach Forest
Sgurr nan Ceannaichean 915
Glencarron and Glenuig Forest
Loch Lundie
Beinn Bhan 896
Balnacra
Coulags
Sgurr na Feartaig 862
Sgurr Choinnich 999
Sgurr a'Chaorachain 1053
Maoile Lunndaidh 1007
Sgurr a' Gharaidh 730
Creag a'Chaorainn
Beinn Tharsuinn 863
West Monar Forest
Strathcarron
Strathcarron Sta
Achintee
Bidean a'Choire Sheasgaich 945
Lurg Mhor 986
Russel
Ardarroch
Lochcarron
Loch Kishorn
An Sgurr
Achintee
Sgeir Fhada
Loch Carron
Carn Geuradainn 594
Attadale
Attadale Forest
Beinn Bheag 619
Meallan Buidhe 555
Achir
Bad a'Chreamha 395
Stromemore
Ardnarff
Airigh-drishaig
Carn nan Iomairean
An Cruachan
A832
A896
A890
B8021
B8056
B8057

178
189
177
166
A
B
C
D
1
2
3
4
5
A835
A832
A890
A831
Braes of Ullapool
Achall
Rhidorroch
Beinn Eilideach
558
Allt na h-Airbhe
Broom
Badr
Blarnalevoch
Loggie
Rhiroy
Leckmelm
Ardcharnich
Ardessie
Eilean Darach
Ardindrean
Letters
Dundonnell
Strath Beag
Dundonnell House
Inverlael
Inverbroom
Auchlunachan
Glackour
Auchindrean
Fasagrianach
Braemore
Corrieshalloch Gorge (NTS)
Strath More
Inverlael Forest
Dundonnell Forest
Fain
Strath na Sealga
Meall an t-Sithe
601
Creag Rainich
807
Loch a'Bhraoin
Beinn Bheag
Groban
Meallan Chuaich
Gleann Tanagaidh
Strath Mulzie
Glen Douchary
Meall nam Bradhan
677
Loch a'Choire Mhoir
Seana Bhraigh
927
Carn Mor
649
Eididh nan Clach Geala
928
Meall nan Ceapraichean
977
1084
Cona' Mheall
980
Beinn Dearg
Beinn Enaiglair
889
Meall Leacachain
618
Creag Dhubh
522
Dirrie More
Lochdrum
Loch Droma
Loch a' Gharbhrain
Allt a' Mhuilinn
Freevater Forest
Bodach Mor
822
Carn Ban
Glenbeg
Gleann Beag
Meall a' Chuaille
628
Tollomuick Forest
Am Faochagach
954
Loch Coire Lair
Strathvaich Forest
Tom Ban Mor
742
Loch Vaich
Loch Glascarnoch
Strath Vaich
Inchbae Forest
Strathrannoch
Strath Rannoch
Carn a'Choin Deirg
701
Amat Forest
Sron Gun Aran
Gleann Mor
Glencalvie
Dunan Liath
691
Diebidale Forest
Beinn Tharsuinn
714
Creag Ruadh
671
Crom Loch
Carn Mor
Loch Bealach Culaidh
Meall a'Chrasgaidh
934
Beinn Liath Mhor Fannaich
954
Beinn Liath Bheag
665
Sgurr nan Clach Geala
1093
Sgurr Mor
1110
A'Chailleach
999
Sgurr Breac
1000
Sgurr nan Each
923
Meall Gorm
949
Beinn Liath Mhor a'Ghiubhais Li
766
Kinlochluichart Forest
Aultguish Inn
Lubfearn
Fannich Forest
An Coileachan
923
Beinn Dearg
687
Meall Mhic Iomhair
607
Corriemoillie Forest
Carn na Dubh Choille
479
Garbat Forest
Garbat
An Cabar
W E S T E R   R O S S
H I G H L A N D S
Beinn nan Ramh
711
Loch Fannich
Strath Chrombuill
Lochrosque Forest
Carn na Beiste
518
An Cabar
558
Carn Daraich
465
Beinn a'Bhric
442
Achnaclerach
Little Wyvis
764
Carn Gorm
556
Strathgarve Forest
Lochluichart
Lochluichart Sta
Gorstan
Garve
Loch Luichart
Loch Garve
Fionn Bheinn
933
Knockban
Meall a'Chaorainn
705
Carn a'Ghlinne
539
Badavanich
Achnasheen
Lubmore
Loch a'Chroisg
An Liathanach
Ledgowan Forest
Carn Beag
550
Carn Chaiseachain
312
S T R A T H   B R A N
Carn na Cre
461
Sgurr Marcasaidh
Tarvie
Falls of Conon
Creag Loch nan Dearcag
536
Little Scatwell
Loch Meig
Milltown
Porin
Torrachilty Wood
Strathconon
Sgurr a'Ghlas Leathaid
844
Sgurr a'Mhuilinn
879
Meallan nan Uan
840
Carn an Leanaidh
574
Gleann Meinich
Meall na Faochaig
680
Glenmeanie
Carn Mhartuin
538
Cnoc an t-Sidhein
372
Scardroy
Loch Beannachan
Carnoch
Inverchoran
Meall Giubhais
662
Carn na Coinnich
Meall nan Damh
671
Carn na Cloiche Moire
591
Sron nan Saobhaidh
408
Glen Orrin
Glen Carron
Moruisg
928
Carn Gorm
875
Carn Liath
857
Sgurr nan Ceannaichean
915
Glencarron and Glenuig Forest
Gleann Fhiodhaig
Bac an Eich
849
Strathconon Forest
Orrin Reservoir
Corriehallie Forest
Gleann Goibhre
Beinn nam Fitheach
494
N O R T H
Maoile Lunndaidh
1007
Sgurr Coire nan Eun
789
Sgurr na Cairbe
Erchless Forest
Sgurr Choinnich
Sgurr a'Chaorachain
1053
Carn Eiteige
882
Sgurr Fhuar-thuill
1049
Sgurr a'Choire Ghlais
1083
Carn nan Gobhar
992
Sgurr na Ruaidhe
993
Meallan Buidhe
766
Sgurr a'Phollain
854
Beinn a'Bha'ach Ard
862
West Monar Forest
East Monar Forest
Sgurr na Muice
891
Carn Ban
736
Culligran
Lurg Mhor
986
Loch Monar
Struy
Erchless Castle
Eskadale
Meallan Odhar
Inchvuilt
Glen Strathfarrar
Loch Beannacharan
Culligran Falls
Mauld
Stuy Forest
Crelevan
Beinn Bheag
619
Meallan Buidhe
555
Meallan Odhar
Sgor na Diollaid
Carn Gorm
An Cruachan
Carnoch
Creag Dubh

Strathcarron
Wester Gruinards
The Craigs
Soyal
Bonar Bridge
Tulloch
Migdale
Clashcoig
Achosnich
Rearquhar
Badninish
Fourpenny
Poles
Kyloag
Lower Gledfield
Ardgay
Kincardine
Ardchronie
Little Creich
Spinningdale
Creagan Asdale
Clashmore Wood
Clashmore
Whiteface
Pulrossie
Skibo
Evelix
Pitgrudy
Carmore
Craft Centre
Lonemore
Cuthill
Dornoch
Dornoch Sands
Dornoch Point
Whiteness Sands
Carn Bhrain 635
Glen Calvie
Coire Bog
Wester Fearn Burn
Easter Fearn
Struie Hill
Struie 371
Dounie
Ardmore
Edderton
Ardjachie Point
Carn Chuinneag 838
Glen Diebidale
Meall Bhenneit 532
Carn Cas nan Gabhar 602
Beinn Clach an Fheadain 477
Cnoc Muigh-bhlaraidh
Aultnamain Inn
St Duthus's Chapel
Morangie
Tain
Balcherry
Balnagall
Morangie Forest
Lairgs of Tain
Glen Aldie
Knockbreck
Aldie
R O S S
Beinn Tharsuinn 692
Braeantra
Kildermorie Forest
Kildermorie Lodge
Loch Morie
Strath Rusdale
Cnoc an t-Sabhail
Strath Rory
Lamington
Scotsburn
Torran
Newfield
Logie Hill
Loandhu
Calrossie
Rhynie
Hill of Fearn
Fearn Abbey
Clay of Allan
Cnoc Corr Guinie
Inchlumpie
Meall Mor 738
Wyvis Lodge
Loch Glass
Boath
Meall an Tuirc 625
Stittenham
Inchindown
Balnagown Castle
Tullich Muir
Kildary
Milton
Anker
Shandwick
Chapelhill
Easter Ardross
Dalnavie
Wester Lealty
Achandunie
Wester Lonvine
Kilmuir
Tarbat Ho.
Sands of Nigg
Nigg
Hill of Nigg
Queen's Cairn
Wyvis Forest
Bendcallt
Cnoc Ceislein 523
Balnaguisich
Rhicullen
Delny
Barbaraville
Nigg Bay
Meall na Drochaide
Kinloch
Contullich
Tomich
Achnagarron
Balintraid
Saltburn
Balnabruaich
Balnapaling
Alness
Rosskeen
Invergordon
Kirkwall, Orkney Is. 9hrs
180
Castlecraig
North Sutor
Ben Wyvis
Glas Leathad Mor
Glen Glass
Dalmore
Redburn
Black Rock Gorge
Alness Bay
Cromarty Firth
Balblair
Newhall Point
Hugh Miller's Cottage (NTS)
Cromarty
Cromarty Court House
Sutor Stacks
Sutors of Cromarty
Meall na Speireig
Swordale
Evanton
Drummond
Balconie Point
Cullicudden
Resolis
Udale Bay
Cromarty Bay
Shoremill
Navity
Cnoc Mhor 482
Strath Sgitheach
Newmills
Jemimaville
Poyntzfield
Muirton
Upper Eathie
Ardullie
The Den
Easter Brae
Glenurquhart
Craighead
Mountgerald
Glensgaich
Heights of Brae
Bottacks
Shoretown
Culbo
Millbuie
Millbuie Forest
Town House
Auchterneed
Fodderty
Findon Mains
Balmungie
Castle Leod
Strath Peffer
Dingwall
Urquhart
Culbokie
Mount Eagle 256
Killen
Janefield
Whiteness Head
Strathpeffer
Loch Ussie
Black Isle
Rosemarkie
Fortrose
Rosemarkie Bay
Fort George
Kirkton
Carse of Ardersier
Hilton of Delnies
Contin
Lochussie
Maryburgh
Alcaig
Duncanston
Belmaduthy
Strathpeffer 1411
Corntown
Conon Bridge
Easter Kinkell
Bogbuie
Knockbain
Easter Suddie
Avoch
Cath
Chanonry Point
Ardersier
Leanaig
Shantullich
Avoch Bay
Moray Firth
Black
Gollanfield
Marybank
Urray
Tore
Munlochy
Munlochy Bay
Muir of the Clans
Brackley
Inverness
Balvaird
Drumderfit
Fisherton
Castle Stuart
Drumine
Clephanton
Cawdor
Falls of Orrin
Faebait
Kilcoy
Bogallan
Muir of Ord
Newton
Redcastle
Milton
Kilmuir
Alturlie Point
Tornagrain
Croy
Dalcross
Cantray
Cawdor
Dallaschyle
Ardnagrask
Windhill
Charlestown
Craigton Point
Cantraywood
Easter Galcantray
Loch nan Eun
Rheindown
Loch nam Bonnach
North Kessock
Urchany and Farley Forest
Ruilick
Beauly
Priory
Made in Scotland
Beauly Firth
South Kessock
Longman Point
Culloden
Balloch
Culloden Forest
Assich Forest
Kirkton of Barevan
Kirkhill
Clachnaharry
INVERNESS
Culloden Muir
Cantraydoune
Achnagairn
Rhinduie
Bunchrew
Battle of Culloden 1746 (NTS)
Cumberland Stone
Drumchardine
Leachkin
Smithton
Leanach
Dalroy
Saddle Hill
Kilmorack
Easter Moniack
Bught Floral Hall and Visitor Cen
Culcabock
Westhill
Clava Cairns
Crask of Aigas
Balchraggan
Mus & Art Gallery
Culloden Visitors Centre
The Aird
Kiltarlity
Belladrum
Cnoc na Moine 316
Bogbain
Castletown
Oldtown of Aigas
Culburnie
An Leacainn
Lagnalean
Knocknagael Boar Stone
Craigdhu
Camault Muir
Tomnacross
Newton of Leys
Beinn Bhuidhe Mhor 548
Druimkinnerras
Dochgarroch
Kirkton
Essich
Craggie
Carn nan Tri-tighearnan 615
Boblainy Forest
Foxhole
Scaniport
Dores
167
Lochend
Carn a'Bhodaich 501
Mains of Faillie
Beinn Bhreac 511
Glen Convinth
Caiplich
Abriachan
Tor Point
Strath
Meall a'Bhreacraibh
Ardblair
Moy Burn

180
191
179
168
A
B
C
D
1
2
3
4
5
Badninish
Fourpenny
Poles
Embo
Embo Street
Evelix
Carmore
A949
Cath
Craft Centre
Dornoch
Lonemore
Cuthill
Dornoch Sands
Dornoch Point
D O R N O C H F I R T H
Whiteness Sands
Innis Mhor
Port Mor
Tarbat Ness
Wilkhaven
Hilton
Bindal
Portmahomack
Innis Bheag
Ardjachie Point
Duthus's Chapel
Tain
Balcherry
Inver Bay
Inver
Rockfield
Tarrel
Balnagall
Lochslin
B9165
Knockbreck
Aldie
A9
Rhynie
Baladie
Geanies Ho.
Loandhu
Hill of Fearn
Fearn Sta
Calrossie
Cadboll
Newfield
Fearn
Tullich
Fearn Abbey
Hilton of Cadboll
Logie Hill
Clay of Allan
B9166
Shandwick
Balintore
Ankerville
Chapelhill
Tarbat Ho.
Sands of Nigg
B9175
Hill of Nigg
Nigg
Nigg Bay
Balnabruaich
Balnapaling
Castlecraig
North Sutor
Hugh Miller's Cottage (NTS)
Cromarty
Cromarty Court House
Sutor Stacks
Sutors of Cromarty
Blue Head
B9163
Newton
Upper Eathie
M O R A Y F I R T H
Whiteness Head
Fort George
Kirkton
Carse of Ardersier
Hilton of Delnies
B9092
Nairn
Tradespark
Househill
Kingsteps
Boath Dovecot (NTS)
Auldearn
Auldearn 1645
Ard
B9006
Blackcastle
Gollanfield
B9091
B9090
B9101
Muir of the Clans
Moss-side
Loch Flemington
Inverness
Brackley
Torrich
Regoul
A939
Laiken Forest
Drumine
Clephanton
Cawdor
Piperhill
Culcharry
Littlemill
A96
Tornagrain
Croy
Dallaschyle
Urchany
Dalcross
Cantray
Easter Galcantray
Achindown
Cantraywood
Culloden Forest
Kirkton of Barevan
Assich Forest
Clunas
Redburn
Cantraydoune
Bruachmary
Balmore
Cumberland Stone
Saddle Hill
Clava Cairns
Castletown
H I G H L A N D
Allt Dearg
Rireach Burn
Carn a'Chrasgie 401
Daltra
Ardclach Bell Tower
Ferness
B9007
Mount
Dulsie
Milltown
Carn Sgumain
Carnoch
Banchor
Beinn Bhuidhe Mhor 548
Carn nan Tri-tighearnan 615
Dalless
Streens
Carn na Sguabaich
Beinn Bhreac 511
Moy Burn
Meall a'Bhreacraibh
Leonach Burn
Hill of Aitnoch
Aitnoch
A939
Cairn Duhie
Dorback Burn
Lochindorb
Carn Ruigh
Dava
Dava Moor
Burghead Well
Hopeman
Burghead
Cummingston
Roseisle Forest
Burghead Bay
B9089
Findhorn
Buthill
Culbin Forest
Findhorn Bay
B9011
Hempriggs
Muirhead
Coltfield
Miltonhill
Wellhill
Kinloss
Alves
The Bar
Kintessack
Inverene
Grange Hall
Cloves
Moy House
Springfield
Toreduff
Forres
Sueno's Stone
Mains of Burgie
Brodie (NTS)
Dyke
Falconer Museum
Monaughty Forest
Heldon Hill 234
Macbeth's Hillock
Newton of Dalvey
A940
B9010
Califer
Blervie Castle
Rafford
Tulloch
Boghole Fm
Darnaway
Loch of Blairs
Black Burn
Whitemire
Old Military Road
Altyre Woods
Briach
Edinvale
Hill of the Wangie 319
Milton
Conicavel
Newtyle Forest
Branchill
Mains of Sluie
Phorp
Dallas
Darnaway Forest
Presley
Romach Hill 313
Ardoch
Fornighty
Logie
Drumine Forest
Mill Buie 371
Craigroy
Lethen Bar
Randolph's Leap
Tomnamoon
Hill of Tomechole 344
Relugas
Loch Dallas
Carnachie 359
M O
Tomdow
Carn Ghiubhais 430
Lossie
Divie
Knock of Braemoray 456
Carn Kitty 521
Slaibh Bainneach 483
Carn Shalag 470
Larig Hill 545
Paul's Hill
Roy's Hill 516
Glen Gheallaidh
Carn Ruighe an Uain 546
Glen Tulchan
Carne na Loine 549
Carn Bad na Caorach
B9102

D
E
F
G
3.2 miles to 1 inch
0
2
4
6
8
10 miles
10 km
2 km to 1 cm
1
2
3
4
5
182
169
Halliman Skerries
Lossiemouth Fisheries and Communities Mus
Covesea Skerries
Clashach Point
Stotfield
Branderburgh
Lossiemouth
B9040
Covesea
Duffus
Gordonstoun
Oakenhead
B9135
St Peter's Church
Salterhill
Duffus
Lossie Forest
Boar's Head Rock
Innes Canal
Innes Links
Spynie Canal
Loch Spynie
Lossie
A941
Findrassie
Palace of Spynie
Quarrywood
Bishopmill
Mus
Old Mills
Cath (ruins)
Elgin
A96
Motor Museum
Johnstons Cashmere Visitor Centre
Palmerscross
New Elgin
Pittendreich
Miltonduff
B9010
B9012
Moss of Barmuckity
Lhanbryde
Urquhart
Lochhill
Kingston
Spey Mouth
Tugnet Icehouse Exhibition
Spey Bay
Garmouth
Nether Dallachy
Portgordon
Bogmoor
Upper Dallachy
Mains of Tannachy
A990
Auchenhalrig
Muir of Lochs
Newton
Baxters Visitor Centre
B9015
B9104
Chapel
Fochabers Folk Mus
Bridge of Tynet
Broadley
Clochan
Mosstodloch
Fochabers
Dipple
Braes of Enzie
Paddockhaugh
Cloddach
Birnie Church
Longmorn
Fogwatt
Auchtertyre
Blackhills
Orbliston
Altonside
B9103
Thomshill
Whitewreath
Ordiequish
Speymouth Forest
Whiteash Hill
264
A96
Crofts of Buinach
Kellas
Leanoch
Glenlatterach
Inchberry
Teindland Forest
Thief's Hill
250
Forgie
Bardon
Findlay's Seat
262
Wood of Dundurcas
Wood of Ordiequish
North Bogbain
Glenlatterach Resr
Leanoch Burn
Brylach Hill
325
Glen of Rothes
Spey
Boat o' Brig
Mill Buie
355
Pikey Hill
355
Auchinroath
Kirkhill
Hill of Mulderie
Cairn Uish
365
The Kettles
B9015
B9103
Mulben
Knock More
356
Auchlunkart
Tauchers
Rosarie
Rothes
Glen Grant & Caperdonich Distillery
Ben Aigan
471
Rosarie Forest
Carn na Cailliche
404
Hill of Stob
Burn of Rothes
Cairn Cattoch
369
Hunt Hill
Whiteacen
Dandaleith
A95
Knockan
372
Hill of Towie
339
Elchies Forest
Maggieknockater
Robertstown
B9102
Telford Bridge
Craigellachie
Drummuir Castle
Loch Park
Archiestown
Ringorm
A941
Upper Knockando
Cardow
Aberlour (Charlestown of Aberlour)
Tullich
Knockando Distillery
Knockando
Carron
Speyview
Parkmore
Daugh of Kinermony
Milltown of Edinvillie
Dufftown
Balvenie
Glenfiddich Distillery
Milltown of Auchindoun
Daugh of Carron
Sheandow
552
Mus
Bakebare
Keithmore
Mortlach Church
Scootmore Forest
Marypark
Glenfarclas Distillery
Bellehiglash
Baby's Hill
Beatshach
Meikle Conval
569
Dullan Water
Laggan
Auchindoun
The Scalp
487
Ben Rinnes
Brigehaugh
Bridge
Towiemore
B9014
B9115
Braehead
Aultnapaddock
Daugh of Invermarkie
Isla
Portknockie
Findochty
A942
Bauds of Cullen
Portessie
Ianstown
Buckie
Seatown
Rathven
Buckie Drifter
A98
Seatown
Cullen House
Cullen Bay
Cullen
Logie Head
Sanden
Bin of Cullen
320
Lintmill
Mains Glassaugh
Clune
Fordy
Slackhead
Arradoul
Drybridge
Hill of Maud
274
Weston
Deskford Church
Milton
Slate Haugh
Berryhillock
Kirktown of Deskford
Ardiec
Hoggie
Black Hill
255
Shiel Muir
Addie Hill
272
Craibstone
Backies
Millstone Hill
301
Aultmore
Burn of Aultmore
Black Hill
262
Lurg Hill
313
Deerhill
Gordonst
Broadrashes
B9016
B9018
Grange Crossroads
Crannach
Knock Hi
430
Aultmore
Garralburn
Sillyearn
Bracobrae
A95
Drumnagorrach
Newmill
B9017
Floors
Knock
Fife Keith
A95
Keith
Isla
Davoch of Grange
Farmtown
Limehillock
Shiel Burn
Tower
Strathisla Distillery
Meikle Balloch Hill
366
B9117
Haughs
Strath Isla
Blackhillock
The Balloch
Balloch Wood
Glen of Coachford
B9022
Edintore
Ruthven
Coachford
A96
Newton
Hillend
Cairnie
Burn of Cairnie
Drumdelgie
The Bin
313
The Bin Forest
Daugh of Cairnborrow
Milton of Cairnborrow
A920
Torry
Huntly
Deveron
Cairnargat
Clashmach Hill
A97
Strathbogie
Glass
Dumeath
Beldorney
Muckle Long Hill
391
Bailiesward
Bridgend
Backside
Succoth
Tillathrowie
Strath Bogie
R
A
Y

A
B
C
D
1
2
3
4
5
3.2 miles to 1 inch
0 2 4 6 8 10 miles
0 2 4 6 8 10 km
2 km to 1 cm
181
170
Portknockie
Scar Nose
Cullen Bay
Logie Head
Findlater Castle
Redhythe Point
Boyne Bay
Bauds of Cullen
Seatown
Cullen
Cullen House
Sandend
Sandend Bay
Portsoy
Boyne
Easter Whyntie
Whitehills
Knock Head
Boyndie Bay
Banff Bay
Banff
Macduff
Head of Garness
Crovie Head
Gamrie Bay
Crovie
Northfield
Troup Head
Lintmill
Mains of Glassaugh
Durn Hill
199
Fordyce
Fordyce Hill
Boyndie
Auds
Blairshinnoch
Duff House
Dounepark
Melrose
Wester Greenskares
Gardenstown
Gamrie
Dubford
Protstonhill
Clune
Milton
Deskford Church
Hill of Maud
274
Weston
Slate Haugh
Berryhillock
Kirktown of Deskford
Ardiecow
Hoggie
Burn of Durn
Wester Culbeuchly
Hill of Culbirnie
156
Kirktown of Alvah
Longmanhill
Cushnie
Minnonie
Black Hill
255
Shiel Muir
Craibstone
Backies
Canterbury
Oldtown of Ord
Fattahead
Greenlaw
Eden
Foulzie
Keilhill
Balgreen
Netherbrae
Overbrae
Bracklamore Hill
Hill of Fishrie
Bogfold
Bracklamore
Black Hill
262
Lurg Hill
313
MORAY
Cornhill
Park
Weachyburn
Linhead
The Pole of Itlaw
Balchers
Gorrachie
Castleton
Milltown of Craigston
Deerhill
Gordonstown
Knock Hill
430
Glen Barry
Milbethill
Kebholes
Plaidy
Craigston
Crannach
Sillyearn
Culvie
Finnygaud
Knowes of Elrick
Gallow Hill
226
Boghead
ABERDEEN
Mountblairy
Muirden
Fintry
Brackens
New Byth
Bracobrae
Drumnagorrach
Wether Hill
Crombie
Cranna
Wrae
Wester Badentyre
Garmond
Floors
Knock
Limehillock
Knabbygates
Auchintoul
Aberchirder
Bogton
Muiryfold
Farmtown
Davoch of Grange
Distillery
Shiel Burn
Old Crombie
Marnoch
Clunie
Carnousie
Turriff
Delgatie
Balthangie
Meikle Balloch Hill
366
Moss-side
Kirkton
Laithers
1639
Cuminestown
Delgaty Forest
West Cairncake
Haughs
Balloch Wood
The Balloch
Milltown of Rothiemay
Mayen
Hillbrae
Southend
Mill of Colp
Little Idoch
Howe of Teuchar
Northburnhill
Glen of Coachford
Ruthven
Redhill
Yonder Bognie
Auchininna
Braefoot
Gask
Darra
Hatton Castle
Waggle Hill
Muirtack
Newton
Fourman Hill
344
Inverkeithny
Bogniebrae
Fortrie
Birkenhills
South Redbriggs
Deer's Hill
178
Maryhill
Cairnie
Glen Dronach Distillery
Hill of Carlincraig
192
Kingsford
Cobairdy
Conland
Feith-hill
Dykeside
Towie Barclay
North Millbrex
The Bin
313
The Bin Forest
Drumblair
Drumdelgie
Corse of Kinnoir
Macterry
Daugh of Cairnborrow
Milton of Cairnborrow
Cruchie
Largue
Steinmanhill
Gourdas
Darnabo
Huntly
Lessendrum
Frendraught
Denmoss
Nether Lenshie
Kirktown of Auchterless
Inverythan
Monkshill
Lethenty
Corse
Aucharnie
Tifty
Cottown
Drumblade
Backhill
Fyvie (NTS)
Cairnargat
Clashmach Hill
Mosshead
Brides
Ythanwells
Badenscoth
Gordonstown
Woodhead
Slioch
Logie Newton
Crofts
Strathbogie
Bailiesward
Denend
Rothiebrisbane
Fyvie
Muckle Long Hill
391
Thomastown
Millburn
Redhill
Greenmyre
Bridgend
Fisherford
Blackford
Rothienorman
Collynie
Illathrowie
A98
A97
A95
A947
A96
A920
B9018
B9022
B9023
B9025
B9139
B9121
B9031
B9123
B9105
B9027
B9170
B9117
B9024
B9001
B992
B9005

D
E
F
G
1
2
3
4
5
Rosehearty
Kinnairds Head
Sandhaven
Broadsea
Museum of Scottish Lighthouses
Fraserburgh
Fraserburgh Bay
Pennan Head
Aberdour Bay
Quarry Head
Pitsligo
Peathill
Cairnbulg Point
Cairnbulg
Inverallochy
Towie
Mid Ardlaw
Pitblae
Coburty
Cardno
Broomhead
Cairnbulg
Whitelinks Bay
Charlestown
St Combs
New Aberdour
Upper Boyndlie
Memsie
Gowanhill
Inzie Head
Windyheads Hill
Woodhead
South Inch
Memsie Cairn
Whitewell
Cairness
Corahill
Strathbeg Bay
Ladysford
Whitebog
Rathen
Craigellie
Nether Glasslaw
Newburgh
Crimonmogate
Hillhead of Auchentumb
Craigmaud
Turclossie
Seatown
Rattray Head
Waughton Hill
Mormond Hill
Dartfield
Loch of Strathbeg
Old Rattray
New Pitsligo
Whitestripe
Crimond
Cairnywhing
Knowhead
Strichen
Blackhill
North Essie
New Leeds
Upper Ridinghill
Rattray Bay
Craigculter
Bonnykelly
Longhill
North Ugie Water
Gas Terminal
Ironside
Leys
Backfolds
Carnichal
Denhead
Hythie
St Fergus Moss
Kirktown
St Fergus
Oldwhat
Fetterangus
Forest of Deer
Toux
Rora Moss
Cuttyhill
Scotstown Head
Rora
Kirkton Head
Mains of Fedderate
Mains of Pitfour
Aberdeenshire Farming Museum
Millbank
Lunderton
Mains of Culsh
Deer Abbey
Aden
Mintlaw
Torterston
Inverugie
Craig Ewen
Maud
Arbuthnot Museum
New Deer
Backhill of Clackriach
Waterhill of Bruxie
Old Deer
Longside
Flushing
Buchanhaven
Peterhead
Peterhead Maritime Heritage Centre
Drymuir
South Ugie Water
Inverquhomery
Thunderton
Keith Inch
Clockhill
Bulwark
Stuartfield
Millbreck
Hillhead of Cocklaw
Peterhead Bay
Moss of Belnagoak
Crichie
Invernettie
Burnhaven
Nethermuir
Sandford Bay
Knaven
Clola
Nether Kinmundy
Little Dens
Buchan Ness
Kinnadie
Blackhill
Stirling
Boddam
South Upper Barrack
Skelmuir
Auchnagatt
Newton
Carse of Balloch
Sandfordhill
Cairnorrie
Hill of Skilmafilly
Mill of Elrick
Kinknockie
Smallburn
Monteach
Skelmuir Hill
Moss of Cruden
Aldie
Coldwells
Skelmonae
Inkhorn
Upper Hawkhillock
Ardallie
Gask
Murdoch Head
Teuchan
171
Quilquox
Loanhead
Hill of Dudwick
Greenheads
North Haven
Muirtack
Auchiries
Bullers of Buchan
Meth.
Drumwhindle
Arthrath
Mains of Dudwick
Hatton
Errollston
Cruden Bay
Tanglandford
Blindburn
Waterloo
Chapel Hill
Slains (ruins)
Ythan
A90
A98
A981
A952
A950
A948
A982
B9031
B9032
B9033
B9093
B9029
B9030
B9106
B9170
B9005
ENSHIRE
UCHAN

A
B
C
D
1
2
3
4
5
186
174
Aird Mhòr Mangurstadh
Cradhlastadh
Camas Uig
Timsgearraidh
Uigen
Vuia Beg
Floday
Cairisiadar
Geis
Loch Sgaslabhat
Mangurstadh
Eadar dha Fhadhail
Suainaval
429
Aird Fenish
Loch Suainaval
Loch Croistean
Einacleit
Islibhig
Mealisval
574
Loch Raonasgail
Tahaval
515
Loch Grunavat
16
Aird Breanais
Breanais
Giosla
Cracaval
514
Skeun
265
Mealasta
Tamanaisval
467
Loch Dibadale
Beinn Mheadhonach
397
Coduinn
241
Loch Morsgail
W E S T
Caolas an Eilein
Maghannan
Mealasta Island
Griomaval
Loch na Craobhaig
Liongam
Loch Tamanavay
Aird Bheag
Loch Bodavat
Loch Benisval
Morsgail Forest
Kearstay
Loch Thealasbhaidh
Gob na h-Airde Moire
Aird Mhòr
Loch Resort
Beinn a'Bhoth
308
Sgeir Moil Duinn
Sron Romul
308
Scarp
Loch Cravadale
Ulladale
Mas a'Chnoic-chuairtich
386
Mullach na Reidheachd
295
Caolas an Scarp
Sgianait
425
Rapaire
453
Loch a'Ghlinne
Loch Voshimid
Stulaval
579
Huisinis
Husival Mòr
489
Tirga Mòr
679
Ullaval
659
Gasker
Hushinish Point
B887
Hushinish Bay
N O R T H
H A R R I S
Arda Beaga
Leosaval
412
Oreval
662
Forest of Harris
(CEANN A TUATH NA HEARADH)
Horsanish
Gobhaig
Abhainnsuidhe
Cleiseval
511
Uisgnaval Mòr
729
Rubha Bhuic
12
Tarransay Glorigs
(NA H-EILEANAN)
Soay Beg
Soay Sound
B887
Soay Mor
Miabhag
Bun Abhainn Eadarra
3.2 miles to 1 inch
0 2 4 6 8 10 miles
0 2 4 6 8 10 km
2 km to 1 cm
West Loch Tarbert
Aird A
3
Ben Raah
267
Beinn Dhubh
506
Taransay (Tarasaigh)
Taobh Siar
Aird Vanish
Paible
Losgaintir
Ceann Reamhar
South Harris Forest
467
287
Rubha Sgeirigin
Sound of Taransay
Corran Seilebost
Seilebost
Rubha Romagi
A859
Rubha Mas a'Chnuic
23
Clett Nisabost
East Stocklett
175
Toe Head
Buirgh
Bulabhall
354
Heileasbhal Mòr
384
An Coileach
386
Aird Mhige
Leac a'Li
339
Chaipaval
365
Sgarasta Mhòr
274
Liceasto
Shillay
Bleaval
398
S O U T H
H A R R I S
(CEANN A DEAS NA HEARADH)
Traigh na Cleavag
Maodal
251
Loch Langavat
Loch Stocklnish
Sound of Shillay
Northton (Taobh Tuath)
Aird Leimhe
Manais
Beinn a'Charnain
196
Bràigh nam Bàgh
Fleoideabhagh
Ard Manish
S O U N D O F H A R R I S
Baile-na-Cille
Pabbay
Carminish Islands
Mas Garbh
Cuidhtinis
Loch Fleoideabhagh
Quinish
Loch Steisevat
Aird Mhighe
Rubha Quidnish
Ensay
Roneval
459
Boirseam
Loch Finsbay
Leverburgh (An T-òb)
A859
Ceann a'Bhàigh
Sound of Pabbay
Cairminis
Strondeval
211
Lingarabay Island
Killegray
Strannda
St Clement's Church
Berneray
(Eilean Bhearnaraigh)
Rodel (Roghadal)
Rubha Vallarip
Massacamber
1½ hrs
Renish Point
Borve Hill
85
Ruisigearraidh
Borgh
Boreray
Bays Loch
Caolas a'Mhorain
Groay
Gilsay
Sound of Berneray
Huilish Point
Lingay
Port nan Long
Lingay
Veilish Point
Scaravay
Baile Mhic Phail
Vallay
Oronsay
B893
Beinn Mhòr
190
Aird Tho
Trumaisge
Stromay

185
187
175
D
E
F
G
1
2
3
4
5
Crulabhig
Kirkibost
Eilean Kearstay
Callanish (Calanais)
Callanish Standing Stones
Ben rovinis
Linsiadar
Teahaval
256
Griomarstaidh
B8011
A858
Achadh Mòr
Eitshal
223
Beinn nan Surrag
200
Beinn a'Bhuna
Loch Vatandip
Loch Urival
Loch Airigh nan Sloc
Loch an Tairbeart
Stornoway
Melbost Pt
Melbost
Garrabost
Seisiadar
Eye Peninsula
Aignis
Cnoc
Suardail
Pabail Iarach
Lews Castle
Creed
Stornoway Harbour
St Columba's Church
Branahuie Banks
Arnish Pt
Arnish Moor
Rubh a'Bhaigh Uaine
Ceann na Circ
Ullapool 2¾ hrs
A859
Loch Orasay
Liurbost
Crosbost
B897
Grimsiadar
Loch Grimsiadar
Raerinish Point
Loch Thota Bridein
Loch nam Falcag
Loch Nisreaval
Loch Cleit Steirmeis
Loch Trealaval
Loch Fada
Laxay
Loch Airigh na h-Airde
Beinn Mohal
207
Loch Fadagoa
228
Roineval
281
Baile Ailein
Lacasaigh
Ceos
Eilean Chaluim Chille
Gleann Ghrabhair
Orasaigh
Tabhaigh Mhor
Torraigh
Loch Erisort
Cearsiadar
Gearraidh Bhaird
Cabharstadh
Tabost
B8060
Marthig
Sleiteachal Mhòr
248
Loch Strandavat
Loch Langavat
Kintarvie
Airidh a'Bhruaich
Malasgair
172
Loch Sgibacleit
Glen Ouirn
Loch Shanndabhat
Calbost
Rubha Iosal
Grabhair
Tom an Fhuadain
Loch Odhairn
Kebock Head
Aird an Troim
Ceann Loch Shiphoirt
Feirihisval
326
Kearnaval
378
Beinn a' Mhuil
370
Liuthaid
492
Sidhean an Airgid
381
Mòr Mhonadh
401
Beinn nah-Uamha
424
389
Muaithabhal
Leumrabhagh
Gob na Milaid
Eisgean
Athlinne
Aird a'Mhulaidh
Seaforth Island
Beinn Mhòr
572
Beannan Mòr
242
Loch Shell
Caolas a' Tuath
Srianach
Eilean Iubhard
Corlabhadh
Clett Ard
Kenmore
Park
Uisenis
371
Mulhagery
Maruig
470
Crionaig
Mol Truisg
A859
Loch Seaforth
Caiteshal
449
Sgaoth Aird
559
Straiaval
389
Toddun
528
Tathas Mhòr
Loch Claidh
Loch Bhrollum
Gob Rubh'Uisenis
Reinigeadal
Bhalamus
Rubha Bhrollum
Laxadale Lochs
Tarbert (An Tairbeart)
Beinn a' Chaolais
Eilean Mòr a' Bhàigh
Sgeir na h-Eigheach
Rubh a' Bhaird
SOUND OF SHIANT
Urgha
Carragrich
Uieseval
334
Kyles Scalpay (Caolas Scalpaigh)
Sgeotasaigh
Sound of Scalpay
Garbh Eilean
161
Eilean Mhuire
Eilean an Tighe
Shiant Islands
East Loch Tarbert
Ben Scoravick
104
Scalpay (Eilean Scalpaigh)
Kennavay
Meall Challibost
Scadabhagh
Rubha Bocaig
Loch Grosebay
Uig 1¾ hrs
Fladda-chuain
Gaeilavore Island
Gearran Island
Rubha Hunish
Eilean Trodday
Loch Hunish
Kilmaluag Bay
The Aird

A
B
C
D
1
2
3
4
5
3.2 miles to 1 inch
0 2 4 6 8 10 miles
0 2 4 6 8 10 km
2 km to 1 cm
WESTERN ISLES
(NA H EILEANAN AN IAR)
Rubh' an Dunain
Bagh Dail Beag
Dail Beag
20
Aird Mhòr
Gearrannan
Dail Mòr
Mullach Charlabhaigh
Craigeam
Borghastan
Carloway (Carlabhagh)
Loch Carlabhagh
Cirbhig
Creag Mhòr
Little Bernera
Carloway Broch
Gallan Head
West Loch Roag
Pabaidh Mòr
Tobson
Tolastadh a' Chaolais
Camas Sandig
East Loch Roag
Geodha Nasavig
Aird Uige
Bhaltos
Great Bernera
Breacleit
Vacsay
Breascleit
Fiavig Bagh
Forsnaval 205
Nisa Mhòr
B8011
Miabhig
Vula Mòr
Barraglom
Kirkibost
Aird Mhòr Mangurstadh
Cradhlastadh
Timsgearraidh
Uigen
Vuia Beg
Tacleit
Crulabhig
Eilean Kearstay
Callanish (Calanais)
Camas Uig
Floday
Ben Drovinish
5
B8059
Callanish Standing Stones
Loch Sgaslabhat
Cairisiadar
Loch Ceann Thulabhig
Mangurstadh
Eadar dha Fhadhail
Geisiadar
Linsiadar
Suainaval 429
Teahaval 256
Griomarstadh
3
Aird Fenish
Loch Suainaval
Loch Croistean
Einacleit
Loch Tungavat
Islibhig
Loch Raonasgail
16
Scealascro
B8011
Aird Breanais
Mealisval 574
Tahaval 515
Little Loch Roag
Loch Cle Steirmeis
Breanais
Loch Grunavat
Giosla
Cracaval 514
Skeun 265
Calltraiseal Bheag 226
Loch an Fhir Mhaoil
Beinn Mohal 207
Mealasta
Tamanaisval 467
Loch Dibadale
Beinn Mheadhonach 397
Coduinn 241
Calltraiseal Mhòr 228
Loch Airigh na h-Airde
Loch Morsgail
Caolas an Eilein
Maghannan
Mealasta Island
Griomaval
Loch na Craobhaig
Roineval 281
Loch Coirigerod
Liongan
184
Loch Tamanavay
Aird Bheag
Scalaval
Sleiteachal Mhòr 248
Loch Bodavat
Loch Benisval
Loch Thealasbhaidh
Morsgail Forest
Loch Langavat
Gob na h-Airde Moire
Aird Mhòr
Loch Resort
Beinn a'Bhoth 308
Aird an Troim
Sgeir Moil Duinn
Sron Romul
Uladale
Kearnaval

D
E
F
G
I
2
3
4
5
Butt of Lewis
(Rubha Robhanais)
Port a' Stoth
Cunndal
Teampull Mholuidh
Eoropaidh
Còig Peighinnean
Bad an Fhithich
Port Nis
Lional
Tabost
Suainebost
Eorodal
Port Skigersta
Aird Dhail
Cros
Sgiogarstaigh
Dail Bho Dheas
Dail Bho Thuath
B8015
Glen Cross
Ness
Meall Geal
Port Alasdair
Toa Galson
A857
Gabhsunn Bho Thuath
Gabhsunn Bho Dheas
Cuidhaseadair
Laimhrig
Broch
Mealabost
Roinn a' Bhuic
15
South Galson
Airigh na Glaice
Dell
Ben Dell
Airighean Beinn nan Caorach
Cellar Head
Còig Peighinnean
Siadar Iarach
Airighean Loch Breihavat
Loch Langavat
Siadar Uarach
Rubha Leathann
Baile an Truiseil
Steinacleit Cairn & Standing Stones
Diaval
Loch Mor Sandavat
Geiraha
Glen Shader
Goile Chroic
Rinn Druim Tallig
Aird Bragair
Port Arnol
A857
Loch Mor Bharabhais
Barvas (Barabhas)
Torray
Loch Gress
Muirneag
248
Port Geiraha
Labost
Bru
Black House
Tolastadh Ùr
Tolsta Head
Tolastadh
Port nam Bothag
Bragar
Arnol
Loch Casgro
Gleann Mòr Bharabhais
Gridis
Loch Mor Sandavit
Siabost
Loch Urrahag
Loch an Tobair
Loch Sgeireach Mor
B895
Loch Breivat
11
Gleann Tholastaidh
Port Bun a' Ghlinne
Glen Bragar
Gleann Bhruthadail
12
Beinn Bragar
261
Beinn Choinnich
210
Griais
Beinn Rahacleit
248
ISLE OF LEWIS
Roishal Mòr
174
(EILEAN LEODHAIS)
Creag Fhraoich
Bac
Loch na Scaravat
Col
Col
Beinn Mholach
292
Breibhig
Rubha Bhataisgeir
Loch Mor an Stuirr
Col Sands
Tiumpan Head
(Rubha an t-Siumpain)
Stacashal
216
Loch nan Stearnag
Loch nam Breac
A857
Aird Thunga
Portnaguran
(Port nan Giùran)
Rubha Deas
Laxdale
Tunga
Sron Ruadh
Newmarket
B895
Loch a' Tuath
A866
Stornoway
(Steornabhagh)
Laxdale
(Lacasdal)
Melbost Sands
Siulaisiadar
East Roisnish
Seisiadar
Loch Vatandip
A858
Melbost Pt
Garrabost
10
Rubha na Gréine
Stornoway
Melbost
Eye Peninsula
(An Rubha)
Loch Airigh nan Sloc
Loch Uraval
Creed
Nan Eilean
Aignis
Loch an Tairbeart
Lewis Castle
Sandwick
(Sanndabhaig)
St Columba's Church
Cnoc
Pabail Uarach
Rubha na Bearnaich
Beinn nan Surrag
13
Stornoway Harbour
Arnish Pt
Branahuie Banks
Suardail
Bagh Phabail
223
200
Beinn a' Bhuna
Pabail Iarach
A858
Eitshal
Arnish Moor
Rubh a'Bhaigh Uaine
Ceann na Circ
Achadh Mòr
Loch Orasay
Ullapool 2¼ hrs
A859
Loch Thota Bridein
6
Loch nam Falcag
Loch Nisreaval
Liurbost
B897
Grimsiadar
Loch Grimsiadar
Loch Trealaval
Crosbost
Loch Fada
Loch Leurbost
Raerinish Point
Laxay
Tabhaigh Mhor
12
Ceos
Eilean Chaluim Chille
Orasaigh
A859
Lacasaigh
Gleann Ghrabhair
Baile Ailein
Loch Erisort
Cearsiadar
Cabharstadh
Torraigh
Gearraidh Bhaird
Tabost
B8060
13
185
Marthig
Airidh a ... ich
Loch Sgibacleit
B8060
Malasgair
172
Calbost
Ceann Loch Shiphoirt
Rubha Iosal
Glen Ouirn
Loch Shanndabhat
Grabhair
Feirihisval

A
B
C
D
1
2
3
4
5
Rubh' Aird an t-Sionnaich
Eilean a'Bhreitheimh
Meall Mor
Meall Beag
Calbha Beag
Eddrachillis Bay
Sgeir nan Gall
Oldany Island
Point of Stoer
Rubha nan Cosan
Cirean Geardail
161
Culkein
Eilean Chrona
Clashnessie Bay
Raffin
Achnacarnin
Cluas Deas
Drumbeg
Nedd
23
B869
Loch Poll
Clashnessie
Balchladich
Loch Poll Dhaidh
Rubh'a' Mhill Dheirg
Stoer
Bay of Stoer
Clachtoll
Loch Crocach
Rubha Leumair
Achmelvich Bay
Rhicarn
Little Assynt
Achmelvich
Rubha Rodha
Ardroe
Baddidarach
Lochinver
Soyea Island
Loch Inver
Kirkaig Point
Loch Culag
A'Chleit
Badnaban
Strathan
Loch Kirkaig
Rubha na Breige
Inverkirkaig
Eilean Mor
Fionn Loch
Falls of Kirkaig
Rhegreanoch
Enard Bay
Loch Sionascaig
3.2 miles to 1 inch
0
2
4
6
8
10 miles
0
2
4
6
8
10 km
2 km to 1 cm
THE MINCH
Rubha Coigeach
Feochag Bay
Camas Eilean Ghlais
Camas Coille
Rubh' a'Choin
Polly Bay
Rubha Mor
Reiff
Loch an Alltain Duibh
Alltan Dubh
Eilean Mullagrach
Aird of Coigach
Inverpolly Forest
Isle Ristol
Loch Osgaig
Stac Pollaidh
613
Loch an Doire Dhuibh
Polbain
Glas-leac Mor
The Hydroponicum
Loch Bad a'Ghaill
Badentarbat Bay
Achiltibuie
Polglass
Cul Beag
769
Tanera Beg
Ardnagoine
An t-Sàil
490
Loch Lurgainn
Garadheancal
Beinn an Eoin
618
Summer Isles
Stornoway 2¾ hrs
Achvraie
Glas-leac Beag
Horse Island
Horse Sound
Ben Mòr Coigach
743
COIGACH
Achduart
Culnacraig
Priest Island
Eilean Dubh
Geodha Mòr
Strathkanaird
Carn nan Sgeir
Bottle Island
Camas Mor
Leac Dhonn
Isle Martin
Loch Kanaird
Greenstone Point
Leac Mhor
Cailleach Head
Rubha Beag
Opinan
Cul a'Bhogha
Ardmair
Rhue
Rubha Mor
Stattic Point
Scoraig
Achmore
Annat Bay
A835
Mellon Udrigle
Gruinard Island
Carnach
Rhireavach
Ullapool
Morefield
Eilean Furadh Mor
Slaggan Bay
Badluarach
Beinn Ghobhlach
635
Ullapool
Achgarve
Gruinard Bay
Little Loch Broom
Cnoc a' Bhaid-rallaich
545
Mungasdale
Durnamuck
Badcaul
Badrallach
Allt na h-Airbhe
Loch Broom
Cove
Laide
Mellon Charles
Second Coast
Coast
30
Blarnalevoch
Loch an Draing
Ormiscaig
A832
Carn na Beiste
302
Ardessie
Loggie
Bualnaluib
Aultbea
177
Little Gruinard
Camusnagaul
Eilean Darach
Rhiroy
296
Drumchork
Isle of Ewe
Loch Ewe
Loch Sguod
Carn nam Buailtean
384
Sail Mhor
A832
Ardindrean
Dundonnell
Inverasdale
Creag-mheall Beag
347
Loch Fada
Gruinard Forest
Dundonnell House
Strath Beag
Bidein
9
Midtown
7
Loch a'Bhaid

192
190
178
D
E
F
G
I
2
3
4
5
HIGHLAND
HIGHLANDS
NORTH WEST
STRATH
Achfary
Reay Forest
Strath Stack
Loch Stack
Ben Stack
721
Ben Auskaird
386
Loch Crocach
A838
A894
A837
A835
A836
A839
B869
Calbha Mor
Ardvar
Kylestrome
Unapool
Newton
Loch Glendhu
Loch Glencoul
Glendhu Forest
Loch an Leathaid Bhuain
Ben Strome
426
Beinn a'Bhutha
547
Loch na Creige Duibhe
Loch More
Aultanrynie
Kinloch
Beinn Lice
470
Strath na Caran
Ben Leoid
792
Ben Aird da Loch
530
Meall na Leitreach
566
Meall a Fheur Loch
613
Mealtan a'Chuail
750
Loch Merkland
Sabhal Beag
729
703
Meallan Liath Coire Mhic Dhughaill
801
796
Carn Dearg
Carn an Tionail
759
Glen Golly
Allnabad
Loch Meadie
Cnoc a'Chraois
348
Druim nam Bad
346
Cnoc an Daimh Mor
295
Allt Coire na Saigh Duibhe
Mudale
Meall na Teanga
365
Ben Hee
873
Meallan Liath Mor
683
Loch Ben Harrald
Loch Fiag
Meall an Fhuarain
473
Cnoc an Alaskie
Crask
266
Cnoc a'Ghiubh
Glen Fiag
Cnoc a'Ghriama
Corrykinloch
Loch a'Ghriama
Overscaig Hotel
Maovally
512
Cnoc a'Bhaid Bhain
367
Loch Shin
Sail Gorm
776
Quinag
808
Gleann Leireag
Spidean Coinich
764
Eas a Chual Aluinn (Waterfall)
Glas Bheinn
776
Beinn Uidhe
740
Loch Assynt
Ardvreck (ruin)
Beinn Gharbh
540
Inchnadamph
Inchnadamph Forest
Gleann Dubh
Ben More Assynt
998
Conival
987
Canisp
846
Stronechrubie
Dubh Loch Mor
715
Breabag
814
Meall a Bhraghaid
688
Benmore Forest
Duchally
Leathad Dail nan Cliabh
329
Strath an Loin
Allt Car
Beinn Sgreamhaidh
435
West Shinnel Lodge
Arscaig
The Airde
Glenmuick
Ben Sgeireach
476
Loch Sgeireach
Badintagairt
Carn nam Bo Maola
424
Glen Cassley
Ledbeg
Ledmore
Elphin
Knockan
Inverpolly
Cul Mòr
849
Loch Urigill
Loch Borralan
Cam Loch
Loch Veyatie
Loch Ailsh
An Stuc
364
Beinn an Eoin
544
Cnoc na Glas Choille
307
Glen Oykel
Loch Craggie
Fionn Bheinn Mhor
330
Drumrunie
Cromalt Hills
516
Meall an Fhuarain
578
Lubcroy
Oykel Bridge
Langwell
Brae
Doune
Rosehall
Invercassley
Glenrossal
Oykel Forest
Achnahanat
Aucharrigill
Altass
Auchintoul
Birchfield
Strath Oykel
Cnoc a'Choire
402
Sallach
Na Dromannan
408
Strath nan Lon
Rappach
Rhidorroch Forest
Rappach Water
Meall Liath Choire
548
Glen Einig
Beinn Ulbhaidh
493
Creag Loisgte
412
Lubachoinnich
Breac-Bheinn
462
Meall Dheirgidh
507
Strathcarron
Rhidorroch
Loch Achall
Glen Achall
Beinn Eilideach
558
Loch an Daimh
Knockdamph
Strath Mulzie
Carn a'Choin Deirg
701
Sgodachail
Croick
The Craigs
Wester Gruinards
Amat Forest
Leckmelm
Ardcharnich
Meall Dubh
642
Meall nam Bradhan
677
Glen Douchary
Seana Bhraigh
927
Bodach Mor
822
Carn Ban
Freevater Forest
Sron Gun Aran
Gleann Mor
Glen Calvie
Carn Bhrain
635
Inverlael Forest
Dunan Liath
Eididh nan
1408

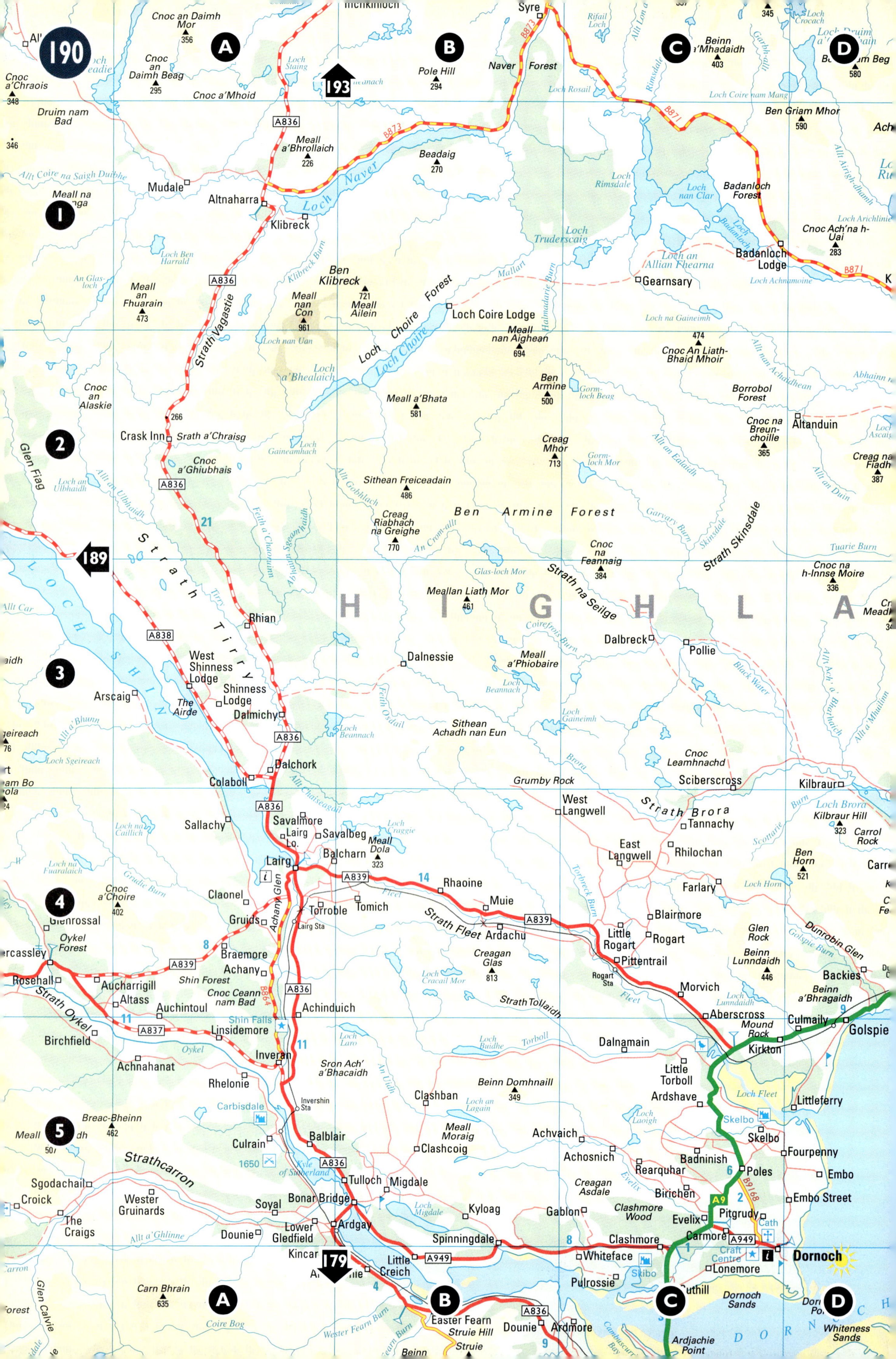
A
B
C
D
193
Syre
Cnoc an Daimh Mor
356
Cnoc an Daimh Beag
295
Cnoc a'Mhoid
Cnoc a'Chraois
348
Druim nam Bad
346
Loch Staing
Pole Hill
294
Naver Forest
Loch Rosail
Rifail Loch
Beinn a'Mhadaidh
403
Loch Coire nam Mang
Ben Griam Mhor
590
580
B873
B871
A836
Meall a'Bhrollaich
226
Beadaig
270
Loch Naver
Mudale
Altnaharra
Klibreck
Meall na
1
Loch Rimsdale
Loch nan Clar
Badanloch Forest
Loch Badanloch
Loch Truderscaig
Loch an Allian Fhearna
Badanloch Lodge
Cnoc Ach'na h-Uai
283
Loch Arichlinie
Gearnsary
Loch Achnamoine
Loch Ben Harrald
An Glas-loch
Meall an Fhuarain
473
Ben Klibreck
721
Meall nan Con
961
Meall Ailein
Loch Choire Forest
Loch Coire Lodge
Mallart
Halmadarie Burn
Meall nan Aighean
694
Loch na Gaineimh
474
Cnoc An Liath-Bhaid Mhoir
Strath Vagastie
Loch nan Uan
Loch a'Bhealaich
Loch Choire
Ben Armine
500
Gorm-loch Beag
Borrobol Forest
Altanduin
Cnoc an Alaskie
Meall a'Bhata
581
Cnoc na Breun-choille
365
266
Crask Inn
Strath a'Chraisg
2
Cnoc a'Ghiubhais
Loch Gaineamhach
Creag Mhor
713
Gorm-loch Mor
Allt an Ealaidh
Creag na Fiadh
387
Glen Fiag
Loch an Ulbhaidh
Allt an Ulbhaidh
Sithean Freiceadain
486
Creag Riabhach na Greighe
770
An Crom-allt
Ben Armine Forest
Garvary Burn
Skinsdale
Strath Skinsdale
Tuarie Burn
21
Strath Tirry
Feith a'Chaorainn
189
Loch Shin
Glas-loch Mor
Cnoc na Feannaig
384
Strath na Seilge
Cnoc na h-Innse Moire
336
Meallan Liath Mor
461
HIGHLA
Rhian
A838
West Shinness Lodge
Shinness Lodge
3
Arscaig
The Airde
Dalmichy
Dalnessie
Meall a'Phiobaire
Loch Beannach
Dalbreck
Pollie
Black Water
Sithean Achadh nan Eun
Loch Gaineimh
Feith Osdail
Loch Beannach
Cnoc Leamhnachd
Allt a'Bhuinn
Loch Sgeireach
Dalchork
Colaboll
Grumby Rock
Sciberscross
Kilbraur
Brora
West Langwell
Strath Brora
Tannachy
Loch Brora
Kilbraur Hill
323
Carrol Rock
Sallachy
Savalmore
Lairg Lo.
Savalbeg
Balcharn
Loch Craggie
Meall Dola
323
Loch na Caillich
Loch na Fuaralaich
East Langwell
Rhilochan
Ben Horn
521
Lairg
A839
14
Rhaoine
Farlary
Loch Horn
Cnoc a'Choire
402
Claonel
Achany Glen
Torroble
Tomich
Muie
Blairmore
4
Glenrossal
Gruids
Lairg Sta
Strath Fleet
Ardachu
Little Rogart
Rogart
Glen Rock
Oykel Forest
Braemore
Achany
8
Creagan Glas
813
Pittentrail
Rogart Sta
Beinn Lunndaidh
446
Dunrobin Glen
Backies
Rosehall
Aucharrigill
Shin Forest
Loch Cracail Mor
Morvich
Beinn a'Bhragaidh
Altass
Cnoc Ceann nam Bad
Achinduich
B864
Strath Tollaidh
Fleet
Aberscross
Culmaily
Golspie
Strath Oykel
11
Auchintoul
Shin Falls
A837
Linsidemore
Birchfield
Loch Laro
Loch Buidhe
Torboll
Dalnamain
Mound Rock
Kirkton
Oykel
Achnahanat
Inveran
Sron Ach' a'Bhacaidh
An Uidh
Little Torboll
Rhelonie
Beinn Domhnaill
349
Ardshave
Loch Fleet
Littleferry
Inverhin Sta
Clashban
Loch an Lagain
Loch Laoigh
Carbisdale
Skelbo
5
Breac-Bheinn
462
Meall
507
Balblair
Meall Moraig
Achvaich
Skelbo
Culrain
Clashcoig
Fourpenny
Strathcarron
1650
Kyle of Sutherland
Achosnich
Badninish
Poles
Embo
6
Rearquhar
Sgodachail
Croick
Wester Gruinards
Tulloch
Migdale
Creagan Asdale
Birichen
B9168
Embo Street
Soyal
Bonar Bridge
Loch Migdale
Kyloag
Gablon
Clashmore Wood
A9
Pitgrudy
The Craigs
Allt a'Ghlinne
Dounie
Lower Gledfield
Ardgay
Evelix
Cath
Spinningdale
Clashmore
Carmore
A949
Kincar
179
Little Creich
Whiteface
Craft Centre
Dornoch
Skibo
Lonemore
Pulrossie
Cuthill
Carn Bhrain
635
Glen Calvie
Dornoch Sands
Coire Bog
Wester Fearn Burn
Easter Fearn
Struie Hill
Dounie
Ardmore
Whiteness Sands
Ardjachie Point
Struie
Beinn
9

191
194
180
D
E
F
G
I
2
3
4
5
Forsinard
Cnoc nan Gall
275
A897
Meall a' Bhealaich
Rumsdale Wat
Loch a' Mhuilinn
Dalganachan
Loch Ruard
Lochan Thulachan
Loch Sand
havanich
Loch Stemster
Stemster H
248
Loch Rangag
Coire na Beinne
226
Sheppardstown
Cnoc Cromuillt
365
Ben Alisky
349
Crofts of Benachielt
Ben-a-chielt
Rumster Forest
Reisgill Burn
Reisgill
toul Forest
Cnocan Conachreag
269
Lochside
Bannock Burn
Cnoc na Saobhaidhe
290
Knockfin Heights
438
Burn of Houstry
Houstry
Nottingh
Gillivoan
Forse
Achentoul
Glutt Water
Achnaclyth
Dunbeath Water
Latheron
Feith Gaineimh Mhor
Smerral
Kinbrace Burn
Badnagie
Latheronwheel
Cnoc Coire na Fearna
437
Gobernuisgeach
Lhaidhay Croft Museum
Heritage Centre
Burnfoot
Braemore
Achorn
Toremore
Dunbeath
Inver
Helmsdale
Maiden Pap
484
Knockally
Dunbeath
Dunbeath Bay
Morven
706
Berriedale Water
Cnoc an Eireannaich
517
Suisgill Burn
Ramscraigs
A897
Scaraben
626
Meall na Caorach
17
Wag
A9
Borgue
Strath of Kildonan
20
Garvery Hill
333
Langwell Forest
Loch Scalabsdale
Creag Scalabsdale
555
Cnoc Salislade
483
Kildonan Burn
Aultibea
Newport
Ceann Leathad nam Bo
Mid Hill
312
330
Langwell Water
Braigh na h-Eaglaise
422
Langwell House
Berriedale
Torrish Burn
Blar a'Ghille Dhomhnaich
Kildonan Lodge
Beinn Dubhain
414
Craggie
Duible
Ousdale
Craggie Water
Kilphedir
Creag Thoraraidh
Badbea
A897
Torrish
Caen
nach
N
D
A9
Ord of Caithness
Eldrable Hill
The Craggan
482
Ben Uarie
Marrel
Navidale
Beinn Dhorain
628
Helmsdale
East Helmsdale
Beinn Mhealaich
592
Meallan Liath Beag
West Helmsdale
Gartymore
Allt Smeorail
Glen Sletdale
Glen Loth
Portgower
Culgower
Creag a'Chrionaich
394
Lothmore
Kilmote
Col-bheinn
538
A9
11
Lothbeg
Gordonbush
Lothbeg Point
Kintradwell
Killin
Achrimsdale
Greenhill
West Clyne
Dalchalm
in Rock
Clynelish
Brora
East Brora
Brora
Doll
A9
Dunrobin Castle
3.2 miles to 1 inch
0
2
4
6
8
10 miles
0
2
4
6
8
10 km
2 km to 1 cm
F I R T H
Tarbat
Port Mor
Innis Mhor
Hilton
Bindal

Duslic
Cape Wrath
Stack Clo Kearvaig
An Garbh-eilean
Kearvaig
Sgribhis-bheinn
371
A'Gholl
Faraid Head
Geodha Ruadh na Fola
Cnoc a'Ghiubhais
297
Balnakeil Bay
Inshore
Loch Inshore
Bay of Keisgaig
299
Maovally
Balnakeil
Durness Old Church
Craft Village
Durness
Sango Bay
Pocan Smoo
Smoo Cave
Eilean Hoan
Loch Keisgaig
Fashven
457
Achiemore
Am Balg
Sandwood Bay
Beinn Dearg
423
Loch Airigh na Beinne
Beinn an Amair
278
Keoldale
Leirinmore
Sangobeg
Am Buachaille
Sandwood Loch
Creag Riabhach
485
Kyle of Durness
Beinn Ceannabeinne
383
Loch Meadaidh
Sarsgrum
Rubh' an Fhir Leithe
An Grianan
467
Meall na Moine
464
Grudie
Meall Meadhonach
422
A838
Loch na Gainimh
Sheigra
Strath Shinary
Ghlas-bheinn
332
15
Port-na-Con
Abhainn an t-Srathain
Drochaid Mhor
Balchrick
Blairmore
Beinn a'Chraisg
257
Meall a'Chraidh
490
Laid
Oldshore Beg
Farrmheall
521
A838
Eilean Choraidh
An Socach
358
Eilean an Roin Mor
Oldshore More
19
Beinn Spionnaidh
772
Loch Eriboll
Loch Clash
Kinlochbervie
Loch na Gainimh
Cranstackie
802
Eriboll
Rubha na Leacaig
B801
Badcall
Loch Tarbhaidh
Bagh Loch an Roin
Achriesgill
Loch Inchard
Strath Dionard
Polla
A838
Strath Beag
Achlyness
Loch Crocach
Loch Dùghaill
An Lean-charn
521
Ardmore Point
Rhiconich
Loch na Claise Carnaich
Ceathramh Garbh
Conamheall
482
Rubha Ruadh
Loch na h-Ula
Loch Uidh an Tuim
Foinaven
915
Loch Laxford
Fanagmore
867
Creag Dionard
778
Loch Dionard
Loch Crocach
Tarbet
Handa Island
Foindle
Sound of Handa
Laxford Bridge
Loch a'Gharbh Bhaid Mhoir
Loch na Tuadh
Feinne-Bheinn Mhor
465
Loch nam Breac
Badnabay
Laxford
Loch an Easain Uaine
Loch an Laig Aird
Arkle
787
Scourie Bay
A894
Gorm Loch
H
Meall a'Chuirn
777
I
G
7
Sabhal Mor
703
Scourie More
Scourie
A838
Loch Stack
Rubh' Aird an t-Sionnaich
Sabhal Beag
729
Glen Golly
Ben Stack
721
Abhainn an Loin
Badcall
Badcall Bay
Ben Auskaird
386
Loch Crocach
Strath Stack
Achfary
Ben Screavie
322
Meallan Liath Coire Mhic Dhughaill
801
796
Carn an Tionail
759
Carn Dearg
Eilean a'Bhreitheimh
Reay Forest
Meall Mor
Rubh' a'Mhucard
10
A894
Loch More
Allt nan Ramh
Loch na Creige Duibhe
Allt a'Chraois
Meall Beag
Calbha Beag
Strath na Caran
Loch an Seilg
Sgeir nan Gall
Calbha Mor
Ben Strome
426
Aultanrynie
Loch Coire na Saighe Duibhe
Rubha nan Cosa
Oldany Island
Eddrachillis Bay
Beinn a'Bhutha
547
Beinn Lice
470
Allt Beithe
Loch a'Chàirn Bhain
Kylestrome
Loch an Leathaid Bhuain
Kinloch
Ben Hee
873
Ardvar
Glendhu Forest
Gleann Dubh
Clashnessie Bay
Drumbeg
Unapool
Loch Glendhu
A838
Mealan Liath Mor
683
23
Loch Nedd
Meall na Leitreach
566
B869
Nedd
B869
Newton
Ben Aird da Loch
530
Loch Glencoul
Meall a Fheur Loch
613
Loch a'Ghorm-choire
Loch Poll
B869
Sail Gorm
776
Loch Merkland
Gleann Leireag
NORTH WEST
Loch Dhaidh
Loch an Leothaid
Quinag
808
Loch na Gainmhich
Beinn Leoid
792
Meallan a'Chuail
750
Loch Fiag
189
7
Loch Dubh a'Chuail
Spidean Coinich
764
A894
Eas a Chual Aluinn (Waterfall)
A
B
C
D
Loch Crocach
9
Loch an Eircill
Loch a'Ghriama
Cnoc a'Ghriama
Rhicarn
Loch Beannach
Little
A837
Loch
776
Beinn Uidhe
740
Gorm Loch Mor
Corrykinloch

D
E
F
G
3.2 miles to 1 inch
0 2 4 6 8 10 miles
0 2 4 6 8 10 km
2 km to 1 cm
I
Strathy Point
Whiten Head
Rubha Thormaid
Cnoc Ard an t-Siuil
183
Geodh' a'Bhrideoin
Eilean Cluimhrig
Port Vasgo
Ben Hutig
408
Midfield
Rabbit Islands
Eilean nan Ron
Neave or Coomb Island
Farr Point
Kirtomy Point
Ardmore Point
Port Allt a'Mhuilinn
Totegan
Strathy Bay
Brawl
Armadale Bay
Aultiphurst
Armadale
Lednagullin
Kirtomy
Swordly
Farr
Kirtomy Bay
Coal Raineach
Skerray
Achtoty
Modsarie
Torrisdale
Torrisdale Bay
Farr Bay
Strathnaver Museum
Bettyhill
Achina
A836
28
Beinn Chuldail
169
Strathy Forest
Bowside Lodge
Talmine
Midtown
A'Mhoine
Strath Melness Burn
Inverhope
Tongue Bay
Skullomie
Coldbackie
Tongue Ho.
22
Moine Ho.
Loch Maovally
A838
Achuvoldrach
Lochside
Druim nan Cliar
262
HIGHLANDS
Borgie
Naver Rock
Invernaver
Leckfurin
Achnabourin
Beinn nam Bo
229
194
Beinn Ru
254
Loch Meadie
Loch Buidhe Mor
Loch Meala
Beinn Bhreac
Tongue
Meall Leathad na Craoibhe
310
Kyle of Tongue
Ribigill
Borgie Forest
Achargary
B871
Naver
Skelpick Burn
Clachan Burn
Loch Mor na Caorach
3
Caol-loch
Loch Hope
Creag Riabhach Bheag
463
Lochan Hakel
Cnoc Craggie
318
Loch Slaim
Loch Craggie
Loch na Moine
Lochan nan Carn
Loch nan Ealachan
Loch nan Clach
The Uair
Cnoc na
Loch na Seilg
Ben Hope
927
Meallan Liath
Kinloch
Ben Hiel
557
Beinn Stumanadh
527
Strathnaver
Duvidean Lochs
Rhifail
Loch a' Ghobha-Dhuibh
Strath More
Ben Loyal
764
Loch an Dherue
Lettermore
Loch Loyal
Meall an Spothaidh
Loch Rifa-gil
Loch na Sgobhaidhe
Loch nam Breac
Loch Strathy
Alltnacaillich
Dun Dornaigil Broch
Cnoc nan Cuilean
557
17
A836
Loch Haluim
Loch Syre
Skail
Creagan Dubha Reidhe Bhig
337
Cnoc nan Tri-chlach
345
4
H L A N D
Inchkinloch
Loch Coulside
Syre
Rifail Loch
Allt Lon a' Chuil
Loch Crocach
Loch Druim a'Chliabhain
Allnabad
Cnoc an Daimh Mor
356
B873
Beinn a'Mhadaidh
403
Ben Griam Beg
580
Loch Meadie
Cnoc an Daimh Beag
295
Loch Staing
Loch Eileanach
Pole Hill
294
Naver Forest
Rimsdale Burn
Cnoc a'Chraois
348
Cnoc a'Mhoid
Loch Rosail
Loch Coire nam Mang
Druim nam Bad
A836
Ben Griam Mhor
590
Ache
346
Meall a'Bhrollaich
226
Beadaig
270
B871
Allt Coire na Saigh Duibhe
Loch Naver
Mudale
Loch Rimsdale
Loch nan Clar
Badanloch Forest
Allt Airigh-dhamh
Meall na Teanga
365
Altnaharra
5
Klibreck
Loch Truderscaig
Loch Badanloch
Cnoc Uai
283
Loch Ben Harrald
Klibreck Burn
Loch an Allain Fhearna
Badanloch Lodge
An Glas-loch
Ben Klibreck
A836
Mallart
Gearnsary
Loch Achnamoine
Meall an Fhuarain
473
Meall nan Con
961
721
Meall Ailein
Loch Choire Forest
Loch Coire Lodge
Halmadarie Burn
Loch na Gaineimh
Strath Vagastie
Loch nan Uan
Meall nan Aighean
694
190
474
Cnoc An Liath-Bhaid Mhoir
Allt nan Achaidhean
Loch a'Bhealaich
Loch Choire
Ben Armine
500
Gorm-loch Beag
Borrobol Forest
Abhainn na
Cnoc an Alaskie
Meall a'Bhata
581
Cnoc na Breun-choille
Altanduin
266
Crask Inn
Strath a'Chraisg
Creag
Loch Ascaig

A
B
C
D
1
2
3
4
5
Stromness 2hrs
Strathy Point
Brims Ness
Ness of Litter
Clett
Holborn Head
Clardon Head
Scrabster
Thurso Bay
Thurso
Crosskirk Bay
Crosskirk
St Mary's Chapel
Lybster
A836
Bridge of Forss
Ormwe
Clardon
Haimer
Port Allt a'Mhuilinn
Totegan
Ardmore Point
Armadale Bay
Strathy Bay
Melvich Bay
Red Point
Sandside Bay
Nuclear Power Exhibition
Dounreay
Buldoo
Achreamie
Viewfield
Janetstown
Lythmore
Glengolly
Brawl
Baligill
Portskerra
Fresgoe
Newlands of Geise
A9
Shalmst
Aultiphurst
Strathy
Melvich
Bighouse
Sandside House
Reay
Isauld
Achvarasdal
Westfield
Lednagullin
Shebster
Forss Water
B874
Buckies
Aimster
A836
28
Beinn Chuldail
169
Strathy Forest
Drum Hollistan
Golval
Kirkton
Forsie
Lieurary
B870
Bowside Lodge
Achridigill Loch
A897
Beinn Ratha
242
Reay Burn
Skinnet
Beinn Ruadh
254
Loch Akran
Broubster
Braal Castle
193
Loch Calder
Calder Mains
Gerston
Halkirk
Loch nan Gall
Loch na Seilge
Achiemore
Shurrery
Bloody Moss
Upper Bighouse
Brawlbin
Loch Olginey
Loch Meala
Craigtown
Smigel Burn
Sandside Burn
Achvarasdal Burn
Shurrery Lodge
Scotscalder Sta
Harpsdale
Loch Scye
Caol-loch
Dalhalvaig
Loch Shurrery
Ben Dorrery
244
Olgrinmore
Achies
Croick
Dorrery
Beinn Nam Bad Mor
290
Trantlemore
Trantlebeg
Cnoc an Fhuarain Bhain
243
Loch Tuim Ghlais
Loch Calum
Cnoc Badaireach na Gaoithe
The Uair
Halladale
Cnocloisgte
Water
Thurso
B870
Westerd
Tor
Forsinain
H I G H L A N
Loch na Sgobhaidhe
Loch nam Breac
Strath Halladale
Sletill Hill
280
Loch Sletill
Lochan Dubh nan Geadh
Loch Eileanach
Loch Meadie
Loch Strathy
Altnabreac Sta
22
Lochdhu Hotel
Loch More
Sleach Water
Loch Crocach
Forsinard
Cnoc nan Gall
275
Loch Druim a' Chliabhain
Garbh-allt
Loch a' Mhuilinn
Loch Ruard
Beinn a'Mhadaidh
403
Ben Griam Beg
580
A897
Meall a' Bhealaich
Lochan Thulachan
Rumsdale Water
Loch Sand
Loch Coire nam Mang
Dalganachan
Ben Griam Mhor
590
Cnoc Cromuillt
365
Achentoul Forest
Ben Alisky
349
Loch an Ruathair
Allt Airigh-dhamh
Bannock Burn
Cnocan Conachreag
269
Loch nan Clar
Badanloch Forest
Lochside
Cnoc na Saobhaidhe
290
Burn of Houstry
Loch Arichlinie
Knockfin Heights
438
Glutt Water
Cnoc Ach'na h-Uai
283
Badanloch Lodge
Achentoul
Achnaclyth
Dunbeath Water
B871
Feith Gaineimh Mhor
Kinbrace
Loch Achnamoine
Kinbrace Burn
Cnoc Coire na Fearna
437
Gobernuisgeach
Braemore
Achorn
Burnfoot
474
Cnoc An Liath-bhaid Mhoir
191
Maiden Pap
484
Knockally
Allt nan Achaidhean
Helmsdale
Morven
706
Berriedale Water
Abhainn
Cnoc an Eireannaich
Borrobol Forest
A897
Suisgill Burn
Scaraben
626
Meall na Caorach
17
Cnoc na Breun-choille
Altanduin
Loch Ascaig
Wag
Garvery
Langwell Forest
20
A9
Borgue

195
196
D
E
F
G
PENTLAND FIRTH
The Tails of Tarf
Swona
Burwick
Liddel
Old Head
Muckle Skerry
Pentland Skerries
Langaton Point
Island of Stroma
Nethertown
Red Head
Mell Head
Uppertown
Inner Sound
Boars of Duncansby
Dunnet Head
Easter Head
Dunnet Hill 121
Skarfskerry Point
Tang Head
Castle of Mey
Men of Mey
St John's Point
Head of Crees
Gills Bay
Ness of Duncansby
Bay of Sannick
Duncansby Head
Stacks of Duncansby
Scarfskerry
Harrow
Loch of Mey
Ham
Brough
Hunspow
The Thirl
St John's Loch
Rattar
Whitebridge
Mey
East Mey
Gills
A836
Huna
John o' Groats
Canisbay
Upper Gills
West Dunnet
Dwarwick Head
Dunnet
Barrock
The Spur
Dunnet Bay
Murkle Bay
Inkstack
Links of Dunnet
Warth Hill 124
Wife Geo
Brabster
Everley
Tofts
Skirza
Skirza Head
Freswick Bay
Gill Burn
Murkle
Castletown
Greenland
Thurdistoft
Loch Heilen
Lochend
Slickly
Freswick
A99
Ness Head
Olrig House
Hayfield
Tain
Lochside
Reaster
Alterwall
Auckengill
Hilliclay
Durran
Hoy
Bowermadden
Kirk Burn
Nybster
B876
Lyth
Sortat
17
Brough Head
Achingills
Stemster
Bowertower
Howe
Knockdee
Tister
Stemster House
Hastigrow
Mireland
Keiss
Tang Head
Roadside
Corsback
Halcro
Burn of Lyth
Stain
B874
Clayock
Loch Scarmclate
Gillock
Georgemas Junc. Sta
A882
North Watten
B870
Kirk
Loch of Wester
Sinclair's Bay
Lynegar
Killimster
Quoys of Reiss
A9
Spittal Hill
Oldhall
Dunn
Loch Watten
Mains of Watten
B874
Houstry of Dunn
Loch of Winless
Reiss
Ackergill Tower
Girnigoe
Noss Head
Newton
Watten
Wick
Winless
Sinclair
Spital
B870
Backlass
15
Whitefield
Ackergill
Bilbster
Sibster
Wick
Staxigoe
Mybster
Strath
Caithness Glass
Loch of Toftingall
Thuster
Haster
North Head
Milton
Burn of Acharole
Strath Burn
Stirkoke House
Wick
Newton
South Head
Whiterow
Northfield
Castle of Old Wick
Badlipster
Achairn Burn
Puldagon
Tannach
Hempriggs House
Camster Burn
Loch Hempriggs
Toftcarl
Tacher
Lower Camster
Thrumster
Ires Geo
Stemster
Ballharn Hill 145
Grey Cairns of Camster
Corbiegoe
Hill of Yarrows 213
Loch of Yarrows
Sarclet
Sarclet Head
Loch Stemster
Achavanich
Stemster Hill 248
Upper Camster
Whiteleen
Stack of Ulbster
Cnoc an Earrannaiche
Loch Rangag
Cairn of Get
Ulbster
Whaligoe
Sheppardstown
Roster
Bruan
East Clyth
Prehistoric Stones
Crofts of Benachielt
Ben-a-chielt
Upper Lybster
Reisgill Burn
Rumster Forest
Mid Clyth
Blackness
Reisgill
Swiney
Occumster
Houstry
Nottingham
Lybster
Gillivoan
Forse
Smerral
Latheron
Badnagie
Latheronwheel
Heritage Centre
Toremore
Inver
Dunbeath
3.2 miles to 1 inch
0 2 4 6 8 10 miles
0 2 4 6 8 10 km
2 km to 1 cm
1
2
3
4
5

A
B
C
D
1
2
3
4
5
198
195
Twatt
Isbister
Outshore Point
Beaquoy
Burn of
B9057
Click
Hillside
Milldoe
221
Wood Wick
Gairsay S
Tingwall
Northdyke
Quoyloo
Skeabrae
Mirbister
A967
A986
A966
B9056
Hackland
Bay of Skaill
Skaill
Skara Brae
Corrigall Farm Museum
Settiscarth
Gorseness
Isbister
Tor Ness
Row Head
Loch of Skaill
B9057
Aith
Loch of Harray
Brough
Netherbrough
Bay of Isbister
Broad Taing
Yesnaby
Voy
Ness of Tenston
Bimbister
A986
WIDE FIRTH
Loch of Wasdale
Neban Point
Hill of Miffia
158
Quholm
Loch of Stenness
B9055
Ring of Brodgar
Maes Howe
Stones of Stenness
Finstown
Bay of Firth
Damsay
Rennibister Earth House
A965
Chambered Cairn
Heddle
Chambered Cairn
Wideford Hill
225
Grainbank Earth House
Clouston
Keelylang Hill
221
Outertown
A965
Breck Ness
Museum
Stromness
Pier Arts Centre
Ireland
St Magnus Cathedral
Loch of Kirbister
Greenigo
Ward Hill
268
Kirbister
Hobbister
A964
A964
Clestrain
Hoy Sound
Clestrain Sound
Graemsay
Kame of Hoy
Murra
Orphir
Gyre
Swanbister Bay
Ve Ness
Waulkmill Bay
Scapa Bay
Long Geo
Houton
Orphir Round Church and Earl's Bu
Midland Ness
Houton Head
St John's Head
Cuilags
433
Ward Hill
479
Linksness
Bring Deeps
The Sow
B9047
Old Man of Hoy
Old Man of Hoy
Dwarfie Stane
Barrel of Butter
SCAPA FLO
Rora Head
Rackwick
Green Head
Cava
Rack Wick
Knap of Trowieglen
399
Lyrawa Burn
Pegal Burn
Rysa Little
354
Calf of Flotta
Roan Head
Hunda
ORKNEY
HOY
Fara
Oil Terminal
Flotta
Sneuk Head
Lyness Naval Base and Interpretation Centre
Lyness
B9045
Rinnigill
Pan
Sound of Hoxa
Hoxa
Bow
Crock Ness
Little Rack Wick
Burn of Ore
Heldale Water
B9047
Widewall Bay
Quindry
B9043
Herston Head
Herston
Martello Towers
Longhope
Hackness
Switha
B9042
North Bay
Melsetter
Hurliness
Cantick Head
Tor Ness
South Walls
Brims Ness
Garth Head
The North Head
Barth Head
Swona
The Tails of Tarf
Burwick
2 hrs
Lerwick 8 hrs
PENTLAND FIRTH
Aberdeen 8 hrs
Langaton Point
Island of Stroma
Nethertown
Red Head
Dunnet Head
Easter Head
Mell Head
Uppertown
Boars of Duncansby
Men of Mey
St John's Point
Inner Sound
B855
Tang Head
Castle of Mey
Skarfskerry Point
Head of Crees
Ness of Duncansby
Bay of Sannick
Duncansby Head
Dunnet Hill
121
Scarfskerry
Harrow
Gills Bay
Ham
Loch of Mey
East Mey
Brough
St John's Loch
Rattar
Gills
A836
Huna
John o' Groats
Stacks of Duncansby
The Thirl
Hunspow
West Dunnet
Whitebridge
Mey
Ness of Litter
Clett
Holborn Head
Dwarwick Head
Barrock
Upper Gills
Canisbay
Scrabster
Clardon Head
The Spur
Dunnet
HIGHLAND
Warth Hill
124
Wife Geo
Thurso Bay
Murkle Bay
Dunnet Bay
Inkstack
A836
Links of Dunnet
Brabster
Everley
Thurso
Murkle
A836
Skirza Head
Forss
Viewfield
Ormwe
Castletown
Greenland
Lochend
Tofts
Skirza
Freswick Bay
A9
Haimer
B876
Thurdistoft
Freswick
Slickly
Janetstown
Glengolly
Olrig House
Hayfield
Tain
Ness Head
A99
Newlands
Lochside
Reaster
Alterwall
Auckengill

ORKNEY ISLANDS
STRONSAY FIRTH
Sweyn Holm
The Galt
Veantrow Bay
Edmonstone
Bay of Furrowend
B9058
Bay of Linton
Shapinsay
B9059
Balfour
Balfour
Helliar Holm
Sandgarth
The Foot
Haco's Ness
Rothiesholm
Rothiesholm Head
Greenli Ness
Grobister
Kirbister
B9060
Dishes
Holland
Burgh Head
Bay of Houseby
Tor Ness
Ingale Skerry
Auskerry Sound
Auskerry
199
Car Ness
Work
Head of Holland
Shapinsay Sound
Berstane
Inganess Bay
Tankerness House Museum
Rerwick Head
Lea Taing
Linksness
Scarva Taing
Mull Head
Deer Sound
Kirkwall
Tankerness
Toab
A960
The Gloup
Skaill
Roand Bay
Mirkady Point
B9051
B9050
Gritley
North Dawn
Foubister
Upper Sanday
Graemshall House
B9052
Newark Bay
Point of Ayre
Camy
Braehead
Corn Holm
St Mary's
Italian Chapel
Cornquoy
South Nevi
Copinsay
Lamb Holm
Holm Sound
Rose Ness
Northtown
Burray
Southtown
Grimness
Grim Ness
B9044
Eastside
South Ronaldsay
Halcro Head
Tomb of the Eagles
Old Head
Pentland Skerries
Invergordon 9 hrs
3.2 miles to 1 inch
0 2 4 6 8 10 miles
0 2 4 6 8 10 km
2 km to 1 cm
D
E
F
G
1
2
3
4
5

A
B
C
D
1
2
3
4
5
3.2 miles to 1 inch
0 2 4 6 8 10 miles
0 2 4 6 8 10 km
2 km to 1 cm
The Bore
Mull Head
Papa Westray
North Hill
Papa Sound
St Boniface Kirk
Bow Head
Aikerness
Westray
Knap of Howar
Papa Westray
Holland
Holm of Papa
Chambered Cairn
St Tredwell's Chapel
Backaskaill
Noup Head
Rackwick
Noup Head
Ouse Ness
Gentlemens' Cave
Noltland
St.Mary's Medieval Church
Broughton
Head of Moclett
Monivey
Pierowall
Bis Geos
Braehead
Spo Ness
Westray
B9066
B9067
Midbea
Bay of Tuquoy
Skelwick
Inga Ness
Cross Kirk
Langskaill
Stanger Head
Berst Ness
Twiness
Rapness
Skea Skerries
WESTRAY FIRTH
Point of Huro
1½ hrs (summer only)
Rapness Sound
Faray
Rusk Holm
Sacquoy Head
Saviskaill Head
Bring Head
Saviskaill Bay
Faraclett Head
Fers Ness
Rousay
Wasbister
B9064
Kili Holm
Eday
Sourin
Mae Ness
Muckle Water
St Magnus Church
Costa Head
Midhowe Broch and Cairn
Skea
Eynhallow
Westness
Blotchnie Fiold 250
Egilsay
Geo Luon
Brough Head
Brough of Birsay
A966
Costa
Eynhallow Church
Knowe of Yarso Chambered Cairn
Brinian
Rousay Sound
Earl's Palace
Birsay
Abune-the-Hill
Loch of Swannay
Broch of Gurness
Muckle Green Holm
Standing Stones
Birsay Bay
Loch of Boardhouse
Eynhallow Sound
Wyre Sound
St Mary's Chapel
Marwick Head
Kitchener's Monument
A967
Loch of Hundland
Evie
Aiker Ness
Cubbie Roo's Castle
Wyre
Marwick
Kirbuster
Redland
1½ hrs (summer only)
Twatt
Burn of
B9057
Wood Wick
Gairsay Sound
Isbister
Outshore Point
B9056
Beaquoy
Click Mill
O
Tingwall
R
Sweyn Holm
K
N
Gairsay
A967
Hillside
A986
Milldoe 221
A966
The Galt
Northdyke
Quoyloo
Skeabrae
Dounby
Hackland
Veantrow Bay
Edmon
Mirbister
Bay of Skaill
Corrigall Farm Museum
Gorseness
Skaill
Tor Ness
Bay of Furrowend
Skara Brae
Settiscarth
Isbister
B9058
Row Head
Loch of Skaill
B9057
Loch of Harray
Brough
Bay of Isbister
Broad Taing
Bay of Linton
Aith
Netherbrough
Yesnaby
Bimbister
B9059
Voy
Ness of Tenston
A986
WIDE FIRTH
Balfour
Balfour
Sandgarth
Loch of Wasdale
Helliar Holm
Haco's N
B9055
Ring of Brodgar
Finstown
Bay of Firth
Damsay
Car Ness
Neban Point
Hill of Miffia 158
A967
Loch of Stenness
Maes Howe
Rennibister Earth House
Bay of Kirkwall
Work
Head of Holland
Shapinsay Sound
Quholm
A965
Heddle
Chambered Cairn
Stones of Stenness
Chambered Cairn
Kirkwall
A965
Wideford Hill 225
Grainbank Earth House
Berstane
Clouston
Chambered Cairn
Keelylang Hill 221
Inganess Bay
Outertown
A965
Tankerness House Museum
Breck Ness
Stromness
Ireland
196
Magnus Cathedral
Linksness
Museum
Loch of Kirbister
Scapa
Pier Arts Centre
Ward Hill 268
Greenigo
Hatspark
Kirkwall
Hoy Sound
Clestrain Sound
A964
A964
Hobbister
Scapa Bay
A961
A960
Toab
Graemsay
Clestrain
Mirkady Point
Kame of Hoy

D
E
F
G
1
2
3
4
5
North Ronaldsay
Point of Sinsoss
Tor Ness
North Ronaldsay
Linklet Bay
Hollandstoun
Bride's Ness
South Bay
Strom Ness
North Ronaldsay Firth
Tofts Ness
3 hrs (summer only)
Whitemill Point
Holms of Ire
Sandquoy
North Loch
Scuthvie Bay
Scar
Burness
Otters Wick
NORTH SOUND
B9068
B9069
North Bay
Bay of Lopness
Start Point
Newark
Red Head
Grey Head
Broughtown
Sanday
Roadside
Sanday
Cata Sand
Overbister
Calf of Eday
B9070
Bay of Newark
Hill Cairn
Calfsound
Kettletoft
Sty Wick
Quoy Ness
Backaskail Bay
Stone of Setter
Eday Sound
Els Ness
Elsness-Quoyness Chambered Tomb
Tres Ness
Braeswick
Millbounds
Stove
SANDAY SOUND
Loth
Eday
Spur Ness
Holm of Huip
B9063
Huip Sound
Huip Ness
Papa Stronsay
Links Ness
Stronsay
Odie
Veness
Whitehall
War Ness
Linga Holm
B9062
B9060
St Catherine's Bay
Mill Bay
Odness
Stronsay
Aith
Everbay
Odin Bay
Bay of Bomasty
B906
Kirbister
Rothiesholm
Grobister
B9060
Bay of Holland
Dishes
Burgh Head
Holland
FIRTH
Rothiesholm Head
Greenli Ness
Tor Ness
Bay of Houseby
Lamb Head
Ingale Skerry
Auskerry Sound
Auskerry
Invergorden 9 hrs
Scarva Taing
Mull Head
197
The Gloup
Skaill
Roana Bay

A
B
C
D
202
1
2
3
4
5
Taing
Isle of Nibon
Sullom
Sullom Voe
Graven
Firth
A968
Mangaster
Trondavoe
B9076
ST MAGNUS BAY
Islesburgh
Mavis Grind
Brae
Button Hills
Collafirth
Colla Firth
Dales Voe
Cunnigill Hill
Erne Stack
Busta
Burravoe
Busta Voe
A970
A968
Strom Ness
Roesound
Wetherstа
Muckle Roe
Olna Firth
Hillside
Laxo
Ve Skerries
Linga
Voe
Papa Stour
Swarbacks Minn
Gonfirth
West Kame
Fogla Skerry
Biggings
Vementry
Papa Little
Gossa Water
Papa Stour
The Rona
Sound of Papa
Aith Voe
East Burrafirth
Mid Kame
Quilva Taing
Melby
West Burrafirth
Brindister
Garth
Scalla Field
281
Sandness
Noonsbrough
Clousta
B9071
East Kame
Sulma Water
Unifirth
Sandness Hill
249
Aith
Aithsting
A971
Bay of Deepdale
Burga Water
Setter
Catfirth
Sand Water
SHETLAND
MAINLAND
Twatt
Weisdale
B9075
12
Mu Ness
Voe of Dale
Dale of Walls
Stourbrough Hill
Bridge of Walls
Effirth
Bixter
A971
Westerfield
Heglibister
Loch of Girlsta
Huxter
Girlsta
Wats Ness
Skarpigarth
A971
Browland
Stanydale
Tresta
Semblister
Sound
Walls
Staneydale Temple
Hellister
Gruting
Sandsound
Braga Ness
Garderhouse
Sand
A971
Vaila Sound
Gruting Voe
Weisdale Voe
A970
Laxfirth
Whiteness
Vaila
Gossa Water
Tingwall
Culswick
Gott
Strom Ness
Easter Skeld
Reawick
Veensgarth
White Ness
Whiteness Voe
Wester Skeld
Loch of Tingwall
Westerwick
Silwick
Roe Ness
North Havra
South Whiteness
Wester Wick
The Deeps
B9074
A970
Holm
Burwick
Skelda Ness
Hildasay
B9073
Scalloway
Cheynies
Papa
Cutts
Uradale
Trondra
Oxna
Easter Quarff
Hamnavoe
B9074
Wester Quarff
3.2 miles to 1 inch
0
2
4
6
8
10 miles
0
2
4
6
8
10 km
2 km to 1 cm
Bridge End
East Burra
West Burra
Muskna Field
292
Fladda
Okraqu
Ukna Skerry
Clift Hills
Clift Sound
Houss Ness
West Voe
A970
Fugla Stack
Starkigarth
Kettla Ness
Royl Field
293
South Havra
Ward of Veester
257
Mail
Lamba
Fair Isle
Dronger
Skroo
Ward Hill
217
Breiti Stack
Bu Ness
Fair Isle
Bird Observatory
Stonybreck
Sheep Rock
Malcolm's Head
Swartz Geo
South Harbour
same scale as main map
Foula
East Hoevdi
Strem Ness
The Kame
The Sneug
418
Wester Hoevdi
Ham
Wick of Mucklabrek
Foula
Hellabrick's Wick
South Ness
same scale as main map
Maywick
Leebo
Hoswick
Channerwick
Sandwick
Griskerry
Ireland
Northpunds
St Ninian's Isle
Bigton
Levenwick
St Ninian's Isle Church
A970
Blovid
Colsay
B9122
Fora
Skelberry
Boddam

D
E
F
G
1
2
3
4
5
Fish Holm
Lunna Ness
Hamnavoe
Muckle Skerry
Bruray
Out Skerries
Housay
203
Filla
Lunna
Taing of Kelswick
$1^1/_2$ hrs
$^1/_4$ hr
Lunning
Vidlin Voe
Lunning Sound
Challister Ness
Skaw
Skaw Taing
Vidlin
Lunnasting
B9071
West Linga
Linga Sound
Brough
Isbister
Marrister
Huxter
Symbister
Whalsay
East Linga
Grif Skerry
$^1/_2$ hr
Dury Voe
Stava Ness
Clett Head
Laxfirth
Neap
The Keen
Bretabister
B9075
South Nesting Bay
SHETLAND ISLANDS
Skellister
Ling Ness
South Nesting
Freester
Moul of Eswick
Gletness
South Isle of Gletness
Hawks Ness
$2^1/_2$ hrs
Kebister Ness
Score Head
Aith Ness
Bressay
Heogan
Gunnista
Loder Head
Isle of Noss
Maryfield
Setter
Shetland Mus
Lerwick
Brough
Sound
Fort Charlotte
Grindiscol
Ward of Bressay
226
Millburn Geo
Feadda Ness
Brei Wick
Kirkabister
Bard Head
Torshavn 13 hrs (summer only)
Seydisfjordur 31 hrs (summer only)
Bergen $12^1/_2$ hrs (summer only)
Helli Ness
Dedda Skerry
Mousa
Broch of Mousa
Stromness 8 hrs & Aberdeen 14 hrs
Ireland
Northpunds
St Ninian's Isle
Bigton
Levenwick
No Ness
St Ninian's Isle Church
Blovid
Colsay
B9122
Fora Ness
Troswick Ness
Scousburgh
Skelberry
Boddam
Wick of Shunni
Loch of Spiggie
Hillwell
Lambhoga Head
Quendale
283
A970
Fitful Head
Exnaboe
Bay of Quendale
Siggar Ness
Toab
Sumburgh
Jarlshof
Grutness
Lady's Holm
Sumburgh
Ness of Burgi
Sumburgh Head
Sumburgh Roost
same scale as main map

A
B
C
D
1
2
3
4
5
3.2 miles to 1 inch
0 2 4 6 8 10 miles
0 2 4 6 8 10 km
2 km to 1 cm
Geo of
Ramna Stacks
Gruney
Point of Fethaland
Garmus Taing
Uyea
Whale Geo
Hellir
YELL SOUND
Isbister
A970
South Wick
North Roe
Burra Voe
Hevdadale Head
North Roe
Muckle Holm
Wes
Sandwic
The Castle
Roer Water
SHETL
The Faither
Muckle Ossa
Housetter
Head of Brough
Ronas Hill
450
Neap of Skea
Collafirth
Colla Firth
Ronas Voe
A970
Quey Firth
Brother Isle
Ness of Soun
The Giants Stones
The Clifts
Lamba
Head of Stanshi
Hamnavoe
Heylor
Voe
Ollaberry
Uynarey
Scarff
Esha Ness
Ure
Braehoulland
Eela Water
Little Roe
A970
Burnside
Urafirth
B9079
Gluss Isle
B9078
Tangwick
Stenness
Brae Wick
Hillswick
Ura Firth
Gluss
Bardister
Orka Voe
Brough
Toft
Sullom Voe Oil Terminal
A970
Burraland
Baa Taing
Firth
Sullom
Sullom Voe
Isle of Nibon
Graven
B9076
Mangaster
Trondavoe
Dales Voe
ST MAGNUS BAY
200
Islesburgh
Brae
Button Hills
Mavis Grind
Colla Firth
Erne Stack
Bus
Burravoe
Busta Voe
Strom Ness
Roesound
A970
A968
A
B
C
D

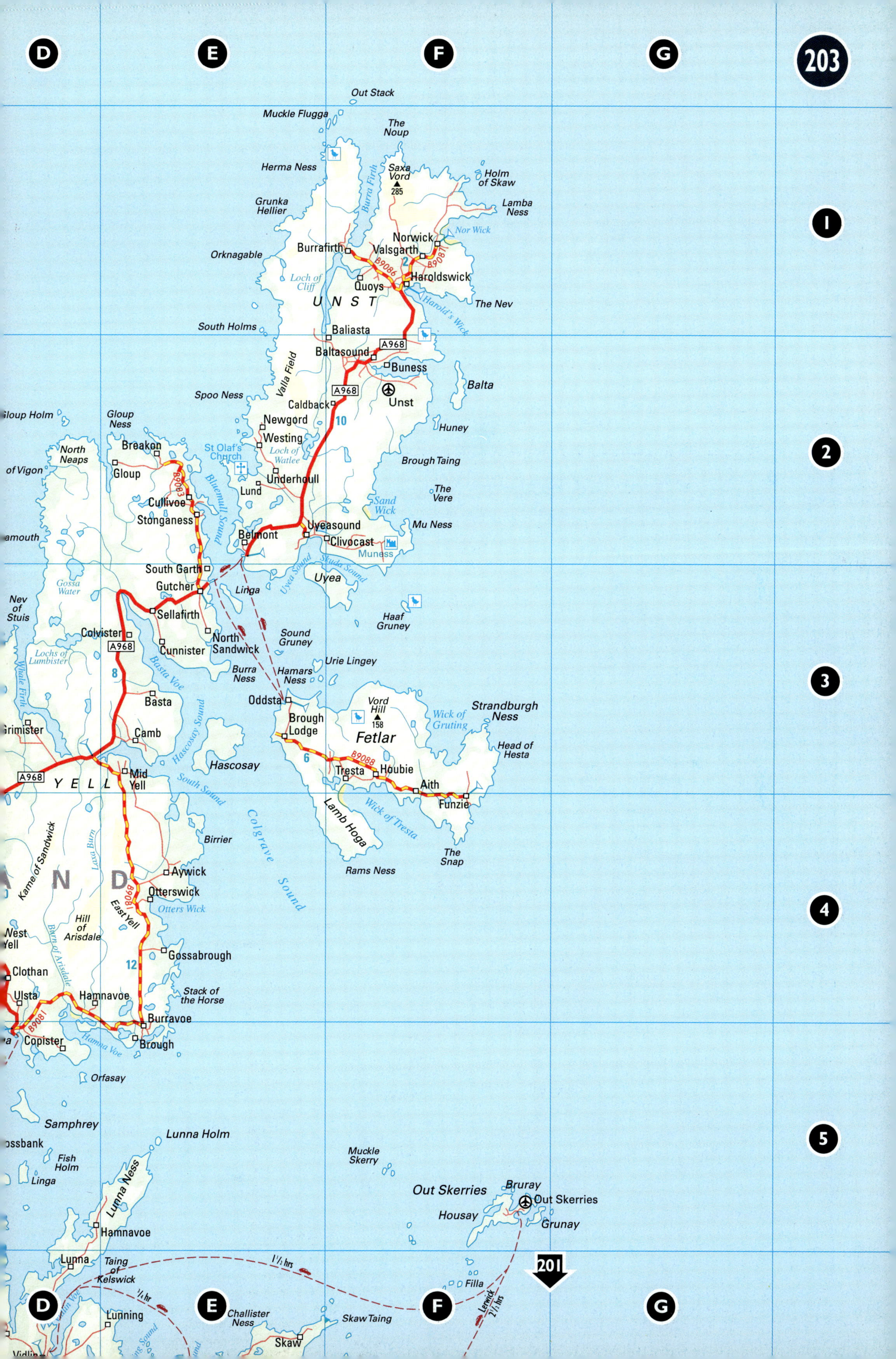
D
E
F
G
1
2
3
4
5
Out Stack
Muckle Flugga
The Noup
Herma Ness
Saxa Vord
285
Holm of Skaw
Lamba Ness
Grunka Hellier
Burra Firth
Norwick
Nor Wick
Orknagable
Burrafirth
Valsgarth
B9086
B9087
Loch of Cliff
Quoys
Haroldswick
Harold's Wick
U N S T
The Nev
South Holms
Baliasta
A968
Baltasound
Buness
Balta
Valla Field
Spoo Ness
Unst
Caldback
Gloup Holm
Gloup Ness
Newgord
10
Huney
North Neaps
Breakon
Westing
St Olaf's Church
Loch of Watlee
Gloup
of Vigon
B9083
Brough Taing
Underhoull
Cullivoe
Lund
The Vere
Bluemull Sound
Sand Wick
Stonganess
Uyeasound
Mu Ness
amouth
Belmont
Clivocast
Muness
South Garth
Uyea Sound
Skuda Sound
Uyea
Gossa Water
Gutcher
Linga
Nev of Stuis
Sellafirth
Haaf Gruney
Colvister
North Sandwick
Sound Gruney
Lochs of Lumbister
Cunnister
Urie Lingey
8
Basta Voe
Burra Ness
Hamars Ness
Whale Firth
Oddsta
Vord Hill
158
Strandburgh Ness
Basta
Wick of Gruting
Brough Lodge
Fetlar
Grimister
Hascosay Sound
Camb
Head of Hesta
B9088
Hascosay
6
Houbie
Mid Yell
Tresta
Aith
Y E L L
South Sound
Funzie
Wick of Tresta
Lamb Hoga
Colgrave Sound
Birrier
The Snap
Rams Ness
Kame of Sandwick
Lumbister Burn
Aywick
N D
B9081
Otterswick
Otters Wick
East Yell
Hill of Arisdale
West Yell
Burn of Arisdale
Gossabrough
12
Clothan
Stack of the Horse
Ulsta
Hamnavoe
Burravoe
Copister
Hamna Voe
Brough
Orfasay
Samphrey
Lunna Holm
ossbank
Fish Holm
Muckle Skerry
Linga
Lunna Ness
Out Skerries
Bruray
Out Skerries
Housay
Grunay
Hamnavoe
Lunna
Taing of Kelswick
1½ hrs
¼ hr
201
Filla
Lerwick 2½ hrs
Lunning
Challister Ness
Skaw Taing
Skaw
Vidlin

Aberdeen • Bath

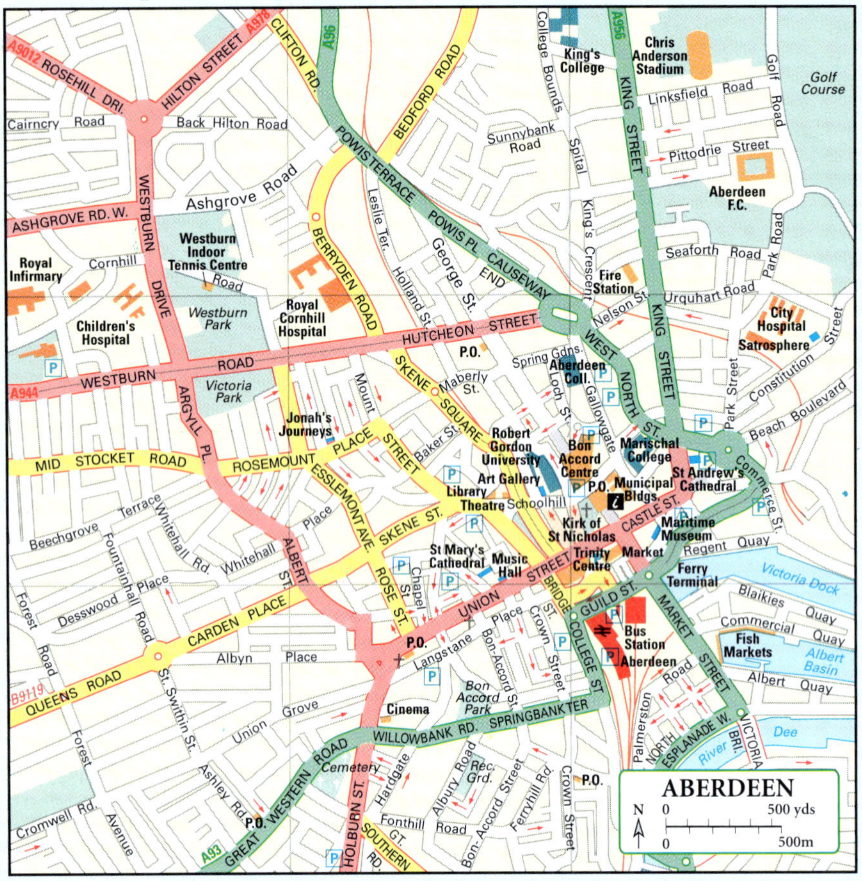

Information Centre: St. Nicholas House, Broad Street
Tel: 01224 632727

Albert Quay	C3
Albert Street	B2
Albury Road	C2
Albyn Place	C1
Argyll Place	B1
Ashgrove Road	A1
Ashgrove Road West	A1
Ashley Road	C1
Back Hilton Road	A1
Baker Street	B2
Beach Boulevard	B3
Bedford Road	A2
Beechgrove Terrace	B1
Berryden Road	A2
Blaikie's Quay	C3
Bon-Accord Street	C2
Bridge Street	B2
Cairncry Road	A1
Carden Place	C1
Castle Street	B3
Causewayend	A2
Chapel Street	B2
Clifton Road	A1
College Bounds	A2
College Street	C3
Commerce Street	B3
Commercial Quay	C3
Constitution Street	B3
Cornhill Road	A1
Cromwell Road	C1
Crown Street	C2
Desswood Place	C1
Esslemont Avenue	B2
Ferryhill Road	C2
Fonthill Road	C2
Forest Road	C1
Forest Avenue	C1
Fountainhall Road	B1
Gallowgate	B3
George Street	A2
Golf Road	A3
Great Southern Road	C2
Great Western Road	C1
Guild Street	C3
Hardgate	C2
Hilton Street	A1
Holburn Street	C2
Holland Street	A2
Hutcheon Street	B2
King's Crescent	A3
King Street	A3
Langstane Place	C2
Leslie Terrace	A2
Linksfield Road	A3
Loch Street	B2
Maberly Street	B2
Market Street	C3
Mid Stocket Road	B1
Mount Street	B2
Nelson Street	B3
North Esplanade West	C3
Palmerston Road	C3
Park Road	A3
Park Street	B3
Pittodrie Street	A3
Powis Place	A2
Powis Terrace	A2
Queens Road	C1
Regent Quay	B3
Rosehill Drive	A1
Rosemount Place	B1
Rose Street	B2
St. Swithin Street	C1
Schoolhill	B2
Seaforth Road	A3
Skene Square	B2
Skene Street	B2
Spital	A3
Springbank Terrace	C2
Spring Gardens	B2
Sunnybank Road	A2
Union Grove	C1
Union Street	C2
Urquhart Road	B3
Victoria Bridge	C3
Westburn Drive	A1
Westburn Road	B1
West North Street	B3
Whitehall Place	B1
Whitehall Road	B1
Willowbank Road	C2

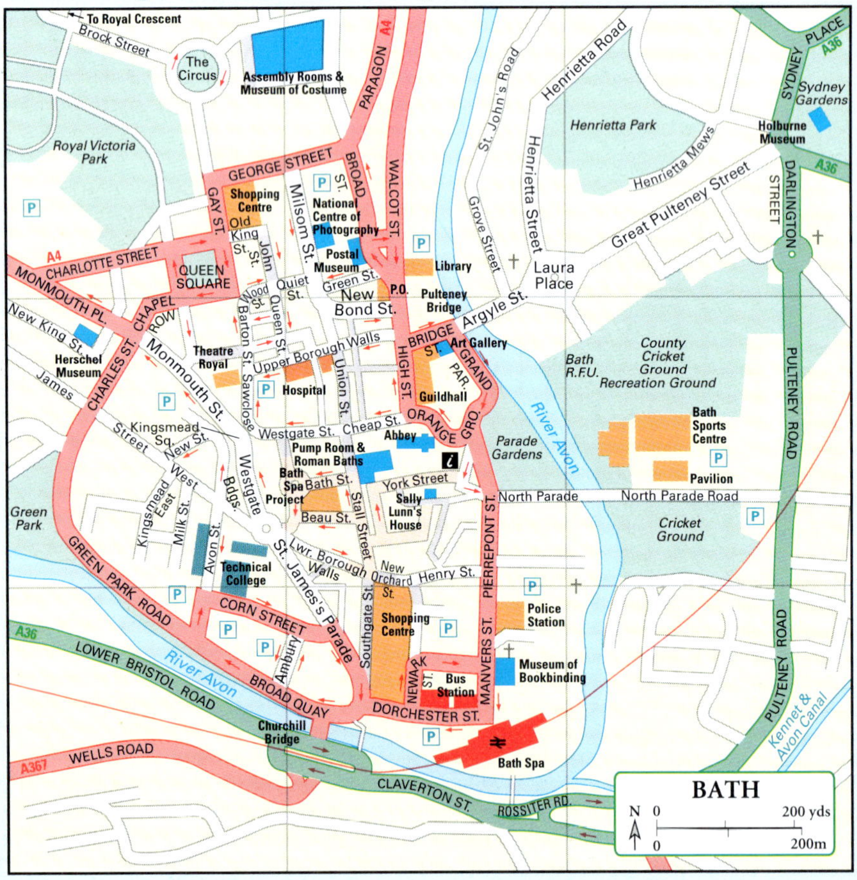

Information Centre: Abbey Chambers, Abbey Churchyard
Tel: 01225 477101

Ambury	C1
Argyle Street	B2
Avon Street	B1
Barton Street	B1
Bath Street	B2
Beau Street	B2
Bridge Street	B2
Broad Quay	C1
Broad Street	A2
Brock Street	A1
Chapel Row	B1
Charles Street	B1
Charlotte Street	A1
Cheap Street	B2
Claverton Street	C2
Corn Street	C1
Darlington Street	A3
Dorchester Street	C2
Gay Street	A1
George Street	A1
Grand Parade	B2
Great Pulteney Street	A3
Green Park Road	B1
Green Street	A2
Grove Street	A2
Henrietta Mews	A3
Henrietta Road	A2
Henrietta Street	A2
Henry Street	B2
High Street	B2
James Street West	B1
John Street	A1
Kingsmead East	B1
Laura Place	A2
Lower Borough Walls	B2
Lower Bristol Road	C1
Manvers Street	C2
Milk Street	B1
Milsom Street	A2
Monmouth Place	A1
Monmouth Street	B1
Newark Street	C2
New Bond Street	B2
New King Street	B1
New Orchard Street	B2
New Street	B1
North Parade	B2
North Parade Road	B3
Old King Street	A1
Orange Grove	B2
Paragon	A2
Pierrepont Street	B2
Pulteney Road	B3
Queen Street	B1
Quiet Street	A1
Rossiter Road	C2
St. James's Parade	B1
St. John's Road	A2
Sawclose	B1
Southgate Street	C2
Stall Street	B2
Sydney Place	A3
The Circus	A1
Union Street	B2
Upper Borough Walls	B1
Walcot Street	A2
Wells Road	C1
Westgate Buildings	B1
Westgate Street	B1
Wood Street	A1
York Street	B2

For Birmingham see page 230

Blackpool • Bournemouth

Information Centre: 1 Clifton Street
Tel: 01253 478222

Abingdon Street	B1
Adelaide Street	B1
Albert Road	C1
Ascot Road	A3
Bank Hey Street	B1
Beech Avenue West	B3
Birchway Avenue	A3
Bonny Street	C1
Boothley Road	A2
Breck Road	C3
Bryan Road	B3
Buchanan Street	B2
Caunce Street	B2/A3
Central Drive	C1
Chapel Street	C1
Charles Street	B2
Charnley Road	C1
Church Street	B2
Clifton Street	B1
Clinton Avenue	C2
Cocker Square	A1
Cocker Street	A1
Collingwood Avenue	A3
Cookson Street	B2
Coronation Street	C1
Corporation Street	B1
Deansgate	B1
Devonshire Road	A2
Devonshire Square	B3
Dickson Road	A1
Egerton Road	A1
Elizabeth Street	A2
Exchange Street	A1
Forest Gate	B3
George Street	B2/A2
Gloucester Avenue	C3
Gorse Road	C3
Gorton Street	A2
Granville Road	B2
Grosvenor Street	B2
High Street	A1
Hornby Road	C1
Hounds Hill	C1
King Street	B1
Laycock Gate	A3
Layton Road	A3
Leamington Road	B2
Leicester Road	B2
Lincoln Road	B2
Liverpool Road	B2
London Road	A3
Lord Street	A1
Market Street	B1
Mather Street	A3
Mere Road	B3
Newton Drive	B3
Palatine Road	C2
Park Road	C2
Peter Street	B2
Pleasant Street	A1
Portland Road	C3
Princess Parade	A1
Promenade	C1
Queens Square	B1
Queen Street	B1
Rathlyn Avenue	A3
Reads Avenue	C2
Regent Road	B2
Ribble Road	C2
Ripon Road	C2
St. Albans Road	C3
Seaside Way	C1
South King Street	B2
Talbot Road	B1/A2
Topping Street	B1
Victory Road	A2
Wayman Road	B3
Whitegate Drive	B3/C3
Woodland Grove	C3
Woolman Road	C2

Information Centre: Westover Road
Tel: 0906 802 0234

Avenue Road	B1
Bath Road	C2
Beechey Road	A3
Bennett Road	A3
Bourne Avenue	B1
Braidley Road	B2
Branksome Wood Road	B1
Cavendish Road	A2
Central Drive	A1
Charminster Road	A2
Christchurch Road	B3
Dean Park Road	B2
Durley Chine Road	C1
Durley Chine Road South	C1
Durley Road	C1
East Avenue	A1
East Overcliff Drive	C3
Elgin Road	A1
Exeter Road	C2
Gervis Place	C2
Gervis Road	C3
Grove Road	C3
Hinton Road	C2
Holdenhurst Road	B3
Knyveton Road	B3
Lansdowne Road	A2
Leven Avenue	A1
Lowther Road	A3
Madeira Road	B2
Malmesbury Park Road	A3
Methuen Road	A3
Meyrick Road	B3
Old Christchurch Road	B2
Ophir Road	A3
Oxford Road	B3
Poole Hill	C1
Portchester Road	A3
Priory Road	C1
Queen's Road	B1
Richmond Hill	B2
Russell Cotes Road	C2
St. Augustin's Road	A2
St. Anthony's Road	A2
St. Leonard's Road	A3
St. Michael's Road	C1
St. Pauls' Road	B3
St. Peter's Road	B2
St. Stephen's Road	B1
St. Swithun's Road	B3
St. Swithun's Road South	B3
St. Winifred's Road	A2
St. Valerie Road	A2
Stewart Raod	A3
Surrey Road	B1
The Lansdowne	B3
The Square	B2
The Triangle	B1
Tregonwell Road	C1
Undercliff Drive	C3
Wellington Road	A2
Wessex Way	B1/A3
West Cliff Promenade	C1
West Cliff Road	C1
West Hill Road	C1
West Overcliff Drive	C1
West Promenade	C1
Westover Road	C2
Wimborne Road	B2

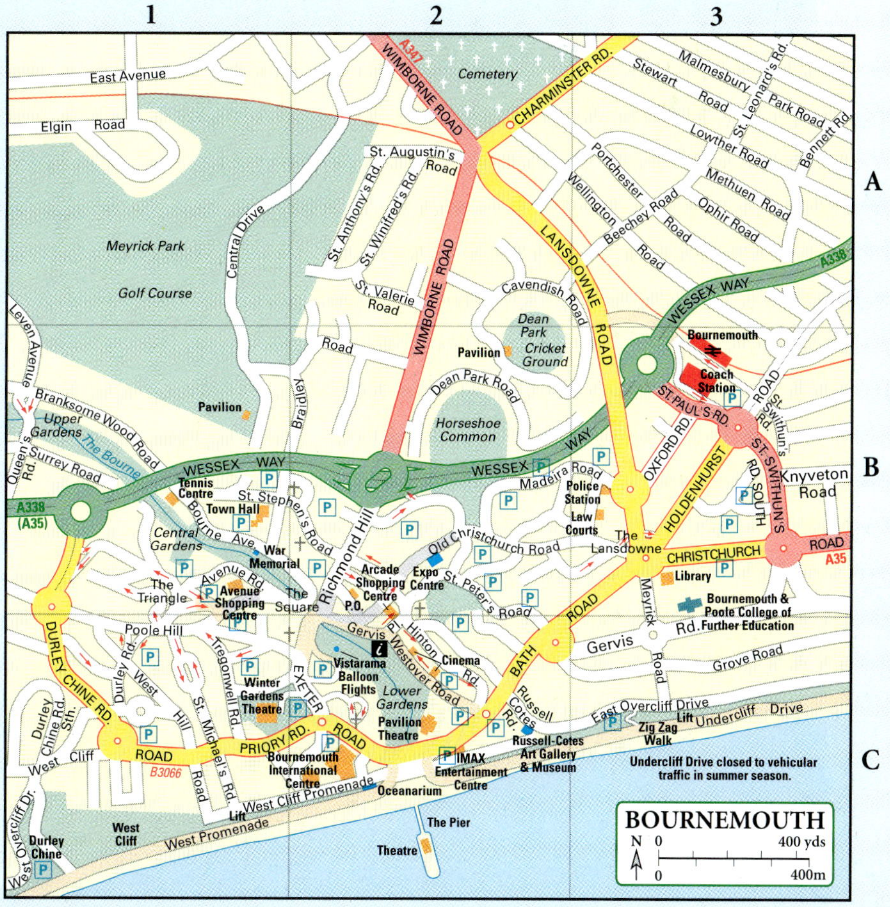

For Bradford see page 238
For Bristol see page 229

Brighton • Cambridge

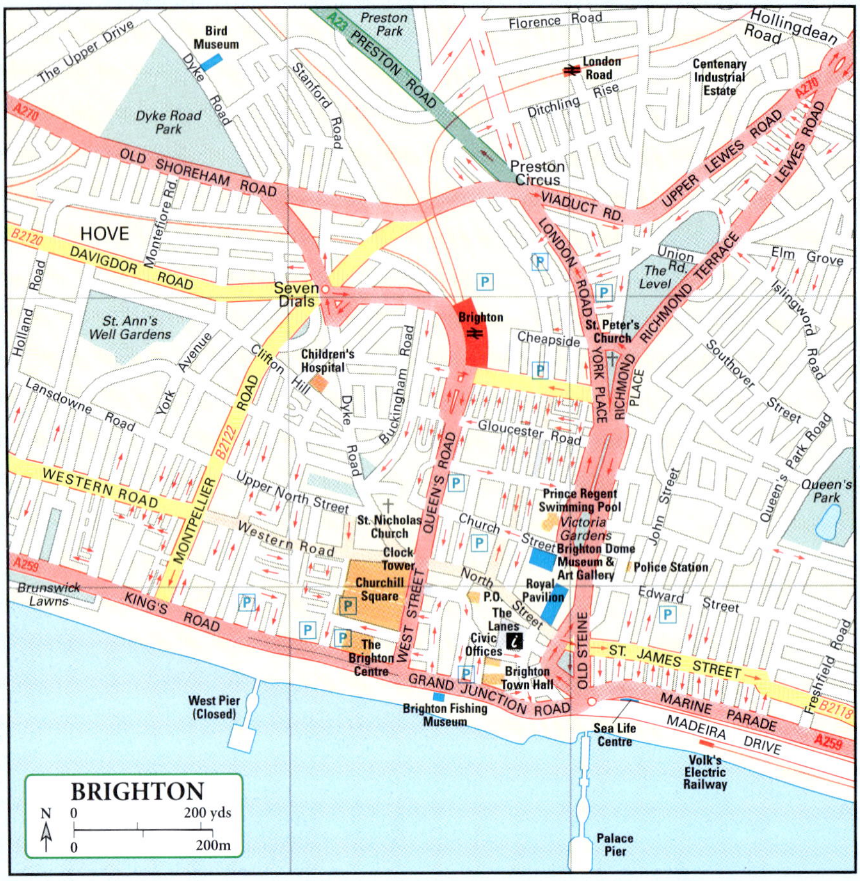

Information Centre:	10 Bartholomew Square
Tel:	0906 711 2255

Buckingham Road	B2
Cheapside	B2
Church Street	B2
Churchill Square	C2
Clifton Hill	B1
Davigdor Road	A1
Ditchling Rise	A2
Dyke Road	B2
Edward Street	C3
Elm Grove	A3
Florence Road	A2
Freshfield Road	C3
Gloucester Road	B2
Grand Junction Road	C2
Holland Road	B1
Hollingdean Road	A3
Islingword Road	A3
John Street	B3
King's Road	C1
Lansdowne Road	B1
Lewes Road	A3
London Road	A2
Madeira Drive	C3
Marine Parade	C3
Montefiore Road	A1
Montpelier Road	B1
North Street	B2
Old Shoreham Road	A1
Old Steine	C3
Preston Circus	A2
Preston Road	A2
Queen's Park Road	B3
Queen's Road	B2
Richmond Place	B3
Richmond Terrace	B3
St. James's Street	C3
Southover Street	B3
Stanford Road	A2
The Lanes	C2
The Upper Drive	A1
Union Road	A3
Upper Lewes Road	A3
Upper North Street	B1
Viaduct Road	A2
West Street	C2
Western Road	B1
York Avenue	B1
York Place	B3

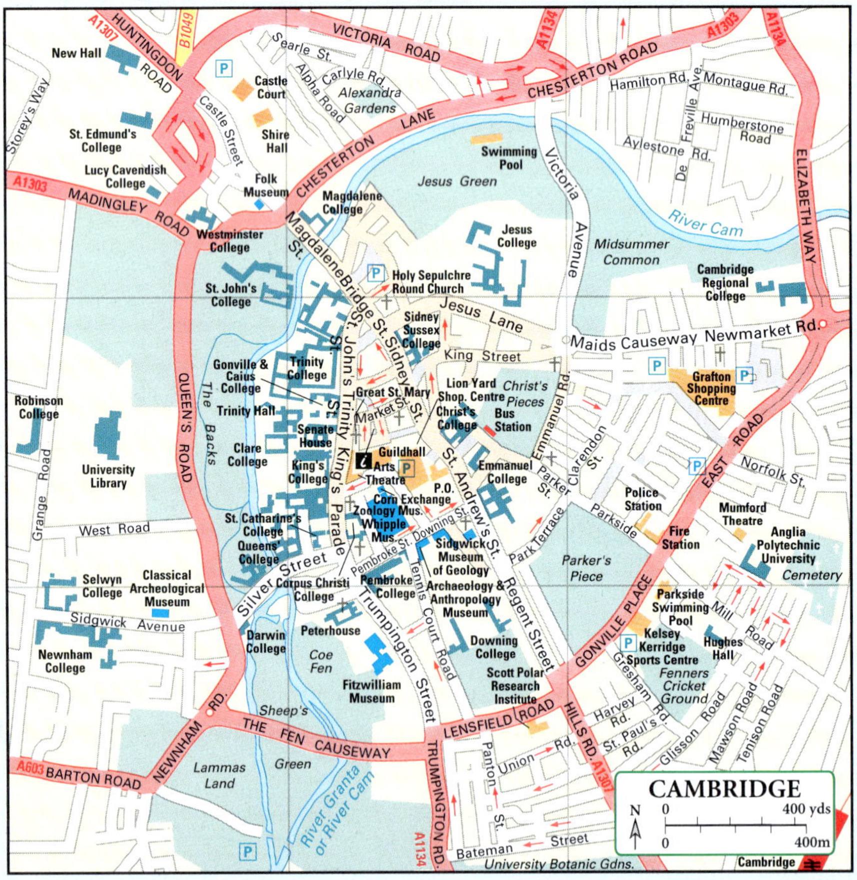

Information Centre:	Wheeler Street
Tel:	01223 322640

Alpha Road	A2	Silver Street	C1
Aylestone Road	A3	Storey's Way	A1
Barton Road	C1	Tenison Road	C3
Bateman Street	C2	Tennis Court Road	B2
Carlyle Road	A2	Trinity Street	B2
Castle Street	A1	Trumpington Road	C2
Chesterton Lane	A2	Trumpington Street	C2
Chesterton Road	A2	Union Road	C2
Clarendon Street	B3	Victoria Avenue	A2
De Freville Avenue	A3	Victoria Road	A2
Downing Street	B2	West Road	B1
East Road	B3		
Elizabeth Way	A3		
Emmanuel Road	B2		
Fen Causeway, The	C1		
Glisson Road	C3		
Gonville Place	C3		
Grange Road	B1		
Gresham Road	C3		
Hamilton Road	A3		
Harvey Road	C3		
Hills Road	C3		
Humberstone Road	A3		
Huntingdon Road	A1		
Jesus Lane	B2		
King's Parade	B2		
King Street	B2		
Lensfield Road	C2		
Madingley Road	A1		
Magdalene Bridge Street	A2		
Maids Causeway	B3		
Market Street	B2		
Mawson Road	C3		
Mill Road	C3		
Montague Road	A3		
Newmarket Road	B3		
Newnham Road	C1		
Norfolk Street	B3		
Panton Street	C2		
Parker Street	B2		
Parkside	B3		
Park Terrace	B2		
Pembroke Street	B2		
Queen's Road	B1		
Regent Street	B2		
St. Andrew's Street	B2		
St. John's Street	B2		
St. Paul's Road	C3		
Searce Street	A1		
Sidgwick Avenue	C1		
Sidney Street	B2		

For Cardiff see page 228

Information Centre: 77 The Promenade
Tel: 01242 522878

Albert Road	A3	Priory Street	C3
Albion Street	B2	Promenade	B2
All Saints Road	B3	St. George's Place	B2
Andover Road	C1	St. George's Road	B1
Bath Road	C2	St. Johns Avenue	B2
Bayshill Road	B1	St. Margaret's Road	A2
Carlton Street	B3	St. Paul's Road	A2
Central Cross Drive	A3	St. Paul's Street North	A2
Christchurch Road	B1	St. Paul's Street South	A2
Christchurch Terrace	B1	St. Stephen's Road	C1
Clarence Road	A2	Sandford Road	C2
College Lawn	C2	Sherborne Street	B3
College Road	C2	Suffolk Road	C1
Dunnally Street	A2	Sun Street	A1
Eldon Road	B3	Swindon Road	A1
Evesham Road	A3	Tewkesbury Road	A1
Fairview Road	B3	Thirlestaine Road	C2
Folly Lane	A2	Townsend Street	A1
Gloucester Road	B1	Vittoria Walk	C2
Grafton Road	C1	Wellington Road	A3
Great Western Road	B1	West Drive	A2
Hale's Road	C3	Whaddon Road	A3
Hanover Street	A2	Winchcombe Street	B2
Henrietta Street	B2		
Hewlett Road	B3		
High Street	A2		
Keynsham Road	C2		
King's Road	B3		
Lansdown Crescent	C1		
Lansdown Road	C1		
London Road	C3		
Malvern Road	B1		
Market Street	A1		
Marle Hill Parade	A2		
Marle Hill Road	A2		
Montpellier Spa Road	B2		
Montpellier Street	C1		
Montpellier Terrace	C1		
Montpellier Walk	C1		
New Street	A2		
North Place	B2		
North Street	B2		
Old Bath Road	C3		
Oriel Road	B2		
Overton Road	B1		
Parabola Road	B1		
Park Place	C1		
Park Street	A1		
Pittville Circus	A3		
Pittville Circus Road	B3		
Portland Street	B2		
Prestbury Road	A3		

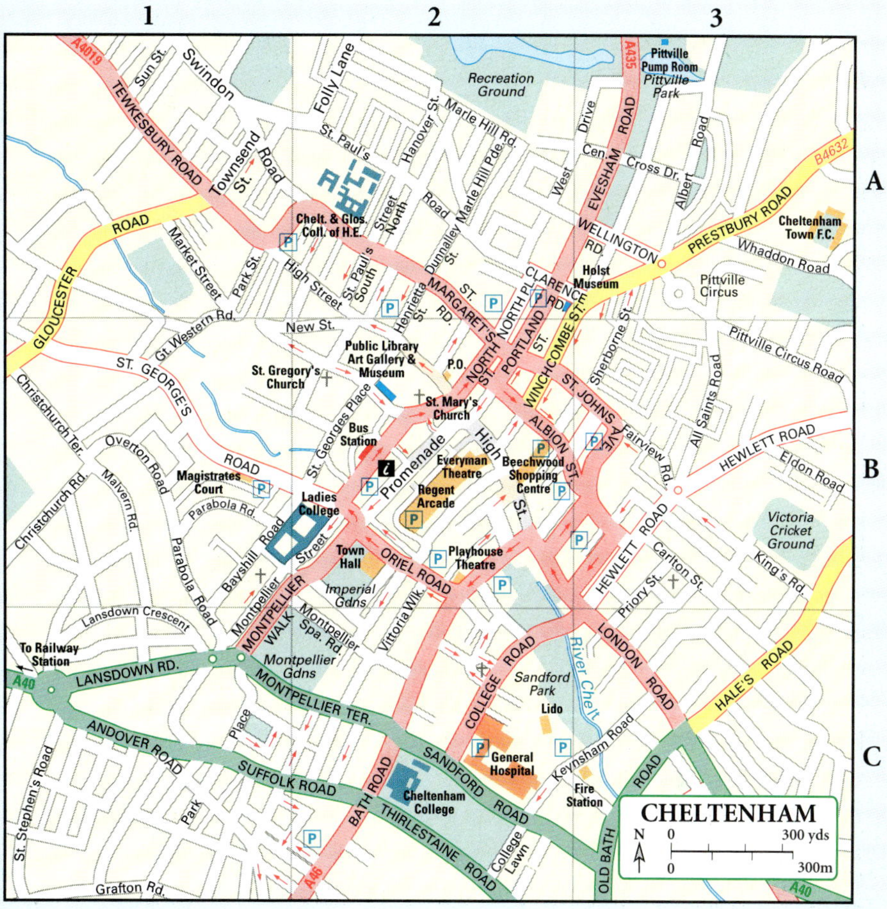

Information Centre: Town Hall, Northgate Street
Tel: 01244 402111

Black Friars	C1
Boughton	B3
Bridge Street	B2
Brook Street	A2
Canal Street	A1
Castle Drive	C1
City Road	B3
City Walls Road	B1
Commonhall Street	B1
Dee Bridge	C2
Dee Lane	B3
Duke Street	C2
Eastgate Street	B2
Foregate Street	B2
Francis Street	A3
Frodsham Street	B2
Garden Lane	A1
George Street	A2
Grosvenor Road	C1
Grosvenor Street	C1
Handbridge	C2
Hoole Road	A2
Hoole Way	A2
Hunter Street	B1
Love Street	B2
Lower Bridge Street	C2
Milton Street	A2
Newgate Street	B2
Nicholas Street	B1
Northgate Street	B1
Nun's Road	C1
Old Dee Bridge	C2
Pepper Street	C2
Princess Street	B1
Queens Park Road	C2
Queen Street	B2
Raymond Street	A1
St. Anne Street	A2
St. John Street	B2
St. Martins Way	A1
St. Oswalds Way	A2
St. Werburgh Street	B2
Souter's Lane	C2
The Bars	B3
The Groves	C2
Union Street	B2
Upper Northgate	A1
Vicar's Lane	B2
Watergate Street	B1
Weaver Street	B1
White Friars	C1

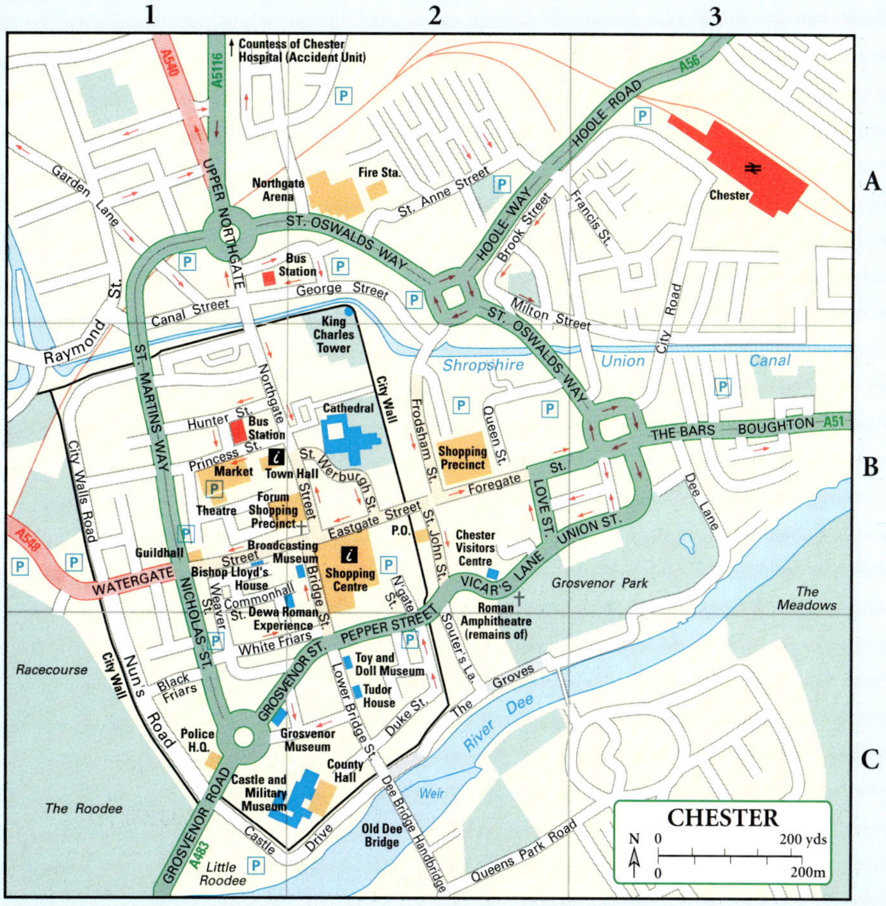

Coventry • Derby

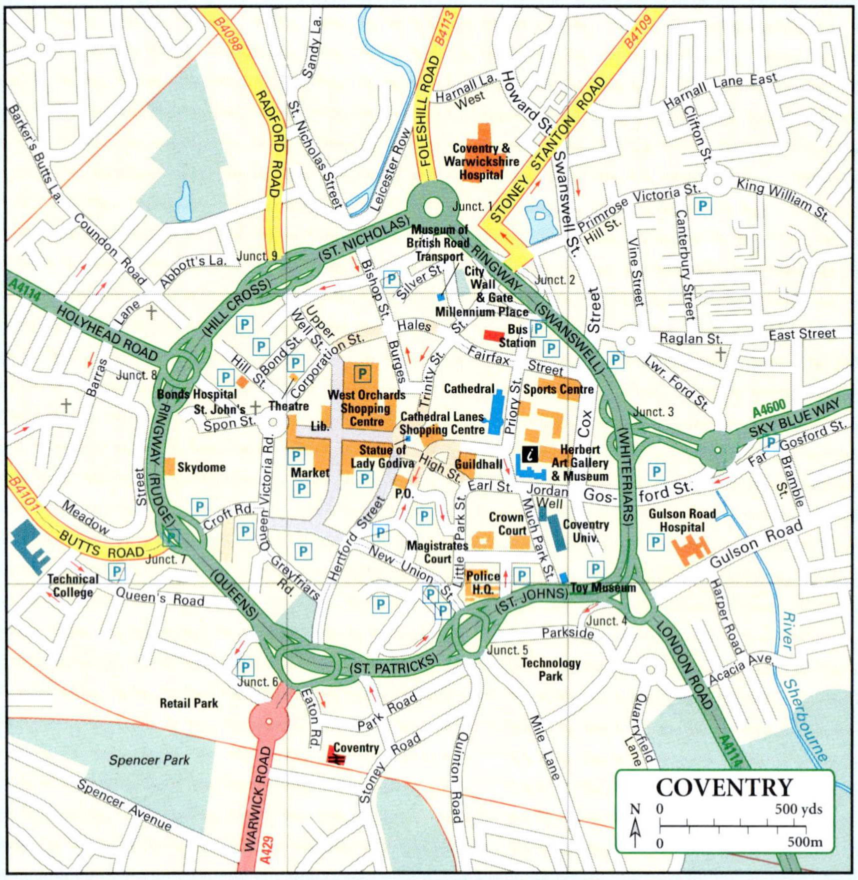

Information Centre: Bayley Lane
Tel: 024 7622 7264

Abbott's Lane	A1
Acacia Avenue	C3
Barker's Butts Lane	A1
Barras Lane	B1
Bishop Street	A2
Bond Street	B1
Bramble Street	B3
Burges	B2
Butts Road	B1
Canterbury Street	A3
Clifton Street	A3
Corporation Street	B2
Coundon Road	A1
Cox Street	B3
Croft Road	B1
Earl Street	B2
East Street	B3
Eaton Road	C2
Fairfax Street	B2
Far Gosford Street	B3
Foleshill Road	A2
Gosford Street	B3
Greyfriars Road	B1
Gulson Road	B3
Hales Street	B2
Harnall Lane East	A3
Harnall Lane West	A2
Harper Road	C3
Hertford Street	B2
High Street	B2
Hill Street	B1
Holyhead Road	B1
Howard Street	A2
Jordan Well	B2
King William Street	A3
Leicester Row	A2
Little Park Street	C2
London Road	C3
Lower Ford Street	B3
Meadow Street	B1
Mile Lane	C2
Much Park Street	B2
New Union Street	B2
Park Road	C2
Parkside	C2
Primrose Hill Street	A3
Priory Street	B2
Quarryfield Lane	C3
Queen's Road	C1
Queen Victoria Road	B1
Quinton Road	C2
Radford Road	A1
Raglan Street	B3
Ringway Hill Cross	B1
Ringway St. Johns	C2
Ringway St. Nicholas	A2
Ringway St. Patricks	C2
Ringway Queens	B1
Ringway Rudge	B1
Ringway Swanswell	B2
Ringway Whitefriars	B3
St. Nicholas Street	A2
Sandy Lane	A2
Silver Street	A2
Sky Blue Way	B3
Spencer Avenue	C1
Spon Street	B1
Stoney Road	C2
Stoney Stanton Road	A2
Swanswell Street	A2
Trinity Street	B2
Upper Well Street	B2
Victoria Street	A3
Vine Street	A3
Warwick Road	C1

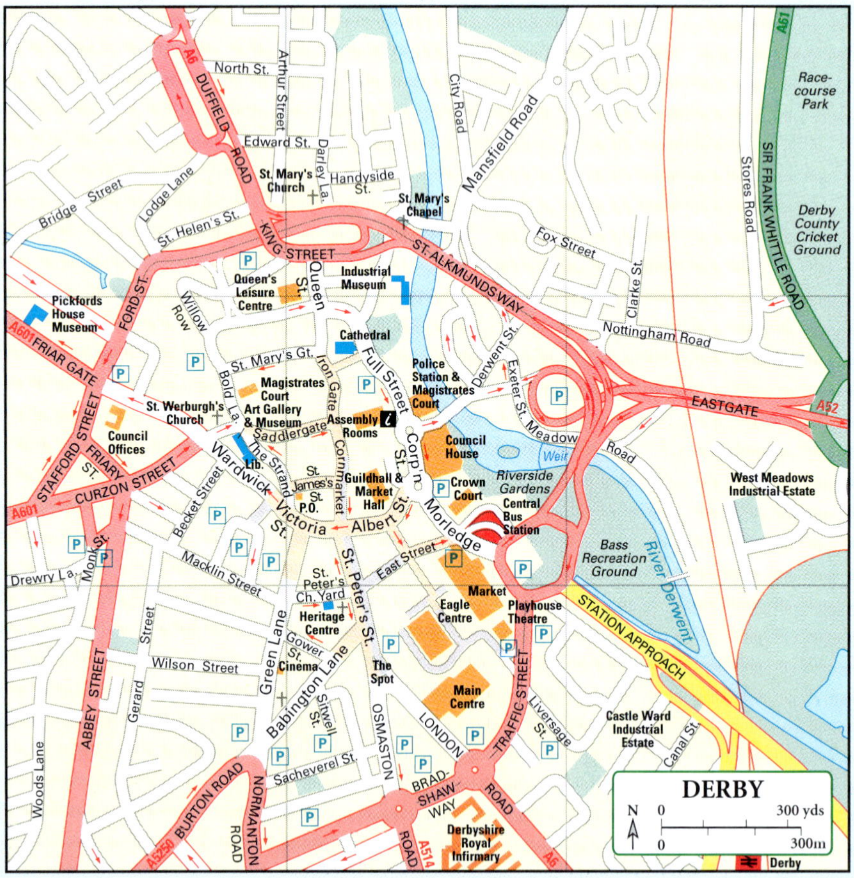

Information Centre: Assembly Rooms, Market Place
Tel: 01332 255802

Abbey Street	C1
Albert Street	B2
Arthur Street	A1
Babington Lane	C1
Becket Street	B1
Bold Lane	B1
Bradshaw Way	C2
Bridge Street	A1
Burton Road	C1
Canal Street	C3
City Road	A2
Clarke Street	B3
Cornmarket	B2
Corporation Street	B2
Curzon Street	B1
Darley Lane	A2
Derwent Street	B2
Drewry Lane	B1
Duffield Road	A1
Eastgate	B3
East Street	B2
Edward Street	A1
Exeter Street	B2
Ford Street	B1
Fox Street	A2
Friar Gate	B1
Friary Street	B1
Full Street	B2
Gerard Street	C1
Gower Street	C2
Green Lane	C1
Handyside Street	A2
Iron Gate	B2
King Street	A1
Liversage Street	C2
Lodge Lane	A1
London Road	C2
Macklin Street	B1
Mansfield Road	A2
Market Place	B2
Meadow Road	B2
Monk Street	B1
Morledge	B2
Normanton Road	C1
North Street	A1
Nottingham Road	B3
Osmaston Road	C2
Queen Street	A2
Sacheverel Street	C1
Saddlergate	B2
St. Alkmunds Way	A2
St. Helen's Street	A1
St. James Street	B2
St. Mary's Gate	B1
St. Peter's Church Yard	C2
St. Peter's Street	B2
Sir Frank Whittle Road	A3
Sitwell Street	C2
Stafford Street	B1
Station Approach	B3
Stores Road	A3
The Strand	B1
Traffic Street	C2
Victoria Street	B1
Wardwick	B1
Willow Row	B1
Wilson Street	C1
Woods Lane	C1

Dover • Dundee

Information Centre: Townwall Street
Tel: 01304 205 108

Astor Avenue	B1
Barton Road	A1
Beaconsfield Avenue	A1
Beaconsfield Road	A1
Biggin Street	B2
Bridge Street	B2
Buckland Avenue	A1
Cannon Street	B2
Canons Gate Road	B2
Castle Hill Road	B2
Castle Street	B2
Cherry Tree Avenue	A1
Connaught Road	A2
Coombe Valley Road	B1
Dover Road	A3
Eaton Road	B1
Folkestone Road	B1
Frith Road	A2
Godwyne Road	B2
Guston Road	A2
High Street	B2
Jubilee Way	A3
Ladywell	B2
Limekiln Street	C2
London Road	A1
Maison Dieu Road	B2
Marine Parade	B2
Military Road	B2
Noah's Ark Road	B1
Northbourne Avenue	B1
North Military Road	B1
Old Charlton Road	A2
Park Avenue	A2
Pencester Road	B2
Priory Hill	B1
Snargate Street	C2
South Road	B1
The Viaduct	C2
Townwall Street	B2
Upper Road	A3
York Street	B2

Information Centre: 21 Castle Street
Tel: 01382 527527

Albany Terrace	A1
Albert Street	B3
Alexander Street	A2
Ann Street	B2
Arbroath Road	B3
Arklay Street	A3
Arthurstone Terrace	B3
Barrack Road	B1
Blackness Road	B1
Blackscroft	B3
Blinshall Street	B1
Brook Street	B1
Broughty Ferry Road	B3
Brown Street	B1
Bruce Street	A1
Byron Street	A1
Canning Street	A2
Constitution Road	B2
Constitution Street	A2
Court Street	A3
Cowgate Street	B2
Dens Road	A2
Douglas Street	B1
Dudhope Street	A1
Dudhope Terrace	A3
Dundonald Street	A3
Dura Street	B3
East Dock Street	B3
East Marketgait	B2
Guthrie Street	B1
Hawkhill	B1
High Street	C2
Hill Street	A2
Hilltown	A2
Kenmore Terrace	A1
Killin Avenue	A1
Kinghorne Road	A1
King Street	B2
Larch Street	B1
Law Crescent	A1
Lawside Avenue	A1
Leng Street	A2
Lochee Road	B1
Mains Road	A2
Main Street	A2
Meadowside	B2
Nelson Street	B2
Nethergate	C1
North Marketgait	B1
Perth Road	C1
Princes Street	B3
Roseangle	C1
Riverside Drive	C1
Seagate	B2
South Marketgait	C2
South Tay Street	C1
Strathmartine Road	A2
Tay Road Bridge	C2
Trades Lane	B2
Upper Constitution Street	A1
Victoria Road	B2
Victoria Street	B3
Ward Road	B1
West Marketgait	B1
West Port	B1

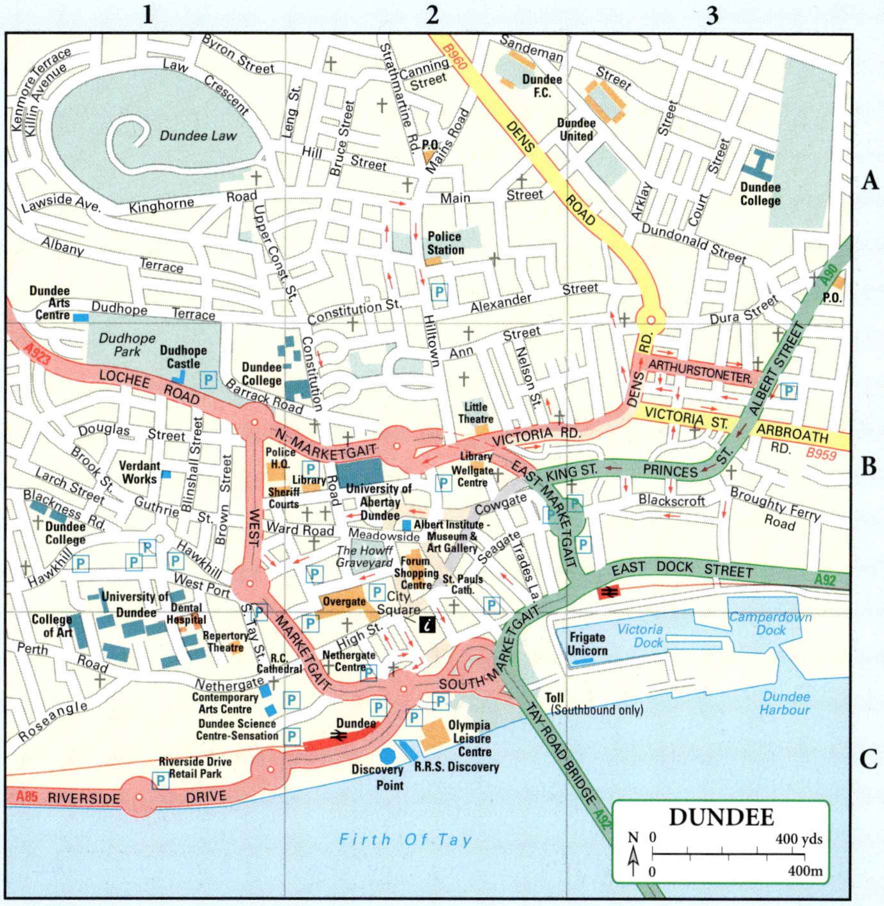

Durham • Exeter

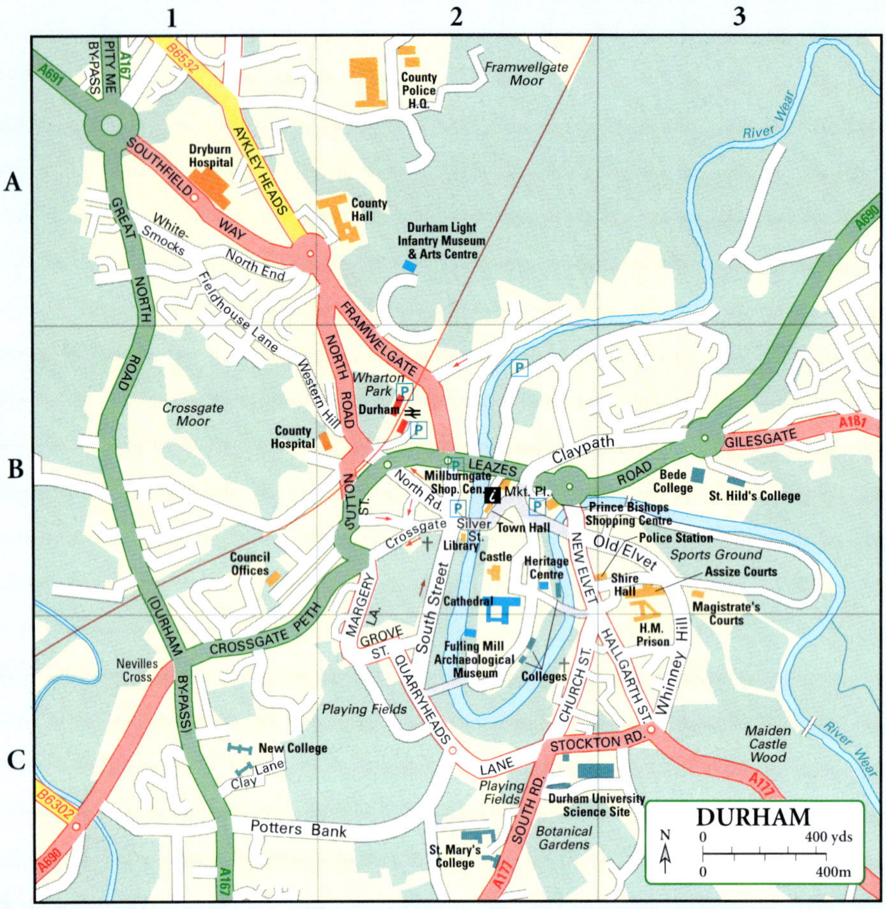

Information Centre: Market Place Tel: 0191 384 3720	
Aykley Heads	A1
Church Street	C2
Clay Lane	C1
Claypath	B2
Crossgate	B2
Crossgate Peth	C1
Durham By-Pass	B1
Fieldhouse Lane	A1
Framwelgate	A2
Gilesgate	B3
Great North Road	A1
Grove Street	C2
Hallgarth Street	C3
Leazes Road	B2
Margery Lane	C2
Market Place	B2
Millburngate Bridge	B2
New Elvet	B2
North End	A1
North Road	B2
Old Elvet	B3
Pity Me By-Pass	A1
Potters Bank	C1
Quarryheads Lane	C2
Silver Street	B2
South Road	C2
South Street	C2
Southfield Way	A1
Stockton Road	C2
Sutton Street	B2
Western Hill	B1
Whinney Hill	C3
Whitesmocks	A1

For Edinburgh see page 241

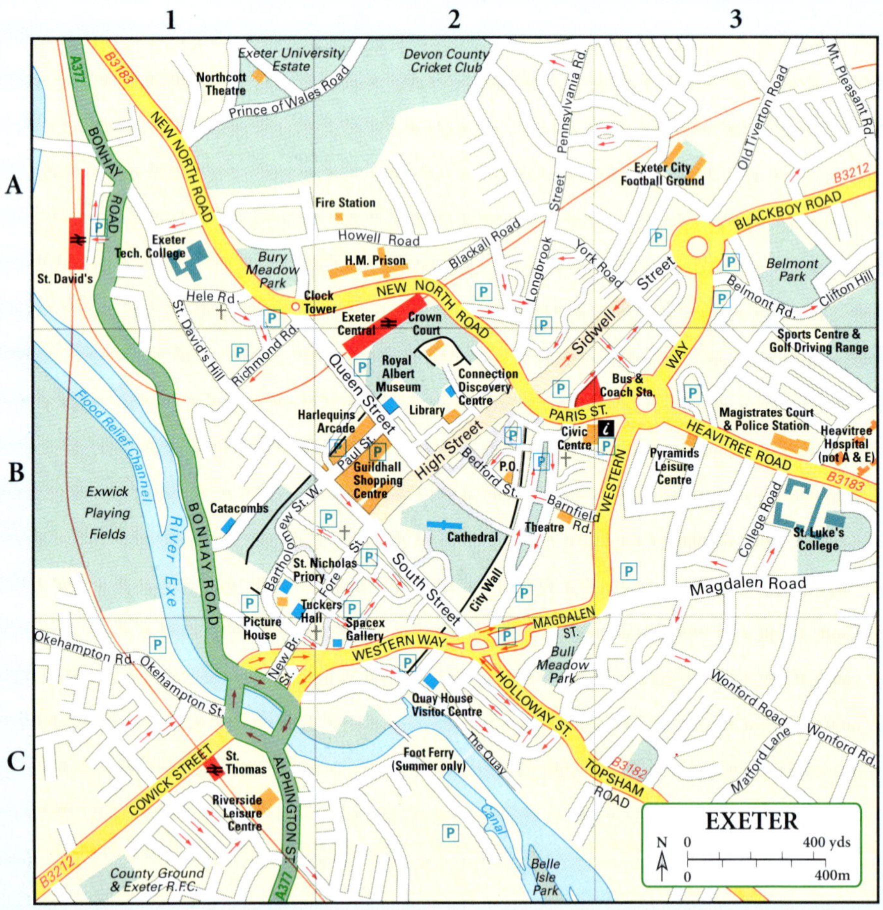

Information Centre: Civic Centre, Paris Street Tel: 01392 265700	
Alphington Street	C1
Barnfield Road	B2
Bartholomew Street West	B1
Bedford Street	B2
Belmont Road	A3
Blackboy Road	A3
Blackall Road	A2
Bonhay Road	B1
Clifton Hill	A3
College Road	B3
Cowick Street	C1
Fore Street	B2
Heavitree Road	B3
Hele Road	A1
High Street	B2
Holloway Street	C2
Howell Road	A2
Longbrook Street	A2
Magdalen Road	B3
Magdalen Street	C2
Matford Lane	C3
Mount Pleasant Road	A3
New Bridge Street	C1
New North Road	A1/A2
Okehampton Road	C1
Okehampton Street	C1
Old Tiverton Road	A3
Paris Street	B2
Paul Street	B2
Pennsylvania Road	A2
Prince of Wales Road	A1
Queen Street	B2
Richmond Road	B1
St. David's Hill	A1
Sidwell Street	B2
South Street	B2
The Quay	C2
Topsham Road	C2
Western Way	B2
Wonford Road	C3
York Road	A2

For Glasgow see page 242

Information Centre: 28 Southgate Street
Tel: 01452 421188

Adelaide Street	C2	Stroud Road	C1
Alma Place	C1	The Quay	B1
Alvin Street	A2	Tredworth Road	C2
Archdeacon Street	A1	Trier Way	C1
Barnwood Road	A3	Upton Street	C2
Barton Street	B2	Victoria Street	B2
Black Dog Way	A2	Wellington Street	B2
Bristol Road	C1	Westgate Street	A1
Brunswick Road	B2	Weston Road	C1
Bruton Way	B2	Wheatstone Road	C2
Calton Road	C2	Worcester Street	A2
Cheltenham Road	A3		
Churchill Road	C1		
Conduit Street	C2		
Dean's Way	A2		
Denmark Road	A2		
Derby Road	B2		
Estcourt Road	A2		
Eastern Avenue	C3		
Eastgate Street	B2		
Gouda Way	A1		
Great Western Road	B2		
Greyfriars	B2		
Hatherley Road	C2		
High Street	C2		
Hopewell Street	C2		
Horton Road	B3		
King Edward's Avenue	C2		
Kingsholm Road	A2		
Linden Road	C1		
London Road	A2		
Lower Westgate Street	A1		
Merevale Road	A3		
Metz Way	B2		
Millbrook Street	B2		
Northgate Street	B2		
Oxford Road	A2		
Oxstalls Lane	A3		
Painswick Road	C3		
Park Road	B2		
Parkend Road	C2		
Pitt Street	A2		
Quay Street	B1		
Ryecroft Street	C2		
St. Ann Way	C1		
St. Oswald's Road	A1		
Secunda Way	C1		
Severn Road	B1		
Seymour Road	C1		
Southgate Street	B1		
Spa Road	B1		
Station Road	B2		

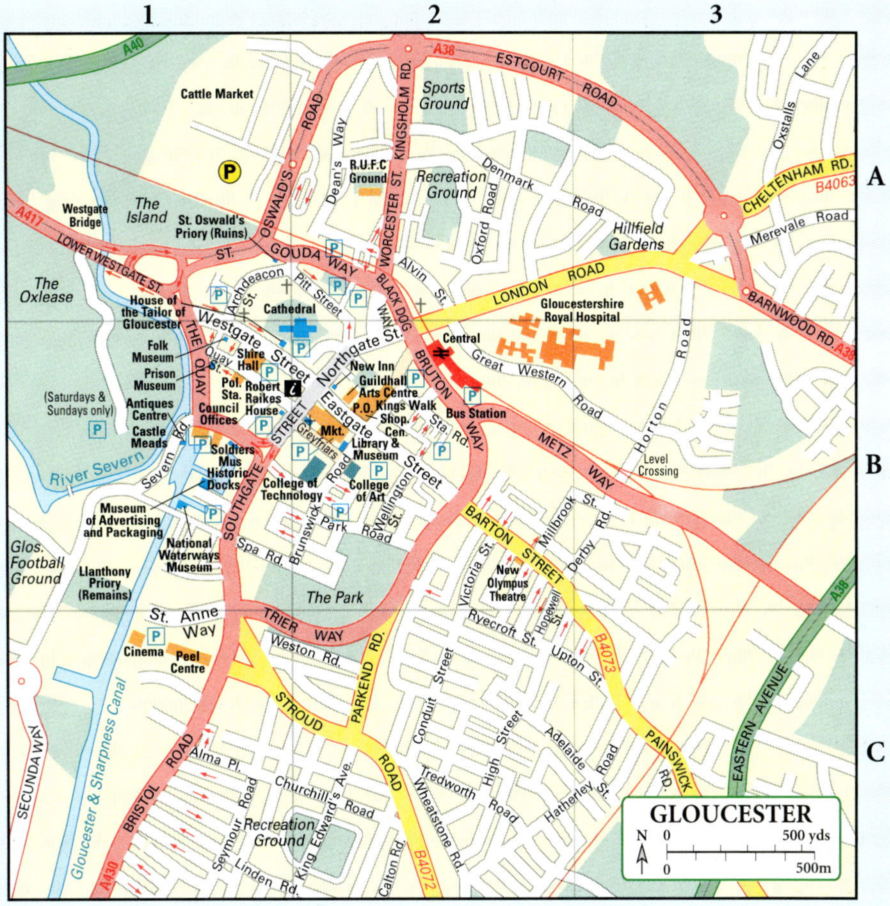

Information Centre: 1 King Street
Tel: 01432 268430

Aubrey Street	B2	Stonebow Road	A3
Barrs Court Road	A3	Symonds Street	B3
Barton Road	B1	The Atrium	A2
Barton Yard	B1	Turner Street	C3
Bath Street	B3	Union Street	B2
Berrington Street	B2	Union Walk	A3
Bewell Street	B2	Victoria Street	B1
Blackfriars Street	A2	West Street	B2
Blueschool Street	A2	Widemarsh Street	B2
Brewers Passage	B2	Wye Street	C2
Bridge Street	B2		
Broad Street	B2		
Canonmoor Street	A1		
Cantilupe Street	B3		
Castle Street	B2		
Catherine Street	A2		
Central Avenue	B3		
Church Street	B2		
Commercial Road	A3		
Commercial Street	B2		
Coningsby Street	A2		
East Street	B2		
Edgar Street	A2		
Eign Gate	B2		
Eign Street	B1		
Friars Street	B1		
Fryzer Court	B2		
Gaol Street	B3		
Green Street	C3		
Grenfell Road	C3		
Greyfriars Avenue	C1		
Greyfriars Bridge	B2		
Grove Road	C3		
Harold Street	C3		
High Street	B2		
High Town	B2		
King Street	B2		
Kyrle Street	B3		
Maylord Street	B2		
Mill Street	C3		
Moorfield Street	A1		
Nelson Street	C3		
Newmarket Street	A2		
Portland Street	A1		
Quay Street	B2		
St. Guthiac Street	B3		
St. James Road	C3		
St. Martin's Avenue	C2		
St. Martin's Street	C2		
St. Owen Street	B3		
Station Approach	A3		
Station Road	B1		

Kingston upon Hull • Leicester

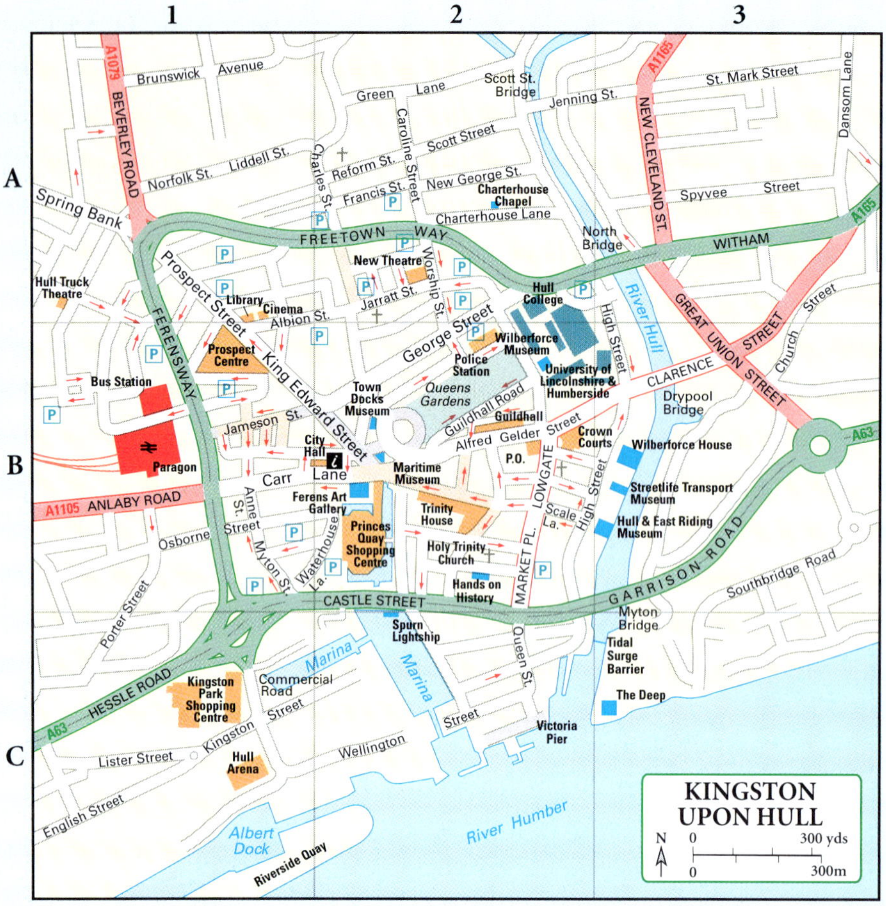

For Leeds see page 238

Information Centre: 1 Paragon Street
Tel: 01482 223559

Albion Street	B1	Waterhouse Lane	B1
Alfred Gelder Street	B2	Wellington Street	C2
Anlaby Road	B1	Witham	A3
Anne Street	B1	Worship Street	A2
Beverley Road	A1		
Brunswick Avenue	A1		
Caroline Street	A2		
Carr Lane	B1		
Castle Street	B2		
Charles Street	A2		
Charterhouse Lane	A2		
Church Street	B3		
Clarence Street	B3		
Cleveland Street	A3		
Dansom Lane	A3		
English Street	C1		
Ferensway	A1		
Francis Street	A2		
Freetown Way	A1		
Garrison Road	B3		
George Street	B2		
Great Union Street	A3		
Green Lane	A2		
Guildhall Road	B2		
Hessle Road	C1		
High Street	A3		
Jameson Street	B1		
Jarratt Street	A2		
Jenning Street	A2		
King Edward Street	B1		
Kingston Street	C1		
Liddell Street	A1		
Lister Street	C1		
Lowgate	B2		
Market Place	B2		
Myton Street	B1		
New Cleveland Street	A3		
New George Street	A2		
Norfolk Street	A1		
North Bridge	A2		
Osborne Street	B1		
Porter Street	C1		
Prospect Street	A1		
Queen Street	C2		
Reform Street	A2		
St. Mark Street	A3		
Scale Lane	B2		
Scott Street	A2		
Scott Street Bridge	A2		
Southbridge Road	B3		
Spring Bank	A1		
Spyvee Street	A3		

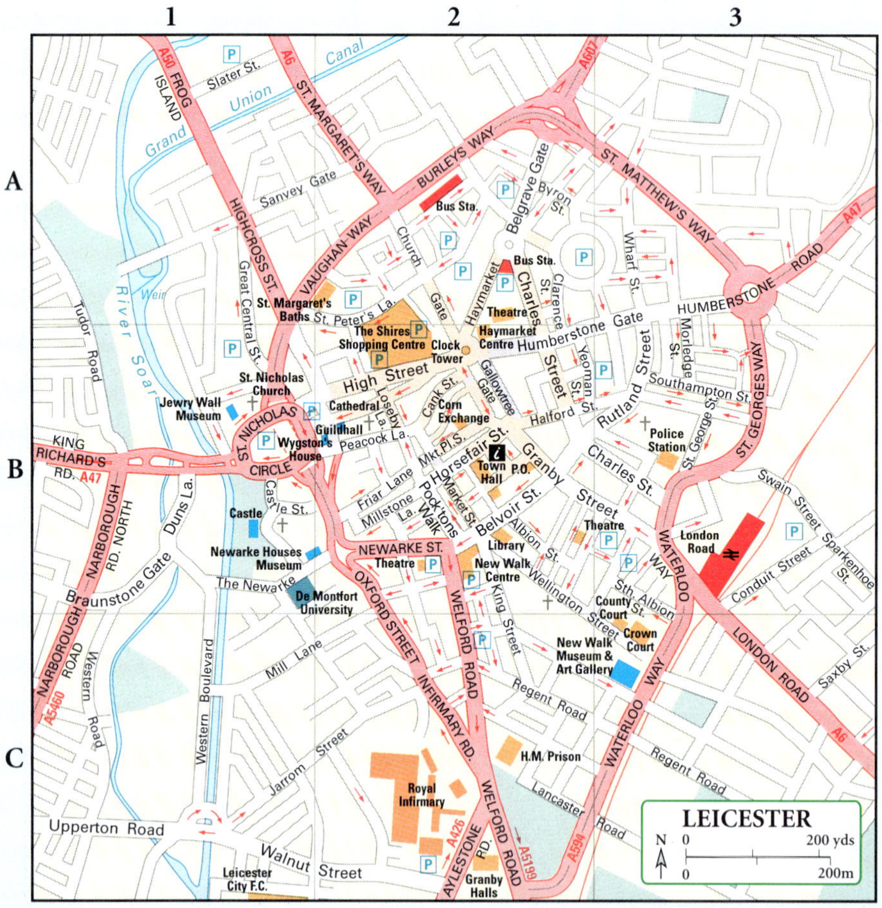

Information Centre: 7-9 Every Street, Town Hall Square
Tel: 0116 299 8888

Albion Street	B2	St. Peter's Lane	A2
Aylestone Road	C2	Sanvey Gare	A1
Belgrave Gate	A2	Saxby Street	C3
Belvoir Street	B2	Slater Street	A1
Braunstone Gate	B1	South Albion Street	B3
Burleys Way	A2	Southampton Street	B3
Byron Street	A2	Sparkenhoe Street	B3
Cank Street	B2	Swain Street	B3
Castle Street	B1	The Newarke	B1
Charles Street	B3	Tudor Road	A1
Church Gate	A2	Upperton Road	C1
Clarence Street	A2	Vaughan Way	A1
Conduit Street	B3	Walnut Street	C1
Duns Lane	B1	Waterloo Way	C3
Friar Lane	B2	Welford Road	B2
Frog Island	A1	Wellington Street	B2
Gallowtree Gate	B2	Western Boulevard	C1
Granby Street	B2	Western Road	C1
Great Central Street	A1	Wharf Street	A3
Halford Street	B2	Yeoman Street	B2
Haymarket	A2		
High Street	B2		
Highcross Street	A1		
Horsfair Street	B2		
Humberstone Gate	B2		
Humberstone Road	A3		
Infirmary Road	C2		
Jarrom Street	C1		
King Richard's Road	B1		
King Street	B2		
Lancaster Road	C2		
London Road	C3		
Loseby Lane	B2		
Market Place South	B2		
Market Street	B2		
Mill Lane	C1		
Millstone Lane	B2		
Morledge Street	B3		
Narborough Road	C1		
Narborough Road North	B1		
Newarke Street	B2		
Oxford Street	B2		
Peacock Lane	B2		
Pocklingtons Walk	B2		
Regent Road	C2		
Rutland Street	B3		
St. George Street	B3		
St. George's Way	B3		
St. Margaret's Way	A1		
St. Matthew's Way	A3		
St. Nicholas Circle	B1		

Lincoln • Middlesbrough

Information Centre: 9 Castle Hill
Tel: 01522 873213

Bailgate	A2
Brayford Way	C1
Beevor Street	C1
Broadgate	B2
Broadway	A2
Burton Road	A1
Canwick Road	C2
Carholme Road	B1
Carline Road	A1
Church Lane	A2
Clasketgate	B2
Croft Street	B2
Cross Street	C2
Drury Lane	B2
East Gate	B2
Firth Road	C1
Great Northern Terrace	C2
Greetwell Road	B3
Gresham Street	B1
High Street	C2
Lee Road	A3
Lindum Road	B2
Lindum Terrace	B3
Long Leys Road	A1
Milman Road	B3
Monks Road	B3
Monson Street	C2
Nettleham Road	A2
Newland	B1
Newport	A2
Northgate	A2
Pelham Bridge	C2
Portland Street	C2
Rasen Lane	A2
Ripon Street	C2
Rope Walk	C1
Ruskin Avenue	A3
St. Anne's Road	B3
St. Mark Street	C2
Saltergate	B2
Sewell Road	B3
Silver Street	B2
Spa Road	C3
Stamp End	C3
Steep Hill	B2
The Avenue	B1
Tritton Road	C1
Upper Long Leys Road	A1
Waterside North	C2
Waterside South	C2
West Parade	B1
Westgate	A2
Wigford Way	B2
Winn Street	B3
Wragby Road	B3
Yarborough Road	A1

For Liverpool see page 235
For Manchester see page 236

Information Centre: 99-101 Albert Road
Tel: 01642 243425/358086

Abingdon Road	B2
Albert Road	A2
Ayresome Green Lane	B1
Ayresome Street	B1
Belle Vue Grove	C3
Bishopton Road	C2
Borough Road	A2/C3
Bridge Street West	A2
Burlam Road	C1
Cargo Fleet Road	A3
Clairville Road	B2
Corporation Road	A2
Crescent Road	B1
Cumberland Road	C2
Dockside Road	A2/A3
Eastbourne Road	C2
Forty Foot Road	A1
Grange Road	A2
Gresham Road	B1
Hartington Road	A1
Heywood Street	B1
Highfield Road	C3
Holwick Road	A1
Linthorpe Road	C2
Longlands Road	B3
Marton Burn Road	C2
Marton Road	B3/C3
Newport Road	A1/A2
North Ormesby Road	A3
Orchard Road	C1
Park Road North	B2
Park Road South	B2
Park Vale Road	B2
Parliament Road	B1
Riverside Park Road	A1
Roman Road	C1
St. Barnabas Road	B1
Scotts Road	A3
Sheperdson Way	A3
Snowdon Road	A2
Southfield Road	B2
The Avenue	C2
The Crescent	C1
Union Street	B1
Valley Road	C2
Victoria Road	B2
Westbourne Grove	B3
Wilson Street	A2
Woodlands Road	B2

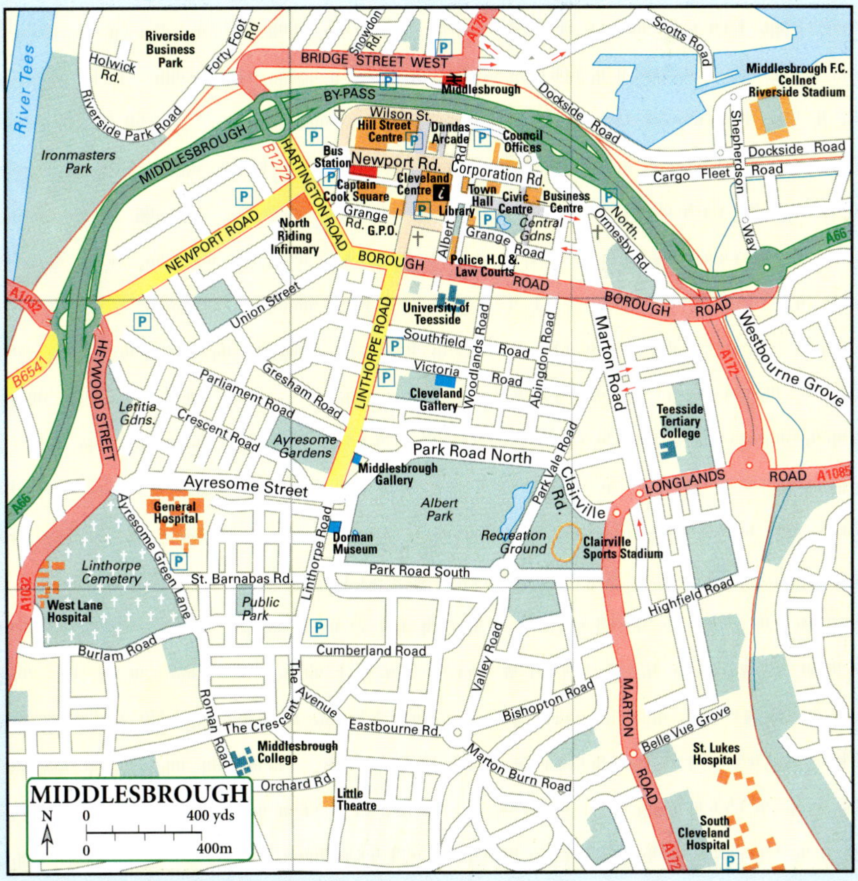

For Newcastle see page 240

Norwich • Oxford

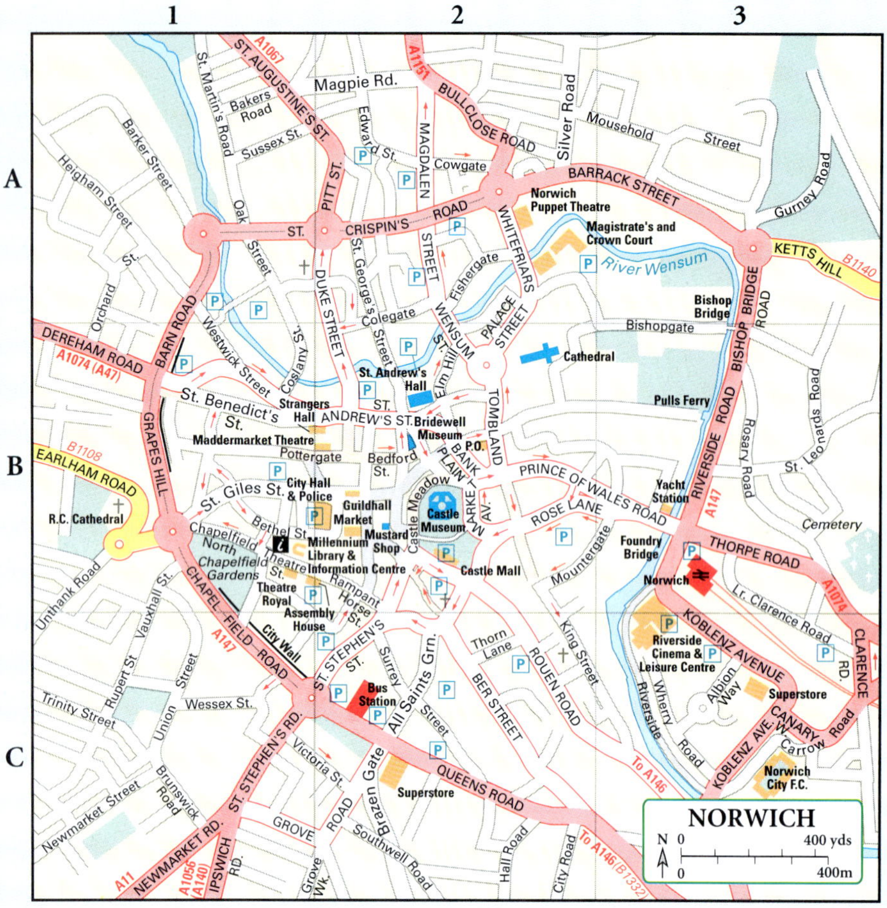

Information Centre: Millennium Library, Bethel Street
Tel: 01603 666071

Albion Way	C3	Pitt Street	A2
All Saints Green	C2	Pottergate	B1
Bakers Road	A1	Prince of Wales Road	B2
Bank Plain	B2	Queens Road	C2
Barker Street	A1	Rampant Horse Street	B2
Barn Road	B1	Riverside	C3
Barrack Street	A2	Riverside Road	B3
Bedford Street	B2	Rosary Road	B3
Ber Street	C2	Rose Lane	B2
Bethel Street	B1	Rouen Road	C2
Bishopbridge Road	B3	Rupert Street	C1
Bishopgate	B3	St. Andrew's Street	B2
Brazen Gate	C2	St. Augustine's Street	A1
Brunswick Road	C1	St. Benedict's Street	B1
Bullclose Road	A2	St. Crispin's Road	A1
Canary Way	C3	St. George's Street	A2
Carrow Road	C3	St. Giles Street	B1
Castle Meadow	B2	St. Leonards Road	B3
Chapel Field Road	B1	St. Martin's Road	A1
Chapelfield North	B1	St. Stephen's Road	C1
City Road	C2	St. Stephen's Street	C2
Clarence Road	C3	Silver Road	A2
Colegate	A2	Southwell Road	C2
Coslany Street	B1	Surrey Street	C2
Cowgate	A2	Sussex Street	A1
Dereham Road	B1	Theatre Street	B1
Duke Street	A2	Thorn Lane	C2
Earlham Road	B1	Thorpe Road	B3
Edward Street	A2	Tombland	B2
Elm Hill	B2	Trinity Street	C1
Fishergate	A2	Union Street	C1
Grapes Hill	B1	Unthank Road	C1
Grove Road	C1	Vauxhall Street	C1
Grove Walk	C1	Victoria Street	C1
Gurney Road	A3	Wensum Street	A2
Hall Road	C2	Wessex Street	C1
Heigham Street	A1	Westwick Street	A1
Ipswich Road	C1	Wherry Road	C3
Ketts Hill	A3	Whitefriars	A2
King Street	C2		
Koblenz Avenue	C3		
Lower Clarence Road	B3		
Magdalen Street	A2		
Magpie Road	A2		
Market Avenue	B2		
Mountergate	B2		
Mousehold Street	A3		
Newmarket Road	C1		
Newmarket Street	C1		
Oak Street	A1		
Orchard Street	A1		
Palace Street	B2		

For Nottingham see page 232

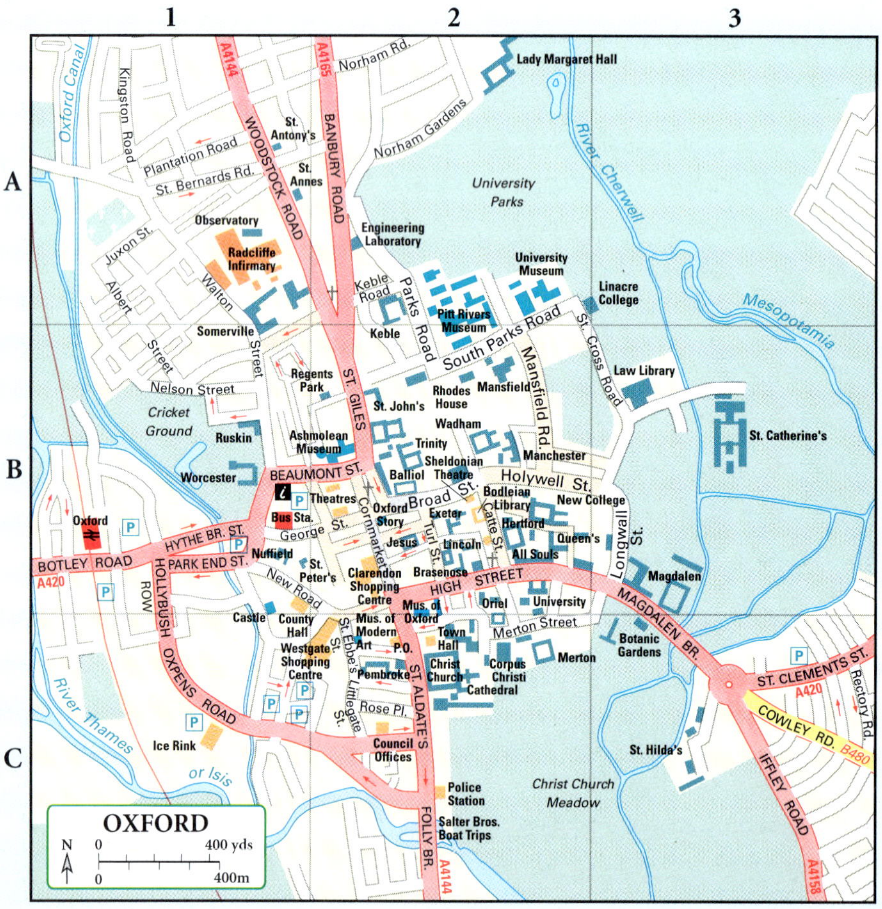

Information Centre: The Old School, Gloucester Green
Tel: 01865 726871

Albert Street	A1
Banbury Road	A2
Beaumont Street	B1
Botley Road	B1
Broad Street	B2
Cattle Street	B2
Cornmarket	B2
Cowley Road	C3
Folly Bridge	C2
George Street	B1
High Street	B2
Hollybush Row	B1
Holywell Street	B2
Hythe Bridge Street	B1
Iffley Road	C3
Juxon Street	A1
Keble Road	A2
Kingston Road	A1
Littlegate Street	C2
Longwall Street	B3
Magdalen Bridge	B3
Mansfield Road	B2
Merton Street	C2
Nelson Street	B1
New Road	B1
Norham Gardens	A2
Norham Road	A2
Oxpens Road	C1
Park End Street	B1
Parks Road	A2
Plantation Road	A1
Rectory Road	C3
Rose Place	C2
St. Aldate's	C2
St. Bernards Road	A1
St. Clements Street	C3
St. Cross Road	A2
St. Ebbe's Street	C2
St. Giles	B2
South Parks Road	B2
Turl Street	B2
Walton Street	A1
Woodstock Road	A1

Plymouth • Reading

Information Centre: Island House, 9 The Barbican
Tel: 01752 264849

Alexandra Road	A3	North Cross	B2
Alma Road	A1	North Hill	B2
Armada Way	B2	North Road East	B2
Ashford Road	A3	North Road West	B1
Barbican Approach	C3	North Street	B2
Beaumont Road	B3	Notte Street	C2
Beechwood Avenue	A2	Oxford Street	B1
Bretonside	B2	Pentillie Road	A2
Buckwell Street	C2	Princess Street	C2
Camden Street	B2	Queen's Road	A3
Cattledown Road	C3	Royal Parade	B2
Cecil Street	B1	Salisbury Road	B3
Central Park Avenue	A1	Saltash Road	A1
Charles Street	B2	Seaton Avenue	A2
Citadel Road	C1	Seymour Avenue	B3
Clarence Place	B1	Southside Street	C2
Cliff Road	C1	Stoke Road	B1
Clifton Place	A2	Stuart Road	A1
Clovelly Road	C3	Sutton Road	B3
Cobourg Street	B2	Sydney Street	B1
Cornwall Street	B2	Teats Hill Road	C3
Dale Road	A2	The Crescent	C1
Drake Circus	B2	Tothill Avenue	B3
East Street	C1	Tothill Road	B3
Eastlake Street	B2	Union Street	B1
Ebrington Street	B2	Vauxhall Street	C2
Elliot Street	C1	West Hoe Road	C1
Embankment Road	B3	Western Approach	B1
Exeter Street	B2	Whittington Street	A1
Ford Park Road	A2	Wilton Street	B1
Gdynia Way	C3	Wyndham Street	B1
Grand Parade	C1		
Greenbank Road	A3		
Grenville Road	B3		
Harwell Street	B1		
Hoe Road	C2		
Houndiscombe Road	A2		
James Street	B2		
King Street	B1		
Lipson Hill	A3		
Lipson Road	B3		
Lisson Grove	A3		
Lockyer Street	C2		
Looe Street	B2		
Madeira Road	C2		
Manor Road	B1		
Martin Street	C1		
Mayflower Street	B2		
Millbay Road	C1		
Mount Gould Road	A3		
Mutley Plain	A2		
New George Street	B1		

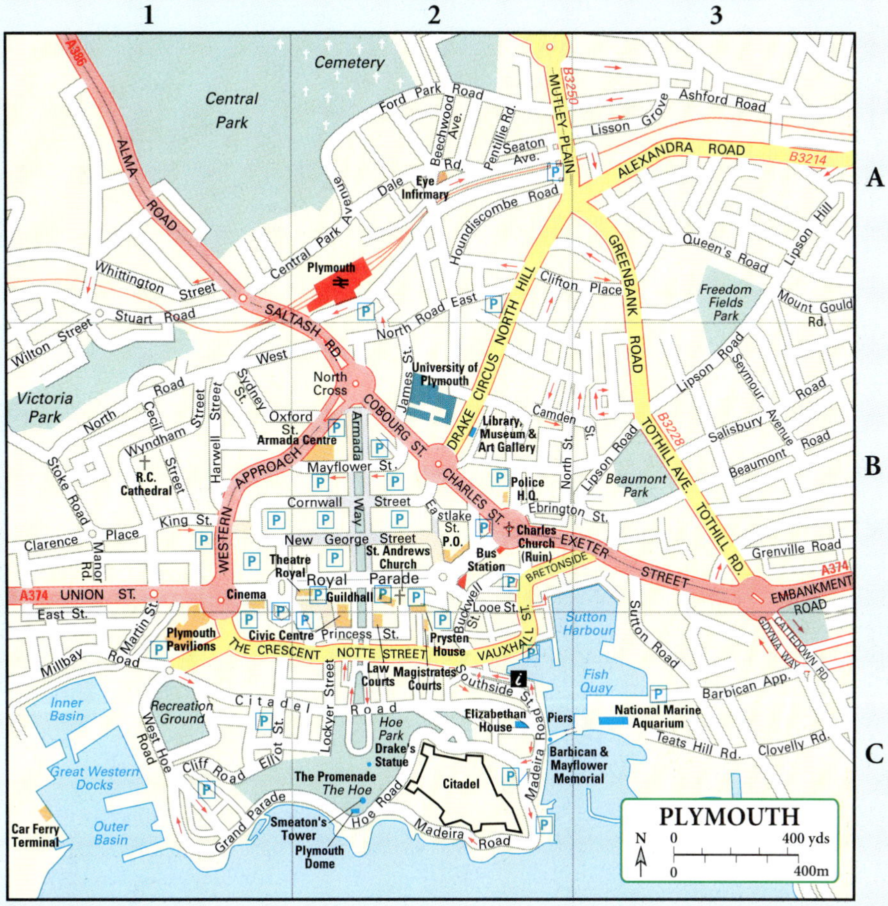

For Portsmouth see page 227

Information Centre: Town Hall, Blagrave Street
Tel: 0118 956 6226

Addington Road	C3	Hill Street	C2
Addison Road	A1	Holybrook Road	C1
Alexandra Road	B3	Kenavon Drive	B3
Allcroft Road	C3	Kendrick Road	C2
Alpine Street	C2	King's Road *Caversham*	A2
Amersham Road	A3	King's Road *Reading*	B2
Amity Road	B3	London Road	B3
Ardler Road	A2	London Street	B2
Audley Street	B1	Lower Henley Road	A3
Basingstoke Road	C2	Mill Road	A3
Bath Road	C1	Millford Road	A1
Bedford Road	B1	Millman Road	C2
Berkeley Avenue	C1	Minster Street	B2
Blagrave Street	B2	Morgan Road	C3
Blenheim Road	B3	Napier Road	B2
Briant's Avenue	A3	Orts Road	B3
Bridge Street	B2	Oxford Road	B1
Broad Street	B2	Pell Street	C2
Cardiff Road	A1	Portman Road	A1
Castle Hill	B1	Priest Hill	A2
Castle Street	B2	Prospect Street *Caversham*	A2
Catherine Street	B1	Prospect Street *Reading*	B1
Caversham Road	B1	Queen's Road *Caversham*	A2
Chatham Street	B1	Queen's Road *Reading*	B2
Cheapside	B1	Redlands Road	C3
Cholmeley Road	B3	Richfield Avenue	A1
Christchurch Road	C2	Rose Kiln Lane	C2
Church Road	A1	Russell Street	B1
Church Street	B2	St. Ann's Road	A2
Coley Avenue	C1	St. John's Road	A3
Cow Lane	B1	St. Mary's Butts	B2
Craven Road	B3	St. Peters Avenue	A1
Crown Place	B3	St. Saviours Road	C1
Crown Street	C2	Silver Street	C2
Cumberland Road	B3	South Street	B2
Curzon Street	B1	Southampton Street	C2
De Beauvoir Road	B3	South View Road	A2
Donnington Road	B3	Star Road	A3
Duke Street	B2	Station Hill	B2
East Street	B2	Station Road	B2
Eldon Road	B3	Swansea Road	A2
Eldon Terrace	B3	Tessa Road	A1
Elgar Road	C2	The Warren	A1
Elgar Road South	C2	Tilehurst Road	B1
Erleigh Road	B3	Upper Redlands Road	C3
Fobney Street	B2	Vastern Road	A2
Forbury Road	B2	Waldeck Street	C2
Friar Street	B2	Waterloo Road	C2
Gas Work Road	B3	Wensley Road	C1
George Street *Caversham*	A2	Western Elms Avenue	B1
George Street *Reading*	B1	Westfield Road	A2
Gosbrook Road	A2	West Street	B2
Gower Street	B1	Whitley Street	C2
Great Knollys Street	B1	Wolsey Road	A2
Greyfriars Road	B2	York Road	A2
Hemdean Road	A2		

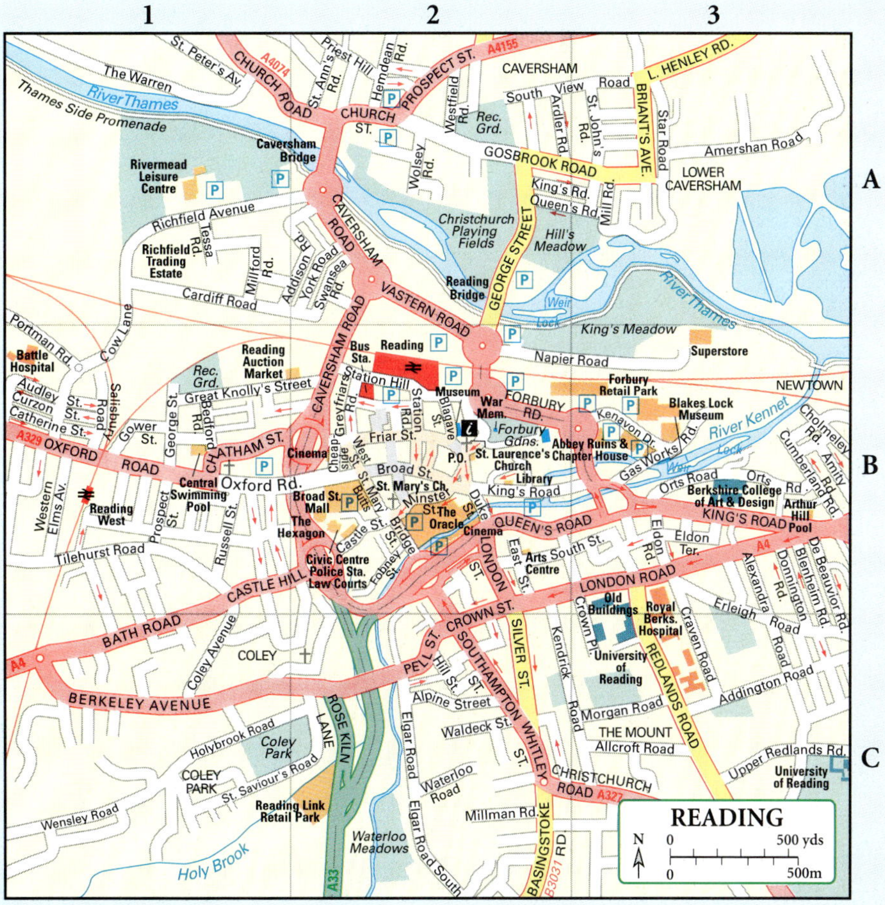

For Sheffield see page 233
For Southampton see page 226

Stoke-on-Trent • Stratford-upon-Avon

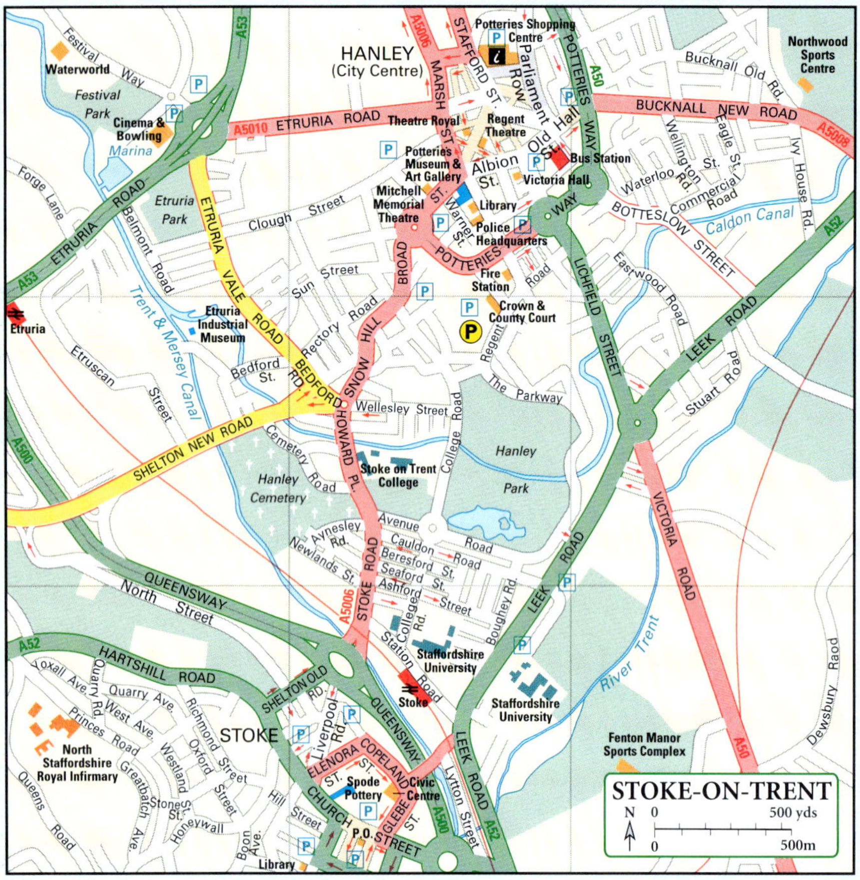

Information Centre: Potteries Shopping Cen, Quadrant Rd
Tel: 01782 236000

Street	Grid
Albion Street	A2
Ashford Street	B2
Avenue Road	B2
Aynsley Road	B2
Bedford Road	B2
Bedford Street	B1
Belmont Road	A1
Beresford Street	B2
Boon Avenue	C1
Botteslow Street	A3
Boughey Road	C2
Broad Street	A2
Bucknall New Road	A3
Bucknall Old Road	A3
Cauldon Road	B2
Cemetery Road	B1
Church Street	C2
Clough Street	A1
College Road	B2
Commercial Road	A3
Copeland Street	C2
Dewsbury Road	C3
Eagle Street	A3
Eastwood Road	A3
Elenora Street	C2
Etruria Road	A1
Etruria Vale Road	A1
Etruscan Street	B1
Festival Way	A1
Forge Lane	A1
Glebe Street	C2
Greatbatch Avenue	C1
Hanley	A2
Hartshill Road	C1
Hill Street	C1
Honeywall	C1
Howard Place	B2
Ivy House Road	A3
Leek Road	C2
Lichfield Street	A3
Liverpool Road	C2
Lytton Street	C2
Marsh Street	A2
Newlands Street	B2
North Street	B1
Old Hall Street	A2
Oxford Street	C1
Parliament Row	A2
Potteries Way	A2
Potters Way	A3
Prince's Road	C1
Quarry Avenue	C1
Quarry Road	C1
Queen's Road	C1
Queensway	B1
Rectory Road	B2
Regent Road	B2
Richmond Street	C1
Seaford Street	B2
Shelton New Road	B1
Shelton Old Road	C1
Snow Hill	B2
Stafford Street	A2
Station Road	C2
Stoke	C2
Stoke Road	C2
Stone Street	C1
Stuart Road	B3
Sun Street	A2
The Parkway	B2
Victoria Road	B3
Warner Street	A2
Waterloo Street	A3
Wellesley Street	B2
Wellington Road	A3
West Avenue	C1
Westland Street	C1
Yoxall Avenue	C1

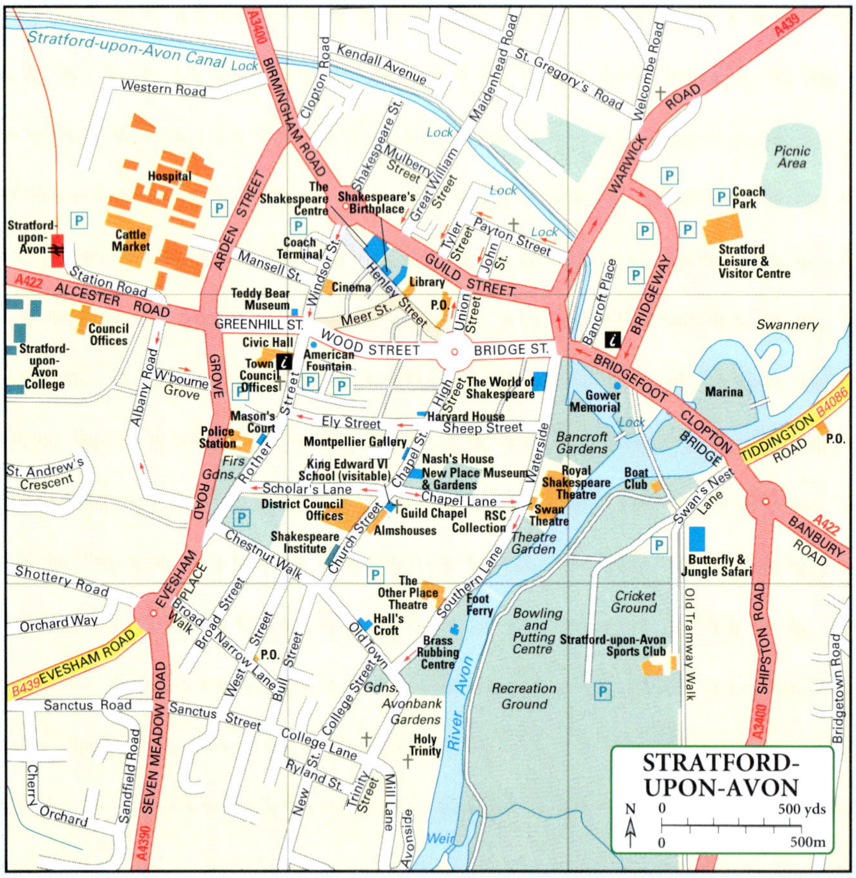

Information Centre: Bridgefoot
Tel: 01789 293127

Street	Grid
Albany Road	B1
Alcester Road	A1
Arden Street	A1
Avonside	C2
Banbury Road	B3
Bancroft Place	B3
Birmingham Road	A1
Bridgefoot	B3
Bridge Street	B2
Bridgeway	B3
Bridgetown Road	C3
Broad Street	C1
Broad Walk	C1
Bull Street	C1
Chapel Lane	B2
Chapel Street	B2
Cherry Orchard	C1
Chestnut Walk	B1
Church Street	B2
Clopton Bridge	B3
Clopton Road	A2
College Lane	C2
College Street	C2
Ely Street	B2
Evesham Place	C1
Evesham Road	C1
Great William Street	A2
Greenhill Street	B1
Grove Road	B1
Guild Street	A2
Henley Street	A2
High Street	B2
John Street	A2
Kendall Avenue	A2
Maidenhead Road	A2
Mansell Street	A1
Meer Street	B2
Mill Lane	C2
Mulberry Street	A2
Narrow Lane	C1
New Street	C2
Old Town	C2
Old Tramway Walk	C3
Orchard Way	C1
Payton Street	A2
Rother Street	B1
Ryland Street	C2
St. Andrews Crescent	B1
St. Gregory's Road	A2
Sanctus Road	C1
Sanctus Street	C1
Sandfield Road	C1
Scholar's Lane	B1
Shakespeare Street	A2
Sheep Street	B2
Shipston Road	C3
Shottery Road	B1
Seven Meadow Road	C1
Southern Lane	C2
Station Road	A1
Swans Nest Lane	B3
Tiddington Road	B3
Trinity Street	C2
Tyler Street	A2
Union Street	B2
Warwick Road	A3
Waterside	B2
Welcombe Road	A3
Westbourne Grove	B1
Western Road	A1
West Street	C1
Windsor Street	B2
Wood Street	B2

Swansea • Swindon

Information Centre: Singleton Street
Tel: 01792 468321

Albert Row	C2
Alexandra Road	B2
Argyle Street	C1
Beach Street	C1
Belle Vue Way	B2
Bond Street	C1
Brooklands Terrace	B1
Brynymor Crescent	C1
Brynymor Road	C1
Burrows Place	C3
Cambrian Place	C3
Carmarthen Road	A2
Castle Street	B2
Clarence Terrace	C2
Constitution Hill	B1
Cromwell Street	B1
De La Beche Street	B2
Delhi Street	B3
Dyfatty Street	A2
Dyfed Avenue	B1
East Burrows Road	C3
Fabian Way	B3
Foxhole Road	A3
Glamorgan Street	C2
Gors Avenue	A1
Grove Place	B2
Gwent Road	A1
Hanover Street	B1
High Street	B2
Islwyn Road	A1
King Edward's Road	C1
Llangyfelach Road	A2
Lower Oxford Street	C1
Mackworth Street	B3
Mansel Street	B1
Mayhill Road	A1
Morris Lane	B3
Mount Pleasant	B2
Mumbles Road	C1
Neath Road	A3
New Cut Road	B3
New Orchard Street	A2
North Hill Road	A2
Orchard Street	B2
Oystermouth Road	C1
Page Street	B2
Pentre Guinea Road	A3
Pen-y-Craig Road	A1
Powys Avenue	A1
Princess Way	B2
Rose Hill	B1
St. Helen's Avenue	C1
St. Helen's Road	C1
St. Mary Street	B2
Singleton Street	C2
Somerset Place	C3
South Guildhall Road	C1
Strand	B3
Terrace Road	B1
The Kingsway	B2
Townhill Road	A1
Vincent Street	C1
Walter Road	C1
Waun-Wen Road	A2
Wellington Street	C2
Westbury Street	C1
Western Street	C1
West Way	C2

Information Centre: 37 Regent Street
Tel: 01793 530328

Bath Road	C2
Beatrice Street	A2
Birch Street	B1
Bridge Street	B2
Broad Street	A3
Canal Walk	B2
Cirencester Way	A3
Clifton Street	C2
Commercial Road	B2
County Road	A3
Courtsknap Court	B1
Cricklade Street	C3
Curtis Street	B2
Dean Street	B1
Drove Road	C3
Eastcott Hill	C2
Edmund Street	B2
Euclid Street	B3
Faringdon Road	B1
Farnby Street	B2
Fleet Street	B2
Fleming Way	B2
Folkstone Road	C2
Great Western Way	A1
Groundwell Road	B3
Hawksworth Way	A1
High Street	C3
Hythe Road	C2
Jennings Street	B1
Kemble Drive	A1
Kent Road	C2
Kingshill Street	C1
Manchester Road	A2
Market Street	B2
Milford Street	B2
Milton Road	B2
Morris Street	A1
Newburn Crescent	B1
North Star Avenue	A2
Ocotal Way	A3
Okus Road	C1
Park Lane	B1
Penzance Drive	B1
Princes Street	B3
Queen Street	B2
Redcliffe Street	B1
Regent Street	B2
Rodbourne Road	A1
Rosebery Way	A3
Spring Gardens	B3
Stafford Street	C2
Station Road	A2
Swindon Road	C2
The Parade	B2
Upham Road	C3
Victoria Road	B3
Westcott Place	C1
Western Street	C3
William Street	C1

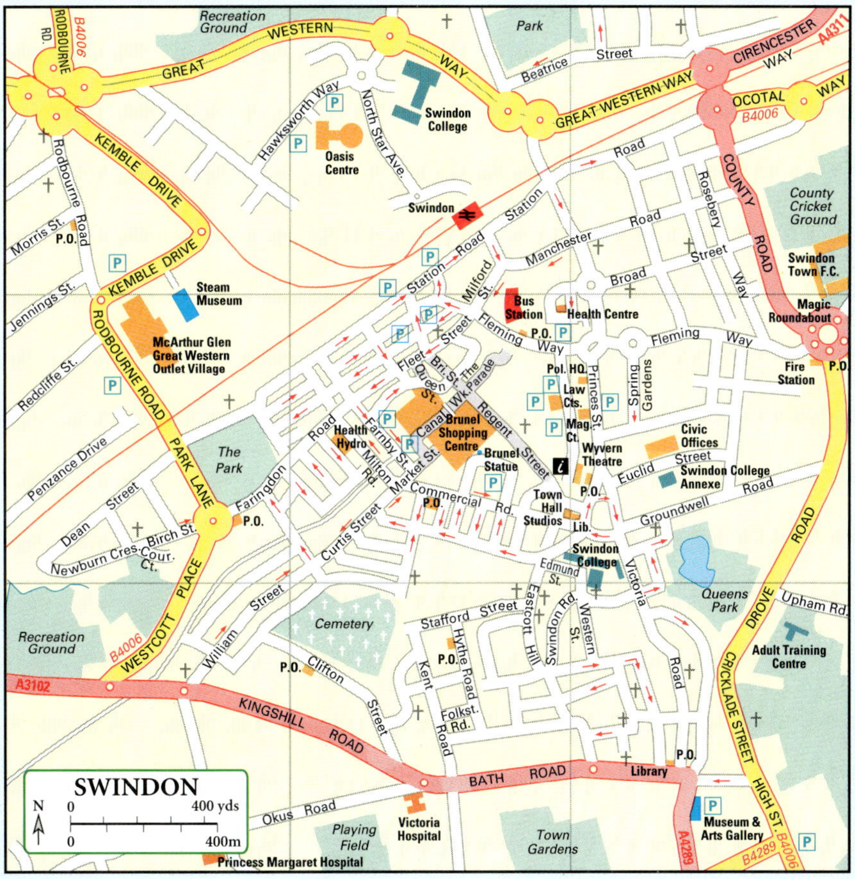

Torquay • Winchester

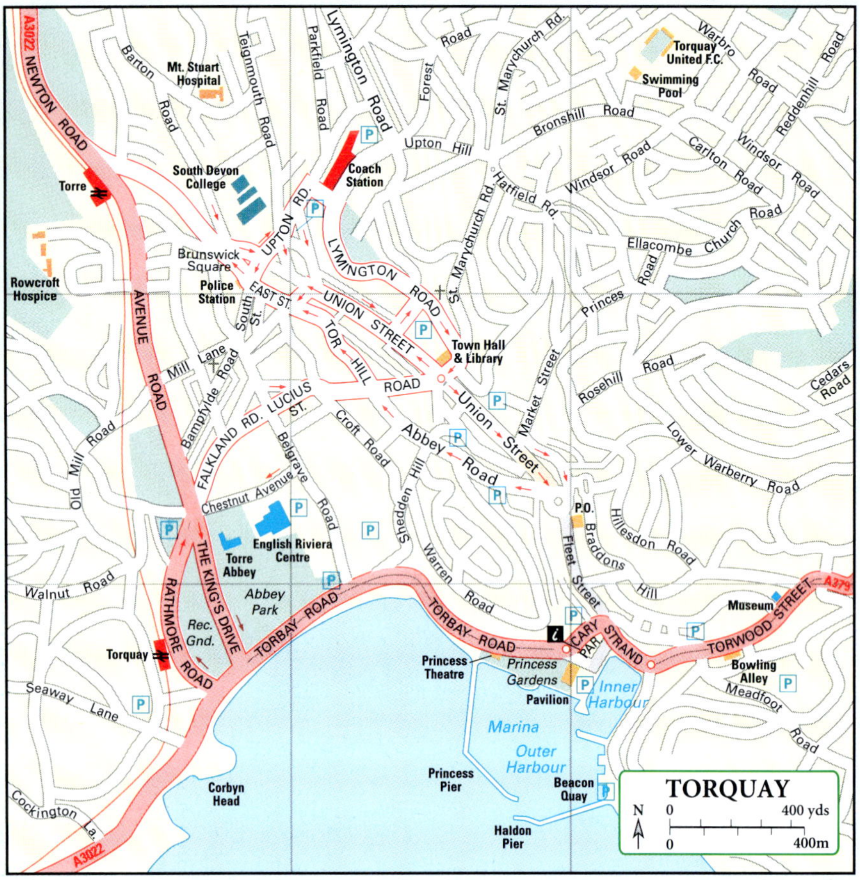

Information Centre: Vaughan Parade
Tel: 01803 297428

Abbey Road	B2
Avenue Road	B1
Bampfylde Road	B1
Barton Road	A1
Belgrave Road	B1
Braddons Hill	B3
Bronshill Road	A2
Brunswick Square	B1
Carlton Road	A3
Cary Parade	C3
Cedars Road	B3
Chestnut Avenue	B1
Cockington Lane	C1
Croft Road	B2
East Street	A1
Ellacombe Church Road	A3
Falkland Road	B1
Fleet Street	B2
Forest Road	A2
Hatfield Road	A2
Hillesdon Road	B3
Lower Warberry Road	B3
Lucius Street	B1
Lymington Road	A2
Market Street	B2
Meadfoot Road	C3
Mill Lane	B1
Newton Road	A1
Old Mill Road	B1
Parkfield Road	A2
Prince's Road	B3
Rathmore Road	C1
Reddenhill Road	A3
Rosehill Road	B3
St. Marychurch Road	B2
Seaway Lane	C1
Shedden Hill	B2
Shiphay Lane	A1
South Street	B1
Strand	C3
Teignmouth Road	A1
The King's Drive	B1
Torbay Road	C1
Tor Hill Road	B2
Torwood Street	C3
Union Street	B2
Upton Hill	A2
Upton Road	A1
Walnut Road	C1
Warbro Road	A3
Warren Road	B2
Westhill Road	A2
Windsor Road	A3

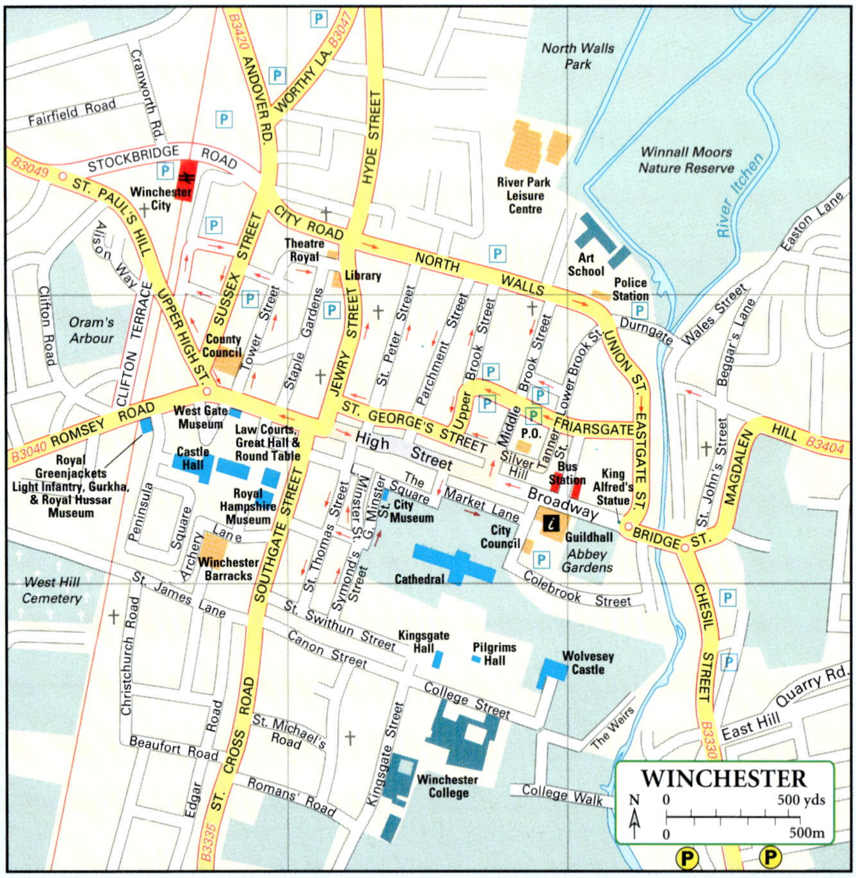

Information Centre: Guildhall, The Broadway
Tel: 01962 840500

Alison Way	A1
Andover Road	A1
Archery Lane	B1
Beaufort Road	C1
Beggar's Lane	B3
Bridge Stret	B3
Broadway	B2
Canon Street	C2
Chesil Street	C3
Christchurch Road	C1
City Road	A1
Clifton Road	A1
Clifton Terrace	B1
Colebrook Street	B2
College Street	C2
College Walk	C2
Cranworth Road	A1
Durngate	B3
Eastgate Street	B3
Easton Lane	A3
East Hill	C3
Edgar Road	C1
Fairfield Road	A1
Friarsgate	B2
Great Minster Street	B2
High Street	B2
Hyde Street	A2
Jewry Street	B2
Kingsgate Street	C2
Little Minster Street	B2
Lower Brook Street	B2
Magdalen Hill	B3
Market Lane	B2
Middle Brook Street	B2
North Walls	A1
Parchment Street	B2
Peninsula Square	B1
Quarry Road	C3
Romans' Road	C1
Romsey Road	B1
St. Cross Road	C1
St. George's Street	B2
St. James Lane	B1
St. John's Street	B3
St. Michael's Road	C1
St. Paul's Hill	A1
St. Peter Street	B2
St. Swithun Street	C2
St. Thomas Street	C2
Silver Hill	B2
Southgate Street	C1
Staple Gardens	B2
Stockbridge Road	A1
Sussex Street	B1
Symond's Street	C2
Tanner Street	B2
The Square	B2
Tower Street	B1
Union Street	B3
Upper Brook Street	B2
Upper High Street	B1
Wales Street	B3
Worthy Lane	A1

Windsor • York

Information Centre: 24 High Street
Tel: 01753 743900

Alexandra Road	C2
Alma Road	B2
Arthur Road	B2
Barry Avenue	A2
Bolton Avenue	C2
Bolton Road	C2
Bulkeley Avenue	C1
Charles Street	B2
Clarence Road	B1
Datchet Road	A3
Eton & Windsor Relief Road	B1
Frances Road	C2
Goslar Way	B1
Green Lane	B1
Grove Road	B2
High Street (Eton)	A2
High Street (Windsor)	B3
Imperial Road	C1
King Edward VII Avenue	A3
Kings Road	C3
Meadow Lane	A2
Osborne Road	C2
Oxford Road	B2
Parsonage Lane	B1
Peascod Street	B2
St. Leonards Road	C2
Sheet Street	B3
Springfield Road	C1
Stovell Road	A1
Thames Street	A3
The Long Walk	C3
Vansittart Road	B2
Victoria Street	B2
York Avenue	C1

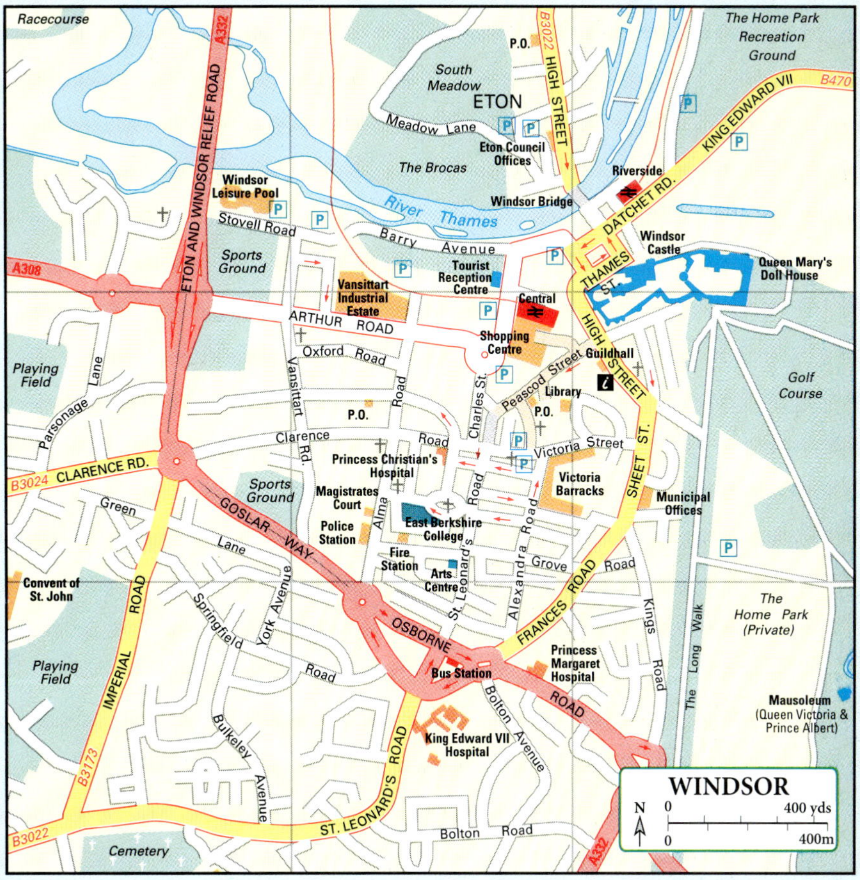

Information Centre: TIC Travel Office, 20 George Hudson St.
Tel: 01904 554488

Albermarle Road	C1
Aldwark	B2
Barbican Road	C3
Bishopthorpe Road	C2
Bishopgate Street	C2
Blossom Street	C1
Bootham	A1
Bull Lane	A3/B3
Burton Stone Lane	A1
Cemetery Road	C3
Church Street	B2
Clarence Street	A2
Clifford Street	B2
Clifton	A1
Coney Street	B2
Dale Street	C1
Dalton Terrace	C1
Dodsworth Avenue	A3
East Parade	A3
Fifth Avenue	A3
Fishergate	C2
Foss Bank	B3
Fossgate	B2
Foss Islands Road	B3
Fourth Avenue	B3
Gillygate	A2
Goodramgate	B2
Grosvenor Road	A1
Grosvenor Terrace	A1
Hallfield Road	B3
Haxby Road	A2
Heslington Road	C3
Heworth Green	A3
Holgate Road	C1
Huntington Road	A3
Lawrence Street	C3
Layerthorpe	B3
Leeman Road	B1
Lendal	B2
Longfield Terrace	B1
Lord Mayor's Walk	A2
Lowther Street	A2
Malton Road	A3
Maurices Road	B2
Micklegate	B1
Monkgate	A2
Moss Street	C1
Museum Street	B2
North Street	B2
Nunnery Lane	C1
Nunthorpe Road	C1
Ousegate	B2
Paragon Street	C2
Park Grove	A2
Penley's Grove Street	A2
Petergate	B2
Piccadilly	B2
Queen Street	B1
Rougier Street	B1
St. Andrewgate	B2
St. John's Street	A2
St. Maurice's Road	B2
Scarcroft Hill	C1
Scarcroft Road	C1
Shambles	B2
Sixon Avenue	A3
Sixth Avenue	A3
Skeldergate	B2
Southlands Road	C1
Station Road	B1
Tadcaster Road	C1
The Mount	C1
The Stonebow	B2
Tower Street	B2
Walmgate	B2
Wigginton Road	A2

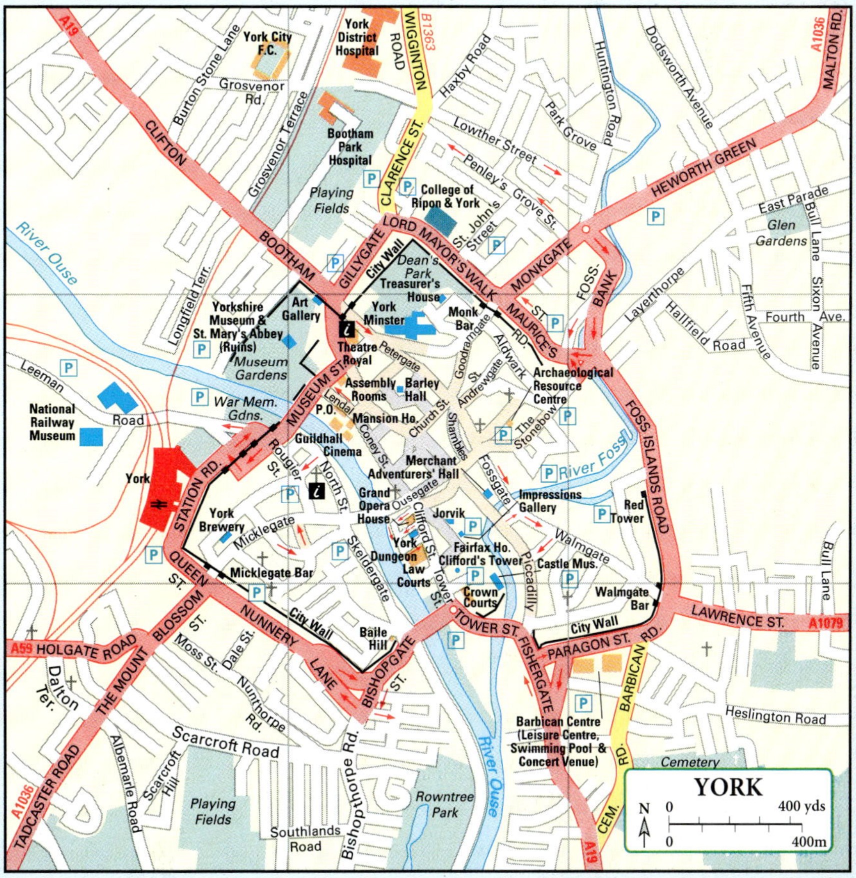

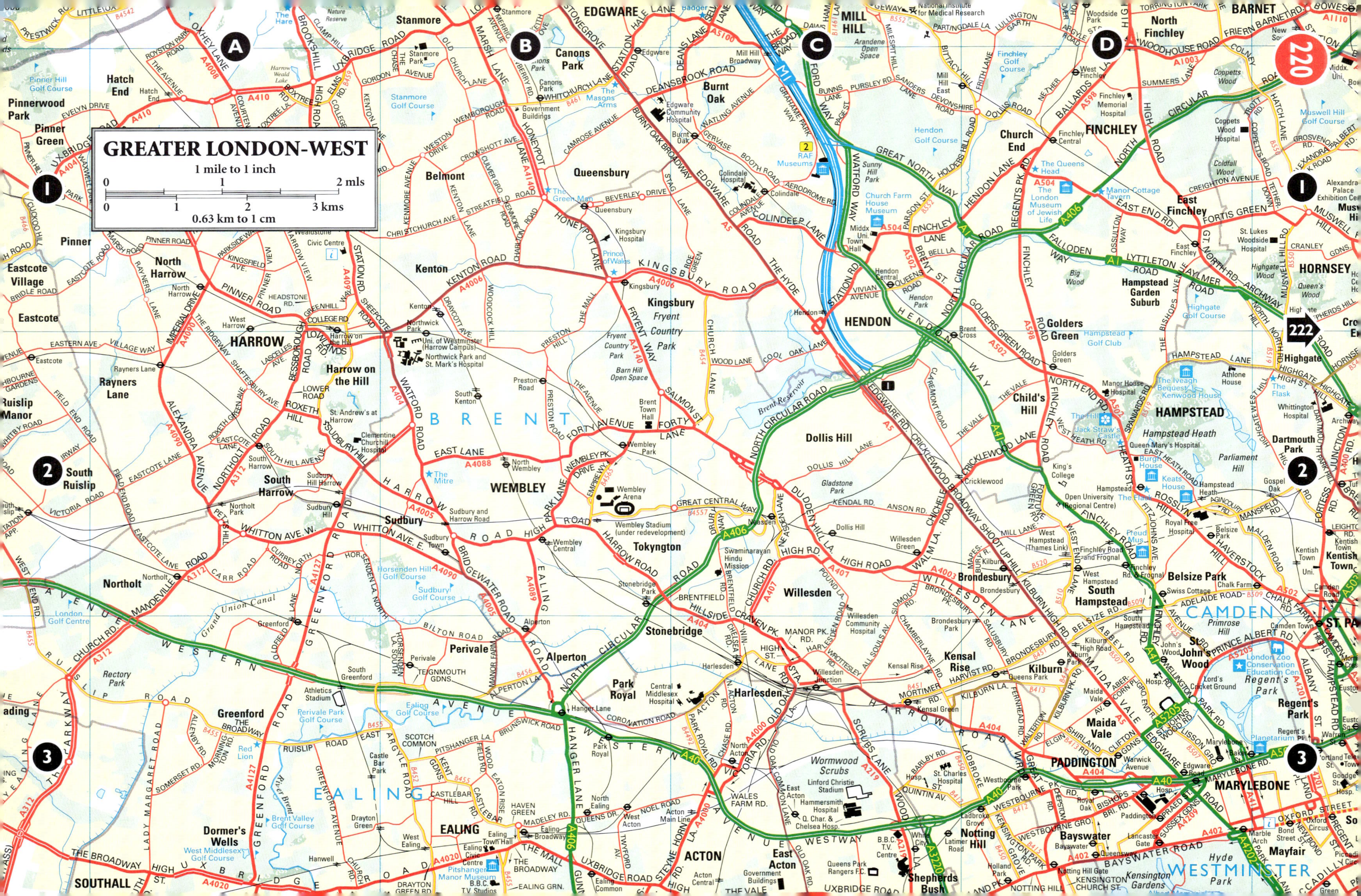
220
GREATER LONDON-WEST
1 mile to 1 inch
0 1 2 mls
0 1 2 3 kms
0.63 km to 1 cm
222
A
B
C
D
1
2
3
Stanmore
EDGWARE
MILL HILL
BARNET
North Finchley
Canons Park
Burnt Oak
FINCHLEY
Church End
East Finchley
HORNSEY
Hatch End
Pinnerwood Park
Pinner Green
Pinner
Eastcote Village
Eastcote
North Harrow
Belmont
Queensbury
Kenton
Kingsbury
HENDON
Hampstead Garden Suburb
Golders Green
Highgate
HARROW
Harrow on the Hill
Rayners Lane
Ruislip Manor
South Ruislip
South Harrow
BRENT
WEMBLEY
Sudbury
Dollis Hill
Child's Hill
HAMPSTEAD
Hampstead Heath
Dartmouth Park
Tokyngton
Willesden
Brondesbury
South Hampstead
Belsize Park
Kentish Town
CAMDEN
St John's Wood
Northolt
Stonebridge
Alperton
Perivale
Park Royal
Harlesden
Kensal Rise
Kilburn
Maida Vale
Regent's Park
Greenford
EALING
PADDINGTON
MARYLEBONE
Dormer's Wells
ACTON
East Acton
Shepherds Bush
Notting Hill
Bayswater
Mayfair
WESTMINSTER
SOUTHALL
Wormwood Scrubs
Hyde Park
Kensington Gardens

KENSINGTON
KENSINGTON & CHELSEA
CHELSEA
Brompton
BATTERSEA
Walham Green
Sands End
Parsons Green
FULHAM
HAMMERSMITH & FULHAM
HAMMERSMITH
WANDSWORTH
Clapham Common
Balham
Upper Tooting
Tooting Graveney
Streatham Park
Furzedown
Earlsfield
Southfields
Summerstown
Wimbledon Park
WIMBLEDON
Wimbledon Common
MERTON
MORDEN
MITCHAM
Collier's Wood
223
Putney
Roehampton
Putney Vale
Kingston Vale
Coombe
Raynes Park
Bushey Mead
New Malden
Norbiton
KINGSTON upon THAMES
KINGSTON UPON THAMES
Richmond Park
RICHMOND
Petersham
Ham
Castelnau
BARNES
Mortlake
East Sheen
North Sheen
Kew
Royal Botanic Gardens Kew
CHISWICK
Grove Park
Bedford Park
South Acton
Gunnersbury
Gunnersbury Park
Little Ealing
Brentford
Spring Grove
ISLEWORTH
Woodlands
TWICKENHAM
Strawberry Hill
Whitton
Teddington
Hampton Wick
Bushy Park
Hampton Court
Hampton Hill
Hampton
East Molesey
West Molesey
HOUNSLOW
Lampton
Osterley Park
HESTON
Norwood Green
North Hyde
Hounslow West
Hounslow Heath
Hanworth
River Thames
A
B
C
D
4
5
6

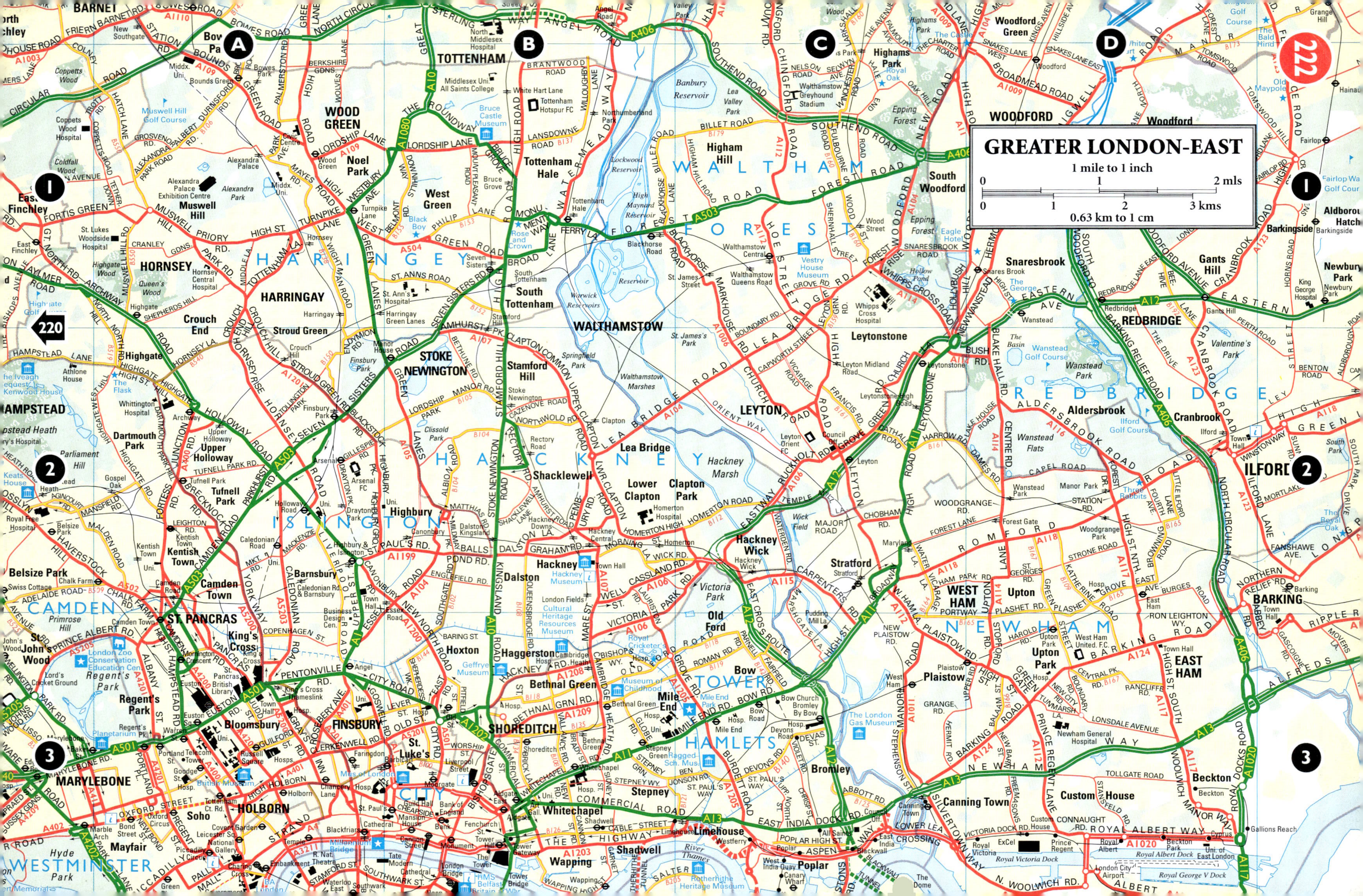
GREATER LONDON-EAST
1 mile to 1 inch
0 1 2 mls
0 1 2 3 kms
0.63 km to 1 cm
A
B
C
D
1
2
3
220
BARNET
East Finchley
HORNSEY
HARRINGAY
Crouch End
Stroud Green
Highgate
HAMPSTEAD
Dartmouth Park
Upper Holloway
Tufnell Park
Kentish Town
Belsize Park
Camden Town
CAMDEN
ST. PANCRAS
King's Cross
St. John's Wood
Regent's Park
MARYLEBONE
Bloomsbury
FINSBURY
HOLBORN
Soho
Mayfair
WESTMINSTER
Hyde Park
CITY
SHOREDITCH
Hoxton
Haggerston
Dalston
Hackney
ISLINGTON
Highbury
STOKE NEWINGTON
Stamford Hill
Shacklewell
HACKNEY
Lower Clapton
Clapton Park
Lea Bridge
Hackney Marsh
Hackney Wick
Victoria Park
Old Ford
Bow
Mile End
Bethnal Green
TOWER HAMLETS
Whitechapel
Stepney
Shadwell
Wapping
Limehouse
Poplar
Bromley
Stratford
LEYTON
Leytonstone
WALTHAMSTOW
South Tottenham
TOTTENHAM
Tottenham Hale
West Green
HARINGEY
WOOD GREEN
Noel Park
Muswell Hill
Higham Hill
WALTHAM FOREST
Highams Park
Woodford Green
WOODFORD
South Woodford
Snaresbrook
Wanstead
Aldersbrook
REDBRIDGE
Gants Hill
Cranbrook
ILFORD
BARKING
EAST HAM
Upton Park
Upton
WEST HAM
NEWHAM
Plaistow
Canning Town
Custom House
Beckton
Barkingside
Newbury Park
Aldborough Hatch

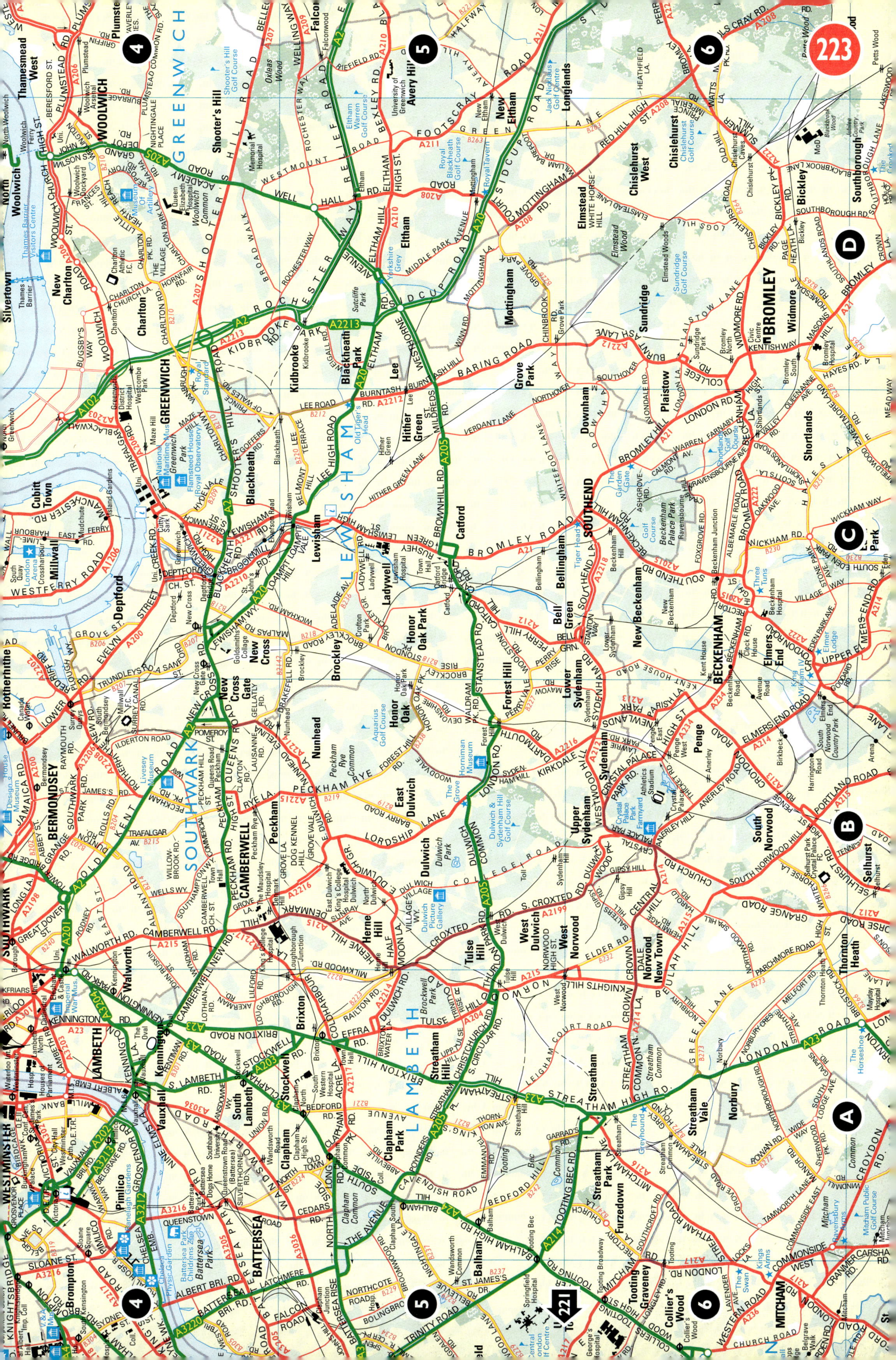
GREENWICH
SOUTHWARK
LEWISHAM
LAMBETH
WOOLWICH
Charlton
Plumstead
Eltham
Mottingham
Chislehurst
Kidbrooke
Blackheath
Deptford
Lewisham
Catford
Lee
Grove Park
BROMLEY
Sundridge
Shortlands
Southend
Bellingham
BECKENHAM
Penge
Sydenham
Forest Hill
Brockley
Nunhead
Peckham
CAMBERWELL
Dulwich
Herne Hill
Tulse Hill
West Norwood
Brixton
Stockwell
Kennington
Vauxhall
Pimlico
BATTERSEA
Clapham
Balham
Tooting
Streatham
Norbury
Thornton Heath
MITCHAM
BERMONDSEY
Walworth
To 221

224
Scale 1 : 12,500 (5.1 inches to 1 mile)
0 km
0.25
0.50
0 miles
1/4
A
B
C
D
E
F
G
H
J
K
NW1
W1
SW1
BOATING LAKE
REGENT'S PARK
EUSTON SQUARE
EUSTON ROAD
MARYLEBONE ROAD
BAKER ST
PADDINGTON ST
GREAT PORTLAND ST
TOTTENHAM COURT RD
GOWER ST
BLOOMSBURY
THE BRITISH MUSEUM
NEW OXFORD ST
OXFORD ST
OXFORD CIRCUS
BOND ST
WIGMORE ST
MARBLE ARCH
SOHO
MAYFAIR
PICCADILLY CIR
HAYMARKET
LEICESTER SQ
NATIONAL GALLERY
TRAFALGAR
PICCADILLY
GREEN PARK
ST. JAMES'S
ST. JAMES'S PARK
THE MALL
PALL MALL
PARK LANE
HYDE PARK CORNER
KNIGHTSBRIDGE
CONSTITUTION HILL
BUCKINGHAM PALACE GARDENS
BUCKINGHAM PALACE
BUCKINGHAM GATE
GROSVENOR PLACE
BELGRAVE SQUARE
BELGRAVIA
SLOANE ST
CHESHAM ST
VICTORIA
VICTORIA ST
WESTMINSTER
ROYAL ACAD. OF ARTS
SELFRIDGES
A4
A40
A501
A4202
A302

K
L
M
N
P
Q
R
S
T
U
1
2
3
4
5
6
7
8
9
10
11
12
13
14
WC1
WC2
EC1
EC4
CLERKENWELL
HOLBORN
BARBICAN
FARRINGDON
STRAND
SOUTHWARK
THE BOROUGH
LAMBETH
RIVER THAMES
WATERLOO
WATERLOO INTERNATIONAL
BLACKFRIARS
EMBANKMENT
WESTMINSTER
CHARING CROSS
CHANCERY LANE
TEMPLE
ST. PAUL'S
MANSION HOUSE
CANNON ST
ELEPHANT & CASTLE
BOROUGH
LAMBETH NORTH
SOUTHWARK
LONDON BRIDGE
GUILFORD STREET
THEOBALD'S ROAD
HOLBORN
CLERKENWELL ROAD
FARRINGDON ROAD
CHARTERHOUSE
NEWGATE ST
VICTORIA EMBANKMENT
STAMFORD STREET
SOUTHWARK STREET
UNION STREET
BLACKFRIARS ROAD
WATERLOO ROAD
WESTMINSTER BRIDGE ROAD
LAMBETH ROAD
ST. GEORGE'S ROAD
BOROUGH ROAD
BOROUGH HIGH ST
LONG LANE
GREAT DOVER ST
NEWINGTON CAUSEWAY
SOUTHWARK BRIDGE
WATERLOO BRIDGE
BLACKFRIARS BRIDGE
MILLENNIUM BRIDGE
HUNGERFORD BRIDGE
LAMBETH BRIDGE
WESTMINSTER BRIDGE
HOUSES OF PARLIAMENT
ST. THOMAS' HOSP
ST. PAUL'S CATHEDRAL
ST. BARTHOLOMEW'S HOSPITAL
TATE MODERN
LINCOLN'S INN FIELDS
GRAY'S INN GARDENS
ROYAL COURTS OF JUSTICE
ROYAL FESTIVAL HALL
QUEEN ELIZABETH HALL & PURCELL ROOM
LONDON EYE
IMAX
ARCHBISHOP'S PARK
GERALDINE MARY HARMSWORTH PARK
IMPERIAL WAR MUS
H.M.S. PRESIDENT
H.Q.S. WELLINGTON
KING'S REACH
SOUTH BANK UNIVERSITY
A4
A40
A201
A301
A302
A3200
A3203
A3036
A23
A5201
A1
A401
A400
A3211
B300
B502
B500
B501

TEST VALLEY DISTRICT
Nutburn
Valley Park
Chandler's Ford
Fryern Hill
Boyatt Wood
Highbridge
Nob's Crook
Fish Pond
Crowdhill
Park Hills Wood
Lower Upham
North Baddesley
Great Covert
Stoke Common
Bishopstoke
Pylehill
EASTLEIGH
Hut Wood
Toothill
Chilworth Old Village
Chilworth
Itchen Vale
Fair Oak
Wintershil
Nightingale Wood
M27
M3
ROWNHAMS SERVICES
Rownhams
Chilworth Common
North Stoneham
EASTLEIGH DISTRICT
Horton Heath
Lord's Wood
Southampton International Airport
River Itchen
Lordswood
Bassett Green
Bassett
Swaythling
Itchen Valley Country Park
Durley
Hillyfields
Lord's Hill
Aldermoor
Hampton Park
Maybush
Coxford
Shirley Warren
Old Shirley
Upper Shirley
Townhill Park
Bitterne Park
Moorgreen
Long Common
Boorley Green
Wimpson
Shirley Park
SOUTHAMPTON
Shirley
Highfield
Portswood
Westwood Park
Bevois Mount
St. Denys
Midanbury
West End
Curdridge
Millbrook
Freemantle
Banister's Park
Bedford Place
Bevois Town
Newtown
Bitterne
Harefield
Wildern
Kitnocks
Botley
Northam
Merry Oak
Thornhill Park
Thornhill
Hedge End
Fourposts
Peartree Green
Sholing Common
Weston Common
Polygon
Itchen
Crosshouse
Sholing
Pleasant View
Botany Bay
High town
Old Netley
Windmill
Lowford
Curbridge
Trotts
Power Station
River Test
Docks
Cracknore Hard
Pooksgreen
Woolston
Newtown
Marchwood
Eastern Docks
Weston
West Wood
Netley Abbey
Butlocks Heath
Bursledon
Swanwick Wood
Burridge
H A M
Swanwick
Whiteley
Lower Swanwick
Marchwood Park
HYTHE MARINA VILLAGE
Hythe
Hound
Badnam Copse
Holly Hill Woodland Park
Sarisbury
Park Gate
Royal Victoria Country Park
Dibden
Applemore
Marchwood Inclosure
NEW FOREST DISTRICT
Dibden Bottom
Southampton Water
West Wood
Hamble-le-Rice
Locks Heath
Dibden Purlieu
Langdown
Frostlane
Warsash
Titchfield Common
Hamble Common
Fleetend
Abshot
Newtown
Hook
Hook Park
FAREHAM DISTRICT
Chilling
Solent Breezes
Brownwich
Meon
Fawley
Ashlett
Stonehills
Fawley Power Station
Ower
Calshot
Hillhead
Eaglehurst
THE SOLENT
Stanswood Bay
Stansore Point
St. Leonards Grange
Horsemoor Copse
Needs Ore Point
Sowley Pond
SOUTHAMPTON
Southampton F.C.
Royal South Hants. Hospital
Northam Industrial Estate
River Itchen
Titanic Memorial
East Park
West Park
BBC Studios
Mayflower Theatre
Police Station
Civic Centre & Art Gallery
Southampton Institute
Southampton Central
Mountbatten Retail Park
Palmerston Park
West Quay Retail Park
West Quay Shopping Centre
Hoglands Park
Southampton City College
Football Ground (under construction)
Dock Gate No.10
City Industrial Park
Leisure World
Bargate Shopping Centre
East St. Shopping Centre
Western Docks
The Quays Leisure Centre
Tudor House Museum
Medieval Merchant's House
Maritime Museum
Tudor Merchant's Hall
Mayflower Park
Dock Gate No.8
The Itchen Bridge (Toll)
Southampton Hall of Aviation
Ocean Village
Marina
Car Ferries to Isle of Wight
Gods House Tower Museum
River Test
Royal Pier (Closed)
Foot passengers to Hythe
Town Quay
Ocean Dock
400 yds
400m

SOUTHAMPTON & PORTSMOUTH
0 1 2 miles
0 1 2 3 kilometres
PORTSMOUTH
500 yds
500m
Upham
Bishop's Waltham
Dean
Droxford
Swanmore
Waltham Chase
Shirrell Heath
Soberton Heath
Newtown
Shedfield
Meon Park
Wickham
Corhampton
Meonstoke
Exton
Brockbridge
Clanfield
Catherington
Cowplain
Waterlooville
Purbrook
Widley
Bedhampton
Cosham
Drayton
Farlington
Highbury
Hilsea
Copnor
Southwick
Fareham
Catisfield
Titchfield
Funtley
Portchester
Port Solent
Paulsgrove
Wymering
Fleetlands
Stubbington
Lee-on-the-Solent
Rowner
Elson
Gosport
Alverstoke
Anglesey
Browndown
Portsea
Old Portsmouth
Southsea
Milton
Eastney
Fratton
Buckland
Kingston
Baffins
PORTSMOUTH
Portsmouth Harbour
Langstone Harbour
Stokes Bay
Gilkicker Point
Browndown Point
Whale Island
Horsea Island
Pewit Island
WINCHESTER DISTRICT
EAST HAMPSHIRE DISTRICT
HAVANT DISTRICT
GOSPORT DISTRICT
PORTSEA ISLAND
H A M P S H I R E
M27
M275
A3(M)
A27
A32
A3
A2030
H. M. Naval Base
Historic Dockyard
Mary Rose
HMS Victory
HMS Warrior
Gunwharf Quays
Millennium Tower
Portsmouth & Southsea Station
Guildhall
Civic Offices
Cascades Shopping Centre
Fratton Station
University of Portsmouth
Round Tower
Square Tower
Clarence Ground
Nelson Statue
Southsea Castle
D-Day Mus.
Sea Life Centre
Royal Naval Hospital (close in 2002)
Fort Nelson
Fort Widley
Fort Purbrook
Fort Brockhurst
HMS Daedalus
HMS Collingwood
HMS Sultan
St. James' Hospital
St. Mary's Hospital
Queen Alexandra Hospital

228
CARDIFF & NEWPORT
0 1 2 miles
0 1 2 3 kilometres
CARDIFF
400 yds
400m
CAERPHILLY
NEWPORT
CARDIFF
RHONDDA CYNON TAFF
VALE OF GLAMORGAN
Caerphilly
Pontymister
Bedwas
Rogerstone
Newport
Cardiff
Llanrumney
St.Mellons
Michaelston-y-Fedw
Castleton
Marshfield
Peterstone Wentlooge
Tongwynlais
Morganstown
Radyr
St. Fagans
Butetown
Grangetown
Bute Park
Cardiff Millennium Stadium

BRISTOL
0 1 2 miles
0 1 2 3 kilometres
BRISTOL
SOUTH
GLOUCESTERSHIRE
NORTH
SOMERSET
BATH &
NORTH
EAST SOMERSET
Avonmouth
Shirehampton
Lawrence Weston
Henbury
Coombe Dingle
Sea Mills
Westbury-on-Trym
Patchway
Bradley Stoke
Stoke Gifford
Filton
Southmead
Horfield
Winterbourne
Frenchay
Fishponds
Staple Hill
Kingswood
Hanham
Clifton
Hotwells
Bedminster
Knowle
Brislington
Long Ashton
Yate
Chipping Sodbury
Frampton Cotterell
Pucklechurch
Lodway
Easton-in-Gordano
Failand
Flax Bourton
Hengrove Park
Hartcliffe
Bishopsworth
Withywood
Stockwood
BRISTOL
0 200 yds
0 200m

WOLVERHAMPTON
WOLVERHAMPTON DISTRICT
WALSALL
STAFFORDSHIRE
SOUTH STAFFORDSHIRE DISTRICT
DUDLEY
DUDLEY DISTRICT
SANDWELL
SANDWELL DISTRICT
STOURBRIDGE
HALESOWEN
WORCESTERSHIRE
BROMSGROVE DISTRICT
Willenhall
Bilston
Wednesbury
Darlaston
Tipton
Sedgley
Wombourne
Kingswinford
Brierley Hill
Oldbury
Smethwick
West Bromwich
Rowley Regis
Blackheath
Cradley Heath
Quinton
Harborne
Northfield
Longbridge
Rubery
Rednal
Frankley
Romsley
Hunnington
Fairfield
Cofton Hackett
M5
M6
FRANKLEY SERVICES
BIRMINGHAM
200 yds
200m

WEST MIDLANDS
0 1 2 miles
0 1 2 3 kilometres
WARWICKSHIRE
NORTH WARKS BOROUGH
WEST MIDLANDS
SOLIHULL DISTRICT
BIRMINGHAM CITY
BIRMINGHAM
SUTTON COLDFIELD
SOLIHULL
Hardwick
Streetly
Roughley
Mere Green
Ley Hill
Little Sutton
Middleton
Doe Bank
Whitehouse Common
Tudor Hill
Falcon Lodge
Pheasey
Banners Gate
Maney
Reddicap Heath
Queslett
Great Barr
Kingstanding
New Oscott
Boldmere
Old Oscott
Perry Beeches
Wylde Green
Walmley
Hamstead
Tower Hill
Perry
Perry Common
Short Heath
Chester Road
Minworth
Curdworth
Perry Barr
Upper Witton
Erdington
Handsworth Wood
Brown's Green
Witton
Tyburn
Castle Vale
Water Orton
Birches Green
Handsworth
Birchfield
Gravelly Hill
Bromford
Castle Bromwich
Nechells
Soho
Gib Heath
Lozells
Washwood Heath
Hodgehill
Shard End
Coleshill
Merry Hill
Winson Green
Hockley
Newtown
Aston
Ward End
Buckland End
Colehall
Vauxhall
Saltley
Kingshurst
Rotton Park
Bacon's End
Glebe Farm
Kitt's Green
Alum Rock
Fordbridge
Stechford
Tile Cross
Chelmsley Wood
Ladywood
Bordesley
Little Bromwich
Lea Hall
Yardley
Garrett's Green
Lee Bank
Digbeth
Chad Valley
Highgate
Small Heath
Lyndon Green
Marston Green
Hay Mills
Gilbertstone
Edgbaston
Balsall Heath
Sparkbrook
South Yardley
Birmingham International Airport
Sheldon
Sparkhill
Tyseley
Acock's Green
Bournbrook
Moseley
Selly Oak
Moor Green
Olton
Wake Green
King's Heath
Hall Green
Kineton Green
Bickenhill
Elmdon Heath
Stirchley
Billesley
Worlds End
Brandwood End
Cotteridge
Lode Heath
Catherine-de-Barnes
Billesley Common
Yardley Wood
Shirley Street
Sharmans Cross
King's Norton
Warstock
Hasluck's Green
Higher's Heath
Shirley
Walkers Heath
Solihull Lodge
Blossomfield
Copt Heath
Hawkesley
Major's Green
Shirley Heath
Hollywood
Trueman's Heath
Drakes Cross
Bateman's Green
Whitlocks End
Knowle
Dickens Heath
Tilehouse Green
Silver Street
Grimes Hill
Tidbury Green
Bentley Heath
Cheswick Green
Wythall
M6
M42
A38(M)

232
NOTTINGHAM
0 1 2 miles
0 1 2 3 kilometres
Calverton
GEDLING BOROUGH
Lambley
Arnold
Redhill
Daybrook
Woodthorpe
Mapperley
Gedling
Porchester
Carlton
Thorneywood
Colwick
Netherfield
Sneinton
Colwick Country Park
Holme Pierrepont
Adbolton
Radcliffe on Trent
Gamston
Edwalton
Tollerton
Nottingham Airport
Clipston
Normanton on-the-Wolds
Plumtree
Plumtree Park
Keyworth
Stanton-on-the-Wolds
Bradmore
RUSHCLIFFE BOROUGH
Bunny
Bunny Hill
NOTTINGHAMSHIRE
Widmer
Wysall
Costock
Willoughby-on-the-Wolds
East Leake
Sutton Bonington
Kegworth
Ruddington
Manor Park
Brook Hill
Mickleborough Hill
Clifton
West Bridgford
Wilford
Meadows
St. Ann's
Lace Market
Radford
Lenton
Dunkirk
Lenton Abbey
Wollaton
Wollaton Park
Bilborough
NOTTINGHAM
Broxtowe
Aspley
Whitemoor
New Basford
Carrington
Mapperley Park
Sherwood
Old Basford
Cinderhill
Bulwell
Highbury Vale
Hempshill Vale
Top Valley
Bestwood
Rise Park
Bestwood Village
Broomhill
Hucknall
Hazelgrove
Ruffs
Beauvale
ASHFIELD DISTRICT
Westville
Moorgreen
Greasley
Beauvale
Newthorpe
Watnall
Giltbrook
Kimberley
Nuthall
Swingate
Awsworth
Babbington
Cossall Marsh
Cossall
BROXTOWE BOROUGH
Strelley
TROWELL SERVICES
Trowell
Stanton Gate
Bramcote Hills
Bramcote
Stapleford
BEESTON
Rylands
Chilwell
Toton
Attenborough
Wilsthorpe
Long Eaton
Trentlock
M1
A52
A60
A610
A6514
A606
A612
A614
A453
A6
Arboretum
Nottingham Trent University
Victoria Shopping Centre
Broad Marsh Shopping Centre
Nottingham Castle
Bus Station
The National Ice Centre
Galleries of Justice Museum
Tales of Robin Hood
Lace Centre
Royal Centre
Playhouse
Nottingham
400 yds
400m

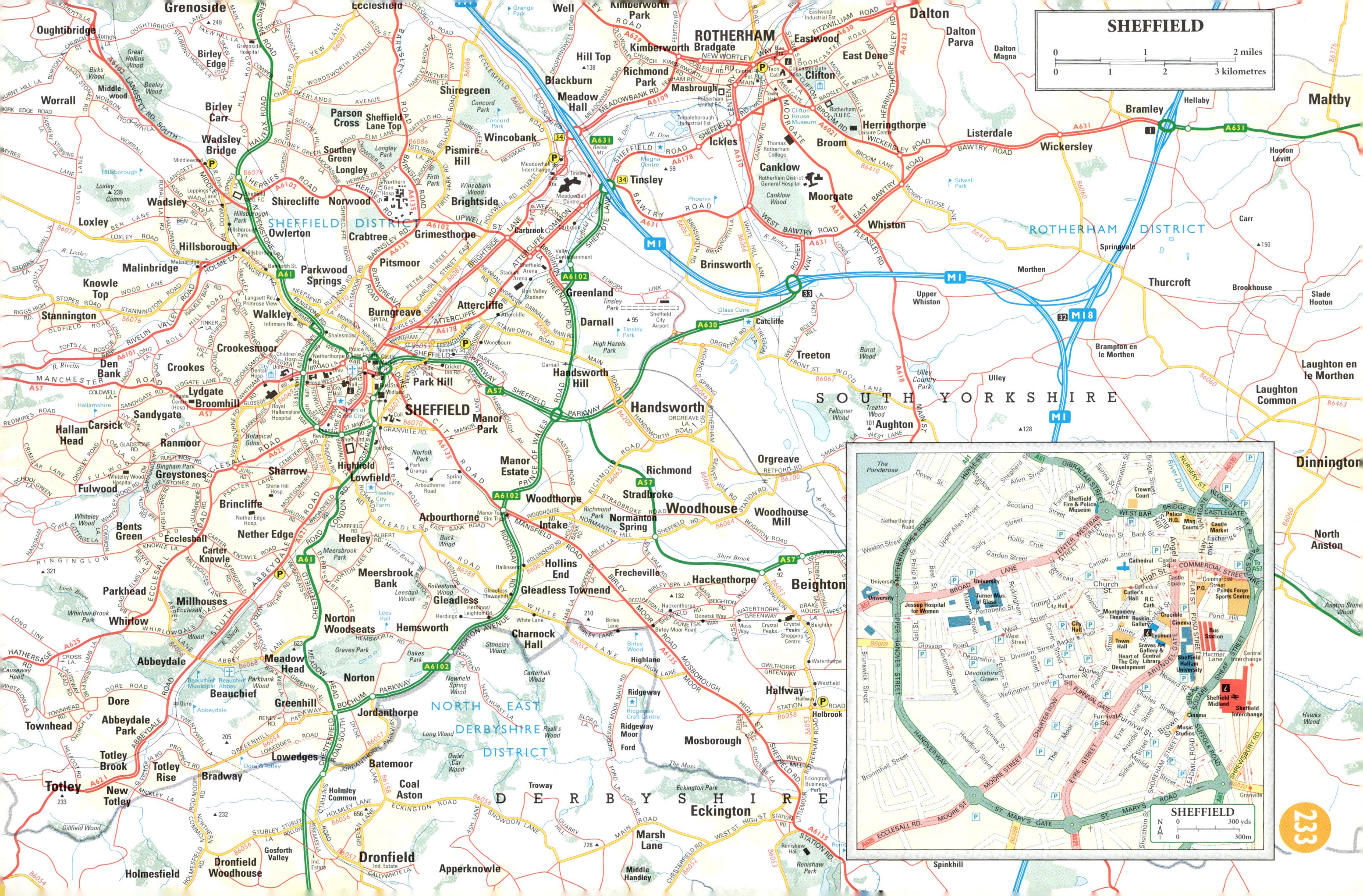
SHEFFIELD
0 1 2 miles
0 1 2 3 kilometres
ROTHERHAM
SHEFFIELD
SHEFFIELD DISTRICT
ROTHERHAM DISTRICT
SOUTH YORKSHIRE
NORTH EAST DERBYSHIRE DISTRICT
DERBYSHIRE
Grenoside
Oughtibridge
Worrall
Loxley
Wadsley
Wadsley Bridge
Hillsborough
Owlerton
Shirecliffe
Norwood
Parson Cross
Shiregreen
Wincobank
Pismire Hill
Brightside
Grimesthorpe
Crabtree
Pitsmoor
Burngreave
Attercliffe
Carbrook
Tinsley
Darnall
Greenland
Handsworth
Handsworth Hill
Park Hill
Manor Park
Manor Estate
Richmond
Woodhouse
Woodhouse Mill
Orgreave
Treeton
Catcliffe
Brinsworth
Whiston
Canklow
Moorgate
Broom
Herringthorpe
Clifton
Eastwood
East Dene
Dalton
Dalton Parva
Dalton Magna
Wickersley
Listerdale
Bramley
Hellaby
Maltby
Hooton Levitt
Thurcroft
Morthen
Upper Whiston
Ulley
Aughton
Brampton en le Morthen
Laughton en le Morthen
Laughton Common
Slade Hooton
Brookhouse
Carr
Dinnington
North Anston
Kimberworth
Kimberworth Park
Bradgate
Masbrough
Richmond Park
Hill Top
Blackburn
Meadow Hall
Ickles
Well
Crookesmoor
Crookes
Walkley
Malinbridge
Knowle Top
Stannington
Den Bank
Lydgate
Broomhill
Sandygate
Hallam Head
Carsick
Ranmoor
Greystones
Fulwood
Sharrow
Brincliffe
Bents Green
Ecclesall
Nether Edge
Carter Knowle
Parkhead
Whirlow
Millhouses
Abbeydale
Beauchief
Dore
Totley
Totley Brook
Totley Rise
New Totley
Abbeydale Park
Townhead
Bradway
Greenhill
Lowedges
Meadow Head
Norton
Norton Woodseats
Hemsworth
Jordanthorpe
Batemoor
Coal Aston
Dronfield
Dronfield Woodhouse
Holmesfield
Apperknowle
Marsh Lane
Middle Handley
Eckington
Mosborough
Halfway
Holbrook
Beighton
Hackenthorpe
Frecheville
Ridgeway
Ridgeway Moor
Ford
Troway
Highlane
Charnock Hall
Gleadless Townend
Gleadless
Hollins End
Intake
Normanton Spring
Stradbroke
Woodthorpe
Arbourthorne
Heeley
Meersbrook Bank
Highfield
Lowfield
Spinkhill
M1
M18
A57
A61
A630
A631
A6102
A6135
A618
A621
A625
A6109
A6178
The Ponderosa
University
Jessop Hospital for Women
Turner Mus. of Glass
Cathedral
City Hall
Town Hall
Crucible
Lyceum
Sheffield Hallam University
Sheffield Midland
Sheffield Interchange
Castle Market
Crown Court
Ponds Forge Sports Centre
West Bar
Castlegate
Commercial Street
Arundel Gate
Furnival Gate
Charter Row
Moore Street
Eyre Street
St. Mary's Gate
Hanoverway
Upper Hanover Street
Netherthorpe Road
Gibraltar Street
Shrewsbury Rd.
Suffolk Road
Sheaf Square
Park Square
Ecclesall Rd.
0 300 yds
0 300m
233

MERSEYSIDE
0 1 2 miles
0 1 2 3 kilometres
SEFTON DISTRICT
LIVERPOOL DISTRICT
KNOWSLEY DISTRICT
WIRRAL DISTRICT
ELLESMERE PORT AND NESTON DISTRICT
LIVERPOOL BAY
Crosby Channel
River Mersey
Stanlow Banks
Blundellsands
Great Crosby
Buckley Hill
CROSBY
Waterloo
Waterloo Park
Litherland
Aintree
Northwood
Westvale
Kirkby
Southdene
Seaforth
Orrell
Fazakerley
Gillmoss
Croxteth
Knowsley
BOOTLE
Walton
Dog and Gun
Norris Green
Kirkdale
Anfield
Clubmoor
Tuebrook
Stoneycroft
Fairfield
Old Swan
Knotty Ash
Everton
LIVERPOOL
New Brighton
WALLASEY
Egremont
Liscard
Poulton
Seacombe
Bidston
BIRKENHEAD
Claughton
Oxton
Prenton
Tranmere
Rock Ferry
Edge Hill
Princes Park
Toxteth
Dingle
St Michael's
Hamlet
Wavertree
Childwall
Mossley Hill
Aigburth
Calderstones
Allerton
Grassendale
Otterspool
Garston
Speke
Woolton
Gateacre
Belle Vale
Netherley
Halewood
Hunts Cross
Fincham
Woolfall Heath
Huyton with Roby
Huyton
Huyton Park
Dovecot
Swanside
Page Moss
Roby
Court Hey
Bowring Park
Higher Bebington
BEBINGTON
Lower Bebington
Woodhey
New Ferry
Bromborough Pool
Port Sunlight
Storeton
Barnston
Brimstage
Poulton
Bromborough
Thornton Hough
Raby Mere
Brookhurst
Raby
Eastham
Willaston
Hooton
Childer Thornton
Overpool
ELLESMERE PORT
Little Neston
Ness
Little Sutton
Greater Sutton
Whitby
Stanlow
CHES
M57
M62
M53
A5036
A580
A59
A57
A562
A561
A41
A550

Rainford
Billinge
Chadwick
Garswood
Ashton in Makerfield
WIGAN DISTRICT
Golborn
Lowto
Moss Bank
Haydock Park Race Course
Haydock Park
Denton's Green
Newtown
Eccleston
ST. HELENS
ST. HELENS DISTRICT
Blackbrook
Haydock
West Park
Parr
Broad Oak
Derbyshire Hill
Newton-le-Willows
Town of Lowton
Wargrave
Vulcan Village
Collins Green
Toll Bar
Ravenhead
Grange Park
Portico
Thatto Heath
Peasley Cross
Sutton Oak
Knowsley Safari Park
Prescot
Eccleston Park
Sutton Heath
Nutgrove
Burtonwood
Winwick
Marshall's Cross
Sutton Leach
Holt
Whiston Cross
Whiston
Rainhill
Rainhill Stoops
Clock Face
Sutton Manor
Windy Arbor
Huyton Quarry
BURTONWOOD SERVICES
Hulme
Cinnamon Brow
Longford
Callands
Dallam
Orford
Bewsey
Old Hall
Bold Heath
Lingley Green
WARRINGTON
Great Sankey
Town End
Cronton
Lunts Heath
Farnworth
Tarbock Green
Penketh
Sankey Bridges
WARRINGTON
Howley
Cuerdley Cross
Crow Wood
Latchford
Hough Green
Appleton
Stockton Heath
Ditton
Ball o' Ditton
Kingsway
Halton
Moss Bank
Lugs Dale
Lower Walton
Hillcliffe
Higher Walton
Woodend
WIDNES
West Bank
Hale Bank
HALTON
Hale
Halton Brook
RUNCORN
Grange
Weston Point
Weston
Beechwood
Higher Whitley
Stretton
Frodsham Marshes
Frodsham Bridge
Frodsham
VALE ROYAL BOROUGH
Marsh Green
Overton
Netherton
Ince Marshes
Ince and Elton
Helsby
Woodhouses
Acton Bridge
LIVERPOOL
Lime St. (Main Line and Underground)
Central (Underground)
Moorfields (Underground)
Walker Art Gallery
Liverpool Museum
Picton Library
St. Georges Hall
St. Johns Garden
Empire Theatre
Royal Court Theatre
Liverpool Playhouse
Neptune Theatre
Bluecoat Arts Centre
Municipal Offices
Conservation Centre
Town Hall
Mercury Court
Cotton Exchange
Royal Liver Building
Cunard Building
Port of Liverpool Building
Mersey Ferry Terminal
Museum of Liverpool Life
Maritime Museum & H.M. Customs Museum
Tate Liverpool
Albert Dock
Salthouse Dock
Canning Dock
Albert Dock Village
Chavasse Park
Queen Elizabeth II Crown Court
Bus Station
Clayton Sq. Shopping Centre
Liverpool John Moores University (JMU)
Mersey Tunnel Entrance (Toll)
Mersey Tunnel Exit
River Mersey
Prince's Dock
M62
M57
M56
M6
A580
A57
A562
A557
A49
A5080
A56
A533
A570
A58
A572
A599
A569
A568
A5300
A5061
A5060
0 200 yds
0 200m

GREATER MANCHESTER
0 1 2 miles
0 1 2 3 kilometres
BOLTON DISTRICT
BURY DISTRICT
SALFORD DISTRICT
WIGAN DISTRICT
TRAFFORD DISTRICT
MACCLESFIELD DISTRICT
G R E A T E R
Deane
Furnhill
Darcy Lever
Burnden
Little Lever
Blackford Bridge
Radcliffe
Rumworth Lodge Resr.
Chew Moor
Hunger Hill
Daubhill
Great Lever
Lever Edge
Moses Gate
Water's Nook
Wingates
Westhoughton
Chequerbent
Edge Fold
Harper Green
Farnworth
New Bury
Dobb Fold
Hollins
Highfield
Prestolee
Stoneclough
Kearsley
Ringley
Cinder Hill
Outwood
Chapel Field
Stand
Park Lane
Daisy Hill
Hag Fold
Atherton
Dangerous Corner
Greenheys
Little Hulton
Hill Top
Kearsley Moss
Clifton
Philips Park
Clifton Junction
Linnyshaw
Walkden
Shakerley
Tyldesley
Hindsford
Howe Bridge
Wardley
Newtown
Clifton Green
Pendlebury
Swinton
Moorside
Parr Brow
Mosley Common
Roe Green
Hazelhurst
Worsley
Ellenbrook
Astley
Boothstown
Gin Pit
Higher Folds
Blackmoor
LEIGH
Firs Lane
Irlams o' th' Height
Dales Brow
Swinton Park
Alder Forest
Ellesmere Park
Brindle Heath
Bedford
Pennington
Lark Hill
Higher Green
Astley Green
Town Lane
Monton
Winton
Seedley
Little Bolton
Patricroft
ECCLES
Weaste
Moss Side
Botany Bay Wood
Worsley Moss
Lately Common
Barton upon Irwell
Peel Green
Barton Airport
Dumplington
Barton Moss
Glazebury
Trafford Park
Chat Moss
Crofts Bank
Davyhulme
URMSTON
STRETFORD
Fowley Common
Twiss Green
Culcheth
Larkhill
Irlam Moss
Higher Irlam
Irlam
Little Woolden Moss
Flixton
WARRINGTON
Risley Remand Centre
Cadishead Moss
Carrington
Sale
Ees
Ashton upon Mersey
SALE
Chemical Works
Carrington Moss
Woodhouses
Brooklands
Sinderland Green
Broadheath
Timperley
Oldfield Brow
Dunham Town
ALTRINCHAM
Dunham Massey
Little Bollington
Bowdon
Hale
Rosehill
Well Green
Davenport Green
Bowgreen
Ashley Heath
Broomedge
Arthill
Big Wood
Booth Bank
Halebarns
Warburton Green
Swarton Heath
Rostherne Mere
Ashley
High Legh
Thorns Green
Hulseheath
M61
M60
M62
M56
M6
A6144(M)
A580
A666
A57
A56
A6
A579
A574
A50
A560
A5081
MANCHESTER
STRANGEWAYS
SALFORD
Salford Town Hall
Cathedral (RC)
M.E.N. Arena
Victoria & Metrolink
Manchester Cathedral
Royal Exchange Theatre
Arndale Centre
Manchester Craft Centre
Salford
The Pump House
Assize Courts
John Rylands Library
Opera House
Police Station
Town Hall
Central Library
Museum of Science & Industry
Air and Space Gallery
G-MEX Centre
Bridgewater Hall
Palace Theatre
Piccadilly & Metrolink
U.M.I.S.T.
Oxford Road
Deansgate
Metropolitan University
Royal Northern College of Music
HULME
0 400 yds
0 400m

OLDHAM DISTRICT
ROCHDALE DISTRICT
MANCHESTER
MANCHESTER DISTRICT
TAMESIDE DISTRICT
STOCKPORT DISTRICT
MACCLESFIELD DISTRICT
CHESHIRE
Hollins
Unsworth
Whitefield
Oak Bank
Kirkhams
Prestwich
Sedgley Park
Hilton Park
Kersal
Lower Kersal
Broughton Park
The Cliff
Higher Broughton
Lower Broughton
Pendleton
Wallness
Ordsall
St. George's
Hulme
Old Trafford
Whalley Range
Chorlton-cum-Hardy
Barlow Moor
West Didsbury
Northern Moor
Northenden
Baguley
Sharston
Benchill
Newall Green
Wythenshawe
Woodhouse Park
Peel Hall
Heald Green
Heyhead
Moss Nook
Manchester Airport
Birch
Bowlee
Simister
Langley
Middleton
Rhodes
Top of Hebers
Hollins
Stanycliffe
Higher Boarshaw
Alkrington
Moor Close
Chadderton
Middleton Junction
Nimble Nook
Higher Blackley
Charlestown
Crumpsall
Blackley
Harpurhey
Cheetham Hill
Cheetham
Moston
Chain Bar
New Moston
White Gate
Failsworth
Woodhouses
Newton Heath
Collyhurst
Miles Platting
Cheetwood
Strangeways
Ancoats
Bradford
Beswick
Ardwick
Brunswick
Clayton
Openshaw
West Gorton
Longsight
Moss Side
Rusholme
Fallowfield
Ladybarn
Withington
Burnage
Levenshulme
Didsbury
East Didsbury
Heaton Mersey
Heaton Moor
Heaton Chapel
Heaton Norris
Lane End
Green End
Gatley
Cheadle
Cheadle Heath
Edgeley
Cheadle Hulme
Adswood
Davenport
Bramhall
Bramhall Park
Smithy Green
Kitt's Moss
Handforth
Thorp
Royton
Haggate
Holden Fold
Long Sight
Heyside
Sholver
Moorside
Higginshaw
Watersheddings
Derker
Spring Hill
Busk
Oldham Edge
Mumps
Greenacres
Austerlands
Scouthead
Grotton
Lees
Springhead
Moorhey
Glodwick
Werneth
Coppice
OLDHAM
Hathershaw
Copster Hill
Alt
Holts
Quick Edge
Brook Bottom
Hollinwood
Lime Side
Bardsley
Park Bridge
Limehurst
Waterloo
Smallshaw
Hurst
Hazelhurst
Mossley Brow
Heyrod
Ridge Hill
Taunton
Crowhill
ASHTON-UNDER-LYNE
Daisy Nook
Littlemoss
Medlock Vale
Clayton Bridge
Droylsden
Guide Bridge
Audenshaw
Dukinfield
Yew Tree
Fairfield
Abbey Hey
Gorton
Debdale
Dane Bank
Denton
Newton
Flowery Field
Kingston
Hyde
Godley
Godley Hill
Backbower
Gee Cross
Haughton Green
North Reddish
Reddish
South Reddish
Brinnington
Woodley
Werneth Low
Greave
Romiley
Compstall
Cherry Tree
Bredbury
Lower Bredbury
Bredbury Green
Portwood
Norris Bank
STOCKPORT
Stockport Little Moor
Bunkers Hill
Offerton Fold
Foggbrook
Offerton Green
Marple Bridge
Ley Hey Park
Marple
Shaw Heath
Heaviley
Great Moor
Cale Green
Woods Moor
Stepping Hill
Bramhall Moor
Hazel Grove
Torkington
Marpleridge
Hawk Green
Windlehurst
Norbury Moor
High Lane
Disley
Poynton
Middlewood
Higher Poynton
M60
M62
M66
M56
M67
A57(M)
A627(M)

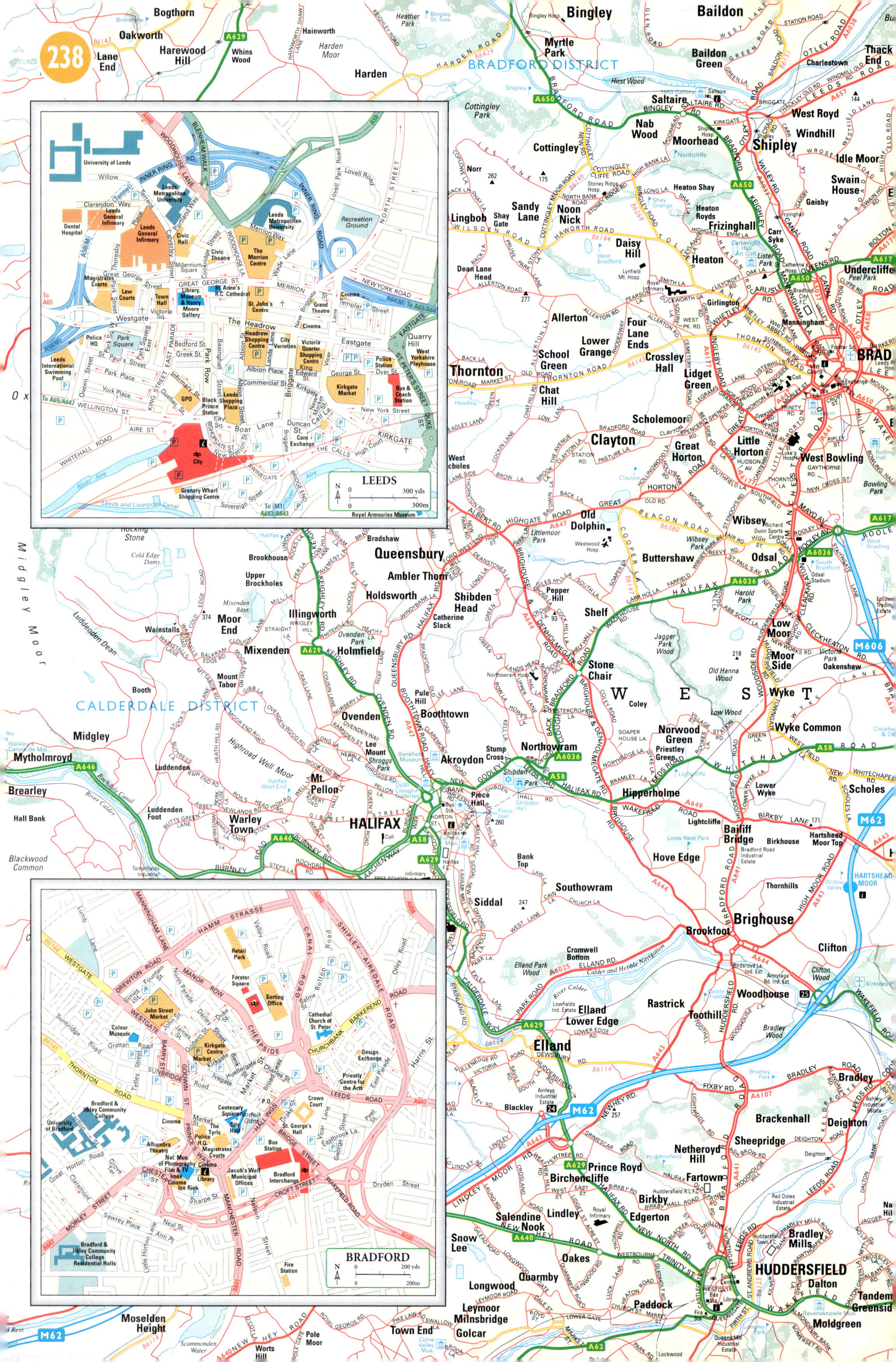
LEEDS
300 yds
300m
Royal Armouries Museum
University of Leeds
Leeds Metropolitan University
Leeds General Infirmary
Dental Hospital
Civic Hall
Civic Theatre
Millennium Square
Leeds Metropolitan University
The Merrion Centre
Recreation Ground
Magistrates Courts
Law Courts
Town Hall
Library, Museum & Henry Moore Gallery
St. Anne's R.C. Cathedral
St. John's Centre
Grand Theatre
Cinema
Headrow Shopping Centre
City Varieties
Victoria Quarter Shopping Centre
Quarry Hill
West Yorkshire Playhouse
Police HQ
Park Square
Leeds International Swimming Pool
GPO
Black Prince Statue
Leeds Shopping Plaza
Kirkgate Market
Police Station
Bus & Coach Station
Corn Exchange
City
Granary Wharf Shopping Centre
Leeds and Liverpool Canal
River Aire
BRADFORD
200 yds
200m
Retail Park
Forster Square
Sorting Office
Cathedral Church of St. Peter
John Street Market
Colour Museum
Kirkgate Centre
Design Exchange
Priestly Centre for the Arts
Bradford & Ilkley Community College
University of Bradford
Centenary Square
City Hall
Crown Court
Police H.Q.
The Tyrls
Magistrates Courts
Alhambra Theatre
Nat. Mus. of Photography Film & TV
Imax Cinema
Library
Jacob's Well Municipal Offices
Bus Station
Bradford Interchange
Ice Rink
St. George's Hall
Fire Station
Bradford & Ilkley Community College Residential Halls
BRADFORD DISTRICT
CALDERDALE DISTRICT
W E S T
Bogthorn
Oakworth
Lane End
Harewood Hill
Whins Wood
Hainworth
Harden Moor
Harden
Heather Park
Bingley
Myrtle Park
Baildon
Baildon Green
Thackley End
Charlestown
Saltaire
Nab Wood
Moorhead
Shipley
West Royd
Windhill
Idle Moor
Swain House
Cottingley Park
Cottingley
Norr
Sandy Lane
Noon Nick
Shay Gate
Lingbob
Heaton Shay
Heaton Royds
Frizinghall
Daisy Hill
Heaton
Carr Syke
Undercliffe
Peel Park
Dean Lane Head
Girlington
Manningham
Allerton
Four Lane Ends
Lower Grange
School Green
Crossley Hall
Lidget Green
Thornton
Chat Hill
BRAD
Scholemoor
Clayton
Great Horton
Little Horton
West Bowling
Bowling Park
West Scholes
Old Dolphin
Littlemoor Park
Wibsey
Wibsey Park
Odsal
Buttershaw
Hocking Stone
Cold Edge Dams
Bradshaw
Queensbury
Ambler Thorn
Brookhouse
Upper Brockholes
Holdsworth
Shibden Head
Catherine Slack
Pepper Hill
Shelf
Harold Park
Midgley Moor
Luddenden Dean
Wainstalls
Mixenden Resr.
Moor End
Mixenden
Illingworth
Ovenden Park
Holmfield
Jagger Park Wood
Low Moor
Moor Side
Oakenshaw
Stone Chair
Mount Tabor
Booth
Pule Hill
Boothtown
Coley
Wyke
Old Hanna Wood
Low Wood
Wyke Common
Ovenden
Norwood Green
Priestley Green
Midgley
Mytholmroyd
Lee Mount
Shroggs Park
Northowram
Stump Cross
Akroydon
Highroad Well Moor
Luddenden
Brearley
Mt. Pellon
Piece Hall
Shibden Park
Hipperholme
Lower Wyke
Scholes
Luddenden Foot
Warley Town
HALIFAX
Hall Bank
Lightcliffe
Crow Nest Park
Bailiff Bridge
Birkhouse
Hartshead Moor Top
Blackwood Common
Bank Top
Hove Edge
Thornhills
HARTSHEAD MOOR
Southowram
Siddal
Brighouse
Brookfoot
Clifton
Cromwell Bottom
Elland Park Wood
Clifton Wood
Woodhouse
Rastrick
Toothill
Bradley Wood
Elland
Lower Edge
Elland
Bradley
Blackley
Brackenhall
Deighton
Sheepridge
Netheroyd Hill
Fartown
Prince Royd
Birchencliffe
Birkby
Edgerton
Lindley
Salendine Nook
Snow Lee
Oakes
Bradley Mills
Quarmby
Longwood
HUDDERSFIELD
Dalton
Tandem
Greensid
Paddock
Leymoor
Milnsbridge
Golcar
Moldgreen
Town End
Moselden Height
Pole Moor
Worts Hill
Scammonden Water
Calder and Hebble Navigation
River Calder
Rochdale Canal
A629
A650
A6038
A657
A658
A6177
A617
A6036
A647
A641
A644
A646
A58
A649
A643
A6025
A6107
A640
A62
M606
M62
M1
B6429
B6143
B6144
B6145
B6146
B6269
B6380
B6147
B6114
B6113

LEEDS & BRADFORD
0 1 2 miles
0 1 2 3 kilometres
LEEDS DISTRICT
KIRKLEES DISTRICT
WAKEFIELD DISTRICT
Y O R K S
Rawdon
Tinshill
Moor Allerton
Moortown
Lawnswood
Low Green
Lane Ends
Rawdon Carrs
Thackley
Simpson Green
Wellroyd
Horsforth
Horsforth Woodside
West Park
Meanwood
Roundhay
Chapel Allerton
Apperley Bridge
Calverley
Newlay Wood
Hawksworth
Weetwood
Gledhow
Greengates
Bank Top
Ravenscliffe
Priesthorpe
Woodhall Hills
Rodley
Bagley
Farsley-Beck Bottom
Whitecote
Moorside
Kirkstall
Headingley
Potternewton
Oakwood
Gipton
Harehills
Fagley
Farsley
Stanningley
Bramley
Hill Top
Upper Armley
Burley
Woodhouse
LEEDS
Burmantofts
Thornbury
Swinnow Moor
Hillfoot
Chapeltown
Laisterdyke
Tyresal
Upper Moor
Pudsey
Gamble Hill
Armley
Osmondthorpe
Wortley
Farnley
Holbeck
Cross Green
Fulneck
Black Carr
Far Royds
Hunslet
Beeston
Beeston Hill
Dudley Hill
Holme Shay
Park Wood
New Farnley
Stourton
Bierley
Tong Street
Tong
Cockers Dale
Upper Moor Side
Mill Shaw
Beeston Park Side
Westgate Hill
East Bierley
Tofts haw
Cockersdale
Moor Head
Churwell
Belle Isle
Gildersome
Drighlington
Adwalton
Rothwell
Daisy Hill
Bantam Grove
Gildersome Street
New Brighton
Middleton
Robin Hood
Birkenshaw
Birkenshaw Bottoms
Moorside
Bruntcliffe
Morley
Hunsworth
Oakwell
Carlton
Merchant Fields
Gomersal
Topcliffe
Thorpe on the Hill
Copley Hill
Birstall
Tingley
Lofthouse
Cleckheaton
Spen
Popeley Fields
Upper Green
Woodkirk
East Ardsley
Carlinghow
Lofthouse Gate
Batley
Hightown Heights
Littletown
Westfield
Hightown
Healey
Haigh Moor
Carr Gate
Stanley
Outwood
Clerk Green
Mount Pleasant
Beggarington Hill
Liversedge
Heckmondwike
Staincliffe
Hanging Heaton
Norristhorpe
Batley Carr
Chidswell
Jaw Hill
Kirkhamgate
Wrenthorpe
Newton Hill
Snow Hill
Roberttown
Dewsbury Moor
DEWSBURY
WAKEFIELD
Hartshead
Boothroyd
Gawthorpe
Alverthorpe
Moor Top
Crossley
Chickenley
Earlsheaton
Flanshaw
Mirfield Moor
Flushdyke
Ossett
Northorpe
Savile Town
Battyeford
Mirfield
Ravensthorpe
Lupset
Thornes Park
Lower Hopton
Thornhill Lees
Ossett Spa
Healey
Upper Heaton
North Moor
South Ossett
Thornes
Combs
Thornhill
Portobello
Horbury
Kirkheaton
Overthorpe
Upper Hopton
Whitley Lower
Thornhill Edge
Horbury Bridge
Horbury Junction
Hill Side
Middlestown
Coxley
Durkar
Houses Hill
Overton
Netherton
Calder Grove
Gawthorpe
Cowmes
Great Cliff
Crigglestone
Fenay Bridge
Lepton
Grange Moor
Painthorpe
Chapelthorpe
Hill Top
M62
M621
M1
A58
A62
A65
A647
A650
A653
A638
A642
A644
A6120
A660
A61
River Calder
Calder and Hebble Navigation
Leeds & Liverpool Canal

NEWCASTLE UPON TYNE
0 1 2 miles
0 1 2 3 kilometres
Tyne and Wear Metro
NEWCASTLE
400 yds
400m
NEWCASTLE UPON TYNE DISTRICT
NORTH TYNESIDE DISTRICT
SOUTH TYNESIDE DISTICT
GATESHEAD DISTRICT
CITY OF SUNDERLAND
NEWCASTLE UPON TYNE
Gateshead
Tynemouth
North Shields
South Shields
Jarrow
Hebburn
Wallsend
Gosforth
Longbenton
Felling
Washington
SUNDERLAND
Whickham
Blaydon
Newcastle International Airport
River Tyne
TYNE & WEAR

EDINBURGH
0 1 2 miles
0 1 2 3 kilometres
FIRTH OF FORTH
EAST LOTHIAN
MIDLOTHIAN
Edinburgh
Leith
Musselburgh
Prestonpans
Dalkeith
Penicuik
Bonnyrigg
Loanhead
Lasswade
Newtongrange
Cramond
Corstorphine
Portobello
Granton
Newhaven
South Queensferry
EDINBURGH
0 400 yds
0 400m

GLASGOW
0 1 2 miles
0 1 2 3 kilometres
WEST DUNBARTONSHIRE
EAST DUNBARTONSHIRE
RENFREWSHIRE
EAST RENFREWSHIRE
Mugdock
Milngavie
Baldernock
Torrance
Balmore
Bardowie
Cadder
Buckhey
Bearsden
Faifley
Duntocher
Hardgate
Old Kilpatrick
Mountblow
Parkhall
Radnor Park
Kilbowie
Dalmuir
Drumry
Drumchapel
Erskine
North Barr
Linburn
Whitecrook
Clydebank
Park Mains
Southbar
Freeland
Inchinnan
Yoker
Knightswood
Temple
Kelvindale
Maryhill
Summerston
Lambhill
Bishopbriggs
Kenmure
Milton
Crowhill
Springburn
Scotstounhill
Anniesland
Kelvinside
Scotstoun
Possil Park
Dowanhill
Partick
Whiteinch
Shieldhall
Renfrew
Dean Park
Shortroods
Gallowhill
Hillington
Cardonald
Govan
Ibrox
Craigton
Dennistoun
Bridgeton
Ferguslie Park
Oldhall
Ralston
Crookston
Pollokshields
GLASGOW
Millarston
PAISLEY
Castlehead
Blackhall
Mosspark
Dumbreck
Oatlands
Hawkhead
Pollok
Govanhill
Polmadie
Rutherglen
Charleston
Thornly Park
Crossmyloof
Shawlands
Langside
Mount Florida
Foxbar
Glenburn
Pollokshaws
Battlefield
Cathcart
King's Park
Hurlet
Nitshill
Priesthill
Mansewood
Newlands
Croftfoot
Muirend
Merrylee
Arden
Carnwadric
Darnley
Thornliebank
Giffnock
Netherlee
Castlemilk
Linn Park
Stamperland
Williamwood
Clarkston
Sheddens
Carmunnock
Crookfur
Whitecraigs
Broom
Busby
Braehead
Thorntonhall
Newton Mearns
Mearns
Waterfoot
Lawmuir
Jackton
Eaglesham
M8
M77
A8
A82
A726
A737
A739
A761
A77
A814
A81
GLASGOW
0 200 yds
0 200m

Milton of Campsie
Twechar
Croy
Craigmarloch
Carrickstone
Westerwood
Kildrum
Cumbernauld
Seafar
Eastfield
Balloch
Carbrain
Birdston
Harestanes
Kirkintilloch
Broadwood
Westfield
Lenziemill
Greenfaulds
Condorrat
Gallowhill
Oxgang
Waterside
Blairlinn
Luggiebank
Lenzie
Strathkelvin Retail Park
Mollinsburn
Greengairs
Gadloch
Auchinloch
Bridgend
Moodiesburn
Annathill
Woodhill
Chryston
Riggend
Wattston
NORTH LANARKSHIRE
Greenfoot
Rigghead
Marnock
Muirhead
Stand
Garnkirk
Glenboig
Stepps
Cardowan
Gartcosh
Johnston Loch
Glenmavis
Millerston
Airdriehill
Hogganfield Loch
Provanmill
Bishop Loch
Gartgill
Townhead
Holehills
Thrashbush
Rawyards
Ruchazie
Woodend Loch
Riddrie
Garthamlock
Lochwood
Gartsherrie
Lochend Loch
Easterhouse
Drumpellier Country Park
Monkland Canal
Airdrie
Craigneuk
Carntyne
Coatbridge
Coatdyke
Springboig
Barlanark
Swinton
Gartlea
Barrachnie
Baillieston
Bargeddie
Greenend
Garrowhill
Shettleston
Crosshill
Kirkwood
Rosehall
Gartness
Muirhead
Woodlands
Old Monkland
Kirkshaws
Shawhead
Carnbroe
Calderbank
Braidfauld
Mount Vernon
Chapelhall
Broomhouse
Carmyle
Birkenshaw
Thorniewood
Newhouse
West
Tannochside
Viewpark
Eastfield
Newton
Kylepark
Fallside
Mossend
Holytown
Uddingston
Bellshill
New Stevenston
Hallside
Bothwell Services
Yett
Cambuslang
Flemington
Kirkfield
Carfin
Low Blantyre
Bothwell
Forgewood
Dalton
North Motherwell
Cleekhimin
SOUTH LANARKSHIRE
Barnhill
Motherwell
Blantyre
Springwells
Whitehill
Craigneuk
Nerston
High Blantyre
Burnbank
Hamilton Services
Strathclyde Loch
Rogerton
Shieldmuir
Stewartfield
Calderwood
Hamilton
Muirhouse
East Mains
Hillhouse
West Mains
EAST KILBRIDE
Auchentibber
Earnock
Laighstonehall
Ferniegair
Low Waters
Silvertonhill
Allanton
Gowkthrapple
Westwood
St. Leonards
Woodhead
Fairhill
Cadzow
The Murray
Birniehill
Meikle Earnock
Eddlewood
Blantyre Moor
Greenhills
River Clyde
M8
M73
M74
M80
A80
A8
A725
A74

246
15.8 miles to 1 inch
0 10 20 30 40 miles
0 10 20 30 40 50 60 km
10 km to 1 cm
Connemara National Park
Joyce's Country
Lough Corrib
Iar Connaght
Galway
Tuam
Athenry
Loughrea
Aran Islands
Inishmore
Inishmaan
Inisheer
North Sound
South Sound
Burren
Ballyvaughan
Lisdoonvarna
Cliffs of Moher
Hag's Head
Slieve Aughty Mts
Gort
Lough Derg
Portumna
Ennistymon
Corofin
Milltown Malbay
Ennis
Clarecastle
Kilkee
Kilrush
Loop Head
Mouth of The Shannon
Shannon
Limerick
Curraghchase Forest Park
Foynes
Tarbert
Ballybunnion
Listowel
Newcastle West
Abbeyfeale
Mullaghareirk Mts
Kerry Hd
Ballyheigue
The Seven Hogs
Brandon Head
Tralee
Tralee Bay
Slieve Mish Mts
Dingle
Castleisland
Castlemaine
Dunquin
Great Blasket I.
Dingle Bay
Killorglin
Killarney
Killarney National Park
Macgillycuddy's Reeks
Iveragh
Cahirciveen
Valencia Island
Kenmare
Derrynane Nat. Hist. Park
Beara
Caha Mts
Glengarriff
Bantry
Bantry Bay
Dursey Island
Castletown Bere
Mizen Head
Crookhaven
Schull
Skibbereen
Clear Island
Cape Clear
Sherkin Island
Galley Head
Clonakilty
Bandon
Kinsale
Old Head of Kinsale
Cork
Cobh
Macroom
Shehy Mts
Gougane Barra Forest Park
Derrynasaggart Mts
Boggeragh Mts
Mallow
Fermoy
Nagles Mts
Ballyhoura Mts
Galtee Mts
Charleville
Rathluirc
Kilmallock
Mitchelstown
Silvermine Mts
Slievefelim Mountains
Arra Mountains
Slieve Bernagh
Killaloe
Newport
Croom
Adare
Rathkeale
Sixmilebridge
Newmarket on-Fergus
KEY TO MAP SYMBOLS
Motorway
under constr.
M1
restricted access
Junction number
dual carriageway
'A'/National primary
N8
'A' /National secondary
N71
'B'/Regional road
B45
Road distances (in miles)
Railway
Car ferry
Airport
International boundary
National park
Regional/Forest park
Urban area
Beach
Canal

247
Mullingar
Athlone
Ballymahon
Uisneach
Kinnegad
Moyvalley
Trim
Hill of Tara
Dunboyne
Rush
Lambay Island
Portrane
Malahide
Ireland's Eye
Howth
DUBLIN
Dublin Bay
Dún Laoghaire
To Douglas 2 3/4 (summer only)
To Liverpool 3 3/4 - 8 hrs
To Holyhead 1 3/4 - 3 3/4 hrs
Leixlip
Celbridge
Lucan
Newcastle
Clane
Naas
Kilteel
Enniskerry
Bray
Kippure
Djouce Mountain
Great Sugar Loaf
Blessington
Blessington Lakes
Mullaghcleevaun
Vartry Res.
Tonelagee
Kilcoole
Newtownmountkennedy
Wicklow Mts. National Park
Wicklow
Wicklow Head
Lugnaquilla Mountain
Rathdrum
Ardmore Point
Brittas Bay
Mizen Head
Aughrim
Avoca
Arklow
Kilmichael Point
Inch
Gorey
Courtown
Ballycanew
Cahore Point
Moate
Clara
Kilbeggan
Edenderry
Bog of Allen
Tullamore
Clonygowan
Rathangan
Newbridge
Kildare
Monasterevan
The Curragh
Kilcullen
Dunlavin
Clogham
Banagher
Kilcormac
Portarlington
Mountmellick
Slieve Bloom Mts
Arderin
Portlaoise
Birr
Stradbally
Athy
Timolin
Mountrath
Castletown
Roscrea
Ballylynan
Baltinglass
Castledermot
Wicklow Mountains
Rathvilly
Abbeyleix
Moneygall
Devils Bit Mountain
Rathdowney
Durrow
Templemore
Templetuohy
Castlecomer
Graigue
Carlow
Tullow
Borrisoleigh
Johnstown
Ballyragget
Freshford
Leighlinbridge
Ballon
Shillelagh
Urlingford
Thurles
Holycross
Whitehall
Muine Bheag
Craanford
Bunclody
Kilkenny
Slieveardagh Hills
Blackstairs Mountains
Mount Leinster
Borris
Dungarvan
Ballymurphy
Ferns
Killenaule
Graiguenamanagh
Callan
Kells
Thomastown
Blackstairs Mountain
Brandon Hill
Enniscorthy
Cashel
Fethard
Knocktopher
Ninemilehouse
Ballyhale
Drummin
Clonroche
Blackwater
Newinn
Slievenamon
Lukeswell
New Ross
Killurin
Wexford Bay
Castlebridge
Booley Hills
Bathkeevin
Cahir
Clonmel
Carrick-on-Suir
John F. Kennedy Park
Wexford
Wexford Harbour
Rosslare Point
Taghmon
Comeragh Mountains
Knockanaffrin
Portlaw
Wellington Bridge
Rosslare
Rosslare Harbour
Greenore Point
To Fishguard 1 3/4 - 3 1/2 hrs
To Pembroke 3 3/4 hrs
To Cherbourg 17 1/2 - 18 hrs & Roscoff 17 hrs (summer only)
Waterford
Cheekpoint
Killinick
Lady's Island
Knockmealdown Mts
Ballymacarberry
Croughaun Hill
Monavullagh Mountains
Seefin
Duncannon
Duncormick
Ballyteige Bay
Carnsore Point
Kilmore Quay
Cappoquin
Tramore
Dunmore East
Lismore
Ballymacmague
Tramore Bay
Waterford Harbour
Hook Head
Saltee Islands
Tallow
Dungarvan
Helvick Head
Clashmore
Grange
Mine Head
Ardmore Bay
Youghal
Youghal Bay
Ballymacoda
Knockadoon Head
Ballycotton Bay
To Swansea 10 hrs
To Roscoff 14-15 hrs (summer only)
RELIEF IN METRES
Over 700m
500-700m
300-500m
200-300m
100-200m
0-100m
DUBLIN
N 0 400 yds
0 200 400 m
Western Way
Dublin Writers Museum
National Wax Museum
James Joyce Centre
Hugh Lane Gallery
Gate Theatre
Parnell Square
Kings Inns
Rotunda Hospital
Constitution Hill
Bolton St.
Dorset St.
Summerhill
McDermott Street
Sean
Gardiner St. Lower
Sheriff Street Lower
Connolly Station
Talbot Street
Police Station
Bus Sta
Amiens
Brunswick Street North
North King Street
Church Street
ILAC Shopping Centre
Henry St.
St. Mary's Cathedral
Abbey Theatre
Custom House
General Post Office
O'Connell Street
Old Jameson Distillery
The Chimney
St. Mary's Lane
Mary Street
Jervis Street
Hot Press Music Hall of Fame
Eden Quay
Custom House Quay
Ceol-Irish Music Centre
Four Courts
Capel Street
Bachelors Wk.
George's Quay
City Quay
Tara Street Station
Burgh Quay
River Liffey
Arran Quay
Inns Quay
Ormond Quay Upper
Ormond Quay Lower
Aston Quay
Wellington Quay
Townsend Street
Police Station
Pearse Street
Temple Bar
Bank of Ireland
Ushers Quay
Merchants Quay
Wood Quay
Essex Quay
Dublin's Viking Adventure
College Green
Dame Street
Trinity College - Book of Kells & The Dublin Experience
Westland Row
Sandwith St.
Pearse Station
Christ Church Cathedral
Dublinia
City Hall
High St.
Thomas St. W.
Civic Museum
South Great George's St.
Nassau St.
Heraldic Museum
Clare St.
Fenian St.
Merrion Sq.
Dublin Castle
Police Station
Westbury Mall
Grafton Arcade
Grafton St.
Dawson St.
Kildare Street
National Library
National Gallery
Leinster House
Mansion House
Francis Street
Meath Street
Patrick Street
St. Patrick's Cathedral
Aungier Street
Gaiety Theatre
St. Stephen's Green
Natural History Museum
National Museum
Government Buildings
The Coombe
Marsh's Library
Police Station
Kevin St. Upper
Bishop St.
York Street
Cuffe St.
St. Stephen's Green Park
New Row South
New St. South
New Bride St.
Ardee St.
Newman House Museum
Grangegorman Upper
Marlborough Street
Gardiner St. Middle

BELFAST
0 200 yds
0 200 m
University of Ulster
St. Anne's Cathedral
Stranraer (Sea Cat) and Isle of Man Ferry Terminals
Odyssey Complex
Library
Smithfield Market
Castle Court Centre
Millfield Technical College
Custom House
Clock Tower
Bus Station
Lookout
Lagan Weir
QUEEN ELIZABETH BRIDGE
QUEEN'S BRIDGE
BRIDGE END
Hipark Centre
Castle Street
Castle Lane
Victoria Centre
Court House
Old Museum Arts Centre
Linen Hall Library
Royal Courts of Justice
Waterfront Hall
River Lagan
COLLEGE SQ. N.
Technical College
Royal Belfast Academical Institution
WELLINGTON PL.
DONEGALL SQ. NORTH
CHICHESTER ST.
City Hall
Spires Mall
MAY STREET
Market
EAST BRIDGE STREET
Central Station
GROSVENOR ROAD
HOWARD ST.
DONEGALL SQ SOUTH
Grand Opera House
Crown Liquor Saloon
Ulster Hall
Group Theatre
Bus Station
Gt. Victoria Street Station
Gt. Northern Mall
BBC
ORMEAU AVENUE
Ormeau Baths Gallery
Cinema
CROMAC STREET
SANDY ROW
DUBLIN RD.
BEDFORD STREET
A B C D
1 2 3 4 5 6
Tory Island
Bloody Foreland
Gweedore
Gola Island
Owey Island
Rosses Bay
The Rosses
Aran Island
Burtonport
Dungloe
Crohy Head
Gweebarra Bay
Dawros Head
Loughros More Bay
Glenties
Ardara
Slievetooey
Glengesh Pass
Rossan Point
Malin Bay
Malin More
Rathlin O'Birne Island
Slieve League
Killybegs
Donegal
Muckross Head
Fintragh Bay
McSwynes Bay
Inver Bay
St John's Point
Doorin Point
Donegal Bay
Mullaghmore Head
Bundoran
Ballyshannon
Inishmurray
Streedagh Point
Cliffoney
Roskeeragh Point
Darty Mts
Glenade Lough
Glencar Lake
Lenadoon Point
Sligo Bay
Aughris Head
Coney I.
Sligo
Manorhamilton
Stags of Broad Haven
Benwee Head
Erris Head
Broad Haven
Downpatrick Head
Belderg
Ballycastle
Killala Bay
Bartragh I.
Belmullet
The Mullet
Carrowmore Lake
Glenamoy
Killala
Dromore West
Knockalongy
Collooney
Drumkeeran
Inishkea North
Inishkea South
Bangor Erris
Owenmore
Lough Dahybaun
Ballina
Easky Lough
Slieve Gamph
Ballymote
Lough Arrow
Lough Key Forest Park
Duvillaun More
Blacksod Bay
Ballycroy
Slieve Car
Nephin Beg
Deel
Mullany's Cross
Templehouse Lake
Tubbercurry
Ballinafad
Boyle
Croaghaun
Dooagh
Slieve More
Owenduff
Nephin Beg Range
Birreencorragh
Nephin
Levally Lough
Lough Conn
Foxford
Pontoon
Charlestown
Knock International
Achill Head
Achill Island
Annagh
Achill
Cushcamcarragh
Lough Feeagh
Beltra Lough
Swinford
Bohola
Lough Gara
Ballaghaderreen
Frenchpark
Corraun Peninsula
Mulrany
Newport
Castlebar
Kiltimagh
Urlaur Lough
Achillbeg Island
Clew Bay
Islandeady Lough
Knock
Mannin Lake
Clare Island
Westport
Murrisk
Croagh Patrick
Ballyhaunis
Castlerea
Tulsk
Louisburgh
Caher Island
Claremorris
Partry
Inishturk
Cregganbaun
Ballindine
Partry Mts
Inishbofin
Inishark
Benbury
Mweelrea
Bengorm
Aasleagh
Benwee
Devils Mother
Ballinrobe
Lough Mask
Kilmaine
Dunmore
Glenamaddy
Roscommon
Ballynakill Bay
Lough Fee
Maumturk Mts
Joyce's Country
Omey Island
Connemara National Park
Benbaun
The Twelve Pins
Bencorr
Inagh
Cong
Lough Corrib
Clonbern
Athleague
Ballygar
Clifden
Tuam
Mannin Bay
Connemara
Recess
Headford
Mount Bellew
Horseleap
Slyne Head
Ballyconneely Bay
Bertraghboy Bay
Connaught
244
Maurrin Lough
Owenboliska
Claregalway
Monivea
Galway
Athenry
Mweenish Island
Gorumna Island
Carraroe
Galway
Oranmore
Kiltullagh
Ballinasloe

E
F
G
H
I
15.8 miles to 1 inch
0 10 20 30 40 miles
0 10 20 30 40 50 60 km
10 km to 1 cm
1
2
3
4
5
6
Sanaigmore
Coul Point
Machir Bay
Portnahaven
Rinns Point
Kintra
Lower Killeyan
The Oa
Mull Of Oa
Port Ellen
Texa
Rubha nan Leacan
Glenegedale
Bridgend
Port Askaig
Feolin Ferry
Small Isles
Rubha na Traille
Ardpatrick Point
Claggain Bay
Gigha
Ardminish
Eilean a'Chuirn
Cara Island
Sound of Gigha
Tayinloan
Carradale
Kintyre
Bellochantuy Bay
Machrihanish Bay
Machrihanish
Campbeltown
Lussa Loch
Ardnacross Bay
Davaar Island
Cnoc Moy
Southend
Mull of Kintyre
Sanda Island
Knapdale
Tarbert
Kames
Rothesay
Ardlamont
Claonaig
Cock of Arran
Lochranza
Garroch Head
Caisteal Abhail
Goat Fell
Brodick
Lamlash
Arran
Lagg
Pladda
Bennan Head
Ailsa Craig
North Channel
Rathlin Island
Bull Point
Fair Head
Ballycastle
Torr Head
Runabay Head
Cushendun
Cushendall
Garron Point
Carnlough Bay
Carnlough
Glenariff Forest Park
Antrim Hills
Trostan
Knocklayd
Armoy
The Maidens
Ballygalley Head
Larne
Island Magee
Black Head
Whitehead
Carrickfergus
Belfast Lough
Newtownabbey
Bangor
Copeland Is.
Donaghadee
Newtownards
Carrowdore
Ards Peninsula
Kircubbin
Portavogie
Strangford Lough
Portaferry
Strangford
Ballyquintin Point
Downpatrick
Ardglass
Dundrum Bay
St John's Point
Newcastle
Tollymore Forest Park
Mourne Mountains
Slieve Donard
Silent Valley Reservoir
Annalong
Kilkeel
Greenore
Cranfield Point
Bullagon Point
Carlingford Lough
Carlingford
Warrenpoint
Newry
Dundalk
Dundalk Bay
Blackrock
Castlebellingham
Dunany Point
Dunleer
Ardee
Clogher Head
Drogheda
Bettystown
Laytown
Balbriggan
Skerries
Rush
Lambay Island
Portrane
Malahide
Swords
Dublin
Ireland's Eye
Howth
DUBLIN
Dublin Bay
Dún Laoghaire
Lucan
Leixlip
Clane
Newcastle
Bog of Allen
Edend
Tullamore
Kilbeggan
Moate
Athlone
Clara
Kinnegad
Moyvalley
Dunboyne
Ashbourne
Navan
Slane
Kells
Trim
Athboy
Delvin
Hill of Tara
Mullingar
Uisneach
Ballymahon
Lough Ree
Longford
Edgeworthstown
Granard
Lough Owel
Ballinalack
Castlepollard
Oldcastle
Lough Sheelin
Lough Derravaragh
Lough Ramor
Virginia
Ballyjamesduff
Bailieborough
Kingscourt
Carrickmacross
Shercock
Cootehill
Cavan
Ballinamore
Mohill
Carrick-on-Shannon
Dromod
Clooneagh
Arvagh
Killykeen Forest Park
Butlers Bridge
Dún a'Rí Forest Park
Nobber
Ballybay
Monaghan
Castleblayney
Crossmaglen
Rossmore Forest Park
Clones
Newtownbutler
Lisnaskea
Rosslea
Enniskillen
Lough Erne
Upper Lough Erne
Lough Macnean Upper
Lough Macnean Lower
Belcoo
Florence Court Forest Park
Blacklion
Glangevlin
Cuilcagh
Iron Mountains
Slieve Anierin
Bencroy
Ballyconnell
Lisbellaw
Fivemiletown
Aughnacloy
Augher
Fintona
Dromore
Pettigo
Boa Island
Lisnarick
Tully
Lough Melvin
Irvinestown
Omagh
Gortin Glen Forest Park
Newtownstewart
Castlederg
Strabane
Lifford
Sion Mills
Raphoe
Letterkenny
Ballybofey
Stranorlar
Lough Mourne
Glenveagh National Park
Creeslough
Milford
Kilmacrenan
Lough Swilly
Buncrana
Carndonagh
Inishowen
Malin Head
Ballygorman
Inishtrahull
Glengad Head
Dunaff Head
Doagh Isle
Fanad Head
Horn Head
Portsalon
Moville
Inishowen Head
Lough Foyle
Carrowkeel
Londonderry
Limavady
Eglinton
Ballykelly
Dungiven
Claudy
Sperrin Mountains
Draperstown
Magherafelt
Moneymore
Cookstown
Davagh Forest Park
Lough Neagh
Coleraine
Portstewart
Portrush
Giant's Causeway
Benbane Head
Bushmills
Magilligan Point
Ballymoney
Ringsend
Kilrea
Garvagh
Dunloy
Ballymena
Cullybackey
Maghera
Glenshane Pass
Slemish
Broughshane
Kells
Ballyclare
Randalstown
Antrim
Belfast International
Crumlin
BELFAST
Belfast City
Dundonald
Comber
Dunmurry
Lisburn
Moira
Lurgan
Craigavon
Portadown
Dungannon
Parkanaur Forest Park
Donaghmore
Pomeroy
Ballygawley
Armagh
Tandragee
Markethill
Gosford Forest Park
Middletown
Keady
Bessbrook
Slieve Gullion Forest Park
Banbridge
Dromore
Hillsborough
Annahilt
Ballynahinch
Saintfield
Killinchy
Crossgar
Castlewellan Forest Park
Ballyward
Rathfriland
Mayo's Corner
Dundrum
Belfast
To Cairnryan 1-2¼ hrs
To Stranraer 1¾-3¼ hrs
To Troon 2½ hrs (summer only)
To Fleetwood 8 hrs
To Douglas 2¾ hrs & Heysham 4 hrs (summer only)
To Liverpool 8½ hrs
To Douglas 2¾-4¾ hrs (summer only)
To Liverpool 3¾ - 8 hrs
To Holyhead 1¾ - 3¾ hrs
245

Index to London street names

General Abbreviations

All	Alley	Circ	Circus	Flds	Fields	Ms	Mews	St	Street
App	Approach	Clo	Close	Gdn/Gdns	Garden/Gardens	N	North	St.	Saint
Arc	Arcade	Cor	Corner	Grd	Ground	Par	Parade	Ter	Terrace
Av/Ave	Avenue	Cres	Crescent	Grn	Green	Pas	Passage	Twr	Tower
Bdy	Broadway	Ct	Court	Gro	Grove	Pk	Park	W	West
Bldgs	Buildings	Ctyd	Courtyard	Ho	House	Pl	Place	Wf	Wharf
Br/Bri	Bridge	Dr	Drive	La	Lane	Rd	Road	Wk	Walk
Cen	Central, Centre	E	East	Lo	Lodge	Ri	Rise	Yd	Yard
Ch	Church	Embk	Embankment	Mans	Mansions	S	South		
Chyd	Churchyard	Est	Estate	Mkt/Mkts	Market/Markets	Sq	Square		

Post Town Abbreviations

Bark.	Barking	Edg.	Edgware	Islw.	Isleworth	Pnr.	Pinner	Twick.	Twickenham
Beck.	Beckenham	Felt.	Feltham	Kings.T.	Kingston upon Thames	Rich.	Richmond	Uxb.	Uxbridge
Brent.	Brentford	Grnf.	Greenford			Ruis.	Ruislip	Walt.	Walton-on-Thames
Brom.	Bromley	Har.	Harrow	Mitch.	Mitcham	Stan.	Stanmore	W.Mol.	West Molesey
Chig.	Chigwell	Hmptn.	Hampton	Mord.	Morden	Sthl.	Southall	Wdf.Grn.	Woodford Green
Chis.	Chislehurst	Houns.	Hounslow	N.Mal.	New Malden	Tedd.	Teddington	Wem.	Wembley
E.Mol.	East Molesey	Ilf.	Ilford	Nthlt.	Northolt	Th.Hth.	Thornton Heath		

A

Abbeville Rd SW4 223 A5
Abbey Orchard St SW1 224 J13
Abbey Rd NW6; NW8 220 D3
Abbey Rd, Bark. IG11 222 D2
Abbey St SE1 223 B4
Abbott Rd E14 222 C3
Abercorn Pl NW8 220 D3
Abingdon St SW1 225 K13
Acacia Rd, Hmptn. TW12 221 A6
Academy Rd SE18 223 D4
Achilles Way W1 224 C10
Acre La SW2 223 A5
Acton La NW10 220 C3
Acton La W3; W4 221 C4
Adam & Eve Ct W1 224 G5
Adam St WC2 225 L8
Adams Row W1 224 C8
Addington St SE1 225 N12
Addle Hill EC4 225 S7
Addle St EC2 225 U4
Adelaide Av SE4 223 C5
Adelaide Rd NW3 220 D2
Adelaide St WC2 225 K8
Adeline Pl WC1 224 J4
Adelphi Ter WC2 225 L8
Aerodrome Rd NW4; NW9 220 C1
Agar St WC2 225 K8
Agdon St EC1 225 R1
Agincourt Rd NW3 220 D2
Air St W1 224 G8
Akerman Rd SW9 223 A4
Alaska St SE1 225 P10
Albany W1 224 F8
Albany Ctyd W1 224 G8
Albany Rd SE5 223 B4
Albany St NW1 222 A3
Albemarle Rd, Beck. BR3 223 C6
Albemarle St W1 224 E8
Albemarle Way EC1 225 R2
Albert Br Rd SW11 221 D4
Albert Embk SE1 223 A4
Albert Gate SW1 224 A11
Albert Rd E16 222 D3
Albert Rd N22 222 A1
Albion Pl EC1 225 R3
Albion Rd N16 222 B2
Albion Way EC1 225 T4
Aldburgh Ms W1 224 C5
Aldermanbury EC2 225 U5
Aldermanbury Sq EC2 225 U4
Alderney Av, Houns. TW5 221 A4
Aldersbrook Rd E11; E12 222 D2
Aldersgate St EC1 225 T5
Aldford St W1 224 B9
Aldwych WC2 225 M7
Alexandra Av W4 221 C4
Alexandra Av, Har. HA2 220 A2
Alexandra Pk Rd N10; N22 222 A1
Alexandra Rd SW19 221 D6
Alfred Ms W1 224 H3
Alfred Pl WC1 224 H3
All Souls Av NW10 220 C3
All Souls Pl W1 224 E4
Allenby Rd, Sthl. UB1 220 A3
Allington St SW1 224 F14
Allsop Pl NW1 224 A2
Alperton La, Grnf. UB6; Wem. HA0 220 B3
Ambassador's Ct SW1 224 G10
Ambrosden Av SW1 224 G14
Amen Cor EC4 225 S6
Amen Ct EC4 225 S5
America St SE1 225 T10
Amhurst Pk N16 222 B2
Amhurst Rd N16 222 B2
Anchor Yd EC1 225 U1
Andrew Borde St WC2 224 J5
Andrewes Ho EC2 225 U4
Andrews Crosse WC2 225 P6
Anerley Hill SE19 223 B6
Anerley Rd SE19; SE20 223 B6
Angel Ct SW1 224 G10
Angel St EC1 225 T5
Ann's Cl SW1 224 A12
Anson Rd NW2 220 C2
Apothecary St EC4 225 R6
Apple Tree Yd SW1 224 G9
Apsley Way W1 224 C11
Aquinas St SE1 225 Q10
Arch St SE1 225 T14
Archer St W1 224 H7
Arches, The WC2 225 L9
Archibald Ms W1 224 C9
Archway Rd N6; N19 220 D1
Argent St SE1 225 S11
Argyle Rd W13; Grnf. UB6 220 B3
Argyll St W1 224 F6
Arlington St SW1 224 F9
Armoury Way SW18 221 D5
Arne St WC2 225 L6
Arneway St SW1 224 J14
Arthur Rd SW19 221 D6
Artillery Pl SW1 224 H14
Artillery Row SW1 224 H14
Arundel Gt Ct WC2 225 N7
Arundel St WC2 225 N7
Ashentree Ct EC4 225 Q6
Ashgrove Rd, Brom. BR1 223 C6
Ashland Pl W1 224 B3
Ashley Gdns SW1 224 G14
Ashley Pl SW1 224 F14
Askew Rd W12 220 C3
Aspen Way E14 222 C3
Audley Sq W1 224 C9
Ave Maria La EC4 225 S6
Avenue, The SW4 223 A5
Avenue, The W4 221 C4
Avenue, The, Hmptn. TW12 221 A6
Avenue, The (Hatch End), Pnr. HA5 220 A1
Avenue, The, Twick. TW1 221 B5
Avenue, The, Wem. HA9 220 B2
Avenue Rd NW8 220 D2
Avery Row W1 224 D7
Avon Pl SE1 225 U12
Avondale Rd, Brom. BR1 223 C6
Avonmouth St SE1 225 T13
Aybrook St W1 224 B4
Aylesbury St EC1 225 R2
Aylmer Rd N2 220 D1
Ayres St SE1 225 U11

B

Babmaes St SW1 224 G8
Back Hill EC1 225 P2
Bainbridge St WC1 224 J5
Baird St EC1 225 U1
Baker St NW1 224 A2
Baker St W1 224 A3
Baker's Ms W1 224 B5
Baker's Row EC1 225 P2
Balaam St E13 222 D3
Balderton St W1 224 C6
Baldwin's Gdns EC1 225 P3
Balfour Ms W1 224 C9
Balfour Pl W1 224 C8
Balham High Rd SW12; SW17 223 A5
Balham Hill SW12 223 A5
Ballards La N3; N12 220 D1
Balls Pond Rd N1 222 B2
Baltic St E EC1 225 T2
Baltic St W EC1 225 T2
Banbury Ct WC2 225 K7
Bank End SE1 225 U9
Bankside SE1 225 T8
Banner St EC1 225 U2
Barbican, The EC2 225 T3
Barbon Cl WC1 225 M3
Barge Ho St SE1 225 Q9
Baring Rd SE12 223 D5
Baring St N1 222 B3
Barking Rd E6; E13; E16 222 C3
Barlby Rd W10 220 C3
Barley Mow Pas EC1 225 S4
Barlow Pl W1 224 E8
Barnard's Inn EC1 225 Q5
Barnes High St SW13 221 C4
Barons Pl SE1 225 Q12
Barrett St W1 224 C6
Barry Rd SE22 223 B5
Barter St WC1 225 L4
Bartholomew Cl EC1 225 T4
Bartholomew Pl EC1 225 T4
Bartholomew Sq EC1 225 U1
Bartlett Ct EC4 225 Q5
Bartletts Pas EC4 225 Q5
Barton St SW1 224 K13
Bastwick St EC1 225 T1
Bateman St W1 224 H6
Bateman's Bldgs W1 224 H6
Bath Ct EC1 225 P2
Bath Rd W4 221 C4
Bath Ter SE1 225 T14
Battersea Br Rd SW11 221 D4
Battersea Pk Rd SW8; SW11 221 D4
Battersea Ri SW11 221 D5
Bayley St WC1 224 H4
Baylis Rd SE1 225 P12
Bayswater Rd W2 220 D3
Beak St W1 224 G7
Bear All EC4 225 R5
Bear Gdns SE1 225 T9
Bear La SE1 225 S9
Bear St WC2 224 J7
Beauchamp St EC1 225 P4
Beaumont Ms W1 224 C3
Beaumont Pl W1 224 G1
Beaumont St W1 224 C3
Beckenham Hill Rd SE6; Beck. BR3 223 C6
Beckenham La, Brom. BR2 223 C6
Beckenham Rd, Beck. BR3 223 C6
Bedford Av WC1 224 J4
Bedford Ct WC2 225 K8
Bedford Hill SW12; SW16 223 A5
Bedford Pl W1 224 G3
Bedford Pl WC1 225 K3
Bedford Rd SW4 223 A5
Bedford Row WC1 225 N3
Bedford Sq WC1 224 J4
Bedford St WC2 225 K7
Bedford Way WC1 224 J2
Bedfordbury WC2 225 K7
Beech St EC2 225 T3
Beehive La, Ilf. IG1, IG4 222 D1
Beeston Pl SW1 224 E14
Belgrave Ms N SW1 224 B12
Belgrave Ms S SW1 224 C13
Belgrave Ms W SW1 224 B13
Belgrave Pl SW1 224 C13
Belgrave Rd SW1 223 A4
Belgrave Sq SW1 224 B13
Belgrave Yd SW1 224 D14
Bell Grn SE26 223 C5
Bell La NW4 220 C1
Bell Wf La EC4 225 U7
Bell Yd WC2 225 P5
Bellevue Rd SW17 221 D5
Belmont Hill SE13 223 C5
Belmont Rd N15 222 B1
Belsize Rd NW6 220 D3
Belvedere Bldgs SE1 225 S12
Belvedere Pl SE1 225 S12
Belvedere Rd SE1 225 N11
Ben Jonson Rd E1 222 C3
Benjamin St EC1 225 R3
Bennet's Hill EC4 225 S7
Bennett St SW1 224 F9
Bennetts Yd SW1 224 J14
Bentinck Ms W1 224 C5
Bentinck St W1 224 C5
Beresford St SE18 223 D4
Berkeley Ms W1 224 A5
Berkeley Sq W1 224 E8
Berkeley St W1 224 E8
Berkshire Gdns N13 222 A1
Bernard St WC1 225 K2
Berners Ms W1 224 G4
Berners Pl W1 224 G5
Berners St W1 224 G4
Berry St EC1 225 S1
Berwick St W1 224 H6
Bessborough Rd, Har. HA1 220 A2
Bethnal Grn Rd E1; E2 222 B3
Bethune Rd N16 222 B2
Betterton St WC2 225 K6
Beulah Hill SE19 223 A6
Beverley Dr, Edg. HA8 220 B1
Beverley Way (Kingston Bypass) SW20 221 C6
Bexley Rd SE9 223 D5
Bickenhall St W1 224 A3
Bickley Pk Rd, Brom. BR1 223 D6
Bickley Rd, Brom. BR1 223 D6
Billet Rd E17 222 B1
Bilton Rd, Grnf. UB6 220 B3
Bingham Pl W1 224 B3
Binney St W1 224 C7
Bird St W1 224 C6
Birdcage Wk SW1 224 G12
Bishops Av, The N2 220 D2
Bishops Br Rd W2 220 D3
Bishop's Ct EC4 225 R5
Bishop's Ct WC2 225 P5
Bishops Way E2 222 B3
Bishopsgate EC2 222 B3
Bittacy Hill NW7 220 C1
Bittern St SE1 225 T12
Black Friars Ct EC4 225 R7
Black Friars La EC4 225 R7
Blackbrook La, Brom. BR1, BR2 223 D6
Blackburne's Ms W1 224 B7
Blackfriars Br EC4 225 R7
Blackfriars Br SE1 225 R7
Blackfriars Pas EC4 225 R7
Blackfriars Rd SE1 225 R12
Blackheath Rd SE10 223 C4
Blackhorse La E17 222 B1
Blackshaw Rd SW17 221 D6
Blackstock Rd N4; N5 222 A2
Blackwall La SE10 223 C4
Blackwall Tunnel E14 222 C3
Blake Hall Rd E11 222 D2
Blandford St W1 224 A5
Bleeding Heart Yd EC1 225 Q4
Blenheim St W1 224 D6
Bloomfield Pl W1 224 E7
Bloomsbury Ct WC1 225 L4
Bloomsbury Pl WC1 225 L3
Bloomsbury Sq WC1 225 L4
Bloomsbury St WC1 224 J4
Bloomsbury Way WC1 225 K5
Blore Ct W1 224 H6
Blue Ball Yd SW1 224 F10
Bolingbroke Gro SW11 221 D5
Bollo La W3; W4 221 B4
Bolsover St W1 224 E2
Bolt Ct EC4 225 Q6
Bolton St W1 224 E9
Book Ms WC2 224 J6
Booth Rd NW9 220 C1
Booth's Pl W1 224 G4
Borough High St SE1 225 T12
Borough Rd SE1 225 R13
Borough Sq SE1 225 T12
Boston Manor Rd, Brent. TW8 221 B4
Boston Rd W7 221 A4
Boswell Ct WC1 225 L3
Boswell St WC1 225 L3
Boundary Rd E13 222 D3
Boundary Rd E17 222 C2
Boundary Row SE1 225 R11
Bounds Grn Rd N11; N22 222 A1
Bourchier St W1 224 H7
Bourdon Pl W1 224 E7
Bourdon St W1 224 D8
Bourlet Cl W1 224 F4
Bourne Est EC1 225 P3
Bouverie St EC4 225 Q6
Bow Chyd EC4 225 U6
Bow La EC4 225 U6
Bow Rd E3 222 C3
Bow St WC2 225 L6
Bowland Yd SW1 224 A12
Bowling Grn La EC1 225 Q1
Boxtree La, Har. HA3 220 A1
Boxtree Rd, Har. HA3 220 A1
Boyce St SE1 225 N10
Boyfield St SE1 225 S12
Boyle St W1 224 F7
Brackley St EC1 225 T3
Brad St SE1 225 Q10
Brady St E1 222 B3
Brantwood Rd N17 222 B1
Bread St EC4 225 U6
Bream's Bldgs EC4 225 P5
Brecknock Rd N7; N19 222 A2
Brent St NW4 220 C1
Brentfield NW10 220 C2
Brentfield Rd NW10 220 C2
Bressenden Pl SW1 224 E13
Brewer St W1 224 G7
Brewer's Grn SW1 224 H13
Brewers Hall Gdns EC2 225 U4
Brewhouse Yd EC1 225 R1
Brick Ct EC4 225 P6
Brick La E1; E2 222 B3
Brick St W1 224 D10
Bride Ct EC4 225 R6
Bride La EC4 225 R6
Bridewell Pl EC4 225 R6
Bridford Ms W1 224 E3
Bridge La NW11 220 D1
Bridge Rd, E.Mol. KT8 221 A6
Bridge Rd, Houns. TW3; Islw. TW7 221 A5
Bridge St SW1 225 K12
Bridgewater Rd, Wem. HA0 220 B2
Bridgewater Sq EC2 225 T3
Bridgewater St EC2 225 T3
Bridle La W1 224 G7
Brinton Wk SE1 225 R10
Briset St EC1 225 R3
Britton St EC1 225 R2
Brixton Hill SW2 223 A5
Brixton Rd SW9 223 A4
Brixton Water La SW2 223 A5
Broad Ct WC2 225 L6
Broad La N15 222 B1
Broad La, Hmptn. TW12 221 A6
Broad Sanctuary SW1 224 J12
Broad Wk SE3 223 D4
Broad Wk W1 224 B9
Broad Yd EC1 225 R2
Broadbent St W1 224 D7
Broadmead Rd, Wdf.Grn. IG8 222 D1
Broadstone Pl W1 224 B4
Broadwall SE1 225 Q9
Broadway E15 222 C2
Broadway SW1 224 H13
Broadway, The SW19 221 D6
Broadway, The W5 220 B3
Broadway, The, Grnf. UB6 220 A3
Broadway, The, Sthl. UB1 220 A3
Broadwick St W1 224 G7
Brockham St SE1 225 U13
Brockley Gro SE4 223 C5
Brockley Ri SE23 223 C5
Brockley Rd SE4 223 C5
Broken Wf EC4 225 T7
Bromley Common, Brom. BR2 223 D6
Bromley Hill, Brom. BR1 223 C6
Bromley Pl W1 224 F3
Bromley Rd SE6; Brom. BR1 223 C5
Bromley Rd, Beck. BR3; Brom. BR2 223 C6
Brompton Rd SW1; SW3; SW7 221 D4
Brondesbury Pk NW2; NW6 220 C2
Brondesbury Rd NW6 220 D3
Brook Dr SE11 225 Q14
Brook Gate W1 224 A8
Brook St W1 224 C7
Brooke St EC1 225 P4
Brooke's Ct EC1 225 P3
Brookes Mkt EC1 225 Q3
Brookmill Rd SE8 223 C4
Brook's Ms W1 224 D7
Broom Rd, Tedd. TW11 221 B6
Broomwood Rd SW11 221 D5
Brown Hart Gdns W1 224 C7
Brownhill Rd SE6 223 C5
Browning Ms W1 224 D4
Browning Rd E12 222 D2
Brownlow Ms WC1 225 N2
Brownlow Rd N11 222 A1
Brownlow St WC1 225 N4
Bruce Gro N17 222 B1
Brunswick Cen WC1 225 K1
Brunswick Ms W1 224 A5
Brunswick Rd W5 220 B3
Brunswick Sq WC1 225 L2
Bruton La W1 224 E8
Bruton Pl W1 224 E8
Bruton St W1 224 E8
Brydges Pl WC2 224 K8
Buckhold Rd SW18 221 D5
Buckingham Arc WC2 225 L8
Buckingham Gate SW1 224 F12
Buckingham Ms SW1 224 F13
Buckingham Pl SW1 224 F13
Buckingham St WC2 225 L8
Buckley St SE1 225 P10
Bucknall St WC2 224 J5
Bugsby's Way SE7; SE10 223 D4
Bull Inn Ct WC2 225 L8
Bull Wf La EC4 225 U7
Bulstrode Pl W1 224 C4
Bulstrode St W1 224 C5
Bunns La NW7 220 C1
Burdett Rd E3; E14 222 C3
Burdett St SE1 225 P13
Burges Rd E6 222 D2
Burgon St EC4 225 S6
Burleigh St WC2 225 M7
Burlington Arc W1 224 F8
Burlington Gdns W1 224 F8
Burlington La W4 221 C4
Burlington Rd, N.Mal. KT3 221 C6
Burnt Ash Hill SE12 223 D5
Burnt Ash La, Brom. BR1 223 D6
Burnt Ash Rd SE12 223 C5
Burnt Oak Bdy, Edg. HA8 220 B1
Burntwood La SW17 221 D5
Burrage Rd SE18 223 D4
Burrell St SE1 225 R9
Burrows Ms SE1 225 R11
Bury Pl WC1 225 K4
Bury St SW1 224 F9
Bush Rd E11 222 D2
Bushey Rd SW20 221 C6
Butler Pl SW1 224 H13
Byng Pl WC1 224 H2
Bywell Pl W1 224 F4

C

Cable St E1 222 B3
Cadogan La SW1 224 B14
Cadogan Pl SW1 224 A14
Cadogan Sq SW1 224 A14
Cahill St EC1 225 U2
Caleb St SE1 225 T11
Caledonian Rd N1; N7 222 A2
Calmont Rd, Brom. BR1 223 C6
Calthorpe St WC1 225 N1
Camberwell Ch St SE5 223 B4
Camberwell New Rd SE5 223 A4
Camberwell Rd SE5 223 B4
Cambridge Circ WC2 224 J6
Cambridge Heath Rd E1; E2 222 B3
Camden High St NW1 222 A3
Camden Rd N7; NW1 222 A2
Camrose Av, Edg. HA8 220 B1
Candover St W1 224 F4
Cannizaro Rd SW19 221 C6
Cannon St EC4 225 T6
Cannon St Rd E1 222 B3
Canon Row SW1 225 K12
Canonbury Rd N1 222 A2
Canvey St SE1 225 S9
Capel Rd E7; E12 222 D2
Capener's Cl SW1 224 B12
Capper St WC1 224 G2
Capworth St E10 222 C2
Carburton St W1 224 E3
Carey La EC2 225 T5
Carey St WC2 225 N6
Carlisle La SE1 225 N14
Carlisle Pl SW1 224 F14
Carlisle St W1 224 H6
Carlos Pl W1 224 C8
Carlton Gdns SW1 224 H10
Carlton Ho Ter SW1 224 H10
Carlton St SW1 224 H8
Carlton Twr Pl SW1 224 A13
Carmelite St EC4 225 Q7
Carnaby St W1 224 F6
Carpenter St W1 224 D8
Carpenters Rd E15 222 C2
Carr Rd, Nthlt. UB5 220 A2
Carrington St W1 224 D10
Carter La EC4 225 S6
Carteret St SW1 224 H12
Carthusian St EC1 225 T3
Carting La WC2 225 L8
Carton St W1 224 A5
Cassland Rd E9 222 B2
Castelnau SW13 221 C4
Castle Baynard St EC4 225 S7
Castle La SW1 224 G13
Castle Yd SE1 225 S9
Castlebar Hill W5 220 B3
Castlebar Rd W5 220 B3
Catford Hill SE6 223 C5
Catford Rd SE6 223 C5
Cathall Rd E11 222 C2
Cathedral Piazza SW1 224 F14
Cathedral Pl EC4 225 T5
Catherine Griffiths Ct EC1 225 Q1
Catherine Pl SW1 224 F13
Catherine St WC2 225 M7
Catherine Wheel Yd SW1 224 F10
Catton St WC1 225 M4
Cavendish Ms N W1 224 E3
Cavendish Ms S W1 224 E4
Cavendish Pl W1 224 E5
Cavendish Rd SW12 223 A5
Cavendish Sq W1 224 E5
Caxton St SW1 224 G13
Cazenove Rd N16 222 B2
Cecil Ct WC2 224 J8
Cedars Rd SW4 223 A5
Cedars Rd W4 221 B4
Centaur St SE1 225 N13
Central Av, Houns. TW3 221 A5
Central Hill SE19 223 B6

Central Mkts EC1 225 S4
Central Pk Rd E6 222 D3
Centre Rd E7; E11 222 D2
Centrepoint WC2 224 J5
Chadwick St SW1 224 J14
Chalk Fm Rd NW1 222 A2
Chamberlayne Rd NW10 220 C3
Chancel St SE1 225 R9
Chancery La WC2 225 P5
Chandos Pl WC2 225 K8
Chandos St W1 224 E4
Chapel Pl W1 224 D6
Chapel St SW1 224 C13
Chaplin Cl SE1 225 Q11
Chapone Pl W1 224 H6
Chapter Ho Ct EC4 225 T6
Charing Cross SW1 224 K9
Charing Cross Rd WC2 224 J5
Charles II St SW1 224 H9
Charles St W1 224 D9
Charlotte Ms W1 224 G3
Charlotte Pl W1 224 G4
Charlotte St W1 224 G4
Charlton Ch La SE7 223 D4
Charlton Pk La SE7 223 D4
Charlton Pk Rd SE7 223 D4
Charlton Rd SE3; SE7 223 D4
Charlton Rd, Har. HA3 220 B1
Charlton Way SE3 223 C4
Charter Rd, The, Wdf.Grn. IG8 222 C1
Charterhouse Bldgs EC1 225 S2
Charterhouse Ms EC1 225 S3
Charterhouse Sq EC1 225 S3
Charterhouse St EC1 225 Q4
Chase, The, Stan. HA7 220 B1
Chase Rd NW10; W3 220 C3
Cheapside EC2 225 U6
Chelsea Embk SW3 223 A4
Chenies Ms WC1 224 H2
Chenies St WC1 224 H3
Chepstow Rd W2 220 D3
Chequer St EC1 225 U2
Cherry Tree Wk EC1 225 U2
Chertsey Rd, Twick. TW1, TW2 221 A5
Chesham Cl SW1 224 B14
Chesham Ms SW1 224 B13
Chesham Pl SW1 224 B14
Chesham St SW1 224 B14
Cheshire Ct EC4 225 Q6
Chester Cl SW1 224 C12
Chester Ms SW1 224 D13
Chester Sq Ms SW1 224 D14
Chester St SW1 224 C13
Chesterfield Gdns W1 224 D9
Chesterfield Hill W1 224 D8
Chesterfield St W1 224 D9
Cheyne Wk SW10 221 D4
Chichele Rd NW2 220 C2
Chicheley St SE1 225 N11
Chichester Rents WC2 225 P5
Chigwell Rd, E18; Wdf.Grn. IG8 222 D1
Chiltern St W1 224 B3
Chinbrook Rd SE12 223 D5
Ching Ct WC2 224 K6
Chingford Rd E4; E17 222 C1
Chislehurst Rd, Brom. BR1; Chis. BR7 223 D6
Chiswell St EC1 225 U3
Chiswick High Rd W4; Brent. TW8 221 B4
Chiswick La W4 221 C4
Chitty St W1 224 G3
Chobham Rd E15 222 C2
Chrisp St E14 222 C3
Christ Ch Pas EC1 225 S5
Christchurch Av, Har. HA3 220 B1
Christchurch Rd SW2 223 A5
Church Entry EC4 225 S6
Church Gro, Kings.T. KT1 221 B6
Church La E11 222 C2
Church La NW9 220 C1
Church La SW17 223 A6
Church Pl SW1 224 G8
Church Rd E10 222 C2
Church Rd NW10 220 C2
Church Rd SE19 223 B6
Church Rd SW13 221 C4
Church Rd SW19 221 C6
Church Rd W7 220 A3
Church Rd (Heston), Houns. TW5 221 A4
Church Rd, Mitch. CR4 221 D6
Church St, Hmptn. TW12 221 A6
City Rd EC1 222 A3
Clapham Common N Side SW4 223 A5
Clapham Common S Side SW4 223 A5
Clapham Pk Rd SW4 223 A5
Clapham Rd SW9 223 A4
Clapton Common E5 222 B2
Clare Mkt WC2 225 M6
Claremont Rd NW2 220 C2
Clarence Av, N.Mal. KT3 221 C6
Clarence La SW15 221 C5
Clarence Ter NW1 224 A1
Clarges Ms W1 224 D9
Clarges St W1 224 E9
Clarke's Ms W1 224 C3
Clay St W1 224 A4
Clayton Rd SE15 223 B4
Clement's Inn WC2 225 N6
Clement's Inn Pas WC2 225 N6
Clennam St SE1 225 U11
Clerkenwell Cl EC1 225 Q1
Clerkenwell Grn EC1 225 Q2
Clerkenwell Rd EC1 225 P2
Cleveland Ms W1 224 F3
Cleveland Pl SW1 224 G9
Cleveland Row SW1 224 F10
Cleveland St W1 224 F2
Clifford Av SW14 221 B5
Clifford St W1 224 F8
Clifford's Inn Pas EC4 225 P6
Clifton Gdns W9 220 D3
Clink St SE1 225 U9
Clipstone Ms W1 224 F2
Clipstone St W1 224 E3
Cloak La EC4 225 U7
Cloth Ct EC1 225 S4
Cloth Fair EC1 225 S4
Cloth St EC1 225 T3
Coach & Horses Yd W1 224 E7
Cock La EC1 225 R4
Cockpit Steps SW1 224 J12
Cockpit Yd WC1 225 N3
Cockspur Ct SW1 224 J9
Cockspur St SW1 224 J9
Coin St SE1 225 P9
Coldbath Sq EC1 225 P1
Coldharbour La SE5; SW9 223 A5
Cole St SE1 225 U12
Coley St WC1 225 N2
Colindale Av NW9 220 C1
Colindeep La NW4; NW9 220 C1
College Hill EC4 225 U7
College Hill Rd, Har. HA3 220 A1
College Ms SW1 225 K13
College Rd SE19; SE21 223 B5
College Rd, Brom. BR1 223 D6
College Rd, Har. HA1 220 A1
Collinson St SE1 225 T12
Collinson Wk SE1 225 T12
Colnbrook St SE1 225 R14
Colney Hatch La N10; N11 220 D1
Colombo St SE1 225 R10
Colonnade WC1 225 K2
Colville Pl W1 224 G4
Commercial Rd E1; E14 222 B3
Commercial St E1 222 B3
Commercial Way SE15 223 B4
Commonside E, Mitch. CR4 223 A6
Commonside W, Mitch. CR4 221 D6
Compton Pas EC1 225 S1
Compton Pl WC1 225 K1
Compton St EC1 225 R1
Concert Hall App SE1 225 N10
Conduit Ct WC2 225 K7
Conduit St W1 224 E7
Coningham Rd W12 220 C3
Connaught Rd E16 222 D3
Cons St SE1 225 Q11
Constitution Hill SW1 224 D11
Conway Ms W1 224 F2
Conway St W1 224 F2
Cool Oak La NW9 220 C2
Coombe La SW20 221 C6
Coombe La W, Kings.T. KT2 221 B6
Coombe Rd, Kings.T. KT2 221 B6
Coombe Rd, N.Mal. KT3 221 C6
Cooper Cl SE1 225 Q12
Copenhagen St N1 222 A3
Copperfield St SE1 225 S11
Coppetts Rd N10 222 A1
Copse Hill SW20 221 C6
Coptic St WC1 224 K4
Coral St SE1 225 Q12
Coram St WC1 224 K2
Cork St W1 224 F8
Cork St Ms W1 224 F8
Corner Ho St WC2 225 K9
Cornwall Rd SE1 225 P9
Cornwall Ter NW1 224 A2
Cornwall Ter Ms NW1 224 A2
Coronation Rd NW10 220 B3
Corporation Row EC1 225 Q1
Cosmo Pl WC1 225 L3
Cosser St SE1 225 P13
Cottenham Pk Rd SW20 221 C6
Cottesloe Ms SE1 225 Q13
County St SE1 225 U14
Court Rd SE9 223 D5
Courtenay Av, Har. HA3 220 A1
Covent Gdn WC2 225 L7
Coventry St W1 224 H8
Cowcross St EC1 225 R3
Cowley St SW1 224 K13
Crab Hill, Beck. BR3 223 C6
Craigs Ct SW1 224 K9
Cramer St W1 224 C4
Cranbourn All WC2 224 J7
Cranbourn St WC2 224 J7
Cranbrook Rd, Ilf. IG1, IG2, IG6 222 D1
Crane Ct EC4 225 Q6
Cranfield Row SE1 225 Q13
Cranley Gdns N10 222 A1
Cranmer Rd, Mitch. CR4 221 D6
Craven Pk NW10 220 C3
Craven Pas WC2 225 K9
Craven St WC2 225 K9
Crawford Pas EC1 225 P2
Creed La EC4 225 S6
Creek Rd SE8; SE10 223 C4
Creighton Av N2; N10 220 D1
Crescent Row EC1 225 T2
Cricklewood Bdy NW2 220 C2
Cricklewood La NW2 220 D2
Cripplegate St EC2 225 T3
Cromwell Rd SW5; SW7 221 D4
Cromwell Twr EC2 225 U3
Cross Deep, Twick. TW1 221 A5
Cross Keys Cl W1 224 C4
Cross Keys Sq EC1 225 T4
Crossway SW20 221 C6
Crouch End Hill N8 222 A2
Crouch Hill N4; N8 222 A1
Crown Ct EC2 225 U6
Crown Ct WC2 225 L6
Crown Dale SE19 223 B6
Crown La SW16 223 A6
Crown La, Mord. SM4 221 D6
Crown Office Row EC4 225 P7
Crown Pas SW1 224 G10
Crown Rd, Twick. TW1 221 B5
Crowshott Av, Stan. HA7 220 B1
Croxted Rd SE21; SE24 223 B5
Croydon Rd SE20 223 B6
Croydon Rd, Beck. BR3 223 C6
Crystal Palace Par SE19 223 B6
Crystal Palace Pk Rd SE26 223 B6
Cubitts Yd WC2 225 L7
Culross St W1 224 B8
Culver Gro, Stan. HA7 220 B1
Currey Rd, Grnf. UB6 220 A2
Cursitor St EC4 225 P5
Curzon Gate W1 224 C10
Curzon Pl W1 224 C10
Curzon St W1 224 C10
Cut, The SE1 225 Q11
Cypress Pl W1 224 G2
Cyrus St EC1 225 S1

D

Dacre St SW1 224 H13
Dallington St EC1 225 S1
Dalston La E8 222 B2
Dames Rd E7 222 D2
Dane St WC1 225 M4
Dansey Pl W1 224 H7
D'Arblay St W1 224 G6
Dartmouth Pk Hill N19; NW5 222 A2
Dartmouth Rd SE23; SE26 223 B5
Dartmouth St SW1 224 H12
David Ms W1 224 A3
Davidge St SE1 225 R12
Davies Ms W1 224 D7
Davies St W1 224 D7
Dawes Rd SW6 221 D4
De Walden St W1 224 C4
Dean Bradley St SW1 225 K14
Dean Farrar St SW1 224 H13
Dean Stanley St SW1 225 K14
Dean St W1 224 H5
Dean Trench St SW1 224 K14
Deanery Ms W1 224 C9
Deanery St W1 224 C9
Deans Ct EC4 225 S6
Deans La, Edg. HA8 220 C1
Deans Ms W1 224 E5
Dean's Yd SW1 224 J13
Deansbrook Rd, Edg. HA8 220 B1
Defoe Ho EC2 225 U3
Denman St W1 224 H8
Denmark Hill SE5 223 B5
Denmark Pl WC2 224 J5
Denmark St WC2 224 J6
Deptford Ch St SE8 223 C4
Derby Gate SW1 225 K11
Derby St W1 224 C10
Dering St W1 224 D6
Devas St E3 222 C3
Devereux Ct WC2 225 P6
Devons Rd E3 222 C3
Devonshire Cl W1 224 D3
Devonshire Ms N W1 224 D3
Devonshire Ms S W1 224 D3
Devonshire Ms W W1 224 D2
Devonshire Pl W1 224 C2
Devonshire Pl Ms W1 224 C2
Devonshire Rd NW7 220 C1
Devonshire Rd SE23 223 B5
Devonshire Row Ms W1 224 E2
Devonshire St W1 224 C3
Diadem Ct W1 224 H6
Diana Pl NW1 224 E1
Dickens Sq SE1 225 U13
Disney Pl SE1 225 U11
Disney St SE1 225 U11
Distaff La EC4 225 T7
Dodson St SE1 225 Q12
Dog Kennel Hill SE22 223 B5
Dolben St SE1 225 R10
Dolby Ct EC4 225 U7
Dollis Hill La NW2 220 C2
Dollis Rd N3; NW7 220 D1
Dombey St WC1 225 M3
Domingo St EC1 225 T1
Doon St SE1 225 P10
Dorrington St EC1 225 P3
Dorset Bldgs EC4 225 R6
Dorset Ms SW1 224 D13
Dorset Ri EC4 225 R6
Dorset Rd SW19 221 D6
Dorset St W1 224 A4
Doughty Ms WC1 225 M2
Doughty St WC1 225 M1
Dover Ho Rd SW15 221 C5
Dover St W1 224 E8
Dover Yd W1 224 F9
Down St W1 224 D10
Down St Ms W1 224 D10
Downham Way, Brom. BR1 223 C6
Downhills Way N17 222 B1
Downing St SW1 224 K11
Doyce St SE1 225 T11
Drake St WC1 225 M4
Drakefell Rd SE4; SE14 223 B5
Draycott Av, Har. HA3 220 B1
Drayton Grn Rd W13 220 B3
Drayton Pk N5 222 A2
Drive, The, Ilf. IG1 222 D2
Drummond St NW1 224 F1
Drury La WC2 225 L6
Drury Way NW10 220 C2
Dryden St WC2 225 L6
Duchess Ms W1 224 E4
Duchess St W1 224 E4
Duchy St SE1 225 Q9
Duck La W1 224 H6
Dudden Hill La NW10 220 C2
Dufferin St EC1 225 U2
Dufour's Pl W1 224 G6
Duke of Wellington Pl SW1 224 C11
Duke of York St SW1 224 G9
Duke St SW1 224 G9
Duke St W1 224 C5
Dukes Av, Rich. TW10; Kings.T. KT2 221 B6
Duke's Ms W1 224 C5
Duke's Yd W1 224 C7
Dulwich Common SE21; SE22 223 B5
Dulwich Rd SE24 223 A5
Dulwich Village SE21 223 B5
Dulwich Wd Pk SE19 223 B6
Duncannon St WC2 225 K8
Dunns Pas WC1 225 L5
Dunraven St W1 224 A7
Dunstable Ms W1 224 C3
Dunton Rd SE1 223 B4
Duplex Ride SW1 224 A12
Durham Ho St WC2 225 L8
Durham Rd SW20 221 C6
Durnsford Rd N11 222 A1
Durnsford Rd SW19 221 D5
Durweston Ms W1 224 A3
Durweston St W1 224 A3
Dyer's Bldgs EC1 225 P4
Dyott St WC1 224 K5

E

Eagle Ct EC1 225 R3
Eagle Pl SW1 224 G8
Eagle St WC1 225 M4
Ealing Grn W5 220 B3
Ealing Rd, Brent. TW8 221 B4
Ealing Rd, Wem. HA0 220 B2
Earlham St WC2 224 J6
Earls Ct Rd SW5; W8 221 D4
Earlsfield Rd SW18 221 D5
Earnshaw St WC2 224 J5
Easley's Ms W1 224 C5
East Av E12 222 D2
East Cross Route E3 222 C2
East Dulwich Gro SE22 223 B5
East Dulwich Rd SE15; SE22 223 B5
East End Rd N2; N3 220 D1
East Ferry Rd E14 223 C4
East Harding St EC4 225 Q5
East Heath Rd NW3 220 D2
East Hill SW18 221 D5
East India Dock Rd E14 222 C3
East La, Wem. HA0 220 B2
East Pas EC1 225 S3
East Poultry Av EC1 225 R4
East Rd N1 222 B3
East St SE17 223 B4
Eastcastle St W1 224 F5
Eastcote La, Har. HA2 220 A2
Eastcote La, Nthlt. UB5 220 A2
Eastern Av E11; Ilf. IG2, IG4 222 D1
Eastway E9; E10; E15 222 C2
Eaton La SW1 224 E14
Eaton Pl SW1 224 B14
Eaton Ri W5 220 B3
Eaton Row SW1 224 D14
Eaton Sq SW1 224 D13
Eccleston Ms SW1 224 C14
Eccleston St SW1 224 D14
Eden Pk Av, Beck. BR3 223 C6
Eden St, Kings.T. KT1 221 B6
Edgware Rd NW2 220 C2
Edgware Rd NW9 220 C1
Edgware Rd W2 220 D3
Edwards Ms W1 224 B6
Effra Rd SW2 223 A5
Elder Rd SE27 223 B6
Elephant & Castle SE1 225 S14
Elgin Av W9 220 D3
Elizabeth Ct SW1 224 J14
Ellesmere Rd W4 221 C4
Elm Ct EC4 225 P7
Elm St WC1 225 N2
Elmers End Rd, SE20; Beck. BR3 223 B6
Elms Rd, Har. HA3 220 A1
Elmstead La, Chis. BR7 223 D6
Eltham High St SE9 223 D5
Eltham Hill SE9 223 D5
Eltham Rd SE9; SE12 223 D5
Ely Ct EC1 225 Q4
Ely Pl EC1 225 Q4
Embankment Pl WC2 225 L9
Emerald St WC1 225 M3
Emerson St SE1 225 T9
Emery Hill St SW1 224 G14
Emery St SE1 225 Q13
Emlyn Rd W12 221 C4
Emmanuel Rd SW12 223 A5
Empire Way, Wem. HA9 220 B2
Endell St WC2 225 K5
Endsleigh Gdns WC1 224 H1
Endsleigh Pl WC1 224 J1
Endsleigh St WC1 224 H1
Endymion Rd N4 222 A2
Englefield Rd N1 222 B2
Errol St EC1 225 U2
Essex Ct EC4 225 P6
Essex Rd N1 222 A3
Essex St WC2 225 P7
Euston Rd NW1 224 E2
Euston St NW1 224 G1
Evelina Rd SE15 223 B4
Evelyn St SE8 223 C4
Evelyn Yd W1 224 H5
Ewer St SE1 225 T10
Excel Ct WC2 224 J8
Exchange Ct WC2 225 L8
Exeter St WC2 225 L7
Exmouth Mkt EC1 225 P1
Exton St SE1 225 P10
Eyre St Hill EC1 225 P2

F

Fairfield Rd E3 222 C3
Fairfield S, Kings.T. KT1 221 B6
Falcon Cl SE1 225 S9
Falcon Ct EC4 225 P6
Falcon Rd SW11 221 D4
Falconberg Ct W1 224 J5
Falconberg Ms W1 224 H5
Falloden Way NW11 220 D1
Falmouth Rd SE1 225 U13
Fann St EC1 225 T2
Fann St EC2 225 T2
Fareham St W1 224 H5
Farm St W1 224 D8
Farnaby Rd, Brom. BR1, BR2 223 C6
Farnham Pl SE1 225 S10
Farringdon La EC1 225 Q2
Farringdon Rd EC1 225 P1
Farringdon St EC4 225 R5
Faulkner's All EC1 225 R3
Fentiman Rd SW8 223 A4
Fern La, Houns. TW5 221 A4
Fernhead Rd W9 220 D3
Ferry La N17 222 B1
Ferry Rd SW13 221 C4
Fetter La EC4 225 Q6
Field Ct WC1 225 N4
Finborough Rd SW10; SW17 221 D4
Finchley La NW4 220 C1
Finchley Rd NW2; NW3; NW8; NW11 220 D2
Finck St SE1 225 N12
Fisher St WC1 225 M4
Fitzhardinge St W1 224 B5
Fitzjohns Av NW3 220 D2
Fitzmaurice Pl W1 224 E9
Fitzroy Ct W1 224 G2
Fitzroy Ms W1 224 F2
Fitzroy Sq W1 224 F2
Fitzroy St W1 224 F2
Flaxman Ct W1 224 H6
Fleet St EC4 225 P6
Flitcroft St WC2 224 J5
Floral St WC2 225 K7
Foley St W1 224 F4
Footscray Rd SE9 223 D5
Fore St EC2 225 U4
Fore St N9; N18 222 B1
Forest Dr E12 222 D2
Forest Hill Rd SE22; SE23 223 B5
Forest La E7; E15 222 C2
Forest Ri E17 222 C1
Forest Rd E17 222 B1
Fortess Rd NW5 222 A2
Fortis Grn N2; N10 220 D1
Fortune Grn Rd NW6 220 D2
Fortune St EC1 225 U2
Forty Av, Wem. HA9 220 B2
Forty La, Wem. HA9 220 B2
Foster La EC2 225 T5
Foubert's Pl W1 224 F6
Foundry Ms NW1 224 G1
Fountain Ct EC4 225 P7
Fourth Av E12 222 D2
Fox & Knot St EC1 225 S3
Foxgrove Rd, Beck. BR3 223 C6
Frances St SE18 223 D4
Francis Rd E10 222 C2
Frazier St SE1 225 P12
Frederic Ms SW1 224 A12
Freemason's Rd E16 222 D3
Friar St EC4 225 S6
Friary Ct SW1 224 G10
Friday St EC4 225 T6
Frith La NW7 220 D1
Frith St W1 224 H6
Fryent Way NW9 220 B1
Fulbourne Rd E17 222 C1
Fulham Palace Rd SW6; W6 221 C4
Fulham Rd SW3; SW10 221 D4
Fulham Rd SW6 221 D4
Fulwood Pl WC1 225 N4
Furnival St EC4 225 P5

G

Gage St WC1 225 L3
Galen Pl WC1 225 L4
Galpins Rd, Th.Hth. CR7 223 A6
Gambia St SE1 225 S10
Ganton St W1 224 F7
Gap Rd SW19 221 D6
Garbutt Pl W1 224 C3
Garden Ct EC4 225 P7
Garden Row SE1 225 R14
Gardners La EC4 225 T7
Garlick Hill EC4 225 U7
Garnet St E1 222 B3
Garrad's Rd SW16 223 A5
Garratt La SW17; SW18 221 D5
Garrett St EC1 225 U1
Garrick St WC2 224 K7
Gate St WC2 225 M5
Gaunt St SE1 225 T13
Gayfere St SW1 224 K14
Gaywood Est SE1 225 S14
Gaywood St SE1 225 S14
Gee St EC1 225 T1
Gees Ct W1 224 C6
Gellatly Rd SE14 223 B4
George Ct WC2 225 L8
George Rd, Kings.T. KT2 221 B6
George St W1 224 A5
George St, Rich. TW9 221 B5
George Yd W1 224 C7
Geraldine St SE11 225 R14
Gerrard Pl W1 224 J7
Gerrard St W1 224 H7
Gerridge St SE1 225 Q12
Gervase Rd, Edg. HA8 220 C1
Gilbert Pl WC1 225 K4
Gilbert St W1 224 C7
Gildea St W1 224 E4
Gillespie Rd N5 222 A2
Giltspur St EC1 225 S5
Gipsy Hill SE19 223 B6
Gipsy Rd SE27 223 B6
Gladstone St SE1 225 R13
Glasshill St SE1 225 S11
Glasshouse All EC4 225 Q6
Glasshouse St W1 224 G8
Glasshouse Yd EC1 225 T3
Glentworth St NW1 224 A2
Globe Rd E1; E2 222 B3
Globe St SE1 225 U13
Globe Yd W1 224 D6
Gloucester Pl W1 224 A3
Gloucester Pl Ms W1 224 A4
Gloucester Rd SW7 221 D4
Gloucester Rd, Kings.T. KT1 221 B6
Goddard Rd, Beck. BR3 223 B6
Godliman St EC4 225 T6
Goffers Rd SE3 223 C4
Golden La EC1 225 T2
Golden La Est EC1 225 T2
Golden Sq W1 224 G7
Golders Grn Rd NW11 220 D1
Goldhawk Rd W6; W12 221 C4
Goldsmith St EC2 225 U5
Goodge Pl W1 224 G4
Goodge St W1 224 G4
Goodwins Ct WC2 224 K7
Gordon Av, Stan. HA7 220 A1
Gordon Sq WC1 224 J2
Gordon St WC1 224 H1
Gosfield St W1 224 F3
Goslett Yd WC2 224 J6
Goswell Rd EC1 225 T2
Gough Sq EC4 225 Q5
Gough St WC1 225 N1
Gower Ct WC1 224 H1
Gower Ms WC1 224 H4
Gower Pl WC1 224 G1
Gower St WC1 224 H2
Grafton Ms W1 224 F2
Grafton St W1 224 E8
Grafton Way W1 224 F2
Grafton Way WC1 224 F2
Graham Rd E8 222 B2
Grahame Pk Way NW7; NW9 220 C1
Grand Av EC1 225 S3
Grand Depot Rd SE18 223 D4
Grand Dr SW20 221 C6
Grange Ct WC2 225 N6
Grange Rd E13 222 C3
Grange Rd SE1 223 B4
Grange Rd SE19; SE25; Th.Hth. CR7 223 B6
Grantham Pl W1 224 D10
Granville Pl W1 224 B6
Grape St WC2 225 K5
Gray St SE1 225 Q12
Gray's Inn WC1 225 N3
Gray's Inn Pl WC1 225 N4
Gray's Inn Rd WC1 222 A3
Gray's Inn Sq WC1 225 N3
Gray's Yd W1 224 C6
Great Cambridge Rd N17 222 B1
Great Castle St W1 224 E5
Great Cen Way NW10; Wem. HA9 220 C2
Great Chapel St W1 224 H5
Great Chertsey Rd W4 221 C4
Great Chertsey Rd (Whitton), Felt. TW13 221 A5
Great College St SW1 224 K13
Great Dover St SE1 225 U12
Great George St SW1 224 J12
Great Guildford St SE1 225 T9
Great James St WC1 225 M2
Great Marlborough St W1 224 F6
Great New St EC4 225 Q5
Great N Rd N2 220 D1
Great N Way NW4 220 C1
Great Ormond St WC1 225 L3
Great Peter St SW1 224 H14
Great Portland St W1 224 E3
Great Pulteney St W1 224 G7
Great Queen St WC2 225 L6
Great Russell St WC1 224 J5
Great St. Thomas Apostle EC4 225 U7
Great Scotland Yd SW1 224 K10
Great Smith St SW1 224 J13
Great Suffolk St SE1 225 S10
Great Sutton St EC1 225 S2
Great Titchfield St W1 224 F5
Great Trinity La EC4 225 U7
Great Turnstile WC1 225 N4
Great W Rd W4; W6 221 C4
Great W Rd, Brent. TW8; Houns. TW5; Islw. TW7 221 A4
Great Western Rd W2; W9; W11 220 D3

Great Windmill St W1 224 H7
Greek Ct W1 224 J6
Greek St W1 224 J6
Greek Yd WC2 224 K7
Green, The, Sthl. UB2 221 A4
Green, The, Twick. TW2 221 A5
Green Arbour Ct EC1 225 R5
Green La SE9; Chis. BR7 223 D5
Green La SW16 223 A6
Green Las N4; N8; N15; N16 222 A1
Green St E7; E13 222 D2
Green St W1 224 B7
Greencoat Row SW1 224 G14
Greenford Av W7 220 A3
Greenford Rd, Grnf. UB6; Sthl. UB1 220 A3
Greengate St E13 222 D3
Greenham Cl SE1 225 P12
Greenhill Way, Har. HA1 220 A1
Greenhill's Rents EC1 225 S3
Green's Ct W1 224 H7
Greenwell St W1 224 E2
Greenwich High Rd SE10 223 C4
Greenwich S St SE10 223 C4
Greet St SE1 225 Q10
Grenville St WC1 225 L2
Gresham St EC2 225 T5
Gresse St W1 224 H4
Greville St EC1 225 Q4
Greycoat Pl SW1 224 H14
Greycoat St SW1 224 H14
Greyfriars Pas EC1 225 S5
Greyhound La SW16 223 A6
Greystoke Pl EC4 225 P5
Grindal St SE1 225 P12
Groom Pl SW1 224 C13
Grosvenor Cres SW1 224 C12
Grosvenor Cres Ms SW1 224 B12
Grosvenor Gdns SW1 224 D13
Grosvenor Gdns Ms E SW1 224 E13
Grosvenor Gdns Ms N SW1 224 D14
Grosvenor Gdns Ms S SW1 224 E14
Grosvenor Gate W1 224 A8
Grosvenor Hill W1 224 D7
Grosvenor Pl SW1 224 C12
Grosvenor Rd N10 222 A1
Grosvenor Rd SW1 223 A4
Grosvenor Sq W1 224 C7
Grosvenor St W1 224 D7
Grotto Pas W1 224 C3
Grove End Rd NW8 220 D3
Grove Grn Rd E11 222 C2
Grove La SE5 223 B4
Grove La, Kings.T. KT1 221 B6
Grove Pk Rd SE9 223 D5
Grove Rd E3 222 C3
Grove Rd E17 222 C1
Grove Rd, Mitch.CR4 223 A6
Grove St SE8 223 C4
Grove Vale SE22 223 B5
Groveland Ct EC4 225 U6
Guilford Pl WC1 225 M2
Guilford St WC1 225 K2
Gunnersbury Av W3; W4; W5 220 B3
Gunnersbury La W3 221 B4
Gunpowder Sq EC4 225 Q5
Gutter La EC2 225 U5

H

Ha-Ha Rd SE18 223 D4
Hackney Rd E2 222 B3
Hale End Rd E4; E17; Wdf.Grn. IG8 222 C1
Half Acre, Brent. TW8 221 B4
Half Moon Ct EC1 225 T4
Half Moon La SE24 223 B5
Half Moon St W1 224 E9
Halkin Arc SW1 224 B13
Halkin Ms SW1 224 B13
Halkin Pl SW1 224 B13
Halkin St SW1 224 C12
Hall Rd, Islw. TW7 221 A5
Hallam Ms W1 224 E3
Hallam St W1 224 E2
Ham Gate Av, Rich. TW10 221 B5
Ham Pk Rd E7; E15 222 C2
Ham St, Rich. TW10 221 B5
Ham Yd W1 224 H7
Hamilton Ms W1 224 D11
Hamilton Pl W1 224 C10
Hammersmith Gro W6 221 C4
Hammersmith Rd W6; W14 221 C4
Hampstead La N6; NW3 220 D2
Hampstead Rd NW1 222 A3
Hampton Ct Rd, E.Mol. KT8; Hmptn. TW12; Kings.T. KT1 221 A6
Hampton Rd, Hmptn. TW12 221 A6
Hampton Rd, Twick. TW2 221 A5
Hampton Rd E, Felt. TW13 221 A6
Hampton Rd W, Felt. TW13 221 A5
Hand Ct WC1 225 N4
Handel St WC1 225 K1
Hanger La W5 220 B3
Hanover Pl WC2 225 L6
Hanover Sq W1 224 E6
Hanover St W1 224 E6
Hans Pl SW1 224 A13
Hans St SW1 224 A14
Hanson St W1 224 F3
Hanway Pl W1 224 H5
Hanway St W1 224 H5
Hanworth Rd, Hmptn. TW12 221 A6
Hanworth Rd, Houns. TW3, TW4 221 A5
Hare Ct EC4 225 P6
Hare Pl EC4 225 Q6
Harewood Pl W1 224 E6
Harlesden Rd NW10 220 C3
Harley Pl W1 224 D4
Harley St W1 224 D4
Harmsworth Ms SE11 225 R14
Harold Rd E13 222 D3
Harold Rd SE19 223 B6
Harp All EC4 225 R5
Harper Rd SE1 225 T13
Harpur Ms WC1 225 M3
Harpur St WC1 225 M3
Harriet St SW1 224 A12
Harriet Wk SW1 224 A12
Harrow Rd E11 222 C2
Harrow Rd NW10; W9; W10 220 C3
Harrow Rd, Wem. HA0 220 B2
Harrow Rd (Tokyngton), Wem. HA9 220 B2
Harrow Vw, Har. HA2, HA3 220 A1
Hartfield Rd SW19 221 D6
Harvist Rd NW6 220 C3
Hat and Mitre Ct EC1 225 S2
Hatfields SE1 225 Q9
Hatton Gdn EC1 225 Q3
Hatton Pl EC1 225 Q2
Hatton Wall EC1 225 P3
Haunch of Venison Yd W1 224 D6
Haven Grn W5 220 B3
Haverstock Hill NW3 220 D2
Hawks Rd, Kings.T. KT1 221 B6
Hay Hill W1 224 E8
Haydons Rd SW19 221 D6
Hayes La, Beck. BR3 223 C6
Hayes Rd, Brom. BR2 223 D6
Haymarket SW1 224 H8
Haymarket Arc SW1 224 H8
Hayne St EC1 225 S3
Hay's Ms W1 224 D8
Hayward's Pl EC1 225 R1
Headfort Pl SW1 224 C12
Headstone Rd, Har. HA1 220 A1
Heath Rd, Houns. TW3 221 A5
Heath Rd, Twick. TW1, TW2 221 A5
Heath St NW3 220 D2
Heathcote St WC1 225 M1
Heathfield Ter W4 221 C4
Heddon St W1 224 F7
Helmet Row EC1 225 U1
Hendon La N3 220 D1
Hendon Way NW2; NW4 220 C1
Henrietta Ms WC1 225 L1
Henrietta Pl W1 224 D6
Henrietta St WC2 225 L7
Herbal Hill EC1 225 Q2
Herbert Cres SW1 224 A13
Herbrand St WC1 224 K1
Hercules Rd SE1 225 N14
Hermit Rd E16 222 C3
Hermitage Rd SE19 223 B6
Hermon Hill E11; E18 222 D1
Herne Hill SE24 223 B5
Hertford Pl W1 224 F2
Hertford St W1 224 D9
Heston Rd, Houns. TW5 221 A4
High Holborn WC1 225 L5
High Rd N2 220 D1
High Rd N15 222 B1
High Rd N22 222 A1
High Rd NW10 220 C2
High Rd, Har. HA3 220 A1
High Rd, Wem. HA0 220 B2
High Rd, Wdf.Grn. IG8 222 C1
High Rd Leyton E10; E15 222 C2
High Rd Leytonstone E11; E15 222 C2
High St E11 222 D1
High St E13 222 D3
High St E15 222 C3
High St N8 222 A1
High St NW10 220 C3
High St SE20 223 B6
High St SE25 223 B6
High St W3 220 B3
High St, Beck. BR3 223 C6
High St, Brent. TW8 221 B4
High St, Brom. BR1 223 D6
High St, Chis. BR7 223 D6
High St, Hmptn. TW12 221 A6
High St (Hampton Wick), Kings.T. KT1 221 B6
High St, N.Mal. KT3 221 C6
High St, Sthl. UB1 220 A3
High St, Tedd. TW11 221 B6
High St, Th.Hth. CR7 223 B6
High St (Whitton), Twick. TW2 221 A5
High St Colliers Wd SW19 221 D6
High St N E6; E12 222 D2
High St S E6 222 D3
High St Wimbledon SW19 221 C6
High Timber St EC4 225 T7
Higham Hill Rd E17 222 C1
Highbury Gro N5 222 A2
Highbury Pk N5 222 A2
Highgate High St N6 222 A2
Highgate Hill N6; N19 222 A2
Highgate Rd NW5 222 A2
Highgate W Hill N6 222 A2
Highway, The E1; E14 222 B3
Hill St W1 224 C9
Hillreach SE18 223 D4
Hills Pl W1 224 F6
Hillside NW10 220 C2
Hind Ct EC4 225 Q6
Hinde St W1 224 C5
Hither Grn La SE13 223 C5
Hobart Pl SW1 224 D13
Hoe St E17 222 C1
Hogarth La W4 221 C4
Holborn EC1 225 P4
Holborn Circ EC1 225 Q4
Holborn Pl WC1 225 M4
Holborn Viaduct EC1 225 Q4
Holders Hill Rd NW4; NW7 220 C1
Holland Pk Av W11 221 C4
Holland Rd W14 221 D4
Holland St SE1 225 S9
Hollen St W1 224 H5
Holles St W1 224 E5
Holloway Rd N7; N19 222 A2
Hollybush Hill E11 222 C1
Holmes Ter SE1 225 P11
Holsworthy Sq WC1 225 N2
Homerton High St E9 222 B2
Homerton Rd E9 222 C2
Homesdale Rd, Brom. BR1, BR2 223 D6
Honduras St EC1 225 T1
Honey La EC2 225 U6
Honeypot La NW9; Stan. HA7 220 B1
Honor Oak Pk SE23 223 B5
Hood Ct EC4 225 Q6
Hop Gdns WC2 224 K8
Hopkins St W1 224 G6
Hopton Gdns SE1 225 S9
Hopton St SE1 225 S9
Horn La W3 220 C3
Hornfair Rd SE7 223 D4
Hornsey La N6; N19 222 A2
Hornsey Ri N19 222 A2
Hornsey Rd N7; N19 222 A2
Horse & Dolphin Yd W1 224 J7
Horse Guards Av SW1 225 K10
Horse Guards Rd SW1 224 J10
Horse Ride SW1 224 H10
Horseferry Rd SW1 224 H14
Horsenden La N, Grnf. UB6 220 A2
Horsenden La S, Grnf. UB6 220 B3
Hosier La EC1 225 R4
Hospital Br Rd, Twick. TW2 221 A5
Houghton St WC2 225 N6
Howard Pl SW1 224 F14
Howberry Rd, Edg. HA8; Stan. HA7 220 B1
Howick Pl SW1 224 G14
Howland Ms E W1 224 G3
Howland St W1 224 F3
Huggin Ct EC4 225 U7
Huggin Hill EC4 225 U7
Hungerford Br SE1 225 L9
Hungerford Br WC2 225 L9
Hungerford La WC2 225 K9
Hunter St WC1 225 L1
Huntley St WC1 224 G2
Hunt's Ct WC2 224 J8
Hurst La, E.Mol. KT8 221 A6
Hurst Rd, E.Mol. KT8; W.Mol. KT8 221 A6
Hutton St EC4 225 Q6
Hyde, The NW9 220 C1
Hyde Pk Cor W1 224 C11
Hyde Vale SE10 223 C4

I

Ilderton Rd SE15; SE16 223 B4
Ilford La, Ilf. IG1 222 D2
Imperial Dr, Har. HA2 220 A2
India Pl WC2 225 M7
Ingestre Pl W1 224 G6
Inigo Pl WC2 225 K7
Inner Temple La EC4 225 P6
Invicta Plaza SE1 225 R9
Ireland Yd EC4 225 S6
Ironmonger Pas EC1 225 U1
Ironmonger Row EC1 225 U1
Irving St WC2 224 J7
Isabella St SE1 225 R10
Ivybridge La WC2 225 L8

J

Jacob's Well Ms W1 224 C5
Jamaica Rd SE1; SE16 223 B4
James St W1 224 C5
James St WC2 225 L7
Jermyn St SW1 224 F9
Jersey Rd, Houns. TW5; Islw. TW7 221 A4
Jerusalem Pas EC1 225 R2
Jervis Ct W1 224 E6
Joan St SE1 225 R10
Jockey's Flds WC1 225 N3
Johanna St SE1 225 P12
John Adam St WC2 225 L8
John Carpenter St EC4 225 R7
John Princes St W1 224 E5
John Ruskin St SE5 223 A4
John St WC1 225 N2
John Wilson St SE18 223 D4
John's Ms WC1 225 N2
Jones St W1 224 D8
Judd St WC1 222 A3
Junction Rd N19 222 A2

K

Katherine Rd E6; E7 222 D2
Kean St WC2 225 M6
Keeley St WC2 225 M6
Kell St SE1 225 S13
Kemble St WC2 225 M6
Kemp's Ct W1 224 G6
Kendal Rd NW10 220 C2
Kendall Pl W1 224 B4
Kenley Rd, Kings.T. KT1 221 B6
Kenmore Av, Har. HA3 220 B1
Kenmore Rd, Har. HA3 220 B1
Kennet Wf La EC4 225 U7
Kennington La SE11 223 A4
Kennington Pk Rd SE11 223 A4
Kennington Rd SE1 225 P13
Kennington Rd SE11 225 P14
Kenrick Pl W1 224 B3
Kensington Ch St W8 220 D3
Kensington High St W8; W14 221 D4
Kensington Pk Rd W11 220 D3
Kensington Rd SW7; W8 221 D4
Kent Gdns W13 220 B3
Kent Ho Rd SE26; Beck. BR3 223 B6
Kentish Way, Brom. BR1 223 D6
Kenton La (Belmont), Har. HA3 220 B1
Kenton La (Harrow Weald), Har. HA3 220 A1
Kenton Rd, Har. HA3 220 B1
Kenton St WC1 225 K1
Keppel Row SE1 225 T10
Keppel St WC1 224 J3
Kew Br Rd, Brent. TW8 221 B4
Kew Rd, Rich. KT9 221 B4
Keyworth St SE1 225 S13
Kidbrooke Pk Rd SE3 223 D4
Kilburn High Rd NW6 220 D2
Kilburn La W9; W10 220 D3
Kilburn Pk Rd NW6 220 D3
King Charles St SW1 224 J11
King Edward St EC1 225 T5
King Edward Wk SE1 225 Q13
King James St SE1 225 S12
King St EC2 225 U6
King St SW1 224 G10
King St W6 221 C4
King St WC2 225 K7
King St, Twick. TW1 221 B5
Kinghorn St EC1 225 T4
Kingly Ct W1 224 F7
Kingly St W1 224 F6
King's Av SW4; SW12 223 A5
Kings Bench St SE1 225 S11
Kings Bench Wk EC4 225 Q6
King's Ms WC1 225 N2
Kings Pl SE1 225 T12
King's Reach Twr SE1 225 Q9
King's Rd SW1; SW3; SW6; SW10 221 D4
Kings Rd, Kings.T. KT2 221 B6
Kings Rd, Rich. TW10 221 B5
Kingsbury Rd NW9 220 B1
Kingscote St EC4 225 R7
Kingsfield Av, Har. HA2 220 A1
Kingsland Rd E2; E8 222 B2
Kingsley Rd, Houns. TW3 221 A4
Kingston Hill, Kings.T. KT2 221 B6
Kingston Rd SW15 221 C5
Kingston Rd SW20 221 C6
Kingston Rd, Kings.T. KT1; N.Mal. KT3 221 B6
Kingston Rd, Tedd. TW11 221 B6
Kingston Vale SW15 221 C6
Kingsway WC2 225 M5
Kinnerton Pl N SW1 224 A12
Kinnerton Pl S SW1 224 A12
Kinnerton St SW1 224 B12
Kinnerton Yd SW1 224 A12
Kirby St EC1 225 Q3
Kirkdale SE26 223 B5
Kirkman Pl W1 224 H4
Kneller Rd, Twick. TW2 221 A5
Knightrider Ct EC4 225 T7
Knights Hill SE27 223 A6
Knightsbridge SW1 224 A12

L

Ladbroke Gro W10; W11 220 D3
Lady Margaret Rd, Sthl. UB1 220 A3
Ladywell Rd SE13 223 C5
Lake Ho Rd E11 222 D2
Lambeth Hill EC4 225 T7
Lambeth Palace Rd SE1 225 M14
Lambeth Rd SE1 225 N14
Lambeth Rd SE11 225 N14
Lambs Conduit Pas WC1 225 M3
Lamb's Conduit St WC1 225 M2
Lamp Office Ct WC1 225 M2
Lampton Rd, Houns. TW3 221 A5
Lancashire Ct W1 224 E7
Lancaster Pl WC2 225 M7
Lancaster St SE1 225 S12
Lanesborough Pl SW1 224 B11
Langham Pl W1 224 E4
Langham St W1 224 E4
Langley Ct WC2 225 K7
Langley St WC2 225 K6
Lansdowne Rd N17 222 B1
Lansdowne Row W1 224 E9
Lansdowne Ter WC1 225 L2
Lansdowne Way SW8 223 A4
Lant St SE1 225 T11
Larden Rd W3 221 C4
Larkshall Rd E4 222 C1
Lascelles Av, Har. HA1 220 A2
Latchmere Rd SW11 221 D4
Latchmere Rd, Kings.T. KT2 221 B6
Lauderdale Twr EC2 225 T3
Launcelot St SE1 225 P12
Lauriston Rd E9 222 B2
Lausanne Rd SE15 223 B4
Lavender Av, Mitch. CR4 221 D6
Lavington St SE1 225 S10
Lawrence La EC2 225 U6
Lawrie Pk Rd SE26 223 B6
Laxton Pl NW1 224 E1
Laystall St EC1 225 P2
Laytons Bldgs SE1 225 U11
Lea Br Rd E5; E10; E17 222 B2
Leake Ct SE1 225 N12
Leake St SE1 225 N11
Leather La EC1 225 Q4
Lee High Rd SE12; SE13 223 C5
Lee Rd SE3 223 C5
Lee Ter SE3; SE13 223 C5
Lees Pl W1 224 B7
Leicester Ct WC2 224 J7
Leicester Pl WC2 224 J7
Leicester Sq WC2 224 J8
Leicester St WC2 224 J7
Leigh Hunt St SE1 225 T11
Leigh Pl EC1 225 P3
Leigh St WC1 224 K1
Leigham Ct Rd SW16 223 A5
Leighton Rd NW5 222 A2
Leo Yd EC1 225 S2
Leopards Ct EC1 225 P3
Lever St EC1 222 B3
Lewisham High St SE13 223 C5
Lewisham Rd SE13 223 C4
Lewisham St SW1 224 J12
Lewisham Way SE4; SE14 223 C4
Lexington St W1 224 G6
Leyton Grn Rd E10 222 C1
Library St SE1 225 R12
Lilford Rd SE5 223 A4
Lillie Rd SW6 221 C4
Lily Pl EC1 225 Q3
Limeburner La EC4 225 R6
Limeharbour E14 223 C4
Lincoln's Inn WC2 225 N5
Lincoln's Inn Flds WC2 225 M5
Lindsey St EC1 225 S3
Lingfield Av, Kings.T. KT1 221 B6
Links Av, Mord. SM4 221 D6
Lisle St WC2 224 J7
Lisson Gro NW1; NW8 220 D3
Litchfield St WC2 224 J7
Little Albany St NW1 224 E1
Little Argyll St W1 224 F6
Little Britain EC1 225 S4
Little Chester St SW1 224 C13
Little College St SW1 225 K13
Little Dean's Yd SW1 224 K13
Little Dorrit Ct SE1 225 U11
Little Ealing La W5 221 B4
Little Essex St WC2 225 P7
Little George St SW1 224 K12
Little Heath SE7 223 D4
Little Ilford La E12 222 D2
Little Marlborough St W1 224 F6
Little New St EC4 225 Q5
Little Newport St WC2 224 J7
Little Portland St W1 224 F5
Little Russell St WC1 224 K4
Little St. James's St SW1 224 F10
Little Sanctuary SW1 224 J12
Little Smith St SW1 224 J13
Little Titchfield St W1 224 F4
Little Trinity La EC4 225 U7
Little Turnstile WC1 225 M4
Liverpool Rd N1; N7 222 A2
Livonia St W1 224 G6
Loampit Hill SE13 223 C4
Loampit Vale SE13 223 C4
Locks La, Mitch. CR4 223 A6
Logs Hill, Brom. BR1; Chis. BR7 223 D6
Loman St SE1 225 S11
Lombard La EC4 225 Q6
Lombard Rd SW11 221 D4
London La, Brom. BR1 223 C6
London Rd SE1 225 R13
London Rd SE23 223 B5
London Rd SW16 223 A6
London Rd, Brent. TW8; Houns. TW3; Islw. TW7 221 A4
London Rd, Brom. BR1 223 C6
London Rd, Kings.T. KT2 221 B6
London Rd, Mitch. CR4 221 D6
London Rd, Twick. TW1 221 B5
London Wall EC2 225 U4
Long Acre WC2 224 K7
Long La EC1 225 S3
Long La SE1 223 B4
Long Rd SW4 223 A5
Long Yd WC1 225 M2
Longford St NW1 224 E1
Longley Rd SW17 221 D6
Long's Ct WC2 224 H7
Longwood Gdns, Ilf. IG5 222 D1
Lonsdale Av E6 222 D3
Lord N St SW1 224 K14
Lordship La N22 222 A1
Lordship La SE22 223 B5
Lordship Pk N16 222 B2
Lothian Rd SW9 223 A4
Loughborough Rd SW9 223 A4
Love La EC2 225 U5
Lover's Wk W1 224 B9
Lower Belgrave St SW1 224 D14
Lower Boston Rd W7 221 A4
Lower Clapton Rd E5 222 B2
Lower Grosvenor Pl SW1 224 D13
Lower James St W1 224 G7
Lower John St W1 224 G7
Lower Lea Crossing E14; E16 222 C3
Lower Marsh SE1 225 P12
Lower Mortlake Rd, Rich. TW9 221 B5
Lower Richmond Rd SW14; Rich. TW9 221 B5
Lower Richmond Rd SW15 221 C5
Lower Rd SE16 223 B4
Lower Rd, Har. HA2 220 A2
Lower Sunbury Rd, Hmptn. TW12 221 A6
Lower Teddington Rd, Kings.T. KT1 221 B6
Lowlands Rd, Har. HA1 220 A2
Lowndes Cl SW1 224 C14
Lowndes Ct W1 224 F6
Lowndes Pl SW1 224 B14
Lowndes Sq SW1 224 A12
Lowndes St SW1 224 A13
Ludgate Bdy EC4 225 R6
Ludgate Circ EC4 225 R6
Ludgate Hill EC4 225 R6
Ludgate Sq EC4 225 S6
Ludlow St EC1 225 T1
Lumley Ct WC2 225 L8
Lumley St W1 224 C6
Luxborough St W1 224 B3
Lyall Ms SW1 224 B14
Lyall Ms W SW1 224 B14
Lyall St SW1 224 B14
Lygon Pl SW1 224 D14
Lyttleton Rd N8 220 D1

M

Macclesfield St W1 224 J7
Macfarren Pl NW1 224 C2
Mackenzie Rd N7 222 A2
Macklin St WC2 225 L5
Maddox St W1 224 E7
Madeley Rd W5 220 B3
Magdalen Rd SW18 221 D5
Magpie All EC4 225 Q6
Maida Vale W9 220 D3
Maiden La SE1 225 U9
Maiden La WC2 225 L8
Maidstone Bldgs SE1 225 U10
Major Rd E15 222 C2
Malden Rd NW5 220 D2
Malet Pl WC1 224 H2
Malet St WC1 224 H2
Mall, The SW1 224 G11
Mall, The W5 220 B3
Mall, The, Har. HA3 220 B1
Malpas Rd SE4 223 C5
Malta St EC1 225 S1
Maltravers St WC2 225 N7
Manchester Ms W1 224 B4
Manchester Rd E14 223 C4
Manchester Sq W1 224 B5
Manchester St W1 224 B4
Mandeville Pl W1 224 C5
Mandeville Rd, Nthlt. UB5 220 A2
Manette St W1 224 J6
Manor Fm Rd, Wem. HA0 220 B3
Manor Pk Rd NW10 220 C3
Manor Rd E16 222 C3
Manor Rd N16 222 B2
Manor Rd, Chig. IG7 222 D1
Manor Rd, Mitch. CR4 223 A6
Manor Rd, Rich. TW9 221 B5
Mansfield Ms W1 224 D4
Mansfield Rd NW3 220 D2
Mansfield St W1 224 D4
Mapesbury Rd NW2 220 D2
Maple Pl W1 224 G2
Maple St W1 224 F3
Marble Arch W1 224 A7
Marchmont St WC1 224 K1
Mare St E8 222 B3
Margaret Ct W1 224 F5
Margaret St W1 224 E5
Marigold All SE1 225 R8
Market Ct W1 224 F5
Market Ms W1 224 D10
Market Pl W1 224 F5
Market Rd N7 222 A2
Markhouse Rd E17 222 C1
Marlborough Ct W1 224 F6
Marlborough Rd SW1 224 G10
Marsh Rd, Pnr. HA5 220 A1
Marsh Wall E14 223 C4
Marshall St W1 224 G6
Marshalsea Rd SE1 225 U11
Marsham St SW1 224 J14
Marshgate La E15 222 C2
Mart St WC2 225 L6
Martin Way SW20; Mord. SM4 221 D6
Martindale Rd, Houns. TW4 221 A5
Martlett Ct WC2 225 L6
Marylebone High St W1 224 C3
Marylebone La W1 224 D6
Marylebone Ms W1 224 D4
Marylebone Pas W1 224 G5
Marylebone Rd NW1 220 D3
Marylebone St W1 224 C4
Masons Arms Ms W1 224 E6
Masons Hill, Brom. BR1 223 D6
Mason's Yd SW1 224 G9
Matthew Parker St SW1 224 J12
Matthews Yd WC2 225 K6
Matthias Rd N16 222 B2
Mayes Rd N22 222 A1
Mayfair Pl W1 224 E9
Mayow Rd SE23; SE26 223 B5
Mays Ct WC2 224 K8

Maze Hill SE3; SE10 223 C4
McAuley Cl SE1 225 P13
McCoid Way SE1 225 T12
Mead Row SE1 225 P13
Meadow Row SE1 225 T14
Meard St W1 224 H6
Mecklenburgh Pl WC1 225 M1
Mecklenburgh Sq WC1 225 M1
Mecklenburgh St WC1 225 M1
Medway St SW1 224 J14
Melbourne Pl WC2 225 N7
Melcombe St NW1 224 A2
Melfort Rd, Th.Hth. CR7 223 A6
Memel Ct EC1 225 T2
Memel St EC1 225 T2
Mepham St SE1 225 N10
Merantun Way SW19 221 D6
Mercer St WC2 224 K6
Merrick Rd, Sthl. UB2 221 A4
Merrick Sq SE1 225 U13
Merton Rd SW18 221 D5
Merton Rd SW19 221 D6
Meymott St SE1 225 R10
Middle La N8 222 A1
Middle Pk Av SE9 223 D5
Middle St EC1 225 T3
Middle Temple EC4 225 P7
Middle Temple La EC4 225 P6
Middlesex Pas EC1 225 S4
Middleton Bldgs W1 224 F4
Midford Pl W1 224 G2
Milcote St SE1 225 R12
Mildmay Pk N1 222 B2
Mile End Rd E1; E3 222 C3
Milford La WC2 225 N7
Milk St EC2 225 U6
Milkwood Rd SE24 223 A5
Mill Hill Rd SW13 221 C4
Mill La NW6 220 D2
Mill St W1 224 F7
Millbank SW1 225 K14
Millennium Mile SE1 225 M10
Miller Wk SE1 225 Q10
Millman Ms WC1 225 M2
Millman St WC1 225 M2
Milroy Wk SE1 225 R9
Mint St SE1 225 T11
Mitcham La SW16 223 A6
Mitcham Rd SW17 221 D6
Mitchell St EC1 225 T1
Mitre Ct EC2 225 U5
Mitre Ct EC4 225 Q6
Mitre Rd SE1 225 Q11
Mogden La, Islw. TW7 221 A5
Monck St SW1 224 J14
Monkwell Sq EC2 225 U4
Monmouth St WC2 224 K6
Montagu Mans W1 224 A3
Montagu Ms N W1 224 A4
Montagu Ms S W1 224 A5
Montagu Ms W W1 224 A5
Montagu Row W1 224 A4
Montagu Sq W1 224 A4
Montagu St W1 224 A5
Montague Pl WC1 224 J3
Montague St EC1 225 T4
Montague St WC1 224 K3
Montreal Pl WC2 225 M7
Montrose Pl SW1 224 C12
Monument Way N17 222 B1
Moor St W1 224 J6
Morden Hall Rd, Mord. SM4 221 D6
Morden Rd SW19 221 D6
Morden Rd, Mitch. CR4 221 D6
Morley St SE1 225 Q13
Morning La E9 222 B2
Mornington Rd, Grnf. UB6 220 A3
Morpeth Ter SW1 224 F14
Mortimer Mkt WC1 224 G2
Mortimer Rd NW10 220 C3
Mortimer St W1 224 F4
Mortlake High St SW14 221 C4
Mortlake Rd, Rich. TW9 221 B4
Morton Pl SE1 225 P14
Morwell St WC1 224 J4
Mostyn Rd SW19 221 D6
Motcomb St SW1 224 A13
Mottingham La SE9; SE12 223 D5
Mottingham Rd SE9 223 D5
Mount Pleasant WC1 225 N2
Mount Pleasant Rd N17 222 B1
Mount Row W1 224 D8
Mount St W1 224 C8
Moxon St W1 224 B4
Mumford Ct EC2 225 U5
Munster Sq NW1 224 E1
Murphy St SE1 225 P12
Museum St WC1 225 K4
Muswell Hill N10 222 A1
Muswell Hill Rd N6; N10 222 A1

N
Nag's Head Ct EC1 225 T2
Nassau St W1 224 F4
Neal St WC2 224 K6
Neal's Yd WC2 224 K6
Neasden La NW10 220 C2
Nelson Rd E4 222 C1
Nelson Rd, Houns. TW4; Twick. TW2 221 A5
Nelson Sq SE1 225 R11
Nether St N3; N12 220 D1
New Barn St E13 222 D3
New Bond St W1 224 E7
New Br St EC4 225 R6
New Burlington Ms W1 224 F7
New Burlington Pl W1 224 F7
New Burlington St W1 224 F7
New Cavendish St W1 224 E3
New Change EC4 225 T6
New City Rd E13 222 D3
New Compton St WC2 224 J6
New Ct EC4 225 P7
New Coventry St W1 224 J8
New Cross Rd SE14 223 B4
New Fetter La EC4 225 Q5
New Globe Wk SE1 225 T9
New Inn Pas WC2 225 N6
New Kent Rd SE1 225 T14
New Kings Rd SW6 221 D4
New N Rd N1 222 B2
New N St WC1 225 M3
New Oxford St WC1 224 J5
New Plaistow Rd E15 222 C3
New Quebec St W1 224 A6
New Rd E1 222 B3
New Rd, W.Mol. KT8 221 A6
New Row WC2 224 K7
New Sq WC2 225 N5
New St Sq EC4 225 Q5
New Turnstile WC1 225 M4
New Wanstead E11 222 C2
Newburgh St W1 224 F6
Newbury St EC1 225 T4
Newcastle Cl EC4 225 R5
Newcastle Row EC1 225 Q1
Newgate St EC1 225 S5
Newham Way E6; E16 222 D3
Newington Causeway SE1 225 S14
Newlands Pk SE26 223 B6
Newman Pas W1 224 G4
Newman St W1 224 G4
Newman Yd W1 224 H5
Newman's Row WC2 225 N4
Newnham Ter SE1 225 P13
Newport Ct WC2 224 J7
Newport Pl WC2 224 J7
Newton St WC2 225 L5
Nicholson St SE1 225 R10
Nightingale La SW4; SW12 221 D5
Nightingale Pl SE18 223 D4
Nine Elms La SW8 223 A4
Noble St EC2 225 T5
Noel Rd W3 220 B3
Noel St W1 224 G6
Norbury Cres SW16 223 A6
Norbury Hill SW16 223 A6
Norris St SW1 224 H8
North Acton Rd NW10 220 C3
North Audley St W1 224 B6
North Ct W1 224 G3
North Cres WC1 224 H3
North End Rd NW11 220 D2
North End Rd SW6; W14 221 D4
North Hill N6 222 A1
North Ms WC1 225 N2
North Rd N6 222 A1
North Row W1 224 A7
North St SW4 223 A5
North Woolwich Rd E16 222 D3
Northampton Rd EC1 225 Q1
Northborough Rd SW16 223 A6
Northburgh St EC1 225 S1
Northcote Rd SW11 221 D5
Northern Relief Rd, Bark. IG11 222 D2
Northfield Av W5; W13 220 B3
Northington St WC1 225 N2
Northolt Rd, Har. HA2 220 A2
Northover, Brom. BR1 223 C5
Northumberland Av WC2 224 K9
Northumberland St WC2 225 K9
Northwold Rd E6; N16 222 B2
Northwood Rd, Th.Hth. CR7 223 B6
Norwich St EC4 225 P5
Norwood High St SE27 223 B5
Norwood Rd SE24; SE27 223 A5
Norwood Rd, Sthl. UB2 221 A4
Notting Hill Gate W11 220 D3
Nottingham Ct WC2 225 K6
Nottingham Pl W1 224 B2
Nottingham St W1 224 B3
Nottingham Ter NW1 224 B2
Nunhead La SE15 223 B5

O
Oak Av, Hmptn. TW12 221 A6
Oak Hill, Wdf.Grn. IG8 222 C1
Oakey La SE1 225 P13
Oakley St SW3 221 D4
Oakwood Av, Beck. BR3 223 C6
Oat La EC2 225 T5
Odhams Wk WC2 225 K6
Ogle St W1 224 F3
Old Bailey EC4 225 S6
Old Barge Ho All SE1 225 P9
Old Barrack Yd SW1 224 B12
Old Bond St W1 224 F8
Old Brewers Yd WC2 225 K6
Old Brompton Rd SW5; SW7 221 D4
Old Bldgs WC2 225 P5
Old Burlington St W1 224 F7
Old Cavendish St W1 224 D5
Old Compton St W1 224 H7
Old Fish St Hill EC4 225 T7
Old Fleet La EC4 225 R5
Old Ford Rd E2; E3 222 B3
Old Gloucester St WC1 225 L3
Old Hill, Chis. BR7 223 D6
Old Kent Rd SE1; SE15 223 B4
Old N St WC1 225 M3
Old Oak Common La NW10; W3 220 C3
Old Oak La NW10 220 C3
Old Oak Rd W3 220 C3
Old Palace Yd SW1 225 K13
Old Pk La W1 224 C10
Old Pye St SW1 224 H13
Old Quebec St W1 224 A6
Old Queen St SW1 224 J12
Old Seacoal La EC4 225 R5
Old Sq WC2 225 N5
Old St EC1 225 T1
Old Town SW4 223 A5
Oldbury Pl W1 224 C3
Oldfield La N, Grnf. UB6 220 A3
O'Meara St SE1 225 U10
Onslow St EC1 225 Q2
Ontario St SE1 225 S14
Orange St WC2 224 H8
Orange Yd W1 224 J6
Orchard St W1 224 B6
Orde Hall St WC1 225 M2
Ormond Cl WC1 225 L3
Ormond Ms WC1 225 L2
Ormond Yd SW1 224 G9
Osnaburgh St NW1 224 E2
Osnaburgh Ter NW1 224 E1
Ossington Bldgs W1 224 B3
Ossulton Way N2 220 D1
Outer Circle NW1 224 B2
Oxendon St SW1 224 H8
Oxford Circ Av W1 224 F6
Oxford St W1 224 B6

P
Paddenswick Rd W6 221 C4
Paddington St W1 224 B3
Page Heath La, Brom. BR1 223 D6
Page St NW7 220 C1
Pageantmaster Ct EC4 225 R6
Pakenham St WC1 225 N1
Palace Pl SW1 224 F13
Palace St SW1 224 F13
Pall Mall SW1 224 G10
Pall Mall E SW1 224 J9
Pall Mall Pl SW1 224 G10
Palmer St SW1 224 H12
Palmerston Rd N22 222 A1
Pancras La EC4 225 U6
Pancras Rd NW1 222 A3
Panton St SW1 224 H8
Panyer All EC4 225 T5
Parchmore Rd, Th.Hth. CR7 223 B6
Pardon St EC1 225 S1
Paris Gdn SE1 225 R9
Parish La SE20 223 B6
Park Av N22 222 A1
Park Cres W1 224 D2
Park Cres Ms E W1 224 E2
Park Cres Ms W W1 224 D3
Park La W1 224 C10
Park La, Wem. HA9 220 B2
Park Pl SW1 224 F10
Park Rd N8 222 A1
Park Rd NW1; NW8 220 D3
Park Rd, Hmptn. TW12 221 A6
Park Rd, Kings.T. KT2 221 B6
Park Rd (Hampton Wick), Kings.T. KT1 221 B6
Park Rd, Tedd. TW11 221 A6
Park Royal Rd NW10; W3 220 C3
Park Sq E NW1 224 D1
Park Sq Ms NW1 224 D1
Park Sq W NW1 224 D1
Park St SE1 225 T9
Park St W1 224 B7
Parker Ms WC2 225 L5
Parker St WC2 225 L5
Parkhurst Rd N7 222 A2
Parkside SW19 221 C5
Parkside Way, Har. HA2 220 A1
Parliament Sq SW1 224 K12
Parliament St SW1 225 K12
Parnell Rd E3 222 C3
Parson St NW4 220 C1
Passing All EC1 225 S2
Paternoster Row EC4 225 T6
Paternoster Sq EC4 225 S5
Paul's Wk EC4 225 S7
Pavilion Rd SW1 224 A14
Pavilion St SW1 224 A14
Peabody Dws WC1 224 K1
Peabody Est EC1 225 U2
Peabody Est SE1 225 Q10
Peabody Sq SE1 225 R12
Peabody Trust SE1 225 T10
Pear Pl SE1 225 P11
Pear Tree Ct EC1 225 Q1
Pear Tree St EC1 225 S1
Pearman St SE1 225 Q13
Peckham High St SE15 223 B4
Peckham Hill St SE15 223 B4
Peckham Pk Rd SE15 223 B4
Peckham Rd SE5; SE15 223 B4
Peckham Rye SE15; SE22 223 B5
Pemberton Row EC4 225 Q5
Pembroke Cl SW1 224 C12
Pembury Rd E5 222 B2
Penge Rd SE20; SE25 223 B6
Penrhyn Rd, Kings.T. KT1 221 B6
Pentonville Rd N1 222 A3
Pepper St SE1 225 T11
Percival St EC1 225 R1
Percy Ms W1 224 H4
Percy Pas W1 224 G4
Percy Rd, Hmptn. TW12 221 A6
Percy Rd, Twick. TW2 221 A5
Percy St W1 224 H4
Perkin's Rents SW1 224 H13
Perkins Sq SE1 225 U9
Perry Hill SE6 223 C5
Perry Ri SE23 223 C5
Perry Vale SE23 223 B5
Perrys Pl W1 224 H5
Perth Rd, Ilf. IG2 222 D1
Peter St W1 224 G7
Peters Hill EC4 225 T7
Peter's La EC1 225 S3
Petersham Rd, Rich. TW10 221 B5
Peto Pl NW1 224 E1
Petts Hill, Nthlt. UB5 220 A2
Petty France SW1 224 G13
Philip La N15 222 B1
Phipp's Ms SW1 224 D14
Phoenix Pl WC1 225 N1
Phoenix St WC2 224 J6
Piccadilly W1 224 E10
Piccadilly Arc SW1 224 F9
Piccadilly Circ W1 224 H8
Piccadilly Pl W1 224 G8
Pickering Pl SW1 224 G10
Pickwick St SE1 225 T12
Picton Pl W1 224 C6
Pilgrim St EC4 225 R6
Pimlico Rd SW1 223 A4
Pine St EC1 225 P1
Pineapple Ct SW1 224 F13
Pinner Rd, Har. HA1 220 A1
Pinner Rd, Pnr. HA5 220 A1
Pinner Vw, Har. HA1, HA2 220 A1
Pitfield St N1 222 B3
Pitshanger La W5 220 B3
Pitt's Head Ms W1 224 C10
Plaistow La, Brom. BR1 223 D6
Plaistow Rd E13; E15 222 C3
Plashet Gro E6 222 D2
Plashet Rd E13 222 D3
Playhouse Yd EC4 225 R6
Pleydell Ct EC4 225 Q6
Pleydell St EC4 225 Q6
Plough La SW17; SW19 221 D6
Plough Pl EC4 225 Q5
Plough Way SE16 223 B4
Plumstead Common Rd SE18 223 D4
Plumstead Rd SE18 223 D4
Plumtree Ct EC4 225 Q5
Pocock St SE1 225 R11
Poland St W1 224 G6
Pollen St W1 224 E6
Pomeroy St SE14 223 B4
Pontypool Pl SE1 225 R11
Pooles Bldgs EC1 225 P2
Popes La W5 221 B4
Poplar High St E14 222 C3
Poppins Ct EC4 225 R6
Porter St SE1 225 U9
Porter St W1 224 A3
Portland Ms W1 224 G6
Portland Pl W1 224 E4
Portland Rd SE25 223 B6
Portman Cl W1 224 A5
Portman Ms S W1 224 B6
Portman Sq W1 224 B5
Portman St W1 224 B6
Portpool La EC1 225 P3
Portsmouth St WC2 225 M6
Portugal St WC2 225 M6
Pound La NW10 220 C2
Powder Mill La, Twick. TW2 221 A5
Powis Pl WC1 225 L2
Poynders Rd SW4 223 A5
Praed St W2 220 D3
Preston Hill, Har. HA3 220 B2
Preston Rd, Har. HA3; Wem. HA9 220 B2
Prestons Rd E14 223 C4
Priest Ct EC2 225 T5
Primrose Hill EC4 225 Q6
Prince Albert Rd NW1; NW8 220 D3
Prince Imperial Rd, Chis. BR7 223 D6
Prince of Wales Rd SE3 223 C4
Prince Regent La E13; E16 222 D3
Prince's Arc SW1 224 G9
Princes Pl SW1 224 G9
Princes St W1 224 E6
Princess St SE1 225 S14
Princeton St WC1 225 M3
Printer St EC4 225 Q5
Printers Inn Ct EC4 225 P5
Priory La SW15 221 C5
Priory Rd N8 222 A1
Procter St WC1 225 M4
Providence Ct W1 224 C7
Prudent Pas EC2 225 U5
Puddle Dock EC4 225 S7
Pump Ct EC4 225 P6
Pursley Rd NW7 220 C1
Putney Br Rd SW15; SW18 221 D5
Putney Heath SW15 221 C5
Putney High St SW15 221 C5
Putney Hill SW15 221 C5

Q
Quadrant Arc W1 224 G8
Quality Ct WC2 225 P5
Quebec Ms W1 224 A6
Queen Anne Av, Brom. BR2 223 C6
Queen Anne Ms W1 224 E4
Queen Anne St W1 224 D5
Queen Anne's Gate SW1 224 H12
Queen Sq WC1 225 L2
Queen Sq Pl WC1 225 L2
Queen St EC4 225 U7
Queen St W1 224 D9
Queen St Pl EC4 225 U8
Queen Victoria St EC4 225 S7
Queenhithe EC4 225 U7
Queens Dr W3; W5 220 B3
Queens Ride SW13; SW15 221 C5
Queens Rd NW4 220 C1
Queens Rd SE14; SE15 223 B4
Queens Rd, Kings.T. KT2 221 B6
Queens Rd, Rich. TW10 221 B5
Queen's Rd, Tedd. TW11 221 A6
Queen's Wk SW1 224 F10
Queens Yd WC1 224 G2
Queensbridge Rd E2; E8 222 B2
Queenstown Rd SW8 223 A4
Quilp St SE1 225 T11

R
Railton Rd SE24 223 A5
Ramillies Pl W1 224 F6
Ramillies St W1 224 F6
Rancliffe Rd E6 222 D3
Rathbone Pl W1 224 H5
Rathbone St W1 224 G4
Ravensbourne Av, Beck. BR3; Brom. BR2 223 C6
Ray St EC1 225 Q2
Ray St Br EC1 225 Q2
Raymond Bldgs WC1 225 N3
Raymouth Rd SE16 223 B4
Rayners La, Har. HA2; Pnr. HA5 220 A1
Rectory La SW17 223 A6
Rectory Rd N16 222 B2
Rectory Rd, Beck. BR3 223 C6
Red Hill, Chis. BR7 223 D6
Red Lion Ct EC4 225 Q5
Red Lion Sq WC1 225 M4
Red Lion St WC1 225 M3
Red Lion Yd W1 224 C9
Red Pl W1 224 B7
Redbridge La E, Ilf. IG4 222 D1
Redcliffe Gdns SW5; SW10 221 D4
Redcross Way SE1 225 U11
Redriff Rd SE16 223 B4
Reeves Ms W1 224 B8
Regent Pl W1 224 G7
Regent St SW1 224 H8
Regent St W1 224 E5
Regents Pk Rd N3 220 D1
Regent's Pl NW1 224 F1
Regnart Bldgs NW1 224 G1
Remnant St WC2 225 M5
Rennie St SE1 225 R9
Repository Rd SE18 223 D4
Rex Pl W1 224 C8
Richardson's Ms W1 224 F2
Richbell Pl WC1 225 M3
Richmond Bldgs W1 224 H6
Richmond Hill, Rich. TW10 221 B5
Richmond Ms W1 224 H6
Richmond Rd, Kings.T. KT2 221 B6
Richmond Rd, Twick. TW1 221 B5
Richmond Ter SW1 225 K11
Ridgeway, The (North Harrow), Har. HA2 220 A1
Ridgmount Gdns WC1 224 H2
Ridgmount Pl WC1 224 H3
Ridgmount St WC1 224 H3
Ridgway SW19 221 C6
Riding Ho St W1 224 F4
Risborough St SE1 225 S11
Rising Sun Ct EC1 225 S4
Riverside Dr, Rich. TW10 221 B5
Riverside Wk SE1 225 M10
Robert Adam St W1 224 B5
Robert St WC2 225 L8
Roberts Ms SW1 224 B14
Robert's Pl EC1 225 Q1
Robin Hood Way (Kingston Bypass) SW15; SW20 221 C5
Rochester St SW1 224 H14
Rochester Way SE3; SE9 223 D5
Rochester Way Relief Rd SE3; SE9 223 D4
Rockingham Est SE1 225 T14
Rockingham St SE1 225 T14
Rocks La SW13 221 C5
Rodmarton St W1 224 A4
Rodney Rd SE17 223 B4
Roe Grn NW9 220 C1
Roehampton La SW15 221 C5
Roehampton Vale SW15 221 C5
Roger St WC1 225 N2
Rolls Bldgs EC4 225 P5
Rolls Pas EC4 225 P5
Rolls Rd SE1 223 B4
Roman Rd E2; E3 222 C3
Romford Rd E7; E15 222 C2
Romilly St W1 224 H7
Romney Ms W1 224 B3
Romney St SW1 224 J14
Ron Leighton Way E6 222 D3
Roscoe St EC1 225 U2
Rose All SE1 225 U9
Rose & Crown Ct EC2 225 T5
Rose & Crown Yd SW1 224 G9
Rose St WC2 225 K7
Rosebery Av EC1 225 P2
Rosebery Sq EC1 225 P2
Rosoman Pl EC1 225 Q1
Rosslyn Hill NW3 220 D2
Rotary St SE1 225 R13
Rotherham Wk SE1 225 R10
Rotherhithe New Rd SE16 223 B4
Rotherhithe Tunnel E1 222 B3
Rotten Row SW1 224 B11
Roundway, The N17 222 B1
Roupell St SE1 225 Q10
Rowan Rd SW16 223 A6
Roxeth Grn Av, Har. HA2 220 A2
Roxeth Hill, Har. HA2 220 A2
Royal Albert Way E16 222 D3
Royal Arc W1 224 F8
Royal Docks Rd E6 222 D3
Royal Hospital Rd SW3 221 D4
Royal Ms, The SW1 224 E13
Royal Opera Arc SW1 224 H9
Royal St SE1 225 N13
Royalty Ms W1 224 H6
Royston Pk Rd, Pnr. HA5 220 A1
Ruckholt Rd E10 222 C2
Rugby St WC1 225 M2
Ruislip Rd E W7; W13; Grnf. UB6 220 A3
Rupert Ct W1 224 H7
Rupert St W1 224 H7
Rushey Grn SE6 223 C5
Rushworth St SE1 225 S11
Russell Ct SW1 224 G10
Russell Sq WC1 224 K2
Russell St WC2 225 L7
Russia Ct EC2 225 U5
Russia Row EC2 225 U6
Rutland Pl EC1 225 T2
Ryder Ct SW1 224 G9
Ryder St SW1 224 G9
Ryder Yd SW1 224 G9
Rye La SE15 223 B4

S
Sackville St W1 224 G8
Saddle Yd W1 224 D9
Saffron Hill EC1 225 Q2
Saffron St EC1 225 Q3
St. Albans St SW1 224 H8
St. Alphage Gdns EC2 225 U4
St. Andrew St EC4 225 Q4
St. Andrew's Hill EC4 225 S7
St. Andrews Pl NW1 224 E1
St. Anne's Ct W1 224 H6
St. Ann's Hill SW18 221 D5
St. Ann's La SW1 224 J13
St. Ann's Rd N15 222 B1
St. Ann's St SW1 224 J13
St. Anselm's Pl W1 224 D6
St. Bride St EC4 225 R5
St. Bride's Pas EC4 225 R6
St. Christopher's Pl W1 224 C5
St. Clement's La WC2 225 N6
St. Cross St EC1 225 Q3
St. Ermin's Hill SW1 224 H13
St. George St W1 224 E6
St. Georges Circ SE1 225 R13
St. Georges Ct EC4 225 R5
St. Georges Rd E7 222 D2
St. Georges Rd SE1 225 Q13
St. Giles High St WC2 224 J5
St. Giles Pas WC2 224 J6
St. James's Ct SW1 224 G13
St. James's Dr SW12; SW17 221 D5
St. James's Mkt SW1 224 H8
St. James's Palace SW1 224 G11
St. James's Pk SW1 224 H11
St. James's Pl SW1 224 F10
St. James's Rd SE1; SE16 223 B4
St. James's Row EC1 225 Q1
St. James's Sq SW1 224 G9
St. James's St SW1 224 F9
St. James's Wk EC1 225 R1
St. John St EC1 225 S2
St. John's Hill SW11 221 D5
St. John's La EC1 225 R2
St. John's Path EC1 225 R2
St. John's Pl EC1 225 R2
St. John's Rd, Islw. TW7 221 A4
St. John's Sq EC1 225 R2
St. John's Wd Rd NW8 220 D3
St. Margaret's Ct SE1 225 U10
St. Margarets Rd, Twick. TW1 221 B5
St. Margaret's St SW1 225 K12
St. Martin's La WC2 224 K7
St. Martin's Ms WC2 224 K8
St. Martin's Pl WC2 224 K8
St. Martin's St WC2 224 J8
St. Martin's-le-Grand EC1 225 T5
St. Mary's Rd SW19 221 D6
St. Mary's Rd W5 221 B4
St. Matthew St SW1 224 H14
St. Mildreds Rd SE12 223 C5
St. Paul's Chyd EC4 225 S6
St. Paul's Way E3; E14 222 C3
St. Quintin Av W10 220 C3
St. Vincent St W1 224 C4
Salisbury Ct EC4 225 R6
Salisbury Sq EC4 225 Q6
Salmon St NW9 220 B2
Salter Rd SE16 223 B4
Salters Hill SE19 223 B6
Salusbury Rd NW6 220 D3
Sanctuary, The SW1 224 J12
Sanctuary St SE1 225 U12
Sandell St SE1 225 P11
Sanders La NW7 220 C1
Sandland St WC1 225 N4
Sandy La, Kings.T. KT1; Tedd. TW11 221 B6
Sandy La, Rich. TW10 221 B5
Sandycombe Rd, Rich. TW9 221 B5
Sanford St SE14 223 C4
Sans Wk EC1 225 Q1
Sardinia St WC2 225 M6
Savile Row W1 224 F7
Savoy Bldgs WC2 225 M8

Savoy Ct WC2 225 L8
Savoy Hill WC2 225 M8
Savoy Pl WC2 225 L8
Savoy Row WC2 225 M7
Savoy St WC2 225 M7
Savoy Way WC2 225 M8
Sawyer St SE1 225 T11
Scala St W1 224 G3
Scoresby St SE1 225 R10
Scotch Common W13 220 B3
Scotland Pl SW1 225 K9
Scotswood St EC1 225 Q1
Scotts La, Brom. BR2 223 C6
Scovell Cres SE1 225 T12
Scovell Rd SE1 225 T12
Scrubs La NW10; W10 220 C3
Secker St SE1 225 P10
Sedley Pl W1 224 D6
Sekforde St EC1 225 R2
Selwyn Av E4 222 C1
Serjeants Inn EC4 225 Q6
Serle St WC2 225 N5
Sermon La EC4 225 T6
Seven Sisters Rd N4; N7; N15 222 A2
Seville St SW1 224 A12
Seward St EC1 225 S1
Seymour Ms W1 224 B5
Shacklewell La E8 222 B2
Shaftesbury Av W1 224 H7
Shaftesbury Av WC2 224 H7
Shaftesbury Av, Har. HA2 220 A2
Shavers Pl SW1 224 H8
Sheen La SW14 221 C5
Sheen Rd, Rich. TW9 221 B5
Sheepcote Rd, Har. HA1 220 A1
Sheffield St WC2 225 M6
Shelton St WC2 224 K6
Shepherd Mkt W1 224 D9
Shepherd St W1 224 D10
Shepherdess Wk N1 222 B3
Shepherds Bush Rd W6 221 C4
Shepherds Hill N6 222 A1
Shepherds Pl W1 224 B7
Sheraton St W1 224 H6
Sherlock Ms W1 224 B3
Shernhall St E17 222 C1
Sherwood Pk Rd, Mitch. CR4 223 A6
Sherwood St W1 224 G7
Shirland Rd W9 220 D3
Shoe La EC4 225 Q5
Shoot Up Hill NW2 220 D2
Shooter's Hill Rd SE3; SE10; SE18 223 C4
Short St SE1 225 Q11
Shortlands Rd, Brom. BR2 223 C6
Shorts Gdns WC2 224 K6
Shropshire Pl WC1 224 G2
Sicilian Av WC1 225 L4
Sidcup Rd SE9; SE12 223 D5
Siddons La NW1 224 A2
Sidford Pl SE1 225 N14
Sidmouth Rd NW2 220 C2
Sidney St E1 222 B3
Silex St SE1 225 S12
Silk St EC2 225 U3
Silver Pl W1 224 G7
Silverthorne Rd SW8 223 A4
Silvertown Way E16 222 C3
Silvester St SE1 225 U12
Skinners La EC4 225 U7
Slingsby Pl WC2 224 K7
Sloane St SW1 224 A13
Smart's Pl WC2 225 L5
Smith Sq SW1 224 K14
Smithfield St EC1 225 R4
Smith's Ct W1 224 G7
Smokehouse Yd EC1 225 S3
Snakes La E, Wdf.Grn. IG8 222 D1
Snakes La W, Wdf.Grn. IG8 222 D1
Snaresbrook Rd E11 222 C1
Snow Hill EC1 225 R4
Snow Hill Ct EC1 225 S5
Soho Sq W1 224 H5
Soho St W1 224 H5
Somerset Rd, Sthl. UB1 220 A3
South Audley St W1 224 C8
South Circular Rd SW2 223 A5
South Cres WC1 224 H4
South Croxted Rd SE21 223 B5
South Ealing Rd W5 221 B4
South Hill Av, Har. HA1, HA2 220 A2
South Lambeth Rd SW8 223 A4
South La, N.Mal. KT3 221 C6
South Lo Av, Mitch. CR4 223 A6
South Molton La W1 224 D6
South Molton St W1 224 D6
South Norwood Hill SE25 223 B6
South Par W4 221 C4
South Rd, Sthl. UB1 221 A4
South Sq WC1 225 P4
South St W1 224 C9
South St, Islw. TW7 221 B5
South Woodford to Barking Relief Rd E11; E12; E18; Bark. IG11; Ilf. IG1 222 D1
Southampton Bldgs WC2 225 P5
Southampton Pl WC1 225 L4
Southampton Row WC1 225 L3
Southampton St WC2 225 L7
Southampton Way SE5 223 B4
Southborough Rd, Brom. BR1 223 D6
Southcroft Rd SW16; SW17 223 A6
Southend La SE6; SE26 223 C6
Southend Rd E4; E17; E18 222 C1
Southend Rd, Beck. BR3 223 C6
Southfield Rd W4 221 C4
Southgate Rd N1 222 B3
Southlands Rd, Brom. BR1, BR2 223 D6
Southover, Brom. BR1 223 D6
Southwark Br EC4 225 U9
Southwark Br SE1 225 U9
Southwark Br Rd SE1 225 S13
Southwark Gro SE1 225 T10
Southwark Pk Rd SE16 223 B4
Southwark St SE1 225 S9
Spa Hill SE19 223 B6
Spafield St EC1 225 P1
Spaniards Rd NW3 220 D2
Spanish Pl W1 224 C4
Spencer Pk SW18 221 D5
Spenser St SW1 224 G13
Spring Gdns SW1 224 J9
Spring Gro Rd, Houns. TW3; Islw. TW7 221 A4
Spring Ms W1 224 A3
Spur Rd SE1 225 P11
Spur Rd SW1 224 F12
Stable Yd SW1 224 F11
Stable Yd Rd SW1 224 F10
Stacey St WC2 224 J6
Stafford Pl SW1 224 F13
Stafford St W1 224 F9
Stag La NW9 220 B1
Stag Pl SW1 224 F13
Staines Rd, Twick. TW2 221 A5
Staining La EC2 225 U5
Stamford Hill N16 222 B2
Stamford St SE1 225 P10
Stanhope Gate W1 224 C9
Stanhope Row W1 224 D10
Stanley Rd, Tedd. TW11; Twick. TW2 221 A6
Stansfeld Rd E6 222 D3
Stanstead Rd SE6; SE23 223 B5
Stanton Way SE26 223 C6
Staple Inn WC1 225 P4
Staple Inn Bldgs WC1 225 P4
Star & Garter Hill, Rich. TW10 221 B5
Star Yd WC2 225 P5
Station App SE1 225 N12
Station Rd E12 222 D2
Station Rd NW4 220 C1
Station Rd NW10 220 C3
Station Rd SW13 221 C4
Station Rd, Edg. HA8 220 B1
Station Rd, Har. HA1 220 A1
Stedham Pl WC1 224 K5
Stephen Ms W1 224 H4
Stephen St W1 224 H4
Stephenson St E16 222 C3
Stephenson Way NW1 224 G1
Stepney Grn E1 222 B3
Stepney Way E1 222 B3
Stew La EC4 225 T7
Steyne Rd W3 220 B3
Stockwell Rd SW9 223 A4
Stoke Newington Rd N16 222 B2
Stondon Pk SE23 223 C5
Stone Bldgs WC2 225 N4
Stone Pk Av, Beck. BR3 223 C6
Stonecutter St EC4 225 R5
Stones End St SE1 225 T12
Stopford Rd E13 222 D3
Store St WC1 224 H4
Storey's Gate SW1 224 J12
Strand WC2 225 K8
Strand La WC2 225 N7
Stratford Pl W1 224 D6
Strathyre Av SW16 223 A6
Stratton St W1 224 E9
Strawberry Vale, Twick. TW1 221 B5
Streatfield Rd, Har. HA3 220 B1
Streatham Common N SW16 223 A6
Streatham High Rd SW16 223 A5
Streatham Hill SW2 223 A5
Streatham Pl SW2 223 A5
Streatham Rd, Mitch. CR4 223 A6
Streatham St WC1 224 J5
Streatham Vale SW16 223 A6
Strone Rd E7; E12 222 D2
Stroud Grn Rd N4 222 A2
Strutton Grd SW1 224 H13
Studio Pl SW1 224 A12
Stukeley St WC2 225 L5
Sturge St SE1 225 T11
Sudbury Hill, Har. HA1 220 A2
Sudrey St SE1 225 T12
Suffolk Pl SW1 224 J9
Suffolk St SW1 224 J9
Summer Hill, Chis. BR7 223 D6
Summer St EC1 225 P2
Summers La N12 220 D1
Sumner St SE1 225 S9
Sunray Av SE24 223 B5
Surbiton Rd, Kings.T. KT1 221 B6
Surrey Canal Rd SE14; SE15 223 B4
Surrey Lo SE1 225 P14
Surrey Quays Rd SE16 223 B4
Surrey Row SE1 225 R11
Surrey St WC2 225 N7
Sussex Gdns W2 220 D3
Sutton La, Houns. TW3 221 A5
Sutton Row W1 224 J5
Sutton's Way EC1 225 U2
Swallow Pas W1 224 E6
Swallow Pl W1 224 E6
Swallow St W1 224 G8
Swan Rd (Hanworth), Felt. TW13 221 A6
Swan St SE1 225 U13
Swandon Way SW18 221 D5
Sycamore St EC1 225 T2
Sydenham Hill SE23; SE26 223 B5
Sydenham Rd SE26 223 B6
Sydney St SW3 221 D4
Syon La, Islw. TW7 221 A4

T

Talgarth Rd W6; W14 221 C4
Tallis St EC4 225 Q7
Tamworth La, Mitch. CR4 223 A6
Tanswell Est SE1 225 Q12
Tanswell St SE1 225 P12
Tarn St SE1 225 T14
Tavistock Pl WC1 224 J1
Tavistock Sq WC1 224 J1
Tavistock St WC2 225 L7
Taviton St WC1 224 H1
Teignmouth Gdns, Grnf. UB6 220 B3
Temple Av EC4 225 Q7
Temple La EC4 225 Q6
Temple Mill La E15 222 C2
Temple Pl WC2 225 N7
Temple W Ms SE11 225 R14
Tenison Ct W1 224 F7
Tenison Way SE1 225 P10
Tennison Rd SE25 223 B6
Tentelow La, Sthl. UB2 221 A4
Tenterden St W1 224 E6
Terminus Pl SW1 224 E14
Terrace, The SW13 221 C4
Tetherdown N10 222 A1
Thames Path SE1 225 Q8
Thavies Inn EC1 225 Q5
Thayer St W1 224 C4
Theed St SE1 225 P10
Theobald's Rd WC1 225 M3
Thicket Rd SE20 223 B6
Thirleby Rd SW1 224 G14
Thomas Doyle St SE1 225 R13
Thornbury Rd, Islw. TW7 221 A4
Thornhaugh Ms WC1 224 J2
Thornhaugh St WC1 224 J3
Thornton Av SW2 223 A5
Thornton Pl W1 224 A3
Thrale St SE1 225 U10
Three Barrels Wk EC4 225 U7
Three Cups Yd WC1 225 N4
Three Kings Yd W1 224 D7
Thurlow Pk Rd SE21 223 A5
Tilney Ct EC1 225 U1
Tilney St W1 224 C9
Timber St EC1 225 T1
Tiverton St SE1 225 T14
Tollgate Rd E16 222 D3
Tollington Pk N4 222 A2
Tolmers Sq NW1 224 G1
Tomswood Hill, Ilf. IG6 222 D1
Tomswood Rd, Chig. IG7 222 D1
Took's Ct EC4 225 P5
Tooting Bec Rd SW16; SW17 223 A5
Tooting High St SW17 221 D6
Topham St EC1 225 P1
Torrington Pl WC1 224 H3
Torrington Sq WC1 224 J2
Tothill St SW1 224 H12
Tottenham Ct Rd W1 224 G2
Tottenham La N8 222 A1
Tottenham Ms W1 224 G3
Tottenham St W1 224 G4
Toulmin St SE1 225 T12
Tower Br Rd SE1 223 B4
Tower Ct WC2 224 K6
Tower Royal EC4 225 U7
Tower St WC2 224 J6
Trafalgar Av SE15 223 B4
Trafalgar Rd SE10 223 C4
Trafalgar Sq SW1 224 J9
Trafalgar Sq WC2 224 J9
Traps La, N.Mal. KT3 221 C6
Trebeck St W1 224 D9
Treveris St SE1 225 R10
Trig La EC4 225 T7
Trinity Ch Sq SE1 225 U13
Trinity Ri SW2 223 A5
Trinity Rd SW17; SW18 221 D5
Trinity St SE1 225 U12
Trio Pl SE1 225 U12
Triton Sq NW1 224 F1
Trott Rd N10 220 D1
Trump St EC2 225 U6
Trundle St SE1 225 T11
Trundleys Rd SE8 223 B4
Tudor Dr, Kings.T. KT2 221 B6
Tudor Pl W1 224 H5
Tudor St EC4 225 Q7
Tufnell Pk Rd N7; N19 222 A2
Tufton St SW1 224 J13
Tulse Hill SW2 223 A5
Tunmarsh La E13 222 D3
Turk's Head Yd EC1 225 R3
Turnagain La EC4 225 R5
Turnmill St EC1 225 Q2
Turnpike La N8 222 A1
Tweezer's All WC2 225 P7
Twickenham Rd (Hanworth), Felt. TW13 221 A5
Twickenham Rd, Islw. TW7 221 B5
Twickenham Rd, Rich. TW9 221 B5
Twickenham Rd, Tedd. TW11 221 B6
Twyford Av W3 220 B3
Twyford Pl WC2 225 M5
Tyburn Way W1 224 A7
Tyler's Ct W1 224 H6

U

Ufford St SE1 225 Q11
Ulster Pl NW1 224 D2
Ulster Ter NW1 224 D1
Union Rd SW4; SW8 223 A4
Union St SE1 225 S10
University St WC1 224 G2
Upper Belgrave St SW1 224 C13
Upper Brook St W1 224 B8
Upper Clapton Rd E5 222 B2
Upper Elmers End Rd, Beck. BR3 223 C6
Upper Grosvenor St W1 224 B8
Upper Grd SE1 225 P9
Upper Ham Rd, Rich. TW10 221 B6
Upper Harley St NW1 224 C1
Upper James St W1 224 G7
Upper John St W1 224 G7
Upper Marsh SE1 225 N13
Upper N St E14 222 C3
Upper Richmond Rd SW15 221 C5
Upper Richmond Rd W SW14; Rich. TW10 221 C5
Upper Rd E13 222 D2
Upper St. Martin's La WC2 224 K7
Upper St N1 222 A3
Upper Sunbury Rd, Hmptn. TW12 221 A6
Upper Thames St EC4 225 S7
Upper Tooting Rd SW17 221 D6
Upper Tulse Hill SW2 223 A5
Upper Wimpole St W1 224 D3
Upton La E7 222 D2
Uxbridge Rd W3; W5 220 B3
Uxbridge Rd W12 220 C3
Uxbridge Rd, Hmptn. TW12 221 A6
Uxbridge Rd, Har. HA3; Pnr. HA5; Stan. HA7 220 A1
Uxbridge Rd, Sthl. UB1 220 A3

V

Vale, The NW11 220 C2
Vale, The W3 220 C3
Valentine Pl SE1 225 R11
Valentine Row SE1 225 R12
Vallance Rd E1; E2 222 B3
Valley Rd, Brom. BR2 223 C6
Vanbrugh Pk SE3 223 C4
Vandon Pas SW1 224 G13
Vandon St SW1 224 G13
Vauxhall Br Rd SW1 223 A4
Verdant La SE6 223 C5
Verdun Rd SW13 221 C4
Vere St W1 224 D6
Vernon Pl WC1 225 L4
Verulam Bldgs WC1 225 N3
Verulam St WC1 225 P3
Vicarage Cres SW11 221 D4
Vicarage La E15 222 C2
Vicarage Rd E10 222 C2
Victoria Dock Rd E16 222 D3
Victoria Embk EC4 225 M8
Victoria Embk SW1 225 L11
Victoria Embk WC2 225 M8
Victoria Pk Rd E9 222 B3
Victoria Rd NW10; W3 220 C3
Victoria Sq SW1 224 E13
Victoria St SW1 224 F14
Vigo St W1 224 F8
Village, The SE7 223 D4
Village Way SE21 223 B5
Village Way, Beck. BR3 223 C6
Village Way, Pnr. HA5 220 A2
Villiers Rd, Kings.T. KT1 221 B6
Villiers St WC2 225 K8
Vine Hill EC1 225 P2
Vine St W1 224 G8
Vine St Br EC1 225 Q2
Vine Yd SE1 225 U11
Vineyard Wk EC1 225 P1
Violet Rd E3 222 C3
Virgil St SE1 225 N13
Viscount St EC1 225 T2
Vivian Av NW4 220 C1

W

Waithman St EC4 225 R6
Wakefield St WC1 225 L1
Waldegrave Rd, Tedd. TW11; Twick. TW1 221 A5
Waldram Pk Rd SE23 223 B5
Wales Fm Rd W3 220 C3
Walkers Ct W1 224 H7
Wallis All SE1 225 U12
Wallside EC2 225 U4
Walm La NW2 220 C2
Walterton Rd W9 220 D3
Walton Rd, E.Mol. KT8; Walt. KT12; W.Mol. KT8 221 A6
Walworth Rd SE1; SE17 223 B4
Wandle Rd, Mord. SM4 221 D6
Wandsworth Br Rd SW6 221 D4
Wandsworth High St SW18 221 D5
Wandsworth Rd SW8 223 A5
Wapping High St E1 222 B3
Wardens Gro SE1 225 T10
Wardour Ms W1 224 G6
Wardour St W1 224 H7
Wardrobe Pl EC4 225 S7
Wardrobe Ter EC4 225 S7
Warner St EC1 225 P2
Warner Yd EC1 225 P2
Warren Av, Brom. BR1 223 C6
Warren Ms W1 224 F2
Warren Rd, Kings.T. KT2 221 C6
Warren St W1 224 F2
Warwick Ct WC1 225 N4
Warwick Ho St SW1 224 J9
Warwick La EC4 225 S6
Warwick Pas EC4 225 S5
Warwick Rd W14 221 D4
Warwick Row SW1 224 E13
Warwick Sq EC4 225 S5
Warwick St W1 224 G7
Warwick Way SW1 223 A4
Warwick Yd EC1 225 U2
Water La E15 222 C2
Water St WC2 225 N7
Waterden Rd E15 222 C2
Watergate EC4 225 R7
Watergate Wk WC2 225 L9
Waterhouse Sq EC1 225 P4
Waterloo Br SE1 225 M8
Waterloo Br WC2 225 M8
Waterloo Pl SW1 224 H9
Waterloo Rd SE1 225 P11
Watermead Way N17 222 B1
Watford Way NW4; NW7 220 C1
Watling Av, Edg. HA8 220 C1
Watling Ct EC4 225 U6
Watling St EC4 225 T6
Watts La, Chis. BR7 223 D6
Waverton St W1 224 C9
Waxwell Ter SE1 225 N12
Webber Row SE1 225 Q13
Webber St SE1 225 Q11
Wedgwood Ms W1 224 J6
Weigall Rd SE12 223 D5
Weighhouse St W1 224 C6
Welbeck St W1 224 D5
Welbeck Way W1 224 D5
Well Ct EC4 225 U6
Well Hall Rd SE9 223 D4
Well St E9 222 B2
Weller St SE1 225 T11
Wellesley Rd W4 221 B4
Wellington Rd NW8 220 D3
Wellington Rd, Hmptn. TW12 221 A6
Wellington Rd N, Houns. TW4 221 A5
Wellington Rd S, Houns. TW4 221 A5
Wellington St SE18 223 D4
Wellington St WC2 225 L7
Wells Ms W1 224 G5
Wells St W1 224 F4
Wells Way SE5 223 B4
Wembley Pk Dr, Wem. HA9 220 B2
Wemborough Rd, Stan. HA7 220 B1
Wesley St W1 224 C4
West Barnes La SW20; N.Mal. KT3 221 C6
West Cen St WC1 225 K5
West End La NW6 220 D2
West Grn Rd N15 222 A1
West Halkin St SW1 224 B13
West Ham La E15 222 C2
West Harding St EC4 225 Q5
West Heath Rd NW3 220 D2
West Hill SW15; SW18 221 D5
West Poultry Av EC1 225 R4
West Side Common SW19 221 C6
West Smithfield EC1 225 R4
West Sq SE11 225 R14
West St WC2 224 J6
Westbourne Gro W2; W11 220 D3
Westbourne Pk Rd W2; W11 220 D3
Westbridge Rd SW11 221 D4
Westbury Av N22 222 A1
Western Av W3; W5; Grnf. UB6; Nthlt. UB5; Ruis. HA4; Uxb. UB8, UB10 220 B3
Western Av, Grnf. UB6; Nthlt. UB5 220 A3
Western Rd SW19; Mitch. CR4 221 D6
Westferry Rd E14 223 C4
Westhorne Av SE9; SE12 223 D5
Westminster Br SE1 225 L12
Westminster Br SW1 225 L12
Westminster Br Rd SE1 225 N12
Westmoreland St W1 224 C4
Westmount Rd SE9 223 D4
Weston Av, W.Mol. KT8 221 A6
Weston Dr, Stan. HA7 220 B1
Westway W2; W9; W10; W12 220 C3
Westwood Hill SE26 223 B6
Weymouth Ms W1 224 D3
Weymouth St W1 224 C4
Wheatley St W1 224 C4
Whetstone Pk WC2 225 M5
Whichcote St SE1 225 P10
Whipps Cross Rd E11 222 C1
Whitchurch La, Edg. HA8 220 B1
Whitcomb St WC2 224 J8
White Horse Ms SE1 225 Q13
White Horse St W1 224 D10
White Lion Hill EC4 225 S7
Whitechapel Rd E1 222 B3
Whitecross St EC1 225 U1
Whitefoot La, Brom. BR1 223 C5
Whitefriars St EC4 225 Q6
Whitehall SW1 224 K9
Whitehall Ct SW1 225 K10
Whitehall Gdns SW1 225 K10
Whitehall Pl SW1 225 K10
Whitehorse Hill, Chis. BR7 223 D6
Whitehorse La SE25 223 B6
Whitfield Pl W1 224 F2
Whitfield St W1 224 H4
Whittlesey St SE1 225 P10
Whitton Av E, Grnf. UB6 220 A2
Whitton Av W, Grnf. UB6; Nthlt. UB5 220 A2
Whitton Dene, Houns. TW3; Islw. TW7 221 A5
Whitton Rd, Houns. TW3 221 A5
Whitton Rd, Twick. TW1 221 A5
Wick Rd E9 222 B2
Wickham Rd SE4 223 C5
Wickham Rd, Beck. BR3 223 C6
Wickham Way, Beck. BR3 223 C6
Wide Way, Mitch. CR4 223 A6
Widmore Rd, Brom. BR1 223 D6
Wightman Rd N4; N8 222 A1
Wigmore Pl W1 224 D5
Wigmore St W1 224 B6
Wilcox Pl SW1 224 G14
Wild Ct WC2 225 M5
Wild St WC2 225 L6
Wilfred St SW1 224 F13
Willesden La NW2; NW6 220 C2
William Barefoot Dr SE9 223 D6
William IV St WC2 224 K8
William Ms SW1 224 A12
William St SW1 224 A12
Willoughby La N17 222 B1
Willoughby St WC1 224 K4
Willowbrook Rd SE15 223 B4
Wilton Cres SW1 224 B12
Wilton Ms SW1 224 C13
Wilton Pl SW1 224 B12
Wilton Rd SW1 224 E14
Wilton Row SW1 224 B12
Wilton St SW1 224 D13
Wilton Ter SW1 224 B13
Wimbledon Hill Rd SW19 221 C6
Wimbledon Pk Rd SW18; SW19 221 D5
Wimbledon Pk Side SW19 221 C5
Wimpole Ms W1 224 D3
Wimpole St W1 224 D5
Winchelsea Rd NW10 220 C3
Winchester Rd E4 222 C1
Winchester St W3 221 C4
Windmill La, Islw. TW7; Sthl. UB2 221 A4
Windmill Rd SW18 221 D5
Windmill Rd W5; Brent. TW8 221 B4
Windmill St W1 224 H4
Windmill Wk SE1 225 Q10
Windsor Pl SW1 224 G14
Wine Office Ct EC4 225 Q5
Winn Rd SE12 223 D5
Winnett St W1 224 H7
Winsley St W1 224 G5
Winston Way, Ilf. IG1 222 D2
Woburn Pl WC1 224 J1
Woburn Sq WC1 224 J2
Wood La NW9 220 C2
Wood La W12 220 C3
Wood La, Islw. TW7 221 A4
Wood St E17 222 C1
Wood St EC2 225 U6
Wood St, Kings.T. KT1 221 B6
Wood Vale SE23 223 B5
Woodbridge St EC1 225 R1
Woodcock Hill, Har. HA3 220 B1
Woodfield Rd W5 220 B3
Woodford Av, Ilf. IG2, IG4; Wdf.Grn. IG8 222 D1
Woodford New Rd E1; E18; Wdf.Grn. IG8 222 C1
Woodford Rd E18 222 D1
Woodgrange Rd E7 222 C2
Woodhayes Rd SW19 221 C6
Woods Ms W1 224 A7
Woodstock Ms W1 224 C4
Woodstock St W1 224 D6
Woolstone Rd SE23 223 C5
Woolwich Ch St SE18 223 D4
Woolwich High St SE18 223 D4
Woolwich Manor Way E6; E16 222 D3
Woolwich Rd SE7 223 D4
Wootton St SE1 225 Q11
Worple Rd SW19; SW20 221 C6
Worship St EC2 222 B3
Worton Rd, Islw. TW7 221 A5
Wren St WC1 225 N1
Wrottesley Rd NW10 220 C3
Wybert St NW1 224 E1
Wyndham Rd SE5 223 A4

Y

Yarmouth Pl W1 224 D10
York Br NW1 224 B1
York Bldgs WC2 225 L8
York Gate NW1 224 B2
York Pl WC2 225 L8
York Rd SE1 225 N12
York Rd SW11; SW18 221 D5
York St W1 224 A3
York St, Twick. TW1 221 B5
York Ter E NW1 224 C2
York Ter W NW1 224 B2
York Way N1; N7 222 A2
Yorkshire Grey Yd WC1 225 M4
Young's Bldgs EC1 225 U1

Z

Zoar St SE1 225 T9

Use of the Index

The letters and numbers around the page edges of the main map section form the referencing system used in this atlas.
To find a place name first turn to the map page shown in bold type in the index, then locate the grid square indicated by the following letter and number.
The following list of abbreviations shows the counties for England and Wales and the councils for Scotland which appear in this atlas.
Where more than one place has the same name, each can be distinguished by the abbreviated county or council name shown after the place name.

Abbreviations

Aber. Aberdeenshire
Arg. & B. Argyll & Bute
B'burn. Blackburn with Darwen
B. & H. Brighton & Hove
B. & N.E.Som. Bath & North East Somerset
B.Gwent Blaenau Gwent
Beds. Bedfordshire
Bourne. Bournemouth
Brack.F. Bracknell Forest
Bucks. Buckinghamshire
Caerp. Caerphilly
Cambs. Cambridgeshire
Carmar. Carmarthenshire
Cere. Ceredigion
Chan.I. Channel Islands
Ches. Cheshire
Cornw. Cornwall
Cumb. Cumbria
D. & G. Dumfries & Galloway
Darl. Darlington
Denb. Denbighshire
Derbys. Derbyshire
Dur. Durham
E.Ayr. East Ayrshire
E.Dun. East Dunbartonshire
E.Loth. East Lothian
E.Renf. East Renfrewshire
E.Riding East Riding of Yorkshire
E.Suss. East Sussex
Edin. Edinburgh
Falk. Falkirk
Flints. Flintshire
Glas. Glasgow
Glos. Gloucestershire
Gt.Lon. Greater London
Gt.Man. Greater Manchester
Gwyn. Gwynedd
Hants. Hampshire
Hart. Hartlepool
Here. Herefordshire
Herts. Hertfordshire
High. Highland
I.o.A. Isle of Anglesey
I.o.M. Isle of Man
I.o.S. Isles of Scilly
I.o.W. Isle of Wight
Inclyde Inverclyde
Lancs. Lancashire
Leic. Leicester
Leics. Leicestershire
Lincs. Lincolnshire
M.K. Milton Keynes
M.Tyd. Merthyr Tydfil
Med. Medway
Mersey. Merseyside
Middbro. Middlesbrough
Midloth. Midlothian
Mon. Monmouthshire
N.Ayr. North Ayrshire
N.E.Lincs. North East Lincolnshire
N.Lan. North Lanarkshire
N.Lincs. North Lincolnshire
N.P.T. Neath Port Talbot
N.Som. North Somerset
N.Yorks. North Yorkshire
Norf. Norfolk
Northants. Northamptonshire
Northumb. Northumberland
Nott. Nottingham
Notts. Nottinghamshire
Ork. Orkney
Oxon. Oxfordshire
P. & K. Perth & Kinross
Pembs. Pembrokeshire
Peter. Peterborough
Plym. Plymouth
Ports. Portsmouth
R. & C. Redcar & Cleveland
R.C.T. Rhondda Cynon Taff
Read. Reading
Renf. Renfrewshire
Rut. Rutland
S'end Southend
S'ham. Southampton
S.Ayr. South Ayrshire
S.Glos. South Gloucestershire
S.Lan. South Lanarkshire
S.Yorks. South Yorkshire
Sc.Bord. Scottish Borders
Shet. Shetland
Shrop. Shropshire
Slo. Slough
Som. Somerset
Staffs. Staffordshire
Stir. Stirling
Stock. Stockton-on-Tees
Stoke Stoke-on-Trent
Suff. Suffolk
Surr. Surrey
Swan. Swansea
Swin. Swindon
T. & W. Tyne & Wear
Tel. & W. Telford & Wrekin
Thur. Thurrock
V. of Glam. Vale of Glamorgan
W'ham Wokingham
W. & M. Windsor & Maidenhead
W.Berks. West Berkshire
W.Dun. West Dunbartonshire
W.Isles Western Isles (Na h-Eileanan an Iar)
W.Loth. West Lothian
W.Mid. West Midlands
W.Suss. West Sussex
W.Yorks. West Yorkshire
Warks. Warwickshire
Warr. Warrington
Wilts. Wiltshire
Worcs. Worcestershire
Wrex. Wrexham

A

A'Chill **163** F4
Ab Kettleby **82** C5
Abbas Combe **25** E5
Abberley **53** G1
Abberton *Essex* **46** D1
Abberton *Worcs.* **54** B2
Abberwick **137** F5
Abbess Roding **45** E1
Abbey Dore **52** C4
Abbey Hulton **79** G3
Abbey St. Bathans **145** E3
Abbey Village **100** C5
Abbey Wood **45** D5
Abbeycwmhir **63** G5
Abbeystead **100** B2
Abbeytown **117** E1
Abbotrule **136** A5
Abbots Bickington **21** D4
Abbots Bromley **80** B5
Abbots Langley **44** A2
Abbots Leigh **39** E5
Abbots Morton **54** C2
Abbots Ripton **70** A5
Abbot's Salford **54** C2
Abbotsbury **12** B4
Abbotsham **21** E3
Abbotskerswell **9** E1
Abbotsley **58** A2
Abbotts Ann **27** E3
Abbottswood **27** E5
Abdon **65** E4
Aber **50** A3
Aber-banc **49** G3
Aber Bargoed **38** A2
Aber Bowlan **50** C4
Aber-Cywarch **63** E1
Aber-llia **37** F1
Aber-Naint **77** E5
Aber-nant **37** G2
Aberaeron **50** A1
Aberaman **37** G2
Aberangell **63** E2
Aberarad **49** G4
Aberarder **157** G1
Aberarder House **167** F2
Aberargie **151** G3
Aberarth **50** A1
Aberavon **37** D4
Aberbeeg **38** B2
Abercanaid **37** G2
Abercarn **38** B3
Abercastle **48** B4
Abercegir **63** E2
Aberchalder **166** C4
Aberchirder **182** B4
Abercorn **143** E2
Abercraf **37** E1
Abercrombie **152** D4
Abercrychan **51** D4
Abercwmboi **37** G2
Abercych **49** F3
Abercynafon **37** G1
Abercynon **37** G3
Aberdalgie **151** F2
Aberdare **37** F2
Aberdaron **74** A5
Aberdaugleddau **34** C2
(Milford Haven)
Aberdeen **171** E4
Aberdeen Airport **171** D3
Aberdesach **74** D2
Aberdour **143** F1
Aberdovey **62** C3
(Aberdyfi)
Aberduhonw **51** G2
Aberdulais **37** D3
Aberdyfi **62** C3
(Aberdovey)
Aberedw **51** G3
Abereiddy **48** B4
Abererch **74** D4
Aberfan **37** G2
Aberfeldy **159** D5
Aberffraw **74** C1
Aberffrwd **62** C5
Aberford **102** D4
Aberfoyle **150** A4
Abergarw **37** F4
Abergavenny **38** C1
(Y Fenni)
Abergele **90** A5
Abergiar **50** B3
Abergorlech **50** B4
Abergwaun **48** C4
(Fishguard)
Abergwesyn **51** E2
Abergwili **50** A5
Abergwydol **63** D2
Abergwynant **62** C1
Abergwynfi **37** E3
Abergwyngregyn **89** E5
Abergynolwyn **62** C2
Aberhafesp **63** G3
Aberhonddu **51** G5
(Brecon)
Aberhosan **63** E3
Aberkenfig **37** E4
Aberlady **144** B1
Aberlemno **160** D4
Aberllefenni **63** D2
Aberlour **181** E5
(Charlestown of
Aberlour)
Abermad **62** B5
Abermaw **62** C1
(Barmouth)
Abermeurig **50** B2
Abermule **64** A3
Abernant **49** G5
Abernethy **151** G3
Abernyte **152** A1
Aberpergwm **37** E2
Aberporth **49** F2
Aberriw (Berriew) **64** A2
Aberscross **190** C4
Abersky **167** E2
Abersoch **74** C5
Abersychan **38** B2
Abertawe **36** C3
(Swansea)
Aberteifi (Cardigan) **49** E3
Aberthin **37** G5
Abertillery **38** B2
Abertridwr *Caerp.* **38** A4
Abertridwr *Powys* **63** G1
Abertysswg **38** A2
Aberuthven **151** E3
Aberyscir **51** F5
Aberystwyth **62** B4
Abhainnsuidhe **184** C3
Abingdon **41** G3
Abinger Common **29** G3
Abinger Hammer **29** F3
Abington **134** A3
Abington Pigotts **58** B3
Abingworth **16** D2
Ablington **40** D2
Abney **93** G5
Aboyne **170** A5
Abram **92** A2
Abriachan **167** E1
Abridge **45** D3
Abronhill **142** B2
Abson **39** F5
Abthorpe **56** B3
Abune-the-Hill **198** A4
Aby **97** E5
Acaster Malbis **103** E3
Acaster Selby **103** E3
Accrington **101** D5
Accurrach **148** D3
Acha **154** A4
Achacha **156** B5
Achadacaie **139** G3
Achadh-chaorrunn **139** F4
Achadh Mòr **187** E5
Achadunan **149** D3
Achagavel **155** G4
Achaglass **139** F5
Achahoish **139** F2
Achalader **159** G5
Achallader **157** F5
Achamore **139** D2
Achandunie **179** F2
Achany **190** A4
Achaphubuil **156** C2
Acharacle **155** F3
Achargary **193** G3
Acharn *Arg. & B.* **148** D1
Acharn *P. & K.* **158** C5
Acharonich **147** D1
Acharosson **140** A2
Achateny **155** E3
Achath **170** C3
Achavanich **195** D4
Achduart **188** C4
Achentoul **194** A5
Achfary **192** B4
Achgarve **188** A5
Achiemore *High.* **192** C2
Achiemore *High.* **194** A3
Achies **194** D3
Achiltibuie **188** C4
Achina **193** G2
Achindown **180** A5
Achinduich **190** A4
Achingills **195** D2
Achintee **177** F5
Achintee House **156** D2
Achintraid **165** E1
Achlean **168** A5
Achleanan **155** E4
Achleek **155** G4
Achlian **148** D2
Achlyness **192** B3
Achmelvich **188** C2
Achmony **167** D1
Achmore *High.* **165** E1
Achmore *High.* **188** C5
Achmore *Stir.* **150** A1
Achnaba **140** A1
Achnabat **167** E1
Achnabourin **193** G3
Achnacairn **148** B1
Achnacarnin **188** C1
Achnaclerach **178** D3
Achnacloich **148** B1
Arg. & B.
Achnacloich *High.* **164** B4
Achnaclyth **194** C5
Achnacraig **155** D5
Achnacroish **156** A5
Achnadrish **155** D4
Achnafalnich **149** E2
Achnafauld **151** D1
Achnagairn **179** E5
Achnagarron **179** F2
Achnaha *High.* **155** F5
Achnaha *High.* **155** D3
Achnahanat **190** A5
Achnahannet **168** B2
Achnalea **156** A3
Achnamara **139** F1
Achnanellan **155** G3
Achnasaul **157** D1
Achnasheen **178** A4
Achnashelloch **148** A5
Achnastank **169** E1
Achorn **194** D5
Achosnich *High.* **190** C5
Achosnich *High.* **154** D3
Achreamie **194** C2
Achriabhach **156** D3
Achriesgill **192** B3
Achrimsdale **191** E4
Achtoty **193** F2
Achurch **69** F4
Achuvoldrach **193** E3
Achvaich **190** C5
Achvarasdal **194** B2
Achvlair **156** B4
Achvraie **188** C4
Ackergill **195** F3
Acklam *Middbro.* **111** D1
Acklam *N.Yorks.* **103** G1
Ackleton **65** G3
Acklington **129** E1
Ackton **102** D5
Ackworth Moor **94** B1
Top
Acle **87** F4
Acock's Green **66** D4
Acol **33** E2
Acomb **119** F1
Northumb.
Acomb *York* **103** E2
Aconbury **53** E4
Acre **101** D5
Acrefair **77** F3
Acrise Place **33** D4
Acton *Ches.* **78** D2
Acton *Gt.Lon.* **44** A5
Acton *Shrop.* **64** C4
Acton *Suff.* **59** G3
Acton *Worcs.* **54** A1
Acton Beauchamp **53** F2
Acton Bridge **91** G5
Acton Burnell **65** E2
Acton Green **53** F2
Acton Pigott **65** E2
Acton Round **65** F3
Acton Scott **65** D4
Acton Trussell **66** B1
Acton Turville **40** A4
Adamhill **132** C2
Adbaston **79** E5
Adber **24** C5
Adderbury **55** G4
Adderley **79** D4
Adderstone **137** F3
Addiewell **143** D3
Addingham **101** G3
Addington *Bucks.* **56** C5
Addington *Gt.Lon.* **30** C2
Addington *Kent* **31** F3
Addlestone **29** F1
Addlethorpe **84** D1
Adel **102** B4
Adeney **65** F1
Adfa **63** G2
Adforton **64** C5
Adisham **33** E3
Adlestrop **55** E5
Adlingfleet **104** A5
Adlington *Ches.* **92** D4
Adlington *Lancs.* **92** A1
Admaston *Staffs.* **80** B5
Admaston **65** F1
Tel. & W.
Admington **55** D3
Adsborough **23** F5
Adstock **56** C4
Adstone **56** A2
Adversane **29** F5
Advie **168** D1
Adwalton **102** B5
Adwell **42** B3
Adwick le Street **94** C2
Adwick upon **94** B2
Dearne
Ae Village **125** D2
Affleck **171** D2
Affpuddle **13** E3
Afon-wen **90** C5
Afton Bridgend **133** E4
Agglethorpe **109** F4
Aigburth **91** E4
Aignis **187** F4
Aike **104** C3
Aikerness **198** C1
Aikers **197** D3
Aiketgate **118** A3
Aikshaw **117** E2
Aikton **117** F1
Aikwood Tower **135** F3
Ailey **52** C3
Ailsworth **69** G3
Aimster **194** D2
Ainderby **110** C4
Quernhow
Ainderby Steeple **110** C3
Aingers Green **47** E1
Ainsdale **91** E1
Ainstable **118** B3
Ainsworth **92** B1
Ainthorpe **111** G2
Aintree **91** E3
Aird **173** F4
Aird a' Mhachair **173** F5
Aird a' Mhulaidh **185** D2
Aird Asaig **184** D3
Aird Dhail **187** F1
Aird Leimhe **184** D5
Aird Mhige **184** D4
Aird Mhighe **184** C5
Aird of Sleat **164** B4
Aird Thunga **187** F4
Aird Uige **186** B4
Airdrie *Fife* **153** D4
Airdrie *N.Lan.* **142** B3
Airidh a' Bhruaich **185** E2
Airieland **124** B5
Airies **122** A4
Airigh-drishaig **165** D1
Airmyn **103** G5
Airntully **151** F1
Airor **164** D4
Airth **142** C1
Airton **101** F2
Airyhassen **115** D2
Aisby *Lincs.* **95** F3
Aisby *Lincs.* **83** F4
Aisgernis **172** C1
Aiskew **110** B4
Aislaby *N.Yorks.* **112** B2
Aislaby *N.Yorks.* **111** G4
Aislaby *Stock.* **110** D1
Aisthorpe **95** G4
Aith *Ork.* **198** A5
Aith *Ork.* **199** E4
Aith *Shet.* **200** C2
Aith *Shet.* **203** F3
Aitnoch **168** B1
Akeld **137** D4
Akeley **56** C4
Akenham **60** C3
Albaston **7** E3
Alberbury **64** C1
Albourne **17** E2
Albrighton *Shrop.* **66** A2
Albrighton *Shrop.* **65** D1
Alburgh **73** D3
Albury *Herts.* **58** C5
Albury *Surr.* **29** F3
Albury Heath **29** F3
Alby Hill **86** C2
Alcaig **179** E4
Alcaston **65** D4
Alcester **54** C2
Alciston **18** A3
Alcombe **22** C3
Alconbury **69** G5
Alconbury Hill **69** G5
Alconbury Weston **69** G5
Aldborough **102** D1
N.Yorks.
Aldborough *Norf.* **86** C2
Aldbourne **41** E5
Aldbrough **105** E4
Aldbrough **110** A1
St. John
Aldburgh **110** B5
Aldbury **43** E1
Aldclune **159** E3
Aldeburgh **61** F2
Aldeby **73** F2
Aldenham **44** A3
Alderbury **26** C5
Alderford **86** C4
Alderholt **14** A1
Alderley **39** G3
Alderley Edge **92** C5
Alderman's Green **67** F4
Aldermaston **27** G1
Aldermaston Soke **28** B1
Aldermaston **28** B1
Wharf
Alderminster **55** E3
Alderney Airport **9** F4
Aldersey Green **78** B2
Aldershot **29** D2
Alderton *Glos.* **54** B4
Alderton **56** C3
Northants.
Alderton *Shrop.* **78** B5
Alderton *Suff.* **61** E3
Alderton *Wilts.* **40** A4
Alderwasley **81** E2
Aldfield **102** B1
Aldford **78** B2
Aldham *Essex* **60** A5
Aldham *Suff.* **60** B3
Aldie *Aber.* **171** F1
Aldie *High.* **179** G1
Aldingbourne **16** B3
Aldingham **107** D5
Aldington *Kent* **32** C5
Aldington *Worcs.* **54** C3
Aldivalloch **169** F2
Aldochlay **149** F5
Aldons **122** C2
Aldreth **70** C5
Aldridge **66** C2
Aldringham **61** F1
Aldro **104** A1
Aldsworth **41** D1
Aldunie **169** F2
Aldville **151** E1
Aldwark *Derbys.* **80** D2
Aldwark *N.Yorks.* **103** D1
Aldwick **16** B4
Aldwincle **69** F4
Aldworth **42** A5
Alexandria **141** E2
Alfardisworthy **20** C4
Alfington **11** E3
Alfold **29** F4
Alfold Crossways **29** F4
Alford *Aber.* **170** A3
Alford *Lincs.* **97** E5
Alford *Som.* **24** D4
Alfreton **81** F2
Alfrick **53** G2
Alfriston **18** A3
Algarkirk **84** A4
Alhampton **24** D4
Alkborough **104** A5
Alkerton **55** F3
Alkham **33** E4
Alkington **78** C4
Alkmonton **80** C4
All Cannings **26** B1
All Saints South **73** E3
Elmham
All Stretton **65** D3
Allaleigh **9** E2
Allanaquoich **168** D5
Allancreich **170** A5
Allangillfoot **126** A2
Allanton *D. & G.* **124** D2
Allanton *N.Lan.* **142** C4
Allanton *S.Lan.* **142** B4
Allanton *Sc.Bord.* **145** F4
Allardice **161** G2
Allathasdal **172** B3
Allendale Town **119** E2
Allenheads **119** E3
Allen's Green **45** D1
Allensford **119** G2
Allensmore **53** D4
Aller **24** A5
Allerby **117** D3
Allerford *Devon* **7** E2
Allerford *Som.* **22** C3
Allerston **112** B4
Allerthorpe **103** G3
Allerton *Mersey.* **91** F4
Allerton *W.Yorks.* **102** A4
Allerton Bywater **102** D5
Allesley **67** E4
Allestree **81** E4
Allexton **68** D2
Allgreave **79** G1
Allhallows **32** A1
Allhallows-on-Sea **32** A1
Alligin Shuas **177** E4
Allimore Green **66** A1
Allington *Lincs.* **83** D3
Allington *Wilts.* **26** D4
Allington *Wilts.* **26** B1
Allithwaite **107** E5
Allnabad **193** D4
Alloa **151** D5
Allonby **117** D2
Alloway **132** B4
Allscot **65** G3
Allt na h-Airbhe **188** D5
Allt-na-subh **165** F2
Alltachonaich **155** G4
Alltan Dubh **188** B3
Alltbeithe **165** G2
Alltforgan **76** C5
Alltmawr **51** G3
Alltnacaillich **193** D4
Alltsigh **167** D3
Alltwalis **50** A4
Alltwen **36** D2
Alltyblaca **50** B3
Almeley **52** C2
Almer **13** F3
Almington **79** D4
Almiston Cross **21** D3
Almondbank **151** F2
Almondbury **93** F1
Almondsbury **39** E4
Alne **103** D1
Alness **179** F3
Alnham **137** D5
Alnmouth **137** G5
Alnwick **137** F5
Alphamstone **59** G4
Alpheton **59** G2
Alphington **10** C3
Alpington **87** D5
Alport **80** D1
Alpraham **78** C2
Alresford **60** B5
Alrewas **67** D1
Alrick **159** G3
Alsager **79** E2
Alsagers Bank **79** F3
Alsop en le Dale **80** C2
Alston *Cumb.* **118** D3
Alston *Devon* **11** G2
Alstone **54** B4
Alstonefield **80** C2
Alswear **22** A5
Altanduin **190** D2
Altarnun **5** G1
Altass **190** A4
Altens **171** E4
Alterwall **195** E2
Altham **101** D4
Althorne **46** C3
Althorpe **95** F2
Alticry **123** D5
Altnafeadh **157** E4
Altnaharra **193** E5
Altofts **102** C5
Alton *Derbys.* **81** E1
Alton *Hants.* **28** C4
Alton *Staffs.* **80** B3
Alton Barnes **26** C1
Alton Pancras **12** C2
Alton Priors **26** C1
Altonside **181** E4
Altrincham **92** B4
Altura **157** E1
Alva **151** D5
Alvanley **91** F5
Alvaston **81** E4
Alvechurch **66** C5
Alvecote **67** E2
Alvediston **26** A5
Alveley **65** G4
Alverdiscott **21** F3
Alverstoke **15** F3
Alverstone **15** E4
Alverton **82** C3
Alves **180** D3
Alvescot **41** E2
Alveston *S.Glos.* **39** F4
Alveston *Warks.* **55** E2
Alvie **168** A4
Alvingham **97** D3
Alvington **39** F2
Alwalton **69** G3
Alweston **12** C1
Alwinton **128** B1
Alwoodley Gates **102** C3
Alyth **160** A5
Amalebra **2** B3
Amber Hill **84** A3
Ambergate **81** E2
Amberley *Glos.* **40** A2
Amberley *W.Suss.* **16** C2
Amble **129** E1
Amblecote **66** A4
Ambleside **107** E2
Ambleston **48** D5
Ambrismore **140** B4
Ambrosden **42** B1
Amcotts **95** F1
Amersham **43** E3
Amesbury **26** C3
Amington **67** E2
Amisfield **125** E2
Amlwch **88** C3
Amlwch Port **88** C3
Ammanford **36** C1
(Rhydaman)
Amotherby **111** G5
Ampfield **27** E5
Ampleforth **111** E5
Ampleforth College **111** E5
Ampney Crucis **40** C2
Ampney St. Mary **40** C2
Ampney St. Peter **40** C2
Amport **27** E3
Ampthill **57** F4
Ampton **71** G5
Amroth **35** E2
Amulree **151** D1
An Tób **184** C5
(Leverburgh)
An Tairbeart **185** D3
(Tarbert)
Anaboard **168** C1
Anaheilt **156** A3
Ancaster **83** E3
Anchor **64** A4
Ancroft **145** G5
Ancrum **136** A4
Ancton **16** B3
Anderby **97** F5
Anderson **13** E3

Anderton **92** A5
Andover **27** E3
Andover Down **27** E3
Andoversford **54** C5
Andreas **98** C2
Anelog **74** A5
Angarrack **2** C3
Angersleigh **11** E1
Angerton **117** F1
Angle **34** B2
Angler's Retreat **62** D3
Angmering **16** C3
Angram **103** E3
Anie **150** A3
Ankerville **180** A2
Anlaby **104** C5
Anmer **85** F5
Anna Valley **27** E3
Annan **125** F4
Annaside **106** B4
Annat *Arg. & B.* **148** C2
Annat *High.* **177** E4
Annbank **132** C3
Annesley **81** G2
Annesley Woodhouse **81** G2
Annfield Plain **120** A2
Annscroft **65** D2
Ansdell **99** G5
Ansford **24** D4
Ansley **67** E3
Anslow **80** D5
Anslow Gate **80** C5
Anstey *Herts.* **58** C4
Anstey *Leics.* **68** A2
Anstruther **153** D4
Ansty *W.Suss.* **17** E1
Ansty *Warks.* **67** F4
Ansty *Wilts.* **26** A5
Anthill Common **15** F1
Anthorn **117** E1
Antingham **87** D2
Anton's Gowt **84** A3
Antony **7** D5
Antrobus **92** A5
Anvil Corner **21** D5
Anwick **83** G2
Anwoth **123** G5
Aoradh **138** A3
Apethorpe **69** F3
Apley **96** B5
Apperknowle **94** A5
Apperley **54** A5
Appin House **156** B5
Appleby **95** G1
Appleby-in-Westmorland **118** C5
Appleby Magna **67** F1
Appleby Parva **67** F2
Applecross **176** D5
Appledore *Devon* **21** E2
Appledore *Devon* **11** D1
Appledore *Kent* **19** E1
Appledore Heath **32** B5
Appleford **42** A3
Appleshaw **27** E3
Applethwaite **117** F4
Appleton **41** G2
Appleton-le-Moors **111** G4
Appleton-le-Street **111** G5
Appleton Roebuck **103** E3
Appleton Thorn **92** A4
Appleton Wiske **110** C2
Appletreehall **135** G4
Appletreewick **101** G1
Appley **23** D5
Appley Bridge **91** G1
Apse Heath **15** E4
Apsley **43** F2
Apsley End **57** G4
Apuldram **16** A3
Arberth (Narberth) **35** E1
Arbirlot **161** D5
Arborfield **28** C1
Arborfield Cross **28** C1
Arborfield Garrison **28** C1
Arbroath **161** E5
Arbuthnott **161** G2
Archdeacon Newton **110** B1
Archiestown **181** E5
Arclid **79** E1
Ard a' Chapuill **140** B2
Ardachearanbeg **140** B1
Ardacheranmor **140** B1
Ardachoil **147** G1
Ardachu **190** B4
Ardachvie **166** A5
Ardailly **139** E4
Ardalanish **146** C3
Ardallie **171** F1
Ardanaiseig **148** C2
Ardaneaskan **165** E1
Ardanstur **148** A3
Ardantiobairt **155** F4
Ardantrive **148** A2
Ardarroch **165** E1
Ardbeg *Arg. & B.* **140** B3
Ardbeg *Arg. & B.* **138** C5
Ardbeg *Arg. & B.* **140** C1
Ardblair **167** D1
Ardbrecknish **148** C2
Ardcharnich **178** A1
Ardchiavaig **146** C3
Ardchonnel **148** B1
Ardchonnell **148** B3
Ardchrishnish **146** D2
Ardchronie **179** F1
Ardchuilk **166** B1
Ardchullarie More **150** A3
Ardchyle **150** A2
Arddlin **64** B1
Ardeley **58** B5
Ardelve **165** E2
Arden **141** E1
Ardencaple House **147** G3
Ardens Grafton **54** D2
Ardentallan **148** A2
Ardentinny **140** C1
Ardeonaig **150** B1
Ardersier **179** G4
Ardery **155** G3
Ardessie **177** G1
Ardfad **147** G3
Ardfern **148** A4
Ardfin **138** C3
Ardgartan **149** E4
Ardgay **190** A5
Ardgenavan **149** D3
Ardgowan **140** D2
Ardgowse **170** B3
Ardgye **180** D3
Ardhallow **140** C2
Ardheslaig **177** D4
Ardiecow **182** A3
Ardinamar **147** G3
Ardindrean **178** A1
Ardingly **17** F1
Ardington **41** G4
Ardintoul **165** E2
Ardkinglas House **149** D3
Ardlair **170** A2
Ardlamont **140** A3
Ardleigh **60** B5
Ardleish **149** F3
Ardler **160** A5
Ardley **56** A5
Ardlui **149** F3
Ardlussa **139** E1
Ardmaddy **148** C1
Ardmair **188** D5
Ardmaleish **140** B3
Ardmay **149** E4
Ardmenish **139** D2
Ardmhór **172** C3
Ardminish **139** E5
Ardmolich **155** G2
Ardmore *Arg. & B.* **138** C5
Ardmore *Arg. & B.* **147** G2
Ardmore *Arg. & B.* **141** E2
Ardmore *High.* **179** G1
Ardnackaig **147** G5
Ardnacross **155** E5
Ardnadam **140** C2
Ardnadrochit **147** G1
Ardnagoine **188** B4
Ardnagowan **148** D4
Ardnagrask **179** E5
Ardnahein **149** E5
Ardnahoe **138** C2
Ardnarff **165** E1
Ardnastang **156** A3
Ardnave **138** A2
Ardno **149** D4
Ardo **171** D1
Ardoch *D. & G.* **133** G5
Ardoch *Moray* **180** D4
Ardoch *P. & K.* **151** F1
Ardochrig **142** A5
Ardoyne **170** B2
Ardpatrick **139** F3
Ardpeaton **140** D1
Ardradnaig **158** C5
Ardrishaig **139** G1
Ardroe **188** C2
Ardrossan **140** D5
Ardscalpsie **140** B4
Ardshave **190** C5
Ardshealach **155** F3
Ardshellach **147** G3
Ardsley **94** A2
Ardslignish **155** E3
Ardtalla **138** C4
Ardtalnaig **150** B1
Ardtaraig **140** B1
Ardteatle **148** D2
Ardtoe **155** F2
Ardtornish **155** G5
Ardtrostan **150** B2
Ardtur **156** B5
Arduaine **148** A4
Ardullie **179** E3
Ardura **147** F1
Ardvar **192** A5
Ardvasar **164** C4
Ardveich **150** B2
Ardverikie **158** A1
Ardvorlich *Arg. & B.* **149** F3
Ardvorlich *P. & K.* **150** B2
Ardwall **123** G5
Ardwell *D. & G.* **114** B2
Ardwell *Moray* **169** F1
Ardwell *S.Ayr.* **122** C1
Areley Kings **66** G5
Arford **28** D4
Argaty **150** C4
Argoed **38** A3
Argoed Mill **51** F1
Argrennan **124** B5
Arichamish **148** B4
Arichastlich **149** E1
Arichonan **147** G5
Aridhglas **146** C2
Arienskill **155** G1
Arileod **154** A4
Arinacrinachd **176** D4
Arinafad Beg **139** F1
Arinagour **154** B4
Arinambane **172** C1
Arisaig **155** F1
Arivegaig **155** F3
Arkendale **102** C1
Arkesden **58** C4
Arkholme **107** G5
Arkleby **117** E3
Arkleside **109** F4
Arkleton **126** B2
Arkley **44** B3
Arksey **94** C2
Arkwright **94** B5
Arlary **151** G4
Arlecdon **116** D5
Arlesey **57** G4
Arleston **65** F1
Arley **92** A4
Arlingham **39** G1
Arlington *Devon* **21** G1
Arlington *E.Suss.* **18** A3
Arlington *Glos.* **40** D2
Arlington Beccott **21** G1
Armadale *High.* **193** G2
Armadale *High.* **164** C4
Armadale *W.Loth.* **142** D3
Armathwaite **118** B3
Arminghall **87** D5
Armitage **66** C1
Armscote **55** E3
Armston **69** F4
Armthorpe **94** D2
Arnabost **154** B4
Arncliffe **109** E5
Arncliffe Cote **109** E5
Arncroach **152** D4
Arne **13** F4
Arnesby **68** B3
Arngask **151** G3
Arngibbon **150** B5
Arngomery **150** B5
Arnhall **161** E3
Arnicle **130** C2
Arnipol **155** G1
Arnisdale **165** E3
Arnish **176** C5
Arniston Engine **144** A3
Arnol **187** E3
Arnold **81** G3
Arnprior **150** B5
Arnside **107** F5
Arowry **78** B4
Arrad Foot **107** E4
Arradoul **181** G3
Arram **104** C3
Arrat **161** E4
Arrathorne **110** A3
Arreton **15** E4
Arrington **58** B2
Arrivain **149** E1
Arrochar **149** F4
Arrow **54** C2
Arscaig **190** A3
Arthington **102** B3
Arthingworth **68** C4
Arthog **62** C1
Arthrath **171** E1
Arthurstone **160** A5
Artrochie **171** F1
Aruadh **138** A3
Arundel **16** C3
Aryhoulan **156** C3
Asby **117** D4
Ascog **140** C3
Ascot **29** E1
Ascott **55** F4
Ascott-under-Wychwood **41** E1
Ascreavie **160** B4
Asenby **110** C5
Asfordby **68** C1
Asfordby Hill **68** C1
Asgarby *Lincs.* **84** B1
Asgarby *Lincs.* **83** G3
Ash *Kent* **33** E3
Ash *Kent* **31** F2
Ash *Som.* **24** B5
Ash *Surr.* **29** D2
Ash Barton **21** F5
Ash Bullayne **10** A2
Ash Magna **78** C4
Ash Mill **22** A5
Ash Priors **23** E5
Ash Thomas **10** D1
Ash Vale **29** D2
Ashampstead **42** A5
Ashbocking **60** C2
Ashbourne **80** C3
Ashbrittle **23** D5
Ashburnham Place **18** B2
Ashburton **9** D1
Ashbury *Devon* **7** F1
Ashbury *Oxon.* **41** E4
Ashby **95** G2
Ashby by Partney **84** C1
Ashby cum Fenby **96** C2
Ashby de la Launde **83** F2
Ashby de la Zouch **67** F1
Ashby Folville **68** C1
Ashby Magna **68** A3
Ashby Parva **68** A4
Ashby Puerorum **96** D5
Ashby St. Ledgers **56** A1
Ashby St. Mary **87** E5
Ashchurch **54** B4
Ashcombe **10** C5
Ashcott **24** B4
Ashdon **59** D3
Ashe **27** G3
Asheldham **46** C2
Ashen **59** F3
Ashenden **32** A5
Ashendon **42** C1
Ashens **139** G2
Ashfield *Arg. & B.* **139** F1
Ashfield *Stir.* **150** C4
Ashfield *Suff.* **60** D1
Ashfield Green **73** D4
Ashfold Crossways **17** E1
Ashford *Devon* **8** C3
Ashford *Devon* **21** F2
Ashford *Hants.* **14** A1
Ashford *Kent* **32** C4
Ashford *Surr.* **43** F5
Ashford Bowdler **65** E5
Ashford Carbonel **65** E5
Ashford Hill **27** G1
Ashford in the Water **80** D1
Ashgill **142** B4
Ashiestiel **135** F2
Ashill *Devon* **11** D1
Ashill *Norf.* **71** G2
Ashill *Som.* **11** G1
Ashingdon **46** B3
Ashington *Northumb.* **129** E3
Ashington *Som.* **24** C5
Ashington *W.Suss.* **16** D2
Ashkirk **135** F3
Ashleworth **54** A5
Ashley *Cambs.* **59** E1
Ashley *Ches.* **92** B4
Ashley *Devon* **21** G4
Ashley *Glos.* **40** B3
Ashley *Hants.* **27** E4
Ashley *Hants.* **14** B3
Ashley *Kent* **33** E4
Ashley *Northants.* **68** C3
Ashley *Staffs.* **79** E4
Ashley *Wilts.* **25** F1
Ashley Green **43** E2
Ashley Heath **14** A2
Ashmanhaugh **87** E3
Ashmansworth **27** F2
Ashmansworthy **20** D4
Ashmore *Dorset* **13** F1
Ashmore *P. & K.* **159** G4
Ashorne **55** F2
Ashover **81** E1
Ashow **67** F5
Ashperton **53** F3
Ashprington **9** E2
Ashreigney **21** G4
Ashtead **29** G2
Ashton *Ches.* **78** C1
Ashton *Cornw.* **2** C4
Ashton *Cornw.* **7** D4
Ashton *Here.* **53** E1
Ashton *Northants.* **69** F4
Ashton *Northants.* **56** C3
Ashton Common **25** F2
Ashton-in-Makerfield **91** G3
Ashton Keynes **40** C3
Ashton under Hill **54** B4
Ashton-under-Lyne **92** D3
Ashton upon Mersey **92** B3
Ashurst *Hants.* **14** C1
Ashurst *Kent* **31** E5
Ashurst *W.Suss.* **17** D2
Ashurstwood **30** D5
Ashwater **7** D1
Ashwell *Herts.* **58** A4
Ashwell *Rut.* **69** D1
Ashwellthorpe **72** C2
Ashwick **24** D3
Ashwicken **71** F1
Ashybank **135** G4
Askam in Furness **106** D5
Askern **94** C1
Askerswell **12** B3
Askett **42** D2
Askham *Cumb.* **118** B5
Askham *Notts.* **95** E5
Askham Bryan **103** E3
Askham Richard **103** E3
Asknish **148** B5
Askrigg **109** E3
Askwith **102** A3
Aslackby **83** F4
Aslacton **72** C2
Aslockton **82** C3
Asloun **170** A3
Aspall **60** C1
Aspatria **117** E2
Aspenden **58** B5
Aspley Guise **57** E4
Aspull **92** A2
Asselby **103** G5
Assington **60** A4
Astbury **79** F1
Astcote **56** B2
Asterby **96** C5
Asterley **64** C2
Asterton **64** C3
Asthall **41** E1
Asthall Leigh **41** F1
Astley *Shrop.* **65** E1
Astley *Warks.* **67** F4
Astley *Worcs.* **53** G1
Astley Abbotts **65** G3
Astley Bridge **92** B1
Astley Cross **54** G1
Astley Green **92** B3
Aston *Ches.* **78** D3
Aston *Ches.* **91** G5
Aston *Derbys.* **93** F4
Aston *Flints.* **78** A1
Aston *Here.* **65** D5
Aston *Herts.* **58** A5
Aston *Oxon.* **41** F2
Aston *S.Yorks.* **94** B4
Aston *Shrop.* **78** C5
Aston *Staffs.* **79** E3
Aston *Tel. & W.* **65** F2
Aston *W'ham* **42** C4
Aston *W.Mid.* **66** C4
Aston Abbotts **42** D1
Aston Botterell **65** F4
Aston-by-Stone **79** G4
Aston Cantlow **54** D2
Aston Clinton **43** D1
Aston Crews **53** F5
Aston Cross **54** B4
Aston End **58** A5
Aston Eyre **65** F3
Aston Fields **66** B5
Aston Flamville **67** G3
Aston Ingham **53** F5
Aston juxta Mondrum **78** D2
Aston le Walls **55** G2
Aston Magna **55** D4
Aston Munslow **65** E4
Aston on Clun **64** C4
Aston on Trent **81** F5
Aston Rogers **64** C2
Aston Rowant **42** C3
Aston Sandford **42** C2
Aston Somerville **54** C4
Aston Subedge **54** D3
Aston Tirrold **42** A4
Aston Upthorpe **42** A4
Astwick **58** A4
Astwood **57** E3
Astwood Bank **54** C1
Aswarby **83** F3
Aswardby **97** D5
Aswick Grange **70** B1
Atch Lench **54** C2
Atcham **65** E2
Athelington **72** D4
Athelney **24** A5
Athelstaneford **144** C2
Atherington **21** F3
Atherstone **67** F3
Atherstone on Stour **55** E2
Atherton **92** A2
Athlinne **185** D2
Atlow **80** D3
Attadale **165** F1
Attenborough **81** G4
Atterby **95** G3
Attleborough *Norf.* **72** B2
Attleborough *Warks.* **67** F3
Attlebridge **86** C4
Atwick **105** D2
Atworth **25** F1
Aubourn **83** E1
Auch **149** F1
Auchairne **122** C2
Auchallater **159** G1
Auchameanach **139** G4
Aucharnie **182** B5
Aucharrigill **189** G4
Auchattie **170** B5
Auchavan **159** G3
Auchbraad **139** G1
Auchbreck **169** E2
Auchenblae **161** F2
Auchenbothie **141** E2
Auchenbrack **124** B1
Auchenbreck **140** B1
Auchencairn **124** C5
Auchencrow **145** F3
Auchendinny **143** G3
Auchendolly **124** B4
Auchenfoyle **141** E2
Auchengray **143** D4
Auchenhalrig **181** F3
Auchenheath **142** C5
Auchenhessnane **124** C1
Auchenlochan **140** A2
Auchenmalg **122** D5
Auchenrivock **126** B3
Auchentiber **141** E5
Auchenvennal **141** D1
Auchessan **149** G2
Auchgourish **168** B3
Auchinafaud **139** F4
Auchincruive **132** B3
Auchindarrach **139** G1
Auchindarroch **156** C4
Auchindrain **148** C4
Auchindrean **178** A1
Auchininna **182** B5
Auchinleck **133** D3
Auchinloch **142** A2
Auchinner **150** B3
Auchinroath **181** E4
Auchintoul *Aber.* **170** A3
Auchintoul *Aber.* **182** B4
Auchintoul *High.* **190** A4
Auchiries **171** F1
Auchleven **170** B2
Auchlochan **133** G2
Auchlunachan **178** A1
Auchlunies **171** D5
Auchlunkart **181** F5
Auchlyne **150** A2
Auchmacoy **171** E1
Auchmair **169** F2
Auchmantle **122** C4
Auchmithie **161** E5
Auchmuirbridge **152** A4
Auchmull **161** D2
Auchnabony **116** A2
Auchnabreac **148** C4
Auchnacloich **150** D1
Auchnacraig **147** G2
Auchnacree **160** C3
Auchnafree **150** D1
Auchnagallin **168** C1
Auchnagatt **183** E5
Auchnaha **140** A1
Auchnangoul **148** C4
Aucholzie **169** F5
Auchorrie **170** B4
Auchraw **150** A2
Auchreoch **149** F2
Auchronie **160** C1
Auchterarder **151** E3
Auchtercairn **177** E2
Auchterderran **152** A5
Auchterhouse **152** B1
Auchtermuchty **152** A3
Auchterneed **179** D3
Auchtertool **152** A5
Auchtertyre *Angus* **160** A5
Auchtertyre *Moray* **181** D4
Auchtertyre *Stir.* **149** F2
Auchtubh **150** A2
Auckengill **195** F2
Auckley **95** D2
Audenshaw **92** D3
Audlem **79** D3
Audley **79** E2
Audley End **58** D4
Auds **182** B3
Aughton *E.Riding* **103** G4
Aughton *Lancs.* **91** E2
Aughton *Lancs.* **100** B1
Aughton *S.Yorks.* **94** B4
Aughton Park **91** F2
Auldearn **180** B4
Aulden **53** D2
Auldhame **144** C1
Auldhouse **142** A4
Aulich **158** B4
Ault a' chruinn **165** F2
Ault Hucknall **81** F1
Aultanrynie **192** C5
Aultbea **177** E1
Aultgrishan **176** D1
Aultguish Inn **178** C2
Aultibea **191** F2
Aultiphurst **194** A2
Aultmore **181** G4
Aultnagoire **167** E2
Aultnamain Inn **179** F1
Aultnapaddock **181** F5
Aulton **170** B2
Aultvoulin **165** D4
Aundorach **168** B3
Aunk **10** D2
Aunsby **83** F4
Auquhorthies **170** D2
Aust **39** E4
Austerfield **95** D3
Austonley **93** F2
Austrey **67** E2
Austwick **101** D1
Authorpe **97** E4
Authorpe Row **97** F5
Avebury **40** C5
Aveley **45** E4
Avening **40** A3
Averham **82** C2
Aveton Gifford **8** C3
Avielochan **168** B3
Aviemore **168** A3
Avington *Hants.* **27** G4
Avington *W.Berks.* **27** E1
Avoch **179** F4
Avon **14** A3
Avon Dassett **55** G2
Avonbridge **142** D2
Avonmouth **39** E5
Avonwick **8** D2
Awbridge **27** E5
Awhirk **122** B5
Awkley **39** E4
Awliscombe **11** E2
Awre **39** G2
Awsworth **81** F3
Axbridge **24** B2
Axford *Hants.* **28** B3
Axford *Wilts.* **41** E5
Axminster **11** F3
Axmouth **11** F3
Aycliffe **120** B5
Aydon **119** G1
Aylburton **39** F2
Ayle **118** D3
Aylesbeare **10** D3
Aylesbury **42** D1
Aylesby **96** C2
Aylesford **31** G3
Aylesham **33** E3
Aylestone **68** A2
Aylmerton **86** C2
Aylsham **86** C3
Aylton **53** F4
Aymestrey **52** D1
Aynho **56** A4
Ayot St. Lawrence **44** A1
Ayot St. Peter **44** B1
Ayr **132** B3
Aysgarth **109** F4
Ayshford **10** D1
Ayside **107** E4
Ayston **69** D2
Aythorpe Roding **45** E1
Ayton *P. & K.* **151** G3
Ayton *Sc.Bord.* **145** G3
Aywick **203** E4
Azerley **110** B5

B

Babbacombe **9** F1
Babbinswood **78** A4
Babcary **24** C5
Babel **51** E4
Babell **90** C5
Babeny **7** G3
Babraham **58** D3
Babworth **95** D4
Bac **187** F3
Back of Keppoch **155** F1
Backaland **199** D3
Backaskaill **198** C1
Backbarrow **107** E4
Backburn **170** A1
Backfolds **183** F4
Backford **91** E5
Backhill **170** C1
Backhill of Clackriach **183** E5
Backhill of Trustach **170** B5
Backies *High.* **190** D4
Backies *Moray* **181** G4
Backlass **195** E3
Backside **169** G1
Backwell **24** B1
Backworth **129** E4
Bacon End **45** E1
Baconsthorpe **86** C2
Bacton *Here.* **52** C4
Bacton *Norf.* **87** E2
Bacton *Suff.* **60** B1
Bacup **101** E5
Badachro **177** D2
Badanloch Lodge **193** G5
Badavanich **178** A4
Badbea **191** F3
Badbury **41** D4
Badby **56** A2
Badcall *High.* **192** A4
Badcall *High.* **192** B3
Badcaul **188** C5
Baddeley Green **79** G2
Badden **139** G1
Baddesley Ensor **67** E3
Baddidarach **188** C2
Badenscoth **170** B1
Badenyon **169** F3
Badger **65** G3
Badgerbank **92** C5
Badgers Mount **31** D2
Badgeworth **40** B1
Badgworth **24** A2
Badicaul **165** D2
Badingham **61** E1
Badintagairt **189** G3
Badlesmere **32** C3
Badley **60** B2
Badlipster **195** E4
Badluarach **188** B5
Badminton **40** A4
Badnaban **188** C2
Badnabay **192** B4
Badnafrave **169** E3
Badnagie **195** D5
Badnambiast **158** C2
Badninish **190** C5
Badrallach **188** C5
Badsey **54** C3
Badshot Lea **29** D3
Badsworth **94** B1
Badwell Ash **60** A1
Badyo **159** E3
Bae Cinmel (Kinmel Bay) **90** A4
Bae Colwyn (Colwyn Bay) **89** G5
Bae Penrhyn (Penrhyn Bay) **89** G4
Bag Enderby **97** D5
Bagby **111** D4
Bagendon **40** C2
Baggrave Hall **68** C2
Baggrow **117** E2
Bagh a' Chaisteil (Castlebay) **172** B4
Baghasdal **172** C2
Bagillt **90** D5
Baginton **67** F5
Baglan **37** D3
Bagley **78** B5
Bagnall **79** G2
Bagnor **27** F1
Bagshot *Surr.* **29** E1
Bagshot *Wilts.* **27** E1
Bagstone **39** F4
Bagthorpe *Norf.* **85** F4
Bagthorpe *Notts.* **81** F2
Baguley **92** C4
Bagworth **67** G2
Bagwyllydiart **52** D5
Baildon **102** A4
Baile a' Mhanaich (Balivanich) **173** F4
Baile Ailein **187** D5
Baile an Truiseil **187** E2
Baile Boidheach **139** F2
Baile Gharbhaidh **173** F5
Baile Glas **173** G4
Baile Mhartainn (Balmartin) **173** F2
Baile Mhic Phail **173** G2
Baile Mòr *Arg. & B.* **146** B2
Baile Mòr *W.Isles* **173** F3
Baile-na-Cille **173** G1
Baile nan Cailleach **173** F4
Baile Raghaill **173** F3
Bailebeag **167** E3
Baileguish **168** A5
Bailetonach **155** F2
Bailiesward **169** G1
Bainbridge **109** E3
Bainsford **142** C1
Bainshole **170** B1
Bainton *E.Riding* **104** B2
Bainton *Peter.* **69** F2
Bairnkine **136** A5
Bakebare **169** F1
Baker Street **45** F4
Baker's End **44** C1
Bakewell **80** D1
Bala **76** C4
Balachuirn **176** B5
Balafark **150** B5
Balaldie **180** A2
Balavil **167** G4
Balbeg *High.* **167** D1
Balbeg *High.* **167** D2
Balbeggie **151** G2
Balbirnie **152** A4
Balbithan **170** C3
Balblair *High.* **179** G3
Balblair *High.* **190** A5
Balcharn **190** A4
Balcherry **180** A1
Balchers **182** C4
Balchladich **188** C1
Balchraggan *High.* **179** E5
Balchraggan *High.* **167** E1
Balchrick **192** A2
Balcombe **30** C5
Balcurvie **152** B4
Baldernock **141** G2
Baldersby **110** C5
Balderstone **100** C4
Balderton **82** D2
Baldhu **4** B5
Baldinnie **152** C3
Baldock **58** A4
Baldovie *Angus* **160** B4
Baldovie *Dundee* **152** C1
Baldrine **98** C3
Baldslow **18** C2
Baldwin **98** B3
Baldwinholme **117** G1
Baldwin's Gate **79** E3
Bale **86** B2
Balelone **173** F2
Balemartine **154** A2
Balendoch **160** A5
Balephuil **154** A2
Balerno **143** F3
Balernock **141** D1
Baleromindubh **146** C5
Balerominmore **146** C5
Balevulin **147** D2
Balfield **160** D3
Balfour *Aber.* **170** A5
Balfour *Ork.* **198** C5
Balfron **141** G1
Balfron Station **141** G1
Balgedie **151** G4
Balgonar **151** F5
Balgove **170** D1
Balgowan *D. & G.* **114** B2
Balgowan *High.* **167** F5
Balgown **175** G3
Balgray **152** C1
Balgreen **182** C4
Balgreggan **122** B5
Balgy **177** E4
Balhaldie **150** D4
Balhalgardy **170** C2
Balhary **160** A5
Balhelvie **152** B2
Balhousie **152** C4
Baliasta **203** F2
Baligill **194** A2
Baligrundle **148** A1
Balindore **148** B1
Balintore **180** A2
Balintraid **179** G2
Balintyre **158** B5
Balivanich (Baile a' Mhanaich) **173** F4
Balkeerie **160** B5
Balkholme **103** G5
Balkissock **122** C2
Ball **78** A5
Ball Haye Green **79** G2
Ball Hill **27** F1
Ballabeg **98** A4
Ballacannell **98** C3

Ballacarnane Beg 98 B3
Ballachulish 156 C4
Balladoole 98 A5
Ballafesson 98 A4
Ballagyr 98 A3
Ballajora 98 C2
Ballakilpheric 98 A4
Ballamodha 98 A4
Ballantrae 122 B2
Ballards Gore 46 C3
Ballasalla *I.o.M.* 98 A4
Ballasalla *I.o.M.* 98 B2
Ballater 169 F5
Ballaterach 169 G5
Ballaugh 98 B2
Ballaveare 98 B4
Ballechin 159 E4
Balleich 150 A4
Ballencrieff 144 B2
Ballidon 80 D2
Balliekine 131 D2
Balliemeanoch 148 D4
Balliemore *Arg. & B.* 148 D5
Balliemore *Arg. & B.* 148 A2
Ballig 98 A3
Ballimeanoch 148 C3
Ballimore *Arg. & B.* 140 A1
Ballimore *Stir.* 150 A3
Ballinaby 138 A3
Ballindean 152 A2
Ballingdon 59 G3
Ballinger Common 43 E2
Ballingham 53 E4
Ballingry 151 G5
Ballinlick 159 E5
Ballinluig *P. & K.* 159 E4
Ballinluig *P. & K.* 159 F4
Ballintuim 159 G4
Balloch *Angus* 160 B4
Balloch *High.* 179 G5
Balloch *N.Lan.* 142 B2
Balloch *W.Dun.* 141 E1
Ballochan 170 A5
Ballochandrain 140 A1
Ballochford 169 F1
Ballochgair 130 C3
Ballochmartin 140 C4
Ballochmorrie 122 D2
Ballochmyle 132 D3
Ballochroy 139 F4
Ballogie 170 A5
Balls Cross 29 E5
Ballyaurgan 139 F2
Ballygown 154 D5
Ballygrant 138 B3
Ballyhaugh 154 A4
Ballymeanoch 148 A5
Ballymichael 131 E2
Balmacara 165 E2
Balmaclellan 124 A3
Balmacneil 159 E4
Balmadies 160 D5
Balmae 115 G2
Balmaha 149 G5
Balmalcolm 152 B4
Balmartin (Baile Mhartainn) 173 F2
Balmeanach *Arg. & B.* 155 F5
Balmeanach *Arg. & B.* 147 D1
Balmedie 171 E3
Balmerino 152 B2
Balmerlawn 14 C2
Balminnoch 123 D4
Balmore *E.Dun.* 142 A2
Balmore *High.* 180 A5
Balmore *High.* 166 C1
Balmore *High.* 175 F5
Balmore *P. & K.* 158 C4
Balmullo 152 C2
Balmungie 179 G4
Balmyle 159 F4
Balnaboth 160 B3
Balnabruaich 179 G2
Balnacra 177 F5
Balnafoich 167 F1
Balnagall 180 A1
Balnagown Castle 179 G2
Balnaguard 159 E4
Balnaguisich 179 F2
Balnahard *Arg. & B.* 146 D5
Balnahard *Arg. & B.* 147 D1
Balnain 166 D1
Balnakeil 192 C2
Balnaknock 176 A3
Balnamoon 160 D3
Balnapaling 179 G3
Balnespick 168 A4
Balquhidder 150 A2
Balsall 67 E5
Balsall Common 67 E5
Balscote 55 F3
Balsham 59 D2
Baltasound 203 F2
Balterley 79 E2
Baltersan 123 F4
Balthangie 182 D4
Balthayock 151 G2
Baltonsborough 24 C4
Baluachraig 148 A5
Balulive 138 C3
Balure *Arg. & B.* 148 C1
Balure *Arg. & B.* 148 A1
Balvaird 179 E4
Balvarran 159 F3
Balvicar 147 G3
Balvraid *High.* 165 E3
Balvraid *High.* 168 A1
Bamber Bridge 100 B5
Bamber's Green 59 D5
Bamburgh 137 F3
Bamff 160 A4
Bamford 93 G4
Bampton *Cumb.* 107 G1
Bampton *Devon* 22 C5
Bampton *Oxon.* 41 F2
Banavie 156 D2
Banbury 55 G3
Banc-y-ffordd 50 A4
Bancffosfelen 36 A1
Banchor 180 B5
Banchory 170 C5
Banchory-Devenick 171 E4
Bancyfelin 35 G1
Bandon 152 A4
Banff 182 B3
Bangor 89 D5
Bangor-is-y-coed 78 A3
Bangor Teifi 49 G3
Banham 72 B3
Bank 14 B2
Bank End 106 D4
Bank Newton 101 F2
Bank Street 53 F1
Bankend *D. & G.* 125 E4
Bankend *S.Lan.* 133 G2
Bankfoot 151 F1
Bankhead *Aber.* 170 B3
Bankhead *Aber.* 170 B4
Bankhead *Aberdeen* 171 D4
Bankhead *D. & G.* 116 A2
Banknock 142 B2
Banks *Cumb.* 118 B1
Banks *Lancs.* 99 G5
Bankshill 125 F2
Banningham 86 D3
Bannister Green 59 E5
Bannockburn 150 D5
Banstead 30 B3
Bantham 8 C3
Banton 142 B2
Banwell 24 A2
Bapchild 32 B2
Baptiston 141 G1
Bar Hill 58 B1
Barabhas (Barvas) 187 E2
Barachander 148 C2
Barassie 132 B2
Barbaraville 179 G2
Barber Booth 93 F4
Barbon 108 B4
Barbrook 22 A3
Barby 68 A5
Barcaldine 156 B5
Barcaple 124 A5
Barcheston 55 E3
Barcombe 17 G2
Barcombe Cross 17 G2
Barden 110 A3
Bardennoch 123 G1
Bardfield End Green 59 E4
Bardfield Saling 59 E5
Bardister 202 C5
Bardney 83 G1
Bardon *Leics.* 67 G1
Bardon *Moray* 181 E4
Bardon Mill 119 D1
Bardsea 107 E5
Bardsey 102 C3
Bardsley 92 D2
Bardwell 72 A4
Barewood 52 C2
Barfad 139 G3
Barford *Norf.* 86 C5
Barford *Warks.* 55 E1
Barford St. John 55 G4
Barford St. Martin 26 B4
Barford St. Michael 55 G4
Barfrestone 33 E3
Bargaly 123 F4
Bargany Mains 132 A5
Bargoed 38 A3
Bargrennan 123 E3
Barham *Cambs.* 69 G5
Barham *Kent* 33 D3
Barham *Suff.* 60 C2
Barharrow 124 A5
Barholm 69 F1
Barholm Mains 123 F5
Barkby 68 B2
Barkby Thorpe 68 B2
Barkestone-le-Vale 82 C4
Barkham 28 C1
Barking *Gt.Lon.* 44 D4
Barking *Suff.* 60 B2
Barking & Dagenham 45 D4
Barkingside 44 D4
Barkisland 93 E1
Barkston *Lincs.* 83 E3
Barkston *N.Yorks.* 103 D4
Barkway 58 B4
Barlae 123 D4
Barlaston 79 F4
Barlavington 16 B2
Barlborough 94 B5
Barlby 103 F4
Barlestone 67 G2
Barley *Herts.* 58 B4
Barley *Lancs.* 101 E3
Barleycroft End 58 C5
Barleyhill 119 G2
Barleythorpe 69 D2
Barling 46 C4
Barlings 96 A5
Barlow *Derbys.* 94 A5
Barlow *N.Yorks.* 103 F5
Barlow *T. & W.* 120 A1
Barmby Moor 103 G3
Barmby on the Marsh 103 F5
Barmer 85 G4
Barmolloch 148 A5
Barmoor Lane End 137 E2
Barmouth (Abermaw) 62 C1
Barmpton 110 C1
Barmston 105 D2
Barnacabber 140 C1
Barnacarry 148 C5
Barnack 69 F2
Barnacle 67 F4
Barnamuc 156 C5
Barnard Castle 109 F1
Barnard Gate 41 G1
Barnardiston 59 F3
Barnard's Green 53 G3
Barnbarroch *D. & G.* 123 E5
Barnbarroch *D. & G.* 124 C5
Barnburgh 94 B2
Barnby 73 F2
Barnby Dun 94 D2
Barnby in the Willows 83 D2
Barnby Moor 95 D4
Barndennoch 124 C2
Barnes 44 B5
Barnet 44 B3
Barnetby le Wold 96 A2
Barney 86 A2
Barnham *Suff.* 71 G5
Barnham *W.Suss.* 16 B3
Barnham Broom 86 B5
Barnhead 161 E4
Barnhill 180 D4
Barnhills 122 A3
Barningham *Dur.* 109 F1
Barningham *Suff.* 72 A4
Barnoldby le Beck 96 C2
Barnoldswick 101 E3
Barns Green 29 G5
Barnsdale Bar 94 C1
Barnsley *Glos.* 40 C2
Barnsley *S.Yorks.* 94 A2
Barnstaple 21 F2
Barnston *Essex* 45 F1
Barnston *Mersey.* 91 D4
Barnstone 82 C4
Barnt Green 66 C5
Barnton 92 A5
Barnwell All Saints 69 F4
Barnwell St. Andrew 69 F4
Barnwood 40 A1
Barr *Arg. & B.* 138 B3
Barr *High.* 155 F4
Barr *S.Ayr.* 123 D1
Barr Hall 59 F4
Barra (Tràigh Mhòr) Airport 172 C3
Barrackan 147 G4
Barraer 123 E4
Barraglom 186 C4
Barrahormid 139 F1
Barran 149 D2
Barrapoll 154 A2
Barrasford 128 B4
Barravullin 148 A4
Barregarrow 98 B3
Barrhead 141 G4
Barrhill 122 D2
Barrington *Cambs.* 58 B3
Barrington *Som.* 11 G1
Barripper 2 D3
Barrisdale 165 E4
Barrmill 141 E4
Barrnacarry 148 A2
Barrock 195 E1
Barrow *Lancs.* 100 D4
Barrow *Rut.* 69 D1
Barrow *Shrop.* 65 F2
Barrow *Som.* 25 E4
Barrow *Suff.* 59 F1
Barrow Gurney 24 C1
Barrow Haven 104 C5
Barrow-in-Furness 99 F1
Barrow Nook 91 F2
Barrow Street 25 F4
Barrow upon Humber 104 C5
Barrow upon Soar 68 A1
Barrow upon Trent 81 E5
Barrowby 83 D4
Barrowden 69 E2
Barrowford 101 E4
Barry *Angus* 152 D1
Barry *V. of Glam.* 23 E1
Barsby 68 C1
Barsham 73 E2
Barskimming 132 C3
Barsloisnoch 148 A5
Barston 67 E5
Bartestree 53 E3
Barthol Chapel 170 D1
Barthomley 79 E2
Bartley 14 C1
Bartlow 59 D3
Barton *Cambs.* 58 C2
Barton *Ches.* 78 B2
Barton *Glos.* 54 C5
Barton *Lancs.* 100 B4
Barton *Lancs.* 91 E2
Barton *N.Yorks.* 110 B2
Barton *Torbay* 9 F1
Barton *Warks.* 54 D2
Barton Bendish 71 F2
Barton Common 87 E3
Barton End 40 A3
Barton Hartshorn 56 B4
Barton in Fabis 81 G4
Barton in the Beans 67 F2
Barton-le-Clay 57 F4
Barton-le-Street 111 G5
Barton-le-Willows 103 G1
Barton Mills 71 F5
Barton on Sea 14 B3
Barton-on-the-Heath 55 E4
Barton St. David 24 C4
Barton Seagrave 69 D5
Barton Stacey 27 F3
Barton Turf 87 E3
Barton-under-Needwood 67 D1
Barton-upon-Humber 104 C5
Barvas (Barabhas) 187 E2
Barway 70 D5
Barwell 67 G3
Barwhinnock 124 A5
Barwick 12 B1
Barwick in Elmet 102 C4
Barwinnock 115 D2
Baschurch 78 B5
Bascote 55 G1
Basford Green 79 G2
Bashall Eaves 100 C3
Bashall Town 100 D3
Bashley 14 B3
Basildon *Essex* 45 G4
Basildon *W.Berks.* 42 B5
Basingstoke 28 B2
Baslow 93 G5
Bason Bridge 24 A3
Bassaleg 38 B4
Bassenthwaite 117 F3
Basset's Cross 21 F5
Bassett 14 D1
Bassingbourn 58 B3
Bassingfield 82 B4
Bassingham 83 E1
Bassingthorpe 83 E5
Basta 203 E3
Baston 69 G1
Bastwick 87 F4
Batavaime 149 G1
Batchworth 43 F3
Batchworth Heath 43 F3
Batcombe *Dorset* 12 C2
Batcombe *Som.* 25 D4
Bate Heath 92 A5
Bath 25 E1
Bathampton 25 E1
Bathealton 23 D5
Batheaston 25 E1
Bathford 25 E1
Bathgate 143 D3
Bathley 82 C2
Bathpool *Cornw.* 5 G2
Bathpool *Som.* 23 F5
Batley 102 B5
Batsford 55 D4
Battersby 111 E2
Battersea 44 B5
Battisborough Cross 8 C3
Battisford 60 B2
Battisford Tye 60 B2
Battle *E.Suss.* 18 C2
Battle *Powys* 51 G4
Battlefield 65 E1
Battlesbridge 45 G3
Battlesden 57 E5
Battleton 22 C5
Battramsley 14 C3
Batt's Corner 28 D3
Bauds of Cullen 181 G3
Baugh 154 B2
Baughton 54 A3
Baughurst 27 G2
Baulds 170 B5
Baulking 41 F3
Baumber 96 C5
Baunton 40 C2
Baveney Wood 65 F5
Baverstock 26 B4
Bawburgh 86 C5
Bawdeswell 86 B3
Bawdrip 24 A4
Bawdsey 61 E3
Bawtry 95 D3
Baxenden 101 D5
Baxterley 67 E3
Baycliff 107 D5
Baydon 41 E5
Bayford *Herts.* 44 C2
Bayford *Som.* 25 E5
Bayfordbury 44 C1
Bayham Abbey 31 F5
Bayles 118 D3
Baylham 60 C2
Baynards Green 56 A5
Baysham 53 E5
Bayston Hill 65 D2
Baythorn End 59 F3
Bayton 65 F5
Beach 155 G4
Beachampton 56 C4
Beacharr 139 E5
Beachborough 33 D5
Beachley 39 E3
Beacon 11 E2
Beacon End 60 A5
Beacon Hill 29 D4
Beacon's Bottom 42 C3
Beaconsfield 43 E3
Beadlam 111 F4
Beadnell 137 G3
Beaford 21 F4
Beal *N.Yorks.* 103 E5
Beal *Northumb.* 137 E2
Bealach 156 B4
Beambridge 78 D2
Beamhurst 80 B4
Beaminster 12 A2
Beamish 120 B2
Beamsley 101 G2
Bean 45 E5
Beanacre 25 F1
Beanley 137 E5
Beaquoy 198 B4
Beardon 7 F2
Beare Green 29 G3
Bearley 55 D1
Bearnie 171 E1
Bearnock 166 D1
Bearnus 154 D5
Bearpark 120 B3
Bearsbridge 119 D2
Bearsden 141 G2
Bearsted 31 G3
Bearwood 13 G3
Beattock 134 B5
Beauchamp Roding 45 E2
Beauchief 94 A4
Beaudesert 55 D1
Beaufort 38 A1
Beaulieu 14 C2
Beauly 179 E5
Beaumaris (Biwmaris) 89 E5
Beaumont *Cumb.* 117 G1
Beaumont *Essex* 60 C5
Beausale 67 E5
Beauworth 27 G5
Beaworthy 7 E1
Beazley End 59 F5
Bebington 91 E4
Bebside 129 E3
Beccles 73 F2
Becconsall 100 A5
Beck Foot 108 B3
Beck Hole 112 B2
Beck Row 71 E5
Beck Side 106 D4
Beckbury 65 G2
Beckenham 30 C2
Beckermet 106 B2
Beckfoot *Cumb.* 106 C2
Beckfoot *Cumb.* 117 D2
Beckford 54 B4
Beckhampton 26 B1
Beckingham *Lincs.* 83 D2
Beckingham *Notts.* 95 E4
Beckington 25 E2
Beckley *E.Suss.* 19 D1
Beckley *Oxon.* 42 A1
Beckton 44 D4
Beckwithshaw 102 B2
Becontree 45 D4
Bedale 110 B4
Bedburn 120 A4
Bedchester 13 E1
Beddau 37 G4
Beddgelert 75 E3
Beddingham 17 G3
Beddington 30 C2
Beddington Corner 30 B2
Bedfield 60 D1
Bedford 57 F3
Bedgebury Cross 31 G5
Bedhampton 15 G2
Bedingfield 60 C1
Bedlington 129 E3
Bedlinog 37 G2
Bedminster 39 E5
Bedmond 44 A2
Bednall 66 B1
Bedol 90 D5
Bedrule 136 G4
Bedstone 64 C5
Bedwas 38 A4
Bedwellty 38 A2
Bedworth 67 F4
Beeby 68 B2
Beech *Hants.* 28 B4
Beech *Staffs.* 79 F4
Beech Hill 28 B1
Beechamwell 71 F2
Beechingstoke 26 B2
Beedon 41 G5
Beeford 104 D2
Beeley 81 D1
Beelsby 96 C2
Beenham 27 G1
Beer 11 F4
Beer Hackett 12 B1
Beercrocombe 24 A5
Beesands 9 E3
Beesby 97 E4
Beeson 9 E3
Beeston *Beds.* 57 G3
Beeston *Ches.* 78 C2
Beeston *Norf.* 86 A4
Beeston *Notts.* 81 G4
Beeston *W.Yorks.* 102 B4
Beeston Regis 86 C1
Beeston St. Lawrence 87 E3
Beeswing 124 C4
Beetham 107 F5
Beetley 86 A4
Began 38 B4
Begbroke 41 G1
Begelly 35 E2
Beggshill 170 A1
Beguildy 64 A5
Beighton *Norf.* 87 E5
Beighton *S.Yorks.* 94 B4
Beith 141 E4
Bekesbourne 33 D3
Belaugh 87 D4
Belbroughton 66 B5
Belchamp Otten 59 G3
Belchamp St. Paul 59 F3
Belchamp Walter 59 G3
Belchford 96 C5
Belford 137 F3
Belgrave 68 A2
Belhaven 145 D2
Belhelvie 171 E3
Belhinnie 169 G2
Bell Bar 44 B2
Bell Busk 101 F2
Bell End 66 B5
Bellabeg 169 F3
Belladrum 179 E5
Bellanoch 148 A5
Bellasize 104 A5
Bellaty 160 A4
Belleau 97 E5
Bellehiglash 169 D1
Bellerby 110 A3
Bellever 7 G3
Belliehill 161 D3
Bellingdon 43 E2
Bellingham 128 A3
Belloch 130 B2
Bellochantuy 130 B2
Bells Yew Green 31 F5
Bellshill *N.Lan.* 142 B4
Bellshill *Northumb.* 137 F3
Bellside 142 C4
Bellsquarry 143 E3
Belluton 24 D1
Belmaduthy 179 F4
Belmesthorpe 69 F1
Belmont *B'burn.* 92 A1
Belmont *Gt.Lon.* 30 B2
Belmont *Shet.* 203 E2
Belowda 5 D3
Belper 81 E3
Belper Lane End 81 E3
Belsay 128 D4
Belsford 9 D2
Belstead 60 C3
Belston 132 B3
Belstone 7 G1
Belstone Corner 7 G1
Belsyde 143 D2
Belthorn 100 D5
Beltinge 33 D2
Beltoft 95 F2
Belton *Leics.* 81 F5
Belton *Lincs.* 83 E4
Belton *N.Lincs.* 95 E2
Belton *Norf.* 87 F5
Belton *Rut.* 68 D2
Beltring 31 F4
Belvedere 45 D5
Belvoir 82 D4
Bembridge 15 F4
Bemersyde 135 G2
Bempton 113 E5
Ben Alder Cottage 157 G3
Ben Alder Lodge 158 A2
Benacre 73 G3
Benbecula (Baile a' Mhanaich) Airport 173 F4
Benbuie 124 B1
Benderloch 148 B1
Bendish 57 G5
Benenden 32 A5
Benfield 123 E4
Bengate 87 E3
Bengeo 44 C1
Benholm 161 G3
Beningbrough 103 E2
Benington *Herts.* 58 A5
Benington *Lincs.* 84 B3
Benington Sea End 84 C3
Benllech 88 D4
Benmore *Arg. & B.* 140 C1
Benmore *Stir.* 149 G2
Bennacott 6 C1
Bennan Cottage 124 A3
Benniworth 96 C4
Benover 31 G4
Benson 42 B3
Benthall *Northumb.* 137 G4
Benthall *Shrop.* 65 F2
Bentham 40 B1
Benthoul 170 D4
Bentley *E.Riding* 104 C4
Bentley *Hants.* 28 C3
Bentley *S.Yorks.* 94 C2
Bentley *Suff.* 60 C4
Bentley *Warks.* 67 E3
Bentley Heath 67 D5
Benton 21 G2
Benton Square 129 F4
Bentpath 126 B2
Bentworth 28 B3
Benvie 152 B1
Benville Lane 12 B2
Benwick 70 B4
Beoley 54 C1
Bepton 16 A2
Berden 58 C5
Bere Alston 8 A1
Bere Ferrers 8 A1
Bere Regis 13 E3
Berea 48 A5
Berepper 3 D4
Bergh Apton 87 E5
Berinsfield 42 A3
Berkeley 39 F3
Berkhamsted 43 E2
Berkley 25 F3
Berkswell 67 E5
Bermondsey 44 C5
Bernera 165 E2
Berners Roding 45 F2
Bernice 148 D5
Bernisdale 176 A4
Berrick Salome 42 B3
Berriedale 191 G2
Berriew (Aberriw) 64 A2
Berrington *Northumb.* 137 E2
Berrington *Shrop.* 65 E2
Berrow 23 F2
Berrow Green 53 G2
Berry Down Cross 21 F1
Berry Hill *Glos.* 39 E1
Berry Hill *Pembs.* 49 D3
Berry Pomeroy 9 E1
Berryhillock 182 A3
Berrynarbor 21 F1
Bersham 78 A3
Berstane 198 C5
Berwick 18 A3
Berwick Bassett 40 C5
Berwick Hill 129 D4
Berwick St. James 26 B4
Berwick St. John 26 A5
Berwick St. Leonard 26 A4
Berwick-upon-Tweed 145 G4
Bescar 91 E1
Besford *Shrop.* 78 C5
Besford *Worcs.* 54 B3
Bessacarr 94 D2
Bessels Leigh 41 G2
Bessingby 105 D1
Bessingham 86 C2
Best Beech Hill 31 F5
Besthorpe *Norf.* 72 B2
Besthorpe *Notts.* 82 D1
Beswick 104 C3
Betchworth 30 B3
Bethania *Cere.* 50 B1
Bethania *Gwyn.* 76 A3
Bethel *Gwyn.* 75 E1
Bethel *Gwyn.* 76 C3
Bethel *I.o.A.* 88 B5
Bethersden 32 B4
Bethesda *Gwyn.* 75 F1
Bethesda *Pembs.* 35 D1
Bethlehem 50 C5
Bethnal Green 44 C4
Betley 79 E3
Betsham 45 F5
Betteshanger 33 F3
Bettiscombe 11 G3
Bettisfield 78 B4
Betton *Shrop.* 64 C2
Betton *Shrop.* 79 D4
Bettws 38 B3
Bettws Bledrws 50 B2
Bettws Cedewain 64 A3
Bettws Evan 49 G3
Bettws Gwerfil Goch 76 D3
Bettws Newydd 38 C2
Bettws-y-crwyn 64 B4
Bettyhill 193 G2
Betws *Bridgend* 37 F4
Betws *Carmar.* 36 C1
Betws Disserth 52 A2
Betws Garmon 75 E2
Betws-y-coed 76 A2
Betws-yn-Rhos 90 A5
Beulah *Cere.* 49 F3
Beulah *Powys* 51 F2
Bevendean 17 F3
Bevercotes 95 E5
Beverley 104 C4
Beverstone 40 A3
Bevington 39 F3
Bewaldeth 117 F3
Bewcastle 127 D4
Bewdley 65 G5
Bewerley 102 A1
Bewholme 105 D3
Bewley Common 26 A1
Bexhill 18 C3
Bexley 45 D5
Bexleyheath 45 D5
Bexwell 71 E2
Beyton 60 A1
Beyton Green 60 A1
Bhalamus 185 E3
Bhaltos 186 B4
Bhatarsaigh (Vatersay) 172 B4
Biallaid 167 G5
Bibury 40 D2
Bicester 56 A5
Bickenhall 11 F1
Bickenhill 67 D4
Bicker 84 A4
Bickerstaffe 91 F2
Bickerton *Ches.* 78 C2
Bickerton *N.Yorks.* 103 D2
Bickford 66 A1
Bickham Bridge 8 D2
Bickham House 10 C4
Bickington *Devon* 21 F2
Bickington *Devon* 10 A5
Bickleigh *Devon* 8 B1
Bickleigh *Devon* 10 C2
Bickleton 21 F2
Bickley 30 D2
Bickley Moss 78 C3
Bickley Town 78 C3
Bicknacre 45 G2
Bicknoller 23 E4
Bicknor 32 A3
Bickton 14 A1
Bicton *Shrop.* 64 D1
Bicton *Shrop.* 64 B4
Bicton Heath 65 D1
Bidborough 31 E4
Biddenden 32 A5
Biddenham 57 F3
Biddestone 40 A5
Biddisham 24 A2
Biddlesden 56 B3
Biddlestone 128 B1
Biddulph 79 F2
Biddulph Moor 79 G2
Bideford 21 E3
Bidford-on-Avon 54 C2
Bidston 91 D3
Bielby 103 G3
Bieldside 171 D4
Bierley *I.o.W.* 15 E5
Bierley *W.Yorks.* 102 A4
Bierton 42 D1
Big Sand 177 D2
Bigbury 8 C3
Bigbury-on-Sea 8 C3
Bigby 96 A2
Bigert Mire 106 C3
Biggar *Cumb.* 99 E1
Biggar *S.Lan.* 134 B2
Biggin *Derbys.* 81 D3
Biggin *Derbys.* 80 C2
Biggin *N.Yorks.* 103 E4
Biggin Hill 30 D3
Biggings 200 A1
Biggleswade 57 G3
Bigholms 126 B3
Bighouse 194 A2
Bighton 28 B4
Biglands 117 F1
Bignor 16 B2
Bigrigg 116 D5
Bigton 200 C5
Bilberry 5 E3
Bilborough 81 G3
Bilbrook *Som.* 22 D3
Bilbrook *Staffs.* 66 A2
Bilbrough 103 E3
Bilbster 195 E3
Bildershaw 120 A5
Bildeston 60 A3
Billericay 45 F3
Billesdon 68 C2
Billesley 54 D2
Billholm 126 A2
Billingborough 83 G4
Billinge 91 G2
Billingford *Norf.* 72 C4
Billingford *Norf.* 86 B3
Billingham 121 D5
Billinghay 83 G2
Billingley 94 B2
Billingshurst 29 F5
Billingsley 65 G4
Billington *Beds.* 57 E5
Billington *Lancs.* 100 D4
Billockby 87 F4
Billy Row 120 A4
Bilsborrow 100 B3
Bilsby 97 E5
Bilsdean 145 E2
Bilsham 16 B3
Bilsington 32 C5
Bilsthorpe 82 B1
Bilston *Midloth.* 143 G3
Bilston *W.Mid.* 66 B3
Bilstone 67 F2
Bilting 32 C4
Bilton *E.Riding* 105 D4
Bilton *N.Yorks.* 103 D2
Bilton *N.Yorks.* 102 C2
Bilton *Northumb.* 137 G5
Bilton *Warks.* 67 G5
Bimbister 198 B5
Binbrook 96 C3

Bincombe 12 C4
Bindal 180 B1
Binegar 24 D3
Bines Green 17 D2
Binfield 42 D5
Binfield Heath 42 C5
Bingfield 128 B4
Bingham 82 C4
Bingham's Melcombe 13 D2
Bingley 102 A4
Binham 86 A2
Binley *Hants.* 27 F2
Binley *W.Mid.* 67 F5
Binniehill 142 C2
Binsoe 110 B5
Binstead 15 E3
Binsted *Hants.* 28 C3
Binsted *W.Suss.* 16 B3
Binton 54 D2
Bintree 86 B3
Binweston 64 B2
Birch *Essex* 46 C1
Birch *Gt.Man.* 92 C2
Birch Green 46 C1
Birch Heath 78 C1
Birch Vale 93 E4
Bircham Newton 85 F4
Bircham Tofts 85 F4
Birchanger 58 D5
Bircher 53 D1
Birchfield 189 G5
Birchgrove *Cardiff* 38 A4
Birchgrove *Swan.* 36 D3
Birchington 33 E2
Birchover 80 D1
Birchwood 92 A3
Bircotes 94 D3
Bird End 66 C3
Birdbrook 59 F3
Birdfield 148 B5
Birdham 16 A4
Birdingbury 55 G1
Birdlip 40 B1
Birdsall 104 A1
Birdsgreen 65 G4
Birdsmoor Gate 11 G2
Birdwell 94 A2
Birdwood 39 G1
Birgham 136 B3
Birichen 190 C5
Birkby 110 C2
Birkdale *Mersey.* 91 E1
Birkdale *N.Yorks.* 109 D2
Birkenhead 91 E4
Birkenhills 182 C5
Birkenshaw 102 B5
Birkhall 169 F5
Birkhill *Angus* 152 B1
Birkhill *Sc.Bord.* 144 C5
Birkhill *Sc.Bord.* 134 D4
Birkin 103 E5
Birkwood 133 G2
Birley 53 D2
Birley Carr 94 A3
Birling *Kent* 31 F2
Birling *Northumb.* 129 E1
Birling Gap 18 A4
Birlingham 54 B3
Birmingham 66 C4
Birmingham International Airport 67 D4
Birnam 159 F5
Birsay 198 A4
Birse 170 A5
Birsemore 170 A5
Birstall 68 A2
Birstall Smithies 102 B5
Birstwith 102 B2
Birthorpe 83 G4
Birtley *Here.* 52 C1
Birtley *Northumb.* 128 A4
Birtley *T.& W.* 120 B2
Birts Street 53 G4
Bisbrooke 69 D3
Bish Mill 22 A5
Bisham 43 D4
Bishampton 54 B2
Bishop Auckland 120 B4
Bishop Burton 104 B4
Bishop Middleham 120 C4
Bishop Monkton 102 C1
Bishop Norton 95 G3
Bishop Sutton 24 C2
Bishop Thornton 102 B1
Bishop Wilton 103 G2
Bishopbridge 96 A3
Bishopbriggs 142 A3
Bishopmill 181 E3
Bishops Cannings 26 B1
Bishop's Castle 64 C4
Bishop's Caundle 12 C1
Bishop's Cleeve 54 B5
Bishop's Frome 53 F3
Bishop's Green 45 F1
Bishop's Hull 23 F5
Bishop's Itchington 55 F2
Bishop's Lydeard 23 E5
Bishop's Nympton 22 A5
Bishop's Offley 79 E5
Bishop's Stortford 58 C5
Bishop's Sutton 28 B4
Bishop's Tachbrook 55 F1
Bishop's Tawton 21 F2
Bishop's Waltham 15 E1
Bishop's Wood 66 A2
Bishopsbourne 33 D3
Bishopsteignton 10 C5
Bishopstoke 15 D1
Bishopston 36 B4
Bishopstone *Bucks.* 42 D1
Bishopstone *E.Suss.* 17 G3
Bishopstone *Here.* 52 D3
Bishopstone *Swin.* 41 E4
Bishopstone *Wilts.* 26 B5
Bishopstrow 25 F3
Bishopswood 11 F1
Bishopsworth 24 C1
Bishopthorpe 103 E3
Bishopton *Darl.* 120 C5
Bishopton *Renf.* 141 F2
Bishton 38 C4
Bisley *Glos.* 40 B2
Bisley *Surr.* 29 E2
Bispham 99 G3
Bissoe 4 B5
Bisterne 14 A2
Bisterne Close 14 B2
Bitchfield 83 E5
Bittadon 21 F1
Bittaford 8 C2
Bittering 86 A4
Bitterley 65 E5
Bitterne 15 D1
Bitteswell 68 A4
Bitton 25 D1
Biwmaris (Beaumaris) 89 E5
Bix 42 C4
Bixter 200 C2
Blaby 68 A3
Black Bourton 41 E2
Black Callerton 120 A1
Black Clauchrie 123 D2
Black Corries Lodge 157 E4
Black Cross 4 D3
Black Dog 10 B2
Black Heddon 128 C4
Black Marsh 64 C3
Black Mount 157 E5
Black Notley 59 F5
Black Pill 36 C3
Black Torrington 21 E5
Blackacre 125 E1
Blackadder 145 F4
Blackawton 9 E2
Blackborough 11 D2
Blackborough End 71 E1
Blackboys 18 A1
Blackbraes *Aber.* 171 D3
Blackbraes *Falk.* 142 D2
Blackbrook 79 E4
Blackburn *Aber.* 170 D3
Blackburn *B'burn.* 100 C5
Blackburn *W.Loth.* 143 D3
Blackbushe 28 C2
Blackcastle 180 A4
Blackchambers 170 C3
Blackcraig *D.& G.* 123 F4
Blackcraig *D.& G.* 124 B2
Blackden Heath 92 B5
Blackdog 171 E3
Blackdown *Devon* 7 F3
Blackdown *Dorset* 11 G2
Blackfield 14 D2
Blackford *Aber.* 170 B1
Blackford *Cumb.* 126 B5
Blackford *P.& K.* 151 D4
Blackford *Som.* 25 D5
Blackford *Som.* 24 B3
Blackfordby 67 F1
Blackgang 15 D5
Blackhall 143 G2
Blackhall Colliery 121 D4
Blackhall Rocks 121 D4
Blackham 31 E5
Blackheath *Essex* 60 A5
Blackheath *Gt.Lon.* 44 C5
Blackheath *Suff.* 73 F4
Blackheath *Surr.* 29 F3
Blackheath *W.Mid.* 66 B4
Blackhill *Aber.* 183 F4
Blackhill *Aber.* 183 F5
Blackhillock 181 G5
Blackhills 181 E4
Blackland 26 B1
Blacklunans 159 G3
Blackmill 37 F4
Blackmoor *Hants.* 28 C4
Blackmoor *Som.* 11 E1
Blackmoor Gate 21 G1
Blackmore 45 F2
Blackmore End *Essex* 59 F4
Blackmore End *Herts.* 44 A1
Blackness *Aber.* 170 B5
Blackness *Falk.* 143 E2
Blackness *High.* 195 E5
Blacknest 28 C3
Blacko 101 E3
Blackpool 99 G4
Blackpool Airport 99 G4
Blackpool Gate 126 D4
Blackridge 142 C3
Blackrock *Arg.& B.* 138 B3
Blackrock *Mon.* 38 B1
Blackrod 92 A1
Blackshaw 125 E4
Blackshaw Head 101 F5
Blacksmith's Corner 60 B4
Blackstone 17 E2
Blackthorn 42 B1
Blackthorpe 60 A1
Blacktoft 104 A5
Blacktop 171 D4
Blacktown 38 B4
Blackwater *Cornw.* 4 B5
Blackwater *Hants.* 29 D2
Blackwater *I.o.W.* 15 E4
Blackwater *Suff.* 73 F4
Blackwaterfoot 131 E3
Blackwell *Darl.* 110 B1
Blackwell *Derbys.* 93 F5
Blackwell *Derbys.* 81 F2
Blackwell *Warks.* 55 E3
Blackwell *Worcs.* 66 B5
Blackwells End 53 G5
Blackwood *Caerp.* 38 A3
Blackwood *D.& G.* 124 D2
Blackwood *S.Lan.* 142 B5
Blackwood Hill 79 G2
Blacon 78 A1
Bladbean 33 D4
Blades 109 E3
Bladnoch 123 F5
Bladon 41 G1
Blaen Dyryn 51 F4
Blaen-y-coed 49 G5
Blaenannerch 49 F3
Blaenau Dolwyddelan 75 F2
Blaenau Ffestiniog 75 F3
Blaenavon 38 B2
Blaenawey 38 B1
Blaencwm 37 F2
Blaenffos 49 E4
Blaengarw 37 F3
Blaengweche 36 C1
Blaengwrach 37 E2
Blaengwynfi 37 E3
Blaenos 51 D4
Blaenpennal 50 C1
Blaenplwyf 62 B5
Blaenporth 49 F3
Blaenrhondda 37 F2
Blaenwaun 49 F5
Blagdon *N.Som.* 24 B2
Blagdon *Torbay* 9 E1
Blagdon Hill 11 F1
Blaich 156 C2
Blaina 38 B2
Blair 141 E5
Blair Atholl 159 D3
Blair Drummond 150 C5
Blairannaich 149 F4
Blairbuie 140 C2
Blairgowrie 159 G5
Blairhall 143 E1
Blairhoyle 150 B4
Blairhullichan 149 G4
Blairingone 151 E5
Blairkip 132 D2
Blairlogie 150 D5
Blairmore *Arg.& B.* 140 C1
Blairmore *High.* 190 C4
Blairmore *High.* 192 A2
Blairnairn 141 E1
Blairnamarrow 169 E3
Blairpark 140 D4
Blairquhan 132 B5
Blairquhosh 141 G1
Blair's Ferry 140 A3
Blairshinnoch 182 B3
Blairuskinmore 149 G4
Blairvadach 141 D1
Blairydryne 170 C5
Blairythan Cottage 171 E2
Blaisdon 39 G1
Blake End 59 E5
Blakebrook 66 A5
Blakedown 66 A5
Blakelaw *Sc.Bord.* 136 B3
Blakelaw *T.& W.* 120 B1
Blakemere 52 C3
Blakeney *Glos.* 39 F2
Blakeney *Norf.* 86 B1
Blakenhall *Ches.* 79 E3
Blakenhall *W.Mid.* 66 B3
Blakeshall 66 A4
Blakesley 56 B2
Blanchland 119 F2
Bland Hill 102 B2
Blandford Camp 13 F2
Blandford Forum 13 E2
Blandford St. Mary 13 E2
Blanefield 141 G2
Blankney 83 F1
Blar a' Chaorainn 156 D3
Blargie 167 F5
Blarglas 141 E1
Blarmachfoldach 156 C3
Blarnalevoch 188 D5
Blashford 14 A2
Blaston 68 D3
Blathaisbhal 173 G2
Blatherwycke 69 E3
Blawith 107 D4
Blaxhall 61 E2
Blaxton 95 D2
Blaydon 120 A1
Bleadney 24 B3
Bleadon 24 A2
Bleak Hey Nook 93 E2
Blean 32 D2
Bleasby 82 C3
Bleatarn 108 C1
Blebocraigs 152 C3
Bleddfa 52 B1
Bledington 55 E5
Bledlow 42 C2
Bledlow Ridge 42 C3
Blencarn 118 C4
Blencogo 117 E2
Blencow 118 A4
Blendworth 15 G1
Blennerhasset 117 E2
Blervie Castle 180 C4
Bletchingdon 42 A1
Bletchingley 30 C3
Bletchley *M.K.* 57 D4
Bletchley *Shrop.* 78 D4
Bletherston 49 D5
Bletsoe 57 F2
Blewbury 42 A4
Blickling 86 C3
Blidworth 81 G2
Blindburn *Aber.* 171 E1
Blindburn *Northumb.* 136 C5
Blindcrake 117 E3
Blindley Heath 30 C4
Blisland 5 F2
Bliss Gate 65 G5
Blissford 14 A1
Blisworth 56 C2
Blithbury 80 B5
Blitterlees 117 E1
Blo Norton 72 B4
Blockley 55 D4
Blofield 87 E5
Blore 80 C3
Blossomfield 66 D5
Blount's Green 80 B4
Bloxham 55 G4
Bloxholm 83 F2
Bloxwich 66 B2
Bloxworth 13 E3
Blubberhouses 102 A2
Blue Anchor *Cornw.* 4 D4
Blue Anchor *Som.* 22 D3
Blue Bell Hill 31 G2
Bluewater 45 E5
Blundeston 73 G2
Blunham 57 G2
Blunsdon St. Andrew 40 D3
Bluntisham 70 B5
Blunts 6 D4
Blyborough 95 G3
Blyford 73 F4
Blymhill 66 A1
Blyth *Northumb.* 129 F3
Blyth *Notts.* 94 D4
Blyth Bridge 143 F5
Blythburgh 73 F4
Blythe Bridge 79 G3
Blythe Marsh 79 G3
Blyton 95 F3
Boarhills 153 D3
Boarhunt 15 F2
Boars Hill 41 G2
Boarshead 31 E5
Boarstall 42 B1
Boarzell 18 C1
Boasley Cross 7 F1
Boat o' Brig 181 F4
Boat of Garten 168 B3
Boath 179 E2
Bobbing 32 A2
Bobbington 66 A3
Bobbingworth 45 E2
Bocaddon 5 F4
Bochastle 150 B4
Bockhampton 41 F5
Bocking 59 F5
Bocking Churchstreet 59 F5
Boconnoc 5 F3
Boddam *Aber.* 183 G5
Boddam *Shet.* 201 G4
Boddington 54 A5
Bodedern 88 B4
Bodelwyddan 90 B5
Bodenham *Here.* 53 E2
Bodenham *Wilts.* 26 C5
Bodenham Moor 53 E2
Bodesbeck 134 C5
Bodewryd 88 B3
Bodfari 90 B5
Bodffordd 88 C5
Bodfuan 74 C4
Bodham Street 86 C1
Bodiam 18 C1
Bodicote 55 G4
Bodieve 5 D2
Bodinnick 5 F4
Bodior 88 A5
Bodle Street Green 18 B2
Bodmin 5 E3
Bodney 71 G3
Bodorgan 74 C1
Bodsham Green 32 D4
Bodwen 5 E3
Bogallan 179 F4
Bogbain 179 G5
Bogbrae 171 F1
Bogbuie 179 E4
Bogend 132 B2
Bogfern 170 A4
Bogfields 170 A4
Bogfold 182 D4
Boghead *Aber.* 182 B4
Boghead *E.Ayr.* 133 E3
Boghead *S.Lan.* 142 B5
Boghole Farm 180 B4
Bogmoor 181 F3
Bogniebrae 182 A5
Bognor Regis 16 B4
Bograxie 170 C3
Bogroy 168 B2
Bogside 151 E5
Bogston 169 F4
Bogton 182 B4
Bogue 124 A2
Bohenie 157 E1
Bohortha 3 F3
Bohuntine 157 E1
Boirseam 184 C5
Bojewyan 2 A3
Bolam 120 A5
Bolberry 8 C4
Bold Heath 91 G4
Bolderwood 14 B2
Boldon 120 C1
Boldre 14 C3
Boldron 109 F1
Bole 95 E4
Bolehill 81 D2
Boleigh 2 B4
Boleside 135 F2
Bolfracks 158 D5
Bolgoed 36 C2
Bolham 10 C1
Bolham Water 11 E1
Bolingey 4 B4
Bollington 92 D5
Bolney 17 E1
Bolnhurst 57 F2
Bolshan 161 E4
Bolsover 94 B5
Bolsterstone 93 G3
Bolstone 53 E4
Boltby 111 D4
Bolter End 42 C3
Bolton *Cumb.* 118 C5
Bolton *E.Loth.* 144 C2
Bolton *E.Riding* 103 G2
Bolton *Gt.Man.* 92 B2
Bolton *Northumb.* 137 F5
Bolton Abbey 101 G2
Bolton Bridge 101 G2
Bolton by Bowland 101 D3
Bolton-le-Sands 100 A1
Bolton Low Houses 117 F2
Bolton-on-Swale 110 B3
Bolton Percy 103 E3
Bolton upon Dearne 94 B2
Boltonfellend 118 A1
Boltongate 117 F2
Bolventor 5 F2
Bombie 124 B5
Bomere Heath 65 D1
Bon-y-maen 36 C3
Bonar Bridge 190 B5
Bonawe 148 C1
Bonawe Quarries 148 C1
Bonby 96 A1
Boncath 49 F4
Bonchester Bridge 135 G4
Bonchurch 15 E5
Bondleigh 21 G5
Bonehill 67 D2
Bo'ness 143 D1
Bonhill 141 E2
Boningale 66 A2
Bonjedward 136 A4
Bonkle 142 C4
Bonnington 32 C5
Bonnybank 152 B4
Bonnybridge 142 C1
Bonnykelly 183 D4
Bonnyrigg 144 A3
Bonnyton *Aber.* 170 B1
Bonnyton *Angus* 153 D1
Bonnyton *Angus* 161 E4
Bonnyton *Angus* 152 B1
Bonsall 81 D2
Bont 38 C1
Bont Dolgadfan 63 E2
Bont-goch (Elerch) 62 C4
Bont Newydd 76 A5
Bontddu 62 C1
Bontnewydd 75 D1
Bontuchel 77 D2
Bonvilston 37 G5
Boohay 9 F2
Booker 42 D3
Booley 78 C5
Boor 177 E1
Boosbeck 111 F1
Boot 106 C2
Booth Wood 93 E1
Boothby Graffoe 83 E2
Boothby Pagnell 83 E4
Boothstown 92 B2
Boothtown 101 G5
Boothville 56 C1
Bootle *Cumb.* 106 C4
Bootle *Mersey.* 91 E3
Booton 86 C3
Boquhan 141 G1
Boraston 65 F5
Bordeaux 9 F4
Borden 32 A2
Bordley 101 F1
Bordon 28 C4
Boreham *Essex* 45 G2
Boreham *Wilts.* 25 F3
Boreham Street 18 B2
Borehamwood 44 A3
Boreland *D.& G.* 125 F1
Boreland *D.& G.* 123 E4
Boreland *Stir.* 150 A1
Boreraig 175 E4
Borgh *W.Isles* 184 B5
Borgh *W.Isles* 172 B3
Borghastan 186 C3
Borgie 193 F3
Borgue *D.& G.* 115 G2
Borgue *High.* 191 G2
Borley 59 G3
Bornais 172 C1
Borness 115 G2
Borough Green 31 F3
Boroughbridge 102 C1
Borras Head 78 A2
Borrowash 81 F4
Borrowby *N.Yorks.* 111 G1
Borrowby *N.Yorks.* 110 D4
Borrowdale 117 F5
Borrowfield 170 D5
Borstal 31 G2
Borth 62 C4
Borth-y-Gest 75 E4
Borthwick 144 A4
Borthwickbrae 135 F4
Borthwickshiels 135 F4
Borve 176 A5
Borwick 107 G5
Bosavern 2 A3
Bosbury 53 F3
Boscastle 6 B1
Boscombe *Bourne.* 14 A3
Boscombe *Wilts.* 26 D4
Boscoppa 5 E4
Bosham 16 A3
Bosherston 34 C3
Bosley 79 G1
Bossall 103 G1
Bossiney 5 E1
Bossingham 32 D4
Bossington *Hants.* 27 E4
Bossington *Som.* 22 B3
Bostock Green 79 D1
Boston 84 B3
Boston Spa 102 D3
Boswinger 5 D5
Botallack 2 A3
Botany Bay 44 B3
Botarua 173 F2
Botcheston 67 G2
Botesdale 72 B4
Bothal 129 E3
Bothamsall 95 D5
Bothel 117 E3
Bothenhampton 12 A3
Bothwell 142 B4
Botley *Bucks.* 43 E2
Botley *Hants.* 15 E1
Botley *Oxon.* 41 G2
Botloe's Green 53 G5
Botolph Claydon 56 C5
Botolphs 17 D3
Bottacks 179 D3
Bottesford *Leics.* 82 D4
Bottesford *N.Lincs.* 95 G2
Bottisham 58 D1
Bottom Head 100 C1
Bottomcraig 152 B2
Botusfleming 8 A1
Botwnnog 74 B4
Bough Beech 31 D4
Boughrood 52 A4
Boughspring 39 E3
Boughton *Norf.* 71 E2
Boughton *Northants.* 56 C1
Boughton *Notts.* 82 B1
Boughton Aluph 32 C4
Boughton Green 31 G3
Boughton Lees 32 C4
Boughton Malherbe 32 A4
Boughton Street 32 C3
Boulby 111 G1
Bouldon 65 E4
Boulmer 137 G5
Boulston 34 C1
Boultenstone Hotel 169 G3
Boultham 83 E1
Bourn 58 B2
Bournbrook 66 C4
Bourne 83 F5
Bourne End *Beds.* 57 E3
Bourne End *Bucks.* 43 D4
Bourne End *Herts.* 43 F2
Bournebridge 45 E3
Bournemouth 13 G3
Bournemouth International Airport 14 A3
Bournes Green 40 B2
Bournheath 66 B5
Bournmoor 120 C2
Bournville 66 C4
Bourton *Dorset* 25 E4
Bourton *N.Som.* 24 A1
Bourton *Oxon.* 41 E4
Bourton *Shrop.* 65 E3
Bourton on Dunsmore 67 G5
Bourton-on-the-Hill 55 D4
Bourton-on-the-Water 55 D5
Bousd 154 B3
Boustead Hill 117 F1
Bouth 107 E4
Bouthwaite 110 A5
Bovain 150 A1
Boveney 43 E5
Boveridge 13 G1
Boverton 22 C1
Bovey Tracey 10 B5
Bovingdon 43 F2
Bovinger 45 E2
Bovington Camp 13 E4
Bow *Devon* 10 A2
Bow *Devon* 9 E2
Bow *Ork.* 196 C3
Bow Brickhill 57 E4
Bow of Fife 152 B3
Bow Street 62 C4
Bowbank 119 F5
Bowburn 120 C4
Bowcombe 15 D4
Bowd 11 E4
Bowden *Devon* 9 E3
Bowden *Sc.Bord.* 135 G2
Bowden Hill 26 A1
Bowdon 92 B4
Bower 127 F3
Bower Hinton 12 A1
Bowerchalke 26 B5
Bowerhill 26 A1
Bowermadden 195 E2
Bowers Gifford 45 G4
Bowershall 151 F5
Bowertower 195 E2
Bowes 109 E1
Bowgreave 100 A3
Bowland Bridge 107 F4
Bowley 53 E2
Bowlhead Green 29 E4
Bowling 141 F2
Bowling Bank 78 A3
Bowlish 24 D3
Bowmanstead 107 E3
Bowmore 138 B4
Bowness-on-Solway 126 A5
Bowness-on-Windermere 107 F3
Bowsden 145 G5
Bowside Lodge 194 A2
Bowthorpe 86 C5
Bowtrees 142 D1
Box *Glos.* 40 A2
Box *Wilts.* 25 F1
Box End 57 F3
Boxbush 39 G1
Boxford *Suff.* 60 A3
Boxford *W.Berks.* 41 G5
Boxgrove 16 B3
Boxley 31 G3
Boxmoor 43 F2
Boxted *Essex* 60 A4
Boxted *Suff.* 59 G2
Boxted Cross 60 B4
Boxworth 58 B1
Boxworth End 58 B1
Boyden Gate 33 E2
Boydston 132 C2
Boylestone 80 C4
Boyndie 182 B3
Boynton 104 D1
Boysack 161 E5
Boyton *Cornw.* 6 D1
Boyton *Suff.* 61 E3
Boyton *Wilts.* 26 A4
Boyton Cross 45 F2
Bozeat 57 E2
Braaid 98 B4
Braal Castle 194 D2
Brabling Green 61 D1
Brabourne 32 C4
Brabourne Lees 32 C4
Brabster 195 F2
Bracadale 163 G1
Braceborough 69 F1
Bracebridge 83 E1
Bracebridge Heath 83 E1
Braceby 83 F4
Bracewell 101 E3
Brachla 167 E1
Brackenber 118 D5
Brackenfield 81 E2
Brackens 182 C4
Bracklach 169 F2
Bracklamore 182 D4
Brackletter 157 D1
Brackley *Arg.& B.* 139 G1
Brackley *High.* 180 A4
Brackley *Northants.* 56 A4
Bracknell 29 D1
Braco 150 D4
Bracobrae 182 A4
Bracon Ash 72 C2
Bracora 164 D5
Bracorina 164 D5
Bradbourne 80 D2
Bradbury 120 C5
Bradda 98 A4
Bradden 56 B3
Bradenham 42 D3
Bradenstoke 40 C4
Bradfield *Devon* 10 D2
Bradfield *Essex* 60 C4
Bradfield *Norf.* 87 D2
Bradfield *W.Berks.* 42 B5
Bradfield Combust 59 G2
Bradfield Green 79 D2
Bradfield Heath 60 C5
Bradfield St. Clare 60 A2
Bradfield St. George 60 A2
Bradford *Devon* 21 E5
Bradford *Northumb.* 137 F3
Bradford *W.Yorks.* 102 A4
Bradford Abbas 12 B1
Bradford Leigh 25 F1
Bradford-on-Avon 25 F1
Bradford-on-Tone 23 E5
Bradford Peverell 12 C3
Brading 15 F4
Bradley *Derbys.* 80 D3
Bradley *Hants.* 28 B3
Bradley *N.E.Lincs.* 96 C2
Bradley *N.Yorks.* 109 F4
Bradley *Staffs.* 66 A1
Bradley *W.Mid.* 66 B3
Bradley Green 54 B1
Bradley in the Moors 80 B3
Bradley Stoke 39 F4
Bradmore *Notts.* 81 G4
Bradmore *W.Mid.* 66 A3
Bradninch 10 D2
Bradnop 80 B2
Bradpole 12 A3
Bradshaw 92 B1
Bradstone 7 D2
Bradwall Green 79 E1
Bradwell *Derbys.* 93 F4
Bradwell *Essex* 59 G5
Bradwell *M.K.* 56 D4
Bradwell *Norf.* 87 G5
Bradwell Grove 41 E2
Bradwell-on-Sea 46 C2
Bradwell Waterside 46 C2
Bradworthy 20 D4
Brae *D.& G.* 124 C3
Brae *High.* 189 G4
Brae *Shet.* 200 C1
Braeantra 179 E2
Braedownie 160 A2
Braefoot 182 C5
Braegrum 151 F2
Braehead *Moray* 181 F5
Braehead *Ork.* 197 E2
Braehead *Ork.* 198 C2
Braehead *S.Lan.* 133 G2
Braehead *S.Lan.* 143 D4
Braehead of Lunan 161 E4
Braehoulland 202 B5
Braeleny 150 B3
Braemar 169 D5
Braemore *High.* 190 A4
Braemore *High.* 194 C5
Braemore *High.* 178 A2
Braenaloin 169 E5
Braes of Enzie 181 F4
Braes of Foss 158 C4
Braes of Ullapool 188 D5
Braeswick 199 E3
Braeval 150 A4
Brafferton *Darl.* 120 B5
Brafferton *N.Yorks.* 110 D5
Brafield-on-the-Green 56 D2
Bragar 187 D3
Bragbury End 58 A5
Bragleenbeg 148 B2
Braichmelyn 75 F1
Braides 100 A2
Braidwood 142 C5
Braigo 138 A3
Brailsford 81 D3
Braintree 59 F5
Braiseworth 72 C4
Braishfield 27 E5
Braithwaite *Cumb.* 117 F4
Braithwaite *S.Yorks.* 94 D1
Braithwell 94 C3
Bramber 17 D2
Brambletye 30 D5
Bramcote 81 G4
Bramdean 28 B5
Bramerton 87 D5
Bramfield *Herts.* 44 B1
Bramfield *Suff.* 73 E4
Bramford 60 C3
Bramhall 92 C4
Bramham 102 D3
Bramhope 102 B3
Bramley *Hants.* 28 B2
Bramley *S.Yorks.* 94 B3
Bramley *Surr.* 29 F3
Bramling 33 E3
Brampford Speke 10 C3
Brampton *Cambs.* 70 A5
Brampton *Cumb.* 118 B1
Brampton *Cumb.* 118 C5
Brampton *Derbys.* 94 A5
Brampton *Lincs.* 95 F5
Brampton *Norf.* 86 D3

Brampton *S.Yorks.* 94 B2
Brampton *Suff.* 73 F3
Brampton Abbotts 53 F5
Brampton Ash 68 C4
Brampton Bryan 64 C5
Brampton en le Morthen 94 B4
Bramshall 80 B4
Bramshaw 14 B1
Bramshill 28 C1
Bramshott 28 D4
Bramwell 24 B5
Bran End 59 E5
Branault 155 E3
Brancaster 85 F3
Brancepeth 120 B4
Branchill 180 C4
Brand Green 53 G5
Branderburgh 181 E2
Brandesburton 104 D3
Brandeston 60 D1
Brandis Corner 21 E5
Brandiston 86 C3
Brandon *Dur.* 120 B4
Brandon *Lincs.* 83 E3
Brandon *Northumb.* 137 E5
Brandon *Suff.* 71 F4
Brandon *Warks.* 67 G5
Brandon Bank 71 E4
Brandon Creek 71 E3
Brandon Parva 86 B5
Brandsby 111 E5
Brandy Wharf 96 A3
Brane 2 A4
Branksome 13 G3
Branksome Park 13 G3
Bransby 95 F5
Branscombe 11 E4
Bransford 53 G2
Bransford Bridge 54 A2
Bransgore 14 A3
Branson's Cross 66 C5
Branston *Leics.* 82 D5
Branston *Lincs.* 83 F1
Branston *Staffs.* 80 D5
Branston Booths 83 F1
Branstone 15 E4
Brant Broughton 83 E2
Brantham 60 C4
Branthwaite *Cumb.* 117 F3
Branthwaite *Cumb.* 117 D4
Brantingham 104 B5
Branton *Northumb.* 137 E5
Branton *S.Yorks.* 94 D2
Brantwood 107 E3
Branxholm Bridgend 135 F4
Branxholme 135 F4
Branxton 136 C3
Brassington 80 D2
Brasted 31 D3
Brasted Chart 31 D3
Brathens 170 B5
Bratoft 84 C1
Brattleby 95 G4
Bratton 26 A2
Bratton Clovelly 7 E1
Bratton Fleming 21 G2
Bratton Seymour 25 D5
Braughing 58 B5
Braunston *Northants.* 56 A1
Braunston *Rut.* 68 D2
Braunstone 68 A2
Braunton 21 E2
Brawby 111 G5
Brawdy 48 B5
Brawl 194 A2
Brawlbin 194 C3
Bray 43 E5
Bray Shop 6 D3
Bray Wick 43 D5
Braybrooke 68 C4
Brayford 21 G2
Brayshaw 101 D2
Brayton 103 F4
Brazacott 6 C1
Breach 33 D4
Breachwood Green 57 G5
Breacleit 186 C4
Breadsall 81 E4
Breadstone 39 G2
Breage 2 D4
Breakon 203 E2
Bream 39 F2
Breamore 14 A1
Brean 23 F2
Breanais 186 A5
Brearton 102 C1
Breascleit 186 D4
Breaston 81 F4
Brechfa 50 B4
Brechin 161 E3
Brecklate 130 B4
Breckles 72 A2
Brecon (Aberhonddu) 51 G5
Breconside 133 G5
Bredbury 92 D3
Brede 18 D2
Bredenbury 53 F2
Bredfield 61 D2
Bredgar 32 A2
Bredhurst 31 G2
Bredicot 54 B2
Bredon 54 B4
Bredon's Hardwick 54 B4
Bredon's Norton 54 B4
Bredwardine 52 C3
Breedon on the Hill 81 F5
Breibhig 187 F4
Breich 143 D3
Breighton 103 G4
Breinton 53 D3
Bremhill 40 B5
Brenachoille 148 C4
Brenchley 31 F4
Brendon *Devon* 22 A3
Brendon *Devon* 21 D4
Brenkley 129 E4
Brent 44 A4
Brent Eleigh 60 A3
Brent Knoll 24 A2
Brent Pelham 58 C4
Brentford 44 A5
Brentingby 68 C1
Brentwood 45 E3
Brenzett 19 F1
Breoch 124 B5
Brereton 66 C1
Brereton Green 79 E1
Brereton Heath 79 F1
Bressingham 72 B3
Bretabister 201 D2
Bretby 81 D5
Bretford 67 G5
Bretforton 54 C3
Bretherdale Head 107 G2
Bretherton 100 A5
Brettenham *Norf.* 72 A3
Brettenham *Suff.* 60 A2
Bretton 78 A1
Brewood 66 A2
Briach 180 C4
Briantspuddle 13 E3
Bricket Wood 44 A2
Bricklehampton 54 B3
Bride 98 C1
Bridekirk 117 E3
Bridell 49 E3
Bridestones 79 G1
Bridestowe 7 F2
Brideswell 170 A1
Bridford 10 B4
Bridge *Cornw.* 4 A5
Bridge *Kent* 33 D3
Bridge End *Lincs.* 83 G4
Bridge End *Shet.* 200 C4
Bridge Hewick 110 C5
Bridge o' Ess 170 A5
Bridge of Alford 170 A3
Bridge of Allan 150 C5
Bridge of Avon 169 D1
Bridge of Balgie 158 A5
Bridge of Bogendreip 170 B5
Bridge of Brewlands 159 G3
Bridge of Brown 168 D2
Bridge of Cally 159 G4
Bridge of Canny 170 B5
Bridge of Craigisla 160 A4
Bridge of Dee *Aber.* 169 D5
Bridge of Dee *Aber.* 170 B5
Bridge of Dee *D. & G.* 124 B4
Bridge of Don 171 E4
Bridge of Dun 161 E4
Bridge of Dye 161 E1
Bridge of Earn 151 G3
Bridge of Ericht 158 A4
Bridge of Feugh 170 B5
Bridge of Forss 194 C2
Bridge of Gairn 169 F5
Bridge of Gaur 158 A4
Bridge of Muchalls 171 D5
Bridge of Muick 169 F5
Bridge of Orchy 149 F1
Bridge of Tilt 159 D3
Bridge of Tynet 181 F3
Bridge of Walls 200 B2
Bridge of Weir 141 E3
Bridge Sollers 52 D3
Bridge Street 59 G3
Bridge Trafford 91 F5
Bridgefoot *Cambs.* 58 C3
Bridgefoot *Cumb.* 117 D4
Bridgehampton 24 C5
Bridgemary 15 E2
Bridgemere 79 E3
Bridgend *Aber.* 170 A1
Bridgend *Angus* 160 D3
Bridgend *Arg. & B.* 138 B3
Bridgend *Arg. & B.* 148 A5
Bridgend (Pen-y-Bont ar Ogwr) *Bridgend* 37 F5
Bridgend *Cornw.* 5 F3
Bridgend *Cumb.* 107 F1
Bridgend *Fife* 152 B3
Bridgend *Moray* 169 F1
Bridgend *P. & K.* 151 G2
Bridgend *W.Loth.* 143 E2
Bridgend of Lintrathen 160 A4
Bridgerule 20 C5
Bridges 64 C3
Bridgeton 170 A3
Bridgetown *Cornw.* 6 D2
Bridgetown *Som.* 22 C4
Bridgeyate 39 F5
Bridgham 72 A3
Bridgnorth 65 G3
Bridgtown 66 B2
Bridgwater 23 F4
Bridlington 105 D1
Bridport 12 A3
Bridstow 53 E5
Brierfield 101 E4
Brierley *Glos.* 39 F1
Brierley *Here.* 53 D2
Brierley *S.Yorks.* 94 B1
Brierley Hill 66 B4
Brig o'Turk 150 A4
Brigehaugh 169 F1
Brigg 96 A2
Brigham *Cumb.* 117 D3
Brigham *E.Riding* 104 C2
Brighouse 102 A5
Brighstone 14 D4
Brightgate 81 D2
Brighthampton 41 F2
Brightling 18 B1
Brightlingsea 47 D1
Brighton *B. & H.* 17 F3
Brighton *Cornw.* 4 D4
Brightons 142 D2
Brightwalton 41 G5
Brightwell *Oxon.* 42 A3
Brightwell *Suff.* 60 D3
Brightwell Baldwin 42 B3
Brignall 109 F1
Brigsley 96 C2
Brigsteer 107 F4
Brigstock 69 E4
Brill *Bucks.* 42 B1
Brill *Cornw.* 3 E4
Brilley 52 B3
Brilley Mountain 52 B2
Brimfield 53 E1
Brimington 94 B5
Brimington Common 94 B5
Brimley 10 B5
Brimpsfield 40 B1
Brimpton 27 G1
Brimscombe 40 A2
Brimstage 91 E4
Brind 103 G4
Brindister *Shet.* 200 D4
Brindister *Shet.* 200 B2
Brindle 100 B5
Brindley Ford 79 F2
Brineton 66 A1
Bringhurst 68 D3
Brington 69 F5
Brinian 198 C4
Briningham 86 B2
Brinkhill 97 D5
Brinkley 59 E2
Brinklow 67 G5
Brinkworth 40 C4
Brinmore 167 F2
Brinscall 100 C5
Brinsley 81 F3
Brinsop 52 D3
Brinsworth 94 B4
Brinton 86 B2
Brisco 118 A2
Brisley 86 A3
Brislington 39 F5
Bristol 39 E5
Bristol International Airport 24 B1
Briston 86 B2
Britannia 101 E5
Britford 26 C5
Brithdir 63 D1
Brithem Bottom 10 D1
Briton Ferry (Llansawel) 36 D3
Britwell Salome 42 B3
Brixham 9 F2
Brixton 8 B2
Brixton Deverill 25 F4
Brixworth 68 C5
Brize Norton 41 E2
Broad Blunsdon 41 D3
Broad Campden 55 D4
Broad Chalke 26 B5
Broad Green *Beds.* 57 E3
Broad Green *Essex* 59 G5
Broad Green *Worcs.* 53 G2
Broad Haven 34 B1
Broad Hill 71 D5
Broad Hinton 40 D5
Broad Laying 27 F1
Broad Marston 54 D3
Broad Oak *Cumb.* 106 C3
Broad Oak *E.Suss.* 18 D2
Broad Oak *E.Suss.* 18 B1
Broad Oak *Here.* 53 D5
Broad Street 32 A3
Broad Street Green 46 B2
Broad Town 40 C5
Broadbottom 93 D3
Broadbridge 16 A3
Broadbridge Heath 29 G4
Broadclyst 10 C3
Broadford 164 C2
Broadford Bridge 29 F5
Broadgate 106 C4
Broadgroves 45 F1
Broadhaugh 135 F5
Broadheath *Gt.Man.* 92 B4
Broadheath *Worcs.* 53 F1
Broadhembury 11 E2
Broadhempston 9 E1
Broadholme 95 F5
Broadland Row 18 D2
Broadlay 35 G2
Broadley *Lancs.* 92 C1
Broadley *Moray* 181 F3
Broadley Common 44 D2
Broadmayne 12 D4
Broadmeadows 135 F3
Broadmere 28 B3
Broadnymett 10 A2
Broadoak *Carmar.* 50 B5
Broadoak *Dorset* 12 A3
Broadoak *Kent* 33 D2
Broadrashes 181 G4
Broadsea 183 E3
Broadstairs 33 F2
Broadstone *Poole* 13 G3
Broadstone *Shrop.* 65 E4
Broadstreet Common 38 C4
Broadwas 53 G2
Broadwater *Herts.* 58 A5
Broadwater *W.Suss.* 16 D3
Broadway *Carmar.* 35 G2
Broadway *Carmar.* 35 F1
Broadway *Pembs.* 34 B1
Broadway *Som.* 11 G1
Broadway *Suff.* 73 E4
Broadway *Worcs.* 54 C4
Broadwell *Glos.* 55 E5
Broadwell *Glos.* 39 E1
Broadwell *Oxon.* 41 E2
Broadwell *Warks.* 55 G1
Broadwell House 119 F2
Broadwey 12 C4
Broadwindsor 12 A2
Broadwood Kelly 21 G5
Broadwoodwidger 7 E2
Brobury 52 C3
Brochel 176 B5
Brochloch 123 G1
Brock 154 B2
Brockbridge 15 F1
Brockdish 72 D4
Brockenhurst 14 C2
Brockfield 103 F2
Brockford Street 60 C1
Brockhall 56 B1
Brockham 29 G3
Brockhampton *Glos.* 54 C5
Brockhampton *Here.* 53 E4
Brockholes 93 F1
Brockhurst 30 D5
Brocklebank 117 G2
Brocklesby 96 B1
Brockley 24 B1
Brockley Green 59 G2
Brockton *Shrop.* 65 E3
Brockton *Shrop.* 65 G2
Brockton *Shrop.* 64 C2
Brockton *Shrop.* 64 C4
Brockweir 39 E2
Brockwood Park 28 B5
Brockworth 40 A1
Brocton 66 B1
Brodick 131 F2
Brodsworth 94 C2
Brogborough 57 E4
Brogyntyn 77 F4
Broken Cross *Ches.* 92 C5
Broken Cross *Ches.* 92 A5
Brokenborough 40 B4
Bromborough 91 E4
Brome 72 C4
Brome Street 72 C4
Bromeswell 61 D2
Bromfield *Cumb.* 117 E2
Bromfield *Shrop.* 65 D5
Bromham *Beds.* 57 F2
Bromham *Wilts.* 26 A1
Bromley 30 D2
Bromley Green 32 B5
Brompton *Med.* 31 G2
Brompton *N.Yorks.* 110 C3
Brompton *N.Yorks.* 112 C4
Brompton on Swale 110 B2
Brompton Ralph 23 D4
Brompton Regis 22 C4
Bromsash 53 F5
Bromsberrow Heath 53 G4
Bromsgrove 66 B5
Bromstead Heath 66 A1
Bromyard 53 F2
Bromyard Downs 53 F2
Bron-y-Gaer 35 G1
Bronaber 76 A4
Brongest 49 G3
Bronington 78 B4
Bronllys 52 A4
Bronnant 50 C1
Bronydd 52 B3
Bronygarth 77 F4
Brook *Carmar.* 35 F2
Brook *Hants.* 14 B1
Brook *Hants.* 27 E5
Brook *I.o.W.* 14 C4
Brook *Kent* 32 C4
Brook *Surr.* 29 E4
Brook Street *Essex* 45 E3
Brook Street *Kent* 32 B5
Brook Street *Suff.* 59 G3
Brook Street *W.Suss.* 17 F1
Brooke *Norf.* 73 D2
Brooke *Rut.* 69 D2
Brookend 39 E3
Brookhouse 100 B1
Brookhouse Green 79 F1
Brookland 19 E1
Brooklands 124 C3
Brookmans Park 44 B2
Brooks 64 A3
Brooks Green 29 G5
Brooksby 68 B1
Brookthorpe 40 A1
Brookwood 29 E2
Broom *Beds.* 57 G3
Broom *Warks.* 54 C2
Broom Hill 13 G2
Broom of Dalreach 151 F3
Broomcroft 65 E2
Broome *Norf.* 73 E2
Broome *Shrop.* 64 C4
Broome *Worcs.* 66 B5
Broome Wood 137 F5
Broomedge 92 B4
Broomer's Corner 29 G5
Broomfield *Aber.* 171 E1
Broomfield *Essex* 45 G1
Broomfield *Kent* 33 D2
Broomfield *Kent* 32 A3
Broomfield *Som.* 23 F4
Broomfleet 104 A5
Broomhaugh 119 G1
Broomhead 183 E3
Broomhill 129 E1
Broom's Green 53 G4
Brora 191 E4
Broseley 65 F2
Brotherlee 119 F4
Brothertoft 84 A3
Brotherton 103 D5
Brotton 121 F5
Broubster 194 C2
Brough *Cumb.* 108 C1
Brough *Derbys.* 93 F4
Brough *E.Riding* 104 B5
Brough *High.* 195 E1
Brough *Notts.* 82 D2
Brough *Ork.* 198 B5
Brough *Shet.* 201 E3
Brough *Shet.* 202 D5
Brough *Shet.* 201 E1
Brough *Shet.* 203 E5
Brough Lodge 203 E3
Brough Sowerby 108 C1
Broughall 78 C3
Brougham 118 B5
Broughton *Cambs.* 70 A5
Broughton *Flints.* 78 A1
Broughton *Hants.* 27 E4
Broughton *Lancs.* 100 B4
Broughton *M.K.* 57 D3
Broughton *N.Lincs.* 95 G2
Broughton *N.Yorks.* 111 G5
Broughton *N.Yorks.* 101 F2
Broughton *Northants.* 68 D5
Broughton *Ork.* 198 C2
Broughton *Oxon.* 55 G4
Broughton *Sc.Bord.* 134 C2
Broughton *V. of Glam.* 37 F5
Broughton Astley 68 A3
Broughton Beck 107 D4
Broughton Gifford 25 F1
Broughton Hackett 54 B2
Broughton in Furness 106 D4
Broughton Mills 106 D3
Broughton Moor 117 D3
Broughton Poggs 41 E2
Broughtown 199 E2
Broughty Ferry 152 C1
Browland 200 B2
Brown Candover 27 G4
Brown Edge *Lancs.* 91 E1
Brown Edge *Staffs.* 79 G2
Brown Lees 79 F2
Brownhill 183 D5
Brownhills *Fife* 152 D3
Brownhills *W.Mid.* 66 C2
Brownieside 137 F4
Brownlow Heath 79 F1
Brownshill Green 67 F4
Brownston 8 C2
Broxa 112 C3
Broxbourne 44 C2
Broxburn *E.Loth.* 145 D2
Broxburn *W.Loth.* 143 E2
Broxholme 95 G5
Broxted 59 D5
Broxton 78 B2
Broxwood 52 C2
Bru 187 E2
Bruachmary 180 A5
Bruan 195 F5
Bruera 78 B1
Bruichladdich 138 A3
Bruisyard 61 E1
Bruisyard Street 61 E1
Brund 80 C1
Brundall 87 E5
Brundish 61 D1
Brundish Street 73 D4
Bruntingthorpe 68 B4
Bruntland 169 G2
Brunton *Fife* 152 B2
Brunton *Northumb.* 137 G4
Brushford *Devon* 21 G5
Brushford *Som.* 22 C5
Bruton 25 D4
Bryanston 13 E2
Brydekirk 125 F3
Brymbo 77 F2
Bryn *Carmar.* 36 B2
Bryn *Gt.Man.* 91 G2
Bryn *N.P.T.* 37 E3
Bryn *Shrop.* 64 B4
Bryn-côch 36 D3
Bryn Gates 91 G2
Bryn-henllan 48 D4
Bryn-teg 88 C4
Bryn-y-maen 89 G5
Brynamman 36 D1
Brynberian 49 E4
Bryncae 37 F4
Bryncethin 37 F4
Bryncir 75 D3
Bryncroes 74 B4
Bryncrug 62 C2
Bryneglwys 77 E3
Brynford 90 C5
Bryngwran 88 B5
Bryngwyn *Mon.* 38 C2
Bryngwyn *Powys* 52 A3
Brynhoffnant 49 G2
Brynmawr 38 A1
Brynmelyn 64 A5
Brynmenyn 37 F4
Brynna 37 F4
Brynog 50 B2
Brynrefail *Gwyn.* 75 E1
Brynrefail *I.o.A.* 88 C4
Brynsadler 37 G4
Brynsiencyn 75 D1
Brynteg 78 A2
Buaile nam Bodach 172 C3
Bualintur 164 A2
Bualnaluib 177 E1
Bubbenhall 67 F5
Bubwith 103 G4
Buccleuch 135 E4
Buchan 124 B4
Buchanan Castle 141 F1
Buchanhaven 183 G5
Buchanty 151 E2
Buchlyvie 150 A5
Buckabank 117 G2
Buckby Wharf 56 B1
Buckden *Cambs.* 57 G1
Buckden *N.Yorks.* 109 E5
Buckenham 87 E5
Buckerell 11 E2
Buckfast 8 D1
Buckfastleigh 8 D1
Buckhaven 152 B5
Buckholm 135 F2
Buckhorn Weston 25 E5
Buckhurst Hill 44 D3
Buckie 181 G3
Buckies 194 D2
Buckingham 56 B4
Buckland *Bucks.* 43 D1
Buckland *Devon* 8 C3
Buckland *Glos.* 54 C4
Buckland *Herts.* 58 B4
Buckland *Kent* 33 E4
Buckland *Oxon.* 41 F3
Buckland *Surr.* 30 B3
Buckland Brewer 21 E3
Buckland Common 43 E2
Buckland Dinham 25 E2
Buckland Filleigh 21 E5
Buckland in the Moor 10 A5
Buckland Monachorum 8 A1
Buckland Newton 12 C2
Buckland St. Mary 11 F1
Buckland-tout-Saints 9 D3
Bucklebury 42 A5
Bucklerheads 152 C1
Bucklers Hard 14 D2
Bucklesham 60 D3
Buckley (Bwcle) 77 F1
Buckman Corner 29 F5
Buckminster 83 D5
Bucknall *Lincs.* 83 G1
Bucknall *Stoke* 79 G3
Bucknell *Oxon.* 56 A5
Bucknell *Shrop.* 64 C5
Buck's Cross 20 D3
Bucks Green 29 F4
Bucks Hill 43 F2
Bucks Horn Oak 28 D3
Buck's Mills 21 D3
Bucksburn 171 D4
Buckspool 34 C3
Buckton *E.Riding* 113 E5
Buckton *Here.* 64 C5
Buckton *Northumb.* 137 E3
Buckworth 69 G5
Budbrooke 55 E1
Budby 82 B1
Buddon 152 D1
Bude 20 C5
Budlake 10 C2
Budle 137 F3
Budleigh Salterton 11 D4
Budock Water 3 E3
Buerton 79 D3
Bugbrooke 56 B2
Bugle 5 E4
Bugthorpe 103 G2
Buildwas 65 F2
Builth Road 51 G2
Builth Wells 51 G2
Buirgh 184 C4
Bulby 83 F5
Buldoo 194 B2
Bulford 26 C3
Bulford Camp 26 C3
Bulkeley 78 C2
Bulkington *Warks.* 67 F4
Bulkington *Wilts.* 26 A2
Bulkworthy 21 D4
Bull Bay 88 C3
Bull Green 32 B5
Bulley 39 G1
Bullington 27 F3
Bullpot Farm 108 B4
Bull's Green 44 B1
Bullwood 140 C2
Bulmer *Essex* 59 G3
Bulmer *N.Yorks.* 103 F1
Bulmer Tye 59 G4
Bulphan 45 F4
Bulverhythe 18 C3
Bulwark 183 E5
Bulwell 81 G3
Bulwick 69 E3
Bumble's Green 44 D2
Bun Abhainn Eadarra 184 D3
Bun Loyne 166 B4
Bunarkaig 157 D1
Bunbury 78 C2
Bunchrew 179 F5
Bundalloch 165 E2
Buness 203 F2
Bunessan 146 C2
Bungay 73 E3
Bunlarie 130 C2
Bunloit 167 E2
Bunnahabhainn 138 C2
Bunny 81 G5
Buntait 166 C1
Buntingford 58 B5
Bunwell 72 C2
Bunwell Street 72 C2
Burbage *Derbys.* 93 E5
Burbage *Leics.* 67 G3
Burbage *Wilts.* 26 D1
Burchett's Green 42 D4
Burcombe 26 B4
Burcot 42 A3
Burcott 57 D5
Burdale 104 A1
Burdocks 29 F5
Bures 60 A4
Bures Green 60 A4
Burford 41 E1
Burgate 72 B4
Burgess Hill 17 F2
Burgh 60 D2
Burgh by Sands 117 G1
Burgh Castle 87 F5
Burgh Heath 30 B3
Burgh le Marsh 84 C1
Burgh next Aylsham 86 D3
Burgh on Bain 96 C4
Burgh St. Margaret 87 F4
Burgh St. Peter 73 F2
Burghclere 27 F1
Burghead 180 D3
Burghfield 28 B1
Burghfield Common 28 B1
Burghfield Hill 28 B1
Burghill 53 D3
Burghwallis 94 C1
Burham 31 G2
Buriton 28 C5
Burland 78 D2
Burlawn 5 D2
Burleigh 29 E1
Burlescombe 11 D1
Burleston 13 D3
Burley *Hants.* 14 B2
Burley *Rut.* 69 D1
Burley Gate 53 E3
Burley in Wharfedale 102 A3
Burley Street 14 B2
Burleydam 78 D3
Burlingjobb 52 B2
Burlow 18 A2
Burlton 78 B5
Burmarsh 32 D5
Burmington 55 E4
Burn 103 E5
Burn Farm 161 E2
Burn Naze 99 G3
Burn of Cambus 150 C4
Burnage 92 C3
Burnaston 81 D4
Burnby 104 A3
Burndell 16 B3
Burnend 182 D5
Burneside 107 G3
Burness 199 E2
Burneston 110 C4
Burnett 25 D1
Burnfoot *High.* 194 A5
Burnfoot *P. & K.* 151 E4
Burnfoot *Sc.Bord.* 135 G4
Burnfoot *Sc.Bord.* 135 F4
Burnham *Bucks.* 43 E4
Burnham *N.Lincs.* 96 A1
Burnham Deepdale 85 G3
Burnham Green 44 B1
Burnham Market 85 G3
Burnham Norton 85 G3
Burnham-on-Crouch 46 C3
Burnham-on-Sea 24 A3
Burnham Overy 85 G3
Burnham Thorpe 85 G3
Burnhaven 183 G5
Burnhead *D. & G.* 123 G2
Burnhead *D. & G.* 124 C1
Burnhervie 170 C3
Burnhill Green 65 G2
Burnhope 120 A3
Burnhouse 141 E4
Burniston 112 D3
Burnley 101 E4
Burnmouth 145 G3
Burnopfield 120 A2
Burnsall 101 G1
Burnside *Aber.* 170 C3
Burnside *Angus* 160 D4
Burnside *E.Ayr.* 133 D4
Burnside *Fife* 151 G4
Burnside *Shet.* 202 B5
Burnside *W.Loth.* 143 E2
Burnside of Duntrune 152 C1
Burnstones 118 C2
Burnswark 125 F3
Burnt Houses 120 A5
Burnt Yates 102 B1
Burntcliff Top 79 G1
Burntisland 143 G1
Burnton *E.Ayr.* 132 C4
Burnton *E.Ayr.* 132 C5
Burntwood 66 C1
Burntwood Green 66 C2
Burpham *Surr.* 29 F2
Burpham *W.Suss.* 16 C3
Burradon *Northumb.* 128 B1
Burradon *T. & W.* 129 E4
Burrafirth 203 F1
Burraland 202 C5
Burras 3 D3
Burravoe *Shet.* 203 E5
Burravoe *Shet.* 200 C1
Burrells 108 B1
Burrelton 151 G1
Burridge 15 E1
Burrill 110 B4
Burringham 95 F2
Burrington *Devon* 21 G4
Burrington *Here.* 64 D5
Burrington *N.Som.* 24 B2
Burrough End 59 E2
Burrough Green 59 E2
Burrough on the Hill 68 C1
Burrow Bridge 24 A4
Burrowhill 29 E1
Burry Port 36 A2
Burscough 91 F1
Burscough Bridge 91 F1
Bursea 104 A4
Burshill 104 C3
Bursledon 15 D2
Burslem 79 F3
Burstall 60 C3
Burstock 12 A2
Burston *Norf.* 72 C3
Burston *Staffs.* 79 G4
Burstow 30 C4
Burstwick 105 E5
Burtersett 109 D4
Burtle 24 B3
Burton *Ches.* 91 E5
Burton *Ches.* 78 C1
Burton *Dorset* 14 A3
Burton *Dorset* 12 C3
Burton *Lincs.* 95 G5
Burton *Northumb.* 137 F3
Burton *Pembs.* 34 C2
Burton *Som.* 23 E3
Burton *Wilts.* 40 A5
Burton Agnes 104 D1
Burton Bradstock 12 A4
Burton Coggles 83 E5
Burton Fleming 113 D5

Burton Green *Warks.* 67 E5
Burton Green *Wrex.* 78 A2
Burton Hastings 67 G3
Burton-in-Kendal 107 G5
Burton in Lonsdale 108 B5
Burton Joyce 82 B3
Burton Latimer 69 E5
Burton Lazars 68 C1
Burton Leonard 102 C1
Burton on the Wolds 81 G5
Burton Overy 68 B3
Burton Pedwardine 83 G3
Burton Pidsea 105 E4
Burton Salmon 103 D5
Burton upon Stather 95 F1
Burton upon Trent 80 D5
Burtonwood 91 G3
Burwardsley 78 C2
Burwarton 65 F4
Burwash 18 B1
Burwash Common 18 B1
Burwash Weald 18 B1
Burwell *Cambs.* 59 D1
Burwell *Lincs.* 97 D5
Burwen 88 C3
Burwick *Ork.* 196 D4
Burwick *Shet.* 200 C3
Bury *Cambs.* 70 A4
Bury *Gt.Man.* 92 C1
Bury *Som.* 22 C5
Bury *W.Suss.* 16 C2
Bury Green 58 C5
Bury St. Edmunds 59 G1
Buryas Bridge 2 B4
Burythorpe 103 G1
Busbridge 29 E3
Busby *E.Renf.* 141 G4
Busby *P. & K.* 151 F2
Buscot 41 E3
Bush Bank 52 D2
Bush Crathie 169 E5
Bush Green 72 D3
Bushbury 66 B2
Bushby 68 B2
Bushey 44 A3
Bushey Heath 44 A3
Bushley 54 A4
Bushton 40 C5
Bussage 40 A2
Busta 200 C1
Butcher's Cross 18 A1
Butcher's Pasture 59 E5
Butcombe 24 C1
Buthill 180 D3
Butleigh 24 C4
Butleigh Wootton 24 C4
Butler's Cross 42 D2
Butler's Hill 81 G3
Butlers Marston 55 F2
Butley 61 E2
Butsfield 120 A3
Butt Green 79 D2
Butt Lane 79 F2
Butterburn 127 E4
Buttercrambe 103 G2
Butterknowle 120 A5
Butterleigh 10 C2
Butterley 81 F2
Buttermere *Cumb.* 117 E5
Buttermere *Wilts.* 27 E1
Butters Green 79 F2
Buttershaw 102 A5
Butterstone 159 F5
Butterton 80 B2
Butterwick *Lincs.* 84 B3
Butterwick *N.Yorks.* 112 C5
Butterwick *N.Yorks.* 111 G5
Buttington 64 B2
Buttonoak 65 G5
Buxhall 60 B2
Buxted 17 G1
Buxton *Derbys.* 93 E5
Buxton *Norf.* 86 D3
Buxton Heath 86 C3
Buxworth 93 E4
Bwcle (Buckley) 77 F1
Bwlch 52 A5
Bwlch-clawdd 49 G4
Bwlch-derwin 75 D3
Bwlch-llan 50 B2
Bwlch-y-cibau 64 A1
Bwlch-y-ddar 77 E5
Bwlch-y-ffridd 63 G3
Bwlch-y-groes 49 F4
Bwlch-y-sarnau 63 G5
Bwlchgwyn 77 F2
Bwlchnewydd 49 G5
Bwlchtocyn 74 C5
Byers Green 120 B4
Byfield 56 A2
Byfleet 29 F1
Byford 52 C3
Bygrave 58 A4
Byker 120 B1
Bylane End 5 G4
Bylchau 76 C1
Byley 79 E1
Bynea 36 B3
Byrness 127 F1
Bythorn 69 F5
Byton 52 C1
Byworth 29 E5

C

Cabharstadh 187 E5
Cabourne 96 B2
Cabrach *Arg. & B.* 138 C3
Cabrach *Moray* 169 F2
Cackle Street 18 D2
Cacrabank 135 E4
Cadboll 180 A2
Cadbury 10 C2
Cadbury Barton 21 G4
Cadbury Heath 39 F5
Cadder 142 A2
Cadderlie 148 C1
Caddington 43 F1
Caddleton 147 G3
Caddonfoot 135 F2
Cade Street 18 B1
Cadeby *Leics.* 67 G2
Cadeby *S.Yorks.* 94 C2
Cadeleigh 10 C2
Cadgwith 3 E5
Cadham 152 A4
Cadishead 92 B3
Cadle 36 C3
Cadley 26 D1
Cadmore End 42 C3
Cadnam 14 C1
Cadney 96 A2
Cadole 77 F1
Cadover Bridge 8 B1
Cadoxton 23 E1
Cadoxton-Juxta-Neath 37 D3
Cae Ddafydd 75 F3
Caeathro 75 E1
Caehopkin 37 E1
Caen 191 F3
Caenby 96 A4
Caenby Corner 95 G4
Caer-Lan 37 E1
Caer Llan 39 D2
Caerau *Bridgend* 37 E3
Caerau *Cardiff* 38 A5
Caerdeon 62 C1
Caerdydd (Cardiff) 38 A5
Caerfarchell 48 A5
Caerfyrddin (Carmarthen) 36 A1
Caergeiliog 88 B5
Caergwrle 78 A2
Caergybi (Holyhead) 88 A4
Caerhun 89 F5
Caerleon 38 C3
Caernarfon 75 D1
Caerphilly 38 A4
Caersws 63 G3
Caerwent 39 D3
Caerwys 90 C5
Caethle Farm 62 C3
Caggan 168 A3
Caio 50 C4
Cairinis 173 G4
Cairisiadar 186 B4
Cairminis 184 C5
Cairnargat 169 G1
Cairnbaan 148 A5
Cairnbeathie 170 A4
Cairnbrogie 171 D2
Cairnbulg 183 F3
Cairncross 145 F3
Cairncurran 141 E3
Cairndoon 115 D3
Cairndow 149 D3
Cairness 183 F3
Cairney Lodge 152 B3
Cairneyhill 143 E1
Cairnhill *Aber.* 171 E2
Cairnhill *Aber.* 170 B1
Cairnie *Aber.* 170 D4
Cairnie *Aber.* 181 G5
Cairnorrie 183 D5
Cairnryan 122 B4
Cairnsmore 123 F4
Caister-on-Sea 87 G4
Caistor 96 B2
Caistor St. Edmund 86 D5
Caistron 128 B1
Cake Street 72 B2
Calanais (Callanish) 186 D4
Calbost 185 G2
Calbourne 14 D4
Calcot 42 B5
Calcott 33 D2
Caldarvan 141 F1
Caldback 203 F2
Caldbeck 117 G3
Caldbergh 109 F4
Caldecote *Cambs.* 58 B2
Caldecote *Cambs.* 69 G4
Caldecote *Herts.* 58 A4
Caldecote *Warks.* 67 F3
Caldecott *Northants.* 57 E1
Caldecott *Rut.* 69 D3
Calder Bridge 106 B2
Calder Mains 194 C3
Calder Vale 100 B3
Calderbank 142 B3
Calderbrook 92 D1
Caldercruix 142 C3
Calderglen 142 A4
Caldermill 142 A5
Caldhame 160 C5
Caldicot 39 D4
Caldwell *Derbys.* 67 E1
Caldwell *N.Yorks.* 110 A1
Caldy 90 D4
Caledrhydiau 50 A2
Calfsound 199 D3
Calgary 154 C4
Califer 180 C4
California *Falk.* 142 D2
California *Norf.* 87 G4
Calke 81 E5
Callakille 176 C4
Callaly 128 C1
Callander 150 B4
Callanish (Calanais) 186 D4
Callerton Lane End 120 A1
Callestick 4 B4
Calliburn 130 C3
Calligarry 164 C4
Callington 7 D4
Callisterhall 126 A3
Callow 53 D4
Callow End 54 A3
Callow Hill *Wilts.* 40 C4
Callow Hill *Worcs.* 65 G5
Callows Grave 53 E1
Calmore 14 C1
Calmsden 40 C2
Calne 40 B5
Calow 94 B5
Calrossie 179 G2
Calshot 15 D2
Calstock 8 A1
Calstone Wellington 26 B1
Calthorpe 86 C2
Calthwaite 118 A3
Calton *N.Yorks.* 101 F2
Calton *Staffs.* 80 C2
Calveley 78 C2
Calver 93 G5
Calver Hill 52 C3
Calverhall 78 D4
Calverleigh 10 C1
Calverley 102 B4
Calvert 56 B5
Calverton *M.K.* 56 C4
Calverton *Notts.* 82 B3
Calvine 158 D3
Calvo 117 E1
Cam 39 G3
Camasnacroise 156 A4
Camastianavaig 164 B1
Camasunary 164 B3
Camault Muir 179 E5
Camb 203 E3
Camber 19 E2
Camberley 29 D1
Camberwell 44 C5
Camblesforth 103 F5
Cambo 128 C3
Cambois 129 F3
Camborne 4 A5
Cambourne 58 B2
Cambridge *Cambs.* 58 C2
Cambridge *Glos.* 39 G2
Cambridge Airport 58 C2
Cambus 151 D5
Cambus o'May 169 G5
Cambusbarron 150 C5
Cambuskenneth 150 D5
Cambuslang 142 A3
Cambusnethan 142 C4
Camden 44 B4
Cameley 24 D2
Camelford 5 F1
Camelon 142 C1
Camelsdale 29 D4
Camer 31 F2
Cameron 141 E1
Camerory 168 C1
Camer's Green 53 G4
Camerton *B. & N.E.Som.* 25 D2
Camerton *Cumb.* 116 D3
Camghouran 158 A4
Camis Eskan 141 E1
Cammachmore 171 E5
Cammeringham 95 G4
Campbeltown 130 C4
Campbeltown (Machrihanish) Airport 130 B3
Camperdown 129 E4
Camphouse 155 E3
Campmuir 152 A1
Camps End 59 E3
Camps Heath 73 G2
Campsall 94 C1
Campsey Ash 61 E2
Campton 57 G4
Camptown 136 A5
Camquhart 140 A1
Camrose 34 C1
Camserney 158 D5
Camstraddan House 149 F5
Camus Croise 164 C3
Camus-luinie 165 F2
Camusnagaul *High.* 156 C2
Camusnagaul *High.* 177 G1
Camusrory 165 E5
Camusteel 176 D5
Camusterrach 176 D5
Camusurich 150 B1
Camusvrachan 158 B5
Canada 14 B1
Candacraig 169 F5
Candlesby 84 C1
Candy Mill 143 E5
Cane End 42 B5
Canewdon 46 B3
Canford Bottom 13 G2
Canford Cliffs 13 G4
Canford Magna 13 G3
Canisbay 195 F1
Cann 25 F5
Cann Common 25 F5
Cannard's Grave 24 D3
Cannich 166 C1
Cannington 23 F4
Cannock 66 B1
Cannock Wood 66 C1
Cannop 39 F1
Canon Bridge 52 D3
Canon Frome 53 F3
Canon Pyon 53 D3
Canonbie 126 B4
Canons Ashby 56 A2
Canon's Town 2 C3
Canterbury *Aber.* 182 A4
Canterbury *Kent* 32 D3
Cantley *Norf.* 87 E5
Cantley *S.Yorks.* 94 D2
Cantlop 65 E2
Canton 38 A5
Cantray 179 G5
Cantraydoune 179 G5
Cantraywood 179 G5
Cantsfield 108 B5
Canvey Island 45 G4
Canwell Hall 66 D2
Canwick 83 E1
Canworthy Water 6 C1
Caol 156 D2
Caolas *Arg. & B.* 154 B2
Caolas *W.Isles* 172 B4
Caolas Scalpaigh (Kyles Scalpay) 185 E4
Caolasnacon 156 D3
Capel *Kent* 31 F4
Capel *Surr.* 29 G3
Capel Bangor 62 C4
Capel Betws Lleucu 50 C2
Capel Carmel 74 A5
Capel Coch 88 C4
Capel Curig 76 A2
Capel Cynon 49 G3
Capel Dewi *Carmar.* 50 A5
Capel Dewi *Cere.* 62 C4
Capel Dewi *Cere.* 50 A3
Capel Garmon 76 B2
Capel Gwyn *Carmar.* 50 A5
Capel Gwyn *I.o.A.* 88 B5
Capel Gwynfe 50 D5
Capel Hendre 36 B1
Capel Isaac 50 B5
Capel Iwan 49 F4
Capel le Ferne 33 E5
Capel Parc 88 C4
Capel St. Andrew 61 E3
Capel St. Mary 60 B4
Capel St. Silin 50 B2
Capel Seion 62 C5
Capel Tygwydd 49 F3
Capel-y-ffin 52 B4
Capeluchaf 74 D3
Capelulo 89 F5
Capenhurst 91 E5
Capernwray 107 G5
Capheaton 128 C3
Caplaw 141 F4
Cappercleuch 134 D3
Capplegill 134 C5
Capstone 31 G2
Capton 9 E2
Caputh 159 F5
Car Colston 82 C3
Carbellow 133 E3
Carbeth 141 G2
Carbis Bay 2 C3
Carbost *High.* 176 A5
Carbost *High.* 163 G1
Carbrain 142 B2
Carbrooke 86 A5
Carburton 94 D5
Carcary 161 E4
Carclew 3 E3
Carco 133 F4
Carcroft 94 C2
Cardenden 152 A5
Cardeston 64 C1
Cardiff (Caerdydd) 38 A5
Cardiff International Airport 23 D1
Cardigan (Aberteifi) 49 E3
Cardington *Beds.* 57 F3
Cardington *Shrop.* 65 E3
Cardinham 5 F3
Cardno 183 E3
Cardoness 123 G5
Cardow 181 D5
Cardrona 135 D2
Cardross 141 E2
Cardurnock 117 E1
Careby 69 F1
Careston 160 D3
Carew 34 D2
Carew Cheriton 34 D2
Carew Newton 34 D2
Carey 53 E4
Carfrae 144 C3
Carfraemill 144 C4
Cargen 125 D3
Cargenbridge 125 D3
Cargill 151 G1
Cargo 117 G1
Cargo Fleet 121 E5
Cargreen 8 A1
Carham 136 B3
Carhampton 22 D3
Carharrack 4 B5
Carie *P. & K.* 158 B4
Carie *P. & K.* 150 B1
Carines 4 B4
Carisbrooke 15 D4
Cark 107 E5
Carkeel 8 A1
Carlabhagh (Carloway) 186 D3
Carland Cross 4 C4
Carlby 69 F1
Carlecotes 93 F2
Carleton *Cumb.* 118 A2
Carleton *Lancs.* 99 G3
Carleton *N.Yorks.* 101 F3
Carleton *W.Yorks.* 103 D5
Carleton Fishery 122 C2
Carleton Forehoe 86 B5
Carleton Rode 72 C2
Carlin How 111 G1
Carlingcott 25 D2
Carlisle 118 A2
Carlops 143 F4
Carloway (Carlabhagh) 186 D3
Carlton *Beds.* 57 E2
Carlton *Cambs.* 59 E2
Carlton *Leics.* 67 F2
Carlton *N.Yorks.* 103 F5
Carlton *N.Yorks.* 109 F4
Carlton *N.Yorks.* 111 F4
Carlton *Notts.* 82 B3
Carlton *S.Yorks.* 94 A2
Carlton *Stock.* 120 C5
Carlton *Suff.* 61 E1
Carlton *W.Yorks.* 102 C5
Carlton Colville 73 G2
Carlton Curlieu 68 B3
Carlton Husthwaite 111 D5
Carlton-in-Cleveland 111 E2
Carlton in Lindrick 94 C4
Carlton-le-Moorland 83 E2
Carlton Miniott 110 C4
Carlton-on-Trent 82 D1
Carlton Scroop 83 E3
Carluke 142 C4
Carlyon Bay 5 E4
Carmacoup 133 F3
Carmarthen (Caerfyrddin) 36 A1
Carmel *Carmar.* 36 B1
Carmel *Flints.* 90 C5
Carmel *Gwyn.* 75 D2
Carmel *I.o.A.* 88 B4
Carmont 161 G1
Carmore 190 C5
Carmunnock 142 A4
Carmyle 142 A3
Carmyllie 160 D5
Carn 138 A4
Carn Brea 4 A5
Carn Dearg 177 D2
Carnaby 104 D1
Carnach *High.* 165 G2
Carnach *High.* 188 C5
Carnassarie 148 A4
Carnbee 152 D4
Carnbo 151 F4
Carnduncan 138 A3
Carne 3 G3
Carnforth 107 F5
Carnhell Green 2 D3
Carnichal 183 E4
Carnmore 138 B5
Carno 63 F3
Carnoch *High.* 166 C1
Carnoch *High.* 178 B4
Carnoch *High.* 180 A5
Carnock 143 E1
Carnon Downs 4 B5
Carnousie 182 B4
Carnoustie 153 D1
Carnwath 143 D5
Carnyorth 2 A3
Carperby 109 F3
Carr Shield 119 E3
Carr Vale 94 B5
Carradale 130 D2
Carragrich 185 D4
Carrbridge 168 B2
Carrefour Selous 8 C5
Carreg-lefn 88 B4
Carrick *Arg. & B.* 149 D5
Carrick *Arg. & B.* 140 A1
Carrick *Fife* 152 C2
Carriden 143 E1
Carrine 130 B5
Carrington *Gt.Man.* 92 B3
Carrington *Lincs.* 84 B2
Carrington *Midloth.* 144 A3
Carroch 124 A1
Carrog 77 E3
Carroglen 150 C2
Carrol 191 D4
Carron *Arg. & B.* 148 B5
Carron *Falk.* 142 C1
Carron *Moray* 181 E5
Carron Bridge 142 B1
Carronbridge 124 C1
Carronshore 142 C1
Carrot 160 C5
Carrutherstown 125 F3
Carruthmuir 141 E3
Carrville 120 C3
Carry 140 A3
Carsaig 147 E2
Carscreugh 122 D4
Carse 139 F3
Carse of Ardesier 180 A4
Carsegowan 123 F5
Carseriggan 123 E4
Carsethorn 125 D5
Carsgoe 194 D2
Carshalton 30 B2
Carsington 81 D2
Carsluith 123 F5
Carsphairn 123 G1
Carstairs 142 D5
Carstairs Junction 143 D5
Carswell Marsh 41 F3
Carter's Clay 27 E5
Carterton 41 E2
Carterway Heads 119 G2
Carthew 5 E4
Carthorpe 110 C4
Cartington 128 C1
Cartmel 107 E5
Cartmel Fell 107 F4
Carway 36 A2
Cascob 52 B1
Cashel Farm 149 G5
Cashlie 157 G5
Cashmoor 13 F1
Casnewydd (Newport) *Newport* 38 C4
Cassencarie 123 F5
Cassington 41 G1
Cassop 120 C4
Castell Gorfod 49 F5
Castell Howell 50 A3
Castell-Nedd (Neath) 37 D3
Castell Newydd Emlyn (Newcastle Emlyn) 49 G3
Castell-y-bwch 38 B3
Castellau 37 G4
Casterton 108 B5
Castle Acre 71 G1
Castle Ashby 57 D2
Castle Bank 79 G5
Castle Bolton 109 F3
Castle Bromwich 66 D4
Castle Bytham 69 E1
Castle Caereinion 64 A2
Castle Camps 59 E3
Castle Carrock 118 B2
Castle Cary 24 D4
Castle Combe 40 A5
Castle Donington 81 F5
Castle Douglas 124 B4
Castle Eaton 40 D3
Castle Eden 120 D4
Castle End 67 E5
Castle Frome 53 F3
Castle Gresley 67 E1
Castle Heaton 145 G5
Castle Hedingham 59 F4
Castle Hill 60 C3
Castle Kennedy 122 C5
Castle Leod 179 D4
Castle Levan 140 D2
Castle Madoc 51 G4
Castle Morris 48 C4
Castle O'er 126 A2
Castle Rising 85 E5
Castle Stuart 179 G4
Castlebay (Bagh a' Chaisteil) 172 B4
Castlebythe 48 D5
Castlecary 142 B2
Castlecraig *High.* 180 A3
Castlecraig *Sc.Bord.* 143 F5
Castlefairn 124 B2
Castleford 102 D5
Castlemartin 34 C3
Castlemilk *D. & G.* 125 F3
Castlemilk *Glas.* 142 A4
Castlemorton 53 G4
Castleside 119 G3
Castlethorpe 56 D3
Castleton *Aber.* 182 C4
Castleton *Angus* 160 B5
Castleton *Arg. & B.* 139 G1
Castleton *Derbys.* 93 F4
Castleton *Gt.Man.* 92 C1
Castleton *N.Yorks.* 111 F2
Castleton *Newport* 38 B4
Castleton *Sc.Bord.* 126 D2
Castletown *High.* 195 D2
Castletown *High.* 179 G5
Castletown *I.o.M.* 98 A5
Castletown *T. & W.* 120 C2
Castleweary 135 F5
Castlewigg 115 E2
Caston 72 A2
Castor 69 G3
Castramont 123 G4
Cat and Fiddle Inn 93 E5
Catbrain 39 E4
Catchall 2 B4
Catcleugh 127 F1
Catcliffe 94 B4
Catcott 24 A4
Caterham 30 C3
Catesby 56 A2
Catfield 87 E3
Catfirth 200 D2
Catford 44 C5
Catforth 100 A4
Cathedine 52 A5
Catherington 15 F1
Catherton 65 F5
Catlow 101 E4
Catlowdy 126 C4
Catmore 41 G5
Caton *Devon* 10 A5
Caton *Lancs.* 100 B1
Cator Court 7 G3
Catrine 132 D3
Catsfield 18 C2
Catshill 66 B5
Cattadale 138 B4
Cattal 102 D2
Cattawade 60 C4
Catterall 100 B3
Catterick 110 B3
Catterick Camp 110 A3
Catterlen 118 A4
Catterline 161 G2
Catterton 103 E3
Catthorpe 68 A5
Cattistock 12 B2
Catton *N.Yorks.* 110 C5
Catton *Norf.* 86 D4
Catton *Northumb.* 119 E2
Catton Hall 67 E1
Catwick 104 D3
Catworth 69 F5
Caudworthy 6 C1
Caulcott 56 A5
Cauldcots 161 E5
Cauldhame *Stir.* 150 B5
Cauldhame *Stir.* 150 D4
Cauldon 80 B3
Caulkerbush 124 D5
Caulside 126 C3
Caundle Marsh 12 C1
Caunsall 66 A4
Caunton 82 C1
Causeway End *D. & G.* 123 F4
Causeway End *Essex* 45 F1
Causewayhead *Cumb.* 117 E1
Causewayhead *Stir.* 150 D5
Causey Park 129 D2
Causeyend 171 E3
Cautley 108 B3
Cavendish 59 G3
Cavenham 59 F1
Cavens 125 D5
Caversfield 56 A5
Caversham 42 C5
Caverswall 79 G3
Cawdor 180 A4
Cawkwell 96 C5
Cawood 103 E4
Cawsand 8 A2
Cawston 86 C3
Cawthorne 93 G2
Cawthorpe 83 F5
Cawton 111 F5
Caxton 58 B2
Caxton Gibbet 58 A2
Caynham 65 E5
Caythorpe *Lincs.* 83 E3
Caythorpe *Notts.* 82 B3
Cayton 113 D4
Ceallan 173 G4
Ceann a' Bhàigh *W.Isles* 173 F3
Ceann a' Bhàigh *W.Isles* 184 C5
Ceann Loch Shiphoirt 185 E2
Cearsiadar 187 E5
Ceathramh Meadhanach 173 F2
Cedig 76 C5
Cefn-brith 76 C2
Cefn Bycharn (Newbridge) 38 B3
Cefn-caer-Ferch 74 D3
Cefn Cantref 51 G5
Cefn Coch 77 E2
Cefn-coch 77 E5
Cefn-coed-y-cymmer 37 G2
Cefn Cribwr 37 E4
Cefn Cross 37 E4
Cefn-ddwysarn 76 C4
Cefn Einion 64 B4
Cefn-gorwydd 51 F3
Cefn-gwyn 64 A4
Cefn Hengoed 38 A3
Cefn-mawr 77 F3
Cefn-y-bedd 78 A2
Cefn-y-pant 49 E5
Cefndeuddwr 76 A5
Cefneithin 36 B1
Cegidfa (Guilsfield) 64 B1
Ceidio 88 C4
Ceidio Fawr 74 B4
Ceinewydd (New Quay) 49 G2
Ceint 88 C5
Cellan 50 C3
Cellardyke 153 D4
Cellarhead 79 G3
Cemaes 88 B3
Cemmaes 63 E2
Cemmaes Road (Glantwymyn) 63 E2
Cenarth 49 F3
Cennin 75 D3
Ceos 187 E5
Ceres 152 B3
Cerne Abbas 12 C2
Cerney Wick 40 C3
Cerrigceinwen 88 C5
Cerrigydrudion 76 C3
Cessford 136 B4
Chaceley 54 A4
Chacewater 4 B5
Chackmore 56 B4
Chacombe 55 G3
Chad Valley 66 C4
Chadderton 92 D2
Chaddesden 81 E4
Chaddesley Corbett 66 A5
Chaddleworth 41 G5
Chadlington 55 F5
Chadshunt 55 F2
Chadwell 82 C5
Chadwell St. Mary 45 F5
Chadwick End 67 E5
Chaffcombe 11 G1
Chagford 10 A4
Chailey 17 F2
Chainhurst 31 G4
Chalbury Common 13 G2
Chaldon 30 C3
Chaldon Herring or East Chaldon 13 D4
Chale 15 D5
Chale Green 15 D5
Chalfont Common 43 F3
Chalfont St. Giles 43 E3
Chalfont St. Peter 43 F3
Chalford 40 A2
Chalgrove 42 B3
Chalk 45 F5
Challacombe 21 G1
Challoch 123 E4
Challock 32 C3
Chalmington 12 B2
Chalton *Beds.* 57 F5
Chalton *Hants.* 15 G1
Chalvington 18 A3
Champany 143 E2
Chandler's Cross 43 F3
Chandler's Ford 27 F5
Channerwick 200 D5
Chantry *Som.* 25 E3
Chantry *Suff.* 60 C3
Chapel 152 A5
Chapel Allerton *Som.* 24 B2
Chapel Allerton *W.Yorks.* 102 C4
Chapel Amble 5 D2
Chapel Brampton 56 C1
Chapel Chorlton 79 F4
Chapel Cross 18 B1
Chapel-en-le-Frith 93 E4
Chapel End 67 F3
Chapel Fields 67 F5
Chapel Haddlesey 103 E5
Chapel Hill *Aber.* 171 F1
Chapel Hill *Lincs.* 84 A2
Chapel Hill *Mon.* 39 E2
Chapel Lawn 64 C5
Chapel-le-Dale 108 C5
Chapel of Garioch 170 C2
Chapel Rossan 114 B2
Chapel Row 27 G1
Chapel St. Leonards 97 F5
Chapel Stile 107 E2
Chapel Town 4 C4
Chapelbank 151 F3
Chapeldonan 131 G5
Chapelgate 84 C5
Chapelhall 142 B3
Chapelhill *High.* 180 A2
Chapelhill *P. & K.* 152 A2
Chapelhill *P. & K.* 151 F1
Chapelknowe 126 B4
Chapelton *Aber.* 161 G1
Chapelton *Angus* 161 E5
Chapelton *S.Lan.* 142 A5
Chapeltown *B'burn.* 92 B1
Chapeltown *Cumb.* 126 C4
Chapeltown *Moray* 169 E2
Chapeltown *S.Yorks.* 94 A3
Chapmans Well 7 D1
Chapmanslade 25 F3

Chapmore End 44 C1
Chappel 59 G5
Chard 11 G2
Chard Junction 11 G2
Chardstock 11 G2
Charfield 39 G3
Charing 32 B4
Charing Heath 32 B4
Charingworth 56 D3
Charlbury 41 F1
Charlcombe 25 E1
Charlcutt 40 B5
Charlecote 55 E2
Charles 21 G2
Charles Tye 60 B2
Charlesfield 135 G3
Charleshill 29 D3
Charleston 160 B5
Charlestown Aber. 183 F3
Charlestown Aberdeen 171 E4
Charlestown Cornw. 5 E4
Charlestown Dorset 12 C5
Charlestown Fife 143 E1
Charlestown High. 177 E2
Charlestown High. 179 F5
Charlestown of Aberlour (Aberlour) 181 E5
Charlesworth 93 E3
Charleton 152 C4
Charlinch 23 F4
Charlton Gt.Lon. 44 D5
Charlton Hants. 27 E3
Charlton Herts. 57 G5
Charlton Northants. 56 A4
Charlton Northumb. 128 A3
Charlton Oxon. 41 G4
Charlton Som. 25 D2
Charlton W.Suss. 16 A2
Charlton Wilts. 26 A5
Charlton Wilts. 40 B4
Charlton Wilts. 26 C2
Charlton Worcs. 54 C3
Charlton Abbots 54 C5
Charlton Adam 24 C5
Charlton-All-Saints 26 C5
Charlton Horethorne 25 D5
Charlton Kings 54 B5
Charlton Mackrell 24 C5
Charlton Marshall 13 E2
Charlton Musgrove 25 E5
Charlton-on-Otmoor 42 A1
Charlwood 30 B4
Charminster 12 C3
Charmouth 11 G3
Charndon 56 B5
Charney Bassett 41 F3
Charnock Richard 91 G1
Charsfield 61 D2
Chart Corner 31 G4
Chart Sutton 32 A4
Charter Alley 28 B2
Charterhouse 24 B2
Charterville Allotments 41 F1
Chartham 32 D3
Chartham Hatch 32 C3
Chartridge 43 E2
Charwelton 56 A2
Chase End Street 53 G4
Chase Terrace 66 C1
Chasetown 66 C2
Chastleton 55 E5
Chasty 20 D5
Chatburn 101 D3
Chatcull 79 E4
Chatham 31 G2
Chathill 137 F4
Chattenden 45 G5
Chatteris 70 B4
Chattisham 60 B3
Chatto 136 B5
Chatton 137 E4
Chawleigh 10 A1
Chawley 41 G2
Chawston 57 G2
Chawton 28 C4
Cheadle Gt.Man. 92 C4
Cheadle Staffs. 80 B3
Cheadle Hulme 92 C4
Cheam 30 B2
Cheapside 29 E1
Chearsley 42 C2
Chebsey 79 F5
Checkendon 42 B4
Checkley Ches. 79 E3
Checkley Here. 53 E4
Checkley Staffs. 80 B4
Chedburgh 59 F2
Cheddar 24 B2
Cheddington 43 E1
Cheddleton 79 G2
Cheddon Fitzpaine 23 F5
Chedglow 40 B3
Chedgrave 73 E2
Chedington 12 A2
Chediston 73 E4
Chedworth 40 C1
Chedzoy 24 A4
Cheeklaw 145 E4
Cheesden 92 C1
Cheeseman's Green 32 C5
Cheetham Hill 92 C2
Cheldon 10 A1
Chelford 92 C5
Chellaston 81 E4
Chelmarsh 65 G4
Chelmondiston 60 D4
Chelmorton 80 C1
Chelmsford 45 G2
Chelsfield 31 D2
Chelsham 30 C3
Chelsworth 60 A3
Cheltenham 54 B5
Chelveston 57 E1
Chelvey 24 B1
Chelwood 24 D1
Chelwood Gate 17 G1
Chelworth 40 B3
Cheney Longville 64 D4
Chenies 43 F3
Chepstow 39 E3
Cherhill 40 C5
Cherington Glos. 40 B3
Cherington Warks. 55 E4
Cheriton Devon 22 A3
Cheriton Hants. 27 G5
Cheriton Kent 33 E5
Cheriton Pembs. 34 C3
Cheriton Swan. 36 A3
Cheriton Bishop 10 A3
Cheriton Cross 10 A3
Cheriton Fitzpaine 10 B2
Cherrington 65 F1
Cherry Burton 104 B3
Cherry Hinton 58 C2
Cherry Willingham 96 A5
Chertsey 29 F1
Cheselbourne 13 D3
Chesham 43 E2
Chesham Bois 43 E3
Cheshunt 44 C2
Cheslyn Hay 66 B2
Chessington 29 G1
Chester 78 B1
Chester-le-Street 120 B2
Chesterblade 25 D3
Chesterfield Derbys. 94 A5
Chesterfield Staffs. 66 D2
Chesters Sc.Bord. 136 A5
Chesters Sc.Bord. 136 A4
Chesterton Cambs. 58 C2
Chesterton Cambs. 69 G3
Chesterton Oxon. 56 A5
Chesterton Shrop. 65 G3
Chesterton Staffs. 79 F3
Chesterton Green 55 F2
Chestfield 32 D2
Cheswardine 79 E5
Cheswick 137 E2
Chetnole 12 C2
Chettiscombe 10 C1
Chettisham 70 D4
Chettle 13 F1
Chetton 65 F3
Chetwode 56 B5
Chetwynd Aston 65 G1
Cheveley 59 E1
Chevening 31 D3
Cheverell's Green 43 F1
Chevington 59 F2
Chevington Drift 129 E2
Chevithorne 10 C1
Chew Magna 24 C1
Chew Stoke 24 C1
Chewton Keynsham 24 D1
Chewton Mendip 24 C2
Chicheley 57 E3
Chichester 16 A3
Chickerell 12 C4
Chickering 72 D4
Chicklade 26 A4
Chickney 59 D5
Chicksands 57 G4
Chidden 15 F1
Chiddingfold 29 E4
Chiddingly 18 A2
Chiddingstone 31 D4
Chiddingstone Causeway 31 E4
Chiddingstone Hoath 31 D4
Chideock 12 A3
Chidham 15 G2
Chieveley 41 G5
Chignall St. James 45 F2
Chignall Smealy 45 F1
Chigwell 44 D3
Chigwell Row 45 D3
Chilbolton 27 E3
Chilcomb 27 G5
Chilcombe 12 B3
Chilcompton 24 D2
Chilcote 67 E1
Child Okeford 13 E1
Childer Thornton 91 E5
Childerditch 45 F4
Childrey 41 F4
Child's Ercall 79 D5
Childswickham 54 C4
Childwall 91 F4
Childwick Green 44 A1
Chilfrome 12 B3
Chilgrove 16 A2
Chilham 32 C3
Chillaton 7 E2
Chillenden 33 E3
Chillerton 15 D4
Chillesford 61 E2
Chillingham 137 E4
Chillington Devon 9 D3
Chillington Som. 11 G1
Chilmark 26 A4
Chilson 41 F1
Chilsworthy Cornw. 7 E3
Chilsworthy Devon 20 D5
Chilthorne Domer 12 B1
Chilton Bucks. 42 B1
Chilton Dur. 120 B4
Chilton Oxon. 41 G4
Chilton Candover 27 G4
Chilton Cantelo 24 C5
Chilton Foliat 41 F5
Chilton Polden 24 A4
Chilton Street 59 F3
Chilton Trinity 23 F4
Chilvers Coton 67 F3
Chilworth Hants. 14 D1
Chilworth Surr. 29 F3
Chimney 41 F2
Chineham 28 B2
Chingford 44 C3
Chinley 93 E4
Chinley Head 93 E4
Chinnor 42 C2
Chipchase Castle 128 A4
Chipley Park 23 E5
Chipnall 79 E4
Chippenham Cambs. 59 E1
Chippenham Wilts. 40 B5
Chipperfield 43 F2
Chipping Herts. 58 B4
Chipping Lancs. 100 C3
Chipping Campden 55 D4
Chipping Hill 46 B1
Chipping Norton 55 F5
Chipping Ongar 45 E2
Chipping Sodbury 39 G4
Chipping Warden 55 G3
Chipstable 22 D5
Chipstead Kent 31 D3
Chipstead Surr. 30 B3
Chirbury 64 B3
Chirk 77 F4
Chirmorrie 122 D3
Chirnside 145 F4
Chirnsidebridge 145 F4
Chirton 26 B2
Chisbury 27 D1
Chiscan 130 B4
Chiselborough 12 A1
Chiseldon 41 D4
Chislehampton 42 A3
Chislehurst 44 D5
Chislet 33 E2
Chiswell Green 44 A2
Chiswick 44 B5
Chisworth 93 D3
Chithurst 28 D5
Chittering 58 C1
Chitterne 26 A3
Chittlehamholt 21 G3
Chittlehampton 21 G3
Chittoe 26 A1
Chivelstone 9 D4
Chobham 29 E1
Choicelee 145 E4
Cholderton 26 D3
Cholesbury 43 E2
Chollerford 128 B4
Chollerton 128 B4
Cholsey 42 A4
Cholstrey 53 D2
Cholwell B. & N.E.Som. 24 D2
Cholwell Devon 7 E3
Chop Gate 111 E2
Chopwell 120 A2
Chorley Ches. 78 C2
Chorley Lancs. 91 G1
Chorley Shrop. 65 F4
Chorley Staffs. 66 C1
Chorleywood 43 F3
Chorlton 79 E2
Chorlton-cum-Hardy 92 C3
Chorlton Lane 78 B3
Chowley 78 B2
Chrishall 58 C4
Chrishall Grange 58 C3
Chrisswell 140 D2
Christchurch Cambs. 70 C3
Christchurch Dorset 14 A3
Christchurch Glos. 39 E1
Christchurch Newport 38 C4
Christian Malford 40 B5
Christleton 78 B1
Christmas Common 42 C3
Christon 24 A2
Christon Bank 137 G4
Christow 10 B4
Chryston 142 A2
Chudleigh 10 B5
Chudleigh Knighton 10 B5
Chulmleigh 21 G4
Chunal 93 E3
Church 100 D5
Church Aston 65 G1
Church Brampton 56 C1
Church Broughton 80 D4
Church Common 61 E2
Church Crookham 28 D2
Church Eaton 66 A1
Church End Beds. 57 G4
Church End Beds. 57 E5
Church End Beds. 57 G2
Church End Cambs. 70 B2
Church End Cambs. 58 C2
Church End Cambs. 70 B5
Church End E.Riding 104 C2
Church End Essex 59 D3
Church End Essex 59 F5
Church End Hants. 28 B2
Church End Herts. 44 A1
Church End Lincs. 84 A4
Church End Lincs. 97 E3
Church End Warks. 67 E3
Church End Wilts. 40 C5
Church Enstone 55 F5
Church Fenton 103 E4
Church Green 11 E3
Church Gresley 67 E1
Church Hanborough 41 G1
Church Houses 111 F3
Church Knowle 13 F4
Church Langley 45 D2
Church Langton 68 C3
Church Lawford 67 G5
Church Lawton 79 F2
Church Leigh 80 B4
Church Lench 54 C2
Church Minshull 79 D1
Church Norton 16 A4
Church Preen 65 E3
Church Pulverbatch 64 D2
Church Stoke 64 B3
Church Stowe 56 B2
Church Street 45 G5
Church Stretton 65 D3
Church Village 37 G4
Church Warsop 81 G1
Churcham 39 G1
Churchdown 54 A5
Churchend Essex 46 D3
Churchend Essex 59 E5
Churchend S.Glos. 39 G3
Churchgate 44 C2
Churchgate Street 45 D1
Churchill N.Som. 24 B2
Churchill Oxon. 55 E5
Churchill Worcs. 54 B2
Churchill Worcs. 66 A5
Churchingford 11 F1
Churchover 68 A4
Churchstanton 11 E1
Churchstow 8 D3
Churchthorpe 96 D3
Churchtown Devon 21 G1
Churchtown I.o.M. 98 C2
Churchtown Lancs. 100 A3
Churchtown Mersey. 91 E1
Churnsike Lodge 127 E4
Churston Ferrers 9 F2
Churt 29 D4
Churton 78 B2
Churwell 102 B5
Chute Cadley 27 E2
Chute Standen 27 E2
Chwilog 74 D4
Chwitffordd (Whitford) 90 C5
Chyandour 2 B3
Cilan Uchaf 74 C5
Cilcain 77 E1
Cilcennin 50 B1
Cilfrew 37 D2
Cilfynydd 37 G3
Cilgerran 49 E3
Cilgwyn Carmar. 50 D5
Cilgwyn Pembs. 49 D4
Ciliau-Aeron 50 B2
Cille Bhrighde 172 C2
Cille Pheadair 172 C2
Cilmery 51 G2
Cilrhedyn 49 F4
Cilrhedyn Bridge 48 D4
Ciltalgarth 76 B3
Cilwendeg 49 F4
Cilybebyll 36 D2
Cilycwm 51 D3
Cinderford 39 F1
Cippyn 49 E3
Cirbhig 186 C3
Cirencester 40 C2
City Dulas 88 C4
City of London 44 C5
City of Westminster 44 B4
Clabhach 154 A4
Clachaig 140 C1
Clachan Arg. & B. 149 D3
Clachan Arg. & B. 156 A5
Clachan Arg. & B. 139 F4
Clachan High. 164 B1
Clachan W.Isles 173 F5
Clachan of Campsie 142 A2
Clachan of Glendaruel 140 B1
Clachan-Seil 147 G3
Clachan Strachur 148 D4
Clachandhu 147 D1
Clachaneasy 123 E3
Clachanmore 114 A2
Clachanturn 169 E5
Clachbreck 139 F2
Clachnabrain 160 B3
Clachnaharry 179 F5
Clachtoll 188 C2
Clackmannan 151 E5
Clacton-on-Sea 47 E1
Cladach a' Chaolais 173 F3
Cladach Chircebost 173 F3
Cladich 148 C2
Claggan High. 156 D2
Claggan High. 155 G5
Claigan 175 F4
Claines 54 A2
Clandown 25 D2
Clanfield Hants. 15 G1
Clanfield Oxon. 41 E2
Clannaborough Barton 10 A2
Clanville 27 E3
Claonaig 139 G4
Claonairigh 148 C4
Claonel 190 A4
Clap Gate 102 C3
Clapgate 13 G2
Clapham Beds. 57 F2
Clapham Gt.Lon. 44 B5
Clapham N.Yorks. 100 D1
Clapham W.Suss. 16 C3
Clapham Hill 32 D2
Clappers 145 G4
Clappersgate 107 E2
Clapton 12 A2
Clapton-in-Gordano 39 D5
Clapton-on-the-Hill 41 D1
Clapworthy 21 G3
Clarach 62 C4
Clarbeston 49 D5
Clarbeston Road 48 D5
Clarborough 95 E4
Clardon 194 D2
Clare 59 F3
Clarebrand 124 B4
Clarencefield 125 E4
Clareton 102 C2
Clarilaw 135 G4
Clarkston 141 G4
Clashban 190 B5
Clashcoig 190 B5
Clashgour 157 E5
Clashindarroch 169 G1
Clashmore 190 C5
Clashnessie 188 C1
Clashnoir 169 E2
Clathy 151 E2
Clatt 170 A2
Clatter 63 F3
Clatterford End 45 E2
Clatterin Brig 161 E2
Clatteringshaws 123 G3
Clatworthy 23 D4
Claughton Lancs. 100 B1
Claughton Lancs. 100 B3
Claverdon 55 D1
Claverham 24 B1
Clavering 58 C4
Claverley 65 G3
Claverton 25 E1
Clawdd-newydd 77 D2
Clawfin 132 D5
Clawthorpe 107 G5
Clawton 7 D1
Claxby Lincs. 97 E5
Claxby Lincs. 96 B3
Claxby Pluckacre 84 B1
Claxton N.Yorks. 103 F1
Claxton Norf. 87 E5
Clay Common 73 F3
Clay Coton 68 A5
Clay Cross 81 E1
Clay of Allan 180 A2
Claybrooke Magna 67 G4
Claybrooke Parva 67 G4
Claydene 31 D4
Claydon Oxon. 55 G2
Claydon Suff. 60 C3
Claygate Kent 31 G4
Claygate Surr. 29 G1
Claygate Cross 31 F3
Clayhanger Devon 22 D5
Clayhanger W.Mid. 66 C2
Clayhidon 11 E1
Clayock 195 D3
Claypole 82 D3
Claythorpe 97 E5
Clayton S.Yorks. 94 B2
Clayton Staffs. 79 F3
Clayton W.Suss. 17 E2
Clayton W.Yorks. 102 A4
Clayton-le-Moors 100 D4
Clayton-le-Woods 100 B5
Clayton West 93 G1
Clayworth 95 E4
Cleadale 155 D1
Cleadon 120 C1
Clearbrook 8 B1
Clearwell 39 E2
Cleasby 110 B1
Cleat 197 D4
Cleatlam 110 A1
Cleatop 101 E1
Cleator 116 D5
Cleator Moor 116 D5
Cleckheaton 102 A5
Clee St. Margaret 65 E4
Cleedownton 65 E4
Cleehill 65 E5
Cleethorpes 96 D2
Cleeton St. Mary 65 F5
Cleeve N.Som. 24 B1
Cleeve Oxon. 42 B4
Cleeve Hill 54 B5
Cleeve Prior 54 C3
Cleghorn 142 D5
Clehonger 52 D4
Cleigh 148 A2
Cleish 151 F5
Cleland 142 B4
Clench Common 26 C1
Clenchwarton 85 D5
Clent 66 B5
Cleobury Mortimer 65 F5
Cleobury North 65 F4
Clephanton 180 A4
Clerklands 135 G3
Clestrain 196 C2
Cleuch Head 135 G4
Cleughbrae 125 E3
Clevancy 40 C5
Clevedon 38 D5
Cleveland Tontine 110 D3
Cleveleys 99 G3
Clevelode 54 A3
Cleverton 40 B4
Clewer 24 B2
Clewer Village 43 E5
Cley next the Sea 86 B1
Cliburn 118 B5
Cliddesden 28 B3
Cliff Carmar. 35 G2
Cliff High. 155 F3
Cliff End 19 D2
Cliffe Med. 45 G5
Cliffe N.Yorks. 103 F4
Cliffe Woods 45 G5
Clifford Here. 52 B3
Clifford W.Yorks. 102 D3
Clifford Chambers 55 D2
Clifford's Mesne 53 G5
Cliffs End 33 F2
Clifton Beds. 57 G4
Clifton Bristol 39 E5
Clifton Cumb. 118 B5
Clifton Derbys. 80 C3
Clifton Lancs. 100 A4
Clifton Northumb. 129 E3
Clifton Nott. 81 G4
Clifton Oxon. 55 G4
Clifton Stir. 149 F1
Clifton Worcs. 54 A3
Clifton Campville 67 E1
Clifton Hampden 42 A3
Clifton Reynes 57 E2
Clifton upon Dunsmore 68 A5
Clifton upon Teme 53 G1
Cliftonville 33 F1
Climping 16 C3
Climpy 142 D4
Clint 102 B2
Clint Green 86 B4
Clinterty 170 D3
Clintmains 136 A3
Clippesby 87 F4
Clipsham 69 E1
Clipston Northants. 68 C4
Clipston Notts. 82 B4
Clipstone 81 G1
Clitheroe 100 D3
Clive 78 C5
Clivocast 203 F2
Clocaenog 77 D2
Clochan 181 G3
Clochtow 171 F1
Clock Face 91 G3
Clockhill 183 D5
Cloddach 181 D4
Clodock 52 C5
Cloford 25 E3
Cloichran 150 B1
Clola 183 F5
Clonrae 124 C1
Clophill 57 F4
Clopton 69 F5
Clopton Green 59 F2
Close Clark 98 A4
Closeburn 124 C1
Closworth 12 B1
Clothall 58 A4
Clothan 203 D4
Clotton 78 C1
Clough Cumb. 108 C3
Clough Gt.Man. 92 D1
Clough Foot 101 F5
Cloughton 112 D3
Cloughton Newlands 112 D3
Clounlaid 155 G4
Clousta 200 C2
Clouston 198 B5
Clova Aber. 169 G2
Clova Angus 160 B2
Clove Lodge 109 E1
Clovelly 20 D3
Clovelly Cross 20 D3
Clovenfords 135 F2
Clovenstone 170 C3
Cloverhill 171 E3
Cloves 180 D3
Clovullin 156 C3
Clowne 94 B5
Clows Top 65 G5
Cloyntie 132 B5
Cluanach 138 B4
Clubworthy 6 C1
Cluer 184 D4
Clun 64 B4
Clunas 180 A5
Clunbury 64 C4
Clune High. 167 G2
Clune Moray 182 A3
Clunes 157 D1
Clungunford 64 C5
Clunie Aber. 182 B4
Clunie P. & K. 159 G5
Clunton 64 C4
Cluny 152 A5
Clutton B. & N.E.Som. 24 D2
Clutton Ches. 78 B2
Clwt-y-bont 75 E1
Clydach Mon. 38 B1
Clydach Swan. 36 C2
Clydach Vale 37 F3
Clydebank 141 G3
Clydey 49 F4
Clyffe Pypard 40 C5
Clynder 140 D1
Clynderwen 35 E1
Clynelish 191 D4
Clynfyw 49 F4
Clynnog-fawr 74 D3
Clyro 52 B3
Clyst Honiton 10 C3
Clyst Hydon 10 D2
Clyst St. George 10 C4
Clyst St. Lawrence 10 D2
Clyst St. Mary 10 C3
Cnewr 51 E5
Cnoc 187 F4
Cnwch Coch 62 C5
Coachford 181 G5
Coad's Green 5 G2
Coal Aston 94 A5
Coalbrookdale 65 F2
Coalbrookvale 38 A2
Coalburn 133 G2
Coalburns 120 A1
Coalcleugh 119 E3
Coaley 39 G2
Coalpit Heath 39 F4
Coalpit Hill 79 F2
Coalport 65 G2
Coalsnaughton 151 E5
Coaltown of Balgonie 152 B5
Coaltown of Wemyss 152 B5
Coalville 67 G1
Coast 188 B5
Coat 24 B5
Coatbridge 142 B3
Coate Swin. 41 D4
Coate Wilts. 26 B1
Coates Cambs. 70 B3
Coates Glos. 40 B2
Coates Lincs. 95 G4
Coates W.Suss. 16 B2
Coatham 121 E5
Coatham Mundeville 120 B5
Cobairdy 182 A5
Cobbaton 21 G3
Coberley 40 B1
Cobham Kent 31 F2
Cobham Surr. 29 G2
Cobleland 150 A5
Cobler's Green 45 F1
Cobnash 52 D1
Coburty 183 E3
Cochno 141 F2
Cock Alley 81 F1
Cock Bridge 169 E4
Cock Clarks 46 B2
Cockayne 111 F3
Cockayne Hatley 58 A3
Cockburnspath 145 E2
Cockenzie and Port Seton 144 B2
Cockerham 100 A2
Cockermouth 117 E3
Cockernhoe 57 G5
Cockett 36 C3
Cockfield Dur. 120 A5
Cockfield Suff. 60 A2
Cockfosters 44 B3
Cocking 16 A2
Cockington 9 E1
Cocklake 24 B3
Cockley Beck 107 D2
Cockley Cley 71 F2
Cockpole Green 42 C4
Cockshutt 78 B5
Cockthorpe 86 A1
Cockwood 10 C4
Codda 5 F2
Coddenham 60 C2
Coddington Ches. 78 B2
Coddington Here. 53 G3
Coddington Notts. 82 D2
Codford St. Mary 26 A4
Codford St. Peter 26 A3
Codicote 44 B1
Codmore Hill 16 C2
Codnor 81 F3
Codrington 39 G5
Codsall 66 A2
Codsall Wood 66 A2
Coed Morgan 38 C1
Coed-y-paen 38 C3
Coed-yr-ynys 52 A5
Coed Ystumgwern 75 E5
Coedcae 38 B2
Coedely 37 G4
Coedkernew 38 B4
Coedpoeth 77 F2
Coelbren 37 E1
Coffinswell 9 E1
Cofton Hackett 66 C5
Cogan 38 A5
Cogenhoe 56 D1
Coggeshall 59 G5
Coggeshall Hamlet 59 G5
Coggins Mill 18 A1
Còig Peighinnean W.Isles 187 E2
Còig Peighinnean W.Isles 187 G1
Coilantogle 150 A4
Coileitir 156 D5
Coilessan 149 E4
Coillaig 148 C2
Coille Mhorgil 166 A4
Coille-righ 165 F2
Coillore 163 G1
Coity 37 F4
Col 187 F3
Colaboll 190 A3
Colan 4 C3
Colaton Raleigh 11 D4
Colbost 175 F5
Colbury 14 C1
Colby Cumb. 118 C5
Colby I.o.M. 98 A4
Colby Norf. 86 D2
Colchester 60 A5
Colcot 23 E1
Cold Ash 27 G1
Cold Ashby 68 B5
Cold Ashton 39 G5
Cold Aston 54 D5
Cold Blow 35 E1
Cold Brayfield 57 E2
Cold Chapel 134 A3
Cold Hanworth 96 A4
Cold Hesledon 120 D3
Cold Higham 56 B2
Cold Kirby 111 E4
Cold Newton 68 C2
Cold Norton 46 B2
Cold Overton 68 D2
Coldbackie 193 F2
Coldblow 45 E5
Coldean 17 F3
Coldeast 10 B5
Colden Common 27 F5
Coldfair Green 61 F1
Coldham 70 C2
Coldharbour 29 G3
Coldingham 145 F3
Coldrain 151 F4
Coldred 33 E4
Coldrey 28 C3
Coldridge 21 G5
Coldrife 128 C2
Coldstream 136 C3
Coldwaltham 16 C2
Coldwells 183 G5
Cole 25 D4
Cole Green 44 B1
Colebatch 64 C4
Colebrook 10 D2
Colebrooke 10 A2
Coleby Lincs. 83 E1
Coleby N.Lincs. 95 G1
Coleford Devon 10 A2
Coleford Glos. 39 E1
Coleford Som. 25 D3
Colehill 13 G2
Coleman's Hatch 31 D5
Colemere 78 B4
Colemore 28 C4
Colenden 151 G2
Coleorton 67 G1
Colerne 40 A5
Cole's Cross 9 D3
Colesbourne 40 C1
Colesden 57 G2
Coleshill Bucks. 43 E3
Coleshill Oxon. 41 E3
Coleshill Warks. 67 E4
Colestocks 11 D2
Colfin 122 B5
Colgate 30 B5
Colgrain 141 E1
Colinsburgh 152 C4
Colinton 143 G3
Colintraive 140 B2
Colkirk 86 A3
Collace 152 A1
Collafirth Shet. 200 D1
Collafirth Shet. 202 C4
Collamoor Head 6 B1

Collaton St. Mary 9 E1
Collessie 152 A3
Colleton Mills 21 G4
Collett's Green 54 A2
Collier Row 45 E3
Collier Street 31 G4
Collier's End 58 B5
Colliery Row 120 C2
Collieston 171 F2
Collin 125 E3
Collingbourne Ducis 26 D2
Collingbourne Kingston 26 D2
Collingham *Notts.* 82 D1
Collingham *W.Yorks.* 102 C3
Collington 53 F1
Collingtree 56 C2
Collins Green 91 G3
Colliston 161 E5
Colliton 11 D2
Collmuir 170 A4
Collycroft 67 F4
Collynie 170 D1
Collyweston 69 F2
Colmonell 122 C2
Colmworth 57 G2
Coln Rogers 40 C2
Coln St. Aldwyns 40 D2
Coln St. Dennis 40 C1
Colnabaichin 169 E4
Colnbrook 43 F5
Colne *Cambs.* 70 B5
Colne *Lancs.* 101 E3
Colne Engaine 59 G4
Colney 86 C5
Colney Heath 44 B2
Colney Street 44 A2
Colonsay 146 C5
Colpy 170 B1
Colquhar 144 A5
Colsterdale 110 A4
Colsterworth 83 E5
Colston Bassett 82 C4
Coltfield 180 D3
Coltishall 87 D4
Colton *Cumb.* 107 E4
Colton *N.Yorks.* 103 E3
Colton *Norf.* 86 C4
Colton *Staffs.* 80 B5
Colva 52 B2
Colvend 124 C5
Colvister 203 E3
Colwall Green 53 G3
Colwall Stone 53 G3
Colwell 128 B4
Colwich 80 B5
Colwick 82 B3
Colwinston 37 F5
Colworth 16 B3
Colwyn Bay (Bae Colwyn) 89 G5
Colyford 11 F3
Colyton 11 F3
Combe *Here.* 52 C1
Combe *Oxon.* 41 G1
Combe *W.Berks.* 27 E1
Combe Cross 10 A5
Combe Down 25 E1
Combe Florey 23 E4
Combe Hay 25 E1
Combe Martin 21 F1
Combe Raleigh 11 E2
Combe St. Nicholas 11 F1
Combeinteignhead 10 C5
Comberbach 92 A5
Comberford 67 D2
Comberton *Cambs.* 58 B2
Comberton *Here.* 53 D1
Combpyne 11 F3
Combrook 55 F2
Combs *Derbys.* 93 E5
Combs *Suff.* 60 B2
Combs Ford 60 B2
Combwich 23 F3
Comer 149 F4
Comers 170 B4
Commercial End 59 D1
Commins Coch 63 E2
Common Edge 99 G4
Common Moor 5 G3
Common Side 94 A5
Commondale 111 F1
Commonside 80 D3
Compstall 93 D3
Compton *Devon* 9 E1
Compton *Hants.* 27 F5
Compton *Surr.* 29 E3
Compton *W.Berks.* 42 A5
Compton *W.Suss.* 15 G1
Compton Abbas 13 E1
Compton Abdale 40 C1
Compton Bassett 40 C5
Compton Beauchamp 41 E4
Compton Bishop 24 A2
Compton Chamberlayne 26 B5
Compton Dando 24 D1
Compton Dundon 24 B4
Compton Martin 24 C2
Compton Pauncefoot 24 D5
Compton Valence 12 B3
Comra 167 E5
Comrie 150 C2
Conchra *Arg. & B.* 140 B1
Conchra *High.* 165 E2
Concraigie 159 G5
Conder Green 100 A2
Conderton 54 B4
Condicote 54 D5
Condorrat 142 B2
Condover 65 D2
Coney Weston 72 A4
Coneyhurst 29 G5
Coneysthorpe 111 G5
Coneythorpe 102 C2
Conford 28 D4
Congash 168 C2
Congdon's Shop 5 G2
Congerstone 67 F2
Congham 85 F5
Congleton 79 F1
Congresbury 24 B1
Conicavel 180 B4
Coningsby 84 A2
Conington *Cambs.* 69 G4
Conington *Cambs.* 58 B1
Conisbrough 94 C3
Conisby 138 A3
Conisholme 97 E3
Coniston *Cumb.* 107 E3
Coniston *E.Riding* 105 D4
Coniston Cold 101 F2
Conistone 101 F1
Conland 182 B5
Connah's Quay 77 F1
Connel 148 B1
Connel Park 133 E4
Connor Downs 2 C3
Conon Bridge 179 E4
Cononish 149 F2
Cononley 101 F3
Cononsyth 161 D5
Consall 79 G3
Consett 120 A2
Constable Burton 110 A3
Constantine 3 E4
Contin 179 D4
Contlaw 170 D4
Contullich 179 F2
Conwy 89 F5
Conyer 32 B2
Cooden 18 C3
Coodham 132 B2
Cookbury 21 E5
Cookham 43 D4
Cookham Dean 43 D4
Cookham Rise 43 D4
Cookhill 54 C2
Cookley *Suff.* 73 E4
Cookley *Worcs.* 66 A4
Cookley Green 42 B4
Cookney 171 D5
Cooksbridge 17 G2
Cookshill 79 G3
Cooksmill Green 45 F2
Cookston 171 E1
Coolham 29 G5
Cooling 45 G5
Coombe *Cornw.* 5 D4
Coombe *Cornw.* 20 C4
Coombe *Cornw.* 4 A5
Coombe *Devon* 9 D3
Coombe *Devon* 10 B4
Coombe Bissett 26 C5
Coombe Hill 54 A5
Coombe Keynes 13 E4
Coombes 17 D3
Coombes Moor 52 C1
Cooper's Corner *E.Suss.* 18 C1
Cooper's Corner *Kent* 31 D4
Cooper's Hill 43 E5
Coopersale Common 45 D2
Cootham 16 C2
Cop Street 33 E3
Copdock 60 C3
Copford Green 60 A5
Copgrove 102 C1
Copister 203 D5
Cople 57 G3
Copley 119 G5
Coplow Dale 93 F5
Copmanthorpe 103 E3
Coppathorne 20 C5
Coppenhall 66 B1
Coppenhall Moss 79 E2
Coppingford 69 G5
Coppleridge 25 F5
Copplestone 10 A2
Coppull 91 G1
Coppull Moor 91 G1
Copsale 29 G5
Copster Green 100 C4
Copston Magna 67 G4
Copt Heath 67 D5
Copt Hewick 110 C5
Copt Oak 67 G1
Copthorne 30 C5
Copy Lake 21 G4
Copythorne 14 C1
Coralhill 183 F3
Corbiegoe 195 F4
Corbridge 119 F1
Corby 69 D4
Corby Glen 83 F5
Cordach 170 B5
Coreley 65 F5
Corfcott Green 6 D1
Corfe 11 F1
Corfe Castle 13 F4
Corfe Mullen 13 F3
Corfton 65 D4
Corgarff 169 E4
Corhampton 28 B5
Corley 67 E4
Corley Ash 67 E4
Corley Moor 67 E4
Cornabus 138 B5
Corney 106 C3
Cornforth 120 C4
Cornhill 182 A4
Cornhill on Tweed 136 C3
Cornholme 101 F5
Cornish Hall End 59 E4
Cornquoy 197 E2
Cornriggs 119 E3
Cornsay 120 A3
Cornsay Colliery 120 A3
Corntown *High.* 179 E4
Corntown *V. of Glam.* 37 F5
Cornwell 55 E5
Cornwood 8 C2
Cornworthy 9 E2
Corpach 156 D2
Corpusty 86 C3
Corrachree 169 G4
Corran *Arg. & B.* 149 E5
Corran *High.* 165 E4
Corran *High.* 156 C3
Corranbuie 139 G3
Corranmore 147 G4
Corrany 98 C3
Corrie 140 B5
Corrie Common 126 A3
Corriechrevie 139 F4
Corriecravie 131 E3
Corriedoo 124 A2
Corrielorne 148 A3
Corrievorrie 167 G2
Corrimony 166 C1
Corringham *Lincs.* 95 F3
Corringham *Thur.* 45 G4
Corris 63 D2
Corris Uchaf 62 D2
Corrlarach 156 B2
Corrour Shooting Lodge 157 G3
Corrow 149 D4
Corry 164 C2
Corrychurrachan 156 C3
Corrykinloch 189 F2
Corrylach 130 C3
Corrymuckloch 151 D1
Corsback 195 E2
Corscombe 12 B2
Corse *Aber.* 182 B5
Corse *Glos.* 53 G5
Corse Lawn 54 A4
Corse of Kinnoir 182 A5
Corsebank 133 G4
Corsehill 125 F2
Corsewall 122 B4
Corsham 40 A5
Corsindae 170 B4
Corsley 25 F3
Corsley Heath 25 F3
Corsock 124 B3
Corston *B. & N.E.Som.* 25 D1
Corston *Wilts.* 40 B4
Corstorphine 143 F2
Cortachy 160 B4
Corton *Suff.* 73 G2
Corton *Wilts.* 26 A3
Corton Denham 24 D5
Coruna (Corunna) 173 G3
Corunna (Coruna) 173 G3
Corwar House 123 D2
Corwen 77 D3
Coryton *Devon* 7 E2
Coryton *Thur.* 45 G4
Cosby 68 A3
Coseley 66 B3
Cosford 65 G2
Cosgrove 56 C3
Cosham 15 F2
Cosheston 34 D2
Coshieville 158 C5
Cossall 81 F3
Cossington *Leics.* 68 B1
Cossington *Som.* 24 A3
Costa 198 B4
Costessey 86 C4
Costock 81 G5
Coston *Leics.* 83 D5
Coston *Norf.* 86 B5
Cote *Oxon.* 41 F2
Cote *Som.* 24 A3
Cotebrook 78 C1
Cotehill 118 A2
Cotes *Cumb.* 107 F4
Cotes *Leics.* 81 G5
Cotes *Staffs.* 79 F4
Cotesbach 68 A4
Cotgrave 82 B4
Cothall 171 D3
Cotham 82 C3
Cothelstone 23 E4
Cothercott 64 D2
Cotheridge 53 G2
Cotherstone 109 F1
Cothill 41 G3
Cotleigh 11 F2
Coton *Cambs.* 58 C2
Coton *Northants.* 68 B5
Coton *Staffs.* 79 G4
Coton *Staffs.* 67 D2
Coton Clanford 79 F5
Coton in the Clay 80 C5
Coton in the Elms 67 E1
Cott 9 D1
Cottam *E.Riding* 104 B1
Cottam *Lancs.* 100 A4
Cottam *Notts.* 95 F4
Cottartown 168 C1
Cottenham 58 C1
Cotterdale 108 D3
Cottered 58 B5
Cotteridge 66 C4
Cotterstock 69 F3
Cottesbrooke 68 C5
Cottesmore 69 E1
Cottingham *E.Riding* 104 C4
Cottingham *Northants.* 68 D3
Cottisford 56 A4
Cotton 60 B1
Cotton End 57 F3
Cottown *Aber.* 170 A2
Cottown *Aber.* 182 D5
Cottown *Aber.* 170 C3
Cotwalton 79 G4
Couch's Mill 5 F4
Coughton *Here.* 53 E5
Coughton *Warks.* 54 C1
Cougie 166 B2
Coulaghailtro 139 F3
Coulags 177 F5
Coulby Newham 111 E1
Coull 170 A4
Coulport 140 D1
Coulsdon 30 C3
Coulston 26 A2
Coulter 134 B2
Coultershaw Bridge 16 B2
Coultings 23 F3
Coulton 111 F5
Coultra 152 B2
Cound 65 E2
Coundon 120 B4
Coundon Grange 120 B5
Countersett 109 E4
Countess 26 C3
Countess Wear 10 C3
Countesthorpe 68 A3
Countisbury 22 A3
County Oak 30 B5
Coupar Angus 160 A5
Coupland *Cumb.* 108 C1
Coupland *Northumb.* 136 D3
Cour 139 G5
Court-at-Street 32 C5
Court Barton 10 B3
Court Henry 50 B5
Court House Green 67 F4
Courteenhall 56 C2
Courtsend 46 D3
Courtway 23 F4
Cousland 144 A3
Cousley Wood 31 F5
Coustonn 140 B2
Cove *Arg. & B.* 140 D1
Cove *Devon* 10 C1
Cove *Hants.* 28 D2
Cove *High.* 188 A5
Cove *Sc.Bord.* 145 E2
Cove Bay 171 E4
Covehithe 73 G3
Coven 66 B2
Coveney 70 C4
Covenham St. Bartholomew 96 D3
Covenham St. Mary 96 D3
Coventry 67 F5
Coverack 3 E5
Coverham 109 F4
Covesea 181 D2
Covington *Cambs.* 69 F5
Covington *S.Lan.* 134 A2
Cowan Bridge 108 B5
Cowbeech 18 B2
Cowbit 70 A1
Cowbridge 37 G5
Cowden 31 D4
Cowden Pound 31 D4
Cowdenbeath 151 G5
Cowes 15 D3
Cowesby 111 D3
Cowfold 17 E1
Cowgill 108 C4
Cowie *Aber.* 161 G1
Cowie *Stir.* 142 C1
Cowlam Manor 104 B1
Cowley *Devon* 10 C3
Cowley *Glos.* 40 B1
Cowley *Gt.Lon.* 43 F4
Cowley *Oxon.* 42 A2
Cowling *N.Yorks.* 101 F3
Cowling *N.Yorks.* 110 B4
Cowlinge 59 F2
Cowmes 93 F1
Cowpen 129 E3
Cowpen Bewley 121 D5
Cowplain 15 F1
Cowshill 119 E3
Cowthorpe 102 D2
Cox Common 73 E3
Coxbank 79 D3
Coxbench 81 E3
Coxheath 31 G3
Coxhoe 120 C4
Coxley 24 C3
Coxtie Green 45 E3
Coxwold 111 E5
Coychurch 37 F5
Coylet 140 C1
Coylton 132 C4
Coylumbridge 168 B3
Coynach 169 G4
Coynachie 169 G1
Coytrahen 37 E4
Crabbet Park 30 C5
Crabbs Cross 54 C1
Crabtree *Plym.* 8 B2
Crabtree *W.Suss.* 17 E1
Crackaig 138 D3
Crackenthorpe 118 C5
Crackington 6 B1
Crackington Haven 6 B1
Crackleybank 65 G1
Crackpot 109 E3
Cracoe 101 F1
Craddock 11 D1
Cradhlastadh 186 B4
Cradley *Here.* 53 G3
Cradley *W.Mid.* 66 B4
Crafthole 7 D5
Cragg 101 G5
Craggan *Moray* 169 D1
Craggan *P. & K.* 150 D3
Cragganruar 158 B5
Craggie *High.* 167 G1
Craggie *High.* 191 D2
Craghead 120 B2
Craibstone *Aberdeen* 171 D3
Craibstone *Moray* 181 G4
Craichie 160 C5
Craig *Arg. & B.* 148 C1
Craig *Arg. & B.* 147 E2
Craig *D. & G.* 124 A4
Craig *High.* 177 D3
Craig *High.* 177 G5
Craig *S.Ayr.* 132 B5
Craig-cefn-parc 36 C2
Craig-y-nos 37 E1
Craigans 148 B5
Craigbeg 157 G1
Craigcleuch 126 B3
Craigculter 183 E4
Craigdallie 152 A2
Craigdam 170 D1
Craigdarroch *D. & G.* 124 B1
Craigdarroch *E.Ayr.* 133 E5
Craigdhu *D. & G.* 115 D2
Craigdhu *High.* 179 D5
Craigearn 170 C3
Craigellachie 181 E5
Craigellie 183 F3
Craigencallie 123 G3
Craigend *Moray* 180 D4
Craigend *P. & K.* 151 G2
Craigendive 140 B1
Craigendoran 141 E1
Craigengillan 132 C5
Craigenputtock 124 B2
Craigens 138 A3
Craigglas 139 G1
Craighall 152 C3
Craighat 141 F1
Craighead *Fife* 153 E4
Craighead *High.* 179 G3
Craighlaw 123 E4
Craighouse 138 D3
Craigie *Aber.* 171 E3
Craigie *P. & K.* 159 G5
Craigie *S.Ayr.* 132 C2
Craigie Brae 171 D1
Craigieburn 134 C5
Craigieholm 151 G1
Craiglockhart 143 G2
Craiglug 170 D5
Craigmaud 183 D4
Craigmillar 143 G2
Craigmore 140 C3
Craigmyle House 170 B4
Craignafeoch 140 A2
Craignant 77 F4
Craignavie 150 A1
Craigneil 122 C2
Craignure 147 G1
Craigo 161 E3
Craigoch 132 B5
Craigow 151 F4
Craigrothie 152 B3
Craigroy 180 D4
Craigroy Farm 169 D1
Craigruie 150 A2
Craigsanquhar 152 B3
Craigton *Aberdeen* 170 D4
Craigton *Angus* 152 D1
Craigton *Angus* 160 B4
Craigton *Stir.* 142 A1
Craigtown 194 A3
Craik *Aber.* 169 G2
Craik *Sc.Bord.* 135 E5
Crail 153 E4
Crailing 136 A4
Crailinghall 136 A4
Crakehill 110 D5
Crambe 103 G1
Cramlington 129 E4
Cramond 143 F2
Cranage 79 E1
Cranberry 79 F4
Cranborne 13 G1
Cranbourne 43 E5
Cranbrook 31 G5
Cranbrook Common 31 G5
Cranfield 57 E3
Cranford *Devon* 20 D3
Cranford *Gt.Lon.* 44 A5
Cranford St. Andrew 69 E5
Cranford St. John 69 E5
Cranham *Glos.* 40 A1
Cranham *Gt.Lon.* 45 E4
Crank 91 G2
Cranleigh 29 F4
Cranmer Green 72 B4
Cranmore *I.o.W.* 14 D3
Cranmore *Som.* 25 D3
Cranna 182 B4
Crannach 181 G4
Cranoe 68 C3
Cransford 61 E1
Cranshaws 145 D3
Cranstal 98 C1
Crantock 4 B3
Cranwell 83 F3
Cranwich 71 F3
Cranworth 86 A5
Craobh Haven 147 G4
Crapstone 8 B1
Crarae 148 B5
Crask Inn 190 A2
Crask of Aigas 179 D5
Craskins 170 A4
Craster 137 G4
Craswall 52 B4
Cratfield 73 E4
Crathes 170 C5
Crathie *Aber.* 169 E5
Crathie *High.* 167 E5
Crathorne 110 D2
Craven Arms 64 D4
Craw 139 G5
Crawcrook 120 A1
Crawford *Lancs.* 91 F2
Crawford *S.Lan.* 134 A3
Crawfordjohn 133 G3
Crawfordton 124 B1
Crawick 133 F4
Crawley *Hants.* 27 F4
Crawley *Oxon.* 41 F1
Crawley *W.Suss.* 30 B5
Crawley Down 30 C5
Crawleyside 119 F3
Crawshawbooth 101 E5
Crawton 161 G2
Crawyn 98 B2
Cray *N.Yorks.* 109 E5
Cray *P. & K.* 159 G3
Cray *Powys* 51 E5
Crayford 45 E5
Crayke 111 E5
Crays Hill 45 G3
Cray's Pond 42 B4
Crazies Hill 42 C4
Creacombe 10 B1
Creag Ghoraidh 173 G5
Creagbheitheachain 156 B3
Creaton 68 C5
Creca 126 A4
Credenhill 52 D3
Crediton 10 B2
Creech Heathfield 23 F5
Creech St. Michael 23 F5
Creed 4 D5
Creedy Park 10 B2
Creekmouth 45 D4
Creeting St. Mary 60 B2
Creeton 83 F5
Creetown 123 F5
Creggans 148 C4
Cregneash 98 A5
Cregrina 52 A2
Creich 152 B2
Creigiau 37 G4
Crelevan 166 C1
Cremyll 8 A2
Cressage 65 E2
Cresselly 35 D2
Cressing 59 F5
Cresswell *Northumb.* 129 E2
Cresswell *Staffs.* 79 G4
Cresswell Quay 35 D2
Creswell 94 C5
Cretingham 60 D2
Cretshengan 139 F3
Crewe *Ches.* 79 E2
Crewe *Ches.* 78 B2
Crewgreen 64 C1
Crewkerne 12 A2
Crewton 81 E4
Crianlarich 149 F2
Cribbs Causeway 39 E4
Cribyn 50 B2
Criccieth 75 D4
Crich 81 E2
Crich Carr 81 E2
Crichie 183 E5
Crichton 144 A3
Crick *Mon.* 39 D4
Crick *Northants.* 68 A5
Crickadarn 51 G3
Cricket Malherbie 11 G1
Cricket St. Thomas 11 G2
Crickheath 77 F5
Crickhowell 38 B1
Cricklade 40 C3
Cridling Stubbs 103 E5
Crieff 151 D2
Criggion 64 B1
Crigglestone 94 A1
Crimdon Park 121 D4
Crimond 183 F4
Crimonmogate 183 F4
Crimplesham 71 E2
Crinan 147 G5
Cringleford 86 C5
Cringletie 143 G5
Crinow 35 E1
Cripplesease 2 B3
Cripp's Corner 18 C1
Crix 45 G1
Croalchapel 124 D1
Croasdale 117 D5
Crock Street 11 G1
Crockenhill 31 E2
Crockernwell 10 A3
Crockerton 25 F3
Crocketford or Ninemile Bar 124 C3
Crockey Hill 103 F3
Crockham Hill 30 D3
Crockhurst Street 31 F4
Crockleford Heath 60 B5
Croes Hywel 38 C1
Croes-lan 49 G3
Croes-y-mwyalch 38 C3
Croes y pant 38 C2
Croesau Bach 77 F5
Croeserw 37 E3
Croesgoch 48 B5
Croesor 75 F3
Croespenmaen 38 A3
Croesyceiliog *Carmar.* 36 A1
Croesyceiliog *Torfaen* 38 C3
Croft *Leics.* 68 A3
Croft *Lincs.* 84 D1
Croft *Warr.* 92 A3
Croft-on-Tees 110 B1
Crofthead 126 B4
Croftmore 159 D3
Crofton *W.Yorks.* 94 A1
Crofton *Wilts.* 27 D1
Crofts 124 B3
Crofts of Benachielt 195 D5
Crofts of Buinach 181 D4
Crofts of Haddo 170 D1
Crofty 36 B3
Crogen 76 D4
Croggan 147 G2
Croglin 118 B3
Croick *High.* 189 G5
Croick *High.* 194 A3
Croig 154 D4
Crois Dughaill 172 C2
Croit e Caley 98 A4
Cromarty 179 G3
Crombie Mill 160 D5
Cromblet 170 C1
Cromdale 168 C2
Cromer *Herts.* 58 A5
Cromer *Norf.* 86 D1
Cromer Hyde 44 B1
Cromford 81 D2
Cromhall 39 F3
Cromhall Common 39 F4
Crompton Fold 93 D2
Cromwell 82 D1
Cronberry 133 E3
Crondall 28 C3
Cronk-y-Voddy 98 B3
Cronton 91 F4
Crook *Cumb.* 107 F3
Crook *Dur.* 120 A4
Crook of Devon 151 F4
Crookedholm 132 C2
Crookham *Northumb.* 136 D3
Crookham *W.Berks.* 27 G1
Crookham Village 28 C2
Crooklands 107 G4
Cropredy 55 G3
Cropston 68 A1
Cropthorne 54 B3
Cropton 111 G4
Cropwell Bishop 82 B4
Cropwell Butler 82 B4
Cros 187 F1
Crosbie 140 D5
Crosbost 187 E5
Crosby *Cumb.* 117 D3
Crosby *I.o.M.* 98 B4
Crosby *Mersey.* 91 E3
Crosby *N.Lincs.* 95 F1
Crosby Court 110 C3
Crosby Garrett 108 C2
Crosby Ravensworth 108 B1
Croscombe 24 C3
Cross 24 B2
Cross Ash 38 D1
Cross-at-Hand 31 G4
Cross Foxes Inn 63 D1
Cross Gates 102 C4
Cross Green *Devon* 7 D2
Cross Green *Suff.* 60 A2
Cross Green *Suff.* 59 G2
Cross Hands *Carmar.* 36 B1
Cross Hands *Pembs.* 35 D1
Cross Hill 81 F3
Cross Hills 101 G3
Cross Houses 65 E2
Cross in Hand 18 A1
Cross Inn *Cere.* 49 G2
Cross Inn *Cere.* 50 B1
Cross Inn *R.C.T.* 37 G4
Cross Keys 40 A5
Cross Lane Head 65 G3
Cross Lanes *Cornw.* 4 B5
Cross Lanes *N.Yorks.* 103 E1
Cross Lanes *Wrex.* 78 A3
Cross o' the Hands 81 D3
Cross of Jackson 170 C1
Cross Street 72 C4
Crossaig 139 G4
Crossapol 154 A4
Crossapoll 154 A2
Crossbush 16 C3
Crosscanonby 117 D3
Crossdale Street 86 D2
Crossens 99 G5
Crossford *D. & G.* 124 C2
Crossford *Fife* 143 E1
Crossford *S.Lan.* 142 C5
Crossgate 84 A5
Crossgatehall 144 A3
Crossgates *Fife* 143 F1
Crossgates *P. & K.* 151 F2
Crossgates *Powys* 51 G1
Crossgill 100 B1
Crosshands 132 C2
Crosshill *Fife* 151 G5
Crosshill *S.Ayr.* 132 B5
Crosshouse 132 B2
Crosskeys 38 B3
Crosskirk 194 C1
Crosslanes *Cornw.* 3 D4
Crosslanes *Shrop.* 64 C1
Crosslee *Renf.* 141 F3
Crosslee *Sc.Bord.* 135 E4
Crosslet 141 F2
Crossmichael 124 B4
Crossmoor 100 A4
Crossroads *Aber.* 170 C5
Crossroads *E.Ayr.* 132 C2
Crossway *Mon.* 38 D1
Crossway *Powys* 51 G2
Crossway Green 54 A1
Crossways *Dorset* 12 D4
Crossways *Glos.* 39 E1
Crosswell 49 E4
Crosthwaite 107 F3
Croston 91 F1
Crostwick 87 D4
Crostwight 87 E2
Crouch 31 F3
Crouch Hill 12 D1
Croughton 56 A4
Crovie 182 D3
Crow 14 A2
Crow Hill 53 F5
Crowan 2 D3
Crowborough 31 E5
Crowcombe 23 E4
Crowdecote 80 C1
Crowdhill 27 F5
Crowfield *Northants.* 56 B3
Crowfield *Suff.* 60 C2
Crowhurst *E.Suss.* 18 C2
Crowhurst *Surr.* 30 C4
Crowhurst Lane End 30 C4
Crowland *Lincs.* 70 A1
Crowland *Suff.* 72 B4
Crowlas 2 C3
Crowle *N.Lincs.* 95 E1
Crowle *Worcs.* 54 B2
Crowle Green 54 B2
Crowmarsh Gifford 42 B4
Crownhill 8 A2
Crownthorpe 86 B5
Crowntown 2 D3
Crows-an-wra 2 A4
Crowthorne 28 D1
Crowton 91 G5
Croxall 67 D1
Croxdale 120 B4
Croxden 80 B4
Croxley Green 43 F3
Croxton *Cambs.* 58 A2
Croxton *N.Lincs.* 96 B1
Croxton *Norf.* 71 G4
Croxton *Staffs.* 79 E4
Croxton Green 78 C2
Croxton Kerrial 82 D5
Croxtonbank 79 E4
Croy *High.* 179 G5
Croy *N.Lan.* 142 B2
Croyde 21 E2
Croydon *Cambs.* 58 B3
Croydon *Gt.Lon.* 30 C2
Cruach 138 B4
Cruchie 182 A5
Cruckmeole 64 D2
Cruckton 64 D1
Cruden Bay 171 F1
Crudgington 65 F1
Crudwell 40 B3
Crug 64 A5
Crugmeer 4 D2
Crugybar 50 C4
Crulabhig 186 C4
Crumlin 38 B3

Crundale *Kent* 32 C4
Crundale *Pembs.* 34 C1
Crutherland 142 A4
Cruwys Morchard 10 B1
Crux Easton 27 F2
Crwbin 36 A1
Cryers Hill 43 D3
Crymlyn 89 E5
Crymych 49 E4
Crynant 37 D2
Crystal Palace 44 C5
Cuaig 176 D4
Cubbington 55 F1
Cubert 4 B4
Cublington 56 D5
Cuckfield 17 F1
Cucklington 25 E5
Cuckney 94 C5
Cuckoo's Nest 78 A1
Cuddesdon 42 A2
Cuddington *Bucks.* 42 C1
Cuddington *Ches.* 92 A5
Cuddington Heath 78 B3
Cuddy Hill 100 A4
Cudham 30 D3
Cudlipptown 7 F3
Cudworth *S.Yorks.* 94 A2
Cudworth *Som.* 11 G1
Cuffley 44 C2
Cuidhaseadair 187 G2
Cuidhir 172 B3
Cuidhtinis 184 C5
Cuidrach 175 G4
Cuil-uaine 148 B1
Cuilmuich 149 D5
Culag 149 F5
Culbo 179 F3
Culbokie 179 F4
Culbone 22 B3
Culburnie 179 D5
Culcabock 179 F5
Culcharan 148 B1
Culcharry 180 A4
Culcheth 92 A3
Culdrain 170 A1
Culduie 176 D5
Culford 59 G1
Culgaith 118 C5
Culgower 191 E3
Culham 42 A3
Culindrach 140 A4
Culkein 188 C1
Culkerton 40 B3
Cullachie 168 B2
Cullen 182 A3
Cullercoats 129 F4
Cullicudden 179 F3
Culligran 178 C5
Cullingworth 101 G4
Cullipool 147 G3
Cullivoe 203 E2
Culloch 150 C3
Culloden 179 G5
Cullompton 10 D2
Culmaily 190 D5
Culmalzie 123 E5
Culmington 65 D4
Culmstock 11 D1
Culnacraig 188 C4
Culnadalloch 148 B1
Culnaknock 176 B3
Culnamean 164 A2
Culpho 60 D3
Culquhirk 123 F5
Culrain 190 A5
Culross 143 D1
Culroy 132 B4
Culsh 169 F5
Culshabbin 123 E5
Culswick 200 B3
Culter Allers Farm 134 B2
Cultercullen 171 E2
Cults *Aber.* 170 A1
Cults *Aberdeen* 171 D4
Cults *D. & G.* 115 E2
Cultybraggan Camp 150 C3
Culverhouse Cross 38 A5
Culverstone Green 31 F2
Culverthorpe 83 F3
Culvie 182 A4
Culworth 56 A3
Cumberhead 133 F2
Cumbernauld 142 B2
Cumberworth 97 F5
Cuminestown 182 D4
Cumloden 123 F4
Cummersdale 117 G1
Cummertrees 125 F4
Cummingstown 180 D3
Cumnock 133 D3
Cumnor 41 G2
Cumrew 118 B2
Cumrue 125 E2
Cumstoun 124 A5
Cumwhinton 118 A2
Cumwhitton 118 B2
Cundall 110 D5
Cunninghamhead 141 E5
Cunnister 203 E3
Cunnoquhie 152 B3
Cupar 152 B3
Cupar Muir 152 B3
Curbar 93 G5
Curbridge *Hants.* 15 E1
Curbridge *Oxon.* 41 F2
Curdridge 15 E1
Curdworth 67 D3
Curland 11 F1
Curload 24 A5
Curridge 41 G5
Currie 143 F3
Curry Mallet 24 A5
Curry Rivel 24 A5
Curteis' Corner 32 A5
Curtisden Green 31 G4
Cury 3 D4
Cushnie 182 C3
Cushuish 23 E4
Cusop 52 B3
Cutcloy 115 E3
Cutcombe 22 C4
Cuthill 179 G1
Cutiau 62 C1
Cutnall Green 54 A1
Cutsdean 54 C4
Cutthorpe 94 A5
Cutts 200 D4
Cuttyhill 183 F4
Cuxham 42 B3
Cuxton 31 G2
Cuxwold 96 B2
Cwm *B.Gwent* 38 A2
Cwm *Denb.* 90 B5
Cwm-Cewydd 63 E1
Cwm Ffrwd-oer 38 B2
Cwm Gwaun 48 D4
Cwm Irfon 51 E3
Cwm-Llinau 63 E2
Cwm-Morgan 49 F4
Cwm-parc 37 F3
Cwm-twrch Isaf 37 D1
Cwm-y-glo 75 E1
Cwm-yr-Eglwys 48 D3
Cwmafan 37 D3
Cwmaman 37 G3
Cwmann 50 B3
Cwmbach *Carmar.* 49 F5
Cwmbach *Powys* 52 A4
Cwmbach *Powys* 51 G2
Cwmbach *R.C.T.* 37 G2
Cwmbelan 63 F4
Cwmbran 38 B3
Cwmbrwyno 62 D4
Cwmcarn 38 B3
Cwmcarvan 39 D2
Cwmcoy 49 F3
Cwmdare 37 F2
Cwmdu *Carmar.* 50 C4
Cwmdu *Powys* 52 A5
Cwmduad 49 G4
Cwmfelin Boeth 35 E1
Cwmfelin Mynach 49 F5
Cwmfelinfach 38 A3
Cwmffrwd 36 A1
Cwmgiedd 37 D1
Cwmgors 36 D1
Cwmgwrach 37 E2
Cwmisfael 36 A1
Cwmllyfri 35 G1
Cwmllynfell 36 D1
Cwmpengraig 49 G4
Cwmsychbant 50 A3
Cwmsymlog 62 C4
Cwmtillery 38 B2
Cwmyoy 52 C5
Cwmystwyth 63 D5
Cwrt 62 C2
Cwrt-newydd 50 A3
Cwrt-y-gollen 38 B1
Cydwelli (Kidwelly) 36 A2
Cyffylliog 77 D2
Cyfronydd 64 A2
Cymmer *N.P.T.* 37 E3
Cymmer *R.C.T.* 37 G3
Cynghordy 51 E4
Cynheidre 36 A2
Cynwyd 77 D3
Cynwyl Elfed 49 G5

D

Dabton 124 C1
Daccombe 9 F1
Dacre *Cumb.* 118 A5
Dacre *N.Yorks.* 102 A1
Dacre Banks 102 A1
Daddry Shield 119 E4
Dadford 56 B4
Dadlington 67 G3
Dafen 36 B2
Daffy Green 86 A5
Dagenham 45 D4
Daggons 14 A1
Daglingworth 40 B2
Dagnall 43 E1
Dail 148 C1
Dail Beag 186 D3
Dail Bho Dheas 187 F1
Dail Bho Thuath 187 F1
Dail Mòr 186 D3
Dailly 132 A5
Dailnamac 148 B1
Dairsie or Osnaburgh 152 C3
Dalabrog 172 C1
Dalavich 148 B3
Dalballoch 167 F5
Dalbeattie 124 C4
Dalblair 133 E4
Dalbog 161 D2
Dalbreck 190 C3
Dalbury 81 D4
Dalby 98 A4
Dalcairnie 132 C5
Dalchalloch 158 C3
Dalchalm 191 E4
Dalchenna 148 C4
Dalchirach 169 D1
Dalchork 190 A3
Dalchreichart 166 B3
Dalchruin 150 C3
Dalcross 179 G5
Dalderby 84 A1
Daldownie 169 E4
Dale *Derbys.* 81 F4
Dale *Pembs.* 34 B2
Dale Head 107 F1
Dale of Walls 200 A2
Dale Park 16 B3
Dalehouse 111 G1
Dalelia 155 G3
Daless 168 A1
Dalestie 169 D3
Dalfad 169 F4
Dalganachan 194 C4
Dalgarven 141 D5
Dalgety Bay 143 F1
Dalgig 133 D4
Dalginross 150 C2
Dalgonar 133 F5
Dalguise 159 E5
Dalhalvaig 194 A3
Dalham 59 F1
Daligan 141 E1
Dalivaddy 130 B4
Daljarrock 122 C2
Dalkeith 144 A3
Dallas 180 D4
Dallaschyle 180 A5
Dallash 123 F4
Dallinghoo 61 D2
Dallington *E.Suss.* 18 B2
Dallington *Northants.* 56 C1
Dalmadilly 170 C3
Dalmally 149 D2
Dalmarnock 159 E5
Dalmary 150 A5
Dalmellington 132 C5
Dalmeny 143 F2
Dalmichy 190 A3
Dalmigavie 167 G3
Dalmore 179 F3
Dalmunzie Hotel 159 F2
Dalnabreck 155 G3
Dalnacarn 159 F3
Dalnaglar Castle 159 G3
Dalnaha 147 F2
Dalnahaitnach 168 A3
Dalnamain 190 C5
Dalnatrat 156 B4
Dalnavie 179 F2
Dalness 157 D4
Dalnessie 190 B3
Dalnigap 122 C3
Dalqueich 151 F4
Dalreoch 122 C2
Dalriech 150 C1
Dalroy 179 G5
Dalrulzian 159 G4
Dalry 141 D5
Dalrymple 132 B4
Dalserf 142 B4
Dalshangan 123 G2
Dalskairth 124 D3
Dalston 117 G1
Dalswinton 124 D2
Daltomach 167 G2
Dalton *D. & G.* 125 F3
Dalton *Lancs.* 91 F2
Dalton *N.Yorks.* 110 D5
Dalton *N.Yorks.* 110 A2
Dalton *Northumb.* 128 D4
Dalton *Northumb.* 119 F2
Dalton *S.Yorks.* 94 B3
Dalton-in-Furness 106 D5
Dalton-le-Dale 120 D3
Dalton-on-Tees 110 B2
Dalton Piercy 121 D4
Daltote 139 F1
Daltra 180 B5
Dalveich 150 B2
Dalvennan 132 B4
Dalvourn 167 F1
Dalwhinnie 158 B1
Dalwood 11 F2
Damerham 14 A1
Damgate 87 F5
Damnaglaur 114 B3
Damside 151 E3
Danbury 45 G2
Danby 111 G2
Danby Wiske 110 C3
Dandaleith 181 E5
Danderhall 144 A3
Dane End 58 B5
Dane Hills 68 A2
Danebridge 79 G1
Danehill 17 G1
Danesmoor 81 F1
Danestone 171 E3
Danskine 144 C3
Darby Green 28 D1
Darenth 45 E5
Daresbury 91 G4
Darfield 94 B2
Dargate 32 C2
Dargues 128 A2
Darite 5 G3
Darlaston 66 B3
Darley 102 B2
Darley Dale 81 D1
Darlingscott 55 E3
Darlington 110 B1
Darliston 78 C4
Darlton 95 E5
Darnabo 182 C5
Darnall 94 A4
Darnconner 133 D3
Darnford 170 C5
Darngarroch 124 A4
Darnick 135 G2
Darowen 63 E2
Darra 182 C5
Darras Hall 129 D4
Darrington 94 B1
Darsham 61 F1
Dartfield 183 F4
Dartford 45 E5
Dartington 9 D1
Dartmeet 7 G3
Dartmouth 9 E2
Darton 94 A2
Darvel 133 D2
Darvell 18 C1
Darwen 100 C5
Datchet 43 E5
Datchworth 44 B1
Datchworth Green 44 B1
Daubhill 92 B2
Daugh of Kinermony 181 E5
Dauntsey 40 B4
Dava 168 C1
Davaar 130 C4
Davan 169 G4
Davenham 92 A5
Daventry 56 A1
Davidstow 5 F1
Davington 134 D5
Daviot *Aber.* 170 C2
Daviot *High.* 167 G1
Davoch of Grange 181 G4
Dawley 65 F2
Dawlish 10 C5
Dawn 89 G5
Daws Heath 46 B4
Dawsmere 84 C4
Daylesford 55 E5
Ddôl 90 C5
Deadwaters 142 B5
Deal 33 F3
Deal Hall 46 D3
Dean *Cumb.* 117 D4
Dean *Devon* 8 D1
Dean *Dorset* 13 F1
Dean *Hants.* 15 E1
Dean *Oxon.* 55 F5
Dean *Som.* 25 D3
Dean Bank 120 B4
Dean Prior 8 D1
Dean Row 92 C4
Dean Street 31 G3
Deanburnhaugh 135 E4
Deane 27 G3
Deanland 13 F1
Deanscales 117 D4
Deanshanger 56 C3
Deanston 150 C4
Dearham 117 D3
Debach 60 D2
Debate 126 A3
Debden 59 D4
Debden Green 59 D4
Debenham 60 C1
Dechmont 143 E2
Deddington 55 G4
Dedham 60 B4
Deecastle 169 G5
Deene 69 E3
Deenethorpe 69 E3
Deepcar 93 G3
Deepcut 29 E2
Deepdale *Cumb.* 108 C4
Deepdale *N.Yorks.* 109 D5
Deeping Gate 69 G2
Deeping St. James 69 G2
Deeping St. Nicholas 70 A1
Deerhill 181 G4
Deerhurst 54 A5
Defford 54 B3
Defynnog 51 F5
Deganwy 89 F5
Degnish 147 G3
Deighton *N.Yorks.* 110 C2
Deighton *York* 103 F3
Deiniolen 75 E1
Delabole 5 E1
Delamere 78 C1
Delavorar 169 D3
Delfrigs 171 E2
Dell Lodge 168 C3
Delliefure 168 C1
Delnabo 169 D3
Delny 179 G2
Delph 93 D2
Delphorrie 169 G3
Delves 120 A3
Delvine 159 G5
Dembleby 83 F4
Denaby 94 B3
Denaby Main 94 B3
Denbigh (Dinbych) 76 D1
Denbury 9 E1
Denby 81 E3
Denby Dale 93 G2
Denchworth 41 F3
Dendron 107 D5
Denend 170 A1
Denford 69 E5
Dengie 46 C2
Denham *Bucks.* 43 F4
Denham *Suff.* 72 C4
Denham *Suff.* 59 F1
Denham Green 43 F4
Denhead *Aber.* 170 C3
Denhead *Aber.* 183 E4
Denhead *Dundee* 152 B1
Denhead *Fife* 152 C3
Denhead of Arbirlot 161 D5
Denholm 135 G4
Denholme 101 G4
Denholme Clough 101 G4
Denio 74 C4
Denmead 15 F1
Denmill 170 D3
Denmoss 182 B5
Dennington 61 D1
Denny 142 C1
Dennyloanhead 142 C1
Denshaw 93 D1
Denside 170 D5
Densole 33 E4
Denston 59 F2
Denstone 80 B3
Dent 108 C4
Denton *Cambs.* 69 G4
Denton *Darl.* 110 B1
Denton *E.Suss.* 17 G3
Denton *Gt.Man.* 92 D3
Denton *Kent* 33 E4
Denton *Lincs.* 83 D4
Denton *N.Yorks.* 102 A3
Denton *Norf.* 73 D3
Denton *Northants.* 56 D2
Denton *Oxon.* 42 A2
Denver 71 E2
Denvilles 15 G2
Denwick 137 G5
Deopham 86 B5
Deopham Green 72 B2
Depden 59 F2
Deptford *Gt.Lon.* 44 C5
Deptford *Wilts.* 26 B4
Derby 81 E4
Derbyhaven 98 A5
Dererach 147 E2
Deri 38 A2
Derringstone 33 D4
Derrington 79 F5
Derry 150 B2
Derry Hill 40 B5
Derrythorpe 95 F2
Dersingham 85 E4
Dervaig 154 D4
Derwen 77 D2
Derwenlas 62 D3
Derwydd 36 C1
Derybruich 140 A2
Desborough 68 D4
Desford 67 G2
Detchant 137 E3
Detling 31 G3
Deuddwr 64 B1
Deunant 76 C1
Deuxhill 65 F4
Devauden 39 D3
Devil's Bridge (Pontarfynach) 62 D5
Devizes 26 B1
Devonport 8 A2
Devonside 151 E5
Devoran 3 E3
Dewar 144 A5
Dewlish 13 D3
Dewsall Court 53 D4
Dewsbury 102 B5
Dhiseig 147 D1
Dhoon 98 C3
Dhoor 98 C2
Dhowin 98 C1
Dhuhallow 167 E2
Dial Post 17 D2
Dibden 14 D2
Dibden Purlieu 14 D2
Dickleburgh 72 C3
Didbrook 54 C4
Didcot 42 A4
Diddington 57 G1
Diddlebury 65 E4
Didley 52 D4
Didling 16 A2
Didmarton 40 A4
Didsbury 92 C3
Didworthy 8 C1
Digby 83 F2
Digg 176 A3
Diggle 93 E2
Digmoor 91 F2
Digswell 44 B1
Dihewyd 50 A2
Dildawn 124 B5
Dilham 87 E3
Dilhorne 79 G3
Dilston 119 F1
Dilton Marsh 25 F2
Dilwyn 52 D2
Dilwyn Common 52 D2
Dinas *Carmar.* 49 F4
Dinas *Gwyn.* 75 D2
Dinas *Gwyn.* 74 B4
Dinas Cross *Pembs.* 48 D4
Dinas Dinlle 74 D2
Dinas-Mawddwy 63 E1
Dinas Powys 38 A5
Dinbych (Denbigh) 76 D1
Dinbych-y-Pysgod (Tenby) 35 E2
Dinder 24 C3
Dinedor 53 E4
Dingestow 39 D1
Dingley 68 C4
Dingwall 179 E4
Dinlabyre 126 D2
Dinnet 169 G5
Dinnington *S.Yorks.* 94 C4
Dinnington *Som.* 12 A1
Dinnington *T. & W.* 129 E4
Dinorwig 75 E1
Dinton *Bucks.* 42 C1
Dinton *Wilts.* 26 B4
Dinvin 122 B5
Dinwoodie Mains 125 F1
Dinworthy 20 D4
Dippen 130 C2
Dippenhall 28 D3
Dippin 131 F3
Dipple *Moray* 181 F4
Dipple *S.Ayr.* 132 A5
Diptford 8 D2
Dipton 120 A2
Dirdhu 168 C2
Dirleton 144 C1
Discoed 52 B1
Diseworth 81 F5
Dishes 199 E4
Dishforth 110 C5
Disley 93 D4
Diss 72 C3
Disserth 51 G2
Distington 116 D4
Ditcheat 24 D4
Ditchingham 73 E2
Ditchley 55 F5
Ditchling 17 F2
Ditteridge 25 F1
Dittisham 9 E2
Ditton *Halton* 91 F4
Ditton *Kent* 31 G3
Ditton Green 59 E2
Ditton Priors 65 F4
Dixton *Glos.* 54 B4
Dixton *Mon.* 39 E1
Dobcross 93 D2
Dobwalls 5 G3
Doc Penfro (Pembroke Dock) 34 C2
Doccombe 10 A4
Dochgarroch 179 F5
Dockenfield 28 D3
Docking 85 F4
Docklow 53 E2
Dockray 117 G4
Doddinghurst 45 E3
Doddington *Cambs.* 70 B3
Doddington *Kent* 32 B3
Doddington *Lincs.* 95 G5
Doddington *Northumb.* 137 D3
Doddington *Shrop.* 65 F5
Doddiscombsleigh 10 B4
Dodford *Northants.* 56 B1
Dodford *Worcs.* 66 B5
Dodington *S.Glos.* 39 G4
Dodington *Som.* 23 E3
Dodington Ash 39 G5
Dodleston 78 A1
Dodworth 94 A2
Doe Lea 81 F1
Dog Village 10 C3
Dogdyke 84 A2
Dogmersfield 28 C2
Dol Fawr 63 E2
Dol-gran 50 A4
Dolanog 63 G1
Dolau 52 A1
Dolbenmaen 75 E3
Dolfach 63 F5
Dolfor 64 A4
Dolgarreg 50 D4
Dolgarrog 76 A1
Dolgellau 62 D1
Dolgoch 62 C2
Doll 191 D4
Dollar 151 E5
Dollarbeg 151 E5
Dolleycanney 52 A3
Dolphinholme 100 B2
Dolphinton 143 F5
Dolton 21 F4
Dolwen *Conwy* 89 G5
Dolwen *Powys* 63 F2
Dolwyddelan 76 A2
Dolybont 62 C4
Dolyhir 52 B2
Dolywern 77 F4
Domgay 64 B1
Doncaster 94 C2
Donhead St. Andrew 26 A5
Donhead St. Mary 26 A5
Donibristle 143 F1
Doniford 23 D3
Donington 84 A4
Donington le Heath 67 G1
Donington on Bain 96 C4
Donisthorpe 67 F1
Donkey Town 29 E1
Donnington *Glos.* 55 D5
Donnington *Here.* 53 G4
Donnington *Shrop.* 65 E2
Donnington *Tel. & W.* 65 G1
Donnington *W.Berks.* 27 F1
Donnington *W.Suss.* 16 A3
Donyatt 11 G1
Dorchester *Dorset* 12 C3
Dorchester *Oxon.* 42 A3
Dordon 67 E2
Dore 94 A4
Dores 167 E1
Dorket Head 81 G3
Dorking 29 G3
Dormans Park 30 C4
Dormansland 30 D4
Dormanstown 121 E5
Dormington 53 E3
Dorney 43 E5
Dornie 165 E2
Dornoch 179 G1
Dornock 126 A5
Dorrery 194 C3
Dorridge 67 D5
Dorrington *Lincs.* 83 F2
Dorrington *Shrop.* 65 D2
Dorsell 170 A3
Dorsington 54 D2
Dorstone 52 C3
Dorton 42 B1
Dorusduain 165 F2
Dosthill 67 E2
Dotland 119 F2
Dottery 12 A3
Doublebois 5 F3
Dougalston 141 G2
Dougarie 131 D2
Doughton 40 A3
Douglas *I.o.M.* 98 B4
Douglas *S.Lan.* 133 G2
Douglas and Angus 152 C1
Douglas Hall 124 C5
Douglas Water 133 G2
Douglastown 160 C5
Doulting 24 D3
Dounby 198 A4
Doune *Arg. & B.* 149 F5
Doune *Arg. & B.* 149 F3
Doune *High.* 168 A3
Doune *High.* 189 G4
Doune *Stir.* 150 C4
Dounepark 182 C3
Douneside 169 G4
Dounie *High.* 179 F1
Dounie *High.* 190 A5
Dounreay 194 B2
Dousland 8 B1
Dovaston 78 A5
Dove Holes 93 E5
Dovenby 117 D3
Dover 33 F4
Dovercourt 60 D5
Doverdale 54 A1
Doveridge 80 C4
Doversgreen 30 B4
Dowally 159 F5
Dowdeswell 54 C5
Dowhill 132 A5
Dowland 21 F4
Dowlands 11 F3
Dowlish Wake 11 G1
Down Ampney 40 D3
Down End 24 A3
Down Hatherley 54 A5
Down St. Mary 10 A2
Down Thomas 8 B3
Downderry 6 D5
Downe 30 D2
Downend *I.o.W.* 15 E4
Downend *S.Glos.* 39 F5
Downend *W.Berks.* 41 G5
Downfield 152 B1
Downfields 71 D5
Downgate 7 D3
Downham *Essex* 45 G3
Downham *Lancs.* 101 D3
Downham *Northumb.* 136 C3
Downham Market 71 E2
Downhead *Cornw.* 5 G1
Downhead *Som.* 25 D3
Downholland Cross 91 E2
Downholme 110 A3
Downies 171 E5
Downing 90 C5
Downley 43 D3
Downside *N.Som.* 24 B1
Downside *Som.* 24 D3
Downside *Surr.* 29 G2
Downton *Devon* 7 F2
Downton *Devon* 9 E2
Downton *Hants.* 14 B3
Downton *Wilts.* 26 C5
Downton on the Rock 64 D5
Dowsby 83 G4
Dowthwaitehead 117 G4
Doynton 39 G5
Draethen 38 B4
Draffan 142 B5
Drakeland Corner 8 B2
Drakes Broughton 54 B3
Drakes Cross 66 C5
Draughton *N.Yorks.* 101 G2
Draughton *Northants.* 68 C5
Drax 103 F5
Draycote 67 G5
Draycott *Derbys.* 81 F4
Draycott *Glos.* 55 D4
Draycott *Som.* 24 B2
Draycott *Worcs.* 54 A3
Draycott in the Clay 80 C5
Draycott in the Moors 79 G4
Drayton *Leics.* 68 D3
Drayton *Lincs.* 84 A4
Drayton *Norf.* 86 C4
Drayton *Oxon.* 55 G3
Drayton *Oxon.* 41 G3
Drayton *Ports.* 15 F2
Drayton *Som.* 24 B5
Drayton *Worcs.* 66 B5
Drayton Bassett 67 D2
Drayton Beauchamp 43 E1
Drayton Parslow 56 D5
Drayton St. Leonard 42 A3
Dre-fach 50 B3
Drebley 101 G2
Dreemskerry 98 C2
Dreenhill 34 C1
Drefach *Carmar.* 49 G4
Drefach *Carmar.* 36 B1
Dreghorn 132 B2
Drellingore 33 E4
Drem 144 C2
Drewsteignton 10 A3
Driby 97 D5
Driffield *E.Riding* 104 C2
Driffield *Glos.* 40 C3
Drigg 106 B3
Drighlington 102 B5
Drimfern 148 C3
Drimlee 148 D3
Drimnin 155 E4
Drimore 162 A1
Drimpton 12 A2
Drimsynie 149 D4
Drimvore 148 A5
Drinan 164 B3
Drinkstone 60 A1
Drinkstone Green 60 A2
Drishaig 149 D3
Drissaig 148 B3
Drointon 80 B5
Droitwich 54 A1
Dron 151 G3
Dronfield 94 A5
Dronfield Woodhouse 94 A5
Drongan 132 C4
Dronley 152 B1
Dropmore 43 E4
Droxford 15 F1
Droylsden 92 D3
Druid 76 D3
Druidston 34 B1
Druimarbin 156 C3
Druimavuic 156 C5
Druimdrishaig 139 F2
Druimindarroch 155 F1
Druimkinnerras 179 D5
Drum *Arg. & B.* 140 A2
Drum *P. & K.* 151 F4
Drumachloy 140 B3
Drumbeg 192 A5
Drumblade 182 A5
Drumblair 182 B5
Drumbuie *D. & G.* 133 F4
Drumbuie *High.* 165 D1
Drumburgh 117 F1
Drumchapel 141 G2
Drumchardine 179 E5
Drumchork 177 E1
Drumclog 133 E2
Drumdelgie 181 G5
Drumderfit 179 F4
Drumeldrie 152 C4
Drumelzier 134 C2
Drumfearn 164 C3
Drumfern 156 B2
Drumgarve 130 C3
Drumgley 160 C5
Drumguish 167 G5
Drumhead 170 B5
Drumin 169 D1
Drumine 179 G4
Drumjohn 123 G1
Drumlamford House 123 D3
Drumlasie 170 B4
Drumlemble 130 B4
Drumlithie 161 F1
Drummond *High.* 179 F3
Drummond *Stir.* 150 B4
Drummore 114 B3
Drummuir Castle 181 F5
Drumnadrochit 167 E1
Drumnagorrach 182 A4
Drumnatorran 156 A3
Drumoak 170 C5
Drumore 130 C3
Drumour 159 E5
Drumrash 124 A3
Drumrunie 189 D4
Drums 171 E2
Drumsturdy 152 C1
Drumuie 176 A5
Drumuillie 168 B2

Drumvaich 150 B4
Drumwhindle 171 E1
Drumwhirn 124 B2
Drunkendub 161 E5
Drury 77 F1
Drws-y-nant 76 B5
Dry Doddington 83 D3
Dry Drayton 58 B1
Dry Harbour 176 C4
Dry Sandford 41 G3
Dry Street 45 F4
Drybeck 108 B1
Drybridge *Moray* 181 G3
Drybridge *N.Ayr.* 132 B2
Drybrook 39 F1
Drygrange 135 G2
Dryhope 135 D3
Drymen 141 F1
Drymuir 183 E5
Drynoch 164 A1
Dryslwyn 50 B5
Dryton 65 E2
Duachy 148 A2
Dubford 182 C3
Dubhchladach 139 G3
Dubheads 151 E2
Dubton 161 D4
Duchal 141 E3
Duchally 189 F3
Duchray 149 G5
Duck End 59 E5
Duckington 78 B2
Ducklington 41 F2
Duck's Cross 57 G2
Duddenhoe End 58 C4
Duddingston 143 G2
Duddington 69 E2
Duddleswell 17 G1
Duddo 145 G5
Duddon 78 C1
Duddon Bridge 106 C4
Dudleston Heath 78 A4
Dudley *T. & W.* 129 E4
Dudley *W.Mid.* 66 B3
Dudley Hill 102 A4
Dudley Port 66 B3
Dudsbury 13 G3
Duffield 81 E3
Duffryn 37 E3
Dufftown 181 F5
Duffus 181 D3
Dufton 118 C5
Duggleby 104 A1
Duiar 168 D1
Duible 191 E2
Duiletter 149 D2
Duinish 158 B3
Duirinish 165 D1
Duisdealmor 164 D3
Duisky 156 C2
Dukestown 38 A1
Dukinfield 92 D3
Dulas 88 C4
Dulax 169 F3
Dulcote 24 C3
Dulford 11 D2
Dull 158 D5
Dullatur 142 B2
Dullingham 59 E2
Dulnain Bridge 168 B2
Duloe *Beds.* 57 G1
Duloe *Cornw.* 5 G4
Dulsie 180 B5
Dulverton 22 C5
Dulwich 44 C5
Dumbarton 141 F2
Dumbleton 54 C4
Dumcrieff 134 C5
Dumeath 169 G1
Dumfin 141 E1
Dumfries 125 D3
Dumgoyne 141 G1
Dummer 27 G3
Dun 161 E4
Dunach 148 A2
Dunalastair 158 C4
Dunan *Arg. & B.* 140 C2
Dunan *High.* 164 B2
Dunans 148 C5
Dunball 24 A3
Dunbar 145 D2
Dunbeath 191 G2
Dunbeg 148 A1
Dunblane 150 C4
Dunbog 152 A3
Duncanston *Aber.* 170 A2
Duncanston *High.* 179 E4
Dunchideock 10 B4
Dunchurch 67 G5
Duncote 56 B2
Duncow 125 D2
Duncraggan 150 A4
Duncrievie 151 G4
Duncroist 150 A1
Duncrub 151 F3
Duncryne 141 F1
Duncton 16 B2
Dundee 152 C1
Dundee Airport 152 B2
Dundon 24 B4
Dundonald 132 B2
Dundonnell 177 G1
Dundraw 117 F2
Dundreggan 166 C3
Dundrennan 116 A2
Dundry 24 C1
Dunearn 143 G1
Dunecht 170 C4
Dunfermline 143 E1
Dunfield 40 D3
Dunford Bridge 93 F2
Dungavel 133 E2
Dunham 95 F5
Dunham-on-the-Hill 91 F5
Dunham Town 92 B4
Dunhampton 54 A1
Dunholme 96 A5
Dunino 152 D3
Dunipace 142 C1
Dunira 150 C2
Dunkeld 159 F5
Dunkerton 25 E2
Dunkeswell 11 E2
Dunkeswick 102 C3
Dunkirk 32 C3
Dunk's Green 31 F3
Dunlappie 161 D3
Dunley 53 G1
Dunlop 141 F5
Dunloskin 140 C2
Dunmere 5 E3
Dunmore *Arg. & B.* 139 F3
Dunmore *Falk.* 142 C1
Dunn 195 D3
Dunnabie 126 A3
Dunnet 195 E1
Dunnichen 160 D5
Dunning 151 F3
Dunnington *E.Riding* 105 D2
Dunnington *Warks.* 54 C2
Dunnington *York* 103 F2
Dunnockshaw 101 E5
Dunoon 140 C2
Dunragit 122 C5
Dunrostan 139 F1
Duns 145 E4
Duns Tew 55 G5
Dunsby 83 G5
Dunscore 124 C2
Dunscroft 95 D2
Dunsdale 111 F1
Dunsden Green 42 C5
Dunsfold 29 F4
Dunsford 10 B4
Dunshelt 152 A3
Dunsinnan 151 G1
Dunsland Cross 21 E5
Dunsley 112 B1
Dunsmore 43 D2
Dunsop Bridge 100 C2
Dunstable 57 F5
Dunstall 80 C5
Dunstall Green 59 F1
Dunstan 137 G4
Dunster 22 C3
Dunston *Lincs.* 83 F1
Dunston *Norf.* 86 D5
Dunston *Staffs.* 66 B1
Dunston *T. & W.* 120 B1
Dunstone *Devon* 9 D3
Dunstone *Devon* 10 A5
Dunstone *Devon* 8 B2
Dunsville 95 D2
Dunswell 104 C4
Dunsyre 143 E5
Dunterton 7 D3
Duntisbourne Abbots 40 B2
Duntisbourne Leer 40 B2
Duntisbourne Rouse 40 B2
Duntish 12 C2
Duntocher 141 F2
Dunton *Beds.* 58 A3
Dunton *Bucks.* 56 D5
Dunton *Norf.* 85 G4
Dunton Bassett 68 A3
Dunton Green 31 E3
Dunton Wayletts 45 F4
Duntulm 176 A2
Dunure 132 A4
Dunure Mains 132 A4
Dunvant 36 B3
Dunvegan 175 F5
Dunwich 73 F4
Dura 152 C3
Durdar 118 A2
Durgates 31 F5
Durham 120 B3
Durinemast 155 F4
Durisdeer 133 G5
Durleigh 23 F4
Durley *Hants.* 15 E1
Durley *Wilts.* 26 D1
Durnamuck 188 C5
Durness 192 C2
Durno 170 C2
Duror 156 B4
Durran *Arg. & B.* 148 B4
Durran *High.* 195 D2
Durrington *W.Suss.* 16 D3
Durrington *Wilts.* 26 C3
Dursley 39 G3
Durston 23 F5
Durweston 13 E2
Dury 201 D1
Duston 56 C1
Duthil 168 B2
Dutlas 64 B5
Duton Hill 59 E5
Dutton 91 G5
Duxford 58 C3
Dwygyfylchi 89 F5
Dwyran 74 D1
Dyce 171 D3
Dyfatty 36 A2
Dyffryn *Bridgend* 37 E3
Dyffryn (Valley) *I.o.A.* 88 A5
Dyffryn *Pembs.* 48 C4
Dyffryn Ardudwy 75 E5
Dyffryn Castell 63 D4
Dyffryn Ceidrych 50 D5
Dyffryn Cellwen 37 E1
Dyke *Devon* 20 D3
Dyke *Lincs.* 83 G5
Dyke *Moray* 180 B4
Dykehead *Angus* 160 B3
Dykehead *N.Lan.* 142 C4
Dykehead *Stir.* 150 A5
Dykelands 161 F3
Dykends 160 A4
Dykeside 182 C5
Dylife 63 E3
Dymchurch 19 F1
Dymock 53 G4
Dyrham 39 G5
Dysart 152 B5
Dyserth 90 B5

E

Eadar dha Fhadhail 186 B4
Eagland Hill 100 A3
Eagle 83 D1
Eaglescliffe 110 D1
Eaglesfield *Cumb.* 117 D4
Eaglesfield *D. & G.* 126 A4
Eaglesham 141 G4
Eaglethorpe 69 F3
Eagley 92 B1
Eairy 98 B4
Eakley 56 D2
Eakring 82 B1
Ealand 95 E1
Ealing 44 A4
Eamont Bridge 118 B5
Earby 101 F3
Earcroft 100 C5
Eardington 65 G3
Eardisland 52 D2
Eardisley 52 C3
Eardiston *Shrop.* 78 A5
Eardiston *Worcs.* 53 F1
Earith 70 B5
Earl Shilton 67 G3
Earl Soham 60 D1
Earl Sterndale 80 B1
Earl Stonham 60 C2
Earle 137 D4
Earlestown 91 G3
Earley 42 C5
Earlham 86 C5
Earlish 175 G3
Earls Barton 57 D1
Earls Colne 59 G5
Earl's Common 54 B2
Earl's Croome 54 A3
Earl's Green 60 B1
Earlsdon 67 F5
Earlsferry 152 C4
Earlsford 170 D1
Earlston 135 G2
Earlswood *Mon.* 39 D3
Earlswood *Warks.* 66 D5
Earnley 16 A4
Earsairidh 172 C4
Earsdon 129 F4
Earsdon Moor 129 D2
Earsham 73 E3
Earswick 103 F2
Eartham 16 B3
Earthcott Green 39 F4
Easby 111 E2
Easdale 147 G3
Easebourne 29 D5
Easenhall 67 G5
Eashing 29 E3
Easington *Bucks.* 42 B2
Easington *Dur.* 120 D3
Easington *E.Riding* 97 E1
Easington *Northumb.* 137 F3
Easington *Oxon.* 42 B3
Easington *R. & C.* 111 G1
Easington Colliery 120 D3
Easington Lane 120 C3
Easingwold 103 E1
Easole Street 33 E3
Eassie and Nevay 160 B5
East Aberthaw 22 D1
East Allington 9 D3
East Anstey 22 B5
East Appleton 110 B3
East Ardsley 102 C5
East Ashey 15 E4
East Ashling 16 A3
East Auchronie 170 D4
East Ayton 112 C4
East Barkwith 96 B4
East Barming 31 G3
East Barnby 112 B1
East Barnet 44 B3
East Barsham 86 A2
East Beckham 86 C2
East Bedfont 43 F5
East Bergholt 60 B4
East Bilney 86 A4
East Blatchington 17 G4
East Boldon 120 C1
East Boldre 14 C2
East Bolton 137 F5
East Bradenham 86 A5
East Brent 24 A2
East Bridge 61 F1
East Bridgford 82 B3
East Brora 191 D4
East Buckland 21 G2
East Budleigh 11 D4
East Burrafirth 200 C2
East Burton 13 E4
East Cairnbeg 161 F2
East Calder 143 E3
East Carleton 86 C5
East Carlton 68 D4
East Chaldon or Chaldon Herring 13 D4
East Challow 41 F4
East Charleton 9 D3
East Chelborough 12 B2
East Chiltington 17 F2
East Chinnock 12 A1
East Chisenbury 26 C2
East Clandon 29 F2
East Claydon 56 C5
East Clyth 195 E5
East Coker 12 B1
East Combe 23 E4
East Cornworthy 9 E2
East Cottingwith 103 G3
East Cowes 15 E3
East Cowick 103 F5
East Cowton 110 C2
East Cranmore 25 D3
East Creech 13 F4
East Croachy 167 F2
East Darlochan 130 B3
East Davoch 169 G4
East Dean *E.Suss.* 18 A4
East Dean *Hants.* 27 D5
East Dean *W.Suss.* 16 B2
East Dereham 86 A4
East Down 21 G1
East Drayton 95 E5
East End *Hants.* 27 F1
East End *Hants.* 14 C3
East End *Herts.* 58 C5
East End *Kent* 32 A5
East End *N.Som.* 39 D5
East End *Oxon.* 41 F1
East End *Poole* 13 F3
East End *Suff.* 60 C4
East Farleigh 31 G3
East Farndon 68 C4
East Ferry 95 F3
East Fortune 144 C2
East Garston 41 F5
East Ginge 41 G4
East Goscote 68 B1
East Grafton 27 D1
East Grimstead 26 D5
East Grinstead 30 C5
East Guldeford 19 E1
East Haddon 56 B1
East Hagbourne 42 A4
East Halton 96 B1
East Ham 44 D4
East Hanney 41 G3
East Hanningfield 45 G2
East Hardwick 94 B1
East Harling 72 A3
East Harlsey 110 D3
East Harptree 24 C2
East Hartford 129 E4
East Harting 15 G1
East Hatch 26 A5
East Hatley 58 A2
East Hauxwell 110 A3
East Haven 153 D1
East Heckington 83 G3
East Hedleyhope 120 A3
East Helmsdale 191 F3
East Hendred 41 G4
East Heslerton 112 C5
East Hoathly 18 A2
East Horndon 45 F4
East Horrington 24 C3
East Horsley 29 F2
East Horton 137 E3
East Huntspill 24 A3
East Hyde 44 A1
East Ilsley 41 G4
East Keal 84 B1
East Kennett 26 C1
East Keswick 102 C3
East Kilbride 142 A4
East Kirkby 84 B1
East Knapton 112 B5
East Knighton 13 E4
East Knoyle 25 F4
East Lambrook 12 A1
East Langdon 33 F4
East Langton 68 C3
East Langwell 190 C4
East Lavant 16 A3
East Lavington 16 B2
East Layton 110 A1
East Leake 81 G5
East Learmouth 136 C3
East Learney 170 B4
East Leigh 10 A2
East Lexham 71 G1
East Lilburn 137 E4
East Linton 144 C2
East Liss 28 C5
East Looe 5 G4
East Lound 95 E3
East Lulworth 13 E4
East Lutton 104 B1
East Lydford 24 C4
East Mains 170 B5
East Malling 31 G3
East March 152 C1
East Marden 16 A2
East Markham 95 E5
East Marton 101 F2
East Meon 28 B5
East Mere 10 C1
East Mersea 47 D1
East Mey 195 F1
East Midlands International Airport 81 F5
East Molesey 29 G1
East Morden 13 F3
East Morton 101 G3
East Ness 111 F5
East Norton 68 C2
East Oakley 27 G3
East Ogwell 10 B5
East Orchard 13 E1
East Ord 145 G4
East Panson 7 D1
East Peckham 31 F4
East Pennard 24 C4
East Portlemouth 9 D4
East Prawle 9 D4
East Preston 16 C3
East Putford 21 D4
East Quantoxhead 23 E3
East Rainton 120 C3
East Ravendale 96 C3
East Raynham 85 G5
East Rigton 102 C3
East Rolstone 24 A1
East Rounton 110 D2
East Rudham 85 G5
East Runton 86 C1
East Ruston 87 E3
East Saltoun 144 B3
East Shefford 41 F5
East Sleekburn 129 E3
East Somerton 87 F4
East Stockwith 95 E3
East Stoke *Dorset* 13 E4
East Stoke *Notts.* 82 C3
East Stour 25 E5
East Stourmouth 33 E2
East Stratton 27 G4
East Studdal 33 F4
East Suisnish 164 B1
East Taphouse 5 F3
East-the-Water 21 E3
East Thirston 129 D2
East Tilbury 45 F5
East Tisted 28 C4
East Torrington 96 B4
East Tuddenham 86 B4
East Tytherley 27 D5
East Tytherton 40 B5
East Village 10 B2
East Wall 65 E3
East Walton 71 F1
East Wellow 27 E5
East Wemyss 152 B5
East Whitburn 143 D3
East Wickham 45 D5
East Williamston 35 D2
East Winch 71 E1
East Wittering 16 A4
East Witton 110 A4
East Woodhay 27 F1
East Worldham 28 C4
East Worlington 10 A1
East Youlstone 20 C4
Eastbourne *Darl.* 110 C1
Eastbourne *E.Suss.* 18 B4
Eastburn 104 B2
Eastbury *Herts.* 44 A3
Eastbury *W.Berks.* 41 F5
Eastby 101 G2
Eastchurch 32 B1
Eastcombe 40 A2
Eastcote *Gt.Lon.* 44 A4
Eastcote *Northants.* 56 B2
Eastcote *W.Mid.* 67 D5
Eastcott *Cornw.* 20 C4
Eastcott *Wilts.* 26 B2
Eastcourt 40 B3
Eastend 55 F5
Easter Ardross 179 F2
Easter Balmoral 169 E5
Easter Boleskine 167 E2
Easter Borland 150 B4
Easter Brae 179 F3
Easter Buckieburn 142 B1
Easter Compton 39 E4
Easter Drummond 167 D3
Easter Dullater 150 A4
Easter Ellister 138 A4
Easter Fearn 179 F1
Easter Galcantray 180 A5
Easter Howlaws 145 E5
Easter Kinkell 179 E4
Easter Knox 161 D5
Easter Lednathie 160 B3
Easter Moniack 179 E5
Easter Ord 170 D4
Easter Poldar 150 B5
Easter Quarff 200 D4
Easter Skeld 200 C3
Easter Suddie 179 F4
Easter Tulloch 161 F2
Easter Whyntie 182 B3
Eastergate 16 B3
Easterton 26 B2
Eastertown 24 A2
Eastfield *N.Lan.* 142 C3
Eastfield *N.Yorks.* 112 D4
Eastfield Hall 129 E1
Eastgate *Dur.* 119 F4
Eastgate *Lincs.* 69 G1
Eastgate *Norf.* 86 C3
Eastham 91 E4
Easthampstead 29 D1
Eastheath 28 D1
Easthope 65 E3
Easthorpe *Essex* 60 A5
Easthorpe *Leics.* 82 D4
Easthorpe *Notts.* 82 C2
Easthouses 144 A3
Eastington *Devon* 10 A2
Eastington *Glos.* 40 D1
Eastington *Glos.* 39 G2
Eastleach Martin 41 E2
Eastleach Turville 41 E2
Eastleigh *Devon* 21 E3
Eastleigh *Hants.* 14 D1
Eastling 32 B3
Eastney 15 F3
Eastnor 53 G4
Eastoft 95 F1
Eastoke 15 G3
Easton *Cambs.* 69 G5
Easton *Cumb.* 126 C4
Easton *Cumb.* 117 F1
Easton *Devon* 10 A4
Easton *Dorset* 12 C5
Easton *Hants.* 27 G4
Easton *I.o.W.* 14 C4
Easton *Lincs.* 83 E5
Easton *Norf.* 86 C4
Easton *Som.* 24 C3
Easton *Suff.* 61 D2
Easton *Wilts.* 40 A5
Easton Grey 40 A4
Easton-in-Gordano 39 E5
Easton Maudit 57 D2
Easton on the Hill 69 F2
Easton Royal 26 D1
Eastrea 70 A3
Eastriggs 126 A5
Eastrington 103 G4
Eastry 33 E3
Eastside 197 D3
Eastville 84 C2
Eastwell 82 C5
Eastwick 44 D1
Eastwood *Notts.* 81 F3
Eastwood *S'end* 46 B4
Eastwood *W.Yorks.* 101 F5
Eathorpe 55 F1
Eaton *Ches.* 79 F1
Eaton *Ches.* 78 C1
Eaton *Leics.* 82 C5
Eaton *Norf.* 86 D5
Eaton *Notts.* 95 E5
Eaton *Oxon.* 41 G2
Eaton *Shrop.* 65 E3
Eaton *Shrop.* 64 C4
Eaton Bishop 52 D4
Eaton Bray 57 E5
Eaton Constantine 65 E2
Eaton Ford 57 G2
Eaton Green 57 E5
Eaton Hall 78 B1
Eaton Hastings 41 E3
Eaton Socon 57 G2
Eaton upon Tern 79 D5
Eavestone 102 B1
Ebberston 112 C4
Ebbesborne Wake 26 A5
Ebbw Vale 38 A2
Ebchester 120 A2
Ebford 10 C4
Ebrington 55 D3
Ecchinswell 27 G2
Ecclaw 145 E3
Ecclefechan 125 F3
Eccles *Gt.Man.* 92 B3
Eccles *Kent* 31 G2
Eccles *Sc.Bord.* 145 E5
Eccles Road 72 B2
Ecclesfield 94 A3
Ecclesgreig 161 F3
Eccleshall 79 F5
Ecclesmachan 143 E2
Eccleston *Ches.* 78 B1
Eccleston *Lancs.* 91 G1
Eccleston *Mersey.* 91 F3
Eccup 102 B3
Echt 170 C4
Eckford 136 B4
Eckington *Derbys.* 94 B5
Eckington *Worcs.* 54 B3
Ecton *Northants.* 56 D1
Ecton *Staffs.* 80 B2
Edale 93 F4
Edburton 17 E2
Edderside 117 E2
Edderton 179 G1
Eddington 27 E1
Eddleston 143 G5
Eddlewood 142 B4
Eden Park 30 C2
Edenbridge 30 D4
Edendonich 149 D2
Edenfield 92 C1
Edenhall 118 B4
Edenham 83 F5
Edensor 81 D1
Edentaggart 149 F5
Edenthorpe 94 D2
Edern 74 B4
Edgarley 24 C4
Edgbaston 66 C4
Edgcott 56 B5
Edgcumbe 3 E3
Edge *Glos.* 40 A2
Edge *Shrop.* 64 C2
Edge End 39 E1
Edgebolton 78 C5
Edgefield 86 C2
Edgeley 78 C3
Edgerley 64 C1
Edgeworth 40 B2
Edginswell 9 E1
Edgmond 65 G1
Edgmond Marsh 79 E5
Edgton 64 C4
Edgware 44 B3
Edgworth 92 B1
Edial 66 C2
Edinample 150 B2
Edinbanchory 169 G3
Edinbane 175 G4
Edinbarnet 141 G2
Edinburgh 143 G2
Edinburgh Airport 143 F2
Edinchip 150 A2
Edingale 67 E1
Edingley 82 B2
Edingthorpe 87 E2
Edington *Som.* 24 A4
Edington *Wilts.* 26 A2
Edintore 181 G5
Edinvale 180 D4
Edistone 20 C3
Edith Weston 69 E2
Edithmead 24 A3
Edlaston 80 C3
Edlesborough 43 E1
Edlingham 128 D1
Edlington 96 C5
Edmondsham 13 G1
Edmondsley 120 B3
Edmondthorpe 69 D1
Edmonstone 198 D4
Edmonton 44 C3
Edmundbyers 119 G2
Ednam 136 B3
Ednaston 80 D3
Edney Common 45 F2
Edra 149 G3
Edradynate 159 D4
Edrom 145 F4
Edstaston 78 C4
Edstone 55 D1
Edvin Loach 53 F2
Edwalton 81 G4
Edwardstone 60 A3
Edwinsford 50 C4
Edwinstowe 82 B1
Edworth 58 A3
Edwyn Ralph 53 F2
Edzell 161 D3
Efail Isaf 37 G4
Efailnewydd 74 C4
Efailwen 49 E5
Efenechtyd 77 E2
Effingham 29 G2
Effirth 200 C2
Efford 10 B2
Egbury 27 F2
Egdean 29 E5
Egerton *Gt.Man.* 92 B1
Egerton *Kent* 32 B4
Egerton Forstal 32 A4
Egerton Green 78 C2
Egg Buckland 8 B2
Eggerness 115 E2
Eggesford Barton 21 G4
Eggington 57 E5
Egginton 81 D5
Egglescliffe 110 D1
Eggleston 119 G5
Egham 43 F5
Egleton 69 D2
Eglingham 137 F5
Egloshayle 5 E2
Egloskerry 5 G1
Eglwys-Brewis 22 D1
Eglwys Cross 78 B3
Eglwys Fach 62 C3
Eglwysbach 89 G5
Eglwyswrw 49 E4
Egmanton 82 C1
Egmere 86 A2
Egremont 116 D5
Egton 112 B2
Egton Bridge 112 B2
Egypt 27 F3
Eight Ash Green 60 A5
Eignaig 155 G5
Eil 168 A3
Eilanreach 165 E3
Eilean Darach 178 A1
Eilean Iarmain (Isleornsay) 164 C3
Einacleit 186 C5
Eisgean 185 F2
Eisingrug 75 F4
Eisteddfa Gurig 63 D4
Elan Village 51 F1
Elberton 39 E4
Elburton 8 B2
Elcho 151 G2
Elcombe 40 D4
Eldernell 70 B3
Eldersfield 53 G4
Elderslie 141 F3
Eldrick 123 D2
Eldroth 101 D1
Eldwick 102 A3
Elerch (Bont-goch) 62 C4
Elford *Northumb.* 137 F3
Elford *Staffs.* 67 D1
Elgin 181 E3
Elgol 164 B3
Elham 33 D4
Elie 152 C4
Elilaw 128 B1
Elim 88 B4
Eling 14 C1
Eliock 133 G5
Elishader 176 B3
Elishaw 128 A2
Elkesley 95 D5
Elkstone 40 B1
Elland 102 A5
Ellary 139 F2
Ellastone 80 C3
Ellemford 145 E3
Ellenborough 116 D3
Ellenhall 79 F5
Ellen's Green 29 F4
Ellerbeck 110 D3
Ellerby 111 G1
Ellerdine Heath 78 D5
Elleric 156 C5
Ellerker 104 B5
Ellerton *E.Riding* 103 G3
Ellerton *N.Yorks.* 110 B3
Ellerton *Shrop.* 79 E5
Ellesborough 42 D2
Ellesmere 78 A4
Ellesmere Port 91 E5
Ellingham *Hants.* 14 A2
Ellingham *Norf.* 73 E2
Ellingham *Northumb.* 137 F4
Ellingstring 110 A4
Ellington *Cambs.* 69 G5
Ellington *Northumb.* 129 E2
Ellisfield 28 B3
Ellistown 67 G1
Ellon 171 E1
Ellonby 118 A4
Ellough 73 F3
Elloughton 104 B5
Ellwood 39 E2
Elm 70 C2
Elm Park 45 E4
Elmbridge 54 B1
Elmdon *Essex* 58 C4
Elmdon *W.Mid.* 67 D4
Elmdon Heath 67 D4
Elmesthorpe 67 G3
Elmhurst 66 D1
Elmley Castle 54 B3
Elmley Lovett 54 A1
Elmore 39 G1
Elmore Back 39 G1
Elmscott 20 C3
Elmsett 60 B3
Elmstead Market 60 B5
Elmstone 33 E2
Elmstone Hardwicke 54 B5
Elmswell *E.Riding* 104 B2
Elmswell *Suff.* 60 A1
Elmton 94 C5
Elphin 189 E3
Elphinstone 144 A2
Elrick *Aber.* 170 D4
Elrick *Moray* 169 G2
Elrig 114 D2
Elrigbeag 148 D3
Elsdon 128 B2
Elsecar 94 A2
Elsenham 58 D5
Elsfield 42 A2
Elsham 96 A1
Elsing 86 B4
Elslack 101 F3
Elson 78 A4
Elsrickle 143 E5
Elstead 29 E3
Elsted 16 A2
Elsthorpe 83 F5
Elstob 120 C5
Elston *Lancs.* 100 B4
Elston *Notts.* 82 C3
Elstone 21 G4
Elstow 57 F3
Elstree 44 A3
Elstronwick 105 E4
Elswick 100 A4
Elsworth 58 B1
Elterwater 107 E2
Eltham 44 D5
Eltisley 58 A2
Elton *Cambs.* 69 F3
Elton *Ches.* 91 F5
Elton *Derbys.* 80 D1
Elton *Glos.* 39 G1
Elton *Here.* 65 D5
Elton *Notts.* 82 C4
Elton *Stock.* 110 D1

Elvanfoot 134 A4
Elvaston 81 F4
Elveden 71 G5
Elvingston 144 B2
Elvington Kent 33 E3
Elvington York 103 G3
Elwick Hart. 121 D4
Elwick Northumb. 137 F3
Elworth 79 E1
Elworthy 23 D4
Ely Cambs. 70 D5
Ely Cardiff 38 A5
Emberton 57 D3
Embleton Cumb. 117 E3
Embleton Northumb. 137 G4
Embo 190 D5
Embo Street 190 D5
Emborough 24 D2
Embsay 101 G2
Emery Down 14 B2
Emley 93 G1
Emmer Green 42 C5
Emmington 42 C2
Emneth 70 C2
Emneth Hungate 70 D2
Empingham 69 E2
Empshott 28 C4
Emsworth 15 G2
Enborne 27 F1
Enchmarsh 65 E3
Enderby 68 A3
Endmoor 107 G4
Endon 79 G2
Enfield 44 C3
Enford 26 C2
Engine Common 39 F4
Englefield 42 B5
Englefield Green 43 E5
Englesea-brook 79 E2
English Bicknor 39 E1
English Frankton 78 B5
Englishcombe 25 E1
Enham Alamein 27 E3
Enmore 23 F4
Ennerdale Bridge 117 D5
Ennochdhu 159 F3
Ensay 154 C5
Ensdon 64 D1
Ensis 21 F3
Enstone 55 F5
Enterkinfoot 133 G5
Enterpen 111 D2
Enville 66 A4
Eolaigearraidh 172 C3
Eorabus 146 C2
Eorodal 187 G1
Eoropaidh 187 G1
Epperstone 82 B3
Epping 45 D2
Epping Green Essex 44 D2
Epping Green Herts. 44 B2
Epping Upland 44 D2
Eppleby 110 A1
Eppleworth 104 C4
Epsom 30 B2
Epwell 55 F3
Epworth 95 E2
Erbistock 78 A3
Erbusaig 165 D2
Erchless Castle 178 D5
Erdington 66 D3
Eredine 148 B4
Eriboll 192 D3
Ericstane 134 B4
Eridge Green 31 E5
Eriff 132 D5
Erines 139 G2
Eriswell 71 F5
Erith 45 E5
Erlestoke 26 A2
Ermington 8 C2
Erpingham 86 C2
Errogie 167 E2
Errol 152 A2
Errollston 171 F1
Erskine 141 F2
Ervie 122 B4
Erwarton 60 D4
Erwood 51 G3
Eryholme 110 C2
Eryrys 77 F2
Escart 139 G3
Escart Farm 139 G4
Escrick 103 F3
Esgair 49 G5
Esgairgeiliog 63 D2
Esh 120 A3
Esh Winning 120 A3
Esher 29 G1
Eshott 129 E2
Eshton 101 F2
Eskadale 166 D1
Eskbank 144 A3
Eskdale Green 106 C2
Eskdalemuir 126 A2
Eskham 97 D3
Esknish 138 B3
Espley Hall 129 D2
Esprick 100 A4
Essendine 69 F1
Essendon 44 B2
Essich 167 F1
Essington 66 B2
Esslemont 171 E2
Eston 111 E1
Etal 136 D3
Etchilhampton 26 B1
Etchingham 18 C1
Etchinghill Kent 33 D5
Etchinghill Staffs. 66 C1
Ethie Mains 161 E5
Eton 43 E5
Eton Wick 43 E5
Etteridge 167 F5
Ettingshall 66 B3
Ettington 55 E3
Etton E.Riding 104 B3
Etton Peter. 69 G2
Ettrick 135 D4
Ettrickbridge 135 E3
Ettrickhill 135 D4
Etwall 81 D4
Eurach 148 A4
Euston 71 G5
Euxton 91 G1
Evanton 179 F3
Evedon 83 F3
Evelix 190 C5
Evenjobb 52 B1
Evenley 56 A4
Evenlode 55 E5
Evenwood 120 A5
Everbay 199 E4
Evercreech 24 D4
Everdon 56 A2
Everingham 104 A3
Everleigh 26 D2
Everley High. 195 F2
Everley N.Yorks. 112 C4
Eversholt 57 E4
Evershot 12 B2
Eversley 28 C1
Eversley Cross 28 C1
Everthorpe 104 B4
Everton Beds. 58 A2
Everton Hants. 14 B3
Everton Notts. 95 D3
Evertown 126 B4
Evesbatch 53 F3
Evesham 54 C3
Evie 198 B4
Evington 68 B2
Ewart Newtown 137 D3
Ewden Village 93 G3
Ewell 30 B2
Ewell Minnis 33 E4
Ewelme 42 B3
Ewen 40 C3
Ewenny 37 F5
Ewerby 83 G3
Ewerby Thorpe 83 G3
Ewhurst E.Suss. 18 C1
Ewhurst Surr. 29 F3
Ewhurst Green 29 F4
Ewloe 77 F1
Ewood 100 C5
Eworthy 7 E1
Ewshot 28 D3
Ewyas Harold 52 C5
Exbourne 21 G5
Exbury 14 D2
Exebridge 22 C5
Exelby 110 B4
Exeter 10 C3
Exeter Airport 10 C3
Exford 22 B4
Exfords Green 65 D2
Exhall Warks. 54 D2
Exhall Warks. 67 F4
Exlade Street 42 B4
Exminster 10 C4
Exmouth 10 D4
Exnaboe 201 G5
Exning 59 E1
Exton Devon 10 C4
Exton Hants. 28 B5
Exton Rut. 69 E1
Exton Som. 22 C4
Exwick 10 C3
Eyam 93 G5
Eydon 56 A2
Eye Here. 53 D1
Eye Peter. 70 A2
Eye Suff. 72 C4
Eye Green 70 A2
Eyemouth 145 G3
Eyeworth 58 A3
Eyhorne Street 32 A3
Eyke 61 E2
Eynesbury 57 G2
Eynort 163 G2
Eynsford 31 E2
Eynsham 41 G2
Eype 12 A3
Eyre 176 A4
Eythorne 33 E4
Eyton Here. 53 D1
Eyton Shrop. 64 C4
Eyton Wrex. 78 A3
Eyton upon the Weald Moors 65 F1
Eywood 52 C2

F

Faccombe 27 E2
Faceby 111 D2
Fachwen 75 E1
Faddiley 78 C2
Fadmoor 111 F4
Faebait 179 D4
Faifley 141 G2
Fail 132 C3
Failand 39 E5
Failford 132 C3
Failsworth 92 C2
Fain 178 A2
Fair Oak Hants. 15 D1
Fair Oak Hants. 27 G1
Fairbourne 62 C1
Fairburn 103 D5
Fairfield Derbys. 93 E5
Fairfield Worcs. 66 B5
Fairford 40 D2
Fairgirth 124 C5
Fairholm 142 B4
Fairley 171 D4
Fairlie 140 D4
Fairlight 19 D2
Fairlight Cove 19 D2
Fairmile 11 D3
Fairmilehead 143 G3
Fairnington 136 A4
Fairoak 79 E4
Fairseat 31 F2
Fairstead Essex 45 G1
Fairstead Norf. 87 D3
Fairwarp 17 G1
Fairy Cross 21 E3
Fairyhill 36 A3
Fakenham 86 A3
Fala 144 B3
Fala Dam 144 B3
Falahill 144 A4
Faldingworth 96 A4
Falfield Fife 152 C4
Falfield S.Glos. 39 F3
Falkenham 61 D4
Falkirk 142 C2
Falkland 152 A4
Falla 136 B5
Fallgate 81 E1
Fallin 150 D5
Falmer 17 F3
Falmouth 3 F3
Falsgrave 112 D4
Falstone 127 F3
Fanagmore 192 A3
Fanans 148 C2
Fancott 57 F5
Fangdale Beck 111 E3
Fangfoss 103 G2
Fanmore 154 D5
Fans 144 D5
Far Cotton 56 C2
Far Forest 65 G5
Far Gearstones 108 C4
Farcet 70 A3
Farden 65 E5
Fareham 15 E2
Farewell 66 C1
Farforth 96 D5
Faringdon 41 E3
Farington 100 B5
Farlam 118 B2
Farlary 190 C4
Farleigh N.Som. 24 B1
Farleigh Surr. 30 C2
Farleigh Hungerford 25 E2
Farleigh Wallop 28 B3
Farlesthorpe 97 E5
Farleton 107 G4
Farley Shrop. 64 C2
Farley Staffs. 80 B3
Farley Wilts. 26 D5
Farley Green 29 F3
Farley Hill 28 C1
Farleys End 39 G1
Farlington 103 F1
Farlow 65 F4
Farmborough 25 D1
Farmcote 54 C5
Farmington 40 D1
Farmoor 41 G2
Farmtown 182 A4
Farnborough Gt.Lon. 30 D2
Farnborough Hants. 29 D2
Farnborough W.Berks. 41 G4
Farnborough Warks. 55 G2
Farnborough Green 29 D2
Farncombe 29 E3
Farndish 57 E1
Farndon Ches. 78 B2
Farndon Notts. 82 C2
Farnell 161 E4
Farnham Dorset 13 F1
Farnham Essex 58 C5
Farnham N.Yorks. 102 C1
Farnham Suff. 61 E2
Farnham Surr. 28 D3
Farnham Common 43 E4
Farnham Green 58 C5
Farnham Royal 43 E4
Farningham 31 E2
Farnley 102 B3
Farnley Tyas 93 F1
Farnsfield 82 B2
Farnworth Gt.Man. 92 B2
Farnworth Halton 91 G4
Farr High. 193 G2
Farr High. 167 F1
Farr High. 168 A4
Farr House 167 F1
Farraline 167 E2
Farringdon 10 D3
Farrington Gurney 24 D2
Farsley 102 B4
Farthinghoe 56 A4
Farthingloe 33 E4
Farthingstone 56 B2
Farway 11 E3
Fasag 177 E4
Fasagrianach 178 A1
Fascadale 155 E2
Faslane 141 D1
Fasnacloich 156 C5
Fasnakyle 166 C2
Fassfern 156 C2
Fatfield 120 C2
Fattahead 182 B4
Faugh 118 B2
Fauldhouse 142 D3
Faulkbourne 45 G1
Faulkland 25 E2
Fauls 78 C4
Faversham 32 C2
Favillar 169 E1
Fawdington 110 D5
Fawdon 120 B1
Fawfieldhead 80 B1
Fawkham Green 31 E2
Fawler 41 F1
Fawley Bucks. 42 C4
Fawley Hants. 15 D2
Fawley W.Berks. 41 F4
Fawley Chapel 53 E5
Fawsyde 161 G2
Faxfleet 104 A5
Faxton 68 C5
Faygate 30 B5
Fazeley 67 E2
Fearby 110 A4
Fearn 180 A2
Fearnan 158 C5
Fearnbeg 176 D4
Fearnhead 92 A3
Fearnmore 176 D3
Fearnoch Arg. & B. 140 B2
Fearnoch Arg. & B. 140 A2
Featherstone Staffs. 66 B2
Featherstone W.Yorks. 94 B1
Featherstone Castle 118 C1
Feckenham 54 C1
Feering 59 G5
Feetham 109 E3
Feith-hill 182 B5
Feizor 101 D1
Felbridge 30 C5
Felbrigg 86 D2
Felcourt 30 C4
Felden 43 F2
Felindre Carmar. 50 D5
Felindre Carmar. 50 B5
Felindre Carmar. 49 G4
Felindre Powys 64 A4
Felindre Swan. 36 C2
Felinfach 51 G4
Felinfoel 36 B2
Felingwmuchaf 50 B5
Felixkirk 111 D4
Felixstowe 61 D4
Felixstowe Ferry 61 E4
Felkington 145 G5
Felldownhead 7 D2
Felling 120 B1
Fellonmore 147 F2
Felmersham 57 E2
Felmingham 87 D3
Felpham 16 B4
Felsham 60 A2
Felsted 59 E5
Feltham 44 A5
Felthorpe 86 C4
Felton Here. 53 E3
Felton N.Som. 24 C1
Felton Northumb. 129 D1
Felton Butler 64 C1
Feltwell 71 F4
Fen Ditton 58 C2
Fen Drayton 58 B1
Fen End 67 E5
Fen Street 72 A4
Fence 101 E4
Fence Houses 120 C2
Fencott 42 A1
Fendike Corner 84 C1
Fenhouses 84 A3
Feniscowles 100 C5
Feniton 11 E3
Fenny Bentley 80 C2
Fenny Bridges 11 E3
Fenny Compton 55 G2
Fenny Drayton 67 F3
Fenny Stratford 57 D4
Fenrother 129 D2
Fenstanton 58 B1
Fenton Cambs. 70 B5
Fenton Lincs. 95 F5
Fenton Lincs. 83 D2
Fenton Northumb. 137 D3
Fenton Stoke 79 F3
Fenwick E.Ayr. 141 F5
Fenwick Northumb. 128 C4
Fenwick Northumb. 137 E2
Fenwick S.Yorks. 94 C1
Feochaig 130 C4
Feock 3 F3
Feolin 138 D3
Feolin Ferry 138 C3
Feorlan 130 B5
Feorlin 148 B5
Ferinquarrie 175 E4
Fern 160 C3
Ferndale 37 F3
Ferndown 13 G2
Ferness 180 B5
Fernham 41 E3
Fernhill Heath 54 A2
Fernhurst 29 D5
Fernie 152 B3
Fernilea 163 G1
Fernilee 93 E5
Fernybank 160 D2
Ferrensby 102 C1
Ferring 16 C3
Ferrybridge 103 D5
Ferryden 161 F4
Ferryhill 120 B4
Ferryside 35 G1
Fersfield 72 B3
Fersit 157 F2
Ferwig 49 E3
Feshiebridge 168 A4
Fetcham 29 G2
Fetterangus 183 E4
Fettercairn 161 E2
Fetternear House 170 C3
Feus of Caldhame 161 E3
Fewcott 56 A5
Fewston 102 A2
Ffair-Rhos 50 D1
Ffairfach 50 C5
Ffarmers 50 C3
Ffawyddog 38 B1
Ffestiniog 76 A3
Ffordd-las 77 E1
Fforest 36 B2
Fforest-fach 36 C3
Ffos-y-ffin 50 A1
Ffostrasol 49 G3
Ffridd Uchaf 75 E2
Ffrith 77 F2
Ffrwdgrech 51 G5
Ffynnon-ddrain 50 A5
Ffynnon Taf (Taff's Well) 38 A4
Ffynnongroyw 90 C4
Fibhig 187 D3
Fichlie 169 G3
Fidden 146 C2
Fiddington Glos. 54 B4
Fiddington Som. 23 F3
Fiddler's Green 53 E4
Fiddlers Hamlet 45 D2
Field 80 B4
Field Broughton 107 E4
Field Dalling 86 B2
Field Head 67 G2
Fife Keith 181 G4
Fifehead Magdalen 25 E5
Fifehead Neville 13 D1
Fifield Oxon. 41 E1
Fifield W. & M. 43 E5
Fifield Bavant 26 B5
Figheldean 26 C3
Filby 87 F4
Filey 113 E5
Filgrave 57 D3
Filkins 41 E2
Filleigh Devon 21 G3
Filleigh Devon 10 A1
Fillingham 95 G4
Fillongley 67 E4
Filmore Hill 28 B5
Filton 39 E5
Fimber 104 B1
Finavon 160 C4
Fincham 71 E2
Finchampstead 28 C1
Finchdean 15 G1
Finchingfield 59 E4
Finchley 44 B3
Findern 81 E4
Findhorn 180 C3
Findhorn Bridge 168 A2
Findhuglen 150 C3
Findo Gask 151 F2
Findochty 181 G3
Findon Aber. 171 E5
Findon W.Suss. 16 D3
Findon Mains 179 F3
Findrassie 181 D3
Findron 169 D3
Finedon 69 E5
Finegand 159 G3
Fingal Street 60 D1
Fingask 170 C2
Fingerpost 65 G5
Fingest 42 C3
Finghall 110 A3
Fingland Cumb. 117 F1
Fingland D. & G. 134 D5
Fingland D. & G. 133 F4
Finglesham 33 F3
Fingringhoe 46 D1
Finlarig 150 A1
Finmere 56 B4
Finnart Arg. & B. 149 E5
Finnart P. & K. 158 A4
Finningham 60 B1
Finningley 95 D3
Finnygaud 182 B4
Finsbury 44 C4
Finstall 66 B5
Finsthwaite 107 E4
Finstock 41 F1
Finstown 198 B5
Fintry Aber. 182 C4
Fintry Stir. 142 A1
Finzean 170 A5
Fionnphort 146 C2
Fir Tree 120 A4
Fir Vale 94 A4
Firbank 108 B3
Firbeck 94 C4
Firgrove 92 D1
Firs Road 26 D4
Firsby 84 C1
Firth 202 D5
Fishbourne I.o.W. 15 E3
Fishbourne W.Suss. 16 A3
Fishburn 120 C4
Fisherford 170 B1
Fisher's Pond 27 F5
Fisher's Row 100 A3
Fisherstreet 29 E4
Fisherton High. 179 G4
Fisherton S.Ayr. 132 A4
Fisherton de la Mere 26 B4
Fishguard (Abergwaun) 48 C4
Fishlake 95 D1
Fishleigh Barton 21 F3
Fishnish 155 F5
Fishpond Bottom 11 G3
Fishponds 39 F5
Fishpool 92 C1
Fishtoft 84 B3
Fishtoft Drove 84 B3
Fishtown of Usan 161 F4
Fishwick Lancs. 100 B4
Fishwick Sc.Bord. 145 G4
Fiskerton Lincs. 96 A5
Fiskerton Notts. 82 C2
Fittleton 26 C2
Fittleworth 16 C2
Fitton End 70 C1
Fitz 64 D1
Fitzhead 23 E5
Fitzwilliam 94 B1
Fiunary 155 F5
Five Ash Down 17 G1
Five Ashes 18 A1
Five Bridges 53 F3
Five Oak Green 31 F4
Five Oaks Chan.I. 8 C5
Five Oaks W.Suss. 29 F5
Five Roads 36 A2
Five Turnings 64 B5
Five Wents 32 A3
Fivehead 24 A5
Fivelanes 5 G1
Flackwell Heath 43 D4
Fladbury 54 B3
Fladdabister 200 D4
Flagg 80 C1
Flamborough 113 F5
Flamstead 43 F1
Flamstead End 44 C2
Flansham 16 B3
Flasby 101 F2
Flash 80 B1
Flashader 175 G4
Flask Inn 112 C2
Flaunden 43 F2
Flawborough 82 C3
Flawith 103 D1
Flax Bourton 24 C1
Flaxby 102 C2
Flaxley 39 F1
Flaxpool 23 E4
Flaxton 103 F1
Fleckney 68 B3
Flecknoe 56 A1
Fleet Hants. 28 D2
Fleet Lincs. 84 B5
Fleet Hargate 84 B5
Fleetwood 99 G3
Flemingston 22 D1
Flemington 142 A4
Flempton 59 G1
Fleoideabhagh 184 C5
Fletchertown 117 F2
Fletching 17 G1
Flete 8 C2
Fleuchats 169 F4
Fleur-de-lis 38 A3
Flexbury 20 C5
Flexford 29 E2
Flimby 116 D3
Flimwell 31 G5
Flint (Y Fflint) 90 D5
Flint Cross 58 C3
Flint Mountain 90 D5
Flintham 82 C3
Flinton 105 E4
Flishinghurst 31 G5
Flitcham 85 F5
Flitton 57 F4
Flitwick 57 F4
Flixborough 95 F1
Flixton Gt.Man. 92 B3
Flixton N.Yorks. 112 D5
Flixton Suff. 73 E3
Flockton 93 G1
Flockton Green 93 G1
Flodden 136 D3
Flodigarry 176 A2
Flookburgh 107 E5
Floors 181 G4
Flordon 72 C2
Flore 56 B1
Flotterton 128 C1
Flowton 60 B3
Flushing Aber. 183 F5
Flushing Cornw. 3 F3
Flyford Flavell 54 B2
Fobbing 45 G4
Fochabers 181 F4
Fochriw 38 A2
Fockerby 95 F1
Fodderletter 168 D2
Fodderty 179 E4
Foel 63 F1
Foggathorpe 103 G4
Fogo 145 E5
Fogorig 145 E5
Foindle 192 A4
Folda 159 G3
Fole 80 B4
Foleshill 67 F4
Folke 12 C1
Folkestone 33 E5
Folkingham 83 F4
Folkington 18 A3
Folksworth 69 G4
Folkton 113 D5
Folla Rule 170 C1
Follifoot 102 C2
Folly Dorset 12 D2
Folly Pembs. 48 C5
Folly Gate 7 F1
Fonthill Bishop 26 A4
Fonthill Gifford 26 A4
Fontmell Magna 13 E1
Fontwell 16 B3
Foolow 93 F5
Foots Cray 45 D5
Forbestown 169 F3
Force Forge 107 E3
Forcett 110 A1
Forches Cross 10 A2
Ford Arg. & B. 148 A4
Ford Bucks. 42 C2
Ford Devon 8 C2
Ford Devon 21 E3
Ford Devon 9 D3
Ford Glos. 54 C5
Ford Mersey. 91 E2
Ford Midloth. 144 A3
Ford Northumb. 136 D3
Ford Pembs. 48 C5
Ford Shrop. 64 D1
Ford Som. 23 D5
Ford W.Suss. 16 B3
Ford Wilts. 40 A5
Ford End 45 F1
Ford Street 11 E1
Fordcombe 31 E4
Fordell 143 F1
Forden 64 B2
Forder Green 9 D1
Fordham Cambs. 71 E5
Fordham Essex 60 A5
Fordham Norf. 71 E3
Fordham Abbey 59 E1
Fordingbridge 14 A1
Fordon 113 D5
Fordoun 161 F2
Fordstreet 60 A5
Fordwells 41 F1
Fordwich 33 D3
Fordyce 182 A3
Forebrae 151 E2
Foreland 138 A3
Forest Gate 44 D4
Forest Green 29 G3
Forest Hall Cumb. 107 G2
Forest Hall T. & W. 120 B1
Forest Head 118 B2
Forest Hill 42 A2
Forest-in-Teesdale 119 E4
Forest Lodge Arg. & B. 157 E5
Forest Lodge P. & K. 159 E2
Forest Mill 151 E5
Forest Row 30 D5
Forest Town 81 G1
Forestburn Gate 128 C2
Forestside 15 G1
Forfar 160 C4
Forgandenny 151 F3
Forgie 181 F4
Formby 91 D2
Forncett End 72 C2
Forncett St. Mary 72 C2
Forncett St. Peter 72 C2
Forneth 159 F5
Fornham All Saints 59 G1
Fornham St. Martin 59 G1
Fornighty 180 B4
Forres 180 C4
Forrest 142 C3
Forrest Lodge 123 G2
Forsbrook 79 G3
Forse 195 E5
Forsie 194 C2
Forsinain 194 B4
Forsinard 194 A4
Forston 12 C3
Fort Augustus 166 C4
Fort George 179 G4
Fort William 156 D2
Forter 159 G3
Forteviot 151 F3
Forth 142 D4
Forthampton 54 A4
Fortingall 158 C5
Forton Hants. 27 F3
Forton Lancs. 100 A2
Forton Shrop. 64 D1
Forton Som. 11 G2
Forton Staffs. 79 E5
Fortrie 182 B5
Fortrose 179 G4
Fortuneswell 12 C5
Forty Green 43 E3
Forty Hill 44 C3
Forward Green 60 B2
Fosbury 27 E2
Foscot 55 E5
Fosdyke 84 B4
Foss 158 C4
Foss Cross 40 C2
Fossdale 109 D3
Fossebridge 40 C1
Foster Street 45 D2
Foster's Booth 56 B2
Foston Derbys. 80 C4
Foston Lincs. 83 D3
Foston N.Yorks. 103 F1
Foston on the Wolds 104 D2
Fotherby 96 D3
Fotheringhay 69 F3
Foubister 197 E2
Foul Mile 18 B2
Foulbog 134 D5
Foulden Norf. 71 F3
Foulden Sc.Bord. 145 G4
Foulridge 101 E3
Foulsham 86 B3
Foulzie 182 C3
Fountainhall 144 B5
Four Ashes Staffs. 66 B2
Four Ashes Suff. 72 A4
Four Crosses Denb. 76 D3
Four Crosses Powys 64 B1
Four Crosses Powys 63 G2
Four Crosses Staffs. 66 B2
Four Elms 31 D4
Four Forks 23 F4
Four Gotes 70 C1
Four Lanes 3 D3
Four Marks 28 B4
Four Mile Bridge 88 A5
Four Oaks E.Suss. 19 D1
Four Oaks W.Mid. 67 E4
Four Oaks W.Mid. 66 D3
Four Roads 36 A2
Four Throws 18 C1
Fourlane Ends 81 E2
Fourlanes End 79 F2
Fourpenny 190 C5
Fourstones 119 E1
Fovant 26 B5
Foveran House 171 E2
Fowey 5 F4
Fowlis 152 B1
Fowlis Wester 151 E2
Fowlmere 58 C3
Fownhope 53 E4
Fox Lane 29 D2
Fox Street 60 B5
Foxcote 40 C1
Foxdale 98 A4
Foxearth 59 G3
Foxfield 106 D4
Foxham 40 B5
Foxhole Cornw. 5 D4
Foxhole High. 167 E1
Foxholes 112 D5
Foxhunt Green 18 A2
Foxley Here. 52 D3
Foxley Norf. 86 B3
Foxley Northants. 56 B2
Foxley Wilts. 40 A4
Foxt 80 B3
Foxton Cambs. 58 C3
Foxton Dur. 120 C5
Foxton Leics. 68 C3
Foxup 109 D5
Foxwist Green 78 D1
Foy 53 E5
Foyers 167 D2
Frachadil 154 C4
Fraddam 2 C3
Fraddon 4 D4
Fradley 67 D1
Fradswell 79 G4
Fraisthorpe 105 D1
Framfield 17 G1
Framingham Earl 87 D5
Framingham Pigot 87 D5
Framlingham 61 D1
Frampton Dorset 12 C3
Frampton Lincs. 84 B4
Frampton Cotterell 39 F4
Frampton Mansell 40 B2
Frampton on Severn 39 G2
Frampton West End 84 B3
Framsden 60 D2
Framwellgate Moor 120 B3
Franche 66 A5
Frankby 90 D4
Frankley 66 B4
Frankton 67 G5
Frant 31 E5
Fraserburgh 183 E3

Frating 60 B5
Fratton 15 F2
Freathy 7 D5
Freckenham 71 E5
Freckleton 100 A5
Freeby 82 D5
Freefolk 27 F3
Freeland 41 G1
Freemantle 14 D1
Freester 201 D2
Freethorpe 87 F5
Freethorpe Common 87 F5
Freiston 84 B3
Freiston Shore 84 B3
Fremington *Devon* 21 F2
Fremington *N.Yorks.* 109 F3
Frenchay 39 F5
Frenchbeer 7 G2
Frendraught 182 B5
Frenich 149 G4
Frensham 28 D3
Fresgoe 194 B2
Freshfield 91 D2
Freshford 25 E1
Freshwater 14 C4
Freshwater East 34 D3
Fressingfield 73 D4
Freston 60 C4
Freswick 195 F2
Frettenham 86 D4
Freuchie 152 A4
Freystrop Cross 34 C1
Friars Carse 124 D2
Friar's Gate 31 D5
Friarton 151 G2
Friday Bridge 70 C2
Friday Street *E.Suss.* 18 B3
Friday Street *Surr.* 29 G3
Fridaythorpe 104 A2
Friern Barnet 44 B3
Friesthorpe 96 A4
Frieston 83 E3
Frieth 42 C3
Frilford 41 G3
Frilsham 42 A5
Frimley 29 D2
Frimley Green 29 D2
Frindsbury 31 G2
Fring 85 F4
Fringford 56 B5
Frinsted 32 A3
Frinton-on-Sea 47 F1
Friockheim 161 D5
Friog 62 C1
Frisby on the Wreake 68 B1
Friskney 84 C2
Friskney Eaudyke 84 C2
Friston *E.Suss.* 18 A4
Friston *Suff.* 61 F2
Fritchley 81 E2
Frith 32 B3
Frith Bank 84 B3
Frith Common 53 F1
Fritham 14 B1
Frithelstock 21 E4
Frithelstock Stone 21 E4
Frithville 84 B2
Frittenden 32 A4
Fritton *Norf.* 72 D2
Fritton *Norf.* 87 F5
Fritwell 56 A5
Frizington 116 D5
Frocester 39 G2
Frochas 64 B1
Frodesley 65 E2
Frodingham 95 F1
Frodsham 91 G5
Frog End 58 C2
Frog Pool 53 G1
Frogden 136 B4
Froggatt 93 G5
Froghall 80 B3
Frogham 14 A1
Frogmore *Devon* 9 D3
Frogmore *Hants.* 28 D2
Frogmore *Herts.* 44 A2
Frolesworth 68 A3
Frome 25 E3
Frome Market 25 F2
Frome St. Quentin 12 B2
Fromes Hill 53 F3
Fron *Gwyn.* 74 C4
Fron *Powys* 64 B2
Fron *Powys* 51 G1
Fron-goch 76 C4
Froncysyllte 77 F3
Frostenden 73 F3
Frosterley 119 G4
Froxfield 27 D1
Froxfield Green 28 C5
Fryerning 45 F2
Fryton 111 F5
Fugglestone St. Peter 26 C4
Fulbeck 83 E2
Fulbourn 58 D2
Fulbrook 41 E1
Fulford *Som.* 23 F5
Fulford *Staffs.* 79 G4
Fulford *York* 103 F3
Fulham 44 B5
Fulking 17 E2
Full Sutton 103 G2
Fuller Street 45 G1
Fuller's Moor 78 B2
Fullerton 27 E4
Fulletby 96 C5
Fullwood 141 F5
Fulmer 43 E4
Fulmodeston 86 A2
Fulnetby 96 B5
Fulready 55 E3
Fulstow 96 D3
Fulwell *Oxon.* 55 F5
Fulwell *T. & W.* 120 C2
Fulwood *Lancs.* 100 B4
Fulwood *S.Yorks.* 94 A4
Fundenhall 72 C2
Funtington 16 A3
Funtley 15 E2
Funzie 203 F4
Furley 11 F2
Furnace *Arg. & B.* 148 C4
Furnace *Cere.* 62 C3
Furnace *High.* 177 F2
Furness Vale 93 E4
Furneux Pelham 58 C5
Furze Platt 43 D4
Furzehill 22 A3
Fyfett 11 F1
Fyfield *Essex* 45 E2
Fyfield *Glos.* 41 E2
Fyfield *Hants.* 27 D3
Fyfield *Oxon.* 41 G3
Fyfield *Wilts.* 26 C1
Fylingthorpe 112 C2
Fyvie 170 C1

G

Gabhsunn Bho Dheas 187 F2
Gabhsunn Bho Thuath 187 F2
Gablon 190 C5
Gabroc Hill 141 F4
Gaddesby 68 B1
Gaddesden Row 43 F1
Gaer *Newport* 38 B4
Gaer *Powys* 52 A5
Gaerllwyd 38 D3
Gaerwen 88 C5
Gagingwell 55 G5
Gaich 168 C2
Gaick 167 F1
Gaick Lodge 158 C1
Gailey 66 B1
Gainford 110 A1
Gainsborough 95 F3
Gairloch 177 E2
Gairlochy 157 D1
Gairney Bank 151 G5
Gairnshiel Lodge 169 E4
Gaitsgill 117 G2
Galabank 144 B5
Galashiels 135 F2
Galdenoch 122 C4
Galgate 100 A2
Galhampton 24 D5
Gallanach 148 A2
Gallantry Bank 78 C2
Gallatown 152 A5
Gallchoille 139 F1
Gallery 161 E3
Galley Common 67 F3
Galleyend 45 G2
Galleywood 45 G2
Gallowfauld 160 C5
Gallowstree Common 42 B5
Gallowstree Elm 66 A4
Gallt Melyd (Meliden) 90 B4
Galltair 165 E3
Galmisdale 155 D1
Galmpton *Devon* 8 C3
Galmpton *Torbay* 9 E2
Galphay 110 B5
Galston 132 D2
Galtrigill 175 E4
Gamble's Green 45 G1
Gamblesby 118 C4
Gamelsby 117 F1
Gamlingay 58 A2
Gammaton Moor 21 E3
Gammersgill 109 F4
Gamrie 182 C3
Gamston *Notts.* 95 E5
Gamston *Notts.* 82 B4
Ganarew 39 E1
Ganllwyd 76 A5
Gannochy 161 E2
Ganstead 105 D4
Ganthorpe 111 F5
Ganton 112 C5
Gaodhail 147 F1
Gara Bridge 8 D2
Garabal 149 F3
Garadheancal 188 B4
Garbat 178 D3
Garbhallt 148 C5
Garboldisham 72 B3
Garden 150 A5
Garden City 78 A1
Gardenstown 182 C3
Garderhouse 200 C3
Gardham 104 B3
Gare Hill 25 E3
Garelochhead 149 E5
Garford 41 G3
Garforth 102 D4
Gargrave 101 F2
Gargunnock 150 C5
Gariob 139 F1
Garlies Castle 123 F4
Garlieston 115 E2
Garlogie 170 C4
Garmond 182 D4
Garmony 155 F5
Garmouth 181 F3
Garnant 36 C1
Garndolbenmaen 75 D3
Garneddwen 63 D2
Garnett Bridge 107 G3
Garnfadryn 74 B4
Garnswllt 36 C2
Garrabost 187 G4
Garrachra 140 B1
Garralburn 181 G4
Garras 3 D4
Garreg 75 F3
Garreg Bank 64 B1
Garrick 150 D3
Garrigill 118 D3
Garroch 123 G2
Garrochty 140 B4
Garros 176 B3
Garrow 150 D1
Garryhorn 123 G1
Garrynahine 186 D4
(Gearraidh na h-Aibhne)
Garsdale Head 108 C3
Garsdon 40 B4
Garshall Green 79 G4
Garsington 42 A2
Garstang 100 A3
Garston 91 F4
Garswood 91 G3
Gartachoil 150 A5
Gartally 167 D1
Gartavaich 139 G4
Gartbreck 138 A4
Gartcosh 142 A3
Garth *Bridgend* 37 E3
Garth *Gwyn.* 89 D5
Garth *I.o.M.* 98 B4
Garth *Powys* 51 F3
Garth *Shet.* 200 B2
Garth *Wrex.* 77 F3
Garthbrengy 51 G4
Gartheli 50 B2
Garthmyl 64 A3
Garthorpe *Leics.* 82 D5
Garthorpe *N.Lincs.* 95 F1
Garths 107 G3
Garthynty 50 D3
Gartincaber 150 B4
Gartly 170 A1
Gartmore 150 A5
Gartnagrenach 139 F4
Gartnatra 138 B4
Gartness 141 G1
Gartocharn 141 F1
Garton 105 E4
Garton-on-the-Wolds 104 B1
Gartymore 191 F3
Garvald 144 C2
Garvamore 167 E5
Garvan 156 B2
Garvard 146 C5
Garve 178 C3
Garveld 130 B5
Garvestone 86 B5
Garvie 140 B1
Garvock *Aber.* 161 F2
Garvock *Inclyde* 141 D2
Garvock *P. & K.* 151 F3
Garwald 134 D5
Garwaldwaterfoot 134 D5
Garway 53 D5
Garway Hill 52 D5
Gask *Aber.* 183 F5
Gask *Aber.* 182 C5
Gask *P. & K.* 151 E3
Gaskan 156 A2
Gass 132 C5
Gastard 25 F1
Gasthorpe 72 A3
Gatcombe 15 D4
Gate Burton 95 F4
Gate Helmsley 103 F2
Gate House 139 D2
Gateacre 91 F4
Gatebeck 107 G4
Gateford 94 C4
Gateforth 103 E5
Gatehead 132 B2
Gatehouse 159 D5
Gatehouse of Fleet 124 A5
Gatelawbridge 124 D1
Gateley 86 A3
Gatenby 110 C4
Gateshaw 136 B4
Gateshead 120 B1
Gatesheath 78 B1
Gateside *Aber.* 170 B3
Gateside *Angus* 160 C5
Gateside *Fife* 151 G4
Gateside *N.Ayr.* 141 E4
Gateslack 133 G5
Gathurst 91 G2
Gatley 92 C4
Gattonside 135 G2
Gatwick (London) Airport 30 B4
Gaufron 51 F1
Gaulby 68 B2
Gauldry 152 B2
Gaunt's Common 13 G2
Gautby 96 B5
Gavinton 145 E4
Gawber 94 A2
Gawcott 56 B4
Gawsworth 79 F1
Gawthrop 108 B4
Gawthwaite 107 D4
Gay Street 29 F5
Gaydon 55 F2
Gayhurst 56 D3
Gayles 110 A2
Gayton *Mersey.* 91 D4
Gayton *Norf.* 71 F1
Gayton *Northants.* 56 C2
Gayton *Staffs.* 79 G5
Gayton le Marsh 97 E4
Gayton le Wold 96 C4
Gayton Thorpe 71 F1
Gaywood 85 E5
Gazeley 59 F1
Geanies House 180 A2
Gearach 138 A4
Gearnsary 193 G5
Gearradh 156 B3
Gearraidh Bhailteas 172 C1
Gearraidh Bhaird 187 E5
Gearraidh na h-Aibhne (Garrynahine) 186 D4
Gearraidh na Monadh 172 C2
Gearrannan 186 C3
Geary 175 F3
Gedding 60 A2
Geddington 69 D4
Gedgrave Hall 61 F3
Gedling 82 B3
Gedney 84 C5
Gedney Broadgate 84 C5
Gedney Drove End 84 C5
Gedney Dyke 84 C5
Gedney Hill 70 B1
Gee Cross 93 D3
Geirinis 173 F5
Geisiadar 186 C4
Geldeston 73 E2
Gell *Conwy* 76 B1
Gell *Gwyn.* 75 D4
Gelli Gynan 77 E2
Gelligaer 38 A3
Gellilydan 75 F4
Gellioedd 76 C3
Gelly 35 D1
Gellyburn 151 F1
Gellywen 49 F5
Gelston 124 B5
Gembling 104 D2
Gemmil 147 G4
Genoch 122 C5
Genoch Square 122 C5
Gentleshaw 66 C1
George Green 43 F4
George Nympton 22 A5
Georgeham 21 E2
Georgetown 141 F3
Gerlan 75 F1
Germansweek 7 E1
Germoe 2 C4
Gerrans 3 F3
Gerrards Cross 43 E4
Gerston 194 D3
Gestingthorpe 59 G4
Geuffordd 64 B1
Geufron 63 E4
Gibbshill 124 B3
Gibraltar 85 D2
Gidea Park 45 E4
Gidleigh 7 G2
Giffnock 141 G4
Gifford 144 C3
Giffordland 141 D5
Giggleswick 101 E1
Gilberdyke 104 A5
Gilchriston 144 B3
Gilcrux 117 E3
Gildersome 102 B5
Gildingwells 94 C4
Gileston 22 D1
Gilfach 38 A3
Gilfach Goch 37 F4
Gilfachrheda 50 A2
Gilgarran 116 D4
Gillamoor 111 F3
Gillen 175 F3
Gillenbie 125 F2
Gillfoot 125 D3
Gilling East 111 F5
Gilling West 110 A2
Gillingham *Dorset* 25 F5
Gillingham *Med.* 31 G2
Gillingham *Norf.* 73 F2
Gillivoan 195 D5
Gillock 195 E3
Gillow Heath 79 F2
Gills 195 F1
Gill's Green 31 G5
Gilmanscleuch 135 E3
Gilmerton *Edin.* 143 G3
Gilmerton *P. & K.* 151 D2
Gilmilnscroft 133 D3
Gilmonby 109 E1
Gilmorton 68 A4
Gilsland 118 C1
Gilsland Spa 118 C1
Gilston 144 B4
Gilston Park 44 D1
Gilwern 38 B1
Gimingham 87 D2
Giosla 186 C5
Gipping 60 B1
Gipsey Bridge 84 A3
Girlsta 200 D2
Girsby 110 C2
Girtford 57 G3
Girthon 124 A5
Girton *Cambs.* 58 C1
Girton *Notts.* 82 D1
Girvan 122 C1
Gisburn 101 E3
Gisleham 73 G3
Gislingham 72 B4
Gissing 72 C3
Gittisham 11 E3
Givons Grove 29 G2
Glackour 178 A1
Gladestry 52 B2
Gladsmuir 144 B2
Glaic 140 B2
Glais 36 D2
Glaisdale 111 G2
Glaister 131 E2
Glame 176 B5
Glamis 160 B5
Glan Conwy 76 B2
Glan-Dwyfach 75 D3
Glan Honddu 51 G4
Glan-y-don 90 C5
Glan-y-llyn 38 A4
Glan-yr-afon *Gwyn.* 76 C3
Glan-yr-afon *Gwyn.* 76 D3
Glanaber Terrace 76 A3
Glanadda 89 D5
Glanaman 36 C1
Glanbran 51 D4
Glanderston 170 A2
Glandford 86 B1
Glandwr *B.Gwent* 38 B2
Glandwr *Pembs.* 49 E5
Glangrwyne 38 B1
Glanllynfi 37 E3
Glanmule 64 A3
Glanrhyd 49 E3
Glanton 137 E5
Glantwymyn (Cemmaes Road) 63 E2
Glanvilles Wootton 12 C2
Glapthorn 69 F4
Glapwell 81 F1
Glasahoile 149 G4
Glasbury 52 A4
Glaschoil 168 C1
Glascoed 38 C2
Glascorrie 169 F5
Glascote 67 E2
Glascwm 52 A2
Glasdrum 156 C5
Glasfryn 76 C2
Glasgow 141 G3
Glasgow Airport 141 F3
Glashmore 170 C4
Glasinfryn 75 E1
Glasnacardoch 164 C5
Glasnakille 164 B3
Glaspant 49 F4
Glaspwll 62 D3
Glassburn 166 C1
Glassel 170 B5
Glassenbury 31 G5
Glasserton 115 E3
Glassford 142 B5
Glasshouse Hill 53 G5
Glasshouses 102 A1
Glassingall 150 C4
Glasslie 152 A4
Glasson *Cumb.* 126 A5
Glasson *Lancs.* 100 A2
Glassonby 118 B4
Glasterlaw 161 D4
Glaston 69 D2
Glastonbury 24 B4
Glatton 69 G4
Glazebury 92 A3
Glazeley 65 G4
Gleadless 94 A4
Gleadsmoss 79 F1
Gleann Ghrabhair 187 E5
Gleann Tholastaidh 187 G3
Gleaston 107 D5
Glecknabae 140 B3
Gledhow 102 C4
Gledrid 77 F4
Glemsford 59 G3
Glen *D. & G.* 124 C3
Glen *D. & G.* 123 G5
Glen Auldyn 98 C2
Glen Parva 68 A3
Glen Trool Lodge 123 F2
Glen Vine 98 B4
Glenae 125 D2
Glenaladale 156 A2
Glenald 149 E5
Glenamachrie 148 B2
Glenapp Castle 122 B2
Glenarm 160 B3
Glenbarr 130 B2
Glenbatrick 138 D2
Glenbeg *High.* 178 C1
Glenbeg *High.* 168 C2
Glenbeg *High.* 155 E3
Glenbeich 150 B2
Glenbervie *Aber.* 161 F1
Glenbervie *Falk.* 142 C1
Glenboig 142 B3
Glenborrodale 155 F3
Glenbranter 148 D5
Glenbreck 134 B3
Glenbrittle 164 A2
Glenbuck 133 F3
Glenbyre 147 E2
Glencaple 125 D4
Glencarse 151 G2
Glencat 170 A5
Glenceitlein 157 D5
Glencloy 131 F2
Glencoe 156 D4
Glenconglass 169 D2
Glencraig 151 G5
Glencripesdale 155 F4
Glencrosh 124 B2
Glencruittein 148 A2
Glencuie 169 G3
Glendearg *D. & G.* 134 D5
Glendearg *Sc.Bord.* 135 G2
Glendessary 165 F5
Glendevon 151 E4
Glendoebeg 166 D4
Glendoick 152 A2
Glendoll Lodge 160 A2
Glendoune 122 C1
Glendrissaig 122 C1
Glenduckie 152 A3
Glenduisk 122 D2
Glendye Lodge 161 E1
Gleneagles Hotel 151 E3
Gleneagles House 151 E4
Glenearn 151 G3
Glenegedale 138 B4
Glenelg 165 E3
Glenfarg 151 G3
Glenfeochan 148 A2
Glenfield 68 A2
Glenfinnan 156 B1
Glenfoot 151 G3
Glengalmadale 156 A4
Glengap 124 A5
Glengarnock 141 E4
Glengarrisdale 147 F5
Glengennet 123 D1
Glengolly 194 D2
Glengrasco 176 A5
Glengyle 149 F3
Glenhead 124 C2
Glenhead Farm 160 A3
Glenhurich 156 A3
Glenkerry 135 D4
Glenkiln 131 F2
Glenkin 140 C2
Glenkindie 169 G3
Glenlair 124 B3
Glenlatterach 181 E4
Glenlean 140 B1
Glenlee *Angus* 160 C1
Glenlee *D. & G.* 124 A2
Glenlichorn 150 C3
Glenlivet 169 D2
Glenlochar 124 B4
Glenluce 122 C5
Glenmallan 149 E5
Glenmanna 133 F5
Glenmavis 142 B3
Glenmaye 98 A3
Glenmeanie 178 B4
Glenmore *Arg. & B.* 140 B3
Glenmore *High.* 176 A5
Glenmore Lodge 168 B4
Glenmoy 160 C3
Glenmuick 189 F3
Glennoe 148 C1
Glenochar 134 A4
Glenogil 160 C3
Glenprosen Village 160 B3
Glenquiech 160 C3
Glenramskill 130 C4
Glenrazie 123 E4
Glenridding 117 G5
Glenrisdell 139 G4
Glenrossal 189 G4
Glenrothes 152 A4
Glensanda 156 A5
Glensaugh 161 E2
Glensgaich 179 D3
Glenshalg 170 A4
Glenshellish 148 D5
Glensluain 148 C5
Glentaggart 133 G3
Glentham 96 A3
Glenton 170 B2
Glentress 135 D2
Glentrool 123 E3
Glentruan 98 C1
Glentworth 95 G4
Glenuachdarach 176 A4
Glenuig 155 F2
Glenure 156 C5
Glenurquhart 179 G3
Glenwhilly 122 C3
Glespin 133 G3
Gletness 201 D2
Glewstone 53 E5
Glinton 69 G2
Glooston 68 C3
Glororum 137 F3
Glossop 93 E3
Gloster Hill 129 E1
Gloucester 40 A1
Gloup 203 E2
Gloweth 4 B5
Glusburn 101 G3
Gluss 202 C5
Glympton 55 G5
Glyn 76 A2
Glyn Ceiriog 77 F4
Glyn-Cywarch 75 F4
Glynarthen 49 G3
Glyncoch 37 G3
Glyncorrwg 37 E3
Glynde 17 G3
Glyndebourne 17 G2
Glyndyfrdwy 77 E3
Glynneath 37 E2
Glynogwr 37 F4
Glyntaff 37 G4
Glynteg 49 G4
Gnosall 79 F5
Gnosall Heath 66 A1
Goadby 68 C3
Goadby Marwood 82 C5
Goatacre 40 C5
Goatfield 148 C4
Goathill 12 C1
Goathland 112 B2
Goathurst 23 F4
Gobernuisgeach 194 B5
Gobhaig 184 C3
Gobowen 78 F4
Godalming 29 E3
Godford Cross 11 E2
Godmanchester 58 A1
Godmanstone 12 C3
Godmersham 32 C3
Godolphin Cross 2 D3
Godor 64 B1
Godre'r-graig 37 D2
Godshill *Hants.* 14 A1
Godshill *I.o.W.* 15 E4
Godstone 30 C3
Goetre 38 C2
Goff's Oak 44 C2
Gogar 143 F2
Gogarth 89 F4
Goginan 62 C4
Goirtean a' Chladaich 156 C2
Goirtein 140 A1
Golan 75 E3
Golant 5 F4
Golberdon 6 D3
Golborne 92 A3
Golcar 93 F1
Gold Hill 70 D3
Goldcliff 38 C4
Golden Cross 18 A2
Golden Green 31 F4
Golden Grove 36 B1
Golden Pot 28 C3
Golden Valley 54 B5
Goldenhill 79 F2
Golders Green 44 B4
Goldhanger 46 B2
Goldielea 124 D3
Golding 65 E2
Goldington 57 F2
Goldsborough *N.Yorks.* 112 B1
Goldsborough *N.Yorks.* 102 C2
Goldsithney 2 C3
Goldthorpe 94 B2
Goldworthy 21 D3
Gollanfield 180 A4
Golspie 190 D5
Golval 194 A2
Gomeldon 26 C4
Gomersal 102 B5
Gometra House 154 C5
Gomshall 29 F3
Gonachan Cottage 142 A1
Gonalston 82 B3
Gonfirth 200 C1
Good Easter 45 F1
Gooderstone 71 F2
Goodleigh 21 G2
Goodmanham 104 A3
Goodnestone *Kent* 33 E3
Goodnestone *Kent* 32 C2
Goodrich 39 E1
Goodrington 9 E2
Goodwick (Wdig) 48 C4
Goodworth Clatford 27 E3
Goodyers End 67 F4
Goole 103 G5
Goonbell 4 B5
Goonhavern 4 B4
Goose Green 31 F3
Gooseham 20 C4
Goosewell 8 B2
Goosey 41 F3
Goosnargh 100 B4
Goostrey 92 B5
Gorcott Hill 54 C1
Gorddinog 89 E5
Gordon 144 D5
Gordonbush 190 D4
Gordonstoun 181 D3
Gordonstown *Aber.* 182 A4
Gordonstown *Aber.* 170 C1
Gore Cross 26 B2
Gore Street 33 E2
Gorebridge 144 A3
Gorefield 70 C1
Gorey 8 D5
Goring 42 B4
Goring-by-Sea 16 D3
Gorleston on Sea 87 G5
Gorllwyn 49 G4
Gornalwood 66 B3
Gorrachie 182 C4
Gorran Churchtown 5 D5
Gorran Haven 5 E5
Gors 62 C5
Gorsedd 90 C5
Gorseinon 36 B3
Gorseness 198 C5
Gorsgoch 50 A2
Gorslas 36 B1
Gorsley 53 F5
Gorsley Common 53 F5
Gorstan 178 C3
Gorstanvorran 156 A2
Gorten 147 G1
Gortenbuie 147 E1
Gorteneorn 155 F3
Gorton *Arg. & B.* 154 A4
Gorton *Gt.Man.* 92 C3
Gosbeck 60 C2
Gosberton 84 A4
Goseley Dale 81 E5
Gosfield 59 F5
Gosforth *Cumb.* 106 B2
Gosforth *T. & W.* 120 B1
Gosmore 57 G5
Gospel End 66 B3
Gosport 15 F3
Gossabrough 203 E4
Gossops Green 30 B5
Goswick 137 E2
Gotham 81 G4
Gotherington 54 B5
Gott 200 D3
Goudhurst 31 G5
Goulceby 96 C5
Gourdas 182 C5
Gourdon 161 G2
Gourock 140 D2
Govan 141 G3
Goveton 9 D3
Govilon 38 B1
Gowanhill 183 F3
Gowdall 103 F5
Gowerton 36 B3
Gowkhall 143 E1
Gowthorpe 103 G2
Goxhill *E.Riding* 105 D3
Goxhill *N.Lincs.* 104 D5
Goytre 37 D4
Grabhair 185 F2
Gradbach 79 G1
Grade 3 E5
Graffham 16 B2
Grafham *Cambs.* 57 G1
Grafham *Surr.* 29 F3
Grafton *Here.* 53 D4
Grafton *N.Yorks.* 102 D1
Grafton *Oxon.* 41 E2
Grafton *Shrop.* 64 D1
Grafton *Worcs.* 53 E1
Grafton Flyford 54 B2
Grafton Regis 56 C3
Grafton Underwood 69 E5
Grafty Green 32 A4
Graianrhyd 77 F2
Graig *Conwy* 89 G5
Graig *Denb.* 90 B5
Graig-fechan 77 E2
Graig Penllyn 37 F5
Grain 32 A1
Grainel 138 A3
Grainhow 183 D5
Grainsby 96 C3
Grainthorpe 97 D3
Graiselound 95 E3
Grampound 4 D5
Grampound Road 4 D4
Gramsdal 173 G4
Granborough 56 C5
Granby 82 C4
Grandborough 55 G1
Grandtully 159 E4
Grange *Cumb.* 117 F5
Grange *High.* 166 C1
Grange *Med.* 31 G2
Grange *N.Yorks.* 111 E3
Grange *P. & K.* 152 A2
Grange Crossroads 181 G4
Grange Hall 180 C3
Grange Hill 44 D3
Grange Moor 93 G1
Grange of Lindores 152 A3
Grange-over-Sands 107 F5
Grange Villa 120 B2
Grangemill 80 D2
Grangemouth 142 D1
Grangemuir 152 D4
Grangeston 122 D1
Grangetown *Cardiff* 38 A5
Grangetown *R. & C.* 121 E5
Granish 168 B3
Gransmoor 104 D2
Granston 48 B4
Grantchester 58 C2
Grantham 83 E4
Grantley 110 B5
Grantlodge 170 C3
Granton House 134 B5

Grantown-on-Spey 168 C2
Grantshouse 145 F3
Grappenhall 92 A4
Grasby 96 A2
Grasmere 107 E2
Grasscroft 93 D2
Grassendale 91 E4
Grassholme 119 F5
Grassington 101 G1
Grassmoor 81 F1
Grassthorpe 82 C1
Grateley 27 D3
Gratwich 80 B4
Graveley Cambs. 58 A1
Graveley Herts. 58 A5
Gravelly Hill 66 D3
Gravels 64 C2
Graven 202 D5
Graveney 32 C2
Gravesend 45 F5
Grayingham 95 G3
Grayrigg 107 G3
Grays 45 F5
Grayshott 29 D4
Grayswood 29 E4
Grazeley 28 C1
Greasbrough 94 B3
Greasby 91 D4
Great Abington 58 D3
Great Addington 69 E5
Great Alne 54 D2
Great Altcar 91 E2
Great Amwell 44 C1
Great Asby 108 B1
Great Ashfield 60 A1
Great Ayton 111 E1
Great Baddow 45 G2
Great Bardfield 59 E4
Great Barford 57 G2
Great Barr 66 C3
Great Barrington 41 E1
Great Barrow 78 B1
Great Barton 59 G1
Great Barugh 111 G5
Great Bavington 128 B3
Great Bealings 60 D3
Great Bedwyn 27 D1
Great Bentley 60 C5
Great Billing 56 D1
Great Bircham 85 F4
Great Blakenham 60 C2
Great Bolas 78 D5
Great Bookham 29 G2
Great Bourton 55 G3
Great Bowden 68 C4
Great Bradley 59 E2
Great Braxted 46 B1
Great Bricett 60 B2
Great Brickhill 57 E4
Great Bridgeford 79 F5
Great Brington 56 B1
Great Bromley 60 B5
Great Broughton Cumb. 117 D3
Great Broughton N.Yorks. 111 E2
Great Budworth 92 A5
Great Burdon 110 C1
Great Burstead 45 F3
Great Busby 111 E2
Great Canfield 45 E1
Great Canney 46 B2
Great Carlton 97 E4
Great Casterton 69 F2
Great Chart 32 B4
Great Chatwell 65 G1
Great Chesterford 58 D3
Great Cheverell 26 A2
Great Chishill 58 C4
Great Clacton 47 E1
Great Clifton 116 D4
Great Coates 96 C2
Great Comberton 54 B3
Great Corby 118 A2
Great Cornard 59 G3
Great Cowden 105 E3
Great Coxwell 41 E3
Great Crakehall 110 B3
Great Cransley 68 D5
Great Cressingham 71 G2
Great Crosby 91 E2
Great Cubley 80 C4
Great Dalby 68 C1
Great Doddington 57 D1
Great Dunham 71 G1
Great Dunmow 59 E5
Great Durnford 26 C4
Great Easton Essex 59 E5
Great Easton Leics. 69 D3
Great Eccleston 100 A3
Great Edstone 111 G4
Great Ellingham 72 B2
Great Elm 25 E3
Great Eversden 58 B2
Great Fencote 110 B3
Great Finborough 60 B2
Great Fransham 71 G1
Great Gaddesden 43 F1
Great Gidding 69 G4
Great Givendale 104 A2
Great Glemham 61 E1
Great Glen 68 B3
Great Gonerby 83 D4
Great Gransden 58 A2
Great Green Norf. 73 D2
Great Green Suff. 60 A2
Great Habton 111 G5
Great Hale 83 G3
Great Hallingbury 45 E1
Great Harrowden 69 D5
Great Harwood 100 D4
Great Haseley 42 B2
Great Hatfield 105 D3
Great Haywood 80 B5
Great Heath 67 F4
Great Heck 103 E5
Great Henny 59 G4
Great Hinton 26 A2
Great Hockham 72 A2
Great Holland 47 F1
Great Horkesley 60 A4
Great Hormead 58 C4
Great Horwood 56 C4
Great Houghton Northants. 56 C2
Great Houghton S.Yorks. 94 B2
Great Hucklow 93 F5
Great Kelk 104 D2
Great Kimble 42 D2
Great Kingshill 43 D3
Great Langton 110 B3
Great Leighs 45 G1
Great Limber 96 B2
Great Linford 56 D3
Great Livermere 71 G5
Great Longstone 93 G5
Great Lumley 120 B3
Great Lyth 65 D2
Great Malvern 53 G3
Great Maplestead 59 G4
Great Marton 99 G4
Great Massingham 85 F5
Great Melton 86 C5
Great Milton 42 B2
Great Missenden 43 D2
Great Mitton 100 D4
Great Mongeham 33 F3
Great Moulton 72 C2
Great Munden 58 B5
Great Musgrave 108 C1
Great Ness 64 C1
Great Notley 59 F5
Great Oak 38 C1
Great Oakley Essex 60 C5
Great Oakley Northants. 69 D4
Great Offley 57 G5
Great Ormside 108 C1
Great Orton 117 G1
Great Ouseburn 102 D1
Great Oxendon 68 C4
Great Oxney Green 45 F2
Great Palgrave 71 G1
Great Parndon 44 D2
Great Paxton 58 A1
Great Plumpton 99 G4
Great Plumstead 87 D5
Great Ponton 83 E4
Great Preston 102 C5
Great Raveley 70 A4
Great Rissington 41 D1
Great Rollright 55 F4
Great Ryburgh 86 A3
Great Ryle 137 E5
Great Ryton 65 D2
Great Saling 59 E5
Great Salkeld 118 B4
Great Sampford 59 E4
Great Sankey 91 G4
Great Saxham 59 F1
Great Shefford 41 F5
Great Shelford 58 C2
Great Smeaton 110 C2
Great Snoring 86 A2
Great Somerford 40 B4
Great Stainton 120 C5
Great Stambridge 46 B3
Great Staughton 57 G1
Great Steeping 84 C1
Great Stonar 33 F3
Great Strickland 118 B5
Great Stukeley 70 A5
Great Sturton 96 C5
Great Sutton Ches. 91 E5
Great Sutton Shrop. 65 E4
Great Swinburne 128 B4
Great Tew 55 F5
Great Tey 59 G5
Great Thurlow 59 E3
Great Torrington 21 F4
Great Tosson 128 C1
Great Totham Essex 46 B1
Great Totham Essex 46 B1
Great Urswick 107 D5
Great Wakering 46 C4
Great Waldingfield 60 A3
Great Walsingham 86 A2
Great Waltham 45 F1
Great Warley 45 E3
Great Washbourne 54 B4
Great Welnetham 59 G2
Great Wenham 60 B4
Great Whittington 128 C4
Great Wigborough 46 C1
Great Wilbraham 58 D2
Great Wishford 26 B4
Great Witcombe 40 B1
Great Witley 53 G1
Great Wolford 55 E4
Great Wratting 59 E3
Great Wymondley 58 A5
Great Wyrley 66 B2
Great Wytheford 65 E1
Great Yarmouth 87 G5
Great Yeldham 59 F4
Greatford 69 F1
Greatgate 80 B3
Greatham Hants. 28 C4
Greatham Hart. 121 D5
Greatham W.Suss. 16 C2
Greatstone-on-Sea 19 F1
Greatworth 56 A3
Green End Beds. 57 G2
Green End Herts. 58 B5
Green Hammerton 103 D2
Green Ore 24 C2
Green Street 44 A3
Green Street Green Gt.Lon. 31 D2
Green Street Green Kent 45 E5
Green Tye 44 D1
Greenburn 152 C1
Greencroft 120 A3
Greendams 170 B5
Greendykes 137 E4
Greenfield Beds. 57 F4
Greenfield (Maes-Glas) Flints. 90 C5
Greenfield Gt.Man. 93 E2
Greenfield High. 166 B4
Greenfield Oxon. 42 C3
Greenford 44 A4
Greengairs 142 B2
Greenhalgh 100 A4
Greenhall 170 B2
Greenham Som. 23 D5
Greenham W.Berks. 27 F1
Greenhaugh 127 F3
Greenhead 118 C1
Greenheads 171 F1
Greenhill Gt.Lon. 44 A4
Greenhill High. 191 E4
Greenhill S.Yorks. 94 A4
Greenhithe 45 E5
Greenholm 132 D2
Greenholme 107 G2
Greenhow Hill 102 A1
Greenigo 196 D2
Greenland 195 E2
Greenlands 42 C4
Greenlaw Aber. 182 B4
Greenlaw Sc.Bord. 145 E5
Greenloaning 150 D4
Greenmount 92 B1
Greenmyre 170 D1
Greenock 141 D2
Greenodd 107 E4
Greens Norton 56 B2
Greenscares 150 C3
Greenside 120 A1
Greenstead Green 59 G5
Greensted 45 E2
Greenway Pembs. 49 D4
Greenway Som. 24 A5
Greenwich Gt.Lon. 44 C5
Greenwich Gt.Lon. 44 C5
Greet 54 C4
Greete 65 E5
Greetham Lincs. 96 D5
Greetham Rut. 69 E1
Greetland 101 G5
Greinetobht 173 G2
Greinton 24 B4
Grenaby 98 A4
Grendon Northants. 57 D1
Grendon Warks. 67 E3
Grendon Common 67 E3
Grendon Green 53 E2
Grendon Underwood 56 B5
Grenoside 94 A3
Greosabhagh 185 D4
Gresford 78 A2
Gresham 86 C2
Greshornish 175 G4
Gressenhall 86 A4
Gressingham 107 G5
Greta Bridge 109 F1
Gretna 126 B5
Gretna Green 126 B5
Gretton Glos. 54 C4
Gretton Northants. 69 E3
Gretton Shrop. 65 E3
Grewelthorpe 110 B5
Greygarth 110 A5
Greylake 24 A4
Greys Green 42 C4
Greysouthen 117 D4
Greystoke 118 A4
Greystone Aber. 169 E5
Greystone Angus 160 D5
Greystone Lancs. 101 E3
Greywell 28 C2
Griais 187 F3
Gribthorpe 103 G4
Gribton 124 D2
Gridley Corner 7 D1
Griff 67 F4
Griffithstown 38 B3
Grigadale 154 D3
Grigghall 107 F3
Grimeford Village 92 A1
Grimethorpe 94 B2
Griminis 173 F4
Grimister 203 D3
Grimley 54 A1
Grimmet 132 B4
Grimness 197 D3
Grimoldby 97 D4
Grimpo 78 A5
Grimsargh 100 B4
Grimsbury 55 G3
Grimsby 96 C2
Grimscote 56 B2
Grimscott 20 C5
Grimsiadar 187 F5
Grimsthorpe 83 F5
Grimston Leics. 82 B5
Grimston Norf. 85 F5
Grimstone 12 C3
Grindale 113 E5
Grindiscol 201 D4
Grindle 65 G2
Grindleford 93 G5
Grindleton 101 D3
Grindley 80 B5
Grindlow 93 F5
Grindon Northumb. 145 G5
Grindon Staffs. 80 B2
Gringley on the Hill 95 E3
Grinsdale 117 G1
Grinshill 78 C5
Grinton 109 F3
Griomarstaidh 186 D4
Grishipoll 154 A4
Gristhorpe 113 D4
Griston 72 A2
Gritley 197 E2
Grittenham 40 C4
Grittleton 40 A4
Grizebeck 106 D4
Grizedale 107 E3
Grobister 199 E4
Groby 68 A2
Groes 76 D1
Groes-faen 37 G4
Groes-lwyd 64 B1
Groesffordd 74 B4
Groesffordd Marli 90 B5
Groeslon 75 D2
Grogport 139 G5
Groigearraidh 162 A1
Gromford 61 E2
Gronant 90 B4
Groombridge 31 E5
Grosmont Mon. 52 D5
Grosmont N.Yorks. 112 B2
Grotaig 167 D2
Groton 60 A3
Groundistone Heights 135 F4
Grouville 8 C5
Grove Dorset 12 C5
Grove Kent 33 E2
Grove Notts. 95 E5
Grove Oxon. 41 G3
Grove Park 44 D5
Grovesend 36 B2
Gruids 190 A4
Gruinart Flats 138 A3
Gruline 147 E1
Grundcruie 151 F2
Grundisburgh 60 D2
Gruting 200 B3
Grutness 201 G5
Gualachulain 156 D5
Guardbridge 152 C3
Guarlford 54 A3
Guay 159 F5
Gubbergill 106 B3
Guernsey Airport 9 E5
Guestling Green 19 D2
Guestling Thorn 19 D2
Guestwick 86 B3
Guide Post 129 E3
Guilden Morden 58 A3
Guilden Sutton 78 B1
Guildford 29 E3
Guildtown 151 G1
Guilsborough 68 B5
Guilsfield (Cegidfa) 64 B1
Guisborough 111 F1
Guiseley 102 A3
Guist 86 A3
Guith 199 D3
Guiting Power 54 C5
Gulberwick 200 D4
Gullane 144 B1
Gulval 2 B3
Gulworthy 7 E3
Gumfreston 35 E2
Gumley 68 B4
Gunby E.Riding 103 G4
Gunby Lincs. 83 E5
Gundleton 28 B4
Gunn 21 G2
Gunnerside 109 E3
Gunnerton 128 B4
Gunness 95 F1
Gunnislake 7 E3
Gunnista 201 D3
Gunter's Bridge 29 E5
Gunthorpe Norf. 86 B2
Gunthorpe Notts. 82 B3
Gunville 15 D4
Gunwalloe 3 D4
Gurnard 15 D3
Gurney Slade 24 D3
Gurnos 37 D2
Gussage All Saints 13 G1
Gussage St. Michael 13 F1
Guston 33 F4
Gutcher 203 E3
Guthrie 161 D4
Guyhirn 70 B2
Guynd 161 D5
Guy's Head 84 C5
Guy's Marsh 25 F5
Guyzance 129 E1
Gwaelod-y-garth 38 A4
Gwaenysgor 90 B4
Gwaithla 52 B2
Gwalchmai 88 B5
Gwaun-Cae-Gurwen 36 D1
Gwaynynog 76 D1
Gwbert 49 E3
Gweek 3 E4
Gwehelog 38 C2
Gwenddwr 51 G3
Gwennap 4 B5
Gwenter 3 E5
Gwernaffield 77 F1
Gwernesney 38 D2
Gwernogle 50 B4
Gwernymynydd 77 F1
Gwersyllt 78 A2
Gwespyr 90 C4
Gwinear 2 C3
Gwithian 2 C2
Gwyddelwern 77 D3
Gwyddgrug 50 A4
Gwystre 51 G1
Gwytherin 76 B1
Gyfelia 78 A3
Gyffin 89 F5
Gyre 196 C2
Gyrn Goch 74 D3

H

Habberley 64 C2
Habrough 96 B1
Haccombe 10 B5
Hacconby 83 G5
Haceby 83 F4
Hacheston 61 E2
Hackenthorpe 94 B4
Hackford 86 B5
Hackforth 110 B3
Hackland 198 B4
Hackleton 56 D2
Hacklinge 33 F3
Hackness N.Yorks. 112 C3
Hackness Ork. 196 C3
Hackney 44 C4
Hackthorn 95 G4
Hackthorpe 118 B5
Hadden 136 B3
Haddenham Bucks. 42 C2
Haddenham Cambs. 70 C5
Haddington E.Loth. 144 C2
Haddington Lincs. 83 E1
Haddiscoe 73 F2
Haddon 69 G3
Hademore 67 D2
Hadfield 93 E3
Hadham Cross 44 D1
Hadham Ford 58 C5
Hadleigh Essex 46 B4
Hadleigh Suff. 60 B3
Hadley 65 F1
Hadley End 80 C5
Hadley Wood 44 B3
Hadlow 31 F4
Hadlow Down 18 A1
Hadnall 78 C5
Hadstock 59 D3
Hadzor 54 B1
Haffenden Quarter 32 A4
Hafod-Dinbych 76 B2
Hafodunos 76 B1
Haggate 101 E4
Haggbeck 126 C4
Haggs 142 B2
Hagley Here. 53 E3
Hagley Worcs. 66 B4
Hagnaby 84 B1
Hagworthingham 84 B1
Haigh 92 A2
Haighton Green 100 B4
Hail Weston 57 G1
Haile 106 B2
Hailes 54 C4
Hailey Herts. 44 C1
Hailey Oxon. 42 B4
Hailey Oxon. 41 F1
Hailsham 18 A3
Haimer 194 D2
Hainault 45 D3
Hainford 86 D4
Hainton 96 B4
Haisthorpe 104 D1
Halam 82 B2
Halbeath 143 F1
Halberton 10 D1
Halcro 195 E2
Hale Gt.Man. 92 B4
Hale Hants. 14 A1
Hale Surr. 28 D3
Hale Bank 91 F4
Hale Street 31 F4
Halebarns 92 B4
Hales Norf. 73 E2
Hales Staffs. 79 E4
Hales Place 32 D3
Halesowen 66 B4
Halesworth 73 E4
Halewood 91 F4
Half Way Inn 11 D3
Halford Shrop. 64 D4
Halford Warks. 55 E3
Halfpenny Green 66 A3
Halfway Carmar. 50 C4
Halfway Powys 51 E4
Halfway S.Yorks. 94 B4
Halfway W.Berks. 27 F1
Halfway House 64 C1
Halfway Houses 32 B1
Halghton Mill 78 B3
Halifax 101 G5
Halistra 175 F4
Halkirk 194 D3
Halkyn 90 D5
Hall 141 F4
Hall Dunnerdale 106 D3
Hall Green 66 D4
Hall of the Forest 64 B4
Halland 18 A2
Hallaton 68 C3
Hallatrow 24 D2
Hallbankgate 118 B2
Hallen 39 E5
Hallin 175 F4
Halling 31 G2
Hallington Lincs. 96 D4
Hallington Northumb. 128 B4
Halloughton 82 B2
Hallow 54 A2
Hallow Heath 54 A2
Hallrule 135 G4
Halls 145 D2
Hall's Green 58 A5
Hall's Tenement 118 B2
Hallsands 9 E4
Hallworthy 5 F1
Halmer End 79 E3
Halmore 39 F2
Halmyre Mains 143 F5
Halnaker 16 B3
Halsall 91 E1
Halse Northants. 56 A3
Halse Som. 23 E5
Halsetown 2 C3
Halsham 105 E5
Halsinger 21 F2
Halstead Essex 59 G4
Halstead Kent 31 D2
Halstead Leics. 68 C2
Halstock 12 B2
Haltham 84 A1
Haltoft End 84 B3
Halton Bucks. 43 D1
Halton Halton 91 G4
Halton Lancs. 100 B1
Halton Northumb. 119 G1
Halton Wrex. 78 A4
Halton East 101 G2
Halton Gill 109 D5
Halton Holegate 84 C1
Halton Lea Gate 118 C2
Halton West 101 E2
Haltwhistle 118 D1
Halvergate 87 F5
Halwell 9 D2
Halwill 7 E1
Halwill Junction 7 E1
Ham Glos. 39 F3
Ham Gt.Lon. 44 A5
Ham High. 195 E1
Ham Kent 33 F3
Ham Shet. 200 B5
Ham Som. 23 F5
Ham Wilts. 27 E1
Ham Green N.Som. 39 E5
Ham Green Worcs. 54 C1
Ham Hill 31 F2
Ham Street 24 C4
Hamble-le-Rice 15 D2
Hambleden 42 C4
Hambledon Hants. 15 F1
Hambledon Surr. 29 E4
Hambleton Lancs. 99 G3
Hambleton N.Yorks. 103 E4
Hambleton Moss Side 99 G3
Hambridge 24 A5
Hambrook S.Glos. 39 F5
Hambrook W.Suss. 15 G2
Hameringham 84 B1
Hamerton 69 G5
Hamilton 142 B4
Hamlet 11 E3
Hammer 29 D4
Hammerpot 16 C3
Hammersmith & Fulham 44 A5
Hammerwich 66 C2
Hammerwood 30 D5
Hammond Street 44 C2
Hammoon 13 E1
Hamnavoe Shet. 200 C4
Hamnavoe Shet. 203 D4
Hamnavoe Shet. 202 B4
Hamnavoe Shet. 203 D5
Hampden Park 18 B3
Hampnett 40 D1
Hampole 94 C2
Hampreston 13 G3
Hampstead 44 B4
Hampstead Norreys 42 A5
Hampsthwaite 102 B2
Hampton Gt.Lon. 29 G1
Hampton Shrop. 65 G4
Hampton Worcs. 54 C3
Hampton Bishop 53 E4
Hampton Heath 78 B3
Hampton in Arden 67 E4
Hampton Lovett 54 A1
Hampton Lucy 55 E2
Hampton on the Hill 55 E1
Hampton Poyle 42 A1
Hamptworth 26 D5
Hamsey 17 G2
Hamstall Ridware 66 D1
Hamstead I.o.W. 14 D3
Hamstead W.Mid. 66 C3
Hamstead Marshall 27 F1
Hamsterley Dur. 120 A4
Hamsterley Dur. 120 A2
Hamstreet 32 C5
Hamworthy 13 F3
Hanbury Staffs. 80 C5
Hanbury Worcs. 54 B1
Hanbury Woodend 80 C5
Hanchurch 79 F3
Handbridge 78 B1
Handcross 17 E1
Handforth 92 C4
Handley 78 B2
Handsacre 66 C1
Handsworth S.Yorks. 94 B4
Handsworth W.Mid. 66 C3
Handy Cross 43 D3
Hanford 79 F3
Hanging Bridge 80 C3
Hanging Langford 26 B4
Hangingshaw 125 F2
Hangleton 17 E3
Hanham 39 F5
Hankelow 79 D3
Hankerton 40 B3
Hankham 18 B3
Hanley 79 F3
Hanley Castle 54 A3
Hanley Child 53 F1
Hanley Swan 54 A3
Hanley William 53 F1
Hanlith 101 F1
Hanmer 78 B4
Hannah 97 E5
Hannington Hants. 27 G2
Hannington Northants. 68 D5
Hannington Swin. 41 D3
Hannington Wick 41 D3
Hanslope 56 D3
Hanthorpe 83 F5
Hanwell Gt.Lon. 44 A5
Hanwell Oxon. 55 G3
Hanwood 64 D2
Hanworth Gt.Lon. 44 A5
Hanworth Norf. 86 C2
Happisburgh 87 E2
Happisburgh Common 87 E3
Hapsford 91 F5
Hapton Lancs. 101 D4
Hapton Norf. 72 C2
Harberton 9 D2
Harbertonford 9 D2
Harbledown 32 D3
Harborne 66 C4
Harborough Magna 67 G5
Harbottle 128 B1
Harbourneford 8 D1
Harbridge 14 A1
Harburn 143 E3
Harbury 55 F2
Harby Leics. 82 C4
Harby Notts. 95 F5
Harcombe 11 E3
Harden 101 G4
Hardenhuish 40 B5
Hardgate 170 C4
Hardham 16 C2
Hardingham 86 B5
Hardings Wood 79 F2
Hardingstone 56 C2
Hardington 25 E2
Hardington Mandeville 12 B1
Hardington Marsh 12 B2
Hardley 14 D2
Hardley Street 87 E5
Hardmead 57 E3
Hardraw 109 D3
Hardstoft 81 F1
Hardway Hants. 15 F2
Hardway Som. 25 E4
Hardwick Bucks. 42 D1
Hardwick Cambs. 58 B2
Hardwick Norf. 72 D2
Hardwick Northants. 57 D1
Hardwick Oxon. 41 F2
Hardwick Oxon. 56 A5
Hardwick Village 94 D5
Hardwicke Glos. 54 B5
Hardwicke Glos. 39 G1
Hardwicke Here. 52 B3
Hardy's Green 46 C1
Hare Green 60 B5
Hare Hatch 42 D5
Hare Street Herts. 58 B5
Hare Street Herts. 58 B5
Hareby 84 B1
Hareden 100 C2
Harefield 43 F3
Harehills 102 C4
Harelaw 142 D5
Haresceugh 118 C3
Harescombe 40 A1
Haresfield 40 A1
Hareshaw 142 A5
Harewood 102 C3
Harewood End 53 E5
Harford 8 C2
Hargate 72 C2
Hargrave Ches. 78 B1
Hargrave Northants. 69 F5
Hargrave Suff. 59 F2
Haringey 44 C4
Harker 126 B5
Harkstead 60 C4
Harlaston 67 E1
Harlaxton 83 D4
Harle Syke 101 E4
Harlech 75 E4
Harlesden 44 B4
Harleston Norf. 72 D3
Harleston Suff. 60 B2
Harlestone 56 C1
Harley 65 E2
Harleyholm 134 A2
Harlington 57 F4
Harlosh 175 F5
Harlow 45 D1
Harlow Hill 119 G1
Harlthorpe 103 G4
Harlton 58 B2
Harman's Cross 13 F4
Harmby 110 A3
Harmer Green 44 B1
Harmer Hill 78 B5
Harmondsworth 43 F5
Harmston 83 E1
Harnham 26 C5
Harnhill 40 C2
Harold Hill 45 E3
Harold Wood 45 E3
Haroldston West 34 B1
Haroldswick 203 F1
Harome 111 F4
Harpenden 44 A1
Harpford 11 D3
Harpham 104 C1
Harpley Norf. 85 F5
Harpley Worcs. 53 F1
Harpole 56 B1
Harprigg 108 B4
Harpsdale 194 D3
Harpsden 42 C4
Harpswell 95 G3
Harpur Hill 93 E5
Harpurhey 92 C2
Harrapool 164 C2
Harrietfield 151 E1
Harrietsham 32 A3
Harrington Lincs. 97 D5
Harrington Northants. 68 C5
Harringworth 69 E3
Harris 163 G5
Harriseahead 79 F2
Harrogate 102 C2
Harrold 57 E2
Harrow Gt.Lon. 44 A4
Harrow High. 195 E1
Harrow on the Hill 44 A4
Harrow Weald 44 A3
Harrowbarrow 7 E3
Harrowden 57 F3
Harston Cambs. 58 C2
Harston Leics. 82 D4
Hart 121 D4
Hartburn Northumb. 128 C3
Hartburn Stock. 110 D1
Hartest 59 G2
Hartfield E.Suss. 31 D5
Hartfield High. 176 D5
Hartford Cambs. 70 A5
Hartford Ches. 92 A5
Hartford End 45 F1
Hartfordbridge 28 C2
Harthill Ches. 78 B2
Harthill N.Lan. 142 D3
Harthill S.Yorks. 94 B4
Hartington 80 C1
Hartland 20 C3
Hartland Quay 20 C3
Hartlebury 66 A5
Hartlepool 121 E4
Hartley Cumb. 108 C2
Hartley Kent 31 F2
Hartley Kent 31 G5
Hartley Northumb. 129 F4
Hartley Wespall 28 C2
Hartley Wintney 28 C2
Hartlip 32 A2
Harton N.Yorks. 103 G1
Harton Shrop. 65 D4
Harton T.&W. 120 C1
Hartpury 53 G5
Hartrigge 136 A4

Hartshill 67 F3
Hartshorne 81 E5
Hartsop 107 F1
Hartwell *Bucks.* 42 C1
Hartwell *E.Suss.* 31 D5
Hartwell *Northants.* 56 C3
Hartwood 142 C4
Harvel 31 F2
Harvington *Worcs.* 54 C3
Harvington *Worcs.* 66 A5
Harwell *Notts.* 95 D3
Harwell *Oxon.* 41 G4
Harwich 60 D4
Harwood *Dur.* 119 E4
Harwood *Gt.Man.* 92 B1
Harwood Dale 112 C3
Harwood on Teviot 135 F5
Harworth 94 D3
Hasbury 66 B4
Hascombe 29 E4
Haselbech 68 C5
Haselbury Plucknett 12 A1
Haseley 55 E1
Haselor 54 D2
Hasfield 54 A5
Hasguard 34 B2
Haskayne 91 E2
Hasketon 60 D2
Hasland 81 E1
Haslemere 29 E4
Haslingden 101 D5
Haslingden Grane 101 D5
Haslingfield 58 C2
Haslington 79 E2
Hassall 79 E2
Hassall Green 79 E2
Hassell Street 32 C4
Hassendean 135 G3
Hassingham 87 E5
Hassocks 17 E2
Hassop 93 G5
Haster 195 F3
Hastigrow 195 E2
Hastingleigh 32 C4
Hastings 18 D3
Hastingwood 45 D2
Hastoe 43 E2
Haswell 120 C3
Hatch *Beds.* 57 G3
Hatch *Hants.* 28 B2
Hatch Beauchamp 23 F5
Hatch End 44 A3
Hatch Green 11 F1
Hatching Green 44 A1
Hatchmere 91 G5
Hatcliffe 96 C2
Hatfield *Here.* 53 E2
Hatfield *Herts.* 44 B2
Hatfield *S.Yorks.* 95 D2
Hatfield Broad Oak 45 E1
Hatfield Heath 45 E1
Hatfield Hyde 44 B1
Hatfield Peverel 45 G1
Hatfield Woodhouse 95 D2
Hatford 41 F3
Hatherden 27 E2
Hatherleigh 21 F5
Hathern 81 F5
Hatherop 41 D2
Hathersage 93 G4
Hatherton *Ches.* 79 D3
Hatherton *Staffs.* 66 B1
Hatley St. George 58 A2
Hatt 7 D4
Hattingley 28 B4
Hatton *Aber.* 171 F1
Hatton *Derbys.* 80 D5
Hatton *Gt.Lon.* 43 F5
Hatton *Lincs.* 96 B5
Hatton *Shrop.* 65 D3
Hatton *Warks.* 55 E1
Hatton *Warr.* 91 G4
Hatton Castle 182 C5
Hatton Heath 78 B1
Hatton of Fintray 170 D3
Hattoncrook 170 D2
Haugh Head 137 E4
Haugh of Glass 169 G1
Haugh of Urr 124 C4
Haugham 96 D4
Haughhead 142 A2
Haughley 60 B1
Haughley Green 60 B1
Haughley New Street 60 B1
Haughs 182 A5
Haughton *Notts.* 95 D5
Haughton *Shrop.* 65 F3
Haughton *Shrop.* 65 E1
Haughton *Shrop.* 78 A5
Haughton *Staffs.* 79 F5
Haughton Green 92 D3
Haughton Le Skerne 110 C1
Haughton Moss 78 C2
Haultwick 58 B5
Haunn 172 C2
Haunton 67 E1
Hauxley 129 E1
Hauxton 58 C2
Havant 15 G2
Haven 52 D2
Haven Side 105 F5
Havenstreet 15 E3
Haverfordwest (Hwlffordd) 34 C1
Haverhill 59 E3
Haverigg 106 C5
Havering 45 E4
Havering-atte-Bower 45 E3
Haversham 56 D3
Haverthwaite 107 E4
Haverton Hill 121 D5
Hawarden 78 A1
Hawbridge 54 B3
Hawbush Green 45 G1
Hawcoat 106 D5
Hawen 49 G3
Hawes 109 D4
Hawford 54 A1
Hawick 135 G4
Hawkchurch 11 G2
Hawkedon 59 F2
Hawkenbury 31 E5
Hawkeridge 25 F2
Hawkerland 11 D4
Hawkes End 67 F4
Hawkesbury 39 G4
Hawkesbury Upton 39 G4
Hawkhill 137 G5
Hawkhurst 31 G5
Hawkinge 33 E4
Hawkley 28 C5
Hawkridge 22 B4
Hawkshead 107 E3
Hawksland 133 G2
Hawkswick 109 E5
Hawksworth *Notts.* 82 C3
Hawksworth *W.Yorks.* 102 A3
Hawkwell *Essex* 46 B3
Hawkwell *Northumb.* 128 C4
Hawley *Hants.* 29 D2
Hawley *Kent* 45 E5
Hawling 54 C5
Hawnby 111 E3
Haworth 101 G4
Hawstead 59 G2
Hawthorn *Dur.* 120 D3
Hawthorn *Wilts.* 25 F1
Hawthorn Hill *Brack.F.* 43 D5
Hawthorn Hill *Lincs.* 84 A2
Hawthorpe 83 F5
Hawton 82 C2
Haxby 103 F2
Haxey 95 E3
Haxted 30 D4
Hay Mills 66 D4
Hay-on-Wye 52 B3
Hay Street 58 B5
Haydock 91 G3
Haydon 12 C1
Haydon Bridge 119 E1
Haydon Wick 40 D4
Haye 6 D4
Hayes *Gt.Lon.* 43 F4
Hayes *Gt.Lon.* 30 D2
Hayfield *Arg. & B.* 148 C2
Hayfield *Derbys.* 93 E4
Hayfield *High.* 195 D2
Hayhillock 160 D5
Haylands 15 E3
Hayle 2 C3
Haynes 57 G3
Haynes Church End 57 F3
Hayscastle 48 B5
Hayscastle Cross 48 C5
Hayton *Cumb.* 118 B2
Hayton *Cumb.* 117 E2
Hayton *E.Riding* 104 A3
Hayton *Notts.* 95 E4
Hayton's Bent 65 E4
Haytor Vale 10 A5
Haywards Heath 17 F1
Haywood Oaks 82 B2
Hazel End 58 C5
Hazel Grove 92 D4
Hazelbank *Arg. & B.* 148 C4
Hazelbank *S.Lan.* 142 C5
Hazelbury Bryan 12 D2
Hazeleigh 46 B2
Hazeley 28 C2
Hazelhead 171 D4
Hazelside 133 G3
Hazelslade 66 C1
Hazelton Walls 152 B2
Hazelwood *Derbys.* 81 E3
Hazelwood *Gt.Lon.* 30 D2
Hazlefield 116 A2
Hazlemere 43 D3
Hazlerigg 129 E4
Hazleton 40 C1
Heacham 85 E4
Head Bridge 21 G4
Headbourne Worthy 27 F4
Headcorn 32 A4
Headington 42 A2
Headlam 110 A1
Headless Cross 54 C1
Headley *Hants.* 28 D4
Headley *Hants.* 27 G1
Headley *Surr.* 30 B3
Headley Down 28 D4
Headon 95 E5
Heads Nook 118 A2
Heage 81 E2
Healaugh *N.Yorks.* 109 F3
Healaugh *N.Yorks.* 103 E3
Heald Green 92 C4
Heale 21 G1
Healey *Lancs.* 92 C1
Healey *N.Yorks.* 110 A4
Healey *Northumb.* 119 G2
Healeyfield 119 G3
Healing 96 C1
Heamoor 2 B3
Heanish 154 B2
Heanor 81 F3
Heanton Punchardon 21 F2
Heanton Satchville 21 F4
Heapey 100 C5
Heapham 95 F4
Hearthstane 134 C3
Heasley Mill 22 A4
Heast 164 C3
Heath 81 F1
Heath and Reach 57 E5
Heath End *Hants.* 27 G1
Heath End *Surr.* 28 D3
Heath Hayes 66 C1
Heath Hill 65 G1
Heath House 24 B3
Heath Town 66 B3
Heathcot 171 D4
Heathcote *Derbys.* 80 C1
Heathcote *Shrop.* 79 D5
Heather 67 F1
Heathfield *Devon* 10 B5
Heathfield *E.Suss.* 18 A1
Heathfield *Som.* 23 E5
Heathton 66 A3
Heatley 92 B4
Heaton *Lancs.* 100 A1
Heaton *Staffs.* 79 G1
Heaton *T. & W.* 120 B1
Heaton Moor 92 C3
Heaverham 31 E3
Heaviley 92 D4
Hebburn 120 C1
Hebden 101 G1
Hebden Bridge 101 F5
Hebden Green 78 D1
Hebing End 58 B5
Hebron *Carmar.* 49 E5
Hebron *Northumb.* 129 D3
Heck 125 E2
Heckfield 28 C1
Heckfield Green 72 C4
Heckfordbridge 60 A5
Heckingham 73 E2
Heckington 83 G3
Heckmondwike 102 B5
Heddington 26 A1
Heddle 198 B5
Heddon-on-the-Wall 120 A1
Hedenham 73 E2
Hedge End 15 D1
Hedgerley 43 E4
Hedging 23 F5
Hedley on the Hill 119 G2
Hednesford 66 C1
Hedon 105 D5
Hedsor 43 E4
Heeley 94 A4
Heglibister 200 C2
Heighington *Darl.* 120 B5
Heighington *Lincs.* 83 F1
Heights of Brae 179 E3
Heilam 193 D2
Heithat 125 F2
Heiton 136 B3
Hele *Devon* 21 F1
Hele *Devon* 10 C2
Hele Bridge 21 F5
Hele Lane 10 A1
Helebridge 20 C5
Helensburgh 141 D1
Helford 3 E4
Helhoughton 85 G5
Helions Bumpstead 59 E3
Helland 5 E2
Hellandbridge 5 E2
Hellesdon 86 C4
Hellidon 56 A2
Hellifield 101 E2
Hellingly 18 A2
Hellington 87 E5
Hellister 200 C3
Helmdon 56 A3
Helmingham 60 C2
Helmsdale 191 F3
Helmshore 101 D5
Helmsley 111 F4
Helperby 110 D5
Helperthorpe 112 C5
Helpringham 83 G3
Helpston 69 G2
Helsby 91 F5
Helston 3 D4
Helstone 5 E1
Helton 118 B5
Helwith Bridge 101 E1
Hemblington 87 E4
Hemborough Post 9 E2
Hemel Hempstead 43 F2
Hemingbrough 103 F4
Hemingby 96 C5
Hemingford Abbots 70 A5
Hemingford Grey 70 A5
Hemingstone 60 C2
Hemington *Leics.* 81 F5
Hemington *Northants.* 69 F4
Hemington *Som.* 25 E2
Hemley 61 D3
Hemlington 111 D1
Hempholme 104 C3
Hempnall 72 D2
Hempnall Green 72 D2
Hempriggs 180 D3
Hempriggs House 195 F4
Hempstead *Essex* 59 E4
Hempstead *Norf.* 87 F3
Hempstead *Norf.* 86 C2
Hempsted 40 A1
Hempton *Norf.* 86 A3
Hempton *Oxon.* 55 G4
Hemsby 87 F4
Hemswell 95 G3
Hemsworth 94 B1
Hemyock 11 E1
Henbury *Bristol* 39 E5
Henbury *Ches.* 92 C5
Henderland 124 C3
Hendersyde Park 136 B3
Hendon *Gt.Lon.* 44 B4
Hendon *T. & W.* 120 C2
Hendy 36 B2
Heneglwys 88 C5
Henfield 17 E2
Henford 7 D1
Henghurst 32 B5
Hengoed *Caerp.* 38 A3
Hengoed *Powys* 52 B2
Hengoed *Shrop.* 77 F4
Hengrave 59 G1
Henham 58 D5
Heniarth 64 A2
Henlade 23 F5
Henley *Shrop.* 65 E5
Henley *Som.* 24 B4
Henley *Suff.* 60 C2
Henley *W.Suss.* 29 D5
Henley Corner 24 B4
Henley-in-Arden 55 D1
Henley-on-Thames 42 C4
Henley Park 29 E2
Henley's Down 18 C2
Henllan *Carmar.* 49 G4
Henllan *Denb.* 76 D1
Henllan Amgoed 49 E5
Henllys 38 B3
Henlow 57 G4
Hennock 10 B4
Henny Street 59 G4
Henryd 89 F5
Henry's Moat 48 D5
Hensall 103 E5
Henshaw 119 D1
Hensingham 116 C5
Henstead 73 F3
Hensting 27 F5
Henstridge 12 D1
Henstridge Ash 25 E5
Henstridge Marsh 25 E5
Henton *Oxon.* 42 C2
Henton *Som.* 24 B3
Henwick 54 A2
Henwood 5 G2
Heogan 201 D3
Heol-ddu 36 B1
Heol Lly Goden 52 A5
Heol Senni 51 F5
Heol-y-Cyw 37 F4
Hepburn 137 E4
Hepple 128 B1
Hepscott 129 E3
Heptonstall 101 F5
Hepworth *Suff.* 72 A4
Hepworth *W.Yorks.* 93 F2
Herbrandston 34 B2
Herdicott 6 D1
Hereford 53 E3
Heriot 144 A4
Hermiston 143 F2
Hermitage *D. & G.* 124 C4
Hermitage *Dorset* 12 C2
Hermitage *Sc.Bord.* 126 D2
Hermitage *W.Berks.* 42 A5
Hermitage *W.Suss.* 15 G2
Hermon *Carmar.* 49 G4
Hermon *I.o.A.* 74 C1
Hermon *Pembs.* 49 F4
Herne 33 D2
Herne Bay 33 D2
Herne Common 33 D2
Herner 21 F3
Hernhill 32 C2
Herodsfoot 5 G3
Herongate 45 F3
Heron's Ghyll 17 G1
Heronsgate 43 F3
Herriard 28 B3
Herringfleet 73 F2
Herring's Green 57 F3
Herringswell 59 F1
Herrington 120 C2
Hersden 33 D2
Hersham *Cornw.* 20 C5
Hersham *Surr.* 29 G1
Herstmonceux 18 B2
Herston *Dorset* 13 G5
Herston *Ork.* 196 D3
Hertford 44 C1
Hertford Heath 44 C1
Hertingfordbury 44 C1
Hesket Newmarket 117 G3
Hesketh Bank 100 A5
Hesketh Lane 100 C3
Heskin Green 91 G1
Hesleden 120 D4
Hesleyside 128 A3
Heslington 103 F2
Hessay 103 E2
Hessenford 6 D5
Hessett 60 A1
Hessle 104 C5
Hest Bank 100 A1
Heston 44 A5
Heswall 91 D4
Hethe 56 A5
Hetherington 128 A4
Hethersett 86 C5
Hethersgill 118 A1
Hethpool 136 C4
Hett 120 B4
Hetton 101 F2
Hetton-le-Hole 120 C3
Heugh 128 C4
Heugh-head *Aber.* 169 F3
Heugh-head *Aber.* 170 A5
Heveningham 73 E4
Hever 31 D4
Heversham 107 F4
Hevingham 86 C3
Hewas Water 5 D5
Hewell Grange 54 C1
Hewell Lane 54 C1
Hewelsfield 39 E2
Hewelsfield Common 39 E2
Hewish *N.Som.* 24 A1
Hewish *Som.* 12 A2
Hewton 7 F1
Hexham 119 F1
Hextable 45 E5
Hexton 57 G4
Hexworthy 7 G3
Heybridge *Essex* 45 F3
Heybridge *Essex* 46 B2
Heybridge Basin 46 B2
Heybrook Bay 8 B3
Heydon *Cambs.* 58 C3
Heydon *Norf.* 86 C3
Heydour 83 F4
Heylipoll 154 A2
Heylor 202 B4
Heysham 100 A1
Heyshaw 102 A1
Heyshott 16 A2
Heyside 92 D2
Heytesbury 26 A3
Heythrop 55 F5
Heywood *Gt.Man.* 92 C1
Heywood *Wilts.* 25 F2
Hibaldstow 95 G2
Hickleton 94 B2
Hickling *Norf.* 87 F3
Hickling *Notts.* 82 B5
Hickling Green 87 F3
Hickling Heath 87 F3
Hickstead 17 E1
Hidcote Boyce 55 D3
High Ackworth 94 B1
High Balantyre 148 C3
High Beach 44 D3
High Bentham 100 C1
High Bickington 21 F3
High Birkwith 108 D5
High Blantyre 142 A4
High Bonnybridge 142 C2
High Borgue 124 A5
High Bradfield 93 G3
High Bray 21 G2
High Brooms 31 E4
High Bullen 21 F3
High Burton 110 B4
High Buston 129 E1
High Callerton 129 D4
High Catton 103 G2
High Cogges 41 F2
High Coniscliffe 110 B1
High Cross *Hants.* 28 C5
High Cross *Herts.* 44 C1
High Cross Bank 67 E1
High Easter 45 F1
High Ellington 110 A4
High Entercommon 110 C2
High Ercall 65 E1
High Etherley 120 A5
High Garrett 59 F5
High Gate 101 F5
High Grange 120 A4
High Green *Norf.* 86 C5
High Green *S.Yorks.* 94 A3
High Green *Worcs.* 54 A3
High Halden 32 A5
High Halstow 45 G5
High Ham 24 B4
High Harrington 116 D4
High Harrogate 102 C2
High Hatton 78 D5
High Hawsker 112 C2
High Heath 79 D5
High Hesket 118 A3
High Hoyland 93 G2
High Hunsley 104 B4
High Hurstwood 17 G1
High Hutton 103 G1
High Ireby 117 F3
High Kilburn 111 E4
High Lane *Derbys.* 81 F3
High Lane *Worcs.* 53 F1
High Laver 45 E2
High Legh 92 B4
High Leven 110 D1
High Littleton 24 D2
High Lorton 117 E4
High Melton 94 C2
High Newton 107 F4
High Newton by-the-Sea 137 G4
High Nibthwaite 107 D3
High Offley 79 E5
High Ongar 45 E2
High Onn 66 A1
High Risby 95 G1
High Roding 45 F1
High Salvington 16 D3
High Shaw 109 D3
High Spen 120 A1
High Street *Cornw.* 5 D4
High Street *Kent* 31 G5
High Street *Suff.* 61 F2
High Street Green 60 B2
High Toynton 84 A1
High Trewhitt 128 C1
High Wollaston 39 E3
High Wray 107 E3
High Wych 45 D1
High Wycombe 43 D3
Higham *Derbys.* 81 E2
Higham *Kent* 45 G5
Higham *Lancs.* 101 E4
Higham *Suff.* 59 F1
Higham *Suff.* 60 B4
Higham Dykes 128 D4
Higham Ferrers 57 E1
Higham Gobion 57 G4
Higham on the Hill 67 F3
Higham Wood 31 F4
Highampton 21 E5
Highbridge 24 A3
Highbrook 30 C5
Highburton 93 F1
Highbury 25 D3
Highbury Vale 81 G3
Highclere 27 F1
Highcliffe 14 B3
Higher Ansty 13 D2
Higher Ashton 10 B4
Higher Ballam 99 G4
Higher Blackley 92 C2
Higher Brixham 9 F2
Higher Cheriton 11 D2
Higher Gabwell 9 F1
Higher Green 92 B3
Higher Kingcombe 12 B3
Higher Tale 11 D2
Higher Thrushgill 100 C1
Higher Town 4 B1
Higher Walreddon 7 E3
Higher Walton *Lancs.* 100 B5
Higher Walton *Warr.* 91 G4
Higher Whatcombe 13 E2
Higher Whitley 92 A4
Higher Wych 78 B3
Highfield *E.Riding* 103 G4
Highfield *N.Ayr.* 141 E4
Highfield *T. & W.* 120 A2
Highfields 58 B2
Highgreen Manor 128 A2
Highlane *Ches.* 79 F1
Highlane *Derbys.* 94 B4
Highlaws 117 E2
Highleadon 53 G5
Highleigh 16 A4
Highley 65 G4
Highmead 50 B3
Highmoor Cross 42 B4
Highmoor Hill 39 D4
Highnam 39 G1
Highstead 33 E2
Highsted 32 B2
Highstreet Green 59 F4
Hightae 125 E3
Hightown *Ches.* 79 F1
Hightown *Mersey.* 91 D2
Highway 40 C5
Highweek 10 B5
Highworth 41 E3
Hilborough 71 G2
Hilcott 26 C2
Hilden Park 31 E4
Hildenborough 31 E4
Hildersham 58 D3
Hilderstone 79 G4
Hilderthorpe 105 D1
Hilfield 12 C2
Hilgay 71 E3
Hill 39 F3
Hill Brow 28 C5
Hill Chorlton 79 E4
Hill Dyke 84 B3
Hill End *Dur.* 119 G4
Hill End *Fife* 151 F5
Hill End *N.Yorks.* 101 G2
Hill Head 15 E2
Hill of Beath 151 G5
Hill of Fearn 180 A2
Hill Ridware 66 C1
Hill Top *Hants.* 14 D2
Hill Top *W.Yorks.* 94 A1
Hill View 13 F3
Hillam 103 E5
Hillbeck 108 C1
Hillberry 98 B3
Hillborough 33 E2
Hillbrae *Aber.* 182 B5
Hillbrae *Aber.* 170 C2
Hillbrae *Aber.* 170 D1
Hillend *Aber.* 181 G5
Hillend *Fife* 143 F1
Hillend *Midloth.* 143 G3
Hillesden 56 B5
Hillesley 39 G4
Hillfarrance 23 E5
Hillhead 9 F2
Hillhead of Auchentumb 183 E4
Hillhead of Cocklaw 183 F5
Hilliard's Cross 67 D1
Hilliclay 195 D2
Hillingdon 43 F4
Hillington 85 F5
Hillmorton 68 A5
Hillockhead *Aber.* 169 F4
Hillockhead *Aber.* 169 G3
Hillowton 124 B4
Hillpound 15 E1
Hills Town 81 F1
Hillsford Bridge 22 A3
Hillside *Aber.* 171 E5
Hillside *Angus* 161 F3
Hillside *Moray* 181 D3
Hillside *Shet.* 200 D1
Hillswick 202 B5
Hillway 15 F4
Hillwell 201 F4
Hilmarton 40 C5
Hilperton 25 F2
Hilsea 15 F2
Hilton *Cambs.* 58 A1
Hilton *Cumb.* 118 D5
Hilton *Derbys.* 80 D4
Hilton *Dorset* 13 D2
Hilton *Dur.* 120 A5
Hilton *High.* 180 B1
Hilton *Shrop.* 65 G3
Hilton *Stock.* 111 D1
Hilton Croft 171 E1
Hilton of Cadboll 180 A2
Hilton of Delnies 180 A4
Himbleton 54 B2
Himley 66 A3
Hincaster 107 G4
Hinckley 67 G3
Hinderclay 72 B4
Hinderwell 111 G1
Hindford 78 A4
Hindhead 29 D4
Hindley 92 A2
Hindley Green 92 A2
Hindlip 54 A2
Hindolveston 86 B3
Hindon 26 A4
Hindringham 86 A2
Hingham 86 B5
Hinstock 79 D5
Hintlesham 60 B3
Hinton *Hants.* 14 B3
Hinton *Here.* 52 C4
Hinton *Northants.* 56 A2
Hinton *S.Glos.* 39 G5
Hinton *Shrop.* 64 D2
Hinton Admiral 14 B3
Hinton Ampner 27 G5
Hinton Blewett 24 C2
Hinton Charterhouse 25 E2
Hinton-in-the-Hedges 56 A4
Hinton Martell 13 G2
Hinton on the Green 54 C3
Hinton Parva 41 E4
Hinton St. George 12 A1
Hinton St. Mary 13 D1
Hinton Waldrist 41 F3
Hints *Shrop.* 65 F5
Hints *Staffs.* 67 D2
Hinwick 57 E1
Hinxhill 32 C4
Hinxton 58 C3
Hinxworth 58 A3
Hipperholme 102 A5
Hirn 170 C4
Hirnant 77 D5
Hirst 129 E3
Hirst Courtney 103 F5
Hirwaen 77 E1
Hirwaun 37 F2
Hiscott 21 F3
Histon 58 C1
Hitcham *Bucks.* 43 E4
Hitcham *Suff.* 60 A2
Hitchin 57 G5
Hither Green 44 C5
Hittisleigh 10 A3
Hixon 80 B5
Hoaden 33 E2
Hoaldalbert 52 C5
Hoar Cross 80 C5
Hoarwithy 53 E5
Hoath 33 D2
Hobarris 64 C5
Hobbister 196 C2
Hobbs Lots Bridge 70 B2
Hobkirk 135 G4
Hobland Hall 87 G5
Hobson 120 A2
Hoby 68 B1
Hockering 86 B4
Hockerton 82 C2
Hockley 46 B3
Hockley Heath 67 D5
Hockliffe 57 E5
Hockwold cum Wilton 71 F4
Hockworthy 10 D1
Hoddesdon 44 C2
Hoddlesden 100 D5
Hodgeston 34 D3
Hodnet 78 D5
Hodthorpe 94 C5
Hoe 86 A4
Hoe Gate 15 F1
Hoff 108 B1
Hoffleet Stow 84 A4
Hoggeston 56 D5
Hoggie 182 A3
Hogha Gearraidh 173 F2
Hoghton 100 C5
Hognaston 80 D2
Hogsthorpe 97 F5
Holbeach 84 B5
Holbeach Bank 84 B5
Holbeach Clough 84 B5
Holbeach Drove 70 B1
Holbeach Hurn 84 B5
Holbeach St. Johns 70 B1
Holbeach St. Marks 84 B4
Holbeach St. Matthew 84 C4
Holbeck 94 C5
Holberrow Green 54 C2
Holbeton 8 C2
Holborough 31 G2
Holbrook *Derbys.* 81 E3
Holbrook *Suff.* 60 C4
Holburn 137 E3
Holbury 14 D2
Holcombe *Devon* 10 C5
Holcombe *Som.* 25 D3
Holcombe Rogus 11 D1
Holcot 56 C1
Holden 101 D3
Holdenby 56 B1
Holdenhurst 14 A3
Holdgate 65 E4
Holdingham 83 F3
Holditch 11 G2
Hole-in-the-Wall 53 F5
Hole Park 32 A5
Hole Street 16 D2
Holford 23 E3
Holker 107 E5
Holkham 85 G3
Hollacombe *Devon* 21 D5
Hollacombe *Devon* 21 G4
Holland *Ork.* 198 C1
Holland *Ork.* 199 E4
Holland *Surr.* 30 D3
Holland-on-Sea 47 E1
Hollandstoun 199 F1
Hollee 126 A5
Hollesley 61 E3
Hollingbourne 32 A3
Hollingbury 17 F3
Hollington *Derbys.* 80 D4
Hollington *E.Suss.* 18 C2
Hollington *Staffs.* 80 B4
Hollingworth 93 E3
Hollins 92 C2
Hollins Green 92 A3
Hollinsclough 80 B1
Hollinswood 65 G2
Hollinwood 78 C4
Holloway 81 E2
Hollowell 68 B5
Holly End 70 D2
Holly Green 54 A3
Hollybush *Caerp.* 38 A2
Hollybush *E.Ayr.* 132 B4
Hollybush *Worcs.* 53 G4
Hollym 105 F5
Holm 126 A2
Holm of Drumlanrig 124 C1
Holmbury St. Mary 29 G3
Holmbush *Cornw.* 5 E4
Holmbush *W.Suss.* 30 B5
Holme *Cambs.* 69 G4
Holme *Cumb.* 107 G5
Holme *Notts.* 82 D2
Holme *W.Yorks.* 93 F2
Holme Chapel 101 E5
Holme Hale 71 G2
Holme Lacy 53 E4
Holme Marsh 52 C2
Holme next the Sea 85 F3
Holme-on-Spalding-Moor 104 A4
Holme on the Wolds 104 B3
Holme Pierrepont 82 B4
Holmebridge 13 E4
Holmer 53 E3
Holmer Green 43 E3
Holmes Chapel 79 E1

Holme's Hill 18 A2
Holmesfield 94 A5
Holmeswood 91 F1
Holmewood 81 F1
Holmfield 101 G5
Holmfirth 93 F2
Holmhead D. & G. 124 B2
Holmhead E.Ayr. 133 D3
Holmpton 105 F5
Holmrook 106 B2
Holmsgarth 201 D3
Holmside 120 B3
Holmston 132 B3
Holmwrangle 118 B3
Holne 8 D1
Holnest 12 C2
Holsworthy 20 D5
Holsworthy Beacon 21 D5
Holt Dorset 13 G2
Holt Norf. 86 B2
Holt Wilts. 25 F1
Holt Worcs. 54 A1
Holt Wrex. 78 B2
Holt End Hants. 28 B4
Holt End Worcs. 54 C1
Holt Fleet 54 A1
Holt Heath Dorset 13 G2
Holt Heath Worcs. 54 A1
Holtby 103 F2
Holton Oxon. 42 B2
Holton Som. 25 D5
Holton Suff. 73 E4
Holton cum Beckering 96 B4
Holton Heath 13 F3
Holton le Clay 96 C2
Holton le Moor 96 A3
Holton St. Mary 60 B4
Holtspur 43 E3
Holtye Common 31 D5
Holwell Dorset 12 D1
Holwell Herts. 57 G4
Holwell Leics. 82 C5
Holwell Oxon. 41 E2
Holwell Som. 25 E3
Holwick 119 F5
Holworth 13 D4
Holy Cross 66 B5
Holy Island 137 F2
Holybourne 28 C3
Holyhead (Caergybi) 88 A4
Holymoorside 81 E1
Holyport 43 D5
Holystone 128 B1
Holytown 142 B3
Holywell Cambs. 70 B5
Holywell Cornw. 4 B4
Holywell Dorset 12 B2
Holywell E.Suss. 18 A4
Holywell Flints. (Treffynnon) 90 C5
Holywell Green 93 E1
Holywell Lake 23 E5
Holywell Row 71 F5
Holywood 124 D2
Hom Green 53 E5
Homer 65 F2
Homersfield 73 D3
Homington 26 C5
Honey Hill 32 D2
Honey Tye 60 A4
Honeyborough 34 C2
Honeybourne 54 D3
Honeychurch 21 G5
Honiley 67 E5
Honing 87 E3
Honingham 86 C4
Honington Lincs. 83 E3
Honington Suff. 72 A4
Honington Warks. 55 E3
Honiton 11 E2
Honley 93 F1
Hoo Med. 45 G5
Hoo Suff. 61 D2
Hooe E.Suss. 18 B3
Hooe Plym. 8 B2
Hooe Common 18 B2
Hook E.Riding 103 G5
Hook Gt.Lon. 29 G1
Hook Hants. 28 C2
Hook Pembs. 34 C1
Hook Wilts. 40 C4
Hook-a-Gate 65 D2
Hook Green Kent 31 F5
Hook Green Kent 31 F2
Hook Green Kent 45 F5
Hook Norton 55 F4
Hooke 12 B2
Hookgate 79 E4
Hookway 10 B3
Hookwood 30 B4
Hoole 78 B1
Hooley 30 B3
Hooton 91 E5
Hooton Levitt 94 C3
Hooton Pagnell 94 B2
Hooton Roberts 94 B3
Hopcrofts Holt 55 G5
Hope Derbys. 93 F4
Hope Devon 8 C4
Hope Flints. 78 A2
Hope Powys 64 B2
Hope Shrop. 64 C2
Hope Bagot 65 E5
Hope Bowdler 65 D3
Hope End Green 45 E1
Hope Mansell 39 F1
Hope under Dinmore 53 E2
Hopehouse 135 D4
Hopeman 180 D3
Hope's Green 45 G4
Hopesay 64 C4
Hopkinstown 37 G3
Hopton Derbys. 81 D2
Hopton Norf. 87 G5
Hopton Shrop. 78 C5
Hopton Staffs. 79 G5
Hopton Suff. 72 A4
Hopton Cangeford 65 E4
Hopton Castle 64 C5
Hopton Wafers 65 F5
Hoptonheath 64 C5
Hopwas 67 D2
Hopwood 66 C5
Horam 18 A2
Horbling 83 G4
Horbury 93 G1
Horden 120 D3
Horderley 64 D4
Hordle 14 B3
Hordley 78 A4
Horeb Carmar. 36 A2
Horeb Cere. 49 G3
Horfield 39 E5
Horham 72 D4
Horkesley Heath 60 A5
Horkstow 95 G1
Horley Oxon. 55 G3
Horley Surr. 30 B4
Horn Hill 43 F3
Hornblotton Green 24 C4
Hornby Lancs. 100 B1
Hornby N.Yorks. 110 B3
Hornby N.Yorks. 110 C2
Horncastle 84 A1
Hornchurch 45 E4
Horncliffe 145 G4
Horndean Hants. 15 G1
Horndean Sc.Bord. 145 F5
Horndon 7 F2
Horndon on the Hill 45 F4
Horne 30 C4
Horniehaugh 160 C3
Horning 87 E4
Horninghold 68 D3
Horninglow 80 D5
Horningsea 58 C1
Horningsham 25 F3
Horningtoft 86 A3
Horningtops 5 G3
Horns Cross Devon 21 D3
Horns Cross E.Suss. 18 D1
Hornsby 118 B3
Hornsby Gate 118 B2
Hornsea 105 E3
Hornsey 44 C4
Hornton 55 F3
Horrabridge 8 B1
Horridge 10 A5
Horringer 59 G1
Horse Bridge 79 G2
Horsebridge Devon 7 E3
Horsebridge Hants. 27 E4
Horsebrook 66 A1
Horsehay 65 F2
Horseheath 59 E3
Horsehouse 109 F4
Horsell 29 E2
Horseman's Green 78 B3
Horseway 70 C4
Horsey 87 F3
Horsford 86 C4
Horsforth 102 B4
Horsham W.Suss. 29 G4
Horsham Worcs. 53 G2
Horsham St. Faith 86 D4
Horsington Lincs. 83 G1
Horsington Som. 25 D5
Horsley Derbys. 81 E3
Horsley Glos. 40 A3
Horsley Northumb. 119 G1
Horsley Northumb. 128 A2
Horsley Cross 60 C5
Horsley Woodhouse 81 E3
Horsleycross Street 60 C5
Horsmonden 31 G4
Horspath 42 A2
Horstead 87 D4
Horsted Keynes 17 F1
Horton Bucks. 43 E1
Horton Dorset 13 G2
Horton Lancs. 101 E2
Horton Northants. 56 D2
Horton S.Glos. 39 G4
Horton Som. 11 G1
Horton Staffs. 79 G2
Horton Swan. 36 A4
Horton W. & M. 43 F5
Horton Wilts. 26 B1
Horton Cross 11 G1
Horton-cum-Studley 42 A1
Horton Grange 129 D4
Horton Green 78 B3
Horton Heath 15 D1
Horton in Ribblesdale 108 D5
Horton Inn 13 G2
Horton Kirby 31 E2
Horwich 92 A1
Horwich End 93 E4
Horwood 21 F3
Hose 82 C5
Hoses 106 D3
Hosh 151 D2
Hosta 173 F2
Hoswick 200 D5
Hotham 104 A4
Hothfield 32 B4
Hoton 81 G5
Houbie 203 F3
Hough 79 E2
Hough Green 91 F4
Hough-on-the-Hill 83 E3
Hougham 83 D3
Houghton Cambs. 70 A5
Houghton Cumb. 118 A2
Houghton Devon 8 C3
Houghton Hants. 27 E4
Houghton Pembs. 34 C2
Houghton W.Suss. 16 C2
Houghton Bank 120 B5
Houghton Conquest 57 F3
Houghton-le-Side 120 B5
Houghton le Spring 120 C3
Houghton on the Hill 68 B2
Houghton Regis 57 F5
Houghton St. Giles 86 A2
Houlsyke 111 G2
Hound 15 D2
Hound Green 28 C2
Houndslow 144 D5
Houndwood 145 F3
Hounsdown 14 C1
Hounslow 44 A5
Hounslow Green 45 F1
Househill 180 A4
Housetter 202 C4
Houston 141 F3
Houstry 195 D5
Houstry of Dunn 195 E3
Houton 196 C2
Hove 17 E3
Hoveringham 82 B3
Hoveton 87 E4
Hovingham 111 F5
How 118 B2
How Caple 53 F4
How End 57 F3
How Man 116 C5
Howden 103 G5
Howden-le-Wear 120 A4
Howe Cumb. 107 F4
Howe High. 195 F2
Howe N.Yorks. 110 C4
Howe Norf. 87 D5
Howe Green 45 G2
Howe of Teuchar 182 C5
Howe Street Essex 45 F1
Howe Street Essex 59 E4
Howell 83 G3
Howey 51 G2
Howgate 143 G4
Howgill 101 G2
Howick 137 G5
Howle 79 D5
Howlett End 59 D4
Howley 11 F2
Hownam 136 B5
Hownam Mains 136 B4
Howpasley 135 E5
Howsham N.Lincs. 96 A2
Howsham N.Yorks. 103 G1
Howtel 136 C3
Howton 52 D5
Howwood 141 F3
Hoxa 196 D3
Hoxne 72 C4
Hoy 195 E2
Hoylake 90 D4
Hoyland 94 A2
Hoyland Swaine 93 G2
Hubberholme 109 E5
Hubbert's Bridge 84 A3
Huby N.Yorks. 103 E1
Huby N.Yorks. 102 B3
Hucclecote 40 A1
Hucking 32 A3
Hucknall 81 G3
Huddersfield 93 F1
Huddington 54 B2
Hudscott 21 G3
Hudswell 110 A2
Huggate 104 A2
Hugglescote 67 G1
Hugh Town 4 B1
Hughenden Valley 43 D3
Hughley 65 E3
Hugmore 78 A2
Huish Devon 21 F4
Huish Wilts. 26 C1
Huish Champflower 22 D5
Huish Episcopi 24 B5
Huisinis 184 B2
Hulcott 43 D1
Hulland 80 D3
Hullavington 40 A4
Hullbridge 46 B3
Hulme End 80 C2
Hulme Walfield 79 F1
Hulver Street 73 F3
Humber 53 E2
Humberside International Airport 96 B2
Humberston 96 D2
Humberstone 68 B2
Humbie 144 B3
Humbleton E.Riding 105 E4
Humbleton Northumb. 137 D4
Humby 83 F4
Hume 145 E5
Humehall 145 E5
Humshaugh 128 B4
Huna 195 F1
Huncoat 101 D4
Huncote 68 A3
Hundalee 136 A5
Hunderthwaite 119 F5
Hundleby 84 B1
Hundleton 34 C2
Hundon 59 F3
Hundred Acres 15 E1
Hundred End 100 A5
Hundred House 52 A2
Hungarton 68 B2
Hungerford Hants. 14 A1
Hungerford W.Berks. 27 E1
Hungerford Newtown 41 F5
Hunglader 175 G2
Hunmanby 113 E5
Hunningham 55 F1
Hunny Hill 15 D4
Hunsdon 44 D1
Hunsingore 102 D2
Hunsonby 118 B4
Hunspow 195 E1
Hunstanton 85 E3
Hunstanworth 119 F3
Hunston Suff. 60 A1
Hunston W.Suss. 16 A3
Hunstrete 24 D1
Hunt End 54 C1
Hunt House 112 B3
Huntercombe End 42 B4
Hunters Forstal 33 D2
Hunter's Inn 21 G1
Hunter's Quay 140 C2
Hunterston 140 C4
Huntford 127 E1
Huntingdon 70 A5
Huntingfield 73 E4
Huntingford 25 F4
Huntington Here. 52 B2
Huntington Staffs. 66 B1
Huntington York 103 F2
Huntingtower 151 F2
Huntley 39 G1
Huntly 182 A5
Huntlywood 144 D5
Hunton Hants. 27 F4
Hunton Kent 31 G4
Hunton N.Yorks. 110 A3
Hunton Bridge 43 F2
Hunt's Cross 91 F4
Huntsham 22 D5
Huntshaw Cross 21 F3
Huntspill 24 A3
Huntworth 24 A4
Hunwick 120 A4
Hunworth 86 B2
Hurdsfield 92 D5
Hurley W. & M. 42 D4
Hurley Warks. 67 E3
Hurley Bottom 42 D4
Hurlford 132 C2
Hurliness 196 B4
Hurn 14 A3
Hursley 27 F5
Hurst Gt.Man. 92 D2
Hurst N.Yorks. 109 F2
Hurst W'ham 42 C5
Hurst Green E.Suss. 18 C1
Hurst Green Lancs. 100 C4
Hurst Green Surr. 30 C3
Hurstbourne Priors 27 F3
Hurstbourne Tarrant 27 E2
Hurstpierpoint 17 E2
Hurstway Common 52 B3
Hurstwood 101 E4
Hurtmore 29 E3
Hurworth-on-Tees 110 C1
Hury 119 F5
Husabost 175 F4
Husbands Bosworth 68 B4
Husborne Crawley 57 E4
Husthwaite 111 E5
Huthwaite 81 F2
Huttoft 97 F5
Hutton Cumb. 118 A5
Hutton Essex 45 F3
Hutton Lancs. 100 A5
Hutton N.Som. 24 A2
Hutton Sc.Bord. 145 G4
Hutton Bonville 110 C2
Hutton Buscel 112 C4
Hutton Conyers 110 C5
Hutton Cranswick 104 C2
Hutton End 118 A4
Hutton Henry 120 D4
Hutton-le-Hole 111 G3
Hutton Magna 110 A1
Hutton Roof Cumb. 107 G5
Hutton Roof Cumb. 117 G3
Hutton Rudby 111 D2
Hutton Sessay 111 D5
Hutton Wandesley 103 E2
Huxley 78 C1
Huxter Shet. 200 C2
Huxter Shet. 201 E1
Huyton 91 F3
Hwlffordd (Haverfordwest) 34 C1
Hycemoor 106 B4
Hyde Glos. 40 A2
Hyde Gt.Man. 92 D3
Hyde Heath 43 E2
Hyde Lea 66 B1
Hydestile 29 E3
Hyndford Bridge 142 D5
Hyndlee 135 G5
Hynish 154 A3
Hyssington 64 C3
Hythe Hants. 14 D2
Hythe Kent 33 D5
Hythe End 43 F5
Hythie 183 F4
Hyton 106 B4

I

Ianstown 181 G3
Ibberton 13 D2
Ible 80 D2
Ibsley 14 A2
Ibstock 67 G1
Ibstone 42 C3
Ibthorpe 27 E2
Ibworth 27 G2
Icelton 24 A1
Ickburgh 71 G3
Ickenham 43 F4
Ickford 42 B2
Ickham 33 E3
Ickleford 57 G4
Icklesham 19 D2
Ickleton 58 C3
Icklingham 71 F5
Ickwell Green 57 G3
Icomb 55 E5
Idbury 55 E5
Iddesleigh 21 F5
Ide 10 C3
Ide Hill 31 D3
Ideford 10 B5
Iden 19 E1
Iden Green Kent 31 G5
Iden Green Kent 32 A5
Idlicote 55 E3
Idmiston 26 C4
Idridgehay 81 D3
Idrigil 175 G3
Idstone 41 E4
Idvies 160 D5
Iffley 42 A2
Ifield or Singlewell Kent 45 F5
Ifield W.Suss. 30 B5
Ifieldwood 30 B5
Ifold 29 F4
Iford 17 G3
Ifton Heath 78 A4
Ightfield 78 C4
Ightham 31 E3
Iken 61 F2
Ilam 80 C2
Ilchester 24 C5
Ilderton 137 E4
Ilford 44 D4
Ilfracombe 21 F1
Ilkeston 81 F3
Ilketshall St. Andrew 73 E3
Ilketshall St. Lawrence 73 E3
Ilketshall St. Margaret 73 E3
Ilkley 102 A3
Illey 66 B4
Illington 72 A3
Illingworth 101 G5
Illogan 4 A5
Illston on the Hill 68 C3
Ilmer 42 C2
Ilmington 55 E3
Ilminster 11 G1
Ilsington 10 A5
Ilston 36 B3
Ilton N.Yorks. 110 A5
Ilton Som. 11 G1
Imachar 139 G5
Immeroin 150 A3
Immingham 96 B1
Immingham Dock 96 C1
Impington 58 C1
Ince 91 F5
Ince Blundell 91 E2
Ince-in-Makerfield 91 G2
Inch of Arnhall 161 E2
Inchbare 161 E3
Inchberry 181 F4
Inchbraoch 161 F4
Inchgrundle 160 C2
Inchindown 179 F2
Inchinnan 141 F3
Inchkinloch 193 F4
Inchlaggan 166 A4
Inchlumpie 179 E2
Inchmarlo 170 B5
Inchnabobart 160 B1
Inchnacardoch Hotel 166 C3
Inchnadamph 189 E2
Inchock 161 E5
Inchrory 169 D4
Inchture 152 A2
Inchvuilt 166 B1
Inchyra 151 G3
Indian Queens 4 D4
Inerval 138 B5
Ingatestone 45 F2
Ingbirchworth 93 G2
Ingerthorpe 102 B1
Ingestre 79 G5
Ingham Lincs. 95 G4
Ingham Norf. 87 E3
Ingham Suff. 71 G5
Ingleby Derbys. 81 E5
Ingleby Lincs. 95 F5
Ingleby Arncliffe 110 D2
Ingleby Barwick 110 D1
Ingleby Cross 110 D2
Ingleby Greenhow 111 E2
Inglesbatch 25 D1
Inglesham 41 E3
Ingleton Dur. 120 A5
Ingleton N.Yorks. 108 B5
Inglewhite 100 B3
Ingmire Hall 108 B3
Ingoe 128 C4
Ingoldisthorpe 85 E4
Ingoldmells 85 D1
Ingoldsby 83 F4
Ingon 55 E2
Ingram 137 E5
Ingrave 45 F3
Ingrow 101 G4
Ings 107 F3
Ingst 39 E4
Ingworth 86 C3
Inistrynich 148 D2
Injebreck 98 B3
Inkberrow 54 C2
Inkhorn 171 E1
Inkpen 27 E1
Inkstack 195 E1
Innellan 140 C3
Innergellie 153 D4
Innerleithen 135 E2
Innerleven 152 B4
Innermessan 122 B4
Innerwick E.Loth. 145 E2
Innerwick P. & K. 158 A5
Inninbeg 155 G5
Innsworth 54 A5
Insch 170 B2
Insh 168 A4
Inshore 192 C2
Inskip 100 A4
Instow 21 E2
Intake 94 A4
Intwood 86 C5
Inver Aber. 169 E5
Inver Arg. & B. 156 B5
Inver High. 180 A1
Inver High. 195 D5
Inver P. & K. 159 F5
Inver Mallie 156 D1
Inverailort 155 G1
Inveralligin 177 E4
Inverallochy 183 F3
Inveran 190 A5
Inveraray 148 C4
Inverardoch Mains 150 C4
Inverardran 149 F2
Inverarish 164 B1
Inverarity 160 C5
Inverarnan 149 F3
Inverasdale 177 E1
Inverbain 177 D4
Inverbeg 149 F5
Inverbervie 161 G2
Inverbroom 178 A1
Inverbrough 168 A2
Invercassley 189 G4
Inverchaolain 140 B2
Invercharnan 156 D5
Inverchorachan 149 E3
Inverchoran 178 B4
Invercreran 156 C5
Inverdruie 168 B3
Inverebrie 171 E1
Invereen 168 A1
Invererne 180 C3
Inveresk 144 A2
Inverey 159 F1
Inverfarigaig 167 E2
Invergarry 166 C4
Invergelder 169 E5
Invergeldie 150 C2
Invergloy 157 E1
Invergordon 179 G3
Invergowrie 152 B1
Inverguseran 164 D4
Inverhadden 158 B4
Inverharroch 169 F1
Inverherive 149 F2
Inverhope 193 D2
Inverie 165 D4
Inverinan 148 B3
Inverinate 165 F2
Inverkeilor 161 E5
Inverkeithing 143 F1
Inverkeithny 182 B5
Inverkip 140 D2
Inverkirkaig 188 C3
Inverlael 178 A1
Inverlauren 141 E1
Inverliever 148 A4
Inverliver 148 C1
Inverlochlarig 149 G3
Inverlochy 149 D2
Inverlussa 139 E1
Invermay 151 F3
Invermoriston 166 D3
Invernaver 193 G2
Inverneil 139 G1
Inverness 179 F5
Inverness Airport 179 G4
Invernettie 183 G5
Invernoaden 148 D5
Inveroran Hotel 157 E5
Inverquharity 160 C4
Inverquhomery 183 F5
Inverroy 157 E1
Inversanda 156 B4
Invershiel 165 F3
Inversnaid Hotel 149 F4
Invertrossachs 150 A4
Inverugie 183 G5
Inveruglas 149 F4
Inveruglass 168 A4
Inverurie 170 C2
Invervar 158 B5
Invervegain 140 B2
Invery House 170 B5
Inverythan 182 C5
Inwardleigh 7 F1
Inworth 46 B1
Iochdar 173 F5
Iping 29 D5
Ipplepen 9 E1
Ipsden 42 B4
Ipstones 80 B2
Ipswich 60 C3
Irby 91 D4
Irby in the Marsh 84 C1
Irby upon Humber 96 B2
Irchester 57 E1
Ireby Cumb. 117 F3
Ireby Lancs. 108 B5
Ireland Ork. 196 C2
Ireland Shet. 200 C5
Ireleth 106 D5
Ireshopeburn 119 E4
Irlam 92 B3
Irnham 83 F5
Iron Acton 39 F4
Iron Cross 54 C2
Ironbridge 65 F2
Ironside 183 D4
Ironville 81 F2
Irstead 87 E3
Irthington 118 A1
Irthlingborough 69 E5
Irton 112 D4
Irvine 132 B2
Isauld 194 B2
Isbister Ork. 198 B5
Isbister Ork. 198 A4
Isbister Shet. 201 E1
Isbister Shet. 202 C3
Isfield 17 G2
Isham 69 D5
Ishriff 147 F1
Islay Airport 138 B4
Islay House 138 B3
Isle Abbotts 24 A5
Isle Brewers 24 A5
Isle of Man Airport 98 A5
Isle of Whithorn 115 E3
Isleham 71 E5
Isleornsay (Eilean Iarmain) 164 C3
Islesburgh 200 C1
Isleworth 44 A5
Isley Walton 81 F5
Islibhig 186 A5
Islington 44 C4
Islip Northants. 69 E5
Islip Oxon. 42 A1
Isombridge 65 F1
Istead Rise 31 F2
Itchen 14 D1
Itchen Abbas 27 G4
Itchen Stoke 27 G4
Itchingfield 29 G5
Itchington 39 F4
Itteringham 86 C2
Itton 7 G1
Itton Common 39 D3
Ivegill 118 A3
Ivelet 109 E3
Iver 43 F4
Iver Heath 43 F4
Iveston 120 A2
Ivinghoe 43 E1
Ivinghoe Aston 43 E1
Ivington 53 D2
Ivington Green 53 D2
Ivy Hatch 31 E3
Ivy Todd 71 G2
Ivybridge 8 C2
Ivychurch 19 F1
Iwade 32 B2
Iwerne Courtney (Shroton) 13 E1
Iwerne Minster 13 E1
Ixworth 72 A4
Ixworth Thorpe 72 A4

J

Jack Hill 102 A2
Jackstown 170 C1
Jackton 141 G4
Jacobstow 6 B1
Jacobstowe 21 F5
Jameston 35 D3
Jamestown D. & G. 126 B2
Jamestown High. 179 D4
Jamestown W.Dun. 141 E1
Janefield 179 G4
Janetstown 194 C2
Jarrow 120 C1
Jarvis Brook 18 A1
Jasper's Green 59 F5
Jawcraig 142 C2
Jayes Park 29 G3
Jaywick 47 E1
Jedburgh 136 A4
Jeffreyston 35 D2
Jemimaville 179 G3
Jersey 142 C3
Jersey Airport 8 B5
Jerviswood 142 C5
Jesmond 120 B1
Jevington 18 A3
Jodrell Bank 92 B5
John o' Groats 195 F1
Johnby 118 A4
John's Cross 18 C1
Johnshaven 161 F3
Johnston 34 C1
Johnston Mains 161 F3
Johnstone 141 F3
Johnstone Castle 141 F3
Johnstonebridge 125 E1
Johnstown Carmar. 35 G1
Johnstown Wrex. 78 A3
Joppa Edin. 144 A2
Joppa S.Ayr. 132 C4
Jordans 43 E3
Jordanston 48 C4
Jordanstone 160 A5
Jump 94 A2
Juniper Green 143 F3
Jura House 138 C3
Jurby East 98 B2
Jurby West 98 B2

K

Kaber 108 C1
Kaimes 143 G3
Kames Arg. & B. 140 A2
Kames Arg. & B. 148 A3
Kames E.Ayr. 133 E3
Kea 4 C5
Keadby 95 F1
Keal Cotes 84 B1
Kearsley 92 B2
Kearstwick 108 B4
Kearton 109 F3
Kearvaig 192 B1
Keasden 100 D1
Kebholes 182 B4
Keckwick 91 G4
Keddington 96 D4
Kedington 59 F3
Kedleston 81 E3
Keelby 96 B2
Keele 79 F3
Keeley Green 57 F3
Keeres Green 45 E1
Keeston 34 C1
Keevil 26 A2
Kegworth 81 F5
Kehelland 4 A5
Keig 170 B3
Keighley 101 G3
Keil Arg. & B. 130 B5
Keil High. 156 B4
Keilhill 182 C4
Keillmore 139 E1
Keillor 160 A5
Keillour 151 E2
Keills 138 C3
Keils 138 D3
Keinton Mandeville 24 C4
Keir House 150 C5
Keir Mill 124 C1
Keisby 83 F5
Keisley 118 D5
Keiss 195 F2
Keith 181 G4
Keithick 152 A1
Keithmore 169 F1
Keithock 161 E3
Kelbrook 101 F3
Kelby 83 F3
Keld Cumb. 107 G1
Keld N.Yorks. 109 D2
Keldholme 111 G4
Keldy Castle 111 G3
Kelfield N.Lincs. 95 F2
Kelfield N.Yorks. 103 E4
Kelham 82 C2
Kellan 155 E5
Kellas Angus 152 C1
Kellas Moray 181 D4
Kellaton 9 E4
Kelleth 108 B2

Kelleythorpe 104 C2
Kelling 86 B1
Kellington 103 E5
Kelloe 120 C4
Kelloholm 133 F4
Kelly Cornw. 5 E2
Kelly Devon 7 D2
Kelly Bray 7 D3
Kelmarsh 68 C5
Kelmscott 41 E3
Kelsale 61 E1
Kelsall 78 C1
Kelsay 138 A4
Kelshall 58 B4
Kelsick 117 E1
Kelso 136 B3
Kelstedge 81 E1
Kelstern 96 C3
Kelston 25 D1
Keltneyburn 158 C5
Kelton 125 D3
Kelton Hill or Rhonehouse 124 B5
Kelty 151 G5
Kelvedon 46 B1
Kelvedon Hatch 45 E3
Kelynack 2 A3
Kemback 152 C3
Kemberton 65 G2
Kemble 40 B3
Kemerton 54 B4
Kemeys Commander 38 C2
Kemeys Inferior 38 C3
Kemnay 170 C3
Kemp Town 17 F3
Kempley 53 F5
Kempley Green 53 F5
Kempsey 54 A3
Kempsford 41 D3
Kempshott 28 B3
Kempston 57 F3
Kempston Church End 57 F3
Kempston Hardwick 57 F3
Kempton 64 C4
Kemsing 31 E3
Kemsley 32 B2
Kenardington 32 B5
Kenchester 52 D3
Kencott 41 E2
Kendal 107 G3
Kenderchurch 52 D5
Kenfig 37 E4
Kenfig Hill 37 E4
Kenilworth 67 E5
Kenknock P. & K. 158 A5
Kenknock Stir. 149 G1
Kenley Gt.Lon. 30 C3
Kenley Shrop. 65 E2
Kenmore Arg. & B. 148 C4
Kenmore High. 177 D4
Kenmore P. & K. 158 C5
Kenmore W.Isles 185 E3
Kenn Devon 10 C4
Kenn N.Som. 24 B1
Kennacraig 139 G3
Kennards House 5 G1
Kennavay 185 E4
Kennerleigh 10 B2
Kennerty 170 B5
Kennet 151 E5
Kennethmont 170 A2
Kennett 59 E1
Kennford 10 C4
Kenninghall 72 B3
Kennington Kent 32 C4
Kennington Oxon. 42 A2
Kennoway 152 B4
Kennyhill 71 E5
Kennythorpe 103 G1
Kensaleyre 176 A4
Kensington & Chelsea 44 B5
Kensworth 43 F1
Kensworth Common 43 F1
Kent Street E.Suss. 18 C2
Kent Street Kent 31 F3
Kentallen 156 C4
Kentchurch 52 D5
Kentford 59 F1
Kentisbeare 11 D2
Kentisbury 21 G1
Kentisbury Ford 21 G1
Kentmere 107 F2
Kenton Devon 10 C4
Kenton Suff. 60 C1
Kenton T. & W. 120 B1
Kentra 155 F3
Kents Bank 107 F5
Kent's Green 53 G5
Kent's Oak 27 E5
Kenwick 78 B4
Kenwyn 4 C5
Kenyon 92 A3
Keoldale 192 C2
Keppanach 156 C3
Keppoch Arg. & B. 141 E2
Keppoch High. 165 E2
Keprigan 130 B4
Kepwick 111 D3
Keresley 67 F4
Kerne Bridge 39 E1
Kerridge 92 D5
Kerris 2 B4
Kerry 64 A4
Kerrycroy 140 C3
Kerry's Gate 52 C4
Kerrysdale 177 E2
Kersall 82 C1
Kersey 60 B3
Kershopefoot 126 C3
Kerswell 11 D2
Kerswell Green 54 A3
Kesgrave 60 D3
Kessingland 73 G3
Kessingland Beach 73 G3
Kestle Mill 4 C4
Keston 30 D2
Keswick Cumb. 117 F4
Keswick Norf. 86 D5
Keswick Norf. 87 E2
Ketsby 97 D5
Kettering 69 D5
Ketteringham 86 C5
Kettins 152 A1
Kettlebaston 60 A3
Kettlebridge 152 B4
Kettlebrook 67 E2
Kettleburgh 61 D2
Ketteholm 125 F3
Kettleness 112 B1
Kettleshulme 93 D5
Kettlesing 102 B2
Kettlesing Bottom 102 B2
Kettlestone 86 A2
Kettlethorpe 95 F5
Kettletoft 199 E3
Kettlewell 109 E5
Ketton 69 E2
Kew 44 A5
Kewstoke 24 A1
Kexbrough 94 A2
Kexby Lincs. 95 F4
Kexby York 103 G2
Key Green 79 F1
Keyham 68 B2
Keyhaven 14 C3
Keyingham 105 E5
Keymer 17 F2
Keynsham 24 D1
Key's Toft 84 C2
Keysoe 57 F1
Keysoe Row 57 F1
Keyston 69 F5
Keyworth 82 B4
Kibblesworth 120 B2
Kibworth Beauchamp 68 B3
Kibworth Harcourt 68 B3
Kidbrooke 44 D5
Kiddal Lane End 102 C4
Kiddemore Green 66 A2
Kidderminster 66 A5
Kiddington 55 G5
Kidlington 41 G1
Kidmore End 42 B5
Kidsdale 115 E3
Kidsgrove 79 F2
Kidstones 109 E4
Kidwelly (Cydweli) 36 A2
Kiel Crofts 148 B1
Kielder 127 E2
Kilbarchan 141 F3
Kilbeg 164 C4
Kilberry 139 F3
Kilbirnie 141 E4
Kilblaan 148 D3
Kilbraur 190 D3
Kilbrennan 154 D5
Kilbride Arg. & B. 148 A2
Kilbride Arg. & B. 140 B3
Kilbride High. 164 B2
Kilbride Farm 140 A3
Kilbridemore 148 C5
Kilburn Derbys. 81 E3
Kilburn N.Yorks. 111 E5
Kilby 68 B3
Kilchattan Arg. & B. 140 C4
Kilchenzie 130 B3
Kilcheran 148 A1
Kilchiaran 138 A4
Kilchoan Arg. & B. 147 G3
Kilchoan High. 155 D3
Kilchoman 138 A3
Kilchrenan 148 C2
Kilchrist 130 B4
Kilconquhar 152 C4
Kilcot 53 F5
Kilcoy 179 E4
Kilcreggan 140 D1
Kildale 111 F2
Kildary 179 G2
Kildavie 130 C4
Kildermorie Lodge 179 E2
Kildonan 131 F3
Kildonan Lodge 191 E2
Kildonnan 155 D1
Kildrochet House 122 B5
Kildrummy 169 G3
Kildwick 101 G3
Kilfinan 140 A2
Kilfinnan 166 B5
Kilgetty 35 E2
Kilgwrrwg Common 39 D3
Kilham E.Riding 104 C1
Kilham Northumb. 136 C3
Kilkenneth 154 A2
Kilkenny 40 C1
Kilkerran Arg. & B. 130 C4
Kilkerran S.Ayr. 132 B5
Kilkhampton 20 C4
Killamarsh 94 B4
Killay 36 C3
Killbeg 155 F5
Killean Arg. & B. 139 E5
Killean Arg. & B. 148 C4
Killearn 141 G1
Killellan 130 B4
Killen 179 F4
Killerby 120 A5
Killichonan 158 A4
Killiechanate 157 E1
Killiechronan 155 E5
Killiecrankie 159 E3
Killiehuntly 167 G5
Killiemor 147 D1
Killilan 165 F1
Killimster 195 F3
Killin High. 191 D4
Killin Stir. 150 A1
Killinallan 138 B2
Killinghall 102 B2
Killington 108 B4
Killingworth 129 E4
Killochyett 144 B5
Killocraw 130 B3
Killunaig 147 D2
Killundine 155 E5
Kilmacolm 141 E3
Kilmaha 148 B4
Kilmahog 150 B4
Kilmalieu 156 A4
Kilmaluag 176 A2
Kilmany 152 B2
Kilmarie 164 B3
Kilmarnock 132 C2
Kilmartin 148 A5
Kilmaurs 141 F5
Kilmelford 148 A3
Kilmersdon 25 D2
Kilmeston 27 G5
Kilmichael 130 B3
Kilmichael Glassary 148 A5
Kilmichael of Inverlussa 139 F1
Kilmington Devon 11 F3
Kilmington Wilts. 25 E4
Kilmington Street 25 E4
Kilmorack 179 D5
Kilmore Arg. & B. 148 A2
Kilmore High. 164 C4
Kilmory Arg. & B. 139 F1
Kilmory Arg. & B. 139 F2
Kilmory High. 163 G4
Kilmory High. 155 E3
Kilmote 191 E3
Kilmuir High. 175 F5
Kilmuir High. 179 F5
Kilmuir High. 179 G2
Kilmuir High. 175 G2
Kilmun 140 C1
Kilmux 152 B4
Kiln Green 42 D5
Kiln Pit Hill 119 G2
Kilnave 138 A2
Kilncadzow 142 C5
Kilndown 31 G5
Kilnhurst 94 B3
Kilninian 154 D5
Kilninver 148 A2
Kilnsea 97 E1
Kilnsey 101 F1
Kilnwick 104 C3
Kiloran 146 C5
Kilpatrick 131 E3
Kilpeck 52 D4
Kilphedir 191 E3
Kilpin 103 G5
Kilrenny 153 D4
Kilsby 68 A5
Kilspindie 152 A2
Kilstay 114 B3
Kilsyth 142 B2
Kiltarlity 179 E5
Kilton R. & C. 111 F1
Kilton Som. 23 E3
Kiltyrie 150 B1
Kilvaxter 175 G3
Kilve 23 E3
Kilverstone 71 G4
Kilvington 82 D3
Kilwinning 141 E5
Kimberley Norf. 86 B5
Kimberley Notts. 81 G3
Kimble Wick 42 D2
Kimblesworth 120 B3
Kimbolton Cambs. 57 G1
Kimbolton Here. 53 E1
Kimcote 68 A4
Kimmeridge 13 F5
Kimmerston 137 D3
Kimpton Hants. 27 D3
Kimpton Herts. 44 A1
Kinaldy 152 D3
Kinblethmont 161 E5
Kinbrace 194 A5
Kinbreack 165 G5
Kinbuck 150 C4
Kincaldrum 160 C5
Kincaple 152 C3
Kincardine Fife 142 D1
Kincardine High. 179 F1
Kincardine O'Neil 170 A5
Kinclaven 151 G1
Kincorth 171 E4
Kincraig Aber. 171 E2
Kincraig High. 168 A4
Kincraigie 159 E5
Kindallachan 159 E5
Kindrogan Field Centre 159 F3
Kinellar 170 D3
Kineton Glos. 54 C5
Kineton Warks. 55 F2
Kineton Green 66 D4
Kinfauns 151 G2
King Sterndale 93 E5
Kingarth 140 B4
Kingcoed 38 D2
Kingerby 96 A3
Kingham 55 E5
Kingholm Quay 125 D3
Kinghorn 143 G1
Kinglassie 152 A5
Kingoodie 152 B2
King's Bromley 66 D1
Kings Caple 53 E5
King's Cliffe 69 F3
King's Coughton 54 C2
King's Green 53 G4
King's Heath 66 C4
King's Hill 66 B3
Kings Langley 43 F2
King's Lynn 85 E5
Kings Meaburn 118 C5
King's Mills 9 E5
Kings Muir 135 D2
King's Newton 81 E5
King's Norton Leics. 68 B2
King's Norton W.Mid. 66 C5
King's Nympton 21 G4
King's Pyon 52 D2
Kings Ripton 70 A5
King's Somborne 27 E4
King's Stag 12 D1
King's Stanley 40 A2
King's Sutton 55 G4
King's Walden 57 G5
Kings Worthy 27 F4
Kingsand 8 A2
Kingsbarns 153 D3
Kingsbridge Devon 8 D3
Kingsbridge Som. 22 C4
Kingsburgh 175 G4
Kingsbury Gt.Lon. 44 A4
Kingsbury Warks. 67 E3
Kingsbury Episcopi 24 B5
Kingscavil 143 E2
Kingsclere 27 G2
Kingscote 40 A3
Kingscott 21 F4
Kingscross 131 F3
Kingsdale 152 B4
Kingsdon 24 C5
Kingsdown 33 F4
Kingseat 151 G5
Kingsey 42 C2
Kingsfold Pembs. 34 C3
Kingsfold W.Suss. 29 G4
Kingsford Aber. 182 C5
Kingsford Aber. 170 A3
Kingsford Aberdeen 170 D4
Kingsford E.Ayr. 141 F5
Kingsford Worcs. 66 A4
Kingsforth 96 A1
Kingsgate 33 F1
Kingsheanton 21 F2
Kingshouse 150 A2
Kingshouse Hotel 157 E4
Kingskerswell 9 E1
Kingskettle 152 B4
Kingsland Here. 52 D1
Kingsland I.o.A. 88 A4
Kingsley Ches. 91 G5
Kingsley Hants. 28 C4
Kingsley Staffs. 80 B3
Kingsley Green 29 D4
Kingsmuir 160 C5
Kingsnorth 32 C5
Kingsnorth Power Station 32 A1
Kingstanding 66 C3
Kingsteignton 10 B5
Kingsteps 180 B4
Kingsthorne 53 E4
Kingsthorpe 56 C1
Kingston Cambs. 58 B2
Kingston Devon 8 C3
Kingston Dorset 12 D2
Kingston Dorset 13 F5
Kingston E.Loth. 144 C1
Kingston Hants. 14 A2
Kingston I.o.W. 15 D4
Kingston Kent 33 D3
Kingston Moray 181 F3
Kingston W.Suss. 16 C3
Kingston Bagpuize 41 G3
Kingston Blount 42 C3
Kingston by Sea 17 E3
Kingston Deverill 25 F4
Kingston Lisle 41 F4
Kingston near Lewes 17 F3
Kingston on Soar 81 G5
Kingston Russell 12 B3
Kingston St. Mary 23 F5
Kingston Seymour 24 A1
Kingston Upon Hull 104 D5
Kingston upon Thames 44 A5
Kingston Warren 41 F4
Kingstone Here. 52 D4
Kingstone Som. 11 G1
Kingstone Staffs. 80 B5
Kingstown 117 G1
Kingswear 9 E2
Kingswell 141 G5
Kingswells 171 D4
Kingswinford 66 A4
Kingswood Bucks. 42 B1
Kingswood Glos. 39 G3
Kingswood Here. 52 B2
Kingswood Kent 32 A3
Kingswood Powys 64 B2
Kingswood S.Glos. 39 F5
Kingswood Surr. 30 B3
Kingswood Warks. 67 D5
Kingthorpe 96 B5
Kington Here. 52 B2
Kington Worcs. 54 B2
Kington Langley 40 B5
Kington Magna 25 E5
Kington St. Michael 40 A5
Kingussie 167 G4
Kingweston 24 C4
Kinharrachie 171 E1
Kinharvie 124 D4
Kinkell 142 A2
Kinkell Bridge 151 E3
Kinknockie 183 F5
Kinlet 65 G4
Kinloch Fife 152 A3
Kinloch High. 192 C5
Kinloch High. 155 F4
Kinloch High. 164 A5
Kinloch High. 179 E2
Kinloch P. & K. 160 A5
Kinloch P. & K. 159 G5
Kinloch Hourn 165 F4
Kinloch Laggan 158 A1
Kinloch Rannoch 158 B4
Kinlochan 156 A3
Kinlochard 149 G4
Kinlocharkaig 165 F5
Kinlochbeoraid 156 A1
Kinlochbervie 192 B3
Kinlocheil 156 B2
Kinlochetive 156 D5
Kinlochewe 177 G3
Kinlochlaich 156 B5
Kinlochleven 157 D3
Kinlochmoidart 155 G2
Kinlochmorar 165 E5
Kinlochmore 157 D3
Kinlochspelve 147 F2
Kinloss 180 C3
Kinmel Bay (Bae Cinmel) 90 A4
Kinmuck 170 D3
Kinnadie 183 E5
Kinnaird 152 A2
Kinneff 161 G2
Kinnelhead 134 B5
Kinnell Angus 161 E4
Kinnell Stir. 150 A1
Kinnerley 78 A5
Kinnersley Here. 52 C3
Kinnersley Worcs. 54 A3
Kinnerton 52 B1
Kinnesswood 151 G4
Kinnettles 160 C5
Kinninvie 119 G5
Kinnordy 160 B4
Kinoulton 82 B4
Kinrara 168 A4
Kinross 151 G4
Kinrossie 151 G1
Kinsbourne Green 44 A1
Kinsham 52 C1
Kinsley 94 B1
Kinson 13 G3
Kintarvie 185 E2
Kintbury 27 E1
Kintessack 180 B3
Kintillo 151 G3
Kintocher 170 A4
Kinton Here. 64 D5
Kinton Shrop. 64 C1
Kintore 170 C3
Kintour 138 C4
Kintra Arg. & B. 138 B5
Kintra Arg. & B. 146 C2
Kintradwell 191 E4
Kintraw 148 A4
Kinuachdrachd 147 G5
Kinveachy 168 B3
Kinver 66 A4
Kiplaw Croft 171 F1
Kiplin 110 B3
Kiplingcotes 104 B3
Kipp 150 A3
Kippax 102 D4
Kippen P. & K. 151 F3
Kippen Stir. 150 B5
Kippenross House 150 C4
Kippford or Scaur 124 C5
Kipping's Cross 31 F4
Kirbister Ork. 196 C2
Kirbister Ork. 199 E4
Kirbuster 198 A4
Kirby Bedon 87 D5
Kirby Cane 73 E2
Kirby Corner 67 E5
Kirby Cross 47 F1
Kirby Grindalythe 104 B1
Kirby Hill N.Yorks. 110 A2
Kirby Hill N.Yorks. 102 C1
Kirby Knowle 111 D4
Kirby le Soken 60 D5
Kirby Misperton 111 G5
Kirby Muxloe 68 A2
Kirby Row 73 E2
Kirby Sigston 110 D3
Kirby Underdale 104 A2
Kirby Wiske 110 C4
Kirdford 29 F5
Kirk 195 E3
Kirk Bramwith 94 D1
Kirk Deighton 102 C2
Kirk Ella 104 C5
Kirk Hallam 81 F3
Kirk Hammerton 103 D2
Kirk Ireton 81 D2
Kirk Langley 81 D4
Kirk Merrington 120 B4
Kirk Michael 98 B2
Kirk of Shotts 142 C3
Kirk Sandall 94 D2
Kirk Smeaton 94 C1
Kirk Yetholm 136 C4
Kirkabister 201 D4
Kirkandrews 115 G2
Kirkandrews-upon-Eden 117 G1
Kirkbampton 117 G1
Kirkbean 125 D5
Kirkbride 117 F1
Kirkbridge 110 B3
Kirkbuddo 160 D5
Kirkburn E.Riding 104 B2
Kirkburn Sc.Bord. 135 D2
Kirkburton 93 F1
Kirkby Lincs. 96 A3
Kirkby Mersey. 91 F3
Kirkby N.Yorks. 111 E2
Kirkby Bellars 68 C1
Kirkby Fleetham 110 B3
Kirkby Green 83 F2
Kirkby in Ashfield 81 F2
Kirkby la Thorpe 83 G3
Kirkby Lonsdale 108 B5
Kirkby Malham 101 E1
Kirkby Mallory 67 G2
Kirkby Malzeard 110 B5
Kirkby Mills 111 G4
Kirkby on Bain 84 A1
Kirkby Overblow 102 C3
Kirkby Stephen 108 C2
Kirkby Thore 118 C5
Kirkby Underwood 83 F5
Kirkby Wharfe 103 E3
Kirkbymoorside 111 F4
Kirkcaldy 152 A5
Kirkcambeck 118 B1
Kirkcolm 122 B4
Kirkconnel 133 F4
Kirkconnell 125 D4
Kirkcowan 123 E4
Kirkcudbright 124 A5
Kirkdale House 123 G5
Kirkdean 143 F5
Kirkfieldbank 142 C5
Kirkgunzeon 124 C4
Kirkham Lancs. 100 A4
Kirkham N.Yorks. 103 G1
Kirkhamgate 102 B5
Kirkharle 128 C3
Kirkhaugh 118 C3
Kirkheaton Northumb. 128 C4
Kirkheaton W.Yorks. 93 F1
Kirkhill Angus 161 E3
Kirkhill High. 179 E5
Kirkhill Moray 181 F4
Kirkhope 135 E3
Kirkibost High. 164 B3
Kirkibost W.Isles 186 C4
Kirkinch 160 B5
Kirkinner 123 F5
Kirkintilloch 142 A2
Kirkland Cumb. 118 C4
Kirkland Cumb. 117 D5
Kirkland D. & G. 124 C1
Kirkland D. & G. 133 F4
Kirkland D. & G. 125 E2
Kirkland of Longcastle 115 D2
Kirkleatham 121 E5
Kirklevington 110 D1
Kirkley 73 G2
Kirklington N.Yorks. 110 C4
Kirklington Notts. 82 B2
Kirklinton 118 A1
Kirkliston 143 F2
Kirkmaiden 114 B3
Kirkmichael P. & K. 159 F3
Kirkmichael S.Ayr. 132 B5
Kirkmuirhill 142 B5
Kirknewton Northumb. 136 D4
Kirknewton W.Loth. 143 F3
Kirkney 170 A1
Kirkoswald Cumb. 118 B3
Kirkoswald S.Ayr. 132 A5
Kirkpatrick Durham 124 B3
Kirkpatrick-Fleming 126 A4
Kirksanton 106 C4
Kirkstall 102 B4
Kirkstead 83 G1
Kirkstile Aber. 170 A1
Kirkstile D. & G. 126 B2
Kirkton Aber. 170 B2
Kirkton Aber. 182 B4
Kirkton Aber. 170 B3
Kirkton Angus 160 C5
Kirkton Arg. & B. 147 G4
Kirkton D. & G. 125 D2
Kirkton Fife 152 B2
Kirkton High. 167 F1
Kirkton High. 190 C5
Kirkton High. 179 G4
Kirkton High. 194 A2
Kirkton High. 165 E2
Kirkton P. & K. 151 E3
Kirkton Sc.Bord. 135 G4
Kirkton Manor 134 D2
Kirkton of Airlie 160 B4
Kirkton of Auchterhouse 152 B1
Kirkton of Barevan 180 A5
Kirkton of Bourtie 170 D2
Kirkton of Collace 151 G1
Kirkton of Craig 161 F4
Kirkton of Culsalmond 170 B1
Kirkton of Durris 170 C5
Kirkton of Glenbuchat 169 F3
Kirkton of Glenisla 160 A3
Kirkton of Kingoldrum 160 B4
Kirkton of Lethendy 159 G5
Kirkton of Logie Buchan 171 E2
Kirkton of Maryculter 171 D5
Kirkton of Menmuir 160 D3
Kirkton of Monikie 152 D1
Kirkton of Rayne 170 B1
Kirkton of Skene 170 D4
Kirkton of Strathmartine 152 B1
Kirkton of Tealing 152 C1
Kirktonhill 161 E3
Kirktown 183 F4
Kirktown of Alvah 182 B3
Kirktown of Auchterless 182 C5
Kirktown of Deskford 182 A3
Kirktown of Fetteresso 161 G1
Kirktown of Slains 171 F2
Kirkwall 198 C5
Kirkwall Airport 197 D2
Kirkwhelpington 128 B3
Kirmington 96 B1
Kirmond le Mire 96 B3
Kirn 140 C2
Kirriemuir 160 B4
Kirstead Green 73 D2
Kirtlebridge 126 A4
Kirtling 59 E2
Kirtling Green 59 E2
Kirtlington 41 G1
Kirtomy 193 G2
Kirton Lincs. 84 B4
Kirton Notts. 82 B1
Kirton Suff. 61 D4
Kirton End 84 A3
Kirton Holme 84 A3
Kirton in Lindsey 95 G3
Kiscadale 131 F3
Kislingbury 56 B2
Kismeldon Bridge 21 D4
Kites Hardwick 55 G1
Kitley 8 B2
Kittisford 23 D5
Kitwood 28 B4
Kiveton Park 94 B4
Klibreck 193 E5
Knabbygates 182 A4
Knaith 95 F4
Knap Corner 25 F5
Knaphill 29 E2
Knapp P. & K. 152 A1
Knapp Som. 23 F5
Knapton Norf. 87 E2
Knapton York 103 E2
Knapton Green 52 D2
Knapwell 58 B1
Knaresborough 102 C2
Knarsdale 118 C2
Knaven 183 D5
Knayton 110 D4
Knebworth 44 B1
Knedlington 103 G5
Kneesall 82 C1
Kneesworth 58 B3
Kneeton 82 C3
Knelston 36 A4
Knettishall 72 A4
Knightacott 21 G2
Knightcote 55 G2
Knighton Devon 8 B3
Knighton Leic. 68 B2
Knighton Powys 64 B5
Knighton Som. 23 E3
Knighton Staffs. 79 E5
Knighton Staffs. 79 E4
Knighton Wilts. 41 E5
Knightwick 53 G2
Knill 52 B1
Knipoch 148 A2
Knipton 82 D4
Knitsley 120 A3
Kniveton 80 D2
Knock Arg. & B. 147 E1
Knock Cumb. 118 C5
Knock Moray 182 A4
Knock of Auchnahannet 168 C1
Knockalava 148 B5
Knockally 191 G2
Knockaloe Moar 98 A3
Knockan 189 E3
Knockandhu 169 E2
Knockando 181 D5
Knockbain 179 F4
Knockban 178 B3
Knockbreck 179 G1
Knockbrex 115 F2
Knockdamph 189 E5
Knockdee 195 D2
Knockdow 140 C2
Knockdown 40 A4
Knockenkelly 131 F3
Knockentiber 132 C2
Knockfin 166 B2
Knockgray 123 G1
Knockholt 31 D3
Knockholt Pound 31 D3
Knockin 78 A5
Knocklearn 124 B3
Knocknaha 130 B4
Knocknain 122 A4
Knocknalling 123 G2
Knockrome 139 D2
Knocksharry 98 A3
Knockville 123 E3
Knockvologan 146 C3
Knodishall 61 F1
Knolls Green 92 C5
Knolton 78 A4
Knook 26 A3
Knossington 68 D2
Knott End-on-Sea 99 G3
Knotting 57 F1
Knotting Green 57 F1
Knottingley 103 E5
Knotty Ash 91 F3
Knotty Green 43 E3
Knowbury 65 E5
Knowe 123 E3
Knowes of Elrick 182 B4
Knowesgate 128 B3
Knoweside 132 A4
Knowetownhead 135 G4
Knowhead 183 E4
Knowl Green 59 F3
Knowl Hill 42 D5
Knowl Wall 79 F4
Knowle Bristol 39 F5
Knowle Devon 10 A2
Knowle Devon 21 E2
Knowle Devon 11 D4
Knowle Shrop. 65 E5
Knowle W.Mid. 67 D5
Knowle Green 100 C4
Knowle Hall 24 A3
Knowlton Dorset 13 G1
Knowlton Kent 33 E3
Knowsley 91 F3
Knowstone 22 B5
Knucklas 64 B5
Knutsford 92 B5
Knypersley 79 F2
Kuggar 3 E5
Kyle of Lochalsh 165 D2
Kyleakin 165 D2
Kylerhea 165 D2
Kyles Scalpay (Caolas Scalpaigh) 185 E4
Kylesbeg 155 F2
Kylesknoydart 165 E5
Kylesmorar 165 E5
Kylestrome 192 B5
Kyloag 190 B5
Kynnersley 65 F1
Kyre Park 53 F1

L

L'Islet 9 F4
Labost 187 D3
Lacasaigh 187 E5
Lacasdal (Laxdale) 187 F4
Laceby 96 C2
Lacey Green 42 D2
Lach Dennis 92 B5
Lackford 71 F5
Lacock 26 A1
Ladbroke 55 G2
Laddingford 31 F4
Lade Bank 84 B2
Ladock 4 C4
Lady Hall 106 C4
Ladybank 152 A3
Ladycross 6 D2
Ladyfield 148 C3
Ladykirk 145 F5
Lady's Green 59 F2
Ladysford 183 E3
Laga 155 F3
Lagalochan 148 A3
Lagavulin 138 C5

Lagg Arg. & B. 139 D2
Lagg N.Ayr. 131 E3
Lagg S.Ayr. 132 A4
Laggan Arg. & B. 138 A4
Laggan High. 166 B5
Laggan High. 167 F5
Laggan Moray 169 F1
Laggan Stir. 150 A3
Lagganulva 155 D5
Lagganvoulin 169 D3
Laglingarten 148 D4
Lagnalean 179 F5
Lagrae 133 F4
Laguna 151 G1
Laid 192 D3
Laide 188 A5
Laig 155 D1
Laight 133 E4
Lainchoil 168 C3
Laindon 45 F4
Lair 159 G3
Lairg 190 A4
Lairg Lodge 190 A4
Lairigmor 156 D3
Laithers 182 B5
Laithes 118 A4
Lake 26 C4
Lakenham 86 D5
Lakenheath 71 F4
Lakesend 70 D3
Lakeside 107 E4
Laleham 29 F1
Laleston 37 E5
Lamancha 143 G4
Lamarsh 59 G4
Lamas 86 D3
Lamb Corner 60 B4
Lamberhurst 31 F5
Lamberhurst Quarter 31 F5
Lamberton 145 G4
Lambeth 44 B5
Lambfell Moar 98 A3
Lambley Northumb. 118 C2
Lambley Notts. 82 B3
Lambourn 41 F5
Lambourn Woodlands 41 F5
Lambourne End 45 D3
Lambs Green 30 B5
Lambston 34 C1
Lamellion 5 G3
Lamerton 7 E3
Lamesley 120 B2
Lamington High. 179 G2
Lamington S.Lan. 134 A2
Lamlash 131 F2
Lamloch 123 G1
Lamonby 118 A4
Lamorran 4 C5
Lampert 127 E4
Lampeter 50 B3
Lampeter Velfrey 35 E1
Lamphey 34 D2
Lamplugh 117 D4
Lamport 68 C5
Lamyatt 25 D4
Lana 6 D1
Lanark 142 C5
Lancaster 100 A1
Lanchester 120 A3
Lancing 17 D3
Landbeach 58 C1
Landcross 21 E3
Landerberry 170 C4
Landewednack 3 E5
Landford 14 B1
Landimore 36 A3
Landkey 21 F2
Landore 36 C3
Landrake 7 D4
Landscove 9 D1
Landshipping 34 D1
Landulph 8 A1
Landwade 59 E1
Landywood 66 B2
Lane-end 5 E3
Lane End Bucks. 42 D3
Lane End Cumb. 106 C3
Lane End Derbys. 81 F1
Lane End Dorset 13 E3
Lane End Kent 45 E5
Lane Green 66 A2
Lane Head Dur. 110 A1
Lane Head Gt.Man. 92 A3
Lane Head W.Yorks. 93 F2
Laneast 5 G1
Laneham 95 F5
Lanehead 127 F3
Laneshawbridge 101 F3
Langais 173 G3
Langamull 154 C4
Langar 82 C4
Langbank 141 E2
Langbar 101 G2
Langcliffe 101 E1
Langdale End 112 C3
Langdon 6 C1
Langdon Beck 119 E4
Langdon Hills 45 F4
Langdon House 10 C5
Langdyke 152 B4
Langenhoe 46 D1
Langford Beds. 57 G3
Langford Devon 10 D2
Langford Essex 46 B2
Langford Notts. 82 D2
Langford Oxon. 41 E2
Langford Budville 23 E5
Langham Essex 60 B4
Langham Norf. 86 B1
Langham Rut. 68 D1
Langham Suff. 60 A1
Langham Moor 60 B4
Langho 100 C4
Langholm 126 B3
Langlands 124 A5
Langlee 136 A5
Langleeford 136 D4
Langley Ches. 92 D5
Langley Derbys. 81 F3
Langley Essex 58 C4
Langley Hants. 14 D2
Langley Herts. 58 A5
Langley Kent 32 A3
Langley Slo. 43 F5
Langley W.Suss. 28 D5
Langley Warks. 55 D1
Langley Burrell 40 B5
Langley Green 81 D4
Langley Heath 32 A3
Langley Marsh 23 D5
Langley Mill 81 F3
Langley Moor 120 B3
Langley Park 120 B3
Langley Street 87 E5
Langney 18 B3
Langold 94 C4
Langore 6 D2
Langport 24 B5
Langrick 84 A3
Langridge B. & N.E.Som. 25 E1
Langridge Devon 21 F3
Langridgeford 21 F3
Langrigg 117 E2
Langrish 28 C5
Langriville 84 A3
Langsett 93 G2
Langshaw 135 G2
Langshawburn 135 D5
Langside 150 C3
Langskaill 198 C2
Langstone 15 G2
Langthorne 110 B3
Langthorpe 102 C1
Langthwaite 109 F2
Langtoft E.Riding 104 C1
Langtoft Lincs. 69 G1
Langton Dur. 110 A1
Langton Lincs. 97 D5
Langton Lincs. 84 A1
Langton N.Yorks. 103 G1
Langton by Wragby 96 B5
Langton Green 31 E5
Langton Herring 12 C4
Langton Long Blandford 13 F2
Langton Matravers 13 G5
Langtree 21 E4
Langwathby 118 B4
Langwell 189 G4
Langwell House 191 G2
Langworth 96 A5
Lanivet 5 E3
Lanlivery 5 E4
Lanner 4 B5
Lanreath 5 F4
Lansallos 5 F4
Lansdown 25 E1
Lanteglos 5 E1
Lanton Northumb. 136 D3
Lanton Sc.Bord. 136 A4
Lapford 10 A2
Laphroaig 138 B5
Lapley 66 A1
Lapworth 67 D5
Larach na Gaibhre 139 F3
Larachbeg 155 F5
Larbert 142 C1
Larden Green 78 C2
Larg 123 E3
Largie 170 B1
Largiemore 140 A1
Largoward 152 C4
Largs 140 D4
Largue 182 B5
Largybaan 130 B4
Largybeg 131 F3
Largymore 131 F3
Lark Hall 59 D2
Larkhall 142 B4
Larkhill 26 C3
Larling 72 A3
Larriston 126 D2
Lartington 109 F1
Lary 169 F4
Lasborough 40 A3
Lasham 28 B3
Lassington 53 G5
Lassintullich 158 C4
Lassodie 151 G5
Lasswade 144 A3
Lastingham 111 G3
Latchford 92 A4
Latchingdon 46 B2
Latchley 7 E3
Lately Common 92 A3
Lathallan Mill 152 C4
Lathbury 57 D3
Latheron 195 D5
Latheronwheel 195 D5
Lathockar 152 C3
Lathones 152 C4
Lathrisk 152 A4
Latimer 43 F3
Latteridge 39 F4
Lattiford 25 D5
Latton 40 C3
Lauchentyre 123 G5
Lauchintilly 170 C3
Lauder 144 C5
Laugharne 35 G1
Laughterton 95 F5
Laughton E.Suss. 18 A2
Laughton Leics. 68 B4
Laughton Lincs. 83 F4
Laughton Lincs. 95 F3
Laughton en le Morthen 94 C4
Launcells 20 C5
Launcells Cross 20 C5
Launceston 6 D2
Launde Abbey 68 D2
Launton 56 B5
Laurencekirk 161 F2
Laurieston D. & G. 124 A4
Laurieston Falk. 142 D2
Lavendon 57 E2
Lavenham 60 A3
Laverhay 125 F1
Lavernock 23 E1
Laversdale 118 A1
Laverstock 26 C4
Laverstoke 27 F3
Laverton Glos. 54 C4
Laverton N.Yorks. 110 B5
Laverton Som. 25 E2
Lavister 78 A2
Law 142 C4
Lawers P. & K. 150 C2
Lawers P. & K. 150 B1
Lawford 60 B4
Lawhitton 7 D2
Lawkland 101 D1
Lawley 65 F2
Lawnhead 79 F5
Lawrenny 34 D2
Laws 152 C1
Lawshall 59 G2
Lawton 52 D2
Laxdale (Lacasdal) 187 F4
Laxey 98 C3
Laxfield 73 D4
Laxfirth Shet. 201 D2
Laxfirth Shet. 200 D3
Laxford Bridge 192 B4
Laxo 200 D1
Laxton E.Riding 103 G5
Laxton Northants. 69 E3
Laxton Notts. 82 C1
Laycock 101 G3
Layer Breton 46 C1
Layer de la Haye 46 C1
Layer Marney 46 C1
Layham 60 B3
Laytham 103 G4
Lazenby 121 E5
Lazonby 118 B4
Lea Derbys. 81 E2
Lea Here. 53 F5
Lea Lincs. 95 F4
Lea Shrop. 64 C4
Lea Shrop. 64 D2
Lea Wilts. 40 B4
Lea Marston 67 E3
Lea Town 100 A4
Lea Yeat 108 C4
Leac a' Li 184 D4
Leachd 148 C5
Leachkin 179 F5
Leadburn 143 G4
Leaden Roding 45 E1
Leadenham 83 E2
Leadgate Cumb. 118 D3
Leadgate Dur. 120 A2
Leadgate T. & W. 120 A2
Leadhills 133 G4
Leafield 41 F1
Leagrave 57 F5
Leake Common Side 84 B2
Leake Hurn's End 84 C3
Lealands 18 A2
Lealholm 111 G2
Lealt Arg. & B. 147 F5
Lealt High. 176 B3
Leamington Hastings 55 G1
Leanach Arg. & B. 148 C5
Leanach High. 179 G5
Leanaig 179 E4
Leanoch 181 D4
Leargybreck 138 D2
Leasgill 107 F4
Leasingham 83 F3
Leask 171 F1
Leatherhead 29 G2
Leathley 102 B3
Leaton 65 D1
Leaveland 32 C3
Leavenheath 60 A4
Leavening 103 G1
Leaves Green 30 D2
Lebberston 113 D4
Lechlade 41 E3
Leck 108 B5
Leckford 27 E4
Leckfurin 193 G3
Leckgruinart 138 A3
Leckhampstead Bucks. 56 C4
Leckhampstead W.Berks. 41 G5
Leckhampton 40 B1
Leckie High. 177 G3
Leckie Stir. 150 B5
Leckmelm 189 D5
Leckroy 166 C5
Leckuary 148 A5
Leckwith 38 A5
Leconfield 104 C3
Ledaig 148 B1
Ledard 149 G4
Ledbeg 189 E3
Ledburn 57 D5
Ledbury 53 G4
Ledcharrie 150 A2
Ledgemoor 52 D2
Ledicot 52 D1
Ledmore Arg. & B. 155 E5
Ledmore High. 189 E3
Lednagullin 193 G2
Ledsham Ches. 91 E5
Ledsham W.Yorks. 103 D5
Ledston 102 D5
Ledwell 55 G5
Lee Arg. & B. 146 D2
Lee Devon 21 E1
Lee Hants. 14 C1
Lee Lancs. 100 B2
Lee Shrop. 78 B4
Lee Brockhurst 78 C5
Lee Clump 43 E2
Lee Mill Bridge 8 B2
Lee Moor 8 B1
Lee-on-the-Solent 15 E2
Leebotten 200 D5
Leebotwood 65 D3
Leece 99 F1
Leeds Kent 32 A3
Leeds W.Yorks. 102 B4
Leeds Bradford International Airport 102 B3
Leedstown 2 D3
Leegomery 65 F1
Leek 79 G2
Leek Wootton 55 E1
Leeming N.Yorks. 110 B4
Leeming W.Yorks. 101 G4
Leeming Bar 110 B3
Lees Derbys. 81 D4
Lees Gt.Man. 93 D2
Leeswood 77 F2
Legars 145 E5
Legbourne 97 D4
Legerwood 144 C5
Legsby 96 B4
Leicester 68 A2
Leideag 172 B4
Leigh Dorset 12 C2
Leigh Glos. 54 A5
Leigh Gt.Man. 92 A2
Leigh Kent 31 E4
Leigh Shrop. 64 C2
Leigh Surr. 30 B4
Leigh Wilts. 40 C3
Leigh Worcs. 53 G2
Leigh Beck 46 B4
Leigh Common 25 E5
Leigh Delamere 40 A5
Leigh Green 32 B5
Leigh-on-Sea 46 B4
Leigh Sinton 53 G2
Leigh upon Mendip 25 D3
Leigh Woods 39 E5
Leighterton 40 A3
Leighton N.Yorks. 110 A5
Leighton Powys 64 B2
Leighton Shrop. 65 F2
Leighton Som. 25 E3
Leighton Bromswold 69 G5
Leighton Buzzard 57 E5
Leinthall Earls 52 D1
Leinthall Starkes 52 D1
Leintwardine 64 D5
Leire 68 A4
Leirinmore 192 D2
Leiston 61 F1
Leitfie 160 A5
Leith 143 G2
Leitholm 145 E5
Lelant 2 C3
Lelley 105 E4
Lem Hill 65 G5
Lemington 120 A1
Lemnas 182 D3
Lempitlaw 136 B3
Lemsford 44 B1
Lenchwick 54 C3
Lendalfoot 122 C2
Lendrick Lodge 150 A4
Lenham 32 A3
Lenham Heath 32 B4
Lenie 167 E2
Lenimore 139 G5
Lennel 145 F5
Lennox Plunton 124 A5
Lennoxtown 142 A2
Lenton 83 F4
Lenwade 86 C4
Lenzie 142 A2
Leoch 152 B1
Leochel-Cushnie 170 A3
Leominster 53 D2
Leonard Stanley 40 A2
Leorin 138 B5
Lepe 15 D3
Lephinchapel 148 B5
Lephinmore 148 B5
Leppington 103 G1
Lepton 93 G1
Lerags 148 A2
Lerryn 5 F4
Lerwick 201 D3
Lesbury 137 G5
Leschangie 170 C3
Lescrow 5 F4
Leslie Aber. 170 A2
Leslie Fife 152 A4
Lesmahagow 133 G2
Lesnewth 6 B1
Lessendrum 182 A5
Lessingham 87 E3
Lessonhall 117 F1
Leswalt 122 B4
Letchmore Heath 44 A3
Letchworth 58 A4
Letcombe Bassett 41 F4
Letcombe Regis 41 F4
Leth Meadhanach 172 C2
Letham Angus 160 D5
Letham Fife 152 B3
Lethanhill 132 C4
Lethenty 182 D5
Letheringham 61 D2
Letheringsett 86 B2
Lettaford 10 A4
Letter Finlay 166 B5
Letterewe 177 F2
Letterfearn 165 E2
Lettermorar 155 G1
Lettermore Arg. & B. 155 E5
Lettermore High. 193 F4
Letters 178 A1
Lettershaws 134 G3
Letterston 48 C5
Lettoch High. 168 C3
Lettoch High. 168 C1
Letton Here. 64 C5
Letton Here. 52 C3
Letty Green 44 B1
Letwell 94 C4
Leuchars 152 C2
Leumrabhagh 185 F2
Levedale 66 A1
Leven E.Riding 104 D3
Leven Fife 152 B4
Levencorroch 131 F3
Levenhall 144 A2
Levens 107 F4
Levenshulme 92 C3
Levenwick 200 D5
Leverburgh (An T-ób) 184 C5
Leverington 70 C1
Leverstock Green 43 F2
Leverton 84 C3
Leverton Outgate 84 C3
Levington 60 D4
Levisham 112 B3
Levishie 166 D3
Lew 41 F2
Lewannick 5 G1
Lewdown 7 E2
Lewes 17 G2
Leweston 48 C5
Lewisham 44 C5
Lewiston 167 E2
Lewknor 42 C3
Leworthy 21 G2
Lewtrenchard 7 E2
Ley Aber. 170 A3
Ley Cornw. 5 F3
Ley Green 57 G5
Leybourne 31 F3
Leyburn 110 A3
Leycett 79 E3
Leyland 100 B5
Leylodge 170 C3
Leys Aber. 183 F4
Leys Aber. 169 G4
Leys P. & K. 152 A1
Leys of Cossans 160 B5
Leysdown-on-Sea 32 C1
Leysmill 161 E5
Leysters 53 E1
Leyton 44 C4
Lezant 6 D3
Lhanbryde 181 E3
Liatrie 166 B1
Libanus 51 F5
Libberton 143 D5
Liberton 143 G3
Liceasto 184 D4
Lichfield 66 D2
Lickey 66 B5
Lickey End 66 B5
Lickfold 29 E5
Liddel 197 D4
Liddesdale 155 G4
Liddington 41 E4
Lidgate Derbys. 94 A5
Lidgate Suff. 59 F2
Lidlington 57 E4
Lidsing 31 G2
Lidstone 55 F5
Lienassie 165 F2
Lieurary 194 C2
Liff 152 B1
Lifton 7 D2
Liftondown 7 D2
Lighthorne 55 F2
Lightwater 29 E1
Lightwood 79 G3
Lightwood Green Ches. 78 D3
Lightwood Green Wrex. 78 A3
Lilbourne 68 A5
Lilburn Tower 137 E4
Lilleshall 65 G1
Lilley Herts. 57 G5
Lilley W.Berks. 41 G5
Lilliesleaf 135 G3
Lillingstone Dayrell 56 C4
Lillingstone Lovell 56 C3
Lillington 12 C1
Lilliput 13 G3
Lilstock 23 E3
Limbrick 92 A1
Limbury 57 F5
Limefield 92 C1
Limehillock 182 A4
Limekilnburn 142 B4
Limekilns 143 E1
Limerigg 142 C2
Limerstone 14 D4
Limington 24 C5
Limpenhoe 87 E5
Limpley Stoke 25 E1
Limpsfield 30 D3
Linbriggs 128 A1
Linby 81 G2
Linchmere 29 D4
Lincoln 95 G5
Lincomb 54 A1
Lincombe 8 D2
Lindal in Furness 107 D5
Lindale 107 F4
Lindean 135 F2
Lindertis 160 B4
Lindfield 17 F1
Lindford 28 D4
Lindifferon 152 B3
Lindley 93 F1
Lindores 152 A3
Lindridge 53 F1
Lindsaig 140 A2
Lindsell 59 E5
Lindsey 60 A3
Linford Hants. 14 A2
Linford Thur. 45 F5
Lingague 98 A4
Lingdale 111 F1
Lingen 52 C1
Lingfield 30 C4
Lingwood 87 E5
Linhead 182 B4
Linhope 135 F5
Linicro 175 G3
Linkenholt 27 E2
Linkhill 18 D1
Linkinhorne 6 D3
Linklater 197 D4
Linksness Ork. 196 B2
Linksness Ork. 198 D5
Linktown 152 A5
Linley 64 C3
Linley Green 53 F2
Linlithgow 143 D2
Linlithgow Bridge 143 D2
Linn of Muick Cottage 160 B1
Linnels 119 F1
Linney 34 B3
Linshiels 128 A1
Linsiadar 186 D4
Linsidemore 190 A5
Linslade 57 E5
Linstead Parva 73 E4
Linstock 118 A2
Linthwaite 93 F1
Lintlaw 145 F4
Lintmill 182 A3
Linton Cambs. 59 D3
Linton Derbys. 67 E1
Linton Here. 53 F5
Linton Kent 31 G4
Linton N.Yorks. 101 F1
Linton Sc.Bord. 136 B4
Linton W.Yorks. 102 C3
Linton-on-Ouse 103 D1
Lintzford 120 A2
Linwood Hants. 14 A2
Linwood Lincs. 96 B4
Linwood Renf. 141 F3
Lionacleit 173 F5
Lional 187 G1
Liphook 28 D4
Liscombe 22 B4
Liskeard 5 G3
Liss 28 C5
Liss Forest 28 C5
Lissett 104 D2
Lissington 96 B4
Liston 59 G3
Lisvane 38 A4
Liswerry 38 C4
Litcham 71 G1
Litchborough 56 B2
Litchfield 27 F2
Litherland 91 E3
Litlington Cambs. 58 B3
Litlington E.Suss. 18 A3
Little Abington 58 D3
Little Addington 69 E5
Little Alne 54 D1
Little Amwell 44 C1
Little Assynt 188 D2
Little Aston 66 C3
Little Atherfield 15 D5
Little Ayton 111 E1
Little Baddow 45 G2
Little Badminton 39 G4
Little Ballinluig 159 E4
Little Bampton 117 F1
Little Bardfield 59 E4
Little Barford 57 G2
Little Barningham 86 C2
Little Barrington 41 E1
Little Barugh 111 G5
Little Bealings 60 D3
Little Bedwyn 27 D1
Little Bentley 60 C5
Little Berkhamsted 44 B2
Little Billing 56 D1
Little Birch 53 E4
Little Bispham 99 G3
Little Blakenham 60 C3
Little Bollington 92 B4
Little Bookham 29 G2
Little Bowden 68 C4
Little Bradley 59 E2
Little Brampton 64 C4
Little Braxted 46 B1
Little Brechin 161 D3
Little Brickhill 57 E4
Little Bridgeford 79 F5
Little Brington 56 B1
Little Bromley 60 B5
Little Broughton 117 D3
Little Budworth 78 C1
Little Burstead 45 F3
Little Burton 104 D3
Little Bytham 69 F1
Little Carlton Lincs. 97 E4
Little Carlton Notts. 82 C2
Little Casterton 69 F2
Little Catwick 104 D3
Little Cawthorpe 97 D4
Little Chalfont 43 E3
Little Chart 32 B4
Little Chesterford 58 D3
Little Cheverell 26 A2
Little Chishill 58 C4
Little Clacton 47 E1
Little Clifton 117 D4
Little Comberton 54 B3
Little Common 18 C3
Little Compton 55 E4
Little Corby 118 A2
Little Cowarne 53 F2
Little Coxwell 41 E3
Little Crakehall 110 B3
Little Creich 179 F1
Little Cressingham 71 G3
Little Crosby 91 E2
Little Cubley 80 C4
Little Dalby 68 C1
Little Dens 183 F5
Little Dewchurch 53 E4
Little Downham 70 D4
Little Driffield 104 C2
Little Dunham 71 G1
Little Dunkeld 159 F5
Little Dunmow 59 E5
Little Easton 59 E5
Little Eaton 81 E3
Little Ellingham 72 B2
Little End 45 E2
Little Eversden 58 B2
Little Fakenham 72 A4
Little Faringdon 41 E2
Little Fencote 110 B3
Little Fenton 103 E4
Little Finborough 60 B2
Little Fransham 86 G1
Little Gaddesden 43 E1
Little Garway 52 D5
Little Gidding 69 G4
Little Glemham 61 E2
Little Glenshee 151 E1
Little Gorsley 53 F5
Little Gransden 58 A2
Little Green 72 B4
Little Grimsby 96 D3
Little Gruinard 177 F1
Little Habton 111 G5
Little Hadham 58 C5
Little Hale 83 G3
Little Hallingbury 45 D1
Little Hampden 43 D2
Little Harrowden 69 D5
Little Haseley 42 B2
Little Hautbois 87 D3
Little Haven 34 B1
Little Hay 66 D2
Little Hayfield 93 E4
Little Haywood 80 B5
Little Heath 67 F4
Little Hereford 53 E1
Little Holtby 110 B3
Little Horkesley 60 A4
Little Hormead 58 C5
Little Horsted 17 G2
Little Horwood 56 C4
Little Houghton 56 D2
Little Hucklow 93 F5
Little Hulton 92 B2
Little Hungerford 42 A5
Little Idoch 182 C5
Little Kimble 42 D2
Little Kineton 55 F2
Little Kingshill 43 D3
Little Langford 26 B4
Little Laver 45 E2
Little Lawford 67 G5
Little Leigh 92 A5
Little Leighs 45 G1
Little Lever 92 B2
Little Ley 170 B3
Little Linford 56 D3
Little London E.Suss. 18 A2
Little London Hants. 27 E2
Little London Hants. 28 B2
Little London I.o.M. 98 B3
Little London Lincs. 84 C5
Little London Lincs. 84 A5
Little London Lincs. 96 D5
Little London Norf. 85 D5
Little London Norf. 71 F3
Little Longstone 93 F5
Little Malvern 53 G3
Little Maplestead 59 G4
Little Marcle 53 F4
Little Marlow 43 D4
Little Massingham 85 F5
Little Melton 86 C5
Little Mill 38 C2
Little Milton 42 B2
Little Missenden 43 E3
Little Musgrave 108 C1
Little Ness 64 D1
Little Neston 91 D5
Little Newcastle 48 C5
Little Newsham 110 A1
Little Oakley Essex 60 D5
Little Oakley Northants. 69 D4
Little Orton 117 G1
Little Ouseburn 102 D1
Little Parndon 44 D2
Little Paxton 57 G1
Little Petherick 4 D2
Little Plumstead 87 E4
Little Ponton 83 E4
Little Raveley 70 A5
Little Ribston 102 C2
Little Rissington 55 D5
Little Rogart 190 C4
Little Ryburgh 86 A3
Little Ryle 137 E5
Little Salkeld 118 B4
Little Sampford 59 E4
Little Saxham 59 F1
Little Scatwell 178 C4
Little Shelford 58 C2
Little Smeaton 94 C1
Little Snoring 86 A2
Little Sodbury 39 G4
Little Somborne 27 E4
Little Somerford 40 B4
Little Stainton 120 C5
Little Stanney 91 F5
Little Staughton 57 G1
Little Steeping 84 C1
Little Stonham 60 C2
Little Stretton Leics. 68 B3
Little Stretton Shrop. 64 D3
Little Strickland 118 B5
Little Stukeley 70 A5
Little Sutton 91 E5
Little Swinburne 128 B4
Little Tew 55 F5
Little Tey 59 G5
Little Thetford 70 D5
Little Thirkleby 111 D5
Little Thorpe 120 D3
Little Thurlow 59 E2
Little Thurrock 45 F5
Little Torboll 190 C5
Little Torrington 21 E4
Little Totham 46 B1
Little Town 117 F5
Little Urswick 107 D5
Little Wakering 46 C4
Little Walden 58 D3
Little Waldingfield 60 A3
Little Walsingham 86 A2
Little Waltham 45 G1
Little Warley 45 F3
Little Weighton 104 B4
Little Welland 54 A4
Little Welnetham 59 G2
Little Wenham 60 B4
Little Wenlock 65 F2
Little Whittingham Green 73 D4
Little Whittington 119 F1
Little Wilbraham 58 D2
Little Witcombe 40 B1
Little Witley 53 G1
Little Wittenham 42 A3
Little Wolford 55 E4
Little Wratting 59 E3
Little Wymondley 58 A5

Little Wyrley 66 C2
Little Yeldham 59 F4
Littlebeck 112 B2
Littleborough Gt.Man. 92 D1
Littleborough Notts. 95 F4
Littlebourne 33 D3
Littlebredy 12 B4
Littlebury 58 D4
Littlebury Green 58 C4
Littledean 39 F1
Littleferry 190 D5
Littleham Devon 21 E3
Littleham Devon 10 D4
Littlehampton 16 C3
Littlehempston 9 E1
Littlehoughton 137 G5
Littlemill E.Ayr. 132 C4
Littlemill High. 180 B4
Littlemore 42 A2
Littleover 81 E4
Littleport 71 D4
Littlestone-on-Sea 19 F1
Littlethorpe 102 C1
Littleton Ches. 78 B1
Littleton Hants. 27 F4
Littleton P. & K. 152 A1
Littleton Som. 24 B4
Littleton Surr. 29 F1
Littleton Drew 40 A4
Littleton-on-Severn 39 E4
Littleton Panell 26 A2
Littletown 120 C3
Littlewick Green 42 D5
Littleworth Oxon. 41 F3
Littleworth Staffs. 66 C1
Littleworth Worcs. 54 A2
Littley Green 45 F1
Litton Derbys. 93 F5
Litton N.Yorks. 109 E5
Litton Som. 24 C2
Litton Cheney 12 B3
Liurbost 187 E5
Liverpool 91 E3
Liverpool Airport 91 F4
Liversedge 102 A5
Liverton Devon 10 B5
Liverton R. & C. 111 G1
Liverton Street 32 A4
Livingston 143 E3
Livingston Village 143 E3
Lixwm 90 C5
Lizard 3 D5
Llaingoch 88 A4
Llaithddu 63 G4
Llan 63 E2
Llan-dafal 38 A2
Llan-faes 89 E5
Llan-y-pwll 78 A2
Llanaber 62 C1
Llanaelhaearn 74 C3
Llanaeron 50 A1
Llanafan 62 C5
Llanafan-fawr 51 F2
Llanafan-fechan 51 F2
Llanallgo 88 C4
Llanarmon 74 D4
Llanarmon Dyffryn Ceiriog 77 E4
Llanarmon-yn-Ial 77 E2
Llanarth Cere. 50 A2
Llanarth Mon. 38 C1
Llanarthney 50 B5
Llanasa 90 C4
Llanbabo 88 B4
Llanbadarn Fawr 62 B4
Llanbadarn Fynydd 63 G5
Llanbadarn-y-garreg 52 A3
Llanbadoc 38 C2
Llanbadrig 88 B3
Llanbeder 38 C3
Llanbedr Gwyn. 75 E5
Llanbedr Powys 52 B5
Llanbedr Powys 52 A3
Llanbedr-Dyffryn-Clwyd 77 E2
Llanbedr-y-cennin 76 A1
Llanbedrgoch 88 D4
Llanbedrog 74 C4
Llanberis 75 E1
Llanbethery 22 D1
Llanbister 64 A5
Llanblethian 37 F5
Llanboidy 49 F5
Llanbradach 38 A3
Llanbrynmair 63 E2
Llancarfan 37 G5
Llancayo 38 C2
Llancynfelyn 62 C3
Llandaff 38 A5
Llandaff North 38 A5
Llandanwg 75 E5
Llandawke 35 F1
Llanddaniel Fab 88 C5
Llanddarog 36 B1
Llanddeiniol 62 B5
Llanddeiniolen 75 E1
Llandderfel 76 C4
Llanddeusant Carmar. 51 D5
Llanddeusant I.o.A. 88 B4
Llanddew 51 G4
Llanddewi 36 A4
Llanddewi-Brefi 50 C2
Llanddewi Rhydderch 38 C1
Llanddewi Velfrey 35 E1
Llanddewi Ystradenni 52 A1
Llanddewi'r Cwm 51 G3
Llanddoged 76 B1
Llanddona 89 D5
Llanddowror 35 F1
Llanddulas 90 A5
Llanddwywe 75 E5
Llanddyfnan 88 D5
Llandefaelog 36 A1
Llandefaelog Fach 51 G4
Llandefaelog-tre'r-graig 52 A5
Llandefalle 52 A4
Llandegfan 89 D5
Llandegla 77 E2
Llandegley 52 A1
Llandegveth 38 C3
Llandegwning 74 B4
Llandeilo 50 C5
Llandeilo Abercywyn 35 G1
Llandeilo Graban 51 G3
Llandeilo'r-Fan 51 E4
Llandeloy 48 B5
Llandenny 38 D2
Llandevenny 38 D4
Llandinabo 53 E5
Llandinam 63 G4
Llandissilio 49 E5
Llandogo 39 E2
Llandough V. of Glam. 38 A5
Llandough V. of Glam. 37 F5
Llandovery 51 D4
Llandow 37 F5
Llandre Carmar. 50 C3
Llandre Carmar. 49 E5
Llandre Cere. 62 C4
Llandrillo 76 D4
Llandrillo-yn-Rhôs 89 G4
Llandrindod Wells 51 G1
Llandrinio 64 B1
Llandudno 89 F4
Llandudno Junction 89 F5
Llandwrog 74 D2
Llandybie 36 C1
Llandyfriog 49 G3
Llandyfrydog 88 C4
Llandygai 89 D5
Llandygwydd 49 F3
Llandyrnog 77 E1
Llandyry 36 A2
Llandysilio 64 B1
Llandyssil 64 A3
Llandysul 50 A3
Llanedeyrn 38 B4
Llanegryn 62 C2
Llanegwad 50 B5
Llaneilian 88 C3
Llaneilian-yn-Rhôs 89 G5
Llanelidan 77 E2
Llanelieu 52 A4
Llanellen 38 C1
Llanelli 36 B2
Llanelltyd 62 D1
Llanelly 38 B1
Llanelly Hill Mon. 38 B1
Llanelwedd 51 G2
Llanelwy (St. Asaph) 90 B5
Llanenddwyn 75 E5
Llanengan 74 B5
Llanerch-y-medd 88 C4
Llanerfyl 63 G2
Llanfachraeth 88 B4
Llanfachreth 76 A5
Llanfaelog 88 B5
Llanfaelrhys 74 B5
Llanfaes Powys 51 G5
Llanfaethlu 88 B4
Llanfaglan 75 D1
Llanfair 75 E5
Llanfair Caereinion 64 A2
Llanfair Clydogau 50 C2
Llanfair Dyffryn Clwyd 77 E2
Llanfair-Nant-Gwyn 49 E4
Llanfair-Orllwyn 49 G3
Llanfair Talhaiarn 90 A5
Llanfair Waterdine 64 B5
Llanfair-yn-neubwll 88 B5
Llanfairfechan 89 E5
Llanfairpwll-gwyngyll 88 D5
Llanfairynghornwy 88 B3
Llanfallteg 35 E1
Llanfallteg West 35 E1
Llanfaredd 51 G2
Llanfarian 62 B5
Llanfechain 77 E5
Llanfechell 88 B3
Llanfendigaid 62 B2
Llanferres 77 E1
Llanfflewyn 88 B4
Llanfigael 88 B4
Llanfihangel ar-arth 50 A4
Llanfihangel Crucorney 52 C5
Llanfihangel Glyn Myfyr 76 C3
Llanfihangel Nant Bran 51 F4
Llanfihangel-nant-Melan 52 A2
Llanfihangel Rhydithon 52 A1
Llanfihangel Rogiet 38 D4
Llanfihangel-Tal-y-llyn 52 A5
Llanfihangel uwch-gwili 50 A5
Llanfihangel-y-Creuddyn 62 C5
Llanfihangel y-pennant Gwyn. 75 E3
Llanfihangel-y-pennant Gwyn. 62 C2
Llanfihangel-yn-Ngwynfa 63 G1
Llanfilo 52 A4
Llanfoist 38 B1
Llanfor 76 C4
Llanfrechfa 38 C3
Llanfrothen 75 F3
Llanfrynach 51 G5
Llanfwrog Denb. 77 E2
Llanfwrog I.o.A. 88 B4
Llanfyllin 64 A1
Llanfynydd Carmar. 50 B5
Llanfynydd Flints. 77 F2
Llanfyrnach 49 F4
Llangadfan 63 G1
Llangadog 50 D5
Llangadwaladr I.o.A. 74 C1
Llangadwaladr Powys 77 E4
Llangaffo 74 D1
Llangain 35 G1
Llangammarch Wells 51 F3
Llangan 37 F5
Llangarron 53 E5
Llangasty-Talyllyn 52 A5
Llangathen 50 B5
Llangattock 38 B1
Llangattock Lingoed 52 C5
Llangattock-Vibon-Avel 39 D1
Llangedwyn 77 E5
Llangefni 88 C5
Llangeinor 37 F4
Llangeitho 50 C2
Llangeler 49 G4
Llangelynin 62 B2
Llangendeirne 36 A1
Llangennech 36 B2
Llangennith 36 A3
Llangenny 38 B1
Llangernyw 76 B1
Llangian 74 B5
Llangiwg 36 D2
Llanglydwen 49 E5
Llangoed 89 E5
Llangoedmor 49 E3
Llangollen 77 F3
Llangolman 49 E5
Llangorse 52 A5
Llangorwen 62 C4
Llangovan 39 D2
Llangower 76 C4
Llangranog 49 G2
Llangristiolus 88 C5
Llangrove 39 E1
Llangua 52 C5
Llangunllo 64 B5
Llangunnor 50 A5
Llangurig 63 F5
Llangwm Conwy 76 C3
Llangwm Pembs. 34 C2
Llangwm-isaf 38 D2
Llangwnnadl 74 B4
Llangwyfan 77 E1
Llangwyllog 88 C5
Llangwyryfon 62 B5
Llangybi Cere. 50 C2
Llangybi Gwyn. 74 D3
Llangybi Mon. 38 C3
Llangyfelach 36 C3
Llangynhafal 77 E1
Llangynidr 38 A1
Llangyniew 64 A2
Llangynin 35 F1
Llangynog Carmar. 35 G1
Llangynog Powys 77 D5
Llangynwyd 37 E4
Llanhamlach 51 G5
Llanharan 37 G4
Llanharry 37 G4
Llanhennock 38 C3
Llanhilleth 38 B2
Llanidloes 63 F4
Llaniestyn 74 B4
Llanigon 52 B4
Llanilar 62 C5
Llanilid 37 F4
Llanishen Cardiff 38 A4
Llanishen Mon. 39 D2
Llanllawddog 50 A5
Llanllechid 75 F1
Llanlleonfel 51 F3
Llanllugan 63 G2
Llanllwch 35 G1
Llanllwchaiarn 64 A3
Llanllwni 50 A3
Llanllyfni 75 D2
Llanllywel 38 C3
Llanmadoc 36 A3
Llanmaes 22 C1
Llanmartin 38 C4
Llanmerewig 64 A3
Llanmihangel 37 F5
Llanmiloe 35 F2
Llanmorlais 36 B3
Llannefydd 90 A5
Llannerch 90 B5
Llannerch-y-Môr 90 C5
Llannon 36 B2
Llannor 74 C4
Llanon 50 B1
Llanover 38 C2
Llanpumsaint 50 A5
Llanreithan 48 B5
Llanrhaeadr 77 D1
Llanrhaeadr-ym-Mochnant 77 E5
Llanrhian 48 B4
Llanrhidian 36 B3
Llanrhos 89 F4
Llanrhyddlad 88 B4
Llanrhystud 50 B1
Llanrothal 39 D1
Llanrug 75 E1
Llanrumney 38 B4
Llanrwst 76 A1
Llansadurnen 35 F1
Llansadwrn Carmar. 50 C4
Llansadwrn I.o.A. 89 D5
Llansaint 35 G2
Llansamlet 36 C3
Llansanffraid Glan Conwy 89 G5
Llansannan 76 C1
Llansannor 37 F5
Llansantffraed 52 A5
Llansantffraed-Cwmdeuddwr 51 F1
Llansantffraed-in-Elvel 51 G2
Llansantffraid 50 B1
Llansantffraid-ym-Mechain 77 F5
Llansawel Carmar. 50 C4
Llansawel (Briton Ferry) N.P.T. 36 D3
Llansilin 77 F5
Llansoy 38 D2
Llanspyddid 51 G5
Llanstadwell 34 C2
Llansteffan Carmar. 35 G1
Llanstephan Powys 52 A3
Llantarnam 38 C3
Llanteg 35 E1
Llanthony 52 B5
Llantilio Crossenny 38 C1
Llantilio Pertholey 38 C1
Llantood 49 E3
Llantrisant Mon. 38 C3
Llantrisant R.C.T. 37 G4
Llantrithyd 37 G5
Llantwit Fardre 37 G4
Llantwit Major 22 C1
Llantysilio 77 E3
Llanuwchllyn 76 B4
Llanvaches 38 D3
Llanvair-Discoed 38 D3
Llanvapley 38 C1
Llanvetherine 38 C1
Llanveynoe 52 C4
Llanvihangel Gobion 38 C2
Llanvihangel-Ystern-Llewern 38 D1
Llanwarne 53 E5
Llanwddyn 63 G1
Llanwenog 50 A3
Llanwern 38 C4
Llanwinio 49 F5
Llanwnda Gwyn. 75 D2
Llanwnda Pembs. 48 C4
Llanwnen 50 B3
Llanwnog 63 G3
Llanwonno 37 G3
Llanwrda 50 D4
Llanwrin 63 D2
Llanwrthwl 51 F1
Llanwrtyd 51 E3
Llanwrtyd Wells 51 E3
Llanwyddelan 63 G2
Llanyblodwel 77 F5
Llanybri 35 G1
Llanybydder 50 B3
Llanycefn 49 E5
Llanychaer Bridge 48 C4
Llanycil 76 C4
Llanycrwys 50 C3
Llanymawddwy 63 F1
Llanymynech 77 F5
Llanynghenedl 88 B4
Llanynys 77 E1
Llanyre 51 G1
Llanystumdwy 75 D4
Llanywern 52 A5
Llawhaden 35 D1
Llawnt 77 F4
Llawr-y-dref 74 B5
Llawryglyn 63 F3
Llay 78 A2
Llechcynfarwy 88 B4
Llechfaen 51 G5
Llechryd Caerp. 38 A2
Llechryd Cere. 49 F3
Llechrydau 77 F4
Lledrod Cere. 62 C5
Lledrod Powys 77 F4
Llethr 48 B5
Llidiadnenog 50 B4
Llidiardau 76 B4
Llithfaen 74 C3
Lloc 90 C5
Llong 77 F1
Llowes 52 A3
Lloyney 64 B5
Llwydcoed 37 F2
Llwydiarth 63 G1
Llwyn 64 B4
Llwyn-Madoc 51 F2
Llwyn-onn 50 A2
Llwyn-y-brain Carmar. 35 F1
Llwyn-y-brain Carmar. 50 D4
Llwyncelyn 50 A2
Llwyndafydd 49 G2
Llwynderw 64 B2
Llwyndyrys 74 C3
Llwyngwril 62 B2
Llwynhendy 36 B3
Llwynmawr 77 F4
Llwynypia 37 F3
Llynclys 77 F5
Llynfaes 88 C5
Llys-y-fran 48 D5
Llysfaen 89 G5
Llyswen 52 A4
Llysworney 37 F5
Llywel 51 E4
Loandhu 180 A2
Loanhead Aber. 171 E1
Loanhead Midloth. 143 G3
Loans 132 B2
Loch Baghasdail (Lochboisdale) 172 C2
Loch Coire Lodge 193 F5
Loch Eil Outward Bound 156 C2
Loch Head D. & G. 114 D2
Loch Head D. & G. 123 F1
Loch na Madadh (Lochmaddy) 174 C3
Loch Sgioport 162 B1
Lochailort 155 G1
Lochaline 155 F5
Lochans 122 B5
Locharbriggs 125 D2
Lochawe 148 D2
Lochboisdale (Loch Baghasdail) 172 C2
Lochbuie 147 F2
Lochcarron 165 E1
Lochdhu Hotel 194 C4
Lochdon 147 G1
Lochdrum 178 B2
Lochearnhead 150 A2
Lochee 152 B1
Lochend High. 195 E2
Lochend High. 167 E1
Lochfoot 124 D3
Lochgair 148 B5
Lochgarthside 167 E3
Lochgelly 151 G5
Lochgilphead 139 G1
Lochgoilhead 149 E4
Lochgoin 141 G5
Lochhill E.Ayr. 133 E4
Lochhill Moray 181 E3
Lochinch Castle 122 C4
Lochinver 188 C2
Lochlair 160 D5
Lochlane 150 D2
Lochlea 132 C3
Lochluichart 178 C3
Lochmaben 125 E2
Lochmaddy (Loch na Madadh) 174 C3
Lochore 151 G5
Lochportain 174 C2
Lochranza 140 A5
Lochside Aber. 161 F3
Lochside High. 193 D3
Lochside High. 194 A5
Lochside High. 195 E2
Lochslin 180 A1
Lochton 123 D2
Lochty 152 D4
Lochuisge 155 G4
Lochurr 124 B2
Lochussie 179 D4
Lochwinnoch 141 E4
Lockengate 5 E3
Lockerbie 125 F2
Lockeridge 26 C1
Lockerley 27 D5
Locking 24 A2
Lockington E.Riding 104 C3
Lockington Leics. 81 F5
Lockleywood 79 D5
Locks Heath 15 E2
Locksbottom 30 D2
Lockton 112 B3
Loddington Leics. 68 C2
Loddington Northants. 68 D5
Loddiswell 8 D3
Loddon 73 E2
Lode 58 D1
Loders 12 A3
Lodsworth 29 E5
Lofthouse N.Yorks. 109 F5
Lofthouse W.Yorks. 102 C5
Loftus 111 G1
Logan D. & G. 114 A2
Logan E.Ayr. 133 D3
Loganlea 143 D3
Loggerheads 79 E4
Loggie 188 D5
Logie Angus 161 E3
Logie Angus 160 B4
Logie Fife 152 C2
Logie Moray 180 C4
Logie Coldstone 169 G4
Logie Hill 179 G2
Logie Newton 170 B1
Logie Pert 161 E3
Logierait 159 E4
Login 49 E5
Lolworth 58 B1
Lonbain 176 C4
Londesborough 104 A3
London 44 C4
London Beach 32 A5
London City Airport 44 D4
London Colney 44 A2
London Heathrow Airport 43 F5
London Luton Airport 57 G5
Londonderry 110 B4
Londonthorpe 83 E4
Londubh 177 E1
Lonemore 179 G1
Long Ashton 39 E5
Long Bennington 82 D3
Long Bredy 12 B3
Long Buckby 56 B1
Long Clawson 82 C5
Long Common 15 E1
Long Compton Staffs. 79 F5
Long Compton Warks. 55 E4
Long Crendon 42 B2
Long Crichel 13 F1
Long Ditton 29 G1
Long Downs 3 E3
Long Drax 103 F5
Long Duckmanton 94 B5
Long Eaton 81 F4
Long Gill 101 D2
Long Hanborough 41 G1
Long Itchington 55 G1
Long Lawford 67 G5
Long Load 24 B5
Long Marston Herts. 43 D1
Long Marston N.Yorks. 103 E2
Long Marston Warks. 55 D3
Long Marton 118 C5
Long Melford 59 G3
Long Newnton 40 B3
Long Preston 101 E2
Long Riston 104 D3
Long Stratton 72 C2
Long Street 56 C3
Long Sutton Hants. 28 C3
Long Sutton Lincs. 84 C5
Long Sutton Som. 24 B5
Long Thurlow 60 B1
Long Waste 65 F1
Long Whatton 81 F5
Long Wittenham 42 A3
Longbenton 120 B1
Longborough 55 D5
Longbridge W.Mid. 66 C5
Longbridge Warks. 55 E1
Longbridge Deverill 25 F3
Longburgh 117 G1
Longburton 12 C1
Longcliffe 80 D2
Longcot 41 E3
Longcroft 142 B2
Longcross Devon 7 E3
Longcross Surr. 29 E1
Longden 64 D2
Longdon Staffs. 66 C1
Longdon Worcs. 54 A4
Longdon upon Tern 65 F1
Longdown 10 B3
Longdrum 171 E3
Longfield 31 F2
Longfield Hill 31 F2
Longfleet 13 G3
Longford Derbys. 80 D4
Longford Glos. 54 A5
Longford Gt.Lon. 43 F5
Longford Shrop. 78 D4
Longford Tel. & W. 65 G1
Longford W.Mid. 67 F4
Longforgan 152 B2
Longformacus 145 D4
Longframlington 128 D1
Longham Dorset 13 G3
Longham Norf. 86 A4
Longhill 183 E4
Longhirst 129 E3
Longhope Glos. 39 F1
Longhope Ork. 196 C3
Longhorsley 128 D2
Longhoughton 137 G5
Longlands Aber. 169 G2
Longlands Cumb. 117 F3
Longlane Derbys. 81 D4
Longlane W.Berks. 42 A5
Longley Green 53 G2
Longmanhill 182 C3
Longmoor Camp 28 C4
Longmorn 181 E4
Longnewton Sc.Bord. 135 G3
Longnewton Stock. 110 C1
Longney 39 G1
Longniddry 144 B2
Longnor Shrop. 65 D2
Longnor Staffs. 80 B1
Longparish 27 F3
Longridge Lancs. 100 C4
Longridge W.Loth. 142 D3
Longridge Towers 145 G4
Longriggend 142 C2
Longrock 2 B3
Longsdon 79 G2
Longside 183 F5
Longslow 79 D4
Longstanton 58 B1
Longstock 27 E4
Longstowe 58 B2
Longstreet 26 C2
Longthorpe 69 G3
Longton Lancs. 100 A5
Longton Stoke 79 G3
Longtown Cumb. 126 B5
Longtown Here. 52 C5
Longville in the Dale 65 E3
Longwell Green 39 F5
Longwick 42 C2
Longwitton 128 C3
Longworth 41 F3
Longyester 144 C3
Lonmore 175 F5
Looe 5 G4
Loose 31 G3
Loosegate 84 B5
Loosley Row 42 D2
Lopcombe Corner 27 D4
Lopen 12 A1
Loppington 78 B5
Lorbottle 128 C1
Lorbottle Hall 128 C1
Lorgill 175 E5
Lorn 141 E1
Lornty 159 G5
Loscoe 81 F3
Losgaintir 184 C4
Lossiemouth 181 E2
Lossit 138 A4
Lostock Gralam 92 A5
Lostock Green 92 A5
Lostock Junction 92 A2
Lostwithiel 5 F4
Loth 199 E3
Lothbeg 191 E3
Lothersdale 101 F3
Lothmore 191 E3
Loudwater 43 E3
Loughborough 68 A1
Loughor 36 B3
Loughton Essex 44 D3
Loughton M.K. 56 D4
Loughton Shrop. 65 F4
Lound Lincs. 69 F1
Lound Notts. 95 D4
Lound Suff. 73 G2
Lount 67 F1
Lour 160 C5
Louth 96 D4
Love Clough 101 E5
Lovedean 15 F1
Lover 26 D5
Loversall 94 C3
Loves Green 45 F2
Loveston 35 D2
Lovington 24 C4
Low 107 F4
Low Ballevain 130 B3
Low Barlay 123 G5
Low Bentham 100 C1
Low Bolton 109 F3
Low Bradfield 93 G3
Low Bradley 101 G3
Low Braithwaite 118 A3
Low Brunton 128 B4
Low Burnham 95 E2
Low Burton 110 B4
Low Catton 103 G2
Low Conscliffe 110 B1
Low Craighead 132 A5
Low Crosby 118 A2
Low Dinsdale 110 C1
Low Eggborough 103 E5
Low Entercommon 110 C2
Low Etherley 120 A5
Low Gate 119 F1
Low Habberley 66 A5
Low Ham 24 B5
Low Hawkser 112 C2
Low Haygarth 108 B3
Low Hesket 118 A3
Low Hesleyhurst 128 C2
Low Hutton 103 G1
Low Laithe 102 A1
Low Leighton 93 E4
Low Marishes 112 B5
Low Mill 111 F3
Low Moor 100 D3
Low Newton-by-the-Sea 137 G4
Low Risby 95 G1
Low Row Cumb. 118 B1
Low Row N.Yorks. 109 E3
Low Santon 95 G1
Low Stillaig 140 A3
Low Street 87 E3
Low Torry 143 E1
Low Toynton 96 C5
Low Waters 142 B4
Low Wood 107 E4
Low Worsall 110 C1
Lowdham 82 B3
Lower Achachenna 148 C2
Lower Aisholt 23 E4
Lower Apperley 54 A5
Lower Ashton 10 B4
Lower Assendon 42 C4
Lower Auchalick 140 A2
Lower Barewood 52 C2
Lower Beeding 17 E1
Lower Benefield 69 E4
Lower Berry Hill 39 E1
Lower Bockhampton 12 D3
Lower Boddington 55 G2
Lower Boscaswell 2 A3
Lower Bourne 28 D3
Lower Brailes 55 F4
Lower Breakish 164 C2
Lower Broadheath 54 A2
Lower Broughton 92 C3
Lower Brynamman 36 D1
Lower Bullingham 53 E4
Lower Burgate 14 A1
Lower Caldecote 57 G3
Lower Cam 39 G2
Lower Camster 195 E4
Lower Chapel 51 G4
Lower Chute 27 E2
Lower Crossings 93 E4
Lower Darwen 100 C5
Lower Dean 57 F1
Lower Diabaig 177 D3
Lower Dicker 18 A2
Lower Dinchope 64 D4
Lower Down 64 C4
Lower Drift 2 B4
Lower Dunsforth 102 D1
Lower Earley 42 C5
Lower Egleton 53 F3
Lower End 57 D1
Lower Everleigh 26 C2
Lower Failand 39 E5
Lower Farringdon 28 C4
Lower Freystrop 34 C1
Lower Froyle 28 C3
Lower Gabwell 9 F1
Lower Gledfield 190 A5
Lower Godney 24 B3
Lower Green Kent 31 F4
Lower Green Norf. 86 A2
Lower Green Staffs. 66 B2
Lower Green Bank 100 B2
Lower Halstow 32 A2
Lower Hardres 32 D3
Lower Hawthwaite 106 D4
Lower Hayton 65 E4
Lower Hergest 52 B2
Lower Heyford 55 G5
Lower Higham 45 G5
Lower Holbrook 60 C4
Lower Hordley 78 A5
Lower Horsebridge 18 A2
Lower Kilchattan 146 C5
Lower Killeyan 138 A5
Lower Kingcombe 12 B3
Lower Kinnerton 78 A1
Lower Langford 24 B1
Lower Largo 152 C4
Lower Lemington 55 E4
Lower Lovacott 21 F3
Lower Lydbrook 39 E1
Lower Lye 52 D1
Lower Machen 38 B4
Lower Maes-coed 52 C4
Lower Moor 54 B3
Lower Nazeing 44 C2
Lower Oakfield 151 G5
Lower Oddington 55 E5
Lower Ollach 164 B1
Lower Penarth 38 A5
Lower Penn 66 A3
Lower Pennington 14 C3
Lower Peover 92 B5
Lower Quinton 55 D3
Lower Seagry 40 B4
Lower Shelton 57 E3
Lower Shiplake 42 C5
Lower Shuckburgh 55 G1
Lower Slaughter 55 D5
Lower Stanton St. Quintin 40 B4
Lower Stoke 32 A1
Lower Stondon 57 G4
Lower Street 18 C2
Lower Sundon 57 F5

Lower Swanwick **15** D2
Lower Swell **55** D5
Lower Tean **80** B4
Lower Thurlton **73** F2
Lower Thurnham **100** A2
Lower Town *I.o.S.* **4** B1
Lower Town *Pembs.* **48** C4
Lower Tysoe **55** F3
Lower Upham **15** E1
Lower Vexford **23** E4
Lower Wallop **64** C2
Lower Walton **92** A4
Lower Weare **24** B2
Lower Welson **52** B2
Lower Whitley **92** A5
Lower Wield **28** B3
Lower (Nether) Winchendon **42** C1
Lower Withington **79** F1
Lower Woodend **42** D4
Lower Woodford **26** C4
Lower Wraxall **12** B2
Lower Wyche **53** G3
Lowesby **68** C2
Lowestoft **73** G2
Lowestoft End **73** G2
Loweswater **117** E4
Lowfield Heath **30** B4
Lowgill *Cumb.* **108** B3
Lowgill *Lancs.* **100** C1
Lowick *Cumb.* **107** D4
Lowick *Northants.* **69** E4
Lowick *Northumb.* **137** E3
Lownie Moor **160** C5
Lowsonford **55** D1
Lowther **118** B5
Lowther Castle **118** B5
Lowthorpe **104** C2
Lowton **92** A3
Lowton Common **92** A3
Loxbeare **10** C1
Loxhill **29** F4
Loxhore **21** G2
Loxley **55** E2
Loxton **24** A2
Loxwood **29** F4
Lubachoinnich **189** G5
Lubcroy **189** F4
Lubenham **68** C4
Lubfearn **178** C2
Lubmore **177** G4
Lubreoch **157** G5
Luccombe **22** C3
Luccombe Village **15** E5
Lucker **137** F3
Luckett **7** D3
Luckington **40** A4
Lucklawhill **152** C2
Luckwell Bridge **22** C4
Lucton **52** D1
Ludag **172** C2
Ludborough **96** C3
Ludchurch **35** E1
Luddenden **101** G5
Luddenden Court **32** B2
Luddesdown **31** F2
Luddington *N.Lincs.* **95** F1
Luddington *Warks.* **55** D2
Luddington in the Brook **69** G4
Ludford **65** E5
Ludford Magna **96** C4
Ludford Parva **96** B4
Ludgershall *Bucks.* **42** B1
Ludgershall *Wilts.* **27** D2
Ludgvan **2** B3
Ludham **87** E4
Ludlow **65** E5
Ludney **97** D3
Ludstock **53** F4
Ludwell **26** A5
Ludworth **120** C3
Luffincott **6** D1
Luffness **144** B1
Lugar **133** D3
Luggiebank **142** B2
Lugton **141** F4
Lugwardine **53** E3
Luib **164** B2
Luibeilt **157** E3
Lulham **52** D3
Lullington *Derbys.* **67** E1
Lullington *Som.* **25** E2
Lulsgate Bottom **24** C1
Lulsley **53** G2
Lulworth Camp **13** E4
Lumb **101** G5
Lumbutts **101** F5
Lumby **103** D4
Lumphanan **170** A4
Lumphinnans **151** G5
Lumsdaine **145** F3
Lumsden **169** G2
Lunan **161** E4
Lunanhead **160** C4
Luncarty **151** F2
Lund *E.Riding* **104** B3
Lund *N.Yorks.* **103** F4
Lund *Shet.* **203** E2
Lundavra **156** C3
Lunderton **183** G5
Lundie *Angus* **152** A1
Lundie *High.* **166** A3
Lundin Links **152** C4
Lunga **147** G4
Lunna **201** D1
Lunning **201** E1
Lunsford's Cross **18** C2
Lunt **91** E2
Luntley **52** C2
Luppitt **11** E2
Lupton **107** G4
Lurgashall **29** E5
Lurignich **156** B4
Lusby **84** B1
Luss **149** F5
Lussagiven **139** E1
Lusta **175** F4
Lustleigh **10** A4
Luston **53** D1
Luthermuir **161** E3
Luthrie **152** B3
Luton *Devon* **11** D2
Luton *Devon* **10** C5
Luton *Luton* **57** F5
Luton *Med.* **31** G2
Lutterworth **68** A4
Lutton *Devon* **8** B2
Lutton *Lincs.* **84** C5
Lutton *Northants.* **69** G4
Luxborough **22** C4
Luxulyan **5** E4
Lybster *High.* **194** C2
Lybster *High.* **195** E5
Lydacott **21** E5
Lydbury North **64** C4
Lydcott **21** G2
Lydd **19** F1
Lydd Airport **19** F1
Lydd-on-Sea **19** F1
Lydden **33** E4
Lyddington **69** D3
Lydeard St. Lawrence **23** E4
Lydford **7** F2
Lydford-on-Fosse **24** C4
Lydgate **101** F5
Lydham **64** C3
Lydiard Millicent **40** C4
Lydiate **91** E2
Lydlinch **12** D1
Lydney **39** F2
Lydstep **35** D3
Lye **66** B4
Lye Green **43** E2
Lyford **41** F3
Lymbridge Green **32** D4
Lyme Regis **11** G3
Lymekilns **142** A4
Lyminge **33** D4
Lymington **14** C3
Lyminster **16** C3
Lymm **92** A4
Lymore **14** C3
Lympne **32** D5
Lympsham **24** A2
Lympstone **10** C4
Lynaberack **167** G5
Lynchat **167** G4
Lyndhurst **14** C2
Lyndon **69** E2
Lyne *Aber.* **170** C4
Lyne *Sc.Bord.* **143** G5
Lyne *Surr.* **29** F1
Lyne of Gorthleck **167** E2
Lyne of Skene **170** C3
Lyne Station **134** D2
Lyneal **78** B4
Lynedale House **175** G4
Lynegar **195** E3
Lyneham *Oxon.* **55** E5
Lyneham *Wilts.* **40** C5
Lyneholmeford **126** D4
Lynemore *High.* **168** C2
Lynemore *Moray* **168** D1
Lynemouth **129** E2
Lyness **196** C3
Lynford **71** G3
Lyng *Norf.* **86** B4
Lyng *Som.* **24** A5
Lynmouth **22** A3
Lynsted **32** B2
Lynton **22** A3
Lyon's Gate **12** C2
Lyonshall **52** C2
Lyrabus **138** A3
Lytchett Matravers **13** F3
Lytchett Minster **13** F3
Lyth **195** E2
Lytham **99** G5
Lytham St. Anne's **99** G5
Lythe **112** B1
Lythe Hill **29** E4
Lythes **197** D4
Lythmore **194** C2

M

Mabe Burnthouse **3** E3
Mabie **124** D3
Mablethorpe **97** F4
Macclesfield **92** D5
Macclesfield Forest **93** D5
Macduff **182** C3
Machan **142** B4
Machany **151** E3
Macharioch **130** C5
Machen **38** B4
Machrie *Arg. & B.* **138** A3
Machrie *Arg. & B.* **138** B5
Machrie *N.Ayr.* **131** E2
Machrihanish **130** B4
Machrins **146** C5
Machynlleth **62** D2
Mackworth **81** E4
Macmerry **144** B2
Macterry **182** C5
Madderty **151** E2
Maddiston **142** D2
Madehurst **16** B2
Madeley *Staffs.* **79** E3
Madeley *Tel. & W.* **65** G2
Madeley Heath **79** E3
Madford **11** E1
Madingley **58** B2
Madjeston **25** F5
Madley **52** D4
Madresfield **54** A3
Madron **2** B3
Maen Porth **3** E4
Maenaddwyn **88** C4
Maenclochog **49** D5
Maendy **37** G5
Maentwrog **75** F3
Maer **79** E4
Maerdy *Carmar.* **50** C5
Maerdy *Carmar.* **50** C5
Maerdy *Conwy* **76** D3
Maerdy *Mon.* **38** C2
Maerdy *R.C.T.* **37** F3
Maes-Glas (Greenfield) **90** C5
Maes-glas **38** B4
Maes-Treylow **52** B1
Maesbrook **77** F5
Maesbury Marsh **78** A5
Maesgwynne **49** F5
Maeshafn **77** F1
Maesllyn **49** G3
Maesmynis **51** G3
Maesteg **37** E3
Maesybont **36** B1
Maesycrugiau **50** A3
Maesycwmmer **38** A3
Magdalen Laver **45** E2
Maggieknockater **181** F5
Magham Down **18** B2
Maghull **91** E2
Magor **38** D4
Maiden Bradley **25** E4
Maiden Law **120** A3
Maiden Newton **12** B3
Maiden Wells **34** C3
Maidencombe **9** F1
Maidenhead **43** D4
Maidens **132** A5
Maiden's Green **43** E5
Maidensgrove **42** C4
Maidenwell *Cornw.* **5** F2
Maidenwell *Lincs.* **96** D5
Maidford **56** B2
Maids' Moreton **56** C4
Maidstone **31** G3
Maidwell **68** C5
Mail **200** D5
Mains of Ardestie **152** D1
Mains of Balgavies **160** D4
Mains of Balhall **160** D3
Mains of Ballindarg **160** C4
Mains of Burgie **180** C4
Mains of Culsh **183** D5
Mains of Dillavaird **161** F1
Mains of Drum **170** D4
Mains of Dudwick **171** E1
Mains of Faillie **167** G1
Mains of Fedderate **183** D5
Mains of Glack **170** C2
Mains of Glassaugh **182** A3
Mains of Glenbuchat **169** F3
Mains of Linton **170** C4
Mains of Melgund **160** D4
Mains of Pitfour **183** E5
Mains of Pittrichie **171** D2
Mains of Sluie **180** C4
Mains of Tannachy **181** F3
Mains of Thornton **161** E2
Mains of Tig **122** C2
Mains of Watten **195** E3
Mainsriddle **124** D5
Mainstone **64** B4
Maisemore **54** A5
Makendon **128** A1
Makerstoun **136** A3
Malacleit **173** F2
Malborough **8** D4
Malden Rushett **29** G1
Maldon **46** B2
Malham **101** F1
Maligar **176** A3
Mallaig **164** C5
Mallaigmore **164** D5
Mallaigvaig **164** C5
Malleny Mills **143** F3
Malletsheugh **141** G4
Malling **150** A4
Malltraeth **74** D1
Mallwyd **63** E1
Malmesbury **40** B4
Malmsmead **22** A3
Malpas *Ches.* **78** B3
Malpas *Cornw.* **4** C5
Malpas *Newport* **38** C3
Maltby *S.Yorks.* **94** C3
Maltby *Stock.* **111** D1
Maltby le Marsh **97** E4
Maltman's Hill **32** B4
Malton **111** G5
Malvern Link **53** G3
Malvern Wells **53** G3
Mambeg **140** D1
Mamble **65** F5
Mamhead **10** C4
Mamhilad **38** C2
Manaccan **3** E4
Manafon **64** A2
Manais **184** D5
Manaton **10** A4
Manby **97** D4
Mancetter **67** F3
Manchester **92** C3
Manchester Airport **92** C4
Mancot Royal **78** A1
Mandally **166** B4
Manea **70** C4
Maneight **132** D5
Manfield **110** B1
Mangaster **202** C5
Mangotsfield **39** F5
Mangurstadh **186** B4
Mankinholes **101** F5
Manley **91** G5
Manmoel **38** A2
Mannal **154** A2
Manningford Abbots **26** C2
Manningford Bohune **26** C2
Manningford Bruce **26** C2
Mannings Heath **17** E1
Mannington **13** G2
Manningtree **60** C4
Mannofield **171** E4
Manorbier **35** D3
Manordeifi **49** F3
Manordeilo **50** C5
Manorowen **48** C4
Mansell Gamage **52** C3
Mansell Lacy **52** D3
Mansergh **108** B4
Mansfield **81** G1
Mansfield Woodhouse **81** G1
Mansriggs **107** D4
Manston *Dorset* **13** E1
Manston *Kent* **33** F2
Manswood **13** F2
Manthorpe *Lincs.* **69** F1
Manthorpe *Lincs.* **83** E4
Manton *N.Lincs.* **95** G2
Manton *Rut.* **69** D2
Manton *Wilts.* **26** C1
Manuden **58** C5
Maolachy **148** A3
Maperton **25** D5
Maple Cross **43** F3
Maplebeck **82** C1
Mapledurham **42** B5
Mapledurwell **28** B2
Maplehurst **29** G5
Mapleton **80** C3
Mapperley **81** F3
Mapperton **12** B3
Mappleborough Green **54** C1
Mappleton **105** E3
Mapplewell **94** A2
Mappowder **12** D2
Mar Lodge **168** C5
Marazion **2** C3
Marbury **78** C3
March **70** C3
Marcham **41** G3
Marchamley **78** C5
Marchington **80** C4
Marchington Woodlands **80** C5
Marchwiel **78** A3
Marchwood **14** C1
Marcross **22** C1
Marcus **160** D4
Marden *Here.* **53** E3
Marden *Kent* **31** G4
Marden *T. & W.* **129** F4
Marden *Wilts.* **26** B2
Marden Beech **31** G4
Marden Thorn **31** G4
Mardy **38** C1
Mare Green **24** A5
Marefield **68** C2
Mareham le Fen **84** A1
Mareham on the Hill **84** A1
Maresfield **17** G1
Marfleet **104** D5
Marford **78** A2
Margam **37** D4
Margaret Marsh **13** E1
Margaret Roding **45** E1
Margaretting **45** F2
Margate **33** F1
Margnaheglish **131** F2
Margreig **124** C3
Margrove Park **111** F1
Marham **71** F2
Marhamchurch **20** C5
Marholm **69** G2
Marian Cwm **90** B5
Marian-Glas **88** D4
Mariansleigh **22** A5
Marishader **176** A3
Maristow House **8** A1
Mark **24** A3
Mark Causeway **24** A3
Mark Cross **31** E5
Markbeech **31** D4
Markby **97** E5
Markdhu **122** C3
Market Bosworth **67** G2
Market Deeping **69** G1
Market Drayton **79** D4
Market Harborough **68** C4
Market Lavington **26** B2
Market Overton **69** D1
Market Rasen **96** B4
Market Stainton **96** C5
Market Street **87** D3
Market Warsop **81** G1
Market Weighton **104** A3
Market Weston **72** A4
Markethill **152** A1
Markfield **67** G1
Markham **38** A2
Markham Moor **95** E5
Markinch **152** A4
Markington **102** B1
Marks Gate **45** D4
Marks Tey **60** A5
Marksbury **25** D1
Markwell **7** D5
Markyate **43** F1
Marlborough **26** C1
Marldon **9** E1
Marlesford **61** E2
Marley Green **78** C3
Marley Hill **120** B2
Marlingford **86** C5
Marloes **34** A2
Marlow **43** D4
Marlpit Hill **30** D4
Marlpool **81** F3
Marnhull **13** D1
Marnoch **182** A4
Marple **93** D4
Marr **94** C2
Marrel **191** F3
Marrick **109** F3
Marrister **201** E1
Marros **35** F2
Marsden *T. & W.* **120** D1
Marsden *W.Yorks.* **93** E1
Marsett **109** E4
Marsh **11** F1
Marsh Baldon **42** A3
Marsh Benham **27** F1
Marsh Chapel **97** D3
Marsh Gibbon **56** B5
Marsh Green *Devon* **10** D3
Marsh Green *Kent* **30** D4
Marsh Green *Tel. & W.* **65** F1
Marsh Lane **94** B5
Marsh Street **22** C3
Marshall's Heath **44** A1
Marshalsea **11** G2
Marsham **86** C3
Marshaw **100** B2
Marshborough **33** E3
Marshbrook **64** D4
Marshfield *Newport* **38** B4
Marshfield *S.Glos.* **39** G5
Marshgate **6** B1
Marshside **91** E1
Marshwood **11** G3
Marske **110** A2
Marske-by-the-Sea **121** F5
Marston *Ches.* **92** A5
Marston *Here.* **52** C2
Marston *Lincs.* **83** D3
Marston *Oxon.* **42** A2
Marston *Staffs.* **79** G5
Marston *Staffs.* **66** A1
Marston *Warks.* **67** E3
Marston *Wilts.* **26** A2
Marston Green **67** D4
Marston Magna **24** C5
Marston Meysey **40** D3
Marston Montgomery **80** C4
Marston Moretaine **57** E3
Marston on Dove **80** D5
Marston St. Lawrence **56** A3
Marston Stannett **53** E2
Marston Trussell **68** B4
Marstow **39** E1
Marsworth **43** E1
Marten **27** D1
Marthall **92** C5
Martham **87** F4
Marthig **185** G2
Martin *Hants.* **13** G1
Martin *Lincs.* **83** G1
Martin Drove End **26** B5
Martin Hussingtree **54** A1
Martinhoe **21** G1
Martinscroft **92** A4
Martinstown **12** C4
Martlesham **60** D3
Martlesham Heath **60** D3
Martletwy **34** D1
Martley **53** G1
Martock **12** A1
Marton *Ches.* **79** F1
Marton *Cumb.* **106** D5
Marton *E.Riding* **105** D4
Marton *Lincs.* **95** F4
Marton *Middbro.* **111** E1
Marton *N.Yorks.* **102** D1
Marton *N.Yorks.* **111** G4
Marton *Shrop.* **64** B2
Marton *Warks.* **55** G1
Marton Abbey **103** E1
Marton-le-Moor **110** C5
Martyr Worthy **27** G4
Martyr's Green **29** F2
Maruig **185** E3
Marwick **198** A4
Marwood **21** F2
Mary Tavy **7** F3
Marybank **179** D4
Maryburgh **179** E4
Maryfield **201** D3
Marygold **145** F3
Maryhill *Aber.* **182** D5
Maryhill *Glas.* **141** G3
Marykirk **161** E3
Marylebone *Gt.Lon.* **44** B4
Marylebone *Gt.Man.* **91** G2
Marypark **169** D1
Maryport *Cumb.* **116** D3
Maryport *D. & G.* **114** B3
Marystow **7** E2
Maryton **161** E4
Marywell *Aber.* **171** E5
Marywell *Aber.* **170** A5
Marywell *Angus* **161** E5
Masham **110** B4
Mashbury **45** F1
Mastrick **171** D4
Matching **45** E1
Matching Green **45** E1
Matching Tye **45** E1
Matfen **128** C4
Matfield **31** F4
Mathern **39** E3
Mathon **53** G3
Mathry **48** B4
Matlaske **86** C2
Matlock **81** E1
Matlock Bank **81** D1
Matlock Bath **81** D2
Matson **40** A1
Matterdale End **117** G4
Mattersey **95** D4
Mattingley **28** C2
Mattishall **86** B4
Mattishall Burgh **86** B4
Mauchline **132** D3
Maud **183** E5
Maufant **8** C5
Maugersbury **55** D5
Maughold **98** C2
Mauld **166** C1
Maulden **57** F4
Maulds Meaburn **108** B1
Maunby **110** C4
Maund Bryan **53** E2
Maundown **23** D5
Mautby **87** F4
Mavesyn Ridware **66** C1
Mavis Enderby **84** B1
Maw Green **66** C3
Mawbray **117** D2
Mawdesley **91** F1
Mawdlam **37** E4
Mawgan **3** E4
Mawla **4** A5
Mawnan **3** E4
Mawnan Smith **3** E4
Maxey **69** G2
Maxstoke **67** E4
Maxton *Kent* **33** E4
Maxton *Sc.Bord.* **136** A4
Maxwellheugh **136** B3
Maxwelltown **125** D3
Maxworthy **6** C1
Maybole **132** B5
Mayen **182** A5
Mayfield *E.Suss.* **18** A1
Mayfield *Midloth.* **144** A3
Mayfield *Staffs.* **80** C3
Mayford **29** E2
Mayland **46** C2
Maylandsea **46** C2
Maynard's Green **18** A2
Maypole *I.o.S.* **4** B1
Maypole *Kent* **33** D2
Maypole Green **73** F2
Maywick **200** C5
Meabhag **185** D4
Mead End **26** B5
Meadle **42** D2
Meadowhall **94** A3
Meadowmill **144** B2
Meadowtown **64** C2
Meal Bank **107** G3
Mealabost **187** F2
Mealasta **186** A5
Meals **97** E3
Mealsgate **117** F2
Meanley **100** D3
Mearbeck **101** E1
Meare **24** B3
Mearns **141** G4
Mears Ashby **56** D1
Measham **67** F1
Meathop **107** F4
Meavy **8** B1
Medbourne **68** D3
Meddon **20** C4
Meden Vale **81** G1
Medmenham **42** D4
Medomsley **120** A2
Medstead **28** B4
Meer End **67** E5
Meerbrook **79** G1
Meesden **58** C4
Meeth **21** F5
Meggethead **134** C3
Meidrim **49** F5
Meifod *Denb.* **76** D2
Meifod *Powys* **64** A1
Meigle **160** A5
Meikle Earnock **142** B4
Meikle Grenach **140** B3
Meikle Kilmory **140** B3
Meikle Rahane **140** D1
Meikle Strath **161** E2
Meikle Tarty **171** E2
Meikle Wartle **170** C1
Meikleour **151** G1
Meinciau **36** A1
Meir **79** G3
Meirheath **79** G4
Melbost **187** F4
Melbourn **58** B3
Melbourne *Derbys.* **81** E5
Melbourne *E.Riding* **103** G3
Melbury **21** D4
Melbury Abbas **13** E1
Melbury Bubb **12** B2
Melbury Osmond **12** B2
Melbury Sampford **12** B2
Melby **200** A2
Melchbourne **57** F1
Melchet Court **27** D5
Melcombe Bingham **13** D2
Melcombe Regis **12** C4
Meldon *Devon* **7** F1
Meldon *Northumb.* **128** D3
Meldreth **58** B3
Melfort **148** A3
Melgarve **167** D5
Melgum **169** G4
Meliden (Gallt Melyd) **90** B4
Melin-y-coed **76** B1
Melin-y-ddol **63** G2
Melin-y-grug **63** G2
Melin-y-Wig **76** D3
Melincourt **37** E2
Melincryddan **37** D3
Melkinthorpe **118** B5
Melkridge **118** D1
Melksham **26** A1
Melksham Forest **26** A1
Melldalloch **140** A2
Melling *Lancs.* **107** G5
Melling *Mersey.* **91** E2
Melling Mount **91** F2
Mellis **72** B4
Mellon Charles **188** A5
Mellon Udrigle **188** A5
Mellor *Gt.Man.* **93** D4
Mellor *Lancs.* **100** C4
Mellor Brook **100** C4
Mells **25** E3
Melmerby *Cumb.* **118** C4
Melmerby *N.Yorks.* **109** F4
Melmerby *N.Yorks.* **110** C5
Melplash **12** A3
Melrose *Aber.* **182** C3
Melrose *Sc.Bord.* **135** G2
Melsetter **196** B4
Melsonby **110** A2
Meltham **93** E1
Melton **61** D2
Melton Constable **86** B2
Melton Mowbray **68** C1
Melton Ross **96** A1
Meltonby **103** G2
Melvaig **176** D1
Melverley **64** C1
Melverley Green **64** C1
Melvich **194** A2
Membury **11** F2
Memsie **183** E3
Memus **160** C4
Menabilly **5** E4
Menai Bridge (Porthaethwy) **89** D5
Mendham **73** D3
Mendlesham **60** C1
Mendlesham Green **60** B1
Menethorpe **103** G1
Menheniot **5** G3
Menie House **171** E2
Mennock **133** G5
Menston **102** A3
Menstrie **150** D5
Mentmore **43** E1
Meoble **155** G1
Meole Brace **65** D1
Meon **15** E2
Meonstoke **15** F1
Meopham **31** F2
Meopham Green **31** F2
Mepal **70** C4
Meppershall **57** G4
Merbach **52** C3
Mercaston **81** D3
Mere *Ches.* **92** B4
Mere *Wilts.* **25** F4
Mere Brow **91** F1
Mere Green **66** D3
Mereworth **31** F3
Mergie **161** F1
Meriden **67** E4
Merkland **124** B3
Merley **13** G3
Merlin's Bridge **34** C1
Merridge **23** F4
Merrifield **9** E3
Merrington **78** B5
Merrion **34** C3
Merriott **12** A1
Merrivale **7** F3
Merrow **29** F2
Merry Hill *Herts.* **44** A3
Merry Hill *W.Mid.* **66** B4
Merrymeet **5** G3
Mersham **32** C5
Merstham **30** B3
Merston **16** A3
Merstone **15** E4
Merther **4** C5
Merthyr **49** G5
Merthyr Cynog **51** F4
Merthyr Dyfan **23** E1
Merthyr Mawr **37** E5
Merthyr Tydfil **37** G2
Merthyr Vale **37** G3
Merton *Devon* **21** F4
Merton *Gt.Lon.* **30** B2
Merton *Norf.* **71** G3
Merton *Oxon.* **42** A1
Mertyn **90** C5
Mervinslaw **136** A5
Meshaw **10** A1
Messing **46** B1
Messingham **95** F2
Metfield **73** D3
Metheringham **83** F1
Methil **152** B5
Methlem **74** A4
Methley **102** C5
Methlick **171** D1
Methven **151** F2
Methwold **71** F3
Methwold Hythe **71** F3
Metrocentre **120** B1
Mettingham **73** E2
Metton **86** C2
Mevagissey **5** E5
Mexborough **94** B3
Mey **195** E1
Meysey Hampton **40** D2
Miabhag **184** C3
Miabhig **186** B4
Mial **177** D2
Michaelchurch **53** E5
Michaelchurch Escley **52** C4
Michaelchurch-on-Arrow **52** B2
Michaelston-le-Pit **38** A5
Michaelston-y-Fedw **38** B4
Michaelstow **5** E2
Micheldever **27** G4
Michelmersh **27** E5
Mickfield **60** C1
Mickle Trafford **78** B1
Mickleby **112** B1
Mickleham **29** G2
Micklehurst **93** D2
Mickleover **81** E4
Micklethwaite **117** F1
Mickleton *Dur.* **119** F5
Mickleton *Glos.* **55** D3
Mickletown **102** C5
Mickley **110** B5
Mickley Square **119** G1
Mid Ardlaw **183** E3
Mid Beltie **170** B4
Mid Cairncross **160** D2
Mid Calder **143** E3
Mid Clyth **195** E5
Mid Lavant **16** A3
Mid Letter **148** C4
Mid Lix **150** A2
Mid Mossdale **108** D3
Mid Sannox **140** B5
Mid Yell **203** E3
Midbea **198** C2
Middle Assendon **42** C4
Middle Aston **55** G5
Middle Barton **55** G5
Middle Claydon **56** C5
Middle Drums **161** D4
Middle Handley **94** B5
Middle Harling **72** A3
Middle Kames **140** A1
Middle Littleton **54** C3
Middle Maes-coed **52** C4
Middle Mill **48** B5
Middle Rasen **96** A4
Middle Rigg **151** F4
Middle Salter **100** C1
Middle Town **4** B1
Middle Tysoe **55** F3
Middle Wallop **27** D4
Middle Winterslow **26** D4
Middle Woodford **26** C4
Middlebie **126** A4
Middleham **110** A4
Middlehill *Aber.* **182** D5
Middlehill *Cornw.* **5** G3
Middlehope **65** D4

Middlemarsh 12 C2
Middlesbrough 121 D5
Middleshaw 107 G4
Middlesmoor 109 F5
Middlestone Moor 120 B4
Middlestown 93 G1
Middleton *Aber.* 170 D3
Middleton *Angus* 161 D5
Middleton *Cumb.* 108 B4
Middleton *Derbys.* 81 D2
Middleton *Derbys.* 80 C1
Middleton *Essex* 59 G3
Middleton *Gt.Man.* 92 C2
Middleton *Hants.* 27 F3
Middleton *Lancs.* 100 A2
Middleton *Midloth.* 144 A4
Middleton *N.Yorks.* 111 G4
Middleton *Norf.* 71 E1
Middleton *Northants.* 68 D4
Middleton *Northumb.* 128 C3
Middleton *Northumb.* 137 E3
Middleton *P.& K.* 151 G4
Middleton *P.& K.* 159 G5
Middleton *Shrop.* 64 B3
Middleton *Shrop.* 65 E5
Middleton *Shrop.* 78 A5
Middleton *Suff.* 61 F1
Middleton *Swan.* 36 A4
Middleton *W.Yorks.* 102 A3
Middleton *W.Yorks.* 102 B5
Middleton *Warks.* 67 D3
Middleton Bank Top 128 C3
Middleton Cheney 55 G3
Middleton Green 79 G4
Middleton Hall 137 D4
Middleton-in-Teesdale 119 F5
Middleton of Potterton 171 E3
Middleton-on-Leven 111 D1
Middleton-on-Sea 16 B4
Middleton on the Hill 53 E1
Middleton-on-the-Wolds 104 B3
Middleton One Row 110 C1
Middleton Park 171 E3
Middleton Priors 65 F4
Middleton Quernhow 110 C5
Middleton St. George 110 C1
Middleton Scriven 65 F4
Middleton Stoney 56 A5
Middleton Tyas 110 B2
Middletown *Cumb.* 106 A2
Middletown *Powys* 64 C1
Middlewich 79 E1
Middlewood 92 D4
Middlewood Green 60 B1
Middleyard 132 D2
Middlezoy 24 A4
Middridge 120 B5
Midfield 193 E2
Midford 25 E1
Midge Hall 100 B5
Midgeholme 118 C2
Midgham 27 G1
Midgley *W.Yorks.* 93 G1
Midgley *W.Yorks.* 101 G5
Midhopestones 93 G3
Midhurst 29 D5
Midlem 135 G3
Midpark 140 B4
Midsomer Norton 25 D2
Midtown *High.* 193 E2
Midtown *High.* 177 E1
Midtown of Barras 161 G1
Midville 84 B2
Migdale 190 B5
Migvie 169 G4
Milarrochy 149 G5
Milber 10 B5
Milbethill 182 B4
Milborne Port 12 C1
Milborne St. Andrew 13 E3
Milborne Wick 25 D5
Milbourne 128 D4
Milburn 118 C5
Milbury Heath 39 F3
Milcombe 55 G4
Milden 60 A3
Mildenhall *Suff.* 71 F5
Mildenhall *Wilts.* 41 E5
Mile Elm 26 A1
Mile End *Essex* 60 A5
Mile End *Glos.* 39 E1
Milebrook 64 C5
Milebush 31 G4
Mileham 86 A4
Milesmark 143 E1
Milfield 136 D3
Milford *Derbys.* 81 E3
Milford *Devon* 20 C3
Milford *Shrop.* 78 B5
Milford *Staffs.* 79 G5
Milford *Surr.* 29 E3
Milford Haven (Aberdaugleddau) 34 C2
Milford on Sea 14 B3
Milkwall 39 E2
Mill Bank 101 G5
Mill End *Bucks.* 42 C4
Mill End *Herts.* 58 B4
Mill End Green 59 E5
Mill Green *Essex* 45 F2
Mill Green *Shrop.* 79 D5
Mill Hill 44 B3
Mill Houses 100 C1
Mill Lane 28 C2
Mill of Camsail 141 D1
Mill of Colp 182 C5
Mill of Elrick 183 E5
Mill of Fortune 150 C2
Mill of Kingoodie 170 D2
Mill of Monquich 171 D5
Mill of Uras 161 G2
Mill Street 86 B4
Milland 28 D5
Millbank 183 F5
Millbeck 117 F4
Millbounds 199 D3
Millbreck 183 F5
Millbridge 28 D3
Millbrook *Beds.* 57 F4
Millbrook *Cornw.* 8 A2
Millbrook *S'ham.* 14 C1
Millburn *Aber.* 170 A2
Millburn *Aber.* 170 B1
Millcombe 9 E3
Millcorner 18 D1
Millden 171 E3
Milldens 160 D4
Millearne 151 E3
Millenheath 78 C4
Millerhill 144 A3
Miller's Dale 93 F5
Millholme 107 G3
Millhouse *Arg. & B.* 140 A2
Millhouse *Cumb.* 117 G3
Millhousebridge 125 F2
Millikenpark 141 F3
Millington 104 A2
Millmeece 79 F4
Millness 166 C1
Millom 106 C4
Millport 140 C4
Millthrop 108 B3
Milltimber 171 D4
Milltown *Aber.* 169 G3
Milltown *D. & G.* 126 B4
Milltown *Derbys.* 81 E1
Milltown *Devon* 21 F2
Milltown *High.* 180 B5
Milltown *High.* 178 C4
Milltown of Aberdalgie 151 F2
Milltown of Auchindoun 181 F5
Milltown of Craigston 182 C4
Milltown of Edinvillie 181 E5
Milltown of Rothiemay 182 A5
Milltown of Towie 169 G3
Milnathort 151 G4
Milngavie 141 G2
Milnrow 92 D1
Milnsbridge 93 F1
Milnthorpe 107 F4
Milovaig 175 E4
Milrig 132 D2
Milson 65 F5
Milstead 32 B3
Milston 26 C3
Milton *Angus* 160 B5
Milton *Cambs.* 58 C1
Milton *Cumb.* 118 B1
Milton *D. & G.* 124 C2
Milton *D. & G.* 124 C3
Milton *Derbys.* 81 E5
Milton *High.* 179 G2
Milton *High.* 180 B4
Milton *High.* 176 D5
Milton *High.* 179 E5
Milton *High.* 195 F3
Milton *High.* 167 D1
Milton *Moray* 182 A3
Milton *N.Som.* 24 A1
Milton *Newport* 38 C4
Milton *Notts.* 95 E5
Milton *Oxon.* 55 G4
Milton *Oxon.* 41 G3
Milton *P.& K.* 151 E1
Milton *Pembs.* 34 D2
Milton *Stir.* 150 A4
Milton *Stir.* 149 G5
Milton *Stoke* 79 G2
Milton *W.Dun.* 141 F2
Milton Abbas 13 E2
Milton Abbot 7 E3
Milton Bridge 143 G3
Milton Bryan 57 E4
Milton Clevedon 25 D4
Milton Combe 8 A1
Milton Damerel 21 D4
Milton Ernest 57 F2
Milton Green 78 B2
Milton Hill 41 G3
Milton Keynes 57 D4
Milton Keynes Village 57 D4
Milton Lilbourne 26 C1
Milton Lockhart 142 C5
Milton Malsor 56 C2
Milton Morenish 150 B1
Milton of Auchinhove 170 A4
Milton of Balgonie 152 B4
Milton of Cairnborrow 181 G5
Milton of Callander 150 A4
Milton of Campfield 170 B4
Milton of Campsie 142 A2
Milton of Coldwells 171 E1
Milton of Cullerlie 170 C4
Milton of Cushnie 170 A3
Milton of Dalcapon 159 E4
Milton of Inveramsay 170 C2
Milton of Noth 170 A2
Milton of Tullich 169 F5
Milton on Stour 25 E5
Milton Regis 32 A2
Milton-under-Wychwood 41 E1
Miltonduff 181 D3
Miltonhill 180 C3
Miltonise 122 C3
Milverton 23 E5
Milwich 79 G4
Minard 148 B5
Minard Castle 148 B5
Minchington 13 F1
Minchinhampton 40 A2
Mindrum 136 C3
Minehead 22 C3
Minera 77 F2
Minety 40 C3
Minffordd *Gwyn.* 62 D1
Minffordd *Gwyn.* 75 E4
Mingearraidh 172 C1
Miningsby 84 B1
Minions 5 G2
Minishant 132 B4
Minley Manor 28 D2
Minllyn 63 E1
Minnes 171 E2
Minnigaff 123 F4
Minnonie 182 C3
Minskip 102 C1
Minstead 14 B1
Minster *Kent* 32 B1
Minster *Kent* 33 F2
Minster Lovell 41 F1
Minsterley 64 C2
Minsterworth 39 G1
Minterne Magna 12 C2
Minting 96 B5
Mintlaw 183 F5
Minto 135 G3
Minton 64 D3
Minwear 34 D1
Minworth 67 D3
Miodar 154 B2
Mirbister 198 B4
Mireland 195 F2
Mirfield 102 A5
Miserden 40 B2
Miskin *R.C.T.* 37 G4
Miskin *R.C.T.* 37 G3
Misson 95 D3
Misterton *Leics.* 68 A4
Misterton *Notts.* 95 E3
Misterton *Som.* 12 A2
Mitcham 30 B2
Mitchel Troy 39 D1
Mitcheldean 39 F1
Mitchell 4 C4
Mitchelland 107 F3
Mitcheltroy Common 39 D2
Mitford 129 D3
Mithian 4 B4
Mitton 66 A1
Mixbury 56 B4
Moar 158 A5
Moat 126 C4
Mobberley 92 B5
Moccas 52 C3
Mochdre *Conwy* 89 G5
Mochdre *Powys* 63 G4
Mochrum 114 D2
Mockbeggar 31 G4
Mockerkin 117 D4
Modbury 8 C2
Moddershall 79 G4
Modsarie 193 F2
Moelfre *I.o.A.* 88 D4
Moelfre *Powys* 77 E5
Moffat 134 B5
Mogerhanger 57 G3
Moin'a'choire 138 B3
Moine House 193 E2
Moira 67 F1
Mol-chlach 164 A3
Molash 32 C3
Mold (Yr Wyddgrug) 77 F1
Molehill Green 59 D5
Molescroft 104 C3
Molesworth 69 F5
Mollance 124 B4
Molland 22 B5
Mollington *Ches.* 91 E5
Mollington *Oxon.* 55 G3
Mollinsburn 142 B2
Monachty 50 B1
Monachyle 149 G3
Moncreiffe 151 G3
Monevechadan 149 D4
Monewden 60 D2
Moneydie 151 F2
Moniaive 124 B1
Monifieth 152 C1
Monikie 152 C1
Monimail 152 A3
Monington 49 E3
Monk Fryston 103 E5
Monk Sherborne 28 B2
Monk Soham 60 D1
Monk Street 59 E5
Monken Hadley 44 B3
Monkhill 117 G1
Monkhopton 65 F3
Monkland 53 D2
Monkleigh 21 E3
Monknash 37 F5
Monkokehampton 21 F5
Monks Eleigh 60 A3
Monk's Gate 17 E1
Monks' Heath 92 C5
Monks Kirby 67 G4
Monks Risborough 42 D2
Monkseaton 129 F4
Monkshill 182 C5
Monksilver 23 D4
Monkstadt 175 G3
Monkswood 38 C2
Monkton *Devon* 11 E2
Monkton *Kent* 33 E2
Monkton *S.Ayr.* 132 B3
Monkton *T. & W.* 120 C1
Monkton Combe 25 E1
Monkton Deverill 25 F4
Monkton Farleigh 25 E1
Monkton Heathfield 23 F5
Monkton Up Wimborne 13 G1
Monkwearmouth 120 C2
Monkwood 28 B4
Monmore Green 66 B3
Monmouth (Trefynwy) 39 E1
Monnington on Wye 52 C3
Monreith 115 D2
Montacute 12 A1
Monteach 183 D5
Montford 64 D1
Montford Bridge 64 D1
Montgarrie 170 A3
Montgomery (Trefaldwyn) 64 B3
Montgreenan 141 E5
Montrave 152 B4
Montrose 161 F4
Monxton 27 E3
Monyash 80 C1
Monymusk 170 B3
Monzie 151 D2
Moodiesburn 142 A2
Moonzie 152 B3
Moor Allerton 102 C4
Moor Cock 100 C1
Moor Crichel 13 F2
Moor End *Cumb.* 107 G5
Moor End *E.Riding* 104 A4
Moor Monkton 103 E2
Moor Nook 100 C4
Moor Row 116 D5
Moor Side 84 A2
Moorby 84 A1
Moorcot 52 C2
Moordown 13 G3
Moore 91 G4
Moorends 95 D1
Moorgreen 81 F3
Moorhall 94 A5
Moorhampton 52 C3
Moorhouse *Cumb.* 117 G1
Moorhouse *Notts.* 82 C1
Moorland or Northmoor Green 24 A4
Moorlinch 24 A4
Moorsholm 111 F1
Moorside 93 D2
Moortown *I.o.W.* 14 D4
Moortown *Lincs.* 96 A3
Morangie 179 G1
Morar 164 C5
Morborne 69 G3
Morchard Bishop 10 A2
Morcombelake 11 G3
Morcott 69 E2
Morda 77 F5
Morden *Dorset* 13 F3
Morden *Gt.Lon.* 30 B2
Mordiford 53 E4
Mordington Holdings 145 G4
Mordon 120 C5
More 64 C3
Morebath 22 C5
Morebattle 136 B4
Morecambe 100 A1
Morefield 188 D5
Moreleigh 9 D2
Morenish 150 B1
Moresby 116 C4
Morestead 27 G5
Moreton *Dorset* 13 E4
Moreton *Essex* 45 E2
Moreton *Here.* 53 E1
Moreton *Mersey.* 91 D4
Moreton *Oxon.* 42 B2
Moreton Corbet 78 C5
Moreton-in-Marsh 55 E4
Moreton Jeffries 53 F3
Moreton Morrell 55 F2
Moreton on Lugg 53 E3
Moreton Pinkney 56 A3
Moreton Say 78 D4
Moreton Valence 39 G2
Moretonhampstead 10 A4
Morfa Bychan 75 E4
Morfa Glas 37 E2
Morfa Nefyn 74 B3
Morgan's Vale 26 C5
Mork 39 E2
Morland 118 B5
Morley *Derbys.* 81 E3
Morley *Dur.* 120 A5
Morley *W.Yorks.* 102 B5
Morley Green 92 C4
Morley St. Botolph 86 B5
Morningside *Edin.* 143 G2
Morningside *N.Lan.* 142 C4
Morningthorpe 72 D2
Morpeth 129 D3
Morphie 161 F3
Morrey 66 D1
Morriston *S.Ayr.* 132 A5
Morriston *Swan.* 36 C3
Morroch 155 F1
Morston 86 B1
Mortehoe 21 E1
Mortimer 28 B1
Mortimer West End 28 B1
Mortimer's Cross 52 D1
Mortlake 44 B5
Morton *Derbys.* 81 F1
Morton *Lincs.* 83 G5
Morton *Lincs.* 95 F3
Morton *Notts.* 82 C2
Morton *S.Glos.* 39 F3
Morton *Shrop.* 77 F5
Morton Bagot 54 D1
Morton-on-Swale 110 C3
Morton on the Hill 86 C4
Morvah 2 A3
Morval 5 G4
Morvich *High.* 165 F2
Morvich *High.* 190 C4
Morvil 48 D4
Morville 65 F3
Morwellham 8 A1
Morwenstow 20 C4
Morwick Hall 129 E1
Mosborough 94 B4
Moscow 141 F5
Mosedale 117 G3
Moselden Height 93 E1
Moseley *W.Mid.* 66 C4
Moseley *Worcs.* 54 A2
Moss *Arg. & B.* 154 A2
Moss *S.Yorks.* 94 C1
Moss *Wrex.* 78 A2
Moss Bank 91 G3
Moss Nook 92 C4
Moss of Barmuckity 181 E3
Moss Side 99 G4
Moss-side *High.* 180 A4
Moss-side *Moray* 182 A4
Mossat 169 G3
Mossbank 203 D5
Mossblown 132 C3
Mossburnford 136 A5
Mossdale 124 A3
Mossend 142 B3
Mossgiel 132 C3
Mosshead 170 A1
Mosside of Ballinshoe 160 C4
Mossley 93 D2
Mossley Hill 91 E4
Mosspaul Hotel 126 C2
Mosstodloch 181 F3
Mosston 160 D5
Mosterton 12 A2
Mostyn 90 C4
Motcombe 25 F5
Motherby 118 A5
Motherwell 142 B4
Mottingham 44 D5
Mottisfont 27 E5
Mottistone 14 D4
Mottram in Longdendale 93 D3
Mottram St. Andrew 92 C5
Mouldsworth 91 G5
Moulin 159 E4
Moulsecoomb 17 F3
Moulsford 42 A4
Moulsham 45 G2
Moulsoe 57 E3
Moulton *Ches.* 79 D1
Moulton *Lincs.* 84 B5
Moulton *N.Yorks.* 110 B2
Moulton *Northants.* 56 C1
Moulton *Suff.* 59 E1
Moulton Chapel 70 A1
Moulton St. Mary 87 E5
Moulton Seas End 84 B5
Mounie Castle 170 C2
Mount *Cornw.* 4 B4
Mount *Cornw.* 5 F3
Mount *High.* 180 B5
Mount Bures 60 A4
Mount Hawke 4 B5
Mount Manisty 91 E5
Mount Oliphant 132 B4
Mount Pleasant *Derbys.* 81 E3
Mount Pleasant *Suff.* 73 F4
Mount Tabor 101 G5
Mountain Ash 37 G3
Mountain Cross 143 F5
Mountain Water 48 C5
Mountbenger 135 E3
Mountblairy 182 B4
Mountfield 18 C1
Mountgerald 179 E3
Mountjoy 4 C3
Mountnessing 45 F3
Mounton 39 E3
Mountsorrel 68 A1
Mountstuart 140 C4
Mousehole 2 B4
Mouswald 125 E3
Mow Cop 79 F2
Mowden 110 B1
Mowhaugh 136 C4
Mowsley 68 B4
Mowtie 161 G1
Moxley 66 B3
Moy *High.* 157 D1
Moy *High.* 157 G1
Moy *High.* 167 G1
Moy House 180 C3
Moyles Court 14 A2
Moylgrove 49 E3
Muasdale 139 E5
Much Birch 53 E4
Much Cowarne 53 F3
Much Dewchurch 53 D4
Much Hadham 44 D1
Much Hoole 100 A5
Much Marcle 53 F4
Much Wenlock 65 F2
Muchalls 171 D5
Muchelney 24 B5
Muchlarnick 5 G4
Muchra 134 D4
Muchrachd 166 B1
Mucking 45 F4
Mucklestone 79 E4
Muckleton 78 C5
Muckletown 170 A2
Muckton 97 D4
Mudale 193 E5
Muddiford 21 F2
Muddles Green 18 A2
Muddleswood 17 E2
Mudeford 14 A3
Mudford 12 B1
Mudgley 24 B3
Mugeary 164 A1
Mugginton 81 D3
Muggleswick 119 G2
Muie 190 B4
Muir 159 F1
Muir of Fowlis 170 A3
Muir of Lochs 181 F3
Muir of Ord 179 E4
Muirden 182 C4
Muirdrum 153 D1
Muirhead *Aber.* 170 A3
Muirhead *Angus* 152 B1
Muirhead *Fife* 152 A4
Muirhead *Moray* 180 C3
Muirhead *N.Lan.* 142 A3
Muirhouses 143 E1
Muirkirk 133 E3
Muirmill 142 B1
Muirtack *Aber.* 171 E1
Muirtack *Aber.* 182 D5
Muirton 179 G3
Muirton of Ardblair 159 G5
Muirton of Ballochy 161 E3
Muirtown 151 E3
Muiryfold 182 C4
Muker 109 E3
Mulbarton 86 C5
Mulben 181 F4
Mulhagery 185 F3
Mullach Charlabhaigh 186 D3
Mullacott Cross 21 F1
Mullion 3 D5
Mumby 97 F5
Munderfield Row 53 F2
Munderfield Stocks 53 F2
Mundesley 87 E2
Mundford 71 F3
Mundham 73 E2
Mundon 46 B2
Mundurno 171 E3
Munerigie 166 B4
Mungasdale 188 B5
Mungoswells 144 B2
Mungrisdale 117 G3
Munlochy 179 F4
Munnoch 140 D5
Munsley 53 F3
Munslow 65 E4
Murchington 7 G2
Murcott 42 A1
Murdostoun 142 C4
Murkle 195 D2
Murlaganmore 150 A1
Murlaggan *High.* 165 G5
Murlaggan *High.* 157 F1
Murra 196 B2
Murroes 152 C1
Murrow 70 B2
Mursley 56 D5
Murston 32 B2
Murthill 160 C4
Murthly 151 F1
Murton *Cumb.* 118 D5
Murton *Dur.* 120 C3
Murton *Northumb.* 145 G5
Murton *York* 103 F2
Musbury 11 F3
Muscoates 111 F4
Musdale 148 B2
Musselburgh 144 A2
Muston *Leics.* 82 D4
Muston *N.Yorks.* 113 E5
Mustow Green 66 A5
Mutford 73 F3
Muthill 151 D3
Mutterton 10 D2
Mybster 195 D3
Myddfai 51 D4
Myddle 78 B5
Myddlewood 78 B5
Mydroilyn 50 A2
Mylor 3 F3
Mylor Bridge 3 F3
Mynachlog-ddu 49 E4
Myndtown 64 C4
Mynydd-bach 39 D3
Mynydd Llandygai 75 F1
Mynytho 74 C4
Myrebird 170 C5
Mytchett 29 D2
Mytholm 101 F5
Mytholmroyd 101 G5
Myton-on-Swale 102 D1

N

Naast 177 E1
Naburn 103 E3
Nackington 33 D3
Nacton 60 D3
Nafferton 104 C2
Nailbridge 39 F1
Nailsea 39 D5
Nailstone 67 G2
Nailsworth 40 A3
Nairn 180 A4
Nancegollan 2 D3
Nancledra 2 B3
Nanhoron 74 B4
Nannau 76 A5
Nannerch 77 E1
Nanpantan 68 A1
Nanpean 5 D4
Nanstallon 5 E3
Nant-ddu 37 G1
Nant-glas 51 F1
Nant Peris 75 F2
Nant-y-derry 38 C2
Nant-y-dugoed 63 F1
Nant-y-groes 51 G1
Nant-y-moel 37 F3
Nant-y-Pandy 89 E5
Nanternis 49 G2
Nantgaredig 50 A5
Nantgarw 38 A4
Nantglyn 76 D1
Nantlle 75 E2
Nantmawr 77 F5
Nantmel 51 G1
Nantmor 75 F3
Nantwich 78 D2
Nantycaws 36 A1
Nantyffyllon 37 E3
Nantyglo 38 A2
Naphill 43 D3
Nappa 101 E2
Napton on the Hill 55 G1
Narberth (Arberth) 35 E1
Narborough *Leics.* 68 A3
Narborough *Norf.* 71 F1
Narrachan 148 B3
Nasareth 75 D2
Naseby 68 B5
Nash *Bucks.* 56 C4
Nash *Here.* 52 C1
Nash *Newport* 38 C4
Nash *Shrop.* 65 E5
Nash *V. of Glam.* 37 F5
Nash Lee 42 D2
Nassington 69 F3
Nasty 58 B5
Nateby *Cumb.* 108 C2
Nateby *Lancs.* 100 A3
Nately Scures 28 C2
Natland 107 G4
Naughton 60 B3
Naunton *Glos.* 54 D5
Naunton *Worcs.* 54 A4
Naunton Beauchamp 54 B2
Navenby 83 E2
Navestock 45 E3
Navestock Side 45 E3
Navidale 191 F3
Navity 179 G3
Nawton 111 F4
Nayland 60 A4
Nazeing 44 D2
Neacroft 14 A3
Neal's Green 67 F4
Neap 201 E2
Near Cotton 80 B3
Near Sawrey 107 E3
Neasham 110 C1
Neath (Castell-Nedd) 37 D3
Neatham 28 C3
Neatishead 87 E3
Nebo *Cere.* 50 B1
Nebo *Conwy* 76 B2
Nebo *Gwyn.* 75 D2
Nebo *I.o.A.* 88 C3
Necton 71 G2
Nedd 192 A5
Nedderton 129 E3
Nedging Tye 60 B3
Needham 72 D3
Needham Market 60 B2
Needingworth 70 B5
Neen Savage 65 F5
Neen Sollars 65 F5
Neenton 65 F4
Nefyn 74 C3
Neilston 141 F4
Nelson *Caerp.* 38 A3
Nelson *Lancs.* 101 E4
Nelson Village 129 E4
Nemphlar 142 C5
Nempnett Thrubwell 24 C1
Nenthall 119 D3
Nenthead 119 D3
Nenthorn 136 A3
Nerabus 138 A4
Nercwys 77 F1
Neriby 138 B3
Nerston 142 A4
Nesbit 137 D3
Ness 91 E5
Ness of Tenston 198 A5
Nesscliffe 64 C1
Neston *Ches.* 91 D5
Neston *Wilts.* 25 F1
Nether Alderley 92 C5
Nether Auchendrane 132 B4
Nether Barr 123 F4
Nether Blainslie 144 C5
Nether Broughton 82 B5
Nether Burrow 108 B5
Nether Cerne 12 C3
Nether Compton 12 B1
Nether Crimond 170 D2
Nether Dalgliesh 135 D5
Nether Dallachy 181 F3
Nether End 93 G5
Nether Exe 10 C3
Nether Glasslaw 183 D4
Nether Handwick 160 B5
Nether Haugh 94 B3
Nether Headon 95 E5
Nether Heselden 109 D5
Nether Heyford 56 B2
Nether Kellet 100 B1
Nether Kinmundy 183 F5
Nether Langwith 94 C5
Nether Lenshie 182 B5
Nether Moor 81 E1
Nether Padley 93 G5
Nether Pitforthie 161 G2
Nether Poppleton 103 E2
Nether Silton 111 D3
Nether Stowey 23 E4
Nether Urquhart 151 G4
Nether Wallop 27 E4
Nether Wasdale 106 C2
Nether Wellwood 133 E3
Nether Whitacre 67 E3
Nether (Lower) Winchendon 42 C1
Nether Worton 55 G4
Netheravon 26 C3
Netherbrae 182 C4
Netherbrough 198 B5
Netherburn 142 C5
Netherbury 12 A3
Netherby *Cumb.* 126 B4
Netherby *N.Yorks.* 102 C3
Nethercott 55 G5
Netherend 39 E3
Netherfield *E.Suss.* 18 C2
Netherfield *Notts.* 82 B3
Netherfield *S.Lan.* 142 B5
Netherhall 140 D3
Netherhampton 26 C4
Netherley 171 D5
Nethermill 125 E2
Nethermuir 183 E5
Netherseal 67 E1
Nethershield 133 D3
Netherstreet 26 A1
Netherthird *D. & G.* 124 B5
Netherthird *E.Ayr.* 133 D4
Netherthong 93 F2
Netherthorpe 94 C4
Netherton *Angus* 160 D4
Netherton *Ches.* 91 G5
Netherton *Devon* 10 B5

Netherton Mersey. 91 E2
Netherton Northumb. 128 B1
Netherton Oxon. 41 G3
Netherton P. & K. 159 G4
Netherton S.Lan. 142 D4
Netherton W.Mid. 66 B4
Netherton W.Yorks. 93 G1
Netherton W.Yorks. 93 F1
Netherton Worcs. 54 B3
Nethertown Cumb. 106 A2
Nethertown Ork. 195 F1
Netherwitton 128 D3
Netherwood D. & G. 125 D3
Netherwood E.Ayr. 133 E3
Nethy Bridge 168 C2
Netley Abbey 15 D2
Netley Marsh 14 C1
Nettlebed 42 C4
Nettlebridge 24 D3
Nettlecombe Dorset 12 B3
Nettlecombe Som. 23 D4
Nettleden 43 F1
Nettleham 96 A5
Nettlestead Kent 31 F3
Nettlestead Suff. 60 B3
Nettlestead Green 31 F3
Nettlestone 15 F3
Nettleton Lincs. 96 B2
Nettleton Wilts. 40 A5
Netton Devon 8 B3
Netton Wilts. 26 C4
Neuadd Cere. 50 A2
Neuadd I.o.A. 88 B3
Neuadd Powys 51 F3
Nevendon 45 G3
Nevern 49 D4
Nevill Holt 68 D3
New Abbey 125 D4
New Aberdour 183 D3
New Addington 30 C2
New Alresford 27 G4
New Alyth 160 A5
New Arley 67 E3
New Ash Green 31 F2
New Barn 31 F2
New Barnet 44 B3
New Belses 135 G3
New Bewick 137 E4
New Bolingbroke 84 B2
New Bradwell 56 D3
New Bridge 124 D3
New Brighton Hants. 15 G2
New Brighton Mersey. 91 E3
New Brinsley 81 F2
New Broughton 78 A2
New Buckenham 72 B2
New Byth 182 D4
New Cheriton 27 G5
New Costessey 86 C5
New Cross 62 C5
New Cumnock 133 E4
New Deer 183 D5
New Duston 56 C1
New Earswick 103 F2
New Edlington 94 C3
New Elgin 181 E3
New Ellerby 105 D4
New Eltham 44 D5
New End 54 C1
New England 69 G2
New Farnley 102 B4
New Ferry 91 E4
New Fryston 103 D5
New Galloway 124 A3
New Gilston 152 C4
New Grimsby 4 A1
New Hartley 129 F4
New Haw 29 F1
New Hedges 35 E2
New Holland 104 C5
New Houghton Derbys. 81 G1
New Houghton Norf. 85 F5
New Houses 108 D5
New Hutton 107 G3
New Hythe 31 G3
New Inn Carmar. 50 A4
New Inn Fife 152 A4
New Inn Mon. 39 D2
New Inn Torfaen 38 B3
New Invention Shrop. 64 B5
New Invention W.Mid. 66 B2
New Lanark 142 C5
New Lane 91 F1
New Leake 84 C2
New Leeds 183 E4
New Leslie 170 A2
New Longton 100 B5
New Luce 122 C4
New Mains 133 G2
New Mains of Ury 161 G1
New Malden 30 B2
New Marske 121 F5
New Marton 78 A4
New Mill Cornw. 2 B3
New Mill Herts. 43 E1
New Mill W.Yorks. 93 F2
New Mill End 44 A1
New Mills Cornw. 4 C4
New Mills Derbys. 93 D4
New Mills Mon. 39 E2
New Mills Powys 63 G2
New Milton 14 B3
New Mistley 60 C4
New Moat 49 D5
New Orleans 130 C4
New Park 5 F1
New Pitsligo 183 D4
New Polzeath 4 D2
New Quay (Ceinewydd) 49 G2
New Rackheath 87 D4
New Radnor 52 B1
New Rent 118 A4
New Romney 19 F1
New Rossington 94 D3
New Row 100 C4
New Sawley 81 F4
New Scone 151 G2
New Silksworth 120 C2
New Town E.Loth. 144 B2
New Town E.Suss. 17 G1
New Town Glos. 54 C4
New Tredegar 38 A2
New Ulva 139 F1
New Walsoken 70 C2
New Waltham 96 C2
New Winton 144 B2
New Yatt 41 F1
New York Lincs. 84 A2
New York T. & W. 129 F4
Newark Ork. 199 F2
Newark Peter. 70 A2
Newark-on-Trent 82 D2
Newarthill 142 B4
Newbarn 33 D4
Newbarns 106 D5
Newbiggin Cumb. 118 A5
Newbiggin Cumb. 118 C5
Newbiggin Cumb. 118 B3
Newbiggin Cumb. 99 F1
Newbiggin Dur. 119 F5
Newbiggin N.Yorks. 109 F4
Newbiggin N.Yorks. 109 E3
Newbiggin Northumb. 119 F1
Newbiggin-by-the-Sea 129 F3
Newbiggin-on-Lune 108 C2
Newbigging Aber. 171 D5
Newbigging Aber. 159 G1
Newbigging Angus 152 C1
Newbigging Angus 152 C1
Newbigging Angus 160 A5
Newbigging S.Lan. 143 E5
Newbold Derbys. 94 A5
Newbold Leics. 67 G1
Newbold on Avon 67 G5
Newbold on Stour 55 E3
Newbold Pacey 55 E2
Newbold Verdon 67 G2
Newborough I.o.A. 74 D1
Newborough Peter. 70 A2
Newborough Staffs. 80 C5
Newbottle 56 A4
Newbourne 61 D3
Newbridge (Cefn Bychan) Caerp. 38 B3
Newbridge Cornw. 2 B3
Newbridge Cornw. 7 D4
Newbridge Edin. 143 F2
Newbridge Hants. 14 C1
Newbridge I.o.W. 14 D4
Newbridge Oxon. 41 G2
Newbridge Pembs. 48 C4
Newbridge Wrex. 77 F3
Newbridge-on-Usk 38 C3
Newbridge on Wye 51 G2
Newbrough 119 E1
Newburgh Aber. 183 E4
Newburgh Aber. 171 E2
Newburgh Fife 152 A3
Newburgh Lancs. 91 F1
Newburgh Sc.Bord. 135 E4
Newburn 120 A1
Newbury 27 F1
Newby Cumb. 118 B5
Newby Lancs. 101 E3
Newby N.Yorks. 111 E1
Newby N.Yorks. 108 C5
Newby Bridge 107 E4
Newby East 118 A2
Newby West 117 G1
Newby Wiske 110 C4
Newcastle Bridgend 37 F5
Newcastle Mon. 38 D1
Newcastle Shrop. 64 B4
Newcastle Emlyn (Castell Newydd Emlyn) 49 G3
Newcastle International Airport 129 D4
Newcastle-under-Lyme 79 F3
Newcastle upon Tyne 120 B1
Newcastleton 126 C3
Newchapel Pembs. 49 F4
Newchapel Stoke 79 F2
Newchapel Surr. 30 C4
Newchurch Carmar. 49 G5
Newchurch I.o.W. 15 E4
Newchurch Kent 32 C5
Newchurch Lancs. 101 E5
Newchurch Lancs. 101 E4
Newchurch Mon. 39 D3
Newchurch Powys 52 B2
Newcott 11 F2
Newcraighall 144 A2
Newdigate 29 G3
Newell Green 43 D5
Newenden 18 D1
Newent 53 G5
Newerne 39 F2
Newfield Dur. 120 B4
Newfield Dur. 120 B2
Newfield High. 179 G2
Newgale 48 B5
Newgate 86 B1
Newgate Street 44 C2
Newgord 203 E2
Newhall Ches. 78 D3
Newhall Derbys. 81 D5
Newham Gt.Lon. 44 C4
Newham Northumb. 137 F4
Newham Hall 137 F4
Newhaven 17 G3
Newhey 92 D1
Newholm 112 B1
Newhouse 142 B3
Newick 17 G1
Newington Kent 33 D5
Newington Kent 32 A2
Newington Oxon. 42 B3
Newington Bagpath 40 A3
Newland Glos. 39 E2
Newland N.Yorks. 103 F5
Newland Worcs. 53 G3
Newlandrig 144 A3
Newlands Northumb. 119 G2
Newlands Sc.Bord. 126 D2
Newland's Corner 29 F3
Newlands of Geise 194 C2
Newlyn 2 B4
Newlyn East 4 C4
Newmachar 171 D3
Newmains 142 C4
Newmarket Suff. 59 E1
Newmarket W.Isles 187 F4
Newmill Aber. 161 F1
Newmill Aber. 183 D5
Newmill Aber. 170 D2
Newmill Moray 181 G4
Newmill Sc.Bord. 135 F4
Newmill of Inshewan 160 C3
Newmills 179 F3
Newmiln P. & K. 151 G1
Newmiln P. & K. 151 F2
Newmilns 132 D2
Newnham Glos. 39 F1
Newnham Hants. 28 C2
Newnham Herts. 58 A4
Newnham Kent 32 B3
Newnham Northants. 56 A2
Newnham Worcs. 53 F1
Newnham Paddox 67 G4
Newnoth 170 A1
Newport Cornw. 6 D2
Newport Devon 21 F2
Newport E.Riding 104 A4
Newport Essex 58 D4
Newport Glos. 39 F3
Newport High. 191 G2
Newport I.o.W. 15 E4
Newport (Casnewydd) Newport 38 C4
Newport Norf. 87 G4
Newport Pembs. 49 D4
Newport Tel. & W. 65 G1
Newport-on-Tay 152 C2
Newport Pagnell 57 D3
Newpound Common 29 F5
Newquay 4 C3
Newquay (Cornwall) Airport 4 C3
Newseat 170 C1
Newsham Lancs. 100 B4
Newsham N.Yorks. 110 A1
Newsham N.Yorks. 110 C4
Newsham Northumb. 129 E4
Newsholme E.Riding 103 G5
Newsholme Lancs. 101 E2
Newstead Northumb. 137 F4
Newstead Notts. 81 G2
Newstead Sc.Bord. 135 G2
Newthorpe 103 D4
Newton Aber. 181 G5
Newton Aber. 183 F5
Newton Arg. & B. 148 C5
Newton Bridgend 37 E5
Newton Cambs. 70 C1
Newton Cambs. 58 C3
Newton Ches. 78 B2
Newton Ches. 91 G5
Newton Cumb. 106 D5
Newton D. & G. 125 F1
Newton Gt.Man. 93 D3
Newton Here. 52 C1
Newton High. 195 F4
Newton High. 179 G5
Newton High. 195 E3
Newton High. 192 B5
Newton High. 179 E4
Newton High. 179 G3
Newton Lancs. 100 C2
Newton Lancs. 107 G5
Newton Lincs. 83 F4
Newton Moray 181 F3
Newton N.Ayr. 140 A4
Newton Norf. 71 G1
Newton Northants. 69 D4
Newton Northumb. 119 G1
Newton Notts. 82 B3
Newton P. & K. 151 D1
Newton Pembs. 48 C5
Newton Pembs. 34 C2
Newton S.Lan. 134 A2
Newton Sc.Bord. 136 A4
Newton Staffs. 80 B5
Newton Suff. 60 A3
Newton Swan. 36 C4
Newton W.Loth. 143 E2
Newton W.Yorks. 103 D5
Newton Warks. 68 A5
Newton Wilts. 26 D5
Newton Abbot 10 B5
Newton Arlosh 117 E1
Newton Aycliffe 120 B5
Newton Bewley 121 D5
Newton Blossomville 57 E2
Newton Bromswold 57 F1
Newton Burgoland 67 F2
Newton by Toft 96 A4
Newton Ferrers 8 B3
Newton Flotman 72 D2
Newton Harcourt 68 B3
Newton Kyme 103 D3
Newton-le-Willows Mersey. 91 G3
Newton-le-Willows N.Yorks. 110 B4
Newton Longville 56 D4
Newton Mearns 141 G4
Newton Morrell 110 B2
Newton Mountain 34 C2
Newton Mulgrave 111 G1
Newton of Affleck 152 C1
Newton of Ardtoe 155 F2
Newton of Balcanquhal 151 G3
Newton of Dalvey 180 C4
Newton of Falkland 152 A4
Newton of Leys 179 F5
Newton-on-Ouse 103 E1
Newton-on-Rawcliffe 112 B3
Newton-on-the-Moor 129 D1
Newton on Trent 95 F5
Newton Poppleford 11 D4
Newton Purcell 56 B4
Newton Regis 67 E2
Newton Reigny 118 A4
Newton St. Cyres 10 B3
Newton St. Faith 86 D4
Newton St. Loe 25 E1
Newton St. Petrock 21 E4
Newton Solney 81 D5
Newton Stacey 27 F3
Newton Stewart 123 F4
Newton Tony 26 D3
Newton Tracey 21 F3
Newton under Roseberry 111 E1
Newton upon Derwent 103 G3
Newton Valence 28 C4
Newtonairds 124 C2
Newtongrange 144 A3
Newtonhill 171 E5
Newtonmill 161 E3
Newtonmore 167 G5
Newtown B.Gwent 38 A1
Newtown Bucks. 43 E2
Newtown Ches. 78 B2
Newtown Cumb. 118 B1
Newtown Derbys. 93 D4
Newtown Hants. 15 F1
Newtown Hants. 27 F1
Newtown Hants. 14 B1
Newtown Hants. 27 E5
Newtown Hants. 15 E1
Newtown Here. 53 G4
Newtown Here. 53 F3
Newtown High. 166 C4
Newtown I.o.M. 98 B4
Newtown I.o.W. 14 D3
Newtown Northumb. 128 C1
Newtown Northumb. 137 E4
Newtown Poole 13 G3
Newtown (Y Drenewydd) Powys 64 A3
Newtown Shrop. 78 B4
Newtown Staffs. 79 G1
Newtown Staffs. 80 B1
Newtown Wilts. 26 A5
Newtown in St. Martin 3 E4
Newtown Linford 68 A1
Newtown St. Boswells 135 G2
Newtown Unthank 67 G2
Newtyle 160 A5
Neyland 34 C2
Nibley Glos. 39 F2
Nibley S.Glos. 39 F4
Nicholashayne 11 E1
Nicholaston 36 B4
Nidd 102 C1
Niddrie 143 G2
Nigg Aberdeen 171 E4
Nigg High. 180 A2
Nightcott 22 B5
Nilig 76 D2
Nimlet 39 G5
Nine Ashes 45 E2
Nine Elms 40 D4
Nine Mile Burn 143 F4
Ninebanks 119 D2
Ninemile Bar or Crocketford 124 C3
Ninfield 18 C2
Ningwood 14 D4
Nisbet 136 A4
Niton 15 E5
Nitshill 141 G3
Nizels 31 E3
No Man's Heath Ches. 78 C3
No Man's Heath Warks. 67 E2
Noak Hill 45 E3
Noblehill 125 D3
Nobottle 56 B1
Nocton 83 F1
Noddsdale 140 D3
Noke 42 A1
Nolton 34 B1
Nomansland Devon 10 B1
Nomansland Wilts. 14 B1
Noneley 78 B5
Nonington 33 E3
Nook Cumb. 126 C4
Nook Cumb. 107 G4
Noonsbrough 200 B2
Noranside 160 C3
Norbiton 29 G1
Norbreck 99 G3
Norbury Ches. 78 C3
Norbury Derbys. 80 C3
Norbury Shrop. 64 C3
Norbury Staffs. 79 E5
Norchard 54 A1
Nordelph 71 D2
Norden 13 F4
Nordley 65 F3
Norham 145 G5
Norland Town 101 G5
Norley 91 G5
Norleywood 14 C3
Norman Cross 69 G3
Normanby N.Lincs. 95 F1
Normanby N.Yorks. 111 G4
Normanby R. & C. 111 E1
Normanby-by-Spital 96 A4
Normanby by Stow 95 F4
Normanby le Wold 96 B3
Normandy 29 E2
Normann's Ruh 154 D5
Norman's Bay 18 B3
Norman's Green 11 D2
Normanton Derby 81 E4
Normanton Leics. 82 D3
Normanton Lincs. 83 E3
Normanton Notts. 82 C2
Normanton Rut. 69 E2
Normanton W.Yorks. 102 C5
Normanton le Heath 67 F1
Normanton on Soar 81 G5
Normanton-on-the-Wolds 82 B4
Normanton on Trent 82 C1
Normoss 99 G4
Norrington Common 25 F1
Norris Hill 67 F1
North Anston 94 C4
North Ascot 29 E1
North Aston 55 G5
North Baddesley 27 E5
North Ballachulish 156 C3
North Balloch 123 E1
North Barrow 24 D5
North Barsham 86 A2
North Benfleet 45 G4
North Bersted 16 B3
North Berwick 144 C1
North Boarhunt 15 F1
North Bogbain 181 F4
North Bovey 10 A4
North Bradley 25 F2
North Brentor 7 E2
North Brewham 25 E4
North Buckland 21 E1
North Burlingham 87 E4
North Cadbury 24 D5
North Cairn 122 A3
North Camp 29 D2
North Carlton Lincs. 95 G5
North Carlton Notts. 94 C4
North Cave 104 A4
North Cerney 40 C2
North Chailey 17 F1
North Charford 26 D5
North Charlton 137 F4
North Cheriton 25 D5
North Cliffe 104 A4
North Clifton 95 F5
North Cockerington 97 D3
North Coker 12 B1
North Connel 148 B1
North Cornelly 37 E4
North Cotes 96 D2
North Cove 73 F3
North Cowton 110 B2
North Crawley 57 E3
North Cray 45 D5
North Creake 85 G4
North Curry 24 A5
North Dallens 156 B5
North Dalton 104 B2
North Dawn 197 D2
North Deighton 102 C2
North Duffield 103 F4
North Elkington 96 C3
North Elmham 86 A3
North Elmsall 94 B1
North End Bucks. 56 D5
North End Essex 45 F1
North End Hants. 27 F1
North End N.Som. 24 B1
North End Norf. 72 B2
North End Northumb. 128 D1
North End Ports. 15 F2
North End W.Suss. 16 D2
North Erradale 176 D1
North Essie 183 F4
North Ferriby 104 B5
North Frodingham 104 D2
North Gorley 14 A1
North Green 72 D3
North Grimston 104 A1
North Hayling 15 G2
North Hazelrigg 137 E3
North Heasley 22 A4
North Heath 29 F5
North Hill 5 G2
North Hinksey 41 G2
North Holmwood 29 G3
North Huish 8 D2
North Hykeham 83 E1
North Johnston 34 C1
North Kelsey 96 A2
North Kessock 179 F5
North Killingholme 96 B1
North Kilvington 110 D4
North Kilworth 68 B4
North Kyme 83 G2
North Lancing 17 D3
North Lee 42 D2
North Leigh 41 F1
North Leverton with Habblesthorpe 95 E4
North Littleton 54 C3
North Lopham 72 B3
North Luffenham 69 E2
North Marden 16 A2
North Marston 56 C5
North Middleton 144 A4
North Millbrex 182 D5
North Molton 22 A5
North Moreton 42 A4
North Mundham 16 A3
North Muskham 82 C2
North Newbald 104 B4
North Newington 55 G4
North Newnton 26 C2
North Newton 23 F4
North Nibley 39 G3
North Oakley 27 G2
North Ockendon 45 E4
North Ormesby 121 E5
North Ormsby 96 C3
North Otterington 110 C3
North Owersby 96 A3
North Perrott 12 A2
North Petherton 23 F4
North Petherwin 5 G1
North Pickenham 71 G2
North Piddle 54 B2
North Poorton 12 B3
North Queensferry 143 F1
North Radworthy 22 A4
North Rauceby 83 F3
North Reston 97 D4
North Rigton 102 B3
North Rode 79 F1
North Roe 202 C4
North Runcton 71 E1
North Sandwick 203 E3
North Scale 99 E1
North Scarle 83 D1
North Seaton 129 E3
North Shian 156 B5
North Shields 120 C1
North Shoebury 46 C4
North Side 70 A3
North Skelton 111 F1
North Somercotes 97 E3
North Stainley 110 B5
North Stainmore 108 D1
North Stifford 45 F4
North Stoke B. & N.E.Som. 25 D1
North Stoke Oxon. 42 B4
North Stoke W.Suss. 16 C2
North Stoneham 14 D1
North Street Hants. 28 B4
North Street Kent 32 C3
North Street W.Berks. 42 B5
North Sunderland 137 G3
North Tamerton 6 D1
North Tarbothill 171 E3
North Tawton 21 G5
North Third 142 B1
North Thoresby 96 C3
North Tidworth 26 D3
North Togston 129 E1
North Town Devon 21 F5
North Town Hants. 29 D2
North Tuddenham 86 B4
North Walsham 87 D2
North Waltham 27 G3
North Warnborough 28 C2
North Watten 195 E3
North Weald Bassett 45 D2
North Wheatley 95 E4
North Whilborough 9 E1
North Wick 24 C1
North Widcombe 24 C2
North Willingham 96 B4
North Wingfield 81 F1
North Witham 83 E5
North Wootton Dorset 12 C1
North Wootton Norf. 85 E5
North Wootton Som. 24 C3
North Wraxall 40 A5
North Wroughton 40 D4
North Yardhope 128 B1
Northacre 72 A2
Northall Green 86 B4
Northallerton 110 C3
Northam Devon 21 E3
Northam S'ham. 14 D1
Northampton 56 C1
Northaw 44 B2
Northay 11 F1
Northborough 69 G2
Northbourne 33 F3
Northbrook 55 G5
Northburnhill 182 D5
Northchapel 29 E5
Northchurch 43 E2
Northcote Manor 21 G4
Northcott 6 D1
Northdyke 198 A4
Northend B. & N.E.Som. 25 E1
Northend Bucks. 42 C3
Northend Warks. 55 F2
Northfield Aber. 182 D3
Northfield Aberdeen 171 D4
Northfield High. 195 F4
Northfield Sc.Bord. 145 G3
Northfield W.Mid. 66 C5
Northfleet 45 F5
Northhouse 135 F5
Northiam 18 D1
Northill 57 G3
Northington 27 G4
Northlands 84 B2
Northleach 40 D1
Northleigh Devon 11 E3
Northleigh Devon 21 G2
Northlew 7 F1
Northmoor 41 G2
Northmoor Green or Moorland 24 A4
Northmuir 160 B4
Northney 15 G2
Northolt 44 A4
Northop 77 F1
Northop Hall 77 F1
Northorpe Lincs. 84 A4
Northorpe Lincs. 95 F3
Northorpe Lincs. 69 F1
Northover 24 C5
Northowram 102 A5
Northpunds 200 D5
Northrepps 86 D2
Northton (Taobh Tuath) 184 B5
Northtown 197 D3
Northway 54 B4
Northwich 92 A5
Northwick 39 E4
Northwold 71 F3
Northwood Gt.Lon. 43 F3
Northwood I.o.W. 15 D3
Northwood Shrop. 78 B4
Northwood Green 39 G1
Norton Glos. 54 A5
Norton Halton 91 G4
Norton Herts. 58 A4
Norton I.o.W. 14 C4
Norton N.Yorks. 111 G5
Norton Northants. 56 B1
Norton Notts. 94 C5
Norton Powys 52 C1
Norton S.Yorks. 94 C1
Norton S.Yorks. 94 A4
Norton Shrop. 65 E2
Norton Shrop. 65 G2
Norton Shrop. 65 D4
Norton Stock. 120 D5
Norton Suff. 60 A1
Norton W.Mid. 66 A4
Norton W.Suss. 16 B3
Norton W.Suss. 16 A4
Norton Wilts. 40 A4
Norton Worcs. 54 A2
Norton Worcs. 54 C3
Norton Bavant 26 A3
Norton Bridge 79 F5
Norton Canes 66 C2
Norton Canon 52 C3
Norton Disney 83 D2
Norton Ferris 25 E4
Norton Fitzwarren 23 E5
Norton Green 14 C4
Norton Hawkfield 24 C1
Norton Heath 45 F2
Norton in Hales 79 D4
Norton in the Moors 79 F2
Norton-Juxta-Twycross 67 F2
Norton-le-Clay 110 C5
Norton Lindsey 55 E1
Norton Malreward 24 C1
Norton Mandeville 45 E2
Norton St. Philip 25 E2
Norton sub Hamdon 12 A1
Norton Subcourse 73 F2
Norton Wood 52 C3
Norwell 82 C1
Norwell Woodhouse 82 C1
Norwich 86 D5
Norwich Airport 86 D4
Norwick 203 F1
Norwood Green 44 A5
Norwood Hill 30 B4
Noseley 68 C3
Noss Mayo 8 B3
Nosterfield 110 B4
Nostie 165 E2
Notgrove 54 D5
Nottage 37 E5
Nottingham High. 195 E5
Nottingham Nott. 81 G3
Notton W.Yorks. 94 A1
Notton Wilts. 26 A1
Nounsley 45 G2
Noutard's Green 53 G1
Nowton 59 G1
Nox 64 D1
Noyadd Trefawr 49 F3
Nuffield 42 B4
Nun Monkton 103 E2
Nunburnholme 104 A3
Nuneaton 67 F3
Nuneham Courtenay 42 A3
Nunney 25 E3
Nunnington 111 F5
Nunnington Park 23 D5
Nunthorpe 111 E1
Nunton 26 C5
Nunwick N.Yorks. 110 C5
Nunwick Northumb. 128 A4
Nup End Bucks. 43 D1
Nup End Glos. 54 A5
Nursling 14 C1
Nursted 28 C5
Nurton 66 A3
Nutbourne W.Suss. 16 C2
Nutbourne W.Suss. 15 G2
Nutfield 30 C3
Nuthall 81 G3
Nuthampstead 58 C4
Nuthurst W.Suss. 29 G5
Nuthurst Warks. 67 D5
Nutley E.Suss. 17 G1
Nutley Hants. 28 B3
Nutwell 94 D2
Nyadd 150 C5
Nybster 195 F2
Nyetimber 16 A4
Nyewood 28 D5

Nymet Rowland 10 A2
Nymet Tracey 10 A2
Nympsfield 40 A2
Nynehead 23 E5
Nythe 24 B4
Nyton 16 B3

O

Oad Street 32 A2
Oadby 68 B2
Oak Cross 7 F1
Oakamoor 80 B3
Oakbank *Arg. & B.* 147 G1
Oakbank *W.Loth.* 143 E3
Oakdale 38 A3
Oake 23 E5
Oaken 66 A2
Oakenclough 100 B3
Oakengates 65 F1
Oakenhead 181 E3
Oakenshaw *Dur.* 120 B4
Oakenshaw *W.Yorks.* 102 A5
Oakford *Cere.* 50 A2
Oakford *Devon* 22 C5
Oakfordbridge 22 C5
Oakgrove 79 G1
Oakham 69 D2
Oakhanger 28 C4
Oakhill 24 D3
Oakington 58 C1
Oaklands *Conwy* 76 B2
Oaklands *Herts.* 44 B1
Oakle Street 39 G1
Oakley *Beds.* 57 F2
Oakley *Bucks.* 42 B1
Oakley *Fife* 143 E1
Oakley *Hants.* 27 G2
Oakley *Suff.* 72 C4
Oakley Green 43 E5
Oakley Park 63 F4
Oakridge Lynch 40 B2
Oaks 64 D2
Oaksey 40 B3
Oakshaw Ford 126 D4
Oakthorpe 67 F1
Oaktree Hill 110 C3
Oakwoodhill 29 G4
Oakworth 101 G4
Oalinlongart 140 C1
Oare *Kent* 32 C2
Oare *Som.* 22 B3
Oare *Wilts.* 26 C1
Oasby 83 F4
Oatfield 130 B4
Oathlaw 160 C4
Oban 148 A2
Obley 64 C5
Oborne 12 C1
Occlestone Green 79 D1
Occold 72 C4
Occumster 195 E5
Ochiltree 132 D3
Ochr-y-Mynydd 37 G2
Ochtermuthill 150 D3
Ochtertyre *P. & K.* 150 D2
Ochtertyre *Stir.* 150 C5
Ockbrook 81 F4
Ockham 29 F2
Ockle 155 E2
Ockley 29 G4
Ocle Pychard 53 E3
Octon 104 C1
Odcombe 12 B1
Odd Down 25 E1
Oddingley 54 B2
Oddington 42 A1
Oddsta 203 E3
Odell 57 E2
Odie 199 E4
Odiham 28 C2
Odstock 26 C5
Odstone 67 F2
Offchurch 55 F1
Offenham 54 C3
Offerton 92 D4
Offham *E.Suss.* 17 G2
Offham *Kent* 31 F3
Offord Cluny 58 A1
Offord D'Arcy 58 A1
Offton 60 B3
Offwell 11 E3
Ogbourne Maizey 41 D5
Ogbourne St. Andrew 41 D5
Ogbourne St. George 41 D5
Ogden 101 G4
Ogil 160 C3
Ogle 128 D4
Ogmore 37 E5
Ogmore-by-Sea 37 E5
Ogmore Vale 37 F3
Oil Terminal 196 C3
Okeford Fitzpaine 13 E1
Okehampton 7 F1
Okehampton Camp 7 F1
Okraquoy 200 D4
Old 68 C5
Old Aberdeen 171 E4
Old Alresford 27 G4
Old Arley 67 E3
Old Basford 81 G3
Old Basing 28 B2
Old Belses 135 G3
Old Bewick 137 E4
Old Bolingbroke 84 B1
Old Brampton 94 A5
Old Bridge of Urr 124 B4
Old Buckenham 72 B2
Old Burghclere 27 F2
Old Byland 111 E4
Old Cleeve 22 D3
Old Clipstone 82 B1
Old Colwyn 89 G5
Old Craig 171 E2
Old Craighall 144 A2
Old Crombie 182 A4
Old Dailly 122 D1
Old Dalby 82 B5
Old Deer 183 E5
Old Ellerby 105 D4
Old Felixstowe 61 E4
Old Fletton 69 G3
Old Glossop 93 E3
Old Goginan 62 C4
Old Goole 103 G5
Old Gore 53 F5
Old Grimsby 4 A1
Old Hall 96 C1
Old Heath 60 B5
Old Hill 66 B4
Old Hutton 107 G4
Old Kea 4 C5
Old Kilpatrick 141 F2
Old Kinnernie 170 C4
Old Knebworth 58 A5
Old Leake 84 C2
Old Leslie 170 A2
Old Malton 112 G5
Old Micklefield 102 D4
Old Milverton 55 E1
Old Montsale 46 D3
Old Netley 15 D1
Old Newton 60 B1
Old Philpstoun 143 E2
Old Poltalloch 148 A4
Old Radnor 52 B2
Old Rattray 183 F4
Old Rayne 170 B2
Old Romney 19 F1
Old Scone 151 G2
Old Shields 142 C2
Old Sodbury 39 G4
Old Somerby 83 E4
Old Stratford 56 C3
Old Sunderlandwick 104 C2
Old Swarland 129 D1
Old Swinford 66 B4
Old Town *Cumb.* 107 G4
Old Town *I.o.S.* 4 B1
Old Town *Northumb.* 128 A2
Old Tupton 81 E1
Old Warden 57 G3
Old Weston 69 G5
Old Windsor 43 E5
Old Wives Lees 32 C3
Old Woking 29 F2
Old Wolverton 56 D3
Old Woods 78 B5
Oldberrow 54 D1
Oldborough 10 A2
Oldbury *Kent* 31 E3
Oldbury *Shrop.* 65 G3
Oldbury *W.Mid.* 66 B3
Oldbury *Warks.* 67 F3
Oldbury Naite 39 F3
Oldbury-on-Severn 39 F3
Oldbury on the Hill 40 A4
Oldcastle 52 C5
Oldcastle Heath 78 B3
Oldcotes 94 C4
Oldfield *W.Yorks.* 101 G4
Oldfield *Worcs.* 54 A1
Oldford 25 E2
Oldhall *Aber.* 169 G5
Oldhall *High.* 195 E3
Oldham 92 D2
Oldhamstocks 145 E2
Oldhurst 70 A5
Oldland 39 F5
Oldmeldrum 170 D2
Oldmill 170 A4
Oldpark 65 F2
Oldridge 10 B3
Oldshore Beg 192 A3
Oldshore More 192 B3
Oldstead 111 E4
Oldtown of Aigas 179 D5
Oldtown of Ord 182 B4
Oldwalls 36 A3
Oldways End 22 B5
Oldwhat 183 D4
Olgrinmore 194 C3
Oliver 134 C3
Oliver's Battery 27 F5
Ollaberry 202 C4
Ollerton *Ches.* 92 B5
Ollerton *Notts.* 82 B1
Ollerton *Shrop.* 78 D5
Olmstead Green 59 E3
Olney 57 D2
Olrig House 195 D2
Olton 66 D4
Olveston 39 E4
Ombersley 54 A1
Ompton 82 B1
Onchan 98 B4
Onecote 80 B2
Ongar Hill 85 D5
Ongar Street 52 C1
Onibury 64 D5
Onich 156 C3
Onllwyn 37 E1
Onneley 79 E3
Onslow Village 29 E3
Opinan *High.* 188 A5
Opinan *High.* 176 D2
Orange Lane 145 E5
Orbliston 181 F4
Orbost 175 F5
Orby 84 C1
Orcadia 140 C3
Orchard 140 C1
Orchard Portman 23 F5
Orchard Wyndham 23 D4
Orcheston 26 B3
Orcop 53 D5
Orcop Hill 53 D5
Ord 164 C3
Ordhead 170 B3
Ordie 169 G4
Ordiequish 181 F4
Ordsall 95 E5
Ore 18 D2
Oreham Common 17 E2
Oreston 8 B2
Oreton 65 F4
Orford *Suff.* 61 F3
Orford *Warr.* 92 A3
Orgreave 66 D1
Orleton *Here.* 53 D1
Orleton *Worcs.* 53 F1
Orleton Common 53 D1
Orlingbury 69 D5
Ormacleit 162 A1
Ormesby 111 E1
Ormesby St. Margaret 87 F4
Ormesby St. Michael 87 F4
Ormiscaig 188 A5
Ormiston 144 B3
Ormsaigmore 155 D3
Ormsdale 140 B1
Ormskirk 91 F2
Ormwe 194 D2
Orphir 196 C2
Orpington 31 D2
Orrell 91 G2
Orrisdale 98 B2
Orrok House 171 E3
Orroland 116 A2
Orsett 45 F4
Orslow 66 A1
Orston 82 C3
Orton *Cumb.* 108 B2
Orton *Northants.* 68 D5
Orton Longueville 69 G3
Orton-on-the-Hill 67 F2
Orton Waterville 69 G3
Orwell 58 B3
Osbaldeston 100 C4
Osbaldwick 103 F2
Osbaston *Leics.* 67 G2
Osbaston *Tel. & W.* 65 E1
Osborne 15 E3
Osbournby 83 F4
Oscroft 78 C1
Ose 175 G5
Osgathorpe 67 G1
Osgodby *Lincs.* 96 A3
Osgodby *N.Yorks.* 103 F4
Osgodby *N.Yorks.* 113 D4
Oskaig 164 B1
Osmaston *Derby* 81 E4
Osmaston *Derbys.* 80 C3
Osmington 12 D4
Osmington Mills 12 D4
Osmotherley 111 D3
Osnaburgh or Dairsie 152 C3
Osney 42 A2
Ospringe 32 C3
Ossett 102 B5
Ossington 82 C1
Ostend 46 C3
Osterley 44 A5
Oswaldkirk 111 F5
Oswaldtwistle 100 D5
Oswestry 77 F5
Otford 31 E3
Otham 31 G3
Othery 24 A4
Otley *Suff.* 60 D2
Otley *W.Yorks.* 102 B3
Otter 140 A2
Otter Ferry 140 A1
Otterbourne 27 F5
Otterburn *N.Yorks.* 101 E2
Otterburn *Northumb.* 128 A2
Otterburn Camp 128 A2
Otterden Place 32 B3
Otterham 6 B1
Otterhampton 23 F3
Ottershaw 29 F1
Otterswick 203 E4
Otterton 11 D4
Ottery St. Mary 11 D3
Ottinge 33 D4
Ottringham 105 E5
Oughterby 117 F1
Oughtershaw 109 D4
Oughtibridge 94 A3
Oulston 111 E5
Oulton *Cumb.* 117 F1
Oulton *Norf.* 86 C3
Oulton *Staffs.* 79 G4
Oulton *Suff.* 73 G2
Oulton *W.Yorks.* 102 C5
Oulton Broad 73 G2
Oulton Street 86 C3
Oundle 69 F4
Ousby 118 C4
Ousdale 191 F2
Ousden 59 F2
Ousefleet 104 A5
Ouston *Dur.* 120 B2
Ouston *Northumb.* 128 C4
Out Newton 105 F5
Out Rawcliffe 100 A3
Outertown 198 A5
Outgate 107 E3
Outhgill 108 C2
Outlands 79 E5
Outlane 93 E1
Outwell 70 D2
Outwood *Surr.* 30 C4
Outwood *W.Yorks.* 102 C5
Ovenden 101 G5
Over *Cambs.* 58 B1
Over *Ches.* 78 D1
Over *S.Glos.* 39 E4
Over Compton 12 B1
Over End 93 G5
Over Haddon 80 D1
Over Kellet 107 G5
Over Kiddington 55 G5
Over Norton 55 F5
Over Peover 92 B5
Over Rankeilour 152 B3
Over Silton 111 D3
Over Stowey 23 E4
Over Stratton 12 A1
Over Tabley 92 B4
Over Wallop 27 D4
Over Whitacre 67 E3
Over (Upper) Winchendon 42 C1
Over Worton 55 G5
Overbister 199 E2
Overbrae 182 D4
Overbury 54 B4
Overcombe 12 C4
Overleigh 24 B4
Overpool 91 E5
Overscaig Hotel 189 G2
Overseal 67 E1
Oversland 32 C3
Oversley Green 54 C2
Overstone 56 D1
Overstrand 87 D1
Overton *Aber.* 170 C3
Overton *Aberdeen* 171 D3
Overton *Hants.* 27 G3
Overton *Lancs.* 100 A2
Overton *N.Yorks.* 103 E2
Overton *Shrop.* 65 E5
Overton *Swan.* 36 A4
Overton *Wrex.* 78 A3
Overtown 142 C4
Overy Staithe 85 G3
Oving *Bucks.* 56 C5
Oving *W.Suss.* 16 B3
Ovingdean 17 F3
Ovingham 119 G1
Ovington *Dur.* 110 A1
Ovington *Essex* 59 F3
Ovington *Hants.* 27 G4
Ovington *Norf.* 86 A5
Ovington *Northumb.* 119 G1
Ower 14 C1
Owermoigne 13 D4
Owlswick 42 C2
Owmby 96 A2
Owmby-by-Spital 96 A4
Owslebury 27 G5
Owston 68 C2
Owston Ferry 95 F2
Owstwick 105 E4
Owthorpe 82 B4
Oxborough 71 F2
Oxcliffe Hill 100 A1
Oxcombe 96 D5
Oxen End 59 E5
Oxen Park 107 E4
Oxenholme 107 G3
Oxenhope 101 G4
Oxenton 54 B4
Oxenwood 27 E2
Oxford 42 A2
Oxhill 55 F3
Oxley 66 B2
Oxley Green 46 C1
Oxley's Green 18 B1
Oxnam 136 A5
Oxnead 86 D3
Oxnop Ghyll 109 E3
Oxshott 29 G1
Oxspring 93 G2
Oxted 30 C3
Oxton *Mersey.* 91 E4
Oxton *Notts.* 82 B2
Oxton *Sc.Bord.* 144 B4
Oxwich 36 B4
Oxwich Green 36 B4
Oxwick 86 A3
Oykel Bridge 189 F4
Oyne 170 B2
Ozleworth 39 G3

P

Pabail Iarach 187 G4
Pabail Uarach 187 G4
Packington 67 F1
Padanaram 160 C4
Padbury 56 C4
Paddington 44 B4
Paddlesworth 33 D4
Paddock Wood 31 F4
Paddockhaugh 181 E4
Paddockhole 126 A3
Paddolgreen 78 C4
Padeswood 77 F1
Padiham 101 D4
Padside 102 A2
Padstow 4 D2
Padworth 28 B1
Pagham 16 A4
Paglesham Churchend 46 C3
Paglesham Eastend 46 C3
Paibeil 173 F3
Paible 184 C4
Paignton 9 E1
Pailton 67 G4
Painscastle 52 A3
Painshawfield 119 G1
Painswick 40 A2
Paisley 141 F3
Pakefield 73 G2
Pakenham 60 A1
Pale 76 C4
Palestine 27 D3
Paley Street 43 D5
Palgowan 123 E2
Palgrave 72 C4
Pallinsburn House 136 C3
Palmerscross 181 E3
Palmerstown 23 E1
Palnackie 124 C5
Palnure 123 F4
Palterton 81 F1
Pamber End 28 B2
Pamber Green 28 B2
Pamber Heath 28 B1
Pamington 54 B4
Pamphill 13 F2
Pampisford 58 C3
Pan 196 C3
Panborough 24 B3
Panbride 153 D1
Pancrasweek 20 C5
Pandy *Gwyn.* 62 C2
Pandy *Mon.* 52 C5
Pandy *Powys* 63 F2
Pandy *Wrex.* 77 E4
Pandy Tudur 76 B1
Panfield 59 F5
Pangbourne 42 B5
Pannal 102 C2
Panpunton 64 B5
Pant *Shrop.* 77 F5
Pant *Wrex.* 77 F3
Pant Glas 75 D3
Pant Gwyn 76 B5
Pant-lasau 36 C2
Pant Mawr 63 E4
Pant-pastynog 76 D1
Pant-y-dwr 63 F5
Pant-y-ffridd 64 A2
Pantasaph 90 C5
Pantglas 63 D3
Pantgwyn 49 F3
Panton 96 B5
Pantperthog 62 D2
Pantyffordd 77 F2
Pantyffynnon 36 C1
Panxworth 87 E4
Papcastle 117 E3
Papple 144 C2
Papplewick 81 G2
Papworth Everard 58 A1
Papworth St. Agnes 58 A1
Par 5 E4
Parbold 91 F1
Parbrook 24 C4
Parc 76 B4
Parc-Seymour 38 D3
Parcllyn 49 F2
Parcrhydderch 50 C2
Pardshaw 117 D4
Parham 61 E1
Parish Holm 133 F3
Park 182 A4
Park Corner 42 B4
Park End 128 A4
Park Gate 15 E2
Park Lane 78 B4
Park Street 44 A2
Parkend *Cumb.* 117 F3
Parkend *Glos.* 39 F2
Parkeston 60 D4
Parkford 160 C4
Parkgate *Ches.* 91 D5
Parkgate *D. & G.* 125 E2
Parkgate *S.Yorks.* 94 B3
Parkgate *Surr.* 30 B4
Parkham 21 D3
Parkham Ash 21 D3
Parkhill *Angus* 161 E5
Parkhill *P. & K.* 159 G5
Parkhouse 39 E2
Parkhurst 15 D3
Parkmill 36 B4
Parkmore 181 F5
Parkneuk 161 F2
Parkstone 13 G3
Parley Cross 13 G3
Parracombe 21 G1
Parrog 48 D4
Parson Drove 70 B2
Parsonby 117 E3
Partick 141 G3
Partington 92 B3
Partney 84 C1
Parton *Cumb.* 116 C4
Parton *D. & G.* 124 A3
Partridge Green 17 D2
Parwich 80 C2
Passenham 56 C4
Passfield 28 D4
Passingford Bridge 45 D3
Paston 87 E2
Patcham 17 F3
Patching 16 C3
Patchole 21 G1
Patchway 39 E4
Pateley Bridge 102 A1
Path of Condie 151 F3
Pathe 24 A4
Pathfinder Village 10 B3
Pathhead *Aber.* 161 F3
Pathhead *E.Ayr.* 133 E4
Pathhead *Fife* 152 A5
Pathhead *Midloth.* 144 A3
Patmore Heath 58 C5
Patna 132 C4
Patney 26 B2
Patrick 98 A3
Patrick Brompton 110 B3
Patrington 105 F5
Patrishow 52 B5
Patrixbourne 33 D3
Patterdale 107 G5
Pattingham 66 A3
Pattishall 56 B2
Pattiswick 59 G5
Paul 2 B4
Paulerspury 56 C3
Paull 105 D5
Paulton 24 D2
Pauperhaugh 128 D2
Pavenham 57 E2
Pawlett 23 F3
Pawston 136 C3
Paxford 55 D4
Paxhill Park 17 F1
Paxton 145 G4
Payhembury 11 D2
Paynes Hall 44 C1
Paythorne 101 E2
Peacehaven 17 G3
Peacemarsh 25 F5
Peachley 54 A2
Peak Dale 93 E5
Peak Forest 93 F5
Peakirk 69 G2
Pean Hill 32 D2
Pearsie 160 B4
Pease Pottage 30 B5
Peasedown St. John 25 E2
Peasemore 41 G5
Peasenhall 61 E1
Peaslake 29 F3
Peasmarsh 19 D1
Peaston 144 B3
Peastonbank 144 B3
Peat Inn 152 C4
Peathill 183 E3
Peatling Magna 68 A3
Peatling Parva 68 A4
Peaton 65 E4
Pebble Coombe 30 B3
Pebmarsh 59 G4
Pebworth 54 D3
Pecket Well 101 F5
Peckforton 78 C2
Peckleton 67 G2
Pedmore 66 B4
Pedwell 24 B4
Peebles 143 G5
Peel 98 A3
Pegswood 129 E3
Peighinn nan Aoireann 162 A1
Peinchorran 164 B1
Peinlich 176 A4
Pelaw 120 B1
Pelcomb Bridge 34 C1
Pelcomb Cross 34 C1
Peldon 46 C1
Pelsall 66 C2
Pelton 120 B2
Pelutho 117 E2
Pelynt 5 G4
Pembrey 36 A2
Pembridge 52 C2
Pembroke (Penfro) 34 C2
Pembroke Dock (Doc Penfro) 34 C2
Pembury 31 F4
Pen-bont Rhydybeddau 62 C4
Pen-clawdd 36 B3
Pen-ffordd 49 D5
Pen-groes-oped 38 C2
Pen-llyn 88 B4
Pen-sarn *Gwyn.* 75 E5
Pen-sarn *Gwyn.* 74 D3
Pen-twyn 39 E2
Pen-y-banc 50 C5
Pen-y-bont *Carmar.* 51 D4
Pen-y-bont *Powys* 63 G1
Pen-y-bont *Powys* 77 F5
Pen-y-Bont ar Ogwr (Bridgend) *Bridgend* 37 F5
Pen-y-bryn 62 C1
Pen-y-cae 37 E1
Pen-y-cae-mawr 38 D3
Pen-y-cefn 90 C5
Pen-y-clawdd 39 D2
Pen-y-coedcae 37 G4
Pen-y-fai 37 E4
Pen-y-garn 50 B4
Pen-y-garreg 51 G3
Pen-y-Gwryd Hotel 75 F2
Pen-y-Park 52 B3
Pen-y-sarn 88 C3
Pen-y-stryt 77 E2
Pen-yr-hoel 38 D1
Penallt 39 E1
Penally 35 E3
Penalt 53 E5
Penare 5 D5
Penarth 38 A5
Penboyr 49 G4
Penbryn 49 F2
Pencader 50 A4
Pencaenewydd 74 D3
Pencaitland 144 B3
Pencarreg 50 B3
Pencelli 51 G5
Pencoed 37 F4
Pencombe 53 E2
Pencoyd 53 E5
Pencraig *Here.* 53 E5
Pencraig *Powys* 76 D5
Pendeen 2 A3
Penderyn 37 F2
Pendine 35 F2
Pendlebury 92 B2
Pendleton 101 D4
Pendock 53 G4
Pendoggett 5 E2
Pendomer 12 B1
Pendoylan 37 G5
Penegoes 63 D2
Penfro (Pembroke) 34 C2
Pengam 38 A3
Penge 44 C5
Pengenffordd 52 A4
Pengorffwysfa 88 C3
Pengover Green 5 G3
Pengwern 90 B5
Penhale 3 D5
Penhallow 4 B4
Penhalvean 3 E3
Penhow 38 D3
Penhurst 18 B2
Peniarth 62 C2
Penicuik 143 G3
Penifiler 176 A5
Peninver 130 C3
Penisa'r Waun 75 E1
Penisarcwn 63 G1
Penistone 93 G2
Penjerrick 3 E3
Penketh 91 G4
Penkill 122 D1
Penkridge 66 B1
Penley 78 B4
Penllech 74 B4
Penllergaer 36 C3
Penllyn 37 F5
Penmachno 76 A2
Penmaen 36 B4
Penmaenmawr 89 F5
Penmaenpool 62 C1
Penmark 23 D1
Penmon 89 E4
Penmorfa 75 E3
Penmynydd 88 D5
Penn *Bucks.* 43 E3
Penn *W.Mid.* 66 A3
Penn Street 43 E3
Pennal 62 C2
Pennan 182 D3
Pennance 4 B5
Pennant *Cere.* 50 B1
Pennant *Powys* 63 E3
Pennant Melangell 76 D5
Pennard 36 B4
Pennerley 64 C3
Penninghame 123 E4
Pennington 107 D5
Pennsylvania 39 G5
Penny Bridge 107 E4
Pennyfuir 148 A1
Pennyghael 147 E2
Pennyglen 132 A4
Pennygown 155 F5
Pennymoor 10 B1
Penparc *Cere.* 49 F3
Penparc *Pembs.* 48 B4
Penparcau 62 B4
Penperlleni 38 C2
Penpillick 5 E4
Penpol 3 F3
Penpoll 5 F4
Penpont *D. & G.* 124 C1
Penpont *Powys* 51 F5
Penprysg 37 F4
Penrherber 49 F4
Penrhiw-llan 49 G3
Penrhiw-pal 49 G3
Penrhiwceiber 37 G3
Penrhiwgoch 36 B1
Penrhos *Gwyn.* 74 C4
Penrhos *I.o.A.* 88 A4
Penrhos *Mon.* 38 D1
Penrhos *Powys* 37 E1
Penrhos-garnedd 89 D5
Penrhyn Bay (Bae Penrhyn) 89 G4
Penrhyn-coch 62 C4
Penrhyn-side 89 G4
Penrhyndeudraeth 75 F4
Penrhys 37 G3
Penrice 36 A4
Penrith 118 B4
Penrose 4 C2
Penruddock 118 A5
Penryn 3 E3
Pensarn *Carmar.* 36 A1
Pensarn *Conwy* 90 A5
Pensax 53 G1
Pensby 91 D4
Penselwood 25 E4
Pensford 24 D1
Pensham 54 B3
Penshaw 120 C2
Penshurst 31 E4
Pensilva 5 G3
Pensnett 66 B4
Pentewan 5 E5
Pentir 75 E1
Pentire 4 B3
Pentireglaze 4 D1
Pentlepoir 35 E2
Pentlow 59 G3
Pentney 71 F1
Penton Mewsey 27 E3
Pentraeth 88 D5
Pentre *Powys* 77 D5
Pentre *Powys* 63 G4
Pentre *Powys* 52 B1
Pentre *Powys* 64 B3
Pentre *R.C.T.* 37 F3
Pentre *Shrop.* 64 C1
Pentre *Wrex.* 77 F3
Pentre-bach 51 F4
Pentre Berw 88 C5
Pentre-bont 76 A2
Pentre-bwlch 77 E3
Pentre-celyn *Denb.* 77 E2
Pentre-celyn *Powys* 63 E2
Pentre-chwyth 36 C3
Pentre-cwrt 49 G4
Pentre-Dolau-Honddu 51 F3
Pentre-dwr 36 C3
Pentre Galar 49 E4
Pentre Gwenlais 36 C1
Pentre Gwynfryn 75 E5
Pentre Halkyn 90 D5
Pentre Isaf 76 B1
Pentre Llanrhaeadr 77 D1
Pentre-Llwyn-Llwyd 51 F2
Pentre-llyn-cymmer 76 C2
Pentre Maelor 78 A3
Pentre-piod 76 B4
Pentre-Poeth 38 B4
Pentre Saron 76 D1
Pentre-tafarn-y-fedw 76 B1
Pentre-ty-gwyn 51 E4
Pentrebach *M.Tyd.* 37 G2
Pentrebach *Swan.* 36 C2
Pentrecagal 49 G3
Pentreclwydau 37 E2
Pentredwr 77 E3
Pentrefelin *Carmar.* 50 B5
Pentrefelin *Cere.* 50 C3
Pentrefelin *Conwy* 89 G5
Pentrefelin *Gwyn.* 75 E4
Pentrefelin *Powys* 77 E5
Pentrefoelas 76 B2
Pentregat 49 G2
Pentreheyling 64 B3
Pentre'r beirdd 64 A1
Pentre'r-felin 51 F4
Pentrich 81 E2
Pentridge 13 G1
Pentwyn 38 B4
Pentyrch 38 A4
Penuwch 50 B1
Penwithick 5 E4
Penwortham 100 B5
Penwyllt 37 E1
Penybont 52 A1
Penybontfawr 77 D5
Penybryn 38 A3
Penycae 77 F3
Penycwm 48 B5
Penyffordd 78 A1
Penygarnedd 77 E5
Penygraig 37 F3
Penygroes *Carmar.* 36 B1
Penygroes *Gwyn.* 75 D2
Penywaun 37 F2
Penzance 2 B3
Penzance Heliport 2 B3
Peopleton 54 B2
Peover Heath 92 B5
Peper Harow 29 E3
Peplow 78 D5
Perceton 141 E5

Percie 170 A5
Perham Down 27 D3
Perivale 44 A4
Perkhill 170 A4
Perkins Beach 64 C2
Perlethorpe 95 D5
Perranarworthal 3 E3
Perranporth 4 B4
Perranuthnoe 2 C4
Perranzabuloe 4 B4
Perry Barr 66 C3
Perry Green 44 D1
Perry Street 45 F5
Pershall 79 F5
Pershore 54 B3
Persie House 159 G4
Pert 161 E3
Pertenhall 57 F1
Perth 151 G2
Perthy 78 A4
Perton 66 A3
Peter Tavy 7 F3
Peterborough 69 G3
Peterburn 176 D1
Peterchurch 52 C4
Peterculter 170 D4
Peterhead 183 G5
Peterlee 120 D3
Peter's Green 44 A1
Peters Marland 21 E4
Petersfield 28 C5
Peterston-super-Ely 37 G5
Peterstone Wentlooge 38 B4
Peterstow 53 E5
Petham 32 D3
Petrockstow 21 F5
Pett 19 D2
Pettaugh 60 C2
Pettinain 143 D5
Pettistree 61 D2
Petton *Devon* 22 D5
Petton *Shrop.* 78 B5
Petty 170 C1
Pettycur 143 G1
Pettymuick 171 E2
Petworth 29 E5
Pevensey 18 B3
Pevensey Bay 18 B3
Pewsey 26 C1
Phesdo 161 E2
Philham 20 C3
Philiphaugh 135 F3
Phillack 2 C3
Philleigh 3 F3
Philpstoun 143 E2
Phoenix Green 28 C2
Phones 167 G5
Phorp 180 C4
Pibsbury 24 B5
Pica 116 D4
Piccadilly Corner 73 D3
Piccotts End 43 F2
Pickerells 45 E2
Pickering 112 B4
Picket Piece 27 E3
Picket Post 14 A2
Pickford Green 67 E4
Pickhill 110 C4
Picklescott 64 D3
Pickletillem 152 C2
Pickmere 92 A5
Pickstock 79 E5
Pickston 151 E2
Pickwell *Devon* 21 E1
Pickwell *Leics.* 68 C1
Pickworth *Lincs.* 83 F4
Pickworth *Rut.* 69 E1
Picton *Ches.* 91 F5
Picton *N.Yorks.* 110 D2
Piddinghoe 17 G3
Piddington *Northants.* 56 D2
Piddington *Oxon.* 42 B1
Piddlehinton 12 D3
Piddletrenthide 12 D3
Pidley 70 B5
Piercebridge 110 B1
Pierowall 198 C2
Pigdon 129 D3
Pikehall 80 C2
Pilgrims Hatch 45 E3
Pilham 95 F3
Pill 39 E5
Pillaton 7 D4
Pillerton Hersey 55 E3
Pillerton Priors 55 E3
Pilleth 52 B1
Pilley *Glos.* 40 B1
Pilley *Hants.* 14 C3
Pilley *S.Yorks.* 94 A2
Pilling 100 A3
Pilling Lane 99 G3
Pillowell 39 F2
Pilning 39 E4
Pilsbury 80 C1
Pilsdon 12 A3
Pilsgate 69 F2
Pilsley *Derbys.* 81 F1
Pilsley *Derbys.* 93 G5
Piltdown 17 G1
Pilton *Devon* 21 F2
Pilton *Northants.* 69 F4
Pilton *Rut.* 69 E2
Pilton *Som.* 24 C3
Pimperne 13 F2
Pinchbeck 84 A5
Pinchbeck Bars 84 A5
Pinchbeck West 84 A5
Pinchinthorpe 111 E1
Pinfold 91 E1
Pinhay 11 G3
Pinhoe 10 C3
Pinkneys Green 43 D4
Pinley Green 55 E1
Pinminnoch 122 C1
Pinmore 122 D1
Pinn 11 E4
Pinner 44 A4
Pinner Green 44 A3
Pinvin 54 B3
Pinwherry 122 C2
Pinxton 81 F2
Pipe and Lyde 53 E3
Pipe Gate 79 E3
Pipe Ridware 66 C1
Piperhall 140 B4
Piperhill 180 A4
Pipers Pool 5 G1
Pipewell 68 D4
Pippacott 21 F2
Pipton 52 A4
Pirbright 29 E2
Pirnmill 139 G5
Pirton *Herts.* 57 G4
Pirton *Worcs.* 54 A3
Pisgah 150 C4
Pishill 42 C4
Pistyll 74 C3
Pitagowan 158 D3
Pitblae 183 E3
Pitcairngreen 151 F2
Pitcairns 151 F3
Pitcaple 170 C2
Pitch Green 42 C2
Pitch Place 29 E2
Pitchcombe 40 A2
Pitchcott 42 C1
Pitchford 65 E2
Pitcombe 25 D4
Pitcot 37 E5
Pitcox 144 D2
Pitcur 152 A1
Pitfichie 170 B3
Pitgrudy 190 C5
Pitinnan 170 C1
Pitkennedy 160 D4
Pitkevy 152 A4
Pitlessie 152 B4
Pitlochry 159 E4
Pitmedden 171 D2
Pitminster 11 F1
Pitmuies 161 D5
Pitmunie 170 B3
Pitnacree 159 E4
Pitney 24 B5
Pitroddie 152 A2
Pitscottie 152 C3
Pitsea 45 G4
Pitsford 56 C1
Pitsford Hill 23 D4
Pitstone 43 E1
Pitstone Green 43 E1
Pitt *Devon* 10 D1
Pitt *Hants.* 27 F5
Pittendreich 181 D3
Pittentrail 190 C4
Pittenweem 152 D4
Pittington 120 C3
Pittodrie House 170 B2
Pitton 26 D4
Pity Me 120 B3
Pityme 4 D2
Pixey Green 72 D4
Place Newton 112 B5
Plaidy 182 C4
Plains 142 B3
Plaish 65 E3
Plaistow 29 F4
Plaitford 14 B1
Plas 50 A5
Plas Gogerddan 62 C4
Plas Gwynant 75 F2
Plas Isaf 77 D3
Plas Llwyd 90 A5
Plas Llwyngwern 63 D2
Plas Llysyn 63 F3
Plas Nantyr 77 E4
Plas-rhiw-Saeson 63 F2
Plas-yn-Cefn 90 B5
Plasisaf 76 C1
Plastow Green 27 G1
Platt 31 F3
Platt Bridge 92 A2
Platt Lane 78 C4
Plawsworth 120 B3
Plaxtol 31 F3
Play Hatch 42 C5
Playden 19 E1
Playford 60 D3
Playing Place 4 C5
Plealey 64 D2
Plean 142 C1
Pleasance 152 A3
Pleasington 100 C5
Pleasley 81 G1
Plenmeller 118 D1
Pleshey 45 F1
Plockton 165 E1
Ploughfield 52 C3
Plowden 64 C4
Ploxgreen 64 C2
Pluckley 32 B4
Pluckley Thorne 32 B4
Plumbland 117 E3
Plumley 92 B5
Plumpton *Cumb.* 118 A4
Plumpton *E.Suss.* 17 F2
Plumpton End 56 C3
Plumpton Green 17 F2
Plumpton Head 118 B4
Plumstead *Gt.Lon.* 44 D5
Plumstead *Norf.* 86 C2
Plumtree 82 B4
Plungar 82 C4
Plush 12 D2
Plwmp 49 G2
Plym Bridge 8 B2
Plymouth 8 A2
Plymouth City Airport 8 B1
Plympton 8 B2
Plymstock 8 B2
Plymtree 10 D2
Pockley 111 F4
Pocklington 104 A3
Pocombe Bridge 10 B3
Pode Hole 84 A5
Podimore 24 C5
Podington 57 E1
Podmore 79 E4
Poffley End 41 F1
Pointon 83 G4
Pokesdown 14 A3
Polanach 156 B4
Polapit Tamar 6 D2
Polbae 123 D3
Polbain 188 B3
Polbathic 7 D5
Polbeth 143 E3
Polchar 168 A4
Poldean 125 F1
Pole Moor 93 E1
Polebrook 69 F4
Polegate 18 A3
Poles 190 C5
Polesworth 67 E2
Polglass 188 C4
Polgooth 5 D4
Polgown 133 F5
Poling 16 C3
Poling Corner 16 C3
Polkerris 5 E4
Poll a' Charra 172 C2
Polla 192 C3
Polldubh 156 D3
Pollie 190 C3
Pollington 94 D1
Polloch 155 G3
Pollokshaws 141 G3
Polmassick 5 D5
Polmont 142 D2
Polnoon 141 G4
Polperro 5 G4
Polruan 5 F4
Polsham 24 C3
Polstead 60 A4
Poltalloch 148 A5
Poltimore 10 C3
Polton 143 G3
Polwarth 145 E4
Polyphant 5 G1
Polzeath 4 D2
Pond Street 58 C4
Ponders End 44 C3
Pondersbridge 70 A3
Ponsanooth 3 E3
Ponsonby 106 B2
Ponsworthy 10 A5
Pont Aber 50 D5
Pont Aberglaslyn 75 E3
Pont Ceri 49 F3
Pont Crugnant 63 E3
Pont Cyfyng 76 A2
Pont Dolgarrog 76 A1
Pont-faen 51 F4
Pont-Henri 36 A2
Pont Nedd Fechan 37 F2
Pont Pen-y-benglog 75 F1
Pont Rhyd-sarn 76 B5
Pont Rhyd-y-cyff 37 E4
Pont-rhyd-y-groes 62 D5
Pont-rug 75 E1
Pont Walby 37 E2
Pont-y-pant 76 A2
Pont yr Alwen 76 C2
Pontamman 36 C1
Pontantwn 36 A1
Pontardawe 36 D2
Pontarddulais 36 B2
Pontarfynach (Devil's Bridge) 62 D5
Pontargothi 50 B5
Pontarsais 50 A5
Pontblyddyn 77 F1
Pontbren Llwyd 37 F2
Pontefract 103 D5
Ponteland 129 D4
Ponterwyd 62 D4
Pontesbury 64 D2
Pontesford 64 D2
Pontfadog 77 F4
Pontfaen 48 D4
Ponthir 38 C3
Ponthirwaun 49 F3
Pontllanfraith 38 A3
Pontlliw 36 C2
Pontllyfni 74 D2
Pontlottyn 38 A2
Pontnewydd 38 B3
Pontnewynydd 38 B2
Pontrhydfendigaid 50 D1
Pontrhydyfen 37 D3
Pontrhydyrun 38 B3
Pontrilas 52 C5
Pontrobert 64 A1
Ponts Green 18 B2
Pontshaen 50 A3
Pontshill 53 F5
Pontsticill 37 G1
Pontwelly 50 A4
Pontyates 36 A2
Pontyberem 36 B1
Pontybodkin 77 F2
Pontyclun 37 G4
Pontycymer 37 F3
Pontygwaith 37 G3
Pontymister 38 B4
Pontypool 38 B2
Pontypridd 37 G4
Pontywaun 38 B3
Pooksgreen 14 C1
Pool *Cornw.* 4 A5
Pool *W.Yorks.* 102 B3
Pool Bank 107 F4
Pool of Muckhart 151 F4
Pool Quay 64 B1
Pool Street 59 F4
Poole 13 G3
Poole Keynes 40 B3
Poolewe 177 E1
Pooley Bridge 118 A5
Poolhill 53 G5
Pope Hill 34 C1
Popeswood 28 D1
Popham 27 G3
Poplar 44 C4
Porchfield 14 D3
Porin 178 C4
Poringland 87 D5
Porkellis 3 D3
Porlock 22 B3
Porlock Weir 22 B3
Port Allen 152 A2
Port Appin 156 B5
Port Askaig 138 C3
Port Bannatyne 140 B3
Port Carlisle 126 A5
Port Charlotte 138 A4
Port Clarence 121 E5
Port Driseach 140 A2
Port e Vullen 98 C2
Port Ellen 138 B5
Port Elphinstone 170 C3
Port Erin 98 A5
Port Erroll 171 F1
Port Eynon 36 A4
Port Gaverne 5 E1
Port Glasgow 141 E2
Port Henderson 177 D2
Port Isaac 5 D1
Port Logan 114 A2
Port Mòr 154 D2
Port Mulgrave 111 G1
Port-na-Con 192 D2
Port na Craig 159 E4
Port nan Giùran (Portnaguran) 187 G4
Port nan Long 173 G2
Port Nis 187 G1
Port o' Warren 124 C5
Port of Menteith 150 A4
Port Penrhyn 89 D5
Port Quin 5 D1
Port Ramsay 156 A5
Port St. Mary 98 A5
Port Solent 15 F2
Port Sunlight 91 E4
Port Talbot 36 D4
Port Wemyss 138 A4
Port William 114 D2
Portachoillan 139 F4
Portavadie 140 A3
Portbury 39 D5
Portchester 15 F2
Portencross 140 C5
Portesham 12 C4
Portessie 181 G3
Portfield 147 G2
Portfield Gate 34 C1
Portgate 7 E2
Portgordon 181 F3
Portgower 191 F3
Porth *Cornw.* 4 C3
Porth *R.C.T.* 37 G3
Porth Colmon 74 A4
Porth Mellin 3 D5
Porth Navas 3 E4
Porth-y-waen 77 F5
Porthaethwy (Menai Bridge) 89 D5
Porthallow *Cornw.* 3 E4
Porthallow *Cornw.* 5 G4
Porthcawl 37 E5
Porthcothan 4 C2
Porthcurno 2 A4
Porthgain 48 B4
Porthkerry 23 D1
Porthleven 2 D4
Porthmadog 75 E4
Porthmeor 2 B3
Portholland 5 D5
Porthoustock 3 F4
Porthpean 5 E4
Porthtowan 4 A5
Porthyrhyd *Carmar.* 50 D4
Porthyrhyd *Carmar.* 36 B1
Portincaple 149 E5
Portington 103 G4
Portinnisherrich 148 B3
Portinscale 117 F4
Portishead 39 D5
Portknockie 181 G3
Portlethen 171 E5
Portlethen Village 171 E5
Portloe 3 G3
Portmahomack 180 B1
Portmeirion 75 E4
Portmore 14 C3
Portnacroish 156 B5
Portnaguran (Port nan Giùran) 187 G4
Portnahaven 138 A4
Portnalong 163 G1
Portnaluchaig 155 F1
Portobello 144 A2
Porton 26 C4
Portpatrick 122 B5
Portreath 4 A5
Portree 176 A5
Portscatho 3 F3
Portsea 15 F2
Portskerra 194 A2
Portskewett 39 E4
Portslade 17 E3
Portslade-by-Sea 17 E3
Portslogan 122 A5
Portsmouth 15 F3
Portsonachan 148 C2
Portsoy 182 A3
Portswood 14 D1
Portuairk 154 D3
Portway *Here.* 52 C3
Portway *Worcs.* 66 C5
Portwrinkle 7 D5
Portyerrock 115 E3
Poslingford 59 F3
Postbridge 7 G3
Postcombe 42 C3
Postling 32 D5
Postwick 87 D5
Potarch 170 B5
Potsgrove 57 E5
Pott Row 85 F5
Pott Shrigley 92 D5
Potten End 43 F2
Potter Heigham 87 F3
Potter Street 45 D2
Potterhanworth 83 F1
Potterhanworth Booths 83 F1
Potterne 26 A2
Potterne Wick 26 A2
Potters Bar 44 B2
Potter's Cross 66 A4
Potters Crouch 44 A2
Potterspury 56 C3
Potterton 171 E3
Potto 111 D2
Potton 58 A3
Poughill *Cornw.* 20 C5
Poughill *Devon* 10 B2
Poulner 14 A2
Poulshot 26 A2
Poulton 40 D2
Poulton-le-Fylde 99 G4
Pound Bank 65 G5
Pound Green 18 A1
Pound Hill 30 B5
Poundffald 36 B3
Poundgate 17 G1
Poundland 122 C2
Poundon 56 B5
Poundsbridge 31 E4
Poundsgate 10 A5
Poundstock 6 C1
Povey Cross 30 B4
Pow Green 53 G3
Powburn 137 E5
Powderham 10 C4
Powerstock 12 B3
Powfoot 125 F4
Powick 54 A2
Powler's Piece 21 D4
Powmill 151 F5
Poxwell 12 D4
Poyle 43 F5
Poynings 17 E2
Poyntington 24 D5
Poynton *Ches.* 92 D4
Poynton *Tel. & W.* 65 E1
Poynton Green 65 E1
Poyntzfield 179 G3
Poys Street 73 E4
Poyston Cross 34 C1
Poystreet Green 60 A2
Praa Sands 2 C4
Pratis 152 B4
Pratt's Bottom 31 D2
Praze-an-Beeble 2 D3
Predannack Wollas 3 D5
Prees 78 C4
Prees Green 78 C4
Prees Higher Heath 78 C4
Preesall 99 G3
Preesgweene 77 F4
Pren-gwyn 50 A3
Prenbrigog 77 F1
Prendergast 34 C1
Prendwick 137 E5
Prenteg 75 E3
Prenton 91 E4
Prescot 91 F3
Prescott 78 B5
Presley 180 C4
Pressen 136 C3
Prestatyn 90 B4
Prestbury *Ches.* 92 C5
Prestbury *Glos.* 54 B5
Presteigne 52 C1
Presthope 65 E3
Prestleigh 24 D3
Prestolee 92 B2
Preston *B. & H.* 17 F3
Preston *Devon* 10 B5
Preston *Dorset* 12 D4
Preston *E.Loth.* 144 C2
Preston *E.Riding* 105 D4
Preston *Glos.* 53 F4
Preston *Glos.* 40 C2
Preston *Herts.* 57 G5
Preston *Kent* 32 C2
Preston *Kent* 33 E2
Preston *Lancs.* 100 B5
Preston *Northumb.* 137 F4
Preston *Rut.* 69 D2
Preston *Sc.Bord.* 145 E4
Preston *Suff.* 60 A2
Preston *T. & W.* 120 C1
Preston *Wilts.* 40 C5
Preston Bagot 55 D1
Preston Bissett 56 B5
Preston Brockhurst 78 C5
Preston Brook 91 G4
Preston Candover 28 B3
Preston Capes 56 A2
Preston Deanery 56 C2
Preston Gubbals 65 D1
Preston on Stour 55 E2
Preston on the Hill 91 G4
Preston on Wye 52 C3
Preston Plucknett 12 B1
Preston-under-Scar 109 F3
Preston upon the Weald Moors 65 F1
Preston Wynne 53 E3
Prestonpans 144 A2
Prestwich 92 C2
Prestwick *Northumb.* 129 D4
Prestwick *S.Ayr.* 132 B3
Prestwick International Airport 132 B3
Prestwold 81 G5
Prestwood 43 D2
Price Town 37 F3
Prickwillow 71 D4
Priddy 24 C2
Priest Hill 100 C4
Priest Hutton 107 G5
Priestland 133 D2
Priestweston 64 B3
Primethorpe 68 A3
Primrose Green 86 B4
Princes End 66 B3
Princes Gate 35 E1
Princes Risborough 42 D2
Princethorpe 67 G5
Princetown *Caerp.* 38 A1
Princetown *Devon* 7 F3
Prior Muir 152 D3
Prior's Frome 53 E4
Priors Hardwick 55 G2
Priors Marston 55 G2
Priory Wood 52 B3
Priston 25 D1
Prittlewell 46 B4
Privett 28 B5
Prixford 21 F2
Proaig 138 C4
Probus 4 C5
Protstonhill 182 D3
Prudhoe 120 A1
Pubil 157 G5
Publow 24 D1
Puckeridge 58 B5
Puckington 11 G1
Pucklechurch 39 F5
Puddinglake 79 E1
Puddington *Ches.* 91 E5
Puddington *Devon* 10 B1
Puddlebrook 39 F1
Puddledock 72 B2
Puddletown 13 D3
Pudleston 53 E2
Pudsey 102 B4
Pulborough 16 C2
Puldagon 195 F4
Puleston 79 E5
Pulford 78 A2
Pulham 12 D2
Pulham Market 72 C3
Pulham St. Mary 72 D3
Pulloxhill 57 F4
Pulrossie 179 G1
Pulverbatch 64 D2
Pumpherston 143 E3
Pumsaint 50 C3
Puncheston 48 D5
Puncknowle 12 B4
Punnett's Town 18 B1
Purbrook 15 F2
Purfleet 45 E5
Puriton 24 A3
Purleigh 46 B2
Purley 30 C2
Purley on Thames 42 B5
Purlogue 64 B5
Purls Bridge 70 C4
Purse Caundle 12 C1
Purslow 64 C4
Purston Jaglin 94 B1
Purton *Glos.* 39 F2
Purton *Wilts.* 40 C4
Purton Stoke 40 C3
Purves Hall 145 E5
Pury End 56 C3
Pusey 41 F3
Putley 53 F4
Putloe 39 G2
Putney 44 B5
Putsborough *Devon* 21 E1
Puttenham *Herts.* 43 D1
Puttenham *Surr.* 29 E3
Puttock End 59 G3
Putts Corner 11 E3
Puxton 24 B1
Pwll 36 A2
Pwll Trap 35 F1
Pwll-y-glaw 37 D3
Pwllcrochan 34 C2
Pwlldefaid 74 A5
Pwllgloyw 51 G4
Pwllheli 74 C4
Pwllmeyric 39 E3
Pye Corner *Herts.* 45 D1
Pye Corner *Newport* 38 C4
Pye Green 66 B1
Pyecombe 17 E2
Pyle *Bridgend* 37 E4
Pyle *I.o.W.* 15 D5
Pylle 24 D4
Pymore 70 C4
Pyrford 29 F2
Pyrton 42 B3
Pytchley 69 D5
Pyworthy 20 D5

Q

Quabbs 64 B4
Quadring 84 A4
Quadring Eaudike 84 A4
Quainton 42 C1
Quarley 27 D3
Quarmby 93 F1
Quarndon 81 E3
Quarr Hill 15 E3
Quarrier's Village 141 E3
Quarrington 83 F3
Quarrington Hill 120 C4
Quarry Bank 66 B4
Quarrybank 78 C1
Quarrywood 181 D3
Quarter 142 B4
Quatford 65 G3
Quatt 65 G4
Quebec 120 A3
Quedgeley 40 A1
Queen Adelaide 71 D4
Queen Camel 24 C5
Queen Charlton 24 D1
Queen Street 31 F4
Queenborough 32 B1
Queen's Head 78 A5
Queensbury 102 A4
Queensferry 78 A1
Queenzieburn 142 A2
Quemerford 40 C5
Quendale 201 F4
Quendon 58 D4
Queniborough 68 B1
Quenington 40 D2
Quernmore 100 B1
Queslett 66 C3
Quethiock 6 D4
Quholm 198 A5
Quidenham 72 B3
Quidhampton *Hants.* 27 G2
Quidhampton *Wilts.* 26 C4
Quilquox 171 E1
Quina Brook 78 C4
Quindry 196 D3
Quine's Hill 98 B4
Quinhill 139 F4
Quinton *Northants.* 56 C2
Quinton *W.Mid.* 66 B4
Quintrell Downs 4 C3
Quoditch 7 E1
Quoig 150 D2
Quoiggs House 150 D4
Quorn 68 A1
Quothquan 134 A2
Quoyloo 198 A4
Quoys 203 F1
Quoys of Reiss 195 F3

R

Raby 91 E5
Rachan 134 C2
Rachub 75 F1
Rackenford 10 B1
Rackham 16 C2
Rackheath 87 D4
Racks 125 E3
Rackwick *Ork.* 196 B3
Rackwick *Ork.* 198 C1
Radbourne 81 D4
Radcliffe *Gt.Man.* 92 B2
Radcliffe *Northumb.* 129 E1
Radcliffe on Trent 82 B4
Radclive 56 B4
Radcot 41 E3
Radford *Oxon.* 55 G5
Radford *W.Mid.* 67 F4
Radford Semele 55 F1
Radipole 12 C4
Radlett 44 A2
Radley 42 A3
Radstock 25 D2
Radstone 56 A3
Radway 55 F3
Radway Green 79 E2
Radwell *Beds.* 57 F2
Radwell *Herts.* 58 A4
Radwinter 59 E4
Radyr 38 A4
Raechester 128 B3
Raemoir House 170 B5
Raffin 188 C1
Rafford 180 C4
Ragdale 68 B1
Raglan 38 D2
Ragnall 95 F5
Rahoy 155 F4
Rainford 91 F2
Rainham *Gt.Lon.* 45 E4
Rainham *Med.* 32 A2
Rainhill 91 F3
Rainhill Stoops 91 G3
Rainow 93 D5
Rainton 110 C5
Rainworth 81 G2
Raisbeck 108 B2
Raise 118 D3
Rait 152 A2
Raithby *Lincs.* 84 B1
Raithby *Lincs.* 96 D4
Rake 28 D5
Raleigh's Cross 22 D4
Ram 50 B3
Ram Lane 32 B4
Ramasaig 175 E5
Rame *Cornw.* 3 E3
Rame *Cornw.* 8 A3
Rampisham 12 B2
Rampside 99 F1
Rampton *Cambs.* 58 C1
Rampton *Notts.* 95 F5
Ramsbottom 92 B1
Ramsbury 41 E5
Ramscraigs 191 G2
Ramsdean 28 C5
Ramsdell 27 G2
Ramsden 41 F1
Ramsden Bellhouse 45 G3
Ramsden Heath 45 G3
Ramsey *Cambs.* 70 A4
Ramsey *Essex* 60 D5
Ramsey *I.o.M.* 98 C2
Ramsey Forty Foot 70 B4
Ramsey Heights 70 A4
Ramsey Island 46 C2
Ramsey Mereside 70 A4
Ramsey St. Mary's 70 A4
Ramsgate 33 F2
Ramsgate Street 86 B2
Ramsgill 110 A5
Ramsholt 61 E3
Ramshorn 80 B3
Ramsnest Common 29 E4
Ranachan 155 G3
Ranby *Lincs.* 96 C5
Ranby *Notts.* 95 D4
Rand 96 B5
Randwick 40 A2
Rangemore 80 C5
Rangeworthy 39 F4
Rankinston 132 C4
Rank's Green 45 G1
Rannoch School 158 A4
Ranochan 156 A1
Ranskill 95 D4
Ranton 79 F5
Ranworth 87 E4
Rapness 198 D2
Rascarrel 116 B2
Raskelf 111 D5
Rassau 38 A1
Rastrick 102 A5
Ratby 68 A2
Ratcliffe Culey 67 F3
Ratcliffe on Soar 81 F5
Ratcliffe on the Wreake 68 B1
Ratford Bridge 34 C1
Rathen 183 F3
Rathillet 152 B2
Rathliesbeag 157 E1
Rathmell 101 E1
Ratho 143 F2
Ratho Station 143 F2
Rathven 181 G3
Ratley 55 F3
Ratlinghope 64 D3
Rattar 195 E1
Ratten Row 100 A3
Rattery 8 D1
Rattlesden 60 A2
Rattray 159 G5
Raughton Head 117 G2
Raunds 69 F5
Ravenfield 94 B3
Ravenglass 106 B3

Raveningham 73 E2
Ravenscar 112 C2
Ravensdale 98 B2
Ravensden 57 F2
Ravenshaw 101 F3
Ravenshayes 10 C2
Ravenshead 81 G2
Ravensmoor 78 D2
Ravensthorpe *Northants.* 68 B5
Ravensthorpe *W.Yorks.* 93 G1
Ravenstone *Leics.* 67 G1
Ravenstone *M.K.* 57 D3
Ravenstonedale 108 C2
Ravenstruther 142 D5
Ravensworth 110 A2
Raw 112 C2
Rawcliffe *E.Riding* 103 F5
Rawcliffe *York* 103 E2
Rawcliffe Bridge 103 F5
Rawdon 102 B4
Rawmarsh 94 B3
Rawreth 45 G3
Rawridge 11 E2
Rawtenstall 101 E5
Rawyards 142 B3
Raxton 171 D1
Raydon 60 B4
Raylees 128 B2
Rayleigh 46 B3
Raymond's Hill 11 G3
Rayne 59 F5
Reach 59 D1
Read 101 D4
Reading 42 C5
Reading Street 32 B5
Reagill 108 B1
Rearquhar 190 C5
Rearsby 68 B1
Rease Heath 78 D2
Reaster 195 E2
Reaveley 137 E5
Reawick 200 C3
Reay 194 B2
Reculver 33 E2
Red Dial 117 F2
Red Hill *Hants.* 15 G1
Red Hill *Warks.* 54 D2
Red Lodge 71 E5
Red Oaks Hill 59 D4
Red Post *Cornw.* 20 C5
Red Post *Devon* 9 E1
Red Rock 91 G1
Red Roses 35 F1
Red Row 129 E2
Red Street 79 F2
Red Wharf Bay 88 D4
Redberth 35 D2
Redbourn 44 A1
Redbourne 95 G2
Redbridge 44 D4
Redbrook 39 E2
Redbrook Street 32 B5
Redburn *High.* 179 E3
Redburn *High.* 180 B5
Redcar 121 F5
Redcastle *Angus* 161 E4
Redcastle *High.* 179 E5
Redcliff Bay 38 D5
Redcloak 161 G1
Reddish 92 C3
Redditch 54 C1
Rede 59 G2
Redenhall 73 D3
Redesmouth 128 A3
Redford *Aber.* 161 F3
Redford *Angus* 161 D5
Redford *Dur.* 119 G4
Redford *W.Suss.* 29 D5
Redgrave 72 B4
Redheugh 160 C3
Redhill *Aber.* 170 B1
Redhill *Aber.* 170 C4
Redhill *Moray* 182 A5
Redhill *N.Som.* 24 B1
Redhill *Notts.* 81 G3
Redhill *Surr.* 30 B3
Redhill *Tel. & W.* 65 G1
Redhill Aerodrome & Heliport 30 B4
Redhouse *Aber.* 170 A2
Redhouse *Arg. & B.* 139 G3
Redhouses 138 B3
Redisham 73 F3
Redland *Bristol* 39 E5
Redland *Ork.* 198 B4
Redlingfield 72 C4
Redlynch *Som.* 25 D4
Redlynch *Wilts.* 26 D5
Redmarley D'Abitot 53 G4
Redmarshall 120 C5
Redmile 82 D4
Redmire 109 F3
Redmoor 5 E3
Rednal *Shrop.* 78 A5
Rednal *W.Mid.* 66 C5
Redpath 135 G2
Redpoint 176 D3
Redruth 4 A5
Redscarhead 143 G5
Redshaw 133 G3
Redstone Bank 35 E1
Redwick *Newport* 38 D4
Redwick *S.Glos.* 39 E4
Redworth 120 B5
Reed 58 B4
Reedham 87 F5
Reedness 103 G5
Reepham *Lincs.* 96 A5
Reepham *Norf.* 86 C3
Reeth 109 F3
Regaby 98 C2
Regil 24 C1
Regoul 180 A4
Reiff 188 B3
Reigate 30 B3
Reighton 113 E5
Reinigeadal 185 E3
Reisgill 195 E5
Reiss 195 F3
Rejerrah 4 B4
Relubbus 2 C3
Relugas 180 B5
Remenham 42 C4
Remenham Hill 42 C4
Remony 158 C5
Rempstone 81 G5
Rendcomb 40 C1
Rendham 61 E1
Rendlesham 61 E2
Renfrew 141 G3
Renhold 57 F2
Renishaw 94 B5
Rennington 137 G5
Renton 141 E2
Renwick 118 B3
Repps 87 F4
Repton 81 E5
Rescobie 160 D4
Resipole 155 G3
Resolis 179 F3
Resolven 37 E2
Resourie 156 A2
Reston 145 F3
Reswallie 160 D4
Retew 4 D4
Retford 95 E4
Rettendon 45 G3
Rettendon Place 45 G3
Retyn 4 C4
Revesby 84 A1
Rew 10 A5
Rewe 10 C3
Reydon 73 F4
Reymerston 86 B5
Reynalton 35 D2
Reynoldston 36 A4
Rezare 7 D3
Rhandirmwyn 51 D3
Rhaoine 190 B4
Rhayader 51 F1
Rhedyn 74 B4
Rhegreanoch 188 C3
Rheindown 179 E5
Rhelonie 190 A5
Rhemore 155 E4
Rhes-y-cae 77 E1
Rhewl *Denb.* 77 E3
Rhewl *Denb.* 77 E1
Rhewl *Shrop.* 78 A4
Rhian 190 A3
Rhicarn 188 C2
Rhiconich 192 B3
Rhicullen 179 F2
Rhidorroch 189 D5
Rhifail 193 G4
Rhigos 37 F2
Rhilochan 190 C4
Rhinduie 179 E5
Rhireavach 188 C5
Rhiroy 178 A1
Rhiw 74 B5
Rhiwargor 76 C5
Rhiwbryfdir 75 F3
Rhiwderin 38 B4
Rhiwlas *Gwyn.* 75 E1
Rhiwlas *Gwyn.* 76 C4
Rhiwlas *Powys* 77 F4
Rhodes Minnis 32 D4
Rhodesia 94 C5
Rhodiad-y-Brenin 48 A5
Rhodmad 62 B5
Rhonadale 130 C2
Rhonehouse or Kelton Hill 124 B5
Rhoose 23 D1
Rhos *Carmar.* 49 G4
Rhos *N.P.T.* 36 D2
Rhos-berse 77 F2
Rhos-ddu 78 A2
Rhos-fawr 74 C4
Rhos-goch 88 C4
Rhos-hill 49 E3
Rhôs-on-Sea 89 G4
Rhos-y-bol 88 C4
Rhos-y-brwyner 77 F1
Rhos-y-garth 62 C5
Rhos-y-gwaliau 76 C4
Rhos-y-llan 74 B4
Rhos-y-mawn 76 B1
Rhos-y-Meirch 52 B1
Rhoscolyn 88 A5
Rhoscrowther 34 C2
Rhosesmor 77 F1
Rhosgadfan 75 E2
Rhosgoch 52 A3
Rhoshirwaun 74 A5
Rhoslan 75 D3
Rhoslefain 62 B2
Rhosllanerchrugog 77 F3
Rhosmaen 50 C5
Rhosmeirch 88 C5
Rhosneigr 88 B5
Rhosnesni 78 A2
Rhossili 36 A4
Rhosson 48 A5
Rhostryfan 75 D2
Rhostyllen 78 A3
Rhu 141 D1
Rhuallt 90 B5
Rhubodach 140 B2
Rhuddlan 90 B5
Rhue 188 C5
Rhulen 52 A3
Rhumach 155 F1
Rhunahaorine 139 F5
Rhuthun (Ruthin) 77 E2
Rhyd *Gwyn.* 75 F3
Rhyd *Powys* 63 F2
Rhyd-Ddu 75 E2
Rhyd-rosser 50 B1
Rhyd-uchaf 76 C4
Rhyd-wen 76 C5
Rhyd-wyn 88 B4
Rhyd-y-clafdy 74 C4
Rhyd-y-foel 90 A5
Rhyd-y-fro 36 D2
Rhyd-y-meirch 38 C2
Rhyd-yr-onnen 62 C2
Rhydaman (Ammanford) 36 C1
Rhydargaeau 50 A5
Rhydcymerau 50 B4
Rhydd 54 A3
Rhydding 37 D3
Rhydlanfair 76 B2
Rhydlewis 49 G3
Rhydlios 74 A4
Rhydlydan *Conwy* 76 B2
Rhydlydan *Powys* 63 G3
Rhydolion 74 B5
Rhydowen 50 A3
Rhydspence 52 B3
Rhydtalog 77 F2
Rhydycroesau 77 F4
Rhydyfelin *Cere.* 62 B5
Rhydyfelin *R.C.T.* 37 G4
Rhydymain 76 A5
Rhydymwyn 77 F1
Rhydywrach 35 E1
Rhyl 90 B4
Rhymney 38 A2
Rhyn 78 A4
Rhynd 151 G2
Rhynie *Aber.* 169 G2
Rhynie *High.* 180 A2
Ribbesford 65 G5
Ribbleton 100 B4
Ribchester 100 C4
Ribigill 193 E3
Riby 96 B2
Riccall 103 F4
Riccarton 132 C2
Richard's Castle 53 D1
Richings Park 43 F5
Richmond 110 A2
Richmond upon Thames 44 A5
Rickarton 161 G1
Rickford 24 B2
Rickinghall 72 B4
Rickling 58 C4
Rickling Green 58 D5
Rickmansworth 43 F3
Riddell 135 G3
Riddings 81 F2
Riddlecombe 21 G4
Riddlesden 101 G3
Ridge *Dorset* 13 F4
Ridge *Herts.* 44 B2
Ridge *Wilts.* 26 A4
Ridge Green 30 C4
Ridge Lane 67 E3
Ridgebourne 51 G1
Ridgeway 94 B4
Ridgeway Cross 53 G3
Ridgewell 59 F3
Ridgewood 17 G1
Ridgmont 57 E4
Riding Mill 119 G1
Ridley 31 F2
Ridleywood 78 A2
Ridlington *Norf.* 87 E2
Ridlington *Rut.* 69 D2
Ridsdale 128 B3
Riechip 159 F5
Rievaulx 111 E4
Rigg *D. & G.* 126 A5
Rigg *High.* 176 B4
Riggend 142 B3
Rigmaden Park 108 B4
Rigsby 97 E5
Rigside 133 G2
Rileyhill 66 D1
Rilla Mill 5 G2
Rillington 112 B5
Rimington 101 E3
Rimpton 24 D5
Rimswell 105 F5
Rinaston 48 C5
Ringford 124 A5
Ringland 86 C4
Ringles Cross 17 G1
Ringmer 17 G2
Ringmore 8 C3
Ringorm 181 E5
Ring's End 70 B2
Ringsfield 73 F3
Ringsfield Corner 73 F3
Ringshall *Herts.* 43 E1
Ringshall *Suff.* 60 B2
Ringshall Stocks 60 B2
Ringstead *Norf.* 85 F3
Ringstead *Northants.* 69 E5
Ringwood 14 A2
Ringwould 33 F4
Rinloan 169 E4
Rinmore 169 G3
Rinnigill 196 C3
Rinsey 2 C4
Ripe 18 A3
Ripley *Derbys.* 81 F2
Ripley *Hants.* 14 A3
Ripley *N.Yorks.* 102 B1
Ripley *Surr.* 29 F2
Riplingham 104 B4
Ripon 110 C5
Rippingale 83 G5
Ripple *Kent* 33 F3
Ripple *Worcs.* 54 A4
Ripponden 93 E1
Risabus 138 B5
Risbury 53 E2
Risby 59 F1
Risca 38 B3
Rise 105 D3
Risegate 84 A4
Riseley *Beds.* 57 F1
Riseley *W'ham* 28 C1
Rishangles 60 C1
Rishton 100 D4
Rishworth 93 E1
Risley *Derbys.* 81 F4
Risley *Warr.* 92 A3
Risplith 102 B1
Rispond 192 D2
Rivar 27 E1
Rivenhall 46 B1
Rivenhall End 46 B1
River 29 E5
River Bank 58 D1
River Bridge 24 A3
Riverford Bridge 9 D1
Riverhead 31 E3
Rivington 92 A1
Roa Island 99 F1
Roade 56 C2
Roadhead 126 D4
Roadside *High.* 195 D2
Roadside *Ork.* 199 E2
Roadside of Kinneff 161 G2
Roadwater 22 D4
Roag 175 F5
Roath 38 B5
Roberton *S.Lan.* 134 A3
Roberton *Sc.Bord.* 135 F4
Robertsbridge 18 C1
Robertstown 181 E5
Roberttown 102 A5
Robeston Cross 34 B2
Robeston Wathen 35 D1
Robin Hood *Derbys.* 93 G5
Robin Hood *W.Yorks.* 102 C5
Robin Hood's Bay 112 C2
Robins 28 D5
Roborough *Devon* 21 F4
Roborough *Plym.* 8 B1
Roby 91 F3
Roby Mill 91 G2
Rocester 80 C4
Roch 48 B5
Rochallie 159 G4
Rochdale 92 C1
Roche 5 D3
Rochester *Med.* 31 G2
Rochester *Northumb.* 128 A2
Rochford *Essex* 46 B3
Rochford *Worcs.* 53 F1
Rock *Caerp.* 38 A3
Rock *Cornw.* 4 D2
Rock *Northumb.* 137 G4
Rock *Worcs.* 65 G5
Rock Ferry 91 E4
Rockbeare 10 D3
Rockbourne 14 A1
Rockcliffe *Cumb.* 126 B5
Rockcliffe *D. & G.* 124 C5
Rockfield *Arg. & B.* 139 G4
Rockfield *High.* 180 B1
Rockfield *Mon.* 39 D1
Rockhampton 39 F3
Rockhead 5 E1
Rockingham 69 D3
Rockland All Saints 72 A2
Rockland St. Mary 87 E5
Rockland St. Peter 72 A2
Rockley 41 D5
Rockside 138 A3
Rockwell End 42 C4
Rockwell Green 11 E1
Rodborough 40 A2
Rodbourne 40 B4
Rodbridge Corner 59 G3
Rodd 52 C1
Roddam 137 E4
Rodden 12 C4
Rode 25 F2
Rode Heath 79 F2
Rodeheath 79 F1
Rodel (Roghadal) 184 C5
Roden 65 E1
Rodhuish 22 D4
Rodington 65 E1
Rodley 39 G1
Rodmarton 40 B3
Rodmell 17 G3
Rodmersham 32 B2
Rodney Stoke 24 B2
Rodsley 80 D3
Rodway 23 F3
Roe Green 58 B4
Roecliffe 102 C1
Roehampton 44 B5
Roesound 200 C1
Roffey 29 G4
Rogart 190 C4
Rogate 28 D5
Rogerstone 38 B4
Roghadal (Rodel) 184 C5
Rogiet 39 D4
Roker 120 D2
Rollesby 87 F4
Rolleston *Leics.* 68 C2
Rolleston *Notts.* 82 C2
Rolleston *Staffs.* 80 D5
Rollestone 26 B3
Rolston 105 E3
Rolvenden 32 A5
Rolvenden Layne 32 A5
Romaldkirk 119 F5
Romanby 110 C3
Romannobridge 143 F5
Romansleigh 22 A5
Romford *Dorset* 13 G2
Romford *Gt.Lon.* 45 E4
Romiley 92 D3
Romney Street 31 E2
Romsey 27 E5
Romsley *Shrop.* 65 G4
Romsley *Worcs.* 66 B4
Ronachan 139 F4
Ronague 98 A4
Ronnachmore 138 B4
Rookhope 119 F3
Rookley 15 E4
Rooks Bridge 24 A2
Rookwith 110 B4
Roos 105 E4
Roosecote 99 F1
Rootpark 143 D4
Ropley 28 B4
Ropley Dean 28 B4
Ropley Soke 28 B4
Ropsley 83 E4
Rora 183 F4
Rorandle 170 B3
Rorrington 64 B2
Rosarie 181 F4
Rose 4 B4
Rose Ash 22 A5
Rose Green 59 G5
Roseacre 100 A4
Rosebank 142 C5
Rosebrough 137 F4
Rosebush 49 D5
Rosedale Abbey 111 G3
Roseden 137 E4
Rosehall 189 G4
Rosehearty 183 E3
Rosehill *Aber.* 170 A5
Rosehill *Shrop.* 79 D4
Roseisle 180 D3
Rosemarket 34 C2
Rosemarkie 179 G4
Rosemary Lane 11 E1
Rosemount *P. & K.* 159 G5
Rosemount *S.Ayr.* 132 B3
Rosepool 34 B1
Rosewarne 2 D3
Rosewell 143 G3
Roseworthy 2 D3
Rosgill 107 G1
Roshven 155 G2
Roskhill 175 F5
Rosley 117 G2
Roslin 143 G3
Rosliston 67 E1
Rosneath 141 D1
Ross *D. & G.* 115 G2
Ross *Northumb.* 137 F3
Ross *P. & K.* 150 C2
Ross-on-Wye 53 F5
Ross Priory 141 F1
Rossdhu House 141 E1
Rossett 78 A2
Rossie Farm School 161 E4
Rossie Ochill 151 F3
Rossie Priory 152 A1
Rossington 94 D3
Rosskeen 179 F3
Roster 195 E5
Rostherne 92 B4
Rosthwaite *Cumb.* 117 F5
Rosthwaite *Cumb.* 106 D4
Roston 80 C3
Rosyth 143 F1
Rothbury 128 C1
Rotherby 68 B1
Rotherfield 18 A1
Rotherfield Greys 42 C4
Rotherfield Peppard 42 C4
Rotherham 94 B3
Rothersthorpe 56 C2
Rotherwick 28 C2
Rothes 181 E5
Rothesay 140 B3
Rothiebrisbane 170 C1
Rothienorman 170 C1
Rothiesholm 199 E4
Rothley *Leics.* 68 A1
Rothley *Northumb.* 128 C3
Rothwell *Lincs.* 96 B3
Rothwell *Northants.* 68 D4
Rothwell *W.Yorks.* 102 C5
Rotsea 104 C2
Rottal 160 B3
Rottingdean 17 F3
Rottington 116 C5
Roud 15 E4
Roudham 72 A3
Rough Close 79 G4
Rough Common 32 D3
Rougham *Norf.* 85 G5
Rougham *Suff.* 60 A1
Rougham Green 60 A1
Roughburn 157 F1
Roughlee 101 E3
Roughley 66 D3
Roughton *Lincs.* 84 A1
Roughton *Norf.* 86 D2
Roughton *Shrop.* 65 G3
Roundhay 102 C4
Roundstreet Common 29 F5
Roundway 26 B1
Rous Lench 54 C2
Rousdon 11 F3
Rousham 55 G5
Rousham Gap 55 G5
Routenburn 140 D3
Routh 104 C3
Row *Cornw.* 5 E2
Row *Cumb.* 107 F4
Row *Cumb.* 118 C4
Row Heath 47 E1
Row Town 29 F1
Rowanburn 126 C4
Rowardennan Lodge 149 F5
Rowberrow 24 B2
Rowchoish 149 F4
Rowde 26 A1
Rowen 89 F5
Rowfoot 118 C1
Rowhedge 60 B5
Rowhook 29 G4
Rowington 55 E1
Rowington Green 67 E5
Rowland 93 G5
Rowland's Castle 15 G1
Rowlands Gill 120 A2
Rowledge 28 D3
Rowley *Devon* 10 A1
Rowley *Dur.* 119 G3
Rowley *E.Riding* 104 B4
Rowley *Shrop.* 64 C2
Rowley Regis 66 B4
Rowlstone 52 C5
Rowly 29 F3
Rowner 15 E2
Rowney Green 66 C5
Rownhams 14 C1
Rowrah 117 D5
Rowsham 43 D1
Rowsley 81 D1
Rowstock 41 G4
Rowston 83 F2
Rowthorne 81 F1
Rowton *Ches.* 78 B1
Rowton *Shrop.* 64 C1
Rowton *Tel. & W.* 65 F1
Roxburgh 136 A3
Roxby *N.Lincs.* 95 G1
Roxby *N.Yorks.* 111 G1
Roxton 57 G2
Roxwell 45 F2
Royal British Legion Village 31 G3
Royal Leamington Spa 55 F1
Royal Tunbridge Wells 31 E5
Roybridge 157 E1
Roydon *Essex* 44 D1
Roydon *Norf.* 72 B3
Roydon *Norf.* 85 F5
Roydon Hamlet 44 D2
Royston *Herts.* 58 B3
Royston *S.Yorks.* 94 A1
Royton 92 D2
Ruabon 78 A3
Ruaig 154 B2
Ruan Lanihorne 4 C5
Ruan Major 3 D5
Ruan Minor 3 E5
Ruanaich 146 B2
Ruardean 39 F1
Ruardean Woodside 39 F1
Rubery 66 B5
Ruckcroft 118 B3
Ruckinge 32 C5
Ruckland 96 D5
Ruckley 65 E2
Rudbaxton 48 C5
Rudby 111 D2
Rudchester 120 A1
Ruddington 81 G4
Ruddlemoor 5 E4
Rudford 53 G5
Rudge 25 F2
Rudgeway 39 F4
Rudgwick 29 F4
Rudhall 53 F5
Rudheath 92 A5
Rudley Green 46 B2
Rudry 38 A4
Rudston 104 C1
Rudyard 79 G2
Rufford 91 F1
Rufforth 103 E2
Ruffside 119 F2
Rugby 68 A5
Rugeley 66 C1
Ruilick 179 E5
Ruishton 23 F5
Ruisigearraidh 184 B5
Ruislip 43 F4
Rumbling Bridge 151 F5
Rumburgh 73 E3
Rumford 4 C2
Rumney 38 B5
Rumwell 23 E5
Runacraig 150 A3
Runcorn 91 G4
Runcton 16 A3
Runcton Holme 71 E2
Rundlestone 7 F3
Runfold 29 D3
Runhall 86 B5
Runham 87 F4
Runnington 23 E5
Runsell Green 45 G2
Runswick 112 B1
Runtaleave 160 A3
Runwell 45 G3
Ruscombe 42 C5
Rush Green 45 E4
Rushall *Here.* 53 F4
Rushall *Norf.* 72 C3
Rushall *W.Mid.* 66 C2
Rushall *Wilts.* 26 C2
Rushbrooke 59 G1
Rushbury 65 E3
Rushden *Herts.* 58 B4
Rushden *Northants.* 57 E1
Rushford 72 A3
Rushlake Green 18 B2
Rushmere 73 F3
Rushmere St. Andrew 60 C3
Rushmoor *Surr.* 29 D3
Rushmoor *Tel. & W.* 65 F1
Rushock 66 A5
Rusholme 92 C3
Rushton *Ches.* 78 C1
Rushton *Northants.* 68 D4
Rushton *Shrop.* 65 F2
Rushton Spencer 79 G1
Rushwick 54 A2
Rushyford 120 B5
Ruskie 150 B4
Ruskington 83 F2
Rusko 123 G5
Rusland 107 E4
Rusper 30 B5
Ruspidge 39 F1
Russel 177 E5
Russell's Water 42 C4
Rusthall 31 E4
Rustington 16 C3
Ruston 112 C4
Ruston Parva 104 C1
Ruswarp 112 B2
Rutherend 142 A4
Rutherford 136 A4
Rutherglen 142 A3
Ruthernbridge 5 E3
Ruthin (Rhuthun) 77 E2
Ruthrieston 171 E4
Ruthven *Aber.* 182 A5
Ruthven *Angus* 160 A5
Ruthven *High.* 168 A1
Ruthven *High.* 167 G5
Ruthvoes 4 D3
Ruthwaite 117 F3
Ruthwell 125 F4
Ruyton-XI-Towns 78 A5
Ryal 128 C4
Ryal Fold 100 C5
Ryall 12 A3
Ryarsh 31 F3
Rydal 107 E2
Ryde 15 E3
Rydon 20 D5
Rye 19 E1
Rye Foreign 19 D1
Rye Harbour 19 E2
Rye Park 44 C2
Ryhall 69 F1
Ryhill 94 A1
Ryhope 120 D2
Ryland 96 A4
Rylstone 101 F2
Ryme Intrinseca 12 B1
Ryther 103 E4
Ryton *Glos.* 53 G4
Ryton *N.Yorks.* 111 G5
Ryton *Shrop.* 65 G2
Ryton *T. & W.* 120 A1
Ryton-on-Dunsmore 67 F5

S

Sabden 101 D4
Sackers Green 60 A4
Sacombe 44 C1
Sacriston 120 B3
Sadberge 110 C1
Saddell 130 C2
Saddington 68 B3
Saddle Bow 71 E1
Sadgill 107 F2
Saffron Walden 58 D4
Sageston 35 D2
Saham Toney 71 G2
Saighdinis 173 G3
Saighton 78 B1
St. Abbs 145 G3
St. Agnes 4 B4
St. Albans 44 A2
St. Allen 4 C4
St. Andrews 152 D3
St. Andrews Major 38 A5
St. Anne 9 G4
St. Anne's 99 G5
St. Ann's 125 E1
St. Ann's Chapel *Cornw.* 7 E3
St. Ann's Chapel *Devon* 8 C3
St. Anthony *Cornw.* 3 E4
St. Anthony *Cornw.* 3 F3
St. Arvans 39 E3
St. Asaph (Llanelwy) 90 B5
St. Athan 22 D1
St. Aubin 8 C5
St. Audries 23 E3
St. Austell 5 E4
St. Bees 116 C5
St. Blazey 5 E4
St. Blazey Gate 5 E4
St. Boswells 135 G2
St. Brelade 8 B5
St. Breock 5 D2
St. Breward 5 E2
St. Briavels 39 E2
St. Brides 34 B1
St. Brides Major 37 E5
St. Brides Netherwent 38 D4
St. Bride's-super-Ely 37 G5
St. Brides Wentlooge 38 B4
St. Budeaux 8 A2
St. Buryan 2 B4
St. Catherine 39 G5
St. Catherines 148 D4
St. Clears 35 F1
St. Cleer 5 G3
St. Clement 4 C5
St. Clether 5 G1
St. Columb Major 4 D3
St. Columb Minor 4 C3
St. Columb Road 4 D4
St. Combs 183 F3
St. Cross South Elmham 73 D3
St. Cyrus 161 F3
St. Davids *Fife* 143 F1
St. David's *P. & K.* 151 E2
St. David's (Tyddewi) *Pembs.* 48 A5
St. Day 4 B5
St. Decumans 23 D3
St. Dennis 5 D4
St. Dogmaels 49 E3
St. Dogwells 48 C5
St. Dominick 8 A1
St. Donats 22 C1
St. Edith's Marsh 26 A1
St. Endellion 5 D2
St. Enoder 4 C4
St. Erme 4 C5
St. Erth 2 C3
St. Erth Praze 2 C3
St. Ervan 4 C2
St. Eval 4 C3
St. Ewe 5 D5
St. Fagans 38 A5
St. Fergus 183 G4
St. Fillans 150 B2
St. Florence 35 D2
St. Gennys 6 B1
St. George 90 A5
St. Georges *N.Som.* 24 A1
St. George's *V. of Glam.* 37 G5
St. Germans 7 D5
St. Giles in the Wood 21 F4
St. Giles on the Heath 7 D1
St. Harmon 63 F5
St. Helen Auckland 120 A5
St. Helena
St. Helen's *E.S*
St. Helens *I.o*
St. Helens *M*

St. Helier 8 C5
St. Hilary Cornw. 2 C3
St. Hilary V. of Glam. 37 G5
St. Hill 30 C5
St. Illtyd 38 B2
St. Ippollitts 58 A5
St. Ishmael 35 G2
St. Ishmael's 34 B2
St. Issey 4 D2
St. Ive 6 D4
St. Ives Cambs. 70 B5
St. Ives Cornw. 2 C2
St. Ives Dorset 14 A2
St. James South Elmham 73 E3
St. John Chan.I. 8 C4
St. John Cornw. 8 A2
St. John's I.o.M. 98 A3
St. John's Surr. 29 E2
St. John's Worcs. 54 A2
St. John's Chapel Devon 21 F3
St. John's Chapel Dur. 119 E4
St. John's Fen End 70 D1
St. Johns Hall 119 G4
St. John's Highway 70 D1
St. John's Kirk 134 A2
St. John's Town of Dalry 124 A2
St. Judes 98 B2
St. Just 2 A3
St. Just in Roseland 3 F3
St. Katherines 170 C1
St. Keverne 3 E4
St. Kew 5 E2
St. Kew Highway 5 E2
St. Keyne 5 G3
St. Lawrence Cornw. 5 E3
St. Lawrence Essex 46 C2
St. Lawrence I.o.W. 15 E5
St. Leonards Bucks. 43 E2
St. Leonards Dorset 14 A2
St. Leonards E.Suss. 18 D3
St. Leonards Grange 14 D3
St. Leonard's Street 31 F3
St. Levan 2 A4
St. Lythans 38 A5
St. Mabyn 5 E2
St. Margaret South Elmham 73 E3
St. Margarets Here. 52 C4
St. Margarets Herts. 44 C1
St. Margaret's at Cliffe 33 F4
St. Margaret's Hope 196 D3
St. Mark's 98 B4
St. Martin Chan.I. 9 F5
St. Martin Chan.I. 8 C5
St. Martin Cornw. 5 G4
St. Martin Cornw. 3 E4
St. Martins P. & K. 151 G1
St. Martin's Shrop. 78 A4
St. Mary Bourne 27 F2
St. Mary Church 37 G5
St. Mary Cray 31 D2
St. Mary Hill 37 F5
St. Mary in the Marsh 19 F1
St. Marychurch 9 F1
St. Mary's 197 D2
St. Mary's Airport 4 B1
St. Mary's Bay 19 F1
St. Mary's Croft 122 B4
St. Mary's Grove 24 B1
St. Mary's Hoo 45 G5
St. Mawes 3 F3
St. Mawgan 4 C3
St. Mellion 7 D4
St. Mellons 38 B4
St. Merryn 4 C2
St. Mewan 5 D4
St. Michael Caerhays 5 D5
St. Michael Penkevil 4 C5
St. Michael South Elmham 73 E3
St. Michaels Kent 32 A5
St. Michaels Worcs. 53 E1
St. Michael's on Wyre 100 A3
St. Minver 5 D2
St. Monans 152 D4
St. Neot 5 F3
St. Neots 57 G2
St. Nicholas Pembs. 48 C4
St. Nicholas V. of Glam. 37 G5
St. Nicholas at Wade 33 E2
St. Ninians 150 C5
St. Osyth 47 E1
St. Ouen 8 B5
St. Owen's Cross 53 E5
St. Paul's Cray 31 D2
St. Paul's Walden 57 G5
St. Peter 8 B5
St. Peter Port 9 F5
St. Peter's 33 F2
St. Petrox 34 C3
St. Pinnock 5 G3
St. Quivox 132 B3
St. Sampson 9 F4
St. Saviour 9 E5
St. Stephen 4 D4
St. Stephens Cornw. 8 A2
St. Stephens Cornw. 6 D2
St. Stephens Herts. 44 A2
St. Teath 5 E1
St. Tudy 5 E2
St. Twynnells 34 C3
St. Veep 5 F4
St. Vigeans 161 E5
St. Wenn 5 D3
St. Weonards 53 D5
Saintbury 54 D3
Salachail 156 C4
Salcombe 8 D4
Salcombe Regis 11 E4
Salcott 46 C1
Sale 92 B3
Sale Green 54 B2
Saleby 97 E5
Salehurst 18 C1
Salem Carmar. 50 C5
Salem Cere. 62 C4
Salem Gwyn. 75 E2
Salen Arg. & B. 155 E5
Salen High. 155 F3
Salesbury 100 C4
Salford Beds. 57 E4
Salford Gt.Man. 92 C3
Salford Oxon. 55 E5
Salford Priors 54 C2
Salfords 30 B4
Salhouse 87 E4
Saline 151 F5
Salisbury 26 C4
Salkeld Dykes 118 B4
Sall 86 C3
Sallachan 156 B3
Sallachry 148 C3
Sallachy High. 190 A4
Sallachy High. 165 F1
Salmonby 96 D5
Salmond's Muir 153 D1
Salperton 54 C5
Salph End 57 F2
Salsburgh 142 C3
Salt 79 G5
Salt Hill 43 E5
Saltash 8 A2
Saltburn 179 G2
Saltburn-by-the-Sea 121 F5
Saltby 83 D5
Saltcoats 140 D5
Saltcotes 99 G5
Saltdean 17 F3
Salterforth 101 E3
Saltergate 112 B3
Salterhill 181 E3
Salterswall 78 D1
Saltfleet 97 E3
Saltfleetby All Saints 97 E3
Saltfleetby St. Clements 97 E3
Saltfleetby St. Peter 97 E4
Saltford 25 D1
Salthaugh Grange 105 E5
Salthouse 86 B1
Saltley 66 C4
Saltmarshe 103 G5
Saltney 78 A1
Salton 111 G4
Saltwick 129 D3
Saltwood 33 D5
Salvington 16 D3
Salwarpe 54 A1
Salwayash 12 A3
Sambourne 54 C1
Sambrook 79 E5
Samhla 173 F3
Samlesbury 100 B4
Samlesbury Bottoms 100 C5
Sampford Arundel 11 E1
Sampford Brett 23 D3
Sampford Courtenay 21 G5
Sampford Peverell 10 D1
Sampford Spiney 7 F3
Samuelston 144 B2
Sanaigmore 138 A3
Sancreed 2 B4
Sancton 104 B4
Sand 200 C3
Sand Hole 104 A4
Sand Hutton 103 F2
Sand Side 106 D4
Sandaig Arg. & B. 154 A2
Sandaig High. 164 D4
Sandaig High. 165 D3
Sandbach 79 E1
Sandbank 140 C1
Sandbanks 13 G4
Sandend 182 A3
Sanderstead 30 C2
Sandford Cumb. 108 C1
Sandford Devon 10 B2
Sandford Dorset 13 F3
Sandford I.o.W. 15 E4
Sandford N.Som. 24 B2
Sandford S.Lan. 142 B5
Sandford-on-Thames 42 A2
Sandford Orcas 24 D5
Sandford St. Martin 55 G5
Sandfordhill 183 G5
Sandgarth 198 D5
Sandgate 33 E5
Sandgreen 123 G5
Sandhaven 183 E3
Sandhead 122 B5
Sandhills Dorset 12 C1
Sandhills Surr. 29 E4
Sandhoe 119 F1
Sandholme E.Riding 104 A4
Sandholme Lincs. 84 B4
Sandhurst Brack.F. 28 D1
Sandhurst Glos. 54 A5
Sandhurst Kent 18 C1
Sandhutton 110 C4
Sandiacre 81 F4
Sandilands 97 F4
Sandiway 92 A5
Sandleheath 14 A1
Sandleigh 41 G2
Sandling 31 G3
Sandness 200 A2
Sandon Essex 45 G2
Sandon Herts. 58 B4
Sandon Staffs. 79 G5
Sandown 15 E4
Sandplace 5 G4
Sandquoy 199 F2
Sandridge Herts. 44 A1
Sandridge Wilts. 26 A1
Sandringham 85 E5
Sandrocks 17 F1
Sandsend 112 B1
Sandside House 194 B2
Sandsound 200 C3
Sandtoft 95 E2
Sanduck 10 A4
Sandway 32 A3
Sandwich 33 F3
Sandwick Cumb. 107 F1
Sandwick Shet. 200 D5
Sandwick (Sanndabhaig) W.Isles 187 F4
Sandwith 116 C5
Sandy 57 G3
Sandy Haven 34 B2
Sandy Lane W.Yorks. 102 A4
Sandy Lane Wilts. 26 A1
Sandycroft 78 A1
Sandygate Devon 10 B5
Sandygate I.o.M. 98 B2
Sandylands 100 A1
Sandyway 53 D5
Sangobeg 192 D2
Sanna 155 D3
Sannaig 138 D3
Sanndabhaig (Sandwick) 187 F4
Sanquhar 133 F5
Santon Bridge 106 C2
Santon Downham 71 G4
Sapcote 67 G3
Sapey Common 53 G1
Sapiston 72 A4
Sapperton Glos. 40 B2
Sapperton Lincs. 83 F4
Saracen's Head 84 B5
Sarclet 195 F4
Sardis 34 C2
Sarisbury 15 E2
Sarn Bridgend 37 F4
Sarn Powys 64 B3
Sarn Bach 74 C5
Sarn Meyllteyrn 74 B4
Sarnau Carmar. 35 G1
Sarnau Cere. 49 G2
Sarnau Gwyn. 76 C4
Sarnau Powys 64 B1
Sarnesfield 52 C2
Saron Carmar. 36 C1
Saron Carmar. 49 G4
Saron Gwyn. 75 E1
Sarratt 43 F3
Sarre 33 E2
Sarsden 55 E5
Sarsgrum 192 C2
Sartfield 98 B2
Satley 120 A3
Satterleigh 21 G3
Satterthwaite 107 E3
Sauchen 170 B3
Saucher 151 G1
Sauchie 151 D5
Sauchieburn 161 E3
Sauchrie 132 B4
Saughall 78 A1
Saughall Massie 90 D4
Saughtree 127 D2
Saul 39 G2
Saundby 95 E4
Saundersfoot 35 E2
Saunderton 42 C2
Saunton 21 E2
Sausthorpe 84 B1
Savalbeg 190 A4
Savalmore 190 A4
Sawbridgeworth 45 D1
Sawdon 112 C4
Sawley Derbys. 81 F4
Sawley Lancs. 101 D3
Sawley N.Yorks. 102 B1
Sawston 58 C3
Sawtry 69 G4
Saxby Leics. 68 D1
Saxby Lincs. 96 A4
Saxby All Saints 95 G1
Saxelbye 82 C5
Saxilby 95 F5
Saxlingham 86 B2
Saxlingham Green 72 D2
Saxlingham Nethergate 72 D2
Saxlingham Thorpe 72 D2
Saxmundham 61 E1
Saxon Street 59 E2
Saxondale 82 B4
Saxtead Green 61 D1
Saxtead Little Green 60 D1
Saxthorpe 86 C2
Saxton 103 D4
Sayers Common 17 E2
Scackleton 111 F5
Scadabhagh 185 D4
Scaftworth 95 D3
Scagglethorpe 112 B5
Scalasaig 146 C5
Scalby E.Riding 104 A5
Scalby N.Yorks. 112 D4
Scaldwell 68 C5
Scale Houses 118 B3
Scaleby 118 A1
Scalebyhill 118 A1
Scales Cumb. 117 G4
Scales Cumb. 107 D5
Scalford 82 C5
Scaling 111 G1
Scallasaig 165 E3
Scallastle 147 G1
Scalloway 200 C4
Scamblesby 96 C5
Scammadale 148 A2
Scamodale 156 A2
Scampston 112 B5
Scampton 95 G5
Scaniport 167 F1
Scapa 196 D2
Scar 199 E2
Scarborough 112 D4
Scarcewater 4 D4
Scarcliffe 81 F1
Scarcroft 102 C3
Scardroy 178 B4
Scarff 202 B4
Scarfskerry 195 E1
Scargill 109 F1
Scarinish 154 B2
Scarisbrick 91 E1
Scarning 86 A4
Scarrington 82 C3
Scarth Hill 91 F2
Scartho 96 C2
Scatraig 167 G1
Scaur D. & G. 124 C3
Scaur or Kippford D. & G. 124 C5
Scawby 95 G2
Scawton 111 E4
Scayne's Hill 17 F1
Scealascro 186 C5
Scethrog 52 A5
Schaw 132 C3
Scholar Green 79 F2
Scholes W.Yorks. 102 C4
Scholes W.Yorks. 93 F2
Sciberscross 190 C3
Scleddau 48 C4
Sco Ruston 87 D3
Scofton 94 D4
Scole 72 C4
Scolpaig 173 F2
Scones Lethendy 151 G2
Sconser 164 B1
Scoor 146 D3
Scopwick 83 F2
Scoraig 188 C5
Scorborough 104 C3
Scorrier 4 B5
Scorriton 8 D1
Scorton Lancs. 100 B3
Scorton N.Yorks. 110 B2
Scotby 118 A2
Scotch Corner 110 B2
Scotforth 100 A2
Scothern 96 A5
Scotland Gate 129 E3
Scotlandwell 151 G4
Scotnish 139 F1
Scots' Gap 128 C3
Scotsburn 179 G2
Scotston Aber. 161 F2
Scotston P. & K. 159 E5
Scotstown 156 A3
Scotter 95 F2
Scotterthorpe 95 F2
Scottlethorpe 83 F5
Scotton Lincs. 95 F3
Scotton N.Yorks. 110 A3
Scotton N.Yorks. 102 C2
Scottow 87 D3
Scoulton 86 A5
Scourie 192 A4
Scourie More 192 A4
Scousburgh 201 F4
Scrabster 194 C1
Scrainwood 128 B1
Scrane End 84 B3
Scraptoft 68 B2
Scratby 87 G4
Scrayingham 103 G1
Scredington 83 F3
Scremby 84 C1
Scremerston 137 E2
Screveton 82 C3
Scriven 102 C2
Scrooby 95 D3
Scropton 80 C4
Scrub Hill 84 A2
Scruton 110 B3
Sculthorpe 85 G4
Scunthorpe 95 F1
Scurlage 36 A4
Sea Palling 87 F3
Seabank 156 B5
Seaborough 12 A2
Seacombe 91 D3
Seacroft Lincs. 85 D1
Seacroft W.Yorks. 102 C4
Seafield Arg. & B. 139 F1
Seafield S.Ayr. 132 B3
Seafield W.Loth. 143 E3
Seaford 17 G4
Seaforth 91 E3
Seagrave 68 B1
Seaham 120 D3
Seahouses 137 G3
Seal 31 E3
Sealand 78 A1
Seale 29 D3
Seamer N.Yorks. 111 D1
Seamer N.Yorks. 112 D4
Seamill 140 D5
Searby 96 A2
Seasalter 32 C2
Seascale 106 B2
Seathwaite Cumb. 117 F5
Seathwaite Cumb. 106 D3
Seatoller 117 F5
Seaton Cornw. 6 D5
Seaton Cumb. 116 D3
Seaton Devon 11 F3
Seaton Dur. 120 D3
Seaton E.Riding 105 D3
Seaton Northumb. 129 F4
Seaton Rut. 69 E3
Seaton Burn 129 E4
Seaton Carew 121 E4
Seaton Delaval 129 F4
Seaton Junction 11 F3
Seaton Ross 103 G3
Seaton Sluice 129 F4
Seatown Aber. 183 G4
Seatown Dorset 12 A3
Seatown Moray 181 G3
Seatown Moray 182 A3
Seave Green 111 E2
Seaview 15 F3
Seaville 117 E1
Seavington St. Mary 12 A1
Seavington St. Michael 12 A1
Seawick 47 E1
Sebastopol 38 B3
Sebergham 117 G2
Seckington 67 E2
Second Coast 188 B5
Sedbergh 108 B3
Sedbury 39 E3
Sedbusk 109 D3
Sedgeberrow 54 C4
Sedgebrook 83 D4
Sedgefield 120 C5
Sedgeford 85 F4
Sedgehill 25 F5
Sedgley 66 B3
Sedgwick 107 G4
Sedlescombe 18 C2
Sedlescombe Street 18 C2
Seend 26 A1
Seend Cleeve 26 A1
Seer Green 43 E3
Seething 73 E2
Sefton 91 E2
Seghill 129 E4
Seifton 65 D4
Seighford 79 F5
Seilebost 184 C4
Seion 75 E1
Seisdon 66 A3
Seisiadar 187 G4
Selattyn 77 F4
Selborne 28 C4
Selby 103 F4
Selham 29 E5
Selkirk 135 F3
Sellack 53 E5
Sellafield 106 B2
Sellafirth 203 E3
Sellindge 32 C5
Selling 32 C3
Sells Green 26 A1
Selly Oak 66 C4
Selmeston 18 A3
Selsdon 30 C2
Selsey 16 A4
Selsfield Common 30 C5
Selside 108 C5
Selstead 33 E4
Selston 81 F2
Selworthy 22 C3
Semblister 200 C2
Semer 60 A3
Semington 25 F1
Semley 25 F5
Send 29 F2
Send Marsh 29 F2
Senghenydd 38 A3
Sennen 2 A4
Sennen Cove 2 A4
Sennybridge 51 F5
Senwick 115 G2
Sequer's Bridge 8 C2
Sessay 111 D5
Setchey 71 E1
Setley 14 C2
Setter Shet. 201 E3
Setter Shet. 200 C2
Settiscarth 198 B5
Settle 101 E1
Settrington 112 B5
Seven Bridges 40 D3
Seven Kings 45 D4
Seven Sisters 37 E2
Seven Springs 40 B1
Sevenhampton Glos. 54 C5
Sevenhampton Swin. 41 E3
Sevenoaks 31 E3
Sevenoaks Weald 31 E3
Severn Beach 39 E4
Severn Stoke 54 A3
Sevington 32 C4
Sewards End 59 D4
Sewardstone 44 C3
Sewerby 105 E1
Seworgan 3 E3
Sewstern 83 D5
Sexhow 111 D2
Sgarasta Mhòr 184 C4
Sgiogarstaigh 187 G1
Sgodachail 189 G5
Shabbington 42 B2
Shackerley 66 A2
Shackerstone 67 F2
Shackleford 29 E3
Shadfen 129 E3
Shadforth 120 C3
Shadingfield 73 F3
Shadoxhurst 32 B5
Shadwell 72 A3
Shaftesbury 25 F5
Shafton 94 A1
Shalbourne 27 E1
Shalcombe 14 D4
Shalden 28 B3
Shaldon 10 C5
Shalfleet 14 D4
Shalford Essex 59 F5
Shalford Surr. 29 F3
Shalford Green 59 F5
Shallowford 22 A3
Shalmsford Street 32 C3
Shalmstry 194 D2
Shalstone 56 B4
Shalunt 140 B2
Shambellie 125 D4
Shamley Green 29 F3
Shandon 141 D1
Shandwick 180 A2
Shangton 68 C3
Shankend 135 G5
Shankhouse 129 E4
Shanklin 15 E4
Shannochie 131 E3
Shantron 141 E1
Shantullich 179 F4
Shanzie 160 A4
Shap 107 G1
Shapwick Dorset 13 F2
Shapwick Som. 24 B4
Shardlow 81 F4
Shareshill 66 B2
Sharlston 94 A1
Sharnbrook 57 F2
Sharnford 67 G3
Sharoe Green 100 B4
Sharow 110 C5
Sharpenhoe 57 F4
Sharperton 128 B1
Sharpham House 9 E2
Sharpness 39 F2
Sharpthorne 30 C5
Sharrington 86 B2
Shatterford 65 G4
Shaugh Prior 8 B1
Shavington 79 D2
Shaw Gt.Man. 92 D2
Shaw Swin. 40 D4
Shaw W.Berks. 27 F1
Shaw Wilts. 25 F1
Shaw Mills 102 B1
Shawbury 78 C5
Shawclough 92 C1
Shawell 68 A4
Shawford 27 F5
Shawforth 101 E5
Shawhead 124 C3
Shawtonhill 142 A5
Sheanachie 130 C4
Sheandow 169 E1
Shear Cross 25 F3
Shearington 125 E4
Shearsby 68 B3
Shebbear 21 E5
Shebdon 79 E5
Shebster 194 C2
Shedfield 15 E1
Sheen 80 C1
Sheepscombe 40 A1
Sheepstor 8 B1
Sheepwash Devon 21 E5
Sheepwash Northumb. 129 E3
Sheepway 39 D5
Sheepy Magna 67 F2
Sheepy Parva 67 F2
Sheering 45 E1
Sheerness 32 B1
Sheet 28 C5
Sheffield 94 A4
Sheffield Bottom 28 B1
Sheffield City Airport 94 B4
Sheffield Green 17 G1
Shefford 57 G4
Shefford Woodlands 41 F5
Sheigra 192 A2
Sheinton 65 F2
Shelderton 64 D5
Sheldon Derbys. 80 C1
Sheldon Devon 11 E2
Sheldon W.Mid. 66 D4
Sheldwich 32 C3
Shelf 102 A5
Shelfanger 72 C3
Shelfield 66 C2
Shelford 82 B3
Shellachan Arg. & B. 148 A3
Shellachan Arg. & B. 148 C2
Shellbrook Hill 78 A3
Shelley Essex 45 E2
Shelley Suff. 60 B4
Shelley W.Yorks. 93 G1
Shellingford 41 F3
Shellow Bowells 45 F2
Shelsley Beauchamp 53 G1
Shelsley Walsh 53 G1
Shelton Beds. 57 F1
Shelton Norf. 72 D2
Shelton Notts. 82 C3
Shelton Shrop. 65 D1
Shelton Green 72 D2
Shelve 64 C3
Shelwick 53 E3
Shenfield 45 F3
Shenington 55 F3
Shenley 44 A2
Shenley Brook End 56 D4
Shenley Church End 56 D4
Shenleybury 44 A2
Shenmore 52 C4
Shennanton 123 E4
Shenstone Staffs. 66 D2
Shenstone Worcs. 66 A5
Shenstone Woodend 66 D2
Shenton 67 F2
Shenval 169 E2
Shepeau Stow 70 B1
Shephall 58 A5
Shepherd's Green 42 C4
Shepherdswell (Sibertswold) 33 E4
Shepley 93 F2
Sheppardstown 195 E5
Shepperdine 39 F3
Shepperton 29 F1
Shepreth 58 B3
Shepshed 67 G1
Shepton Beauchamp 12 A1
Shepton Mallet 24 D3
Shepton Montague 25 D4
Shepway 31 G3
Sheraton 120 D4
Sherborne Dorset 12 C1
Sherborne Glos. 41 D1
Sherborne St. John 28 B2
Sherbourne 55 E1
Sherburn Dur. 120 C3
Sherburn N.Yorks. 112 C5
Sherburn in Elmet 103 D4
Shere 29 F3
Shereford 85 G5
Sherfield English 27 D5
Sherfield on Loddon 28 B2
Sherford 9 D3
Sheriff Hutton 103 F1
Sheriffhales 65 G1
Sheringham 86 C1
Sherington 57 D3
Shernborne 85 F4
Sherramore 167 E5
Sherrington 26 A4
Sherston 40 A4
Sherwood Green 21 F3
Shettleston 142 A3
Shevington 91 G2
Shevington Moor 91 G1
Sheviock 7 D5
Shiel Bridge 165 F3
Shieldaig High. 177 E4
Shieldaig High. 177 E2
Shieldhill 142 C2
Shielfoot 155 F2
Shielhill 160 C4
Shiels 170 B4
Shifford 41 F2
Shifnal 65 G2
Shilbottle 129 D1
Shildon 120 B5
Shillingford Devon 22 C5
Shillingford Oxon. 42 A3
Shillingford St. George 10 C4
Shillingstone 13 E1
Shillington 57 G4
Shillmoor 128 A1
Shilstone 21 F5
Shilton Oxon. 41 E2
Shilton Warks. 67 G4
Shimpling Norf. 72 C3
Shimpling Suff. 59 G2
Shimpling Street 59 G2
Shincliffe 120 B3
Shiney Row 120 C2
Shinfield 28 C1
Shingay 58 B3
Shingle Street 61 E3
Shinner's Bridge 9 D1
Shinness Lodge 190 A3
Shipbourne 31 E3
Shipdham 86 A5
Shipham 24 B2
Shiphay 9 E1
Shiplake 42 C5
Shipley Northumb. 137 F5
Shipley Shrop. 66 A3
Shipley W.Suss. 29 G5
Shipley W.Yorks. 102 A4
Shipley Bridge Devon 8 C1
Shipley Bridge Surr. 30 C4
Shipmeadow 73 E2
Shippon 41 G3
Shipston on Stour 55 E3
Shipton Glos. 40 C1
Shipton N.Yorks. 103 E2
Shipton Shrop. 65 E3
Shipton Bellinger 26 D3
Shipton Gorge 12 A3
Shipton Green 16 A4
Shipton Moyne 40 A4
Shipton-on-Cherwell 41 G1
Shipton-under-Wychwood 41 E1
Shiptonthorpe 104 A3
Shira 149 D3
Shirburn 42 B3
Shirdley Hill 91 E1
Shire Oak 66 C2
Shirebrook 81 G1
Shirehampton 39 E5
Shiremoor 129 F4
Shirenewton 39 D3
Shireoaks 94 C4
Shirl Heath 52 D2
Shirland 81 F2
Shirley Derbys. 80 D3
Shirley Gt.Lon. 30 C2
Shirley Hants. 14 A3
Shirley S'ham. 14 D1
Shirley W.Mid. 66 D5
Shirrell Heath 15 E1
Shirwell 21 F2
Shirwell Cross 21 F2
Shiskine 131 E3
Shobdon 52 C1
Shobrooke 10 B2
Shocklach 78 B3
Shoeburyness 46 C4
Sholden 33 F3
Sholing 15 D1
Shoot Hill 64 D1
Shooter's Hill 44 D5
Shop Cornw. 4 C2
Shop Cornw. 20 C4
Shop Corner 60 D4
Shoreditch 44 C4
Shoreham 31 E2
Shoreham-by-Sea 17 E3
Shoremill 179 G3
Shoresdean 145 G5
Shoreswood 145 G5
Shoretown 179 F3
Shorncote 40 C3
Shorne 45 F5
Shorne Ridgeway 45 F5
Short Cross 64 B2
Short Green 72 B3
Short Heath Derbys. 67 F1
Short Heath W.Mid. 66 C3
Shortacombe 7 F2
Shortgate 17 G2
Shortgrove 58 D4
Shortlanesend 4 C5
Shorwell 15 D4
Shoscombe 25 E2
Shotesham 72 D2
Shotgate 45 G3
Shotley 60 D4
Shotley Bridge 119 G2

Shotley Gate 60 D4
Shotleyfield 119 G2
Shottenden 32 C3
Shottermill 29 D4
Shottery 55 D2
Shotteswell 55 G3
Shottisham 61 E3
Shottle 81 E2
Shottlegate 81 E3
Shotton *Dur.* 120 D4
Shotton *Flints.* 78 A1
Shotton *Northumb.* 136 C3
Shotton Colliery 120 C3
Shotts 142 C3
Shotwick 91 E5
Shoughlaige-e-Caine 98 B3
Shouldham 71 E2
Shouldham Thorpe 71 E2
Shoulton 54 A2
Shover's Green 31 F5
Shrawardine 64 C1
Shrawley 54 A1
Shrewley 55 E1
Shrewsbury 65 D1
Shrewton 26 B3
Shripney 16 B3
Shrivenham 41 E4
Shropham 72 A2
Shroton (Iwerne Courtney) 13 E1
Shrub End 60 A5
Shucknall 53 E3
Shudy Camps 59 E3
Shurdington 40 B1
Shurlock Row 42 D5
Shurrery 194 C3
Shurrery Lodge 194 C3
Shurton 23 E3
Shustoke 67 E3
Shut Heath 79 F5
Shute 11 F3
Shutford 55 F3
Shuthonger 54 A4
Shutlanger 56 C2
Shuttington 67 E2
Shuttlewood 94 B5
Shuttleworth 92 C1
Siabost 187 D3
Siadar Iarach 187 E2
Siadar Uarach 187 E2
Sibbaldbie 125 F2
Sibbertoft 68 B4
Sibdon Carwood 64 D4
Sibertswold (Shepherdswell) 33 E4
Sibford Ferris 55 F4
Sibford Gower 55 F4
Sible Hedingham 59 F4
Sibsey 84 B2
Sibson *Cambs.* 69 F3
Sibson *Leics.* 67 F2
Sibster 195 F3
Sibthorpe 82 C3
Sibton 61 E1
Sicklesmere 59 G2
Sicklinghall 102 C3
Sidbury *Devon* 11 E3
Sidbury *Shrop.* 65 F4
Sidcot 24 B2
Sidcup 45 D5
Siddington *Ches.* 92 C5
Siddington *Glos.* 40 C3
Sidemoor 66 B5
Sidestrand 87 D2
Sidford 11 E3
Sidlesham 16 A4
Sidley 18 C3
Sidlow 30 B4
Sidmouth 11 E4
Sigford 10 A5
Sigglesthorne 105 D3
Sigingstone 37 F5
Silchester 28 B1
Sileby 68 B1
Silecroft 106 C4
Silfield 72 C2
Silian 50 B2
Silk Willoughby 83 F3
Silkstone 93 G2
Silkstone Common 93 G2
Silksworth 120 C2
Silloth 117 E1
Sills 128 A1
Sillyearn 182 A4
Silpho 112 C3
Silsden 101 G3
Silsoe 57 F4
Silton 25 E5
Silver End 46 B1
Silver Hill *E.Suss.* 18 C1
Silverburn 143 G3
Silvercraigs 139 G1
Silverdale *Lancs.* 107 F5
Silverdale *Staffs.* 79 F3
Silverhill 18 D2
Silverley's Green 73 D4
Silvermoss 170 D1
Silverstone 56 B3
Silverton 10 C2
Silvington 65 F5
Silwick 200 B3
Simonburn 128 A4
Simonsbath 22 A4
Simonstone 101 D4
Simprim 145 F5
Simpson 57 D4
Sinclair's Hill 145 F4
Sinclairston 132 C4
Sinderby 110 C4
Sinderhope 119 E2
Sindlesham 28 C1
Singdean 135 G5
Singleton *Lancs.* 99 G4
Singleton *W.Suss.* 16 A2
Singlewell or Ifield 45 F5
Sinnahard 169 G3
Sinnington 111 G4
Sinton Green 54 A1
Sipson 43 F5
Sirhowy 38 A1
Sisland 73 E2
Sissinghurst 31 G5
Siston 39 F5
Sithney 2 D4
Sittingbourne 32 B2
Siulaisiadar 187 G4
Six Ashes 65 G4
Six Mile Bottom 59 D2
Sixhills 96 B4
Sixmile Cottages 32 D4
Sixpenny Handley 13 F1
Sizewell 61 F1
Skail 193 G4
Skaill *Ork.* 198 A5
Skaill *Ork.* 197 E2
Skares *Aber.* 170 B1
Skares *E.Ayr.* 132 D4
Skarpigarth 200 A2
Skateraw 145 E2
Skaw 201 E1
Skeabost 176 A5
Skeabrae 198 A4
Skeeby 110 A2
Skeffington 68 C2
Skeffling 97 D1
Skegby 81 G1
Skegness 85 D1
Skelberry 201 G4
Skelbo 190 C5
Skeldon 132 B4
Skeldyke 84 B4
Skellingthorpe 95 G5
Skellister 201 D2
Skellow 94 C1
Skelmanthorpe 93 G1
Skelmersdale 91 F2
Skelmonae 171 D1
Skelmorlie 140 C3
Skelmuir 183 E5
Skelton *Cumb.* 118 A4
Skelton *E.Riding* 103 G5
Skelton *N.Yorks.* 109 F2
Skelton *N.Yorks.* 102 C1
Skelton *R. & C.* 111 F1
Skelton *York* 103 E2
Skelton Green 111 F1
Skelwick 198 C2
Skelwith Bridge 107 E2
Skendleby 84 C1
Skenfrith 53 D5
Skerne 104 C2
Skeroblingarry 130 C3
Skerray 193 F2
Sketty 36 C3
Skewen 36 D3
Skewsby 111 F5
Skeyton 86 D3
Skidbrooke 97 E3
Skidby 104 C4
Skilgate 22 C5
Skillington 83 E5
Skinburness 117 E1
Skinflats 142 D1
Skinidin 175 F5
Skinnet 194 D2
Skinningrove 121 G5
Skipness 140 A4
Skipsea 105 D2
Skipton 101 F2
Skipton-on-Swale 110 C4
Skipwith 103 F4
Skirbeck 84 B3
Skirlaugh 104 D4
Skirling 134 B2
Skirmett 42 C4
Skirpenbeck 103 G2
Skirwith *Cumb.* 118 C4
Skirwith *N.Yorks.* 108 C5
Skirza 195 F2
Skulamus 164 C2
Skullomie 193 F2
Skye of Curr 168 B2
Slack 170 A1
Slackhall 93 E4
Slackhead 181 G3
Slad 40 A2
Slade 21 F1
Slade Green 45 E5
Slaggyford 118 C2
Slaidburn 100 D2
Slains Park 161 G2
Slaithwaite 93 E1
Slaley 119 F2
Slamannan 142 C2
Slapton *Bucks.* 57 E5
Slapton *Devon* 9 E3
Slapton *Northants.* 56 B3
Slate Haugh 181 G3
Slatenber 108 C5
Slattadale 177 E2
Slattocks 92 C2
Slaugham 17 E1
Slaughden 61 F2
Slaughterford 40 A5
Slawston 68 C3
Sleaford *Hants.* 28 D4
Sleaford *Lincs.* 83 F3
Sleagill 107 G1
Sleapford 65 F1
Sledge Green 54 A4
Sledmere 104 B1
Sleights 112 B2
Slepe 13 F3
Slickly 195 E2
Sliddery 131 E3
Sliemore 168 C2
Sligachan 164 A2
Slimbridge 39 G2
Slindon *Staffs.* 79 F4
Slindon *W.Suss.* 16 B3
Slinfold 29 G4
Slingsby 111 F5
Slioch 170 A1
Slip End *Beds.* 43 F1
Slip End *Herts.* 58 A4
Slipton 69 E5
Slochd 168 A2
Slockavullin 148 A5
Slogarie 124 A4
Sloley 87 D3
Slongaber 124 C3
Sloothby 97 E5
Slough 43 E5
Sluggan 168 A2
Slyne 100 A1
Smailholm 136 A3
Small Dole 17 E2
Small Hythe 32 A5
Smallbridge 92 D1
Smallburgh 87 E3
Smallburn *Aber.* 183 F5
Smallburn *E.Ayr.* 133 E3
Smalley 81 F3
Smallfield 30 C4
Smallridge 11 F2
Smallthorne 79 F2
Smallworth 72 B3
Smannell 27 E3
Smardale 108 C2
Smarden 32 A4
Smaull 138 A3
Smeale Farm 98 C1
Smeatharpe 11 E1
Smeeth 32 C5
Smeeton Westerby 68 B3
Smelthouses 102 A1
Smerral 195 D5
Smethwick 66 C4
Smirisary 155 F2
Smisby 67 F1
Smith End Green 53 G2
Smithfield 118 A1
Smithincott 11 D1
Smith's Green 59 D5
Smithton 179 G5
Smithy Green 92 B5
Smug Oak 44 A2
Smyrton 122 C2
Smythe's Green 46 C1
Snailbeach 64 C2
Snailwell 59 E1
Snainton 112 C4
Snaith 103 F5
Snape *N.Yorks.* 110 B4
Snape *Suff.* 61 E2
Snape Green 91 E1
Snarestone 67 F2
Snarford 96 A4
Snargate 19 E1
Snave 32 C5
Sneachill 54 B2
Snead 64 C3
Sneaton 112 B2
Sneatonthorpe 112 C2
Snelland 96 A4
Snellings 106 A2
Snelston 80 C3
Snetterton 72 A2
Snettisham 85 E4
Snibston 67 G1
Snishival 162 A1
Snitter 128 C1
Snitterby 95 G3
Snitterfield 55 E2
Snitton 65 E5
Snodhill 52 C3
Snodland 31 G2
Snowshill 54 C4
Soar *Carmar.* 50 C5
Soar *Devon* 8 D4
Soberton 15 F1
Soberton Heath 15 F1
Sockburn 110 C2
Sodylt Bank 78 A4
Soham 71 D5
Solas 173 G2
Soldon Cross 20 D4
Soldridge 28 B4
Sole Street *Kent* 32 C4
Sole Street *Kent* 31 F2
Solihull 67 D5
Solihull Lodge 66 C5
Sollers Dilwyn 52 D2
Sollers Hope 53 F4
Sollom 91 F1
Solsgirth 151 E5
Solva 48 A5
Solwaybank 126 B4
Somerby 68 C1
Somercotes 81 F2
Somerford Keynes 40 C3
Somerley 16 A4
Somerleyton 73 F2
Somersal Herbert 80 C4
Somersby 96 D5
Somersham *Cambs.* 70 B5
Somersham *Suff.* 60 B3
Somerton *Oxon.* 55 G5
Somerton *Som.* 24 B5
Somerton *Suff.* 59 G2
Sompting 17 D3
Sonning 42 C5
Sonning Common 42 C4
Sonning Eye 42 C5
Sopley 14 A3
Sopworth 40 A4
Sorbie 115 E2
Sordale 194 D2
Sorisdale 154 B3
Sorn 133 D3
Sornhill 132 D2
Soroba 148 A2
Sortat 195 E2
Sotby 96 C5
Sots Hole 83 G1
Sotterly 73 F3
Soudley 79 E5
Soughton 77 F1
Soulbury 57 D5
Soulby 108 C1
Souldern 56 A4
Souldrop 57 E1
Sound *Ches.* 78 D3
Sound *Shet.* 201 D3
Sound *Shet.* 200 C2
Soundwell 39 F5
Sourhope 136 C4
Sourin 198 C3
Sourton 7 F2
Soutergate 106 D4
South Acre 71 G1
South Allington 9 D4
South Alloa 151 D5
South Ambersham 29 E5
South Anston 94 C4
South Ascot 29 E1
South Ballachulish 156 C4
South Balloch 123 E1
South Bank 121 E5
South Barrow 24 D5
South Beddington 30 B2
South Bellsdyke 142 D1
South Benfleet 45 G4
South Bersted 16 B4
South Blackbog 170 C1
South Bowood 12 A3
South Brent 8 C1
South Brentor 7 E2
South Brewham 25 E4
South Broomhill 129 E2
South Burlingham 87 E5
South Cadbury 24 D5
South Cairn 122 A4
South Carlton 95 G5
South Cave 104 B4
South Cerney 40 C3
South Chard 11 G2
South Charlton 137 F4
South Cheriton 25 D5
South Cliffe 104 A4
South Clifton 95 F5
South Cockerington 97 D4
South Common 17 F2
South Cornelly 37 E5
South Corrygills 131 F2
South Cove 73 F3
South Creagan 156 B5
South Creake 85 G4
South Croxton 68 B1
South Dalton 104 B3
South Darenth 31 E2
South Duffield 103 F4
South Elkington 96 C4
South Elmsall 94 B1
South End *Bucks.* 57 D5
South End *Cumb.* 99 F1
South End *N.Lincs.* 96 B1
South Erradale 176 D2
South Fambridge 46 B3
South Fawley 41 F4
South Ferriby 104 B5
South Flobbets 170 C1
South Garth 203 E3
South Godstone 30 C4
South Gorley 14 A1
South Green *Essex* 45 F3
South Green *Norf.* 86 B4
South Hall 140 B2
South Hanningfield 45 G3
South Harting 15 G1
South Hayling 15 G3
South Hazelrigg 137 E3
South Heath 43 E2
South Heighton 17 G3
South Hetton 120 C3
South Hiendley 94 A1
South Hill 6 D3
South Hinksey 42 A2
South Hole 20 C4
South Holmwood 29 G3
South Hornchurch 45 E4
South Hourat 141 D4
South Huish 8 C3
South Hykeham 83 E1
South Hylton 120 C2
South Kelsey 96 A3
South Kessock 179 F5
South Killingholme 96 B1
South Kilvington 110 D4
South Kilworth 68 B4
South Kirkby 94 B1
South Kirkton 170 C4
South Kyme 83 G3
South Lancing 17 D3
South Ledaig 148 B1
South Leigh 41 F2
South Leverton 95 E4
South Littleton 54 C3
South Lopham 72 B3
South Luffenham 69 E2
South Malling 17 G2
South Marston 41 D4
South Milford 103 D4
South Milton 8 D3
South Mimms 44 B2
South Molton 22 A5
South Moor 120 A2
South Moreton 42 A4
South Mundham 16 A3
South Muskham 82 C2
South Newbald 104 B4
South Newington 55 G4
South Newton 26 B4
South Normanton 81 F2
South Norwood 30 C2
South Nutfield 30 C4
South Ockendon 45 E4
South Ormsby 97 D5
South Otterington 110 C4
South Oxhey 44 A3
South Park 30 B4
South Perrott 12 A2
South Petherton 12 A1
South Petherwin 6 D2
South Pickenham 71 G2
South Pool 9 D3
South Queensferry 143 F2
South Radworthy 22 A4
South Rauceby 83 F3
South Raynham 85 G5
South Redbriggs 182 C5
South Reston 97 E4
South Runcton 71 E2
South Scarle 82 D1
South Shian 156 B5
South Shields 120 C1
South Somercotes 97 E3
South Stainley 102 C1
South Stoke *Oxon.* 42 B4
South Stoke *W.Suss.* 16 C3
South Street *E.Suss.* 17 F2
South Street *Kent* 31 F2
South Tawton 7 G1
South Thoresby 97 E5
South Tidworth 26 D3
South Town 28 B4
South Upper Barrack 183 E5
South Walsham 87 E4
South Warnborough 28 C3
South Weald 45 E3
South Weston 42 C3
South Wheatley *Cornw.* 6 C1
South Wheatley *Notts.* 95 E4
South Whiteness 200 C3
South Widcombe 24 C2
South Wigston 68 A3
South Willesborough 32 C4
South Willingham 96 B4
South Wingate 120 D4
South Wingfield 81 E2
South Witham 69 E1
South Wonston 27 F4
South Woodham Ferrers 46 B3
South Wootton 85 E5
South Wraxall 25 F1
South Yardley 66 D4
South Zeal 7 G1
Southall 44 A5
Southam *Glos.* 54 B5
Southam *Warks.* 55 G1
Southampton 14 D1
Southampton International Airport 15 D1
Southbar 141 F3
Southborough 31 E4
Southbourne *Bourne.* 14 A3
Southbourne *W.Suss.* 15 G2
Southburgh 86 B5
Southburn 104 B2
Southchurch 46 C4
Southcott 7 F1
Southdean 127 E1
Southease 17 G3
Southend *Aber.* 182 C5
Southend *Arg. & B.* 130 B5
Southend *W.Berks.* 42 B5
Southend-on-Sea 46 B4
Southerndown 37 E5
Southerness 125 D5
Southery 71 E3
Southfleet 45 F5
Southgate *Gt.Lon.* 44 B3
Southgate *Norf.* 86 C3
Southgate *Norf.* 85 E4
Southgate *Swan.* 36 B4
Southill 57 G3
Southington 27 G3
Southleigh 11 F3
Southminster 46 C3
Southmuir 160 B4
Southoe 57 G1
Southolt 60 C1
Southorpe 69 F2
Southowram 102 A5
Southport 91 E1
Southrepps 87 D2
Southrey 83 G1
Southrop 41 D2
Southrope 28 B3
Southsea *Ports.* 15 F3
Southsea *Wrex.* 77 F2
Southstoke 25 E1
Southtown *Norf.* 87 G5
Southtown *Ork.* 197 D3
Southwaite *Cumb.* 108 C2
Southwaite *Cumb.* 118 A3
Southwark 44 C5
Southwater 29 G5
Southway 24 C3
Southwell *Dorset* 12 C5
Southwell *Notts.* 82 C2
Southwick *Hants.* 15 F2
Southwick *Northants.* 69 F3
Southwick *T. & W.* 120 C2
Southwick *W.Suss.* 17 E3
Southwick *Wilts.* 25 F2
Southwold 73 G4
Southwood *Norf.* 87 E5
Southwood *Som.* 24 C4
Sowerby *N.Yorks.* 110 D4
Sowerby *W.Yorks.* 101 G5
Sowerby Bridge 101 G5
Sowerby Row 117 G2
Sowton 10 C3
Soyal 190 A5
Spa Common 87 D2
Spadeadam 127 D4
Spalding 84 A5
Spaldington 103 G4
Spaldwick 69 G5
Spalefield 153 D4
Spalford 82 D1
Spanby 83 F4
Sparham 86 B4
Spark Bridge 107 E4
Sparkford 24 D5
Sparkwell 8 B2
Sparrowpit 93 E4
Sparrow's Green 31 F5
Sparsholt *Hants.* 27 F4
Sparsholt *Oxon.* 41 F4
Spartylea 119 E3
Spaunton 111 G3
Spaxton 23 F4
Spean Bridge 157 E1
Speddoch 124 C2
Speen *Bucks.* 42 D2
Speen *W.Berks.* 27 F1
Speeton 113 E5
Speke 91 F4
Speldhurst 31 E4
Spellbrook 45 D1
Spelsbury 55 F5
Spen Green 79 F1
Spencers Wood 28 C1
Spennithorne 110 A4
Spennymoor 120 B4
Spetchley 54 A2
Spetisbury 13 F2
Spexhall 73 E3
Spey Bay 181 F3
Speybridge 168 C2
Speyview 181 E5
Spilsby 84 C1
Spindlestone 137 F3
Spinkhill 94 B5
Spinningdale 190 B5
Spirthill 40 B5
Spital *High.* 195 D3
Spital *W. & M.* 43 E5
Spital in the Street 95 G3
Spitalbrook 44 C2
Spithurst 17 G2
Spittal *D. & G.* 123 F4
Spittal *D. & G.* 123 E5
Spittal *E.Loth.* 144 B2
Spittal *Northumb.* 137 E1
Spittal *Pembs.* 48 C5
Spittal of Glenmuick 160 B1
Spittal of Glenshee 159 G3
Spittalfield 159 G5
Spixworth 86 D4
Spofforth 102 C2
Spondon 81 F4
Spooner Row 72 B2
Spoonley 79 D4
Sporle 71 G1
Sportsman's Arms 76 C2
Spott 145 D2
Spratton 56 C1
Spreakley 28 D3
Spreyton 7 G1
Spridlington 96 A4
Springburn 142 A3
Springfield *Arg. & B.* 140 B2
Springfield *D. & G.* 126 B5
Springfield *Fife* 152 B3
Springfield *Moray* 180 C4
Springfield *P. & K.* 151 G1
Springfield *W.Mid.* 66 C4
Springholm 124 C4
Springkell 126 A4
Springleys 170 C1
Springside 132 B2
Springthorpe 95 F4
Springwell 120 B2
Sproatley 105 D4
Sproston Green 79 E1
Sprotbrough 94 C2
Sproughton 60 C3
Sprouston 136 B3
Sprowston 86 D4
Sproxton *Leics.* 83 D5
Sproxton *N.Yorks.* 111 F4
Spurstow 78 C2
Square Point 124 B3
Squires Gate 99 G4
Sròndoire 139 G2
Sronphadruig Lodge 158 C2
Stableford 79 F4
Stackhouse 101 E1
Stackpole 34 C3
Stacksteads 101 E5
Staddiscombe 8 B2
Staddlethorpe 104 A5
Stadhampton 42 B3
Stadhlaigearraidh 162 A1
Staffield 118 B3
Staffin 176 A3
Stafford 79 G5
Stagden Cross 45 F1
Stagsden 57 E3
Stagshaw Bank 119 F1
Stain 195 F2
Stainburn 102 B3
Stainby 83 E5
Staincross 94 A2
Staindrop 120 A5
Staines 43 F5
Stainfield *Lincs.* 83 F5
Stainfield *Lincs.* 96 B5
Stainforth *N.Yorks.* 101 E1
Stainforth *S.Yorks.* 94 D1
Staining 99 G4
Stainland 93 E1
Stainsacre 112 C2
Stainton *Cumb.* 107 G4
Stainton *Cumb.* 118 A5
Stainton *Dur.* 109 F1
Stainton *Middbro.* 111 D1
Stainton *N.Yorks.* 109 F3
Stainton *S.Yorks.* 94 C3
Stainton by Langworth 96 A5
Stainton le Vale 96 B3
Stainton with Adgarley 107 D5
Staintondale 112 C3
Stair *Cumb.* 117 F4
Stair *E.Ayr.* 132 C3
Staithes 111 G1
Stake Pool 100 A3
Stakeford 129 E3
Stalbridge 12 D1
Stalbridge Weston 12 D1
Stalham 87 E3
Stalham Green 87 E3
Stalisfield Green 32 B3
Stalling Busk 109 E4
Stallingborough 96 C1
Stalmine 99 G3
Stalybridge 93 D3
Stambourne 59 F4
Stamford *Lincs.* 69 F2
Stamford *Northumb.* 137 G5
Stamford Bridge 103 G2
Stamfordham 128 C4
Stanborough 44 B1
Stanbridge *Beds.* 57 E5
Stanbridge *Dorset* 13 G2
Stanbridge Earls 27 E5
Stanbury 101 G4
Stand 142 B3
Standburn 142 D2
Standeford 66 B2
Standen 32 A4
Standford 28 D4
Standish 91 G1
Standlake 41 F2
Standon *Hants.* 27 F5
Standon *Herts.* 58 B5
Standon *Staffs.* 79 F4
Stane 142 C4
Stanfield 86 A3
Stanford *Beds.* 57 G3
Stanford *Kent* 32 D5
Stanford Bishop 53 F2
Stanford Bridge 53 G1
Stanford Dingley 42 A5
Stanford in the Vale 41 F3
Stanford-le-Hope 45 F4
Stanford on Avon 68 A5
Stanford on Soar 81 G5
Stanford on Teme 53 G1
Stanford Rivers 45 E2
Stanghow 111 F1
Stanground 70 A3
Stanhoe 85 G4
Stanhope *Dur.* 119 F4
Stanhope *Sc.Bord.* 134 C3
Stanion 69 E4
Stanley *Derbys.* 81 F3
Stanley *Dur.* 120 A2
Stanley *P. & K.* 151 G1
Stanley *Staffs.* 79 G2
Stanley *W.Yorks.* 102 C5
Stanley *Wilts.* 40 B5
Stanley Common 81 F3
Stanmer 17 F3
Stanmore *Gt.Lon.* 44 A3
Stanmore *W.Berks.* 41 G5
Stannersburn 127 F3
Stanningfield 59 G2
Stannington *Northumb.* 129 E4
Stannington *S.Yorks.* 94 A4
Stansbatch 52 C1
Stansfield 59 F2
Stanstead 59 G3
Stanstead Abbotts 44 C1
Stansted 31 F2
Stansted Airport 58 D5
Stansted Mountfitchet 58 D5
Stanton *Derbys.* 67 E1
Stanton *Glos.* 54 C4
Stanton *Northumb.* 128 D2
Stanton *Staffs.* 80 C3
Stanton *Suff.* 72 A4
Stanton by Bridge 81 E5
Stanton by Dale 81 F4
Stanton Drew 24 C1
Stanton Fitzwarren 41 D3
Stanton Harcourt 41 G2
Stanton Hill 81 F1
Stanton in Peak 80 D1
Stanton Lacy 65 D5
Stanton Long 65 E3
Stanton-on-the-Wolds 82 B4
Stanton Prior 25 D1
Stanton St. Bernard 26 B1
Stanton St. John 42 A2
Stanton St. Quintin 40 B4
Stanton Street 60 A1
Stanton under Bardon 67 G1
Stanton upon Hine Heath 78 C5
Stanton Wick 24 D1
Stanwardine in the Fields 78 B5
Stanway *Essex* 60 A5
Stanway *Glos.* 54 C4
Stanwell 43 F5
Stanwell Moor 43 F5
Stanwick 69 E5
Stanwix 118 A2
Stanydale 200 B2
Staoinebrig 162 A1
Stape 111 G3
Stapehill 13 G2
Stapeley 79 D3
Staple 33 E3
Staple Fitzpaine 11 F1
Staplecross 18 C1
Staplefield 17 E1
Stapleford *Cambs.* 58 C2
Stapleford *Herts.* 44 C1
Stapleford *Leics.* 68 D1
Stapleford *Lincs.* 83 D2
Stapleford *Notts.* 81 F4
Stapleford *Wilts.* 26 B4
Stapleford Abbotts 45 D3
Stapleford Tawney 45 E3
Staplegrove 23 F5
Staplehurst 31 G4
Staplers 15 E4
Stapleton *Bristol* 39 E5
Stapleton *Cumb.* 126 D4
Stapleton *Here.* 52 C1
Stapleton *Leics.* 67 G3
Stapleton *N.Yorks.* 110 B1
Stapleton *Shrop.* 65 D2
Stapleton *Som.* 24 B5
Stapley 11 E1
Staploe 57 G1
Staplow 53 F3
Star *Fife* 152 B4
Star *Pembs.* 49 F4
Star *Som.* 24 B2
Starbotton 109 E5
Starcross 10 C4
Starkigarth 200 D5
Starling's Green 58 C4
Starr 123 F1
Starston 72 D3
Startforth 109 F1

Startley 40 B4
Statham 92 A4
Stathe 24 A5
Stathern 82 C4
Station Town 120 D4
Staughton Green 57 G1
Staughton Highway 57 G1
Staunton Glos. 39 E1
Staunton Glos. 53 G5
Staunton Harold Hall 81 E5
Staunton on Arrow 52 C1
Staunton on Wye 52 C3
Staveley Cumb. 107 F3
Staveley Derbys. 94 B5
Staveley N.Yorks. 102 C1
Staveley-in-Cartmel 107 E4
Staverton Devon 9 D1
Staverton Glos. 54 A5
Staverton Northants. 56 A1
Staverton Wilts. 25 F1
Staverton Bridge 54 A5
Stawell 24 A4
Stawley 23 D5
Staxigoe 195 F3
Staxton 112 D5
Staylittle 63 E3
Staynall 99 G3
Staythorpe 82 C2
Stean 109 F5
Steane 56 A4
Stearsby 111 F5
Steart 23 F3
Stebbing 59 E5
Stebbing Green 59 E5
Stedham 29 D5
Steel Cross 31 E5
Steele Road 126 D2
Steen's Bridge 53 E2
Steep 28 C5
Steep Marsh 28 C5
Steeple Dorset 13 F4
Steeple Essex 46 C2
Steeple Ashton 26 A2
Steeple Aston 55 G5
Steeple Barton 55 G5
Steeple Bumpstead 59 E3
Steeple Claydon 56 B5
Steeple Gidding 69 G4
Steeple Langford 26 B4
Steeple Morden 58 A3
Steeton 101 G3
Stein 175 F4
Steinmanhill 182 C5
Stella 120 A1
Stelling Minnis 32 D4
Stemster High. 195 D2
Stemster High. 195 D4
Stemster House 195 D2
Stenalees 5 E4
Stenhousemuir 142 C1
Stenigot 96 C4
Stenness 202 B5
Stenscholl 176 A3
Stenton E.Loth. 144 D2
Stenton P. & K. 159 F5
Steornabhagh (Stornoway) 187 F4
Stepaside 35 E2
Stepney 44 C4
Steppingley 57 F4
Stepps 142 A3
Sternfield 61 E1
Sterridge 21 F1
Stert 26 B2
Stetchworth 59 E2
Stevenage 58 A5
Stevenston 141 D5
Steventon Hants. 27 G3
Steventon Oxon. 41 G3
Stevington 57 E2
Stewartby 57 F3
Stewarton D. & G. 115 E2
Stewarton E.Ayr. 141 F5
Stewkley 57 D5
Stewton 97 D4
Steyning 17 D2
Steynton 34 C2
Stibb 20 C4
Stibb Cross 21 E4
Stibb Green 26 D1
Stibbard 86 A3
Stibbington 69 F3
Stichill 136 B3
Sticker 5 D4
Stickford 84 B1
Sticklepath 7 G1
Stickney 84 B2
Stiffkey 86 A1
Stifford's Bridge 53 G3
Stillingfleet 103 E3
Stillington N.Yorks. 103 E1
Stillington Stock. 120 C5
Stilton 69 G4
Stinchcombe 39 G3
Stinsford 12 D3
Stirchley Tel. & W. 65 G2
Stirchley W.Mid. 66 C4
Stirkoke House 195 F3
Stirling Aber. 183 G5
Stirling Stir. 150 C5
Stirton 101 F2
Stisted 59 F5
Stithians 3 E3
Stittenham 179 F2
Stivichall 67 F5
Stix 158 C5
Stixwould 83 G1
Stoak 91 F5
Stobo 134 C2
Stoborough 13 F4
Stoborough Green 13 F4
Stobwood 143 D4
Stock 45 F3
Stock Green 54 B2
Stock Lane 41 E5
Stock Wood 54 C2
Stockbridge Hants. 27 E4
Stockbridge Stir. 150 C4
Stockbury 32 A2
Stockcross 27 F1
Stockdalewath 117 G2
Stockerston 68 D3
Stocking Pelham 58 C5
Stockingford 67 F3
Stockland 11 F2
Stockland Bristol 23 F3
Stockleigh English 10 B2
Stockleigh Pomeroy 10 B2
Stockley 26 A1
Stocklinch 11 G1
Stockport 92 C4
Stocksbridge 93 G3
Stocksfield 119 G1
Stockton Here. 53 E1
Stockton Norf. 73 E2
Stockton Shrop. 65 G3
Stockton Warks. 55 G1
Stockton Wilts. 26 A4
Stockton Heath 92 A4
Stockton-on-Tees 120 D5
Stockton on Teme 53 G1
Stockton on the Forest 103 F2
Stockwood 12 B2
Stodday 100 A2
Stodmarsh 33 E2
Stody 86 B2
Stoer 188 C2
Stoford Som. 12 B1
Stoford Wilts. 26 B4
Stogumber 23 D4
Stogursey 23 F3
Stoke Devon 20 C3
Stoke Hants. 27 F2
Stoke Hants. 15 G2
Stoke Med. 32 A1
Stoke W.Mid. 67 F5
Stoke Abbott 12 A2
Stoke Albany 68 D4
Stoke Ash 72 C4
Stoke Bardolph 82 B3
Stoke Bliss 53 F1
Stoke Bruerne 56 C2
Stoke by Clare 59 F3
Stoke-by-Nayland 60 A4
Stoke Canon 10 C3
Stoke Charity 27 F4
Stoke Climsland 7 D3
Stoke D'Abernon 29 G2
Stoke Doyle 69 F4
Stoke Dry 69 D3
Stoke Ferry 71 E3
Stoke Fleming 9 E3
Stoke Gabriel 9 E2
Stoke Gifford 39 F5
Stoke Golding 67 F3
Stoke Goldington 56 D3
Stoke Hammond 57 D5
Stoke Heath 79 D5
Stoke Holy Cross 86 D5
Stoke Lacy 53 F2
Stoke Lyne 56 A5
Stoke Mandeville 42 D2
Stoke Newington 44 C4
Stoke on Tern 78 D5
Stoke-on-Trent 79 F3
Stoke Orchard 54 B5
Stoke Poges 43 E4
Stoke Prior Here. 53 E2
Stoke Prior Worcs. 54 B1
Stoke Rivers 21 G2
Stoke Rochford 83 E5
Stoke Row 42 B4
Stoke St. Gregory 24 A5
Stoke St. Mary 23 F5
Stoke St. Michael 25 D3
Stoke St. Milborough 65 E4
Stoke sub Hamdon 12 A1
Stoke Talmage 42 B3
Stoke Trister 25 E5
Stoke Wake 13 D2
Stokeford 13 E4
Stokeham 95 E5
Stokeinteignhead 10 C5
Stokenchurch 42 C3
Stokenham 9 E3
Stokesay 64 D4
Stokesby 87 F4
Stokesley 111 E2
Stolford 23 F3
Ston Easton 24 D2
Stonar Cut 33 F2
Stondon Massey 45 E2
Stone Bucks. 42 C1
Stone Glos. 39 F3
Stone Kent 45 E5
Stone Kent 19 E1
Stone Staffs. 79 F4
Stone Worcs. 66 A5
Stone Allerton 24 A2
Stone Cross E.Suss. 18 B3
Stone Cross Kent 32 C5
Stone Cross Kent 31 E5
Stone House 108 C4
Stone Street Kent 31 E3
Stone Street Suff. 73 E3
Stonebridge E.Suss. 18 A1
Stonebridge Warks. 67 E4
Stonebroom 81 F2
Stoneferry 104 D4
Stonefield Arg. & B. 139 G2
Stonefield S.Lan. 142 A4
Stonegate 18 B1
Stonegrave 111 F5
Stonehaugh 127 F4
Stonehaven 161 G1
Stonehouse D. & G. 124 C4
Stonehouse Glos. 40 A2
Stonehouse Northumb. 118 C2
Stonehouse Plym. 8 A2
Stonehouse S.Lan. 142 B5
Stoneleigh 67 F5
Stonely 57 G1
Stoner Hill 28 C5
Stones Green 60 C5
Stonesby 82 D5
Stonesfield 41 F1
Stonestreet Green 32 C5
Stonethwaite 117 F5
Stoney Cross 14 B1
Stoney Middleton 93 G5
Stoney Stanton 67 G3
Stoney Stoke 25 E4
Stoney Stratton 25 D4
Stoney Stretton 64 C2
Stoneyburn 143 D3
Stoneygate 68 B2
Stoneyhills 46 C3
Stoneykirk 122 B5
Stoneywood 171 D3
Stonganess 203 E2
Stonham Aspal 60 C2
Stonnall 66 C2
Stonor 42 C4
Stonton Wyville 68 C3
Stony Houghton 81 F1
Stony Stratford 56 C3
Stonybreck 200 A5
Stoodleigh 10 C1
Stopham 16 C2
Stopsley 57 G5
Stoptide 4 D2
Storeton 91 E4
Stornoway (Steornabhagh) 187 F4
Stornoway Airport 187 F4
Storridge 53 G3
Storrington 16 C2
Storth 107 F4
Storwood 103 G3
Stotfield 181 E2
Stotfold 58 A4
Stottesdon 65 F4
Stoughton Leics. 68 B2
Stoughton Surr. 29 E2
Stoughton W.Suss. 16 A2
Stoul 165 D5
Stoulton 54 B2
Stour Provost 25 E5
Stour Row 25 F5
Stourbridge 66 A4
Stourpaine 13 E2
Stourport-on-Severn 66 A5
Stourton Staffs. 66 A4
Stourton Warks. 55 E4
Stourton Wilts. 25 E4
Stourton Caundle 12 D1
Stove 199 E3
Stoven 73 F3
Stow Lincs. 95 F4
Stow Sc.Bord. 144 B5
Stow Bardolph 71 E2
Stow Bedon 72 A2
Stow cum Quy 58 D1
Stow Longa 69 G5
Stow Maries 46 B3
Stow-on-the-Wold 55 D5
Stowbridge 71 E2
Stowe Glos. 39 E2
Stowe Shrop. 64 C5
Stowe Staffs. 80 B5
Stowell Glos. 40 C1
Stowell Som. 25 D5
Stowey 24 C2
Stowford 7 E2
Stowlangtoft 60 A1
Stowmarket 60 B2
Stowting 32 D4
Stowupland 60 B2
Stracathro 161 E3
Strachan 170 B5
Stradbroke 72 D4
Stradishall 59 F2
Stradsett 71 E2
Stragglethorpe 83 E2
Straiton Edin. 143 G3
Straiton S.Ayr. 132 B5
Straloch Aber. 171 D2
Straloch P. & K. 159 F3
Stramshall 80 B4
Strang 98 B4
Strannda 184 C5
Stranraer 122 B4
Strata Florida 50 D1
Stratfield Mortimer 28 B1
Stratfield Saye 28 B1
Stratfield Turgis 28 B2
Stratford 54 A4
Stratford St. Andrew 61 E2
Stratford St. Mary 60 B4
Stratford sub Castle 26 C4
Stratford Tony 26 B5
Stratford-upon-Avon 55 D2
Strath 195 E3
Strathan High. 188 C2
Strathan High. 165 F5
Strathaven 142 B5
Strathblane 141 G2
Strathcarron 177 F5
Strathdon 169 F3
Strathgirnock 169 F5
Strathkanaird 188 D4
Strathkinness 152 C3
Strathmiglo 152 A4
Strathpeffer 179 D4
Strathrannoch 178 C2
Strathtay 159 E4
Strathwhillan 131 F2
Strathy 194 A2
Strathyre 150 A3
Stratton Cornw. 20 C5
Stratton Dorset 12 C3
Stratton Glos. 40 C2
Stratton Audley 56 B5
Stratton-on-the-Fosse 25 D2
Stratton St. Margaret 41 D4
Stratton St. Michael 72 D2
Stratton Strawless 86 D3
Stravanan 140 B4
Stravithie 152 D3
Streat 17 F2
Streatham 44 B5
Streatley Beds. 57 F5
Streatley W.Berks. 42 A4
Street Lancs. 100 B2
Street N.Yorks. 111 G2
Street Som. 24 B4
Street Dinas 78 A4
Street End Kent 32 D3
Street End W.Suss. 16 A4
Street on the Fosse 24 D4
Streethay 66 D1
Streetlam 110 C3
Streetly 66 C3
Strefford 64 D4
Strensall 103 F1
Strensham 54 B3
Stretcholt 23 F3
Strete 9 E3
Stretford 92 B3
Stretford Court 52 D2
Strethall 58 C4
Stretham 70 D5
Strettington 16 A3
Stretton Ches. 78 B2
Stretton Derbys. 81 E1
Stretton Rut. 69 E1
Stretton Staffs. 66 A1
Stretton Staffs. 81 D5
Stretton Warr. 92 A4
Stretton en le Field 67 F1
Stretton Grandison 53 F3
Stretton Heath 64 C1
Stretton-on-Dunsmore 67 G5
Stretton-on-Fosse 55 E4
Stretton Sugwas 53 D3
Stretton under Fosse 67 G4
Stretton Westwood 65 E3
Stribers 107 E4
Strichen 183 E4
Stringston 23 E3
Strixton 57 E1
Stroat 39 E3
Stromeferry 165 E1
Stromemore 165 E1
Stromness 196 B2
Stronachlachar 149 G4
Strone Arg. & B. 140 C1
Strone High. 167 E2
Strone High. 156 D1
Strone Stir. 149 G3
Stronechrubie 189 E3
Stronenaba 157 E1
Stronlonag 140 C1
Stronmilchan 149 D2
Strontian 156 A3
Strontoiller 148 B2
Stronvar 150 A3
Strood 31 G2
Strood Green 29 F5
Stroquhan 124 C2
Stroud Glos. 40 A2
Stroud Hants. 28 C5
Stroud Common 29 F3
Stroud Green 40 A2
Stroul 141 D1
Stroxton 83 E4
Struan High. 163 G1
Struan P. & K. 158 D3
Strubby 97 E4
Strumpshaw 87 E5
Struthers 152 B4
Struy 178 D5
Stryt-issa 77 F3
Stryt-yr-hwch 78 A3
Stuartfield 183 E5
Stub Place 106 B3
Stubbington 15 E2
Stubbins 92 B1
Stubhampton 13 F1
Stubley 94 A5
Stubton 83 D3
Stuck Arg. & B. 140 B2
Stuck Arg. & B. 148 D5
Stuckbeg 149 E5
Stuckgowan 149 F4
Stuckindroin 149 F3
Stuckreoch 148 C5
Stuckton 14 A1
Stud Green 43 D5
Studdon 119 E2
Studfold 108 D5
Studham 43 F1
Studholme 117 F1
Studland 13 G4
Studley Warks. 54 C1
Studley Wilts. 40 B5
Studley Common 54 C1
Studley Roger 110 B5
Stuggadhoo 98 B4
Stump Cross 58 D3
Stuntney 71 D5
Stunts Green 18 B2
Sturbridge 79 F4
Sturmer 59 F3
Sturminster Common 13 D1
Sturminster Marshall 13 F2
Sturminster Newton 13 D1
Sturry 33 D2
Sturton by Stow 95 F4
Sturton le Steeple 95 E4
Stuston 72 C4
Stutton N.Yorks. 103 D3
Stutton Suff. 60 C4
Styal 92 C4
Styrrup 94 D3
Suainebost 187 G1
Suardail 187 F4
Succoth Aber. 169 G1
Succoth Arg. & B. 149 E4
Succothmore 148 D4
Suckley 53 G2
Sudborough 69 E4
Sudbourne 61 F2
Sudbrook Lincs. 83 E3
Sudbrook Mon. 39 E4
Sudbrooke 96 A5
Sudbury Derbys. 80 C4
Sudbury Gt.Lon. 44 A4
Sudbury Suff. 59 G3
Sudgrove 40 B2
Suffield N.Yorks. 112 C3
Suffield Norf. 86 D2
Sugarloaf 32 B5
Sugnall 79 E4
Suie Lodge Hotel 149 G2
Sulby 98 B2
Sulgrave 56 A3
Sulham 42 B5
Sulhamstead 28 B1
Sullington 16 C2
Sullom 202 C5
Sullom Voe Oil Terminal 202 C5
Sully 23 E1
Sumburgh 201 G5
Sumburgh Airport 201 G5
Summer Bridge 102 B1
Summercourt 4 C4
Summerfield 85 F4
Summerhill 78 A2
Summerhouse 110 B1
Summerleaze 38 D4
Summerseat 92 B1
Summertown 42 A2
Summit 92 D1
Sunadale 139 G5
Sunbury 29 G1
Sundaywell 124 C2
Sunderland Cumb. 117 E3
Sunderland T. & W. 120 C2
Sunderland Bridge 120 B4
Sundhope 135 E3
Sundon Park 57 F5
Sundridge 31 D3
Sundrum Mains 132 C3
Sunhill 40 D2
Sunipol 154 C4
Sunk Island 96 C1
Sunningdale 29 E1
Sunninghill 29 E1
Sunningwell 41 G3
Sunniside Dur. 120 A4
Sunniside T. & W. 120 B2
Sunny Bank 107 D3
Sunnylaw 150 C5
Sunnymead 42 A2
Sunnyside Aber. 171 D5
Sunnyside Northumb. 119 F1
Sunnyside W.Suss. 30 C5
Sunwick 145 F4
Surbiton 29 G1
Surfleet 84 A5
Surfleet Seas End 84 A5
Surlingham 87 E5
Sustead 86 C2
Susworth 95 F2
Sutcombe 20 D4
Suton 72 B2
Sutors of Cromarty 180 A3
Sutterton 84 A4
Sutton Beds. 58 A3
Sutton Cambs. 70 C5
Sutton Gt.Lon. 30 B2
Sutton Kent 33 F4
Sutton Lincs. 83 D2
Sutton Norf. 87 E3
Sutton Notts. 82 C4
Sutton Notts. 95 D4
Sutton Oxon. 41 G2
Sutton Pembs. 34 C1
Sutton Peter. 69 G3
Sutton S.Yorks. 94 C1
Sutton Shrop. 65 G4
Sutton Shrop. 79 D4
Sutton Shrop. 65 E1
Sutton Staffs. 79 E5
Sutton Suff. 61 E3
Sutton W.Suss. 16 B2
Sutton Abinger 29 G3
Sutton at Hone 45 E5
Sutton Bassett 68 C4
Sutton Benger 40 B5
Sutton Bonington 81 G5
Sutton Bridge 84 C5
Sutton Cheney 67 G2
Sutton Coldfield 66 D3
Sutton Courtenay 42 G3
Sutton Crosses 84 C5
Sutton Grange 110 B5
Sutton Green 29 F2
Sutton Holms 13 G1
Sutton Howgrave 110 C5
Sutton in Ashfield 81 F2
Sutton-in-Craven 101 G3
Sutton in the Elms 68 A3
Sutton Lane Ends 92 D5
Sutton le Marsh 97 F4
Sutton Leach 91 G3
Sutton Maddock 65 G2
Sutton Mallet 24 A4
Sutton Mandeville 26 A5
Sutton Montis 24 D5
Sutton-on-Hull 104 D4
Sutton on Sea 97 F4
Sutton-on-the-Forest 103 E1
Sutton on the Hill 80 D4
Sutton on Trent 82 C1
Sutton Poyntz 12 D4
Sutton St. Edmund 70 B1
Sutton St. James 70 C1
Sutton St. Nicholas 53 E3
Sutton Scarsdale 81 F1
Sutton Scotney 27 F4
Sutton-under-Brailes 55 E4
Sutton-under-Whitestonecliffe 111 D4
Sutton upon Derwent 103 G3
Sutton Valence 32 A4
Sutton Veny 25 F3
Sutton Waldron 13 E1
Sutton Weaver 91 G5
Sutton Wick 41 G3
Swaby 97 D5
Swadlincote 67 F1
Swaffham 71 G2
Swaffham Bulbeck 59 D1
Swaffham Prior 59 D1
Swafield 87 D2
Swainby 111 D2
Swainshill 53 D3
Swainsthorpe 86 D5
Swainswick 25 E1
Swalcliffe 55 F4
Swalecliffe 32 D2
Swallow 96 B2
Swallow Beck 83 E1
Swallowcliffe 26 A5
Swallowfield 28 C1
Swalwell 120 B1
Swampton 27 F2
Swan Street 59 G5
Swanage 13 G5
Swanbach 79 D3
Swanbourne 56 D5
Swanbridge 23 E1
Swancote 65 G3
Swanland 104 B5
Swanlaws 136 B5
Swanley 31 E2
Swanmore 15 E1
Swannington Leics. 67 G1
Swannington Norf. 86 C4
Swanscombe 45 F5
Swansea (Abertawe) 36 C3
Swanton Abbot 87 D3
Swanton Morley 86 B4
Swanton Novers 86 B2
Swanwick Derbys. 81 F2
Swanwick Hants. 15 E2
Swarby 83 F3
Swardeston 86 C5
Swarkestone 81 E5
Swarland 129 D1
Swaton 83 G4
Swavesey 58 B1
Sway 14 B3
Swayfield 83 E5
Swaythling 14 D1
Swaythorpe 104 C1
Sweetshouse 5 E3
Sweffling 61 E1
Swell 24 A5
Swepstone 67 F1
Swerford 55 F4
Swettenham 79 F1
Swffryd 38 B3
Swiftsden 18 C1
Swilland 60 C2
Swillbrook 100 A4
Swillington 102 C4
Swimbridge 21 G3
Swimbridge Newland 21 G2
Swinbrook 41 E1
Swincliffe 102 B2
Swinderby 83 D1
Swindon Staffs. 66 A3
Swindon Swin. 41 D4
Swindon Village 54 B5
Swine 104 D4
Swinefleet 103 G5
Swineshead Beds. 57 F1
Swineshead Lincs. 84 A3
Swineshead Bridge 84 A3
Swiney 195 E5
Swinford Leics. 68 A5
Swinford Oxon. 41 G2
Swingfield Minnis 33 E4
Swinhoe 137 G4
Swinhope 96 C3
Swining 201 D1
Swinithwaite 109 F4
Swinscoe 80 C3
Swinside Hall 136 B5
Swinstead 83 F5
Swinton Gt.Man. 92 B2
Swinton N.Yorks. 111 G5
Swinton N.Yorks. 110 B4
Swinton S.Yorks. 94 B3
Swinton Sc.Bord. 145 F5
Swintonmill 145 F5
Swithland 68 A1
Swordale 179 E3
Swordland 165 D5
Swordle 155 E3
Swordly 193 G2
Sworton Heath 92 A4
Swyddffynnon 50 C1
Swyncombe 42 B3
Swynnerton 79 F4
Swyre 12 B4
Syde 40 B1
Sydenham Gt.Lon. 44 C5
Sydenham Oxon. 42 C2
Sydenham Damerel 7 E3
Syderstone 85 G4
Sydling St. Nicholas 12 C3
Sydmonton 27 F2
Syerston 82 C3
Syke 92 C1
Sykehouse 94 D1
Sykes 100 C2
Sylen 36 B2
Symbister 201 E1
Symington S.Ayr. 132 B2
Symington S.Lan. 134 A2
Symonds Yat 39 E1
Symondsbury 12 A3
Synod Inn 50 A2
Syre 193 F4
Syreford 54 C5
Syresham 56 B3
Syston Leics. 68 B1
Syston Lincs. 83 E3
Sytchampton 54 A1
Sywell 56 D1

T

Taagan 177 G3
Tabost W.Isles 185 F2
Tabost W.Isles 187 G1
Tacher 195 D4
Tackley 41 G1
Tacleit 186 C4
Tacolneston 72 C2
Tadcaster 103 D3
Tadden 13 F2
Taddington 93 F5
Taddiport 21 E4
Tadley 28 B1
Tadlow 58 A3
Tadmarton 55 F4
Tadworth 30 B3
Tafarn-y-bwlch 49 D4
Tafarn-y-Gelyn 77 E1
Tafarnaubach 38 A1
Taff's Well (Ffynnon Taf) 38 A4
Tafolwern 63 E2
Tai-bach 77 E5
Tai'n Lôn 74 D2
Taibach 37 D4
Taicynhaeaf 62 C1
Tain High. 195 E2
Tain High. 179 G1
Tai'r Bull 51 F5
Tairgwaith 36 D1
Tairlaw 132 C5
Takeley 59 D5
Takeley Street 58 D5
Tal-sarn 50 B2
Tal-y-bont Conwy 76 A1
Tal-y-bont Gwyn. 75 E5
Tal-y-bont Gwyn. 89 E5
Tal-y-Cae 75 F1
Tal-y-cafn 89 F5
Tal-y-llyn 62 D2
Tal-y-wern 63 E2
Talachddu 51 G4
Talacre 90 C4
Talardd 76 B5
Talaton 11 D3
Talbenny 34 B1
Talbot Green 37 G4
Talerddig 63 F2
Talgarreg 50 A2
Talgarth 52 A4
Taliesin 62 C3
Talisker 163 G1
Talke 79 F2
Talkin 118 B2
Talla Linnfoots 134 C3
Talladale 177 F2
Talladh-a-Bheithe 158 A4
Tallarn Green 78 B3
Tallentire 117 E3
Talley 50 C4
Tallington 69 F2
Talmine 193 E2
Talog 49 G5
Talsarnau 75 F4
Talskiddy 4 D3
Talwrn I.o.A. 88 C5
Talwrn Wrex. 77 F3
Talybont 62 C4
Talybont-on-Usk 52 A5
Talyllyn 52 A5
Talysarn 75 D2
Tamavoid 150 A5
Tamerton Foliot 8 A1
Tamworth 67 E2
Tan-lan 75 F3
Tan-y-fron 76 C1
Tan-y-graig 74 C4
Tan-y-groes 49 F3
Tan-y-pistyll 77 D5
Tandridge 30 C3
Tanerdy 50 A5
Tanfield 120 A2
Tangiers 34 C1
Tanglandford 171 D1
Tangley 27 E2
Tangmere 16 B3
Tangwick 202 B5
Tangy 130 B3
Tankerness 197 E2
Tankersley 94 A2
Tannach 195 F4
Tannachie 161 F1
Tannachy 190 C4
Tannadice 160 C4
Tannington 60 D1
Tannochside 142 B3
Tansley 81 E2
Tansor 69 F3
Tantobie 120 A2
Tanton 111 E1
Tanworth in Arden 66 D5
Tanygrisiau 75 F3
Taobh a' Deas Loch Baghasdail 172 C2
Taobh Siar 184 D3
Taobh Tuath (Northton) 184 B5
Tapeley 21 E3
Taplow 43 E4
Taraphocain 156 C5
Tarbat House 179 G2
Tarbert Arg. & B. 139 G3
Tarbert Arg. & B. 139 E4
Tarbert Arg. & B. 139 E1
Tarbert High. 155 F3
Tarbert (An Tairbeart) W.Isles 185 D3
Tarbet Arg. & B. 149 F4
Tarbet High. 165 D5
Tarbet High. 192 A4
Tarbolton 132 C3
Tarbrax 143 E4
Tardebigge 54 B1
Tardy Gate 100 B5
Tarfside 160 C1
Tarland 169 G4
Tarleton 100 A5
Tarlscough 91 F1
Tarlton 40 B3
Tarnbrook 100 B2
Tarnock 24 A2
Tarporley 78 C1
Tarr 23 E4
Tarrant Crawford 13 F2
Tarrant Gunville 13 F1
Tarrant Hinton 13 F1
Tarrant Keyneston 13 F2
Tarrant Launceston 13 F2
Tarrant Monkton 13 F2

Tarrant Rawston 13 F2
Tarrant Rushton 13 F2
Tarrel 180 A1
Tarring Neville 17 G3
Tarrington 53 F3
Tarrnacraig 131 E2
Tarsappie 151 G2
Tarskavaig 164 B4
Tarves 171 D1
Tarvie *High.* 178 D4
Tarvie *P. & K.* 159 F3
Tarvin 78 B1
Tarvin Sands 78 B1
Tasburgh 72 D2
Tasley 65 F3
Taston 55 F5
Tatenhill 80 D5
Tatham 100 C1
Tathwell 96 D4
Tatsfield 30 D3
Tattenhall 78 B2
Tatterford 85 G5
Tattersett 85 G5
Tattershall 84 A2
Tattershall Bridge 83 G2
Tattershall Thorpe 84 A2
Tattingstone 60 C4
Tatworth 11 G2
Tauchers 181 F4
Taunton 23 F5
Tavelty 170 C3
Taverham 86 C4
Tavernspite 35 E1
Tavistock 7 E3
Taw Bridge 21 G5
Taw Green 7 G1
Tawstock 21 F3
Taxal 93 E5
Tayburn 141 G5
Taychreggan 148 C2
Tayinloan 139 E5
Taylors Cross 20 C4
Taynafead 148 C3
Taynish 139 F1
Taynton *Glos.* 53 G5
Taynton *Oxon.* 41 E1
Taynuilt 148 C1
Tayock 161 E4
Tayovullin 138 A2
Tayport 152 C2
Tayvallich 139 F1
Tealby 96 B3
Team Valley 120 B1
Teanamachar 173 F3
Teangue 164 C4
Teasses 152 C4
Tebay 108 B2
Tebworth 57 E5
Tedburn St. Mary 10 B3
Teddington *Glos.* 54 B4
Teddington *Gt.Lon.* 44 A5
Tedstone Delamere 53 F2
Tedstone Wafre 53 F2
Teesside International Airport 110 C1
Teeton 68 B5
Teffont Evias 26 A4
Teffont Magna 26 A4
Tegryn 49 F4
Teigh 69 D1
Teigngrace 10 B5
Teignmouth 10 C5
Telford 65 F2
Telham 18 C2
Tellisford 25 E2
Telscombe 17 G3
Telscombe Cliffs 17 G3
Tempar 158 B4
Templand 125 E2
Temple *Cornw.* 5 F2
Temple *Midloth.* 144 A4
Temple Bar 50 B2
Temple Cloud 24 D2
Temple Ewell 33 E4
Temple Grafton 54 D2
Temple Guiting 54 C5
Temple Hirst 103 F5
Temple Normanton 81 F1
Temple Sowerby 118 C5
Templecombe 25 E5
Templeton *Devon* 10 B1
Templeton *Pembs.* 35 E1
Templeton Bridge 10 B1
Templewood 161 E3
Tempsford 57 G2
Ten Mile Bank 71 D3
Tenbury Wells 53 E1
Tenby (Dinbych-y-Pysgod) 35 E2
Tendring 60 C5
Tenga 155 E5
Tenterden 32 A5
Tepersie Castle 170 A2
Terally 114 B2
Terling 45 G1
Ternhill 78 D4
Terregles 124 D3
Terrington 111 F5
Terrington St. Clement 85 D5
Terrington St. John 70 D1
Tervieside 169 E1
Teston 31 G3
Testwood 14 C1
Tetbury 40 A3
Tetbury Upton 40 A3
Tetchill 78 A4
Tetcott 6 D1
Tetford 96 D5
Tetney 96 D2
Tetney Lock 96 D2
Tetsworth 42 B2
Tettenhall 66 A2
Tettenhall Wood 66 A3
Tetworth 58 A2
Teuchan 171 F1
Teversal 81 F1
Teversham 58 C2
Teviothead 135 F5
Tewel 161 G1
Tewin 44 B1
Tewkesbury 54 A4
Teynham 32 B2
Thainston 161 E2
Thainstone House 170 C3
Thakeham 16 D2
Thame 42 C2
Thames Ditton 29 G1
Thames Haven 45 G4
Thamesmead 45 D4
Thanington 32 D3
Thankerton 134 A2
Tharston 72 C2
Thatcham 27 G1
Thatto Heath 91 G3
Thaxted 59 E4
The Apes Hall 71 D4
The Bage 52 B3
The Balloch 150 D3
The Banking 170 C1
The Bar 29 G5
The Belfry 67 D3
The Birks 170 C4
The Bog 64 C3
The Bourne 28 D3
The Bratch 66 A3
The Bryn 38 C2
The Burf 54 A1
The Burn 161 D2
The Camp 40 B2
The Chequer 78 B3
The City 42 C3
The Common 27 D4
The Craigs 189 G5
The Cronk 98 B2
The Den 141 E4
The Dicker 18 A3
The Drums 160 B3
The Eaves 39 F2
The Flatt 127 D4
The Folly 44 A1
The Grange *Shrop.* 78 A4
The Grange *Surr.* 30 C4
The Green *Arg. & B.* 154 A2
The Green *Wilts.* 25 F4
The Haven 29 F4
The Headland 121 E4
The Hermitage 30 B3
The Howe 98 A5
The Isle 65 D1
The Knowle 31 F4
The Laurels 73 E2
The Leacon 32 B5
The Lee 43 E2
The Lhen 98 B1
The Lodge 149 D5
The Marsh 64 C3
The Moor *E.Suss.* 18 D2
The Moor *Kent* 18 C1
The Mumbles 36 C4
The Mythe 54 A4
The Neuk 170 C5
The Node 44 B1
The Oval 25 E1
The Rhos 34 D1
The Rowe 79 F4
The Sands 29 D3
The Shoe 40 A5
The Smithies 65 F3
The Stocks 19 E1
The Vauld 53 E3
The Wrythe 30 B2
The Wyke 65 G2
Theakston 110 B4
Thealby 95 F1
Theale *Som.* 24 B3
Theale *W.Berks.* 42 B5
Thearne 104 C4
Theberton 61 F1
Thedden Grange 28 B4
Theddingworth 68 B4
Theddlethorpe All Saints 97 E4
Theddlethorpe St. Helen 97 E4
Thelbridge Barton 10 A1
Thelnetham 72 B4
Thelveton 72 C3
Thelwall 92 A4
Themelthorpe 86 B3
Thenford 56 A3
Therfield 58 B4
Thetford 71 G4
Theydon Bois 44 D3
Thickwood 40 A5
Thimbleby *Lincs.* 96 C5
Thimbleby *N.Yorks.* 110 D3
Thirkleby 111 D5
Thirlby 111 D4
Thirlestane 144 C5
Thirn 110 B4
Thirsk 110 D4
Thistleton *Lancs.* 100 A4
Thistleton *Rut.* 69 E1
Thistley Green 71 E5
Thixendale 104 A1
Thockrington 128 B4
Tholomas Drove 70 B2
Tholthorpe 103 D1
Thomas Chapel 35 E2
Thomastown 170 A1
Thompson 72 A2
Thomshill 181 E4
Thong 45 F5
Thoralby 109 F4
Thoresby 94 D5
Thoresway 96 B3
Thorganby *Lincs.* 96 C3
Thorganby *N.Yorks.* 103 F3
Thorgill 111 G3
Thorington 73 F4
Thorington Street 60 B4
Thorlby 101 F2
Thorley 45 D1
Thorley Street *Herts.* 45 D1
Thorley Street *I.o.W.* 14 C4
Thormanby 111 D5
Thorn Falcon 23 F5
Thornaby-on-Tees 111 D1
Thornage 86 B2
Thornborough *Bucks.* 56 C4
Thornborough *N.Yorks.* 110 B4
Thornbury *Devon* 21 E5
Thornbury *Here.* 53 F2
Thornbury *S.Glos.* 39 F4
Thornby 68 B5
Thorncliff 80 B2
Thorncombe 11 G2
Thorncombe Street 29 F3
Thorncote Green 57 G3
Thorndon 60 C1
Thorndon Cross 7 F1
Thorne 95 D1
Thorne St. Margaret 23 D5
Thorner 102 C3
Thornes 66 C2
Thorney *Bucks.* 43 F5
Thorney *Notts.* 95 F5
Thorney *Peter.* 70 A2
Thorney *Som.* 24 B5
Thorney Hill 14 B2
Thornford 12 C1
Thorngrove 24 A4
Thorngumbald 105 E5
Thornham 85 F3
Thornham Magna 72 C4
Thornham Parva 72 C4
Thornhaugh 69 F2
Thornhill *Cardiff* 38 A4
Thornhill *D. & G.* 124 C1
Thornhill *Derbys.* 93 F4
Thornhill *S'ham.* 15 D1
Thornhill *Stir.* 150 B4
Thornhill *W.Yorks.* 93 G1
Thornholme 104 D1
Thornicombe 13 E2
Thornley *Dur.* 120 C4
Thornley *Dur.* 120 A4
Thornliebank 141 G4
Thorns 59 F2
Thornsett 93 E4
Thornthwaite *Cumb.* 117 F4
Thornthwaite *N.Yorks.* 102 A2
Thornton *Angus* 160 B5
Thornton *Bucks.* 56 C4
Thornton *E.Riding* 103 G3
Thornton *Fife* 152 A5
Thornton *Lancs.* 99 G3
Thornton *Leics.* 67 G2
Thornton *Lincs.* 84 A1
Thornton *Mersey.* 91 E2
Thornton *Middbro.* 111 D1
Thornton *Northumb.* 145 G5
Thornton *P. & K.* 159 F5
Thornton *Pembs.* 34 C2
Thornton *W.Yorks.* 102 A4
Thornton Curtis 96 A1
Thornton Hough 91 E4
Thornton-in-Craven 101 F3
Thornton-le-Beans 110 C3
Thornton-le-Clay 103 F1
Thornton-le-Dale 112 B4
Thornton le Moor *Lincs.* 96 A3
Thornton-le-Moor *N.Yorks.* 110 C4
Thornton-le-Moors 91 F5
Thornton-le-Street 110 D4
Thornton Park 145 G5
Thornton Rust 109 E4
Thornton Steward 110 A4
Thornton Watlass 110 B4
Thorntonhall 141 G4
Thorntonloch 145 E2
Thornwood Common 45 D2
Thornyhill 161 E2
Thornylee 135 F2
Thoroton 82 C3
Thorp Arch 102 D3
Thorpe *Derbys.* 80 C2
Thorpe *E.Riding* 104 C3
Thorpe *Lincs.* 97 E4
Thorpe *N.Yorks.* 101 G1
Thorpe *Norf.* 73 F2
Thorpe *Notts.* 82 C2
Thorpe *Surr.* 29 F1
Thorpe Abbotts 72 C4
Thorpe Acre 81 G5
Thorpe Arnold 82 C5
Thorpe Audlin 94 B1
Thorpe Bassett 112 B5
Thorpe Bay 46 C4
Thorpe by Water 69 D3
Thorpe Constantine 67 E2
Thorpe Culvert 84 C1
Thorpe End Garden Village 87 D4
Thorpe Green 60 A2
Thorpe Hall 111 E5
Thorpe Hesley 94 A3
Thorpe in Balne 94 C1
Thorpe in the Fallows 95 G4
Thorpe Langton 68 C3
Thorpe Larches 120 C5
Thorpe-le-Soken 60 C5
Thorpe le Street 104 A3
Thorpe Malsor 68 D5
Thorpe Mandeville 56 A3
Thorpe Market 86 D2
Thorpe Morieux 60 A2
Thorpe on the Hill *Lincs.* 83 E1
Thorpe on the Hill *W.Yorks.* 102 C5
Thorpe St. Andrew 87 D5
Thorpe St. Peter 84 C1
Thorpe Salvin 94 C4
Thorpe Satchville 68 C1
Thorpe Thewles 120 C5
Thorpe Tilney Dales 83 G2
Thorpe Underwood 103 D2
Thorpe Waterville 69 F4
Thorpe Willoughby 103 E4
Thorpeness 61 F2
Thorpland 71 E2
Thorrington 47 D1
Thorverton 10 C2
Thrandeston 72 C4
Thrapston 69 F5
Threapland 101 F1
Threapwood 78 B3
Three Bridges 30 B5
Three Burrows 4 B5
Three Chimneys 32 A5
Three Cocks 52 A4
Three Crosses 36 B3
Three Cups Corner 18 B1
Three Holes 70 D2
Three Leg Cross 31 F5
Three Legged Cross 13 G2
Three Mile Cross 28 C1
Threekingham 83 F4
Threemilestone 4 B5
Threlkeld 117 G4
Threshers Bush 45 D2
Threshfield 101 F1
Threxton Hill 71 G2
Thriepley 152 B1
Thrigby 87 F4
Thringarth 119 F5
Thringstone 67 G1
Thrintoft 110 C3
Thriplow 58 C3
Throcking 58 B4
Throckley 120 A1
Throckmorton 54 B2
Throphill 128 D3
Thropton 128 C1
Throwleigh 7 G1
Throwley 32 B3
Thrumpton 81 G4
Thrumster 195 F4
Thrunton 137 E5
Thrupp *Glos.* 40 A2
Thrupp *Oxon.* 41 G1
Thrushelton 7 E2
Thrussington 68 B1
Thruxton *Hants.* 27 D3
Thruxton *Here.* 52 D4
Thrybergh 94 B3
Thulston 81 F4
Thundergay 139 G5
Thundersley 46 B4
Thunderton 183 F5
Thundridge 44 C1
Thurcaston 68 A1
Thurcroft 94 C4
Thurdistoft 195 E2
Thurgarton *Norf.* 86 C2
Thurgarton *Notts.* 82 B3
Thurgoland 93 G2
Thurlaston *Leics.* 68 A3
Thurlaston *Warks.* 67 G5
Thurlbear 23 F5
Thurlby *Lincs.* 69 G1
Thurlby *Lincs.* 83 E1
Thurleigh 57 F2
Thurlestone 8 C3
Thurloxton 23 F4
Thurlstone 93 G2
Thurlton 73 F2
Thurmaston 68 B2
Thurnby 68 B2
Thurne 87 F4
Thurnham 32 A3
Thurning *Norf.* 86 B3
Thurning *Northants.* 69 F4
Thurnscoe 94 B2
Thurrock Lakeside 45 E5
Thursby 117 G1
Thursford 86 A2
Thursley 29 E4
Thurso 194 D2
Thurstaston 90 D4
Thurston 60 A1
Thurstonfield 117 G1
Thurstonland 93 F1
Thurton 87 E5
Thurvaston 80 D4
Thuster 195 E3
Thuxton 86 B5
Thwaite *N.Yorks.* 109 D3
Thwaite *Suff.* 60 C1
Thwaite Head 107 E3
Thwaite St. Mary 73 E2
Thwing 104 C1
Tibbermore 151 F2
Tibberton *Glos.* 53 G5
Tibberton *Tel. & W.* 79 D5
Tibberton *Worcs.* 54 B2
Tibbie Shiels Inn 134 D3
Tibenham 72 C2
Tibertich 148 A4
Tibshelf 81 F1
Tibthorpe 104 B2
Ticehurst 31 F5
Tichborne 27 G4
Tickencote 69 E2
Tickenham 39 D5
Tickhill 94 C3
Ticklerton 65 D3
Ticknall 81 E5
Tickton 104 C3
Tidcombe 27 D2
Tiddington *Oxon.* 42 B2
Tiddington *Warks.* 55 E2
Tidebrook 18 B1
Tideford 7 D5
Tidenham 39 E3
Tidenham Chase 39 E3
Tideswell 93 F5
Tidmarsh 42 B5
Tidmington 55 E4
Tidpit 13 G1
Tidworth 26 D3
Tiers Cross 34 C1
Tiffield 56 B2
Tifty 182 C5
Tigerton 160 D3
Tigh a' Gearraidh 173 F2
Tighachnoic 155 F5
Tighnablair 150 C3
Tighnabruaich 140 A2
Tighnacomaire 156 B3
Tigley 9 D1
Tilbrook 57 F1
Tilbury 45 F5
Tile Cross 67 D4
Tile Hill 67 E5
Tilehurst 42 B5
Tilford 29 D3
Tillathrowie 169 G1
Tillers' Green 53 F4
Tillery 171 E2
Tilley 78 C5
Tillicoultry 151 E5
Tillingham 46 C2
Tillington *Here.* 53 D3
Tillington *W.Suss.* 29 E5
Tillington Common 53 D3
Tillyarblet 160 D3
Tillybirloch 170 B4
Tillycairn Castle 170 B3
Tillycorthie 171 E2
Tillydrine 170 B5
Tillyfar 183 D5
Tillyfour 170 A3
Tillyfourie 170 B3
Tillygreig 171 D2
Tillypronie 169 G4
Tilmanstone 33 E3
Tilney All Saints 71 D1
Tilney High End 71 D1
Tilney St. Lawrence 71 D1
Tilshead 26 B3
Tilstock 78 C4
Tilston 78 B2
Tilstone Fearnall 78 C1
Tilsworth 57 E5
Tilton on the Hill 68 C2
Tiltups End 40 A3
Timberland 83 G2
Timberland Dales 83 G1
Timbersbrook 79 F1
Timberscombe 22 C3
Timble 102 A2
Timperley 92 B4
Timsbury *B. & N.E.Som.* 25 D2
Timsbury *Hants.* 27 E5
Timsgearraidh 186 B4
Timworth Green 59 G1
Tincleton 13 D3
Tindale 118 C2
Tingewick 56 B4
Tingley 102 B5
Tingrith 57 F4
Tingwall 198 C4
Tinhay 7 E2
Tinney 6 C1
Tinshill 102 B4
Tinsley 94 B3
Tinsley Green 30 B5
Tintagel 5 E1
Tintern Parva 39 E2
Tintinhull 12 A1
Tintwistle 93 E3
Tinwald 125 E2
Tinwell 69 F2
Tippacott 22 A3
Tipperty *Aber.* 161 F1
Tipperty *Aber.* 171 E2
Tiptoe 14 B3
Tipton 66 B3
Tipton St. John 11 D3
Tiptree 46 B1
Tiptree Heath 46 B1
Tir-y-dail 36 C1
Tirabad 51 E3
Tirdeunaw 36 C3
Tiree Airport 154 B2
Tirindrish 157 E1
Tirley 54 A5
Tirphil 38 A2
Tirril 118 B5
Tisbury 26 A5
Tissington 80 C2
Tister 195 D2
Titchberry 20 C3
Titchfield 15 E2
Titchmarsh 69 F5
Titchwell 85 F3
Tithby 82 B4
Titley 52 C1
Titsey 30 D3
Titson 20 C5
Tittensor 79 F4
Tittleshall 85 G5
Tiverton *Ches.* 78 C1
Tiverton *Devon* 10 C1
Tivetshall St. Margaret 72 C3
Tivetshall St. Mary 72 C3
Tixall 79 G5
Tixover 69 E2
Toab *Ork.* 197 E2
Toab *Shet.* 201 G5
Tobermory 155 E4
Toberonochy 147 G4
Tobha Mòr 162 A1
Tobson 186 C4
Tocher 170 B1
Tockenham 40 C5
Tockenham Wick 40 C4
Tockholes 100 C5
Tockington 39 F4
Tockwith 103 D2
Todber 25 E5
Toddington *Beds.* 57 F5
Toddington *Glos.* 54 C4
Toddington *W.Suss.* 16 C3
Todenham 55 E4
Todhills *Angus* 152 C1
Todhills *Cumb.* 126 B5
Todlachie 170 B3
Todmorden 101 F5
Todwick 94 B4
Toft *Cambs.* 58 B2
Toft *Lincs.* 69 F1
Toft *Shet.* 202 D5
Toft Hill 120 A5
Toft Monks 73 F2
Toft next Newton 96 A4
Toftcarl 195 F4
Toftrees 85 G5
Tofts 195 F2
Toftwood 86 A4
Togston 129 E1
Tokavaig 164 C3
Tokers Green 42 C5
Tolastadh 187 G3
Tolastadh a' Chaolais 186 C4
Tolastadh Úr 187 G3
Toll of Birness 171 F1
Tolland 23 E4
Tollard Royal 13 F1
Tollcross 142 A3
Toller Down Gate 12 B2
Toller Fratrum 12 B3
Toller Porcorum 12 B3
Toller Whelme 12 B2
Tollerton *N.Yorks.* 103 E1
Tollerton *Notts.* 82 B4
Tollesbury 46 C2
Tollesby 111 E1
Tolleshunt D'Arcy 46 C1
Tolleshunt Knights 46 C1
Tolleshunt Major 46 B1
Tolpuddle 13 D3
Tolvah 168 A5
Tolworth 29 G1
Tom an Fhuadain 185 F2
Tomatin 168 A2
Tombreck 167 F1
Tomchrasky 166 B3
Tomdoun 166 A4
Tomdow 180 C5
Tomich *High.* 166 C2
Tomich *High.* 179 F2
Tomich *High.* 190 B4
Tomintoul 169 D3
Tomnacross 179 E5
Tomnamoon 180 C4
Tomnaven 169 G1
Tomnavoulin 169 E2
Tomvaich 168 C1
Ton Pentre 37 F3
Ton-teg 37 G4
Tonbridge 31 E4
Tondu 37 E4
Tonfanau 62 B2
Tong 65 G2
Tong Norton 65 G2
Tong Street 102 A4
Tonge 81 F5
Tongham 29 D3
Tongland 124 B5
Tongue 193 E3
Tongue House 193 E3
Tongwynlais 38 A4
Tonna 37 D3
Tonwell 44 C1
Tonypandy 37 F3
Tonyrefail 37 G4
Toot Baldon 42 A2
Toot Hill 45 E2
Toothill 14 C1
Top End 57 F1
Topcliffe 110 C5
Topcroft 73 D2
Topcroft Street 73 D2
Toppesfield 59 F4
Toppings 92 B1
Topsham 10 C4
Topsham Bridge 8 D2
Torastan 154 B3
Torbain 169 D3
Torbeg *Aber.* 169 F4
Torbeg *N.Ayr.* 131 E3
Torbryan 9 E1
Torcastle 156 D2
Torcross 9 E3
Tordarroch 167 F1
Tore 179 F4
Toreduff 180 D3
Toremore *High.* 168 D1
Toremore *High.* 195 D5
Torgyle 166 C3
Torksey 95 F5
Torlum 173 F4
Torlundy 156 D2
Tormarton 39 G5
Tormisdale 1138 A4
Tormore 131 D2
Tormsdale 194 D3
Tornagrain 179 G4
Tornahaish 169 E4
Tornaveen 170 B4
Torness 167 E2
Torpenhow 117 E3
Torphichen 143 D2
Torphins 170 B4
Torpoint 8 A2
Torquay 9 F1
Torquhan 144 B5
Torr 8 B2
Torran *Arg. & B.* 148 A4
Torran *High.* 179 G2
Torran *High.* 176 B5
Torrance *E.Dun.* 142 A2
Torrance *S.Lan.* 142 A4
Torrancroy 169 F3
Torrich 180 A4
Torridon 177 F4
Torrin 164 B2
Torrisdale *Arg. & B.* 130 C2
Torrisdale *High.* 193 F2
Torrish 191 E3
Torrisholme 100 A1
Torroble 190 A4
Torry *Aber.* 181 G5
Torry *Aberdeen* 171 E4
Torryburn 143 E1
Torsonce 144 B5
Torterston 183 F5
Torthorwald 125 E3
Tortington 16 B3
Tortworth 39 G3
Torvaig 176 A5
Torver 107 D3
Torwood 142 C1
Torworth 95 D4
Tosberry 20 C3
Toscaig 164 D1
Toseland 58 A1
Tosside 101 D2
Tostarie 154 C5
Tostock 60 A1
Totaig 175 F4
Totamore 154 A4
Tote 176 A5
Totegan 194 A2
Totford 27 G4
Tothill 97 E4
Totland 14 C4
Totley 94 A4
Totnes 9 E1
Toton 81 G4
Totronald 154 A4
Tottenham 44 C3
Tottenhill 71 E1
Totteridge 44 B3
Totternhoe 57 E5
Tottington *Gt.Man.* 92 B1
Tottington *Norf.* 71 G3
Totton 14 C1
Touchen-End 43 D5
Toulton 23 E4
Toux 183 E4
Tovil 31 G3
Tow Law 120 A4
Toward 140 C3
Towcester 56 B3
Towednack 2 B3
Tower Hamlets 44 C4
Towersey 42 C2
Towie *Aber.* 183 D3
Towie *Aber.* 170 A2
Towie *Aber.* 169 G3
Towiemore 181 F5
Town End *Cambs.* 70 C3
Town End *Cumb.* 107 F4
Town Green 91 F2
Town Row 31 E5
Town Street 71 F4
Town Yetholm 136 C4
Townend 141 F2
Townhead 115 G2
Townhead of Greenlaw 124 B4
Townhill 143 F1
Townshend 2 C3
Towthorpe *E.Riding* 104 B1
Towthorpe *York* 103 F2
Towton 103 D4
Towyn 90 A5
Toynton All Saints 84 B1
Toynton Fen Side 84 B1
Toynton St. Peter 84 C1
Toy's Hill 31 D3
Trabboch 132 C3
Traboe 3 E4
Tradespark *High.* 180 A4
Tradespark *Ork.* 197 D2
Trafford Centre 92 B3
Trafford Park 92 B3
Trallong 51 F5
Trallwn *Swan.* 36 C3
Tranch 38 B2
Tranent 144 B2
Trantlebeg 194 A3
Trantlemore 194 A3
Tranwell 129 D3
Trap 36 C1
Traprain 144 C2
Traquair 135 E2
Trawden 101 F4
Trawsfynydd 76 A4
Tre-ddiog 48 B5
Tre-groes 50 A3
Tre-Rhys 49 E3
Tre-vaughan 50 A5
Trealaw 37 F3
Treales 100 A4
Trearddur 88 A5
Treaslane 175 G4
Trebanog 37 G3
Trebanos 36 D2
Trebarrow 6 C1
Trebartha 5 G2
Trebarwith 5 E1
Trebetherick 4 D2
Treborough 22 D4
Trebudannon 4 C3
Trebullett 6 D3
Treburley 7 D3
Trebyan 5 E3
Trecastle 51 E5
Trecwn 48 C4
Trecynon 37 F2
Tredavoe 2 B4
Tredegar 38 A2
Tredington *Glos.* 54 B5
Tredington *Warks.* 55 E3
Tredinnick *Cornw.* 4 D2
Tredinnick *Cornw.* 5 G4
Tredomen 52 A4
Tredrissi 49 D3
Tredunnock 38 C3
Treen 2 A4
Treeton 94 B4
Trefaldwyn (Montgomery) 64 B3
Trefasser 48 B4
Trefdraeth 88 C5
Trefecca 52 A4
Trefeglwys 63 F3
Trefenter 50 C1
Treffgarne 48 C5
Treffynnon (Holywell) *Flints.* 90 C5
Treffynnon *Pembs.* 48 B5
Trefgarn Owen 48 B5
Trefil 38 A1
Trefilan 50 B2
Treflach 77 F5
Trefnanney 64 B1
Trefnant 90 B5
Trefonen 77 F5
Trefor *Gwyn.* 74 C3
Trefor *I.o.A.* 88 B4
Treforest 37 G4
Treforest Industrial Estate 38 A4
Trefriw 76 A1

Trefynwy 39 E1
(Monmouth)
Tregadillett 6 D2
Tregaian 88 C5
Tregare 38 D1
Tregaron 50 C2
Tregarth 75 F1
Tregavethan 4 B5
Tregear 4 C4
Tregeare 5 G1
Tregeiriog 77 E4
Tregele 88 B3
Tregidden 3 E4
Treglemais 48 B5
Tregolds 4 C2
Tregole 6 B1
Tregonetha 5 D3
Tregony 4 D5
Tregoyd 52 A4
Treguff 37 G5
Tregurrian 4 C3
Tregynon 63 G3
Trehafod 37 G3
Treharris 37 G3
Treherbert 37 F3
Trekenner 6 D3
Treknow 5 E1
Trelash 6 B1
Trelassick 4 C4
Trelawnyd 90 B5
Trelech 49 F4
Trelech a'r Betws 49 G5
Treleddyd-fawr 48 A5
Trelewis 38 A3
Treligga 5 E1
Trelights 5 D2
Trelill 5 E2
Trelissick 3 F3
Trelleck 39 E2
Trelleck Grange 39 D2
Trelogan 90 C4
Trelystan 64 B2
Tremadog 75 E3
Tremail 5 F1
Tremain 49 F3
Tremaine 5 G1
Tremar 5 G3
Trematon 7 D5
Tremeirchion 90 B5
Tremethick Cross 2 B3
Trenance 4 C3
Trenarren 5 E5
Trench Tel. & W. 65 F1
Trench Wrex. 78 A4
Treneglos 5 G1
Trenewan 5 F4
Trent 12 B1
Trentham 79 F3
Trentishoe 21 G1
Treoes 37 F5
Treorchy 37 F3
Tre'r-ddol 62 C3
Trerulefoot 6 D5
Tresaith 49 F2
Trescott 66 A3
Trescowe 2 C3
Tresham 39 G3
Treshnish 154 C5
Tresillian 4 C5
Tresinney 5 F1
Tresinwen 48 C3
Treskinnick Cross 6 C1
Tresmeer 5 G1
Tresparrett 6 B1
Tresparrett Posts 6 B1
Tressait 158 D3
Tresta Shet. 203 F3
Tresta Shet. 200 C2
Treswell 95 E5
Trethurgy 5 E4
Tretio 48 A5
Tretire 53 E5
Tretower 52 A5
Treuddyn 77 F2
Trevalga 5 E1
Trevalyn 78 A2
Trevanson 5 D2
Trevarren 4 D3
Trevarrick 5 D5
Trevaughan 35 F1
Trevellas 4 B4
Trevelmond 5 G3
Treverva 3 E3
Trevescan 2 A4
Trevethin 38 B2
Trevigro 6 D4
Trevine Arg. & B. 148 C2
Trevine Pembs. 48 B4
Treviscoe 4 D4
Trevone 4 C2
Trevor 77 F3
Trewalder 5 E1
Trewarmett 5 E1
Trewarthenick 4 D5
Trewassa 5 F1
Trewellard 2 A3
Trewen 5 G1
Trewern 64 B1
Trewidland 5 G4
Trewilym 49 E3
Trewint 6 B1
Trewithian 3 F3
Trewoon 5 D4
Treworan 5 D2
Treyarnon 4 C2
Treyford 16 A2
Triangle 101 G5
Trickett's Cross 13 G2
Trimdon 120 C4
Trimdon Colliery 120 C4
Trimdon Grange 120 C4
Trimingham 87 D2
Trimley St. Martin 61 D4
Trimley St. Mary 61 D4
Trimpley 65 G5
Trimsaran 36 A2
Trimstone 21 F1
Trinafour 158 C3
Trinant 38 B3
Tring 43 E1
Trinity 161 E3
Trislaig 156 C2
Trispen 4 C4
Tritlington 129 E2
Trochry 159 E5
Troedyraur 49 G3
Troedyrhiw 37 G2
Trondavoe 202 C5
Troon Cornw. 3 D3
Troon S.Ayr. 132 B2
Trosaraidh 172 C2
Troston 71 G5
Troswell 6 C1
Trottiscliffe 31 F3
Trotton 28 D5
Troughend 128 A2
Troustan 140 B2
Troutbeck 107 F2
Troutbeck Bridge 107 F2
Trow Green 39 E2
Trowbridge 25 F2
Trowle Common 25 F2
Trowley Bottom 43 F1
Trows 136 A3
Trowse Newton 86 D5
Trudernish 138 C4
Trudoxhill 25 E3
Trull 23 F5
Trumaisge 173 G2
Arraidh
Trumpan 175 F3
Trumpet 53 F4
Trumpington 58 C2
Trunch 87 D2
Trunnah 99 G3
Truro 4 C5
Trusham 10 B4
Trusley 81 D4
Trusthorpe 97 F4
Truthan 4 C4
Trysull 66 A3
Tubney 41 G3
Tuckenhay 9 E2
Tuckingmill 4 A5
Tuddenham Suff. 60 C3
Tuddenham Suff. 71 F5
Tudeley 31 F4
Tudhoe 120 B4
Tudweiliog 74 B4
Tuffley 40 A1
Tufton Hants. 27 F3
Tufton Pembs. 48 D5
Tugby 68 C2
Tugford 65 E4
Tughall 137 G4
Tuirnaig 177 E1
Tulchan 151 E2
Tullibody 151 D5
Tullich Arg. & B. 148 C3
Tullich Arg. & B. 148 A3
Tullich High. 180 A2
Tullich High. 167 F2
Tullich Moray 181 F5
Tullich Stir. 150 A1
Tullich Muir 179 G2
Tulliemet 159 E4
Tulloch Aber. 170 D1
Tulloch High. 190 B5
Tulloch Moray 180 C4
Tullochgorm 148 B5
Tullochgribban 168 B2
High
Tullochvenus 170 A4
Tulloes 160 D5
Tullybannocher 150 C2
Tullybelton 151 F1
Tullyfergus 160 A5
Tullymurdoch 159 G4
Tullynessle 170 A3
Tumble 36 B1
Tumby 84 A2
Tumby Woodside 84 A2
Tummel Bridge 158 C4
Tundergarth 125 F2
Mains
Tunga 187 F4
Tunstall E.Riding 105 F4
Tunstall Kent 32 A2
Tunstall Lancs. 108 B5
Tunstall N.Yorks. 110 B3
Tunstall Norf. 87 F5
Tunstall Stoke 79 F2
Tunstall Suff. 61 E2
Tunstead 87 E3
Tunworth 28 B3
Tupsley 53 E3
Tupton 81 E1
Tur Langton 68 C3
Turbiskill 139 F1
Turclossie 183 D4
Turgis Green 28 B2
Turin 160 D4
Turkdean 40 D1
Turnastone 52 C4
Turnberry 132 A5
Turnchapel 8 A2
Turnditch 81 D3
Turner's Green 67 D5
Turners Hill 30 C5
Turners Puddle 13 E3
Turnford 44 C2
Turnworth 13 E2
Turret Bridge 166 C5
Turriff 182 C4
Turton Bottoms 92 B1
Turvey 57 E2
Turville 42 C3
Turville Heath 42 C3
Turweston 56 B4
Tutbury 80 D5
Tutnall 66 B5
Tutshill 39 E3
Tuttington 86 D3
Tuxford 95 E5
Twatt Ork. 198 A4
Twatt Shet. 200 C2
Twechar 142 A2
Tweedmouth 145 G4
Tweedsmuir 134 B3
Twelveheads 4 B5
Twenty 83 G5
Twerton 25 E1
Twickenham 44 A5
Twigworth 54 A5
Twineham 17 E1
Twinhoe 25 E2
Twinstead 59 G4
Twiss Green 92 A3
Twitchen Devon 22 A4
Twitchen Shrop. 64 C5
Twizell House 137 F4
Two Bridges 7 G3
Two Dales 81 D1
Two Gates 67 E2
Twycross 67 F2
Twyford Bucks. 56 B5
Twyford Derbys. 81 E5
Twyford Dorset 13 E1
Twyford Hants. 27 F5
Twyford Leics. 68 C2
Twyford Norf. 86 B3
Twyford Oxon. 55 G4
Twyford W'ham 42 C5
Twyford 53 E4
Common
Twyn-y-Sheriff 38 D2
Twyn-yr-odyn 38 A5
Twynholm 124 A5
Twyning 54 A4
Twyning Green 54 A4
Twynllanan 51 D5
Twywell 69 E5
Ty-hen 74 A4
Ty-Mawr 76 C3
Ty-mawr 77 E3
Ty-nant Conwy 76 C3
Ty-nant Gwyn. 76 C5
Ty-uchaf 76 C5
Tyberton 52 C4
Tyburn 66 D3
Tycroes 36 C1
Tycrwyn 64 A1
Tydd Gote 70 C1
Tydd St. Giles 70 C1
Tydd St. Mary 70 C1
Tyddewi 48 A5
(St. David's)
Tye Common 45 F3
Tye Green 59 F5
Tyldesley 92 A2
Tyle-garw 37 G4
Tyler Hill 32 D2
Tylers Green 43 E3
Bucks.
Tyler's Green 45 E2
Essex
Tylorstown 37 G3
Tylwch 63 F5
Tyn-y-cefn 77 D3
Tyn-y-Cwm 63 E4
Tyn-y-ffridd 77 E4
Tyn-y-graig 51 G3
Ty'n-y-groes 89 F5
Tyndrum 149 F1
Tyneham 13 E4
Tynehead 144 A4
Tynemouth 120 C1
Tynewydd 37 F3
Tyninghame 144 D2
Tynribbie 156 B5
Tynron 124 C1
Tynygraig 50 C1
Tyringham 57 D3
Tythegston 37 E5
Tytherington 92 D5
Ches.
Tytherington 39 F4
S.Glos.
Tytherington 25 E3
Som.
Tytherington 26 A3
Wilts.
Tytherleigh 11 G2
Tytherton Lucas 40 B5
Tywardreath 5 E4
Tywardreath 5 E4
Highway
Tywyn 62 B2

U

Uachdar 173 G4
Uags 164 D1
Ubbeston Green 73 E4
Ubley 24 C2
Uckerby 110 B2
Uckfield 17 G1
Uckinghall 54 A4
Uckington 54 B5
Uddingston 142 A3
Uddington 133 G2
Udimore 19 D2
Udny Green 171 D2
Udny Station 171 E2
Udstonhead 142 B5
Uffcott 40 D5
Uffculme 11 D1
Uffington Lincs. 69 F2
Uffington Oxon. 41 F4
Uffington Shrop. 65 E1
Ufford Peter. 69 F2
Ufford Suff. 61 D2
Ufton 55 F1
Ufton Nervet 28 B1
Ugborough 8 C2
Uggeshall 73 F4
Ugglebarnby 112 B2
Ugley 58 D5
Ugley Green 58 D5
Ugthorpe 111 G1
Uig Arg. & B. 154 A4
Uig Arg. & B. 140 C1
Uig High. 175 G3
Uig High. 175 E4
Uigen 186 B4
Uiginish 175 F5
Uigshader 176 A5
Uisgebhagh 173 G5
Uisken 146 C3
Ulbster 195 F4
Ulcat Row 118 A5
Ulceby Lincs. 97 E5
Ulceby N.Lincs. 96 B1
Ulceby Cross 97 E5
Ulcombe 32 A4
Uldale 117 F3
Uldale House 108 C3
Uley 39 G3
Ulgham 129 E2
Ullapool 188 D5
Ullenhall 54 D1
Ullenwood 40 B1
Ulleskelf 103 E3
Ullesthorpe 68 A4
Ulley 94 B4
Ullingswick 53 E3
Ullinish 163 G1
Ullock 117 D4
Ulpha 106 C3
Ulrome 105 D2
Ulsta 203 D4
Ulting 46 B2
Uluvalt 147 E2
Ulverston 107 D5
Ulwell 13 G4
Ulzieside 133 F5
Umberleigh 21 G3
Unapool 192 B5
Underbarrow 107 F3
Underhoull 203 E2
Underriver 31 E3
Underwood 38 C4
Newport
Underwood Notts. 81 F2
Undy 38 D4
Unifirth 200 B2
Union Croft 170 D5
Union Mills 98 B4
Unstone 94 A5
Unthank 118 A4
Up Cerne 12 C2
Up Exe 10 C2
Up Hatherley 54 B5
Up Holland 91 G2
Up Marden 15 G1
Up Nately 28 C2
Up Somborne 27 E4
Up Sydling 12 C2
Upavon 26 C2
Upchurch 32 A2
Upcott Devon 7 E1
Upcott Here. 52 C2
Upend 59 E2
Uphall Dorset 12 B2
Uphall W.Loth. 143 E2
Uphall Station 143 E2
Upham Devon 10 B2
Upham Hants. 27 G5
Uphampton 54 A1
Uphill 24 A2
Uplawmoor 141 F4
Upleadon 53 G5
Upleatham 121 F5
Uplees 32 C2
Uploders 12 B3
Uplowman 10 D1
Uplyme 11 G3
Upminster 45 E4
Upottery 11 E2
Upper Affcot 64 D4
Upper 140 B3
Ardroscadale
Upper Arley 65 G4
Upper Arncott 42 B1
Upper Aston 66 A3
Upper Astrop 56 A4
Upper Basildon 42 B5
Upper Beeding 17 D2
Upper Benefield 69 E4
Upper Bighouse 194 A3
Upper Boat 38 A4
Upper Boddington 55 G2
Upper Borth 62 C4
Upper Boyndlie 183 E3
Upper Brailes 55 F3
Upper Breakish 164 C2
Upper Breinton 53 D3
Upper Broughton 82 B5
Upper Bucklebury 27 G1
Upper Burgate 14 A1
Upper Burnhaugh 170 D5
Upper Caldecote 57 G3
Upper Camster 195 E4
Upper Catshill 66 B5
Upper Chapel 51 G3
Upper Chute 27 D2
Upper Clatford 27 E3
Upper Coberley 40 B1
Upper Cound 65 E2
Upper Cwmbran 38 B3
Upper Dallachy 181 F3
Upper Dean 57 F1
Upper Denby 93 G2
Upper Derraid 168 C1
Upper Diabaig 177 E3
Upper Dicker 18 A2
Upper Dovercourt 60 D5
Upper Dunsforth 102 D1
Upper Eastern 67 E4
Green
Upper Eathie 179 G3
Upper Elkstone 80 B2
Upper End 93 E5
Upper Farringdon 28 C4
Upper Framilode 39 G1
Upper Froyle 28 C3
Upper Gills 195 F1
Upper 165 F5
Glendessarry
Upper Godney 24 B3
Upper Gornal 66 B3
Upper Gravenhurst 57 G4
Upper Green 58 C4
Essex
Upper Green Mon. 38 C1
Upper Green 27 E1
W.Berks.
Upper Gylen 148 A2
Upper Hackney 81 D1
Upper Halliford 29 F1
Upper Halling 31 F2
Upper Hambleton 69 E2
Upper Hardres 32 D3
Court
Upper Hartfield 31 D5
Upper Hawkhillock 171 F1
Upper Hayton 65 E4
Upper Heath 65 E4
Upper Helmsley 103 F2
Upper Hergest 52 B2
Upper Heyford 55 G5
Upper Hill 53 D2
Upper Hopton 93 F1
Upper Horsebridge 18 A2
Upper Hulme 80 B1
Upper Inglesham 41 E3
Upper Kilchattan 146 C5
Upper Killay 36 B3
Upper Knockando 181 D5
Upper Lambourn 41 F4
Upper Langwith 81 G1
Upper Largo 152 C4
Upper Lochton 170 B5
Upper Longdon 66 C1
Upper Longwood 65 F2
Upper Ludstone 66 A3
Upper Lybster 195 E5
Upper Lydbrook 39 F1
Upper Maes-coed 52 C4
Upper Midhope 93 G3
Upper Minety 40 C3
Upper Mitton 66 A5
Upper Muirskie 170 D5
Upper North Dean 43 D3
Upper Norwood 44 C5
Upper Obney 151 F1
Upper Oddington 55 E5
Upper Ollach 164 B1
Upper Poppleton 103 E2
Upper Quinton 55 D3
Upper Ridinghill 183 F4
Upper Rissington 55 E5
Upper Rochford 53 F1
Upper Sanday 197 E2
Upper Sapey 53 F1
Upper Scolton 48 C5
Upper Seagry 40 B4
Upper Shelton 57 E3
Upper 86 C1
Sheringham
Upper Skelmorlie 140 D3
Upper Slaughter 55 D5
Upper Sonachan 148 C2
Upper Soudley 39 F1
Upper Stoke 67 F4
Upper Stondon 57 G4
Upper Stowe 56 B2
Upper Street 14 A1
Hants.
Upper Street 87 E4
Norf.
Upper Street 60 C4
Suff.
Upper Sundon 57 F5
Upper Swell 55 D5
Upper Tean 80 B4
Upper Thurnham 100 A2
Upper Tillyrie 151 G4
Upper Tooting 44 B5
Upper Town 24 C1
Upper Tysoe 55 F3
Upper Upham 41 E5
Upper Upnor 45 G5
Upper Victoria 152 D1
Upper Wardington 55 G3
Upper Weald 56 D4
Upper Weedon 56 B2
Upper Welson 52 B2
Upper Wield 28 B4
Upper (Over) 42 C1
Winchendon
Upper Woodford 26 C4
Upper Wootton 27 G2
Upper Wraxall 39 G5
Upper Wyche 53 G3
Uppermill 93 D2
Upperthong 93 F2
Upperton 29 E5
Uppertown 195 F1
Uppingham 69 D3
Uppington Dorset 13 G2
Uppington 65 E2
Shrop.
Upsall 110 D4
Upsettlington 145 F5
Upshire 44 D2
Upstreet 33 E2
Upton Bucks. 42 C1
Upton Cambs. 69 G5
Upton Ches. 78 B1
Upton Cornw. 5 G2
Upton Devon 11 D2
Upton Devon 8 D3
Upton Dorset 13 F3
Upton Hants. 27 E2
Upton Hants. 14 C1
Upton Lincs. 95 F4
Upton Mersey. 91 D4
Upton Norf. 87 E4
Upton Northants. 56 C1
Upton Notts. 95 E5
Upton Notts. 82 C2
Upton Oxon. 42 A4
Upton Peter. 69 G2
Upton Slo. 43 E5
Upton Som. 22 C5
Upton W.Yorks. 94 B1
Upton Bishop 53 F5
Upton Cheyney 25 D1
Upton Cressett 65 F3
Upton Cross 5 G2
Upton End 57 G4
Upton Green 87 E4
Upton Grey 28 B3
Upton Hellions 10 B2
Upton Lovell 26 A3
Upton Magna 65 E1
Upton Noble 25 E4
Upton Pyne 10 C3
Upton 40 A1
St. Leonards
Upton Scudamore 25 F3
Upton Snodsbury 54 B2
Upton upon 54 A3
Severn
Upton Warren 54 B1
Upwaltham 16 B2
Upware 58 D1
Upwell 70 D2
Upwey 12 C4
Upwood 70 A4
Uradale 200 D4
Urafirth 202 C5
Urchany 180 A5
Urchfont 26 B2
Urdimarsh 53 E3
Ure 202 B5
Urgha 185 D4
Urlay Nook 110 C1
Urmston 92 B3
Urquhart High. 179 E4
Urquhart Moray 181 E3
Urra 111 E2
Urray 179 E4
Ushaw Moor 120 B3
Usk 38 C2
Usselby 96 A3
Utley 101 G3
Uton 10 B3
Utterby 96 D3
Uttoxeter 80 B4
Uwchmynydd 74 A5
Uxbridge 43 F4
Uyeasound 203 E2
Uzmaston 34 C1

V

Valley (Dyffryn) 88 A5
Valley Truckle 5 F1
Valleyfield 124 A5
D. & G.
Valleyfield Fife 143 E1
Valsgarth 203 F1
Vange 45 G4
Vardre 36 C2
Varteg 38 B2
Vatersay 172 B4
(Bhatarsaigh)
Vatten 175 F5
Vaul 154 B2
Vaynor 37 G1
Vaynor Park 64 A2
Veaullt 52 A2
Veensgarth 200 D3
Velindre Pembs. 49 E4
Velindre Powys 52 A4
Vellow 23 D4
Veness 199 D4
Venn 8 D3
Venn Ottery 11 D3
Vennington 64 C2
Ventnor 15 E5
Vernham Dean 27 E2
Vernham Street 27 E2
Vernolds Common 65 D4
Verwood 13 G2
Veryan 3 G3
Vicarage 11 F4
Vickerstown 99 E1
Victoria 5 D3
Vidlin 201 D1
Viewfield 194 C2
Viewpark 142 B3
Vigo 66 C2
Vigo Village 31 F2
Villavin 21 F4
Vinehall Street 18 C1
Vine's Cross 18 A2
Viney Hill 39 F2
Virginia Water 29 E1
Virginstow 7 D1
Virley 46 C1
Vobster 25 E3
Voe Shet. 200 D1
Voe Shet. 202 C4
Vowchurch 52 C4
Voy 198 A5

W

Wackerfield 120 A5
Wacton 72 C2
Wadborough 54 B3
Waddesdon 42 C1
Waddingham 95 G3
Waddington 100 D3
Lancs.
Waddington Lincs. 83 E1
Waddingworth 96 B5
Wadebridge 5 D2
Wadeford 11 G1
Wadenhoe 69 F4
Wadesmill 44 C1
Wadhurst 31 F5
Wadshelf 94 A5
Wadsley Bridge 94 A3
Wadworth 94 C3
Wadworth Hill 105 E5
Waen 77 E1
Waen-fach 64 B1
Waen-wen 75 E1
Wag 191 F2
Wainfleet All 84 C2
Saints
Wainfleet Bank 84 C2
Wainhouse Corner 6 B1
Wainscott 45 G5
Wainstalls 101 G5
Waitby 108 C2
Wakefield 102 C5
Wakerley 69 E3
Wakes Colne 59 G5
Walberswick 73 F4
Walberton 16 B3
Walcot Lincs. 83 F4
Walcot Lincs. 83 G2
Walcot N.Lincs. 104 A5
Walcot Shrop. 64 C4
Walcot Tel. & W. 65 E1
Walcot Green 72 C3
Walcote Leics. 68 A4
Walcote Warks. 54 D2
Walcott 87 E2
Walcott Dales 83 G2
Walden 109 F4
Walden Head 109 E4
Walden Stubbs 94 C1
Walderslade 31 G2
Walderton 15 G1
Walditch 12 A3
Waldley 80 C4
Waldridge 120 B2
Waldringfield 61 D3
Waldron 18 A2
Wales 94 B4
Walesby Lincs. 96 B3
Walesby Notts. 95 D5
Walford Here. 64 C5
Walford Here. 53 E5
Walford Shrop. 78 B5
Walgherton 79 D3
Walgrave 68 D5
Walhampton 14 C3
Walk Mill 101 E4
Walkden 92 B2
Walker 120 B1
Walker Fold 100 C3
Walkerburn 135 E2
Walkeringham 95 E3
Walkerith 95 E3
Walkern 58 A5
Walker's Green 53 E3
Walkhampton 8 B1
Walkington 104 C4
Walkwood 54 C1
Wall Northumb. 119 F1
Wall Staffs. 66 D2
Wall Bank 65 E3
Wall Heath 66 A4
Wall under 65 E3
Heywood
Wallacehall 126 A4
Wallacetown 132 A5
Wallasey 91 D3
Wallbottle 120 A1
Wallend 32 A1
Waller's Green 53 F4
Wallingford 42 B4
Wallington 30 B2
Gt.Lon.
Wallington Hants. 15 E2
Wallington Herts. 58 A4
Wallis 48 D5
Wallisdown 13 G3
Walliswood 29 G4
Walls 200 B3
Wallsend 120 C1
Wallyford 144 A2
Walmer 33 F3
Walmer Bridge 100 A5
Walmersley 92 C1
Walmley 66 D3
Walpole 73 E4
Walpole Cross 70 D1
Keys
Walpole Highway 70 D1
Walpole 70 D1
St. Andrew
Walpole St. Peter 70 D1
Walsall 66 C3
Walsall Wood 66 C2
Walsden 101 F5
Walsgrave on 67 F4
Sowe
Walsham le 72 B4
Willows
Walsoken 70 C1
Walston 143 E5
Walsworth 57 G4
Walterstone 52 C5
Waltham Kent 32 D4
Waltham 96 C2
N.E.Lincs.
Waltham Abbey 44 C2
Waltham Chase 15 E1
Waltham Cross 44 C2
Waltham Forest 44 C3
Waltham on the 82 D5
Wolds
Waltham 42 D5
St. Lawrence
Walthamstow 44 C4
Walton Bucks. 42 D1
Walton Cumb. 118 B1
Walton Derbys. 81 E1
Walton Leics. 68 A4
Walton M.K. 57 D4
Walton Mersey. 91 E3
Walton Peter. 69 G2
Walton Powys 52 B2
Walton Som. 24 B4
Walton Staffs. 79 F4
Walton Suff. 61 D4
Walton Tel. & W. 65 E1
Walton W.Yorks. 94 A1
Walton W.Yorks. 102 D3
Walton Warks. 55 E2
Walton Cardiff 54 B4
Walton East 48 D5
Walton- 38 D5
in-Gordano
Walton-le-Dale 100 B5
Walton-on-Thames 29 G1
Walton-on-the-Hill 79 G5
Staffs.
Walton on the Hill 30 B3
Surr.
Walton on the 60 D5
Naze
Walton on the 68 A1
Wolds
Walton-on-Trent 67 E1
Walton Park 124 B3
Walton West 34 B1
Walwen Flints. 90 C5
Walwen Flints. 90 D5
Walwick 128 B4
Walworth 110 B1
Walwyn's Castle 34 B1
Wambrook 11 F2
Wanborough Surr. 29 E3
Wanborough 41 E4
Swin.
Wandel 134 A3
Wandon 137 E4
Wandsworth 44 B5
Wandylaw 137 F4
Wangford Suff. 73 F4
Wangford Suff. 71 F4
Wanlip 68 B1
Wanlockhead 133 G4
Wannock 18 A3
Wansford 104 C2
E.Riding
Wansford Peter. 69 F3
Wanstead 44 D4
Wanstrow 25 E3
Wanswell 39 F2
Wantage 41 F4
Wapley 39 G5
Wappenbury 55 F1
Wappenham 56 B3
Warblebank 117 F2
Warbleton 18 B2
Warborough 42 A3
Warboys 70 B5
Warbstow 6 C1
Warburton 92 A4
Warcop 108 C1
Ward End 66 D4
Ward Green 60 B1
Warden Kent 32 C1
Warden 119 F1
Northumb.

Wardgate 81 D3
Wardhouse 170 A1
Wardington 55 G3
Wardle *Ches.* 78 D2
Wardle *Gt.Man.* 92 D1
Wardley 68 D2
Wardlow 93 F5
Wardy Hill 70 C4
Ware *Herts.* 44 C1
Ware *Kent* 33 E2
Wareham 13 F4
Warehorne 32 B5
Waren Mill 137 F3
Warenford 137 F4
Warenton 137 F3
Wareside 44 C1
Waresley 58 A2
Warfield 43 D5
Wargrave 42 C5
Warham 86 A1
Wark *Northumb.* 128 A4
Wark *Northumb.* 136 C3
Warkleigh 21 G3
Warkton 69 D5
Warkworth *Northants.* 55 G3
Warkworth *Northumb.* 129 E1
Warlaby 110 C3
Warland 101 F5
Warleggan 5 F3
Warley 66 C4
Warley Town 101 G5
Warlingham 30 C3
Warmfield 102 C5
Warmingham 79 E1
Warminghurst 16 D2
Warmington *Northants.* 69 F3
Warmington *Warks.* 55 G3
Warminster 25 F3
Warmlake 32 A3
Warmley 39 F5
Warmsworth 94 C2
Warmwell 13 D4
Warndon 54 A2
Warnford 28 B5
Warnham 29 G4
Warningcamp 16 C3
Warninglid 17 E1
Warren *Ches.* 92 C5
Warren *Pembs.* 34 C3
Warren House 7 G2
Warren Row 42 D4
Warren Street 32 B3
Warrenby 121 E5
Warrington *M.K.* 57 D2
Warrington *Warr.* 92 A4
Warroch 151 F4
Warsash 15 D2
Warslow 80 B2
Warter 104 A2
Warthill 103 F2
Wartle 170 A4
Wartling 18 B3
Wartnaby 82 C5
Warton *Lancs.* 107 G5
Warton *Lancs.* 100 A5
Warton *Northumb.* 128 C1
Warton *Warks.* 67 E2
Warwick *Cumb.* 118 A2
Warwick *Warks.* 55 E1
Warwick Bridge 118 A2
Wasbister 198 B3
Wash Common 27 F1
Washaway 5 E3
Washbourne 9 D2
Washfield 10 C1
Washfold 109 F2
Washford 22 D3
Washford Pyne 10 B1
Washingborough 96 A5
Washington *T. & W.* 120 C2
Washington *W.Suss.* 16 D2
Washmere Green 60 A3
Wasing 27 G1
Waskerley 119 G3
Wasperton 55 E2
Wass 111 E5
Watchet 23 D3
Watchfield *Oxon.* 41 E3
Watchfield *Som.* 24 A3
Watchgate 107 G3
Watendlath 117 F5
Water 101 E5
Water Eaton 42 A1
Water End *Herts.* 44 B2
Water End *Herts.* 43 F1
Water Newton 69 G3
Water Orton 67 D3
Water Stratford 56 B4
Water Yeat 107 D4
Waterbeach 58 C1
Waterbeck 126 A4
Waterfall 80 B2
Waterfoot *E.Renf.* 141 G4
Waterfoot *Lancs.* 101 E5
Waterford 44 C1
Waterhead *Cumb.* 107 E2
Waterhead *D. & G.* 124 B2
Waterhill of Bruxie 183 E5
Waterhouses *Dur.* 120 A3
Waterhouses *Staffs.* 80 B2
Wateringbury 31 F3
Waterloo *Aber.* 171 F1
Waterloo *Mersey.* 91 E3
Waterloo *N.Lan.* 142 C4
Waterloo *Norf.* 86 D4
Waterloo *P. & K.* 151 F1
Waterloo *Pembs.* 34 C2
Waterloo *Poole* 13 G3
Waterloo Cross 11 D1
Waterloo Port 75 D1
Waterlooville 15 F1
Watermeetings 134 A4
Watermillock 118 A5
Waterperry 42 B2
Waterrow 22 D5
Waters Upton 65 F1
Watersfield 16 C2
Waterside *Aber.* 169 F3
Waterside *Aber.* 171 F2
Waterside *Bucks.* 43 E2
Waterside *E.Ayr.* 132 C5
Waterside *E.Ayr.* 141 F5
Waterside *E.Dun.* 142 A2
Waterstock 42 B2
Waterston 34 C2
Waterthorpe 94 B4
Watford *Herts.* 44 A3
Watford *Northants.* 56 B1
Wath *N.Yorks.* 110 C5
Wath *N.Yorks.* 102 A1
Wath Brow 116 D5
Wath upon Dearne 94 B2
Watlington *Norf.* 71 E1
Watlington *Oxon.* 42 B3
Watnall 81 G3
Watten 195 E3
Wattisfield 72 B4
Wattisham 60 B2
Watton *E.Riding* 104 C3
Watton *Norf.* 86 A5
Watton at Stone 44 C1
Watton Green 86 A5
Wattston 142 B3
Wattstown 37 G3
Wattsville 38 A3
Waun Fawr 62 C4
Waun y Clyn 36 A2
Waunarlwydd 36 C3
Waunclynda 50 C4
Waunfawr 75 E2
Wavendon 57 E4
Waverbridge 117 F2
Waverton *Ches.* 78 B1
Waverton *Cumb.* 117 F2
Wawne 104 C4
Waxham 87 F3
Waxholme 105 F5
Way Gill 101 F1
Way Village 10 B1
Wayford 12 A2
Waytown 12 A3
Wdig (Goodwick) 48 C4
Weachyburn 182 B4
Weald 41 F2
Wealdstone 44 A4
Weare 24 B2
Weare Giffard 21 E3
Wearhead 119 E3
Wearne 24 B5
Weasenham All Saints 85 G5
Weasenham St. Peter 85 G5
Weathercote 108 C5
Weatheroak Hill 66 C5
Weaverham 92 A5
Weaverthorpe 112 C5
Webheath 54 C1
Webton 52 D4
Wedderlairs 171 D1
Weddington 67 F3
Wedhampton 26 B2
Wedmore 24 B3
Wednesbury 66 B3
Wednesfield 66 B2
Weedon 42 D1
Weedon Bec 56 B2
Weedon Lois 56 B3
Weeford 66 D2
Week 10 A1
Week Orchard 20 C5
Week St. Mary 6 C1
Weekley 69 D4
Weeley 60 C5
Weeley Heath 47 E1
Weem 158 D5
Weeping Cross 79 G5
Weethley 54 C2
Weeting 71 F4
Weeton *E.Riding* 105 F5
Weeton *Lancs.* 99 G4
Weeton *N.Yorks.* 102 B3
Weir *Essex* 46 B4
Weir *Lancs.* 101 E5
Weirbrook 78 A5
Welbeck Abbey 94 C5
Welborne 86 B5
Welbourn 83 E2
Welburn 103 G1
Welbury 110 C2
Welby 83 E4
Welches Dam 70 C4
Welcombe 20 C4
Weldon 69 E4
Welford *Northants.* 68 B4
Welford *W.Berks.* 41 G5
Welford-on-Avon 54 D2
Welham *Leics.* 68 C3
Welham *Notts.* 95 E4
Welham Green 44 B2
Well *Hants.* 28 C3
Well *Lincs.* 97 E5
Well *N.Yorks.* 110 B4
Well End 43 D4
Well Hill 31 D2
Well Town 10 C2
Welland 53 G3
Wellbank 152 C1
Wellesbourne 55 E2
Wellhill 180 B3
Welling 45 D5
Wellingborough 57 D1
Wellingham 85 G5
Wellingore 83 E2
Wellington *Cumb.* 106 B2
Wellington *Here.* 53 D3
Wellington *Som.* 23 E5
Wellington *Tel. & W.* 65 F1
Wellington Heath 53 G3
Wellington Marsh 53 E3
Wellow *B. & N.E.Som.* 25 E2
Wellow *I.o.W.* 14 C4
Wellow *Notts.* 82 B1
Wells 24 C3
Wells-next-the-Sea 86 A1
Wellsborough 67 F2
Wellwood 143 E1
Welney 70 D3
Welsh Bicknor 39 E1
Welsh End 78 C4
Welsh Frankton 78 A4
Welsh Hook 48 C5
Welsh Newton 39 E1
Welsh St. Donats 37 G5
Welshampton 78 B4
Welshpool (Y Trallwng) 64 B2
Welton *B. & N.E.Som.* 25 D2
Welton *Cumb.* 117 G2
Welton *E.Riding* 104 B5
Welton *Lincs.* 96 A4
Welton *Northants.* 56 A1
Welton le Marsh 84 C1
Welton le Wold 96 C4
Welwick 105 F5
Welwyn 44 B1
Welwyn Garden City 44 B1
Wem 78 C5
Wembdon 23 F4
Wembley 44 A4
Wembury 8 B3
Wembworthy 21 G5
Wemyss Bay 140 C3
Wenallt 76 C3
Wendens Ambo 58 D4
Wendlebury 42 A1
Wendling 86 A4
Wendover 43 D2
Wendron 3 D3
Wendy 58 B3
Wenhaston 73 F4
Wenlli 76 B1
Wennington *Cambs.* 70 A5
Wennington *Gt.Lon.* 45 E4
Wennington *Lancs.* 108 B5
Wensley *Derbys.* 81 D1
Wensley *N.Yorks.* 109 F3
Wentbridge 94 B1
Wentnor 64 C3
Wentworth *Cambs.* 70 C5
Wentworth *S.Yorks.* 94 A3
Wentworth Castle 94 A2
Wenvoe 38 A5
Weobley 52 C2
Weobley Marsh 52 D2
Wepham 16 C3
Wepre 77 F1
Wereham 71 E2
Wergs 66 A2
Wernyrheolydd 38 C1
Werrington *Cornw.* 6 D2
Werrington *Peter.* 69 G2
Werrington *Staffs.* 79 G3
Wervil Brook 49 G2
Wervin 91 F5
Wesham 100 A4
Wessington 81 E2
West Aberthaw 22 D1
West Acre 71 F1
West Allerdean 145 G5
West Alvington 8 D3
West Amesbury 26 C3
West Anstey 22 B5
West Ashby 96 C5
West Ashling 16 A3
West Ashton 25 F2
West Auckland 120 A5
West Ayton 112 C4
West Bagborough 23 E4
West Barkwith 96 B4
West Barnby 112 B1
West Barns 144 D2
West Barsham 86 A2
West Bay 12 A3
West Beckham 86 C2
West Benhar 142 C3
West Bergholt 60 A5
West Bexington 12 B4
West Bilney 71 F1
West Blatchington 17 E3
West Boldon 120 C1
West Bradenham 86 A5
West Bradford 100 D3
West Bradley 24 C4
West Bretton 93 G1
West Bridgford 81 G4
West Bromwich 66 C3
West Buckland *Devon* 21 G2
West Buckland *Som.* 23 E5
West Burrafirth 200 B2
West Burton *N.Yorks.* 109 F4
West Burton *W.Suss.* 16 B2
West Butterwick 95 F2
West Byfleet 29 F1
West Cairncake 182 D5
West Caister 87 G4
West Calder 143 E3
West Camel 24 C5
West Cauldcoats 142 A5
West Challow 41 F4
West Charleton 9 D3
West Chelborough 12 B2
West Chevington 129 E2
West Chiltington 16 C2
West Chiltington Common 16 C2
West Chinnock 12 A1
West Chisenbury 26 C2
West Clandon 29 F2
West Cliffe 33 F4
West Clyne 191 D4
West Coker 12 B1
West Compton *Dorset* 12 B3
West Compton *Som.* 24 C3
West Cross 36 C4
West Curry 6 C1
West Curthwaite 117 G2
West Dean *W.Suss.* 16 A2
West Dean *Wilts.* 27 D5
West Deeping 69 G2
West Derby 91 E3
West Dereham 71 E2
West Ditchburn 137 F4
West Down 21 F1
West Drayton *Gt.Lon.* 43 F5
West Drayton *Notts.* 95 E5
West Dullater 150 A4
West Dunnet 195 E1
West Edington 129 D3
West Ella 104 C5
West End *Beds.* 57 E2
West End *E.Riding* 104 C1
West End *Hants.* 15 D1
West End *Kent* 32 D2
West End *Lancs.* 100 A1
West End *Lincs.* 97 D3
West End *N.Som.* 24 B1
West End *N.Yorks.* 102 A2
West End *Norf.* 87 F4
West End *Oxon.* 41 G2
West End *S.Lan.* 143 D5
West End *Suff.* 73 F3
West End *Surr.* 29 G1
West End *Surr.* 29 E1
West End Green 28 B1
West Farleigh 31 G3
West Farndon 56 A2
West Felton 78 A5
West Firle 17 G3
West Fleetham 137 F4
West Garforth 102 C4
West Ginge 41 G4
West Glen 140 B2
West Grafton 26 D1
West Green 28 C2
West Grimstead 26 D5
West Grinstead 29 G5
West Haddlesey 103 E5
West Haddon 68 B5
West Hagbourne 42 A4
West Hagley 66 B4
West Hall 118 B1
West Hallam 81 F3
West Halton 104 B5
West Ham 44 D4
West Handley 94 A5
West Hanney 41 G3
West Hanningfield 45 G3
West Hardwick 94 B1
West Harptree 24 C2
West Harting 28 C5
West Hatch 23 F5
West Heath *Hants.* 29 D2
West Heath *W.Mid.* 66 C5
West Helmsdale 191 F3
West Hendred 41 G4
West Heslerton 112 C5
West Hill *Devon* 11 D3
West Hill *N.Som.* 39 D5
West Hoathly 30 C5
West Holme 13 E4
West Horndon 45 F4
West Horrington 24 C3
West Horsley 29 F2
West Horton 137 E3
West Hougham 33 E4
West Huntspill 24 A3
West Hyde 43 F3
West Hythe 32 D5
West Ilsley 41 G4
West Itchenor 16 G2
West Keal 84 B1
West Kennett 26 C1
West Kilbride 140 D5
West Kingsdown 31 E2
West Kington 40 A5
West Kirby 90 D4
West Knapton 112 B5
West Knighton 12 D4
West Knoyle 25 F4
West Kyloe 137 E2
West Lambrook 12 A1
West Langdon 33 F4
West Langwell 190 B4
West Lavington *W.Suss.* 29 D5
West Lavington *Wilts.* 26 B2
West Layton 110 A1
West Leake 81 G5
West Lexham 71 G1
West Lilling 103 F1
West Lingo 152 C4
West Linton 143 F4
West Littleton 39 G5
West Lockinge 41 G4
West Looe 5 G4
West Lulworth 13 E4
West Lutton 104 B1
West Lydford 24 C4
West Lyng 24 A5
West Lynn 71 E1
West Mains 137 E2
West Malling 31 F3
West Malvern 53 G3
West Marden 15 G1
West Markham 95 E5
West Marsh 96 C2
West Marton 101 E2
West Melton 94 B2
West Meon 28 B5
West Meon Hut 28 B5
West Mersea 46 D1
West Milton 12 B3
West Minster 32 B1
West Molesey 29 G1
West Monkton 23 F5
West Moors 13 G2
West Mostard 108 C3
West Muir 161 D3
West Ness 111 F5
West Newton *E.Riding* 105 E4
West Newton *Norf.* 85 E5
West Norwood 44 C5
West Ogwell 10 B5
West Orchard 13 E1
West Overton 26 C1
West Park *Aber.* 170 C5
West Park *Mersey.* 91 G3
West Parley 13 G3
West Peckham 31 F3
West Pennard 24 C4
West Pentire 4 B3
West Perry 57 G1
West Porlock 22 B3
West Putford 21 D4
West Quantoxhead 23 E3
West Rainton 120 C3
West Rasen 96 A4
West Raynham 85 G5
West Rounton 110 D2
West Row 71 E5
West Rudham 85 G5
West Runton 86 C1
West Saltoun 144 B3
West Sandwick 203 D4
West Scrafton 109 F4
West Shinness Lodge 190 A3
West Somerton 87 F3
West Stafford 12 D4
West Stockwith 95 E3
West Stoke 16 A3
West Stonesdale 109 D2
West Stoughton 24 B3
West Stour 25 E5
West Stourmouth 33 E2
West Stow 71 G5
West Stowell 26 C1
West Stratton 27 G3
West Street 32 B3
West Tanfield 110 B5
West Taphouse 5 F3
West Tarbert 139 G3
West Tarring 16 D3
West Thorney 15 G2
West Thurrock 45 E5
West Tilbury 45 F5
West Tisted 28 B5
West Tofts *Norf.* 71 G3
West Tofts *P. & K.* 151 G1
West Torrington 96 B4
West Town *Hants.* 15 G3
West Town *N.Som.* 24 B1
West Tytherley 27 D4
West Walton 70 C1
West Walton Highway 70 C1
West Wellow 27 D5
West Wemyss 152 B5
West Wick 24 A1
West Wickham *Cambs.* 59 E3
West Wickham *Gt.Lon.* 30 C2
West Williamston 34 D2
West Winch 71 E1
West Winterslow 26 D4
West Wittering 15 G3
West Witton 109 F4
West Woodburn 128 A3
West Woodhay 27 E1
West Woodlands 25 E3
West Worldham 28 C4
West Worlington 10 A1
West Worthing 16 D3
West Wratting 59 D2
West Wycombe 42 D3
West Yell 203 D4
Westbere 33 D2
Westborough 83 D3
Westbourne *Bourne.* 13 G3
Westbourne *W.Suss.* 15 G2
Westbrook 41 G5
Westbury *Bucks.* 56 B4
Westbury *Shrop.* 64 C2
Westbury *Wilts.* 25 F2
Westbury Leigh 25 F2
Westbury-on-Severn 39 G1
Westbury on Trym 39 E5
Westbury-sub-Mendip 24 C3
Westby 99 G4
Westcliff-on-Sea 46 B4
Westcombe 25 D4
Westcote 55 E5
Westcott *Bucks.* 42 C1
Westcott *Devon* 10 D2
Westcott *Surr.* 29 G3
Westcott Barton 55 G5
Westdean 18 A4
Westdowns 5 E1
Wester Aberchalder 167 E2
Wester Badentyre 182 C4
Wester Culbeuchly 182 B3
Wester Dechmont 143 E2
Wester Fintray 170 D3
Wester Foffarty 160 C5
Wester Greenskares 182 C3
Wester Gruinards 190 A5
Wester Lealty 179 F2
Wester Lonvine 179 G2
Wester Newburn 152 C4
Wester Ord 170 D4
Wester Quarff 200 D4
Wester Skeld 200 B3
Westerdale *High.* 194 D3
Westerdale *N.Yorks.* 111 F2
Westerfield *Shet.* 200 C2
Westerfield *Suff.* 60 C3
Westergate 16 B3
Westerham 30 D3
Westerleigh 39 F5
Westerton *Aber.* 170 C5
Westerton *Angus* 161 E4
Westerton *Dur.* 120 B4
Westerton *P. & K.* 151 D3
Westerwick 200 B3
Westfield *Cumb.* 116 C4
Westfield *E.Suss.* 18 D2
Westfield *High.* 194 C2
Westfield *Norf.* 86 A5
Westfield *W.Loth.* 142 D2
Westgate *Dur.* 119 F4
Westgate *N.Lincs.* 95 E2
Westgate *Norf.* 86 A1
Westgate *Northumb.* 128 D4
Westgate Hill 102 B5
Westgate on Sea 33 F1
Westhall *Aber.* 170 B2
Westhall *Suff.* 73 F3
Westham *Dorset* 12 C5
Westham *E.Suss.* 18 B3
Westham *Som.* 24 A3
Westhampnett 16 A3
Westhay 24 B3
Westhead 91 F2
Westhide 53 E3
Westhill *Aber.* 170 D4
Westhill *High.* 179 G5
Westhope *Here.* 53 D2
Westhope *Shrop.* 65 D4
Westhorpe *Lincs.* 84 A4
Westhorpe *Suff.* 60 B1
Westhoughton 92 A2
Westhouse 108 B5
Westhouses 81 F2
Westhumble 29 G2
Westing 203 E2
Westlake 8 C2
Westleigh *Devon* 21 E3
Westleigh *Devon* 11 D1
Westleigh *Gt.Man.* 92 A2
Westleton 61 F1
Westley *Shrop.* 64 C2
Westley *Suff.* 59 G1
Westley Heights 45 F4
Westley Waterless 59 E2
Westlington 42 C1
Westlinton 126 B5
Westloch 143 G4
Westmarsh 33 E2
Westmeston 17 F2
Westmill 58 B5
Westmuir 160 B4
Westness 198 B4
Westnewton *Cumb.* 117 E2
Westnewton *Northumb.* 136 C3
Weston *B. & N.E.Som.* 25 E1
Weston *Ches.* 79 E2
Weston *Devon* 11 E4
Weston *Dorset* 12 C5
Weston *Halton* 91 G4
Weston *Hants.* 28 C5
Weston *Herts.* 58 A4
Weston *Lincs.* 84 A5
Weston *Moray* 181 G3
Weston *N.Yorks.* 102 A3
Weston *Northants.* 56 A3
Weston *Notts.* 82 C1
Weston *Shrop.* 78 C5
Weston *Shrop.* 65 E3
Weston *Staffs.* 79 G5
Weston *W.Berks.* 41 G5
Weston Beggard 53 E3
Weston by Welland 68 C3
Weston Colville 59 E2
Weston Corbett 28 B3
Weston Coyney 79 G3
Weston Favell 56 C1
Weston Green *Cambs.* 59 E2
Weston Green *Norf.* 86 C4
Weston Green *Surr.* 29 G1
Weston Heath 65 G1
Weston Hills 84 A5
Weston-in-Gordano 38 D5
Weston Jones 79 E5
Weston Longville 86 C4
Weston Lullingfields 78 B5
Weston-on-the-Green 42 A1
Weston-on-Trent 81 F5
Weston Patrick 28 B3
Weston Point 91 F4
Weston Rhyn 77 F4
Weston Subedge 54 D3
Weston-super-Mare 24 A1
Weston Turville 43 D1
Weston-under-Lizard 66 A1
Weston under Penyard 53 F5
Weston under Wetherley 55 F1
Weston Underwood *Derbys.* 81 D3
Weston Underwood *M.K.* 57 D3
Westonbirt 40 A4
Westoning 57 F4
Westonzoyland 24 A4
Westow 103 G1
Westport *Arg. & B.* 130 B3
Westport *Som.* 11 G1
Westrigg 142 D3
Westruther 144 D4
Westry 70 B3
Westside 171 D5
Westward 117 F2
Westward Ho! 21 E3
Westwell *Kent* 32 B4
Westwell *Oxon.* 41 E1
Westwell Leacon 32 B4
Westwick *Cambs.* 58 C1
Westwick *Dur.* 109 F1
Westwick *Norf.* 87 D3
Westwood *Devon* 10 D3
Westwood *Wilts.* 25 F2
Westwood Heath 67 E5
Westwoodside 95 E3
Wether Cote Farm 111 F4
Wetheral 118 A2
Wetherby 102 D3
Wetherden 60 B1
Wetheringsett 60 C1
Wethersfield 59 F4
Wethersta 200 C1
Wetherup Street 60 C1
Wetley Rocks 79 G3
Wettenhall 78 D1
Wettenhall Green 78 D1
Wetton 80 C2
Wetwang 104 B2
Wetwood 79 E4
Wexcombe 27 D2
Weybourne 86 C1
Weybread 72 D3
Weybridge 29 F1
Weycroft 11 G2
Weydale 194 D2
Weyhill 27 E3
Weymouth 12 C5
Whaddon *Bucks.* 56 D4
Whaddon *Cambs.* 58 B3
Whaddon *Glos.* 40 A1
Whaddon *Wilts.* 26 C5
Whaddon Gap 58 B3
Whale 118 B5
Whaley 94 C5
Whaley Bridge 93 E4
Whaligoe 195 F4
Whalley 100 D4
Whalton 128 D3
Wham 101 D1
Whaplode 84 B5
Whaplode Drove 70 B1
Whaplode St. Catherine 70 B1
Wharfe 101 D1
Wharles 100 A4
Wharncliffe Side 94 A3
Wharram le Street 104 A1
Wharram Percy 104 A1
Wharton *Ches.* 79 D1
Wharton *Here.* 53 E2
Whashton 110 A2
Whatcote 55 E3
Whatfield 60 B3
Whatley 25 E3
Whatlington 18 C2
Whatstandwell 81 E2
Whatton 82 C4
Whauphill 115 E2
Whaw 109 E2
Wheatacre 73 F2
Wheatenhurst 39 G2
Wheathampstead 44 A1
Wheathill 65 F4
Wheatley *Hants.* 28 C4
Wheatley *Oxon.* 42 B2
Wheatley Hill 120 C4
Wheatley Lane 101 E4
Wheaton Aston 66 A1
Wheddon Cross 22 C4
Wheedlemont 169 G2
Wheelerstreet 29 E3
Wheelock 79 E2
Wheelton 100 C5
Wheen 160 B2
Wheldrake 103 F3
Whelford 41 D3
Whelpley Hill 43 F2
Whelpo 117 G3
Whenby 103 F1
Whepstead 59 G2
Wherstead 60 C3
Wherwell 27 E3
Wheston 93 F5
Whetley Cross 12 A2
Whetsted 31 F4
Whetstone 68 A3
Whicham 106 C4
Whichford 55 F4
Whickham 120 B1
Whiddon Down 7 G1
Whifflet 142 B3
Whigstreet 160 C5
Whilton 56 B1
Whim 143 G4
Whimple 10 D3
Whimpwell Green 87 E2
Whin Lane End 99 G3
Whinburgh 86 B5
Whinnyfold 171 F1
Whippingham 15 E3
Whipsnade 43 F1
Whipton 10 C3
Whisby 83 E1
Whissendine 68 D1
Whissonsett 86 A3
Whistley Green 42 C5
Whiston *Mersey.* 91 F3
Whiston *Northants.* 57 D1
Whiston *S.Yorks.* 94 B4
Whiston *Staffs.* 80 B3
Whiston *Staffs.* 66 A1
Whitbeck 106 C4
Whitbourne 53 G2
Whitburn *T. & W.* 120 D1
Whitburn *W.Loth.* 142 D3
Whitby *Ches.* 91 E5
Whitby *N.Yorks.* 112 B1
Whitchurch *B. & N.E.Som.* 24 D1
Whitchurch *Bucks.* 56 D5
Whitchurch *Cardiff* 38 A5
Whitchurch *Devon* 7 E3
Whitchurch *Hants.* 27 F3
Whitchurch *Here.* 39 E1
Whitchurch *Pembs.* 48 B5
Whitchurch *Shrop.* 78 C3
Whitchurch Canonicorum 11 G3
Whitchurch Hill 42 B5
Whitchurch-on-Thames 42 B5
Whitcombe 12 D4
Whitcott Keysett 64 B4
White Colne 59 G5
White Coppice 92 A1
White Cross *Cornw.* 4 C4
White Cross *Devon* 10 D3
White Cross *Here.* 53 D3
White End 54 A5
White Lackington 12 D3
White Ladies Aston 54 B2
White Mill 50 A5
White Moor 81 E3
White Notley 45 G1
White Pit 97 D5

White Roding 45 E1
White Waltham 43 D5
Whiteacen 181 E5
Whiteash Green 59 F4
Whitebog 183 E4
Whitebridge High. 195 E1
Whitebridge High. 167 D3
Whitebrook 39 E2
Whiteburn 144 C5
Whitecairn 122 D5
Whitecairns 171 E3
Whitecastle 143 E5
Whitechapel 100 B3
Whitechurch 49 E4
Whitecraig 144 A2
Whitecroft 39 F2
Whitecrook 122 C5
Whitecross 2 C3
Whiteface 179 G1
Whitefield Aber. 170 C2
Whitefield Gt.Man. 92 C2
Whitefield High. 167 E2
Whitefield High. 195 E3
Whitefield P. & K. 151 G1
Whiteford 170 C2
Whitegate 78 D1
Whitehall 199 E4
Whitehaven 116 C5
Whitehill Hants. 28 C4
Whitehill Kent 32 B3
Whitehill N.Ayr. 141 D4
Whitehills 182 B3
Whitehouse Aber. 170 B3
Whitehouse Arg. & B. 139 G3
Whitekirk 144 C1
Whitelackington 11 G1
Whitelaw 145 F4
Whiteleen 195 F4
Whitelees 132 B2
Whiteley 15 E2
Whiteley Bank 15 E4
Whiteley Village 29 F1
Whiteleys 122 B5
Whitemans Green 17 F1
Whitemire 180 B4
Whiteparish 27 D5
Whiterashes 171 D2
Whiterow 195 F4
Whiteshill 40 A2
Whiteside Northumb. 118 D1
Whiteside W.Loth. 143 D3
Whitesmith 18 A2
Whitestaunton 11 F1
Whitestone Aber. 170 B5
Whitestone Arg. & B. 130 C2
Whitestone Devon 10 B3
Whitestripe 183 E4
Whiteway 40 B1
Whitewell Aber. 183 E3
Whitewell Lancs. 100 C3
Whiteworks 7 G3
Whitewreath 181 E4
Whitfield Here. 52 D4
Whitfield Kent 33 E4
Whitfield Northants. 56 B3
Whitfield Northumb. 119 D2
Whitfield S.Glos. 39 F3
Whitford Devon 11 F3
Whitford (Chwitffordd) Flints. 90 C5
Whitgift 104 A5
Whitgreave 79 F5
Whithorn 115 E2
Whiting Bay 131 F3
Whitkirk 102 C4
Whitlam 171 D2
Whitland 35 F1
Whitland Abbey 35 F1
Whitletts 132 B3
Whitley N.Yorks. 103 E5
Whitley Read. 28 C1
Whitley Wilts. 25 F1
Whitley Bay 129 F4
Whitley Chapel 119 F2
Whitley Lower 93 G1
Whitley Row 31 D3
Whitlock's End 66 D5
Whitminster 39 G2
Whitmore Dorset 13 G2
Whitmore Staffs. 79 F3
Whitnage 10 D1
Whitnash 55 F1
Whitney 52 B3
Whitrigg Cumb. 117 F1
Whitrigg Cumb. 117 F3
Whitsbury 14 A1
Whitsome 145 F4
Whitson 38 C4
Whitstable 32 D2
Whitstone 6 C1
Whittingham 137 E5
Whittingslow 64 D4
Whittington Derbys. 94 A5
Whittington Glos. 54 C5
Whittington Lancs. 108 B5
Whittington Norf. 71 F3
Whittington Shrop. 78 A4
Whittington Staffs. 67 D2
Whittington Staffs. 66 A4
Whittington Worcs. 54 A2
Whittle-le-Woods 100 B5
Whittlebury 56 B3
Whittlesey 70 A3
Whittlesford 58 C3
Whitton N.Lincs. 104 B5
Whitton Northumb. 128 C1
Whitton Powys 52 B1
Whitton Shrop. 65 E5
Whitton Stock. 120 C5
Whitton Suff. 60 C3
Whittonditch 41 E5
Whittonstall 119 G2
Whitway 27 F2
Whitwell Derbys. 94 C5
Whitwell Herts. 57 G5
Whitwell I.o.W. 15 E5
Whitwell N.Yorks. 110 B3
Whitwell Norf. 86 C3
Whitwell Rut. 69 E2
Whitwell-on-the-Hill 103 G1
Whitwick 67 G1
Whitwood 102 D5
Whitworth 92 C1
Whixall 78 C4
Whixley 102 D2
Whorlton Dur. 110 A1
Whorlton N.Yorks. 111 D2
Whygate 127 F4
Whyle 53 E1
Whyteleafe 30 C3
Wibdon 39 E3
Wibsey 102 A4
Wibtoft 67 G4
Wichenford 53 G1
Wichling 32 B3
Wick Bourne. 14 A3
Wick High. 195 F3
Wick S.Glos. 39 G5
Wick V. of Glam. 37 F5
Wick W.Suss. 16 C3
Wick Wilts. 26 C5
Wick Worcs. 54 B3
Wick Airport 195 F3
Wick Hill Kent 32 A4
Wick Hill W'ham 28 C1
Wick St. Lawrence 24 A1
Wicken Cambs. 71 D5
Wicken Northants. 56 C4
Wicken Bonhunt 58 C4
Wickenby 96 A4
Wickerslack 108 B1
Wickersley 94 B3
Wickford 45 G3
Wickham Hants. 15 E1
Wickham W.Berks. 41 F5
Wickham Bishops 46 B1
Wickham Heath 27 F1
Wickham Market 61 D2
Wickham St. Paul 59 G4
Wickham Skeith 60 B1
Wickham Street Suff. 59 F2
Wickham Street Suff. 60 B1
Wickhambreaux 33 E3
Wickhambrook 59 F2
Wickhamford 54 C3
Wickhampton 87 F5
Wicklewood 86 B5
Wickmere 86 C2
Wickwar 39 G4
Widdington 58 D4
Widdop 101 F4
Widdrington 129 E2
Wide Open 129 E4
Widecombe in the Moor 10 A5
Widegates 5 G4
Widemouth Bay 20 C5
Widewall 196 D3
Widford Essex 45 F2
Widford Herts. 44 D1
Widmerpool 82 B5
Widnes 91 G4
Widworthy 11 F3
Wigan 91 G2
Wiggaton 11 E3
Wiggenhall St. Germans 71 E1
Wiggenhall St. Mary Magdalen 71 E1
Wiggenhall St. Mary the Virgin 71 D1
Wiggenhall St. Peter 71 E1
Wiggington 103 F2
Wigginton Herts. 43 E1
Wigginton Oxon. 55 F4
Wigginton Staffs. 67 E2
Wigglesworth 101 E2
Wiggonby 117 F1
Wiggonholt 16 C2
Wighill 103 D3
Wighton 86 A2
Wightwizzle 93 G3
Wigmore Here. 52 D1
Wigmore Med. 32 A2
Wigsley 95 F5
Wigsthorpe 69 F4
Wigston 68 B3
Wigston Parva 67 G3
Wigthorpe 94 C4
Wigtoft 84 A4
Wigton 117 F2
Wigtown 123 F5
Wilbarston 68 D4
Wilberfoss 103 G2
Wilburton 70 C5
Wilby Norf. 72 B2
Wilby Northants. 57 D1
Wilby Suff. 72 D4
Wilcot 26 C1
Wilcott 64 C1
Wilcrick 38 D4
Wildboarclough 79 G1
Wilden Beds. 57 F2
Wilden Worcs. 66 A5
Wildhern 27 E2
Wildhill 44 B2
Wildsworth 95 F3
Wilford 81 G4
Wilkesley 78 D3
Wilkhaven 180 B1
Wilkieston 143 F3
Willand 10 D1
Willaston Ches. 91 E5
Willaston Ches. 79 D2
Willen 57 D3
Willenhall W.Mid. 66 B3
Willenhall W.Mid. 67 F5
Willerby E.Riding 104 C5
Willerby N.Yorks. 112 D5
Willersey 54 D3
Willersley 52 C3
Willesborough 32 C4
Willesborough Lees 32 C4
Willesden 44 B4
Willesley 40 A4
Willett 23 E4
Willey Shrop. 65 F3
Willey Warks. 67 G4
Williamscot 55 G3
Williamthorpe 81 F1
Willian 58 A4
Willimontswick 119 D1
Willingale 45 E2
Willingdon 18 A3
Willingham Cambs. 58 C1
Willingham Lincs. 95 F4
Willington Beds. 57 G3
Willington Derbys. 81 D5
Willington Dur. 120 A4
Willington T. & W. 120 C1
Willington Warks. 55 E4
Willington Corner 78 C1
Willisham 60 B2
Willitoft 103 G4
Williton 23 D3
Willoughby Lincs. 97 E5
Willoughby Warks. 56 A1
Willoughby-on-the-Wolds 82 B5
Willoughby Waterleys 68 A3
Willoughton 95 G3
Willows Green 45 G1
Willsworthy 7 F2
Wilmcote 55 D2
Wilmington Devon 11 F2
Wilmington E.Suss. 18 A3
Wilmington Kent 45 E5
Wilmslow 92 C4
Wilnecote 67 E2
Wilpshire 100 C4
Wilsden 101 G4
Wilsford Lincs. 83 F3
Wilsford Wilts. 26 C3
Wilsford Wilts. 26 B2
Wilsill 102 A1
Wilsley Green 31 G5
Wilson 81 F5
Wilstead 57 F3
Wilsthorpe 69 F1
Wilstone 43 E1
Wilton Cumb. 116 D5
Wilton N.Yorks. 112 B4
Wilton R. & C. 121 E5
Wilton Sc.Bord. 135 F4
Wilton Som. 23 F5
Wilton Wilts. 27 D1
Wilton Wilts. 26 B4
Wimbish 59 D4
Wimbish Green 59 E4
Wimblebury 66 C1
Wimbledon 44 B5
Wimblington 70 C3
Wimborne Minster 13 G2
Wimborne St. Giles 13 G1
Wimbotsham 71 E2
Wimpole 58 B3
Wimpstone 55 E3
Wincanton 25 E5
Wincham 92 A5
Winchburgh 143 E2
Winchcombe 54 C5
Winchelsea 19 E2
Winchelsea Beach 19 E2
Winchester 27 F5
Winchet Hill 31 G4
Winchfield 28 C2
Winchmore Hill Bucks. 43 E3
Winchmore Hill Gt.Lon. 44 C3
Wincle 79 G1
Wincobank 94 A3
Windermere 107 F3
Winderton 55 F3
Windhill 179 E5
Windlesham 29 E1
Windley 81 E3
Windley Meadows 81 E3
Windmill Hill E.Suss. 18 B2
Windmill Hill Som. 11 G1
Windrush 41 D1
Windsor 43 E5
Windy Yet 141 F4
Windygates 152 B4
Wineham 17 E1
Winestead 105 F5
Winewall 101 F3
Winfarthing 72 C3
Winford 24 C1
Winforton 52 B3
Winfrith Newburgh 13 E4
Wing Bucks. 57 D5
Wing Rut. 69 D2
Wingate 120 D4
Wingates Gt.Man. 92 A2
Wingates Northumb. 128 C2
Wingerworth 81 E1
Wingfield Beds. 57 F5
Wingfield Suff. 72 D4
Wingfield Wilts. 25 F2
Wingham 33 E3
Wingmore 33 D4
Wingrave 43 D1
Winkburn 82 C2
Winkfield 43 E5
Winkfield Row 43 D5
Winkhill 80 B2
Winkleigh 21 G5
Winksley 110 B5
Winksley Banks 110 B5
Winkton 14 A3
Winlaton 120 A1
Winlaton Mill 120 A1
Winless 195 E3
Winmarleigh 100 A3
Winnards Perch 4 D3
Winnersh 42 C5
Winscombe 24 B2
Winsford Ches. 79 D1
Winsford Som. 22 C4
Winsh-wen Swan. 36 C3
Winsham 11 G2
Winshill 81 D5
Winskill 118 B4
Winslade 28 B3
Winsley 25 E1
Winslow 56 C5
Winson 40 C2
Winsor 14 C1
Winster Cumb. 107 F3
Winster Derbys. 80 D1
Winston Dur. 110 A1
Winston Suff. 60 C1
Winstone 40 B2
Winswell 21 E4
Winterborne Came 12 D4
Winterborne Clenston 13 E2
Winterborne Houghton 13 E2
Winterborne Kingston 13 E3
Winterborne Monkton 12 C4
Winterborne Stickland 13 E2
Winterborne Whitechurch 13 E2
Winterborne Zelston 13 E3
Winterbourne S.Glos. 39 F4
Winterbourne W.Berks. 41 G5
Winterbourne Abbas 12 C3
Winterbourne Bassett 40 C5
Winterbourne Dauntsey 26 C4
Winterbourne Earls 26 C4
Winterbourne Gunner 26 C4
Winterbourne Monkton 40 C5
Winterbourne Steepleton 12 C4
Winterbourne Stoke 26 B3
Winterburn 101 F2
Wintercleugh 134 A4
Winteringham 104 B5
Winterley 79 E2
Wintersett 94 A1
Wintershill 15 E1
Winterslow 26 D4
Winterton 95 G1
Winterton-on-Sea 87 F4
Winthorpe Lincs. 85 D1
Winthorpe Notts. 82 D2
Winton Bourne. 13 G3
Winton Cumb. 108 C1
Wintringham 112 B5
Winwick Cambs. 69 G4
Winwick Northants. 68 B5
Winwick Warr. 92 A3
Wirksworth 81 D2
Wirswall 78 C3
Wisbech 70 C2
Wisbech St. Mary 70 C2
Wisborough Green 29 F5
Wiseton 95 E4
Wishaw N.Lan. 142 B4
Wishaw Warks. 67 D3
Wisley 29 F2
Wispington 96 C5
Wissett 73 E4
Wissington 60 A4
Wistanstow 64 D4
Wistanswick 79 D5
Wistaston 79 D2
Wiston Pembs. 34 D1
Wiston S.Lan. 134 A2
Wistow Cambs. 70 A4
Wistow N.Yorks. 103 E4
Wiswell 100 D4
Witcham 70 C5
Witchampton 13 F2
Witchburn 130 C4
Witchford 70 D5
Witcombe 24 B5
Witham 46 B1
Witham Friary 25 E3
Witham on the Hill 69 F1
Withcote 68 D2
Witherenden Hill 18 B1
Witherhurst 18 B1
Witheridge 10 B1
Witherley 67 F3
Withern 97 E4
Withernsea 105 F5
Withernwick 105 E3
Withersdale Street 73 D3
Withersfield 59 E3
Witherslack 107 F4
Witherslack Hall 107 F4
Withiel 5 D3
Withiel Florey 22 C4
Withington Glos. 40 C1
Withington Gt.Man. 92 C3
Withington Here. 53 E3
Withington Shrop. 65 E1
Withington Staffs. 80 B4
Withington Green 92 C5
Withleigh 10 C1
Withnell 100 C5
Withybrook 67 G4
Withycombe 22 D3
Withycombe Raleigh 10 D4
Withyham 31 D5
Withypool 22 B4
Witley 29 E4
Witnesham 60 C2
Witney 41 F1
Wittering 69 F2
Wittersham 19 D1
Witton 161 D3
Witton Bridge 87 E2
Witton Gilbert 120 B3
Witton-le-Wear 120 A4
Witton Park 120 A4
Wiveliscombe 23 D5
Wivelsfield 17 F1
Wivelsfield Green 17 F2
Wivenhoe 60 B5
Wiveton 86 B1
Wix 60 C5
Wixford 54 C2
Wixoe 59 F3
Woburn 57 E4
Woburn Sands 57 E4
Wokefield Park 28 B1
Woking 29 F2
Wokingham 28 D1
Wolborough 10 B5
Wold Newton E.Riding 112 D5
Wold Newton N.E.Lincs. 96 C3
Woldingham 30 C3
Wolfelee 135 G5
Wolferlow 53 F1
Wolferton 85 E5
Wolfhampcote 56 A1
Wolfhill 151 G1
Wolfpits 52 B2
Wolf's Castle 48 C5
Wolfsdale 48 C5
Woll 135 F3
Wollaston Northants. 57 E1
Wollaston Shrop. 64 C1
Wollaston W.Mid. 66 A4
Wollerton 78 D5
Wolsingham 119 G4
Wolstenholme 92 C1
Wolston 67 G5
Wolvercote 41 G2
Wolverhampton 66 B3
Wolverley Shrop. 78 B4
Wolverley Worcs. 66 A5
Wolverton Hants. 27 G2
Wolverton M.K. 56 D3
Wolverton Warks. 55 E1
Wolvesnewton 39 D3
Wolvey 67 G4
Wolviston 120 D5
Wombleton 111 F4
Wombourne 66 A3
Wombwell 94 B2
Womenswold 33 E3
Womersley 94 C1
Wonastow 39 D1
Wonersh 29 F3
Wonson 7 G2
Wonston 27 F4
Wooburn 43 E4
Wooburn Green 43 E4
Wood Burcote 56 B3
Wood Dalling 86 B3
Wood End Beds. 57 F3
Wood End Herts. 58 B5
Wood End Warks. 67 E3
Wood End Warks. 66 D5
Wood Enderby 84 A1
Wood Green 44 C3
Wood Hayes 66 B2
Wood Norton 86 B3
Wood Street Village 29 E2
Woodale 109 F5
Woodbastwick 87 E4
Woodbeck 95 E5
Woodbine 34 C1
Woodborough Notts. 82 B3
Woodborough Wilts. 26 C1
Woodbridge 61 D3
Woodbury 10 D4
Woodbury Salterton 10 D4
Woodchester 40 A2
Woodchurch Kent 32 B5
Woodchurch Mersey. 91 D4
Woodcote Oxon. 42 B4
Woodcote Tel. & W. 65 G1
Woodcott 27 F2
Woodcroft 39 E3
Woodcutts 13 F1
Woodditton 59 E2
Woodeaton 42 A1
Woodend Aber. 170 B3
Woodend Cumb. 106 C3
Woodend High. 167 G2
Woodend High. 155 G3
Woodend Northants. 56 B3
Woodend P. & K. 158 C5
Woodend W.Suss. 16 A3
Woodfalls 26 D5
Woodford Cornw. 20 C4
Woodford Glos. 39 F3
Woodford Gt.Lon. 44 D3
Woodford Gt.Man. 92 C4
Woodford Northants. 69 E5
Woodford Bridge 44 D3
Woodford Green 44 D3
Woodford Halse 56 A2
Woodgate Norf. 86 B4
Woodgate W.Mid. 66 B4
Woodgate W.Suss. 16 B3
Woodgate Worcs. 54 B1
Woodgreen 14 A1
Woodhall 109 E3
Woodhall Spa 83 G1
Woodham Dur. 120 B5
Woodham Surr. 29 F1
Woodham Ferrers 45 G3
Woodham Mortimer 46 B2
Woodham Walter 46 B2
Woodhaven 152 C2
Woodhead 170 C1
Woodhill 65 G4
Woodhorn 129 E3
Woodhouse Cumb. 107 G4
Woodhouse Leics. 68 A1
Woodhouse S.Yorks. 94 B4
Woodhouse Eaves 68 A1
Woodhouses 67 D1
Woodhuish 9 F2
Woodhurst 70 B5
Woodingdean 17 F3
Woodland Devon 9 D1
Woodland Dur. 119 G5
Woodlands Dorset 13 G2
Woodlands Hants. 14 C1
Woodlands Shrop. 65 G4
Woodlands Park 43 D5
Woodleigh 8 D3
Woodlesford 102 C5
Woodley 42 C5
Woodmancote Glos. 40 C2
Woodmancote Glos. 54 B5
Woodmancote W.Suss. 17 E2
Woodmancote W.Suss. 15 G2
Woodmancott 27 G3
Woodmansey 104 C4
Woodmansterne 30 B3
Woodminton 26 B5
Woodmoor 64 B2
Woodnesborough 33 E3
Woodnewton 69 F3
Woodplumpton 100 B4
Woodrising 86 A5
Woodseaves Shrop. 79 D4
Woodseaves Staffs. 79 E5
Woodsend 41 E5
Woodsetts 94 C4
Woodsford 13 D3
Woodside Aberdeen 171 E4
Woodside Brack.F. 43 E5
Woodside D. & G. 125 E3
Woodside Fife 152 C4
Woodside Fife 152 A4
Woodside Herts. 44 B2
Woodside N.Ayr. 141 E4
Woodside P. & K. 151 G1
Woodside Shrop. 64 C5
Woodside W.Mid. 66 B4
Woodstock 41 G1
Woodstock Slop 48 D5
Woodston 69 G3
Woodthorpe Derbys. 94 B5
Woodthorpe Leics. 68 A1
Woodton 73 D2
Woodtown 21 E3
Woodville 67 F1
Woodwalton 70 A4
Woodyates 13 G1
Woofferton 53 E1
Wookey 24 C3
Wookey Hole 24 C3
Wool 13 E4
Woolacombe 21 E1
Woolaston 39 E3
Woolavington 24 A3
Woolbeding 29 D5
Wooler 137 D4
Woolfardisworthy Devon 10 B2
Woolfardisworthy Devon 20 D3
Woolfords Cottages 143 E4
Woolhampton 27 G1
Woolhope 53 F4
Woollage Green 33 E4
Woolland 13 D2
Woollard 24 D1
Woollaton 21 E4
Woolley B. & N.E.Som. 25 E1
Woolley Cambs. 69 G5
Woolley W.Yorks. 94 A1
Woolmer Green 44 B1
Woolmere Green 54 B1
Woolmersdon 23 F4
Woolpit 60 A1
Woolscott 55 G1
Woolstaston 65 D3
Woolsthorpe Lincs. 82 D4
Woolsthorpe Lincs. 83 E5
Woolston S'ham. 14 D1
Woolston Shrop. 78 A5
Woolston Shrop. 64 D4
Woolston Warr. 92 A4
Woolston Green 9 D1
Woolstone M.K. 57 D4
Woolstone Oxon. 41 E4
Woolton 91 F4
Woolton Hill 27 F1
Woolverstone 60 C4
Woolverton 25 E2
Woolwich 44 D5
Woonton 52 C2
Wooperton 137 E4
Woore 79 E3
Wootton Beds. 57 F3
Wootton Hants. 14 B3
Wootton Kent 33 E4
Wootton N.Lincs. 96 A1
Wootton Northants. 56 C2
Wootton Oxon. 41 G1
Wootton Oxon. 41 G2
Wootton Shrop. 65 D5
Wootton Staffs. 79 F5
Wootton Staffs. 80 C3
Wootton Bassett 40 C4
Wootton Bridge 15 E3
Wootton Common 15 E3
Wootton Courtenay 22 C3
Wootton Fitzpaine 11 G3
Wootton Green 57 F3
Wootton Rivers 26 C1
Wootton St. Lawrence 27 G2
Wootton Wawen 55 D1
Worcester 54 A2
Worcester Park 30 B2
Wordsley 66 A4
Wordwell 71 G5
Worfield 65 G3
Work 198 C5
Workington 116 D4
Worksop 94 C5
Worlaby 96 A1
Worlds End Hants. 15 F1
World's End W.Berks. 41 G5
Worle 24 A1
Worleston 79 D2
Worlingham 73 F2
Worlington 71 E5
Worlingworth 60 D1
Wormbridge 52 D4
Wormegay 71 E1
Wormelow Tump 53 D4
Wormhill 93 F5
Wormiehills 153 E1
Wormingford 60 A4
Worminghall 42 B2
Wormington 54 C4
Worminster 24 C3
Wormiston 153 E4
Wormit 152 B2
Wormleighton 55 G2
Wormley Herts. 44 C2
Wormley Surr. 29 E4
Wormshill 32 A3
Wormsley 52 D3
Worplesdon 29 E2
Worrall 94 A3
Worsbrough 94 A2
Worsley 92 B2
Worstead 87 E3
Worsted Lodge 58 D2
Worsthorne 101 E4
Worston 101 D3
Worswell 8 B3
Worth Kent 33 F3
Worth W.Suss. 30 C5
Worth Matravers 13 F5
Wortham 72 B4
Worthen 64 C2
Worthenbury 78 B3
Worthing Norf. 86 B4
Worthing W.Suss. 16 D3
Worthington 81 F5
Wortley Glos. 39 G3
Wortley S.Yorks. 94 A3
Worton 26 A2
Wortwell 73 D3
Wotherton 64 B2
Wotton 29 G3
Wotton-under-Edge 39 G3
Wotton Underwood 42 B1
Woughton on the Green 57 D4
Wouldham 31 G2
Wrabness 60 C4
Wrae 182 C4
Wrafton 21 E2
Wragby 96 B5
Wragholme 97 D3
Wramplingham 86 C5
Wrangham 170 B1
Wrangle 84 C2
Wrangle Lowgate 84 C2
Wrangway 11 E1
Wrantage 24 A5
Wrawby 96 A2
Wraxall N.Som. 39 D5
Wraxall Som. 24 D4
Wray 100 C1
Wray Castle 107 E2
Wraysbury 43 F5
Wrea Green 99 G4
Wreay Cumb. 118 A5
Wreay Cumb. 118 A3
Wrecclesham 28 D3
Wrecsam (Wrexham) 78 A3
Wrekenton 120 B2
Wrelton 111 G4
Wrenbury 78 C3
Wreningham 72 C2
Wrentham 73 F3
Wrenthorpe 102 C5
Wrentnall 64 D2
Wressle 103 G4
Wrestlingworth 58 A3
Wretham 72 A3
Wretton 71 E3
Wrexham (Wrecsam) 78 A3
Wrexham Industrial Estate 78 A3
Wribbenhall 65 G5
Wrightington Bar 91 G1
Wrightpark 150 B5
Wrinehill 79 E3
Wrington 24 B1
Writhlington 25 D2
Writtle 45 F2
Wrockwardine 65 F1
Wroot 95 E2
Wrotham 31 F3
Wrotham Heath 31 F3
Wrotham Hill 31 F2
Wrotham Park 44 B3
Wroughton 40 D4
Wroxall I.o.W. 15 E5
Wroxall Warks. 67 E5
Wroxeter 65 E2
Wroxham 87 E4
Wroxton 55 G3
Wstrws 49 G3
Wyaston 80 C3
Wyberton 84 B3
Wyboston 57 G2
Wybunbury 79 D3
Wych Cross 30 D5
Wychbold 54 B1
Wyck 28 C4
Wyck Rissington 55 D5
Wycliffe 110 A1
Wycoller 101 F4
Wycomb 82 C5
Wycombe Marsh 43 D3
Wyddial 58 B4
Wye 32 C4
Wyke Dorset 25 E5
Wyke Shrop. 65 F2
Wyke W.Yorks. 102 A5
Wyke Regis 12 C5
Wykeham N.Yorks. 112 C4

Wykeham *N.Yorks.* 112 B5
Wyken 65 G3
Wykey 78 A5
Wylam 120 A1
Wylde Green 66 D3
Wyllie 38 A3
Wylye 26 B4
Wymering 15 F2
Wymeswold 82 B5
Wymington 57 E1
Wymondham *Leics.* 69 D1
Wymondham *Norf.* 86 C5
Wyndham 37 F3
Wynford Eagle 12 B3
Wynnstay Park 78 A3
Wynyard 120 D5
Wyre Piddle 54 B3
Wyresdale lower 100 C2
Wysall 82 B5
Wyson 53 E1
Wythall 66 C5
Wytham 41 G2
Wythburn 117 G5
Wyton 70 A5
Wyverstone 60 B1
Wyverstone Street 60 B1
Wyville 83 D5
Wyvis Lodge 179 D2

Y
Y Bryn 76 B5
Y Drenewydd (Newtown) 64 A3
Y Fan 63 F4
Y Felinheli 75 E1
Y Fenni (Abergavenny) 38 C1
Y Fflint (Flint) 90 D5
Y Ffôr 74 C4
Y Trallwng (Welshpool) 64 B2
Yaddlethorpe 95 F2
Yafford 15 D4
Yafforth 110 C3
Yalding 31 F4
Yanworth 40 C1
Yapham 103 G2
Yapton 16 B3
Yarburgh 96 D3
Yarcombe 11 F2
Yardley 66 D4
Yardley Gobion 56 C3
Yardley Hastings 57 D2
Yardro 52 B2
Yarkhill 53 F3
Yarlet 79 G5
Yarley 24 C3
Yarlington 25 D5
Yarm 110 D1
Yarmouth 14 C4
Yarnacott 21 G2
Yarnbrook 25 F2
Yarnfield 79 F4
Yarnscombe 21 F3
Yarnton 41 G1
Yarpole 53 D1
Yarrow 135 E3
Yarrow Feus 135 E3
Yarrowford 135 F3
Yarsop 52 D3
Yarwell 69 F3
Yate 39 G4
Yateley 28 D1
Yatesbury 40 C5
Yattendon 42 A5
Yatton *Here.* 52 D1
Yatton *N.Som.* 24 B1
Yatton Keynell 40 A5
Yaverland 15 F4
Yaxham 86 B4
Yaxley *Cambs.* 69 G3
Yaxley *Suff.* 72 C4
Yazor 52 D3
Yeading 44 A4
Yeadon 102 B3
Yealand Conyers 107 G5
Yealand Redmayne 107 G5
Yealmpton 8 B2
Yearby 121 F5
Yearsley 111 E5
Yeaton 64 D1
Yeaveley 80 C3
Yedingham 112 B5
Yelford 41 F2
Yelland *Devon* 21 E2
Yelland *Devon* 7 F1
Yelling 58 A1
Yelvertoft 68 A5
Yelverton *Devon* 8 B1
Yelverton *Norf.* 87 D5
Yenston 25 E5
Yeo Vale 21 E3
Yeoford 10 A3
Yeolmbridge 6 D2
Yeomadon 20 D5
Yeovil 12 B1
Yeovil Marsh 12 B1
Yeovilton 24 C5
Yerbeston 35 D2
Yesnaby 198 A5
Yetlington 137 E5
Yetminster 12 B1
Yettington 11 D4
Yetts o'Muckhart 151 F4
Yielden 57 F1
Yiewsley 43 F5
Ynys 75 E4
Ynysboeth 37 G3
Ynysddu 38 A3
Ynyshir 37 G3
Ynyslas 62 C3
Ynysmeudwy 36 D2
Ynystawe 36 C2
Ynysybwl 37 G3
Yockenthwaite 109 E5
Yockleton 64 C1
Yokefleet 104 A5
Yoker 141 G3
Yonder Bognie 182 A5
York 103 F2
Yorkletts 32 C2
Yorkley 39 F2
Yorton 78 C5
Youldon 20 D5
Youldonmoor Cross 20 D5
Youlgreave 80 D1
Youlthorpe 103 G2
Youlton 103 D1
Young's End 45 G1
Yoxall 66 D1
Yoxford 61 E1
Yr Wyddgrug (Mold) 77 F1
Ysbyty Cynfyn 63 D5
Ysbyty Ifan 76 B3
Ysbyty Ystwyth 62 D5
Ysceifiog 90 C5
Ysgubor-y-coed 62 C3
Ystalyfera 37 D2
Ystrad 37 F3
Ystrad Aeron 50 B2
Ystrad Meurig 50 D1
Ystrad Mynach 38 A3
Ystradfellte 37 F1
Ystradffin 51 D3
Ystradgynlais 37 D1
Ystradowen *N.P.T.* 36 D1
Ystradowen *V. of Glam.* 37 G5
Ythanwells 170 B1
Ythsie 171 D1

Z
Zeal Monachorum 10 A2
Zeals 25 E4
Zelah 4 C4
Zennor 2 B3

Index to place names in Ireland

Abbreviations

Ant.	Antrim	*Kilk.*	Kilkenny	*Tyr.*	Tyrone	*Wexf.*	Wexford
Dub.	Dublin	*Tipp.*	Tipperary	*Water.*	Waterford		

A
Aasleagh 246 B6
Abbeyfeale 244 C3
Abbeyleix 245 F2
Achill 246 B5
Adare 244 C2
Annahilt 247 G4
Annalong 247 H5
Antrim 247 G3
Ardara 246 D3
Ardee 247 G5
Ardglass 247 H4
Arklow (An tInbhear Mór) 245 G2
Armagh 247 G4
Armoy 247 G2
Arvagh 247 E5
Ashbourne 247 G6
Athboy 247 F6
Athenry 244 D1
Athleague 246 D6
Athlone (Baile Átha Luain) 247 E6
Athy 245 F1
Augher 247 F4
Aughnacloy 247 F4
Aughrim 245 G2
Avoca 245 G2

B
Balbriggan 247 G6
Balieborough 247 F5
Ballaghaderreen 246 D5
Ballina (Béal an Átha) 246 C5
Ballinafad 246 D5
Ballinalack 247 E6
Ballinamore 247 E5
Ballinasloe (Béal Átha na Sluaighe) 244 D1
Ballindine 246 C6
Ballinrobe 246 C6
Ballon 245 F2
Ballybay 247 F5
Ballybofey 247 E3
Ballybrack 244 A4
Ballybunnion 244 B3
Ballycanew 245 G2
Ballycastle *Ant.* 247 G2
Ballycastle *Mayo* 246 C4
Ballyclare 247 G3
Ballyconnell 247 E5
Ballycroy 246 B5
Ballydesmond 244 C3
Ballygar 246 D6
Ballygawley 247 F4
Ballygorman 247 F2
Ballyhale 245 F3
Ballyhaunis 246 D6
Ballyheigue 244 B3
Ballyjamesduff 247 F5
Ballykelly 247 F3
Ballylynan 245 F2
Ballymacarberry 245 E3
Ballymacmague 245 E4
Ballymacoda 245 E4
Ballymahon 247 E6
Ballymakeery 244 C4
Ballymena 247 G3
Ballymoney 247 G3
Ballymote 246 D5
Ballymurphy 245 F2
Ballynahinch 247 H4
Ballyragget 245 F2
Ballyshannon 246 D4
Ballyvaughan 244 C1
Ballyward 247 G4
Baltinglass 245 G2
Banagher 245 E1
Banbridge 247 G4
Bandon 244 D4
Bangor 247 H4
Bangor Erris 246 B5
Banteer 244 C3
Bantry 244 B5
Belcoo 247 E4
Belderg 246 B4
Belfast 247 H4
Belfast City Airport 247 H4
Belfast International Airport 247 G4
Belmullet 246 B5
Beragh 247 F4
Bessbrook 247 G5
Bettystown 247 G6
Birr 245 E1
Blackrock 247 G5
Blackwater 245 G3
Blarney 244 D4
Blessington 245 G1
Bohola 246 C5
Borris 245 F2
Borrisokane 244 D1
Borrisoleigh 245 E2
Boyle 246 D5
Bray (Bré) 245 G1
Broadford 244 C3
Broughshane 247 G3
Bunbeg 246 D3
Bunclody 245 G2
Buncrana 247 E2
Bundoran 246 D4
Burtonport 246 D3
Bushmills 247 G2
Butlers Bridge 247 F5
Buttevant 244 D3

C
Cahermore 244 B5
Cahir 245 E3
Cahirciveen 244 A4
Callan 245 F3
Cappoquin 245 E3
Carlingford 247 G5
Carlow (Ceatharlach) 245 F2
Carndonagh 247 F2
Carnlough 247 G3
Carraroe 244 B1
Carrick-on-Shannon 247 E5
Carrick-on-Suir (Carraig na Siúire) 245 F3
Carrickfergus 247 H3
Carrickmacross 247 F5
Carrigallen 247 E5
Carrigtwohill 244 D4
Carrowdore 247 H4
Carrowkeel 247 F2
Cashel 245 E3
Castlebar (Caisleán an Bharraigh) 246 C5
Castlebellingham 247 G5
Castleblayney 247 F5
Castlebridge 245 G3
Castlecomer 245 F2
Castleconnell 244 D2
Castlederg 247 E3
Castledermot 245 F2
Castlegregory 244 B3
Castleisland 244 B3
Castlemaine 244 B3
Castlemartyr 245 E4
Castlepollard 247 F6
Castlerea 246 D6
Castletown 245 E1
Castletown Bere 244 B5
Catherdaniel 244 A4
Cavan 247 F5
Celbridge 245 G1
Charlestown 246 D5
Cheekpoint 245 F3
City of Derry Airport 247 F3
Clady 247 E3
Clane 245 G1
Clara 245 E1
Clarecastle 244 C2
Claregalway 244 C1
Claremorris 246 C6
Clashmore 245 E4
Claudy 247 F3
Clifden 246 B6
Cliffonoy 246 D4
Cloghan 245 E1
Clogheen 245 E3
Clonakilty 244 C5
Clonbern 246 D6
Clones 247 F5
Clonmel (Cluain Meala) 245 E3
Clonroche 245 G3
Clonygowan 245 F1
Cloonbannin 244 C3
Clooneagh 247 E5
Cobh (An Cóbh) 244 D4
Coleraine 247 F2
Collooney 246 D5
Comber 247 H4
Cong 246 C6
Cookstown 247 F4
Cootehill 247 F5
Cork (Corcaigh) 244 D4
Cork Airport 244 D4
Corofin 244 C2
Courtmacsherry 244 D5
Courtown 245 G2
Craanford 245 G2
Craigavon 247 G4
Creeslough 247 E2
Cregganbaun 246 B6
Crookhaven 244 B5
Croom 244 D3
Crossgar 247 H4
Crosshaven 244 D4
Crossmaglen 247 G5
Crumlin 247 G4
Crusheen 244 C2
Cullybackey 247 G3
Cushendall 247 G3
Cushendun 247 G2

D
Delvin 247 F6
Dingle 244 A3
Donaghadee 247 H4
Donaghmore 247 F4
Donegal 246 D4
Donoughmore 244 D4
Dooagh 246 B5
Downpatrick 247 H4
Draperstown 247 F3
Drimoleague 244 C5
Drogheda (Droichead Átha) 247 G6
Dromod 247 E5
Dromore *Down* 247 G4
Dromore *Tyr.* 247 E4
Dromore West 246 C5
Drumfree 247 E2
Drumkeeran 246 D5
Drummin 245 F3
Dublin (Baile Átha Cliath) 245 G1
Dublin Airport 247 G6
Dún Laoghaire 245 G1
Dunboyne 247 G6
Duncannon 245 F3
Duncormick 245 G3
Dundalk (Dún Dealgan) 247 G5
Dundonald 247 H4
Dundrum 247 H4
Dungannon 247 F4
Dungarvan *Kilk.* 245 F2
Dungarvan (Dún Garbhán) *Water.* 245 E4
Dungiven 247 F3
Dungloe 246 D3
Dunlavin 245 G1
Dunleer 247 G5
Dunloy 247 G3
Dunmanway 244 C4
Dunmore 246 D6
Dunmore East 245 F3
Dunmurry 247 G4
Dunquin 244 A3
Durrow 245 F2

E
Edenderry 245 F1
Edgeworthstown 247 E6
Eglinton 247 F3
Ennis (Inis) 244 C2
Enniscorthy (Inis Córthaidh) 245 G3
Enniskean 244 C4
Enniskerry 245 G1
Enniskillen 247 E4
Ennistymon 244 C2

F
Farranfore 244 B3
Fermoy 244 D3
Ferns 245 G2
Fethard 245 E3
Fintona 247 F4
Fintown 246 D3
Fivemiletown 247 F4
Foxford 246 C5
Foynes 244 C2
Frenchpark 246 D5
Freshford 245 F2

G
Galbally 244 D3
Galway (Gaillimh) 244 C1
Galway Airport 244 C1
Garvagh 247 F3
Glenamaddy 246 D6
Glengarriff 244 B4
Glengavlen 247 E5
Glenties 246 D3
Gorey 245 G2
Gort 244 C1
Gortahork 246 D2
Graigue 245 F2
Graiguenamanagh 245 F2
Granard 247 E6
Grange 245 E4
Greenore 247 G5
Gweedore 246 D3

H
Halfway 244 D4
Headford 246 C6
Holycross 245 E2
Horseleap 246 D6
Hospital 244 D3
Howth 247 G6
Hurler's Cross 244 C2

I
Inch *Kerry* 244 B3
Inch *Wexf.* 245 G2

J
Johnstown 245 E2

K
Kanturk 244 C3
Keady 247 F5
Kells *Kilk.* 245 F3
Kells (Ceanannus Mór) *Meath* 247 F6
Kenmare 244 B4
Kerry Airport 244 B3
Kilbeggan 245 E1
Kilcolgan 244 C1
Kilcommon 245 E3
Kilcoole 245 G1
Kilcormac 245 E1
Kilcullen 245 F1
Kildare 245 F1
Kilkee 244 B2
Kilkeel 247 G5
Kilkenny (Cill Chainnigh) 245 F2
Killala 246 C5
Killaloe 244 D2
Killarney (Cill Airne) 244 B4
Killenaule 245 E2
Killimor 244 D1
Killinchy 247 H4
Killinick 245 G3
Killorglin 244 B4
Killurin 245 G3
Killybegs 246 D4
Kilmacrenan 247 E3
Kilmaine 246 C6
Kilmallock 244 D3
Kilmona 244 D4
Kilmore Quay 245 G3
Kilrea 247 G3
Kilrush 244 B2
Kilteel 245 G1
Kiltimagh 246 C5
Kiltullagh 244 D1
Kingscourt 247 F5
Kinnegad 247 F6
Kinsale 244 D4
Kinvara 244 C1
Kircubbin 247 H4
Knock 246 C6
Knock International Airport 246 C5
Knockalough 244 C2
Knocktopher 245 F3

L
Lanesborough 247 E6
Larne 247 H3
Lauragh 244 B4
Laytown 247 G6
Leap 244 C5
Leighlinbridge 245 F2
Leixlip 245 G1
Letterkenny 247 E3
Lifford 247 E3
Limavady 247 F3
Limerick (Luimneach) 244 D2
Lisbellaw 247 E4
Lisburn 247 G4
Lisdoonvarna 244 C1
Lismore 245 E3
Lisnarrick 247 E4
Lisnaskea 247 E5
Listowel 244 B3
Londonderry (Derry) 247 F3
Longford 247 E6
Loughrea 244 D1
Louisburgh 246 B6
Lucan 245 G1
Lukeswell 245 F3
Lurgan 247 G4

M
Macroom 244 C4
Maghera 247 G3
Magherafelt 247 G3
Malahide 247 G6
Malin More 246 D3
Mallow (Mala) 244 D3
Manorhamilton 246 D4
Markethill 247 G4
May's Corner 247 G4
Middletown 247 F4
Midleton 244 D4
Milestone 245 E2
Milford 247 E3
Millstreet 244 C4
Milltown Malbay 244 C2
Mitchelstown 244 D3
Moate 245 E1
Mohill 247 E5
Moira 247 G4
Monaghan (Muineachán) 247 F5
Monasterevan 245 F1
Moneygall 245 E2
Moneymore 247 G3
Monivea 244 D1
Mount Bellew 246 D6
Mountmellick 245 F1
Mountrath 245 E1
Mountshannon 244 D2
Moville 247 F2
Moyvalley 247 F6
Muine Bheag 245 F2
Mullany's Cross 246 C5
Mullingar (An Muileann gCearr) 247 F6
Mulrany 246 B5
Murrisk 246 B6
Murroogh 244 C1

N
Naas (An Nás) 245 G1
Navan (An Uaimh) 247 G6
Nenagh (An tAonach) 244 D2
New Ross 245 F3
Newbridge (Droichead Nua) 245 F1
Newcastle *Down* 247 H5
Newcastle *Dub.* 245 G1
Newcastle West 244 C3
Newinn 245 E3
Newmarket 244 C3
Newmarket-on-Fergus 244 C2
Newport *Mayo* 246 B5
Newport *Tipp.* 244 D2
Newry 247 G5
Newtown 244 D3
Newtownabbey 247 H4
Newtownards 247 H4
Newtownbutler 247 F5
Newtownmount-kennedy 245 G1
Newtownstewart 247 F3
Ninemilehouse 245 E3
Nobber 247 F5

O
Oldcastle 247 F6
Omagh 247 F4
Oranmore 244 C1

P
Pallas Green 244 D2
Park 247 F3
Partry 246 C6
Pettigo 247 E4
Pomeroy 247 F4
Pontoon 246 C5
Portadown 247 G4
Portaferry 247 H4
Portarlington 245 F1
Portavogie 247 H4
Portlaoise 245 F1
Portlaw 245 F3
Portmagee 244 A4
Portrane 247 G6
Portrush 247 G2
Portsalon 247 E2
Portstewart 247 F2
Portumna 244 D1
Poulgorm Bridge 244 C4

R
Randalstown 247 G3
Raphoe 247 E3
Rathangan 245 F1
Rathdowney 245 E2
Rathdrum 245 G2
Rathfriland 247 G5
Rathkeale 244 C3
Rathkeevin 245 E3
Rathluirc (Charleville) 244 D3
Rathvilly 245 G2
Recess 246 B6
Ringsend 247 F3
Roscommon 246 D6
Roscrea 245 E2
Ross Carbery 244 C5
Rosslare 245 G3
Rosslare Harbour 245 G3
Rosslea 247 F5
Rush 247 G6

S
Saintfield 247 H4
Schull 244 B5
Shanacrane 244 C4
Shannon Airport 244 C2
Shercock 247 F5
Shillelagh 245 G2
Sion Mills 247 E3
Sixmilebridge 244 D2
Sixmilecross 247 F4
Skerries 247 G6
Skibbereen 244 C5
Slane 247 G6
Sligo (Sligeach) 246 D4
Sneem 244 B4
Strabane 247 E3
Stradbally 245 F1
Strangford 247 H4
Stranorlar 247 E3
Strokestown 246 D6
Swinford 246 C5
Swords 247 G6

T
Taghmon 245 G3
Tallow 245 E4
Tandragee 247 G4
Tarbert 244 C2
Templemore 245 E2
Templetuohy 245 E2
Thomastown 245 F3
Thurles (Durlas) 245 E2
Timolin 245 F1
Tipperary 244 D3
Tower 244 D4
Tralee (Trá Lí) 244 B3
Tramore (Trá Mhór) 245 F3
Trim 247 F6
Tuam 246 C6
Tubbercurry 246 D5
Tulla 244 D2
Tullamore (Tulach Mhór) 245 E1
Tullow 245 F2
Tully 247 E4
Tulsk 246 D6

U
Urlingford 245 E2

V
Virginia 247 F5

W
Warrenpoint 247 G5
Waterford (Port Láirgé) 245 F3
Waterford Airport 245 F3
Watergrasshill 244 D4
Wellington Bridge 245 F3
Westport 246 B6
Wexford (Loch Garman) 245 G3
Whitehall 245 F2
Whitehead 247 H3
Wicklow (Cill Mhantáin) 245 H1

Y
Youghal (Eochaill) 245 E4